IUS COMMUNE CASEBOOKS
FOR THE COMMON LAW OF EUROPE

CASES, MATERIALS AND TEXT ON

PROPERTY LAW

IUS COMMUNE CASEBOOKS
FOR THE COMMON LAW OF EUROPE

Series General Editor
Walter van Gerven

Cases, Materials and Text on National, Supranational and International Property Law

Editors
Sjef (JHM) van Erp (Maastricht University)
Bram Akkermans (Maastricht University)

Series Managing Editor
Dimitri Droshout (University of Leuven and Maastricht University)

Chapter Authors

Bram Akkermans (Maastricht University)
Alexandra Braun (University of Oxford)
Sjef (JHM) van Erp (Maastricht University)
Monika Hinteregger (University of Graz)
Caroline Lebon (University of Leuven, member of the Brussels Bar)
Michael Milo (University of Utrecht)
Vincent Sagaert (Universities of Leuven and Antwerp, member of the Brussels Bar)
William Swadling (University of Oxford)
Lars van Vliet (Maastricht University)

•HART•
OXFORD • LONDON • NEW YORK • NEW DELHI • SYDNEY

HART PUBLISHING
Bloomsbury Publishing Plc
Kemp House, Chawley Park, Cumnor Hill, Oxford, OX2 9PH, UK
1385 Broadway, New York, NY 10018, USA
29 Earlsfort Terrace, Dublin 2, Ireland

HART PUBLISHING, the Hart/Stag logo, BLOOMSBURY and the Diana logo are trademarks of Bloomsbury Publishing Plc

First published in Great Britain 2012
Reprinted 2013 (twice), 2014, 2016, 2017, 2018, 2020 (twice), 2021 (twice), 2022, 2023

A catalogue record for this book is available from the British Library.

Library of Congress Cataloging-in-Publication data
A catalogue record for this book is available from the Library of Congress.

ISBN: PB: 978-1-84113-750-6

Typeset by Compuscript Ltd, Shannon
Printed and bound in Great Britain by CPI Group (UK) Ltd, Croydon CR0 4YY

MIX
Paper | Supporting responsible forestry
FSC® C013604

IUS COMMUNE CASEBOOKS FOR THE COMMON LAW OF EUROPE

www.casebooks.eu

S (JHM) van Erp and B Akkermans (eds), *Cases, Materials and Text on National, Supranational and International Property Law* (Oxford, Hart Publishing, 2012)

H Beale, B Fauvarque-Cosson, J Rutgers, D Tallon and S Vogenauer, *Cases, Materials and Text on Contract Law*, Second Edition, (Oxford, Hart Publishing, 2010)

H Micklitz, J Stuyck and E Terryn (eds), *Cases, Materials and Text on National and European Consumer Law* (Oxford, Hart Publishing, 2010)

D Schiek, L Waddington and M Bell (eds), *Cases, Materials and Text on National, Supranational and International Non-Discrimination Law* (Oxford, Hart Publishing, 2007)

J Beatson and E Schrage (eds), *Cases, Materials and Text on Unjustified Enrichment* (Oxford, Hart Publishing, 2003)

H Beale, H Kötz, A Hartkamp and D Tallon (eds), *Cases, Materials and Text on Contract Law* (Oxford, Hart Publishing, 2002)

W van Gerven, P Larouche and J Lever, *Cases, Materials and Text on National, Supranational and International Tort Law* (Oxford, Hart Publishing, 2000)

W van Gerven (ed), *Tort Law – Scope of Protection* (Oxford, Hart Publishing, 1998)

Companion Website

The reader's attention is drawn to a companion website, with additional information about the Ius Commune Casebook series as well as original language versions of and hyperlinks to the full text versions of the excerpted materials reproduced in this casebook:

www.casebooks.eu/propertylaw/

ACKNOWLEDGEMENTS

The author and publisher gratefully acknowledge the authors and publishers of extracted material which appears in this book and in particular the following:

ABC-CLIO, *Boston Law Journal*, *California Law Review*, Cambridge University Press, CH Beck, Christian Von Bar and Ulrich Drobnig, Dalloz, De Gruyter, Die Keure, Duncker and Humblot, François-Xavier Licari, Gouda Quinta/WHM Reehuis, *Harvard Law Review*, Ivan Peeters, Kluwer Law International, Larcier (Groupe De Boeck), LexisNexis (Paris), *LGDJ*, Manz'sche, Marie-Andree Rakotovahiny, *Modern Law Review*, Mohr Siebeck, Otto Seller, Oxford University Press, Penguin, Sellier, Story, Sweet and Maxwell, The Estate of Pr. Jean Marc Mousseron, T*ulane Law Review*, and *Yale Law Journal*.

While every care has been taken to establish and acknowledge copyright, and to contact copyright owners, the publishers apologise for any accidental infringement and would be pleased to come to a suitable agreement with the rightful copyright owners in each case.

PREFACE

This casebook is the eighth publication in the Casebook series for the Common Law of Europe under the general editorship of Professor Walter van Gerven. We are greatly indebted to him for his continuous interest and relentless support for our team. This Casebook fits within the broader objectives of the *Ius Commune* Casebook Project, which is a joint undertaking on the part of the Universities of Leuven (KU Leuven, Belgium) and Maastricht (Maastricht University, the Netherlands). The project fosters co-operation among legal scholars from all over Europe, allowing them to join forces to undertake in-depth research in various areas of comparative and European law. One of its main aims is to enable scholars and students across Europe and beyond to study and discuss the same leading cases and materials. More information on the project is available at www.casebooks.eu.

Set-up and aims of the Casebook on Property Law

This is a casebook on property law: the first ever casebook on comparative and European property law. A major difficulty consisted in identifying appropriate cases. Sometimes this proved nearly impossible and we then had to turn to other sources, such as legislation and excerpts from scholarly writings. This 'casebook' – or rather this 'sourcebook' – unites materials from common law and civil law systems, especially from England and Wales, France, Germany and the Netherlands. Moreover, excerpts were taken from Austrian, Belgian, Scots, Irish, United States and European Union sources.

Property law systems are generally held to differ greatly from one another. This casebook respects those differences, but seeks at the same time to uncover commonalities and similarities between the legal systems. The casebook therefore prefers a functional approach, as far as possible grouping excerpts from different systems together under a single topical heading: whenever an area showed such convergence that an integrated approach proved possible, legal systems are discussed as various modes of thought leading to the same or comparable solutions to a given problem. But whenever this proved impossible or undesirable, a more classical, consecutive country-by-country approach had to be adhered to. Indeed, the European law traditions are sometimes so diverse that only a consecutive approach seemed feasible. Where this is the case, topics (problem areas) are first introduced and then followed by materials accompanied by explanatory notes from the various legal systems. At the end of the sequence, comparative notes are provided. The decision to choose the 'consecutive' or the 'integrated' approach was based on rather pragmatic arguments and depended upon the particular area of property law. However, throughout the casebook no bias is to be found towards integration or non-integration of property law in Europe. This is a casebook offering materials for further reflection, not a textbook. Of course, underlying the casebook is a particular theoretical structure, necessary to present the materials in an orderly fashion; but it is a very general and open structure that is common to the various property traditions.

The structure of the casebook itself is therefore a prime example of an integrated comparative approach, whereas, for instance, Chapter 9 on destruction provides a clear example of the consecutive approach.

The book is intended, first and foremost, for all those who study property law. Hence it is a book that can be used to teach courses on comparative and European property law, both within and beyond the European Union. At the same time it is directed towards scholars who seek to acquire a more profound knowledge of property law in another country. In addition the casebook may offer help to all those practising law and seeking information about a particular legal system or looking for a solution to a particular case. And, last but not least, this volume may prove especially useful for policy makers and legislators as it provides an overview of alternative solutions to particular problems.

The emerging field of comparative property law

As already stated, property law is an area of law with respect to which it is traditionally held that there are many and deeply rooted differences between legal systems which are difficult to overcome. This firm conviction not only concerns the traditional divide between common law and civil law, but also persists with respect to systems within the civil law family. In this respect, property law is rather different from other areas of law such as contract and tort, or constitutional law, where similarities were discovered earlier and comparative research has really gained ground. In comparison to those fields, comparative property law still finds itself in an emerging state and remains rather small, precisely because of said – often real, but, as it will appear, in many cases also unduly perceived – differences.

Nonetheless the number of academics devoting their time to the comparative study of property law is increasing. Although they must take fundamental differences into account, there is indeed an increasing consensus that property law systems do share many similarities. These similarities, we would submit, do not exist at a technical level, ie at the level of the actual rules that serve to solve disputes, but are rather to be found in the realm of common thought-patterns and approaches. When property law is analysed at such a level, underlying values and policy questions prove to be the same. The question 'who should be allowed to create new types of property rights?' could serve as a prime example, since its answer – enshrined in the principle of *numerus clausus* – is present in all legal systems: generally speaking no legal system permits parties to freely create new types of property rights and therefore the list of property rights is limited in all property law systems.

The genesis of the Casebook

It is the above-sketched type of analysis that made it possible to embark on this project in the area of property law, especially in the framework of the casebook series which offers a natural habitat for such an endeavour. With the above-described mind-set, a team of nine authors from different EU Member States set to work. From England, representing the common law tradition, William Swadling (Brasenose

College, University of Oxford) and Alexandra Braun (formerly St John's College, now Lady Margaret Hall, University of Oxford) took part. From Belgium, representing the Romanistic civil law tradition, Vincent Sagaert (Universities of Leuven and Antwerp and member of the Brussels bar) as well as Caroline Lebon (University of Leuven and member of the Brussels bar) joined in. From Austria, representing the Germanic civil law tradition, Monika Hinteregger (University of Graz) reinforced the team. And finally, from the Netherlands, representing a civil law tradition straddling the Romanistic and the Germanic traditions, Sjef van Erp (Maastricht University, Deputy-Justice Court of Appeals and Adviser for European law to the Netherlands Royal Society of Notaries), Bram Akkermans (Maastricht University), Lars van Vliet (Maastricht University) and Michael Milo (University of Utrecht) were involved.

This team conceived the casebook around six essential questions:

1. What is property law? – addressed in Chapters 1 and 2, which respectively set the scene and discuss the degree of protection enjoyed by property rights; and eventually revisited in the final Chapter 10 on harmonisation efforts in the area of property law.
2. What are property rights? – unravelled in Chapters 3–5, respectively dealing with property rights that can be held in respect of immovables and movables, property rights that can be held in respect of claims, and property security rights.
3. How can these rights be held? – described in Chapter 6 on management devices and the holding of property rights.
4. How can these rights be created? – dealt with in Chapter 7 on creation.
5. How can these rights be transferred? – analysed in Chapter 8 on transfer.
6. How can these rights be destroyed? – discussed in Chapter 9 on destruction.

This will not come as a surprise: writing a casebook is teamwork. It is in essence a collaborative effort.

This casebook is the fruit of regular author meetings. During these meetings the casebook took shape: its structure was set, authors suggested materials from their jurisdictions and fields of expertise, contextualised their suggestions and explained their importance to their fellow team members, materials were pondered before selection, draft chapters were presented, debated and refined. However, different authors stem from different backgrounds; different personal styles and inclinations remain as well. The latter is of course reflected in the eventual text of the chapters for which they took final responsibility. Therefore we thought it appropriate to make plain who contributed to which chapter at the outset of each chapter.

Throughout the process, we were able to draw on the invaluable experience and insights of our advisory committee which consisted of Madeleine Cantin-Cumyn (McGill University), Marius de Waal (University of Stellenbosch), Susan French (UCLA Law School), Kenneth Reid (University of Edinburgh) and Reinhard Zimmermann (Max Planck Institute for Comparative and International Private Law). We are very grateful for their continuous involvement and support.

Sincere thanks are also due to all those who assisted the authors in the making and revising of translations of excerpts taken from non-English sources. Utmost efforts have been taken in the making and revising of translations for this casebook.

As far as terminology is concerned, all involved endeavoured to achieve as much consistency as possible. However, in view of the number of persons involved and the complexity of the subject matter, some inconsistencies seem unavoidable and may have escaped the eye of the editors. In addition to translations by the authors themselves, many translations were prepared by students who either followed the courses on European and/or comparative property law that we teach within the European Law School programme at Maastricht University or who were employed as student assistants at the same university. Dozens contributed, but special words of thanks are due to Almaz Teffara, Anna Berlee, Lee-An Geerman, Laura Guteirrez Gomez, Tessel Kuijten, Eveline Ramaekers, Bonnie Witvliet, Willem Loof and, above all, Hanna Schebesta. They translated substantial parts of the French, Dutch and German materials in this book. We are also indebted to Manuela Weissenbacher (wissenschaftlicher Mitarbeiterin of Professsor Monika Hinteregger at the University of Graz) for translating large German excerpts. Last but not least, we extend sincere thanks to editors, Philipp Kiiver and Nicole Kornet, of 'The Maastricht Collection: Selected National, European and International Provisions from Public and Private Law', who allowed us to reproduce many of their excellent translations of French and German civil code provisions, as well as to professional translator, Filip Ameloot, for organising the swift translation of the excerpts that still remained to be taken care of at the end of the editing process. The translation process could not have been organised without the help of our former student assistant, Ton Rosenboom, who uploaded all original source materials to our intranet system, and student assistants, Sophie von Wedel, and, again, Hanna Schebesta, who kept the necessary overview of the translation process. Sincere thanks are also due to Christina Lienen for setting up the accompanying website.

The technical editing was expertly taken care of by former student assistant, Eveline Ramaekers, when she started working as a PhD researcher at Maastricht University. Mention should also be made of the support which, throughout the project, was readily offered by the Maastricht European Institute for Transnational Legal Studies (METRO), and especially by Yleen Simonis and Chantal Kuypers. At the proofreading stage we relied on the eyes of Beatrix van Erp-Jacobs, professor of legal history at Tilburg University. And, this casebook would never have been in front of you without the efforts of Hart Publishing: sincere thanks are due to its managing director, Richard Hart and managing editor, Mel Hamill.

Last but not least, we are indebted to Dimitri Droshout, managing editor of the *Ius Commune* Casebook series, who was very much involved in the preparation of the present volume. From the very beginning, he offered his guidance and advised our team on the many methodological and organisational questions we encountered on our way to completion of the process. All authors, and the undersigned in particular, are grateful for his support and friendship without which this casebook could not have appeared.

www.casebooks.eu/property

A digital companion to this casebook is to be found on the website of the casebook series: www.casebooks.eu/property. Every excerpt in this casebook has a threefold number. For example, the number '1.2 (NL)' identifies the second excerpt of the first chapter and informs you that the excerpt relates to Dutch law. On the website the same numbers are to be found. They will lead you to a page where either a link to the original source can be found or where the original language version of the excerpt has been reproduced. Whenever possible the website will lead you to or offer the full text from which an excerpt has been taken, thereby enabling those who master its original language to study the case in its entirety. In addition the website allows readers to leave comments on the structure of a chapter or on the selection or translation of a particular excerpt. Moreover, it enables registered readers to submit materials from their own legal system, thereby complementing the materials in the casebook. We do invite our readers to consult the website and to make use of its interactive features. The editors undertake to actively follow the property law section of the casebook website. They hope to establish an online community of comparative property lawyers as cooperation and teamwork are pivotal to enhancing fundamental and comparative legal analyses in this area of the law.

In conclusion . . .

We have immensely enjoyed working on this casebook and hope that the enthusiasm of the entire casebook team is reflected in its text. Suggestions and questions on (the making of) the casebook are most welcomed. The editors can be reached at s.vanerp@maastrichtuniversity.nl and b.akkermans@maastrichtuniversity.nl.

Sjef van Erp and Bram Akkermans
Maastricht and Brussels, April 2012

CONTENTS

CHAPTER SIX
MANAGEMENT: TRUST, *TREUHAND* AND *FIDUCIE* 553

COUNTRY CODES

AT	Austria
BE	Belgium
DE	Germany
E&W	England and Wales
EU	European Union
FR	France
INT	International
NL	The Netherlands
SC	Scotland
US	United States of America

TABLE OF CASES

Cases are ordered alphabetically by name except where otherwise indicated. Citations and page numbers in bold indicate verbatim quotations from court reports. For the convenience of the reader, the instruments and provisions have been listed in the same language in which they apear in this casebook and have been ordered alphabetically.

EUROPEAN COURT OF HUMAN RIGHTS

COURT OF JUSTICE OF THE EUROPEAN UNION (CJEU)

NATIONAL

AUSTRALIA

AUSTRIA (ORDERED BY DATE)

BELGIUM (ORDERED BY DATE)

CANADA

FRANCE (ORDERED BY DATE)

GERMANY (ORDERED BY DATE)

NETHERLANDS (ORDERED BY DATE)

NEW ZEALAND

UNITED KINGDOM

UNITED STATES

UNITED STATES

TABLE OF LEGISLATION

Citations and page numbers in bold indicate verbatim quotations from the instrument/provision in question.

INTERNATIONAL

COUNCIL OF EUROPE

EUROPEAN UNION

AUSTRIA

BELGIUM

CANADA

FRANCE

GERMANY

IRELAND

ITALY

LUXEMBOURG

NETHERLANDS

NEW ZEALAND

SAN MARINO

SWITZERLAND

UNITED KINGDOM

UNITED STATES

INTRODUCTION
ESSENTIAL DIRECTIONS ON USING THE CASEBOOK

*Bram Akkermans, Vincent Sagaert and William Swadling**

This introduction deals, first of all, with the nature of a casebook, followed by a short introduction to differences in court structures, styles of judgments and legislative styles. It offers essential directions on using the casebook before we can enter into the six essential questions of property law. Moreover, it offers an introduction into German, French, Belgian, Dutch and English property law. As such, the chapter therefore offers a general overview of the subject matter and approach.

The *Ius Commune* Casebooks for the Common Law of Europe are no ordinary casebooks. Unlike casebooks on national law, they comprise materials from different legal systems. Different legal systems require different approaches, and this chapter seeks to introduce the general aspects of the legal systems dealt with herein. Moreover, this casebook takes a different approach to property law. It is structured around six essential questions, which are explained below (I).[1]

This chapter will not so much focus on the differences in content between the legal systems—in property law these differences can be, unlike in contract law, substantial—but on the general structure of the legal systems.

This casebook deals with French, German, Dutch and English law, and, to some extent, the law of Belgium and Austria. In other words, the casebook focuses on the main civil law and common law traditions in Europe. French and German law represent the dominant approaches of the civil law tradition, with the property laws of systems such as Italian law, Spanish law, Polish law and Hungarian law based, albeit not entirely, on either French or German law. Dutch law is of interest because of the coming into force in 1992 of a new part of the Civil Code dealing with, amongst other things, property law. The law of England and Wales represents the common law tradition in this book. Although there are more common law systems in Europe, the law of Northern Ireland and the law of the Republic of Ireland have their roots in the English system.

* Sections I.A.2 and I.B.1.d. on English law were written by William Swadling, section II.A was written by Vincent Sagaert. All other text was written by Bram Akkermans.

[1] See, on these questions, also the preface to this casebook.

This chapter introduces various characteristics of the four legal systems. To begin, we will look at the various models of case law. For example, a French decision by the highest court in the country, the Cour de cassation, can be, in total, only five sentences long, whereas a decision by the highest court in Germany, the Bundesgerichtshof, or in England, the Supreme Court (formerly the House of Lords), can be tens of pages. Moreover, the way in which a common law court deals with the law may differ from a civil law court.

Secondly, we turn to the property law itself and provide short introductions to the sources of property law in the four legal systems. We start, whenever possible, with the civil law, and the common law then follows. At the end of each chapter a short comparative overview is provided.

I. THE CONTENT AND STRUCTURE OF THE CASEBOOK

This casebook deals with the law of property. It is structured around six essential questions as outlined in the preface. These questions are the six essential questions a property lawyer asks him or herself. For example, person A wants to buy a piece of land with a house on it. Property law applies to this because property law is the law relating to things (question 1). When person A buys the land and the house on it, he or she acquires a property right, a right which can be enforced against everyone else. There are many property rights and person A will come across the most important of these when researching what property right he or she is about the acquire, but also what property rights are already created on the piece of land (question 2). Moreover, some of these property rights may be held directly or by someone on behalf of someone else (question 3). These property rights can be created (question 4) or already exist having been acquired from someone else (question 5). There can also be property rights that cease to exist (question 6).

In case of our example, the seller is likely to have created a limited property security right (see chapter 5) on his property right on the land (see Chapter 3), which will cease to exist upon payment of his debt (see Chapter 9), so that the property right on the land can be transferred to the buyer (see chapter 8), who in his turn can create a limited property security right on the land again to secure the financing of the acquisition (see Chapter 7).

In short the six essential questions in property law are:

1. What is property law?
2. What are property rights?
3. How can these rights be held?
4. How are these rights created?
5. How are these rights transferred?
6. How are these rights destroyed?

This casebook is structured along the lines of these questions.

Chapter 1 will introduce the issues; it will explain the concept of property law and the method of analysis this casebook uses. It will explain concepts and definitions used in property law, and common thought patterns, and it will offer an outline of the basic principles and ground rules of property law. (Question 1)

Chapter 2 will deal with the protection of property rights. The protection of property rights is one of the most fundamental aspects of property law and separates property law from the law of obligations. (Question 1)

Chapter 3 will outline the types of property rights that can be held in respect to immovables (land) and movables (goods). (Question 2)

Chapter 4 will outline the types of property rights that can be held in respect to claims. These are dealt with in a separate chapter as claims occupy a special and sometimes controversial position in property law. (Question 2)

Chapter 5 will deal with property security rights. This area of property law is closely related to insolvency law and offers such different questions that a separate chapter allows an exclusive focus on these issues. (Question 2)

Chapter 6 will deal with management devises and will explain how property rights can be held. Prominent in this chapter will be the English trust, but civil law systems will also be dealt with extensively. (Question 3)

Chapter 7 deals with the creation of property rights. This includes the ways a right of ownership is created, as well as the creation of limited property rights. (Question 4)

Chapter 8 deals with the transfer of property rights and will extensively explain what transfer systems exist and will illustrate how these operate. (Question 5)

Chapter 9 deals with the destruction of property rights, not only the destruction of objects on which property rights are created, but also the destruction of the property rights itself. (Question 6)

Chapter 10 will deal with harmonisation efforts in the area of property law and provide an overview of the most important existing and pending harmonisation efforts, both at an international and at a European level.

II. LEGAL SYSTEMS IN GENERAL

As already mentioned, the legal systems dealt with in this book are French law, German law, Dutch law and the law of England and Wales. The first three of these four systems represent the civil law tradition. By civil law is meant the fact that in these legal systems a civil code is used in which the majority of the rules on private law are contained. England and Wales represents the common law, so called because the law in that system is not always made by the legislature but also by judges through a case law system.

Courts therefore have a different function in the two legal traditions. At the risk of oversimplification, in civil law systems, the role of the court is to apply the law enacted by the legislature to concrete cases. However, in doing so, the courts must not create any new law, the theory being that, under the doctrine of separation of powers, the lawmaking power is with the legislature, not the judiciary. The philosopher Montesquieu, the founder of the *Trias Politica*, the separation-of-powers doctrine, said that the judiciary should be nothing more that the mouth of the law (*la bouche de la loi*). Courts in legal systems which adhere to the common law tradition fulfil a different function. Although these courts also recognise the supremacy of parliament, they have lawmaking powers.

A decision of a case in a civil law jurisdiction must be looked at differently from one by a court in a common law tradition. We should be aware of this difference at all times and not try to interpret civil law cases in the way of common law cases, and vice versa. Knowing and understanding the difference between the legal traditions will help in interpreting the scope and meaning of a certain decision. Sometimes a certain subject will be dealt with by a court decision elaborately in one jurisdiction, while in other systems courts have remained silent on this subject, or another power, the legislature for example, has dealt with this point.

The differences between these traditions are such that this chapter will explain some of the fundamental characteristics in these systems. In so far as possible, this section will focus on private law. We will divide not only between civil law and common law, but the civil law systems will also be further divided. The reason for this is that the differences between French and German law can sometimes be as significant as the differences between the civil law and the common law tradition. We will start by looking at the sources of law and the hierarchy of these sources. We will then look at the court system and finally at the case law method used in French, German, Dutch and English and Welsh law.

II.A SOURCES OF LAW

How do we know what is the law? In order to find that answer we must look at the sources of law. Sources of law are the materials and processes from which the law is developed. One of the first of these that comes to mind might be a constitution from which fundamental rights follow. Another might be a criminal code that proscribes offences such as theft, robbery and murder. In private law the sources of law are not so much constitutional sources, although there is a constitutional dimension to private law, but rather legislation, case law and customary law. Moreover, the writings of private law scholars, to a certain degree and depending on the legal system, provide a source of law.

In some situations, different sources of law might each have something to say about a certain topic. Of course, the views on a certain subject matter may differ. In order to resolve conflicts, legal systems recognise a hierarchy of sources, though this may differ between legal systems.

II.A.1 CIVIL LAW

II.A.1.a Source: different forms of legislation

Introductory Notes

(a) As stated above, civil law systems are so called because they generally have a civil code that contains the main rules of private law. If there are other rules of private law, these will generally also be included in a legislative document. An example of such is the French Consumer Code, which contains special rules on consumer law, or the German Law on Apartment Rights, which deals with a specific property right not mentioned in the German Civil Code.

(b) Civil law systems tend to have legislation in other areas of law as well. This includes specific legislation such as an insolvency code, but generally, and that is the most important for now, a constitution. A constitution is generally a system of government, by which is meant that it is the organisation of a country. In civil law systems this organisation is, like private law, codified in a document known as a constitution. The constitution will provide rules on the separation of powers, the organisation of the state, fundamental rights and much more. Of our concern here is the separation of powers and the organisation of the state.

A civil law constitution will generally mention what office or institution holds the legislative, executive and judiciary power. Moreover, the Constitution might say something, either explicitly or implicitly, on the sources of law and the order of the sources of law.

(c) France and the Netherlands each have a document known as a constitution. Germany uses the term basic law (*Grundgesetz*) to describe the constitutional document in its legal order.

French Constitution **1 (FR)**

Article 24 Parliament shall pass statutes. It shall monitor the actions of the government. It shall assess public policies.
Parliament shall comprise the National Assembly and the Senate.
Article 34 Statutes shall determine the rules concerning:
—civil rights and the fundamental guarantees granted to citizens for the exercise of their civil liberties; freedom, pluralism and the independence of the media; the obligations imposed for the purposes of national defense upon the person and objects of citizens. ...
Statutes shall also lay down the basic principles of: ... systems of ownership, property rights and civil and commercial obligations.

Note

These excerpts from the French constitution show the assignment of parliament to deal with private law and property law in particular. Parliament, the institution of the state that is authorised to pass statutes, ie legislation, is therefore solely entitled to regulate matters of private law. The French Civil Code, the Code civil, should be considered in this perspective.

German Basic Law **2 (DE)**

Article 70 (1) The states [*Länder*] shall have the right to legislate insofar as this Basic Law does not confer legislative power on the Federation.
(2) The division of authority between the Federation and the *Länder* shall be governed

by the provisions of this Basic Law concerning exclusive and concurrent legislative powers.

Article 72 (1) On matters within the concurrent legislative power, the Länder shall have power to legislate so long as and to the extent that the Federation has not exercised its legislative power by enacting a law.

Article 74 (1) Concurrent legislative power shall extend to the following matters:

1. civil law, criminal law, court organisation and procedure (except for the correctional law of pre-trial detention), the legal profession, notaries, and the provision of legal advice; …

15. the transfer of land, natural resources, and means of production to public ownership or other forms of public enterprise; …

18. urban real estate transactions, land law (except for laws regarding development fees), and the law on rental subsidies, subsidies for old debts, home building loan premiums, miners' homebuilding and homesteading;

Notes

(1) The situation in Germany is more complicated than that in France, as Germany is a federation. Therefore, the legislative powers in Germany are divided between the Federal legislature and the legislature of the states, which are known as *Länder* (a single state is known as a *Land*).

(2) The legislative competences in the area of private law are shared competences between the federation and the states, but the federation has acted by enacting a civil code, the Bürgerliches Gesetzbuch (BGB), in 1900. Therefore, the main legislative power in respect to private law is with the federal legislature. Nonetheless, some states do use their powers under the basic law to regulate additional aspects of private law themselves. A full overview of German law therefore requires a check in the legal system of the relevant state as well. However, as most private law, property law in particular, concerns federal legislation, this casebook will focus only on federal legislation, the BGB and some special legislation.

Dutch Constitution **3 (NL)**

Article 81 Acts of Parliament shall be passed jointly by the Government and the Parliament.

Article 107 (1) Civil law, criminal law and civil and criminal procedure shall be regulated by Act of Parliament in general legal codes without prejudice to the power to regulate certain matters in separate Acts of Parliament.

Note

Like in France, the Netherlands parliament, comprising of two houses, is the sole legislature. Moreover, the Dutch constitution prescribes that regulating matters of private law belongs to the power of parliament, as parliament is the only institution of the state that may adopt Acts of Parliament.

Comparative Notes

(1) Some constitutions make it more explicit than others, but, as stated above, legislation enacted by parliament is the primary source of private law in French, German and Dutch law. The acts of parliament in each of these countries have taken the form of a civil code. In chronological order these are the Code civil français (Cciv) (1804), the Bürgerliches Gesetzbuch (BGB) (1900), and the Burgerlijk Wetboek (BW) (1992).

(2) Apart from these general codes of private law, there are many specific statutes that deal with private law. Examples of these are the French Consumer Code, Commercial Code, Rural Code, and Monetary and Financial Code, the German Law on Apartment Ownership and the Law on the Right of Superficies, as well as the Dutch law on the transfer of money, and the law on consumer credit. These other statutes often contain more specific rules on aspects that have been generally dealt with in the civil codes, or contain rules that have not been dealt with by the civil codes at all.

(3) When there is a conflict between the special rules and the more general rules the general principle of *lex specialis derogat legi generali* applies. This principle determines that the specific rule always goes before the general rule. Therefore specific rules in a statute can apply before the civil code.

II.A.1.b Source: court decisions

A second source, besides legislation, is court decisions. These decisions are almost as important as legislation as they clarify the application of legislation in practice. Moreover, in some legal systems legislation leaves room for courts to make decisions and develop the law further. One example of these may be provided.

Burgerlijk Wetboek **4 (NL)**

Article 3:4 (1) Everything which according to public opinion forms part of an object, is part of that object.
(2) An object which is connected to a principal object in such a way that it cannot be separated without considerable damage to one of the objects, becomes part of the principal object.

Notes

(1) The above Article illustrates how the Dutch legislature deliberately left room for the judiciary to develop the law on this point. The term public opinion and the role it places on determining which elements form part of a thing are left for the judiciary to apply in practice. This is exactly what has happened.[2] We shall return to Article 3:4 BW and the case law applying it in Chapter 7.

Another example of court activity, but without explicit room allowed by the legislature, can be seen in French law. The French Civil Code is one of the oldest

[2] HR 15 November 1991, NJ 1993/316. See also HR 26 March 1936, NJ 1936/757; HR 11 December 1953, NJ 1954/115; HR 27 November 1992, NJ 1993/317; HR 28 June 1996, NJ 1997/397.

civil codes in Europe. The French Supreme Court has more than once taken the provisions in the Civil Code as a guideline to develop the law further. Examples of this can be found in the area of tort law, but also in respect to property security rights. Only in 2006 did the French legislature codify the existing case law. This will be dealt with in Chapter 5 dealing with security rights.

II.A.1.c Source: customary law

A less important, but still present, source of law is custom. Sometimes, legislation and case law are silent on a certain point, or a certain point can only be decided when taking custom into account. For example, Chapter 7 of this casebook deals with the question whether a building is movable or immovable, a question relevant to determine who has a right of ownership over the building. In order to determine whether the building is immovable, the courts look at whether it is customary to perceive the building as connected to the land on which it stands. Custom, in other words, is used to help determine a criterion provided by legislation or case law.

II.A.1.d Source: doctrine

In some legal systems more than others, the writings of academics are also of importance. In German law, German courts, in order to give authority to their reasoning, often quote the writings of academics in commentaries to the German Civil Code. In French and Dutch law, the courts do not generally refer to doctrine, but the advocate general, a court official who advises supreme courts on how and what to decide, may refer to scholarly writings.

Doctrine is the most inferior source of law, as writers may change their opinions and it is not their primary task to provide assistance to the courts. On the contrary, most academic writers develop critical views on the development of law, and often disagree with case law or legislation. However, depending on the legal system, doctrine sometimes takes an important position, such as in German law.

II.A.1.e Hierarchy of sources of law

Generally speaking the hierarchy between the sources of law in civil law countries is:

1. Legislation
   (a) Constitution
   (b) Civil codes
   (c) Special statutes
   (d) Other acts of legislation and implementing instruments (ministerial decrees, etc)
2. Case law (following the hierarchy between courts discussed below)
3. Customary law
4. Doctrine

Depending on the legal system, international law takes place before or after the level of the constitution (1a). European Union law, because of its primacy over national law, generally takes its place above the national constitution (1a), although this is debated.[3]

II.A.2 COMMON LAW

The sources of law in English law are no different from the sources of law in civil law jurisdictions. However, the content of these sources as well as the hierarchy between them differs considerably.

Although there is now a document guaranteeing the protection of human rights, there is no constitutional document dealing with the organisation of the state in English law.[4] Moreover, English law is made up of a mixture of legislation and judge-made law.

Case law, therefore, is an important source of law in England. Within that case law, and somewhat confusingly, are two jurisdictions: common law and equity. Equity is a separate system often correcting the strict application of the rules of common law. The term common law, as used in the heading of this paragraph and in this chapter so far to contrast it with civil law, should be understood to include both the sub-systems of common law and equity.

II.A.2.a Common law and equity

The difference between common law and equity in a common law system can only be understood as a matter of history; it has no logical foundation. For certain political reasons, essentially a contest between the royal (ie common law) courts and those lower down the feudal chain (ie local courts), the jurisdiction of the royal courts was limited to areas on which they had already pronounced. No new types of issue could be adjudicated on: these were to be the preserve of the local courts. As time went on, these local courts fell out of favour with litigants, who preferred royal justice. In response to these demands, a further royal court was set up, the Court of Chancery, administering the jurisdiction known as equity. Not long afterwards, the common law courts regained their jurisdiction to try novel disputes, with the result that England and Wales have both courts of common law and equity, though since 1873, the administration of the two jurisdictions has been merged.

II.A.2.b Source: case law and the rule of precedent

Courts in England and Wales follow a strict hierarchical structure. Decisions of first instance courts bind no one save the parties to the dispute. In private law (or civil law) cases, appeal is generally to the Court of Appeal, the decisions of which bind all first instance courts and the Court of Appeal itself. Appeals from the Court of Appeal are made to the Supreme Court (formerly the House of Lords). Decisions of the Supreme Court bind the Court of Appeal and all first instance courts and, until

[3] See Case 26/62 *Van Gend en Loos v Nederlandse Administratie der Belastingen* [1963] ECR 1 and Case 6/64 *Costa v ENEL* [1964] ECR 585. On the debate see, inter alia, P Craig and G de Búrca, *EU Law, Text Cases and Materials*, 5th edn (Oxford, Oxford University Press, 2011) ch 4.

[4] Human Rights Act 1998.

1966, the Supreme Court (then the House of Lords) itself. Since 1966, the Supreme Court can depart from its own decisions, but only under limited circumstances.

What is binding about any decision of either the Court of Appeal or the Supreme Court is the *ratio decidendi*. Things said by the way (*obiter dicta*) are of persuasive value only. Also of persuasive value are decisions of the Privy Council on appeal from Commonwealth jurisdictions, and decisions of common law courts from other countries, eg the High Court of Australia and the Supreme Court of Canada.

II.A.2.c Source: legislation

In many areas of law, the rules governing the resolution of disputes do not arise as a result of rules generated by previous disputes but by rules enacted by the legislature. These rules in English law are called 'statutes'. There may also be a power given to certain officials by statute to make further rules, thus allowing, by what are called 'statutory instruments', a form of delegated legislation. The application of rules laid down in statutes and statutory instruments is of course a matter for the courts, and case law can arise on the interpretation of such legislation.

II.A.2.d Source: academic commentary

Although they have no status as laying down rules, and do not constitute 'authority', the writings of academic commentators are nevertheless an important part of English lawmaking. Judges are willing to listen to the views of commentators cited to them by counsel. Indeed, in a celebrated instance in the 1980s, the House of Lords in *R v Shipuri* [1987] reversed its own decision in a criminal matter within six months largely because of criticisms heaped on the case by an academic writer, Professor Glanville Williams.

II.A.2.e Hierarchy of sources

In the common law system, rules laid down by the legislature trump rules laid down by the courts. Parliament, in other words, is supreme.

II.B TYPES OF CASE LAW

In private law, court cases arise because of a dispute between parties that are unwilling to settle themselves. The state is therefore generally not involved in the proceedings, except when the state appears as a party. Besides resolving concrete disputes, court cases clarify the law, whether in civil law it is to apply legislation in a particular situation, or, in common law, to clarify the rule of law that is to be applied in a certain situation or to state or restate a point of law. However, a court will not generally make a decision without a case at hand: a fact pattern is needed to make a decision. A judgment is a decision that is made in a case between two or more parties appearing in front of an organ of the judiciary.

The decision is binding on the parties. As was stated above, a case can also be binding on persons not party to the proceedings. This effect, the binding nature of case law, can have different forms. First of all, a case decided on the basis of a certain fact pattern will be generally applicable to all cases with a similar pattern of facts. Moreover the decision made can sometimes also set a line of decision making, but this depends on the legal system and the type of court involved.

The content of the case law will depend on the judiciary system that is used. There are two types of case law. First, there are judgments that decide on the facts. These cases resolve a dispute between parties by applying the law. Second, there are judgments that decide on the law. These cases do resolve a dispute between parties, but indirectly by stating or restating the content of the law.

All legal systems use the decisions of fact to resolve disputes (in appeal known as *appel* in French and *Berufung* in German). Some legal systems apply a system of decisions of law on top of that. These systems, which are civil law systems, allow the parties to launch an appeal in law to the highest court in the jurisdiction. This system is known as cassation (*cassation* in French, *cassatie* in Dutch) in French-oriented systems (France, Belgium and The Netherlands) and revision (*Revision*) in Germanic-oriented systems (Germany, Austria).[5]

As a general principle of law, court decisions in private matters are not taken by one single court. Although the system is aimed at resolving disputes, it is considered part of fair procedure that parties have a right to appeal against a decision made against them or with which they are not satisfied. Generally speaking there are three levels in a procedure: lower level, appeal and a supreme court. The proportion of cases dealt with by these courts can best be visualised as a pyramid, where the supreme court is confronted with or takes (depending on the system) the smallest number of cases.

Lower courts function as courts with original jurisdiction, meaning they are authorised to hear cases for the first time, or as courts of appeal to lower courts.

In most legal systems there are certain disputes, usually with a low financial interest, which have no appeal or only appeal in one instance available. The organisation of the court system is a complicated matter that will be dealt with more elaborately in another casebook.[6] However, some elementary information is necessary to understand the excerpts of cases that will follow in this casebook. Therefore, this section will deal with the court organisation and the types of appeal that are available. Some short notes will further highlight some particular national aspects of case law that are necessary to understand some of the court decisions.

II.B.1. FRENCH LAW

Introductory Notes

(a) The French judicial system comprises three levels. The *tribunal de première instance* (tribunal of first instance) is the first court that generally hears civil disputes. Representation is not necessary and procedure is simply based on oral arguments. The court will hear claims up until €10,000 and in specific matters such as labour

[5] See R Youngs, *English, French and German Comparative Law* (London and Sydney, Cavendish Publishing, 1998) 65, 69.

[6] See CH van Rhee and P Oberhammer (eds), *Ius Commune Casebook for the Common Law of Europe. Text, Cases and Materials on Civil Procedure* (Oxford, Hart Publishing, forthcoming)

disputes.[7] Other private law disputes will start proceedings at the *tribunal de grande instance* (court of first instance).[8] This court hears disputes representing a value starting from €10,000. The courts comprise a president and several judges that may also as an individual judge be sent to sit alone on a tribunal of first instance.[9] Against decisions taken by the tribunals and courts of first instance (they are organised by region), appeal in fact (*appel*) is possible.

(b) What follows is a full translation of a case decided by a French Court of Appeal. In the rest of the casebook we will use excerpts, ie fragments from court decisions. It is important to see a full decision once, as the Court of Appeal also deals with the facts of the case. A decision of the Cour the cassation, the French Supreme Court, will only deal with matters of law and therefore be shorter and structured in a very different manner.

Code de l'organisation judiciaire **5 (FR)**

Article L111-1 The judiciary renders its decisions in the name of the people of France.

Article L311-1 The Court of Appeal deals with, taking into account the compentences awared to other courts in the judiciary, legal decisions in civil and criminal matters taken at first instance. The Court of Appeal adjudicates the substance of the matter in final instance.

Cour d'appel de Montpellier, 15 March 2005 **6 (FR)**

SPOUSES X ... AND SCI LA RECHE V SPOUSES Y

Prescription of a common wall

A common wall placed wrongfully on the land of one of the neighbours becomes owned by these after the prescription period has ended.

Facts: In 1974 the spouses X constructed a wall separating their land from the land of their neighbours, the spouses Y. After some time, the spouses Y discovered that the wall was not placed on the border between their lands, but on their land only. Moreover, in 1988 the wall was strengthened and elevated. The spouses Y claimed that the wall was on their land and that they suffered damages as a consequence. Moreover, they claimed that strengthening of the wall resulted in a loss of light on their land and that they had to surrender more land to strengthen the new construction. Spouses X claimed that the spouses Y have become owners of the wall by acquisitive prescription[10] and therefore cannot claim damages.

Held: The spouses Y have no claim through prescription and must pay damages to the applicants.[11]

Judgment: Given the judgment of the Court of first instance of Montpellier of 17 June 2002, that stated that François X ... incorrectly relied on the requirement of

[7] Arts L221-4 and L221-5 Code de l'organisation judiciaire.

[8] Art L211-1 Code de l'organisation judiciaire.

[9] Arts L212-3 and L221-3 Code de l'organisation judicaire.

[10] On acquisitive prescription, the gaining of land through possession for a certain period of time, see Chapter 7.

[11] Note that this case uses the version of the Civil Code and the Code of Civil Procedure of 2004. Both codes were amended substantially after this period and the Article numbers in the Civil Code no longer correspond.

Article 2270-1 of the Civil Code and the prescription of Article 2265, and ordered an expert to determine the size of each of the properties and the price applicable to m., i.e. if the elevation of the common wall is consistent with legislation and if it causes damage to any of the parties;

Considering the regular appeal brought by the spouses X ... and the SCI La Reche, and their conclusions of 10 December 2004 seeking to declare that the action has prescribed, alternatively is inadmissible because it is contrary to the transfer of the land on 14 May 1974; more alternatively, assuming that there is encroachment, this is prescribed and seeking to declare the action unfounded; in any case to hold the spouses Y ... jointly liable to pay 6000 euro for damages and 2000 euro on the basis of Article 700 of the New Civil Procedure Code (NCPC) and all the costs;

Considering the findings reported by the spouses Y ... on 19 January 2005, seeking to declare the appeal inadmissible, alternatively, confirming the decision in lower instance; order the appellants to pay 1000 euro on the bases of Article 700 NCPC and all the costs;

I—On the admissibility of the appeal

To declare the appeal inadmissible, the respondents argue that the acquisitive prescription rejected by the judge of first instance is not of a substantive nature but q plea of non-admissibility foreseen in Article 2265 of the Civil Code, itself inserted in Section III titled 'of prescription of ten or twenty years' in the same title as Article 2270-1; that moreover, Article 122 of the New Code of Civil Procedure that defines the plea of non-admissibility as each means which purpose it is to have the adversary's claim declared inadmissible without entering into the substantive nature of the case, makes reference to 'prescription', without distinguishing between acquisitive and extinctive prescription

Yet, invoking acquisitive prescription, as this leads to the recognition of a property right on an immovable for the benefit of he who invokes it, is a substantive matter, and not an plea of non-admissibility without examining the substantive nature of the action invoked by him against another party.

It follows that in rejecting the claim of the spouses X ... in holding that they have become owners through prescription of the wall in issue, the judge in first instance ruled on a principal issue within the meaning of Article 544 New Code of Civil Procedure, and the appeal is therefore admissible.

II—On the demand for the payment of damages

The spouses Y ..., who claim that the wall bordering their premises that was constructed in 1974 by the spouses X ... encroaches on their land, do not seek its destruction, but a compensation for their disadvantage that results from this:

—First, this intrusion would have generated a loss of use of 28m of land during a period of 26 years and the impossibility to obtain a certificate of compliance for their home.

—Second, the enhancement of the wall and the raising of the ground level in 1988 resulted in a loss of sunlight and light, as well as the need to reinforce the wall by providing land.

They are based on Articles 659, 662 and 1382 of the Civil Code, specifically referred to in their assignment of 2 February 2001.

Contrary to what they claim, the second type of injury for which they seek damages is not an aggravation of the first. These grounds for damages are totally distinct from the nature of their cause. Indeed, the first would be a loss of surface and rights of residence created by a wrong placement of a wall, whereas the second is a deprivation of sunlight and an obligation to reinforce the structure, caused byt he fact that in 1988, the wall was wired, raised and strengthened with stone.

These claims are governed by different legal rules and should be considered in turn.

On the compensation for damage caused by the wrongful construction of the wall.

Seeking compensation for damage resulting from a fault, and not from the demolition of work improperly executed, this is a claim exclusively dealt with by civil non-contractual liability of the common rules governed by article 1382 of the Civil Code. As such, it is subject to a ten-year limitation of Article 2270-1 to be calculated from the 'manisfestation of the damage'.

In this case, it is the date on which the spouses Y ... knew that the wall build by the spouses X ... encroached on their property.

In a letter dated 14 November 1984 addressed to Mr X ... through his council, Mr Y ... 'confirms in a definite way that the wall was constructed on his land'.

This correspondence shows in clear and incontestable terms the fact that at that date he was aware of the encroachment, which is sufficient to start the prescription period of Articler 2270-1 of the Civil Code, the text of which does not require that the person suffering the damage at that stage has a complete overview of the nature and the extent of the damage, both in respect to the land lost and its implications in respect to planning regulations.

Moreover, it should be noted that the spouses Y ... do not report evidence that in 2003 they did not know the refusal for building permits of 16 May 1975, or even that this decision is related to the creation of the wall under dispute.

The ten-year prescription period expired on 14 November 1994. It is clear, without any need to examine the other claims, that the acquisitive prescription had taken effect in the assignment of 2 February 2001.

On the compensation for damage caused by the elevation of the wall.

Seen the provisions of Article 659 Civil Code, and subject to the prescription of thirty years of the common rules in Article 2262 Code civil, this claim is admissible.

It appears from the bailiff's report of 13 October 2003, made on the request of the spouses Y ..., that the hight of the wall is approximately 2 metres at the side at the entrance and on the side of the house, to reach 2,20 metres on the level of the terrace with a maximum height of 2,60 metres at the end of it.

However, the bailiff has not recorded a loss of sunlight or light and the spouses Y ... have made no complaints about this to him. Neither the photographs attached to the report, nor any any objective evidence does allow them to provide proof.

Similarly, they produce no evidence of a professional technical finding of a risk of collapse of the wall and the need to strengthen it by pillars or the supply of land.

In the absence of evidence resulting from the enhancement of the wall, they are accordingly dismissed in their claims for damages.

Succumbing, the spouses Y ... pay the spouses X ... and the SCI La reche a sum of 2000 euro on the basis of Article 700 of the NCPC, however established their share of abuse in the exercise of the procedure to be compensable.

Decides

Reverses the judgment, and states again:

Declares the claim of the spouses Y ... for compensation for damage resulting from the encroachment of the wall inadmissible through prescription.

Rejects their request for damages resulting from the raising of the wall.

Orders to pay to the spouses X ... and the SCI La reche the sum of 2000 euro on the basis of Article 700 of the New Code of Civil Procedure.

Dismisses the parts of the claims for or against this.

Orders the spouses Y ... to pay all costs, ...

Notes

(1) The *appel* is an appeal in both fact and in law, meaning that the court of appeal (known as Cour d'appel) will redecide the case, taking into account the judgment of the *tribunal* or court of first instance. Its judgment has more authority for other courts of appeal as well as for all the lower courts and will generally be followed.

(2) The decision taken, as can be seen from the example, is the final decision on the facts. After this decision, parties may only appeal on a question of law, ie an appeal in cassation and no longer a regular appeal. Instead of claiming the decision was wrongly decided, they may state their grievances on the treatment of the law by the court of appeal to the court of cassation, which will be dealt next.

Code de l'organisation judiciaire **7 (FR)**

Article L411-1 There is, for the Republic, one Court of cassation.

Article L411-2 The Court of cassation renders decisions on appeals in cassation against rulings and judgments of the courts of substance in final instance. The Court of cassation does not examine the substance of the case unless otherwise specified by law.

Article L411-3 The Court of cassation may quash the judgment in substance in final instance without referring the case back, if there is no need to rule again on the substance of the case.

It may also, in cassation proceedings without referring back, decide on the facts of the litigation, if these were recognised and agreed to in final instance and allow the Court to apply the relevant provision of law.

In these cases, it rules on the burden of the costs of the civil proceedings before the courts of substance.

The ruling carries force of execution.

The ways of implementing this article shall be decided by degree of the Council of State (*Conseil d'Etat*).

Article L421-1 The Court of cassation comprises chambers dealing with civil law and a chamber dealing with criminal law.

Article L421-3 The judgments of the Court of cassations are made by one of the chambers, or by a mixed chamber or by a general assembly of justices.

Cour de cassation 3ème Civ 27 June 2007 **8 (FR)**
Spouses X v Spouses Y

RENEWAL OF A LEASE

The bakery-patisserie

A stipulation in a lease contract that the premises may only be used as a bakery must be interpreted strictly.

Facts: The spouses X are owners of a very old building that is used as a bakery-patisserie in Montpellier. Spouses Y are lessees of the building and operate a bakery-patisserie there. They applied for a renewal of the contract of lease, which was refused by spouses X on the grounds that the contract of the lease states that bread and pastry must be made on the premises. In reality, spouses Y sell bread and pastry made in other premises that they hold. On appeal the Court of Appeal of Montpellier had held that the lease must be renewed as the clause was not fulfilled because bread and pastry were sold at the premises.

Held: The clause must be interpreted strictly as bread and pastry is still sold on the premises. The case is referred back to the court of appeal, in a different composition, to decide on the facts of the case.

Judgment: Considering Article L145-8 of the Commercial Code, together with Article 1134 of the Civil Code.

Whereas the right to a renewal of a lease can be invoked by the owner of land that is used, the land changes, if applicable, as provided in Section VIII of Chapter V of title IV of the Commercial Code, shall, unless legitimate reasons exist, been the object of effective utilisation for a period of three years preceding the date of expiry of the lease or its renewal as provided in Article L145-9;

Whereas, according to the decision in cassation (Montpellier, 15 March 2005) that, by act of 24 July 2001, the spouses X ..., lessees of commercial buildings owned by the spouses Y ..., have requested a renewal of their lease as of 1 July 2002; That by act of 14 September 2001, the spouses Y ..., have refused consent for renewal on the grounds that no bakery-patisserie was operated in the leased premises in accordance with the purpose intended by the lease, then were assigned in denial of the right under the statute of commercial leases;

Whereas, to accommodate the request of the lessees, the decision holds, for specific reasons adopted, it appears from the evidence produced in the debate as bread and pastries sold in the leased premises are manufactured in another bakery operated by the lessees, as the premised leased by them no longer serve as storage and sale and they are no longer engaged in the business of bakery and patisserie as contractually stipulated;

So holding, while the clause in the contract relating to the purpose of the bakery-patisserie did not require, in the absence of special provisions, the handmade creation and sale of bread and pastry in the same space leased, the Court of appeal violated the above texts.

For these reasons:

Quashes and voids, in all its provisions, the decision of 15 March 2005, between the parties, by the Court of Appeal of Montpellier; reinstates, therefore, the situation and the parties as they were before the decision and, to do justice, refers the case to the Court of appeal of Montpellier, with a different composition.[12]

Notes

(1) The court of cassation (Cour de cassation) decides on questions of law. It decides, in other words, whether the court of appeal has interpreted and applied the law in a correct way. However, the court of cassation does not conclude this in an extensive review of the decision on appeal, but by answering the grievances of the parties. As a result, the judgment of the court of cassation is not an elaborate document filled with logical reasoning and arguments, but rather a short statement on the law taken into account (the 'considering' parts) and a concise answer to the question, followed by a decision to uphold or destroy the judgment on appeal. French decisions are therefore, especially compared to English and German cases, extremely short.

(2) Because of this concise nature of the judgments, there is an important role for the annotator of the judgment. In France, judgments are reported in print, together with annotations made by renowned law professors. In these notes, the professors explain the relevance of the case and the reasoning of the court. Because of the lack of information of the court's motives, the annotations are sometimes almost just as important as the case.

(3) When a decision of the court of appeal on appeal in cassation is held to be correct, this generally ends the procedure between the parties. A higher court in the French legal system is not available, although parties may try and appeal to the European Court of Human Rights, a part of the Council of Europe, situated in Strasbourg, France.

(4) When a decision of the court of appeal is overturned on appeal in cassation, the case needs to be decided on the facts again. As the court of cassation is a supreme court of appeal dealing with questions of law only, it will refer the case back to a court of appeal, in a city other than that where the court of appeal overturned the judgment, to redecide the matter. Appeal against this decision is again possible in cassation.

Finally, as the article above shows, the court, like all French courts, decides as one. It is therefore not known how opinions in the court were divided, or whether the decision was unanimous. The judges are sworn to secrecy in respect to the deliberations in chamber. Revealing the secrets of the meetings in chamber is a criminal offence.

II.B.2 GERMAN LAW

Introductory Notes

(a) Germany is a federal state and therefore its court structure is more complicated than that of France. In Germany the organisation of the judiciary is a state competence

[12] The decision of the Court of Appeal in Montpellier after this decision by the Cour de cassation can be found under no 06/7156. Cour d'Appel de Montpellier 1st chamber, 5 March 2008.

as well as a federal competence. The basic law allows states, the *Bundesländer* or *Länder*, to have their own judiciary. At the same time, at a federal (*Bund*) level there is a federal supreme court, the Bundesgerichtshof, and a constitutional court, the Bundesverfassungsgericht. The German basic law provides the general structure of the organisation of the courts, which are further dealt with by special federal and state legislation.[13] In general, there are four levels in the court system.

(b) As a general principle of German procedural law, the names of the parties in a case are made anonymous.[14] It is therefore impossible to refer to German cases by the name of the parties. Throughout the casebook the effort is made to refer to all cases by the nickname of the case, rather than the names of the parties.

(c) The lowest courts in Germany are the local courts (Amtsgerichte). In the German court organisation only one judge hears smaller civil law disputes up to a value of €5,000.[15] Generally, the first instances and first appeal in private law matters take place at the *Land* (state) level. Against decisions taken by the local courts, appeal (*Berufung*) is open to the state court (Landesgericht).[16]

Gerichtsverfassungsgesetz **9 (DE)**

§1 The judiciary powers is exercised by independent Courts, created exclusively by law.

§12 The judiciary power is exercised by the district courts (*Amtsgerichte*), state courts (*Landgerichte*), State Courts of Appeal (*Oberlandesgerichte*) and by the Federal Supreme Court (*Bundesgerichtshof*) (the highest Court of the Federation for the exercise of the judiciary power).

§60 The state courts comprise chambers of civil law and criminal law.

§71 (1) The civil law chambers, including the chamber for commercial affairs, will deal with all private law disputes, safe those awarded to the district courts.

§72 (1) The civil law chambers, ..., are the courts of appeal and complaints for the civil law cases decided by district courts, in so far as the State Courts of Appeal do not have jurisdiction ...

Notes

(1) The private law chambers of the regional courts comprise a president and usually two other judges.[17] The courts have original jurisdiction, ie the right to hear cases on first instance, in all matters not falling within the scope of the local courts. Moreover, the state courts function as a court of appeal for decisions made by the local courts.

(2) The state courts will decide the case on appeal, which is aimed to end the dispute between the parties.[18] Against the decision taken by the state court appeal is open to a state appellate court (Oberlandesgericht).

[13] Art 92 Basic Law, and the Gerichtsverfassungsgesetz (GVG) (Law on the organisation of the courts).
[14] See paras 169 *et seq* GVG.
[15] Paras 22 and 23 GVG.
[16] Para 59 GVG.
[17] Para 59 GVG.
[18] In some situations the case can be referred back to the local court, see para 522 ZPO.

Gerichtsverfassungsgesetz **10 (DE)**

§119 (1) The State Courts of Appeal have jurisdiction in civil law matters for the hearing and descision on the appeal: …
(2) the appeal and complaints against the decisions of the State Courts.

Oberlandesgericht München 4 September 2003[19] **11 (DE)**

SECURITY-SERVITUDES

Beer purchase agreement

A right of real servitude can be created to strengthen the performance of an obligation, if there is no strong link between the obligation and the limited property right.

Facts: In 1970 the second defendant made an agreement with the legal predecessor of the claimant, a brewery, that the defendant needed permission to serve beverages from the brewery, combined with a purchase obligation to buy beverages from the claimant-brewery. The permission requirement was made part of a right of real servitude. The second defendant conveyed the land to the first defendant. The defendant seeks to get rid of the need to have permission as well as the purchase obligation. The claimant seeks to enforce the servitude.

Held: The right of real servitude was validly created and therefore the claimant can force the defendant to keep to the content of the servitude. This is possible as there is no strong link between the purchase obligation and the right of servitude, eg by way of a condition in the content of the servitude itself.

Judgment: About the facts of the case:
The claimant claims from the defendants, that run a department store, the ceasing of the serving of beverages on the land of the first defendant. He bases his claim on a right of servitude that was registered to his benefit, that burdens the parcel of land of the first defendant. The former owner, the second defendant, had acquired the parceld of land from the legal predecessor of the claimant and thereby, in section V (paragraph 3) of the contract of sale of 15 May and 10 September 1970 created the following right of real servitude: 'On the parcel of land on which a department store will be created a restaurant or pub or a serving installation of any kind respectively, may only be operated and only serve, sell, market and provide fermented and bottom-fermented beers, nourishment beers (*Nährbiere*), soft drinks or other such drinks, juices, cola-drinks, soda-drinks and mineral water, with the approval of G-Brewery, occupant of G2 as owner of … parcel number YY …' By way of a counterclaim the first defendant requests the claimant permission for the termination of the right of real servitude, because it is permanent and was made to secure an obligation to purchase beverages; and according to the rules governing it, is immoral.

The lower court (*Landesgericht*) ordered the defendant to cease the operation of the restaurant or pub or a serving installation of any kind respectively, may only be operated and only serve, sell, market and provide fermented and bottom-fermented beers, nourishment beers (*Nährbiere*), soft drinks or other such drinks, juices, cola-drinks, soda-drinks and mineral water, and dismissed the remainder of the claim as well as the counter claim. The appeal of the defendant was unsuccessful.

[19] NJW-RR 2004, 164.

On the grounds:
1. The claimant was allowed to prohibit the defendant from the dispute serving of beverages on the parcel of land of the defendant; he is, on the basis of his right of real servitude, entitled to an injunction against the defendant. The real servitude has a permissible content and was created effectively (§1018 BGB). The conveyance of the parcel of land from the second to the first defendant has not changed the effectiveness of the right of real servitude.

(a) The lawfulness of a prohibitive real servitude (Verbotsgrunddienstbarkeit) subject to authorisation was determined by the BGH in its decision of 25 March 1980 (NJW 1981, NJW Year 1981 page 343). Although a purchase-obligation (*Bezugsbindung*), ie the obligation of an owner of a parcel of land to purchase no other goods than those of a particular manufacturer on the land, cannot be the subject of a right of real servitude, because the right of free choice of suppliers of goods is not a part of the right of ownership of land. (cf BGH, NJW 1959, NJW Year 1959 page 670—Gas Station Servitude; NJW 1979, NJW Year 1979 page 2150). The present right of servitude is allowed, because the ban on an owner to operate a restaurant on this land, or to sell drinks, is something different then the forced commitment to a supplier. (cf BGH, NJW 1962, NJW Year 1962 page 486; NJW 1980, NJW Year 1980 page 179; MDR 1975, MDR Year 1975 page 399).

The same applies to §16 Nr 2 GWB and Article EWGVO198483 Article 8 EWGVO198483 Article 8 paragraph I lit c of the EEC-Regulation 1984/83. The security agreement does not contain an agreement on the exclusivity. Its contents cannot even in the light of §18 GWB be criticised (cf BGH, NJW 1988, NJW Year 1988 page 2364 = GRUR 1988, GRUR Year 1988 page 854).

(b) The lower court (LG) has rightfully left open whether the servitude is only for the purpose of a purchase-obligation or securement of the purchase of beverages. It would be even be admissible (cf BGH, GRUR 1985, GRUR Year 1985 Page 994 mw Nachw), when this would indirectly lead to a intereference with the right of free choice of suppliers. Such a 'security-servitude' is regularly void because of a violation of the good morals (*guten Sitten*), nor does it create an inpermissible circumvention of the law or a sham-transaction (*Scheingeschäft*) under §117 BGB, §117 paragraph I BGB (cf BGH, NJW 1979, NJW Year 1979 page 2150; NJW 1981, NJW Year 1981 page 343). The BGH has dealt several times with the criticism of the defendant, especially by Joost (cf ia Joost, in: MünchKomm, 2 Aufl, §1090 Rdnrn 15-20), and has maintained its line of case law (recently NJW 1988, NJW Year 1988 page 2364 = GRUR 1988, GRUR Year 1988 page 854).

(c) The right of servitude is therefore not ineffective, because it was created for an unlimited period of time. In that regard the BGH has changed its case law; the first time with the cited decision of 29 January 1988 it partially deviated from its case law, that in case of the securing of a purchase-obligation with a prohibitive-servitude a difference must be made, as in case of a security-Grundschuld, between the contractual purchase obligation, the contractual security agreement and, finally, the right of servitude. This property right is abtract and essentially independent of the underlying contractual arrangements, for which a time-limit may be necessary. It would only be different when the contractual arrangements would as a condition, become content of the property right. (§158 BGB; cf BGH, NJW 1979, NJW Year 1979 page 2149), or when there is a legal connection between the contractual and the property relations (§139 BGB; BGH, NJW 1988, NJW Year 1988 page 2364 = GRUR 1988, GRUR Year 1988 page 854).

These exceptions do not apply here; the parties have not created a temporary right of servitude and made no condition linked to the contractual purchase obligation. There is otherwise no legal connection between the contractual and the property relations. With regard to the prevailing principle of abstraction (*Abstraktionsprinzip*) in German law such a link can only be accepted in exceptional circumstances and requires the finding of concrete evidence, what have not been provided in this dispute. A practically always existing relation or summary of grounds for creation in a deed are not sufficient for this. (cf BGH, NJW 1967, NJW Year 1967 page 1128). The alleged—by the defendant—*de facto* connection to the holder of the right of servitude is inherent to the principle of abstraction, that must have been avoided by the agreement of an obligation or limitation when the right of servitude was created (BGH, NJW-RR 1992, NJW-RR Year 1992 page 593; OLG Zweibrücken, OLG-Report 2000, 499).

(d) Even when the causal relation, which underlies the creation of the servitude, would be void under §138 BGB paragraph I BGB, it would not—different from the voidance under §138 paragrah II BGB—without anything else result in the voidness of the abstract creation of the right of servitude, because it is neither established, nor argued, that the performance of the obligation would be immoral, or would, with the creation of a property right, pursue an immoral objective or underlie an immoral creation. (cf BGH, NJW 1988, NJW Year 1988 page 2364 = GRUR 1988, GRUR Year 1988 page 854; NJW-RR 1989, NJW-RR Year 1989 page 519).

(e) Paragraphs §7 bis GEWO §10 GewO are not applicable, as these provisions deal with the exchange of goods and not with the exercise of the right of ownership or other situations (cf BGH, NJW 1984, NJW Year 1984 page 924).

(f) The servitude is also not void for violation of Article 85 EEC Treaty. It does need to be decided, if the creation of servitudes are can fulfil the requirements of Article 85 paragaph I EC-Treaty at all. At the moment of creation and registration of the disputed servitude the excusive purchasing agreements were under Article 67 paragraph I of Regulation 65/67/EEC exempted from the scope of Article 85 paragraph I EEC Treaty. (cf eg Paulusch, *Höchstrichterliche Rechtsprechung zum Brauerei- und GaststättenR*, 6 Aufl, S 114ff, 118f; EuGH, Slg 1977, EUGH-SLG Year 1977 page 65 = WuW/E EWG/MUV 413—*Brauerei C*). That must apply to all servitudes. Regulation 1984/83 of 22 June 1983 (ABlEG v 30 6 1983 Nr L 173/5), that only applies to beverage purchasing obligations (cf Art 6, 15 II, 3), that does not include the creation of servitudes (see above), does not affect the existence of already effective real servitudes. (cf BGH, NJW-RR 1992, NJW-RR Year 1992 page 593). Also, there would be no appreciable effect on the trade between Member States (cf EuGH, Slg 1991 I, EUGH-SLG Year 1991 I page 935 Nr 27, in juris/CELEX—Delimitis/Henninger).

(g) The claimant can also use his right under the servitude. He is not affected by the defendant's claim of abuse of his right (*Schikaneeinwand*) (§226 BGB). The claimant does with his claim not at all seek to damage the defendant. The pressure on the defendant, either to conclude an agreement with the claimant on the distribution of beer or to establish a restaurant on the department store parcel of land, is a consequence of this effective right of servitude (cf also BGH, WM 1984, WM Year 1984 page 820—Heating distribution obligation). The defendant does not have an actual need to operate a restaurant. A department store can also function with a profit without a restaurant, as the lower court has already established.

2. The counterclaim has no effect. A claim of the first defendant for the termina-

tion of the servitude does not exist (§894 BGB). It was legally created, and the land register (*Grundbuch*) is consistent with the legal relations. The servitude is still valid, as it was not created for a limited period of time and the end of the beverage purchasing obligation will not have any effect on its existence. The first defendant therefore cannot ask the claimant for consent to the amendment of the land register under §894 BGB, because its conent is in conformity with the actual legal situation.

(a) The servitude itself does not contain a time limit or a link to the beer supply agreement, nor was an agreement for refund or cancellation made at the moment of creation of the right of servitude. As a part of a deed, there is the presumption of completeness and and correctness.

(b) The, from today's viewpoint, immorality or at least the elapsed time period of the beer purchase agreement has—as explained above—no impact on the effectiveness of the creation of the right of servitude. It can also be left open whether the objective of the servitude lies exclusively in the enforcement of the beverage purchasing obligation, or if another objective, such as the protection from competitors, played a role in the creation of the right (cf BGH, WM 1973, WM Year 1973 page 900; NJW 1977, NJW Year 1977 page 38). The property agreement (§873 BGB) would only be void as well if the immorality lies in the performance of the obligation, where also the objective of the use of the property right would be immoral or be founded on immoral grounds.

(c) The claimant is not obliged to agree to the termination of the right of real servitude. A subsequent adjustment to the timeframe of the beer supply agreement is not considered. It was not agreed, either explicit or implied, with the creation of the right of servitude that the obligor would have a claim for restitution at the end of the purchase obligation (cf BGH, NJW 1983, NJW Year 1983 page 2502; NJW 1998, NJW Year 1998 page 2286). The real servitude also pursues at least the objective to prevent undesirable competition. (BGH, NJW 1988, NJW Year 1988 page 2362). The defendants have not rebutted the claim of the claimant that the servitude was part of the purchase price and therewith was the counter-performance for the conveyance of the parcel of land. Such an objective would give rise to a personal claim for early termination of the servitude (OLG Karlsruhe, WuW 1991, WUW Year 1991 page 49). In relation to the abstractness (see above) of the servitude the arguments of a 'factual purchase obligation' cannot give rise to a claim for the defendant to terminate the servitude (cf BGH, NJW-RR 1992, NJW-RR Year 1992 page 593; OLG Zweibrücken, OLG-Report 2000, 499).

Notes

(1) The state appellate courts (Oberlandesgerichte) are divided into senates. A senate will usually comprise three judges and will either deal with private law or criminal law matters.[20] As the example shows, the decisions will deal with both issues of fact and of law and are duly motivated.

(2) Against a decision taken by the state appellate court, appeal is open to the German Federal Supreme Court (Bundersgerichtshof).

[20] Para 122 GVG.

Gerichtsverfassungsgesetz **12 (DE)**

§130 (1) Civil and criminal senates will be formed at the Federal Supreme Court and investigating justices will be appointed. The number of justices shall be determined by the Federal Minister of Justice.

§132 (1) A Grand Senate for civil law courts and a criminal Grand Senate will be created at the Federal Supreme Court. The Grand Senates together form the Joined Grand Senate. …

(3) A submission to the Grand Senate or the Joined Grand Senate can only be admissible, when the Senate, which judgment should be departed from, on the request of the currently competent Senate, declared it will retain its opinion of the law. If the Senate, whose decision should be deviated from, can no longer adjudicate the question of law due to a reallocation of tasks, then that Senate takes its place, that became competent after the reallocation of tasks. …

(4) The Senate may ask the Grand Senate to answer a question of fundamental importance, if that is necessary in its opinion for the development of the law or to ensure uniformity of decisions.

(5) The Grand Senate in private law cases comprises the presidents and a member of the civil Senates.

§133 The Federal Supreme Court is responsible for the hearing and decision on appeal of the revision (*Revision*) the leap appeal (*Sprungrevision*) the legal complaint (*Rechtsbeschwerde*) and the leap complaint (*Sprungrechtsbeschwerde*).

Zivilprozessordnung (ZPO) **13 (DE)**

§543 (1) The revision takes place, only when

1. the appeal court allowed it in its judgment or
2. the court of revision has authorised a complaint against the refusal.

(2) The revision is allowed when

1. the case is of fundamental importance or
2. the development of the law or the ensuring of a uniform line of case law of the judiciary requires a decision of the court of revision.

The court of appeal must approve the access to the court of revision.

BGH, 13 January 1994[21] **14 (DE)**

OVER-SECURITISATION AND RELEASE CLAUSES

Over-securitisation

The security transfer by standardised form-contract of a collection of objects, the content of which stays essentially the same, is in such cases effective also without a release clause.

Facts: A company transferred a collection of objects, mostly carpentry machines, for security purposes to

[21] BGHZ 124, 371.

a bank. The standardised contract was extended by the parties to include a replacement clause obliging the company to replace objects if necessary. The company came into financial difficulties and was declared insolvent. The trustee in bankruptcy, the claimant in this case, argues that the security agreement is void as there was no clause protecting the company from over-securitisation.

Held: The security transfer by standardised form-contract of a collection of objects, the content of which stays essentially the same, is in such cases effective also without a release clause. The claim is therefore rejected.

Judgment: The transfer for security purposes by form of a collection of objects must not contain a release clause for when a certain rate of coverage is reached, when the contents of the collection of objects—apart from the replacement of individual parts—is already established by agreement (limitation to BGHZ 117,374).
AGBG §9; BGB §930

IX. Senate in Civil Matters, judgment of 13 January 1994 [13.01.94]
i. SS (claimant) v St (defendant).
I. Court of Karlsruhe
II. Court of Appeal Karlsruhe

The claimant is trustee in bankruptcy of the patrimony of RSGJ Gmbh (further: debtor). Using a form of the German Savings Bank, the debtor on 3 May 1991 transferred 54 parts of her inventory for security purposes—mostly carpentry machines—to the defendant savings bank. Under number 1b ('information about the transferred objects') the standard text was stricken through and by typewriter the following text was added: 'for the calculation of the lower value limit, the calculation of the savings banks prevails.'

Number 2 ('security purposes') states: 'the objects serve as security for all existing and future, including conditional and temporary, claims of the savings bank on the ... debtor ... arising from their business relationship' Number 8 ('right of realisation of the savings bank') is mentioned: 'the entitlement also arises, when (the following is again added by typewriter) the savings bank considers it necessary based on grounds of valuation.

Under Number 9 ('changes to the security object, replacement') the debtor obliges herself to 'replace those objects that were transferred that are lost, destroyed, seized or damaged or which value decreased for any other reason'. For these replacement objects the debtor agreed with the defendant on an anticipated transfer for security purposes under agreement of an anticipated fictive transfer of possession.

Number 10 ('release of security') states the following in section 1: 'As soon as all the claims of the savings bank on the debtor are satisfied, she is obliged to release the object of security. She is already prepared to do so, in so far as she decides at her discretion, that they are no longer needed.'

Under Number 13 the terms and conditions of savings banks are taken into account.

The secured object is—at least in part—realised by way of execution. The claimant, who claims the invalidity of the security transfer, seeks to establish with her claim that the defendant cannot hold the rights it claims on the objects now that the contract is annulled. The state court and the court of appeal have rejected the claim. The appeal of the claimant had no effect

On these grounds:

I, II

The court of appeal has argued that, in case of a transfer of ownership of a collection of goods, that no longer changes in content, the provider of security should not be protected in the same way in case of a general assignment or security transfer of a stock with a changing content. There is therefore no reason to apply the developed case law to this extent, under which a security transfer is effective only when a release clause with a numerical limitation prevents a situation of over-securitisation of the creditor, the to the present situation.

These considerations remain upheld in a legal reconsideration

The applied establishment, that the defendant does not have any rights on the value of the object that was sold by way of realisation, cannot be made. Although the security contract of 3 May 1991 does not contain a release clause with a numerical coverage limit, this does not result in the ineffectiveness of the security transfer.

1. The security transfer must be tested to §9 sec 1 of the law on the general terms and conditions (AGBG).

(a) if the additions made by typewriter in numbers 1b and 8 of the contract are dependent additions to the contract (cf on this BGHZ 99,203,205 with note Clemente EWiR 1987, 593; BGHZ 102, 152, 158; BGH, Judgment of 19 June 1991—VIII ZR 244/90, ZIP 1991, 997; Wolf/Horn/Lindacher, AGBG 2nd edition §1 number 39) or have an independent character, can remain open. The security transfer as such with unchanged clauses 9 and 10 and the clause in number 2 dealing exclusively with the company of the debtor was made by way of general terms and conditions.

(b) Section 2, number 1 of §9 AGBG does not interfere, because the transfer of ownership for security purposes is not dealt with by legislation. This case concerns a so-called provisional credit security (*kautelarische Kreditsicherheit*), that finds its basis in case law and doctrine. The requirements of Section 2, number 2, only apply, when actual rights or duties, that arise from the nature of the contract, are limited in such a way, that the purpose of the contract is in danger. That is, when a provision is missing that specifies the rights of the debtor in case of over-securitisation of the creditor, not simply the case. The starting point is therefore the general provision in section 1.

2. The control of the content of the security contract does not provide reasons that lead to the ineffectiveness of the security transfer.

(a) Leading is whether the clauses of the security contract, when considered from the perspective of the specific interests of the parties lead to an unreasonable disadvantage of the contracting party (BGHZ 98,303,308). When there is a chance of such a disadvantage, this must be dealt in advance with by specific design of the general conditions (cf BGHZ 98, 303, 308; 108, 98, 105; 109, 240, 248 f; 117, 374, 379; BGH, Judgment of 19 June 1991—VIII ZR 244/90, ZIP 1991, 997, 998). When these are not there, the security contract is ineffective. A transfer for security purposes agreed on in the general terms and conditions can lead to the danger of over-securitisation. Such an over-securitisation is the case when the value of the security not only temporarily exceeds the value of the outstanding claim for which security was provided and therefore there is no carefully weighted balance between the security and the claim, that exist from the point of view of the rights of the parties to the contract. (BGH, Judgment of 19 Juni 1991—VIII ZR 244/90, aaO; Löwe/v Westphalen/Trinkner, AGBG Bd III 2nd edition Tz 34.1 number 59). In such case the security provider is disproportionally disadvantaged (BGHZ 94, 105, 112; 98, 303, 308; 108, 98, 106; 109, 240, 246; 117, 374, 379; Löwe/v Westphalen/Trinkner aaO Tz 12.2 number 6; Ulmer/Brandner/Hensen, AGBG 7th edition Anh §§9–11 number 658; Wolf/Horn/Lindacher aaO §9 number S 117; Wolf, Festschrift Baur 1981 S 147,166; ders EWiR 1988,525; Kohte ZIP 1988, 1225, 1236), because the over-securitisation prevents a the reasonable and protection-worthy interests of both contractual parties and therefore is also contrary to the parity of contract that governs private law (cf BVerfG ZIP 1993, 1774, 1780), without a valid reason to deviate from this. Generally, the existence of a release claim for the security provider prevents the danger of a disproportionate relationship between security and claim. This release-claim does not generally need to be agreen upon by contract. It follows already from the security transfer (cf BGHZ 110, 241, 246; BGH, Judgment of 30 May 1960—VII ZR 257/ 59, WM 1960, 855, 856, in so far in BGHZ 32,357 not printed; 4 October 1965—VII ZR 185/63, WM 1966, 13, 15; v 3. November 1965—Ib ZR 137/63, WM 1966, 115, 118; 10 June 1983—V ZR 252/80, WM 1983, 961, 963; v 8 December 1989—V ZR 53/88, WM 1990, 423, 424; Serick, Eigentumsvorbehalt und Sicherungsübertragung 2nd edition III §37 IV 2 = S 438; MünchKomm/Eickmann 2nd edition §1191 Rdnr 81; Erman/Räfle, BGB 9th edition §1191 number 25; Scholz/Lwowski, Das Recht der Kreditsicherung 6th edition number 230; Huber, Die Sicherungsgrundschuld 1965 S 180; Gaberdiel, Kreditsicherung durch Grundschulden 5th edition number 13.62; Wolf, Festschrift Baur S 147,164; Derleder JuS 1971,90,92). In so far as the secured objects surpass the limit of coverage their stay with the security-creditor is no longer justified by the security purpose. Then it is the will of reasonable parties (§§133, 157, 242 BGB), that the security objects should be released, ie that they are re-transferred to the security provider. When such an interpretation was not possible, §812 BGB would interfere, because the security purpose is the legal ground for the security transfer (cf Serick aaO II §18 I 1 (S 44 ff); Soergel/Mühl, BGB 12th edition §930 number 29; Palandt/Bassenge, BGB 5th edition §930 number 14; Westermann/Westermann, Sachenrecht 6th edition §44 III 2 = S 316 u 4 a S 317; Jauernig NJW 1982,268).

The consideration of this release claim does not result (but see BGHZ 98, 303, 311) in a so-called validity-preserving reduction (on a permissible content of the transfer clauses), that is prohibited under the case law of the Federal Supreme Court (cf BGHZ 84, 109, 114 ff; 92, 312, 314 f; 115, 324, 326). The release claim is not the still permissible content of the transfer clausus; it is more independent on these. Therefore the absence of a release-clause does not necessarily result in the ineffectiveness of a security transfer. When the security contract contains clauses that exclude or limited the release clause, or which make it more complicate to use the claim, these clauses are generally ineffective (§6 section 1 AGBG). The ineffectiveness of these specific clauses effects the complete contract, when it would be undue hardship to keep one of the contracting parties to the contract (§6 section 3 AGBG).

(b) Exceptionally, a release clause is necessary to compensate for effects on the security provider specifically related to the security transfer that are particularly disadvantageous. Here the clauses will facilitate the security provider to enforce his already existing release claim, when she agrees to this specifically in the contract. In particular the valuation of the security-objects will not be made single-handedly by the security creditor at his complete discretion (§315 BGB). There must rather be an agreement on a numerically specified coverage limit, under which objects no longer needed in case of over-securement are released

The Federal Supreme Court has decided this for the normal assignment of surplus of the security creditor in relation to an extended reservation of ownership (BGHZ 94, 105, 113 ff; 98, 303, 308; 120, 300), assignment by form for a lending bank (BGHZ 98, 303, 316; 109, 240, 245 ff; BGH, Judgment of 26 April 1990—VII ZR 39/89, ZIP 1990, 852, 853; v 6 December 1990–VII ZR 334/89, NJW-RR 1991,625; v 18 April 1991—IX ZR 149/90, ZIP 1991, 807, 811; v 19 June 1991—VIII ZR 244/90, ZIP 1991, 997, 998), assignment of salaries (BGHZ 108, 98, 106 ff) and the transfer by form of stock with a changing content (BGHZ 117, 374, 377 ff). For the last mentioned case the Court required that the form-contract contains a reference to the calculation of strocks, which makes it possible to determine whether the coverage limit is exceeded.

All these cases had in common that collectives of objects or rights were transferred to the security creditor. In this rights or objects were regularly included, that did not belong to the patrimony of the security provider at the time of agreement. In such a case the burden of their development cannot be overseen by the security creditor (BGHZ 109, 240, 247; OLG Hamm ZIP 1993, 1301, 1302; Bülow ZBB 1990, 29, 31; Wolf/Horn/Lindacher aaO §9 number S 102).

An over-securitisation following from that results in any case an element of gagging (*Knebelung*). When a future object is involved, it is at the disposal of new creditors not even when the current creditor (security creditor) does not need it anymore as security object. A strong limitation on the economic freedom of the security provider follows from this.

This is especially so in case of the danger that security objects unduly increase. When in case of extended reservation of ownership on the proceeds of the sale encompass the value of the labour of the security provider, and certainly incudes his profit, when 'global' outstanding debts or stock transferred in its entirety or the salary for dependent labour is assigned, this shows the 'chosen security-automatic' (Serick aaO III §37 IV 1 [S 437]), that the security creditor acquirers new objects, or at least could acquire new objects, that are more numerous or have more value then expected. The increase in security objects for the security creditor is uncontrollable. The height of the stock of securities at the end of the contractual term—especially in case of default by the debtor—can again not be estimated for the security creditor (as is the case with extended reservation of ownership, 'global' assignment, security transfer of a stock with changing content) or only in terms of the—mostly unknown to the security provider—time-factor.

The uncontrollable increase of security objects has, moreover, the effect that its value must be determined in case of default for the first time. This brings great difficulties with it. At the moment of agreement of the contract it is fully open which securities will be available to the security provider in the course of the business relationship. In case of a security-transfer of a stock with changing content it is unknown, which products were included in the security transfer and how their entry on the market and their replacement should be dealt with. In case of default of payment by the debtor all these circumstances must be clarified. When the security creditor has a power to value the objects under §315 BGB, long explanations are to be reckoned with.

(c) The complications described here do not apply to a security transfer in which the content of objects stays the same. Here, the security provider known which security objects he entrusted the security creditor with, and can completely oversee the situation.

This is also guaranteed in case a sold security object must be replaced. The security provider cannot, however, assume at the time of conclusion of the contact that the body of security objects will not change during the period the contract runs. Changes, however, only effect specific objects transfer for security purposes and normally do not include an increase in number of value. Moreover, such changer are caused by the security provider and are effected under his control. He knows when he 'causes replacement', which object he replaces and so has a complete overview at any moment during the timeframe of the contract. Furthermore, parties can decide in case of a transfer of existing security objects whether the proceeds must be used as security or that the security on this can be waived. The security provider is therefore able to keep an eye on the balance between the secured claim and the value of the security objects and the decrease of the secured claim and the release-claim that follows from that.

In case of security transfer of existing objects and in case of object that belong to the security provider it rarely happens that these increase in value. The security provider must calculate that the value stays the same, because the objects are inherently stable in value, or that the security provider, as in the current case, by way of 'addition-' or 'replacement clauses' he must provide additional or replacement objects in case of a loss of value.

An over-securitisation can also occur here when the secured credit is reduced and the secured object is stable in value or by way of a 'replacement-clause' must be kept stable in value, or when the credit is paid back earlier than foreseen, if the value of the security object decreases. Contrary to the over-securitisation in case of increase of security objects, the over-securitisation in case of a decrease of the secured claim is something that each security provider must take into account and does take into account.

Also the valuation is—even is the security transfer concerns a large number of objects—usually less difficult if the parties, at the moment of transfer, already considered whether the security objects cover the secured claim.

Admittedly, also the security transfer of a set collection of objects or a single object can give rise to a dispute on which degree of over-securitisation of the security creditor can be allowed by the security provider. However, defining a numerical coverage limit—that would have avoided this dispute almost for certain—cannot be required. In so far the dispute is not solved by the application of the general conditions. The question to the degree of over-securitisation is independent whether it was agreed upon in the general conditions or in the agreement itself. When the security creditor did not substantially extent the standard form-contract, the interests of the security provider are adequately protected as in case of an individual contract. Securities existing with the transfer, without any securities that cannot be overseen, do not require protection to the same degree as is the case in a complicated security transfer including such securities, that are acquired only later. In so far as the Senate has expressed that a situation of over-securitisation can arise already from the decrease of the secured claim, when a release clause with a numerical coverage limit is missing (BGHZ 117, 374, 379), it does not continue to hold this. The security transfer by standardised form-contract of a collection of objects, which content stays essentially the same, is in such cases effective also without a release clause.

Notes

(1) The appeal to the Federal Supreme Court is an appeal in law (*Revision*). The senate deciding the matter will comprise of five justices, the grand senates comprise nine justices.

(2) The *Revision* procedure is not automatically granted. The state court (Landesgericht) or court of appeal (appellate court (Oberlandesgericht)) must grant permission to the procedure. Against the decision to allow a *Revision*, a complaint procedure may be launched at the Federal Supreme Court. Upon decision of that court the appeal in law may be allowed.

(3) Although there is one even higher court in Germany, the Federal Constitutional Court (Bundesverfassungsgericht), the decisions of the Federal Supreme Court form the highest authority in private law matters. The rules of procedure of the Federal Constitutional Court set forth a procedure that is separated from the normal civil procedure rules.

(4) The Federal Supreme Court accepts appeals from both the state and the state appellate courts because there is generally only one step of appeal. A decision by the local court, appealed against to the state court will be open for *Revision* to the Federal Supreme Court.

II.B.3 DUTCH LAW

The system in the Netherlands is the same as in France. Local tribunals, which are part of the local courts and known as *kantongerechten*, are authorised to hear private law disputes up to €25,000.[22] Local courts are known as *rechtbanken* and have original jurisdiction on all other private law matters. An appeal, both in law and in fact, against a decision taken by the local tribunal or court is open to a *gerechtshof*.[23] These courts of appeal will deal with the appeal and will attempt to decide conclusively the matter before them. Finally, an appeal in law, termed a *cassatie*, against a decision of the court of appeal is possible to the Hoge Raad (Supreme Court).[24] The Hoge Raad will, like the French Cour de cassation, only deal with the grievances put before it and will give a short and concise decision.[25] In the Netherlands decisions are generally longer and more detailed than the decisions of the Cour de cassation in France. As in France, the Dutch Hoge Raad may refer the case back to a court of appeal to decide on the matters of fact.

II.B.4 THE LAW OF ENGLAND AND WALES

There are three types of trial court, or courts of first instance, in England and Wales, small claims courts, county courts and the High Court of Judicature. Which court the case goes to depends on the sums involved. An avenue of appeal is available to the Court of Appeal, and from there to the Supreme Court (formerly the House

[22] Art 93 Wetboek van Burgerlijke Rechtsvordering.
[23] Arts 332 *et seq* Wetboek van Burgerlijke Rechtsvordering.
[24] Arts 398 *et seq* Wetboek van Burgerlijke Rechtsvordering.
[25] Arts 419 *et seq* Wetboek van Burgerlijke Rechtsvordering.

of Lords). It should be noted that there is no right of appeal. Leave must be given either by the court appealed from or the court appealed to. Unlike a jurisdiction such as Germany's, therefore, only a comparatively small number of cases go to appeal.

Issues of fact are found by the court of first instance, with appeals to the higher courts being solely on matters of law. Unlike Germany and Austria, the cases are not anonymous and are referred to by practitioners, judges, and academics by the names of the parties.

II.B.5 THE ROLE OF INTERNATIONAL COURTS

In addition to these national procedures, there are two international legal orders with a direct effect on substantive national law: the Council of Europe and the European Union. With respect to the Council of Europe, the European Convention on Human Rights (ECHR) is especially important. The European Court of Human Rights in Strasbourg can be appealed to by individuals from any Contracting State. The European Court of Justice (ECJ) is the highest court of the European Union (there is also the Court of First Instance) and is located in Luxembourg.

European Convention on Human Rights **15 (ECHR)**

Article 1 The High Contracting Parties shall secure to everyone within their jurisdiction the rights and freedoms defined in Section I of this Convention.

Article 19 To ensure the observance of the engagements undertaken by the High Contracting Parties in the Convention and the Protocols thereto, there shall be set up a European Court of Human Rights, hereinafter referred to as 'the Court'. It shall function on a permanent basis.

Article 32 1 The jurisdiction of the Court shall extend to all matters concerning the interpretation and application of the Convention and the protocols thereto which are referred to it as provided in Articles 33, 34 and 47.

Article 34 The Court may receive applications from any person, non-governmental organisation or group of individuals claiming to be the victim of a violation by one of the High Contracting Parties of the rights set forth in the Convention or the protocols thereto. The High Contracting Parties undertake not to hinder in any way the effective exercise of this right.

Article 35 1 The Court may only deal with the matter after all domestic remedies have been exhausted, according to the generally recognised rules of international law, and within a period of six months from the date on which the final decision was taken.

Treaty on the functioning of the European Union **16 (EU)**

Article 267 The Court of Justice of the European Union shall have jurisdiction to give preliminary rulings concerning:

(a) the interpretation of the Treaties;

(b) the validity and interpretation of acts of the institutions, bodies, offices or agencies of the Union;

Where such a question is raised before any court or tribunal of a Member State, that court or tribunal may, if it considers that a decision on the question is necessary to enable it to give judgment, request the Court to give a ruling thereon.

Where any such question is raised in a case pending before a court or tribunal of a Member State against whose decisions there is no judicial remedy under national law, that court or tribunal shall bring the matter before the Court.

If such a question is raised in a case pending before a court or tribunal of a Member State with regard to a person in custody, the Court of Justice of the European Union shall act with the minimum of delay.

Notes

(1) The effects of the jurisdiction of these two international courts on national law are very far reaching. After all national remedies have been exhausted, and when a case falls within the rights guaranteed by the European Convention on Human Rights, appeal remains open to the Court of Human Rights in Strasbourg. Decisions by that court are decisions on the facts and must be accepted in national law.

(2) The effect of the case law of the ECJ under Article 267 TFEU is even more far reaching. The article refers to the preliminary question procedure. Any matter which concerns the interpretation of the TEU or TFEU treaty as well as any matter of EU law can be posed to the ECJ. Exclusive interpretation power in these matters therefore belongs to the ECJ. The preliminary questions are asked by the national court dealing with the case, which will have to stay proceedings until an answer from the ECJ is received. The ECJ will therefore not decide on the facts of the case, but merely on an aspect of the case dealing with EU law. The national court will decide the case on the facts, or on the law when the referring court is a supreme court on an appeal in law, after the decision of the ECJ.

(3) Both of these jurisdictions are also relevant to property law. The first protocol to the European Convention on Human Rights guarantees the right of ownership and protects individuals from expropriation. The EU Treaty creates an internal market in which there is free movement of goods, persons, services and capital. Divergences of national property law can create problems with each of these freedoms. These issues will be dealt with further in Chapter 10.

II.C PROPERTY LAW

In the most general terms, the law of property is the law dealing with things. These things may either be tangible (corporeal) or intangible (incorporeal). This casebook will describe the basic principles and rules of the property law systems of France, Germany, the Netherlands and England and Wales.[26] In order to get started, some background knowledge on these legal systems is necessary.

[26] The casebook will also contain aspects of other European and international legal systems, if these are of interest to the discussion. This includes Austrian, Belgium, Scots, American and European Union law.

II.C.1 FRANCE

In French law, property law is part of the larger concept of patrimonial law. Patrimonial law means that it is the law dealing with patrimony, the complete body of assets and debts a person has. Patrimonial law is dealt with in three books of the French Civil Code (Code civil (Cciv)): (1) the law of obligations, (2) the law of property and (3) intellectual property law. The latter was introduced in the second half of the twentieth century because of economic developments. The distinction between the first two categories determines the structure of the French Civil Code.

The French Civil Code came into force in 1804 and contains five books.[27] Of the most interest to this casebook are book 2 titled 'Of Things and of the Various Modifications of Ownership', book 3 'Of the Various Ways in which Ownership is Acquired', and book 4 titled 'Of Securities'.

The central concept in the French Civil Code is the concept of ownership. The first book, titled 'Of Persons' is perceived as the answer to the question about who can be entitled to ownership, the third book is seen as an amalgam of different subject matters (successions, gift and wills, law of obligations, liability, matrimonial property law, specific contracts, and prescription). Therefore, the definition of ownership in Art 544 Cciv is the key provision in the Code: 'Ownership is the right to enjoy and dispose of objects in the most complete manner, provided they are not used in a way prohibited by statutes or regulations.'

The rules on property law in the Civil Code of 1804 are especially focused on land, which was the only object of value in the agricultural society of the beginning of the nineteenth century. Movable objects, or just movables, were, from an economic point of view, considered of no value. Social and economic developments have reoriented society towards the economic value of movables, but for a very long time the French Civil Code has remained the same. Only in recent years have projects been started to modernise the law of persons and obligations. Even more recently, the French Civil Code was changed by adding a book on security rights, both personal and property security rights, as well as chapters on a trust-like instrument named the *fiducie*.[28] However, changes to property law have not been made, although in 2009 a proposal was made to update some aspects of the law of property. As a consequence, the current statutory provisions are criticised because they do not provide answers to the current legal problems with regard to property law.

The property law rules remain highly determined by historical circumstances prevailing at the beginning of the nineteenth century, and more specifically by the reaction against the social, political, economic and legal structures of the *ancien régime*, the period before the French Revolution. The *ancien régime* was built on perpetual charges on land, which have been abolished by the introduction of the French Civil Code, with the exception of servitudes. The mixture of property law and the law of obligations was the legal basis for the social, economic and political structure of the feudal regime. The distinction between property law and the law of

[27] Originally, there were only three books. The books dealing with security rights (book 4) and special provisions for Mayotte (book 5) have been added later.

[28] The security rights will be dealt with in Chapter 5. Fiducie is dealt with in Chapter 6.

obligations was therefore one of the basic principles in the introduction of the Civil Code. These foundations of the Civil Code have remained unchanged since then.

The French Civil Code mentions the property rights which were recognised in 1804, as Article 543 Cciv provides that 'on an object one may have a right of ownership, a mere right of enjoyment or only a right of servitude'. It is, however, certain that, nowadays, this enumeration is not sufficiently accurate to be exhaustive. Setting apart the right of *emphyteusis* and superficies (which were reintroduced afterwards), the Civil Code does not mention accessory property rights (property security rights) and co-ownership.[29]

Other limited property rights than those mentioned in the Civil Code were not recognised, as the French legislature feared that they would cause too heavy a burden on the right of ownership, and would entail the risk of a restoration of feudal concepts. This can be illustrated by the developments with regard to the right of *emphyteusis*, sometimes also known as the right of long-lease. This right was recognised under Roman law and the feudal regime, but no longer under the Civil Code. However, case law has continued to recognise the proprietary nature of the existence.[30] The legislature has reintroduced the property right in the Act of 25 June 1902, which was inserted in Article 937 and further of the Rural Code. In revising the Rural Code, these provisions have been renumbered as Article L451-1 and further, but the content has not been subject to amendments. Hence, even though the legislature in 1804 tried to protect the right of ownership from bearing too heavy a burden, some of these burdens were reintroduced after a period of time.[31]

Very few amendments have been introduced in the second book of the French Civil Code. A major amendment is situated in the field of co-ownership. The original Civil Code only dealt with co-ownership of apartments in one provision (Article 664 Cciv). This provision was amended in 1938 (Act of 28 June 1938), which was replaced to a large extent by the Act of 10 July 1965 and the Decree of 17 March 1967. The current regulation of co-ownership dates from the Act of 31 December 1976, which has been introduced in Article 815 and further of the Civil Code.

A major amendment within the field of property security rights has been introduced much more recently. The Ordonnance of 23 March 2006 introduced a completely new system of the security rights, including property security rights. This result was achieved by introducing a fourth book in the French Civil Code, entitled 'Of Security Rights', which contained two divisions: (1) personal security rights and (2) property security rights. As far as the second category is concerned, the statutory reform includes both property security rights on movables (new Articles 2329 and further) and real security rights on immovables (new Articles 2373 and further).[32]

Finally, in 2008 the Association Henri Capitant des amis de la culture juridique Française, launched an *avant-projet* to reform book 2 of the Civil Code. Some of

[29] These rights will be dealt with in Chapter 3.

[30] Cass 24 August 1857, DP 1857, I, 326.

[31] The issue of the closed system of property rights, also known as the *numerus clausus* of property rights, will be returned to in Chapters 1 and 3.

[32] These rights will be dealt with in Chapter 5.

these proposals will be dealt with in the casebook, but the proposals have not been taken on in the legislative process yet.

II.C.2 GERMANY

The German Civil Code, the Bürgerliches Gesetzbuch (BGB), dates from 1 January 1900. After that period, no significant changes have been made to the law of property. In 2002, the law of obligations was thoroughly reformed to bring the rules in line with modern ideas on especially contract law as well as with various international developments.

Even stricter than the French Civil Code, the BGB operates on a sharp distinction between the law of obligations and the law of property. This distinction—which, like in French law, should be seen as a rejection of the law of the *ancien régime*—is so important in Germany that is known as the principle of separation or *Trennungsprinzip*.

German law is, like French law, heavily based on Roman law. The property rights that are recognised are therefore largely a repetition of the Roman catalogue of property rights. They include ownership as the most important right and usufruct and servitudes, pledge and hypothec as the main limited property rights.[33] However, compared to French law, there are also additional property rights recognised such as the right of *Grundschuld*, a special property security right.[34] Moreover, German law has, from the beginning of the introduction of the Civil Code, made use of a trust-like instrument known as *Treuhand*.[35]

German property law is a very abstract and theoretical system that is not always in line with reality. Therefore, sometimes the theory of property law is severely criticised and the practice of property law treats the rules of property law very creatively. Increasingly, the law of contract is used to achieve effects that cannot be achieved by property law alone.[36] As a result, the distinction between the law of contract and the law of property, the *Trennungsprinzip*, is sometimes difficult to maintain.[37]

Because of their common basis in Roman law, the content of German property law is very similar to the content of French law. There is a primary property right in the form of the right of ownership. Unlike French law, paragraph 903 of the German Civil Code restricts ownership to corporeal objects only. As a result of that, ownership of claims is impossible, creating complicated theoretical problems when dealing with claims. Especially in the area of property security rights (see Chapter 5), the transfer of claims for security purposes, *fiducia cum creditore*, is the principal form of security in German law.

The German BGB strictly adheres to the *numerus clausus* of property rights. German property law scholars generally hold that only property rights dealt with by

[33] These rights will be dealt with in Chapters 3 and 5.

[34] The right of Grundschuld is dealt with more elaborately in Chapter 5.

[35] *Treuhand* will be dealt with in Chapter 6.

[36] See, for an example of this, the security-servitudes in German law in Chapter 3.

[37] See, on this, JT Fuller, *Eigenständiges Sachenrecht?* Jus Privatum. Beitrage zum Privatrecht, 104 (Tubingen, Mohr Siebeck, 2006) 8 *et seq*.

the Civil Code can be property rights. At the same time, the courts are developing alternative property rights, leading to fierce debates as to who has the authority to recognise new property rights. As mentioned above, the list of property rights in German law is longer then the French list and there are also management devices in the form of a *Treuhand*.

The book on property law in the German Civil Code has not been subject to major reform since the introduction of the Code in 1900. There is, however, an increasing debate on the role of the very strict and heavily regulated area of property law and the connection to legal practice. There is an important role for property law doctrine that seeks to bridge the gap that exists between theory and practice.

II.C.3 THE NETHERLANDS

The law of the Netherlands occupies an intermediate position between French and German law. In 1838 the Netherlands received its own civil code, heavily modelled after the French Code civil, but with some Dutch additions and changes. This Civil Code, which is no longer in force, provided the Netherlands with a strong French tradition. It used a concept of ownership that extended to both corporeal and incorporeal objects, and copied the property rights available in the French Civil Code, though it continued to accept some additional property relations dating from the *ancien régime*.

After the Second World War Professor EM Meijers from the University of Leiden received royal assent to draft a new civil code for the Netherlands. Meijers died soon after he presented his first draft to the Dutch parliament. His work was taken over by a commission of three, which managed to continue the work and produce the first draft for Book 5 dealing with property law, but not to finish it. The work of the Commission was taken over by the government assisted by special commissioners. A lengthy procedure and debate followed so that only on 1 January 1992 did the parts on the law of obligations and property (*vermogensrecht*, patrimonial law) of the New Dutch Civil Code enter into force.

Meijers and the members of the commission, who were very much influenced by him, strongly followed the German tradition. They therefore proposed a property law that turned away from the French tradition towards German traditions, but sought more flexibility than the German Civil Code offered. The German influence is very visible in the Dutch Civil Code in the restriction of ownership to corporeal objects, and the explicit statements in the explanatory memoranda that only the legislature is entitled to create new property rights. At the same time, however, the New Dutch Civil Code also contains innovations that deviate from the French and German tradition. This includes the introduction of a non-possessory right of pledge, combined with a prohibition to use the right of ownership for security purposes.

In Dutch law there is therefore also a strict *numerus clausus* of property rights, although as in French and German law, legal practice is very creative in the way in which property law is used.

Finally, because the Dutch Civil Code only entered into force in 1992, it has not yet seen any substantial reform. There is, since 2011, a pending proposal to change the prohibition of the transfer of ownership for security purposes (*fiducia cum creditore*), which is combined with a prohibition of the transfer for management purposes (*fiducia cum amico*), and to introduce a trust-like instrument. Moreover, under pressure from European Union law some modifications in the use of this prohibition have already been made.

II.C.4 ENGLAND AND WALES

England and Wales have no civil codes, and thus no code of property law. Instead, the law of property is an amalgam of statutory and judge-made rules. The main division in English law is between real property and personal property. At the risk of some simplification, real property, at least nowadays, is the property law relating to land, while personal property is the property law relating to things other than land. It is a matter of some debate whether the word 'things' extends to claims, though textbooks on personal property are content to assume that it does. The topic of intellectual property is generally considered as *sui generis*, not part of either real or personal property.

Real property in England and Wales has a feudal structure, though the content of the law bears little trace today of that system, as it has been gradually ripped out by statute over the centuries. The system is, however, essentially one that is judge-made, though the statutory interventions, especially those made in 1925, make this subject incomprehensible without a detailed knowledge of the appropriate legislation. This is especially so with regard to the registration system for land introduced in 1925, and overhauled in 2002,

Personal property, by contrast, at least that relating to physical things, has had little statutory intervention, and thc vast majority of the law is to be gleaned from the cases. Nor does it have a feudal basis, chattels never being subject to that system.

As will be seen, the common law is similar to the civil law in having a *numerus clausus*, where that phrase means a closed list of property rights. Where it fundamentally differs, however, is in having nothing as ambitious as a concept of ownership, preferring instead to deal in rights to possession. Where claims are concerned, a common lawyer would likewise eschew the language of ownership and speak only of 'having' or 'holding' a claim.

The final point of difference is the trust. The trust, a product of the jurisdiction called 'equity', is a device by which rights, either personal or proprietary, can be held for the benefit of other persons or certain purposes. Trusts involve no division of rights, but the subjection of the right-holder to certain duties in the way that right is exercised. Much ink has been spilt on the question whether the rights of the beneficiary of a trust are *in rem* or *in personam*. The truth is that they do not fall neatly into either category and are best thought of as in a class of their own.

CHAPTER ONE
GENERAL ISSUES: SETTING THE SCENE

*Sjef van Erp**

This chapter deals with the first of the six leading essential questions: what is property law? In doing so, it deals with several complicated matters. When we study the law of property, especially from a comparative perspective, a considerable divergence between legal systems can be found. However, there are also many similarities. This chapter seeks to explain what is property law and to raise awareness of the most important pitfalls when comparing property law systems, such as the use of English terminology to describe non-English legal systems. Finally, the chapter provides a framework for analysis of property law systems by introducing the fundamental principles of *numerus clausus* and transparency, as well as some ground rules that are present in all property law systems.

I. INTRODUCTORY REMARKS

Property law is the law that deals with entitlements to property. Property in this sense means an object such as a car or a table, but also land and buildings such as houses constructed on that land. Moreover, it also concerns intangible or incorporeal 'objects' such as intellectual property and rights to performance by another party arising from a contract (claims). In general, there is always demand for these objects, creating what economists refer to as scarcity of resources. Because of this scarcity, there are rules on the entitlement to these objects individuals may hold and on how these entitlements are created, transferred and destroyed.

Moreover, these entitlements, or better, rights to objects, are different from other

* Section III on the principle of *numerus clausus* was written together with Bram Akkermans.

rights as they are created in respect to an object and not vis-à-vis specific other persons. Property rights, to put it differently, have effect against third parties by their nature. Personal rights, which are rights arising from a contract, and even though they also concern an object (the 'performance' of that contract), are generally only binding between two or more specific parties. This is something that is shared universally between systems of property law.

However, the answer to the question as to what precisely is included in property law differs from country to country, or better from legal system to legal system. Property lawyers hold that because of their different historical orgins and development, legal systems have chosen different routes and have ended up with different results. The outcome is that, unlike other areas of private law, such as contract law, there are more pronounced differences between systems of property law.

This casebook focuses on German, French, Dutch and English law. We will soon discover that even though many similarities exist between these four systems, there are also many differences. Occasionally we will take an excursion into other legal systems, such as Austrian, Belgian, Scots and US law, which will complicate the picture even further.

Property lawyers traditionally use an historical approach to illustrate how a certain system of property law came about and how it has developed over time. This casebook certainly adheres to this method of explanation. Increasingly, however, there are also other areas, such as law and economics, that seek to offer explanations of what constitutes property law and how differences between property law systems have come about.[1]

This chapter will first introduce the question of what is property law (I.A), but will also offer insights into the complications created by using English terminology (I.B) and by using the concept of a property right (I.C). Furthermore, this chapter will deal with the importance of understanding the historical development of property law, especially in the light of modern developments (II).

Most important of all, this chapter will offer a framework for analysis of property law systems that can be used to describe and explain all the systems of property law dealt with in this casebook.[2] This framework consists of two fundamental principles of property law. The principle of *numerus clausus* which limits the number and content of property rights that are available in a property law system (III), and the principle of transparency, which ensures that third parties can determine which person(s) hold a property right and as to which object(s) a property right is held (IV). Besides these fundamental principles (III and IV), the framework contains a

[1] See eg K Ayotte and HE Smith, *Research Handbook on the Economics of Property Law* (Cheltenham and Northampton, Edward Elgar, 2011).

[2] On this framework analysis and its general application, see JHM van Erp, *European and National Property Law: Osmosis or Growing Antagonism?, Sixth Walter van Gerven Lecture* (Groningen, Europa Law Publishing, 2006); JHM van Erp, 'From "Classical" to Modern European Property Law', in *Essays in Honour of Konstantinos D Kerameus/Festschrift für Konstantinos D. Kerameus*, vol I (Athens/Brussels, Ant A Sakkoulas/Bruylant, 2009) 1517–33. On this approach and its relevance see also B Akkermans, 'The European Union Development of European Property Law', in C Godt (ed), *Hanse Law School in Perspective—Legal Teaching and Cross Border Research after Lisbon* (The Hague, Kluwer, 2012).

set of four ground rules, which are also present in all property law systems dealt with. These are discussed in the final section of this chapter (V).

I.A WHAT IS 'PROPERTY' LAW?

In this casebook property law is used in a very wide sense: it concerns rights that a person has against a considerable group of other persons concerning an object. Property law includes land law, the law of personal property, and the law relating to claims, trust law and the law on security rights. All of these terms, as well as their corresponding legal areas, will be more fully explained in the following chapters of this casebook.

In English law the term 'property law' still frequently only refers to land law. In continental European legal systems, property law sometimes covers land law as well as personal property law, but not the law relating to claims, whereas in some civil law systems it does cover claims. In English law, property and trust are intimately connected, but as the continental legal systems do not know the so-called 'common law trust', trust law in the English legal sense of the word is unknown in the civil law. In general, the law on security rights is everywhere considered to be a part of property law.

Traditionally, land has always been an object of property law, later also movables and sometimes claims. However, 'new' forms of property are also being discussed: entitlements to social security benefits, the right to an unpolluted environment, the right to 'roam' in forests and fields, public law licenses (eg emission rights) and 'virtual' property (eg e-mail accounts, objects in virtual worlds).

I.A.1 CLASSIC APPROACHES

KH Schwab and H Prütting, Property Law—Physical Things as Objects of Property Law[3] **1.1 (DE)**

1. The concept of an object is the essential foundation of property law, which is defined in §90 as a physical thing. With this the law considers the concept of a thing to be an overarching notion which encompasses the (corporeal) objects and (incorporeal) rights. Finally, in addition to individual things sometimes also unities of objects (*Sachgesamtheiten*) or even an entire patrimony can be subject to legal regulations ... All of these notions are covered by the overarching concept of 'legal subject' (*Rechtssubjekt*). The concept of an object is therefore primarily determined by its 'physicality' feature. Here, it is not the physical state (solid, liquid, gas) that is important. In the negative sense, the concept of an object is limited in the meaning that everything that is an individual or his right is not an object. There are some boundary issues (after natural consideration) regarding incorporeal objects. For instance, electric energy is not considered an object, ... On the other hand it is possible for a computer program (that is, the software) to be an object, if it is saved on a data carrier. ...

[3] KH Schwab and H Prütting, *Sachenrecht*, 34th new edn (München, CH Beck, 2010) 1 *et seq*.

3. Animals were always treated as objects in the German Civil Code (BGB). Since 1.9.1990 they have been withdrawn from the concept of objects in property law, but remain legal objects (*Rechtsobjekte*), ie they cannot be bearers of rights and obligations (as can legal subjects). Ultimately they are treated in accordance with the rules on moveables (§90a).
4. The *human body* of a living person is not an object. By contrast, parts of the human body that are separated from a living body (for example cut off hair, donated blood, transplanted organs) are objects. Once separated they are owned, analogous to §953, by the 'donor'. A controversial question is to what extent a *human corpse* can be considered an object. One will have to answer in the affirmative. The (continuing) deceased's right to individuality (*Persönlichkeitsrecht)* and the power of decision of the next of kin (which does not have to coincide with that of the heirs) lead, however, to the fact that a human corpse is not marketable, and cannot be sold nor transferred. ...
5. Objects for public use, such as public roads, streets or the beach are commonly owned by public sector bodies. They can, however, also be privately owned as well as transferred and burdened by private law means. Private ownership of these objects can however be superimposed and limited by public law competence.

Ch Atias, Private Law. Property Law—Patrimony[4] **1.2 (FR)**

The first feature of the composition of a patrimony is that it is limited to economic values. As diverse as these values might be, all patrimonial components share the possibility of being converted into money. The elements belonging to a patrimony, especially its active side display complementary characteristics, both individually and cumulatively. They have a pecuniary value. They can be taken from their owner in order to be transferred *inter vivos*, which means they can be sold or donated. Consequently, they can be seized by the unpaid creditor who will recover the debt by the sale of the object. Finally, upon the death of the owner, they pass to his heirs: they are transmissible *mortis causa*. In the analysis of patrimony, one must forget any personal implications. All the rights which cannot be converted into money thus escape the patrimony, and the same is true for all values which are too intimately linked to the person to be able to participate in the economic traffic. Political rights of the citizen, as well as personal rights (honor, name, affection ...), are extra-patrimonial. The patrimonial and extra-patrimonial categories seem to be divided in opposition. In reality, intermediary categories are far from being excluded: there are 'possible degrees of patrimony'. For instance, physical integrity tends to become a patrimonial value when its violation can be compensated or repaired by the allocation of a sum of money. ...

The second feature of the composition of the patrimony is that it is as general as possible. A patrimony combines all rights and all obligations of any one person. A patrimony cannot be defined and its content cannot be identified without reference to its owner. On the active side, one must add, without any exclusion, all rights, whatever their nature or purpose. The generality of the existing assets of a person are included in his patrimony. Because the patrimony is the pecuniary representation of a person, and not of his fortune upon a given moment, the active part of the

[4] C Atias, *Droit Civil. Les biens*, 11th edn (Paris, Lexis Nexis, 2011) 14 *et seq.*

patrimony is extended to all future assets. That which will not belong to the owner until a later time, already has a certain presence in his patrimony. This composition is never legally non-existent: better yet, it cannot be accurately evaluated.
From the perspective of its passive side, the patrimony presents the same general feature: it comprises all the debs of its owner. All of the latter must be placed next to his assets. Debts are patrimonial, whatever their object may be, some can consist of money, but there are also obligations to procuring a thing or a service. The debt appears in the patrimony of the debtor when it has arisen: it is sufficient, for instance, that the seller and the buyer agree over the thing and the price. In that moment, the payment obligation is created and it gives rights to the creditor. It is present in the patrimony of the buyer, even if it is not yet due, because a delay has been granted for payment (debt to be performed after a specific time period), even if it is not yet certain, because the existence of the contract is conditioned by the occurrence of an event (conditional debt), and even if it is not yet liquid, which is to say not yet valued or convertible.

Ch Atias, Private Law. Property Law—Movables, Going Concern as Object of Property Law[5] **1.3 (FR)**

Tangible movable things generally have a legal regime that is less precise and developed than that of immovable things. The free circulation of movable things has only been maintained because of legislative and doctrinal discretion. These goods are only seized by law in the moment when they become objects of contracts (sale, rent, ...) or more generally of transfer; it is still the common contractual law that applies. Consumer protection policy has only led to the creation of several special rules. Above all, the principles governing tangible movable goods can seem inconsistent by any analysis. There are no common aspects as to the legal provisions governing instruments for work, household property, vehicles, weapons, boats and ships, aircraft, medicines. The difficulties left to be resolved share a certain connection. This is user safety, the security of the purchasers of rights over these goods, the fight against theft, fiscal controls. ...

The *fonds de commerce* can be defined as the intangible movable thing created by the reunion of the necessary elements of attraction and conservation of a commercial clientele in the patrimony of the commercial owner. This context recognizes in *fonds de commerce* a type of existence which is similar to that granted to all things governed by law. For this reason, authors generally blame the French legistator: for a long, very long time, it has demonstrated blindness or unrealism, since the first laws relating to the *fonds* date from the XXth century, although the *fonds* existed well before.

C Lebon, The Proprietary Nature of Claims[6] **1.4 (BE)**

In classical doctrinal legal thinking personal rights are given (a usually undifferentiated) relative character, whereas property rights are considered to be of an absolute nature. The distinction between property rights and personal rights is, therefore, that

[5] *Ibid*, 419.
[6] C Lebon, *Het goederenrechtelijk statuut van schuldvorderingen*, Diss (Leuven, 2008) 34–35.

personal rights do not bind every other person (they are not effective *erga omnes*). A personal right only has effect between parties (*inter partes*): it concerns a duty ('obligation') for one or more specific debtors vis-à-vis one or more creditors and only from those specific debtors performance of that duty can be demanded. A third person cannot be held bound to satisfy a debtor's debt.

A second difference regarding the various legal consequences of, on the one hand, property rights and, on the other hand, personal rights, concerns the right to follow and the right of preference. These rights are, so it is argued by the proponents of classical legal thinking, only connected with property rights. A property right rests immediately and direct on the physical thing which is its object and remains resting on that thing, wherever it is located and in whose hands it may have passed from a substantive law viewpoint. The person entitled to a property right has a right to follow the object of his right and, generally speaking, derives from this right the possibility to demand the thing by a property *actio* from who holds the thing in his hands. A property right is also endowed with a right of preference. The right of preference implies that a person entitled to a property right that rests on a specific thing has priority over all property rights of a later date on that same thing (*prior tempore, potior iure*) and over all creditors whose claims are not secured by a property security right. The right of preference is important when the patrimony of the debtor is insufficient to pay all debts.

FH Lawson and B Rudden, Law of Property[7] **1.5 (E&W)**

But all of us all the time take peacefully for granted the business of getting things and then keeping and utilizing them. A person may acquire something by making it, but is more likely to get it from something else and to have to pay for it. Buyers want to be sure that they get what they are paying for, but are normally far more concerned with quality and suitability than with worrying whether it was the seller's to sell. They are able to take this for granted in most cases because the law is working, virtually unnoticed, to protect them.

The buyer may prefer to pay for the goods or the house by instalments, and in such cases no one would provide credit without security. By means of such devices as mortgage and hire purchase, the law enables the creditor to obtain this security. It thus reduces the risk of giving credit and tends to improve the terms offered, typically by increasing the amount of a loan, by extending the period for which it is made, or by lowering the interest rate. Having got the thing, its owner may keep and use it, or keep and forget about it, or may want to sell it or give it away. The thing may have been acquired for its own sake, like a shirt or a dwelling, or may be merely an investment such as a savings certificate or block of shares. Furthermore—especially if the thing is of a fairly permanent nature like a house or shares—the owner may want to distribute it among others either commercially by charging a rent or by way of gift or bequest to family and friends.

All these, and similar, transactions are entirely normal, peaceful, and useful. The law of property underlies them. Some of its provisions are 'default' rules, which operate unless we expressly design our own scheme, but there are a number of important mandatory rules whose application we cannot avoid—many of them

[7] FH Lawson and B Rudden, *Law of Property*, 3rd edn (Oxford, Clarendon Press, 2002) 3–4.

concern the use of transfer of land, especially by way of lease. In general, however, the function of the law relating to private property is to provide us with a bag of tools with which to achieve our wishes.

First of all, it ways what counts as property, that is to say what can be the object of its powers and protections. We cannot, for instance, effectively sell, lease, or bequeath our reputation, or our surname, or our job: these may be ours, and may be valuable, but they do not count as property so as to form the subject matter of dispositions. The law of property also determines the types of interest which will be treated as proprietary, that is as being more than merely personal, familial, or contractual, and it spells out the consequences of a finding that a particular interest is proprietary. It says what we can do with these interests—anything we like, if we like; and it says what others can do with them—nothing, unless we let them. So in conjunction with other branches of law—especially the law of obligations—property law protects the rights of the holders of these interests—owners, co-owners, lessees, charge-holders, trustees, and so on. And, again along with other branches of law, it deals with the transfer of property and the repackaging of proprietary interests whether *inter vivos* or on death. Here we find the formalities needed for certain transactions, and the methods used for altering and amalgamating the various components of, and interests in, property, and for creating complex, if fairly standard, structures of control and enjoyment (leases, co-ownership, security interests, trusts, and so on) …

I.A.2 MODERN APPROACHES

Introductory Note

The following three excerpts are meant to be a starting point for a first reflection on the concept of property law today.

Ch Reich, The New Property—Government Largess, Wealth and Property[8] **1.6 (US)**

The highly organized, scientifically planned society of the future, governed for the good of its inhabitants, promises the best life that men have ever known. In place of the misery and injustice of the past there can be prosperity, leisure, knowledge, and rich opportunity open to all. In the rush of accomplishment, however, not all values receive equal attention; some are temporarily forgotten while others are pushed ahead. We have made provision for nearly everything, but we have made no adequate provision for individual man.

This article is an attempt to offer perspective on the transformation of society as it bears on the economic basis of individualism. The effort has been to show relationships; to bring together drivers' licenses, unemployment insurance, membership in the bar, permits for using school auditoriums, and second class mail privileges, in order to see what we are becoming. Government largess is only one small corner of a far vaster problem. There are many other new forms of wealth: franchises in private businesses, equities in corporations, the right to receive privately furnished utilities and services, status in private organizations. These too may need added safeguards

[8] Ch Reich, 'The new property' [1964] *Yale Law Journal* 733, 787–88.

in the future. Similarly, there are many sources of expanded governmental power aside from largess. By themselves, proposals concerning government largess would be far from accomplishing any fundamental reforms. But, somehow, we must begin. At the very least, it is time to reconsider the theories under which new forms of wealth are regulated, and by which governmental power over them is measured. It is time to recognize that 'the public interest' is all too often a reassuring platitude that covers up sharp clashes of conflicting values, and hides fundamental choices. It is time to see that the 'privilege' or 'gratuity' concept, as applied to wealth dispensed by government, is not much different from the absolute right of ownership that private capital once invoked to justify arbitrary power over employees and the public. Above all, the time has come for us to remember what the framers of the Constitution knew so well-that 'a power over a man's subsistence amounts to a power over his will.' We cannot safely entrust our livelihoods and our rights to the discretion of authorities, examiners, boards of control, character committees, regents, or license commissioners. We cannot permit any official or agency to pretend to sole knowledge of the public good. We cannot put the independence of any man-least of all our Barskys and our Anastaplos wholly in the power of other men. If the individual is to survive in a collective society, he must have protection against its ruthless pressures. There must be sanctuaries or enclaves where no majority can reach. To shelter the solitary human spirit does not merely make possible the fulfilment of individuals; it also gives society the power to change, to grow, and to regenerate, and hence to endure. These were the objects which property sought to achieve, and can no longer achieve. The challenge of the future will be to construct, for the society that is coming, institutions and laws to carry on this work. Just as the Homestead Act was a deliberate effort to foster individual values at an earlier time, so we must try to build an economic basis for liberty today—a Homestead Act for rootless twentieth century man. We must create a new property.

Emission Trading Directive (2003/87/EC)[9] 1.7 (EU)

Article 1 Subject matter

This Directive establishes a scheme for greenhouse gas emission allowance trading within the Community (hereinafter referred to as the 'Community scheme') in order to promote reductions of greenhouse gas emissions in a cost-effective and economically efficient manner.

Article 2 Scope

(1) This Directive shall apply to emissions from the activities listed in Annex I and greenhouse gases listed in Annex II.

(2) This Directive shall apply without prejudice to any requirements pursuant to Directive 96/61/EC.

Article 3 Definitions

For the purposes of this Directive the following definitions shall apply:

(a) 'allowance' means an allowance to emit one tonne of carbon dioxide equivalent during a specified period, which shall be valid only for the purposes of meeting

[9] Directive 2003/87/EC of the European Parliament and of the Council of 13 October 2003 establishing a scheme for greenhouse gas emission allowance trading within the Community and amending Council Directive 96/61, OJ L275/32.

the requirements of this Directive and shall be transferable in accordance with the provisions of this Directive ...

Article 12 Transfer, surrender and cancellation of allowances

(1) Member States shall ensure that allowances can be transferred between:

(a) persons within the Community;

(b) persons within the Community and persons in third countries, where such allowances are recognised in accordance with the procedure referred to in Article 25 without restrictions other than those contained in, or adopted pursuant to, this Directive.

(2) Member States shall ensure that allowances issued by a competent authority of another Member State are recognised for the purpose of meeting an operator's obligations under paragraph 3.

(3) Member States shall ensure that, by 30 April each year at the latest, the operator of each installation surrenders a number of allowances equal to the total emissions from that installation during the preceding calendar year as verified in accordance with Article 15, and that these are subsequently cancelled.

(4) Member States shall take the necessary steps to ensure that allowances will be cancelled at any time at the request of the person holding them.

JAT Fairfield, Virtual Property[10] **1.8 (US)**

Should computer code that is designed to act like real world property be regulated and protected like real world property? This article contends that it should.

Much computer code is just one step removed from a pure idea. It is non-rivalrous; that is, one person's use of the code does not stop another person from using it. This kind of code is, correctly, protected by the law of intellectual property. Intellectual property protects the creative interest in non-rivalrous resources. If intellectual property did not exist, creators would not be able to recoup the costs of creation.

But there is another kind of code, rarely discussed in the technical or legal literature. This kind of code is designed to act more like land or chattel than ideas. It pervades the internet and comprises many of the most important online resources. Often, this kind of code makes up the structural components of the internet itself. Domain names, URLs (uniform resource locators), websites, email accounts, and entire virtual worlds are all examples of this second type of code. They are rivalrous. If one person owns and controls them, others do not. They are persistent. Unlike the software on your computer, they do not go away when you turn your computer off. And they are interconnected. Other people can interact with them. This kind of code I term 'virtual property.'

There is, however, a problem. In general, we continue to govern virtual property through the law of intellectual property. Even where there has been some recognition that virtual property is somehow 'different,' no clear articulation of that difference has been offered. As a result, holders of intellectual property rights have been systematically eliminating emerging virtual property rights by the use of contracts called End User License Agreements ('EULAs'). Despite (or perhaps because of) these contracts,

[10] JH Fairfield, 'Virtual property' (2005) 85 *Boston University Law Review* 1047, 1048–52. Recently the Netherlands Supreme Court accepted the notion of virtual property in a criminal law case concerning theft—HR 31 January 2012, *Rechtspraak van de Week* 2012, 259, also accessible at www.rechtspraak.nl.

no distinct protection for property rights in virtual property has appeared in the United States, even though millions of people and billions of dollars are involved in gray-market transactions in such property. In comparison, China, Taiwan, and Korea have already made significant steps toward protecting ownership interests in virtual property, hoping to attract the burgeoning industry of virtual worlds.

Why is it important that we have a theory of virtual property? The common law of property works to ensure that resources are used well. If we do not have a good theory of virtual property, then virtual property will be poorly used. For example, a key step in the development of the internet was the adoption of a property-style regime in the form of the International Corporation for Assigned Names and Numbers ('ICANN'), an organization that acts as a recording system for internet addresses. Property law also lowers search costs associated with the sale of resources by permitting a limited number of property forms that are easier to search. For example, a title search on a house is less expensive because there are a fixed and limited set of ways in which the house could be encumbered. Similarly, property law lowers negotiation costs by limiting fragmentation of property rights. To give an example of fragmentation, if property rights in a tractor were split such that one person owned the wheels while another owned the chassis, you would have to negotiate with both people to be able to use the tractor as a whole, which would be more expensive. Thus, a theory of virtual property is critical to ensure efficient use of internet resources, lower search costs, and reduce negotiation costs that would otherwise prevent the flow of high-value resources to high-value uses.

A good theory of virtual property is also important to the future of the internet. If we protect virtual property, the internet could become a three-dimensional global virtual environment. The possibilities for medical, commercial, social, military, artistic, and cultural advancement offered by such a virtual environment have just begun to be explored. Thus, we should care about the protection of virtual property not only because markets already value it immensely, but because we will all come to value it more due to the potential it offers for societal advancement.

Finally, a theory of virtual property is important to maintain the equilibrium of the law as it adapts to new contexts. The common law is a complex system that has evolved over time to encode many different factors into its rules. In particular, the law of contract and the law of property traditionally balance each other. The law of contract permits parties to realize the value of idiosyncratic preferences through trades. The law of property traditionally limits the burdens that parties may place on the productive use or marketability of high-value resources by means of contract. For example, unreasonable contractual restraints on alienation are eliminated by the law of property. But currently in the context of the internet, we have imported the common law of contract wholesale, without the counterbalance of property law. As a result, emergent useful property forms are being eliminated by contract.

This article will therefore set forth a theory of virtual property, will demonstrate the relevance of the common law of property to cyberspace, and will address challenges to the model of virtual property.

I.B TERMINOLOGY AND THE USE OF ENGLISH

This casebook is, as all the other *Ius Commune* casebooks, in English. The use of English is sometimes highly problematic when describing civil property law concepts.

The definition of what constitutes 'property law' is only one example. Legal English is so intimately connected with English law that, given the fundamental differences between common law and civil law, explaining civil law concepts in English sometimes creates a serious risk of misunderstanding. *Caveat comparator!* To avoid as much as possible misunderstanding the technical terms used are explained in each chapter. Nevertheless, it might be useful to explain here some of the difficulties. We have tried to define a term as precisely as possible to avoid a term having more than one meaning. However, sometimes this proved to be impossible as a particular expression was already an established term and it would have caused even more uncertainty to create neologisms. An example of such an established legal term with various meanings is 'title'. Title may mean 'legal ground' when discussing whether a system of transfer is causal or abstract. However, title means 'ownership' when examining retention of title (reservation of ownership) clauses. It should be realised further that the term 'ownership' also has an ambivalent meaning in English! Civil law ownership is not the same as, for example, ownership in the recent Irish Land and Conveyancing Law Reform Act 2009 which abolished the feudal system. The translation in English of specific civil law terms sometimes proves to be highly problematic. How to translate the whole of a person's assets and debts for which the civil law developed the term 'patrimony'? The best equivalent in English seems to be 'estate', but this term—again—has various meanings in English. A further example is the term for the person who administers an insolvent estate. We used the terms 'trustee in bankruptcy', 'administrator in insolvency' and curator.

JH Merryman, Ownership and Estate—Variations on a Theme by Lawson[11] **1.9 (US)**

Several conclusions emerge from this brief comparison of ownership and estate. The first is that they are different in application as well as in theory; they are not alternate names for the same or similar things. A legal system in which ownership is a basic legal concept might conceivably have developed institutions and interests paralleling those of the common law, and perhaps during the Middle Ages substantial similarities existed, but the emphasis on a Napoleonic version of Roman ownership since codification and reform has led to a quite different body of property law in the civil law nations.

Second, the attitude that ownership is indivisible has played an important role in this development; occasionally, it may even have become an end in itself, without reference to discoverable social or economic functions. It has the lure of certainty, the attraction of simplicity, the ease of generality. The commitment to it in Italy and a number of other civil law nations seems to be unshakeable at the present time. This both inhibits improvisation in the system of property interests and requires the use of fictions to explain how those that are allowed can be made consistent with theory.

Third, the Italian land law has been reformed and defeudalized. It is consequently a good deal simpler to understand, at least on first acquaintance, than our own land law. Many of our legal terms and institutions can only be comprehended in the

[11] JH Merryman, 'Ownership and Estate (Variations on a Theme by Lawson)' [1974] *Tulane Law Review* 916, 943 *et seq*. Reprinted by permission of the *TLR*.

light of a very complex historical development, beginning with the establishment of Norman feudalism in England in the eleventh century. History is not, of course, irrelevant to a proper understanding of Italian property law, but the process of reform and defeudalization has greatly simplified the task of the Italian student by removing many feudal, and some Roman and Germanic, terms, notions, and institutions from the area of contemporary significance.

Fourth, the Italian law of property in land is codified. Hence, it is more systematic than ours is. There is a uniform terminology. Basic concepts are defined, and relationships are described in these terms. Rules are based on these concepts and relationships. The code was drafted with simplicity, inner consistency, and comprehensiveness as accepted values, and, although these can never be fully realized in practice, the resulting Italian law comes far closer to their realization than our own highly diffuse 'system.'

Fifth, the variety and flexibility of devices for preserving and disposing of property interests are much greater in the common law jurisdictions than in Italy. There are historical (the antifeudal, democratic spirit in which reform and codification were undertaken) and formal (the dogma of indivisible ownership and the concept of the *numerus clausus*) explanations for the extremely limited range of opportunities given the Italian man of property in planning his estate. But we would greatly underestimate the quality of European legal scholarship were we to assume that a balanced social and economic judgment did not play an important role in arriving at the present juridical scheme. The remarkable thing is that their judgment has been so different from our own.

In part, the distance between their system and ours is attributable to the extremes of rationalism and anti-feudalism that colored property law reform in nineteenth century Europe. Extreme positions were rigorously taken with respect to fiduciary substitutions, successive usufructs, and so on, though there has been a noticeable tendency toward relaxation of these positions in more recent times. Still, the greater reason for the lack of similarity in the two property systems lies on the common law side, in the peculiarity—better, the idiosyncracy—of our law of property. Much of the complexity that we tolerate, and even glorify, is fun for the antiquarian and profitable for the lawyer versed in the black arts of property, but society pays a high price for these dubious benefits. Unlike civil law nations, the United States had no property revolution. The process has been evolutionary, and the pace has been unconscionably slow. Fifty years ago, when the British abolished all legal estates except the fee simple absolute and the term of years (while leaving unaffected equitable interests and estates), an important step was taken that American jurisdictions have, inexplicably, failed to emulate. That, and a few other measures of comparable scope and audacity, would make our property law a good deal simpler and more efficient without any loss of sensitivity.

Whether the notion of 'estate' would or should survive fundamental reform in the law of property is not likely to be a very important question. Some central concept is necessary, and it is not clear that 'ownership,' at least as it is employed in modern civil law systems, is a particularly good one for the purpose. The meanings attributed to 'estate' in our law, when contrasted with the meanings attributed to 'ownership' in theirs, seem more sophisticated, more richly and variously useful, and freer from extra-legal cultural baggage. If these values could be retained while ridding our property law of the useless antiquarianism and arcane complexity that now characterize it, then it might be preferable to stay with 'estate'.

J Gordley, The Common Law in the Twentieth Century. Some Unfinished Business[12] **1.10 (US)**

It is not surprising that, with a few exceptions, the law of property was not remodelled along the lines of civil law. Property was at the core of older English law. Moreover, wherever civil law has spread, the local rules of property usually have been one of the last areas to be assimilated.

Nevertheless, there has been a great deal of parallel evolution. One distinctive feature of English property law was the so-called common law estates in land: fee simple, fee tail, life estate, and leasehold. Of these, fee tail has been abolished in all but a few American jurisdictions. Fee simple and life estate look very much like the 'ownership' and 'usufruct' of civil law. Lease admittedly is different, and I will discuss the difference shortly.

Another traditional difference concerned the role of courts of equity in protecting the 'equitable title' of purchasers of land. These rules grew up before there was a recording system. Today, however, in virtually every state, transfer of land is governed by a land transfer act, which varies considerably from state to state. Moreover, virtually every state has a recording act that prescribes what should happen if the seller conveys the land twice. The old rules governing the equitable title of the prior purchasers apply only in rare cases in which an interest in land cannot be recorded.

Moreover, the acquisition of title by adverse possession resembles civil law prescription, even though it seems to have developed independently.

The problem of *'immissioni'* in Italy, *'Immissionen'* in Germany, or *'troubles de voisinage'* in France looks much like that of nuisance in the United States. The rule that the government must pay just compensation when it takes private property was adopted by the American Constitution in the eighteenth century. The problems that rule raises are much like those of similar provisions in continental Europe. In this case, the similarity may be due to a common source in the natural law school of the seventeenth and eighteenth centuries. In any event, the institutions and rules are much the same.

There are, of course, differences. Some say that one difference is fundamental: the common law does not recognize 'ownership' in the civil law sense. We will consider this claim, and then turn to some practical differences.

A. Ownership

Supposedly, the civil law and common law take radically different views of the relationship between ownership and possession. While the common law blurs these concepts, '[c]ontinental law makes a sharp distinction'. The accounts that continental and Anglo-American jurists give of these institutions seem to be polar opposites. Typically, continental jurists say that the owner has the right to possession while the mere possessor does not. Then they try to explain why the law protects someone who is acting without right. In contrast, Anglo-American jurists—particularly the English—say that the common law 'never bothered much with the idea of ownership', 'never applied the conception of ownership to land', and 'never really disentangled [the concept of ownership] from that of possession'. In the common law, supposedly, ownership or title to land is based on the fact of possession or the best right to

[12] J Gordley, 'The Common Law in the Twentieth Century. Some Unfinished Business' (2000) 88 *California Law Review* 1815, 1859 *et seq*. Reprinted by permission of the *CLR*.

possession. Title is therefore relative. The person with possession has title against anyone who does not have a 'better right', or a right based on still earlier possession. Supposedly, the reason that title is relative is that the common law never protected ownership as such. The medieval actions to recover land protected 'seizin', which was something like possession. One who had been seized and was dispossessed would bring an action called 'novel disseizin' to get back his land. The heir of someone who had been 'seized' of land would bring an action called *'mort d'ancestor'*. The closest thing to an action based on ownership was the 'writ of right', but even this was an action to protect seizin, since the party who prevailed was the party who could trace his claim to the earliest person to have had seizin.

JH Baker, An Introduction to English Legal History[13] **1.11 (E&W)**

Movable wealth could not be settled on a succession of owners, because the common law did not allow future estates to be created in chattels. A gift of a chattel for an hour was a gift for ever. But a lesser kind of interest could be conferred by the contract of hire, as on a lease of sheep or furniture. There is analogy here with the lease of land, which conferred possession but not freehold or seisin; and later lawyers explained it in similar terms as a separation of ownership from possession. It is unclear how far this dichotomy was known in medieval times. To some extent ownership and possession coincided in the medieval concept of 'property' (*proprietas*), a word which for a time was used only in connection with movables. Property arose from occupation and was generally transferred by delivery; it went hand in hand with possession. There was no such thing as *dominium*, absolute abstract ownership or right. The most a person out of possession could claim was a better right to possession than the person in possession. …

The relationship between property and mere possession was seen most clearly when there was some dealing between two parties. There is a natural distinction between handing over a thing with the intention that all the property should pass to the recipient (gift or sale), and handing it over with the intention that the recipient should have only temporary use or profits of the thing (loan or hire) or should hold it passively as a pawn or deposit. These latter transactions were all forms of 'bailment', the common-law name for a transaction whereby a thing is delivered (*baillé*) on the basis that the bailor shall retain his property. But a similar separation of property and possession could occur without a bailment; for instance, where goods were stolen, or lost and then found by a stranger. Even in these cases, however, the terms 'property' and 'possession' can describe no more than the relative position of the people involved. They mean only that someone may have a right which is superior to one based on bare possession.

[13] JH Baker, *An Introduction to English Legal History*, 4th edn (Oxford, Oxford University Press, 2005) 389–90.

J Gordley, Foundations of Private Law. Property, Tort, Contract, Unjust Enrichment[14] **1.12 (US)**

Most jurists would say that the common law and civil law rules of property differ in two fundamental respects. One is that the civil law recognises a limited number of types of interests in property—it has a *numerus clausus*—whereas the common law allows private parties considerably more freedom in the types of interests which they can create. The second is that the civil law recognizes 'ownership' or 'absolute ownership' whereas the common law does not clearly distinguish ownership and possession. ... We will see that while the common law is more flexible in allowing such interests to be created, this flexibility is to be understood as a means to purposes which civil law systems are also trying to achieve, and that civil law systems themselves differ in the degree of flexibility that they permit to achieve these purposes. ... It is a difference, and only a difference in degree, in techniques employed to accomplish common ends. ... The rights of a person with full ownership in civil law are much the same as those of one who holds a fee simple at common law. What can it mean to speak of a basic structural difference between the civil law and common law approach? To be taken more seriously is the idea that civil law and common law take a radically different view of the relationship between ownership and possession. Supposedly, while the common law blurs those concepts, '[c]ontinental law makes a sharp distinction' The accounts that continental and Anglo-American jurists give of these institutions do seem to be polar opposites. Typically, continental jurists say that the owner has the right to possession while the mere possessor does not. They then try to explain why the law protects someone who is acting without right. In contrast, Anglo-American jurists—and particularly the English—say that the common law 'never bothered much with the idea of ownership' 'never applied the conception of ownership to land', 'never really disentangled (the concept of ownership) from that of possession'. In the common law, supposedly, ownership to title to land is based on the fact of possession or the best right to possession. Title is therefore relative. The person with possession has title against anyone who does not have a better right. A 'better right' is a right based on still earlier possession.

I.C THE NATURE OF PROPERTY RIGHTS

Stating which legal areas are covered by this casebook still does not answer the question of what the rights are that property law confers on people relating to those objects. Which rights are 'property rights' and what do we mean when we call certain rights 'property rights'? What we mean is that these rights are stronger than (1) contractual rights, (2) the right by an injured party to claim damages on the basis of a tort or (3) the right to repayment of, for example, a certain amount of money as a result of unjustified enrichment. Contractual rights, rights to payment of damages or to undo an unjustified enrichment are personal: these are rights that someone has against one or more specific other persons. More on these personal rights can be found in the casebooks on contract law, tort law and unjustified enrich-

[14] J Gordley, *Foundations of Private Law. Property, Tort, Contract, Unjust Enrichment* (Oxford, Oxford University Press, 2006) 3.

ment. Property rights are not personal, but are rights 'against the world' or *erga omnes*. Their external effect is that they are absolute, binding upon every person or, at least, binding against more than just one or several specific other persons. Personal rights correspond with personal duties ('obligations' in civil law terminology), but property rights correspond with duties resting on everyone (or at least, as already mentioned, more than just one or several specific other persons). Property rights have, what in French is called, *droit de suite* (the right can be claimed against anyone who is in control of the object) and *droit de préférence* (the right is stronger than any personal right with regard to the object).

The development of property law, and in particular the dividing line between personal and property rights, can frequently only be explained by taking into account the law's historical development. On the other hand, from the perspective of positive law, it seems that legal systems will only accept that a particular right is a property right if a justification exists. Property law is seen as exceptional. A right is presumed to be personal, unless the legal system accepts that it is of a proprietary nature. Given the far-reaching effect of property rights and their exceptional nature, the law of property is therefore generally mandatory law, limiting the parties' freedom to shape the content of proprietary relationships. A further limitation with regard to the ambit of property law can be found when looking at what can be an object of property law. Historically, land was seen as the most valuable asset a person could have and it will be no surprise that in many legal systems property law originally developed as land law. This changed as a result of the Industrial Revolution. During that period movable assets became of growing importance, together with claims on debtors. The main reason behind this development was the need for secured financing: movables and claims represented value that could secure the repayment of a loan. We have seen that during the last century (partially as the result of the Information Revolution) other objects of property law were also recognised (so-called 'new' property). Examples are licenses, emission rights and virtual property. These new objects are generally immaterial.

Given the strength of property rights and considering their exceptional nature, legal systems limit the number and content of these rights (the *numerus clausus* principle) and require that third parties must be adequately informed about their existence. It must be clear as to which object a property right is claimed and third parties should be adequately informed about both the object and the right (principles of specificity and publicity). These principles function as filters through which a legal relationship must pass before it can be qualified as being of a proprietary nature.

The application of these principles is guided by legal policies. A legal policy can be, eg, to give priority to the protection of owners (thus limiting rules which validate transfers *a non-domino*), to give protection to commerce (thus protecting third parties who acquire property rights in good faith from a non-owner), to aim at *ex ante* security (by limiting the freedom of parties to shape their property relations according to their own wishes) or to aim at *ex post* security by allowing parties freedom to shape their property relationships, though within a confined area to be controlled by courts.

Once a right has been qualified as proprietary, certain general ground rules apply.

The first ground rule is that one cannot transfer more than one has (the *nemo dat* or *nemo plus iuris* rule). The second is that older property rights have priority over younger property rights (the *prior tempore* rule), with the exception of a younger property right created with the consent of the older property right. The final general ground rule is that any property right is given special protection, given its strong nature. If a property right is securing the repayment of a loan, a further ground rule applies: the existence of the security rights depends upon the existence of an underlying debt (accessority rule). Accessority is reached either by property law itself (no loan, no security) or by (standard) contracts in which accessority is stipulated and which forbid enforcement of a security right after a loan has been paid (in German law this is sometimes called *Ersatzakzessorietät*).

Property law, when analysed from both a historical-comparative and a functional viewpoint, shows that not only can certain general characteristics (leading principles, legal policies and ground rules) be detected, but also certain shared concepts (or perhaps better, shared notions). Of course, differences can and will be found as well as exceptions to the above-mentioned general characteristics, legal policies, leading principles and ground rules. It should also be borne in mind that concepts, which appear to be the same, may be completely different when examined in greater depth. A notorious example is the concept of 'ownership'. For civil lawyers the term ownership refers to a concept with a clear, unitary, content, whereas common lawyers use this term almost in a more colloquial way and without reference to any clearly defined concept. Nevertheless, it seems that every legal system has property rights which follow a basic order: a primary right, which confers the most extensive property right on a person, secondary rights, which confer lesser property rights on persons, and tertiary rights that are an intermediary category between personal and property rights, representing property rights *in statu nascendi*.

II. IMPORTANCE OF UNDERSTANDING THE HISTORY OF PROPERTY LAW

Frequently, property law can only be understood, not as the result of logical reasoning, but as the result of historical development. Although property law certainly is everywhere seen as a system (that is to say, as a coherent body of values, policies, principles, concepts and rules), these systems are nevertheless, at least in part, not the result of (academic) logical reasoning, but of the way the law has developed over time. This applies particularly to English common law, but it also applies to the civil law tradition. To give but one example: property law in both common law as well as civil law cannot be understood without having studied feudalism. The feudal system was at the same time a system of governance (we would nowadays call it public or constitutional law) and a system of land holding (what we would now call private law). From the perspective of property law it is important to know that under the feudal system a lord would grant land use rights to a person he relied on, who in return would render services, such as providing soldiers for an army. At the top of the feudal pyramid stood the king as the 'lord paramount', all others were (sub)tenants, as they 'held' land from a lord. The relationship between a lord and a tenant is an 'estate'. It can be said that this led to a fragmentation of ownership. Various persons had land rights of such strength that each could be seen as 'owner'. It could also be said that various types of ownership were recognised.

The feudal system could be found everywhere in Europe. It was abolished on the continent of Europe as a result of the French Revolution. In Scotland it was only abolished on 28 November 2004 by the Abolition of Feudal Tenure etc (Scotland) Act. In Ireland the feudal system was abolished on 1 December 2009 by the Land and Conveyancing Law Reform Act 2009, although feudal concepts such as tenure and estate are maintained. Remnants of the feudal system of the Duchy of Normandy, the basis of the feudal system in England as it was this system that was transplanted by William the Conqueror when he established himself in England, can still be found on the Channel Islands of, eg, Guernsey and Jersey.

Before the French Revolution, on the continent of Europe concepts stemming from the feudal system were reformulated in Roman law terminology, as a result of the study of rediscovered Roman law sources. This led to the concept of *duplex dominium* to explain that both the lord had certain rights with regard to the land (*dominium directum*) as well as the tenant (*dominium utile*). After the French Revolution ownership became a unitary concept, at the apex of all other absolute rights. Fragmentation of ownership was seen as a relic of the *ancien régime* and as a violation of the new liberal freedoms of the *citoyen*. Remarkable though it may seem, an understanding of the feudal system is still important to an understanding of civil law systems. Property law in civil law systems can sometimes only be explained by becoming aware of the fact that the relevant rules are the result of a *rejection* of the feudal system. This explains, to give but one example, why civil law systems hesitate to accept a general security right as exists under English law with regard to immovables, movables and claims in the form of a floating charge. General mortgages were well known under the feudal system and created serious problems for third parties who gave credit while being unaware of the existence of such a general mortgage. Although in England the feudal system has not been abolished, the system was nevertheless transformed and a modern system of property law resulted. The feudal roots of modern English property law can still be found in the terminology used (in land law the concepts of 'tenure' and 'estate'), but the content has changed considerably. If someone has the 'estate in fee simple absolute' (or 'freehold estate') of a parcel of land, that person, for all practical purposes, is in the same position as the owner of land in a civil law system, because the freeholder is free to do with the land as he or she pleases. That person is certainly no longer the Crown's vassal. It could be said that in English land law the concept of 'freehold' functions as the apex of all other estates and rights in land. The same can be said of the concept of 'title' in personal property law. It seems as if each property law system, irrespective of whether it is common law or civil law based, needs a starting point: one right to express the maximum of—to put it in Hohfeldian terminology—the rights, powers, privileges and immunities a person can have with regard to an object.[15] Such maximum is called ownership in the civil law, freehold and title in the common law. All other rights are lesser rights. It will be obvious that at the level of legal technique major differences exist between common law and civil law and even, for that matter, within each legal tradition, as will be seen in the various chapters of this casebook. However, these differences are not (or perhaps one should say, no longer) the result of any fundamental divergence with regard to the political system or ideology. All European property law systems are founded on market economies where individual freedom of ownership is seen as a fundamental right. This becomes even clearer when looking at the laws of the Member States of the European Union, the European Free Trade Association and the European Economic Area, because in these integrated economic areas the creation of an internal market based on this individual freedom of ownership is one of the corner-stones.

Historically, land law developed earlier than the law of personal property. Land is at the heart of the feudal system. Personal property only became really important during and after the Industrial Revolution with its mass production and consumption of goods. A further development, characteristic of what can be seen today, is the growing importance of money claims, immaterial property, such as intellectual property rights, and what is sometimes called 'new' property (government licenses, emission rights).

A highly important historical development in the common law tradition, the understanding of which is vital to understanding its system of property law, is the existence of two legal orders, a *duplex ordo*: next to the common law in a strict sense, equity was developed as a subsidiary system of law. Equity and its relationship with the common law are governed by the so-called 'principles of equity'. Two well-known principles are that equity follows the law (first a common law analysis must be conducted, before solutions based on the law of equity can be introduced) and that equity considers as done what ought to be done (if, at common law, a formal act is necessary, the intention to perform the act suffices for its performance under equity). The understanding of the relevance of equity is of utmost importance for the understanding of English property law. The best example to show this is the trust, a mechanism to separate management of property from benefit. As a result of the existence of the *duplex ordo* of common law and equity, a distinction can be made between a 'legal' and an 'equitable' owner in which both have property rights with regard to the object of the trust: the 'trustee' (manager of property) is entitled to it under common law and the 'beneficiary' (person in whose interest the property is managed) is entitled to it under equity.

[15] *Cf* WN Hohfeld, *Fundamental Legal Conceptions As Applied in Judicial Reasoning*, ed W Wheeler Cook (Union, NJ, The Lawbook Exchange, 2000).

R Helmholz and R Zimmermann, Trust and Treuhand in Historical Perspective[16] **1.13 (DE)**

'I do not understand your law of trusts'—so *Otto von Gierke* is said to have remarked about this characteristic English institution. His words were long remembered by the great English legal historian, *FW Maitland*, who quoted them more than once. According to this view—the traditional view and probably still the prevailing one—the trust is a distinctive institution of Anglo-American law. It is a special child of the English common law. Nothing like it elsewhere.

In *Maitland's* hands, *Gierke's* puzzlement about the trust became an example, and eventually a symbol, of a wall of incomprehension that separated the English common law from the law of the Continent. Indeed trusts were only the most dramatic example of a quite fundamental divide. No matter the possible coincidence in origins of the Germanic *Salmann* and the English feoffee to uses, trusts were strange creatures to lawyers versed in the civil law. *Maitland* concluded that trusts always required substantial modification, as well as an extended period of adjustment, whenever they were taken over into a civilian legal system.

Maitland would have been surprised to find that in recent times the trust has been adopted in many civil law countries, and apparently without fundamental difficulty. ...

Much, of course, depends upon definition. Just what is a trust? *Maitland* wrestled with the question, and German scholars have themselves found that defining *Treuhand* is a task not free from ambiguity. The question is important. Some definition is required; otherwise a trust will be indistinguishable from a bailment or an agency relationship. Too strict a definition, however, will inevitably exclude all possibility of establishing intellectual relationships between trust-like institutions across legal and geographical boundaries. That would not be realistic. Absorption of an institution or a legal rule from without has undeniably occurred, and it virtually always changes the institution or legal rule itself. Such changes should not keep us from seeing the realities.

Today English law assumes that the trust requires that legal ownership of the trust property be vested in the trustee. A divided title between beneficiary and trustee appears to some to constitute the essence of the trust, and Anglo-American lawyers have continued to speak easily of legal title and equitable title long after the amalgamation of legal and equitable jurisdiction. For purposes of this volume, however, we have purposely avoided a definition tied to the modern English trust. In our view, the English trust has itself been the product of evolution. It was a practical device, evolved out of the needs of clients, not fixed by its modern definition.

Too narrow a definition would, moreover, be false to the protean nature of institutions that have always been acknowledged to be trusts. It would be false to the flexible nature of the institutions and to the wide variety of purposes the trust and *Treuhand* have served. It would, for instance, preclude the possibility of influence simply because the trust was so closely connected in England with the equitable jurisdiction of the Court of Chancery, a court that had no exact analogue on the Continent. Moreover, within English law itself, adopting too narrow a definition of trusts would make it difficult to find any relationship between a charitable trust and the dynamic trust that was part of a family settlement. The latter required

[16] R Helmholz and R Zimmermann, 'Views of Trust and Treuhand: An Introduction', in *Itinera Fiduciae. Trust and Treuhand in Historical Perspective* (Berlin, Duncker and Humblot, 1998) 27 and 37–39.

that beneficiaries be named; the former did not. Yet we know that a connection between them did exist.

This [International Working Group on Trusts] has therefore thought it right to adopt a relatively general definition. Such a choice accords with that repeatedly made by most modern writers. It is essentially the approach adopted by *Helmut Coing*. It is at one in its major particulars with the definition adopted by the American Restatement of Trusts, and also with the Hague Convention on Private International Law in 1985. Individual contributors to the volume have added to or adduced from this definition, according to the special needs of their subject. But they have made their exceptions clear.

With these exceptions, a trust is defined in this volume as a relationship in which one or more persons (the trustees) hold property, but administer it either for the benefit of someone else (the beneficiary) or to further some particular purpose. No special terminology is required, as long as the substance is present. Properly speaking, the relationship must have more than a momentary duration, for otherwise it serves a purely remedial purpose. Some specific asset (real property or chattels) is also required before one can speak of a trust; an obligation to act in the interests of another person may be an agency relationship or even a partnership. A trust must have a lawful purpose, though lawful purposes may be widely conceived and may vary over time. There must also be a remedy against the trustee for breach of his duties as a fiduciary. Under the definition adopted, a moral duty to hold property for another does not qualify as a trust unless there is a realistic way of enforcing it. Finally, it may be useful to state that the object of our investigations has been the express trust, not the constructive or resulting trust. These are remedial devices.

Report on the Proposal of Law (N 3385) introducting the fiducie—Introduction of fiducie in French law, difference with English trust[17] **1.14 (FR)**

After several failed attempts, the Parliament is finally ready to introduce the *fiducie* in our law. The initiative is not initiated by the Government, even if the latter had constituted a working group on the question in February 2005, but by the general rapporteur of the Senate's finance commission, M Philippe Marini, author of a bill that was adopted at first reading by the senators, on 17 October 2006, and over which henceforth, the National Assembly must decide. ...

Of Roman origin, the *fiducie* is one of the oldest real contracts regarding either the administration of a patrimony (*fiducie cum amico*), or the security of a claim (*fiducie cum creditore*). Even if it has developed beyond its original shape, its principles remain fundamentally unchanged: the owner of the rights over a patrimony (*constituant*) must consent to the transfer of a part or the entirety of his rights to the patrimony of another party (*fiduciaire*), for the benefit of a third party (*bénéficiaire*).

In France, the *fiducie* has known a certain success in the Middle Ages, particularly in the era of crusades, since it allowed crusaders to transfer the property of their domains to third parties, with the obligation incumbent on the latter to return

[17] Rapport fait au nom de la Commission des Lois Constitutionnelles, de la Législation et de l'Administration Générale de la République sur la Proposition de Loi (No 3385), adoptée par le Sénat, instituant la fiducie, par M Xavier de Roux, Député, 7 *et seq*.

property upon their comeback, or, if they perished in the Holy Land, to transfer the property to their heirs.

It was later maintained under the form of fideicommissary substitutions, which oblige the heir or the legatee, to conserve the transmitted goods and to transfer them upon the death of the constituent to a third party designated in advance. It was however knowingly forgotten by the drafters of the Napoleonic Civil Code, who saw in it a feudal instrument designed to avoid the division of the largest patrimonies.

Today, France remains one of the rare European countries not to apply the fiduciary institution or its Anglo-Saxon common law equivalent, the trust, which differentiates itself from the *fiducie* by the separation it establishes between the control of goods and their enjoyment. The mechanism of Roman law, as well as that of the Anglo-Saxon common law proves to be greatly flexible in its use, particularly efficient in a commercial setting or for international financing. The splendid French isolation only appears to be more damaging.

The European as well as international legal context already supports the development of our national law. Firstly, France, which has signed the Hague Convention of 1 July 1985 regarding the law applicable to trusts and on their recognition, will not be able to eternally discard the due date of the ratification of this international legal instrument. Secondly, on 15 November 2001 the European Parliament adopted a resolution inviting the Member States to harmonise their law in different fields, including the trust. Finally, on 2 May 2003, the European Commission has put forward a model trust contract applicable to mergers of groups subject to authorization of its Directorate General for Competition, so that the French companies called upon to restructure at the European level are given opportunities which they do not have at the national level.

It would yet be unfair to consider that the successive French governments have not grasped the necessity of developing our legislation in view of allowing recourse to mechanisms of a fiduciary type, or similar to those. On the one hand, in 1989, 1992 and 1994 several bills or bill proposals were prepared to establish a general fiduciary regime, but they have not delivered any results because of multiple precautions linked to fiscal and legal considerations. The *fiducie* has been considered for a long time a means of tax evasion and of money laundering, resulting from insufficiently solid security. We can see that this is no longer the case, especially with respect to the provisions envisaged in the present bill. On the other hand, French law has progressively incorporated the legal mechanisms which closely relate to the *fiducie* without these institutions bearing that name. Compelling economic need created the following instruments, belonging to 'unnamed' *fiducies*: the sale with right to repurchase, the transfer 'Dailly', securities lending or even the provision of financial instruments. The fact remains that these very specific instruments do not cover the same vast range of situations as the *fiducie*.

II.A THE FRENCH REVOLUTION

A major ideological distinction between common law and civil law came into existence as a result of the French Revolution, with its expression of equality and liberty, which abolished the feudal system and created laws (codes) that applied to everyone equally.

Decree Abolishing the Feudal System of 11 August 1789 **1.15 (FR)**

Article 1 The National Assembly hereby completely abolishes the feudal system. It decrees that, among the existing rights and dues, both feudal and censuel, all those originating in or representing real or personal serfdom shall be abolished without indemnification. All other dues are declared redeemable, the terms and mode of redemption to be fixed by the National Assembly. Those of the said dues which are not extinguished by this decree shall continue to be collected until indemnification shall take place.

Note

By this decree the French National Assembly abolished the feudal system as it still existed. It did not, however, lay down which rules would replace the abolished system. That would only come later after a period of uncertainty. In later times, such uncertainty was avoided when the feudal system was ended.

II.B ABOLISHING THE FEUDAL SYSTEM DOES NOT ALWAYS MEAN ABOLISHING FEUDAL CONCEPTS

In Scotland, a so-called mixed jurisdiction in which uncodified civil law, rooted in Roman law, is applied together with English common law, the existing feudal system has been abolished with almost the same terminology as used in France 200 years earlier. The abolition of feudal tenure in Scotland was not the result of a revolutionary mood to change the existing system of governance, but the result of a legislative process to change and modernise property law, although it could be argued that it was also intended to (re-)establish Scottish law as an independent jurisdiction separate from England. Not only was the feudal system abolished, it was also immediately replaced with a new system of rules. This was different in France where, after the abolition of the feudal system, for some time it was unclear what the new rules were. Ireland shows yet another example of how feudal tenure can be abolished without leaving a vacuum. It also shows, however, that such termination does not necessarily imply leaving the common law tradition.

Ireland maintained feudal concepts such as 'estate', provoking questions as to whether substance can be changed without changing form. The feudal system was, on the continent as well as in Great Britain and Ireland, originally both a system of governance and a system of land holding. We would now say that it belonged to both public as well as private law. Over the centuries the public law side of the feudal system declined until it was no more than a relic of the past. Abolishing the feudal system as a system of governance does not, therefore, have to mean that the private law side of the system also has to be abolished. Irish law is an example of the latter development. That France and other countries following the civil law tradition in the area of property law, such as Scotland, have chosen a different approach is due to the influence of Roman law based legal thinking.

Abolition of Feudal Tenure etc (Scotland) Act 2000 **1.16 (SC)**

Article 1 Abolition on appointed day

The feudal system of land tenure, that is to say the entire system whereby land is held by a vassal on perpetual tenure from a superior is, on the appointed day, abolished.

Article 2 Consequences of abolition

(1) An estate of dominium utile of land shall, on the appointed day, cease to exist as a feudal estate but shall forthwith become the ownership of the land and, in so far as is consistent with the provisions of this Act, the land shall be subject to the same subordinate real rights and other encumbrances as was the estate of dominium utile.

(2) Every other feudal estate in land shall, on that day, cease to exist.

(3) It shall, on that day, cease to be possible to create a feudal estate in land.

Land and Conveyancing Law Reform Act 2009 **1.17 (IR)**

PART 2 Ownership of Land

9—

(1) From the commencement of this Part, ownership of land comprises the estates and interests specified in this Part.

(2) In so far as it survives, feudal tenure is abolished.

(3) Subsection (2) does not affect—

(a) the position of the State under—

(i) the State Property Act 1954,

(ii) section 73 of the Act of 1965,

(b) the concept of an estate under section 10,

(c) any fee farm grant made in derogation of the Statute Quia Emptores 1290,

(d) any surviving customary right or franchise.

(4) A fee simple remains freely alienable.

10—

(1) The concept of an estate in land is retained and, subject to this Act, continues with the interests specified in this Part to denote the nature and extent of land ownership.

(2) Such an estate retains its pre-existing characteristics, but without any tenurial incidents.

(3) All references in any enactment or any instrument (whether made or executed before or after the commencement of this Part) to tenure or estates or interests in land, or to the holder of any such estate or interest, shall be read accordingly.

11—(1) The only legal estates in land which may be created or disposed of are the freehold and leasehold estates specified by this section.

(2) For the purposes of subsection (1), a 'freehold estate' means a fee simple in possession and includes—

(a) a determinable fee,

(b) a fee simple subject to a right of entry or of re-entry,

(c) a fee simple subject only to—

(i) a power of revocation,

(ii) an annuity or other payment of capital or income for the advancement, maintenance or other benefit of any person, or

(iii) a right of residence which is not an exclusive right over the whole land.

(3) For the purposes of subsection (1), a 'leasehold estate' means, subject to sections 12 and 14, the estate which arises when a tenancy is created for any period of time or any recurring period and irrespective of whether or not the estate—

(a) takes effect in immediate possession or in future, or

(b) is subject to another legal estate or interest, or

(c) is for a term which is uncertain or liable to termination by notice, re-entry or operation of law or by virtue of a provision for cessor on redemption or for any other reason.

(4) The only legal interests in land which may be created or disposed of are—

(a) an easement,

(b) a freehold covenant,

(c) an incumbrance,

(d) a rent payable under a tenancy,

(e) a possibility of reverter,

(f) a profit à prendre, including a mining right,

(g) a public or customary right,

(h) a rentcharge,

(i) a right of entry or of re-entry attached to a legal estate,

(j) a wayleave or other right to lay cables, pipes, wires or other conduits,

(k) any other legal interest created by any statutory provision.

(5) A legal estate or legal interest under this section has, subject to this Act, the same attributes as the corresponding legal estates and interests existing at the commencement of this Part and may exist concurrently with, or subject to, any other legal estate or interest in the same land.

(6) Subject to this Act, estates and interests other than those referred to in subsections (1) to (4) take effect as equitable interests only, but this does not prevent the creation of the estates and interests referred to in those subsections as equitable interests.

(7) Nothing in this Act affects judicial recognition of equitable interests.

(8) Subject to this Act, a power of attorney, power of appointment or other power to dispose of a legal estate or interest in land operates with the same force and effect as such powers had before the commencement of this Part.

(9) All estates and interests in land, whether legal or equitable, may be disposed of.

12—

(1) The creation of a fee farm grant at law or in equity is prohibited.

(2) Any instrument executed after the commencement of this Part purporting to—

(a) create a fee farm grant, or

(b) grant a lease for life or lives renewable for ever or for any period which is perpetually renewable, vests in the purported grantee or lessee a legal fee simple or, as the case may be, an equitable fee simple and any contract for such a grant entered into after such commencement operates as a contract for such a vesting.

(3) A fee simple which vests under subsection (2) is freed and discharged from any covenant or other provision relating to rent, but all other covenants or provisions continue in force so far as consistent with the nature of a fee simple.

(4) Subsection (2) does not apply to any contract or instrument giving effect to a contract entered into before the commencement of this Part.

(5) Notwithstanding section 11(2), any fee simple held under a fee farm grant existing at law at the commencement of this Part continues as a legal estate and may be disposed of.

(6) Notwithstanding section 11(4), any fee farm rent existing at law at the commencement of this Part continues as a legal interest and may be disposed of.

13—

(1) The creation of a fee tail of any kind at law or in equity is prohibited.

(2) Any instrument executed after the commencement of this Part purporting to create a fee tail in favour of any person vests in that person a legal fee simple or, as the case may be, an equitable fee simple and any contract for such a creation entered into before or after such commencement operates as a contract for such vesting.

(3) Where—

(a) immediately before the commencement of this Part, a person was entitled to a fee tail at law or in equity, or

(b) after such commencement, a person becomes entitled to such a fee tail, a legal or, as the case may be, an equitable fee simple vests in that person on such commencement or on that person becoming so entitled provided any protectorship has ended.

(4) In subsection (3) 'fee tail' includes—

(a) a base fee provided the protectorship has ended,

(b) a base fee created by failure to enrol the disentailing deed, but does not include the estate of a tenant in tail after possibility of issue extinct.

(5) A fee simple which vests under subsection (2) or subsection

(3) is—

(a) not subject to any estates or interests limited by the instrument creating the fee tail to take effect after the termination of the fee tail,

(b) subject to any estates or interests limited to take effect in defeasance of the fee tail which would be valid if limited to take effect in defeasance of a fee simple.

14— The grant of a lease for—

(a) a life or lives,

(b) a life or lives combined with a concurrent or reversionary term of any period,

(c) any term coming to an end on the death of a person or persons, and any contract for such a grant made after the commencement of this Part is void both at law and in equity.

PART 3 Future Interests

15—

(1) Subject to subsection (2), all future interests in land, whether vested or contingent, exist in equity only.

(2) Subsection (1) does not apply to—

(a) a possibility of reverter, or

(b) a right of entry or of re-entry attached to a legal estate.

Explanatory and Financial Memorandum to the Land and Conveyancing Law Reform Bill 2006[18] **1.18 (IR)**

The Bill provides for the repeal—in whole or in part—of about 150 pre-1922 statutes and their replacement, where appropriate, with statutory provisions more suited to modern conditions. It also repeals certain provisions in Acts of the Oireachtas which will no longer be required following its enactment. Apart from these statutory provisions, much current law and practice relating to land ownership and land transactions is based on the system introduced to Ireland by the Normans from the 12th century onwards. A key feature was the feudal notion of land tenure whereby all land was held from the Crown. The Bill abolishes feudal tenure in so far as it survives and updates the law relating to land ownership. It also abolishes various common law rules resulting from court decisions and conveyancing practices over the centuries. Another significant feature of land and conveyancing law as it has evolved has been the development of equitable jurisdiction by the courts in order to temper the harshness or rigidity of the common law. This has led to the important distinction between 'legal' ownership of land and 'equitable' or, as it is often referred to, 'beneficial' ownership. A good illustration of this distinction is the trust under which the legal title to property is vested in a trustee (or trustees) who is obliged to hold or use the property entirely for the benefit of others ie the 'beneficiaries'. Under the Bill's provisions, the courts will remain free to exercise their equitable jurisdiction to develop the law in order to accommodate changing circumstances and conditions.

While this Bill introduces many changes to the common law relating to land ownership and land transactions, it recognises that it will otherwise continue to operate and to develop. A consequence of this is that well-established concepts which are still of relevance in modern times are retained, though often subject to modifications set out in the Bill and explained later. …

Sections 9 to *14* contain provisions to reform and modernise the ownership of land. They remove the remaining vestiges of the old feudal system of landholding introduced by the Normans to Ireland in the 12th century. In particular, the concept of tenure, whereby all land was held from the Crown is abolished. This concept is not compatible with the relationship between the State and its citizens as prescribed by the Constitution. Also abolished are methods of landholding developed by conveyancers over the centuries to meet the needs of earlier times but which are no longer of relevance to modern conditions or will cease to be of significance as a result of other provisions of the Bill. This applies to creation of a fee tail, fee farm grants and leases for lives. The Bill retains the concept of an 'estate' in land which was also part of the feudal system, because this remains a central feature of the modern system of land ownership. The notion of dividing ownership according to different periods of time is what makes land ownership under a common law system flexible. It enshrines the fundamental principle that what is owned is not the physical entity, the land, but rather some estate (giving substantial rights in respect of the land such as the right to occupy it) or interest (giving less substantial rights such as the limited use given by an easement comprising, for example, a right of way over a road on the land, or a *profit à prendre* comprising a right to cut and take away turf) in the land. The full ownership of any particular parcel of land comprises

[18] Land and Conveyancing Law Reform Bill 2006, Explanatory and Financial Memorandum, 1, 3 and 4.

these various estates and interests, including equitable interests, such as those existing under a trust of the land. Article 10.1 of the Constitution refers expressly to 'estates and interests' (in the context of natural resources). How many of the various estates and interests will exist in respect of a particular parcel of land will vary from case to case. As part of its objective of simplifying the law, the Bill reduces substantially the number of estates which can be created in future.

Section 10 confirms that the concept of 'estates' and 'interests' is being retained as denoting the nature and extent of land ownership. As explained earlier, this is the fundamental principle of ownership under the common law system which applies to Ireland and many other parts of the world, but which distinguishes it from civil law systems which apply elsewhere. It is also confirms that estates will retain their long-established characteristics apart from any derived from the concept of tenure.

II.C A FRAGMENTED OR A UNIFIED SYSTEM OF PROPERTY LAW?

JH Baker, An Introduction to English Legal History[19] **1.19 (E&W)**

The common law relating to movable property was quite separate from that relating to real property. The reason is not that movables were once of minimal importance: 'Not even in the feudal age', jested Maitland, 'did men eat or drink land'. There was, nevertheless, a marked difference in value and permanence between land, which was a capital asset producing a continuous livelihood or income, and most ordinary chattels, such as grain or cattle, which were consumable. Until the Industrial Revolution, land was the chief source of wealth, and litigation about landed property was one of the principal concerns of the royal courts. ...

The learning of real property dominated the readings and moots of the medieval Inns of Court, and no book comparable with Littleton was written about chattels.

Notes

(1) One of the major structural differences between common law and civil law is that the civil law knows a uniform approach towards property law, whereas the common law follows a—historically determined—fragmented approach. In the common law 'property law' comprises several legal areas: land law, trust law, personal property law and claims. All these areas follow their own paths. The differences may even result from a lawyer's background: personal property law and claims are particularly relevant in commercial transactions and commercial lawyers tend to follow their own terminology and definitions. This is different in the civil law where, after the French Revolution and the abolishment of the feudal system, a Roman law based structure was introduced in the newly enacted civil codes. Nevertheless, fragmentation can also be found in the civil law. An example are the formalities for transfer: delivery of movables requires the passing of possession; delivery of immovables generally requires registration in the land registry of an authentic (notarial) deed.

[19] JH Baker, *An Introduction to English Legal History*, 4th edn (Oxford, Oxford University Press, 2005).

(2) A new type of fragmentation can be found in the European Union, where, as a result of legal integration, uniform European property law exists next to the law of the Member States. This new European property law does not have to fit in nicely with existing national law.

III. *NUMERUS CLAUSUS*

Property rights are rights that have effects against third parties. In civil law systems this effect is generally characterised as against the world or *erga omnes*. Parties are not completely free in the creation of these rights; in any legal system some limitation can be found with regard to (a) the number and content of property rights as well as to (b) the way in which these rights can be created, transferred or destroyed. This is called the principle of *numerus clausus*. The first mentioned aspect of the *numerus clausus* principle, which is more of a substantive nature, will be introduced below. The second aspect, which is more of a procedural nature, will be discussed in Chapters 7, 8 and 9.

III.A *NUMERUS CLAUSUS* IN THEORY

Introductory Notes

(a) The law of property needs a method to decide which legal relations belong to the law of property and which do not. The latter are then, as a consequence, part of the law of obligations (contract, tort, unjustified enrichment). In fact, the law of obligations seems to function as the default regime when it comes to qualifying a particular right as belonging to the law of property or not.

(b) The application of the *numerus clausus* principle differs from country to country. Basically, in German law the *numerus clausus* is best developed doctrinally. For reasons of clarity this paragraph will therefore start with a statement from German law, after which other legal systems will follow.

Explanation to the Draft of a Civil Code for the German Nation—Property Law (1888)[20] **1.20 (DE)**

Property law must, to ensure its independence, deal with the creation of property rights according to its own principles. ... The parties involved cannot be free to create any right, which sees to an object, and provide property effect to it. The starting point of the freedom of contract, that governs the law of obligations, does not apply to the law of property. Here, the opposite applies: the parties involved can only create those rights, which are allowed by the law. The number of property rights is therefore necessarily closed.

[20] *Motive zu dem Entwurfe eines Bürgerlichen Gesetzbuches für das Deutsche Reich—Sachenrecht* (Berlin, Verlag von J Guttentag, 1888) 3.

M Treilhard in Complete Collection of Preparatory Works of the Civil Code[21] **1.21 (FR)**

See here, in effect, the only modifications to which the owners can be susceptible in our political and social organisation. There can be no other rights on any object than a right of ownership, full and complete, including the right to use and enjoy and to dispose; or a simple right of use and enjoyment, without the right to dispose of a piece of land; or, finally, a right of servitude on the object of another.

Parliamentary History, Book 5[22] **1.22 (NL)**

In continental legal systems the system of property law is, different from contract law ..., a closed system.

Lord Chancellor's Division, 18, 20, 21 and 29 January 1834[23] **1.23 (E&W)**

Keppel v Bailey

Limestone quarry

Parties are not free to create new, as yet unknown, property rights by themselves.

Facts: In 1795 an ironworks company was created that constructed a railway to enable limestone to be transported from a lime quarry to the company more efficiently and at lower cost than had been possible before. Upon construction of the railway the company and the lime quarry entered into a covenant that the company and its 'heirs, executors, administrators, and assigns' would procure all the limestone they might want from the lime quarry. In 1833 part of the ironworks company came, after a few changes in titleholders, into the hands of Joseph and Crawshay Bailey with full notice of the covenant. The Baileys started construction of a railway to other quarries in the area. Upon this the shareholders of the lime quarry brought an action to prevent the Baileys from constructing the railway and to force them to use the existing railway.

Held: The covenant did not create a property right and therefore Mr and Mr Bailey, not having been part to the covenant, were not bound by its terms.

Judgment: Lord Brougham LC—There are certain known incidents to property and its enjoyment; among others, certain burthens werewith it may be affected, or rights which may be created and enjoyed over it by parties other than the owner; all which incidents are recognized by the law. In respect of possession the property may be in one, while the reversion is in another ; in respect of interest, the life estate in one, the remainder in tail in a second, and the fee in reversion in a third. So in respect of enjoyment, one may have the possession and the fee simple, and another may have a rent issuing out of it, or the tithes of its produce, or an easement, as a right of way upon it, or of common over it. ... All these kinds of property, however, all these holdings, are well known to the law and familiarly dealt with by its principles. But it must not therefore be supposed that incidents of a novel kind

[21] PA Fenet, *Recueil complet des travaux préparatoires du code civil*, 11 (Osnabrück, Otto Zeller 1968; repr of the 1827 edn) 33.

[22] Parlementaire Geschiedenis van het Nieuwe Burgerlijk Wetboek (Deventer, Kluwer, 1981) 3.

[23] (1834) 2 Myl & K 517 39 Eng Rep 1042.

can be devised and attached to property, at the fancy or caprice of any owner. It is clearly inconvenient both to the science of law and to the public weal, that such a latitude should be given. There can be no harm in allowing the fullest latitude to men in binding themselves and their representatives, that is, their assets, real and personal, to answer in damages for breach of their obligations. This tends to no mischief, and is reasonable liberty to bestow; but great detriment would arise and much confusion of rights, if parties were allowed to invent new modes of holding and enjoying real property, and to impress upon their lands and tenements a peculiar character, which should follow them into all hands, however remote. Every close, every messuage, might thus be held in a several fashion; and it would hardly be possible to know what rights the acquisition of any parcel conferred, or what obligations it imposed.

Notes

(1) The *numerus clausus* is a filter through which legal relations must pass for property law to apply. When a legal relation does not pass the filter, it consequently belongs to the law of obligations. When it does pass through the filter, we know the law of property applies and we can apply other principles and rules. These other principles and rules include the transparency principle dealt with in section IV, and the rules of *nemo dat*, *potior iure*, that limited rights have priority over fuller rights and the rule of special protection (section V).

(2) Property law is mandatory law, which means that parties will have to respect its rules. Party autonomy is therefore—and this is a major difference with contract law—not the starting point in property law.

(3) First and foremost, the *numerus clausus* limits party autonomy, but it is also a rule of 'constitutional' property law in that it decides on who has authority to create new property rights. In civil law systems this authority is, at least as a starting point, given to the legislator, which does not exclude occasional development of new property rights through case law. In common law systems this authority rests primarily with the judiciary, although through legislation new types of property rights can also be created.[24]

III.B LIMITATIONS ON PARTY AUTONOMY

Now that we have seen that the *numerus clausus* of property rights limits party autonomy, we can look at how this party autonomy is limited. These limitations are twofold and concern the number of property rights from which the parties may choose as well as the mandatory content of the selected property right.

[24] See eg the so-called commonhold scheme, which is a special type of holding a fee simple introduced by the Commonhold and Leasehold Reform Act 2002.

III.B.1 TYPENZWANG

Staudinger-Seiler, Third Book—Property Law. Introduction to Property Law, §§854–82[25] **1.24 (DE)**

The *principle of numerus clausus* also denotes the general characteristics of absolute rights: rights on objects are standardised in their nature and content by the law and custom. Only those rights dealt with by these sources of law, so a limited number, can exist. Therefore there is numerus clausus of property rights. Parties must use the types of property rights available to them, hence the *Typenzwang*.

Cour de cassation civ 3e, 18 January 1984[26] **1.25 (FR)**

Association of owners v Spouses Olive and others

NUMERUS CLAUSUS: TYPENZWANG

Right to put up posters

The right to put up posters is neither a right of servitude nor usufruct.

Facts: The owners, named David-Chaux, of a building sold their building to several owners in an apartment co-ownership regime. As a part of the sale the former owners reserved themselves the perpetual right to put up posters on one of the walls of the building. The regulations of the association of owners described the right as a right of servitude. The association of owners contested the right and in lower instance it was recognised as a property right of the former owners, but as a right of usufruct and not as servitude. The association of co-owners appealed this decision, claiming that, as the right was phrased as a perpetual right, it could not be a usufruct or, if it was a usufruct, the right would only exist for the duration of the lifetime of the former owners.

Held: The right to put up posters as reserved by the former owners of the building is—contrary to earlier classifications—not a right of usufruct.

Judgment: Regarding the single argument of the incidental appeal:

Article 578 Civil Code

Whereas the usufruct is the right to enjoy things, the ownership of which is held by someone else, like the owner himself, but under the obligation to preserve the substance;

Whereas after having taken note that the parties David-Chaux had placed under co-ownership regime, considering its sale by land parcel, an immovable, the object of that co-ownership, they had reserved 'in perpetuity the right to post' on one of the walls of the immovable, with the possibility to 'transfer this right to third parties', in the appealed decision it was held that this right should have been qualified as a right of usufruct; Holding that the act reserved to the parties David-Chaux, a perpetual posting right, the Court of Appeal has infringed the text referred to above,

For these reasons, and without any need to rule on the main appeal, overrules ..., sends back before the Appeal Court of Nîmes.

[25] *Staudinger-Seiler, Drittes Buch—Sachenrecht. Einleitung zum Sachenrecht* (München, Sellier, de Gruyter, 2001) §§854–82, pp 24–25

[26] D 1985, 504.

Note

These cases illustrate the principle known as *Typenzwang*. When parties wish to create a property right, they must choose from the available property rights. A perpetual right cannot therefore take the form of a right of usufruct, which by its nature can only exist for the duration of the life of the right-holder. See Chapter 4 on the content of the property rights mentioned.

III.B.2 TYPENFIXIERUNG

F Baur, JF Baur, and R Stürner, Property Law[27] **1.26 (DE)**

Already from the necessity of such delimitations the legislature cannot but limit the types, and in two ways:

(a) The possible rights *in rem* in property law have to be enshrined in law; hence there is the so-called numerus clausus of property rights (*Typenzwang*).

(b) At least the outlines of the content of a possible right *in rem* have to be laid down by mandatory law (*Typenfixierung*).

Court of Appeal, 26 and 27 October 1936[28] **1.27 (E&W)**

Clore v Theatrical Properties

CONTENT OF A RIGHT OF LEASE

Front-of-house theatre rights

The granting of front-of-house rights does not grant exclusive possession to a right-holder and therefore cannot constitute a lease.

Facts: On 7 November 1899 an agreement was made between Bruce and Leigh granting the latter the 'front-of-house rights', a set of rights entitling Leigh to the use of the refreshment area of the theatre as well as the right to sell refreshments there. To this extent the agreement stated that 'the lessor doth hereby demise and grant unto the lessee the free and exclusive use of all the refreshment rooms of the theatre for the purpose only of the supply to and the accommodation of the visitors to the theatre and for no other purpose whatsoever'. The lessor, Bruce, then assigned his interest and the new right-holder tried to prevent the lessee from exercising his rights under the lease. In addition, the lessee had assigned his rights under the lease.

Held: The agreement is a mere personal covenant as it does not grant exclusive possession. Because the new lessor is not party to the contract, he is not bound by its terms.

Judgment: Lord Wright MR—The case to which reference must be made is *Daly v Edwardes*. It was held in that case that a document similar in character and effect to the document in the present case was not a lease or a grant of part of an interest in land, but was merely a personal contract or as it was sometimes said a licence. In the Court of Appeal, Rigby LJ seems to have held that the matter was not free from doubt. He says, at pp 550, 551:

[27] F Baur, JF Baur and R Stürner, *Sachenrecht*, 18th edn (München: CH Beck'sche Verlagsbuchhandlung, 2009) 3, discussing delimitiations of rights in one and the same object.

[28] [1936] 3 All ER 483.

'Not only does the form of this agreement naturally give rise to the arguments that have been presented to us on the part of the appellant, but I must say that at the first sight of the agreement I was very much inclined to take the view for which they have contended. It is only after consideration, and careful consideration, that I have come to the conclusion that a licence instead of a lease of the hereditament was really what was intended. It looks very much like a lease of land. But I do not think that any of those considerations, or all of those considerations put together, should take us away from the real substance of the matter as I deduce it from the words used; not only, however, from those words, but first of all from those words, and afterwards from the rest of the agreement. It is the free and exclusive licence and right to use. Those are not words prima facie of a demise of land, although they may, under certain circumstances, have the effect of a demise of land. But what are Frank Warr & Co. to have the use of? The refreshment rooms, bars and smoke rooms. I stop there because that is enough for my purpose. They are to have the same right in the bars, for instance, that they are to have in the refreshment rooms and smoke rooms. I cannot get over the fact that they never imagined that they were to have a lease of the refreshment rooms and the smoke rooms, and if not of those then not of the bars. Let us look at the state of the admitted facts. The smoke room was to be used by those persons who paid for places in the theatre, or were admitted by the order of the lessee of the theatre. The refreshment rooms were to be used in like manner by the same class of people, and it did not follow that they were going there for refreshments. They might obviously not intend that at all; they might go to obtain a change of atmosphere and of scene, and, if they did not smoke, at any rate to get relief from the tedium of their places in the theatre. No doubt the bars were peculiarly required for the purpose of serving out refreshment. But I cannot see how in any other way they differed from the rest of the rooms, the refreshment rooms, and the smoke rooms. No doubt the persons who had got a licence to sell refreshments had a perfect right to say to others: "You must not come behind our bars, because you will interfere with us, not because you would be a trespasser." They would say, whether to the lessee of the theatre, or to anybody else "You must not come here, because we have the right by contract to do everything that is required for serving refreshments, and we cannot do that effectually and properly if you come behind the bars." That is not treating them as trespassers on land. I cannot see that that was in their minds. I asked a question which probably was a very small matter, but it seemed to me not immaterial: "Who lights the rooms?" and it appears that the lessee of the theatre does so. That lighting probably would not involve much interference. If the lights were turned on once, probably it would not be likely that they would have to be interfered with during the whole of the entertainment that was then going on. But still, without a reservation for that purpose in the lease as a mere consequence of his ownership, I apprehend that if there had been any difficulty about the electric lights during the performance, it would have been the lessee of the theatre who would have been entitled to see that the lights were put right. At any rate, if any catastrophe had happened, it would be set right by him and not by the alleged lessees of these refreshment rooms. On the whole, I think that the proper conclusion is that Frank Warr & Co. took no estate or interest in land, but that they were entitled, for all reasonable purposes,

> to consider themselves as having an exclusive licence to provide refreshments and all that follows from that privilege, and nothing else at all.'

This case went to the House of Lords, and the Earl of Halsbury LC gives judgment to the same effect and points out, at p 652, that:

> 'Those who drew up the documents have used words inappropriate to the particular thing with which they were dealing. But they are not words of art, and it is frankly and most properly conceded that we must, if we can, find out from the language of the instrument, having regard to the relations between the parties and the object which was on the face of the instrument apparent, what were the real intentions of the parties. And really but for the extremely confused and inaccurate use of technical words from time to time in the course of those instruments the object is clear enough. The lessee of a theatre is making a bargain with a refreshment contractor, and he wants proper accommodation for those whom he invites to his theatre to be provided by some person who shall preside over and have the command and the profits of the refreshment department of the theatre. The mode in which the parties have contracted is that which really makes the difficulty. But when one looks at the whole thing there is not one word which necessarily, as a matter of art, decides the question. Then let us see what the words are that they did use. They did not say that they demise, for instance, but they say that the person with whom the contract is made is to have the use of certain parts of the premises, and—I confess that I follow the language and the reasoning of the Lord Chief Justice very much—if you look through the whole thing you see what is the object of it. No doubt both parties intended that the one should be the exclusive refreshment contractor, and that the other person who was the lessee of the theatre should have certain control and certain powers of dealing with that part of the theatre which was reserved for refreshment—the refreshment bars, cupboards, &c. If that is the real meaning of the parties, is there anything in the language which they have used which prevents that intention from being carried out? I think not. I think the instrument most unfortunately framed—framed apparently by attempting to adapt a common form of lease of land to the contract into which the parties were entering; and from time to time language is used—I think the strongest case is where you find the covenant for quiet enjoyment, and the payment of rent and so on—which is more appropriate to the ordinary transactions by way of conveyance and lease and covenants in a lease. But still, when I look at the whole and see the relations between the parties, and that which both parties were contemplating to be done respectively by one and the other, I come to the conclusion that the decision which was arrived at by the courts below is correct, and I also come to the conclusion that there is nothing in the language of the instrument in question which prevents us from carrying out the real intention of the parties.' ...

Now, it is perfectly true that the construction of one contract is not necessarily a guide to the construction of another contract, and that is true certainly when there are differences of language in the documents to be construed. But where there is no such difference in language as would justify a court of law refusing to apply to the documents the construction which the court applied to the other cases, then the court should apply that construction. The language of the instrument in the case before this court, in some respects is more favourable to being construed as a demise of an interest in land than in the other cases to which I have referred. In some respects it is the other way. Words which include in the term "lessee, his executors, administrators and assigns" are not prima facie applicable when what is dealt with is a personal contract or a mere licence. I cannot attach to these words any meaning which would import the sense that what was being transferred was an interest in land. I think, on the contrary, that this is not a document which creates an estate in land, but merely one which is a personal contract between the parties named therein and is only enforceable among parties between whom there is privity of contract. For example, the assignees of Bruce, the lessee, would be entitled to enforce this contract but only against the actual contracting parties. The obligation as a whole goes beyond a mere licence. It involves an obligation to fulfil the terms of the indenture and involves a liability to damages if there is a breach. This obligation may be revoked by the covenantor, but if he does so he will break the conditions and be liable in damages. The defendants who seek to establish their rights under this document are not seeking to establish them against Mr Leigh but against the plaintiff, the assigned of Mr Leigh—which is not possible at common law as there is no privity of contract between the plaintiff and the defendants, and as the defendants can only enforce these rights on the contract the defence must fail. ...

I do not think that a personal covenant as in the present case can be binding on a third party with notice, and this appeal must fail.

Notes

(1) Although parties enjoy some freedom to modify their property rights to their liking, the parties must stay within the boundaries of the property right they have selected. When parties attempt to create a property right which does not fit within the set criteria, the right cannot be a property right and must be a personal right. The case of the 'front-of-house rights' illustrates the consequences this might have.

(2) Furthermore, the French case on the right to put up posters above offers illustration on how contents of a property right may alter its qualification as a different type of property right, or, in the end, cause the right to be a personal right altogether.

III.C LEGAL PROVISIONS ON *NUMERUS CLAUSUS*

Code Civil **1.28 (FR)**

Article 543 One can have, in relation to things, either a right of ownership, or a simple right of enjoyment, or merely a land burden.

Burgerlijk Wetboek **1.29 (NL)**

Article 3:81(1) He who is entitled to an independent and transferable right can, within the limits of that right, establish the limited rights that are prescribed by law.

Law of Property Act 1925 **1.30 (E&W)**

Section 1 Legal Estates and Equitable Interests (1) The only estates in land which are capable of subsisting or of being conveyed or created at law are—

(a) An estate in fee simple absolute in possession;
(b) A term of years absolute.

(2) The only interests or charges in or over land which are capable of subsisting or of being conveyed or created at law are—

(a) An easement, right, or privilege in or over land for an interest equivalent to an estate in fee simple absolute in possession or a term of years absolute;
(b) A rentcharge in possession issuing out of or charged on land being either perpetual or for a term of years absolute;
(c) A charge by way of legal mortgage;
(d) ... and any other similar charge on land which is not created by an instrument;
(e) Rights of entry exercisable over or in respect of a legal term of years absolute, or annexed, for any purpose, to a legal rentcharge.

(3) All other estates, interests, and charges in or over land take effect as equitable interests.

Notes

(1) The principle of *numerus clausus* of property rights is mainly developed by doctrine. However, in France and the Netherlands, the principle also finds reflection in the civil codes. In Germany the principle of *numerus clausus* is not explicitly mentioned, but could be derived from the fact that property rights are dealt with by legislation. See Chapter 4 on the catalogue of property rights in these civil law systems.

(2) In English law, the recognition of the *numerus clausus* is somewhat more difficult. As can be seen above, in the eyes of the judiciary, the list of property rights in English law is closed so that parties cannot create new property rights at their 'fancy or caprice'. With regard to land, the Law of Property Act 1925 standardised the available property rights at common law. In equity, the list is somewhat longer and it could be discussed whether that list is not open.

(3) Depending on the legal system the rights mentioned in these provisions are exhaustive. In French law, Article 543 Cciv, was originally intended to be exhaustive, but, as can be seen in Chapter 3, new property rights have been introduced by legislation. In English law too the property rights mentioned in section 1 of the Law of Property Act 1925 have been modified by later legislation—eg the rentcharge which was modified by the Rentcharges Act 1977.

III.D IS THE LIST OF PROPERTY RIGHTS REALLY CLOSED?

As seen above, the principle of *numerus clausus* of property rights allows parties limited freedom but does not mean they may create new property rights themselves. In most legal systems, however, the judiciary has allowed the recognition of new property rights. These new property rights are dealt with in Chapter 3. Here two excerpts illustrate how the judiciary has interpreted *numerus clausus*.

Cour de cassation, 13 February 1834[29] **1.31 (FR)**

Caquelard v Lemoine

NUMERUS CLAUSUS?

Caquelard case

Two parties can very well be co-owners, even with an unfamiliar division of rights.

Facts: This case concerned a situation in which one party, Caquelard, owned a riverbank and the grass and plants on top of that, and another party, Lemoine, was owner of the trees which grew on that land. A lower court in Rouen had decided that both parties were owners, or at least co-owners, of the riverbank, but that Caquelard had to respect the rights of Lemoine over the trees.[30] Lemoine's rights, the court of Rouen held, were recognised as a servitude.[31] Caquelard argued that the court of Rouen had violated the Civil Code's principles of ownership.

Held: The Cour de cassation rejected the appeal and ruled that the two parties could very well be co-owners, even with an unfamiliar division of rights as in this case. The court stated that Articles 544, 546 and 552 Cciv represent the general law on ownership, but are not prohibitive.[32]

Judgment: On the first ground of appeal, derived from the violation of articles 544, 546, 552 and 691 of the Civil Code and article 607 of the Custom of Normandy;

Considering, as to fact, that, after having formally by its motives recognised to Caquelard and Lemoine an absolute co-estate in the verge or the bank concerned, and after having explained the nature and the respective limits of this estate, according to the facts and circumstances of the title and notably the common origin of the settlements, the reciprocal possession, the common interest in the conservation of the meadow, the burden of maintenance and the appreciation of certain documents, the contested judgment recognises and declares once more, in its decision, the same concurrence of owners and the respective limits of their estates; which precludes the application of the articles 691 of the Civil Code and 607 of the Custom of Normandy;

Considering as to law, that the articles 544, 546 and 552 of the Civil Code are declaratory on the proper law related to the nature and to the effects of the estate, but that they are not prohibitive;

That neither these articles, nor any other law exclude the different modifications and decompositions of which the ordinary law of property is susceptible;

[29] DP 1834.I.218, S.1834.I.205.

[30] Cour royale de Rouen, 14 March 1832, A Hervieu, *De la limitation des droits réels. Contribution a l'étude de la distinction des droits réels et personnels*, Diss (Caen, 1981) 57.

[31] *Servitude discontinue, non établie par titre*, S 1834.I.205. See also AM Patault, 'La propriété non exclusive au XIXe siècle: histoire de la dissociation juridique de l'immeuble' [1983] *Revue historique de droit français et étranger* 222–23.

[32] The Court states 'Attendue, en droit, que les articles 544, 546 et 552 du Code civil, sont déclaratifs du droit commun relativement à la nature et aux effets de la propriété, mais ne sont pas prohibitifs.'

House of Lords, 13 May 1965[33] **1.32 (E&W)**

National Provincial Bank v Ainsworth

NUMERUS CLAUSUS?

Criteria for new property rights

New property rights cannot be added to the list.

Facts: A wife had been deserted by her husband, but had a right to continue to live in the matrimonial home. However, the husband had charged the matrimonial home and defaulted on his payments. The question before the House of Lords was whether the wife had a property right to live in the house which would bind the bank as a chargee.

Held: The right in question is not a property right because it does not fulfil the criteria of a property right.

Judgement: Lord Wilberforce—On any division, then, which is to be made between property rights on the one hand, and personal rights on the other hand, however broad or penumbral the separating band between these two kinds of rights may be, there can be little doubt where the wife's rights fall. Before a right or an interest can be admitted into the category of property, or of a right affecting property, it must be definable, identifiable by third parties, capable in its nature of assumption by third parties, and have some degree of permanence or stability. The wife's right has none of these qualities, it is characterised by the reverse of them.

Notes

(1) Although the Cour de cassation does not explicitly state it, the general opinion in French law is that the decision by the court should be taken as to say that Article 543 Cciv is not exhaustive and that, theoretically, new property rights can be added to the list. With this decision, the Cour de cassation has held itself competent to recognise new property rights, and the court has done so with the recognition of the rights of retention and real or property suretyship as property rights.[34]

(2) Following the English case it could be possible to argue that in English law the list of property rights is not closed after all. Also, in English law the courts have been known to recognise new property rights, as can be seen in Chapter 3. These include, for example, restrictive covenants.

IV. TRANSPARENCY: SPECIFICITY AND PUBLICITY

Passing the *numerus clausus* test is not sufficient for the qualification of a right as a property right. Passing a second test is required: the right should be transparent to everybody concerned. Transparency has two aspects: specificity and publicity. First of all, the object of the property right must be precise enough. The strength of a property right is such that it must be clear which objects are controlled by that right. Furthermore, again given the strength of any property right, third parties

[33] *National Provincial Bank Ltd v Ainsworth* [1965] AC 1175.
[34] See Chapter 5.

must be able to obtain information about such a right: publicity is vital in property relations. In the following excerpts examples of both aspects of the transparency principle will be given. It will be seen that frequently the decision as to whether or not a particular right can be qualified as a property right is the outcome of a balancing test based upon both the principle of *numerus clausus* and the transparency principle.

KH Schwab and H Prütting, Property Law[35] **1.33 (DE)**

I. The principle of certainty and the principle of specificity. All property rights can only exist on individual and specified objects. Property rights on a kind of certain object do not exist. One speaks of the so-called principle of certainty and the principle of specificity or specialty.

1. The principle of specificity. Legal acts in property law must concern certain specified objects; a parallel to unspecified debts is impossible. It is possible to enter into a contract, which refers only to the type, etc of certain things on delivery, however no one can transfer the ownership of non-ascertained objects. A right to control as to possibly existing, though not yet ascertained, goods is unthinkable. The single object is in its entirety, but also when it changes, governed by a property right. For, according to §93 essential components of an object cannot be the subject of specific rights, ie rights in rem as opposed to mere obligations for example, it is impossible for several people to own parts of a house (with the exception of apartment-ownership (*Wohnungseigentum*); ...

2. The principle of certainty. While there is certain overlap between the two, one can distinguish the aforementioned principle of specifity from the principle of certainty. Typical expressions of the principle of specifity are the ... examples of transfer of ownership of a warehouse, library or other collection of objects. In property law every single 'specific' thing is transferred. In contrast, the emphasis in the certainty principle is in particular that each disposal makes it exactly clear which 'ascertained' thing is concerned by the disposal. Typical expressions for this problem of certainty are transfers of security with abstract features. ... If in such a case the principle of certainty is loosened—by the case law on security transfers of unities of objects—and only requires the objects to be determinable [*Bestimmbarkeit*], it is not apparent that this loosening also extends to the principle of specificity. All the arrangements that have property effects must, above all, have a precise content (ie the exact definition of the content of a servitude or a real burden; the exact determination of the amount of each sum of money or the interest rate on the mortgage).

II. The principle of separation [*Trennungsgrundsatz*] and the principle of abstraction. 1. Principle of separation. The strict separation that the German Civil Code makes between the legal act creating a duty and the legal act by which the duty is fulfilled is very important. Both are agreements but with differing contents. By concluding a sales agreement the seller obliges himself to transfer the ownership; by his consent to transfer he fulfils that obligation by transferring the ownership to the buyer. The real [or property] agreement is usually only made pursuant to, and to the fulfilment of, an agreement of a binding nature. Nobody enters into a real

[35] Schwab and Prütting, above n 3, 9 *et seq.*

agreement without at least assuming being bound by a contract. This is the legal foundation, the *causa*, of the real transaction. Therefore, the underlying contract is also referred to as the causal transaction. That is why the contract from which obligations arise is also called the causal legal act. Terminologically it is not uncommon to find the separation between legal acts giving rights to obligations and real agreements under the heading 'principle of abstraction' [*Abstraktionsprinzip*]. On closer inspection, however, the separation of both transactions and the special abstraction of real transactions ... can again be distinguished.

2. Principle of abstraction. The separation of both agreements is further sharpened, in the sense that the real contract is abstract, ie its effect is independent of the effect of the causal transaction. The real agreement consequently has effect (to be precise: its effect is independently determinable), also when the causal transaction has not been established, void, or became void after having been successfully challenged. The same holds true when both contracts have been concluded simultaneously and are recorded in a deed.

III. The principle of publicity (principle of public knowledge). The absolute nature of property rights is derived from the desire of property law to make clearly known to anybody the legal relationships in property law and changes thereto.

Privy Council, 25 May 1994[36] **1.34 (E&W)**

Re Goldcorp Exchange Ltd (in receivership)

AN OBJECT OF PROPERTY LAW MUST BE SPECIFIED

Re Goldcorp

No passing of property without appropriation.

Facts: In this New Zealand case a company dealing in gold and other precious metals had sold bullion for future delivery to numerous purchasers. The bullion was not appropriated to the individual contracts, but was instead stored en masse as part of the company's overall stock of bullion. Subsequently the company became insolvent and a bank holding a debenture secured by a floating charge appointed receivers. The purchasers contend, inter alia, that under the contracts of sale ownership of the bullion has passed to them, so that the bullion purchased is not subject to the bank's charge.

Held: The purchasers have not acquired ownership of the bullion, since no bullion has been appropriated to their individual contracts.

Judgment: II. The issues.

As already seen, by the time the judgment in the Court of Appeal had been delivered the proprietary claims of the customers had been widened to comprise not only bullion but also the general assets of the company, to an extent representing the sums originally paid by way of purchase price. The following issues now arise for consideration:

(i) Did the property in any bullion pass to the customers immediately upon the making of the purchases—

(a) simply by virtue of contract of purchase itself, or

(b) by virtue of the written and oral statements made in the brochures and by the company's employees? (Although these were referred to in argument as repre-

[36] [1995] 1 AC 74.

sentations their Lordships believe them to be more in the nature of contractual undertakings, and therefore call them 'the collateral promises').

(ii) Did the property in any bullion subsequently acquired by the company pass to the customer upon acquisition?

(iii) When the customers paid over the purchase monies under the contract of sale, did they retain a beneficial interest in them by virtue of an express or constructive trust?

(iv) Should the court now grant a restitutionary remedy of a proprietary character in respect of the purchase moneys?

If the answer to any of these questions is in the affirmative it will be necessary to consider the extent to which the customer's rights in the relevant subject matter can be applied to the bullion or other assets now in the possession of the company.

III. Title to bullion: the sale contracts

Their Lordships begin with the question whether the customer obtained any form of proprietary interest, legal or equitable, simply by virtue of the contract of sale, independently of the collateral promises. In the opinion of their Lordships the answer is so clearly that he did not that it would be possible simply to quote section 18 of the Sale of Goods Act 1908 (New Zealand) and one reported case and turn to more difficult issues. It is however convenient to pause for a moment to consider why the answer must inevitably be negative, because the reasons for this answer are the same as those which stand in the way of the customers at every point of the case. It is common ground that the contracts in question were for the sale of unascertained goods. For present purposes, two species of unascertained goods may be distinguished. First, there are generic goods. These are sold on terms which preserve the seller's freedom to decide for himself how and from what source he will obtain goods answering the contractual description. Secondly, there are 'goods sold ex-bulk'. By this expression their Lordships denote goods which are by express stipulation to be supplied from a fixed and a pre-determined source, from within which the seller may make his own choice (unless the contract requires it to be made in some other way) but outside which he may not go. For example, 'I sell you 60 of the 100 sheep now on my farm'.

Approaching these situations *a priori* common sense dictates that the buyer cannot acquire title until it is known to what goods the title relates. Whether the property then passes will depend upon the intention of the parties and in particular on whether there has been a consensual appropriation of particular goods to the contract. On the latter question the law is not straightforward, and if it had been decisive of the present appeal it would have been necessary to examine cases such as *Carlos Federspiel & Co SA v Charles Twigg & Co Ltd* ... and other cases cited in argument. In fact, however, the case turns not on appropriation but on ascertainment, and on the latter the law has never been in doubt. It makes no difference what the parties intended if what they intend is impossible: as is the case with an immediate transfer of title to goods whose identity is not yet known. As Lord Blackburn wrote in his treatise on The Effect of the Contract of Sale ... a principal inspiration of the Sale of Goods Act 1893:—

> 'The first of the rules that the parties must be agreed as to the specific goods on which the contract is to attach before there can be a bargain and sale, is one that is founded on the very nature of things. Till the parties are agreed on the specific individual goods the contract can be no more than a contract to supply

goods answering a particular description, and since the vendor would fulfil his part of the contract by furnishing any parcel of goods answering that description, and the purchaser could not object to them if they did answer the description, it is clear there can be no intention to transfer the property in any particular lot of goods more than another, till it is ascertained which are the very goods sold.'

'This rule has existed at all times; it is to be found in the earliest English law books ... It makes no difference, although the goods are so far ascertained that the parties have agreed that they shall be taken from some specified larger stock. In such a case the reason still applies: the parties did not intend to transfer the property in one portion of the stock more than in another, and the law which only gives effect to their intention, does not transfer the property in any individual portion.'

Their Lordships have laboured this point, about which there has been no dispute, simply to show that any attempt by the non-allocated claimants to assert that a legal title passed by virtue of the sale would have been defeated, not by some arid legal technicality but by what Lord Blackburn called 'the very nature of things'. The same conclusion applies, and for the same reason. to any argument that a title in equity was created by the sale, taken in isolation from the collateral promises. It is unnecessary to examine in detail the decision of the Court of Appeal in *re Wait* for the facts were crucially different. There, the contract was for a sale ex-bulk. The 500 tons in question formed part of a larger quantity shipped on board a named vessel; the seller could supply from no other source; and once the entire quantity had been landed and warehoused the buyer could point to the bulk and say that his goods were definitely there although he could not tell which part they were. It was this feature which prompted the dissenting opinion of Sargant LJ that the sub purchasers had a sufficient partial equitable interest in the whole to found a claim for measuring-out and delivery of 500 tons. No such feature exists here. Nevertheless, the reasoning contained in the judgment of Atkin LJ ... which their Lordships' venture to find irresistible, points unequivocally to the conclusion that under a simple contract for the sale of unascertained goods no equitable title can pass merely by virtue of the sale.

This is not, of course, the end of the matter. As Atkin LJ himself acknowledged at page 636:—

'[The rules in the statute] have, of course, no relevance when one is considering rights legal or equitable, which may come into existence *dehors* the contract for sale. A seller or a purchaser may, of course, create any equity he pleases by way of charge, equitable assignment or any other dealing with or disposition of goods, the subject matter of sale: and he may, of course, create such an equity as one of the terms expressed in the contract of sale. ...'

Their Lordships therefore turn to consider whether there is anything in the collateral promises which enables the customers to overcome the practical objections to an immediate transfer of title. The most direct route would be to treat the collateral promises as containing a declaration of trust by the company in favour of the customer. The question then immediately arises—What was the subject matter of the trust? The only possible answer, so far as concerns an immediate transfer of title on sale. Is that the trust related to the company's current stock of bullion answering the contractual description; for there was no other bullion to which the trust could relate. Their Lordships do not doubt that the vendor of goods sold ex-bulk can effectively declare himself trustee of the bulk in favour of the buyer, so as to confer *pro tanto* an equitable title. But the present transaction was not of this type. The company cannot have intended to create an interest in its general stock of gold which would have inhibited any dealings with it otherwise than for the purpose of delivery under the non-allocated sale contracts. Conversely the customer, who is presumed to have intended that somewhere in the bullion held by or on behalf of the company there would be stored a quantity representing 'his' bullion, cannot have contemplated that his rights would be fixed by reference to a combination of the quantity of bullion of the relevant description which the company happened to have in stock at the relevant time and the number of purchasers who happened to have open contracts at that time for goods of that description. To understand the transaction in this way would be to make it a sale of bullion ex-bulk, which on the documents and findings of fact it plainly was not.

Nor is the argument improved by re-shaping the trust, so as to contemplate that the property in the *res vendita* did pass to the customer, albeit in the absence of delivery, and then merged in a general equitable title to the pooled stock of bullion. Once again the argument contradicts the transaction. The customer purchased for the physical delivery on demand of the precise quantity of bullion fixed by his contract, not a shifting proportion of a shifting bulk, prior to delivery. It is of course true that a vendor may agree to retain physical possession of the goods on behalf of his purchaser after the sale has been completed, and that there may be a constructive delivery and redelivery of possession, so as to transform the vendor into a bailee or pledgee without the goods actually changing hands: See per Lord Atkinson in *Dublin City Distillery Ltd v Doherty*. Lord Atkinson was there contemplating a situation, such as existed in the *Dublin City* case itself, where the goods held in the warehouse were already identified (by numbers on the casks: see page 825), so that the contract was one for the sale of specific goods under which the property would pass at once to the vendee. The case is, however, quite different where the sale is of generic goods. Even if the present contract had been a sale ex-bulk, in the sense that the contractual source was the bulk of bullion in the store, section 18 of the 1908 Act would have prevented the property from passing on sale: see *Laurie v Dudin & Sons* and *Whitehouse v Frost*. The present case is even more clear, since the customers contracted to purchase generic goods without any stipulation as to their source.

The next group of arguments for the non-allocated claimants all turn on an estoppel, said to derive from the collateral promises. Their Lordships derive no assistance from cases such as *Waltons Stores (Interstate) Ltd v Maher* and *Commonwealth of Australia v Verwayen* which show that on occasion a party may estop himself from relying on the protection of the statute. No such estoppel could assist the customers here, for the problem facing them at every turn is not section 18, but the practical reality underlying it which Lord Blackburn called 'the very nature of things': namely that it is impossible to have a title to goods, when nobody knows to which goods the title relate. The same objection rules out reliance on cases such as in *re Sharpe* concerning what is called a proprietary estoppel.

A more plausible version of the argument posits that the company, having represented to its customers that they had title to bullion held in the vaults, cannot now be heard to say that they did not. At first sight this argument gains support from a small group of cases, of which *Knights v Wiffen* is the most prominent. Wiffen had a large quantity of barley lying in sacks in his granary, close to a railway station. He agreed to sell 80 quarters of this barley to Maris, without appropriating any particular sacks. Maris sold 60 quarters to Knights, who paid for them and received in exchange a document signed by Maris addressed to the station master, directing him to deliver 60 quarters of barley. This was shown by the station master to Wiffen who told him that when he got the forwarding note the barley would be put on the line. Knights gave a forwarding note to the station master for 60 quarters of barley. Maris became bankrupt, and Wiffen, as unpaid vendor, refused to part with the barley. Knights sued Wiffen in trover, to which Wiffen pleaded that the barley was not the property of the plaintiff. A very strong court of Queen's Bench found in favour of the plaintiff. Blackburn J explained the matter thus, at pages 655–666:

> 'No doubt the law is that until an appropriation from a bulk is made, so that the vendor has said what portion belongs to him and what portion belongs to the buyer, the goods remain *in solido,* and no property passes. But can Wiffen here be permitted to say, "I never set aside any quarters?". ... The defendant knew that, when he assented to the delivery order, the plaintiff, as a reasonable man would rest satisfied— ... The plaintiff may well say, "I abstained from active measures in consequence of your statement, and I am entitled to hold you precluded from denying that what you stated was true".'

There may perhaps be a shadow over this decision, notwithstanding the high authority of the court: see the observations of Brett LJ in *Simm v Anglo-American Telegraph Co*. Assuming that the decision was nevertheless correct the question is whether it applies to the present case. Their Lordships consider that, notwithstanding the apparent similarities, it does not. The agreement for sale in *Knights v Wiffen* (*supra*) was a sale ex-bulk, or at least it must have been seen as such, for otherwise Blackburn J's judgment would have contradicted his treatise in the passage above quoted.

On this view, the bulk was the whole of the stock in Wiffen's warehouse. This stock was therefore committed to the purchase to the extent that Wiffen could not properly have sold the whole of it without making delivery of part to his buyer. Another and more important aspect of the same point is that the bulk actually existed. The effect of Wiffen's representation was to preclude him from denying to the sub-purchaser, Knights, that he had made a sufficient appropriation from the fixed and identified bulk to give the intermediate purchaser, and hence Knights himself, the proprietary interest sufficient to found a claim in trover. The present case is quite different, for there was no existing bulk and therefore nothing from which a title could be carved out by a deemed appropriation. The reasoning of *Knights v Wiffen* (*supra*) does not enable a bulk to be conjured into existence for this purpose simply through the chance that the vendor happens to have some goods answering the description of the *res vendita* in its trading stock at the time of the sale—quite apart, of course, from the fact that if all the purchasers obtained a deemed title by estoppel there would not be enough bullion to go around.

All this aside, there is another reason why the argument founded on estoppel cannot prevail. The answer is given by Mellor J in *Knights v Wiffen* itself where quoting from Blackburn's Contract of Sale page 162 he says:—

> 'This is a rule [ie the estoppel], which, within the limits applied by law, is of great equity; for when parties have agreed to act upon an assumed state of facts, their rights between themselves are justly made to depend on the conventional

state of facts and not on the truth. The reason of the rule ceases at once when a stranger to the arrangement seeks to avail himself of the statements which were not made as a basis for him to act upon. They are for a stranger evidence against the party making the statement, but no more than evidence which may be rebutted; between the parties they form an estoppel in law.'

Later, Brett LJ was to observe in *Simm v Anglo-American TeLegraph Co* (*supra*):—

'It seems to me that an estoppel gives no title to that which is the subject matter of estoppel. The estoppel assumes that the reality is contrary to that which the person is estopped from denying, and the estoppel has no effect at all upon the reality of the Circumstances. ... A person may be estopped from denying that certain goods belong to another; he may be compelled by a suit in the nature of an action of trover to deliver them up, if he has them in his possession under his control; but if the goods, in respect of which he has estopped himself, really belonged to someone else, it seems impossible to suppose that ... he can be compelled to deliver over another's goods to the person in whose favour the estoppel exists against him. ... That person cannot recover the goods, because no property has really passed to him, he can recover only damages. In my view estoppel only creates a cause of action between the person in whose favour the estoppel exists and the person who is estopped.'

Similar statements can be found in several texts, such as for example NE Palmer, 'Bailment' 2nd Edn (1991), page 1374.

To this the customers respond that they are not obliged to assert the same proprietary interest against the bank as they would do if their opponents were strangers to the entire relationship. By taking a floating rather than an immediate fixed charge the bank accepted the risk of adverse dealings by the company with its assets, and when the charge crystallised the bank 'stood in the shoes' of the company, taking those assets with all the detrimental features which the company had attached to them. If the estoppel binds the company, then it must bind the bank as well.

Attractive as this argument has been made to seem, their Lordships cannot accept it. The chargee does not become on the crystallisation of the charge the universal successor of the chargor, in the same way as the trustee, in bankruptcy or personal representative, who is as much subject to the personal claims of third parties against the insolvent as he is entitled to the benefit of personal claims of which the insolvent is the obligee. Rather, the chargee becomes entitled to a proprietary interest which he asserts adversely to the company, personified by the liquidator and all those general creditors who share in the assets of the company. The freedom of the chargor to deal with its assets pending the crystallisation of the charge does not entail that the chargee's right to the assets is circumscribed by an indebtedness of a purely personal nature. The most that the *Knights v Wiffen* line of authority can give to the purchaser is the pretence of a title where no title exists. Valuable as it may be where one party to the estoppel asserts as against the other a proprietary cause of action such as trover, this cannot avail the purchaser in a contest with a third-party creditor possessing a real proprietary interest in a real subject matter, whereas the purchaser has no more than a pretence of a title to a subject matter which does not actually exist.

Similar obstacles stand in the way of a more elaborate version of the same argument. This seeks to combine two principles: the first that a person who represents (by attornment or otherwise) that he has goods in his possession which he holds for a third party is in certain circumstances precluded from denying to that third party that he does so possess and hold the goods even if in tact he does not; the second that a bailee of goods is precluded, as against the bailor, from denying that the bailor has a good title. The result is said to be that by acknowledging itself to be a bailee the company gave its customers a good title to that which they had agreed to purchase. Whilst acknowledging the ingenuity of this argument their Lordships are unable to accept it. If correct, it would entail that a customer, who chose to bring a proprietary action (such as trover, under the former law) rather than simply claiming damages for non-delivery would be entitled to an order for delivery-up of the goods which he had purchased. But which goods? Not a portion of the goods in store, for there was no representation and the customers cannot have believed that it was from these goods alone that by a process of separation their own orders would be fulfilled. And if not these goods, there were no others to which the title could attach since the source of supply was completely at large.

Their Lordships must also reject a further variant of the argument, whereby a trust in respect of bullion came into existence as an aspect of a bailment, so that even if title *stricto sensu* did not pass nevertheless the fruits of the breach of trust may be traced into the existing stock of bullion. In other circumstances it might be necessary to look more closely at those elements of the argument which seek to attach the characteristics of a trust to a relationship of bailment, which does not ordinarily have this character, and also at the feasibility of tracing. There is no need for this, however, since there was never any bailment, and no identifiable property to which any trust could attach.

IV. Title to after-acquired bullion

Having for these reasons rejected the submission that the non-allocated claimants acquired an immediate title by reason of the contract of sale and the collateral promises their Lordships turn to the question whether the claimants later achieved a proprietary interest when the company purchased bullion and put it into its own stock. Broadly speaking, there are two forms which such an argument might take.

According to the first, the contracts of sale were agreements for the sale of goods afterwards to be acquired. It might be contended that quite independently of any representation made by the company to the non-allocated claimants, as soon as the company acquired bullion answering the contractual description the purchaser achieved an equitable title, even though the passing of legal title *was* postponed until the goods were ascertained and appropriated at the time of physical delivery to the purchaser. In the event this argument was not separately pursued, and their Lordships mention it only by way of introduction. They will do so briefly, since it was bound to fail. The line of old cases, founded on *Holroyd v Marshall* and discussed in Benjamin on Sale of Goods, 3rd Edn (1987), pages 80, 218–219, at paras 106 and 357 which might be said to support it, was concerned with situations where the goods upon acquisition could be unequivocally identified with the individual contract relied upon. As Lord Hanworth MR demonstrated in *re Wait, supra,* the reasoning of these cases cannot be transferred to a situation like the present where there was no means of knowing to which, if any, of the non-allocated sales a particular purchase by the company was related. Since this objection on its own is fatal, there is no need to discuss the other obstacles which stand in its way.

The second category of argument asserts, in a variety of forms, that the collateral promises operated to impress on the bullion, as and when it was acquired by the company, a trust in favour of each purchaser. Before looking at the arguments in detail it is necessary to mention a problem which is very little discussed in the judgments and arguments. It will be seen that the analysis to date has involved two markedly different assumptions. The first relates to the expectation of the customer in the light of the collateral promises. The customer is assumed to have believed that it would make no difference whether he took immediate delivery of the bullion and put it in a bank, or left it with the company—except that in the latter case he would avoid the trouble, risk and expense of storage. In law this expectation could be fulfilled only by a system under which the company obtained bullion either by an outside purchase or by transfer from its own stock, and immediately stored it separately in the name of the customer, leaving it untouched until the moment of delivery or re-purchase. The second assumption relates to the obligations which the company actually undertook. It has not been suggested that this matched the customer's expectation, for there is nothing in the collateral promises, either written or oral, entitling the customer to separate and individual appropriation of goods. Instead, as shown by the passage already quoted from the judgment of McKay J, the arguments proceed on the basis that the company promised to maintain bullion, separate from its own trading stock, which would in some way stand as security, or reassurance, that the bullion would be available when the customer called for delivery. But what kind of security or reassurance? If the scheme had contemplated that, properly performed, it would have brought about a transfer of title to the individual customer before that customer's appropriated bullion was mixed in the undifferentiated bulk, analogies could have been drawn with decisions such as *Spence v Union Maine Insurance Co Ltd*, *South Australia Insurance Co v Rendell*, *Indian Oil Corporation Ltd v Greenstone Shipping SA (Panama)*, and the *United States silo cases* of which *Savage v Salem Mills Co* is an example. Since, however, even if the company had performed its obligations to the full there would have been no transfer of title to the purchaser before admixture, these cases are not in point. The only remaining alternative, consistently with the scheme being designed to give the customer any title at all before delivery, is that the company through the medium of the collateral promises had declared itself a trustee of the constantly changing undifferentiated bulk of bullion which should have been set aside to back the customers' contracts. Such a trust might well be feasible in theory, but their Lordships find it hard to reconcile with the practicalities of the scheme, for it would seem to involve that the separated bulk would become the source from which alone the sale contracts were to be supplied: whereas, as already observed, it is impossible to read the collateral promises as creating a sale ex-bulk.

This being so, whilst it is easy to see how the company's failure to perform the collateral obligations has fuelled the indignation created by its failure to deliver the bullion under the sales to non-allocated purchasers, their Lordships are far from convinced that this particular breach has in fact made any difference.

Let it be assumed, however, as did McKay J in his dissenting judgment, that the creation of a separate and sufficient stock would have given the non-allocated purchasers some kind of proprietary interest, the fact remains that the separate and sufficient stock did not exist.

The customers' first response to this objection is that even if the concept of an immediate trust derived from a bailment arising at the time of the original transactions cannot be sustained, the collateral promises created a potential or incomplete or (as it was called in argument) 'floating' bailment, which hovered above the continuing relationship between each purchaser and the company, until the company bought and took delivery of bullion corresponding to the claimant's contract, whereupon the company became bailee of the bullion on terms which involved a trust in favour of the purchaser. Their Lordships find it impossible to see how this ingenious notion, even if feasible in principle, could be put into practice here, given that the body of potential beneficiaries was constantly changing as some purchasers called for and took delivery whilst others came newly on the scene, at the same time as the pool of available bullion waxed and waned (sometimes to zero as regards some types of bullion) with fresh deliveries and acquisitions. Even if this is left aside, the concept simply does not fit the facts. True, there is no difficultly with a transaction whereby B promises A that if in the future goods belonging to A come within the physical control of B he will hold them as bailee for A on terms fixed in advance by the agreement. But this has nothing to do with a trust relationship, and it has nothing to do with the present case, since in the example given A has both title to the goods and actual or constructive possession of them before their receipt by B, whereas in the present case the non-allocated claimants had neither. The only escape would be to suggest that every time the company took delivery of bullion of a particular description all the purchasers from the company of the relevant kind of bullion acquired both a higher possessory right than the company (for such would be essential if the company was to be a bailee) and a title to the goods, via some species of estoppel derived from this notional transfer and re-transfer of possession, Their Lordships find it impossible to construct such a contorted legal relationship from the contracts of sale and the collateral promises.

Next, the claimants put forward an argument in two stages. First, it is said that because the company held itself out as willing to vest bullion in the customer and to hold it in safe custody on behalf of him in circumstances where he was totally dependent on the company, and trusted the company to do what it had promised without in practice there being any means of verification, the company was a fiduciary, From this it is deduced that the company as fiduciary created an equity by inviting the customer to look on and treat stocks vested in it as his own, which could appropriately be recognised only by treating the customer as entitled to a proprietary interest in the stock.

To describe someone as a fiduciary, without more is meaningless. As Justice Frankfurter said in *SEC v Chenery Corporation* cited in Goff and Jones on Restitution, 4th Edn at page 644:—

> 'To say that a man is a fiduciary only begins analysis it gives direction to further inquiry. To whom is he a fiduciary? What obligations does he owe as a fiduciary? In what respect has he failed to discharge these obligations? And what are the consequences of his deviation from duty?'

Here, the argument assumes that the person towards whom the company was fiduciary was the non-allocated claimant. But what kind of fiduciary duties did the company owe to the customer? None have been suggested beyond those which the company assumed under the contracts of sale read with the collateral promises; namely to deliver the goods and meanwhile to keep a separate stock of bullion (or, more accurately, separate stocks of each variety of bullion) to which the customers could look as a safeguard for performance when delivery was called for. No doubt the fact that one person is placed in a particular position vis-à-vis another through the medium of a contract does not necessarily mean that he does not also owe fiduciary duties to that other by virtue of being in that position. But the essence of a fiduciary relationship is that it creates obligations of a different character from those deriving from the contract itself. Their Lordships have not heard in argument any submission which went beyond suggesting that by virtue of being a fiduciary the company was obliged honestly and conscientiously to do what it had contract promised to do. Many commercial relationships involve just such a reliance by one party on the other, and to introduce the whole new dimension into such relationships which would flow from giving them a fiduciary character would (as it seems to their Lordships) have adverse consequences far exceeding those foreseen by Atkin LJ in *re Wait*. It is possible without misuse of language to say that the customers put faith in the company, and that their trust has not been repaid. But the vocabulary is misleading; high expectations do not necessarily lead to equitable remedies.

Let it be assumed, however, that the company could properly be described as a fiduciary and let it also be assumed that notwithstanding the doubts expressed above the non-allocated claimants would have achieved some kind of proprietary interest if the company had done what it said. This still leaves the problem, to which their Lordships can see no answer, that the company did not do what it said. There never was a separate and sufficient stock of bullion in which a proprietary interest could be created. What the non-allocated claimants are really trying to achieve is to attach the proprietary interest, which they maintain should have been created on the non-existent stock, to wholly different assets. It is understandable that the claimants, having been badly let down in a transaction concerning bullion should believe that they must have rights over whatever bullion the company still happens to possess. Whilst sympathising with this notion their Lordships must reject it, for the remaining stock, having never been separated, is just another asset of the company, like its vehicles and office furniture. If the argument applies to the bullion it must apply to the latter as well, an obviously unsustainable idea.

Finally it is argued that the court should declare in favour of the claimants a remedial constructive trust, or to use another name a restitutionary proprietary interest, over the bullion in the company's vaults. Such a trust or interest would differ fundamentally from those so far discussed, in that it would not arise directly from the transaction between the individual claimants, the company and the bullion, but would be created by the court as a measure of justice after the event. Their Lordships must return to this topic later when considering the Walker & Hall claimants who, the trial judge has held, did acquire a proprietary interest in some bullion, but they are unable to understand how the doctrine in any of its suggested formulations could apply to the facts of the present case. By leaving its stock of bullion in a non-differentiated state the company did not unjustly enrich itself by mixing its own bullion with that of the purchasers: for all the gold belonged to the company. It did not act wrongfully in acquiring, maintaining and using its own stock of bullion, since there was no term of the sale contracts or of the collateral promises, and none could possibility be implied, requiring that all bullion purchased by the company should be set aside to fulfil the unallocated sales. The conduct of the company was wrongful in the sense of being a breach of contract, but it did not involve any injurious dealing with the subject-matter of the alleged trust. Nor, if some wider equitable principle is involved, does the case become any stronger. As previously remarked the claimants' argument really comes to this, that because the company broke its contract in a way which had to do with bullion the court should call into existence a proprietary interest in whatever bullion happened to be in the possession and ownership of the company at the time when the competition between the non-allocated claimants and the other secured and unsecured creditors first arose. The company's stock of bullion had no connection with the claimants' purchases, and to enable the claimants to reach out and not only abstract it from the assets available to the body of creditors as a whole, but also to afford a priority over a secured creditor, would give them an adventitious benefit devoid of the foundation in logic and justice which underlies this important new branch of the law.

V. Conclusion on property in bullion

For these reasons their Lordships reject, in company with all the judges in New Zealand, the grounds upon which it is said that the customers acquired a proprietary interest in bullion. In the light of the importance understandably attached to this dispute in the courts of New Zealand, and the careful and well-researched arguments addressed on this appeal, the Board has thought it right to approach the question afresh in some little detail. The question is not, however, novel since it has been discussed in two English authorities very close to the point.

The first is the Judgment of Oliver J (as he then was) in *re London Wine Co (Shippers) Ltd*. The facts of that case were not precisely the same as the present, and the arguments on the present appeal have been more far-reaching than were there deployed. Nevertheless their Lordships are greatly fortified in their opinion by the close analysis of the authorities and the principles by Oliver J, and in other circumstances their Lordships would have been content to do little more than summarise it and express their entire agreement. So also with the judgment delivered by Scott LJ in *Mac-Jordan Construction Ltd v Brookmount Erostin Ltd* which is mentioned by Gault J, but not discussed since it was not then reported in full. This was a stronger case than the present, because the separate fund which the contract required the insolvent company to maintain would have been impressed with a trust in favour of the other party, if in fact it had been maintained and also because the floating charge which, as the Court of Appeal held, took priority over the contractual claim, expressly referred to the contract under which the claim arose. Once again their Lordships are fortified in their conclusion by the fact that the reasoning of Scott LJ conforms entirely with the opinion at which they have independently arrived.

Note

Publicity is reached through attaching importance to possession (particularly in the case of movables) and through registration (land, houses and movables of considerable value such as aircraft and ships). The person who possesses a movable is in a far stronger position to argue that he or she has a property right (eg ownership or title) than a non-possessor. Registration is not only a prime source of publicity with regard to land, etc, but sometimes also with regard to security rights on movables.

Hoge Raad, 3 March 1905[37] **1.35 (NL)**

Blaauboer cs v Berlips and Van Aalst

SHARP DISTINCTION BETWEEN CONTRACT LAW AND PROPERTY LAW

Blaauboer/Berlips

A contractual duty cannot limit the right of ownership itself.

Facts: In 1881 the brothers Berlips sold land to various buyers. The land was to be developed for housing. The brothers Berlips retained the ownership of a neighbouring parcel of land. They concluded a contract with the buyers that they would construct a public road on that parcel of land. Thirty years later most houses had been built on the estate, but the road had not been constructed. A buyer (Blaauboer) and an heir of a buyer claimed damages from the surviving brother for non-performance. As a defence, Berlips stated that he was no longer bound by the contract, as in 1887 the land on which the road was to be constructed had been transferred to a new owner. Only the new owner could, according to Berlips, be sued for non-performance.

Held: A contract obliging the owner of land to construct a public road on his land does not bind successive owners of that land.

Judgment: Considering that as a result of the argument made against this decision, the question has to be answered whether an obligation, taken on by the owner of an immovable with regard to that immovable, is passed to him, whom he has transferred ownership of the immovable as a result of a contract of sale, with the consequence that the obligor is relieved of that obligation;

Considering that it has to be placed in the forefront, that an obligation, arisen out of an agreement, also when this obligation is taken on by the obligor with regard to an immovable that he owns, nevertheless is a personal obligation, to which must be applied that what is laid down with regard to such obligations, unless the opposite is apparent beyond any doubt from any statutory provision;

that as such, it cannot be held in concurrence with the Court of Appeal, unless in case of the above-mentioned, that the owner, who has taken on an obligation with regard to his object, is limited in the enjoyment and free disposal of his object 'in such a way that in case of an alienation that object can only be transferred to the new owner under the same limitation or condition';

that it must surely be held that personal obligations do not limit the right of ownership itself;

Considering that, in accordance with the rule of article 1376 of the Civil Code, agreements can only be valid between the parties to it and their successors under universal title, who continue them as persons, but cannot—outside of a situation that does not present itself in this case—bring any advantage or disadvantage to third parties;

that if the obligation, which is taken on by somebody with regard to his object, would be passed to the new owner in case of a transfer of ownership of the object, then the agreement by which the obligation was created, contrary to the aforementioned provision, would be disadvantageous to the transferee, who is a third party with regard to that agreement, in as far that he is neither a party that has acted to that agreement, nor a party that has succeeded an ancestor in title to that agreement;

Considering furthermore, that, wherever the obligation would rest on each succes-

[37] 1905, Weekblad van het Recht 8191.

sive owner, as such the right to performance of that obligation would become proprietary in nature, though arising out of an agreement, something which, without a statutory provision permitting such, cannot be accepted, because this would erase the existing, sharp distinction between the law of property and the law of obligations in our civil law;

Considering that the passing of an obligation on each successive owner would also be in conflict with the system of the law concerning servitudes;

that the law, in article 721 and 722 of the Civil Code, permits placing a permanent burden on a piece of land, be it within certain boundaries, that is, solely to use in enjoyment of the servient land and solely, with regard to burdens, consisting in the obligation to tolerate something or refrain from doing something;

that as such, the legislature could not have wanted, and according to the parliamentary history did not want to, allow that on an owner, NB by agreement, any further-reaching burdens—namely to act (construct a road)—could be placed and such to the benefit of a person;

Considering that such a passing of an obligation, by which great insecurity would be created, with regard to burdens that rest on things, cannot be reconciled with the system of publicity, adopted by the law—with the exception of the acquisition by prescription—for the creation of rights *in rem*, as was already noticed for the Old Dutch law by Voet no 1 tit of the Dig Communia (8.4) and Groenewegen on the last paragraph of the Inst de Serv praed II.3;

that finally relief of a personal obligation by way of passing from one to another debtor is only possible with the cooperation or consent of the creditor, who derives from the agreement a right against him, whom he agreed with, and consequently also against his assets, and without whose consent the debtor and that security cannot be taken away from;

Considering however, that from the above-mentioned the incorrectness of the decision of the Court of Appeal cannot be derived, in case the passing of the obligation to the new owner could be based on article 1354 of the Civil Code;

that this is nonetheless not the case, because the expression of that article 'to have stipulated' does not include the committing of oneself to an obligation;

Considering on that subject:

that from the meaning, in which the noun 'stipulation' is used in certain articles of the law, no conclusions can be drawn as to the meaning to be conferred to the verb 'stipulate';

that the meaning of the latter in article 1354 is made clear by article 1351 of the Civil Code, that is in close connection to the former article, and which puts 'stipulate' as distinct from 'committing oneself', out of which must be deduced that also in article 1354 'stipulate' does not include 'committing oneself';

that Poithier—from whose Traité des Obligations, nos 53-73, the French legislature has derived articles 1119–1122 of the [Civil] Code, from which in our code, articles 1351–1354, have been adopted—uses the word 'stipuler', of which our 'stipulate' is the translation, constantly in distinction from 'promettre' as is already apparent from the heading of §II, which deals with the subject, while in connection to this it must be noted that Pothier in nos 61 and 66, in reference to heirs, uses 'stipuler' and 'promettre' but in reference to legal successors, in no 67 as well as in no 68, which are both dedicated to the *ayants cause, successeurs à titre singulier à une chose*, only uses the word 'stipuler';

that in the judgment, to the benefit of the explanation given there to article

1354, the attention is directed to the circumstance, that both obligations and rights of the testator are transferred to the heirs and therefore the same should apply to legal successors;

that, however, in considering the importance of this circumstance one should not lose sight of the fact that the obligations of the testator do not pass to the heirs on the ground of article 1354, but because heirs are, 'en quelque façon la continuation de nous-mêmes', as Pothier, no 61 states, who, in accordance with that, does not consider the stipulating for or the committing of the heirs as essentially an exception to the principle that is now expressed in article 1351 of the Civil Code;

that the mentioning of heirs in article 1354 is principally meant to determine the exception, namely that the opposite may explicitly be stipulated and will be assumed, if it arises out of the nature of the agreement; in addition, it is remarkable that the exceptions, mentioned by Pothier in no 63, only concern that which the testator had stipulated for, not that to which he had committed himself;

that, as also these exceptions did not require a special mention in the law, article 1354, for as far heirs are concerned, cannot be awarded a special meaning, but also an inference of article 1354 from heirs to legal successors, successors under particular title, with respect to whom the article does have a meaning, because it gives the ability to make stipulations at their behest, is too daring to be held permissible;

Considering, therefore, that the defendant was not relieved of his obligation by the sale and transfer of the road, the argument must be held well founded;

Notes

(1) The case shows how courts struggle when they have to decide on whether a right is of a personal or proprietory (also called real) nature.[38] In other words: whether or not a right has *erga omnes* effect (a right 'binding against the world'). From a positive side the decision shows that contract law and property law are distinct legal areas. The decision shows negatively that a right, although it relates to land is, as such, not by definition a right that passes with the ownership of the land. It is, therefore, not an absolute right. It is also not a, what might be called, qualitative right, as it also does not pass immediately together with the passing of ownership. The court uses a combination of historical, comparative and systematic arguments to reach this result.

(2) Reference is made to the law as it was applied in the province of Holland before the French Revolution. The court mentions Voet and Groenewegen. These two authors are still authoritative in South African law, where Roman-Dutch law is still the basis of property law. A further reference is made to French pre-code law: Pothier, *Traité des Obligations*, which influenced the French Civil Code and, given the enormous influence of the French Civil Code on the old Dutch Civil Code, also Dutch law. It should be noted that at the time of the decision, given the strong intellectual influence of French legal thinking on Dutch law, historical analysis in fact also meant comparative analysis, as the legal history of the old Civil Code still was young.

(3) Not only did the court look at historical (and hence comparative) arguments,

[38] In this casebook we use the term property right and not real right. However, occassionally the term real right can occur in excerpts that have not been translated.

which can be qualified as being external to the national legal system, it also approached the matter from within the national legal system itself: systematic and teleological arguments.

(4) The first systematic argument deals with the concept of contract. A contract can only bind those who are parties to the contract, as well as third parties 'under general title' (eg heirs). As a matter of principle contracts cannot benefit (except when this has been stipulated explicitly) nor burden third parties. The principle that contracts cannot benefit nor burden third parties is justified by the 'sharp separation' between the law of contract and the law of property. The binding nature of a contract implies that only by consent from the creditor can the debtor pass his duty to another person. The second systematic argument deals with the concept of servitude. The law gives mandatory requirements as to what a servitude is. A servitude is a burden for the benefit of a parcel of land (dominant tenement) and burdening a neighbouring parcel of land (servient tenement). This burden can only be passive (negative: a duty to accept/abstain or not to do something); it cannot be positive, such as constructing a street. A third systematic argument deals with the principle of transparency. Duties burdening third parties must be made public. This is also, states the court, in accordance with pre-codified law. Finally, the court states that a debtor's entire patrimony is the security for the performance of his contractual obligations. The debtor cannot take this security away from the creditor unilaterally, eg by selling and transferring the land. The creditor must give his permission. Hence, the duty to construct a road will remain the obligation of the original debtor.

Hoge Raad, 17 May 1985[39] **1.36 (NL)**

Het Eilandgebied Curaçao v Wilhelm Ascension Boyé, Johanita Elizabeth Maria Boyé and Lurdus Dionisia Boyé

PROPRIETARY EFFECT OF A CHAIN CLAUSE

Curaçao v Heirs Boyé

A chain (or perpetual) clause in a contract for the sale of land does not bind third parties, unless explicitly accepted by a third party or unless a third party commits a tort by provoking the non-performance of the duty to pass the clause on to that party.

Facts: By notarial deed of 10 March 1880 a certain Mr Sprock sold a parcel of land called 'Plantation Hermanus' to Hellmund. The deed contained a clause, creating a contractual rent, which obliged the buyer to pay a certain sum of money to the seller, his heirs or assignees depending upon the proceeds of the sale of certain minerals taken from the land. Hellmund sold the land in 1891 to WE Boyé under the same conditions as he had bought it. On 21 November 1893 WE Boyé sold the plantation to Correa. In the notarial deed of sale the duty of the new buyer towards Sprock was inserted, but also a new clause creating a comparable rent for the benefit of Boyé, his heirs and assignees, which was created as a duty for Correa, his heirs and assignees. The Plantation Hermanus was sold several times. Each time the rent clauses were inserted into the sales agreements. However, in the last deed of sale of 6 November 1974 between the the seller AR-CU and the buyer, the island of Curaçao, the clause

[39] NJ 1986, 760.

containing the passing of the rent burdens to the buyer was no longer included. The island demanded a declaration from the court that it was not bound to accept the ground rents.

Held: The buyer only commits the tort of taking advantage of the non-performance of the seller under strict conditions. Knowledge of the buyer that the clause existed and the possibility of damage to the heirs of Boyé are not sufficient grounds for accepting such a tort. Otherwise, the clause would be given an effect that would violate its contractual nature.

Judgment: As such the Court of Appeal has grounded its decision in the conclusion that the *Eilandgebied* [island of Curaçao], by profiting of the non-performance of AR-CU NV, has committed a tort against the heirs of Boyé. For the assessment of this conclusion it is important that the unlawfulness of profiting from a tort, that was accepted by the Court, necessarily includes that the *Eilandgebied*, on the punishment of being liable for tort, was obliged to abide by the clause and refrain from, for instance,—in the words of the Court of First Instance—exporting the minerals mentioned in the clause from the plantation without paying the amounts mentioned in the clause to the heirs of Boyé. The decision of the Court, therefore, leads to the result that the *Eilandgebied*, purely on the grounds of the aforementioned cognoscibility and the threat of damage, would be bound by the clause, as if passed to the Eilandgebied as successor of AR-CU NV and as if accepted by the *Eilandgebied*. As such, the Court has conferred upon the clause an effect that cannot be reconciled with its obligatory character.

It is against this judgment that the subdivision of the argument is—justifiably—aimed. Whether the *Eilandgebied* was obliged to honour the clause can only be determined by considering the subsequent circumstances of the case, such as the answer to the questions whether the *Eilandgebied* at the time of the purchase of the plantation in 1974 was aware of the clause and aware of the purpose of the clause, as later interpreted by the Court of Appeal and whether in respect thereof a duty of investigation existed on the part of the *Eilandgebied*, while the seriousness of the detriment suffered by the heirs of Boyé as a consequence of the breach of the clause and the foreseeability of this detriment at the time of the purchase, as well as the extent to which the *Eilandgebied* has influenced the non-performance by AR-CU NV and the role that the possibility of profiting of that non-performance has played for *Eilandgebied* in purchasing the object, could also be of importance.

Note

A contractual clause cannot be strengthened by a tort claim in order to compel third parties to accept this clause. If this were the case, the law of tort would function as a vehicle to create new property rights outside the *numerus clausus*. In certain specific situations a tort claim is possible, especially if the buyer provoked the seller in excluding the chain clause from the contract. Such a situation should, however, be exceptional. The court explicitly refers to the principle of publicity: simple knowledge about the clause as such is insufficient.

V. GROUND RULES

Once a relationship has been qualified as having a proprietary nature, certain ground rules apply.

S van Erp, European and National Property Law: Osmosis or Growing Antagonism?[40] **1.37 (NL)**

Once it has been established that a right can be fitted into the numerus clausus of property rights and is transparent enough towards third parties for it to be justified that these third parties are nolens volens bound by it, the ground rules of property law apply. These ground rules concern the further consequences of the conclusion that the right in question is a property right and focus on how property rights relate among themselves. In Europe, these ground rules are the following: the nemo dat (or nemo plus) rule (i), the prior tempore rule (ii), limited rights have priority over fuller rights (iii), protection rules such as the right to (re)claim the object of the property right (iv).

(i) According to the nemo dat rule, one cannot give away more than one has. A transfer of the right of ownership, to give an example, is only effective if the transferor has the power to dispose, because he or she is the owner. This is a highly logical ground rule. It would be unacceptable if one were able to alienate the property rights of others, which would violate the absolute nature of such a property right. Of course, the nemo dat rule is counterbalanced by rules on third party protection. A third party in good faith, who paid for the right, is frequently protected against the original owner, who claims his right of ownership. A major reason for such an exception can be that in day-to-day business a buyer should be allowed to rely, if justified, on the outward appearance that a seller is also the owner, to safeguard ordinary commercial dealings. If the original owner could always reclaim the right of ownership, this could jeopardize commerce and would affect various third parties in good faith.

(ii) If various persons claim property rights with regard to an object, the oldest property right has priority over a younger property right: prior tempore, potior iure. This ground rule is connected, first of all, with the absolute nature of the pre-existing property right. A property right can only be impaired by a new property right if the holder of the existing property right is a party to the creation of the new property right. If not, the absolute nature of the pre-existing property right protects the holder of such a property right against later property rights. This explains, for instance, why a mortgage which was created after another mortgage had already been created, ranks second and its holder will only be entitled to the proceeds of any public auction after the first mortgagee has been fully paid.

(iii) Nevertheless, if a new property right has been created with the consent of the holder of the first property right, such a second right will limit the first right. In such a case the first right holder (sometimes in civil law terminology called the holder of the 'mother right') then must accept that the holder of the second property right has a stronger position and can enforce its right (the 'daughter right') against the mother right, although the 'daughter right' is younger than the 'mother right'. For that reason, a right of mortgage is stronger than the right of ownership which is burdened by the right of mortgage.

(iv) Finally, the fourth ground rule is that, once a property right has been accepted as such it is given special protection. This could be with a special remedy, such as revindication (the owner can claim the object of the right of ownership from any person who has such object under his control), or with the help of

[40] Van Erp, above n 2 (2006) 16.

claims based upon tort. It could be contended that some circularity of reasoning may be detected here, because it could be argued that whenever a right is given special protection through for instance a revindication claim, such a right must be a property right. In my view this is incorrect. If a special claim is given to a right holder or if such right holder is given a protected status in insolvency proceedings, allowing him or her to separate the object of the right from the insolvent estate, this means that it must have been decided previously that the right to be protected is a property right.

Notes

(1) Like the fundamental principles of property law, *numerus clausus* (III) and transparency (IV), the ground rules are present in all systems of property law under discussion in this casebook.[41] Together they offer a framework for analysis of property law systems that enable us to overcome differences we might discover at first sight.

(2) For example, when we—as we will do in Chapter 3—look at the content of property law systems and discover the property rights that are available in a property law system, there are many differences. Nevertheless, each of these systems adheres to the principles of *numerus clausus*, the principle that limits the availability and content of property rights for private parties (see above, section III). When property law systems are compared with a focus on the fundamental principles of *numerus clausus* and transparency, as well as the above-mentioned ground rules, rather then the different technical provisions or cases dealing with various property rights, there are many similarities to be discovered.[42]

(3) Other rules in a property law system are known as technical rules. They are equally important to the study of property law. However, it is at this level that many differences between systems exist. Technical rules are the result of underlying policy issues such as the system of transfer of ownership or the connection between property security rights and the claim that they aim to secure (accessority, see Chapter 5).

CONCISE BIBLIOGRAPHY

B Akkermans, *The Principle of Numerus Clausus in European Property Law* (Antwerp, Intersentia, 2008).JHM (Sjef) van Erp, *European and National Property Law: Osmosis or Growing Antagonism*, 6th Walter van Gerven Lecture (Groningen, Europalaw Publishers, 2006).

JHM (Sjef) van Erp, 'From "Classical" to Modern European Property Law', in *Essays in*

[41] On the universal nature of this approach, see JHM van Erp, 'Deconstruction and Reconstruction of European Property law: A Research Agenda', in E Cashin Ritaine (ed), *Legal Engineering and Comparative law/L'ingénierie juridique et le droit comparé. Rapports du colloque du 25e anniversaire de l'Institut Suisse de Droit Comparé du 29 août 2008 à Lausanne* (Zurich/Basel, Schultess, 2009) 105–21.

[42] See eg THD Struycken, *De numerus clausus in het goederenrecht* (The Hague, Kluwer, 2007); B Akkermans, *The Principle of Numerus Clausus in European Property Law* (Antwerp, Intersentia, 2008).

Honour of Konstantinos D Kerameus/Festschrift für Konstantinos D Kerameus, bol I (Athens/Brussels, Ant A Sakkoulas/Bruylant, 2009) 1517–33.

JHM (Sjef) van Erp, 'Deconstruction and Reconstruction of European Property Law: A Research Agenda', in E Cashin Ritaine (ed), *Legal Engineering and Comparative Law/L'ingénierie juridique et le droit comparé. Rapports du colloque du 25e anniversaire de l'Institut Suisse de Droit Comparé du 29 août 2008 à Lausanne* (Zurich/Basel, Schultess, 2009) 105–21.

CHAPTER 2
THE PROTECTION OF PROPERTY RIGHTS

Monika Hinteregger

This chapter deals with the special nature of property rights. It not only deals with the first of the six essential questions—what is property law?—but also with the second question: what are property rights? Property rights are special types of rights that have effect against third parties by their nature. The holder of such a right can therefore enforce his right against those third parties. Moreover, holders of a property right can also take action against third parties when these parties interfere with the holders' property rights. This chapter deals, in other words, with the protection of property rights.

Due to the technical nature of the subject matter, unlike from the rest of this casebook, some parts of the chapter are emphasised to stress the most important issues.

Introductory Note

Property rights enjoy comprehensive protection against interference from third parties. This chapter deals with the private law instruments that protect property rights. The protection of ownership from interference by the state and the obligation of the state to guarantee the existence and the protection of private ownership, as provided by Article 1 First Protocol of the European Convention of Human Rights,[1] has become the domain of the public law. It is interesting to note that the old codifications (Article 545 Cciv, §365 ABGB) still contain special provisions for the protection of the owner from expropriation:

> Article 545 Cciv: 'No one may be compelled to yield his ownership, unless for public purposes and for a fair and previous indemnity.'
>
> §365 ABGB: 'If the public good so requires, a citizen of the state must cede even the complete ownership of property for a suitable compensation.'

In Germany this is provided by constitutional law (Article 14 Grundgesetz):

[1] See Chapter 10.

> Property, inheritance, expropriation:
> Property and the right of inheritance shall be guaranteed. Their content and limits shall be defined by the laws.
> Property entails obligations. Its use shall also serve the public good.
> Expropriation shall only be permissible for the public good. It may only be ordered by or pursuant to a law that determines the nature and extent of compensation. Such compensation shall be determined by establishing an equitable balance between the public interest and the interests of those affected. In case of dispute respecting the amount of compensation, recourse may be had to the ordinary courts.

Comprehensive protection of property rights entails the protection of the holder of the right against all sorts of interference. When property is illegally attacked, the owner may even be allowed to defend it by use of reasonable force.[2] If an object is harmed or destroyed by the tortious behaviour of another, the holder of a property right is entitled to damages[3] and, where another uses the object without consent, the holder of the right may recover the obtained profits or claim a decent price for the use of the object. The protection of property rights against such interference is the objective of tort law and the law of unjust enrichment in the civil law and for the restitution for wrongdoing in the common law, respectively.[4]

For a casebook on property law, two types of interference are of primary interest: (1) the protection of the holder of a property right against dispossession; and (2) the protection against disturbance of the enjoyment of possession. Although all the legal systems provide for special claims to protect the holder of a property right against such interference, there are fundamental differences between the civil law countries and the common law. As a result of their basis in Roman law, the civil law countries distinguish between ownership and possession.[5] They provide for specific actions for the protection of ownership and possession which, clearly separated from tort law instruments, allow for specific recovery and injunctive relief. For English law, which has no concept of ownership,[6] the protection of property rights means primarily the protection of possession. In contrast to the civil law, English law did not develop such specific unitary property actions, but follows a fragmented approach differentiating between the property rights in respect to land and the property rights in goods.

For the discussion of the protection of property rights it is, thus, feasible to distinguish between the civil law systems on the one hand and the common law on the other. Accordingly, this chapter is divided into two parts. The first part describes the instruments for the protection of property rights in civil law countries and the second part is dedicated to the common law. The discussion of the civil law starts with a

[2] See eg §§227, 229, 230 BGB, which regulate necessity, self-defence and self-help.

[3] Very well exemplified by §823(1) BGB, which explicitly defines ownership as an absolutely protected right the infringement of which obliges to liability in tort.

[4] See W van Gerven, J Lever and P Larouche, *Common Law of Europe Casebooks, Cases, Materials and Text on National, Supranational and International Tort Law* (Oxford, Hart Publishing, 2000) 169 *et seq* and J Beatson, EJH Schrage (eds), *Common Law of Europe Casebooks, Cases, Materials and Texts on Unjustified Enrichment* (Oxford, Hart Publishing, 2003).

[5] See Chapter 1.

[6] See Chapter 3.

short description of the notion of possession and then continues with the discussion of the instruments for the protection of possession and the protection of ownership.

I. CIVIL LAW

I.A POSSESSION AND POSSESSORY CLAIMS

Based on the Roman law distinction between *possessorium* and *petitorium*, all the civil law systems analysed in this casebook distinguish between ownership and possession. Whilst ownership and the limited property rights deal with the legal entitlements a person may have with respect to an object (see Chapter 3), possession relates primarily to the factual control of an object. In civil law systems possession serves several important functions. Possession of an object indicates the existence of a property right and thus makes it public. Accordingly, French and German law provide for a legal presumption that the possessor of a movable object is also its owner (Article 2276 Cciv, §1006 BGB) and §323 ABGB presumes that the possessor has a valid title, meaning that he is a lawful possessor. This *publicity function* of possession is one of the reasons that possession plays an important role in the acquisition and the transfer of property rights on movables (see Chapters 7 and 8). Moreover, the civil law systems provide for specific instruments for the protection of possession which are granted regardless of the legal entitlement the possessor enjoys with respect to the object. Possessory protection serves to prevent unlawful and violent behaviour and thus shall enhance the *preservation of peace* in a society. In the following we will start with a short description of the main features of possession, and then analyse in depth the instruments of possessory protection.

I.A.1 POSSESSION

I.A.1.a France

Code civil **2.1 (FR)**

Article 2255 Possession is the detention or enjoyment of an object or of a right which we hold or exercise by ourselves, or by another who holds and exercises it in our name.

Article 2261 To be able to prescribe, one must have a continuous and uninterrupted, peaceful, public and unequivocal possession, exercised in the capacity of an owner.

Article 2256 One is always presumed to possess for oneself, and in the capacity of an owner, where it is not proved that one has started possession by possessing for another.

Article 2257 Where one has started possession by possessing for another, one is always presumed to possess in the same capacity, unless there is proof to the contrary.

Article 2262 Acts which are merely allowed or simply tolerated may not give rise to possession or prescription.

Article 2263 Acts of duress may not give rise to a possession capable of bringing about prescription either.

Possession begins to produce effects only from the time the duress has ceased.

Article 2264 A present possessor who proves that he has formerly possessed, is presumed to have possessed during the intervening time, unless there is proof to the contrary.

Article 2265 To complete a prescription, one may join to one's possession that of one's predecessor, in whatever manner one may have succeeded to him, whether by virtue of a universal or specific title, or for value or gratuitously.

Article 2266 Those who possess for another never acquire ownership by prescription, whatever the time elapsed may be.

Thus a farm tenant, a depositary, a usufructuary, and all those who precariously hold the object of an owner, may not prescribe it.

Notes

(1) The Code civil does not provide for a comprehensive regulation of possession. The main rules on possession are Articles 2255 Cciv *et seq*, which primarily deal with the role of possession as a prerequisite of acquisitive prescription. The protection of possession is regulated in Articles 2278 and 2279 Cciv and Articles 1264–67 of the Nouveau Code de Procedure Civile (NCPC).[7]

(2) Article 2255 Cciv contains the definition of possession. Possession relates to *corporeal objects* and to claims which are incorporated in a corporeal title (eg bearer instruments). Whether Article 2255 Cciv, by referring to the 'enjoyment of an object or a right', also encompasses mere claims is contested.[8] Possession extends to movables and immovable property alike, although with quite different effects.

(3) Possession requires two factors: (i) the actual control of the object (*corpus*) and (ii) the will to hold the object as an owner respectively as the holder of a limited property right (*animus domini* or *animus rem sibi habendi*; Article 2261 Cciv). To hold an object for another does not amount to possession but constitutes only detention (*détention précaire*). Accordingly, a farm tenant or a depository[9] holds the object not as a possessor, but for lack of the *animus domini*, as an intermediary of the possessor (*in corpore alieno*). The distinction between possession and detention plays an important role for the acquisition of property rights, as the detentor cannot acquire ownership of the object by way of acquisitive prescription (Article 2266 Cciv).[10]

[7] As provided by Loi 75-596 of 9 July 1975.

[8] *Cf* S Ginosar, *Droit réel, propriété et créance—élaboration d'un système rationnel des droits patrimoniaux* (Paris, Librarie Générale de Droit et de Jurisprudence (LGDJ), 1960); F Zenati-Castaing and Th Revet, *Les biens*, 3rd edn (Paris, Presse Universitaires de France, 2008) 647, para 441. J Bergel, M Bruschi and S Cimamonti, *Traité de droit civil: Les biens*, 2nd edn (Paris, LGDJ, 2010) 147 *et seq*, 158 and 159, however, reject this view. They see the wording of Art 2255 Cciv merely as a reference to the distinction between the enjoyment of an object as the owner (*jouissance d'une chose*) or as the holder of a limited property right (*jouissance d'un droit*).

[9] See Art 2266(2) Cciv. The usufructuary, however, has a double position. In respect of ownership he is a detentor, but with respect to his limited property right he holds the object as a possessor.

[10] See in detail Chapter 7.

(4) According to Article 2256 Cciv, one is always presumed to possess for oneself and in the capacity of an owner. It is therefore up to the person who contests the possession of another with actual control of the object to prove that this person has started possession by possessing for another. If, however, this is proved, it is then up to the presumed detentor to prove a change of title in order to reach the position as possessor (Article 2257 Cciv; *inversion du titre de détention*).

(5) Possession is terminated when either the *animus* or the *corpus* is lost. As provided by Article 2255 Cciv, it is, however, sufficient to exercise the actual control of the object by an intermediary (*in corpore alieno*) in order to become a possessor, and, despite the loss of actual control, possession may be maintained under certain conditions only by the will to possess (*solo animo*).

I.A.1.b Germany

Bürgerliches Gesetzbuch (BGB) **2.2 (DE)**

§854 Acquisition of possession

(1) Possession of an object is acquired by obtaining actual control of the object.

(2) Agreement between the previous possessor and the acquirer is sufficient for acquisition if the acquirer is able to exercise control over the object.

§855 Servant in possession

If a person exercises actual control over an object for another in the other's household or business or in a similar relationship, by virtue of which he has to follow the other's directives relating to the object, so only the other is possessor.

§856 Termination of possession

(1) Possession is terminated as a result of the possessor giving up, or losing in another way, actual control of the object.

(2) As a result of a, in its nature, temporary prevention to exercise control possession is not terminated.

§857 Transferability of possession by succession

Possession devolves on the heir.

§858 Unlawful interference

(1) Whoever deprives the possessor against his will of the possession or interferes with the possession acts, except where the deprivation or interference is permitted by law, unlawfully (unlawful interference).

(2) The possession obtained as a result of unlawful interference is defective. The successor in possession must allow the defectiveness to be asserted against him if he is the heir of the possessor or if he knows when he acquires possession of the defectiveness of his predecessor's possession.

§859 Self-help by the possessor

(1) The possessor may ward off unlawful interference by use of force.

(2) If a moveable object is taken away from the possessor by means of unlawful interference, the possessor may use force to remove the object from the perpetrator caught in the act or pursued.

(3) The possessor of a parcel who is deprived of possession by unlawful interference

may recover possession immediately after the deprivation by dispossession of the perpetrator.

(4) The possessor has the same rights against a person who under §858(2) must allow the defectiveness of the possession to be asserted against him.

§860 Self-help by the servant in possession

The rights to which the possessor is entitled under §859 may also be exercised by the person who exercises actual control for the possessor under §855.

§861 Claim on account of deprivation of possession

(1) If the possessor is deprived of possession by unlawful interference, he may request the person who in relation to him possesses defectively to restore possession.

(2) The claim is excluded if the removed possession was defective in relation to the interferer [*Störer*] or his predecessor and if the possession was obtained in the last year before the deprivation of possession.

§862 Claim on account of interference with possession

(1) If the possessor is disturbed in his possession by unlawful interference he may request the interferer to remove the disturbance. If further disturbances are to be concerned the possessor may sue for an injunction.

(2) The claim is excluded if the possessor possesses defectively in relation to the interferer or his predecessor and if the possession was obtained in the last year before the disturbance.

§863 Defences of the dispossessor or interferer

Against the claims set out in §861 and §862 a right to possession or to perform the interfering act may be put forward only to establish the assertion that the deprivation or disturbance of the possession is not unlawful interference.

§864 Extinction of possessory claims

(1) A claim under §§861, 862 expires one year after the performance of the unlawful interference, unless the claim is enforced by way of legal action before this date.

(2) Extinction also occurs if it is established after the performance of the unlawful act by a final judgment not subject to appeal that the interferer holds a right to the object by virtue of which he may claim the establishment of a possessory status that corresponds to his act.

§865 Part possession

The provisions of §§858 to 864 apply also in favour of a person who possesses only part of a object, particularly separate rooms for housing purposes or rooms for other purposes.

§866 Co-possession

If several persons share the possession of a object, in relation to each other no protection of possession takes place insofar as it concerns the limits of the use to which each of them is entitled.

§867 Right of pursuit of the possessor

If an object in the control of the possessor gets on a plot of land in the possession of another, the possessor of the plot of land must permit the possessor of the object to locate and remove the object unless the object has meanwhile been taken into possession. The possessor of the plot of land may claim compensation for the damage caused by the locating and removal. He may refuse the permission if causation of damage is to be concerned until he is given security; the refusal is impermissible if delay entails danger.

§868 Indirect possession

If a person possesses an object as a usufructuary, a pledgee, a lessee [*Pächter*], a tenant [*Mieter*], a depositary or in a similar relationship, by virtue of which he is as against another entitled, or obliged, to have possession for a period of time, the other person is also a possessor (indirect possession).

§869 Claim of the indirect possessor

If unlawful interference is exercised against a possessor, the claims set out under §861, 862 also apply to the indirect possessor. In case of deprivation of possession the indirect possessor is entitled to claim that possession is restored to the previous possessor; if the latter cannot or does not wish to retake possession, the indirect possessor may claim that possession is restored to him. Under the same condition he, in the case of §867, may require that he is permitted to locate and remove the object.

§870 Transfer of indirect possession

Indirect possession may be transferred to another by assigning the claim for restoration of property.

§871 Multistage indirect possession

If the indirect possessor is with a third party in a relationship as set out in §868, the third party is also indirect possessor.

§872 Possession as owner [*Eigenbesitz*]

A person who possesses an object as belonging to him is a self-possessor [*Eigenbesitzer*].

§1007 Claims of the former possessor, exclusion in case of knowledge

(1) A person who has had a movable object in his possession may require the possessor to return the object if the possessor was not in good faith when he acquired possession.

(2) If the object was stolen from the former possessor or if it was lost or went astray in another way, the former possessor may require return even from a possessor in good faith, unless the latter is the owner of the object or has lost possession before the former owner acquired possession. This provision does not apply to money and bearer instruments.

(3) The claim is excluded if the former possessor was not in good faith on the acquisition of possession or if he has given up possession. Apart from this, the provisions of §§986 to 1003 apply mutatis mutandis.

Mugdan, The Collected Materials for the Civil Code for the German Nation[11] **2.3 (DE)**

A. Applications 1 and 2 were both based on the same idea, that it is recommended in the interest of the clarity of the law to restrict the provisions of this chapter to possession as a condition of possessory protection, on the other hand to cut out at

[11] Mugdan, *Die gesamten Materialien zum bürgerlichen Gesetzbuch für das deutsche Reich*, vol III (Aalen, Scientia Verlag, 1979) 502.

least for the time being those provisions which relate to possession as a condition for other legal provisions, in particular with respect to property. This main thought of the applications has been approved without contradiction, ...

B. The applications furthermore terminologically differed from the draft to that effect, as they proposed to characterise as 'possession' each possessory protected relationship of the person to the object. This recommendation, due to the reasons advanced by the critique, met with approval from all sides.

Notes

(1) Contrary to the French Code civil and the Austrian ABGB, the BGB does not provide for a general definition of possession, but rather concentrates on the aspect of the *protection of possession*.

(2) Accordingly, possession is understood in a very broad sense as the *actual control* of a *corporeal object*.[12] It comprises movables as well as immovable property and, as is explicitly provided by §865 BGB, may also extend only to an integral part of a object, eg one room of a house or apartment. Possession can be shared by several persons (§866 BGB, co-possession). If all the co-possessors can use the object only together, one speaks of joint possession (*gesamthänderischer Mitbesitz*).

(3) German law distinguishes between different *types of possession*, namely between *Eigenbesitz* and *Fremdbesitz* and direct (*unmittelbarer*) and indirect possession (*mittelbarer Besitz*). The distinction between *Eigenbesitz* and *Fremdbesitz* depends on the intention of the possessor. A person who holds an object for himself is *Eigenbesitzer* (§872 BGB), no matter whether he is the rightful owner or even a thief, while a person who holds an object for another is a *Fremdbesitzer*. Examples for a *Fremdbesitzer* are the tenant, the depositary or the borrower of a object. Accordingly, the finder of an object is *Eigenbesitzer*, if he wants to keep the object for himself, or *Fremdbesitzer*, if he has the intention to return it. *Eigenbesitzer* and *Fremdbesitzer* are possessors and thus enjoy the legal protection of possession. This distinction, however, plays a role with regard to other provisions, such as the presumption of ownership (§1006 BGB) or the preconditions of acquisitive prescription (§937 BGB) which both only apply to the *Eigenbesitzer*. The old distinction between *Sachbesitz* and *Rechtsbesitz*, as still provided by Austrian law, is rejected by German doctrine as being misleading[13] and only accepted with regard to the rare case of the exercise of an easement that does not comprise actual control of the parcel (§1029 and §1090(2) BGB).[14]

The *direct possessor* has actual control of the object, whilst the *indirect possessor* exercises his possession not in person, but by an intermediary. This intermediary is called *Besitzmittler*. §868 BGB enumerates some examples of indirect possession. Contrary to the servant in possession (*Besitzdiener*, §855 BGB), who is only an

[12] D Joost in FJ Säcker *et al* (eds), *Münchener Kommentar zum Bürgerlichen Gesetzbuch*, vol VI, 5th edn (München, Beck, 2009) before §854 at 14, para 6; J Baur and R Stürner, *Sachenrecht*, 18th edn (München, Beck, 2009) §7 at 67, para 1; M Wolf and M Wellenhofer, *Sachenrecht*, 26th edn (München, Beck, 2010) 39, paras 1 *et seq*.

[13] Joost, above n 12, before §854 at 15, para 7.

[14] *Ibid*, before §854 at 14, para 5; Wolf and Wellenhofer, above n 12, 39, para 1 and at 479, para 13.

agent without any right of his own, the *Besitzmittler* has the position of a possessor and enjoys, as well as the indirect possessor, possessory protection. He is direct possessor and, as he does not possess the object as an owner, but only according to a specific entitlement, he is a *Fremdbesitzer*.

(4) Direct possession is *acquired* by gaining actual control of the object (§854(1) BGB). This can be done by way of original acquisition or by way of transfer (derivative acquisition). In both cases the acquisition of possession must be perceptible to the outside world and, according to the majority opinion of legal doctrine,[15] the acquirer must have the 'natural' will to acquire possession of the object. For this it is sufficient that the acquirer has the factual capacity to obtain actual control of the object. Legal capacity or even knowledge of the existence of the object by the acquirer is not necessary.[16] In case of transfer of possession, the transferor must also have the 'natural' will to transfer the possession to the acquirer. In order to facilitate the acquisition of possession, §854(2) BGB lets the agreement[17] between the former possessor and the acquirer suffice, provided that the acquirer is able to exercise actual control over the object. According to the BGH,[18] the transfer of possession, however, only takes place, if the transferor gives his possession up. In cases of universal succession, such as succession by inheritance or the merger of two companies, possession is transferred by operation of law without a need to acquire actual control (§857 BGB). The legal person acquires possession through its organs.[19]

While direct possession is primarily acquired in a factual way, the creation of indirect possession is the result of a legal transaction (eg the creation of a lease and delivery of possession of the leased object). The transfer of indirect possession can also be performed by assigning the claim for restoration of property (§870 BGB).

Direct possession is *terminated* by the loss of the actual control over the object (§856 BGB), be it by a wilful act of the possessor to give up possession or, without the will of the possessor, by the final loss of the object. Only temporary prevention to exercise control is not sufficient. Indirect possession is terminated if the direct possessor loses the possession, or if the direct possessor shows by way of a perceptible act that he no longer accepts the position of the indirect possessor, or if the indirect possessor loses the claim for restoration of property.

I.A.1.c Austria

Allgemeines Bürgerliches Gesetzbuch (ABGB) **2.4 (AT)**

§309 Holder, possessor

He who has an object in his power or custody is called the holder of it. If the holder of an object has the intention of keeping it as his own, then he is the possessor.

[15] A Stadler in Th Soergel (ed), *Kommentar zum Bürgerlichen Gesetzbuch*, vol XIV, 13th edn by W Siebert *et al* (Stuttgart, Kohlhammer, 2002) §854 at 33, para 9-111; Baur and Stürner, above n 12, §7 at 70, para 15; Joost, above n 12, §854 at 22, paras 8 *et seq*.

[16] Joost, above n 12, §854 at 22, paras 9 *et seq*.

[17] The nature of this agreement, whether legal or not, is contested: ibid, §854 at 28 *et seq*, paras 31 *et seq*.

[18] BGH, 10 January 1979, NJW 1979, 714.

[19] Joost, above n 12, §854 at 25 *et seq*, paras 17 *et seq*.

§311 Objects of possession

All corporeal and incorporeal objects which are the objects of legal commerce are subject to possession.

§316 Lawful and unlawful possession

The possession of property is called lawful if it rests on a valid title, that is on a lawful cause of its acquisition. In a contrary case, it is called unlawful.

§317 Title to lawful possession

The title for unattached property exists in the inborn liberty to perform acts by which the rights of other persons are not infringed; for other property, the title exists in the will of the former possessor, or in the decision of a judge, or the law, by which the right of possession is given.

§326 Bona fide and mala fide possessor

A possessor who has reasonable cause to believe that the property he possesses is his own is a bona fide possessor. A mala fide possessor is one who knows or should have known from the circumstances that the property in his possession belongs to another. Because of errors in facts or ignorance of the legal provisions one can be an unlawful (§316) but still a bona fide possessor.

§328 Decision about the bona fides

For purposes of legal proceedings, whether the possession is bona fide or mala fide must be decided by adjudication. In case of doubt the possession is presumed bona fide.

§345 Legal remedy against the spurious possessor

If someone trespasses or enters secretly, by fraud or by entreaty, into possession or endeavours to change a temporary permission into a continuous right, his possession, unlawful and mala fide, is also spurious; in contrary cases the possession is not considered spurious.

Notes

(1) The Austrian ABGB provides for a comprehensive regulation of possession (§§309–52 ABGB). As expressed in §309 ABGB, Austrian law distinguishes between detention, which is the actual control of an object (*Innehabung*, so-called 'corpus'), and possession, which, in addition to mere actual control, requires the will to hold the object as an owner (so-called *animus*). Only a person who fulfils both requirements (*corpus* and *animus*) is a possessor and enjoys possessory protection. Austrian doctrine distinguishes between many different types of possession. Besides the distinction between *Eigenbesitzer* and *Fremdbesitzer*, *unmittelbarer* and *mittelbarer Besitzer, Besitzmittler* and *Besitzdiener* that are used in the same sense as in German law, Austrian law, as provided in §311 ABGB, also distinguishes between *Sachbesitz*, the possession of corporeal objects, and the possession of a right (*Rechtsbesitz*). This wide understanding of possession is based on the comprehensive definition of the object in §285 ABGB[20] encompassing both corporeal objects and rights. Not all rights are, however, capable of being the object of possession. It

[20] §285 ABGB: 'Everything that is different from a person and serves to the use of man, is called in the legal sense an object.'

is generally accepted that only rights in objects which (i) are transferable by legal commerce and (ii) that allow for permanent use can be possessed. This excludes family rights and personality rights, and also mere claims which aim at the performance of a singular act, such as the paying of a sum of money or the rendering of a service. A possessor of a right is the holder of a servitude, of a building right, or a real burden (*Reallast*), the person who buys an object under retention of title, the pledgee of a movable object, the lessee or the borrower of a object, but not to the depositary, as he does not exercise a right to control the object.[21] With the argument that the primary goal of possession is the entitlement to make use of the instruments for possessory protection, several authors[22] claim as a further condition for the possession of a right that the right must be connected with the detention or the use of a corporeal object. According to this view, only rights that entitle the holder to the actual control of a corporeal object can be the object of possession. This restriction is, however, disputed.[23]

(2) Contrary to German law, Austrian law does not provide for joint possession, and the legal admissibility of possession of an integral part of an object in the form of *Sachbesitz* is rather disputed.[24] Acquisition of possession requires at least limited legal capacity. Persons who are without legal capacity (children under 7 years and mentally disabled persons) can, with the exception of the acquisition of minor objects of daily life, only acquire possession via their legal representative.

(4) Austrian law distinguishes between lawful und unlawful (§316 ABGB), *bona fide* and *mala fide* (§326 ABGB), and spurious and not spurious possession (§345 ABGB). These classifications are of importance concerning the right of the possessor to acquire the fruits of the object, for the relationship between possessor and owner, for prescriptive acquisition of ownership and with regard to the protection of possession.

I.A.2 PROTECTION OF POSSESSION

I.A.2.a France

Code civil[25] **2.5 (FR)**

Article 2278 Possession is protected, regardless of the substance of the right, against disturbance which affects or threatens it. Protection of possession is also granted to a person who holds a thing for another [*detenteur*] against any other person than the one from whom he derives his rights.

Article 2279 Claims for the protection of possession may be brought under the

[21] H Koziol and R Welser, *Grundriss des Bürgerlichen Rechts*, vol I, 13th edn (Wien, Manz, 2006) 259.

[22] *Ibid.* G Iro, *Sachenrecht*, vol IV, 4th edn (Wien, Springer, 2010) 21, para 2/7; Th Klicka in M Schwimann (ed), *Praxiskommentar ABGB*, vol II, 3rd edn (Wien, Orac, 2005) §311 at 43, para 4.

[23] See comprehensively G Kodek, *Die Besitzstörung* (Wien, Manz, 2002) 102 *et seq*.

[24] *Pro* A Ehrenzweig, *System des österreichischen allgemeinen Privatrechts: Das Sachenrecht*, vol I/2, 2nd edn (Wien, Manz, 1957) §171 at 60; *contra* J Schey in H Klang (ed), *Kommentar zum ABGB*, vol II, 2nd edn (Wien, Österreichische Staatsdruckerei, 1950) §311 at 71 *et seq*; G Kodek in H Klang (ed), *Kommentar zum ABGB*, §§285–352, 3rd edn (Wien, Verlag Österreich, 2011) §311 at 38.

[25] Inserted by Loi 75-596 of 9 July 1975, JO 10 July 1975.

conditions provided by the Code of Civil Procedure by those who possess or hold for another peacefully.

Nouveau Code de Procedure Civile (NCPC)[26] **2.6 (FR)**

Article 1264 Subject to compliance with the rules relating to public property, the possessory actions are open within the year during which the interference occurred to those who peacefully possess or hold the property for at least a year; however, an action of restitution [*l'action en réintégration*] against the person who causes an interference may be brought even when the victim of the dispossession has possessed or held the property for less than a year.
Article 1265 The protection of possession and the consideration of the right may never be combined. The judge may, however, examine the titles in order to ensure whether the conditions of the protection of possession are satisfied. The investigation measures may not relate to the consideration of the right.
Article 1266 The one who initiates an action on the right will not be admissible to initiate a possessory action.
Article 1267 The defendant in a possessory action may bring an action on the right only after having put an end to the disturbance.

Notes

(1) Articles 2278 and 2279 Cciv and Articles 1264–67 NCPC regulate the protection of possession.[27] Although not explicitly provided by the law, it is common opinion that possessory protection relates only to *immovable objects*.[28] The possession of a movable object is regarded to be sufficiently protected by Article 2276 Cciv (*en fait de meubles, la possession vaut titre*), according to which the possessor of a corporeal movable is irrefutably regarded to be its owner. Unlawful interference with movables is remedied by the vindication. Since the 1975 amendment of the rules on the protection of possession, the detentor of an immovable property also enjoys possessory protection against interference by third persons (Article 2278 Cciv).[29] Before this amendment, case law, in order to protect the social peace, already accepted the admissibility of the *action en réintégration*, which provides for possessory protection in case of violent dispossession.[30] The detentor, however, cannot rely on possessory protection against the person from whom he received his

[26] Decree no 81-500 of 12 May 1981, Arts 5 and 52, JO, 14 May 1981 amendment JORF of 21 May 1981 in force on 1 January 1982.

[27] See H Mazeaud and F Chabas, *Leçons de droit civil, droit de propriété et ses démembrements; licence et maîtrise en droit*, vol II/2, 8th edn (Paris, Montchrestien, 1994) 218 *et seq*; C Larroumet, *Droit civil: Les biens droits réel principaux*, vol II, 5th edn (Paris, Economica, 2006) 70; P Malaurie and L Aynès, *Les biens*, 4th edn (Paris: Defrénois, 2010) 153; C Atias, *Droit civil. Les biens*, 11th edn (Paris, Litec, 2011) 411; J Bergel, M Bruschi and S Cimamonti, *Traité de droit civil: Les biens*, 2nd edn (Paris: LGDJ, 2010) 485 *et seq*.

[28] Bergel, Bruschi and Cimamonti, above n 27, 486.

[29] See comprehensively G Goubeaux, 'L'extension de la protection possessoire au bénéfice des detenteurs' Defrenois 1976, 374–87.

[30] Cass civ, 22 January 1878, *Contant v Coutin,* D 78.I.316.

rights (eg the tenant against the landlord), but is restricted to the rights deriving from the underlying obligatory relationship (eg tenancy contract).

(2) Although not explicitly laid down in the wording of the law, French doctrine[31] traditionally distinguishes between three different *types of possessory actions*: *complainte*, *dénonciation de nouvel ouvre* and, explicitly mentioned in Article 1264 NCPC, *action en réintégration*. The action for a *complainte* is available in case of actual disturbance or dispossession by a non-violent act, while *dénonciation de nouvel ouvre* can be claimed against imminent future interference caused by construction works. Prerequisite for both actions is that the claimant has been enjoying possession or detention for at least one year. The action for restoration (*action en réintégration*) covers the loss of actual control by a violent act of the dispossessor. Contrary to the other two actions this action is also available if possession, or detention, lasted for less than one year (Article 1264 NCPC). The competent court for a possessory action is the Tribunal de grande instance (Article R211-4 Code de l'organisation judiciare). In order to prevent imminent damage or to end an obvious unlawful interference, the president of the Tribunal de grande instance is entitled to issue an interim injunction (Articles 809, 849 NCPC).[32]

(3) Possessory protection is irrespective of an underlying entitlement to the property (Article 1265 NCPC). The possessor who is also the owner of the property, or the holder of a limited property right, can choose between possessory protection and vindication of the object. When he decides to raise an action for vindication, the possessory claim, however, becomes inadmissible (Article 1266 NCPC). Objections based on the entitlement to the object cannot be raised in the possessory proceedings. The defendant may only bring an action based on the right after the end of the possessory proceedings and after having put an end to the disturbance (Article 1267 NCPC).

(4) Only possession or detention which is free of defaults is protected. The actions for interference (*complainte*, *dénonciation de nouvel ouvre*) require that the possession or detention is continuous and unequivocal and that the possessor or detentor did not, in relation to the interferer, acquire possession or detention violently, or that he is holding the property in a clandestine way. The action for restoration (*action en réintégration*) is only prohibited in case of violent acquisition or furtiveness of the possession respectively detention. The (former) possessor or detentor must claim for possessory protection within one year from the interference or loss of actual control (Article 1264 NCPC).

(5) With the action of *complainte* the possessor, or detentor, may claim for the abatement of the interference and the preservation of the previous status of possession. It also covers the removal of erected constructions. The action for *dénonciation de nouvel ouvre* only allows claiming the cessation of the works. The *action en réintégration* is for recovery of possession and restoration to the original condition, including the removal of erected constructions and restoration of damaged constructions. As French law is generally very open with regard to the entitlement

[31] Bergel, Bruschi and Cimamonti, above n 27, 486 *et seq*.

[32] On the French court structure, see Chapter 11.

to bring an action in tort, the possessor and detentor may also be awarded damages in possessory proceedings.

Cour de Cassation, 6 February 1996[33] **2.7 (FR)**

Harhouz v Kherif

PROTECTION OF POSSESSION COVERS ONLY IMMOVABLES

Money in the envelope

The rules on possessory protection do not apply to movables.

Facts: Liazib and Mustapha Kherif acted as the garantors of Harhouz's bank loan; in exchange, Harhouz had agreed to pay them the sum of FRF50,000. At the time of the conclusion of the guarantee, Harhouz showed an envelope to the Kherifs containing FRF50,000 in real banknotes. However, after the signature of the deed, Harhouz, gave the Kherifs another envelope, which only contained pieces of paper cut in the shapes of banknotes. After a brawl erupted between the protagonists, the police intervened and the envelope containing the sum of FRF50,000 was eventually given to Liazib Kherif. Harhouz sought the restitution of this sum as well as damages. The lower court demanded Liazib Kherif return the FRF50,000 to Harhouz.

Held: The protection of possession only applies to immovable property.

Judgment: Considering that the spouses Kerif appealed against the contested judgment (Paris, 15 October 1993) on the grounds that it condemned Liziad Kherif to return the sum of FRF50,000 to Mr Harhouz, further that the possessory claim was prescribed by application of Article 1265 of the New Code of Civil Procedure; and further that, on the one hand, the claim in reintegration is only open to the holder of a peaceful possession which Mr Harhouz, who tried to keep the funds by the use of a deceptive method, is not; and further that, on the other hand, the court of appeal did not apply the rule against Mr Harhouz that no one can invoke his own turpitude;

But considering that, first, the possessory protection applies only to immovables and that these rules, including the one on the annual prescription of the action, do not apply to claims on movables; and considering that ... the court of appeal has adroitly decided that the possession of Mr Kherif was vitiated by violence with respect to the circumstances in which he acquired it; that the challenged decision is legally grounded; on these reasons appeal dismissed.

Notes

(1) This decision raises several questions. Libchaber R, D 1996, Somm 331 rejects the view of the court of appeal that the money must be restored to Harouz. According to the French consensual transfer system (see Chapter 8 on transfer of property rights), Harouz already lost his ownership on the envelope and the banknotes to the Kherifs when he concluded the contract with them. The Kherifs were thus entitled to the envelope with the money. Moreover, according to Libchaber, the Court of Appeal was wrong to oblige the Kherifs to return the sum of FRF50,000 to Harouz in an action of vindication. The action of vindication can

[33] Bull civ 1996.I.57.

only be directed to the restoration of a object, ie the envelope with the banknotes, but not to a sum of money.

(2) The ruling of the Cour de cassation that the action for restoration (*l'action en réintégration*) does not apply to movables is rejected by F Zenati, RTD 1996, 932 (943 *et seq*). Zenati indicates that this rule, which is not explicitly provided by the law, cannot be based on legal tradition either, as the old action of '*réintégrande*' could also be applied to movables. That movables were, historically, excluded from the other possessory actions of the old law found its justification in the fact that movables were then of comparatively low value, which made special judicial protection for such objects not worthwhile. Today, this view has totally changed, as movable property plays an important role in modern society. The practical need for possessory protection of movable property is shown by the fact that courts try to evade the rule by extending the notion of immovable property to so-called *immovables per destination*, or to movables accessory to immovables, in order to grant possessory protection. Zenati thus calls on the Cour de cassation, who created the rule, to abandon it.

Cour de cassation, 9 March 1982[34] **2.8 (FR)**

Machicoisne v Thomas

THE CO-OWNER IS ENTITLED TO RAISE A POSSESSORY ACTION

The yard window

Each co-owner is entitled to claim for possessory protection.

Facts: The co-owners of a court and a passage, Machicoisne and Roncin, filed a possesory action (*complainte*) against Thomas, the owner of a neighbouring piece of land, claiming that Thomas should remove the windows which he had built without obeying the distance requirements provided by law. During the proceedings Roncin died and his successors, the couple Roncin, discontinued the action. Machicoisne, however, upheld the claim.

Held: Article 815-3 of the Civil Code[35] only relates to the pecuniary administration of the undivided property and does not prevent the individual co-owner from filing a possessory action against a third party who unlawfully interferes with the property.

Judgment: ... but considering that the provision contained in the first subparagraph of Article 815-3 Civil Code, which only concerns the management of the undivided property, does not prohibit a co-owner of undivided property from acting individually by complaining against a third party who is disturbing his possession of the property held in undivided ownership; considering that the challenged judgment points

[34] Bull civ 1982.III.63.

[35] Art 815-3 (Act no 76-1286 of 31 Dec 1976): 'Acts of administration and disposition relating to undivided property require the consent of all the undivided co-owners. They may give to one or several of them general authority for administration. A special authority is required for any act which does not belong to a normal management of the undivided property, as well as for the conclusion and renewal of leases. Where one undivided owner takes up the management of the undivided property, with the knowledge of the others and nevertheless without opposition on their part, he is deemed to have received an implied authority, covering acts of administration, but not acts of disposition or conclusion or renewal of contracts.' Art 815-3 was modified by Act no 2006-728 from 23 June 2006.

out that Mr Machicoisne has given evidence of actual long-standing possession of both the court and passageway which are held in undivided common ownership by him and Roncin's heirs; and that the court of appeal ruled, within the limits of its sovereign authority, that Mr Thomas had no rights over these properties and that the openings he made on the building, constituted a disturbance of Mr Machicoisne's quiet possession; that in the light of those findings, the judgment, which is properly justified, specifically states that Mr Machicoisne was entitled to act alone in order to protect his possession even if he enjoyed it in common with the Roncins; that, accordingly, the ground of appeal is unfounded.

On those grounds, the challenge made against the judgment of 29 May 1980 decided by the Court of Appeal of Orléans is dismissed.

Note

The judgment holds that each co-possessor is entitled to raise a possessory action against a third party. According to persistent case law, between the co-owners of the same building, however, a possessory action is not possible (eg Cour de cassation, 6 March 1991, D 1993, jur, 655, note Souleau).

Cour de Cassation, 7 June 1990[36] **2.9 (FR)**

Pelletier v SCI

DEFINITION OF INTERFERENCE

Demolition works

The mere performance of construction works on one's own land does not amount to an interference with possession.

Facts: Pelletier sued his neighbour, the association SCI, for interference with possession. The SCI pulled down a building adjacent to a wall which separated the two pieces of land. The demolition works destabilized the boundary wall belonging to Pelletier.

Held: The Cour de cassation quashed the judgment of the lower court and ruled that the lower court judgment which held that demolition works on the neighbouring land destabilised the boundary wall of the claimant did not establish relevant facts demonstrating the validity of an adverse claim against Mr Pelletier's possession.

Judgment: On the single ground: on the basis of Article 2282 (now 2278) Civil Code; considering that, in upholding the possessory action brought by Mr Pelletier against the real estate partnership Melle Lettings SCI following the demolition of a building belonging to Melle Lettings and abutting a wall separating their properties, the challenged judgment (Poitiers, 1 June 1988) ruled on grounds concurring with those of the court of first instance, that the demolition works had weakened that wall by exposing the fastening cavities for the joinery of the demolished building and by laying bare mullions and masonry that were neither jointed nor mortared;

In so deciding, without establishing any fact which would imply a conflicting claim against Mr Pelletier's right of possession, the court of appeal failed to provide its decision with a legal basis;

[36] Bull civ 1990.III.135.

On those grounds: the Cour de cassation quashes and annuls the judgment delivered on 1 June 1988 by the Court of Appeal, Poitiers, in regard to all its provisions; consequently replaces the parties in the situation in which they were before the date of that judgment and refers the case and the parties to the Court of Appeal, Limoges.

Note

This judgment is commented by Souleau, Defrenois 1991, 368:

> It is taught that 'possessory actions protect the possessor of a right *in rem* or the holder at will against the act of a third party which not only causes them material damage but chiefly evidences assertion of a claim conflicting with the *de facto* power that they exercise over the *res*.' What is a conflicting claim? Is it a voluntary act of encroachment on another's property? It is certainly that, yet not only that. Is it acting voluntarily in one's own interest and ignoring possession by the neighbour? That does not seem entirely to answer the point. There is therefore an area within which the action of the person causing the disturbance in itself conflicts with peaceful possession by the neighbour. In the case that gave rise to the judgment being commented on there was doubtless no assertion of claim conflicting with possession of the wall by the neighbour. The property company carried out demolition works on its land which laid bare the fastening cavities for the joinery and masonry that was not mortared. That does not conflict with possession by another person: it is simply the exercise by the owner of his legitimate right to demolish. In the absence of specific damage, no claim may be made by the possessor of the wall. If, conversely, the wall were to collapse, an action might lie on the basis of the concept of neighbourhood disturbances, which is a personal action for reparation and not an action *in rem*, seeking to remedy the disturbance.

Cour de cassation, 15 February 1995[37] **2.10 (FR)**

Cornillie v Pierson

RIGHT OF WAY AND POSSESSORY ACTION

The wall

The holder of a servitude granting a right of way is entitled to ward off interference by possessory action.

Facts: The Piersons constructed a wall in order to prevent their neighbours, Mr and Mrs Cornillie, from entering their land. The Cornillies invoked the existence of a contractual right of way and claimed that the wall had to be removed.

Held: The servitude of right of way grants a claim for restoration (*action en réintégration*).

Judgment: On the single ground: Having regard to Article 1264 of the New Code of Civil Procedure; considering that a possessory action may be brought within one year of the interference by any person who has been enjoying peaceful possession or has been holding the property for at least one year; that nonetheless a claim for restoration against a person committing the actionable act may be brought even

[37] Bull civ 1995.III.45.

where the dispossessed person was in possession for less than one year; considering that, according to the challenged judgment (Bastia, 30 November 1992), in 1990 Mr and Mrs Pierson built a wall preventing their neighbours, Mr and Mrs Cornillie, from gaining access to their land; that they, relying on a contractual right of way which has been granted under a private agreement dated 27 June 1927 and alleging that the construction of the wall amounted to an actionable act, demanded the demolition of the wall by way of a possessory action; considering that, in dismissing the claim of Mr and Mrs Cornillie, the judgment decided that a claim for restoration cannot lie in respect of a right of way; that in so deciding the court of appeal breached the statutory provision mentioned above.

On those grounds: the Cour de cassation quashes and sets aside the judgment delivered on 30 November 1992 by the Court of Appeal, Bastia, in regard to all its provisions; consequently restores the cause and the parties to the situation in which they were before the date of that judgment and refers the case and the parties to the Court of Appeal, Aix-en-Provence, for adjudication.

Note

In this landmark decision the Cour de cassation granted an action for restoration (*action en réintégration*) to the beneficiary of a right of way. It thereby abandoned the prevailing view that only servitudes that are apparent and continuous can be the object of possessory protection, and that the holder of even such servitude is not entitled to the action of restoration. The servitude of right of way is, according to French doctrine, a discontinuous servitude because it does not exist by itself, like, for instance the servitude of view, but must be exercised by human acts.[38] It can be apparent or not apparent depending on whether there are buildings or other structures that document the existence of the servitude. Both restrictions, the exclusion of the action of restoration and the continuity requirement, were based on the inaccurate opinion (i) that the holder of a non-apparent and discontinuous servitude is not in possession of the land and, therefore, cannot be dispossessed, and (ii) that the holder of an apparent and continuous servitude cannot be dispossessed in the violent or furtive way required by the action of restoration.[39]

Zenati, RTD 1995, 927:

> There seems no reason why the possession of servitudes should be subject to requirements of varying intensity depending on the action envisaged. Either the servitude is the subject-matter of possession or it is not. The possession of rights has been recognised by the civil law since the days of Roman law and its institution of *quasi-possessio*. The Napoleonic Code, which is still in force on this point, pays tribute to possession in Article 2228 (now 2255), defining it as the holding or enjoyment of a thing or a right. The Cour de cassation is here under the sway of the classic theory of possession: quasi-possession as possession of the thing analogous to an owner's possession but exercised under a right over another person's property (possession by right). Hence the prejudice that possession by the owner is stronger, in that it is palpable whereas possession of a right over another person's property is tenuous or theoretical. Plainly, possession of a right relates to an intangible item but that does not prevent it from being genuine possession and from giving

[38] Bergel, Bruschi and Cimamonti, above n 27, 379.
[39] Larroumet, above n 27, 550 *et seq*; Zenati, RTD 1995, 925.

rise to a genuine dispossession. The holder of a right of way deprived of his prerogative is not merely dispossessed theoretically of a right but is in fact prevented from exercising it substantively. Theoretical dispossession results in a tangible disturbance which satisfies the requirement of an actionable act necessary to found an action for restoration.

I.A.2.b Germany

(i) Self-help

German law attributes important legal consequences to the actual control over a object, over and above the interdiction of unlawful interference (see the definition in §858 BGB) by another, and grants the possessor the right to defend his position. Actual interference entitles the possessor to *self-help*. German law distinguishes two sorts of self-help, the *Besitzwehr* (§859(1) BGB) and the *Besitzkehr* (§859(2) and (3) BGB). *Besitzwehr* is a specific form of self-defence (§227 BGB) against actual force, whilst *Besitzkehr* entitles the possessor to recover the object from the dispossessor immediately after the interfering act. The right to exercise self-help applies to the direct possessor and the servant in possession (§860 BGB). Although not expressly provided by the BGB, it is held by the majority of legal doctrine that this right also extends to the indirect possessor.[40]

OLG Koblenz, 8 July 1977[41] **2.11 (DE)**

BESITZWEHR

Fight for the parking space

Self-help of the possessor must be proportionate.

Facts: The claimant, who had leased a restaurant including the lay-by (parking space) situated in front of it to the defendant, tried to embed several iron poles in concrete to block this lay-by. All attempts efforts by the defendant to make the claimant liberate the parking space proved ineffective. Finally the defendant slapped the neck of the 68-year-old claimant hard; this blow knocked the claimant to the ground, and the defendant then struck the prostrate claimant again.

Held: A possessor who strikes the trespasser in order to make him leave his premises acts unlawfully, unless he initially has exercised without success more modest remedies, which seemed to be suitable according to the circumstances.

Judgment: The defendant's blow on the neck and his subsequent blows on the claimant himself, lying on the ground, were neither justified by self-defence (§227 BGB, §32 StGB) nor by 'Besitzkehr' nor by 'Besitzwehr' (§859 BGB). Self-defence is already therefore inapplicable, because the claimant was not attacking the defendant at the moment when the defendant hit his neck. As far as the claimant's abidance on the parking space was an immediate attack to the defendant's possession, the defendant's blows could not in any case be considered as an 'act called for by self-defence'.

However, since the claimant exercised unlawful interference with the possession

[40] Baur and Stürner, above n 12, §9 at 98, para 23.

[41] MDR 1978, 141.

of another, the defendant was basically entitled to remove the claimant, who had not complied with the oral demand to abandon the premises, from the premises by force, relying on his right of self-help. This entitlement was not dependent on the fact that the defendant could not have obtained help from the authorities in good time. According to the common legal opinion he who exercises his right with respect to the protection of possession must not go beyond the measures which are necessary to reject the trespass. Following the self-defence provision ('essential defence') this restriction of the right of protection of possession is partly described as unwritten constituent fact of §859 BGB and it is partly derived from the general right of self-help (§229 BGB), which according to §230(1) BGB may not extend further than is necessary to ward off the danger on the grounds that the right of protection of possession is a case of self-help. Thus the possessor may oppose a trespass with the demanded means only within the scope of the absolute necessary and may use more severe means only in as far as appropriate more modest means do not work. If the possessor goes beyond these limits of his right of protection of possession, his actions turn unlawful and he becomes himself liable for damages, provided that he is at fault. ...

Considering these principles the defendant's blow on the claimant's neck was no longer within the limits of §859 BGB. According to the circumstances, which did not demand an immediate solution, the defendant would at least have had to try to use more modest means as appropriate. There is no use in discussing whether he could be expected simply to safeguard the iron poles already torn out and to make it—as a result—impossible for the claimant to continue his plan. The defendant, though, would have been in the position, for instance, to further update the previously uttered threat to release the German shepherd dog by approaching the claimant threateningly with the leashed dog. Besides, before hitting his neck brutally, the defendant had not even tried to persuade the claimant to leave the premises on threat of force. Yet, the claimant is liable for contributory fault.

BGH, 19 October 1966[42] **2.12 (DE)**

BESITZKEHR

Advertising space

Time limit for the recovery of possession by way of self-help.

Facts: Over the course of several years, the claimant had been putting up advertising panels on the surfaces of buildings to which the defendant, an advertising firm, had already attached advertising panels. The defendant derived this right from contracts the defendant had concluded with the owners of the buildings. According to these contracts, third parties should not be allowed to use the walls for advertising. As the claimant did not stop his behaviour upon written request by the defendant, the defendant started to remove the claimant's advertising panels. The defendant was only ready to return the removed panels upon reimbursement of the removal and storage costs. In the filed action the claimant demanded (inter alia) that the defendant be prohibited from removing the claimant's advertising panels.

Held: An advertisement contractor whom the owner of the building has granted the exclusive right to place advertisements on the building can become co-possessor of this part of the building. He is entitled to remove the advertisements placed by another enterprise, but only immediately after their attachment.

[42] NJW 1967, 46.

Judgment: ... the arbitrary removal of the panels can be authorised from the point of view of the protection of possession. The possessor may ward off unlawful interference by use of force (§859(1) BGB); unlawful interference is also an infringement of possession (§858(1) BGB). The claimant's advertising panels can be considered as an interference with the possession on the relevant building surface. Therefore the court of appeal has to examine the question whether the defendant has obtained possession on these surfaces ... .

The question whether an ... enterprise obtains direct possession—at least co-possession with the building owner—of the whole building surface by concluding a contract with the building owner on the exclusive use of the surface as advertising space and by attaching an advertising panel in exercising this contractual right must be based on the common opinion [*Verkehrsauffassung*] which constitutes a matter of fact. ... The court of appeal, however, did not ascertain the contents of this common opinion or the circumstances in this field which influence the common opinion. ...

If the court of appeal, after re-examination of the case, finds that the defendant has direct possession on the entire building surface, then the claimant's claim which is directed at the unrestricted injunction of the removal of the advertising panels attached by the claimant must be rejected. Because at least when the defendant removed the panels 'immediately' after their attachment, that is as fast as it was possible to act under the given circumstances, the defendant's acting keeps within the limits of its right to self-help [*Besitzkehr*] against unlawful interference (§859(3) BGB). The so far filed application for an injunction makes no difference whether the defendant removes the panels 'immediately' or only later.

For the re-examination of the case, it is emphasised with respect to the extent of the defendant's possessory protection that there are reservations against a temporarily unlimited right of the defendant to remove arbitrarily the panels attached by the claimant. If the attachment of the advertising panels by the claimant is considered a partial deprivation of the defendant's possession (on the part of the wall surface occupied by the claimant), then the inadmissibility of the not immediately occurring arbitrary removal by the defendant arises from the provision of §859(3) BGB. Such an attachment of advertising panels is also considered to be a disturbance of the defendant's possession on the remaining partial area that is left at his disposal; this interference originates from the negative impact on the advertising effect. Therefore, in principle, to the benefit of the defendant the provision concerning the arbitrary warding off of a disturbance of possession which does not provide for a time limit would come into consideration. But if the measure taken to ward off a disturbance of possession constitutes at the same time the recovery of the deprived possession on a real part of the parcel, it seems imperative to the senate to apply the temporary limits of the 'Besitzkehr' ... .

LG Frankfurt, 22 June 1983[43] **2.13 (DE)**

BESITZKEHR

The removed car

Towing away a vehicle four hours after it has been unlawfully parked on another's parking space is an act of immediate self-help.

Facts: The claimant claimed DM1468.82 as compensation because the defendant had her vehicle towed away from a parking space on the top storey of car-park M on 20 May 1982 at 00.15 h. The claimant had parked her car in the defendant's car-park on 19 May 1982 at 20.00 h. On the morning of 20 May 1982, she reported the car as stolen to the police and did not retrieve it until 28 June 1982 at L Street, whereto the car had been towed.

Held: The county court held that the suit was founded in the amount of DM792. The defendant's appeal was successful, while the claimant's cross-appeal was rejected. The BGH held that the defendant was entitled to remove the car on the basis of self-help (*Besitzkehr*).

Judgment: From the reasons:

... The claimant is not entitled to compensation according to §823(1) BGB, because the defendant lawfully had the car towed away from the parking space. The defendant did not act unlawfully, because he was entitled to ward off the unlawful interference with his possession of the parking space and the unlawful interference (§858 BGB) of the claimant by having the claimant's car towed. Both in literature and jurisdiction there is unity regarding the fact that cases like the present are subject to §859(3) BGB, according to which the possessor of a parking space as possessor of a part of a piece of land is entitled to recover possession immediately after deprivation of possession by towing away the unlawfully parked car. This the claimant admits herself ... But as far as she holds in this connection the view that there can be no immediate 'Besitzkehr', as required by §859(3) BGB, if the car is towed only about four hours after the parking and the bonnet has cooled down, the chamber is not in a position to follow.

'Immediately' must be interpreted to the effect that the 'Besitzkehr' has to take place as fast as possible according to objective standards without consideration of the subjective knowledge of the deprivation. ... That does not mean, according to the unanimous opinion of the jurisdiction and literature, as the claimant alleges, that dispossession of the tortfeasor has to take place instantaneously after deprivation of possession and as long as the bonnet is still warm. ... On the contrary, not excessively strict requirements, but a balanced interpretation based on the ratio of the provision must be applied, whereas it has to be taken into consideration that the possessor of the parking space, when he finds his space occupied, usually is unable to determine at what time the car has been parked and for how long it is already there. Already the genesis of §859(3) BGB shows that, according to the legislator's will, 'immediately' may not be understood in the sense of instantaneous respectively like a flash of lightning, because such a strict interpretation would impair the right for repossession too much (cf Prot III 39, 40). Therefore, both in literature and jurisdiction, it is equally accepted that the dispossession of the trespasser 'at the same day', or 'in the same evening', but even within 'the next day', has to be considered to be in direct and temporal connection with the trespass and therefore to be

[43] NJW 1984, 183.

immediate in the sense of §859(3) BGB. ... Since the defendant indisputably arrived at the parking space only a few hours after the claimant had parked the car and, after some attributable time for information, consideration and preparation ..., set without delay in the same evening to arrange the removal of the car, he has acted immediately in the sense of §859(3) BGB.

The claimant cannot claim that the defendant acted unlawfully because towing away the car was an excessive remedy. He was not obliged to park the car on another parking space on the parking deck, since by doing so he would have run the risk of committing an unlawful interference with respect to other parking space possessors, as the defendant could not know which other parking spaces on the parking deck were not leased or would remain unoccupied. The defendant also cannot be blamed that he arranged that the car was towed to the vicinity of the competent 10th police station rather than parking it in the close vicinity to the parking space on public ground. To this argument the defendant alleged that this was not possible, respectively indicated, because of the tight parking situtation throughout the residential area M and the fact that it is generally known that many cars are forced open and stolen there. Since the defendant was obliged, according to his duty, to minimise the loss, to provide for a parking space that was as safe as possible, it cannot be criticised that, upon the recommendation of the towing company and the police, he parked the car in the vicinity of the police station. Finally, the defendant cannot be accused of having culpably violated his obligation under §242 BGB to take reasonable measures to minimise the loss ... within the frame of §859 BGB. To inform the caretaker, who was not available at night-time, about the towing process on the next day was not necessary, since the defendant on his part could assume that the claimant would appropriately be informed by the police or that she would herself ask the caretaker to get the name of the tenant or owner of the parking space where she had parked the car.

Note

Using another's parking space constitutes an act of dispossession while the blocking of an entrance or drive amounts to a disturbance of possession. In both cases the possessor of the parking space is entitled to remove the car. In the first case, however, he must obey the time limit set by §859(3) BGB that allows recovery of possession only immediately after the dispossession. In the annotated judgment the LG Frankfurt holds that a possessor who waits for four hours before the removal is still within the time limit, but, according to the AG München, 23 November 1995, NJW 1996, 853, waiting for seven hours is too long. It is disputed whether the possessor is obliged to wait for a reasonable period of time before he removes the car: *pro* AG Frankfurt/M, 7 April 1988, NJW-RR 1989, 83, *contra* AG München, 11 May 2001, NJW-RR 2002, 200. See also OLG Brandenburg 14 May 1996, NJW 1998, 1717, 1718: the house owner who waits for two weeks to remove squatters has lost his right to self-help.

(ii) Possessory actions

§§861–67 BGB regulate the protection of the direct and indirect (§869 BGB) possessor against dispossession (§861 BGB) and disturbance of possession (§862 BGB) by way of *judicial action*. In case of dispossession, the action is for recovery of possession and in case of disturbance of possession either for abatement of the interference or an injunction. These possessory actions protect the possession as such. Whether the possessor is legally entitled to have or to use the object is not relevant. In possessory proceedings, the dispossessor or interferer cannot therefore claim that he is the owner of the object, but is only entitled to raise the 'possessory' objection that the possessor's possession is defective as against him (§861(2) BGB). The rightful owner must assert his ownership by a separate action based on §985 BGB. According to case law and the majority opinion of legal doctrine, this action, however, can be filed as a counterclaim to the possessory action.[44] The right to file for possessory protection under §§861 and 862 BGB expires after one year after the performance of the unlawful interference (§864(1) BGB). In order to achieve fast judicial protection, possessory claims can be secured by an interim injunction (§§935, 940 ZPO).

BGH, 7 March 1956[45] **2.14 (DE)**

DEFINITION OF DISTURBANCE OF POSSESSION

Unfounded action

Not only material interference, but also immaterial interference (eg contesting the possession of another, uttering threats or prohibitions) may constitute a disturbance of possession.

Facts: In 1939, the defendant sold a part of his parcel of land to the claimant. After several legal disputes between the defendant and the claimant and her husband, the defendant had to transfer the parcel to the claimant. On 24 June 1948, the defendant filed another action against the claimant denying the effectiveness of the last court decision and claiming damages. The action was dismissed. In March 1952, the claimant sued the defendant and claimed damages. She alleged that the defendant's refusal to transfer the parcel and the subsequent numerous judicial actions triggered by the defendant delayed her plans to construct a factory building from 1941 to 1951, thus increasing the building costs by DM50,000. The claim was rejected in all three instances.

Held: Not only material interference, but also immaterial interference (eg contesting the possession of another, uttering threats or prohibitions) may constitute a disturbance of possession. To take lawful legal action, however, does not amount to a disturbance of possession.

Judgment: ... The RG was of the opinion that a disturbance of possession by unlawful interference in the sense of §858 BGB could be exerted not only by material but also by mental intervention, by verbal denial of the possession and by prohibitions and threats (RG in JW 08, 274; 31, 2904 [2906]; BGB RGRK, NB 5 to §858 BGB). ... The present case, however, is different in the facts from the decided cases by the RG. The defendant did not influence the claimant by arbitrary activities like threats and prohibitions and induce her to refrain from the intended use of her parcel, but has lawfully taken legal action and has placed her claims which she assumed to be entitled to as against the claimant under the control of the court. In doing so she made use of a remedy that is provided in a state in which the rule of law prevails

44 Baur and Stürner, above n 12, §9 at 96 *et seq*, para 17 *et seq*; Joost, above n 12, §863 at 71 *et seq*, paras 9 *et seq*.

45 NJW 1956, 787.

for the decision and disentanglement of disputes between private persons. Its very use cannot constitute unlawful interference, but is the pure opposite of arbitrary acting, even if the enforced claim afterwards turns out to be without foundation. ...

BGH, 14 October 1994[46] **2.15 (DE)**

UNLAWFULNESS OF NOISE BY AN INDUSTRIAL UNDERTAKING

Paper factory

Noise may constitute a disturbance of possession.

Facts: The claimant had been a tenant of a house on a hill since the beginning of the 1970s. The house was constructed in the 1950s. In the valley below, at a distance of 50–60 meters from the claimant's land, lies the defendant's paper factory. The factory, in operation since 1867, contains several paper machines, storage depots, three firing systems and a gas tank. On 20 October 1988, the Trade Supervisory Office issued two administrative orders prohibiting the defendant from emitting from the installations of his plant, be they subject to authorisation according to the Federal Emission Control Act or not, noise above the level of 45 dB(A) measured at the claimant's land between 10 pm and 6 am. Alleging that the defendant's factory is regularly emitting noise exceeding this level during the night, the claimants applied for an injunction. The claimant indicated that the interference could be reduced by economically reasonable measures, or that the defendant could adopt protective measures. The court of first instance (LG) allowed the claim. The court of appeal (OLG) dismissed the appeal.

Held: The BGH held that interference by noise may constitute a disturbance of possession. It applied §906 BGB and §14 BImSchG (Federal Immission Control Act) that regulate the right of the owner of a parcel of land to abate such interference to possessory claims under §862 BGB and stated that in case of a permanent interference the one-year period of §864 BGB starts with the ending of the interference.

Judgment: I. The court of appeal admits the claimant's claim for the injunction of noise emissions according to §862(1) BGB. This claim neither has become extinct according to §864(1) BGB nor statute-barred, because noise emissions constitute repeated interferences with possession. The noise emitted from the defendant's premises interferes with the claimant's use of his house not only marginally; the noise interferences are not customary under local conditions and, moreover, can be prevented by economically reasonable measures. The claimant's claim is not excluded by §242 BGB or §14 sentence 1 BImSchG.

II. These findings cannot be upheld in some fundamental aspects. The court of appeal is in principle correct when it assumes that the claimant as possessor of the parcel is entitled to an injunction according to §862(1) BGB against the defendant as the operator of the interfering paper factory. It rightly examines the admissibility of the noise impact by the standards laid down by §906 BGB because the possessor's right to ward off interference cannot go further than that of the owner ... .

1. Contrary to the view of the notice of appeal, such a claim is also not statute-barred (§864(1) BGB) when the noise pollution has been persisting for many years. In respect to repeated interferences of the same kind the expiry of the time limit starts to run only with the completion of the last act of interference ... . Whether it is permissible in the present case to assume repeated interference must be left open. In case of permanent noise impact the unlawful interference, which, according to the law, starts the running of the time limit, not only lies in the beginning of

[46] NJW 1995, 132.

the interference. It is not a completed occurrence that lies in the past and has only continuing effects, but the interfering activity itself, which herein consists of the operation of the paper factory, continues and solely ends upon closure of the factory. It is not acceptable that the running of the preclusive period restarts in case of an interrupted—even if only for a short time—and therefore repeated interference, but with respect to a permanent interference should be aligned with the beginning of the interference.

2. …

3. The court of appeal is right not to apply the exclusion of the claim provided by §14(1) BImSchG. … In principle, §14(1) BImSchG is also applicable in the context of claims of possessory protection … . The court of first instance (LG) denies, with incomplete reasoning, the exclusion of the claim because the claimant did not ask for the closure of the factory and because it is up to the defendant to decide how to stop the interference. According to the spirit of the provision, all applications for an injunction based on interference that lead necessarily to a closure of the factory must not be allowed. But that is not the case here. Although the defendant has argued that the noise which led to the violation of the limit stems solely from the firing system which was approved according to pollution law, he stated at the same time that there is the—obviously from an economic point of view reasonable—possibility to construct a noise barrier which would reduce the noise emissions to an admissible amount. That means that the claimant's main application is also not a priori excluded (§14 BImSchG).

Note

This decision states three important points of possessory protection: (i) 'emissions' (interference by noise, water, smell, etc) may constitute a disturbance of possession according to §862 BGB; (ii) §906 BGB and §14 BImSchG which regulate the right of the owner of a parcel to abate such interference also apply to the right of the possessor under §862 BGB; (iii) in the case of a permanent interference the one-year period of §864 BGB starts with the ending of the interference.

BGH, 21 February 1979[47] **2.16 (DE)**

ACTION FOR DISPOSSESSION AND COUNTERCLAIM OF THE OWNER UNDER §985 BGB

Disputed horse

If the action for dispossession filed by the former possessor and the counterclaim of the owner under §985 BGB are both founded and ready for decision, the court has to dismiss the possessory action and to grant the counterclaim.

Facts: In November 1975, the claimant bought from the defendant, a horse trader, horse D for DM17,500, but reserved the right to exchange it after its presentation. As the claimant was not satisfied with D, the parties entered into negotiations during which the defendant exchanged horse D for mare F to give the claimant the option to try mare F. The price of the mare F was DM13,500. In a letter dated 5 July 1976 the claimant informed the defendant that he wanted to keep mare F and that the defendant should

[47] NJW 1979, 1358, BGHZ 73, 355.

refund him the price difference of DM3,500. On 8 July 1976, the defendant took mare F without the claimant's knowledge. The claimant obtained a temporary injunction according to which the mare was handed over to a bailiff as sequestrator. Meanwhile the mare foaled. Both parties claim that the other party should agree that mare F be returned from the sequestrator. The claimant also claims compensation for use of the mare by the defendant since 9 July 1976, the payment of DM3,500 from the, according to his opinion, concluded barter deal and—since the appellate instance—the recovery of the foal.

Held: If the action for dispossession filed by the former possessor and the counterclaim of the owner under §985 BGB are both founded and ready for decision, the court has to dismiss the possessory action and to grant the counterclaim.

Judgment: I. The reciprocally asserted claim to release the mare.

1. With his claim the claimant has asserted both a (so-called possessory) claim for protection of possession (§861 BGB) and a (so-called petitory) claim for restoration according to §§985, 1007 BGB. Before the appellate court the defendant filed a (petitory) counterclaim founded exclusively on his right to possess the mare because of his ownership.

(a) The admissibility of the counterclaim has been answered in the affirmative by the appeal court; the notice of appeal does not object to this. In BGHZ 53, 166 (169) = NJW 1970, 707, the division for civil matters at the BGH has decided that §33 ZPO or §863 BGB give rise to doubts regarding the admissibility of a petitory counterclaim against a possessory action. The Senate agrees with this decision, which has received approval by literature. …

(b) The court of appeal thinks—and insofar no error of law is recognisable—that the claimant has a claim for restoration of possession because the defendant committed unlawful interference when taking the mare on 8 July 1976 (§§858, 861(1) BGB). It, however, regards itself unable to confirm the defendant's conviction by the court of first instance since the defendant's counterclaim for restitution is founded according to §985 and ready for decision; claim and counterclaim cannot be successful at the same time; because that would mean that both the defendant and the claimant must agree to surrender possession of the horse to the opponent; as far as the interferer's right to possession has been—even though not yet legally binding—adjudicated or will be adjudicated at the same time, a claim based on possessory protection in application of §864(2) BGB must be dismissed. At any rate this legal viewpoint is correct for the present case.

(aa) With respect to the claims for possessory protection under §§861, 862 BGB it is, according to §863 BGB, not admissble to plead the right to possess based on a material entitlement of the interferer. This restriction of objection serves to enable the possessor to quickly regain his possession impaired by unlawful interference; the judicial enforcement of the claims for possessory protection should not be delayed by the necessity to discuss at first the defendant's alleged right to possess and to gather evidence in possibly protracted proceedings. … But the rule of §863 BGB applies not without exception. According to §864(2) BGB, a claim founded on §§861, 862 BGB is terminated, if it becomes ascertained by final judgment after the perpetration of the unlawful interference that the interferer has a right to the object, which allows him to claim that the situation of possession is established which is in conformity with his actions.

2. The appeal court regards the counterclaim under §985 BGB as justified. The 'presumption that arises out of the former possession of the claimant according to §1006 BGB' is 'invalided' by the evidence that no transfer of ownership to him has taken place. Since the claimant should have exercised his right to exchange D, which

was bought in November 1975, within a reasonable, short—in May 1976 lapsed—period of time, it must be assumed that the parties entered into new negotiations which have not yet led to a contractual agreement; the reciprocal delivery of the horses was only effected in order to prepare the intended conclusion of the contract, because both parties—not just the claimant as he alleges—should get the opportunity to check the consigned animals with respect to capability and value; furthermore there has not been any price agreement.

(a) …

(b) … As the appeal court has found without any error of law that the negotiations between the parties in May 1976 did not lead to a conclusion of the contract, it can rest upon itself, whether insofar the onus of proof actually would lie with the defendant, as the appeal means; whether a presumption of the claimant's ownership of F can be deduced from §1006 BGB—also assumed by the appeal court—is doubtful, because it is obvious that the claimant acquired only indirect possession (*Fremdbesitz*) by the delivery of the horse for testing purposes; if the possessor later on acts like an *Eigenbesitzer*, he has to prove that his *Fremdbesitz* changed in a lawful way into direct possession (*Eigenbesitz*). …

(c) In the absence of a binding exchange agreement, the legal relationship between the parties concerning the horses reciprocally delivered in May 1976 is exhausted to the effect that each party can—for the purposes of approval—use a horse belonging to another. That is why the appeal court's opinion can be confirmed insofar, as it denies a still existing (material) right of the claimant to possess F, which he can oppose to the defendant's claim for restoration according to §985 BGB (§986(1) BGB). The defendant could unilaterally terminate the claimant's right to possess F, which arose from the fact that the defendant left the mare to him for testing purposes, at least when from his viewpoint the contractual negotiations had been frustrated; according to the findings of the appeal court, this was the case when he picked up the mare on 8 July 1976.

II. The claimant's claim for compensation for lost use

1. The appeal court denies such a claim because the claimant was not entitled to possess F at the moment (9 July 1976) as of which he claims for compensation for lost use and therefore did not have a right to use it anymore. This opinion holds up in legal review too.

2. As a basis for the claim only §823(1) BGB—namely the direct possession as a protected legal interest—as well as §§823(2), 858 BGB can be taken into consideration. The question whether also the non-entitled—like here—or only the entitled possessor is entitled to demand compensation is controversial. … Here the claimant demands the damage resulting from the impairment to use the object. A party who has no right of use cannot claim compensation for such damage from somebody who has a right of use even if the latter deprived him of possession by unlawful interference. In such a case the possessor was obliged to abstain from use and to grant the entitled person the possibility of use. From the provisions on possessory protection (§§858 *et seq* BGB) which should only prevent the entitled person from arbitrarily establishing the state he is entitled to, nothing to the contrary can be deduced.

III. The court of appeal rightly also denies the claimant's claim for payment of DM3,500 on the basis that the agreement on exchange of D against F combined with an obligation of repayment of DM3,500 which has been alleged by the claimant, could not be established.

IV. The claimant's claim for return of the foal.

As the female belongs to the defendant, the claimant could have acquired ownership of the foal only on the basis of good faith possession of the mare according to §955(1) BGB. The court of appeal denies that because the claimant either knew about the lack of his right to possess F as an owner before the foal was born or—with respect to the pending lawsuit–grossly negligently did not know it. In any case, the outcome is correct. Thereby it may rest on itself, whether the appeal court was right to assume that the claimant was the direct possessor of the mare—at that time she was located at the sequestrator—when the foal was born.

Notes

(1) This decision on the coincidence of the possessory action for dispossession and the *rei vindicatio* of the owner confirms the landmark decision BGHZ 53, 166 = NJW 1970, 707. In BGH, 9 November 1998, NJW 1999, 425 the BGH applied the same reasoning to the reverse constellation of a possessory action as counterclaim to the *rei vindicatio* of the owner. The issue is rather disputed as it endangers the fundamental aim of possessory protection which is to grant the possessor a quick tool with which to protect his possession irrespective of the underlying right in order to prevent violence (critical therefore Staudinger–Bund, §863 at 184 *et seq*, para 8; P. Spieß. 'Die Auswirkungen der petitorischen Widerklage auf die Besitzklage' JZ 1979, 717; K Gursky 'Die neuere höchstrichterliche Rechtsprechung zum Mobiliarsachenrecht' JZ 1984, 604 (605); A Amend, 'Aktuelles und Historisches zur richterlichen Anerkennung des possessorischen Besitzschutzes—BGH, NJW 1999, 425' JuS 2001, 124). J Baur and R Stürner, *Sachenrecht*, §9 at 87, para 18; Münchener Kommentar—Joost, VI §864 at 72 *et seq*, para 10 *et seq*, agree with the BGH with the reservation that the possessory action may only be dismissed if the decision of the counterclaim is not appealable.

(2) The annotated judgment discusses two further important issues of possession: (i) the right of the possessor to damages in tort as compensation for the lost uses caused by the unlawful dispossession and (ii) the distribution of ownership of the fruits of the object (*in concreto*: the foal) between owner and possessor. Both issues are discussed below.

(iii) Claim for restoration of possession

§1007 BGB only applies to movables. It provides for a specific claim according to which the former possessor of the object is entitled to claim restoration of possession from the actual holder of the object.

(iv) Protection in tort and unjust enrichment

BGH, 21 January 1981[48] **2.17 (DE)**

DAMAGE CLAIM OF THE POSSESSOR

The locked-out subtenant

The subtenant who lost the right to use the object is not entitled to claim damages for the lost uses from the lessor who unlawfully dispossessed him.

Facts: The claimant let part of a commercial building (a hall with a ramp) to A, who sublet the main part of the building to the defendant. On 24 May 1974, the claimant terminated the contract with A and urged the defendant to conclude a lease contract or to vacate the building. On 4 June 1974, as the defendant did not react, the claimant closed the hall and ramp entrances and denied the defendant's workers access to the building. On 19 June 1974, the defendant regained possession of the building by way of an interim injunction. In 27 November 1974, the defendant was ordered by a final court decision to vacate the building. The claimant requires the payment of several positions (rent, costs for heating, electricity and repairs, etc). The defendant claims, inter alia, damages for the lost use during 4 June and 19 June 1974 by way of set-off and counterclaim.

Held: The one who had no right of use cannot claim compensation for the impairment of the possibility to use the object from the one who is entitled to the right of use, even if the latter deprived him of the possession by unlawful interference.

Judgment: ... The question, whether in cases of unlawful dispossession or impairment of possession only the legitimate possessor is entitled to claim for compensation for damage thereby caused or whether in such cases even the non-entitled possessor can claim compensation, is controversial, but need not to be answered in the present case no more than in the case decided on 9 March 1976.[49] Here, like then, the claim for loss of uses, the diminution is asserted, which lies in the impairment of the possibility to use the object. The 8th Senate for civil matters at the BGH was able to leave this question open also. In the quoted decision it says after all that there are many reasons for the assumption that someone who is impaired in his possession can claim compensation for loss of use only 'if he was entitled to a right to use'. It is extremely doubtful whether a non-entitled impaired possessor can claim compensation for loss of use from the holder of the right to use. The Senate of decision approved in its judgment from 21 February 1979 the point of view adopted in this matter by the court of appeal that the claimant in that case had, at the point in time from which he claimed the compensation for lost uses, no right to possession with respect to the arbitrarily taken horse and, therefore, no longer any right of use. As cause of action for this claim only §823(1) BGB or §823(2) in conjunction with §858 BGB (infringement of direct possession by unlawful interference) could be taken into consideration. The one who had no right of use cannot claim compensation for the impairment of the possibility to use the object (to ride the horse) from the one who is entitled to the right of use, even if the latter deprived him of the possession by unlawful interference. In such a case the possessor is obligated to abstain from use and to grant the beneficiary the possibility to use. From the rules on possessory protection, which—as already mentioned—should only prevent the beneficiary from arbitrarily establishing the situation to which he is entitled,

[48] NJW 1981, 865, BGHZ 79, 232.
[49] See above NJW 1979, 1358, BGHZ 73, 355 (disputed horse).

nothing different can be derived. This view is upheld here. ... Even from the rules regarding the relationship between owner and possessor in §§987 *et seq* BGB, ... a right of the unauthorised possessor to use cannot be deduced. The benefit, that the law leaves the drawn fruits to the unauthorised possessor who is in good faith, does not mean that he has a right of use, the impairment of which would oblige the owner to compensate him. ...

Notes

(1) While it is common opinion that lawful possession constitutes 'another right' under §823(1) BGB and is thus protected by tort law, it is contested whether this extends to the possession as such.[50] In the annotated judgment the BGH restrained from a definitive decision on this issue. It, however, denied the unauthorised possessor the right to claim compensation for lost uses. Under certain circumstances the possessor may also be entitled to compensation under §906(2) BGB (BGH, 23 February 2001, NJW 2001, 1865).

(2) The lawful possessor is entitled to claim under the rules of unjust enrichment (BGH, 18 June 1979, NJW 1979, 2034).

BGH, 18 June 1979[51] **2.18 (DE)**

UNJUST ENRICHMENT

Gravel pit

The lawful possessor (lessee) is entitled to claim under the rules of unjust enrichment.

Facts: Both parties obtained permission from farmer K to extract gravel from different areas of his parcel of land. After the claimant had removed the 'overburden', ie the humus and loam/gravel layer, from part of the area assigned to her, the public authority ordered the immediate cessation of the gravel mining. While the claimant did not do anything against this, the defendant obtained permission for dry mining, and proceeded to mine gravel down to the ground-water level from the area the claimant had cleared. The claimant alleges that the defendant had mined 10,000 m^3 gravel from the area she had leased and cleared. She claims payment of DM20,000, the expenses she had incurred in vain for the development of the area.

Held: The lawful possessor is entitled to claim under the rules of unjust enrichment.

Judgment: I. ... Essential for the caused damage suffered by the claimant is here not the value of her expenditures, which turned out to be useless, but the possible depreciation the possession of the area leased by the claimant could have suffered through the disturbance or the deprivation of the possession by the defendant. For this, the value of possession is represented by the right of lease, which lies behind it. The damage consists of the depreciation of the value which the claimant's right to exploit the area sustained after the impairment by the gravel mining. ... This damage, however, the claimant did not request in her claim.

[50] Baur and Stürner, above n 12, §9 at 100, paras 31 *et seq*; Joost, above n 12, before §854 at 17, para 14.

[51] NJW 1979, 2034.

II. The court of appeal also rejects the claimant's claim for compensation for (alleged) expenses on the basis of unjust enrichment. It holds that all the expenses were incurred for the parcel and remained there. By this, the development of the gravel pit had been facilitated; but this is compensated by the fact that the mining costs are reflected in the value or the price of the gravel quarried by the defendant. With her claim the claimant, however, did not request the—here possible—refund according to §818(2) or §816 BGB. The notice of appeal rightly objects to this view. The claimant was not obliged to calculate her claim on unjust enrichment according to the mode considered by the appeal court. She can already found her claim on the fact that the defendant saved the expenses for the development of the area—incurred by the claimant—which he would have had under normal circumstances. With respect to the saving of these necessary costs, he is enriched. Had he commissioned the claimant or a third party to undertake the removal works, he would have been obliged to pay an adequate fee. In the fact that he saved these expenses, lies his enrichment. ... He cannot claim that if he had known of this obligation, he would not have mined the area ... .

I.A.2.c Austria

(i) Possessory protection

Allgemeines Bürgerliches Gesetzbuch (ABGB) **2.19 (AT)**

§339 Judicial remedy of the possessor in case of disturbance of possession
Of whatever quality the possession may be, no one is entitled to disturb it arbitrarily. The person disturbed is entitled to claim by order of the court the interdiction of the interference and compensation for provable damage.

§344 Judicial remedy for the preservation of possession in case of urgent danger
The right of possession includes the right to protect oneself in one's possession, and in case that timely judicial assistance would unavailable, to ward off force with adequate force (§19).

ZPO—Special provisions for the proceedings of possessory protection **2.20 (AT)**

§454 (1) In proceedings concerning actions for interference with possession of objects and rights, in which the relief sought is only directed at the protection and restoration of the last status of possession and which must be brought within 30 days after the claimant became aware of the interference, the following special provisions (§455–§460) must be applied.

(2) Actions filed in writing are to be designated as actions for disturbance of possession.

§457 (1) The court hearing is restricted to the discussion and proof of the fact of the last status of possession and the occurrence of the interference, and all discussion of the right to possession, the title, of bona or male fide possession or of compensation claims are excluded.

§459 The decision must be rendered immediately after the closing of the hearing by way of court order (final order) and it must be restricted to set a temporary rule for the factual status of possession or to provisionally provide, according to the law (§340–§343 ABGB), an interdiction or security. The subsequent judicial assertion of the right to possession and of the claims derived thereof is not inhibited ...

Notes

(1) §344 ABGB allows the possessor to defend his possession by way of *self-help*. Self-help, however, is only a means of last resort, if judicial help is not available.

(2) §§454 *et seq* ZPO provide for a specific, expeditious procedure for the *judicial protection of possession*. It is of a provisional character and ends with a court order, not a judgment. The action must be brought within a time limit of 30 days from the day when the claimant received notice of the interference and covers interference by dispossession and disturbance of possession. The claim is directed at the restoration of the original condition (recovery of possession and/or abatement of the interference) and the interdiction of future interference. Possessory claims can be secured by an interim injunction (§458 ZPO). Possessory proceedings aim to protect the last peaceful possession and do not allow for a discussion of the underlying right or of compensation claims. Like in German law, the interferer is thus only entitled to raise the objection that the claimant's possession is defective as against him (§345 ABGB, spurious possession).

(3) §§340–43 ABGB provide special rules for the protection of the possessor of immovable property or of a limited property right in case of endangerment by construction works or dangerous buildings.

(ii) *Actio Publiciana*

Allgemeines Bürgerliches Gesetzbuch (ABGB)—Revindication based upon legally presumed ownership of the claimant **2.21 (AT)**

§372 If the claimant cannot sufficiently prove that he acquired ownership of an object withheld from him, but has established the valid title and the not spurious manner by which he acquired possession, he shall be considered the real owner in regard to every possessor who is unable to allege a superior title.

§373 If hereto the defendant possesses the object in mala fide or unlawful manner; if he can disclose no or only a suspicious predecessor; or, if he has received the object without payment but the claimant has received it for payment, he must surrender the object to the claimant.

§374 If the defendant and the claimant have an equal title to their not spurious possession, the defendant is to have the preference by virtue of the factual possession.

§375 Whoever possesses an object in the name of another can defend himself against a revindication by disclosing the name of his predecessor and alleging the proof therefore.

Note

The *actio publiciana* is based on the *right to possession* and protects the person who can show the better title to the object against dispossession and disturbance of possession. The order of prevalence of title is described in §373 ABGB. In case of equivalence of title the defendant, for being in possession of the object, prevails. The *actio publiciana* is also available to the possessor of a right (*Rechtsbesitzer*).

OGH, 25 June 1958[52] **2.22 (AT)**

ACTIO PUBLICIANA

The contested plastic floor covering

*The person who bought an object under retention of title is entitled to claim recovery of the object from a third person under §372 ABGB (*actio publiciana*).*

Facts: Based on a lease contract dated 16 January 1956, Anna W, a tradeswoman, rented several offices in house W, P-Gasse 5. In these rooms she had put down a plastic floor covering of 2.4 mm thickness. The floor-seller, Josef T, retained the title in this covering, which cost about ATS9,000. Anna W had not at the time of proceedings paid anything. On 25 March 1957, bankruptcy proceedings were instituted against her assets. Just before the institution of bankruptcy proceedings she terminated the lease contract, whereupon the house owner, Hedwig M, let the offices to the defendants. Now the liquidator requests from the defendants the restitution of the floor covering or payment of ATS9,000.

Held: The person who bought an object under retention of title is entitled to claim recovery of the object from a third person under §372 ABGB (*actio publiciana*).

Judgment: As regards the subject matter, the appellants oppose the opinion of the court of appeal, that the claiming party as conditional buyer is—besides the seller—entitled to claim the return of the object on the basis of the action of legally presumed ownership (*actio publiciana*). They hold that it would be legally impossible that both the seller as true owner with the revindication and the purchaser with the action of legally presumed ownership (*actio publiciana*) can claim the restitution of the object. With these pleadings the appellants misjudge the nature of this claim. Regarding the derivative acquisition of ownership, the proof of the ownership is sometimes very difficult, since the acquisition of ownership also requires the ownership of the predecessor, from whom the object was acquired. The ABGB as well as Roman law also grants the possibility to base the claim for recovery of an object merely on the claimant's stronger right compared to the defendant's weaker right instead of on the ownership. Even if the provision of §372 ABGB only has the case of the possessor who acquires by acquisitive prescription in mind, he who has acquired the object upon a valid title and to whom it was also handed over, he who is the lawful, bona fide and real possessor, this right to sue can also be granted to the conditional buyer by analogy without hesitation, who is entitled to the right of possession and use as well as to a conditional expectancy right upon the ownership, as the court of appeal appropriately argued. In this case the proof of ownership is not necessary, the action, however, does not have the same comprehensive effect against everybody, either, like the revindication (§366 ABGB). Its relevance is that of a complementary legal remedy, which—besides the right of action of the true owner—is granted to the one who is able to prove his title but not the acquisition of ownership and who should at least be successful against the third party, who has nothing but the fact of the actual possession or whose entitlement with respect to

[52] 5 Ob 197/58 SZ 31/91.

the possession is less justified than that of the claimant. The legal situation is not different from the action of the previous against the subsequent lessee, which was likewise admitted by the courts by way of analogy to §372 ABGB and which exists irrespective of the landlord's right of action. Hence, the appellants' argument that two persons could not be entitled to claim restitution at the same time is not valid.

Finally the appellants' reference to the provision of §375 ABGB, with which they obviously contest their legitimation as regards the subject matter, is wrong. If they did not want to enter the legal proceedings, they would have been able to defend themselves against the action by revealing their predecessor, the landlady, according to this provision. Since they failed to do so, their legitimation as regards the subject matter is to be approved, because the possession of the object is sufficient for the position of the defendant, and because it does not matter whether they possess the object on behalf of another person.

Note

The annotated judgment gives a clear account of the contents and conditions of the *actio publiciana* (only possession and no ownership required, applies also to *Rechtsbesitz*) and shows the relationship between the *actio publiciana* and the *rei vindicatio* of §366 ABGB.

I.B PROTECTION OF OWNERSHIP

As the most extensive property right, ownership also enjoys comprehensive protection. All the civil law systems covered by this casebook provide specific claims for the assertion of ownership. Based on Roman law, the civil law systems provide for the *rei vindicatio*, comprising the right of the owner to assert his right of ownership and to claim the return of the object from any third party who holds the object without sufficient entitlement. On the other hand, the owner is granted the right to protect his object from negative interference. As we will see in the following there are, however, fundamental differences between the legal systems.

I.B.1 FRANCE

Although the Code civil does not explicitly provide for the *rei vindicatio*, it is generally accepted that the Code civil, by using the word *revendication* in several provisions (eg Articles 549, 1653 Cciv), implicitly recognises this right. In principle, the *rei vindicatio* covers movable and immovable property. Due to Article 2276 Cciv, according to which the possession of a movable object usually also establishes ownership, its importance, however, lies with the protection of immovable property.[53] As registration in the French land register has no constitutive effect and does not presume or prove ownership (see Chapter 8), the crucial issue in French law with regard to the *rei vindicatio* is the proof of ownership. The competent court for the

[53] Bergel, Bruschi and Cimamonti, above n 27, 439; F Terré and Ph Simler, *Droit civil. Les biens*, 8th edn (Paris, Dalloz, 2010) 408, para 520.

revendication is the tribunal de grande instance where the parcel of land is situated (Code de l'organisation judiciaire R211-4, 5).[54]

Besides requesting the return of the object by way of the *rei vindicatio*, the owner is also entitled to claim damages for harm caused to the object on the basis of general tort law. For the restoration of the fruits of the object, the Code civil provides for a specific rule in Article 549 Cciv, according to which the possessor in good faith becomes the owner of the fruits, while the possessor in bad faith is obliged to return the fruits, or if he is unable to do so, must compensate the owner for their value. The possessor who is obliged to return the object may claim the reimbursement of the expenses incurred for the object depending on the type of expenses (necessary, useful and luxury expenses). For plantings, constructions or works made by the possessor, Article 555 Cciv provides for specific rules.

Further specific actions relating to the assertion of a property right (*actions pétitoires*) are the *action en bornage*, by which the land owner can request his neighbour to set the boundaries of their contiguous tenements (Article 646 Cciv). Moreover, the holder of servitude or usufruct is entitled to assert his right and to ward off unlawful interference by a specific type of revindication, *l'action confessoire*, whilst the *action négatoire de servitude* refers to the specific claim of the land owner to ward off an unjustified claim of servitude.[55]

Unlike German law, French law does not provide for an explicit comprehensive right of the owner to ward off unlawful interference by third parties (§1004 BGB, *actio negatoria*). Such claims are partly covered by the *revindication*. With respect to excessive interference by noise or polluting substances between neighbours, case law attributes to the troubled neighbour specific compensatory claims against the interfering neighbour on the basis of tort law (*abus de droits* and *troubles de voisinage*).[56]

I.B.1.a Immovable objects

(i) Right to removal

Cour de cassation, 22 April 1823[57] **2.23 (FR)**

Hellot v Leclerc Morlet

REMOVAL OF A BUILDING

The building on the neighbour's land

The owner of a parcel is entitled to request the removal of a building encroaching onto his land which was constructed without his consent.

Facts: Hellot and Leclerc Morlet owned two adjacent buildings separated by a wall. In 1819, Leclerc Morlet demolished the wall and erected a new building. When the building was eight or nine feet high,

[54] See Introduction on the court systems in France.

[55] Bergel, Bruschi and Cimamonti, above n 27, 439; Atias, above n 27, 407; Larroumet, above n 27, 551, 559 *et seq.*

[56] Larroumet, above n 27, 114 *et seq.*

[57] S 1822-1824.I.234.

Hellot demanded Leclerc Morlet stop the construction work, indicating that the building encroached on his land. Despite this request, Leclerc Morlet continued the construction and completed it. Hellot sued Leclerc Morlet before the court of Rouen alleging (i) that the new building invaded his land by more than 14 inches; (ii) that Leclerc Morlet had lopped a stair and a balk of his building; and (iii) that Leclerc Morlet had destabilised his building. Hellot demanded that Leclerc Morlet remove the new building, fix the destabilised building and pay FRF3,000 damages. Leclerc Morlet did not challenge the allegations put forward by Hellot, which were also verified by an expert, but alleged that Hellot's building had fallen into ruin and could not be repaired because of public building restrictions. According to his view, Hellot had suffered only minimal loss while the obligation to remove his building would cause him considerable prejudice. He requested Hellot's claim for compensation be rejected. The lower courts followed the reasoning of the defendant.

Held: The rulings of the lower court violated Articles 545 and 555 CCiv. Hellot is entitled to request the removal of the encroaching building.

Judgment: Having regard to Articles 545 and 555 of the Civil Code; considering that the provisions contained in those articles honour the enshrined right of property which must always be scrupulously observed, except where the public good permits an exception; as to undermine that right is not only to disturb, but even to destroy the society of which it is the cornerstone; considering that it is common ground that it was against the consent of Mr Hellot, and in spite of his opposition formally expressed in the summons of 31 January 1820, that Mr Leclerc Morlet in his private interest built on the land of Mr Hellot; that thus the Royal Court, in dismissing the application for demolition brought by Mr Hellot, infringed the articles referred to above.

The Cour de cassation therefore quashed the judgment under appeal.

Note

This judgment was reaffirmed by the Cour de cassation, 21 November 1969,[58] where that court added the view that the right of the landowner to claim the removal of the construction encroaching on his land is not affected by whether the constructor acted in good or bad faith. In Cour de cassation, 16 December 1998[59] the court granted the right to sue for the removal even to a landowner who knowingly delayed action until the completion of construction.

Cour de cassation, 20 March 2002[60] **2.24 (FR)**

Houssin v Legrasse

RIGHT TO REMOVAL

The fence

The landowner is entitled to claim the removal of a fence which extends 0.5 cm onto his land, but not an abuse of rights.

Facts: Mr Legrasse erected a fence which extended 0.5 cm into his neighbour's property. The neighbour, Ms Houssin, sued Mr Legrasse.

[58] D 1970.426, annotated by R Lindon.
[59] D 1998.810, annotated by C Atias.
[60] D 2002.2075, annotated by Ch Caron.

Held: The court of appeal, Paris, infringed Article 545 Cciv by dismissing a claim by a landowner founded on an encroachment by the owner of a neighbouring property on the basis that such encroachment was negligible.

Judgment: Having regard to Article 545 Civil Code: considering that no person may be compelled to cede his property, except if the public good so requires and subject to equitable prior compensation; considering that, according to the contested judgment (Paris, 16 March 2000), that Mrs X and Mr Y, owners of adjoining properties, agreed to erect a shared fence; that Mrs X issued a summons against Mr Y for failure to observe that agreement and breach of her property rights; that the court-appointed expert found that a part of the fence encroached by 0.5 cm onto Mrs X's property; considering that, in dismissing Mrs X's claims, the court of appeal ruled that the encroachment was negligible; considering that in so deciding the case, as the degree of encroachment is of no relevance, the court of appeal infringed the above-mentioned provision.

On those grounds the Cour de cassation quashed the judgment and referred the case to the Court of Appeal, Versailles.

(ii) Proof of ownership

Cour de cassation, 22 June 1864[61] **2.25 (FR)**

Lepére v Leprovost

PROOF OF OWNERSHIP

The contested hedge

The claimant can establish his ownership by producing deeds to which the defendant is not a party.

Facts: Z (Lepère) claimed ownership of a parcel of land separating his land from Y's (Leprovost) land. In order to establish his ownership, Z produced two deeds: the settlement of inheritance and the court order conferring title resulting from a judicial sale. The defendant Y and his predecessors were not parties to either of those instruments.

Held: An applicant who claims ownership of a building on the basis of documents that he produces may rely on those documents even if the defendant is a third party to the document. To allow the production of such documents does not violate the principle of privacy of contracts provided by Article 1165 Cciv as it does not infringe the rights of third parties.

Judgment: Having regard to Articles 711 and 1165 of the Napoleonic Code; considering that it has been clearly established by the two first instance judgments and confirmed by the challenged judgment that both the deed of partition of 15 October 1812 and the adjudication of 25 November 1855, produced by Z, demonstrated his property over the hedge separating his land from that of Y and that, accordingly, his claim should be upheld; considering that, on the basis that Y and his predecessors were not parties at the deed of partition of 1812, the preparatory judgment considered that the deed could not be opposed to them, and, consequently, the preparatory judgment invited the parties to adduce further evidence establishing their possession and prescription over the disputed land; considering that the definitive judgment, though deciding that both parties had occupied the disputed land,

[61] Bull civ 1864.101.

declared that the claimant's deeds were irrelevant, and gave a stronger weight to the factual possession of Y, thereby ruling that Z's claim was unfounded; considering that it derives from neither the operative part nor the reasoning of that judgment that Y's possession, or that of his predecessors, was continuous, uninterrupted, peaceful, public, unequivocal and by way of ownership over a period of thirty years; considering that Y's possession could have prevailed over the documentary evidence produced by Z only if it had had that origin, or that duration, that neither of those characteristics is attributed to it by the contested judgment, that on the basis of the factual situation that emerges from that judgment, the sole question that remains to be examined is whether the documentary evidence produced by Z, was rightly disregarded on the ground that Y and his predecessors were not parties at the instruments; considering that under Article 711 of the Napoleonic Code title to property is acquired and transferred by the conclusion of the contract and that the contracts, which serve as title and evidence of ownership, are made between the purchaser and the vendor; considering that the right of property would be permanently weakened if the contracts, intended to establish ownership, could only be opposed to the persons who were parties to them, as it would be impossible to persuade third parties to enter into contracts which do not concern them, it would be impossible to acquire titles protecting ownership from third parties; considering that deciding that regular property deeds can be relied upon against third parties does in no way mean that those deeds may alter the rights of third parties; and consequently the rule in Article 1165, which provides that contracts have only effect between the parties concerned, is not applicable here; hence, in deciding that the evidence as to possession of Y should prevail over the documentary evidence produced by Z, and thus rejecting Z's claim, the challenged judgment wrongly applied Article 1165 of the Code Napoleon and breached that statutory provision as well as Article 711 of the same code.

The Cour de cassation (Civil Chamber) quashed the judgment.

Cour de cassation, 27 December 1865[62] **2.26 (FR)**

Tercinet v Tripier

PROOF OF OWNERSHIP

Ownership of a lake

Even a judgment that has only relative effect can serve as a means to prove ownership.

Facts: In legal proceedings against the inhabitants of the village of Colletières, the joined parties Tercinet were attributed ownership of Lake Paladru by the court decision of 28 August 1851. In the following case, the Tercinets filed an action in revindication against father and son Tripier by which the claimants sought to forbid the defendants from use the contested part of the lake for fishing and boating. The court of first instance ruled that the judicial decision of 28 August 1851 could not be applied to the defendants, as the defendants did not participate in the court proceedings.

Held: An application for judicial protection of property rights, in order to obtain a declaration that certain individuals shall have no fishing rights over a lake, cannot be rejected on the basis that the claimant was unable to demonstrate that his property title was applicable to the defendants when the claimant

[62] D 1866.I.5.

produces a judgment delivered in a previous trial between a third party and himself in which he was judicially declared as the owner of the lake. In fact, this first judgment amounts to a title. It is true that that judgment does not have the authority of *res judicata* against the defendant, but it suffices to serve as a basis for the action, so long as it has not been challenged; the defendants can only nullify the authority of that previous judgment by establishing a property right in their favour that would prevail over the right declared in favour of the claimant under the judgment relied on.

Judgment: Considering that since, in a legal sense, ownership is a right *in rem,* the judgment declaring an individual to have ownership necessarily equates to a title which may, like any other title, be invoked *erga omnes* by the person who has acquired it; that since Article 1351 of the Napoleonic Code undoubtedly limits the authority of *res judicata* to the parties to the case, such a judgment cannot be invoked against third parties with the force of *res judicata*; but that it is nonetheless a valid title and that, even if the third parties against whom it is invoked can challenge it either indirectly, by means of a third party opposition, or even directly, cannot destroy the evidence resulting from it unless they can establish an evidence to the contrary in their favour, demonstrating either their prior right of property, or their prior possession, amounting to the legal acquisition of title; considering that, in the present case as Mr and Mrs Tercinet provided evidence by producing the judgment of 1851 in which they were declared to be the owners of the whole of Paladru lake, their action against Mr Tripier and his son could only be dismissed if the latter had nullified that evidence by producing evidence to the contrary; that, however, the contested judgment declared the action inadmissible solely on the basis that the claimants could not demonstrate any proprietary title and consequently had not the legal status to prohibit the defendants to assert their right to fish and keep a boat on the disputed part of the lake; and that in so deciding the case, the above-mentioned judgment breached the statutory provisions mentioned above, either directly or by misapplication.

On those grounds, and without finding necessary to analyse the other grounds of the appeal, the Cour de cassation quashed the challenged judgment.

Cour de cassation, 26 December 1921[63] **2.27 (FR)**

Epoux Charlin v Consorts Sorin

FREE EVALUATION OF EVIDENCE

Cutting of trees

If none of the parties is able to demonstrate any title or any acquisitive prescription, the court must assess the question of ownership on the merits of the facts put forward by the parties.

Facts: The Sorins sued the Charlins, who were the owners of an adjoining piece of land, in order to force the latter to restore destroyed ditches and to obtain damages for the removal of a hedge and the cutting of trees. The court of first instance decided for the claimants. It held that the defendants were only able to adduce the contested cutting of the trees as an evidence of their possession and that, furthermore, they had not been in possession of the disputed piece of land for at least one year. The claimants on the other hand, though unable to demonstrate acquisitive prescription of 30 years, were

[63] D 1925.1.140, S 1923.I.297.

able to show that they were in possession of the land for a long time and that their possession was well characterised.

Held: If none of the parties is able prove title or acquisitive prescription, the court must assess the question of ownership on the merits of the facts put forward by the parties.

Judgment: Considering that, by upholding the judgment of the first instance in the light of those findings, the challenged judgment did not breach the statutory provisions relevant to the case. Considering that, when in a property matter the parties cannot show title or demonstrate any prescriptive rights and that, furthermore, the defendant to a claim involving property matters cannot demonstrate any legal, exclusive and serious possession, it is for the court to rule on the question of ownership on the basis of the factual presumptions put forward by the parties.

The Cour de cassation dismissed the appeal.

Cour de cassation, 23 April 1981[64] **2.28 (FR)**

Bertrand v Volpinac

PROOF OF OWNERSHIP

Common passage

The settlement of inheritance, even if not published in the land registry, can be opposed by third parties

Facts: The court of first instance, seised by the motion of the landowner Bertrand, found against the Volpinac, concerning the existence of a common passage. The passage was created by the settlement of inheritance dated 24 May 1897 to which a map was attached. This document was referred to in the acquisitive instrument of Bertrand dated 18 January 1967, as well as in the sales contract between Mme Guillaume and the Volpinac of May 1973. The settlement of inheritance had not been published in the land registry.

Held: The settlement of inheritance can be opposed by third parties, even if it is not published in the land registry. In an action of *revindication*, the court evaluates freely the evidence put forward by the parties.

Judgment: On the ground that, on the one hand, judicial documents and decisions subject to the requirement of publication in the land registry can only be opposed by third parties if they have been duly published in the land registry; and that that requirement includes documents altering or establishing property rights and, in particular, deeds of partition, and that the lower court did not establish that the Act of 24 May 1897 had been entered in the register and thus did not provide his decision with a legal basis; and that, on the other hand, the court of appeal did not respond to the submissions claiming that in order for the alleged common right of way to be opposed to third parties, it had to be published under a special number in the registry and that, in the present case, it had not been so registered; that it is further submitted that agreements only have effect between the contracting parties, and they cannot affect third parties unless it is for their benefit under the hypothesis provided by Article 1121 of the Civil Code; that the reference to the common right of way at stake, either in the Bertrand's deed of purchase or in the deed of purchase by Mr and Mrs Volpilhac, could not produce any effect in regard to legal

[64] Bullciv 1981.III.80.

relations between Bertrand and Mr and Mrs Volpilhac, since there is no finding by the courts that neither of them were parties to the deeds of purchase; that finally, the land registry is a mere record enabling titles to be identified and the corresponding physical extent of properties to be determined for fiscal or administrative purposes; that, however, in regard to third parties, the land register does not provide the evidence of co-ownership under a deed which is not registered and cannot be opposed by them; considering, however, that deeds of partition deriving from an inheritance, even if they are not published, can be opposed by third parties; and that furthermore in property matters the courts are entitled to assess the merits of the case on the basis of the evidence submitted to them and that the rules governing the land registry are irrelevant in this case as they fulfil other and distinct purposes, it is in the limits of its sovereign authority that the challenged judgment relied on the deed of partition of 24 May 1897 with the map which was joined to and on the references made in both Bertrand's and Volpilhac's deeds of purchase, and on presumptions based on the earlier register on which the path appeared, that it follows that the judgment did not have to deal with the submissions that would have rendered it inoperable and that the plea is therefore unfounded.

On those grounds the Cour de cassation dismissed the appeal.

Notes

(1) As registration in the land register does not prove or even presume ownership, the claimant in an action for *revendication* must prove his entitlement to the object according to Articles 1315 Cciv *et seq*, which provide for a complex series of rules concerning evidence.[65] One important principle is that the possessor of the object is presumed to be the owner. With respect to immovable objects this presumption is rebuttable. The burden of proof lies with the person who contests the right. The claimant is obliged to prove his own entitlement to the land (positive proof). It is not sufficient to show that the defendant is not the owner of the land. Usually both claimant and defendant will forward all available evidence that establishes ownership and the court must make its decision by evaluating this evidence (principle of free evaluation of evidence). It is important to note that the judgment has only relative effect between the litigants, which means that the winning party can still be challenged by a third party who proves to have an even better entitlement to the object.

(2) The annotated judgments show some important methods and typical constellations of the proof of ownership.

[65] Larroumet, above n 27, 387 *et seq*.

(iii) Troubles de voisinage (neighbour law)

Cour de cassation, 3 November 1977[66] **2.29 (FR)**

Camys et Lavoye v Mercier

NEGATIVE INTERFERENCE

The high wall

To deprive the neighbour of sunlight may constitute an unlawful interference and create an obligation to pay damages.

Facts: Camys and Lavoye were owners of houses with gardens adjoining the weaving mill of the company Detant-Delplace. The claimants sued Mercier, the trustee of the group in bankruptcy, to obtain damages. They alleged that they were disturbed by noise stemming from the operation of looms and that raising the height of the factory wall had deprived them of sunlight.

Held: The right of an owner to enjoy his property in the most absolute manner, save for the use prohibited by statutory or regulatory provisions, is limited by the requirement that an owner shall not cause to another person's property any prejudice going beyond the normal inconveniences inherent in neighbourly proximity. A claim for damages resulting from the prejudice suffered as the consequence of the reduction in sunshine to his property, due to the increase in height of a factory wall, was dismissed by the lower court, on the ground that no right of servitude, or any legislative or regulatory provisions had been breached and the claimant had failed to demonstrate any loss of income or any depreciation of his property. This judgment was quashed by the Cour de cassation which ruled that, in so deciding, the court of appeal had failed to evaluate whether the alleged prejudice, which was not merely constituted by the reduction in value of his real estate, exceeded the normal inconveniences inherent in neighbourly proximity.

Judgment: Considering that the challenged judgment is criticised on the ground that, for reducing the amount of the damages awarded to Camys and Lavoye due to the disturbances caused by the operation of the factory, the court found that those disturbances were of only relative importance given the noise level to be expected in an industrial area, and that, according to the motion, that the distinction between a residential area, where a strict assessment of the disturbances occurring there is justified, and an industrial area, where people have to adjust to the nuisances occurring there, does not derive from any legal provision and that, therefore, the assessment of the abnormality of neighbourhood disturbances according to the characteristics of the area, is contrary to the law which confers on all the same rights to use the amenities of the area, whatever their place of residence may be, subject only to the differences introduced by the town planning legislation which, in the present case, classified the area at stake within an area reserved for residential use; that moreover in order to assess whether the noises were only of relative importance for the concerned area, the court of appeal should have ascertained what was the appropriate noise level consistent with the normal inconveniences inherent in the neighbourly proximity at stake; but considering that the court hearing the case on its merits has sovereign discretion to assess with respect to time and location the limit of the normalality of neighbourhood disturbances; that, in the present case, the judges of first instance did assess, within the limits of their sovereign discretion, the damage suffered by Camys and Lavoye; and that consequently, this ground

[66] D 1978, jur., 434.

of appeal is not well founded; the Cour de cassation dismisses the second ground; but, concerning the first ground of appeal, having regard to Articles 544 and 1382 of the Civil Code, considering that an owner's right to enjoy his property in the most absolute manner, save for use prohibited by law or regulation, is limited by the requirement not to cause to another person's property a prejudice going beyond the normal inconveniences inherent in the neighbourly proximity; considering that, in dismissing the claimant's action for reparation of the prejudice suffered as a result of the reduction of the sunshine in their properties, the court of appeal held that such reduction, which was due to the heightening of the factory wall belonging to Detant-Delplace company, was not breaching any right of servitude, nor any legislative or regulatory provisions, neither any customs and that, furthermore, Camys and Lavoye had failed to demonstrate any loss of income or any depreciation of their assets; considering that in so deciding, without ascertaining whether the prejudice alleged, which was not limited to a mere depreciation in value of the real estate, went beyond the normal inconveniences inherent in neighbourly proximity, the court of appeal provided no legal justification for its decision; ... on those grounds, quashed and annulled, but only as regards the first and third grounds.

Cour de cassation, 31 May 2000[67] **2.30 (FR)**

Chardonnet v Consorts Docet

DEFINITION OF NUISANCE

The noisy fairground

The owner of a piece of land can be held liable for the excessive noise caused by his lessee.

Facts: Ms Chardonnet, the owner of a house in Guérande, complained of disturbance due to noise coming from an amusement park situated about 500 metres from her house. The park belonged to the Docets who, each summer since 26 June 1990, had leased the park to the National Syndicate of Fairgrounds who put it at the disposition of diverse fairground owners. Ms Chardonnets claimed damages from the Docets. The defendants alleged that, in recent years, they had required the lessee provide in its leasing contracts with the fairground owners a clause that the latter should abstain from music and the use of microphones.

Held: A court of appeal is acting within the limits of discretion when deciding that the owners, who regularly let their land for the purpose of a fairground are obliged, irrespective of fault on their part, to pay reparation for the harm neighbours sustain because of noise emissions.

Judgment: Considering that the challenged judgment, ... found that the noise level caused by the fairground was largely above the authorised level and ... that the noise was emanating at night time from Mr and Mrs Docet's land.. and that this noise had subsisted until 1997, thereby causing serious disturbance to Mrs Chardonnet, going beyond what would be normally tolerable in a neighbourhood.

Considering that, secondly, Mr and Mrs Docet were aware of those nuisances, and yet nevertheless, they renewed the letting of their property each summer and, thirdly, that the mere fact of mentioning in the lease agreement that they had requested their lessee to discontinue the use of microphones and music from their lessee in

[67] Bull civ 2000.II.94.

the previous year, was not sufficient to demonstrate that they had placed their lessee on notice to observe the noise regulations; nor could they show that any particular checks had been made to ensure that their lessee was respecting their obligations.

Therefore, given the matters set forth above, the court of appeal, acting within the limits of discretion in assessing the abnormal neighbourhood disturbances emanating from the property let by Mr and Mrs Docet, has correctly decided that, irrespective of any fault on their part, the owners were obliged to afford reparation of the prejudicial consequences suffered by a third party.

Accordingly the ground of appeal is unfounded. On those grounds, the Cour de cassation dismissed the appeal.

Cour de cassation, 15 November 1978[68] **2.31 (FR)**

Epoux Clavel-Fargier v SCI Étoile-Trocadéro and others

DEFINITION OF NUISANCE

The fire

The owner of a piece of land from where a fire spreads to neighbouring land is only liable in case of fault

Facts: On 16 November 1971 a fire started in a building site belonging to the SCI Étoile-Trocadéro in Paris and damaged the apartment of the Clavel-Fargiers. The Clavel-Fargiers sued for damages.

Held: Under Article 1384(2) Cciv, the owner of a building or movable property in which a fire starts shall be liable to third parties only if fault on his part is proven. The notion of neighbourhood nuisance cannot be extended to the case where a fire spreads to adjoining properties.

Judgment: Considering that under Article 1384(2) of the Civil Code a person who holds, under whatever title, the whole or part of a building or movable property in which a fire starts, shall be liable to third parties for damages caused by that fire only if fault is proven on his part, or on the part of persons for whom he is responsible; considering that the court of appeal was right to hold that the concept of neighbourhood disturbance could not be extended to the case where a fire spreads to adjoining properties and that, consequently, Mr and Mrs X, had to show that the Etoile-Trocadéro Property partnership had committed a fault that gave rise to the fire or its subsequent spreading. Thus, the challenged judgment legally justified its decision; on those grounds appeal brought against the judgment of the Court of Appeal of Paris on 9 February 1977 is dismissed.

[68] Bull civ 1978.III.345.

Cour de cassation, 28 June 1995[69] **2.32 (FR)**

Consorts Ficarelli v Société Laiterie Harrand

RIGHT TO SUE

Noisy neighbours

A landowner can claim cessation of interference by noise even if he does not live on that piece of land.

Facts: The Ficarellis, the owners of a piece of land with a building, brought an action against a dairy, Laiterie Harrand, because of excessive interference stemming from the factory. They demanded the cessation of works and the shutting down of the factory. The defendant alleged that the claimant only owned the affected parcel, but did not live on it.

Held: Even the owner of a parcel who does not live on the parcel is entitled to claim the cessation of interference by way of judicial action.

Judgment: Having regard to the principle that no person may cause another an abnormal neighbourhood disturbance and considering that, in dismissing the claims made by Mr and Mrs Ficarelli, the judgment notes that since they are no longer resident at the property of which they are the owners they can no longer complain of the nuisances attributed to the Harrand Dairy so that their claim concerning the carrying out of works and for the closure of the undertaking must be dismissed.

In so deciding, even though it is admissible for an owner, even if not resident on his property, to claim that abnormal neighbourhood disturbances should cease where they come from an adjoining property, the court of appeal infringed the above-mentioned principle.

On those grounds the Cour de cassation quashed and set aside the judgment.

I.B.1.b Movable objects

Code civil **2.33 (FR)**

Article 2276 With respect to movables, possession is equivalent to a title.

Nevertheless, the person who has lost or from whom an object has been stolen, may claim restoration during three years, from the day of the loss or of the theft, from the person in whose hands he finds it; irrespective of the recourse of the latter against the person from whom he received it.

Article 2277 If the present possessor of a lost or stolen object has bought it at a fair or market, or at a public sale, or from a merchant selling such objects, the original owner may have it returned to him only by reimbursing the possessor for the price which it has cost him.

A lessor who, under Article 2332, resumes possession of movables displaced without his consent and which have been bought in the same conditions, must likewise reimburse the buyer for the price which they have cost him.

[69] Bull civ 1995.II.222.

Note

With respect to movables, French law only provides for one sort of real action, the *revendication*, which allows the owner to require the restoration of the object from a third party who holds it without sufficient entitlement. In order to recover the object, the claimant must prove his ownership, but as a consequence of the rules governing the proof of ownership, it suffices to show that he has a better entitlement to the object than the defendant. Thus the *revendication* is not a *rei vindicatio* in the strict sense, but comparable to the specific actions of restoration provided by §1007 BGB and §372 ABGB (*actio publiciana*). The right to claim restoration of a movable object is, however, restricted by Article 2276 Cciv, which, to a very large extent, protects the actual possessor (see Chapter 9).

I.B.2 GERMANY

I.B.2.a Assertion of ownership (*rei vindicatio*)

In German law the owner of an object has the right to request the return of the object from any person who holds the object without sufficient entitlement (unlawful possessor). This specific claim is provided by §985 BGB and extends equally to movable and immovable property. In order to recover the object the owner must prove his ownership and that the defendant has direct or indirect possession of the object. According to §986, it is then up to the possessor to prove his right to possession.

In order to prove ownership the owner can rely on the presumption of ownership as provided by §891 BGB for parcels and by §1006 for movables. The right to recovery also obtains to the co-owner of an object (§1011 BGB). The co-owner may either claim the granting of joint possession, or the recovery of the whole object. If the co-owner claims recovery of the whole object he must demand performance to all co-owners (§432 BGB). The right to claim recovery of the object applies, mutatis mutandis, to the holder of a hereditary building right (§11 ErbBauRG), a right of usufruct (§1065 BGB) or a right of pledge (§1227 BGB).

The possessor is not obliged to return the object if he has a right to possession. This right may derive from a property right (eg usufruct, servitude, pledge or an acquisition right), a contract (eg sale, tenancy agreement) or another legal obligation (eg the spouse's right to use the matrimonial home).[70] The right to claim the return of the object is also blocked by a retention right under §273 or §1003 BGB.[71]

The right to claim the return of the object is complemented by a series of provisions that regulate the reciprocal rights and obligations of the owner and the possessor (the 'owner-possessor–relationship': *Eigentümer-Besitzer-Verhältnis*). §§987–93 BGB describe the claims the owner may raise against the possessor (right to compensation under tort law or unjust enrichment, entitlement to the fruits of the object), and §§994–1003 BGB define the rights of the possessor against the

[70] Even lawful possession may suffice: BGH, 2 March 1984, NJW 1984, 1960, BGHZ 90, 269 (limitation of the right to claim transfer of ownership).

[71] See Wolf and Wellenhofer, above n 12, 311 *et seq*, paras 28, 29.

owner (right to reimbursement of expenses made on the object). With respect to these entitlements the law makes a fundamental difference between the possessor in good faith, the possessor in bad faith (§990 BGB) and the wrongful possessor (§992 BGB) who gained possession by way of unlawful interference or criminal offence. From the time when litigation is pending the possessor is subject to the rules applying to the possessor in bad faith (§989 BGB). In case of loss or deterioration of the object during the time of the possession, accordingly, the possessor in good faith is not liable at all (§993 BGB), the possessor in bad faith is liable when at fault (§990 BGB), and the wrongful possessor is even liable for accidental damage (§848, §992 BGB). The same pattern applies to the obligation of the possessor to restore any gained uses or fruits of the object. While the possessor in good faith must only return the fruits if he has obtained possession without payment (§988) or gained the fruits by way of excessive management (§993 BGB), the law obliges the possessor in bad faith to restore all gained uses, to compensate the owner for all the fruits he cannot return and for the profits and benefits the possessor negligently failed to gain from the object (§990, §987 BGB). The wrongful possessor, again, is fully liable in tort (§992 BGB). The rules concerning the right of the possessor to claim the reimbursement of the expenses incurred for the object (§§994–1003 BGB) not only distinguish between these different types of possessors but also between the types of expenses (necessary, useful and other expenses). The rules on the *Eigentümer-Besitzer-Verhältnis* are very comprehensive and complex and therefore cannot be dealt with in detail in this casebook.

Ownership is also protected when the object is included in an execution or insolvency proceeding of another. §771 ZPO and §47 InsO (Insolvency Act) allow the owner to assert his ownership.

In respect to the basic features, the *Austrian rules on the rei vindicatio* are rather similar to German law. The *rei vindicatio* is explicitly provided in §366 ABGB. The rules on the *Eigentümer-Besitzer-Verhältnis* are less complex than in German law, but also distinguish between the good or bad faith of the holder and the types of expenses (necessary, useful and luxury expenses, see §§330 *et seq* ABGB). The right of the owner to assert his ownership in execution or insolvency proceeding of another are provided in 37 EO (Execution Act) and 44 IO (Insolvency Act).

Bürgerliches Gesetzbuch **2.34 (DE)**

§985 Recovery of property

The owner may claim from the possessor the return of the object.

§986 Defenses of the possessor

(1) The possessor may refuse the return of the object, if he or the indirect possessor from whom he derives a right to possession is entitled to possession as against the owner. If the indirect possessor is not authorised as against the owner to grant possession to the possessor, the owner may require the possessor to deliver the object to the indirect possessor or, if the indirect possessor cannot or does not wish to resume possession, to the owner himself.

(2) The possessor of an object that has been alienated under §931 by assignment

of the claim of restoration may put forward against the new owner any defence available against the assigned claim.

§891 Legal presumption

(1) If a right has been entered in the Land Register for a person, it is presumed that the person is entitled to the right.

(2) If a registered right is cancelled in the Land Register, it is presumed that the right does not exist.

§1006 Presumption of ownership for the possessor

(1) It is presumed that the possessor of a movable object is the owner of the object. This, however, does not apply as against a former possessor who lost possession because the object was stolen, lost or otherwise went astray unless it concerns money or bearer instruments.

(2) With respect to a former possessor it is presumed that during the period of his possession he was the owner of the object.

(3) In the case of indirect possession the presumption applies to the indirect possessor.

BGH, 30 September 1964[72] **2.35 (DE)**

MONEY INSTEAD OF RECOVERY OF THE OBJECT

Upholsterer

*The claim under §985 BGB (*rei vindicatio*) only covers recovery of the object, not monetary compensation for lost value.*

Facts: The claimant conducted in H in rented premises an upholstery workshop. He sold the business to firm E which entered into the tenancy agreement of the premises. At the end of August 1959, firm E relocated—according to the claimant's assertions without his knowledge—its business enterprise to R. There defendant 1, a former supplier and creditor of firm E, took over a large stock in credit against a claim. In September 1959 the firm E was shut down. The claimant claimed that the goods (upholstery material amounting to DM7,863.60) taken over by the defendant were identical with material that firm E took over from him with the business in H. He had reserved title on this material until full payment of the purchase price. These circumstances had been well known by defendant 2, the managing partner of the defendant firm. The defendant 1 (the firm) had therefore not become owner of the material. The claimant claimed payment of DM7,863.60. The contested material essentially no longer existed. Furthermore, the claimant alleged that he was not interested in the restitution of the material because it was meanwhile out of date and unsaleable. The court of first intance admitted the claim for DM7,863.60. The defendant's appeal to the court of appeal remained unsuccessful, whilst the defendant's appeal to the BGH led to the repeal and remittal of the case.

Held: The claim under §985 BGB (*rei vindicatio*) only covers recovery of the object, not monetary compensation for lost value.

Judgment: The defendants have asserted and given proof that the material which the claimant reclaimed is 'to a large extent' stored by defendant 1. At a meeting on 19 October 1961, they offered the claimant to surrender the material to him. The claimant refused the offer. The court of appeal did not take evidence whether and which material still remains with defendant 1. It assumes, contrary to the court of first instance, that the claimant is entitled, as far as the material still exists, to

[72] NJW 1964, 2414.

restoration according to §985 BGB and not to compensation according to §§989, 990 BGB, because the material is meanwhile out of date and of diminished value; ...

Contrary to the opinion of the court of first instance, §251(1) BGB, according to which the liable person must compensate the creditor in money as far as restitution in kind does not compensate the creditor sufficiently, is not—also not by analogy—applicable. §985 BGB is not a claim for restitution in kind, and §§990, 989 BGB are not a case of application of §25 BGB1. Therefore the claimant is obliged to claim the restitution of the still existing material, even as far as it is depreciated, in addition he can claim the damage caused by the delay of the possessor to restore the material according to §§985, 286 BGB. The holding of the court of appeal must insofar be confirmed.

As far as the defendants have disposed of the material, the court of appeal considers the defendant as liable for damage according to §§989, 990 BGB. Also in this regard—the existence of the retention of title clause assumed—there are no legal reasons to raise reservations.

Notes

(1) The revindication is directed to the restoration of the object and does not include the right of the owner to claim compensation for sustained harm. Such claims must be based on §§989 *et seq* BGB, which provide for specific tort law rules.

(2) The possessor in good faith is not obliged to deliver the object which must be restored to the owner. He is only obligated to make it ready for collection by the owner. Costs that are caused by this must be borne by the possessor (BGH, 26 May 1988, NJW 1988, 3264, BGHZ 104, 304—wood moulders: costs of separation of the object which is object of the revindication from the possessor's estate in case of bankruptcy of the possessor). According to tort law, the possessor in bad faith, however, is obliged to bring the object to the owner. A possessor who changed the location of the object after he started to be in bad faith must restore it at the place where it was situated at the point in time when the possessor started to be in bad faith (BGH, 12 January 1981 NJW 1981, 752, BGHZ 79, 211—the sold vehicles). This rule is derived from §269(1) BGB which defines the place of performance of obligational duties.

BGH, 29 October 1969[73] **2.36 (DE)**

RECOVERY OF THE OBJECT FROM THE INDIRECT POSSESSOR

Bowling alley

The owner may claim recovery of the object from the indirect possessor either by claiming the assignment of the indirect possessor's claim for restoration of property or directly by claiming recovery of the object. Direct recovery may not, however, be claimed if the indirect possessor is unable to return the object unless the indirect possessor is liable to the owner under §§989 et seq *BGB.*

Facts: The defendant was the owner of a hotel which, in 1969, she leased to G for a period of 10

[73] NJW 1970, 241, BGHZ 53, 29.

years. Attached to the hotel was a bowling alley. At the beginning of 1964, the claimants delivered several parts of the alley to G. The buyer, G, was allowed to pay in instalments and the claimants retained the title of the parts. G then failed to pay. The defendant terminated the tenancy prematurely and leased the hotel, including the bowling alley, to L. The claimants claimed from the defendant, the hotel owner, the restoration of the delivered parts. The court of first instance allowed the claim. The court of appeal dismissed the claim.

Held: The owner may claim recovery of the object from the indirect possessor either by claiming the assignment of the possessor's claim for restoration of property or directly by claiming recovery of the object. Direct recovery may, however, not be claimed if the indirect possessor is unable to return the object unless the indirect possessor is liable to the owner under §§989 *et seq* BGB.

Judgment: From the reasons:

1. The court of appeal holds that the claimants are, due to the retention of title, still owners of the objects: they have not lost their title to the defendant, not because of §§93, 94, 946, 947 BGB nor by good faith acquisition pursuant to §932 BGB by the defendant from the former leaseholder G, because the latter had no intention to transfer the ownership of objects not belonging to him. Under the given circumstances, however, the claim for restoration based on §985 BGB must be dismissed, as the defendant is only indirect possessor of the object.

2. Thereby the court of appeal does not fail to appreciate that ... the claim under §985 BGB can also be directed against the indirect possessor. According to the prevailing opinion in literature, which the Senate of decision follows ..., the owner is thereby not restricted to claim from the indirect possessor the assignment of his claim of restoration against the direct possessor; the owner—according to the wording of §985 BGB—is rather entitled, in principle, to direct the claim for restoration against the indirect possessor. Such a conclusion—and this speaks for this solution—has for the owner the advantage that the enforceability is independent of a possible termination of the relationship which is the basis of the indirect possession. If this relationship still exists at the time of the enforcement, then the owner is able to enforce the judgment according to §886 ZPO by requesting the assignment of the indirect possesor's claim for restoration against the direct possessor; he can then instead of the indirect possessor enforce the claim according to §836 ZPO against the direct possessor. But if the relationship establishing the indirect possession has been terminated in the meantime by return of the object to the direct possessor, then the owner can directly enforce the claim by taking of the object according to §883 ZPO (or—if it concerns an immovable—according to §885 ZPO). The court of appeal also correctly based its decision on this legal evaluation.

3. ...

4. The principle that, according to §985 BGB, the owner can also sue the indirect possessor for restoration of the object must, however, be limited—as has also correctly been pointed out by the court of appeal— ... in order to prevent the owner from obtaining unjustified compensation on the basis of §283 BGB. Consequently, the owner is not entitled to the claim of restoration if the indirect possessor is unable to surrender the object because he left it to the direct possessor, unless he is obliged to compensate the owner according to §§989 *et seq* BGB.

Note

§283 BGB gives the owner, who has obtained a legally binding judgment for restoration, the right to claim monetary compensation when the possessor does not deliver the object within the time limit set by the owner or the trial court. §283 BGB is part of the law of obligations, but is also applied to the claim of restoration according to §985 BGB. In the annotated judgment the BGH solved the conflict between §283 BGB, which grants the right to compensation in case of non-performance of an obligation, and the specific liability rules of §§989 *et seq*, which regulate the right of the owner to claim compensation from the possessor in a more restrictive way. The BGH holds that the claimant was entitled to sue the hotel owner as indirect possessor for restoration of the alley parts, but only if the hotel owner is liable according to §§989 *et seq* BGB. In the annotated judgment such liability is perceivable, although not yet established, as the hotel owner left the parts of the bowling alley to the new tenant although they still belonged to the claimant.

I.B.2.b Injunction (*actio negatoria*) and right to removal

Bürgerliches Gesetzbuch **2.37 (DE)**

§1004 BGB Claim for removal and injunction (1) If the ownership is impaired in another way than by removal or retention of possession, the owner may require the disturber to remove the interference. If further interferences are to be feared, the owner may sue for an injunction.

(2) The claim is excluded if the owner is obliged to tolerate the interference.

Notes

(1) In §1004 BGB German law explicitly provides for the right of the owner of an object to ward off impairment caused by third parties by way of judicial action. It thus complements §985 BGB which enables the owner to regain possession of the object. §1004 BGB provides for two claims: (i) the right to removal of actual interference (*Beseitigungsanspruch*) and (ii) the right to an injunction (*Unterlassungsanspruch*) in order to prevent the occurrence of future interference. For this the owner must prove that the interference is either imminent, or that there is the concrete danger that the interferer who already caused an interference will repeat the interference (*Wiederholungsgefahr*). Both claims cover movable and—practically more important—immovable objects.

(2) The entitlement lies with the owner of the object including the co-owner (§1011 BGB). In respect to claims one co-owner raises against the other, the claimant, however, must observe the obligations deriving from their internal relationship and the mutual obligation of each co-owner to consider the rights and interests of the other (§745 BGB, §15 WEG). §1004 BGB applies also to the holder of other property rights, such as the holder of a right of servitude (§1027, §1090(2) BGB), the usufructuary (§1065 BGB), the pledgee (§1227 BGB), the holder of a security interest in land (§1134 BGB) and the holder of a right of superficies (§11 ErbBauRG).[74] The right to claim for an injunction or the removal of interference, whether explicitly provided by statutory provisions or not, applies not only to prop-

[74] On these property rights, see Chapter 3.

erty rights, but to all rights with absolute effect towards third parties (eg intangible property rights, personality rights).[75]

(3) The action must be addressed to the interferer (*Störer*). German law distinguishes between the *Handlungsstörer* and the *Zustandsstörer*, which is also called 'indirect interferer' (*mittelbarer Störer*). While the *Handlungsstörer* is the person who causes the interference by his own active behaviour, the *Zustandsstörer* is liable under §1004 BGB due to his responsibility for the impairing condition of the object or undertaking. The owner is not entitled to claim an injunction or the removal, if the owner is obliged to tolerate the interference. Such an obligation may derive from a property right (eg a right of servitude) or an obligatory right of the interferer or be directly provided by law (eg public use of a privately owned object).

(i) Definition of interference

BGH, 23 April 1993[76] **2.38 (DE)**

INTERFERENCE BY NATURAL EVENTS

The blown over tree

§1004 BGB only covers interference by human behaviour.

Facts: The parties were owners of adjoining premises in H, where they live with their spouses. In the evening of 26 February 1990, during an unusually strong thunderstorm with squalls of storm force 9–10, two mature spruces were blown over from the defendant's premises to the claimant's premises, where they damaged the roof of the garage and the porch of the front door. The claimant holds that the defendant should have removed the two spruces in time, as they have visibly contracted a certain sickness which was the reason that they did not withstand the wind forces. He claimed DM11,018.69 from the defendant and her spouse, which according to him had to be spent in order to repair the damages. The claim was rejected.

Held: §1004 BGB only covers interference by human behaviour.

Judgment: From the reasons:

II. The claimant is not entitled to claim no-fault compensation from the defendant pursuant to §906(2) sentence 2 BGB.

1. The analogous application of this provision would be adequate, if because of specific reasons the claimant was legally or actually inhibited to enforce some primary relief to which he is entitled. ... Insofar the compensation claim in accordance with neighbour law replaces the primary right for injunctive relief pursuant to §1004 (1) BGB, which is directed towards the abatement or omission of the interferences, but it has a precondition that the defendant has been exposed to such an injunction by the claimant. But this is not the case here.

2. The claim for injunctive relief under §1004(1) BGB requires the defendant to be responsible as interferer. According to the jurisdiction of the BGH, the mere position as owner of the premises, from which the interference originates, does not suffice for this purpose ...; rather, the interference must at least indirectly go back to the will of the owner. Interferences which are caused by natural phenomena can be attributed to him as interferer only then, if he has made them possible by his own

[75] Wolf and Wellenhofer, above n 12, 376, para 44; Baur and Stürner, above n 12, §12 at 108, para 3.
[76] NJW 1993, 1855, BGHZ 122, 283.

acts or if they were induced by unlawful nonfeasance. ... The attribution of interference also implies that the situation created or owed by the owner has generated a special source of danger with respect to the neighbouring premises. ...

In general, the mere planting and raising of robust trees does not cause such a hazardous situation. The fact that in case of natural disasters damage cannot be prevented does not change anything, as the court of appeal has rightly held. Such quite unusual incidents stemming from outside are imaginable, but are normally not to be expected; prior to their occurrence there does not emanate any serious danger with respect to the neighbouring premises from the trees, which are planted on the premises and which are sufficiently robust against normal external hazards of natural forces. ... Thus, the owner of the premises is only responsible within the scope of §1004(1) BGB, when the trees, which were maintained by him, have lost this resistibility due to disease or ageing. The latter question, however, does not need to be deepened here, because it is irrelevant for the ruling on the case.

(a) According to the findings of the court of appeal ... the claimant did not suffer any additional noteworthy detriment due to the breakdown of the smaller spruce which was suffering from decay [Rotfäule]. The bigger tree, however, was not impaired with respect to its stability and therefore did not represent any serious danger for the neighbouring premises until the beginning of the thunderstorm on 26 February 1990, which would amount to an interference in the sense of §1004(1) sentence 1 BGB.

(b) The situation only changed during the unusually strong storm, when the trunk broke and the spruce fell down on the neighbouring premises. At that moment the defendant was no longer able to eliminate the danger, as the court of appeal has remarked appropriately. Hence, the interference on the neighbouring premises could not be attributed to her as interferer.

(c) As far as the notice of appeal holds that this conclusion was inconsistent with other decisions of the senate, it is not to be followed there. First of all this is true for the cases involving the penetration of roots of trees located on streets into the sewerage of neighbouring premises (BGHZ 97, 231 *et seq* = NJW 1986, 2640 = LM §1004 BGB Nr 168; BGHZ 106, 142 *et seq* = NJW 1989, 1032 = LM §1004 BGB Nr 183). Because in those cases the interference had solely emanated from the natural development of the rhizosphere, from the natural growth, which was sustained by the owner's will (see Senate, NJW 1993, 925 = LM H 5/1993 §823 (Dd) BGB Nr 22 = ZIP 1993, 200 (205)); the penetration of the roots into the neighbouring premises already constituted an interference of the property, which basically the owner can repulse (§§1044, 910 BGB). In this case, in contrast, the interference of the neighbouring premises was caused by an additional special natural event coming from outside, which cannot be attributed to the defendant's will even indirectly.

In the 'pellets'-case (BGHZ 111, 158 (162) = NJW 1990, 1910 = LM §906 BGB Nr 84) the interference by pellets was at least indirectly based also upon the will of the operator of the shooting range, without requiring an additional natural event. The same is insofar true for other decisions, which admit a compensation claim because of interferences, against which the owner either was not allowed to proceed pursuant to §1004(1) BGB on legal grounds or against which he was not able to proceed on factual grounds.

Notes

(1) The right to claim an injunction or removal of an interference under §1004 BGB only covers interference that can be sufficiently linked to human behaviour and does not extend to interference from the neighbouring parcel of land caused solely by a natural event (eg rainwater: BGH, 18 April 1991, NJW 1991, 2770; or natural bugs: BGH, 7 July 1995, NJW 1995, 2633). It thus clearly covers positive acts, which negatively interfere with the owner's entitlement in respect of the object, such as causing damage to the object, entering a house or a garden without consent or even planting a tree and thus setting the cause for the damage to the neighbour's watercourse by penetrating roots (BGH, 21 October, NJW 1995, 395) or causing noise from frog croaking by erecting a garden pond (BGH, 20 November 1992, NJW 1993, 925). As the BGH states in the annotated judgment, the unlawful omission to prevent damage by a diseased tree can also amount to unlawful interference, if the tree falls on the neighbour's land.

(2) The unlawfulness of emissions (interference by noise, gas, smell, dust, etc, from one parcel of land to another) is concretised by the special provisions of private neighbourhood law (§§906–24 BGB) according to which the landowner is only allowed to claim for an injunction if the interference is significant. Even significant interference cannot be prohibited if the interference is caused by the use of the land that is customary under local conditions (*ortsübliche Benutzung*) and if it cannot be prevented by measures that are financially reasonable for users of this kind. In this case, however, the owner of the impaired land is entitled to compensation, if the interference impairs a use of the land which is customary under local conditions or if it impairs the revenue of the land to an intolerable extent. This specific compensation claim (§906(2) BGB: *nachbarrechtlicher Ausgleichsanspruch*) is irrespective of fault on behalf of the interferer. Such a compensatory claim is also granted by way of analogy in respect to unlawful interferences which need not be tolerated if the owner of the impaired land was impeded by factual circumstances from raising the injunction in time (BGH, 20 November 1998, NJW 1999, 1029: blasting; BGH, 30 May 2003, NJW 2003, 2377: burst of a water pipe). In the annotated judgment the owner of the impaired land raised such a compensatory claim in analogous application of §906(2) BGB. The BGH, however, rejected the claim as the landowner was not entitled to claim for an injunction in the first place.

BGH, 12 July 1985[77] **2.39 (DE)**

NO RIGHT TO AN INJUNCTION AGAINST MORAL INTERFERENCE

Brothel

§1004 BGB does not cover interference of a genuine moral nature.

Facts: The claimant was the owner of a parcel of land with a house. The defendant let the neighbouring premises to the spouses T. According to the claimant's allegation, Mrs T is, approved and tolerated by the defendant, running a brothel in the house. The claimant believed that his under-age daughter and

[77] NJW 1985, 2823, BGHZ 95, 307.

the under-age children of other neighbours were morally endangered and that the value of his property was debased. Moreover, the claimant alleged that the visitors of the brothel caused a significant noise pollution. The claimant demanded the defendant terminate commercial sex-working in his house. The claim was rejected in all three instances.

Held: §1004 BGB does not cover interference of a genuine moral nature.

Judgment: From the reasons:

1. The court of appeal correctly holds that the defendant can be held responsible for interferences of her tenant within the scope of §1004(1) BGB; because it has not been shown so far that the defendant would not be able to deter her tenant from using the rental property in a way which violates the property of a third party … .

2. Nevertheless the court of appeal denies the injunction pursuant to §1004 BGB by primarily quoting case law of the Supreme Court of the German Reich [Reichsgericht], according to which interferences of a moral nature, which emanate from a property, do not qualify for a nuisance violating the property of neighbouring premises in the sense of §§1004, 906 BGB.

It can be agreed with the contested judgement therein, that the claimant is not able to successfully claim the action for an injunction because of the 'brothel-like' incidents in the neighbouring house solely because the moral sensation of the neighbourhood is violated. §1004(1) BGB requires a detriment of the property. When applying this provision in relation to real estate neighbours the Supreme Court of the German Reich already followed the notion of nuisance pursuant to §906 BGB and argued that the property owner, who feels disturbed, could prohibit only such interferences emerging from the neighbouring premises, which either have a harmful impact on the premises or on the objects situated on it or which annoy the people staying on the premises in such a way, that their physical well-being is disturbed or they feel some corporal discomfort; whereas §§1004(1), 906 BGB shall not be applied if incidents occur on the neighbouring premises which solely violate the sense of shame or the aesthetic sensation (see basically RGZ 76, 130 (131, 132)). Continuing this judicature the Senate has decided that in any case the feature of a sight which simply violates the aesthetic sensation of the neighbour cannot be stopped according to §1004(1) BGB (BGHZ 51, 396 (398, 399) = NJW 1969, 1208 = LM §906 BGB Nr 32a). Despite critical voices uttered by legal doctrine it adhered to it in the following (BGHZ 54, 56 (60) = NJW 1970, 1541 = LM §906 BGB Nr 39a; BGH, NJW 1975, 170; in the last-mentioned decision the Senate left open whether this was invariably valid in particular with respect to very grave cases).

The particular case does not give any reason to deviate from the principles as defined in the cited decisions. An ideal—moral or simply aesthetic—interference requires that the objectionable state or activity can be sensually perceived from the neighbouring premises. This aspect is precisely emphasised by the former decisions of the courts of appeal, in which a view is held which differs from the later judicature of the Supreme Court of the Third Reich with regard to 'moral' interferences (OLG Colmar, OLGE 5, 386 (387); OLG Celle, SeuffA 60, 18 (19)). That is why an injunction of the neighbour according to §1004(1) BGB does not exist even with incidents which violate the sense of shame, if his mental sensation is not affected by the perception of these incidents, but only because he is aware of it. … This is true, even if the premises of the owner, who feels disturbed, should suffer from general depreciation after these incidents, which are not accessible to the sensory perception, got known …. The objected incident or situation on the neighbouring premises, which is imperceptible, does not turn into a nuisance in the sense of §906

BGB and an interference in the sense of §1004 BGB solely because it results in a depreciation of the object. The court of appeal did not establish that the rooms, in which the tenant T is said to operate a brothel, can be viewed from the claimant's premises or that the incidents in the house can be observed from outside otherwise. Furthermore there are no findings that the 'clients' of Mrs T or herself display an objectionable or shameless behaviour outside of the home. In this regard the appeal does not show any missed statement of facts either.

3. …

4. The court of appeal also appropriately denied a claim of the claimant pursuant to §§906, 1004 BGB because of noise emanating from the premises. As far as from the judgment on appeal could be gathered, that it was the claimant's obligation to allege and prove, that his parcel of land was impaired substantially, this would be incorrect. The fact that a parcel of land is solely impaired insignificantly must be pleaded and proved by the interferer. … The owner of the property, who is affected by the noise, is only obliged to demonstrate an interference with noise. The judgment on appeal can be confirmed anyway, since the court of appeal appropriately denied a substantiate demonstration of the alleged noise annoyance by the claimant. In this case there is no use to discuss, whether the suit comprises a demand for relief against interference by noise.

BGH, 22 February 1991[78] **2.40 (DE)**

NEGATIVE INTERFERENCE

Frozen vines

§1004 BGB does not cover negative interference. The right to claim an injunction may, however, derive from the principle of good faith under §242 BGB.

Facts: The defendants stored excavation material, which had accrued in the course of constructing a tunnel, at an officially authorised intermediate dumpsite, which had been created on premises that adjoined the lower edge of the vineyard of the claimant. The dimensions of the dumpsite were contested by the parties. According to the claimant, the dumpsite (4.5 metres high, 25 metres wide and 200 metres long) blocked the drain of cold air from his vineyard. That is why in January/February 1985 a lake of cold air developed at the bottom of the vineyard, which caused considerable frost damage to the vines. The claimant claimed damages in the amount of DM42,960.94 (expenses for repair work, material and expert costs as well as compensation for loss in revenue in the years 1985–87). The court of first instance ordered the defendants to pay jointly and severally DM19,966.47 to the claimant together with interest by partial judgment, and for the rest it dismissed the claim. On the appeal of the defendants the court of appeal annulled the judgment of the court of first instance and dismissed the claim. The claimant's appeal resulted in the annulment and the matter was referred back to the court of first instance.

Held: §1004 BGB does not cover negative interference. The right to claim an injunction may, however, derive from the principle of good faith under §242 BGB.

Judgment: From the reasons:

1. According to the prevailing view in judicature and legal doctrine, the notion of 'unlawful interference' in the sense of §906 BGB is derived from the general provisions on ownership and neighbour law, in particular §§903, 905, 906 BGB. Thus, the owner of a parcel can only request the removal of such installations, which are able

[78] NJW 1991, 1671, BGHZ 113, 384.

to interfere directly and actively with the neighbouring premises beyond the border of the land in a perceivable manner. In contrast, installations, which remain within the area of the premises on which they have been erected and which do not interfere with the territory of the neighbouring premises directly and actively, but which interfere with it solely in an indirect way, must be tolerated. ...

According to the claimant, the natural drain of cold air from his premises to the lower-lying neighbouring premises was blocked because of the intermediate dumpsite. This corresponds to the findings of the expert opinion, which was obtained in the first instance, according to which cold air drains off down in sloping terrain, following gravitation because of its lower specific weight. This process can be retarded or totally stopped by barriers. As a consequence the cold air accumulates in front of the barrier; a so-called cold air lake is formed. This is not to be considered an active interference with the premises of the claimant, because no perceivable substances were conducted from the intermediate dumpsite across the border of the land to the premises of the claimant. There is no use in discussing whether in the strict sense there could be talked about a mere indirect interference as is the case with the privation of light, air, water or the shading of radio or television waves. In any case the blocking of the natural drain of cold air cannot be treated differently. It simply is a matter of a physical process, which does not emanate from the dumpsite, but is based upon an effect of a law of nature; the earthwork solely appears to be protective and does not actively interfere itself with the premises of the claimant across the border. These facts of the case are comparable to cases wherein a building impairs the movement of the wind to the prejudice of the neighbouring premises, because a wind surge emerges ..., or where the rising of the groundwater level of the neighbouring premises is affected due to simple fills ..., or where radio or television waves are shaded or reflected by a multi-storey building ....

2. Neither a claim for damages exists against the defendants pursuant to §823(2) icw §1004 (1) BGB. §1004 BGB is applicable only if the property is impaired by active external hazards. ... That is why indirect interferences cannot be combated pursuant to §1004 BGB. ... Also with a view to an 'impairment', the case cannot be adjudicated differently than under the concept of 'interference' in the sense of §907 BGB. ...

3. Indeed, the court of appeal in principle sees the possibility of a claim under §242 BGB, 'which in the particular case could give relief in case of unbearable results'; it denies, however, the application of this provision, because the claimant could have indicated his concerns during the licensing procedure. If he was still oblivious of them at that time, a clear result, which was achieved according to law and the prevailing interpretation of §907 BGB, cannot be overruled by §242 BGB.

These arguments do not hold when reviewed in the proceedings on appeal. ... Although the rights and duties of neighbouring landowners primarily result from the provisions of neighbourhood law and they are regulated specially and in detail there. Thus, as a general rule, the notion of good faith does not constitute an independent claim, but it primarily has an effect as a limit to the exercise of legal rights. ... From the 'nachbarrechtliche Gemeinschaftsverhältnis' emanates, according to bona fide, an obligation to increased mutual respect which in exceptional cases may result in the total or partial inadmissibility of the exercise of certain rights derived from ownership. ... This can be the case here as well. According to the claimant, he was hit very hard by the impact of the intermediate dumpsite. Such a dumpsite in a landscape conservation area normally was not to be anticipated, it could only be obtained by means of a special approval (follow-up measures on the basis of a plan decided on by the Bundesbahn). If it was possible to technically configure (eg by the creation of gaps or the installation of pipes) the intermediate dumpsite already in the course of its installation with economically reasonable measures (see the insofar generalisable principle in §906(2) sentence 1 BGB), so that the cold air lake which caused the claimant unreasonable damage could not accrue, the claimant could have insisted on this consideration pursuant to §242 BGB ..., especially since in this case it was not the question of a permanent installation on the neighbouring premises and the intermediate dumpsite had to be eliminated again later anyway. The court of appeal has not reviewed the case in this direction so far. On the basis of such a limited injunctive relief there can also result a compensation claim for the claimant after the occurrence of the damage.

Note

Negative interference (blocking the drain of cold air by an earthwork) does not amount to an interference under §1004 and §906 BGB. The BGH held, however, that the defendants may nevertheless be liable for the damage to the vines if they had been able to take financially reasonable measures to prevent the damage. The basis for this claim is the so-called *nachbarrechtliche Gemeinschaftsverhältnis*, methodically derived from the principle of good faith (§242 BGB), which obliges neighbours to mutual respect for the interests of the other. In principle, the *nachbarrechtliche Gemeinschaftsverhältnis* functions as a limitation for the exercise of a right (eg the right to impose an injunction). In the decided case, the BGH went one step further and granted the impaired landowner the right to claim an injunction and, as the injunction came too late, compensation under the conditions set by §906(2) BGB. In legal doctrine this view is rather contested (pro Münchener–Medicus, VI §1004 at 1418, para 49; contra Wolf, at 146, para 309; Staudinger–Gursky, at 518 *et seq*, paras 65 *et seq*).

(ii) Definition of interferer

BGH, 11 June 1999[79] **2.41 (DE)**

DEFINITION OF INTERFERER

Fire

*The owner of a house is responsible as indirect interferer (*mittelbarer Störer *or* Zustandsstörer*) for the fire damage on the neighbour's house caused by a technical defect of the electrical installations.*

Facts: In the morning of 3 January 1996 a fire developed in the hallway of the defendant's dwelling house, the cause of which remained unsolved. Natural forces as well as malicious or negligent arson of a third party can be eliminated. The house was burned to the ground. The thatched timbered house of the owner V, who is insured by the claimant, is located on the neighbouring premises. The owner requested compensation for the damage of the house from the claimant, which, according to his statement, had been caused by the fire. The claimant paid compensation in the amount of DM17,610.69.

[79] NJW 1999, 2896, BGHZ 142, 66, JABl 2000, 357 (Heiderhoff), LM H.12/1999, §906 BGB Nr 101 (Roth).

Since the right was transferred to him by law, the claimant requests this amount under neighbourhood law. The court of first instance found against the defendant; the court of appeal released an affirmative, basic judgment. The defendant's appeal was not successful.

Held: The owner of the house is responsible as indirect interferer for the damages caused by the fire to the neighbour's house.

Judgment: From the reasons:

I. The court of appeal considers the prerequisites of no-fault compensation according to the neighbour law under §906(2) BGB to be valid. The insured person, who suffered loss because of the fire, was hindered by factual reasons to enforce the injunction to which he was entitled against the defendant. The defendant's capacity of interfering results from the fact, that the impairment caused by the fire was at least indirectly attributed to his will. The fire could only be caused by a technical defect of the electrical installations or devices of his house, for which he was responsible. …

II. These arguments withstand the attacks of the appeal.

1. The court of appeal lawfully supports the prerequisites of a right to compensation according to neighbour law under §906(2) sentence 2 BGB which was transferred to the claimant by law. … According to the settled case law of the BGH, in particular of the Senate, such a claim, which is aimed at a reasonable pecuniary compensation, is lawful, if interferences emanate from a premise in the course of its private use to another premise, which exceed the reasonable degree of a nuisance, which must be accepted without compensation, provided that the affected owner was hindered because of particular reasons to stop these interferences pursuant to §1004(1) BGB in due time … . The notice of appeal does not question either that accordingly a claim with respect to an unlawful interference is suitable, which could not be prevented in due time because of a factual duty to tolerate … . It argues, though, that the claim predominantly failed due to the fact, that the defendant could not be sued for an injunction as interferer in the sense of §1004(1) BGB. This argument goes astray.

(a) Without success it turns against the assumption of the court of appeal that the fire could only be caused by a technical defect of the electrical installations or devices. The court of appeal has come to this conclusion by excluding each other theoretically suitable cause. The Senate is bound to this appreciation by the trier of facts. … It is—within the scope of the concrete circumstances—free in its valuation. The appeal does not point out that in the present case the court of appeals has entirely disregarded imaginable possibilities or that it has denied the causes excluded by it for reasons, which are not supported by the remaining findings.

(b) Contrary to the appeal's view, it is not objectionable by law that the court of appeal has considered the defendant as interferer in the sense of §1004(1) BGB, based on a defect of the electrical installations or devices. In any case, the very fact of the ownership of the premises, from which the nuisance emanates, does not qualify for the capacity as interferer; the interference must at least indirectly go back to the will of the owner. … This was not misjudged by the court of appeal and the court appropriately found for the responsibility of the defendant on this requirement.

The question if the owner of a premise can be held responsible as interferer because of interferences emanating thereof, cannot be resolved on the basis of terminology, but can only be answered by an evaluation on a case to case basis. … Accordingly, the fact that the defendant as owner has acted within the usual use of his premises contradicts the assumption that he acted as interferer … . Such circumstances, however, do not generally exonerate from liability. As the jurisdiction of the

Senate regarding the penetration of water into the shower room of the neighbour as a result of a burst pipe (WM 1985, 1041), or of roots into the sewerage of the neighbouring premises shows, liability according to §1004(1) BGB can even be possible when the own premises are used in accordance with the law and not in a hazardous way, if interference with respect to the neighbouring premises are to be suspected or have occurred … . The crucial point is, whether there are factual reasons, which even in such cases make the owner of the premises, from which the interferences emanate, liable. In the case of the penetration of water or the encroaching of roots, the Senate has derived this from the statutory right of the neighbour to abate any interference with his premises (§§836, 907 *et seq* BGB). In the present case of an imminent spread of fire, such a right to abate the interference must be supported as well for the following reasons. According to the findings of the court of appeal, the fire was not … the result of a natural phenomenon, which could not be controlled by anybody. Thus it did not constitute a general risk, which could have materialised—like a stroke of lightning for instance—just as well with respect to the house of the neighbour as with the one of the defendant and the consequences of which must be born by the affected person itself. It was rather due to circumstances, which in principle solely the defendant could influence, even though there might have been no reason to take preventive measures in the present case. If a fire breaks out on the premises under such circumstances, it is up to him to provide for the prevention of its expansion, for its containment and elimination. If the fire spreads, the affected neighbour can take measures of defence, while accepting the damage of the house, from which the fire emanates (§228 BGB). Therefore it is justified to consider the defendant as interferer in the sense of §1004 BGB.

(c) That the compensation under neighbour law and in accordance with §906(2) BGB does not mandatorily result in the complete compensation of the damage as claimed, but—as the appeal points out—in a reasonable pecuniary compensation according to the principles of the compensation in the case of expropriation …, does not contradict the contested basic judgment. If the nuisance results in a damage of the substance, the compensation claim can definitely be directed towards full compensation.

Note

In this judgment the BGH considered the owner of a house from which a fire emanated as indirect interferer (*mittelbarer Störer* or *Zustandsstörer*) and held him liable for the damage the fire caused to the neighbour according to §906(2) BGB, the special compensation under neighbourhood law (*nachbarrechtlicher Ausgleichsanspruch*). This decision is in line with many other cases where liability was attributed to a person, not because of harmful behaviour (act or unlawful omission) but because of his general responsibility for the impairing condition of the object or undertaking. This responsibility typically applies to the lessor of a parcel of land. In BGH 7 April 2000, NJW 2000, 2901 the operator of a drug rehabilitation centre and the lessor of the land whereon the center was situated were held responsible as indirect interferer for the nuisance caused by drug-related activity on the public street in front of the neighbouring building. In this decision the BGH further held that the right of the neighbour to claim an injunction under §1004 BGB can be excluded for reasons of public interest in the operation of the centre. If this is the case the neighbour, however, is also entitled to damages under §906(2) BGB.

BGH, 1 December 1995[80] **2.42 (DE)**

RIGHT TO REMOVAL

Contaminated soil

The operator of a facility that caused soil contamination on a neighbouring piece of land remains responsible after the shutdown of the facility, to the extent of the right of the owner of the contaminated land to claim the removal of the contaminants under §1004 BGB.

Facts: In 1990 the claimants purchased a parcel of land from the spouses R, which was situated next to the factory premises of the defendant, and erected there an office building with underground car-park and appurtenant structures. Excavation works were started at the beginning of 1991. On 5 February 1991, the construction company detected considerable pollution by chemical substances. The disposal of the excavation waste led to high costs. The claimants sued for the payment of the disposal costs against the spouses R under the sales contract and settled on an amount payable of DM1.3 million. In the present lawsuit the claimants requested the payment of additional disposal costs (DM610,693.85 plus interest) from the defendant company (respectively the liquidator in bankruptcy), arguing that the contamination of the soil was caused by the defendant's factory premises. They also filed for a declaratory judgment that the defendant was bound to pay all additional costs emanating from the removal and disposal of the contaminated soil.

Held: The operator of a facility that caused soil contamination on a neighbouring parcel of land remains responsible after the shutdown of the facility according to §1004 BGB. The owner of the contaminated land is entitled to claim removal of the contaminants.

Judgment: From the reasons:

1. The appeal does not raise any reprimands, as far as the court of appeal denies a claim of the claimants regarding the compensation for their expenses pursuant to §823(1) BGB, §823(2) BGB icw the Federal Waste Act [*Bundesabfallgesetz*], applying the Environmental Liability Act, the Product Liability Act, the Soil Protection Act [*Bodenschutzgesetz*] of Baden-Württemberg as well as good neighbourly conduct, and the compensation obligation pursuant to §426 BGB and §22(1) WHG. In this respect the judgment does not reveal any substantive error of law.

2. The court of appeal denies in an error of law a liability for unjust enrichment (§812 BGB; ...) and a possible claim under *negotiorum gestio* arguing that the claimants have not yet been entitled to claim the removal of the contaminants against the defendant company (§1004(1) BGB).

Though it assumes that the contaminants have invaded from the factory premises of the defendant company to the premises of the claimants, it holds that the defendant was not a direct or indirect interferer [*Handlungsstörer* or *Zustandsstörer*], since he had already shut down his facility several years ago, thereby stopping the interference with the neighbouring premises for the future and eliminating the cause of the interference. The claim regarding the removal of the interference [*Beseitigungsanspruch*] was basically aimed at stopping the nuisance for the future; the removal of the consequences of the nuisance was not required. Insofar one had to distinguish

[80] NJW 1996, 845.

between the injunction and the claim for damages. There no longer emanated any further interference from the premises of the defendant, and the expenses incurred by the claimants have accrued in order to remove the consequences of a former interference emanating from the premises of the defendant.

The Senate cannot follow these findings. The holding of the court of appeal contradicts both the jurisdiction of the BGH and the prevailing opinion of the literature. If in the appeal procedure there can be assumed, that the contaminants in the premises of the claimants originate from the facility of the defendant, the claimants were entitled to claim the removal of these contaminants against the defendant, which in fact impair their property as long as they existed in the soil. The court of appeal does not doubt, either, that the defendant was a direct interferer [*Handlungsstörerin*] 'in the past'. It cannot be comprehended why this capacity as interferer would have ceased to exist with respect to a continuing impairment. A once established liability cannot be altered by the behaviour of the liable person … . The reasoning of the court of appeal would result in the rule that somebody who, for instance, throws stones at a parcel of land, is not obliged to remove them pursuant to §1004(1) BGB, because he has stopped throwing. This cannot be right. If any objects or substances came onto a parcel of land by interference, they impair the right of the property owner, which entails the right to keep away alien substances from his premises. Until they are removed they constitute the source of the violation of ownership, even independent from the fact, whether the annoying substances belong to the interferer or not … . His liability for an injunction is solely based on the fact that these substances have penetrated the premises of another due to a behaviour, which can be attributed to him, even if he is not at fault … . In the reply to the notice of appeal, it is argued, that the interferer were only obliged to 'stop the factual usage of the property of another and to retreat behind the border of his legal circle', which misjudges the difference, stated by the law itself, between the right to removal of the interference (§1004(1) sentence 1 BGB) and the right to an injunction (§1004(1) sentence 2 BGB).

The opinion of the court of appeal cannot be justified by arguing with respect to the extent of the right to removal either. Drawing up the limits between the right to removal and the compensation claim in tort law belongs to the unsolved problems of §1004 BGB. … At least to a certain point, the claim for removal has the same effect to restore as the compensation claim has, and the risk that the tort law, which is based on the principle of fault liability, is avoided by a strict liability to removal, must be combated. The Senate need not try to solve this difficult problem generally.

The question is—which shall be clarified with a repeatedly discussed example—whether the person who breaks a window glass with a stone is liable to simply remove the stone or to replace the window glass as well. The present case, however, is not primarily about impediments and damages, which result as a consequence from the interference of the property, but first of all about the substances themselves, which have arrived on the premises of the claimants (removal of the stone). Even if one takes up a narrower position in this respect, there is common opinion in the literature to a large extent that the interferer is obliged to remove them pursuant to §1004(1) BGB. … This is consistent with the judicature of the Supreme Court of the German Reich (RGZ 51, 408 (411): slid down debris and rock masses; RGZ 127, 29 (35): burning waste dump, which encroached on an embankment of a railway) and with the jurisdiction of the BGH. As far as the literature partly disagrees just with respect to soil contamination …, the Senate cannot follow. That the interferer shall be obliged to remove objects, which are located unlawfully on the premises of the claimants ..., but that on the other hand such a duty to remove invaded substances (oil et al) shall not exist, is a distinction which does not make sense ... . The BGH has also basically decided on the assumption of a right to removal pursuant to §1004(1) BGB in the case of a soil contamination by seeped oil and has considered it to be time-barred only due to the particular circumstances of that case.

The Senate does not misconceive that there is a close relationship between the soil and the invaded substances in cases of soil contamination, as a result of which this situation could appear as consequential damage resulting from the interference into the property. The claim to removal, however, cannot fail because of the fact that the isolated removal of the present substances is technically not manageable and that this can only be achieved by earth-moving works plus appropriate disposal. The impaired owner cannot accordingly lose his claim under §1004(1) BGB, because the interferer must render a more extensive performance according to the technical conditions than it would be necessary to remedy the mere interference as such. If one is not possible without the other, the right to removal must also extend to the removal of the soil and its disposal ... .

After all this, there is no use to discuss, if the claimants are entitled to a pecuniary claim pursuant to §906(2) sentence 2 BGB by analogy or in the sense of so-called loss minimisation costs ... under §22 sentence 2 WHG.

I.B.3 AUSTRIA

Allgemeines Bürgerliches Gesetzbuch 2.43 (AT)

§364(2) The owner of land may prohibit the neighbour from causing interference by wastewater, smoke, gases, heat, smells, noise, vibration and similar from the neighbour's land insofar as they exceed the level customary under local conditions and significantly impair the use of the land customary under local conditions. Direct interference with the property of another without a special legal title is not permissible under any circumstances.

§523 In regard to servitudes, there is double right of action. One may claim against the owner the right of servitude, or the owner may complain of the arrogation of a servitude. In the former case, the claimant must prove the acquisition or, at least, the possession of it as a property right, and in the latter case, the claimant must prove the arrogation of the servitude upon his property.

Note

The ABGB does not contain a general regulation concerning the *actio negatoria*. §523 ABGB only provides for injunctive relief with regard to servitudes and §364(2) ABGB for interference by pollutants. Despite this somewhat meagre legal basis, Austrian doctrine[81] acknowledges a general right of the holder of a property right to injunctive relief against any unlawful interference. The claim is directed at the restoration of the original condition (recovery of possession and/or abatement of

[81] Iro, above n 22, §7/12 at 160; Koziol and Welser, above n 21, 350.

the interference) and the interdiction of future interference. According to case law[82] this right to an *actio negatoria* also applies to the lessee of immovable property.

II. COMMON LAW

English law deals with the protection of property interests mainly by tort law, which provides for a number of specific property-related torts, the so-called *property torts*. Damage to property, both land and movable property, may also give rise to an action under other torts, not specifically related to property, especially under the tort of negligence which is available when damage is caused by the breach of a duty of care. The tort of negligence is extensively dealt with in the tort law casebook,[83] and therefore will not be explored further in the following.

The primary remedy for the protection of property rights is the attribution of *damages*. When property is harmed, damages are awarded to compensate for the sustained loss.[84] In property torts, however, even the mere infringement of a property right without inflicting any actual damage may oblige the tortfeasor to pay a certain sum of money for the violation of the right per se (nominal damages). Contrary to the vindication in the civil law systems, English law has no concept of a general right to claim the compulsory return of the object. This, however, does not mean that such a remedy is totally unavailable. Quite the contrary: with regard to land, as is shown in the following, the common law traditionally recognises a specific action for *specific recovery* of possession of land and in respect to goods, specific recovery may be attributed as a tort law remedy upon discretion of the court.

The right to claim an *injunction* is in English law also part of tort law. Historically, the remedy of an injunction was developed by the courts of equity which, originally, could not award damages, while the courts of common law could only give damages, but no prospective relief in form of an injunction. This changed in the middle of the nineteenth century, when the courts of common law received the power to grant an injunction (Common Law Procedure Act 1854), and the Court of Chancery the power to award damages (Chancery Amendment Act 1858, Lord Cairns' Act).[85] The issue of an injunction is still an equitable relief and thus in the discretion of the court. In respect to the torts of trespass to land and nuisance it is, however, usually granted.[86] The concept of the injunction is rather broad. It comprises the right to claim that the defendant refrain from committing breaches of legal obligations in the future (prohibitory or negative injunction) and the right to force the defendant to observe a legal obligation or to undo the effects of a past

[82] OGH, 14 December 1989, SZ 62/204; B Eccher in H Koziol, P Bydlinski and R Bollenberger (eds), *Kurzkommentar zum ABGB*, 3rd edn (Wien, Springer, 2010) §364 at 341, para 14; P Oberhammer in M Schwimann (ed), *Praxiskommentar ABGB*, vol II, 3rd edn (Wien, Orac, 2005) §364 at 103, para 11.

[83] W van Gerven, J Lever and P Larouche, *Common Law of Europe Casebooks, Cases, Materials and Text on National, Supranational and International Tort Law* (Oxford, Hart Publishing, 2000) 44 *et seq*.

[84] This is extensively dealt with in the tort law casebook: *ibid*, 169 *et seq*.

[85] See JA Jolowicz, 'Damages in Equity—A Study of Lord Cairns' Act' [1975] CLJ 224.

[86] For further details, especially for the power of the court to grant damages instead of an injunction for future wrongs, see the discussion of *Shelfer v City of London Electric Lighting Co*.

breach of legal obligation (mandatory injunction). Further types are the interlocutory injunction, which gives provisional relief until the hearing of the case on the merits, and the *quia timet* injunction to prevent an imminent future wrong.[87]

The following part of this chapter explores primarily the availability of specific recovery to the holder of a property right in case of dispossession and his right to claim for an injunction. Due to the sharp division between property rights in respect to land and goods in English law, it is necessary to distinguish between the remedies applicable to the protection of immovable and movable property.

II.A LAND

II.A.1 DISPOSSESSION

Introductory Notes

(a) The holder of a title to land which enables exclusive possession[88] has the right to recover possession from a person who entered the land without his consent. The dispossessed title-holder may either retake the land himself by way of self-help, or obtain an order from the court that possession of the land be given up to him.

(b) Recovery of possession by judicial action has a long history in English law. Feudal law developed special actions ('writs') for the recovery of land, the so-called 'real actions',[89] which were later complemented by the 'action of ejectment'. The action of ejectment, originally invented for the protection of leaseholders who could not make use of the feudal real actions, evolved from the personal tort of trespass into a real action during the sixteenth century. The action of ejectment gradually replaced the ancient real actions, which were formally abolished by the Real Property Limitation Act 1833 and the Common Law Procedure Act 1860. Further reforms of civil procedure law removed the formalities originally required for the action, but did not change the substantive law, which means that an 'action for recovery of land is still in essence an action of trespass'.[90]

(c) Today the Civil Procedure Rules provide for special rules on the recovery of possession of land, the Summary Proceedings for Possession of Land[91] and the Interim Possession Order.[92] The Summary Proceedings for Possession of Land contain a summary procedure by which a person entitled to possession of land can obtain a court order for possession against a person who entered into or remained in occupation without his consent. The Interim Possession Order[93] is an expeditious

[87] WVH Rogers, *Winfield and Jolowicz on Tort*, 18th edn (London, Sweet & Maxwell, 2010) 22–48 *et seq*.

[88] The types of property rights in the common law are described in detail in Chapter 3. For a discussion of the right to sue, see the note to *Hunter v Canary Wharf* below.

[89] JH Baker, *An Introduction to English Legal History*, 4th edn (London, Butterworths, 2002) 389–400. For a short summary, see Ch Harpum, *The Law of Real Property*, 8th edn (London, Sweet & Maxwell, 2012) 93 *et seq*.

[90] Ch Harpum, *The Law of Real Property*, 8th edn (London: Sweet & Maxwell, 2012) 98.

[91] CPR Sched 1, R 113 (High Court) and CPR Sched 2, C 24 (County Court).

[92] CPR Sched 2, C24.8-C24.15.

[93] CPR Sched 2, C24.8-C24.15.

form of summary proceeding enforced by criminal sanctions.[94] Both remedies are also available against unknown persons.

The Civil Procedure Rules 1998 (No 3132 L 17)—Schedule 1, R 113—Summary Proceedings for Possession of Land 2.44 (E&W)

Proceedings to be brought by claim form

Rule 1 (1) Where a person claims possession of land which he alleges is occupied solely by a person or persons (not being a tenant or tenants holding over after the termination of the tenancy) who entered into or remained in occupation without his licence or consent or that of any predecessor in title of his, the proceedings shall be brought by claim form in accordance with the provisions of this Order.

(2) Where proceedings of the type referred to in paragraph (1) are brought, the court will fix a day for the hearing when it issues the claim form.

Jurisdiction of Masters

Rule 1A Proceedings under this Order may be heard and determined by a master, who may refer them to a judge if he thinks they should properly be decided by the judge.

Forms of claim form

Rule 2 (1) The claim form shall be as set out in the relevant practice direction and no acknowledgment of service of it shall be required.

(2) The claim form shall be endorsed with or contain a statement showing whether possession is claimed in respect of residential premises or in respect of other land.

Witness statement or affidavit in support

Rule 3 The claimant shall file in support of the claim form a witness statement or affidavit stating—

(a) his interest in the land;

(b) the circumstances in which the land has been occupied without licence or consent and in which his claim to possession arises; and

(c) that he does not know the name of any person occupying the land who is not named in the claim form;

and, unless the Court directs, any such witness statement or affidavit may contain statements of information or belief with the sources and grounds thereof.

Service of claim form

Rule 4 (1) Where any person in occupation of the land is named in the claim form, the claim form together with a copy of the witness statement or affidavit in support shall be served on him—

(a) personally; or

(b) by leaving a copy of the claim form and of the witness statement or affidavit or sending them to him, at the premises; or

[94] Ch Harpum, *The Law of Real Property*, 8th edn (London, Sweet & Maxwell, 2012) 98.

(c) in such other manner as the Court may direct.

(2) Where any person not named as a defendant is in occupation of the land, the claim form shall be served (whether or not it is also required to be served in accordance with paragraph (1)), unless the court otherwise directs, by—

(a) affixing a copy of the claim form and a copy of the witness statement or affidavit to the main door or other conspicuous part of the premises and, if practicable, inserting through the letter-box at the premises a copy of the claim form and a copy of the witness statement or affidavit enclosed in a sealed transparent envelope addressed to 'the occupiers', or

(b) placing stakes in the ground at conspicuous parts of the occupied land, to each of which shall be affixed a sealed transparent envelope addressed to 'the occupiers' and containing a copy of the claim form and a copy of the witness statement or affidavit.

(2A) Every copy of a claim form for service under paragraph (1) or (2) shall be sealed with the seal of the Office of the Supreme Court out of which the claim form was issued.

Application by occupier to be made a party

Rule 5 Any person not named as a defendant who is in occupation of the land and wishes to be heard on the question whether an order for possession should be made may apply at any stage of the proceedings to be joined as a defendant.

Order for possession

Rule 6—(1) A final order for possession in proceedings under this Order shall, except in case of emergency and by permission of the court, not be made—

(a) in the case of residential premises, less than five clear days after the date of service, and

(b) in the case of other land, less than two clear days after the date of service.

(2) An order for possession in proceedings under this Order shall be in Form No. 42A.

(3) Nothing in this Order shall prevent the Court from ordering possession to be given on a specified date, in the exercise of any power which could have been exercised if possession had been sought in a claim begun in accordance with CPR Part 7.

Writ of possession

Rule 7 (1) Order 45, rule 3 (2) shall not apply in relation to an order for possession in a possession claim against trespassers under Part 55 but no writ of possession to enforce such an order shall be issued after the expiry of three months from the date of the order without the permission of the Court. An application for permission may be made without notice being served on any other party unless the Court otherwise directs.

(2) The writ of possession shall be in Form No. 66A.

Setting aside order

Rule 8 The court may, on such terms as it thinks just, set aside or vary any order made in proceedings under this Order.

Note

Nearly identical rules apply to the proceeding before the County Court: CPR, Schedule 2, C 24. The second part of Schedule 2 (rules 8–15) contains the rules concerning the Interim Possession Order.

Court of Appeal, 24 May 1973[95] **2.45 (E&W)**

McPhail v persons, names unknown and Bristol Corporation v Ross and another

SELF-HELP

The homeless squatters

The 'owner' of a house occupied by squatters may use reasonable force to turn them out without aid of the courts of law or apply for an order for possession. The court has no discretion to suspend the order.

Facts: The defendants, who were homeless, broke into unoccupied premises of the claimants and made their home there. As squatters in the premises the defendants were trespassers. They were also guilty of the criminal offence of forcible entry. The claimants took proceedings for possession against the defendants under CPR, R 113. On the hearing of the summons the judge made an order, enforceable forthwith, that the claimant 'do recover' possession of the premises. The defendants appealed, asking for a stay of execution of four weeks or so. The appeal was dismissed.

Held: The court has no discretion to suspend the order.

Judgment: Lord Denning MR—Introduction ... In both cases the squatters appeal to the courts. They admit that they have no defence in law, but they ask the court to give them time. They only ask for four weeks, or so. Can the court give it to them? The case raises this question: when the owner of the house asks for an order for possession, is the judge bound to make an order which is enforceable forthwith? or can he suspend it for a while?

The law as to squatters

What is a squatter? He is one who, without any colour of right, enters on an unoccupied house or land, intending to stay there as long as he can. He may seek to justify or excuse his conduct. He may say that he was homeless and that this house or land was standing empty, doing nothing. But this plea is of no avail in law. ...

(i) The remedy of self-help.

Now I would say this at once about squatters. The owner is not obliged to go to the courts to obtain possession. He is entitled, if he so desires, to take the remedy into his own hands. He can go in himself and turn them out without the aid of the courts of law. This is not a course to be recommended because of the disturbance which might follow. But the legality of it is beyond question. The squatters were themselves guilty of the offence of forcible entry contrary to the statute of 1381 [The Forcible Entry Act 1381]. When they broke in, they entered 'with strong hand' which the statute forbids. They were not only guilty of a criminal offence. They were guilty of a civil wrong. They were trespassers when they entered, and they continued to be trespassers so long as they remained there. The owner never acquiesced in their presence there. So the trespassers never gained possession. The

[95] [1973] Ch 447, [1973] 3 All ER 393, [1973] 3 WLR 71, 72 LGR 93, 227 EG 985, [1973] EGD 328.

owner, being entitled to possession, was entitled forcibly to turn them out... . Even though the owner himself should use force, then so long as he uses no more force than is reasonably necessary, he is not himself liable either criminally or civilly.

(ii) The remedy by action.

Although the law thus enables the owner to take the remedy into his own hands, that is not a course to be encouraged. In a civilised society, the courts should themselves provide a remedy which is speedy and effective; and thus make self-help unnecessary. The courts of common law have done this for centuries. The owner is entitled to go to the court and obtain an order that the owner 'do recover' the land, and to issue a writ of possession immediately. That was the practice in the old action of ejectment ... . So far as I can discover, the courts of common law never suspended the order for possession. Once the order was made, the owner could straightaway get a writ of possession for the sheriff to cause the owner to be put into possession. Sometimes the owner, although he got an order, might not wish to get the sheriff to turn out the trespassers, because the sheriff was known to charge extortionate fees. In that case the owner was entitled to take possession at once by his own hand ... . Seeing that the owner could take possession at once without the help of the courts, it is plain that, when he does come to the courts, he should not be in any worse position. The courts should give him possession at once, else he would be tempted to do it himself. So the courts of common law never suspended the order for possession.

It was suggested by counsel for the defendants that, although the courts of common law never suspended the order for possession, nevertheless, the courts of equity might do so; because they had power to issue an injunction to restrain the owner from proceeding with his action at law or with the enforcement of his order ... . I am satisfied that a court of equity would never intervene in aid of a wrongdoer.

By the Supreme Court of Judicature Act 1875 the old action of ejectment was replaced by an action for the recovery of land; but the practice remained the same, although the machinery was different ... . The judgment was, as before, that the plaintiff 'do recover' possession. No time was mentioned. No date was given. The plaintiff could at once issue a writ of possession which was executed against the premises themselves. The sheriff's officers turned out everyone who was there. If there was someone else there, in addition to the defendant, he too would be turned out unless he applied to come in and defend ... .

(iii) The remedy by summons.

... A summons can be issued for possession against squatters even though they cannot be identified by name and even though, as one squatter goes, another comes in. Judgment can be obtained summarily. It is an order that the plaintiffs 'do recover' possession. That order can be enforced by a writ of possession immediately. It is an authority under which anyone who is squatting on the premises can be turned out at once. There is no provision for giving any time. The court cannot give any time. It must, at the behest of the owner, make an order for recovery of possession. It is then for the owner to give such time as he thinks right to the squatters. They must make their appeal to his goodwill and consideration, and not to the courts.

Notes

(1) In this case Lord Denning explains very vividly that the owner of a house dispossessed by squatters may exercise self-help and evict the squatters by use of reasonable force. Unreasonable force against an intruder, however, may give rise to liability in tort for the harm sustained by the intruder (see *Revill v Newberry* [1996] QB 567, where the owner of a shed, by mistake albeit in a reckless manner, shot a burglar). The exercise of unreasonable force may also constitute a criminal act under section 3 of the Criminal Law Act 1967. But, according to the Criminal Law (Amendment) (Householder Protection) Act 2005, which amended section 3 of the Criminal Law Act 1967, the use of force against a trespasser only constitutes a criminal offence if (i) the degree of force used was grossly disproportionate, and (ii) this was or ought to have been apparent to the person using such force.

(2) The landlord is not allowed to evict his overstaying tenant without a court order (section 3 of the Protection from Eviction Act 1977), but self-help remedies are provided in the Animal Act 1971 in relation to trespassing livestock (sections: detention and sale of trespassing livestock) and the protection of livestock against dogs (section 9).

(3) In the annotated judgment Lord Denning also explains the judicial remedy of a possession order. In this regard the judgment is important for the holding that the court has no discretion to suspend the order on grounds of social considerations.

Queen's Bench Division, 3 November 1865[96] **2.46 (E&W)**

Asher and wife v Whitlock

NO DEFENCE OF JUS TERTII (RIGHT OF ANOTHER)

The occupied land

A person in possession of land without other title has a devisable interest; and the heir of his devisee can claim for ejectment against a person who has entered upon the land and cannot show title or possession prior to the testator.

Facts: Whitlock in 1842 enclosed some waste land; in 1850 he enclosed more land adjoining, and built a cottage; he occupied the whole until 1860, when he died, having devised it to his wife, so long as she remained unmarried, with the remainder to his daughter in fee. On his death, the widow and daughter continued to reside on the property, and in 1861 the defendant married the widow, and came to reside with them. Early in 1863 the daughter died, aged 18 years, and the mother died soon after. The defendant continued to occupy the property, and in 1865 the daughter's heir-at-law brought ejectment against him.

Held: The claimant was entitled to recover the whole property.

Judgment: Cockburn CJ—The defendant, on the facts, is in this dilemma; either his possession was adverse, or it was not. If it was not adverse to the devisee of the person who inclosed the land, and it may be treated as a continuance of the possession which the widow had and ought to have given up, on her marriage with the

[96] [1865] LR 1 QB 1.

defendant, then, as she and the defendant came in under the will, both would be estopped from denying the title of the devisee and her heir-at-law. But assuming the defendant's possession to have been adverse, we have then to consider how far it operated to destroy the right of the devisee and her heir-at-law. Mr Merewether was obliged to contend that possession acquired, as this was, against a rightful owner, would not be sufficient to keep out every other person but the rightful owner. But I take it as clearly established, that possession is good against all the world except the person who can shew a good title; and it would be mischievous to change this established doctrine. In *Doe v Dyeball* one year's possession by the plaintiff was held good against a person who came and turned him out; and there are other authorities to the same effect. Suppose the person who originally inclosed the land had been expelled by the defendant, or the defendant had obtained possession without force, by simply walking in at the open door in the absence of the then possessor, and were to say to him, 'You have no more title than I have, my possession is as good as yours', surely ejectment could have been maintained by the original possessor against the defendant. All the old law on the doctrine of disseisin was founded on the principle that the disseisor's title was good against all but the disseisee. It is too clear to admit of doubt, that if the devisor had been turned out of possession he could have maintained ejectment. What is the position of the devisee? There can be no doubt that a man has a right to devise that estate, which the law gives him against all the world but the true owner. Here the widow was a prior devisee, but *durante viduitate* only, and as soon as the testator died, the estate became vested in the widow; and immediately on the widow's marriage the daughter had a right to possession; the defendant however anticipates her, and with the widow takes possession. But just as he had no right to interfere with the testator, so he had no right against the daughter, and had she lived she could have brought ejectment; although she died without asserting her right, the same right belongs to her heir. Therefore I think the action can be maintained, inasmuch as the defendant had not acquired any title by length of possession. The devisor might have brought ejectment, his right of possession being passed by will to his daughter, she could have maintained ejectment, and so therefore can her heir, the female plaintiff. We know to what extent encroachments on waste lands have taken place; and if the lord has acquiesced and does not interfere, can it be at the mere will of any stranger to disturb the person in possession? I do not know what equity may say to the rights of different claimants who have come in at different times without title; but at law, I think the right of the original possessor is clear. On the simple ground that possession is good title against all but the true owner, I think the plaintiffs entitled to succeed, and that the rule should be discharged.

Note

Whether or not *jus tertii* is a defence in an action of ejectment is, however, rather disputed (see WVH Rogers, *Winfield and Jolowicz on Tort*, at 13–17).

II.A.2 OTHER INTERFERENCE

II.A.2.a Trespass to land

Interference other than dispossession allows for a remedy in tort. Apart from the more general, not specifically property related tort of negligence, the torts of trespass to land and *nuisance* may apply. *Trespass to land* is available where the defendant has entered the land without consent of the title-holder, or actual possessor, and leads to an entitlement to claim for damages and an injunction to prevent future interference.

High Court, Chancery Division, 27 March 1987[97] **2.47 (E&W)**

Anchor Brewhouse Developments Ltd and Others v Berkley House (Docklands Developments) Ltd

DEFINITION OF INTERFERENCE

The overhanging crane

The tort of trespass represents an interference with the possession or right to possession. Trespass does not depend on the balancing of rights.

Facts: The defendants (Berkley House) were owners of a development site on which building work was being carried out. The three claimants (Anchor, Dual and Ironacre) each owned three neighbouring sites. Berkley House's contractors had erected a number of tower cranes at different points on the site. Since January 1986 the defendant's cranes repeatedly oversailed the claimant's sites. The claimants issued a writ on 2 March 1987 and subsequently sought interlocutory injunctions to restrain Berkley House from further trespass by reason of the oversailing. The Chancery Division granted the injunction.

Held: The tort of trespass represents an interference with the possession or right to possession. Trespass does not depend on the balancing of rights.

Judgment: Scott J—What is complained of in the present case is infringement of air space by a structure positioned upon a neighbour's land. The defendant has erected tower cranes on its land. Attached to each tower crane is a boom which swings over the plaintiffs' land. The booms invade the air space over the plaintiffs' land. Each boom is part of the structure on the defendant's land. The tort of trespass represents an interference with possession or with the right to possession. A land-owner is entitled, as an attribute of his ownership of the land, to place structures on his land and thereby to reduce into actual possession the air space above his land. If an adjoining owner places a structure on his (the adjoining owner's) land that overhangs his neighbour's land, he thereby takes into his possession air space to which his neighbour is entitled. That, in my judgment, is trespass. It does not depend upon any balancing of rights.

... In my view, the defendant is committing trespass by its use of its oversailing cranes. ... The plaintiffs are, in my judgment, entitled now to the injunctive relief to which, in accordance with the view of the law that I take, they would be entitled at trial.

Note

The tort of trespass requires the unauthorised or otherwise unjustified entry into, or interference with, another's land. Trespass to land covers already small interfer-

[97] 38 Build LR 82.

ences with another's land. The interference must be direct and immediate.[98] It need not be persistent, however, or cause harm to the land itself or to property on the land.[99] Fault need not be established, but an involuntary act is not sufficient. Accordingly, liability for trespass was denied in *Smith v Stone*,[100] where the defendant was carried upon the claimant's land by force, and attributed in *Basely v Clarkson*,[101] where the defendant by mistake cut and obtained his neighbour's grass. As Stanton, *The Modern Law of Tort* (1994) 377 puts it: 'In so far trespass is a tort based on intentional acts, the required intention is that of being on the land, rather than that of infringing another person's rights.'

Court of Appeal, 28 January 1987[102] **2.48 (E&W)**

Patel and others v WH Smith (Eziot) Ltd and another

INTERLOCUTORY INJUNCTION

Parking space

A landowner whose title is not at issue is prima facie entitled to an (interlocutory) injunction to restrain a trespass whether or not the trespass harmed him. The claimant is entitled to damages or an injunction, but special circumstances might justify withholding an injunction.

Facts: The claimants were the freehold owners of a yard over which the defendants had a right of way, which included a right to park vehicles for the purposes of loading and unloading. Since 1948 the defendants and their predecessors in title had parked vehicles along a wall of the yard adjoining the claimants' premises. A licence which permitted the defendants so to park was revoked by the claimants in March 1986. Thereafter, the defendants continued to park along the wall, and the claimants sought an interlocutory injunction restraining them from so doing and damages for trespass. The defendants pleaded a prescriptive right to park their vehicles for purposes beyond loading and unloading in the exercise of their right of way. The judge refused the interlocutory injunction. The claimants' appeal was allowed.

Held: A landowner whose title is not at issue is prima facie entitled to an (interlocutory) injunction to restrain a trespass whether or not the trespass harmed him. The claimant is entitled to damages or an injunction, but special circumstances might justify withholding an injunction.

Judgment: Balcombe LJ—What, then, are the principles which a court should apply in a case of this type? It seems to me that, first, prima facie a landowner whose title is not in issue is entitled to an injunction to restrain trespass on his land whether or not the trespass harms him. In support of that proposition there are two comparatively recent cases at first instance. The first is *Woollerton & Wilson Ltd v Richard Costain Ltd* [1970] 1 All ER 483, [1970] 1 WLR 411, ... Stamp J said (at 413):

> 'It is in my judgment well established that it is no answer to a claim for an injunction to restrain a trespass that the trespass does no harm to the plaintiff. Indeed, the very fact that no harm is done is a reason for rather than against

[98] Rogers, above n 87, 13-4.
[99] *Ibid*, 13-1.
[100] [1647] Style 65.
[101] Common Pleas [1681] 3 Lev 37, 83 ER 565.
[102] [1987] 2 All ER 569, [1987] 1 WLR 853.

> the granting of an injunction for if there is no damage done the damage recovered in the action will be nominal and if the injunction is refused the result will be no more nor less than a licence to continue the tort to trespass in return for a nominal payment.'

To the like effect is the decision, also at first instance, of Walton J in *John Trenberth Ltd v National Westminster Bank Ltd*, and I cite a short passage from the judgment (at 108) where the judge accepted a submission by counsel for the plaintiffs in that case that—

> 'when one is dealing with the direct physical invasion of a right of property by a trespass one is very close to the line of cases stemming from *Doherty v Allman* which decide that an injunction to enforce a negative stipulation in a contract goes almost as of course. The parties, having agreed that something shall not be done, the court simply says that what the parties have agreed shall not be done.'

When the court resumed this morning, argument having been concluded, counsel for the defendants drew our attention to the case which I have mentioned of *Behrens v Richards*. This is a decision of Buckley J and the headnote states quite accurately that the effect of the decision was: 'The Court may refuse to grant an injunction to restrain persons from trespassing on land if the landowner is not injured thereby.' That was a case relating to exercise by the public of claimed rights of way over a path where it was clear there could have been no damage of any kind done to the landowner.

If it came to a choice between these two lines of authority, for my part I think I would prefer the more recent authority, but I do not think it necessary to go to the extent of saying that this court must choose to follow one line of authority rather than another. In normal circumstances the prima facie test should be that indicated by Stamp J in the *Woollerton & Wilson Ltd* case, but there may be exceptional circumstances, such as those considered by the court in *Behrens v Richards*, when the court will not think it appropriate to grant an injunction.

Court of Appeal, 18 December 1894[103] **2.49 (E&W)**

Shelfer v City of London Electric Lighting Company

RIGHT TO AN INJUNCTION ('DAMAGES IN LIEU OF INJUNCTION')

Electric power engines

It may be stated as a good working rule that damages may be given in substitution for an injunction in cases where there are found in combination the four following requirements, namely where the injury to the claimant's legal rights is (i) small, (ii) capable of being estimated in money, (iii) can be adequately compensated by a small money payment, and (iv) where the case is one in which it would be oppressive to the defendant to grant an injunction (per L Smith LJ).

Facts: The City of London Electric Lighting Company erected powerful engines and other works on land near to a house which was subject to a lease. Owing to excavations for the foundations of the

[103] [1895] 1 Ch 287.

engines, and to vibration and noise from the working of them, structural injury was caused to the house, and annoyance and discomfort to the lessee. The lessee and the reversioners brought separate actions against the company for an injunction and damages in respect of the nuisance and injury thus occasioned. Kekewich J held that both the lessee and the reversioners were entitled to relief, but, under the circumstances, by way of damages and not of injunction. The claimants in both actions appealed against the refusal of the injunction. The Court of Appeal allowed the appeal.

Held: Under certain circumstances damages may be awarded instead of an injunction. The assessment must be left to the good sense of the tribunal which deals with each case as it comes up for adjudication.

Judgment: AL Smith LJ—Many Judges have stated, and I emphatically agree with them, that a person by committing a wrongful act (whether it be a public company for public purposes or a private individual) is not thereby entitled to ask the Court to sanction his doing so by purchasing his neighbour's rights, by assessing damages in that behalf, leaving his neighbour with the nuisance, or his lights dimmed, as the case may be.In such cases the well-known rule is not to accede to the application, but to grant the injunction sought, for the plaintiff's legal right has been invaded, and he is prima facie entitled to an injunction.

There are, however, cases in which this rule may be relaxed, and in which damages may be awarded in substitution for an injunction as authorized by this section.

In any instance in which a case for an injunction has been made out, if the plaintiff by his acts or laches has disentitled himself to an injunction the Court may award damages in its place. So again, whether the case be for a mandatory injunction or to restrain a continuing nuisance, the appropriate remedy may be damages in lieu of an injunction, assuming a case for an injunction to be made out.

In my opinion, it may be stated as a good working rule that—

(1) If the injury to the plaintiff's legal rights is small,

(2) And is one which is capable of being estimated in money,

(3) And is one which can be adequately compensated by a small money payment,

(4) And the case is one in which it would be oppressive to the defendant to grant an injunction [emphasis added]:—

then damages in substitution for an injunction may be given.

There may also be cases in which, though the four above-mentioned requirements exist, the defendant by his conduct, as, for instance, hurrying up his buildings so as if possible to avoid an injunction, or otherwise acting with a reckless disregard to the plaintiff's rights, has disentitled himself from asking that damages may be assessed in substitution for an injunction.

It is impossible to lay down any rule as to what, under the differing circumstances of each case, constitutes either a small injury, or one that can be estimated in money, or what is a small money payment, or an adequate compensation, or what would be oppressive to the defendant. This must be left to the good sense of the tribunal which deals with each case as it comes up for adjudication. For instance, an injury to the plaintiff's legal right to light to a window in a cottage represented by £15 might well be held to be not small but considerable; whereas a similar injury to a warehouse or other large building represented by ten times that amount might be held to be inconsiderable. Each case must be decided upon its own facts; but to escape the rule it must be brought within the exception. In the present case it appears to me that the injury to the plaintiff is certainly not small, nor is it in my judgment capable of being estimated in money, or of being adequately compensated by a small money payment.

For nineteen years the plaintiff is saddled with his lease, and for that period, upon the hypothesis of the nuisance continuing, he is to suffer whatever annoyance, inconvenience, and personal discomfort other than by steam may be created by the user of the works of the defendants, and the cracks in the walls of the house already made by the defendants' works are to be increased, and it may be that his wife and daughter throughout that period are to continue to be made ill as heretofore. Can any one truly say that that is a small injury to the Plaintiff's legal rights?

Moreover, how are these injuries to be put into money, and upon what principle are these damages to be assessed so as to represent the continuing injury to the plaintiff? To guess at them is not assessing them at all.

In order to constitute a real assessment it appears to me that the principle of purchasing the plaintiff's interest in his lease for the unexpired term will have to be adopted as the basis upon which the assessment is to be made, and, as I have before stated, this is never sanctioned by the Court at the instance of a tortfeasor. The assessment upon the facts proved will manifestly not result in a small money payment.

In my judgment, for the reasons above, this is clearly not a case in which damages should be granted to the plaintiff in substitution for the injunction which he asks for, which is an injunction to restrain the continuance of the existing nuisance... .

As regards the case of the reversioners, Meux's Brewery Company, that appears to me to give rise to a discussion of somewhat an academic description, so far as the defendants are concerned, assuming that an injunction is granted against them, as it is in the case of the tenant Shelfer. It may, however, be of moment to the plaintiff reversioners, for the reasons pointed out by Mr Warmington, and more especially as the works of the defendants, as regards engine power, are about to be enormously increased, which obviously will increase the present continuing injury to the fabric of the house. There is evidence that the defendants are committing and are proposing to continue to commit acts which are injurious to the fabric of the plaintiffs' house of a permanent character, and from which a jury would be well warranted in finding an injury to the reversioners.

I agree with what Lord Halsbury and Lord Justice Lindley have said upon these matters, and that an injunction should go in this case as in the case of the tenant.

For the reasons above given, these appeals must be allowed.

Notes

(1) Section 2 of Lord Cairns' Act[104] enabled the courts of equity to award damages for unlawful conduct in the past as well as an injunction to restrain unlawful conduct in the future, but also to award damages instead of granting an injunction to restrain unlawful conduct in the future. In *Shelfer v City of London Electric Lighting Co*,

[104] Chancery Amendment Act 1858 (Lord Cairn's Act), s 2: 'In all cases in which the Court of Chancery has jurisdiction to entertain an application for an injunction against a breach of any covenant, contract, or agreement, or against the commission or continuance of any wrongful act, or for the specific performance of any covenant, contract, or agreement, it shall be lawful for the same Court, if it shall think fit, to award damages to the party injured, either in addition to or in substitution for such injunction or specific performance; and such damages may be assessed in such manner as the Court shall direct.' Today the power of the courts to award damages is provided by Section 50 of the Supreme Court Act 1981: 'Where the Court of Appeal or the High Court has jurisdiction to entertain an application for an injunction or specific performance, it may award damages in addition to, or in substitution for, an injunction or specific performance.'

Lord Justice Smith stated that although in principle a person committing a wrongful act should not be entitled to purchase his neighbours' rights by asking the court to grant damages instead of an injunction, there are certain circumstances where this rule may be relaxed, and he outlined the circumstances where damages instead of an injunction may be rewarded. This 'good working rule'—(1) If the injury to the claimant's legal rights is small, (2) And is one which is capable of being estimated in money, (3) And is one which can be adequately compensated by a small money payment, (4) And the case is one in which it would be oppressive to the defendant to grant an injunction—became known as the 'Shelfer rule' and has been applied in many later cases. In *Jaggard v Sawyer*[105] the defendants constructed a driveway on part of their garden in breach of a restrictive covenant in order to provide access to their newly built house. The claimants were refused the injunction, but received damages instead, which were measured by the amount which the claimant could reasonably have expected to receive for the release of the covenant.

(2) The court has the power to award damages instead of an injunction also when a *mandatory injunction* (removal of the trespass) is sought. This was the case in *Wrotham Park Estate Company v Parkside Homes Ltd* and others,[106] while in *Daniells v Mendonca*[107] the Court of Appeal rejected the application of the defendant, who had secretly built an extension to his property which encroached on the claimant's land, to grant damages instead of the mandatory injunction issued by the trial judge on the basis of the Shelfer rule.

(3) It is apparent that in such cases the claimant cannot be limited to nominal damages. In *Jaggard v Sawyer* and in *Wrotham Park* the courts took an economic view and assessed the attributed damages according to the sum of money the claimant might reasonably have been demanded from the defendant as a quid pro quo for relaxing the covenant and also taking into account the profits the tortfeasor gained from the tortious interference.

II.A.2.b Nuisance

Introductory Notes

(a) Nuisance can be invoked in case of indirect interference when pollutants (eg smoke, wastewater, smells, noises or other indirect interference) cause a disturbance to the use and enjoyment of land. Fault need not to be established.[108] In *Cambridge Water Co Ltd v Eastern Counties Leather*[109] the House of Lords held that liability in nuisance, like in negligence, requires foreseeability of the harm. This ruling was reaffirmed and further explained in *Graham and Graham v Re-Chem International Limited*[110] and in *Savage and Another v Fairclough and Others*[111] where a pig farmer had contaminated neighbouring land with nitrates. In nuisance three remedies are

[105] [1995] 1 WLR 269, CA.
[106] [1974] 1 WLR 798, [1974] 2 All ER 321.
[107] [1999] 78 P & CR 401, CA.
[108] See *Jan de Nul (UK) Ltd v NV Royale Belge* [2000] 2 Lloyd's Rep 700.
[109] [1994] 2 AC 264, [1994] 1 All ER 53, [1994] 2 WLR 53, [1994] 1 Lloyd's Rep 261, 144 NLJ 15.
[110] [1996] Env LR 158 (contamination of land by a waste incinerator).
[111] [2000] Env LR 183 (191), CA.

available: damages, injunction and abatement of nuisance, which is a very limited form of self-help.

(b) Where damage to land is caused by the non-natural use of land, the rule in *Rylands v Fletcher*[112] may also apply, which provides for a special strict liability tort for hazardous activities. This landmark decision concerned the flooding of a mine caused by the works on an artificial millpond. In the decision[113] Blackburn J stated:

> We think that the rule of law is, that the person who, for his own purposes, brings onto his land and collects and keeps there something likely to do mischief if it escapes, must keep it in at his peril, and if he does not do so, he is prima facie liable for the damage, which is the natural consequence of its escape.

(c) Liability under *Rylands v Fletcher* requires: (i) a non-natural use of the land by the tortfeasor, (ii) a dangerous thing or substance and (iii) the escape of this thing or substance onto the land of another. In *Cambridge Water Co Ltd v Eastern Counties Leather* the House of Lords held that liability under *Rylands v Fletcher* also requires foreseeability of damage and, furthermore, gave some explanation on the interpretation of the non-natural use of land by holding that the storage of chemicals in substantial quantities cannot be regarded as ordinary use of land. Liability under *Rylands v Fletcher* covers primarily damage to the land itself and to other property on the land.

House of Lords, 24 April 1997[114] **2.50 (E&W)**

Hunter v Canary Wharf

DEFINITION OF NUISANCE AND RIGHT TO SUE

London docklands

Interference with television reception caused by the mere presence of a building ('negative interference') does not constitute an actionable private nuisance. Only a person with a right to exclusive possession of the land affected has the right to sue in nuisance. Damages for nuisance are measured by the diminution in value of the land or, in the case of interference with quiet enjoyment, by loss of amenity value. There is no cause of action in nuisance for personal injury or for interference with personal enjoyment.

Facts: In 1993 a large number of residents (690) in the vicinity of the former London docklands, which were undergoing huge reconstruction, commenced two actions. The first action against Canary Wharf Ltd, the owner of a new office tower 250 metres high, complained of interference with television reception. The second action, originally brought by 513 residents against the London Docklands Development Corporation (LDDC), complained of damage and annoyance caused by dust from the construction of a new 1,800-metre-long link road. Many claimants were the sole or joint owners or tenants of houses, but many of the claimants had no proprietary interests in land at all. They were wives living in houses owned by or let to their husbands, or children living with their parents, or relations or lodgers having

[112] [1866] LR 1 Ex 265, ExCh, [1868] LR 3 HL 330.
[113] [1866] LR 1 Ex 265, ExCh.
[114] [1997] AC 655, [1997] 2 All ER 426, [1997] 2 WLR 684, [1997] 2 FLR 342.

the use of a room. The Court of Appeal ([1996] 1 All ER 482, [1996] 2 WLR 348 and [1996] 1 All ER 482, [1996] 2 WLR 348) allowed an appeal by the claimants in the dust action and declared that a claimant need not have an interest in property, and it allowed an appeal by the defendant in the television action and declared that the interference with television alleged in this case was not capable of constituting an actionable nuisance.

Held: Interference with television reception caused by the mere presence of a building ('negative interference') does not constitute an actionable private nuisance. Only a person with a right to exclusive possession of the land affected has the right to sue in nuisance. Damages for nuisance are measured by the diminution in value of the land or, in the case of interference with quiet enjoyment, by loss of amenity value. There is no cause of action in nuisance for personal injury or for interference with personal enjoyment.

Judgment: Lord Goff of Chieveley—I turn first to consider the question whether interference with television signals may give rise to an action in private nuisance. ...

As a general rule, a man is entitled to build on his own land, though nowadays this right is inevitably subject to our system of planning controls. Moreover, as a general rule, a man's right to build on his land is not restricted by the fact that the presence of the building may of itself interfere with his neighbour's enjoyment of his land. The building may spoil his neighbour's view (see *A-G (ex rel Gray's Inn Society) v Doughty and Fishmongers' Co v East India Co*); in the absence of an easement, it may restrict the flow of air onto his neighbour's land (see *Bland v Mosely*, cited in Aldred's Case); and, again in the absence of an easement, it may take away light from his neighbour's windows (*Dalton v Henry Angus & Co, Comrs of HM Works and Public Buildings v Henry Angus & Co* per Lord Selborne LC and Lord Blackburn): nevertheless his neighbour generally cannot complain of the presence of the building, though this may seriously detract from the enjoyment of his land. As Lindley LJ said in *Chastey v Ackland* [1895] 2 Ch 389 at 402 (a case concerned with interference with the flow of air):

> '... speaking generally, apart from long enjoyment, or some grant or agreement, no one has a right to prevent his neighbour from building on his own land, although the consequence may be to diminish or alter the flow of air over it on to land adjoining. So to diminish a flow of air is not actionable as a nuisance.'

From this it follows that, in the absence of an easement, more is required than the mere presence of a neighbouring building to give rise to an actionable private nuisance. Indeed, for an action in private nuisance to lie in respect of interference with the plaintiff's enjoyment of his land, it will generally arise from something emanating from the defendant's land. Such an emanation may take many forms—noise, dirt, fumes, a noxious smell, vibrations, and suchlike. Occasionally, activities on the defendant's land are in themselves so offensive to neighbours as to constitute an actionable nuisance, as in *Thompson-Schwab v Costaki*, where the sight of prostitutes and their clients entering and leaving neighbouring premises were held to fall into that category. Such cases must, however, be relatively rare. ... At all events the mere fact that a building on the defendant's land gets in the way and so prevents something from reaching the plaintiff's land is generally speaking not enough for this purpose. ...

For these reasons, I would dismiss the appeal of the plaintiffs in the first action on this issue.

Right to sue in private nuisance

... Since the tort of nuisance is a tort directed against the plaintiff's enjoyment of his rights over land, an action of private nuisance will usually be brought by the person in actual possession of the land affected, either as the freeholder or tenant of the land in question, or even as a licensee with exclusive possession of the land (see *Newcastle-under-Lyme Corp v Wolstanton Ltd* per Evershed J); though a reversioner may sue in respect of a nuisance of a sufficiently permanent character to damage his reversion. It was however established, in *Foster v Warblington UDC* that, since *jus tertii* is not a defence to an action of nuisance, a person who is in exclusive possession of land may sue even though he cannot prove title to it. That case was concerned with a nuisance caused by the discharge of sewage by the defendant council into certain oyster beds. The plaintiff was an oyster merchant who had for many years been in occupation of the oyster beds which had been artificially constructed on the foreshore, which belonged to the lord of the manor. The plaintiff excluded everybody from the oyster beds, and nobody interfered with his occupation of the oyster beds or his removal and sale of oysters from them. It was held by the Court of Appeal that he could sue the defendant council in nuisance, notwithstanding that he could not prove his title....

This decision was followed and applied by Mahon J in *Paxhaven Holdings Ltd v A-G* [1974] 2 NZLR 185 at 189. He said:

> 'In my opinion, however, the matter is clear in principle. In an action for nuisance the defence of ius tertii is excluded, and it is no answer for the respondent to contend in the present case that the nuisance was committed on an area of land mistakenly included in the grant of lease to the appellant from its landlord. De facto possession is sufficient to give the appellant his remedy: *Foster v Warblington Urban District Council*.'

Subject to this exception, however, it has for many years been regarded as settled law that a person who has no right in the land cannot sue in private nuisance. For this proposition, it is usual to cite the decision of the Court of Appeal in *Malone v Laskey*. In that case, the manager of a company resided in a house as a licensee of the company which employed him. The plaintiff was the manager's wife who lived with her husband in the house. She was injured when a bracket fell from a wall in the house. She claimed damages from the defendants in nuisance and negligence, her claim in nuisance being founded upon an allegation, accepted by the jury, that the fall of the bracket had been caused by vibrations from an engine operating on the defendants' adjoining premises. The Court of Appeal held that she was unable to succeed in her claim in nuisance. ...

Fletcher Moulton LJ said (at 306):

> 'So far as the plaintiff's case is based upon nuisance, the contention on her behalf appears to me to be supported by no authority. Witherby & Co were the tenants and occupiers of these premises, and if the premises had been injured or the enjoyment of them interfered with by the vibration it was open to them to take any one of three courses—they might come to the courts for an injunction to stop the vibration, or they might simply have tolerated it, or they might have authorized its continuance either gratuitously or for a valuable consideration. A person in the position of the plaintiff, who was in the premises as a mere licensee, had no right to dictate to Witherby & Co which course they should take, and they seem to have voluntarily permitted the vibration to continue. Indeed, if it is permissible to conjecture, I have very little doubt that the proximity of the

engine was by no means an unmixed evil to them, for it may well have affected the amount of rent paid by them for the premises. But, whether that be so or not, it was a matter entirely for the tenant, and a person who is merely present in the house cannot complain of a nuisance which has in it no element of a public nuisance.'...

It follows that, on the authorities as they stand, an action in private nuisance will only lie at the suit of a person who has a right to the land affected. Ordinarily, such a person can only sue if he has the right to exclusive possession of the land, such as a freeholder or tenant in possession, or even a licensee with exclusive possession. Exceptionally however, this category may include a person in actual possession who has no right to be there; and in any event a reversioner can sue in so far his reversionary interest is affected. But a mere licensee on the land has no right to sue [emphasis added].

... For private nuisances of this kind, the primary remedy is in most cases an injunction, which is sought to bring the nuisance to an end, and in most cases should swiftly achieve that objective. The right to bring such proceedings is, as the law stands, ordinarily vested in the person who has exclusive possession of the land. ... [A]ny such departure from the established law on this subject, such as that adopted by the Court of Appeal in the present case, faces the problem of defining the category of persons who would have the right to sue. The Court of Appeal adopted the not easily identifiable category of those who have a 'substantial link' with the land, regarding a person who occupied the premises 'as a home' as having a sufficient link for this purpose. But who is to be included in this category? It was plainly intended to include husbands and wives, or partners, and their children, and even other relatives living with them. But is the category also to include the lodger upstairs, or the au pair girl or resident nurse caring for an invalid who makes her home in the house while she works there? If the latter, it seems strange that the category should not extend to include places where people work as well as places where they live, where nuisances such as noise can be just as unpleasant or distracting. *In any event, the extension of the tort in this way would transform it from a tort to land into a tort to the person, in which damages could be recovered in respect of something less serious than personal injury and the criteria for liability were founded not upon negligence but upon striking a balance between the interests of neighbours in the use of their land. This is, in my opinion, not an acceptable way in which to develop the law* [emphasis added]. ...

For all these reasons, I can see no good reason to depart from the law on this topic as established in the authorities ... .

Lord Lloyd of Berwick—Private nuisances are of three kinds. They are (1) nuisance by encroachment on a neighbour's land; (2) nuisance by direct physical injury to a neighbour's land; and (3) nuisance by interference with a neighbour's quiet enjoyment of his land. In cases (1) and (2) it is the owner, or the occupier with the right to exclusive possession, who is entitled to sue. It has never, so far as I know, been suggested that anyone else can sue, for example, a visitor or a lodger; and the reason is not far to seek. For the basis of the cause of action in cases (1) and (2) is damage to the land itself, whether by encroachment or by direct physical injury.

In the case of encroachment the plaintiff may have a remedy by way of abatement. In other cases he may be entitled to an injunction. But where he claims damages, the measure of damages in cases (1) and (2) will be the diminution in the value of the land. This will usually (though not always) be equal to the cost of reinstatement. The loss resulting from diminution in the value of the land is a loss suffered by the owner or occupier with the exclusive right to possession (as the case may be) or both, since it is they alone who have a proprietary interest, or stake, in the land. So it is they alone who can bring an action to recover the loss … .

… On the first point I would allow the appeal, …

I need add very little on the second point, since I agree with the unanimous decision of the Court of Appeal that interference with television reception is not capable of constituting an actionable private nuisance. I lay stress on the word 'actionable'. For I would not want it to be thought for one moment that I regard television reception as being of little or no moment. The annoyance caused by the erection of Canary Wharf and the consequential interference with television reception must have been very considerable. But unfortunately the law does not always afford a remedy for every annoyance, however great. …

Lord Hoffmann—Up to about 20 years ago, no one would have had the slightest doubt about who could sue. Nuisance is a tort against land, including interests in land such as easements and profits. A plaintiff must therefore have an interest in the land affected by the nuisance. …

Is there any reason of policy why the rule should be abandoned? Once nuisance has escaped the bounds of being a tort against land, there seems no logic in compromise limitations, such as that proposed by the Court of Appeal in this case, requiring the plaintiff to have been residing on land as his or her home. This was recognised by the Court of Appeal in Khorasandjian's case, where the injunction applied whether the plaintiff was at home or not. There is a good deal in this case and other writings about the need for the law to adapt to modern social conditions. But the development of the common law should be rational and coherent. It should not distort its principles and create anomalies merely as an expedient to fill a gap.

The perceived gap in Khorasandjian's case was the absence of a tort of intentional harassment causing distress without actual bodily or psychiatric illness. … The law of harassment has now been put on a statutory basis (see the Protection from Harassment Act 1997) and it is unnecessary to consider how the common law might have developed. But as at present advised, I see no reason why a tort of intention should be subject to the rule which excludes compensation for mere distress, inconvenience or discomfort in actions based on negligence (see *Hicks v Chief Constable of the South Yorkshire Police*). The policy considerations are quite different. I do not therefore say that Khorasandjian's case was wrongly decided. But it must be seen as a case on intentional harassment, not nuisance.

So far as the claim is for personal injury, it seems to me that the only appropriate cause of action is negligence. It would be anomalous if the rules for recovery of damages under this head were different according as to whether, for example, the plaintiff was at home or at work. It is true, as I have said, that the law of negligence gives no remedy for discomfort or distress which does not result in bodily or psychiatric illness. But this is a matter of general policy and I can see no logic in making an exception for cases in which the discomfort or distress was suffered at home rather than somewhere else…

I would therefore allow the appeal of the defendants in the dust case and their cross-appeal in the television case and restore the declaration made on this point by the judge.

Interference with television

In the television action, the plaintiffs complain that Canary Wharf Tower has diminished the amenity of their houses by interfering with television reception. ... The general principle is that at common law anyone may build whatever he likes on his land. If the effect is to interfere with the light, air or view of his neighbour, that is his misfortune. The owner's right to build can be restrained only by covenant or the acquisition (by grant or prescription) of an easement of light or air for the benefit of windows or apertures on adjoining land. ...

I would therefore agree with the Court of Appeal on this point and dismiss the plaintiffs' appeal in the television action.

Lord Hope of Craighead—delivered a concurring judgment.

Lord Cooke of Thorndon—(dissented on the question of title to sue): ... Private nuisance is commonly said to be an interference with the enjoyment of land and to be actionable by an occupier. But 'occupier' is an expression of varying meanings, ... Where interference with an amenity of a home is in issue there is no a priori reason why the expression should not include, and it appears natural that it should include, anyone living there who has been exercising a continuing right to enjoyment of that amenity.

Notes

(1) Besides explaining what sort of interference may give rise to a claim in nuisance, *Hunter v Canary Wharf* makes clear that nuisance is a land-related tort which only covers interference with land or the enjoyment of land. Accordingly, an action of private nuisance can only be brought by a person who has the right to exclusive possession of the land, such as a freeholder or tenant in possession, or even a licensee with exclusive possession. Exceptionally this category may include a person in actual possession, but not to a mere licensee on the land.

(2) This view also applies to the *right to sue in trespass to land*. It is well established by case law that the holder of an exclusive right to possession (an estate holder or a lessee) is entitled to raise a claim under the old action of ejectment and the action of trespass to land.[115] Furthermore, a person in actual possession also has legal standing (see *Harper v Charlesworth*, [1825] 4 B&C 574: 'Generally speaking, actual possession is sufficient to entitle a party to maintain trespass against a wrongdoer'). Actual possession, however, is only sufficient to support an action against a third party, an intruder. As Tucker LJ held in *Delaney v TP Smith Ltd*, [1946] KB 393: '[I]t is not sufficient as against the lawful owner, and in an action against the freeholder, the claimant must at some stage of the pleadings set up a title derived from the defendant.' In order to be entitled to sue in trespass, the actual possessor must control the land and have the will to exclude others from its possession. He is then protected against everybody who cannot show a better right to possession.[116]

(3) Quite in contrast to this established rule, the Court of Appeal extended in

[115] Eg Rogers, above n 87, 13-2, 13-16. See also the judgment of Lord Chadwick in *Manchester Airport v Dutton and others*.

[116] Rogers, above n 87, 13-2.

Manchester Airport plc v Dutton and Others[117] the scope of the Summary Proceedings for Possession of Land, as provided by CPR Schedule 1, R 113, to the holder of a licence, who was entitled to occupy the land, but had not yet acquired possession. While Chadwick LJ held the opinion, that CPR Schedule 1, R 113 only provides for a special procedural rule that does not affect the substantive law, which thus remains unchanged, the majority, Laws and Kennedy LJJ, felt free to define the scope of application by an independent interpretation of the statute itself. This decision was heavily critised[118] for granting the holder of a contractual right a remedy hitherto restricted to a right *in rem*. In *Countryside Residential (North Thames) Ltd v Tugwell and others*, [2000] 34 EG 87 the Court of Appeal slightly restructured the ruling and held that a licence that grants a right to access the land, but not to occupy it, is not sufficient. Whether or not the ruling in *Manchester Airport v Dutton and Others* will be upheld by the House of Lords is very doubtful. Australian courts at any rate refused to follow it.[119]

House of Lords, 5 July 1865[120] **2.51 (E&W)**

St Helen's Smelting Co v Tipping

DEFINITION OF INTERFERENCE

The copper smelter

To be actionable in nuisance, the interference with enjoyment of land must be 'unreasonable'.

Facts: The claimant, Mr Tipping, in 1860 acquired a valuable estate, containing a dwelling-house and premises, with gardens, parks and lands adjoining. In 1862 the defendants erected and started to use certain smelting works upon land near to the said dwelling-house and lands of the claimant, and caused large quantities of noxious gases, vapours and other noxious matter to issue from the said works and diffuse themselves over the land and premises of the claimant, whereby the hedges, trees, shrubs, fruit and herbage were greatly injured and the cattle were rendered unhealthy. The claimant sued for damages. The jury found a verdict for the claimant (with damages of about £361). The defendants moved for a new trial on the ground of misdirection of the jury, but were not successful in the Queen's Bench [1863] 122 ER 588 and in the Court of Exchequer Chamber [1864] 122 ER 591. The House of Lords affirmed the judgment of the Court of Exchequer.

Held: To be actionable in nuisance, the interference with enjoyment of land must be 'unreasonable'.

Judgment: At the trial, Mellor J instructed the jury as follows—Gentlemen, a man has no doubt a right to exercise certain rights, and to act upon his own property. He has certain rights of property, and within the limits of those rights he may do

[117] [2000] 1 QB 133.

[118] WJ Swadling, 'Opening the *Numerus Clausus*' (2000) 116 *Law Quarterly Review* 354.

[119] *Georgeski v Owners Corporation SP49833 and Others* [2005] 12 BPR 22, 573, Supreme Court of New South Wales. In *Bropho v Western Australia* [2007] FCA 519 Nicholson J (at [474]) held that '[i]n my view the reliance which the applicant places on the majority reasoning in Manchester Airport [2000] 1 QB 133 finds no support in Australian law and should not be followed here'. For a further discussion of the issue from an Australian viewpoint see B Edgeworth, 'The *Numerus Clausus* Principle in Contemporary Australian Property Law' (2006) 32 *Monash University Law Review* 387–419.

[120] [1865] 11 HLC 642, [1861-1873] All ER Rep Ext 1389.

any act which is not unlawful; when I say unlawful, I mean any act which is not wrong; he may erect a lime-kiln, if it is in a convenient place; but the meaning of the word 'convenient' I shall venture to interpret to you as being that it must be plain that he will not do an actionable injury to another, because a man may not use his own property so as to injure his neighbour. When he sends on the property of his neighbour noxious smells, or smokes, or vapours, then he is not doing an act on his own property only, but he is doing an act on his neighbour's property also, because every man, by common law, has a right to the pure air, and to have no noxious smells sent on his land, unless by a period of time a man has, by what is called a prescriptive right, obtained the power of throwing a burden upon his neighbour's property. If a man for twenty-one years or more has carried on in a particular district a work which is noxious to his neighbours, and has for a period of time sent noxious smells and impure air over the neighbourhood, and that has been submitted to for twenty years, he gets in time what is called a prescriptive right to do what he has done; but here you have no prescriptive right act all; there is nothing of that sort in the case. ... But when you are coming to the question of facts, there is no doubt you must take into consideration a variety of circumstances. Whether or not a man's property has been sensibly injured by the actions of another person on his own land, of course you will consider the place, the circumstances, and the whole nature of the thing. It would not be sufficient merely to say that noxious vapours have come on the man's property, but you must consider to what degree and to what extent they have come, and whether they have come from the premises of the defendants. Now, with respect to that, I do not think I can lay it down in better words that I find expressed in a note to a very admirable book edited by a gentleman, now dead, who was an eminent lawyer, and whose loss is a loss to be deplored. He says, on the question of fact: 'Whether a nuisance has been caused by the defendants at all, the nature of the locality, the work, and every other fact in the case, must be taken into consideration'; and so Erle, J says, in a case which has been handed up to me: 'The time, the locality, and so on, are all circumstances to be taken into consideration upon the question of fact whether an actionable injury has been occasioned by a man to his neighbour or not.' Now, gentlemen, you must apply your common sense to the question on the one side and the other. The defendants say, 'If you do not mind you will stop the progress of works of this description.' I agree that that is so, because, no doubt, in the county of Lancaster above all other counties, where great works have been created and carried on, and are the means of developing the national wealth, you must not stand on extreme rights, and allow a person to say, I will bring an action against you for this and that and so on. Business could not go on if that were so. Everything must be looked at from a reasonable point of view, therefore the law does not regard trifling and small inconveniences, but only regards sensible inconveniences, injuries which sensibly diminish the comfort, enjoyment, or value of the property which is affected. ...

The learned judge asked first, whether the enjoyment of the claimant's property was sensibly diminished? to which the jury answered, yes. Secondly, was the business there carried on an ordinary business for smelting copper? to which the jury answered that they considered it an ordinary business, and conducted in a proper manner, in as good a manner as possible. Thirdly, was it carried on in a proper place? to which the jury answered that it was not.

The Lord Chancellor (Westbury)—In matters of this description it appears to me that it is a very desirable thing to mark the difference between an action brought for a nuisance upon the ground that the alleged nuisance produces material injury to the property, and an action brought for a nuisance on the ground that the thing alleged to be a nuisance is productive of sensible personal discomfort. With regard to the latter, namely the personal inconvenience, and interference with one's enjoyment, one's quiet, one's personal freedom, anything that discomposes or injuriously affects the senses or the nerves, whether that may or may not be denominated a nuisance, must undoubtedly depend greatly on the circumstance where the thing complained of actually occurs. If a man lives in a town, of necessity he should subject himself to the consequences of those operations of trade which may be carried on in his immediate locality, which are actually necessary for trade and commerce, also for the enjoyment of property, and for the benefit of the inhabitants of the town and of the public at large. If a man lives in a street where there are numerous shops, and a shop is opened next door to him which is carried on in a fair and reasonable way, he has no ground for complaint because to himself individually there may arise much discomfort from the trade carried on in that shop; but when an occupation is carried on by one person in the neighbourhood of another, and the result of that trade or occupation or business is a material injury, there unquestionably arises a very different consideration, and I think that in a case of that description the submission which is required from persons living in society to that amount of discomfort which may be necessary for the legitimate and free exercise of the trade of their neighbours, and would not apply to circumstances, the immediate result of which is sensible injury to the value of the property. Now, in the present case, it appears that the plaintiff purchased a very valuable estate, which lies within a mile and a half from large smelting works. What the occupation of these copper-smelting premises was anterior to the year 1860 does not clearly appear. The plaintiff became the proprietor of an estate of great value in the month of June 1860. In the month of September 1860 very extensive smelting operations began on the property of the present appellant, the works at St Helens. Of the effect of the vapours exhaling from these works upon the plaintiff's property, and the injury done to the trees and shrubs there is abundance of evidence. The action has been brought for that. The jury have found the existence of the injury, and the only ground upon which your Lordships are asked to set aside that verdict and to direct a new trial is this, that the whole neighbourhood where these copper-smelting works were carried on is a neighbourhood more or less devoted to manufacturing purposes, and therefore it is said that, inasmuch as this copper-smelting is carried on in what the appellant contends is a fit place, it may be carried on with impunity, although the result may be the utter destruction, or the very considerable diminution of the value of the plaintiff's property. I apprehend that that is not the meaning of the word 'suitable', or the meaning of the word 'convenient', when the law is laid down on the subject. The word suitable unquestionably cannot carry with it this consequence, that a trade may be carried on in a particular locality, the consequence of which trade may be injury and destruction to the neighbouring property. Of course I except the cases where any prescriptive right has been acquired by a lengthened user of the place. On these grounds, therefore, shortly, without dilating further upon them, they are sufficiently unfolded by the judgment of the learned judges in the court below. I advise that your Lordships to affirm the decision of the court below, and to refuse this appeal, and refuse it with costs.

Court of Appeal, 31 July 1979[121] **2.52 (E&W)**

Leakey and others v National Trust for Places of Historic Interest or Natural Beauty

DEFINITION OF INTERFERER (NATURAL EVENT)

The landslide

Liability under nuisance does not cover harm caused by mere natural events. A landowner is under a duty, if he knew or ought to have known of the risk, to do what was reasonable in all the circumstances to prevent or minimise the risk of the known or foreseeable damage or injury to the other person or his property, and is liable in nuisance if he did not.

Facts: The defendants owned and occupied a parcel of land consisting of a conical shaped hill composed of soil which made it peculiarly liable to cracking and slipping as a result of weathering. The claimants were the owners of two houses at the base of the hill, the hill rising in a steep bank from a narrow strip of land lying at the back of the houses. The boundary between the defendants' land and the houses ran along the bottom of the bank, so that the bank formed part of the defendants' property, For many years there had from time to time been slides of soil, rocks, tree roots and other debris from the bank onto the claimants' land caused by the effect of natural weathering on the land. In 1976 a prolonged summer drought followed by an unusually wet autumn aggravated the process of natural weathering and in September 1976 one of the claimants pointed out to the defendants that a large crack had opened up in the bank above her house and that there was a grave danger of a major collapse of the bank onto her house. The defendants replied that they were not obliged to do anything about it because it was caused by the natural movement of the earth. Some weeks later there was a large fall of the bank onto the land of the claimant who had complained, extending up against the house and, it was alleged, putting it at risk if there were further falls. The defendants were asked to clear the fallen earth and debris but they refused, saying they were not responsible for what had occurred. The cost of clearing the material and subsequent protective works amounted to some £60,000. In January 1977 the claimants brought an action against the defendants: (i) an injunction restraining them from permitting soil, earth and tree stumps to move from the defendants' land onto land adjoining thereon owned by the claimants; (ii) an order that the defendants take all necessary steps to remove and stop and prevent soil, earth and tree stumps moving from their land onto the claimants' land; and (iii) damages for nuisance. There was no express pleading of negligence. The injunction was refused, but the judge held the defendants liable in damages. The defendants' appeal was dismissed, the claimant's cross-appeal abandoned.

Held: A landowner is under no liability in respect of any damage which might be caused to neighbouring property in consequence of the natural condition of their property and the operation of natural forces thereon. A person, however, on whose land a hazard naturally occurred and which encroached or threatened to encroach onto another's land thereby causing or threatening to cause damage, is under a duty, if he knew or ought to have known of the risk of encroachment, to do what was reasonable in all the circumstances to prevent or minimise the risk of the known or foreseeable damage or injury to the other person or his property, and is liable in nuisance if he did not.

Judgment: Megaw LJ—This appeal from the judgment of O'Connor J ([1978] QB 849) raises questions which are of importance in the development of English law. The learned judge held that the defendants are liable to the plaintiffs in damages, on a claim framed in nuisance, based on the fact that soil and other detritus had fallen from property owned and occupied by the defendants onto the plaintiffs' properties. It was accepted by the parties that the instability of the defendants' land which made it labile, and which had caused, and was likely to continue to cause, falls of

[121] [1980] QB 485, [1980] 1 All ER 17, [1980] 2 WLR 65, 78 LGR 100.

detritus on the plaintiffs' land, was not caused by, nor was it aggravated by, any human activities on the defendants' land. It was caused by nature: the geological structure, content and contours of the land, and the effect thereon of sun, rain, wind and frost and suchlike natural phenomena. It was held by the learned judge, and is not now in dispute, that, at least since 1968, the defendants knew that the instability of their land was a threat to the plaintiffs' property because of the possibility of falls of soil and other material. Although requested by the plaintiffs to take steps to prevent such falls, the defendants had not taken any action, because they held the view, no doubt on legal advice, that in law they were under no liability in respect of any damage which might be caused to neighbouring property in consequence of the natural condition of their own property and the operation of natural forces thereon.

O'Connor J has held that that view of the law is wrong. He based his decision on the judgment of the Judicial Committee of the Privy Council in *Goldman v Hargrave*. The main issue in this appeal is whether *Goldman v Hargrave* accurately states the law of England. If it does, the appeal fails, and the defendants are liable. ...

The relevant facts of *Goldman v Hargrave* were simple. A redgum tree, 100 feet high, on the defendant's land was struck by lightning and caught fire. The defendant caused the land around the burning tree to be cleared and the tree was then cut down and sawn into sections. So far there could be no complaint that the defendant had done anything which he ought not to have done or left undone anything which he ought to have done, so as in any way to increase the risk which had been caused by this act of natural forces setting fire to the tree. Thereafter the defendant (this was the state of the facts on which the Judicial Committee based their decision) did not do anything which he ought not to have done. He took no positive action which increased the risk of the fire spreading. But he failed to do something which he could have done without any substantial trouble or expense, which would, if done, have eliminated or rendered unlikely the spreading of the fire, that is, to have doused with water the burning or smouldering sections of the tree as they lay on the ground. Instead, the defendant chose to allow or encourage the fire to burn itself out. Foreseeably (again it was the forces of nature and not human action), the weather became even hotter and a strong wind sprang up. The flames from the tree spread rapidly through the defendant's land to the land of neighbours where it did extensive damage to their properties.

The judgment of the Board was delivered by Lord Wilberforce. It was held that the risk of the consequence which in fact happened was foreseeable. This, it is said, 'was not really disputed'. The legal issue was then defined:

> '... the case is not one where a person has brought a source of danger on to his land, nor one where an occupier has so used his property as to cause a danger to his neighbour. It is one where an occupier, faced with a hazard accidentally arising on his land, fails to act with reasonable prudence so as to remove the hazard. The issue is therefore whether in such a case the occupier is guilty of legal negligence, which involves the issue whether he is under a duty of care, and, if so, what is the scope of that duty'.

I return to the judgment in *Goldman v Hargrave* (at 657). The law of England as it used to be is set out in the following passage:

> '... it is only in comparatively recent times that the law has recognised an occu-

> pier's duty as one of a more positive character than merely to abstain from creating, or adding to, a source of danger or annoyance. It was for long satisfied with the conception of separate or autonomous proprietors, each of which was entitled to exploit his territory in a "natural" manner and none of whom was obliged to restrain or direct the operations of nature in the interest of avoiding harm to his neighbours.'

The judgment of the Board then goes on to review the development of the law which, as the Board held, had changed the law so that there now exists 'a general duty on occupiers in relation to hazards occurring on their land, whether natural or man-made' (at 661–662).

That change in the law, in its essence and in its timing, corresponds with, and may be viewed as being a part of, the change in the law of tort which achieved its decisive victory in *Donoghue v Stevenson*, though it was not until eight years later, in the House of Lords decision in *Sedleigh-Denfield v O'Callagan*, that the change as affecting the area with which we are concerned was expressed or recognised in a decision binding on all English courts, and, even then, the full, logical effect of the decision in altering what had hitherto been thought to be the law was not immediately recognised. But *Goldman v Hargrave* has now demonstrated what that effect was in English law. ...

In the *Sedleigh-Denfield* case, a local authority had trespassed on the defendant's land, without the defendant's knowledge or consent, and had placed a culvert in a ditch on that land. By the improper placing of a grid at the mouth of the culvert, instead of further back, those who did the work created a danger of flooding which would be likely to spread to the plaintiff's land. The defendant, through his servants, came to know what had been done. He should have realised that it created a real risk of flooding of his neighbour's land. He did nothing. A heavy rainstorm caused the ditch to flood, because of the trespassers' work. The plaintiff's land was damaged. The House of Lords held that the defendant was liable. The defendant himself had not done anything which was an 'unnatural use' of his land. He had not himself brought anything 'unnatural' onto his land. But when he knew or ought to have known of the risk of flood water from his land encroaching on his neighbour's land he had done nothing towards preventing it. Prevention could have been achieved without any great trouble or expense.

The approval by the House of Lords in the *Sedleigh-Denfield* case of Scrutton LJ's judgment in the Job Edwards case meant, ... that it was thereafter the law of England that a duty existed under which the occupier of land might be liable to his neighbour for damage to his neighbour's property as a result of a nuisance spreading from his land to his neighbour's land, even though the existence and the operative effect of the nuisance were not caused by any 'non-natural' use by the defendant of his own land. But the liability was not a strict liability such as that which was postulated by the House of Lords in *Rylands v Fletcher* as arising where damage was caused to another by an 'unnatural' user of land. The obligation postulated in the *Sedleigh-Denfield* case, in conformity with the development of the law in *Donoghue v Stevenson*, was an obligation to use reasonable care. A defendant was not to be liable as a result of a risk of which he neither was aware nor ought, as a reasonable careful landowner, to have been aware.

... A passage in Lord Wright's speech [1940] 3 All ER 349 at 365, [1940] AC 880 at 904 gives, I believe, a fair reflection of the attitude of their Lordships:

'The liability for a nuisance is not, at least in modern law, a strict or absolute liability. If the defendant, by himself or those for whom he is responsible, has created what constitutes a nuisance, and if it causes damage, the difficulty now being considered does not arise; but he may have taken over the nuisance, ready made as it were, when he acquired the property, or the nuisance may be due to a latent defect or to the act of a trespasser or stranger. Then he is not liable unless he continued or adopted the nuisance, or, more accurately, did not without undue delay remedy it when he became aware of it, or with ordinary and reasonable care should have become aware of it. This rule seems to be in accord with good sense and convenience.'

I am confident that Lord Wright's words 'latent defect' were intended to include a defect in the land itself. Lord Wright was making the same point, the lack of any valid distinction, in this context, between a trespasser's act and an act of nature, as he had made when he was Wright J, in *Noble v Harrison* [1926] 2 KB 332 at 341, [1926] All ER Rep 284 at 288. There … he said:

'The nuisance in that case was caused by the act of a trespasser, but I think the same principle applies to a nuisance (in this case the latent crack in the branch with the resulting risk that some day it would fall) caused by a secret and unobservable operation of nature.'

So long as the defect remains 'latent' there is no duty on the occupier, whether the defect has been caused by a trespasser or by nature. Equally, once the latent becomes patent, a duty will arise, whether the causative agent of the defect is man or nature. But the mere fact that there is a duty does not necessarily mean that inaction constitutes a breach of the duty.

… Suppose that we are not bound by *Rylands v Fletcher* or any other authority to hold in favour of the defendants where the nuisance arises solely from natural forces; but suppose also that we are not bound by the decision in *Sedleigh-Denfield* or other binding authority to hold that there is a duty on the defendants in a case such as the present. Ought we as a matter of policy to develop the law by holding that there is a duty in a case such as the present?

If, as a result of the working of the forces of nature, there is, poised above my land, or above my house, a boulder or a rotten tree, which is liable to fall at any moment of the day or night, perhaps destroying my house, and perhaps killing or injuring me or members of my family, am I without remedy? (Of course the standard of care required may be much higher where there is risk to life or limb as contrasted with mere risk to property, but can it be said that the duty exists in the one case and not in the other?) Must I, in such a case, if my protests to my neighbour go unheeded, sit and wait and hope that the worst will not befall? If it is said that I have in such circumstances a remedy of going on my neighbour's land to abate the nuisance, that would, or might, be an unsatisfactory remedy. But in any event, if there were such a right of abatement, it would, as counsel for the plaintiffs rightly contended, be because my neighbour owed me a duty. There is, I think, ample authority that, if I have a right to abatement, I have also a remedy in damages if the nuisance remains unabated and causes me damage or personal injury. …

In the example which I have given above, I believe that few people would regard it as anything other than a grievous blot on the law if the law recognises the existence of no duty on the part of the owner or occupier. But take another example, at the other end of the scale, where it might be though that there is, potentially, an equally serious injustice the other way. If a stream flows through A's land, A being a small farmer, and there is a known danger that in times of heavy rainfall, because of the configuration of A's land and the nature of the stream's course and flow, there may be an overflow, which will pass beyond A's land and damage the property of A's neighbours: perhaps much wealthier neighbours. It may require expensive works, far beyond A's means, to prevent or even diminish the risk of such flooding. Is A to be liable for all the loss that occurs when the flood comes, if he has not done the impossible and carried out these works at his own expense?

In my judgment, there is, in the scope of the duty as explained in *Goldman v Hargrave*, a removal, or at least a powerful amelioration, of the injustice which might otherwise be caused in such a case by the recognition of the duty of care. Because of that limitation on the scope of the duty, I would say that, as a matter of policy, the law ought to recognise such a duty of care.

This leads on to the question of the scope of the duty. This is discussed, and the nature and extent of the duty is explained, in the judgment in *Goldman v Hargrave*. The duty is a duty to do that which is reasonable in all the circumstances, and no more than what, if anything, is reasonable, or prevent or minimise the known risk of damage or injury to one's neighbour or to his property. ...

I would dismiss the appeal.

Shaw LJ (read by Cumming-Bruce LJ)—Why should a nuisance which has its origin in some natural phenomenon and which manifests itself without any human intervention cast a liability on a person who has no other connection with that nuisance than the title to the land on which it chances to originate? This view is fortified inasmuch as a title to land cannot be discarded or abandoned. Why should the owner of land in such a case be bound to protect his neighbour's property and person rather than that the neighbour should protect his interests against the potential danger?

The old common law duty of a landowner on whose land there arose a nuisance from natural causes only, without any human intervention, was to afford a neighbour whose property or person was threatened by the nuisance a reasonable opportunity to abate that nuisance. This entailed (1) that the landowner should on becoming aware of the nuisance give reasonable warning of it to his neighbour, (2) that the landowner should give to the neighbour such access to the land as was reasonably requisite to enable him to abate the nuisance.

The principle was relatively clear in its application and served in broad terms to do justice between the parties concerned. The development of 'the good neighbour' concept has however blurred the definition of rights and liabilities between persons who stand in such a relationship as may involve them in reciprocal rights and liabilities.

It has culminated in the judgment of the Privy Council in *Goldman v Hargrave*. Though not binding on this court, it is of great persuasive authority. It might have been possible to explain the result of that case in the context of its special facts, for the defendant had added his own ill-directed exertions to what the forces of nature had initiated. However, the judgment of the Board is in general terms and expounds a universal principle. It is for this reason that it has to be seen as powerful support for a development in the law relating to the liability of a landowner for nuisance. It is to be observed that the judgment was expressly stated to be founded on negligence and it repudiated any necessity to resolve jurisprudential distinctions between a liability arising from a duty to take care on the one hand and on the other a liability not directly related to any duty of care but absolute in its character as in the case of what is understood as nuisance in the English common law. It is readily understandable that the scope of absolute liability must be bounded by relatively narrow limits, and that it is right to hesitate before adopting a principle which will have the effect of extending those limits in the law of nuisance. I do not for myself, if I may respectfully venture to say so, see how the difficulty is disposed of by transmuting a liability in nuisance (howsoever occasioned) into a duty to do what can reasonably be done in the circumstances of a particular case to prevent or to diminish the consequences of a nuisance. This formulation may, so it seems to me, create fresh problems, and the derivative problems may defy resolution.

However, a judgment based on general principle and given by a tribunal so commanding of attention and esteem must, even though not authoritative in the courts of England, be regarded as relating to the law of England and as being an induction of that law.

Seen in the light of Megaw LJ's analysis and exposition of the long line of cases, the judgment in *Goldman v Hargrave* may represent the climax of a movement in the law of England expanding that part of the law which relates to liability for nuisance.

It is in this attitude of mind that I find myself in agreement with the conclusions which Megaw LJ has stated.

Accordingly, albeit with diffident reluctance, I would dismiss the appeal.

Queen's Bench Division, 12 May 1876[122] **2.53 (E&W)**

Harris v James and another

DEFINITION OF INTERFERER (LANDLORD)

Lime quarry

If land is let for a definite purpose, the landlord is liable for any nuisance caused by the tenant which arises as the natural and necessary result of such use.

Facts: A landlord demised a field for the express purpose of it being worked as a lime quarry, and the tenant erected limekilns on the field for the purpose of burning limestone taken from the field. The smoke and vapours arising from this kiln spread over the lands of the claimant, and injured the herbage and lessened the value of the land. This injury was partly the natural and necessary result of limekilns being used in the said field, and partly the result of the improper manner in which the kiln has been worked.

Held: The landlord is liable for any mischief that arises from the natural and necessary result of what the landlord authorised and required, or even authorised and did not require.

Judgment: Blackburn J—Where one person authorises and requests a person to do certain things, he is liable for any consequences that arise therefrom. If the authority is given in a lease, the person who gives that authority is no less liable on that account. I do not think that the lessor can be said to require everything the occupier may do; for example, if a man devises certain land on an agricultural lease, and requires that it should be cultivated in the best manner possible, and the tenant, exercising his discretion, brings on to the farm an enormous quantity of most odiferous manure so as to create a nuisance to the neighbourhood, I do not think in

[122] [1874–80] All ER Rep 1142.

a case of that kind that the landlord would be liable, because I do not think that he could be said in any way to request or authorise what had been done. So, too, in the case of a lease of building land, the lessee might so build as to obstruct a neighbour's lights, but the lessor would not be liable, for, although he may have enabled the lessee so to build, he did not request him to do it. But in the case before us the lime field was let for the very purpose of burning lime. No doubt, for any mischief arising from a careless or negligent use of the field, the landlord would not be liable, but for any mischief that arises from the natural and necessary result of what the landlord authorised and required, or even authorised and did not require, I think that the landlord must be held liable ...

I do not think that the landlord is responsible for what has been negligently and improperly done ... .

Lush J—I am of the same opinion.

Court of Appeal, 31 July 1981[123] **2.54 (E&W)**

Sampson v Hodson-Pressinger and another

DEFINITION OF INTERFERER AND AVAILABLE REMEDY

The badly sound-proofed terrace

The landlord who lets an apartment that is not fit to be used in a normal way without interfering with the reasonable use of another is liable in nuisance. If the award of damages would produce a satisfactory result, achieve finality and is not against the will of the claimant, it is appropriate to award damages in lieu of an injunction.

Facts: The claimant was the tenant of a flat under a 99-year lease. The lease contained the usual covenant for quiet enjoyment. Between 1974 and 1978 the flat above the claimant's flat, flat 7, was empty while conversion work was being carried out. In particular the flat roof situated immediately above the claimant's sitting-room, kitchen and bathroom was converted into an attractive tiled terrace of some 30 feet by 19 feet and French windows were put in the wall of the sitting room of flat 7 so that it opened onto the terrace. On 11 August 1978 the first defendant moved into flat 7 under a lease in similar terms to that of the claimant granted by the same landlord. Thereafter the first defendant used the terrace in a normal way; she invited friends onto it and occasionally gave a party there. However, because the tiles had been improperly laid, whenever anyone walked on the roof terrace the noise of treading feet penetrated to the claimant's flat below and in particular his sitting-room and the claimant could hear conversations to such an extent that it interfered with his use and enjoyment of his premises. The claimant complained to the first defendant and to the landlord. In May 1979 the second defendant showed an interest in buying the freehold of the entire house. The claimant told him about the noise from the terrace and showed him an architect's report in which the noise was described as excessive and in which remedies were advocated. The second defendant nevertheless bought the property from the landlord and thereafter denied any responsibility for the noise resulting from the use of the terrace. The claimant brought an action against the defendants claiming damages against the second defendant in nuisance and seeking an injunction against both defendants to restrain them from causing or permitting the terrace to be used in such a manner as to cause a nuisance to the claimant. The judge in the county court held that the disturbance to the claimant from the use by the first defendant of her roof terrace amounted to a nuisance for which the second defendant was liable. The judge awarded the claimant £2,000 damages against the second defendant, but he refused an injunction. The second defendant appealed. The appeal was dismissed.

[123] [1981] 3 All ER 710, 261 EG 895, [1982] EGD 482, 12 HLR 40.

Held: The landlord who lets an apartment that is not fit to be used in a normal way without interfering with the reasonable use of another is liable in nuisance. If the award of damages would produce a satisfactory result, achieve finality and is not against the will of the claimant, it is appropriate to award damages in lieu of an injunction.

Judgment: Eveleigh LJ—It was … contended that the second defendant could not be guilty of a nuisance, because the first defendant was using residential property in a normal way. The flaw in this argument, in my opinion, is that the property itself was not fit to be used in a normal way in so far as the terrace was concerned. It could not so be used without interfering with the reasonable enjoyment by the plaintiff of his flat. The use of the terrace put a strain on the plaintiff that normal use in a normal building would not have done.

The first landlord is not a party to these proceedings. However, it is helpful to consider what his position would have been had he continued to be the landlord. He clearly would have been liable in nuisance to the plaintiff. He let the premises to be used for residential purposes and those purposes, in my opinion, included the use of the terrace in the way in which the first defendant used it. It must have been contemplated by the landlord that the tenant of flat 7 would walk on the terrace wearing ordinary footwear and that she would invite others to do so and to converse while there. He had himself been responsible for the condition of the premises, which were not in fact suitable for use in the manner contemplated without causing a nuisance.

In these circumstances, what remedies are available? There could be an injunction against the first and second defendants. Alternatively, it is possible to award damages for prospective nuisance in exercise of the court's power first introduced by Lord Cairns's Act (the Chancery Amendment Act 1858). In addition, damages could be granted to cover the period up to the date of trial. It is not clear on what precise legal basis the learned judge awarded the sum of £2,000. I do not think it matters for the purpose of this appeal provided this court is satisfied that the award can be justified in law.

To grant an injunction against both defendants is likely to produce a situation which will be very unsatisfactory from the first defendant's point of view and probably unfair to her. If the court were to grant an injunction against her an injunction against the landlord would be unnecessary. However, the first defendant would then no doubt consider whether or not she had any remedy against the second defendant or against the original landlord. She did serve a notice in the present case claiming contribution against the second defendant in respect of any damages and costs which she might be ordered to pay to the plaintiff and in respect of her own costs of defending the action. In the event the plaintiff withdrew his claim for damages against the first defendant hoping to remain on good terms with her, but the judge did grant her an indemnity in respect of her costs of defending the action. As drafted, the contribution notice is not in such terms as would enable the court to determine issues which might arise under the terms of the first defendant's lease if the court were to grant an injunction against the first defendant. For example, there might be a contention that, as the injunction resulted from the act of a person claiming under the landlord (ie the plaintiff himself), the landlord was in breach of his covenant with the first defendant for quiet enjoyment. Moreover, the court has been told that the plaintiff would prefer to uphold the judgment which he has obtained rather than to seek injunctions. The figure of £2,000 may not be enough to carry out the necessary remedial works, but, while the court has not been given any details, it does appear that, at least as between the plaintiff and the first defendant, something can be done to remedy the situation. As we are told that, it seems to me that this really is a case where an award of damages would produce a satisfactory result and achieve finality. However, on behalf of the landlord, it was contended that the court should not make such an award. It was said that the court should only grant damages for a prospective nuisance in exceptional circumstances and in very simple cases, which it was said this case was not.

A common argument against the award of damages as opposed to an injunction is that to do so would legalise or license the commission of future torts. In my opinion, while this argument may have merit when submitted by the plaintiff, it has much less strength when involved by a defendant. ...

In the present case we would not be granting damages against the will of the plaintiff. That is an important consideration. ... I for my part ... would regard the present case as an appropriate one in which to award damages in lieu of an injunction. It is unnecessary to state a specific figure in respect of the nuisance for the period preceding the trial and to give detailed reasons to justify any particular figure in respect of prospective nuisance. This is because the evidence establishes, as the learned judge himself thought, that an appropriate figure would exceed that which could be awarded in the county court.

Strictly speaking, there could be an award in damages against both defendants. Had the plaintiff not withdrawn his claim against the first defendant I would have made an award against her. However, I regard this as a case in which she would have been entitled to a complete indemnity from the original landlord. ...

As I would uphold an award of damages against the second defendant it follows that it would be inappropriate to grant an injunction against the first defendant. The plaintiff is accepting damages in lieu of his right to complain of nuisance in the future. There is, therefore, no basis on which an injunction can be granted against the first defendant. I would dismiss this appeal.

Brandon LJ and O'Connor LJ—agreed.

Notes

(1) Both cases, *Harris v James* and *Sampson v Hodson-Pressinger*, show that not only the person who creates an interference is liable in nuisance, but also the person, in the annotated cases the landlord, who authorised it, either by way of implied or express consent (*Harris v James*) or as a result of the responsibility a landlord has for the construction of the house (*Sampson v Hodson-Pressinger*). This view was upheld by the Queen's Bench Division in *Tetley and others v Chitty and others* [1986] 1 All ER 663, where the landlord was held liable in nuisance for the noise of his tenant's go-kart track.

(2) In *Sampson v Hodson-Pressinger* and *Tetley v Chitty*, the court discussed the remedy available in nuisance. While it is apparent that the claimant must be entitled to claim damages for the harm he has actually sustained (physical damage to property, depreciation in the value of land, and lost profits), the claim of an injunction against future continuance of the interference depends on the discretion of the court. See *Tetley v Chitty* [1986] 1 All ER 663 per McNeill J:

> It is clear that the decision whether or not to grant an injunction requires a balancing of interest and may, as here, involve balancing the interests of individuals, such as the

plaintiffs, against the public interest in the provision of recreational facilities. I approach the question on this basis and, of course, on the principle that an injunction should not be ordered if an award of damages would be a sufficient remedy.

II.B GOODS

Introductory Notes

(a) The right to exclusive possession of goods (movable objects) is protected by various torts, primarily by the torts of conversion (also called trover), trespass to goods and negligence. While negligence deals with the entitlement to compensatory damages when property is harmed in breach of a duty of care, conversion and trespass constitute legal instruments to protect the holder of movable property against misappropriation or other interference. In 1977, these historically developed torts were then systematised by the Torts (Interference with Goods) Act 1977. The act formally abolished the historic tort of detinue, which was committed when the person who had actual control of an object refused to deliver it to the person with a better right to it, and transferred its contents to the tort of conversion.[124] The torts of conversion and trespass only apply to corporeal objects, not to choses in action.[125]

(b) Historically, the common law did not allow for recovery of the good by way of judicial action and courts could only award damages in tort against the person who interfered. The defendant, thus, had the option to deliver the good to the claimant or to pay him its value. This has changed during the centuries[126] and nowadays, according to section 3(2) of the Tort (Interference with Goods) Act 1977, which specifies the available relief in case of wrongful interference with goods, the court may at its discretion, besides attributing damages, also issue an order for delivery of the good.

(c) Contrary to negligence the torts of conversion and trespass do not require that damage is shown or fault is established.

(d) The time limit to bring an action of conversion is six years (Limitation Act 1980, sections 2 and 3).

Torts (Interference with Goods) Act 1977[127] **2.55 (E&W)**

Preliminary

1. Definition of 'wrongful interference with goods'.

In this Act 'wrongful interference', or 'wrongful interference with goods', means—

(a) conversion of goods (also called trover),

(b) trespass to goods,

(c) negligence so far at it results in damage to goods or to an interest in goods.

[124] Torts (Interference with Goods) Act 1977, s 2.

[125] See also Torts (Interference with Goods) Act 1977, s 14(1). On the term 'chose in action', see Chapter 4.

[126] See above.

[127] 22 July 1977, c 32.

(d) subject to section 2, any other tort so far as it results in damage to goods or to an interest in goods.

Detention of goods

2. Abolition of detinue

(1) Detinue is abolished.

(2) An action lies in conversion for loss or destruction of goods which a bailee has allowed to happen in breach of his duty to his bailor (that is to say it lies in a case which is not otherwise conversion, but would have been detinue before detinue was abolished).

3. Form of judgment where goods are detained

(1) In proceedings for wrongful interference against a person who is in possession or in control of the goods relief may be given in accordance with this section, so far as appropriate.

(2) The relief is—

(a) an order for delivery of the goods, and for payment of any consequential damages, or

(b) an order for delivery of the goods, but giving the defendant the alternative of paying damages by reference to the value of the goods, together in either alternative with payment of any consequential damages, or

(c) damages.

(3) Subject to rules of court—

(a) relief shall be given under only one of paragraphs (a), (b) and (c) of subsection (2),

(b) relief under paragraph (a) of subsection (2) is at the discretion of the court, and the claimant may choose between the others.

(4) If it is shown to the satisfaction of the court that an order under subsection (2)(a) has not been complied with, the court may—

(a) revoke the order, or the relevant part of it, and

(b) make an order for payment of damages by reference to the value of the goods.

(5) Where an order is made under subsection (2)(b) the defendant may satisfy the order by returning the goods at any time before execution of judgment, but without prejudice to liability to pay any consequential damages.

(6) An order for delivery of the goods under subsection (2)(a) or (b) may impose such conditions as may be determined by the court, or pursuant to rules of court, and in particular, where damages by reference to the value of the goods would not be the whole of the value of the goods, may require an allowance to be made by the claimant to reflect the difference.

For example, a bailor's action against the bailee may be one in which the measure of damages is not the full value of the goods, and then the court may order delivery of the goods, but require the bailor to pay the bailee a sum reflecting the difference.

(7) Where under subsection (1) or subsection (2) of section 6 an allowance is to be made in respect of an improvement of the goods, and an order is made under subsection (2)(a) or (b), the court may assess the allowance to be made in respect of the improvement, and by the order require, as a condition for delivery of the goods, that allowance to be made by the claimant.

(8) This section is without prejudice—

(a) to the remedies afforded by section 133 of the Consumer Credit Act 1974, or

(b) to the remedies afforded by sections 35, 42 and 44 of the Hire-Purchase Act 1965, or to those sections of the Hire-Purchase Act (Northern Ireland) 1966 (so long as those sections respectively remain in force), or

(c) to any jurisdiction to afford ancillary or incidental relief.

4. Interlocutory relief where goods are detained

(1) In this section 'proceedings' means proceedings for wrongful interference.

(2) On the application of any person in accordance with rules of court, the High Court shall, in such circumstances as may be specified in the rules, have power to make an order providing for the delivery up of any goods which are or may become the subject matter of subsequent proceedings in the court, or as to which any question may arise in proceedings.

(3) Delivery shall be, as the order may provide, to the claimant or to a person appointed by the court for the purpose, and shall be on such terms and conditions as may be specified in the order.

(4) …

(5) …

Damages

5. Extinction of title on satisfaction of claim for damages

(1) Where damages for wrongful interference are, or would fall to be, assessed on the footing that the claimant is being compensated—

(a) for the whole of his interest in the goods, or

(b) for the whole of his interest in the goods subject to a reduction for contributory negligence, payment of the assessed damages (under all heads), or as the case may be settlement of a claim for damages for the wrong (under all heads), extinguishes the claimant's title to that interest.

(2) …

(3) It is hereby declared that subsection (1) does not apply where damages are assessed on the footing that the claimant is being compensated for the whole of his interest in the goods, but the damages paid are limited to some lesser amount by virtue of any enactment or rule of law.

(4) Where under section 7(3) the claimant accounts over to another person (the 'third party') so as to compensate (under all heads) the third party for the whole of his interest in the goods, the third party's title to that interest is extinguished.

(5) This section has effect subject to any agreement varying the respective rights of the parties to the agreement, and where the claim is made in court proceedings has effect subject to any order of the court.

6. Allowance for improvement of the goods

(1) If in proceedings for wrongful interference against a person (the 'improver') who has improved the goods, it is shown that the improver acted in the mistaken but honest belief that he had a good title to them, an allowance shall be made for the extent to which, at the time as at which the goods fall to be valued in assessing damages, the value of the goods is attributable to the improvement.

(2) If, in proceedings for wrongful interference against a person (the 'purchaser') who has purported to purchase the goods—

(a) from the improver, or

(b) where after such a purported sale the goods passed by a further purported sale on one or more occasions, on any such occasion,

it is shown that the purchaser acted in good faith, an allowance shall be made on the principle set out in subsection (1).

For example, where a person in good faith buys a stolen car from the improver and is sued in conversion by the true owner the damages may be reduced to reflect the improvement, but if the person who bought the stolen car from the improver sues the improver for failure of consideration, and the improver acted in good faith, subsection (3) below will ordinarily make a comparable reduction in the damages he recovers from the improver.

(3) If in a case within subsection (2) the person purporting to sell the goods acted in good faith, then in proceedings by the purchaser for recovery of the purchase price because of failure of consideration, or in any other proceedings founded on that failure of consideration, an allowance shall, where appropriate, be made on the principle set out in subsection (1).

(4) This section applies, with the necessary modifications, to a purported bailment or other disposition of goods as it applies to a purported sale of goods.

Liability to two or more claimants

7. Double liability

(1) In this section 'double liability' means the double liability of the wrongdoer which can arise—

(a) where one of two or more rights of action for wrongful interference is founded on a possessory title, or

(b) where the measure of damages in an action for wrongful interference founded on a proprietary title is or includes the entire value of the goods, although the interest is one of two or more interests in the goods.

(2) In proceedings to which any two or more claimants are parties, the relief shall be such as to avoid double liability of the wrongdoer as between those claimants.

(3) On satisfaction, in whole or in part, of any claim for an amount exceeding that recoverable if subsection (2) applied, the claimant is liable to account over to the other person having a right to claim to such extent as will avoid double liability.

(4) Where, as the result of enforcement of a double liability, any claimant is unjustly enriched to any extent, he shall be liable to reimburse the wrongdoer to that extent.

For example, if a converter of goods pays damages first to a finder of the goods, and then to the true owner, the finder is unjustly enriched unless he accounts over to the true owner under subsection (3); and then the true owner is unjustly enriched and becomes liable to reimburse the converter of the goods.

8. Competing rights to the goods

(1) The defendant in an action for wrongful interference shall be entitled to show, in accordance with rules of court, that a third party has a better right than the plaintiff as respects all or any part of the interest claimed by the plaintiff, or in right of which he sues, and any rule of law (sometimes called jus tertii) to the contrary is abolished.

(2) Rules of court relating to proceedings for wrongful interference may—

(a) require the plaintiff to give particulars of his title,

(b) require the plaintiff to identify any person who, to his knowledge, has or claims any interest in the goods,

(c) authorise the defendant to apply for directions as to whether any person should be joined with a view to establishing whether he has a better right than the plaintiff, or has a claim as a result of which the defendant might be doubly liable,

(d) where a party fails to appear on an application within paragraph (c), or to comply with any direction given by the court on such an application, authorise the court to deprive him of any right of action against the defendant for the wrong either unconditionally, or subject to such terms or conditions as may be specified.

(3) Subsection (2) is without prejudice to any other power of making rules of court.

9. Concurrent actions

(1) This section applies where goods are the subject of two or more claims for wrongful interference (whether or not the claims are founded on the same wrongful act, and whether or not any of the claims relates also to other goods).

(2) Where goods are the subject of two or more claims under section 6 this section shall apply as if any claim under section 6(3) were a claim for wrongful interference.

(3) If proceedings have been brought in a county court on one of those claims, county court rules may waive, or allow a court to waive, any limit (financial or territorial) on the jurisdiction of county courts in [the County Courts Act 1984] or the County Courts [(Northern Ireland) Order 1980] so as to allow another of those claims to be brought in the same county court.

(4) If proceedings are brought on one of the claims in the High Court, and proceedings on any other are brought in a county court, whether prior to the High Court proceedings or not, the High Court may, on the application of the defendant, after notice has been given to the claimant in the county court proceedings—

(a) order that the county court proceedings be transferred to the High Court,

(b) order security for costs or impose such other terms as the court thinks fit.

Conversion and trespass to goods

10. Co-owners

(1) Co-ownership is no defence to an action founded on conversion or trespass to goods where the defendant without the authority of the other co-owner—

(a) destroys the goods, or disposes of the goods in a way giving a good title to the entire property in the goods, or otherwise does anything equivalent to the destruction of the other's interest in the goods, or

(b) purports to dispose of the goods in a way which would give a good title to the entire property in the goods if he was acting with the authority of all co-owners of the goods.

(2) Subsection (1) shall not affect the law concerning execution or enforcement of judgments, or concerning any form of distress.

(3) Subsection (1)(a) is by way of restatement of existing law so far as it relates to conversion.

11. Minor amendments

(1) Contributory negligence is no defence in proceedings founded on conversion, or on intentional trespass to goods.

(2) Receipt of goods by way of pledge is conversion if the delivery of the goods is conversion.

(3) Denial of title is not of itself conversion.

...

14. Interpretation

(1) In this Act, unless the context otherwise requires—

"goods" includes all chattels personal other than things in action and money. ...

II.B.1 TRESPASS

Trespass to goods (trespass *de bonis asportatis* and trespass on the case) requires a direct physical interference with the good of another. As the tort is directed at the invasion of possession, the right to sue lies with the person who is in possession of the good at the time of the interference.[128] Trespass to goods may occur in many different forms, such scratching another person's coach panel,[129] killing another's animals[130] or removing a car from a garage.[131] It is not necessary that the interference causes material damage.[132] See Latham CJ in *Penfold Wines v Elliott*:[133]

> A mere taking or asportation of a chattel may be a trespass without the infliction of any material damage. The handling of a chattel without authority is a trespass. ... Unauthorized user of goods is a trespass; unauthorized acts of riding a horse, driving a motor car, using a bottle, are all equally trespasses, even though the horse may be returned unharmed or the motor car unwrecked or the bottle unbroken. The normal use of a bottle is as a container, and the use of it for this purpose is a trespass if, ... it is not authorized by a person in possession or entitled to immediate possession'.

Indirect interference, such as putting out poison for an animal to take,[134] or a mere accidental and not wilful act does not constitute trespass.[135]

[128] B Markesinis and S Deakin, *Markesinis and Deakin's Tort Law*, 6th edn (New York, Oxford University Press, 2008) 484; Rogers, above n 87, 17-4.

[129] *Fouldes v Willowby* [1841] 8 M & W 538, 549.

[130] *Sheldrick v Abery* [1793] 1 Esp 55.

[131] *Wilson v Lombank Ltd* [1963] 1 WLR 1294.

[132] Rogers, above n 87, 17-3; MG Bridge, *Personal Property Law*, 3rd edn (Oxford, Oxford University Press, 2002) 49.

[133] [1946] 74 CLR 204, High Court of Australia at 215.

[134] Rogers, above n 87, 17-3.

[135] *National Coal Board v Evans* [1951] 2 KB 861, CA: accidental damage to an electrical cable by construction workers.

II.B.2 CONVERSION

House of Lords, 6 July 1875[136] **2.56 (E&W)**

Hollins and others v Fowler and others

THE ACT OF CONVERSION

The sold cotton

Any person who, however innocently, obtains possession of the goods of a person who has been fraudulently deprived of them, and disposes of those goods for his own benefit, or for that of another person, is guilty of a conversion.

Facts: The appellants, Hollins and others, bought cotton from Bayley, intending to act as brokers and resell the cotton to any of their customers whom it might suit, charging only a commission, but having no immediate principal at the time of the purchase. Subsequently, they sold the cotton to M Bayley who had obtained the cotton from the respondents (Fowlers and others) by fraud, but the appellants were not aware of this. The respondents brought an action of trover against the appellants to recover the value of the cotton. The appeal was dismissed.

Held: Any person who, however innocently, obtains possession of the goods of a person who has been fraudulently deprived of them, and disposes of them, whether for his own benefit or that of any other person, is guilty of a conversion.

Judgment: Lord Chelmsford—The question upon the facts is whether the appellants were guilty of a conversion. There can be no doubt that the property and legal right of possession of the cotton remained in the respondents, and Bayley, who had fraudulently obtained possession of it, could not give a title to anyone to whom he transferred the possession, however ignorant the transferee might be of the means by which Bayley acquired it. A great deal of argument was directed to the question of what amounts in law to a conversion. ... [T]he proposition which fits this case is that any person who, however innocently, obtains possession of the goods of a person who has been fraudulently deprived of them, and disposes of them, whether for his own benefit or that of any other person, is guilty of a conversion.

The Court of Queen's Bench, in their judgment in this case, thought that it was not distinguishable from *Hardman v Booth*. In that case the plaintiffs were worsted manufacturers near Manchester. One of the partners, being in London, called at the place of business of a firm of Gandell & Co, for orders. At that time the firm, which had been long established, and was well known, consisted only of Thomas Gandell, whose son, Edward Gandell, was his clerk, and managed the business. On inquiring for Messrs Gandell, one of the workmen directed the plaintiff to the counting house, where he saw Edward Gandell, who led him to believe he was one of the firm of Gandell & Co, and under that belief the plaintiffs sent goods to the place of business of Gandell & Co, and invoiced them to Edward Gandell & Co. Edward Gandell who, unknown to the plaintiffs, carried on business with one Todd, pledged the goods with the defendant Booth for advances bona fide made to Gandell and Todd, and the defendant afterwards sold the goods under a power of sale. It was held by the Court of Exchequer that the defendant was liable for a conversion on the ground that there was no contract of sale, inasmuch as the plaintiffs believed they were

[136] [1874-1880] All ER Rep 118.

contracting with Gandell & Co, and not with Edward Gandell personally, and Gandell & Co never authorised Edward Gandell to contract for them, and, consequently no property passed by the sale, and the defendant, though ignorant of Gandell and Todd's want of title to the goods, was liable in trover for the amount realised by the sale. I agree with the Court of Queen's Bench that *Hardman v Booth* is not to be distinguished from the present case.

I may also advert to *Stephens v Elwall* mentioned by Blackburn J in his opinion delivered to your Lordships in this case. There a bankrupt, after his bankruptcy, sold goods to Deane to be paid for by bills on Heathcote, for whom Deane bought the goods Heathcote was in America, and the defendant Elwall was his clerk, and conducted the business of his house in London. Deane informed the defendant of the purchase, and, the goods being afterwards delivered to him, he sent them to America to Heathcote. This was held to be a conversion by the defendant Lord Ellenborough CJ said (4 M & S at p 261):

> 'The clerk acted under an unavoidable ignorance, and for his master's benefit, when he sent the goods to his master, but nevertheless his acts may amount to a conversion, for a person is guilty of a conversion who intermeddles with my property and disposes of it, and it is no answer that he acted under the authority of another, who had himself no authority to dispose of it.'

This case was decided sixty years ago, and I do not find that its authority has ever been disputed I think that the judgments of the Court of Queen's Bench and of the Exchequer Chamber are right, and ought to be affirmed.

Lord Cairns LC, Lord Hatherley and Lord O'Hagan delivered concurring opinions.

Notes

(1) The tort of conversion covers a wide range of acts. This was expressed by Lord Nicholls of Birkenhead in *Kuwait Airways v Iraqi Airways Co*[137] as follows: 'Conversion of goods can occur in so many different circumstances that framing a precise definition of universal application is well nigh impossible.' And he continues:

> In general, the basic features of the tort are threefold. First, the defendant's conduct was inconsistent with the rights of the owner (or other person entitled to possession). Second, the conduct was deliberate, not accidental. Third, the conduct was so extensive an encroachment on the rights of the owner as to exclude him from use and possession of the goods. The contrast is with lesser acts of interference. If these cause damage they may give rise to claims for trespass or in negligence, but they do not constitute conversion.

Typical acts of conversion are thus the taking, detention or disposition of a chattel in a way that is inconsistent with the claimant's title.

(2) In the annotated judgment the court held that even a broker may be liable in conversion and in *Marcq v Christie Manson & Woods Ltd*,[138] a case concerning a stolen painting, the Court of Appeal held that an auctioneer who merely redelivered the good to the consignor when they were unsold, was not liable in conversion, provided that he had acted in good faith and without knowledge of any adverse

[137] [2002] UKHL 19 at 39.

[138] [2003] EWCA Civ 731, [2003] 3 All ER 561, [2003] 2 WLR 980, CA.

claim to the goods. But if the auctioneer sold the goods, he would incur liability if he delivered them to the buyer.

Court of King's Bench, Hilary Term, 1722[139] **2.57 (E&W)**

Armory v Delamirie

RIGHT TO SUE (FINDER)

The chimney-sweep's boy

The finder of an object has such a property as would enable him to keep it against all but the rightful owner.

Facts: The claimant, a chimney-sweep's boy, found a jewel and took it to the shop of the defendant, a goldsmith, to find out what it was. The goldsmith delivered it into the hands of an apprentice who, under pretence of weighing it, took out the stones, and called to the defendant to let him know its value came to three halfpence; the defendant offered the claimant that money. The claimant refused to take it and insisted on having the jewel back, whereupon the apprentice gave him back the socket without the stones. The claimant sued the defendant for trover. The claim was approved.

Held: The finder of a jewel, though he does not by such finding acquire an absolute property or ownership, yet he has such a property as will enable him to keep it against all but the rightful owner, and consequently may maintain trover.

Judgment: Sir John Pratt, CJ—Ruled the following points: (i) That the finder of a jewel, though he does not by such finding acquire an absolute property or ownership, yet he has such a property as will enable him to keep it against all but the rightful owner, and consequently may maintain trover. (ii) That the action well lay against the master who gives a credit to his apprentice and is answerable for his neglect. (iii) As to the value of the jewel, several of the trade were examined to prove what a jewel of the finest water that would fit the socket would be worth; and Sir John Pratt, CJ, directed the jury that, unless the defendant did produce the jewel and show it not to be of the finest water, they should presume the strongest against him and make the value of the best jewels the measure of their damages, which they accordingly did.

[139] [1558–1774] All ER Rep 121.

Court of Appeal, 22 March 2001[140] **2.58 (E&W)**

Costello v Chief Constable of Derbyshire Constabulary

RIGHT TO SUE (THIEF)

The stolen car

Possession of an object vests in the possessor a possessory title which is good against the world save as against anyone setting up or claiming under a better title. In the case of theft the title is frail, and likely to be of limited value, but it remains none the less a title to which the law affords protection.

Facts: In July 1996 the police lawfully seized a car in the belief that it was stolen. The car was then in the possession of the claimant, Costello, who was registered as its keeper. No criminal proceedings were brought against Costello. The statutory purposes for which the police held the car were exhausted on 5 January 1997, and Costello subsequently asked for its return. The police, however, continued to hold the car, contending that Costello had been aware that it had been stolen and that accordingly they were entitled to refuse his request, even though the true owner of the car was unknown. Costello brought proceedings against the police for the return of the car and damages for wrongful detention. The trial judge dismissed the claim. The Court of Appeal allowed the appeal.

Held: Possession means the same object and is entitled to the same legal protection whether or not it has been obtained lawfully or by theft or by other unlawful means. It vests in the possessor a possessory title which is good against the world save as against anyone setting up or claiming under a better title.

Judgment: Lightman J—Three general propositions of law are clearly established ... : (i) The fact of possession of a chattel of itself gives to the possessor a possessory title and the possessor is entitled to rely on such title without reference to the circumstances in which such possession was obtained: his entitlement to do so is not prejudiced by the fact that he obtained such possession unlawfully or under an illegal transaction. His claim can only be defeated by proof of a title superior to his possessory title. (ii) In the case of competing claims to ownership (in the case of personalty as in the case of realty), titles are relative and the issue falls to be determined by reference to the relative strengths of the two claims and the party with the better title (however frail it may be) is entitled to succeed. (iii) The statutory power of the police conferred by section 19 of the 1984 Act to seize goods and by section 22 of that Act to retain them so long as is necessary in all the circumstances places in suspension or temporarily divests all existing rights to possession over the period of the detention, but does not otherwise affect those rights or vest in the police any permanent entitlement to retain the property in the police. The limited right of the police to retain property for the statutory purpose and their obligation thereupon to return it to the 'owner' is unaffected by any perceived public policy consideration that the fruits of his criminal activities ought to be withheld from a criminal.

For completeness I should add two qualifications. First there is a limited statutory qualification to the second of these principles created by section 8 of the Torts (Interference with Goods) Act 1977 which permits a defendant in an action for wrongful interference to show in accordance with rules of court that a third party has a better right than the claimant as respect all or any part of the interest claimed by the claimant or in right of which he sues. It is clear from the terms of the Law Commission Report to which this section gives effect and the provisions

[140] [2001] EWCA Civ 381, [2001] 3 All ER 150, [2001] 1 WLR 1437, [2001] 2 Lloyd's Rep 216.

of the section for joinder of such third party as a party to the proceedings that the third party must be identified and that the purpose is to have the issue of his title and any claim he may have against the defendant resolved once and for all in the existing proceedings. ... This statutory provision has no application in this case since the police cannot identify any third party with a better title than the claimant. Secondly a party cannot assert a right to immediate possession against a defendant if his possession of the goods would be illegal or it would be illegal for the defendant to give him possession. ...

In my view on a review of the authorities, (save so far as legislation otherwise provides) as a matter of principle and authority possession means the same object and is entitled to the same legal protection whether or not it has been obtained lawfully or by theft or by other unlawful means. It vests in the possessor a possessory title which is good against the world save as against anyone setting up or claiming under a better title. In the case of a theft the title is frail, and of likely limited value (see eg *Rowland v Divall*), but none the less remains a title to which the law affords protection. ...

I accordingly hold that the claimant was entitled to the return of the Ford on 5 January 1997 and that he is entitled to an order for its delivery up and for damages for the wrongful failure to deliver it up to him since 5 January 1997 to be assessed by the district judge. The claim to exemplary damages made in the claimant's reply has no basis in law or fact, and accordingly the assessment is not to include any element of exemplary damages.

Keene LJ and Robert Walker LJ agreed.

Note

The torts of conversion and trespass deal with the protection of possession. According to the principle of relativity of title, the party in possession has a title good against any person who cannot show a better title. In the annotated judgment the court did not give in to the public policy deliberations and did not deny the unlawful possessor the right to sue in conversion. Traditionally, as shown in *Armory v Delamirie*, the wrongdoer was not allowed to plead that a third party had a better right to the object than the claimant (no defence of *jus tertii*). Section 8(1) of the Torts (Interference with Goods) Act 1977 abolished this rule. The annotated judgment reduced the application of this rule to cases where the third person can be named. As the police was not able to identify the lawful owner of the car, they were obliged to return it to the claimant. Whether or not this finding of the court can be upheld under the Proceeds of Crime Act 2002, however, is unclear and remains to be seen.[141]

[141] Markesinis and Deakin, above n 128, 487.

Court of Appeal, 26 June 1990[142] **2.59 (E&W)**

IBL Ltd v Coussens

ASSESSMENT OF DAMAGES

The director's cars

Damages awarded under section 3 of the 1977 Act for conversion as an alternative to the return of the goods are not to be arbitrarily assessed as at either the date of the conversion or the date of judgment but ought to be such as fairly compensated the owner for the loss of the goods.

Facts: The claimant company bought two cars, an Aston Martin and a Rolls Royce, for the use of the defendant while he was its chairman and managing director. In February 1988 the defendant was dismissed and he was given the option of returning the two cars or purchasing the Rolls Royce for £25,000 and the Aston Martin for £37,000. The defendant failed to return the cars or purchase them and on 19 February 1988 the company wrote to the defendant asking him to return the cars. When he still failed to do so the company issued a writ on 18 August 1988 seeking, inter alia, delivery up of the cars and damages for breach of contract and/or conversion. The master made an order under section 3(2)(a) of the Torts (Interference with Goods) Act 1977 requiring the defendant to give the claimant possession of the two cars within 28 days without the option of retaining the cars on payment of the assessed value thereof. The defendant appealed and before the hearing returned the Rolls Royce. The judge dismissed the appeal but varied the master's order by making an order under section 3(2)(b) of the 1977 Act giving the defendant the option of returning the Aston Martin or retaining both cars on payment of £62,000 and interest from 1 March 1988. The company appealed against that part of the order and contended, inter alia, (i) that £62,000 was not the assessed value of the cars but merely represented the figure at which it had been prepared to sell the cars to the defendant in February 1988, which offer had been refused, (ii) that the value of the cars, particularly the Aston Martin, had risen substantially since January 1988 and (iii) that there had been a continuing conversion of the cars and therefore the damages should be assessed, as in detinue, on the basis of the value of the goods at the date of judgment. The defendant contended (i) that the cars were converted in February 1988 when he declined to return them to the company and the value of the goods was to be assessed, in accordance with the normal rule in conversion, as at the date of the conversion, (ii) that £62,000 was the value of the cars at that time and (iii) that the company, had it wanted to replace the cars at that time, could have gone into the market to buy replacements at that price. The Court of Appeal allowed the appeal, set the order aside and remitted the matter to a master for damages to be assessed.

Held: Damages in tort are awarded by way of monetary compensation for loss or losses which a claimant has actually sustained, and the measure of damages awarded on this basis may vary infinitely according to the individual circumstances of any particular case.

Judgment: Neill LJ—In considering any award of damages in an action in tort it is necessary to bear in mind the general principle which was restated by Brandon LJ in *Brandeis Goldschmidt & Co v Western Transport Ltd* [1982] 1 All ER 28 at 31–32, [1981] QB 864 at 870:

> 'Damages in tort are awarded by way of monetary compensation for loss or losses which a plaintiff has actually sustained, and the measure of damages awarded on this basis may vary infinitely according to the individual circumstances of any particular case.'

In the Brandeis case the Court of Appeal substituted an award of £5 nominal damages in an action in detinue where the goods had been recovered and the

[142] [1991] 2 All ER 133.

plaintiffs had failed to show that they had suffered any quantifiable loss by reason of an adverse interference with their business operations.

At the same time it is necessary to bear in mind that where the goods are irreversibly converted and are not recovered the general rule is that the measure of damages is the value of the goods at the time of conversion. This general rule has been recently reaffirmed by the Privy Council in *BBMB Finance (Hong Kong) Ltd v Eda Holdings Ltd*.

An examination of the provisions of the 1977 Act in the light of the existing rules of the common law indicates that when making an award of damages under section 3 of the 1977 Act the court is faced with a number of competing considerations. These considerations include: (a) the fact that the tort of detinue has been abolished (b) the fact that the remedies now available for the tort of conversion (hitherto a purely personal action) have in effect extended the scope of the tort so that a proprietary claim can be asserted (c) the general rule that where goods have been irreversibly converted their value is assessed at the date of conversion. It may be noted, however, that even where goods are articles of ordinary commerce the damages may be assessed by reference to the cost of replacement goods if the cost has increased between the date of conversion and the date when the plaintiff, acting reasonably, ought to have obtained the replacement: cf *Emp Exportadora de Azucar v Industria Azucarera Nacional SA, The Playa Larga and Marble Islands* (d) the former general rule that in detinue the value of the goods detained was assessed at the date of judgment (e) the fact that after conversion the value of goods may fall instead of rise.

I have come to the conclusion that if one takes account of all these considerations and the fact that several different remedies are available under section 3 of the 1977 Act it is not possible, or indeed appropriate, to attempt to lay down any rule which is intended to be of universal application as to the date by reference to which the value of goods is to be assessed. The method of valuation and the date of valuation will depend on the circumstances.

I return to the facts of the present case where we are concerned with an order made under section 3(2)(b) of the 1977 Act.

In my judgment when the damages are assessed it will be necessary for the court to proceed as follows: (1) to decide whether if the cars had not been converted IBL would have kept and used the cars or have disposed of them elsewhere (2) to decide whether if the cars would have been kept and used IBL could and should have obtained replacement cars and, if so, when (3) if (a) the cars would have been kept and used and (b) it is decided either that IBL were under no obligation to obtain replacements or that they would have been unable to do so, the court will assess the damages in the light of those findings. It seems to me that the damages on this basis are likely to be assessed by reference to the value of the cars at the date of judgment, 3 November 1989. Such an assessment would take account of the value of the option which the judge's order gave to Mr Coussens (4) if the court decides that the cars would not have been kept and used or replacements could and should have been obtained it seems clear that an earlier date should be used for the calculation of the damages (5) to calculate any damages suffered by reason of the loss of the use of the cars between the date of conversion and the date ascertained in accordance with (3) and (4).

Accordingly, I would allow the appeal and order that the matter should be referred to a master for the calculation of the damages. It may be that in the light of the guidance which we have given the parties will be able to reach some agreement. If this is not possible I anticipate that evidence as well as argument will be necessary before the master.

Nicholls LJ delivered a concurring judgment and Butler-Sloss LJ agreed.

III. COMPARATIVE OVERVIEW

This chapter describes the protection of property rights in civil law (section I) and common law (section II). Although there are fundamental differences between civil law (section I) and common law (section II) there are also similarities between the approaches. This final section will make some comparative remarks to highlight similarities and differences among the civil law countries and between the civil law and the common law.

III.A CIVIL LAW AND COMMON LAW: THE FUNDAMENTAL DIFFERENCE

As regards the protection of property rights there are fundamental differences between civil law and common law countries. The civil law countries, based on the common heritage of Roman law, distinguish between ownership and possession and provide for specific actions for the protection of possession and ownership. These actions allow, apart from tort law instruments, for specific recovery and injunctive relief in case of dispossession and disturbance of possession.

In the common law, which has no comparable unitary concept of ownership, the protection of property rights is dealt with under the notion of the protection of possession. Contrary to the civil law, the common law did not develop such specified unitary property actions, but provides for the protection of property rights by tort law.

III.B PROTECTION OF PROPERTY RIGHTS IN CIVIL LAW

III.B.1 POSSESSION

The rules on the *protection of possession* in the civil law have primarily the function to enhance the preservation of peace. Hence their use does not depend on the legal entitlement towards the object, and in all three legal systems the defendant cannot raise objections based on the proprietary entitlement to the object.

The rules on possession of the French Code civile and the Austrian ABGB, which stem from the same time period, have much in common. In both countries the notion of possession extends to movable and immovable property and covers corporeal objects and claims which are incorporated in a corporeal title (eg bearer instruments). Although the wordings of both codes also allow the inclusion of mere claims, this broad view is contested. In particular, Austrian doctrine seeks to restrict the application of the rules on possession to claims which are transferable by legal commerce and allow for permanent use, which excludes family rights and personality rights, and also mere claims which aim at the performance of a singular act, such as the paying of a sum of money or the rendering of a service.

The German BGB primarily regulates the possession under the aspect of the protection of possession. Contrary to Austria and France, only corporeal objects can be the object of possession. German law provides for a comprehensive definition of the possessor which leaves no room for the distinction between possessor and detentor still existent in the two other countries. Accordingly, a person who holds an object for another is considered a detentor under French law, a detentor in Austria if he has no permanent right to the object and a possessor (*Fremdbesitzer*) in Germany. This difference is mitigated by the fact that since 1975 French law has granted possessory protection against interference by third parties also to the detentor of an immovable property.

All three countries provide specific actions for the protection of possession which in case of dispossession allow for recovery of possession and in case of disturbance of possession for the abatement of the interference or an injunction. The most complex picture is provided by French law where legal doctrine still preserves the traditional distinction between three possessory actions (*complainte*, *dénonciation de nouvel ouevre* and *l'action en réintégration*) with specific fields of application. Although the possessory actions have the aim to provide fast judicial protection against interference, all three countries provide that possessory claims can be secured by an interim injunction. A major difference, however, lies in the fact that in France possessory protection relates only to immovable property, while German and Austrian law do not differentiate between movable and immovable property.

French law does not explicitly discuss *self-help* of the possessor. Austrian, German and English law admit it under certain restricted preconditions. The most extensive regulation is provided by German law which distinguishes between two types of self-help, the defence against actual force (*Besitzwehr*) and the right of the possessor to recover the object immediately after the interference (*Besitzkehr*).

III.B.2 OWNERSHIP

Again based on Roman law, the civil law systems provide specific claims for the *protection of ownership* and the protection of limited property rights. The *rei vindicatio* gives the owner the right to assert his right and to claim the return of the object from any third party who holds the object without sufficient entitlement. The *rei vindicatio* applies to movable and immovable property alike. In France, however, its main importance lies with the protection of immovable property, as, according to Article 2276 Cciv, possession of a movable object usually establishes ownership. All three civil law systems provide for rules regarding the reciprocal rights and obligations of the possessor and the owner when the object is vindicated (damage claims, right to the enjoyment of fruits and reimbursement of expenses). The most complex rules in this regard are provided by German law (*Eigentümer-Besitzer-Verhältnis*).

In §1004 BGB German law explicitly provides for the right of the owner of an object to ward off impairment caused by third parties by way of judicial action (*actio negatoria*). It comprises the right to removal of actual interference (*Beseitigungsanspruch*) and the right to an injunction (*Unterlassungsanspruch*) in order to prevent the occurrence of future interference. For this, the owner must prove that the interference is either imminent or that there is the concrete danger that the interferer who already caused an interference will repeat the interference (*Wiederholungsgefahr*). Both claims cover movable and—in practice more important—immovable property and also apply to the holder of other property rights (servitude, the usufruct, the pledge, etc). These claims are also available under Austrian law, although the ABGB itself does not contain a general regulation concerning the *actio negatoria*. French law does not provide for a specific *actio negatoria*, but deals with such claims under the *rei vindicatio*.

All three countries have rules concerning the protection of a neighbour against excessive interference by noise and polluting substances. In Germany and Austria this is explicitly regulated in the respective code. In France it is provided by case law on the basis of tort law (*abus de droits* and *troubles de voisinage*).

III.C THE PROTECTION OF PROPERTY RIGHTS IN ENGLISH LAW

In England the protection of property rights is primarily achieved by tort law. Thus the primary remedy for the infringement of property rights is the attribution of damages. Apart from the more general tort of negligence which is available when property is harmed in breach of a duty of care, English law provides for several specific property related torts, the so-called *property torts*. Unlike negligence, these torts do not require that damage is shown or fault is established and allow the attribution of nominal damages. According to the fragmented approach of English tort law, the available instruments vary with respect to land and goods.

Interference with the *possession of land* may give rise to the torts of trespass to land and nuisance. *Trespass to land* is available where the defendant has entered the land without consent of the title-holder or actual possessor. *Nuisance* can be invoked in case of indirect interference, when pollutants (eg smoke, wastewater, smells, noises or other indirect interference) cause a disturbance to the use and enjoyment of land. The tort of nuisance apparently constitutes an equivalent to the instruments provided by the provisions of neighbourhood law in Austria and Germany. Like in France (*troubles de voisinage*), it is, however, part of tort law.

The right to exclusive *possession of goods* (movable property) is protected by the torts of *conversion* (also called trover) and *trespass to goods*. Conversion and trespass constitute legal instruments to protect the holder of movable property against misappropriation or other interference. In 1977, these historically developed torts were systematised by the Torts (Interference with Goods) Act 1977. The act formally abolished the historic tort of detinue, which was committed when the person who had actual control of an object refused to deliver it to the person with a better right to it, and transferred its contents to the tort of conversion. The torts of conversion and trespass only apply to corporeal property, not to objects in action.

Although English law has no comprehensive claim comparable to the *rei vindicatio* of the civil law, *specific recovery* is also obtainable. With regard to land, specific recovery can be obtained under the Civil Procedure Rules which provide for special rules on the recovery of possession of land (Summary Proceedings for Possession of Land and Interim Possession Order). The Summary Proceedings for Possession of Land contain a summary procedure by which a person entitled to possession of land can obtain a court order for possession against a person who entered into or remained in occupation without his consent. The Interim Possession Order is an expeditious form of summary proceeding enforced by criminal sanctions. Contrary to the civil law *rei vindicatio*, both remedies are also available against unknown persons. In respect of goods, specific recovery may be attributed as a tort law remedy upon discretion of the court (section 3(2) of the Tort (Interference with Goods) Act 1977).

The tort law remedies also comprise the right to claim for an *injunction*. The right to an injunction thus forms part of tort law and, contrary especially to German law (followed by Austrian law), has not evolved to a separate property law remedy. The main difference between the two concepts is the fact that in English law the granting of an injunction, like specific recovery, lies in the discretion of the courts.

CONCISE BIBLIOGRAPHY

Austria

P Apathy, *Die publizianische Klage* (Wien, Österreichische Staatsdruckerei, 1981).

F Kerschner and E Wagner in H Klang (ed), *Kommentar zum ABGB*, §§353–379, 3rd edn (Wien, Verlag Österreich, 2011) §364 at 134 *et seq*, §366 at 551 *et seq*.

Th Klicka in M Schwimann (ed), *Praxiskommentar ABGB*, vol II, 3rd edn (Wien, Orac, 2005) §339 at 59 *et seq*, §366 at 158 *et seq*.

G Kodek, *Die Besitzstörung* (Wien, Manz, 2002).

P Oberhammer in M Schwimann (ed), *Praxiskommentar ABGB*, vol II, 3rd edn (Wien, Orac, 2005) §364 at 95 *et seq*.

J Schey in H Klang (ed), *Kommentar zum ABGB*, vol II, 2nd edn (Wien, Österreichische Staatsdruckerei, 1950) §339 at 104 *et seq*.

K Spielbüchler in P Rummel (ed), *Kommentar zum ABGB*, vol I, 3rd edn (Wien, Manz, 2000) §339 at 493 *et seq*, §364 at 536 *et seq*, §366 at 573 *et seq*.

E Wagner, *Gesetzliche Unterlassungsansprüche im Zivilrecht* (Wien, Manz, 2006)

France

J Djoudi, 'Revendication' in P Raynoud (ed), *Encyclopédie Juridique, Répertoire de droit civil*, vol IX, 2nd edn (Paris, Dalloz, 1999).

J Djoudi, 'Action possessoire' in P Raynoud (ed), *Encyclopédie Juridique, Répertoire de droit civil*, vol I, 2nd edn (Paris, Dalloz, 2001).

G Goubeaux, 'L´extension de la protection possessoire au bénéfice des détenteurs' Défrenois 1976, 374.

V Grellière, 'La protection possessoire' AJPI 1982, 589.

Germany

C Baldus in FJ Säcker *et al* (eds), *Münchener Kommentar zum Bürgerlichen Gesetzbuch*, vol VI, 5th edn (München, Beck, 2009) §1004 at 1403 *et seq*.

P Bassenge in O Palandt (ed), *Bürgerliches Gesetzbuch*, 70th edn by P Bassenge *et al*

(München, Beck, 2011) §861 at 1423 *et seq*, §862 at 1424 *et seq*, §985 at 1522 *et seq*, §1004 at 1535 *et seq*.

F Baur, 'Der Beseitigungsanspruch nach §1004 BGB' (1961) 160 *AcP* 465.

E Bund in E Bund *et al* (eds), *J von Staudingers Kommentar zum Bürgerlichen Gesetzbuch: Einleitung zum Sachenrecht, §§854–882*, vol III (Berlin, Sellier de Gruyter, 2007) §861 at 167 *et seq*, §862 at 177 *et seq*.

H Dedek, 'Der Besitzschutz im römischen, deutschen und französischen Recht—gesellschaftliche Gründe dogmatischen Wandels' [1997] *ZEuP* 342.

KH Gursky in KH Gursky (ed), *J von Staudingers Kommentar zum Bürgerlichen Gesetzbuch, §§985–1011*, vol III (Berlin, Sellier de Gruyter, 2006) §985 at 9 *et seq*, §1004 at 464 *et seq*.

E Herrmann, *Der Störer nach §1004 BGB* (Berlin, Duncker & Humblot, 1987).

O Jauernig, 'Zivilrechtlicher Schutz des Grundeigentums in der neueren Rechtsentwicklung' [1986] *JZ* 605.

D Joost in FJ Säcker *et al* (eds), *Münchener Kommentar zum Bürgerlichen Gesetzbuch*, vol VI, 5th edn (München, Beck, 2009) §861 at 62 *et seq*, §862 at 66 *et seq*, §865 at 75 *et seq*.

F Klinkhammer, *Der Besitz als Gegenstand des Bereicherungsanspruchs* (Berlin, Duncker & Humblot, 1997).

O Mühl in Th Soergel (ed), *Kommentar zum Bürgerlichen Gesetzbuch*, vol VI, 12th edn by W Siebert *et al* (Stuttgart, Berlin and Köln, Kohlhammer, 1989) §985 at 591 *et seq*, §1004 at 666 *et seq*.

E Picker, *Der negatorische Beseitigungsanspruch*, 2nd edn (Bonn, Mohr Siebeck, 2007).

H Roth, 'Das Eigentümer-Besitzer-Verhältnis' [2003] *JuS* 937.

A Stadler in Th Soergel (ed), *Kommentar zum Bürgerlichen Gesetzbuch*, vol XIV, 13th edn by W Siebert et al (Stuttgart, Kohlhammer, 2002) §861 at 61 *et seq*, §862 at 63 *et seq*.

England

P Birks 'Personal Property: Proprietory Rights and Remedies' KLJ 2000, 1–18.

JA Jolowicz, 'Damages in Equity—A Study of Lord Cairns'Act' [1975] CLJ 224–252.

B Markesinis and S Deakin, *Markesinis and Deakin's Tort Law*, 6th edn (New York, Oxford University Press, 2008) 483–564.

WVH Rogers, *Winfield and Jolowicz on Tort*, 18th edn (London, Sweet & Maxwell, 2010) 619–725, 745–784.

W Swadling 'Unjust delivery' in A Burrows and A Rodger (eds), *Mapping the Law. Essays in memory of Peter Birks* (Oxford, Oxford University Press, 2006) 277–298.

A Tettenborn 'Trust property and conversion: An equitable confusion' [1996] CLJ 36–42.

CHAPTER THREE
TYPES OF PROPERTY RIGHTS—IMMOVABLES AND MOVABLES (GOODS)

*Bram Akkermans and William Swadling**

This chapter deals with the second of the six essential questions: what are property rights? The chapter offers an overview of the property rights available in German, French, Dutch and English law. The overview can be provided because of the existence of the principle of *numerus clausus* that was dealt with in Chapter 1, the principle that helps to decide which rights are personal and which are proprietary. The chapter also deals with the most important borderline cases between personal and property rights.

Introductory Note

This chapter deals with the property rights over immovables and movables (goods) recognised by the major civil and common law systems. The first section deals with the civil law, the second with the common law. As will be seen, both operate a closed system of property rights.[1]

The civil law part of this chapter approaches the list of property rights from a view that assumes a basic similarity. Because the main civil law systems share a historical basis in Roman law and, to some extent, in the development of the *ius commune* in the Middle Ages, the property rights these systems use and recognise are broadly the same. Where a system does recognise a distinct property right, it is dealt with separately or a specific difference is noted.

* Bram Akkermans wrote the section on civil law, William Swadling wrote the section on common law. The comparative notes are a combined effort.

[1] Above, Chapter 1.

The common law part of this chapter divides the treatment of the various property rights between land and goods. Land has always been treated separately in English law, not least because goods were never subject to the feudal system which still obtains, albeit in an attenuated form, in English land law.

The chapter concludes with comparative remarks underlining the differences and similarities between the civil and the common law.

I. CIVIL LAW

Introductory Notes

Three civil law systems are described in this section: France, Germany and the Netherlands. French and German law are examples of the two major civil law traditions in Europe, the Romanist and Germanic traditions. The Netherlands, with its new Civil Code of 1992, takes an intermediate position between these two.[2]

This chapter is concerned with property rights in respect of immovables, mainly land and buildings or constructions on land, and property rights in respect of movables. As we saw in Chapter 1, civilian systems use a *numerus clausus* of property rights. The result is that the number and, to a certain extent, the content of the available property rights are defined by legislation or, in some exceptional cases, by case law. Any other right cannot be a property right and thus can only form part of the law of obligations. And because the lease has never formed part of the civilian *numerus clausus*, it necessarily falls under the law of obligations. As we will see, this provides a major difference between the civil and the common law, and may be the reason why civilian systems rely so heavily on rights of usufruct. Moreover, the proprietary status of the lease is the subject of much debate.[3]

When the systems of property law in civil law systems were created, immovables, ie land, were the most important resource. Movables were of less value and therefore not as extensively dealt with as land. However, in the civil law, many property law concepts apply to both movables and immovables. When, therefore, the law needed to be clarified, most cases dealt with immovables. However, the rules laid down by these cases are equally applicable to movables.

This section describes the main elements of the various property rights. Each entitles the right-holder to use and enjoy an object to some degree. However, in certain situations property rights can also be used to secure performance of an obligation, usually the payment of a debt.[4] These rights, known as security rights, are mentioned only briefly in this chapter, receiving a detailed treatment in the chapter on security rights.

Civil law systems recognise the right of ownership, defined as the most extensive entitlement a person can have with regard to an object. From this right of owner-

[2] See K Zweigert and H Kötz, *Introduction to Comparative Law*, trans Tony Weir, 3rd rev edn (Oxford, Clarendon Press, 1998) 63 *et seq*.

[3] Below, I.I.2.

[4] In other words, the security right then secures a claim; below Chapter 5.

ship, other property rights are derived. These divide into three main groups: rights of real servitude; rights of personal servitude; and rights of *emphyteusis* and superficies. However, each legal system also recognises some additional property rights. These include the construction lease in French law,[5] the limited personal servitude in German law[6] and the apartment right in Dutch law.[7]

The most extensive property right, the right of ownership, will be dealt with first, after which we will examine servitudes, both real[8] and personal,[9] the right of *emphyteusis*,[10] the right of superficies[11] and apartment rights.[12] Finally, some borderline cases will be discussed.[13]

I.A OWNERSHIP

Introductory Notes

(a) The right of ownership functions as the starting point for all civil law property law systems. It is this right which has fascinated lawyers, philosophers and theologians throughout time, and is a concept which has been subjected to much theoretical analysis. Unlike common law, civilian systems use a doctrinal concept of ownership to explain the system of property law. This doctrinal basis derives mainly from academic writings, though it at times surfaces, or can be deduced from, case law. In order to understand the doctrinal bases, this section first deals with the foundations of the right of ownership, after which the various practical applications of the right of ownership are examined.

(b) The right of ownership is the most extensive property right known to civil law systems. For that reason, the rights of the owner are also the most extensive. The rights of the owner can be seen from two different perspectives.[14] The first concerns the relationship of the owner towards the object owned. Each of the civilian systems deals with this issue in their definition of the right of ownership.

The German definition in §903 BGB allows the owner to use the object as he thinks fit. Ownership is seen as an indivisible power over an object.[15] The right of

[5] Below, I.D.4.
[6] Below, I.C.4.
[7] Below, I.F.3.
[8] Below, IB.
[9] Below, I.C.
[10] Below, I.D.
[11] Below, I.E.
[12] Below, I.F.
[13] Below, I.I.
[14] German doctrine distinguishes a positive and a negative side of the right of ownership. See BJH Windscheid and Th Kipp, *Lehrbuch Des Pandektenrechts—I*, 9th with BGB compared edn (Frankfurt am Main, Literarische Anstalt Rütten & Loenig, 1906) 856–57; M Wolf, *Sachenrecht*, 21st edn (München, Verlag CH Beck, 2005) 24–25; KH Schwab and H Prütting, *Sachenrecht. Ein Studienbuch*, 31st edn (München, Verlag CH Beck, 2003) 138–39; K Müller, *Sachenrecht*, 4th rev edn (Köln,Berlin,Bonn and München, Carl Heymanns Verlag KG, 1997) 97–99.
[15] W Wiegand, 'Die Entwicklung Des Sachenrechts', *Archiv für die civilistische Praxis,* 190. Band (1990) 112, at 117; EB Rank-Berenschot, *Over de Scheidslijn tussen Goederen- en Verbintenissenrecht* (Deventer, Kluwer, 1992) 243.

ownership cannot therefore be separated out into more limited types of ownership. Instead, another person holding a property right over the same asset will hold it as a *ius in re aliena* (right in the land of another) or limited property right, and not as an owner. In such a case, the right of ownership remains whole, though with another property right burdening it.

German law offers one complication to this system in that, unlike other civil law systems, it allows a person to have some limited property rights on his own object of ownership.[16] In such a situation, which can only concern a property right on an immovable, a person is both owner and holder of a limited property right over the same object at the same time.

The French doctrine on ownership distinguishes three powers of the owner: the right to use (*usus*), the right to enjoy, particularly the fruits (*fructus*), and the right to alienate (*abusus*). This division, which is derived from the Glossators, is still used today to explain the content of the right of ownership.[17] These three elements can be seen in Article 544 Cciv. The right of ownership is the right to enjoy, which should be read as to include the right to use, and the right to transfer the right of ownership to someone else or to establish a limited property right.[18] So, for example, it is possible to grant a right of usufruct which allows its holder the use the object and to take its fruits.[19]

The Dutch concept of ownership should be understood in the light of the French doctrine. The old Dutch Civil Code defined ownership in an almost identical way to Article 544 Cciv, and included the division into *usus*, *fructus* and *abusus*.[20] The new definition of ownership in Article 5:2 BW focuses more on the nature of the right than on the powers of the owner. Nevertheless the powers of the owner remain of importance and take a central place in doctrinal discussions of the right of ownership.[21]

(c) The second perspective concerns the rights of the owner against third parties, in other words, the right of the owner to stop others interfering with the object of his ownership. The various definitions of the right of ownership also focus on

[16] §889 BGB: see M Wolff and L Raiser, *Sachenrecht. Ein Lehrbuch*, 10th edn (Tübingen: JCB Mohr (Paul Sibeck) 1957) 128; Schwab and Prütting, above n 14, 10.

[17] PJ Carbonnier, *Droit Civil 3/Les Biens: Monnaie, Immeubles, Meubles*, 19th edn (Paris, Presses Universitaires de France (PUF) 2000) 128–31; P Jourdain, G Marty and P Raynaud, *Les Biens* (Paris, Dalloz, 1995) 46.

[18] C Demolombe, *Traité de la distinction des biens; de la propriéte; de l'usufruit de l'usage et de l'habitation; Tome Premier*, 4th edn (Paris, Auguste Durand/L Hachette et Cie, 1870) n 543 at 462; Jourdain, Marty and Raynaud, above n 17, 47; F Terré and Ph Simler, *Droit Civil—Les Biens*, 5th edn (Paris, Dalloz, 1998) 93–98; Ph Malaurie and L Aynès, *Les Biens* (Droit Civil; Paris, Defrénois, 2003) 111–13; Carbonnier, above n 17, 128–31; F Chabas, *Biens: Droit de Propriété et ses Démembrements*, tome 2, 8th edn (Paris, Montchrestien, 1994) 84–85.

[19] Art 543 Cciv, §1030 BGB and Art 3:201 BW.

[20] Art 625 Old BW stated: 'eigendom is het regt om van eene zaak het vrij genot the hebben en daarover op de volstrekste wijze te beschikken, mits men er geen gebruik van make, strijdende tegen de wetten of de openbare verordeningen, daargesteld door zoodanige magt, die daartoe volgens de Grondwet, de bevoegdheid heeft, en mits men aan de regten van anderen geen hinder toebrenge; alles behoudens de onteigening ten algemeenen nutte tegen behoorlijke schadeloosstelling, ingevolge de Grondwet.'

[21] The old Dutch Civil Code also allowed, after the French example, ownership of incorporeal objects: C Asser *et al*, *Goederenrecht 3—II Zakelijke Rechten*, 14th edn (Deventer, Kluwer, 2002) 20 *et seq.*

this right of an owner. There are basically two possible remedies available against those who interfere, either an order for the return of the object itself, known as a vindication, or the award of an injunction against a third party restraining them from interfering with the object. The latter remedy is commonly known as the *actio negatoria*.[22] This second perspective, being concerned with protection of the right of ownership, was dealt with in Chapter 2.[23]

I.A.1 LEGISLATION ON OWNERSHIP

Code civil **3.1. (FR)**

Article 544 Ownership is the right to enjoy and dispose of objects in the most complete manner, provided they are not used in a way prohibited by statutes or regulations.

Bürgerliches Gesetzbuch **3.2 (DE)**

§903 The owner of a corporeal object can, when this does not interfere with the law or other rights of third parties, do with the object what he wishes and exclude others from interfering. The owner of an animal must, in the exercise of his powers, obey the special provisions for the protection of animals.

Burgerlijk Wetboek **3.3 (NL)**

Article 5:1 (1) Ownership is the most extensive right which a person can have in a corporeal object. (2) To the exclusion of all others, the owner is free to use the object provided that this use does not violate the rights of others and that it respects the limitations based upon statutory rules and rules of unwritten law.
(3) Without prejudice to the rights of others, the owner of the object becomes owner of the fruits the object produces once separated.

Presentation to the legislative body, and clarification of the motives by Portalis[24] **3.4 (FR)**

Also you will need to hurry, lawmakers, to devote your votes to the grand principle of ownership, presented in the Act as *the right to enjoy and dispose of objects in the most complete manner*. However, as man lives in society and under the law, he cannot have the right to violate laws that govern society.

It is well-arranged legislation that regulates the exercise of the right to ownership in the way one regulates the exercise of all other rights. Independence is another

[22] The *actio negatoria* was a Roman law action. On this action see R Feenstra, *Romeinsrechtelijke Grondslagen van het Nederlands Privaatrecht*, 5th edn (Leiden, EJ Bril/Universitaire Pers Leiden, 1990) 90–91; M Kaser and R Knütel, *Römisches Privatrecht*, 17th renewed and extended edn (München, CH Beck, 2003) 171. See above, Chapter 2.

[23] Above, Chapter 2.

[24] *Présentation au corps législatif, et exposé des motifs*, par M Portalis in PA Fenet, *Recueil Complet Des Travaux Préparatoires Du Code Civil, Tome 11* (Osnabrück, Otto Zeller, 1968) 116–17.

matter, as is freedom. One does not achieve true freedom but through the sacrifice of independence.

The people that live together in the state of nature are independent, but not free. They are always forcing or being forced. Citizens are free without being independent, because they are subjected to the laws that protect them against the others and against themselves.

True freedom consists of a sensible balance of rights and individual powers with the common good. When everyone can do as he pleases, he can do that which hinders another; he can do that which hinders the many. The prerogative of each individual would inescapably promote the misfortune of all.

So we need laws to govern actions in respect to the use of objects, as they exist to govern those that are in respect to the use of personal means.

We must be free with the laws, and never against them. Therefore, although we recognise the right of the owner to enjoy and dispose of his ownership in the most complete manner, we have added, *provided it is not used in a manner prohibited by law or by regulation.*

Explanation to the draft of a Civil Code for the German Nation, Book III[25] **3.5 (DE)**

The draft wants not so much to provide a definition, but more to establish the actual content of the rights that is at the disposal of the owner. The positive side of this is not as important as the negative side, namely that the right of the owner to exclude others from his use and enjoyment cannot be restricted to one limitation. The separate powers of the owner are, even without a general provision, derived from the provisions on the protection of ownership and the provisions on the way in which the owner may dispose of his right; they cannot be described exhaustively; the exercise of making such an exhaustive list is not necessary because the right of ownership is not a sum of powers. Because of that the right of ownership cannot be fragmented in such as way that the powers contained in ownership are attributed to one and another person, and the typical character of the right of ownership is maintained by both. The acceptance of the right of co-ownership is not affected by this.

TM Art 5.1.1 Parliamentary History, Book 5[26] **3.6 (NL)**

TM. In the general description, which is provided in the first subsection, it is held that ownership is the most comprehensive right that a person can have in respect to a corporeal object. 'Corporeal objects' are, in the terminology of the draft 'tangible material things, which are suitable for possesion' (art 3.1.1). Thus, a right on other things does not fall under the concept of ownership …

When the second subsection holds that the owner is entitled to use the corporeal object 'at his own discretion', this does not imply that the draft takes an individualistic concept of ownership as its starting point. In all known legal systems the

[25] *Motive zu dem Entwurfe eines Bürgerlichen Gesetzbuches für das Deutsche Reich—Sachenrecht*, vol III (Berlin, Verlag von J. Guttentag, 1888) 262.

[26] CJ Van Zeben and JW Du Pon, *Boek 5—Zakelijke Rechten, Parlementaire Geschiedenis Van Het Nieuwe Burgerlijk Wetboek* (Deventer, Kluwer, 1981) 18–19.

legal-technical basic principle is that the owner is free to do with the object as he pleases; to what extent the owner in a certain legal system, in exercising his right of ownership, has to comply with a social purpose, depends on the restrictions that have been imposed on him in respect to the interest of other persons and the common good.

Regarding all three powers mentioned in the second subsection, the owner may be limited in exercising these powers by law and by the rights of others.

Notes

(1) The concept of ownership forms the foundation of the legal systems of France, Germany and the Netherlands. Each of these systems has received the Roman law concept of *dominium* and given it a central place in their legal system.[27] However, not only do the definitions differ greatly, but also the way in which the right of ownership is approached in legal literature and case law. French and Dutch law focus on the content of the right of ownership as the most complete and extensive right available, whereas German law is much more focused on the powers of the owner, or, in other words on the actions the owner may take to protect his right of ownership.

The modern definitions of ownership go back to those of the medieval scholar Bartolus, who said that ownership is 'the right in a corporeal object to have it completely at ones disposal, unless forbidden by law'.[28] This definition of Bartolus, specifically the part stating 'completely at one's disposal', focuses on the powers of the owner. However, the product of Bartolus' definition is not an unlimited power on the part of the owner.[29] In fact, Bartolus recognised three different types of ownership, *dominium directum* (direct ownership), *dominium utile* (ownership to use) and quasi-*dominium* (quasi-ownership), which makes it difficult to explain the powers of one owner as unlimited.[30] So, for example, the *dominium directum* of a feudal lord and the *dominium utile* of a feudal tenant or vassal would be in respect of the same plot of land.[31]

The definition in the French Civil Code of a right of ownership as a right to enjoy and to dispose of objects in the most complete manner should be seen as a

[27] See also §364(1) ABGB.

[28] … *ius in re corporali perfecte disponendi nisi lege prohibeatur*, quote and translation from EJH Schrage, '*Ius in Re Corporali Perfecte Disponendi*: Property from Bartolus to the New Dutch Civil Code of 1992' in GE van Maanen and AJ van der Walt (eds), *Property Law on the Threshold of the 21st Century* (Antwerpen, MAKLU, 1996) 35–67, at 43.

[29] See, inter alia, AJ van der Walt, 'Bartolus se omkrywing van dominium an die interpretasis daarvan sedert die vyftiende eeu' [1986] *Tydskrif vir hedendaagse Romeins-Hollandse reg* 305–21 (in Afrikaans); AJ van der Walt and D Kleyn, 'Duplex Dominium: The History and Significance of the Concept of Divided Ownership' in DP Visser (ed), *Essays on the History of Law* (Cape Town, Juta & Co, 1989); H Coing, 'Zur Eigentumslehre des Bartulus', *Zeitschrift der Savigny-Stiftung für Rechtsgeschichte, Romanistische Abteilung,* 70. Band (1953) 348–71.

[30] For a modern discussion on the division of ownership, see D Heirbaut, 'Feudal Law: The Real *Ius Commune* of Property in Europe, or: Should we Reintroduce *Duplex Dominium*' (2003) 3 *European Review of Private Law* 301–20. See also Schrage, above n 28, 44.

[31] On the history and functioning of the feudal system, see KE Digby and WM Harrison, *An Introduction to the History of the Law of Real Property*, 5th edn (Oxford, Clarendon Press, 1897); H Coing, *Europäisches Privatrecht, Band I* (München, CH Beck'sche Verlagsbuchhandlung, 1985).

development from Bartolus' definition,[32] as should the object of ownership. As to the latter, Bartolus said: 'I ask what property might be. And it can be termed in the widest sense for every incorporeal right.'[33]

The German definition of ownership can also be seen as an evolution from that of Bartolus.[34] At its heart is the conception of ownership advocated by, inter alia, von Savigny: the right of ownership is considered the most absolute and total power over a corporeal object.[35] Objects other than corporeal objects (*Sache*) are excluded from the scope of property rights. Under this approach, ownership is seen as an indivisible power over corporeal objects.[36]

An echo of Bartolus can also be seen in the Dutch definition of ownership.[37] That contained in the old Civil Code closely resembled the French definition. Although the definition in the new BW moves away from an emphasis on the powers of the owner and focuses more on the nature of the right itself, in content the powers of the owner remain of importance and are further qualified in section 2 of Article 5:1 BW. Furthermore, under the influence of German law, the concept of ownership in Dutch law is restricted to corporeal objects (*zaak*).[38]

(2) The explanatory memoranda also illustrate that French, German and Dutch law share common views on the position of ownership in the legal system, the meaning of the 'most comprehensive' nature of the right, and, connected with that, the rights and powers of the owner.

(3) A final issue is the nature of the right of ownership with respect to the object on which it is established. In modern doctrine, the right of ownership is unitary. The result is that the right of ownership remains the same, regardless of whether it is established on a movable, immovable or even, in the case of French law, on an incorporeal object. Nevertheless, different rules apply to rights of ownership on immovable objects than movable objects. With respect to immovables, legal systems generally require more amounts of publication than in case of movables.[39]

[32] See A Bürge, *Das Französische Privatrecht im 19 Jahrhundert. Zwischen Tradition und Pandektenwissenschaft, Liberalismus und Etatismus* (Frankfurt am Main, Vittorio Klostermann, 1991) 3–63; Schrage, above n 28, 35–67, at 45; GCJJ Van Den Bergh, *Eigendom. Grepen uit de Geschiedenis van een Omstreden Begrip*, 2nd edn (Deventer, Kluwer, 1988) 39–50.

[33] Bartolus on D 41,2,17 (4); see Schrage, above n 28, 35–67, at 44.

[34] However, the restriction of the right of ownership to corporeal objects does not follow from the definition provided by Bartolus. W Wiegand, 'Zur Theoretischen Begründung der Boedenmobilisierung in Der Rechtswissenschaft: Der Abstracte Eigentumsbegriff', in H Coing and W Wilhelm (eds), *Wissenschaft und Kodification des Privatrechts im 19 Jahrhundert—III Die Rechtliche und Wirtschaftliche Entwicklung Des Grundeigentums und Grundkredits* (Frankfurt am Main, Vittorio Klostermann, 1976) 118–57, at 121.

[35] Wiegand, above n 15, 117; FK von Savigny, *System Des Heutigen Römischien Rechts*, vol 1 (Aalen, Scienta Verlag, 1981) §53, at 338 *et seq.*

[36] Wiegand, above n 15, at 117; Rank-Berenschot, above n 15, 243.

[37] The article in the Dutch Civil Code from 1838 resembled Article 544 Cciv and also spoke of 'to dispose in the most complete manner'.

[38] Therefore, like the German definition, the restriction to corporeal objects does not follow from Bartolus' definition. See Art 5:1 BW.

[39] Below, Chapter 8, II.

I.A.2 'MOST COMPREHENSIVE' NATURE OF THE RIGHT OF OWNERSHIP

Introductory Notes

(a) If the right of ownership is the most comprehensive right a person can have over an object, there is no better entitlement a person can have than being owner. The most comprehensive right means that the content of the right of ownership is such that the owner may do with the object as he wishes. In civil law case law the most comprehensive nature of the right of ownership as such is not dealt with. Instead, legal scholarship derives this theoretical approach from case law which limits the rights of the owner.

(b) As a general principle, it is possible to say that the right of ownership only stops where the rights of another begin. When the right of ownership interferes with other rights, in particular with other rights of ownership, legal systems provide limitations on the powers of the owner. Most of these limitations are imposed through the abuse of rights doctrine, of which this section will provide some examples.

OLG Düsseldorf, 4 September 2000[40] **3.7 (DE)**

MOST COMPREHENSIVE NATURE OF THE RIGHT OF OWNERSHIP

The forest road

The owner cannot, if he accepts the general use of part of his land as a road, refuse the access of others.

Facts: The claimants owned a piece of land and a house in a forest. The defendants owned two other pieces of land, which were situated such that the house of the claimants could only be reached through a public road running between the two pieces of the defendants' land. At some point in the past, the municipality had widened the road, using part of the defendants' land. Therefore the road ran over public, but also privately owned, land. The parties were in dispute over the use of another plot of land, and as a result, the defendants placed obstructions preventing anyone but themselves from reaching the road leading to the claimants' house.

The claimants sought the removal of the obstructions. At issue was the question whether the actions of the defendants constituted an abuse of their right of ownership.

Held: The court allowed the claim, holding that the actions by the defendants constituted an abuse of right under §226 BGB because they could only be interpreted as intended to cause damage to the claimants.

Judgment: A claim according to §226 BGB requires objectively that the exercise of a legal right has no other purpose than to cause damage on another.

The Senate is convinced that the installation of the steel poles and the subsequent depositing of the boulders on the opposite part of the road served no other purpose than to cut off the claimant's access with his passenger car as well as the access for supply vehicles to his piece of land, thereby inflicting significant disadvantage on him. …

The defendants admittedly have placed the corresponding obstacles on their land. According to §903 BGB, the owner is, in principle, entitled to designate who may use his piece of land; if necessary he may prevent third parties from any interfer-

[40] NJW-RR 2001, 162.

ence. The defendants make parts of their pieces of land available for the use by adjacent owners and hikers for decades. ... The installation of the contested steel poles, however, did not serve the purpose of returning back to an exclusively used piece of land that which before had been accessible to the common public.As the Senate had already recognised ... the defendants are not hindered by §226 BGB to make optimal use of their land and to, by moving the boulders, protect the border of their land with the public road.

Cour de cassation Req, 3 August 1915[41] **3.8 (FR)**

Coquerel v Clément-Bayard

MOST COMPREHENSIVE NATURE OF THE RIGHT OF OWNERSHIP

The 15-metre 'spiked' wall

The powers of the owner and therefore the most comprehensive nature of the right of ownership do not go as far as to allow the owner to use his ownership purely to cause a nuisance to his neighbour.

Facts: A person named Clément-Bayard built a hangar for airships on his land. Because of a dispute between himself and his neighbour, Coquerel, the latter placed a 15-metre-wide, 10-metre-high wooden frame on the border of his land facing the entrance to the hangar to hinder the airships on their way into and out of the hanger. At the top of the frame, Coquerel placed four iron spikes, each of 2–3 metres in length. The wooden frame had no other function than to obstruct Clément-Bayard's use of the hangar. When one of his airships was damaged, Clément-Bayard sought damages based on an abuse of rights. Against an affirmative decision at first instance ordering Coquerel to remove the frame and spikes, he appealed in cassation. Clément-Bayard, the defendant in cassation, argued in defence that Coquerel had abused his right of ownership.

Held: That building a wall for the sole purpose of causing a nuisance to a neighbour is an abuse of the right of ownership. The claimant had therefore to remove the spikes.

Judgment: Considering, that it follows from the contested judgment that Coquerel has placed on his land, adjoining that of Clément-Bayard, a wooden framework of 10 metres in height on which iron spikes are placed; that this structure did not serve any purpose for the exploitation of the land of Coquerel and that it had not been constructed but for the sole objective of causing a nuisance to Clément-Bayard, ... that, given such factual circumstances, it could be held in the judgment that Coquerel had abused his right, and, on the one hand, to order him to pay compensation for the damage caused to an airship of Clément-Bayard, on the other hand, to order the removal of the iron spikes from the wooden framework.

[41] DP 1917.1.79.

Hoge Raad, 13 March 1936[42] **3.9 (NL)**

Stolk v Van der Goes

MOST COMPREHENSIVE NATURE OF THE RIGHT OF OWNERSHIP

Water tower of 'Berg en Dal'

The abuse-of-rights doctrine does not apply simply because the act of an owner could have been conducted in such a way as to cause less damage.

Facts: Because of a dispute over the use of a path, Stolk placed on his land two poles with canvas stretched between them so as to block the view of Van der Goes, his neighbour. These had to be removed after a court held that their placement constituted an abuse of rights by Stolk. However, two weeks later, Stolk began construction of a water tower, which also obstructed the view of the Van der Goes. Although designed to water the garden of Stolk, it was not connected to any water supply. A court order was then made ordering Stolk to take down the tower on the ground that its construction constituted an abuse of rights. Stolk thereupon connected the tower to a water supply. Van der Goes again sought its removal on the same ground. This time, however, the court of first instance refused to accept the abuse-of-rights argument. Its decision was, however, overturned by the court of appeal, which held that Stolk could have constructed the tower anywhere on his land, not just in that place obstructing the defendant's view, and that therefore Stolk's actions constituted an abuse of rights. Against this decision Stolk appealed in cassation claiming the water tower now served a purpose for the land.

Held: That because the tower might be necessary for the use of the defendant's land, it was sufficient to show that it could have been placed elsewhere on the land. The case was referred back to the court of appeal to decide whether there were other grounds on which this might be held to be an abuse of rights.

Judgment: Considering, that the court of appeal, not deciding on these matters in dispute but only announcing that it questions the usefulness of the tower in respect to the objective pursued by Stolk, is of the opinion that the claimant did not exercise the due care towards his neighbour required from him in society by placing the tower exactly in this place, while his land fully allows the tower to be placed in such a way that it does not obstruct the view of van der Goes; that the grievance presented by the claimant correctly holds that the court of appeal has violated Art 1401 of the Dutch Civil Code, because when several ways of exercising a right can be undertaken, one is not obliged—irrespective of other considerations which could determine the choice—to refrain from a certain way of acting just because this could be disadvantageous—without violating any particular right of this person—for a third person, whereas another way of acting would not have this negative effect.

Baur, Baur and Stürner, Property Law, 562 **3.10 (DE)**

I. In respect of ownership of movable objects, the possiblity of general conflicts and conflicts with the rights of others are less likely than in respect to the ownership of land; whose effects are so strong, that—as we know—the description of the content of the right (almost naturally) also includes gereral limitations and the limits and limitations in respect of neighbours. Contrary to that, the use of the right of ownership on movable objects takes place—to use a catchphrase—in the 'intimate spheres' of the owner, the rights of specific others or all others are not really effected by its

[42] NJ 1936, 415.

use. When this is the case, the conflict of interests is not altogether clear, and is, therefore, much more difficult to solve.

Demolombe, Course, treatise on the differentiation of things; of ownership; of usufruct, use and habitation, no 544–45[43] **3.11 (FR)**

To let it decline, and even to degrade or to destroy it. 'For example,' says Pothier, 'the owner of a good piece of tillable earth has the right, as he sees fit, to turn it into untilled land, which only serves for the grazing of cattle; like the owner of a painting, has the right to cover it with a colour in order to erase it, or the owner of a book who has the right to throw it onto the fire, if that seems right to him, or to tear it up' (About Ownership, n 5).

The owner is in fact free to commit these kinds of excessive acts in respect to the object.

But he nevertheless elicits remarks that these excessive acts, which are actually the inevitable consequence of his most comprehensive right of ownership, nevertheless do not, by themselves, constitute a manner of exercising this right, which the laws recognise and approve of.

The Roman word *abuti* only expressed … the idea of *disposal*, not of *destruction…*

In this regard, the French word *abuser*, which is a synonym for misuse, does not at all represent the Roman concept of the word *abuti*; and we can certainly proclaim among us this maxim: that it touches upon the interest of society, that private persons properly govern their wealth instead of misusing it. We even know that in cases of this kind of excess, the owner could either, according to the circumstances, be barred, or brought before a judicial assembly …

But in the end, one must recognise that ownership, being the most comprehensive right, confers, if not in law, then at least necessarily in fact, on the owner, the right to misuse his object; for it would not be the most comprehensive without that; and every preventive restriction, by infringing the right to ownership itself, would thus have entailed much more of a danger than an advantage.

MVA II Art 5.1.3. Parlimentary History, Book 5[44] **3.12 (NL)**

[In discussing Article 5:3 BW, which allows an owner to exclude others from his enjoyment of the object of his ownership, the legislative commission examines the meaning of the word 'use' in Article 5:1 (2) BW]

However, concerning the editorial objections rightfully raised by the Commission against the term 'to avail oneself of', for the amended draft, the present writer has given preference to the expression 'that another makes use of the object in any way'. This expression, as well as the one in the new version of Article 1 subsection 2, in which 'to make use of' is mentioned, refers to its use in the broadest sense of the word, including to use up, to damage, to alter, etc.

[43] Demolombe, above n 18, 464–65.

[44] CJ Van Zeben and JW Du Pon, *Boek 5—Zakelijke Rechten, Parlementaire Geschiedenis van het nieuwe Burgerlijk Wetboek* (Deventer, Kluwer, 1981) 69.

Notes

(1) Although the basic starting point of all civil law systems is that the owner is free to do with the object under his ownership as he wishes, all legal systems recognise limits. So, for example, in French law, where the Civil Code describes the right of ownership as including the power to dispose of an object in the most complete manner, a fierce debate has been conducted as to the question of how unlimited the right of ownership really is.[45]

The final part of Article 544 Cciv provides for limitations on the powers of the owner. These include limitations that the drafters of the Civil Code, although influenced by the natural law doctrine of unlimited powers of the owner, had foreseen, but also limitations imposed, particularly also by case law, in the course of the nineteenth and twentieth centuries.[46] In the second half of the nineteenth century, both the French legislature and the courts started to impose general restrictions on the powers of the owner by making use of the doctrine of abuse of rights (*abus de droit*).[47] The French case cited above is a good example of the doctrine. If a party acts with the sole intent of causing a nuisance to his neighbour, this will constitute an abuse of his right of ownership.

The abuse-of-rights jurisprudence is particularly relevant in the area of the law concerning the relations between neighbours. Damage caused by the act of the owner, through use, enjoyment or disposal, with intent to disadvantage another without any benefit for the owner can constitute an abuse of the right of ownership and will lead to an obligation to remove or stop the disturbance to the third party and pay damages.[48]

(2) The rights of the owner are interpreted so as to give the owner maximum freedom. This maximum freedom of the owner should not be limited easily. There-

[45] Req 12 July 1905, DP 109.1.141, S 1907.1.273; K-S Zachariae, G Massé and Ch Vergé, *Le Droit Civil Français*, tome 2 (Paris, Auguste Durand, 1855) 55 *et seq*; Aubry et al, *Cours de droit civil Français d'après la méthode de Zachariae*, tome 2 (Paris, Imprimerie et librairie générale de jurisprudence, 1897) 255–56; G Baudry-Lacantinerie and M Chauveau, *Traité théorique et pratique de droit civil. Des Biens*, tome 6, 3rd edn (Paris, Librarie de la société recueil J-B Sirey et du journal du palais, 1905) 152; Demolombe, above n 18, 462 *et seq*. On these authors see also Bürge, above n 32, 29, 42–43, 55; P Crocq, *Propriété et Garantie* (Paris, Librarie Générale de Droit et de Jurisprudence, 1995) 68 *et seq*.

[46] Terré and Simler, above n 18, 108–09; Chabas, above n 18, 87 *et seq*. Chabas uses the term sovereignty of the owner in this respect. However, the importance of the second part of Art 544 Cciv should not be underestimated. Also in 1804 the drafters of the Civil Code knew and foresaw many exceptions to the sovereignty of the owner. RJ Pothier, *Traité du droit de domaine de propriété, Tome premier* (Paris,Orléans, Debure pere/La veuve Rouzeau-Montaut, 1772) 14; JEM Portalis, *Discours rapports et travaux inédits sur le Code civil* (Paris; Joubert, Libraire de la Cour de cassation, 1844) 219; see Portalis in PA Fenet, *Recueil Complet Des Travaux Préparatoires Du Code Civil*, tome 11 (Osnabrück, Otto Zeller, 1968) 116–17. For an overview, see R Derine, *Grenzen van het eigendomsrecht in de negentiende eeuw. Bijdrage tot de geschiedenis van het moderne privaatrecht* (Antwerpen, De Sikkel, 1955) 15–18, 40–43, 90 *et seq*.

[47] See apart from Req 3 August 1915, DP 1917.1.79, also Cass 20 January 1964, D 1964. 518, but also Cass 30 October 1972, Bull civ III, no 576; Chabas, above n 18, 89, Terré and Simler, above n 18, 108–09; K Zweigert and H Kötz, *Introduction to Comparative Law*, trans T Weir, 3rd rev edn (Oxford, Clarendon Press, 1998) 95; P Crocq, above n 45, 77. It should be emphasised that the doctrine of abuse of rights was not new, but merely became more applied after 1855. On this development, see Derine, above n 46, 178 *et seq*.

[48] The abuse of the right of ownership is a specific abuse of right, see *Req* 3 August 1915, DP 1917.1.79; Carbonnier, above n 17, 272–73. Below, I.A.4.c.

fore, an abuse of the right of ownership is not accepted easily. A party claiming that an owner abused his right of ownership must prove not only the effects of an act of the owner, but that it was the intention of the owner to harm him or at least cause a nuisance. It is this second requirement in particular which limits the application of the doctrine of abuse of rights.

I.A.3 UNITARY NATURE

Introductory Note

Civil law doctrine distinguishes between, on the one hand, the most comprehensive nature of the right of ownership, and, on the other, the unitary nature of the right. Whereas the former refers to the content of the right, the latter refers to the right itself. A unitary right cannot be divided, or at least cannot be divided so as to lose its status. It is this latter idea which can be found in the various definitions of the right of ownership given above.[49] Dutch law refers to this concept as *ondeelbaarheid*, German law as *Unteilbarkeit*. The French have no specific term, but refer to the right of ownership as having 'an exclusive character'.[50]

Parlimentary History, 17–18[51] **3.13 (NL)**

Final report 1

Question

Is it advisable, following the monograph of WJ Slagter, to make a distinction between legal and economic ownership in the Civil Code?

Answer

This question seems to refer to the lecture Slagter gave in 1968, entitled Legal and Economic Ownership on the occasion of the *dies natalis* (foundation day) of the Dutch School of Economics in Rotterdam. In this lecture it is assumed that someone is the economic owner of an object when he keeps the object without also being the legal owner and he carries the benefits and burdens of the object. This last case

[49] See JM Smits, 'Van partijen en derden; over interpretaties van de *Numerus Clausus* van zakelijke rechten' (1996) XIII *Groninger Opmerkingen en Mededelingen: magazijn voor leerstellige rechtsvergelijking op historische grondslag* 41–64, at 57; SCJJ Kortmann, 'Eigendom onder voorwaarde', in E Hondius et al (eds), *Quod Licet; Kleijn-Bundel* (Deventer, Kluwer, 1992) 199–211, at 211.

[50] Or *exclusivité*. On German law see *Motive zu dem Entwurfe eines Bürgerlichen Gesetzbuches für das Deutsche Reich—Sachenrecht*, vol III (Berlin, Verlag von J Guttentag, 1888) 262; see also GF Puchta, *Vorlesungen über das Heutige Römische Recht*—I, 6th edn (Leipzig, Verlag von Bernhard Tauchnitz, 1873) 324–26; Wiegand, above n 34, 117, at 139 *et seq*, H Hattenhauer, 'Über vereintes und entzweites Eigentum', in JF Baur (ed), *Das Eigentum. Vorträge gehalten auf der Tagung des Joachim Jungius-Gesellschaft der Wissenschaften Hamburg am 10, 11 und 12 December 1987.* (Göttingen, Vandenhoeck & Ruprecht, 1989) 83–101, at 90–91. On French law, see Portalis, above n 46 (1844), 209 *et seq*; see also R Libchaber, 'La recodification du droit des biens', *Le Code Civil 1804–2004; Livre Du Bicentenaire* (Paris, Dalloz/Lexis Nexis Litec, 2004) 297–372, at 305, 352; Crocq, above n 45, 64 *et seq*; Terré and Simler, above n 18, 65; Malaurie and Aynès, above n 18, 103 *et seq*; Carbonnier, above n 17, 143–44, Jourdain, Marty and Raynaud, above n 17, 37; Chabas, above n 18, 87; Baudry-Lacantinerie and Chauveau, above n 45, 13.

[51] CJ Van Zeben and JW Du Pon, *Boek 5—Zakelijke Rechten*, *Parlementaire Geschiedenis van het Nieuwe Burgerlijk Wetboek* (Deventer, Kluwer, 1981).

can be the result of a contractual agreement, such as lease or an instalment plan, but it can also be the result of a limited property right, such as a right of usufruct or a right of *emphyteusis*.

It is not advisable to introduce economic ownership into the Civil Code. The position of someone who is the holder of an object on the basis of a contractual agreement or a limited property right needs to be determined by rules concerning the aforementioned agreement or property right and not by other rules attached to economic ownership, whatever is meant by that expression. Moreover, it is not insignificant that this concept originated in tax law where it has worked well, ... Whereas, because legal ownership, meaning the right of ownership in private law, is not relevant to these tax questions, there is no need for any distinction in private law between legal and economic ownership.

Cour de cassation, civ 1er, 1 December 1964[52] **3.14 (FR)**

Pochiola v Ferouillet

UNITARY NATURE OF OWNERSHIP

Leased apartment

The right of ownership of a plot of land comprises the land and any building erected upon it.

Facts: The claimant granted a lease over a plot of land to the defendant. The defendant erected a building on the land, which was destroyed during the Second World War. The parties were in dispute over the cost of the repairs and, as a subsidiary point, over the ownership of the building.

Held: In the absence of any agreement to the contrary, the building formed part of the ownership of the lessor. However, during currency of the lease, the lessee was the owner of the buildings he constructed.

Judgment: But considering that, in the absence of an agreement between the parties, the buildings constructed by the lessee are dealt with at the end of the lease agreement by Art 555, first and second paragraph, of the Civil Code, the lessee remains owner, for the duration of the lease, of the buildings he erected on the land of the lessor.

Notes

(1) In many parts of continental Europe, most, if not all, land was held in feudal tenure.[53] The result was that most land was also held in both *dominium directum* and in *dominium utile*, a form of fragmented ownership. When, as a result of the French Revolution, the feudal system was abolished and a unitary concept of ownership was established, a choice then had to be made between *dominium directum* and

[52] JCP 1965, II, nr 14213.

[53] A French maxim states *nulle terre sans seigneur* or no land without a feudal lord. Exceptions were possible and known as allodial land: see J-P Lévy and A Castaldo, *Histoire du droit civil* (Paris, Dalloz, 2002) 434; FCJ Ketelaar, *Oude zakelijke rechten—vroeger, nu en in de toekomst* (Leiden/Zwolle, Universitaire pers Leiden/WEJ Tjeenk Willink, 1978) 18. It should be noted that it was particularly France where most of the land was in feudal tenure. Other territories, such as the Germanic countries, knew much more allodial land.

dominium utile. It was *dominium utile* which eventually prevailed and which, with the Decree Abolishing the Feudal System of 11 August 1789, became the remaining right of ownership.[54] The rights of the *dominus directum* were abolished, with or without compensation.[55] It is because of this development that only one type of ownership prevailed. Any other property right could be a property right, but not a right of ownership.[56]

(2) The modern concept of ownership still bears its historical roots, in particular concerning the unitary nature of the right. Each of the civil law systems under discussion struggles with the recognition of legal relations which challenge the unitary nature of ownership. These difficulties surface particularly in relation to the recognition of trusts and trust-like devices, which are often, though possibly wrongly, seen as causing a fragmentation of ownership, or in relation to the use of ownership as a security device, which may have a similar result.[57]

Other fragmentations of ownership are also rejected. In most civil law systems, a division is made between economic and legal ownership.[58] Economic ownership, often a concept developed in tax law, is seen as that part of the right of ownership which comprises the actual use of an object. Legal ownership, by contrast, is seen as the entitlement to that object and the ability to protect it against other parties. The answer of the Minister of Justice from the Dutch parliamentary history cited above is a direct response to a call by a Dutch academic, Slagter, for the inclusion of such a fragmentation of the right of ownership in the Dutch Civil Code.[59]

However, because of the unitary nature of the right of ownership, legal systems, including Dutch law, although recognising the importance of the concept, do not conceive economic ownership as a property right but usually only as a set of personal rights and claims.[60] Further discussion on economic ownership is therefore complicated and mostly a matter of tax law.

I.A.4 LIMITATIONS ON THE RIGHTS OF THE OWNER

Introductory Notes

(a) Although the rights of an owner are said to be the most comprehensive powers over an object it is possible to have, there are limitations on what an owner may

[54] 'The Decree Abolishing the Feudal System' (1789) Arts III, IV, V, IX and XI; Lévy and Castaldo, above n 53, 433.

[55] Ketelaar, above n 53, 18; Lévy and Castaldo, above n 53, 432–34.

[56] Any other right which was not recognised as a property right either must be a personal right under the *numerus clausus* of property rights. Above, Chapter 1.

[57] See, inter alia, Art 3:84(3) BW, and on that Art HR 19 May 1995, NJ 1996/119 (*Sogelease*) which prohibits transfers of ownership for security purposes. Below, Chapters 5 and 6.

[58] See C Asser, FHJ Mijnssen and P De Haan, *Goederenrecht 3—I Algemeen Goederenrecht*, 14th edn (Deventer, WEJ Tjeenk Willink, 2001) 483; Crocq, above n 45, 191–201.

[59] See WJ Slagter, *Juridische en economische eigendom—Rede uitgesproken op vrijdag 8 november 1968 ter gelegenheid van de 55e Dies Natalis der Nederlandse economische hogeschool, hogeschool voor maatschappijwetenschappen* (Deventer, Kluwer, 1968).

[60] Asser, Mijnssen and De Haan, above n 58, 491; WJ Slagter, 'Eigendom En Pseudo-Eigendom', in E Hondius *et al* (eds), *Quod Licet; Kleijn-Bundel* (Deventer, Kluwer, 1992) 357–74, at 357 *et seq*; WG Huijgen, *Economische Eigendom* (Zwolle, WEJ Tjeenk Willink, 1995). See Crocq, above n 45, 191–201.

do. There are two ways in which the owner can be limited in his rights over an object. First, there are certain limitations which are imposed through public law. These limitations are imposed by the state, usually in order to provide for certain services. Examples can be found in the area of public planning or zoning law in respect of immovables[61] and in rules on the protection of special movables such as pieces of art or animals.[62]

(b) Other limitations are provided through private law. These private law limitations, mostly imposed through case law, impose a standard of reasonableness on the owner. As a starting point the owner may do with the object of his ownership as he wishes, but when the exercise of his right of ownership is unreasonable or interferes with the right of ownership of another person, civil law systems provide limitations.

I.A.4.a Limitations by law

Cour de cassation civ 3e, 21 November 1969[63] **3.15 (FR)**

Samuel v Monlon and others

SCOPE OF POWERS OF THE OWNER

Wall in the wrong place

An owner can compel demolition of a building built on his land without consent.

Facts: The defendant was the manager of a co-owned piece of land on which there was an apartment block. One wall of the building was on the claimant's land. Relying on Article 545 Cciv, which provides that no one can be compelled to give up his ownership, the claimant sought its removal. The removal would result in the destruction of the building.

Held: That an owner may, without restriction, claim the demolition of a building built on his land without his consent. In this case the defendant had to remove the building.

Judgment: The court, on the first grievance—Considering that a complaint has been made against the confirmative judgment (Rouen 12 December 1976), for condemning Samuel, in his capacity as the manager of the co-owned 'Ilot 27 au Have', of which the wall of the building infringes on the land of Monlon, to proceed, under threat of a penalty imposed on a daily basis in case of non-compliance, with all activities of destruction in order to bring an end to the infringement on the right of ownership of Monlon, without researching whether the builder had or had not acted in good faith, while, even in case of a simple infringement on a construction on a neighbouring land, the owner of the latter cannot pursue the demolition of the contravening work, if the builder has acted in good faith;—However, considering that according to the provisions of Article 545 Civil Code, no one can be forced to give up his or her right of ownership, unless it is for public purposes; that the court

[61] Eg Art 10 Wet op de Ruimtelijke Ordening; Art L111-1-2 Code de l'urbanisme and §9 Bundesfernstraßengesetz (FStrG).

[62] Art L111-7 Code du patrimoine, §16 KultgSchG, Art 7(1) and 9 Wet tot behoud van cultuurbezit. On animals, see explicitly §903 BGB; Carbonnier, above n 17, 353–54; C Larroumet, *Les Biens. Droits réels principaux*, 4th edn (Paris: Economica, 2004) 563–64.

[63] D 1970.426, note M Lindon.

of appeal, having realised the existence of an infringement on the land of another under the circumstances provided for by Article 555 Civil Code, has, for this reason only, and without having researched whether the builder acted in good faith, justified its decision in a legal manner; that the first grievance is without foundation; for these reasons, rejects …

OLG Düsseldorf, 9 August 1989[64] **3.16 (DE)**

POWERS OF THE OWNER

The overhanging crane

An owner of a plot of land with a house on it does not have to tolerate a 20-metre high crane hanging partly over his land.

Facts: The defendant owned a piece of land which he used for the storage of building materials, which included a 24-metre-long, 20-metre-high crane. The crane overhung the claimant's land by approximately 5 metres, and moved over approximately 29 m^2 of the claimant's land. The claimant sought to restrain the defendant from bringing the crane into the airspace above his land.

Held: The claim was allowed. The owner of a piece of land with a house on it does not have to tolerate a crane used by a neighbouring company swinging through the airspace over his land.

Judgment: The defendant is not authorised to use the crane installed on his piece of land in a way that its extension arm rotates up to 4.95 m above the piece of land of the claimant. In fact, he is obliged to refrain from violating the right of ownership of the claimant (§1004(1) (2) BGB). §905(1) BGB extends the right protected by §1004(1) BGB of the owner to 'do with the object what he wishes and exclude others from interfering' (§903 BGB) also to the airspace above the surface below his piece of land. The defendant interferes in this area—meanwhile undisputed and determined through an expert report—with his revolving crane on a surface of approximately 29 m^2 and in a length of (from the border) up to 4.95 m, whenever the extension arm of the revolving crane rotates across the piece of land of the claimant. However, the owner of a piece of land cannot, according to §905(2) BGB, prohibit interferences that are undertaken at such a height (or depth) that he has no interest in their interference with his right.

In this case, the absence of an interest in prohibiting the interference constitutes, as arising out of the 'however' [from §905 2nd sentence], an exception to sentence 1, that is from the principle of the unlimited dominion of the owner. Whoever undertakes interferences therefore has to demonstrate and must, if necessary, prove that the owner does not have an interest in the prohibition thereof. The limitation of the right of ownership according to §905(2) BGB only begins there, where every interest of the owner to the excercise of ownership rights above his piece of land stops. Therefore, every interest worthy of protection is to be taken into consideration, even a mere future interest of the owner of land, which can be recognised as such; the interest does not have to be of a proprietary nature but may also be an aesthetic interest. The interest merely has to be based upon a connection to the use of the piece of land.

[64] NJW 1975, 1313 = BGHZ 64, 273.

In this respect it is a consideration that in this case a user of the piece of land of the claimant may feel endangered or still disturbed by the swivelling extension arm. Fears and emotions of this kind can, even if they are in the end not objectively and factually founded, at any rate also be shared by rational persons, which are on their part not offhand capable of forming their own opinion on whether and in how far the dangers connected and imaginable with such rotation have been prevented through special security arrangements and measures. Partly because of this it may not depend on whether the revolving crane of the defendant has been approved by the TÜV, whether he has been regularly unduly maintained and how high the security risks are in the end to be objectively assessed.

Burgerlijk Wetboek **3.17 (NL)**

Article 5:54 (1) Where part of a building or construction has been constructed on, over or under the land of another person and where removal of the protruding part would be disproportionately more prejudicial to the owner of the building or work than its preservation would be to the owner of the land, the owner of the building or work may at any time demand that, in return for compensation, a right of servitude be granted to him in order to preserve the existing situation or that, at the option of the owner of the land, the required part of the land is transferred to him.
(2) The preceding paragraph applies, *mutatis mutandis*, to a building or work which over time has begun to lean over the land of another person.
(3) The preceding paragraphs do not apply if this is the result of an obligation, arising from the law or a judicial act, to tolerate the existing situation or if the owner of the building or work can be held to have been in bad faith or grossly negligent with respect to the construction or his acquisition of the building or work.

Notes

The first case shows the scope of the powers of the owner. The article quoted by the Cour de cassation, Article 545 Cciv, states that no owner may be compelled to give up his ownership. As a general principle the owner has the power to decide what goes on and what does not regarding his own right of ownership.[65] This includes the possibility to claim the removal of a building which was placed either partly or in full on his land by another unauthorised party.[66] Seen from the side of the ownership of the neighbour this case illustrates the natural limitations on the rights of the owner; when one owner extends the object of ownership onto the land of another party, that other party has a right to prevent that first owner from doing so.

This right is not restricted to the soil itself. The second case shows that, in German law, the owner also has power over the space below and above the object of his ownership. Here the starting point of the OLG is that an owner may do with

[65] See also Cass 22 April 1823, S 1822–1824, I, 234.

[66] This also includes a minimum violation. See Cour de cassation 20 March 2002, D 2002, 2075 on a violation of 0.5 cm.

his land as he wishes. Generally this right extends to the space above and below his land. However, §905(2) BGB limits this.

I.A.4.b Limitations by contract

Introductory Notes

(a) Another way to limit the right of ownership and the exercise of the right of ownership is through agreement. The owner can agree with another person that he will not transfer the asset he owns. A non-transferability clause enables an owner to limit the powers of the owner to which he transfers the object under ownership. These limitations concern the right to dispose of the owner and can include a prohibition to transfer in general and a prohibition to transfer partially, ie create other property rights.

(b) The validity of a non-transferability clause can be in direct conflict with the concept of ownership and the provisions on ownership in civil law systems. As a general starting point in these systems all objects are generally transferable and the owner may do with these as he wishes. Therefore, it depends on the legal system whether such an agreement has effect against third parties.

Cour de cassation civ, 20 April 1858[67] **3.18 (FR)**

Crémieux v Régnard and others

ACCEPTANCE OF NON-TRANSFERABILITY CLAUSE

The donation

A donation with a non-transferability clause can be made, but only when the effect of the clause is temporary.

Facts: Mr Saint-Colombe gave all his assets to his children though retaining a right of usufruct. The gift of assets meant that the children became bare owners. As part of the contract of donation a clause stipulated that during his life the assets could not be transferred or made subject of a security right.

Later, Mr Saint-Colombe borrowed FRF100,000 from a Mr Régnard, wanting to create a property security right on his right of usufruct on some of the assets. However, the children intervened and created a security right on their bare ownership instead. After the death of Mr Saint-Colombe, one of the children, Ms Pons, borrowed money from a Mr Crémieux and created a security right on one of her assets of which she was bare owner.

When the debtor defaulted on his loans both creditors tried to make use of their security rights and sell the assets. Crémieux argued that the security right of Régnard was not validly created because of the clause in the donation.

Held: A non-transferability clause will be valid if it is limited in time and made in the interest of one of the parties. In this case, because the clause was limited to the duration of the life of Saint-Colombe, and the clause was made in his interest as holder of a usufruct, the clause was valid, and the security right of the defendant rendered invalid.

Judgment: Considering that ownership is the right to enjoy and dispose of assets in the most complete manner, provided that it is not used in a manner prohibited by statute or regulation.—That no law prevents the father of the family (*père de*

[67] DP 58. 1. 154, S 58.1.589.

famille), who donates his things to his children, from reserving the right of usufruct, and, be it in the interest of his right as usufructuary, be it to assure the exercise of his right of repossession, to which he could be entitled one day, to impose upon his children the condition not to dispose of or burden with a hypothec, during his lifetime, the donated things;—That this temporary prohibition, imposed in the interest of the donating father, cannot be turned into an absolute and indefinite prohibition to dispose, which would have as a result to put the things out of circulation for a long period of time;—That by declaring valid the hypothec granted by Ms Pons to Régnard, for the sole reason that the condition imposed by the donating father to Ms Pons was void for being contrary to the law, the mentioned judgment has been wrongly applied, and, as a consequence, has formally infringed the abovementioned clause; ...

Code civil **3.19 (FR)**

Article 900-1 Non-transferability clauses concerning an object donated or bequeathed are valid only where they are temporary and justified by a serious and legitimate aim. Even in that case, a donee or legatee may be judicially authorised to dispose of the object if the aim which justified the clause has disappeared or if it happens that a more important interest so requires.

Bürgerliches Gesetzbuch **3.20 (DE)**

§137 The power to dispose over a transferable right cannot be limited or excluded by legal act.

Baur, Baur and Stürner, Property Law, 22 **3.21 (DE)**

Moreover, the right of ownership can be transferred to someone else by fiduciary transfer [*zu treuen Händen*]; this leads to a fragmentation of 'economic' and 'legal' ownership.

It is characteristic that the *Treuhänder* is full owner to the outside, but that in the internal relation to the *Treugeber* he is bound by contract, to only exercise his right (his '*Treuhand*-ownership') in the way that parties agreed.

Burgerlijk Wetboek **3.22 (NL)**

Article 3:83 (1) Ownership, limited property rights and claims are transferable, unless this is prohibited by law or the nature of the right resists a transfer.
(2) The transferability of claims can also be excluded through agreement between the creditor and the debtor of that claim.

TM Art 3.4.2.1 (now 3:83 BW), Parliamentary History, Book 3[68] **3.23 (NL)**

This article regulates which rights are transferable. In principle all property rights and all claims are transferable. They are nevertheless not transferable when they have a personal character. Property rights only have this in very exceptional cases; claims by contrast have this each time the performance is connected to the creditor personally. Moreover, there is a difference between property rights and claims in that a transfer of a claim can be specifically excluded by agreement, and that this is not possible with property rigths.

Notes

(1) The original French Civil Code of 1804 did not provide rules on non-transferability clauses.[69] When the clauses arose in practice, also the courts were very reluctant to allow the use of these clauses, having the *ancien régime*, where non-transferability had been one of the main elements of the feudal system, still in their minds. Many courts refused to accept the validity of such clauses, particularly because they were usually made perpetual.[70] The landmark case is the first example where the Cour de cassation recognised the validity of a non-transferability clause in certain circumstances.

(2) It was not until 1971 that the legislator included provisions in the French Civil Code affirming this case law of the Cour de cassation.[71] The effect of a valid non-transferability clause is that the owner cannot dispose of the object. This can include the impossibility to establish a property right on the object, particularly a property security right.[72]

The effect of a transfer of an object for which a non-transferability claim is valid is debated in France.[73] It is clear that the effect of a valid non-transferability clause in operation is and should be a void transfer. Furthermore it should be emphasised that only the person in whose interest the clause was made is able to invoke the voidness.[74] The debate centres on the question how this voidability comes about.

(3) German law and Dutch law are much more reluctant to allow contractual arrangements to limit the right of ownership on movable assets. In German law an

[68] CJ Van Zeben and JW Du Pon, *Boek 3—Vermogensrecht, Parlementaire Geschiedenis van het Nieuwe Burgerlijk Wetboek* (Deventer, Kluwer, 1981); TM Art 3.4.2.1 (now 3:83 BW) 314.

[69] Terré and Simler, above n 18, 100.

[70] See, inter alia, Civ 6 June 1853, D 1.191, on perpetuity issues see Req 20 May 1879, DP 79.1.431, on the former case see Th Huc, *Commentaire théorique & practique du Code civil*, 4 (Paris, Librarie Cotillon, 1893) 107; on the latter, see Terré and Simler, above n 18, 101.

[71] Loi no 71-526 of 3 July 1971 that inserted Art 900-1 Cciv.

[72] Terré and Simler, above n 18, 103. However, a property security right coming into operation by force of law and not by agreement between parties will be able to exist since such a security right comes into existence and exists regardless of the power to dispose of the owner. See Carbonnier, above n 17, 162–63.

[73] See Carbonnier, above n 17, 151–53; Terré and Simler, above n 18, 103–05; Jourdain, Marty and Raynaud, above n 17, 75–77. See Crocq, above n 45, 200-201.

[74] Terré and Simler, above n 18, 104–05; Jourdain, Marty and Raynaud, above n 17, 75–76.

exception is offered through the use of *Treuhand*, a trust-like device.[75] A *Treuhand* can limit the owner in his powers for a certain period of time as well. *Treuhand* law is dealt with in Chapter 6 dealing with trust law.[76] Dutch law is strict when it comes to this subject by prohibiting the restriction of powers of the owner by contract other than the creation of the recognised limited property rights.[77]

I.A.4.c Limitations in neighbour law

Introductory Notes

(a) There can be situations where the powers of the owner also extend into the ownership of a neighbour. Although the principal rule is that the powers of the owner end where the powers of another owner begin as can be seen from the 'wall in the wrong place' case above,[78] the borderline between these powers can sometimes shift. If part of a building is placed on a piece of land owned by another, the person owning the bulk of the land on which the building is placed can, under certain conditions, be forced to tolerate the building. This can be done either by allowing the creation of a limited property right burdening the ownership of the latter owner or by recognising a legal duty to tolerate. The latter is a common solution in disputes between neighbours. The following section provides some examples of neighbour law problems.

(b) The law of neighbours is an area of law which by its nature only applies to immovables, in particular to land. These rules, therefore, find no application in the law dealing with movables.

Hoge Raad, 1 April 2005[79] **3.24 (NL)**

RIGHT TO A PATH

Road between greenhouses

When land is enclosed by other land (landlocked) and the public road cannot be reached, the owner of the enclosed piece of land may demand a path to the public road over the land of one of the neighbours.

Facts: The defendant landowner owned land with greenhouses on it. The claimant owned a neighbouring piece of land. In 1996 the defendant acquired another piece of land which was isolated from a public road neighbouring both his own land as well as the land of the claimant. The previous owner of this isolated piece of land had made use of a right to a path under Article 5:57 BW over the claimant's

[75] See in general HG Ganter, 'Die Rechtsprechung des Bundesgerichtshofs zu Treuhandkonten in der Insolvenz des Treuhänders', in Haarmeyer et al (eds), *Verschulding, Haftung, Vollstreckung, Insolvenz. Festschrift Für Gerhart Kreft Zum 65 Geburtstag* (Kevelaer, Bercker, 2004) 251–66, at 260; H. Kötz, *Trust und Treuhand. Eine rechtsvergleichende Darstellung des anglo-amerikanishen trust und funktionsverwandter Institute des deutschen Rechts* (Göttingen, Vandenhoeck & Ruprecht, 1963); J Marwede, *Rechtsnatur und aussenschutz des trust und der treuhand. Zugleich ein Beitrag zur Dinglichkeit und zum System subjectiver Privatrechte* (Bonn, Rheinische Friedrich-Wilhelms-Universität, 1972).

[76] Below, Chapter 6.

[77] This is the application of the *numerus clausus* principle.

[78] See case 3.15 (FR).

[79] HR 1 April 2005, no C03/302HR.

land. The claimant now argued, by virtue of Article 5:57 BW, that the right to the path was extinguished because the defendant could now access the public road from the isolated land across his own land through a small space between the greenhouses. The defendant in turn argued that the path was still necessary because the path between the greenhouses on his original plot was too small to drive through with heavy machinery.

Held: That the term 'parcel of land' in Article 5:57 BW does not only cover a single parcel, but can also cover a complex of adjoined pieces of land. However, even if these pieces of land are owned by the same person, there can still be factual circumstances which allow for the existence of a right to a path. In this case, the right remained in existence because the need to use it remained, even though the defendant could theoretically reach the public road over his own land.

Judgment: 3.3 The court of appeal has upheld the judgment, which was brought by the claimant. The court of appeal decided to that end, as far as this is significant in cassation, that the term 'parcel of land' in Art 5:57(1) Dutch Civil Code not only covers a parcel of land, but can also cover a complex of connected parcels of land which to a considerable degree appear outwardly as a unit. If that unit is situated next to a public road, then in principle there is no enclosed parcel of land. According to the court of appeal this does not impede the possibility that even if two adjoined parcels of land are used by the same person, where only one parcel of land is situated next to a public road, the factual circumstances with regard to the other parcel of land can be so different that there is no unity in the aforementioned sense. Although the piece of land without greenhouses situated in the back, as well as the piece of land with greenhouses situated in the front, are used for an agricultural purpose, these pieces of land cannot be considered a unit in the afore-mentioned sense. Moreover, it is impracticable to drive machinery of common size between the greenhouses to the piece of land in the back …

3.4.2 The opinion of the court of appeal that the defendant can claim the upholding of the path over the claimant's land is not only based on the disputed ground, but also on the self-supporting ground that it is impracticable for the defendant to drive machinery of standard size through the greenhouses to the piece of land without greenhouses in the back, which he acquired in 1966. The court of appeal used this opinion to express that, with a view to the normal exploitation of the parcel of land in the back, there is no proper acces possible to that piece of land over the parcels of land (owned by the defendant) situated at a public road. This opinion is not disputed in cassation. The conclusion must therefore be that the grievances in section 1 cannot lead to cassation for lack of significance.

…

3.6.2 In this case, whether the defendant has a right to a path is not the crucial question, but rather whether the claimant could justly take the position that the right to a path over his parcel of land for the benefit of the parcels of land [A] [005] and [A] [006], which together form the parcel of land in the back owned by the defendant, was lapsed because the path was no longer needed. … This crucial question is answered in the negative.

BGH, 15 April 1964[80] 3.25 (DE)

RIGHT TO A PATH MAY ALSO APPLY TO WATERWAYS

The waterway

An enclosed piece of land that needs a path out can be granted such a path under certain conditions. The rules applicable on the recognition of a path may also apply to a sewer and waterway.

Facts: The parties were neighbours. On the land was a stone construction which allowed drain water to flow from the claimant's land over the defendant's land. In 1959 the defendant took away this waterway. The claimant claimed that she had a right to demand the defendant to tolerate the waterway and, furthermore, that she could claim the reinstatement of the waterway.

Before the court, whether an agreement between parties could be reached was no longer at issue. Instead, the claimant argued to make use of the right to a path in case of enclosure of the land of §242 BGB (*Notwegrecht*). The defendant claimed that there was another way in which a waterway could technically be constructed allowing the drain water of the claimant to flow somewhere else. Therefore, the defendant argued the claimant had no right to make use of §242 BGB.

Held: The BGH held that a waterway could be allowed in the same sense as a path, but under strict conditions. When another connection to the public road or waterway is possible, the acceptance of the right to a path, in this case a waterway or sewer, depends on the normal use of the land. When the costs of the direct connection to the public road or waterway are disproportionate to the general profit coming from the land, all in relation to the normal use of the land, the waterway can be allowed. In this case the way was allowed, but only for drain water.

Judgment: 2. The applicant only invoked a duty to tolerate the sewer, which directly follows from the law (§917 BGB) in second instance of the proceedings,—triggered by the decision of the respective senate which was published around that time v 4. 11. 1959, V ZR 49/58 (WM 59, 1461 = NJW 60, 93 [L]; partially published LM Nr 3 zu §917 BGB und MDR 60, 124). According to that judgment a right to a path can contain a duty for a neighbour to tolerate an underground sewer on his piece of land. The claimant assumes that the preconditions for such a right are met in the case at hand.

The court of appeal did not follow this. According to this court, rights to a path are a far-reaching limitation on the right of ownership; they therefore only need to be tolerated when the neighbour cannot help himself by other means; he would, in order to gain a different access, need to accept higher expenditures. The claimant—whose piece of land is characterised by a relatively high amount of sewage due to the number of visitors of an average of 60 persons daily—would have the possibility, to connect a sewer pipeline to the sewer pipe of the municipality under the *Dorfstraße*. However, she would be able, since the back part of her piece of land features a slight downward slope, only to transport to the public pipe the largest part of her sewage through the use of a pumping installation. However, the costs of such an installation, which amounted to a maximum of DM12,000 for the one-time purchase and yearly DM136 for the operation of the pump, would be expected of the claimant; the profitability of her factory and living space would thereby be neither eliminated, nor seriously jeopardised.3. The revision accuses the judge on appeal of contradicting the principles developed by the Senate in the afore-mentioned judgment of 4.11.1959, as well as the RG-judgment RGZ 157, 305 to which it referred. It

[80] NJW 1964, 1321.

would not be possible only to grant a right to a path, when the profitability of the piece of land would be eliminated or seriously jeopardised. Rather, already disproportional disadvantages should be enough. The revision attempt is unfounded. Whether or not the defendant had to tolerate the claim of the claimant for private canalisation purposes is not answered, contrary to what the revision seems to assume, on the basis of §242 BGB. Indeed, the principle of good faith is also applicable in property law, and it can be of relevance for questions of neighbours living together in particular. However, its task in this area of law is, since the mutual rights and duties know detailed special provisions (§§905 *et sequ* BGB), mainly of a limiting and compensatory nature; generally it does not give rise to independent claims and is only applied in exceptions whose specific features seem to necessitate a fair compensation which goes beyond the statutory provisions, whereby it mostly serves as a limit to the exercise of legal rights. The obligation lodged by the claim of the defendant to tolerate the sewer line from the neighbouring piece of land onto her own therefore has to be examined as to whether the conditions of §917 BGB are fulfilled.

This provision—whose applicability to sewer pipes is beyond doubt due to the earlier judgment of the Senate—allows the claim to a neighbouring piece of land, which is in other ownership, to a right to a path where the relevant piece of land lacks the ,connection that is necessary for a normal use'; intended is the connection to a public road or, if a waterway or sewer is at stake, to public pipelines. The claim to a right to a path therefore presupposes a lack of an external connection of a piece of land.

To this lack of an external connection, stringent requirements are to be made. It does not exist where another possibility to connect is possible that also assures a normal use of the piece of land. Whether or not the latter is the case is determined along objective criteria; practical economic reasons serve as a standard for the assessment of normal use of the land, whereby this depends on the type of usage, the size of the piece of land, its surrounding and other circumstances of a specific case. That the use of another possibility of connection is more cumbersome, less comfortable or more expensive than the claim to a neighbouring piece of land for a right to a path does not alone justify the demand to such a path. Such difficulties further have to be accepted regularly. Only where they exceptionally would be so as to remove the profitability of the use of the piece of land or if they would limit the use of the land in an unacceptable manner, the neighbour is required to provide a way on his own land. Only in this context can the question of acceptability rise in disputes relating to the right to a path.

... Whether or not an expense is within boundaries which can be accepted by the owner of the piece of land is determined, as the challenged judgment remarks correctly, not by comparing the costs of the demanded right to a path on the one piece of land and those of a direct connection on another piece of land, but rather it is the relationship of the latter costs to the profitability of the use of the piece of land as such which is decisive. Otherwise the legal provision that the piece of land lacks a connection necessary for a normal usage according (§917(1) sentence 1 BGB) would be deprived of its practical significance and the neighbour would already have to tolerate the claim on his own piece of land where in such a way smaller expenses would be incurred than by installation and maintenance of a direct access. This would amount to a disadvantage for the neighbour of the piece of land that was not intended by the law and therefore would not be legal.

In the end, the decision made on appeal that the defendant would have to tolerate the sewer according to §242 BGB, since the sewer pipe runs along the outher border of the piece of land, is only 20 m long and does not come within 3 m of the buildings on to neighbouring piece of land, fails. The attempt of the revision to derive here a duty to tolerate of the defendant 'from the point of view of proportionality' cannot be maintained. It is not the smaller or bigger limitation of the neighbouring piece of land in this context, the right to a path according to §917 BGB rather depends on whether the piece of land of the claimant lacks the connection, which is necessary for a normal use. This is, as the court of appeal has held correctly, not the case.

Cour de cassation, 22 November 1937[81] **3.26 (FR)**

Delafoy v Verly

RIGHT TO A PATH MAY ALSO APPLY TO ELECTRICITY LINES AND GAS AND WATER PIPES

Gas, electricity and water

The owner of a landlocked piece of land needing a path for access can be granted such a path under certain circumstances. This rule can also apply to pipelines.

Facts: The claimant owned a piece of land which was enclosed by other pieces of land in such a way that no public road could be reached from the land itself. The only access was over the land of the defendant. The claimant claimed not only to have a right to a path over the land of the defendant through Article 682 Cciv, but that this right also included the right to have gas and electricity lines as well as a water pipe for drainage.

Held: The right of way given by Article 682 Cciv extends to the space below the way including the possibility of a way for gas, electricity and water.

Judgment: In view of Article 682 Civil Code;—Considering that the right to a path envisaged by this text should be interpreted in the sense that the words 'on the ground of his neighbours' does not only envisage the surface of the ground, but can include up to 'the subsoil', in order to ensure means of communication strictly necessary for the average use of the enclosed land: that also applies to pipelines in the subsoil indispensable to this effect;—considering that mademoiselle Delafoy, owner of a house in Trouville-sur-Mer having access to the public road only by way of an alley belonging to monsieur Verly, has opened up in this alley trenches for the supply of water, gas, electricity, as well as for drainage, but that the judgment in appeal has held that, for the reason of the enclosed state, she possessed a right to a path, this right permitting her only passage on foot, on horse or by car, but that the provisions of Article 682 Civil Code did not encompass the establishment of permanent works for any other use; However, considering that thus stating, instead of researching, on the one hand, if the planned works would be of such nature to influence the amount of compensation provided for by the aforementioned article, and, on the other hand, if the works could be effectuated in a way less damaging for the servient property and at the same time appropriate for

[81] D 1938, 62, note M Voirin.

the needs of exploitation of the dominant property, the judgment has not given a legal basis to its decision;—for these reasons, quashes the judgment.

Notes

(1) The right to a path is a primary part of neighbour law. As the lower court in the German case states, the recognition of a right to a path has a severe impact on the right of ownership. The recognition of a right to a path is a clear limitation on the powers of the owner, although in German and Dutch law it is not constructed as a limited property right.[82] An owner is generally entitled to do with his land as he desires, including the right to keep others from interfering with its use. However, in case of the acceptance of a right to a path, the owner is forced by law to tolerate a neighbouring owner entering his land. The concept of a right to a path is known in German law as *Notweg*, in Dutch law as *Noodweg*.

Such restrictions on the right of ownership are strictly controlled. Where land is fully enclosed by other pieces of land and no public area, usually a road, can be reached, the owner of the enclosed land is entitled to a path to the public area. Although the civil law systems all recognise such a right, and even apply very similar rules to them, the way in which they construe the right itself differs.

(2) In German and in Dutch law, the right to a path is found through a limitation on the right of ownership imposed by law.[83] The civil codes of these legal systems create a right which can be exercised against neighbouring owners.[84] Legislation imposes rules to which the right is subject. However, in French law the right to a path is constructed by the recognition of a limited property right. By force of law, a right of servitude comes into existence creating the possibility for the owner of the enclosed land having access to the public area.[85] The concept used in French law is known as a legal servitude.[86] The law of servitudes applies to the legal servitude as well, but at the same time parts of the law dealing with the right of ownership also apply.[87]

The two different approaches achieve similar results. In neither case is an agreement between the parties necessary. Where, however, they do reach agreement, the need for a right to a path ceases to exist. Where in German and Dutch law the right of ownership of the neighbour over which the path must run is limited by

[82] At least not in German or Dutch law. French law takes a different approach here. In French law this problem is solved through the recognition of a right of servitudes which comes into existence by operation of the law. Below, I.B.2.

[83] See F Baur, J Baur and R Stürner, *Sachenrecht*, 17th edn (München, CH Beck'sche Verlagsbuchhandlung, 1999) n 25.15, at 280; A Pitlo et al, *Goederenrecht*, 11th edn (Deventer, Gouda Quint, 2001) n 575, at 412.

[84] §917 BGB and Art 5:57 BW; see Baur, Baur and Stürner, above n 83, 280; CJ Van Zeben and JW Du Pon, *Boek 5—Zakelijke Rechten, Parlementaire Geschiedenis van het nieuwe Burgerlijk Wetboek* (Deventer, Kluwer, 1981) 214–17.

[85] On the creation of these types of servitude, see below, Chapter 8.

[86] See in general Terré and Simler, above n 18, 192 *et seq*, 656.

[87] *Ibid*, 194.

law, in French law the limitation of the same right of ownership is achieved by the recognition of a right of servitude, created and enforced by law.[88]

I.A.5 CO-OWNERSHIP

Co-ownership in general

BGH, 14 February 1962[89] **3.27 (DE)**

CO-OWNERSHIP IN SHARES

Community in Marriage

Co-ownership is not a separate property right, but is part of the concept of ownership.

Facts: The parties were married. The defendant acquired a piece of land and was registered as owner. On this land, he and his spouse, the claimant, built a house and later an extension. These were partly financed with the money of the claimant. When the marriage ended in divorce, the claimant sought DM30,000 or at least a 50% share of the ownership of the land and house, including the extension.

Held: The claim was allowed. Co-ownership is not a specific right but should be seen as an appearance of the right of ownership. In this case, the right claimed by the claimant is therefore not a separate property right, but a share in the right of ownership which is held jointly. The claimant was entitled to at least half of the ownership.

Judgment: The right of co-owners in shares is according to the case law of the *Reichsgericht* not a separate right to a share that burdens the right of ownership, but a share in the right of ownership which is held jointly. Rather, it is of a similar nature to the right of ownership of corporeal objects, ie ownership and a separate right of the same nature as the right as a whole. … The right of co-ownership to which a person is entitled is, except in specific cases, a unitary right. The thereby indicated share of co-ownership merely specifies the scope of this right.

Then, only the requested higher share would have been submitted to the court's decision. However, here it was the co-ownership as such that was object of the procedural claim. Though a claim to grant co-ownership in accordance with the provision of §47 GBO can only be granted in a manner of awarding a fraction in a co-ownership. When according to a management agreement a right of co-ownership is requested under §667, then usually the share acquired and demanded by the claimant is awarded. The claimant must explicitly state, when he exceptionally demands a fraction above that, and wishes to receive a share in the co-ownership in accordance with that fraction. … This does not conflict with the explanations in those judgments that the claimant is entitled to half of the co-ownership.

[88] After all, in French law a limited property right is a *démembrement* of the right of ownership. See B Akkermans, 'Concurrence of Ownership and Limited Property Rights' [2010] *European Review of Private Law* 259–84.

[89] BGHZ 36, 365.

Hoge Raad, 30 March 2001[90] **3.28 (NL)**
LISV v Grifhorst

LEGAL QUALIFICATION OF SHARES IN A CO-OWNERSHIP

Seizure of a co-owned home

A seizure executed on a co-owned house is void.

Facts: Following the claimant's divorce, assets which had been part of the community of property were divided between the former spouses, apart from a house, the consequence of which meant that the house remained co-owned. Because of an outstanding debt, the claimant, a creditor of the former husband of the claimant, seized the house. The claimant argued that the seizure was void and should be lifted, at least partially, because the house was co-owned.

Held: The seizure of the full ownership of the house was void since the seizure included a part of the house which was not owned by the former husband of the claimant. The creditor should have seized the share in the community of the former husband. Because the seizure could not be altered, it was declared to be void.

Judgment: 3.3. In considering the grievance the following must be assumed.

(1) The share of a participant in a community is a patrimonial right of a different nature than the ownership of corporeal objects belonging to that community. The question of which rights and powers he can derive from his share in the community cannot be answered on the basis of Article 5:1 Civil Code. He does not, on the basis of his share, have the rights and powers laid down in Article 5:1 Civil Code. It follows from Article 3:178 Civil Code that he has the right to claim the division of the community, whereas the question whether he has the enjoyment of a common object and the question whether he is entitled to the use and/or the management of it, must be answered on the basis of Article 3:168 *et seq*.

(2) The present community should be qualified as a special community as referred to in Article 3:189 Civil Code. Indeed only one object belonged to the community, but for the answer to the question whether the community should be qualified as a special one, as referred to in the last-mentioned provision, it is the legal relationship between the holders of the shares, which has led to the existence of the community, that is decisive, not the circumstance that only one object belongs to the community.

(3) LISV could recover its claim against D, on, in principle, all of his objects, on the basis of Article 3:191(1) as well as on the share of D in the dissolved community in marriage; the latter though having had regard to the reservation made in the aforementioned provision. As a preparation of this seizure, LISV could seize this share provisionally. The point of departure should be that when seizing, it is specified which patrimonial right is seized. After all, when realising the seizure, the object that is to be sold must be specified. The record of seizure serves in part to establish which object of the debtor will eventually be sold. It cannot be accepted that the seizure, that, as is evident from the record, encompasses a right on an object not belonging to the debtor, could be altered into the seizure of a right indeed belonging to the debtor.

[90] NJ 2002/380.

Code civil[91] **3.29 (FR)**

Article 815 No one can be forced to remain in co-ownership and the division can at any time be invoked, unless it has been suspended by court decision or agreement.

Article 815-1 The co-owners can make agreements concerning the exercise of their co-ownership rights in conformity with Articles 1873-1 to 1873-18.

Article 1873-3 The agreement can be concluded for a limited duration not over five years. The agreement is renewable through an explicit decision of the parties involved. The division cannot be invoked before the agreed period, except when there are rightful reasons for it.

The agreement can equally be concluded for an undetermined duration. The division can, in that case, be invoked at any point in time, provided that this will not be in bad faith or at the wrong moment.

It can be decided that the agreement for determined duration will be tacitly renewed for either a determined or an undetermined duration. In the absence of such arrangement, the co-ownership will be governed by Articles 815 *et seq* the expiration of an agreement for determined duration.

Notes

(1) In general, civil law systems all use a similar approach to co-ownership.[92] The reason is not surprising, as they all share a common concept of ownership. A unitary concept of ownership does not allow for a fragmentation of ownership, at least not in such a way that two different rights of ownership can come into existence.[93] The general resistance to fragmentation of the right of ownership can be seen in the specific way in which co-ownership is dealt with. Instead of fragmenting the right of ownership itself, co-ownership results in several shares of that one and complete right of ownership to which the 'co-owners' are entitled.[94] These shares are not to be seen as a fragmentation of the right of ownership and therefore not as a distinct property right; each share entitles its holder to the whole of the right of ownership. Only when the right of ownership is expressed into monetary value, eg in case of sale, does the share entitle its holder to a certain part of the value. Depending on the relationship between the holders of these shares, the ratio will differ. In the first of the cases above a marriage is used to create a community, ie a special co-ownership regime, of objects. As the case concerns spouses, a general division of shares will be 50-50. However, other divisions are possible, usually dependent on the input of the parties.[95]

(2) In French and Dutch law the concept of co-ownership is constructed through the use of a general concept of co-entitlement. In French law this concept is known

[91] Art 815 modified by Art 2 Loi 2006-728 of 23 June 2006.

[92] The principal difference can be seen in the division of buildings into apartments. In French and Belgian law this is done by using a special co-ownership regime, whereas German and Dutch law recognise separate property rights for this purpose.

[93] At least no fragmentation other than a fragmentation particularly prescribed by law.

[94] Chabas, above n 18, 35; Carbonnier, above n 17, 144–45; Wolf, above n 14, 26–27; Asser, Mijnssen and De Haan, above n 58, n 445 *et seq*, at 441 *et seq*; Asser et al, above n 21, n 343, at 367.

[95] A share in a co-ownership is expressed in a fraction (eg ½) or a percentage (eg 50%) As the final sentence of the excerpt shows, the claimant was eventually only awarded 50%.

as *indivision* and in Dutch law as *gemeenschap*. This concept, best described as a community, is not only used for purposes of co-ownership but also to share different types of entitlement. This can include other property rights, such as a right of usufruct. Personal rights can also be shared. Furthermore, the general concept of community enables the legal system to use communities in more ways than those just created by simple agreement. The concept is also used in cases of inheritance and marriage to denote the joint entitlement of the right holders. In case of a marriage these right-holders are the spouses; in case of an inheritance, these are the heirs.[96]

In Dutch law the general concept of co-ownership is dealt with by Article 3:166 BW. This provision provides rules on a concept known as a community. The community comes into existence by operation of law, eg in case of marriage, or by agreement between parties. The term co-ownership may be used when the right of ownership is subject to a community of shares.

(3) German law recognises a form of co-ownership similar to Dutch law, but additionally a second type. This similar type is a right of co-ownership in equal, undivided shares. This ownership in undivided shares or *Miteigentum nach Bruchteilen* is dealt with in §§741 *et seq* BGB and §§1008 *et seq* BGB.

The second type of co-ownership is a pure type of co-ownership or *Gesamthandseigentum* and is characterised by an undividable community over which the owners can only acting together exercise their powers.[97] This second type of co-ownership only exists where specifically provided for by legislation. These are partnerships in company law, a marriage, or the receipt of an inheritance.[98]

(4) In French law co-ownership is seen as an exception to normal ownership. While the co-ownership regime is in force, the exclusivity of a single owner is compromised on behalf of the co-owners. A co-ownership regime can arise either by law or through agreement.[99] As a general rule the co-owners each have the right to use and enjoy, *usus* and *fructus*, the object under co-ownership but, because of the nature of their relation, must share the object between them.[100]

The parties are bound to each other through the community. So, for example, unless otherwise provided, unanimity is required when one co-owner intends to sell and transfer an object in the community or his share in the community.[101] However, Article 1873-3 Cciv expressly allows parties to deviate from these provisions. Furthermore, Article 815 Cciv does not provide a maximum duration.

Comparative Note

In general the approach to co-ownership is similar in the civil law systems under review. Differences can, however, be seen in the German restriction to the right of

[96] See, eg, Art 3:189 BW.

[97] Baur, Baur and Stürner, above n 83, 19; Wolf, above n 14, 27.

[98] §§718, 105 *et seq*, 161 *et seq*, §1405 *et seq* and §2032 *et seq* BGB, as mentioned by Baur, Baur and Stürner, above n 83, 18–19. See also Wolf, above n 14, 26–27.

[99] Terré and Simler, above n 18, 397–98.

[100] Art 815-9 Cciv: Chabas, above n 18, 42; Malaurie and Aynès, above n 18, 195, 199; Terré and Simler, above n 18, 415–16.

[101] Art 1873-8 Cciv: Chabas, above n 18, 45.

ownership and the French and Dutch concept of community applying to rights other than the right of ownership. Furthermore, both French and German law provide a basic regime in which co-owners are completely dependent on each other. However, in each of these systems, agreements by the parties can change the application of these mandatory rules, either by choosing another type of co-ownership or using the contractual freedom left by legislation.

Nevertheless each civil law system adheres to the unitary concept of ownership and therefore refuses to accept a fragmentation of the right of ownership. Instead, an abstract concept of a share is created which allows doctrine to deal with co-ownership without having to change the unitary nature of the right of ownership. What exactly is the legal nature of a share in a co-ownership regime could be subject of debate. Is the share a property right in itself? Arguments in favour of that could be that it is a right which can be enforced against third parties, assigned on its own and only gives an entitlement to limited access to the object of co-ownership, ie the holder of a share cannot, without co-operation of the holders of the other shares, transfer the object under co-ownership to a third party. Arguments against could focus on the unitary nature of ownership and the fact that as a general principle no two types of ownership may exist at the same time.[102] A share in a co-ownership is not generally recognised as a limited property right and, in this approach, therefore an unlawful fragmentation of the right of ownership.

I.A.6 SECURITY OWNERSHIP

Security ownership will be dealt with in Chapter 5.

I.B REAL SERVITUDES

Introductory Notes

(a) Where an owner of a piece of land wants to grant a neighbour access to his land he can do so by agreement, which would create a right personal to that neighbour. However, the owner may also establish a property right on behalf of the neighbour which would connect the property right to the ownership of the land. Once established, the property right would burden the right of ownership and therefore bind the right of ownership in the hands of a transferee. Such a right would increase the value of the neighbouring land. A property right granting access to a neighbour over an owner's land is known as a real servitude.

(b) The law on real servitudes has its basis in Roman law.[103] Since the civil

[102] However, see Req 13 February 1834, DP 1834.I.218, S 1834.I.205. Above, Chapter 1.

[103] WM Gordon and OF Robinson, *The Institutes of Gaius*, Texts in Roman Law, ed Peter Birks (London, Duckworth, 1988) 127–31; B Nicholas, *An Introduction to Roman Law* (New York, Oxford University Press, 1962) 143; DL Carey Miller, 'Property', in E Metzger (ed), *A Companion to Justinian's Institutes* (Ithaca, NYm Cornell University Press, 1998) ch 3, 96; Wolff and Raiser, above n 16, 430; J von Staudinger et al, *Buch 3 Sachenrecht—Erbb Vo; §§1018–1112* (Berlin, Sellier de Gruyter, 2002) 205; M Kaser and FBJ Wubbe, *Romeins Privaatrecht*, trans FBJ Wubbe, 2nd edn (Zwolle, Tjeenk Willink, 1971) 93–55, at 137.

law systems of France, Germany and the Netherlands base their property law on Roman law ideas, many rules on servitudes are common to all three. As we will see, even the English law on easements closely resembles the Roman-law-based general criteria for servitudes.[104] The common rules of civilian systems form the subject-matter of the first section. At the end, a comparative note provides an overview of the civil law systems.

(c) As real servitudes are property rights which burden a piece of land, there are no real servitudes on movable objects.

I.B.1 RULES COMMON TO FRENCH, GERMAN AND DUTCH LAW.

Code civil **3.30 (FR)**

Article 637 A right of servitude is a charge on an immovable object for the use and utility of an immovable object of another owner.

Article 686 Owners may create on their land or in favour of their land those servitudes as they seem fit, provided however that the duties the servitude creates are not imposed on a person, nor in favour of a person, but solely on a piece of land and on behalf of a piece of land, and provided that these duties are not contrary to public policy.

The use and the extent of the servitude are established by the title that creates it; without a title by the rules that follow after this Article.

Bürgerliches Gesetzbuch **3.31 (DE)**

§1018 A piece of land can, for the benefit of an owner of another piece of land, be burdened in such a way, in which the owner may use this piece of land for specific purposes or in which on the piece of land certain action cannot be taken or a certain right which follows from the burdened piece of land against the other piece of land cannot be exercised.

Burgerlijk Wetboek **3.32 (NL)**

Article 5:70(1) The right of real servitude is a burden, with which an immovable object—the servient land—for the benefit of another immovable object—the dominant land—is burdened.

Article 5:71(1) A burden that a right of real servitude places on the servient land, entails the obligation to on, over or under one of either pieces of land, allow something or not to do something. In the deed of creation it can be determined that the burden furthermore entails an obligation to install buildings, works or plantings, necessary for the exercise of the right of real servitude, provided that these buildings, works or plantings will be located entirely or in part on the servient land.

[104] Below, II.A.4.

Notes

(1) First and foremost, a real servitude is a property right which comes into existence between two owners of a piece of land. The right of real servitude limits the ownership of the owner over which the burden runs and not the owner himself. In that respect, both the Dutch and German versions refer to *Erf* (parcel) and *Grund* (land).[105] In principle, a right of servitude burdens the land alone and only requires the owner of that land to tolerate or not to do something.[106]

(2) A right of servitude requires two pieces of land. Traditionally these pieces are known as the dominant and servient land.[107] The owner of the servient land must tolerate a specific act of the owner of the dominant land over his land.

(3) Another requirement which follows from the definitions provided by the civil codes is that it is the dominant land which should benefit from the existence of the servitude and not just the owner himself. This requirement of benefit restricts the content of the servitude. When one piece of land must benefit from another piece of land, the law considers that these two pieces of land must be near each other.[108] What exactly this benefit can be is very wide and can include, besides a monetary value which is most common, aesthetic value.[109] However, as French law shows, where the right benefits the owner in only his personal capacity, it cannot amount to a servitude. Thus, rights to pick fruits or to hunt have been excluded from this category.[110]

(4) The connection, ie the requirement of benefit, between the owners of the dominant and the servient land also underlines one of the most fundamental principles of real servitude law. Not only must the owner of the dominant land benefit in his capacity as an owner, but the owner of the servient land can only be burdened in his capacity as owner. In other words, in principle, the owner of the servient land cannot be compelled to do something. A positive duty can therefore not be the subject of a real servitude. This principle, already known to Roman law, but in particular connected to the rejection of the *ancien régime*, protects the ownership of the servient land.[111] A positive duty would force the owner to do something and hence decrease the value of his ownership in an unacceptable manner.

(5) A final restriction to the content of a right of servitude is that though it may restrict the owner from doing something on the land itself, it cannot restrict the

[105] Ie, *Erfdienstbaarheid* and *Grunddienstbarkeit*.

[106] The French Civil Code even uses the term *service foncier* or land service in order to avoid the term servitude which had become connected to this feudal form. See Chabas, above n 18, 425.

[107] See Terré and Simler, above n 18, 648–49; Malaurie and Aynès, above n 18, 329–30; von Staudinger et al, above n 103, 236; Asser et al, above n 21, n 172, at 198.

[108] C Asser et al, *Zakenrecht 3—II Eigendom en beperkte zakelijke genotsrechten*, 12th edn (Zwolle, WEJ Tjeenk Willink, 1990) n 210, 211, at 203–04; JTh Smalbraak, *Erfdienstbaarheden en kwalitatieve verbintenissen (huidig en wordend recht)* (Preadviezen uitgebracht ter behandeling in de algemene vergadering van de Broederschap Van Candidaat-Notarissen, 1966) 90; WJM Davids, *Burenrecht, Mandeligheid en Erfdienstbaarheden*, 3rd edn (Deventer, Kluwer, 1988) 138; Baur, Baur and Stürner, above n 83, 369; Terré and Simler, above n 18, 653.

[109] Baur, Baur and Stürner, above n 83, 369.

[110] See Art 686 Cciv: Terré and Simler, above n 18, 650.

[111] A restriction to negative duties is phrased in the Roman maxim *servitus in faciendo consistere nequit*.

owner's exercise of his right to dispose of the land.[112] Furthermore, a total restriction on the powers of the owner is not allowed.

BGH, 25 February 1959[113] **3.33 (DE)**

SECONDARY DUTIES IN REAL SERVITUDES MAY CONTAIN POSITIVE DUTIES

The safety bridges

The content of a right of real servitude is determined by what the parties have agreed. A positive duty may be connected to a right of servitude as a secondary duty.

Facts: The parties were neighbours. In 1900 agreements had been made concerning the crossing of a street which ran up a hill, which had meanwhile become a cableway. These agreements dealt with the construction of safety bridges for pedestrians. However, no agreements concerning the costs of these had been made.

The claimant owned a piece of land which entitled her, through a right of real servitude, to access a cableway. The defendant, however, owned another piece of land on which the cableway ran. When the land was not used very much, the construction of bridges had not been a safety issue. However, with the increase in the use of the land by persons and animals, the need for safety measure, in particular safety bridges, arose. At issue between the parties was whether the servitude contained a positive duty to construct the safety bridges and who should pay for the construction.

Held: The BGH held that a positive duty, in this case the construction of the safety bridges, can only be part of a right of servitude as a secondary duty. As the duty to construct these safety bridges can be seen as a secondary duty, the claimant is under the obligation to construct the bridges at her own cost.

Judgment: A servitude, be it a real servitude or as in this case a limited personal servitude, grants its holder, according to its nature, a right of usage of the piece of land limited in content and imposes on the owner of the piece of land ... the duty to tolerate or refrain from doing something (§§1018, 1090 BGB).

Positive duties are incumbent neither on the holder nor on the person that is burdened. They can, however, exist for any of the two as a secondary duty; this results in respect to the holder out of his general duty to a conservative exercise of his legal rights (§1020 BGB, see below), in the case of the burdened land out of the statutory special provisions of §1021 (duty of maintenance through an agreement), §1022 (again by virtue of statute) and §1023 BGB (duty to bear costs out of the relocation of the facilities). This is not a matter of subsidiary legal obligations, which exist next to the servitude, but of the demarcation of the servitude itself. (Wolff-Raiser, Sachenrecht, 10 Edition, §106 under footnote 38). ...

Hereafter, the claimant owed the construction of the safety bridges according to the content of the servitude to the defendant at her own expense. A limitation of the servitude in the sense of §§1090, 1027, 1004 BGB does not arise; a reimbursement claim exists neither from the point of view of an action for damages ... nor from compensation for expenses.

112 BGH 14 March 2003: Asser et al, above n 21, n. 174, at 201; Terré and Simler, above n 18, 649; Malaurie and Aynès, above n 18, 332–33.

113 *Deutsche Notar-Zeitschrift* (DNotZ) 1959, 240.

Burgerlijk Wetboek **3.34 (NL)**

Article 5:70 (2) The burden that the right of real servitude places on the servient land can also entail the obligation of maintenance of the servient land or of buildings, works or plantings that are or will be located entirely or in part on the servient land.

Notes

(1) Although a fundamental principle of the law of real servitudes, the rule that positive burdens cannot be placed on the owner of land admits of two exceptions.

In very specific circumstances parties may agree to the creation of a right of real servitude containing a positive duty. Coming originally from Roman law, there is in existence a real servitude of support in the case where one building supports another. Here, the owner of the supporting building is under the positive duty to maintain and uphold the building so that the owner of the second building does not lose his building.

The second exception concerns the distinction between primary and secondary duties. The annotated German case shows how the right of real servitude concerned access to the cableway, but the case dealt with the placement of safety features and the question of whether this duty to place safety features could be part of the right of real servitude. This case illustrates how a negative primary duty, the access, can be combined with a positive secondary duty, ie the duty to construct safety bridges. In other words, though a primary duty must be negative, a secondary duty may contain a positive duty.

(2) This category of secondary duties is recognised in all civil law systems. However, not every system treats them in the same way. Other positive duties may be maintenance obligations in order to ensure that the right of servitude can be exercised.[114] Article 5:70(2) of the Dutch BW expressly mentions these obligations.[115] In Dutch law these secondary obligations are part of the right of servitude only as long as the content the parties attempt to give the servitude is not contrary to the nature of the right of real servitude.[116] In French law it is generally held that these positive obligations are accessory to the property right of servitude containing a negative duty.[117] In German law a specific relation between the current owners of the dominant and servient land is recognised. This relation is seen as to create

[114] See Req 22 February 1814, DP 1881, I, 111 and Cass civ 9 January 1901, DP 1901, I, 451, S 1901, I, 169.

[115] See Pitlo et al, above n 83, 201.

[116] HR 16 March 1977, NJ 1977, 399, although this case concerns a right of *emphyteusis,* the doctrine following from this decision applies to all property rights. WB Plantenga and WC Treurniet, *Erfpacht en erfpachtsvoorwaarden* (Preadviezen uitgebracht ter behandeling in de algemene vergadering van de Broederschap Van Candidaat-Notarissen, 1957) 177; AA van Velten, 'Privaatrechtelijke Aspecten van Stedelijke Erfpacht', *Erfpacht* (Preadvies uitgebracht voor de jaarlijkse algemene ledenvergadering van de Koninklijke Notariële Broederschap te houden te Nijmegen op 22 september 1995; Lelystad, Koninklijke Vermande BV, 1995) 17–88, at 47; J De Jong, *Erfpacht en Opstal*, 2nd edn (Deventer, Kluwer, 1995) 17; Rank-Berenschot, above n 15, 110–11.

[117] See Arts 696–97 Cciv, 22 February 1814, DP 1881, I, 111 and Cass civ 9 January 1901, DP 1901, I, 451, S 1901, I, 169; see V Sagaert, 'Real Rights and Real Obligations in Belgian and French Law', in SE Bartels and JM Milo (eds), *Contents of Real Rights* (Nijmegen, Wolf Legal Publishers, 2004) 47–70, at 56–59; V Sagaert, 'Les interferences entre le droit des biens et le droit des obligations: une

obligations and not property rights. Because the law of obligations applies, the content of this secondary obligation can be a positive duty, even a positive duty not directly arising from a specific legal provision.[118]

Cour de cassation, civ 3, 24 May 2000[119] **3.35 (FR)**

Sté Leva v Pierrel

CONTENT OF REAL SERVITUDE

The apartment extension right

A real servitude may not comprise a prohibition to make use of a piece of land.

Facts: Land was subdivided by a couple and sold to the société Toute Transactions Immobilières (TTI). TTI sold one of these parcels to a 'société Immobilière Bust' and the other to a 'société Natiocrédibail-Sicomi'. When a building developer, the claimant in this case, wanted to begin the construction of a building on the second of the pieces of land, its owner, Natiocrédibail-Sicomi, discovered a restriction had been imposed by the couple, which had not been mentioned in the contract of sale.

The couple had stipulated that on the other piece of land a building could be constructed which reached the border to the next piece. Furthermore, the owner of the apartment on the ground floor in this building would be entitled to extend his apartment on the piece of land now owned by Natiocrédibail-Sicomi, or use the extension right to construct a septic tank on that other piece of land.

The right to extend the apartment hindered the construction plans of the defendant, because the extension right covered the full piece of land on which the defendant wanted to build. The defendant therefore claimed the right to extend could not be enforced against them because it had not been mentioned in the contract of sale. The defendant was lessor of the ground floor apartment. He argued that he had an exclusive right to use a part of the neighbouring land and that this right was part of a right of servitude.

Held: A servitude taking away the full right of the owner to use and enjoy his land could not be a right of servitude. The court of appeal deciding that this was possible has misjudged the case.

Judgment: Considering Article 544 of the Civil Code, together with Article 637 of this Code;—Considering that ownership is the right to enjoy and dispose of objects in the most complete manner, provided it is not used in a manner prohibited by statute or by regulation, that a servitude is a burden imposed for the use and utility of land of another owner; …

Considering that by saying that the société Immobilière Bust disposes of a right of enjoyment of the parcel, supporting the building under litigation, which is owned by the société Natiocrédibail, and that the lease granted to the société Cabinet Fabre d'Eglantine, which includes these premises, can be invoked against the société Natiocrédibail, the judgment holds that the continuous and apparent infringement, preceding the division of the parcels and maintained in the same state by the holders of the two parcels, led to a right of servitude *du père de famille* for the parties jointly, of an exclusive right of enjoyment resting on parcel A to the benefit of parcel B, of the territory incorporated in the business premises of parcel B given in lease

analyse de l'evolution depuis le Code civil', in P Wery (ed), *Le droit des obligations contractuelles et le bicentenaire du Code civil* (Brugge, die Keure, 2004) 353–96, n. 16.

[118] See von Staudinger et al, above n 103, 277.

[119] D 2001, 151.

by the holder and that it entails a definitive character, considering the configuration of the premises previously walled in and sealed from the side of the servient land and open and accessible only from the side of the dominant land henceforward the parcel to which the servitude is attached; that by ruling as such, that a servitude cannot but be constituted by an exclusive right prohibiting the owner of the serving land any enjoyment of his ownership, the court of appeal has infringed the aforementioned texts.

Note

The real servitude in this case is a peculiar feature of French law, but the decision, ie the limitations the court imposes on the content of a real servitude to protect the content of the right of ownership, applies to all servitudes. When an owner of a single piece of land gives a specific use to his land, known in French law as *destination du père de famille*, similar to that of an exercise of a servitude, eg a path or waterway, upon separation of the land a right of real servitude will come into existence.[120] This type of servitude is unknown in German and Dutch law.

I.B.2 FRENCH LAW: LEGAL SERVITUDES

In a standard situation, rights of real servitude come into existence after an agreement has been reached between an owner or right-holder of a dominant piece of land and an owner or right-holder of a servient piece of land. However, in French law a right of real servitude can also come into existence by operation of the law. These servitudes are property rights and therefore have effect against third parties, even without registration.[121] How these rights come into existence is dealt with in the chapter on acquisition of property rights.[122]

In other legal systems, similar solutions to the difficulties solved by the use of natural servitudes in French law exist, though without making use of the law of real servitudes.[123] The law of neighbours, a separate and distinct area of law, gives actions to the owner who may demand a solution from his neighbouring owners.[124] Resort to the law of servitudes is unnecessary.

Legal servitudes

Code civil **3.36 (FR)**

Article 640 Lower pieces of land are subjected to those that are situated higher, to receive waters which naturally flow from them without the hand of man having contributed thereto.

An owner of the lower piece of land may not raise dams that prevent that flow.

[120] Art. 692 Cciv: Malaurie and Aynès, above n 18, 350 *et seq.*

[121] Malaurie and Aynès, above n 18, 339.

[122] Below, Chapter 7.

[123] Above, I.B.

[124] Asser et al, above n 21, n 127, at 144–48; Baur, Baur and Stürner, above n 83, 280.

An owner of the higher piece of land may not do anything to the detriment of the servitude of the owner of the lower piece of land.

Cour de cassation, 1 June 1965[125] **3.37 (FR)**
Commune de Bersee v Dupire

NATURAL SERVITUDE

The blocked aqueduct

A natural servitude created by application of Article 640 Cciv only concerns that water which is naturally produced, not water produced by acts of mankind.

Facts: The defendant, owned a piece of land situated lower than a piece of land owned by the claimant, the community of Bersee. A natural servitude allowing water to flow through a water pipe from the higher piece of land owned by the claimant over the land of the defendant had been created through Article 640 Cciv, the existence of which had been recognised in an earlier court ruling. Also above the defendant's land was a public road from which water also flowed through the pipe. On the draining point of this public road, the claimant dumped the community's waste water, which also flowed through the water pipe over the defendant's land.

The question was who should pay for the cleaning and maintenance of the pipe. The claimant argued that because the natural servitude was in place, the defendant had to undertake the cleaning and maintenance work. The defendant argued that the natural servitude extended only to the water coming from the claimant's land and not to that coming from the public road or that dumped there by the claimant.

Held: The natural servitude only covered the natural flow of water, meaning primarily rain. It did, however, also extend to water coming from the public road. It did not, however, cover the waste water, which did not come directly from nature but was produced by the claimant. The claim was accordingly rejected.

Judgment: As laid down by Article 640 of the Civil Code, upon the instructions of which the community of Bersee has exclusively founded its claim, and which only concerns waters the flow of which is the natural result of the specific situation and in particular rainwater, to the exclusion of domestic or waste waters, the appeal judges rightly note that the owner of the lower premises is not held to get rid of obstacles to the natural flow of waters which are there as a consequence of a fact for which he is not accountable, and that hence the existence at the property of Dupire of works operated by those who made them is not sufficient to oblige him to undertake cleaning work;

That the disputed judgment moreover maintains that the observations of the expert provide the evidence that the share of domestic waters coming from the public road has, at the very least, contributed to the blockage of the aqueduct and that that flow of water continues, without the community offering to make it stop;

That, in those circumstances, the court of appeal has rightly considered that Dupire should not be held to possibly participate in the costs of a cleaning, the effect of which would be to make him tolerate the flow upon his land and that it is first up to the community to conduct the necessary works to put an end to a state of affairs which is contrary to the instructions of Article 640 of the Civil Code.

[125] Bull Civ 1965, I, n 362.

Notes

(1) This case shows how a right of servitude comes into existence by operation of Article 640 Cciv and functions as a normal right of real servitude.[126] As far as possible, the normal provisions on servitudes apply. This includes the requirement of a servient and a dominant land, an owner of the dominant land and the owner of the servient land and the negative content of the primary obligation imposed by the servitude.

(2) Apart from this example, there are other legal servitudes. These include a right to use public water for irrigation of the owner's land, and the right to set boundaries between neighbouring pieces of land, and the right for an owner to enclose his land with a fence or wall.[127] Again, circumstances force the creation of a legal servitude. The first situation, the right to take water, can easily be constructed as a right of servitude. The public waterway functions as the servient land from which the owner of the dominant land may take water. The owner of the servient land, ie the state, is forced to tolerate the taking of the water, which constitutes a negative obligation.

However, the latter two examples, ie the right to set boundaries or close off land with a fence or wall, are more difficult to conceive as a right of servitude.[128] Nevertheless, the general provisions on servitudes can also be imposed on these situations. The owner of one piece of land is entitled to bring an action against the other owner of the land who is forced to tolerate that action.

Comparative Note

Of course, other legal systems are faced with similar difficulties. The natural servitude of water as dealt with in the annotated French case is contained in Article 5:38 of the Dutch BW,[129] which states that a lower piece of land is forced to tolerate natural water flowing from a higher piece of land. German law uses a very broadly formulated paragraph, §906 BGB, in which an owner is forced to allow emissions of neighbouring pieces of land, including natural water such as rainwater, in so far as they do not affect the use of his own land.[130]

Other similar problems are dealt with in Dutch and German law. Article 5:40 BW allows an owner to take water from public water flowing next to his land. Further, Articles 5:47 and 5:48 BW provide an owner with a claim to set the boundaries between his and his neighbour's land and a power for an owner to enclose his land.[131] Finally, German law allows the owner to demand from a neighbouring owner that he co-operate in the setting of boundaries between their two pieces of

[126] See Aubry et al, *Droit Civil Français*, vol 3, 7th edn (Paris, Libraries Techniques, 1968) 23 *et seq.*

[127] Arts 644, 646 and 647 Cciv: see Terré and Simler, above n 18, 195–203; Malaurie and Aynès, above n 18, 287–89.

[128] See Terré and Simler, above n 18, 201.

[129] See Asser et al, above n 21, n 133, at 154 *et seq.*

[130] Baur, Baur and Stürner, above n 83, 283–85.

[131] Asser et al, above n 21, n 138–41, at 159–63.

land by, for instance, placing a border post or clearing a border post which had been previously placed.[132]

Code civil **3.38 (FR)**

Article 649 The servitudes created by the law have as a purpose a public or local interest, or a private interest.

Article 650 Those created for a public or local interest have as purposes the footpaths along the state streams of water, the construction or reparation of paths and other public or local duties.

Everything concerning this kind of servitudes is determined by statutes or special acts.

Article 682 The owner of which the lands are enclosed and from which there is no exit by public road, or only an insufficient exit, either for the agricultural, industrial or commercial exploitation of his ownership, or for the realisation of undertaking constructions or allotments, is entitled to demand a sufficient passageway over the grounds of the neighbours to ensure a connection of his land to the public space, on condition of a proportional compensation to the loss that it may cause.

Notes

(1) Because of this method of creation, a legal servitude can arise even when there is no dominant or servient land.[133] For an example see excerpt 3.FR.37. Nevertheless, a legal servitude is still a property right with effect against third parties and the general rules on real servitudes apply.[134]

Article 649 Cciv divides legal servitudes into two categories. Legal servitudes for private purposes include the earlier-mentioned servitudes, but also a right to a path as seen from the annotated case which was already used to illustrate limitations on the right of ownership.[135] In such a situation, ie an enclosed piece of land, there is a dominant and a servient land.

(2) Servitudes for public purposes should be distinguished from normal real servitudes. These public legal servitudes arise from specific legislation and have no dominant land. Instead, a public legal person benefits from the existence of the public legal servitude.[136] Furthermore, the fundamental restriction to the negative content of servitudes does not apply to public legal servitudes.[137] The public legal servitudes are used by the French state to regulate public roads and public transmission lines. The latter category includes electricity and telecommunication lines.[138]

[132] §919 BGB: Baur, Baur and Stürner, above n 83, 291.

[133] Cass civ 3e 11 December 1970, Bull civ, III, n 699.

[134] Terré and Simler, above n 18, 650; Malaurie and Aynès, above n 18, 343–44.

[135] See Cass 22 November 1937.

[136] Terré and Simler, above n 18, 238–39.

[137] *Ibid*, 239.

[138] See Art L114-1 Code voirie routière; Art 11 Décr no 70-492 du 11 juin 1970; Art L45-1 Code des postes et télécommunications.

I.C PERSONAL SERVITUDES

A personal servitude is a property right established on behalf of a person as such and not in his capacity as owner. The property right is therefore connected to the person holding the right. Because these rights are property rights, the term personal servitude may sound confusing. In general, when the person holding the right ceases to exist, the right also ceases to exist. Because of this connection to a person, the word 'personal' is added to the general word 'servitude'.[139]

The category of personal servitudes comprises the right of usufruct, and the rights of use and habitation. Unlike real servitudes, these rights can, with one exception, also be held on movable assets.

These rights all share the same basis. Usufruct, as the most important amongst the personal servitudes, serves as a model for the other property rights and will be dealt with first.

German law additionally recognises two further personal servitudes, the limited personal servitudes and the so-called real burdens or *Reallasten*. These are dealt with at the end

I.C.1 USUFRUCT

A right of usufruct is a property right which grants the holder the right to use and enjoy a thing of the owner as well as a right to take the fruits this thing produces. When a right of usufruct is created, the owner of the asset can no longer exercise his right to use and enjoy the asset. In fact, the only power the owner has is the right to transfer ownership of the asset to another person. For this reason the right of ownership in these situations is known as bare ownership and the owner is known as the bare owner.[140] However, at the end of the usufruct, the right of ownership will become full and complete again.

Rules common to French, German and Dutch law

Code civil **3.39 (FR)**

Article 578 The right of usufruct is the right to use and enjoy an object of another in the same way as an owner himself, but on condition that the substance of the object is preserved.

[139] The approach taken here is also followed in German law, which uses the term *persönliche Dienstbarkeiten*. French and Dutch law generally do not use this specific term. However, from a comparative viewpoint it should cover the rights of usufruct, use, habitation and limited personal servitudes as well as real burdens.

[140] Note that in some legal systems ownership of other assets than movable things, such as claims is not possible. Then the terminology is different. Below, Chapter 4.

Bürgerliches Gesetzbuch **3.40 (DE)**

§1030 (1) An object can be burdened in such a way, that the person for whose benefit this burdening occurs is entitled to the use of the object and to take the fruits. (Usufruct)
(2) The usufruct can be limited by the exclusion of certain powers of use.

Burgerlijk Wetboek **3.41 (NL)**

Article 3:201 Usufruct provides the right to use and take the fruits of objects which belong to someone else.

Article 3:216 The usufructary is entitled to all fruits that are produced during the right of usufruct or that become due. In the deed of creation it can be further determined what should, with respect to the right of usufruct, be considered as a fruit.

RG, 27 June 1940[141] **3.42 (DE)**

USUFRUCT ON IMMOVABLE ASSETS

The inheritance

A usufruct can be established on an immovable object, but not on a particular part of such an object.

Facts: The parties were brother and sister. In a will, the parents intended to leave the ownership of the land on which their house stood to their son. The house contained a small rifle construction factory and store which had also been owned and run by the parents. The will provided for the creation of a right of usufruct on the factory and store on behalf of the son, but only from the right side of the entrance. The usufruct was also to include the second floor of the house. By the same will, the daughter was given a right of usufruct on the left side of the factory and store and the first floor of the house.

When the father died the mother agreed with the daughter on the transfer of the factory's machines and other facilities as well as the construction department. Furthermore, the mother agreed to transfer the land to the daughter, the defendant in this case. The son, as claimant, claimed the voidance of this agreement on the basis that his mother was not entitled to transfer against her consent which she had already given in the testament. Furthermore he argued the mother could not transfer the objects because of his right of usufruct on the left half of the company. At issue was whether such a right of usufruct on the company and on the second floor in the house could exist.

Held: The court held that, although a usufruct can be established on immovable assets, the object of establishment must be identifiable. A mere description of the object is not enough. The object itself must be distinct and separated from the rest of the building in the meaning of §93 BGB. As this was not the case, no right of usufruct had been created, but the will continued to bind the mother, and also her heirs, to dispose of the land and house in the manner provided.

Judgment: 1. ... In the testamentary clause over the rights of usufruct for both of the heirs the provision of legacies, but not a general sharing arrangement (§2048 BGB) can be found. Actual rights of usufruct, not just proprietary or personal housing rights, were intended. The creation of a right of usufruct on land is legally permissible. The circumstance that the piece of land—at the time of succession—did no longer economically belong to the inheritance does not make the legacy void, since

[141] RGZ 164, 196.

we may assume that the testators, had they imagined the acquisition of the land by one of the heirs, would have maintained the legacies nonetheless. The creation of the right of usufruct does not pose difficulties to the heirs or to he who is burdened with the legacy, because piece of land was acquired by one of the heirs.

2. If the revision turns against the establishment of a claim for the creation of the right of usufruct, because clarifying a legal question important for the later division of the inheritance cannot be the subject of a declaratory action under §256 ZPD, then this attempt is unfounded. Here, not only the decision of a purely legal question is concerned, but also a specific legal relation, ie the contentious question between the parties, whether in the pending division of the inheritance in favour of the claimant an entitlement from the provisions on the usufruct mey be derived. An interest of the claimant in the immediate declaration of this legal relation is therefore to be recognised because thereby the argument is appropriately prepared.

3. The revision states that the creation of a rights of usufruct on a space in a house, which is a substantial component part of the land, contradicts the provision that such a space cannot be the subject-matter of special rights (§93 BGB). Therefore the claimant claims a performance that is not legally possible. The concern raised in the revision is to be agreed to. The court of appeal correctly holds that a usufruct can be created in respect to a fraction of an object, which in §981 of the first draft of the Civil Code was expressly stated, but later removed as apparent (minutes of the commission for the second reading of the draft of the Civil Code Book II, at 384 under II). The store and a floor in the house however are not such a (theoretical) fraction of ownership of land in the meaning of §741 BGB *et seq*, but are parts of the house, which are distinct from other parts of the land by tangible (physical) borders. A contradiction in itself exists, if the court of appeal speaks of the 'actual fraction of a piece of land', which could be the subject-matter of a right of usufruct. The usufruct of an object includes basically all usages of the encumbered object. However, specific ways of usage can be excluded according to special legal provisions (§1030(2) BGB.). A right of usufruct cannot be restricted to specific uses only. The use of a part of the house can also not be regarded as total use with permissible exception. A right to use only certain specific parts of a house represents no permission to a proportionate practice of usages resulting from the whole piece of land, as the case would be with a division of the land into fractions, which could be content of a usufruct.

Somewhat completely different than this is a right of use, which is limited to certain, in reality—and not only proportionately (theoretically)—defined parts of a piece of land. If such, for a certain person as property right, directly relating to the object, is created, then this can only happen in the form of a limited personal servitude under §§1090, 1093 BGB.

Notes

(1) The case shows that a right of usufruct is not only used to provide another with a right to use and enjoy during the lifetime of the owner, but that the right of usufruct can also be created by a will so as to distribute the right to use and enjoy to another person for the duration of that person's life.[142] In fact, the many

[142] See W Schön, *Der Nießbrauch und Sachen. Gesetzliche Struktur und Rechsgeschäftliche Gestaltung* (Köln, Verlag Dr Otto Schmidt KG, 1992) 29–30; Schwab and Prütting, above n 14, 421; Baur,

succession laws in Europe make use of the right of usufruct to allow parties to deal with their assets after their death.[143] In this case the right of usufruct allowed the parents to separate the ownership of the land and house from the right to use. The advantage of the right of usufruct as an estate planning device is that it enables a permanent transfer to a person who becomes owner, and whose heirs will further inherit the object, and a temporary transfer to someone who, for the duration of his life, is entitled to use the object, but whose heirs do not inherit his right to use.

(2) The case also illustrates how a usufruct on an immovable object needs a different approach than the same right on a movable object. This different approach does not only concern registration but also the nature of the immovable object itself.[144] In a Dutch case similar to the case above, the Hoge Raad allowed a right of usufruct of a separate and distinct part of a building used as a dental practice. The Dutch court held that, if parties wanted, they could transfer ownership of the residential part separate from the ownership of the dental practice part. Because of this possible separation, a right of usufruct could be established on each part.[145]

(3) Apart from the right to use an asset, a right of usufruct also entitles the right-holder to take the fruits the asset produces. What exactly are fruits is dealt with in Chapter 7.[146]

Code civil **3.43 (FR)**

Article 600 The usufructuary takes the objects in the state in which they are, but he cannot commence their enjoyment until after having drawn up, in the presence of the owner, or after duly summoning him, an inventory of the movable objects and a record of the immovables subject to the usufruct.

Article 601 He shall provide security to enjoy as a good housefather (*bon père de famille*), unless he is exempted thereof by the act creating the right of usufruct; however, the father and mother having the legal usufruct of the objects of their children, and the seller or the donor, who reserved the right of usufruct, are not compelled to provide security.

Bürgerliches Gesetzbuch **3.44 (DE)**

§1036 (1) The holder of a right of usufruct is entitled to possession of the object.
(2) In the exercise of his right to use the holder must maintain the economic purpose for which the object was used and must exercise his right in a normal economic way

§1037 The holder of a right of usufruct is not entitled to transform or actually change the object.

Baur and Stürner, above n 83, 360; Terré and Simler, above n 18, 597–98, 600; Malaurie and Aynès, above n 18, 258–59.

[143] JHM van Erp, 'New developments in succession law', in K Boele-Woelki and JHM van Erp (eds), *General reports of the XVIIth congress of the International Academy of Comparative Law/Rapports Généraux du XViie congrès de l'Académie Internationale de Droit Comparé* (Bruxelles, Utrecht, Bruylant/Eleven International Publishing, 2007) 73 *et seq.*

[144] On registration see below, Chapter 8.

[145] HR 29 May 1985, NJ 1986/274.

[146] Below, Chapter 7.

Burgerlijk Wetboek **3.45 (NL)**

Article 3:207 (1) A holder of a right of usufruct can use and consume the objects under usufruct in accordance with the agreement made upon creation, or when such agreement is missing, in accordance with the nature of the objects in respect to the practice of use and consume.

(2) Furthermore, a holder of a right of usufruct is entitled to perform all acts needed in the course of duty of a good usufructuary. In respect of all other acts the holder of the usufruct and the holder of the right from which the usufruct was derived can only act together.

(3) In respect of the holder of the right from which the usufruct was derived the holder of the right of usufruct muse take care of the objects and manage them under the standard of a good usufructuary.

Article 3:215 When with creation of a usufruct, or after that, the power partially or completely to alienate or consume the objects under usufruct is given to the usufructuary, the holder of the right from which the right of usufruct was derived may demand the retro-transfer of the objects under usufruct or the objects substituted for these, unless the holder of the usufruct or acquirers of his right prove that the objects were consumed or vanished by coincidence.

Notes

(1) Although the holder of a usufruct may use things for the duration of his property right, he is under the obligation to take care of them. The standard all of these legal systems impose is that of a good usufructuary.[147] For example, when assets have decreased in value and the holder of the usufruct could have prevented this, he can be liable.[148]

(2) When the usufruct is created, an inventory is drafted to establish which assets fall under the right of usufruct. This requirement is a duty in French and Dutch law. In German law parties may choose to do so.[149] Other duties of the holder of a usufruct are the obligation to provide security when the usufruct is established and to provide insurance for the assets under his care.[150] The usufructuary will also be liable to pay the costs of repair and maintenance of the assets.[151]

(3) The right of usufruct is a property right which is connected to the life of a person. Traditionally a right of usufruct cannot be assigned to another person. In German law this has remained the case.[152] In French and in Dutch law the right of usufruct can be assigned.[153] When the right is assigned to another person the exist-

[147] See Art 601 Cciv, §1036(2) BGB and Art 3:207(3) BW.

[148] Baur, Baur and Stürner, above n 83, 365; Pitlo et al, above n 83, 523–24.

[149] Art 600 Cciv, Art 3:205 BW and §1034 BGB.

[150] On the providing of security: Art 601 Cciv, §1051 BGB and Art 3:206 BW. On the providing of insurance: Art 608 Cciv, §1045 BGB and Art 3:209 BW.

[151] Art 608 Cciv, §§1047, 1045 and 1048(2) BGB and Art. 3:220 BW.

[152] §1059 BGB.

[153] Art 595 Cciv, Art 3:223 BW; Terré and Simler, above n 18, 616–17.

ence of the right remains connected to the life of the person on whose behalf the right was established or the duration which was agreed upon.[154]

(4) The holder of the right of usufruct is under an obligation to preserve the assets he has been entrusted with. To this rule Dutch law has made an exception. Article 3:215 BW allows the possibility of creating a usufruct on assets which are perishable or can be consumed combined with a power for the holder of the usufruct to allow those assets to perish or to consume the assets.[155] French law and German law strongly oppose this use of the right of usufruct. Instead these latter systems use a quasi-usufruct to solve this problem.

Cour de cassation, 5 December 1968[156] **3.46 (FR)**

SARL Le Grand Verger v Widow Cozon and others

CONTENT OF THE RIGHT OF USUFRUCT

Conservation of the object under usufruct

A usufructuary may use the object under usufruct, but must take care of the object as well as retain the same use of the object.

Facts: Dorel owned a very large house. He left ownership of the house to a lady named Cozon and a right of usufruct to his widow. The widow subsequently leased the house to a party named Aubry who intended to use it as a children's lodging. On 7 December 1951 the lease was renewed with the intention of using it as a hotel-restaurant, family lodging, children's lodging or another similar commercial purpose. This commercial lease was renewed by the widow Dorel on 5 January 1959. In the period between the conclusion of the two lease agreements, Aubry transferred his rights under the lease to a limited company, Le Grand Verger, the claimant in this case.

When the widow died, Cozon, as owner, claimed that the lease was void on the ground that a usufructuary is obliged to preserve the purpose of the land. The court of appeal allowed this claim and held that the widow violated Article 578 Cciv. Against this decision Le Grand Verger appealed in cassation, claiming the widow Dorel as right-holder of a usufruct was allowed to change the use of the building into a hotel-restaurant.

Held: The house was originally a house to live in. A holder of a usufruct has no power to change the use of the building from habitation to a commercial use.

Judgment: Considering that an grievance was brought to the court of appeal upholding that the consensual lease exceeded the rights of the usufructuary, therefore, according to the grievance, 'that on the one hand, the awarding of a lease only constitutes an administrative act of the powers of the usufructuary and that, on the other hand, it appears from own findings in the judgment that the lease had resulted in, in this instance, significant improvements to the leased object and corresponding to the nature of the leased object, which makes it impossible to argue that the usufructuary had altered the substance';—But considering that the usufructuary should manage the object in due diligence, according to the purpose for

[154] Cass civ 3e 26 January 1972, D 1975, at 22; JCP 1972, éd G, II, 17104; Art 3:223 BW; Pitlo et al, above n 83, 523–24.

[155] See Asser et al, above n 21, n 261, at 289; EB Rank-Berenschot, 'Enige aspecten van de plaats van het vruchtgebruik in het vermogensrechtelijk systeem' (1985) 5730 *WPNR* 170–79, at 178; MS van Gaalen, *Vruchtgebruik* (Deventer, Kluwer, 2001) 23, 118–22.

[156] D 1969, 274–75.

which it was intended, on condition that the subject-matter is preserved and that he does not change the nature of the object under usufruct; that pronouncing that agreeing to 'commercial leases which permit the holder of the usufruct to establish and exploit a business in the accomodations which, until now, were intended to be used as a residential building, and by transforming a countryhouse into a commercial building, the widow Dorel has changed the purpose of the building on which held a right of usufruct' and adding 'that the widow Dorel has violated the privisions of Article 578 Cciv, which require her to preserve the subject-matter...', the court of appeal has not violated any of the provisions referred to in the grievance, the changes to the substance of the object do not exist except in the the improvements involved to the leased object made by the lessee.

Notes

(1) The right of usufruct has an important impact on the right of ownership, which, following the creation of the usufruct, becomes known as 'bare ownership'. The usufructuary is limited in what he may do with the object under usufruct. In general the usufructuary is awarded the right to use and to enjoy the object of the owner, who, for the duration of the usufruct, is not entitled to do so. The right to use includes the right to lease the object, although the Cour de cassation has held on another occasion that the right to lease is restricted to a maximum duration of nine years.[157]

(2) In a later judgment, the Cour de cassation stated that a lease with another purpose than the purpose for which the right of usufruct was established constituted an abuse of the right to use of the holder of the right of usufruct. Moreover, the court held that because of this abuse, the bare owner could claim that the right of usufruct should come to an end.[158]

Kammergericht, 23 July 1991[159] **3.47 (DE)**

CONTENT OF THE RIGHT OF USUFRUCT

Building duty

An agreement to build upon a piece of land cannot be made the content of a right of usufruct.

Facts: A person X had established a right of usufruct on a piece of land on behalf of person Y. The deed establishing the usufruct contained a clause which stated 'the usufructuary is entitled, in the scope of his right to use, to create, in accordance with the legal requirements, a factory building and the necessary parking spaces, access roads etc'. When the deed was send for registration, the registrar refused to register this deed establishing a right of usufruct.

The registrar referred to §1037 BGB, which creates an obligation to maintain the object under usufruct, and stated a right to build would allow the usufructuary to alter the object and not to maintain it.

The parties X and Y to the deed establishing a right of usufruct, claimants in this case, claimed

[157] See Cass civ 3e 4 October 1972, Bull Civ III, n 498.

[158] Cass civ 4 June 1975, Bull civ III, n 194.

[159] KG (Kammergericht) Beschl vom 23.7.1991—1 W 7919/89, DNotZ 1992, 675 mit Anm Frank.

the deed constituted a valid right of usufruct including the building right as a part of it. The registrar, the defendant, persisted in refusing registration because a usufruct could not include a building right.

Held: The court held that §1037 BGB could not be deviated from and that the agreement did not have effect against third parties. Therefore, a right of usufruct cannot include a building right.

Judgment: … Since the usufruct grants the right to make use of an object (§1030(1) BGB), the owner is drastically limited by the creation of a right of usufruct. While before he held a comprehensive power to use and to dispose, after the creation of the usufruct he does not dispose over the fruits of the object and over the advantages that the use of the object grants (see §100 BGB), and the usufructuary acquires the right to possession of the object (§1036(1) BGB). Thus the owner transfers substantial parts of his full right to the usufructuary upon the creation of a right of usufruct and at the same time gives up—to a large extent—his direct influence on the object. Because of this extensive limitation on the owner in his legal position the legislature imposed the usufructuary not only with the obligation, to maintain the object under usufruct and to use object in the ordinary economic function in accordance with the rules of a normal economy (§1036(2) BGB), but it has above all forbidden, to transform the thing and substantially change it (§1037(1) BGB). With this prohibition, which was only limited for plants for the production of soil components (§1037(2) BGB), it is to be guaranteed that the substance of the object remains the same for the owner as it was at the time of the creation of the right of usufruct (see Planck, BGB 5th edn, §1037 notes 1). This provision in §1037(1) BGB thus aims at the protection of the owner from the consequences of a transformation or a substantial change which secure, would because of the property effect of the usufruct a later owner, who is not also legal successor to the personal relations, subject to the unpredictable risk, not to get the object back in changed condition.

Accordingly, the usufructuary is even forbidden from making a transformation or a substantial change, if thereby the object becomes more valuable or more lucrative (see Staudinger/Promberger, BGB, 12th edn, §1037 Rdn 1; MünchKommBGB/Petzoldt, 2nd edn, §1037 Rdn. 2). Only if the substance of the object in its total character is not affected, transformations and changes are reasonable for the respective owner and therefore permitted (see Petzoldt, aaO; BGB RGRK/Rothe, 12th edn, §1037 Rdn.1). The duty of the usufructuary to preserve of the object is corresponding to the loss of the owner's right of use the object, which follows from his right of ownership, which is why the duty to preserve the substance of the usufructuary standardized in §1037(1) BGB belongs to the nature of the right of usufruct and so that §1037(1) BGB cannot be claimed with property effect. … However if the maintaining of the subject-matter belongs to the nature of the usufruct, then the claim of §1037(1) BGB with property effect cannot be justified either by the consideration that the usufructuary must meet the obligation to maintain the economic purpose of the object. …

A legally inadmissible deviation of §1037(1) of the BGB with property effect is present only if the owner permits the usufructuary, after specific agreement with the owner, to transform the object according to his liking. Rather, such a violation is to be affirmed if the usufructuary is to be entitled according to the agreement with the owner in case of a usufruct in respect to an empty piece of land, to erect a building. … Such a freeing from the obligation to the maintaining of the subject-matter with property effect cannot be justified under the condition that the parties are considering the creation of a right of usufruct on an undeveloped piece of land or consider the intention to construct a building as a possibility (so, however,

Staudinger/Promberger, aaO, Rdn 4). The argument, in maintaining the subject-matter of a substantial change of form, but a use of property in the framework of its 'composition objectively shaped and by the will of the parties' (so Staudinger/Promberger, aaO), does not justify any other evaluation. The substance of an object in the sense of §1037(1) of the BGB is shaped not by an act of will of the owner or of the parties to the contract for the creation of the right of usufruct, but is an objectively ascertainable thing. Also the consideration that in the current case the land development served the maintenance of the economic purpose of the land desired by the owner, ie the development of the land, and that therefore the corresponding agreement was not in breach of the prohibition of transformation in the sense of §1037 BGB, is not able not to convince. Because of that the legal provision, which prohibit interferences by the usufructuary with the substance of an object, is not only a concretisation of the principle laid down in §1036(2) BGB that the usufructuary has to continue the past economical regular management.

A transformation or a substantial change of an object can be present also if this transformation corresponds to an economic purpose supported by the will of the owner. ... It is obvious that the owner may grant the right to develop a vacant piece of land to another. Because of §1037(1) BGB, which cannot be deviated from with property effect, this power cannot be granted to a usufructuary as a part of the property right.

Note

The maintenance duty for a right-holder is therefore used to limit the agreement the owner and the holder of a usufruct can make on the rights of the latter. However, when parties stay within the maintenance duty, eg give the holder of a usufruct the power to assign his right of usufruct, this agreement becomes part of the usufruct itself and therefore will have effect against third parties.

I.C.2 QUASI-USUFRUCT

Introductory Note

Where a right of usufruct is established on assets which are perishable or which are intended to be consumed, the holder of the usufruct cannot fulfil his obligation as a good usufructuary to preserve the assets. In those situations, with the exception of the Netherlands as dealt with in the previous section, a right of usufruct cannot be created. Instead, French and German law recognise a quasi-usufruct—a device that originated in Roman law

Code civil **3.48 (FR)**

Article 587 When a right of usufruct is established on objects which cannot be used without being consumed, such as money, grain, liquors, the usufructuary has a right to use them, but with the obligation to, at the end of the usufruct, return either objects of the same quantity and quality or their value estimated at the date of return.

Bürgerliches Gesetzbuch **3.49 (DE)**

§1067 (1) If objects that can be consumed or used up are subject to a right of usufruct, the holder of the usufruct becomes owner of these objects; after the termination of the right of usufruct the value of these objects, that they had at the moment of creation of the right, must be returned. Both the person creating the right of usufruct as well as the holder of the right can, at his own costs, ask an expert to determine the value of the objects.
(2) The person creating the right of usufruct may demand security, when the claim to the value of the object is endangered.

Note

The quasi-usufruct is not really a right of usufruct as such, but more a transfer of ownership of a thing. However, as in the Dutch solution above, the usufructuary is under the obligation to return either similar objects or the value of those objects. The right of quasi-usufruct can be combined with a normal usufruct.[160]

I.C.3 USE AND HABITATION

Rules common to French, German and Dutch law

Introductory Note

Another Roman law inspired distinction is between the right of usufruct and the lesser personal servitudes of use and habitation.[161] These rights are similar to the right of usufruct but more restricted in content. The right of use is used for immovable objects more than for movable objects, mainly because it only awards the rights to use, which is particularly used to give another the right to use land rather than use an object. The right of habitation can only be created on an immovable object.

Code civil **3.50 (FR)**

Article 625 The rights of use and of habitation are created and destroyed in the same ways as a right of usufruct.

[160] Terré and Simler, above n 18, 599–601.

[161] On Roman law, see A Watson, *The Law of Property in the Later Roman Republic* (Oxford, Oxford University Press, 1968) 220-221; E Bund, 'Begriff und Einteilung der Servituten im Römishen Recht' (1956) 367 *Zeitschrift der Savigny-Stiftung für Rechtsgeschichte, Romanistische Abteilung* 155–219, at 167; JAC Thomas, *Textbook of Roman Law* (Amsterdam, North-Holland Publishing Company, 1976) 195–210, at 207–08; M Kaser, *Das Römische Privatrecht; 1. Abschnitt*, 2nd edn (München, CH Beck'sche Verlagsbuchhandlung, 1971) 454.

Cour de cassation, 3 January 1978[162] **3.51 (FR)**

Grenot v Richardot

NATURE OF THE RIGHT OF USE

The expropriated land

The right of use is a property right and should be distinguished from a right of real servitude.

Facts: A couple named Gallard divided and transferred land with a house on it between several parties. As a party of this transfer, the couple reserved to themselves grazing rights for their cattle over a specific period, including as a part of the grazing right a general right to use the land. Through a series of transactions Grenot, the claimant, acquired this grazing right, including the right to use, on 6 January 1923. Meanwhile, the land had become owned by Richardot, the defendant.

On 4 April 1973 the French government expropriated the land. The claimant sought compensation from the defendant as owner, as well as from the French state. The claimant could do so because of a specific provision allowing them to claim for compensation in case their right to use had been affected. If the right of use were to be recognised the claimant would have a property right on the land and therefore be entitled to compensation. At issue was the legal nature of the grazing right as well as the claim for compensation.

Held: The grazing right constituted a right to use and this right was a property right. However, such a right is strictly connected to the person to whom it was granted, and thus cannot be transferred. Therefore, the claimant had not become holder of the right of use, and consequently he was not entitled to compensation.

Judgment: ... That in fact, always according to the appellant, the holders of the grazing right did not resort to any other action as against the compensated owner than the action for unjust enrichment, not having, in turn, the possibility to obtain compensation from the part of the expropriator, that is is the same fact, the expropriation, which was originally for the enrichment of the owner and for the impoverishment of the holder of the right of use;

But considering, first, that when analysing the sense and the extent of the clause through which the partners Gallard had reserved the grazing right, the judges in first instance have considered that it created a property right, which may not be considered as a right of servitude, as defined by Article 637 of the Civil Code;

That furthermore the right of use, created and destroyed in the same manner as a right of usufruct and consequently, being constituted as a result of a right for life, not capable of being transferred at death, the court of appeal did consider whether the heirs Grenot could use them as such.

Burgerlijk Wetboek **3.52 (NL)**

Article 3:226 (1) To the right of use and the right of habitation, the rules of usufruct apply in the same way, except according to the following provisions.

(2) In case only the right of use is created, the holder of the right has the competence to use and enjoy the fruits of the corporeal objects subject to his right, which he needs for himself and his family.

[162] Bull civ III, n 3, at 3.

(3) In case only the right of habitation is granted, the holder of the right has the competence to occupy with his family the house subject to his right.

(4) He who has one of the rights specified in this Article cannot transfer or burden his right, nor let another use the corporeal object or let another occupy the house.

Notes

(1) The right to use includes the same right of use as a usufructuary, but does not include the right to take the fruits, except when needed for private use.[163] The right of habitation is a right to use a building to live in and therefore should be seen as a restricted property right of use. The rights of use and habitation are strictly connected to the person to whom the right was granted and cannot be assigned. This prohibition of assignment also means that the right-holder cannot allow another access to the exercise of the right.[164] The right of use and habitation can therefore only be used in a very limited sense,

The right-holders of a right to use or habitation are under the same obligations as a usufructuary. These include the duty to take care of the land as well as to preserve its value. As the French case illustrates, the right of use is a property right. The right will bind third parties. The same is true for rights of habitation.

(2) In respect to the right of habitation German law uses a specific right which can be seen as a part of limited personal servitudes, and which is dealt with in the next paragraph. §1093 BGB stipulates that a limited personal servitude can have a specific right to use a building or part of a building as its object. The right is known as a *Wohnungsrecht*.[165] For the creation, duration and cessation of this right the rules of limited personal servitudes apply in a similar fashion as the rules on usufruct to the rights of use and habitation.

I.C.4 GERMANY: LIMITED PERSONAL SERVITUDES

(i) Regular servitudes

Introductory Note

German law recognises a type of property right which is established on behalf of a person, as in the case of a right of usufruct, but which burdens the use of land of another person, as in the case of a right of real servitude. This property right is known as a limited personal servitude or *beschränkte persönliche Dienstbarkeit*. This right shares many characteristics with the usufruct as it does with the real servitude. This section shortly deals with these limited personal servitudes and provides one specific example of its application in practice.

[163] On French law see Art 630 Cciv; Malaurie and Aynès, above n 18, 275–76.

[164] Art 3:226 (4) BW, Art 631 and 634 Cciv.

[165] See von Staudinger et al, above n 103, 728.

Bürgerliches Gesetzbuch **3.53 (DE)**

§1090 A piece of land can be burdened in such a way that a person, to whose benefit the right is created, is entitled to a specific use of the land or which awards him a power, which can be the subject of a real servitude.

BGH, 14 March 2003[166] **3.54 (DE)**

CONTENT OF LIMITED PERSONAL SERVITUDE

Holiday apartment

Reserving the right to lease a building, provide heat and deal with television and electricity companies for the right-holder of a right to have a holiday home in a bungalow park can constitute a limited personal servitude.

Facts: On 31 August 1997 the claimant bought a right to have a holiday home in a bungalow park from the owner of the park, the defendant. Before the conclusion of the transfer, the defendant confronted the claimant with a deed in which a limited personal servitude had been established for an unlimited duration.

The limited personal servitude was established on behalf of the defendant and contained a provision that the apartment could only be used as a holiday apartment. Furthermore the servitude provided that only the defendant could lease and manage the apartment. The power to manage included the right to provide heat, television and electricity as well as a telephone line.

The claimant claimed they did not know of the existence of the limited personal servitude and that they were not informed of its existence by the notary. The claimant therefore argued the limited personal servitude was not validly created.*Held:* The content which the defendant attempted to give to the limited personal servitude was permissible and the servitude was properly registered. It is the content of the servitude which determines whether a limited personal servitude is validly established and not the lack of information of the claimant. In order to determine what a content of a limited personal servitude can be the same requirements as for real servitudes are used.

Judgment: … [B]ecause the right to operate a holiday park is a permissible content of the effectively created right of servitude. Which of the two claims would otherwise be relevant can therefore remain open. There are no considertions against the validity of content of the servitude.

(a) The subject of a limited personal servitude can be, under §1090 BGB, each power, which can form the content of a right of servitude under §1018 BGB. Accordingly the servitude can be directed to a specific usage of the burdened land, toward the omission of certain action on the burdened land as well as on the exclusion of the exercise of a right. On the other hand, the content of a servitude cannot be a positive duty to perform and also not a positive act of the owner himself … the servitude may also not contain restrictions of the freedom to dispose over the burdened land of the owner; rather the dity to refrain imposed on the owner must be aimed towards a restriction of the actual use of piece of land. …

(b) The servitude of the defendant does not oblige the claimant to a positive act. The subject-matter of the property right is not also a direct obligation on the claimant to perform, to conclude contracts with the defendant on the management and lease, on the supply of heat or on the operation of cable television and a hotel telephone system. The entry in the land entry and the authorisation for registration recorded

[166] V ZR 304/02=NJW-RR 2003, 733.

therein merely state that the apartment can be used as a vacation home only and that it may be offered to a changing group of persons for leisure purposes and that the defendant may deliver the aforementioned services. The servitude is thus aimed at the use of the separate ownership of the claimant (§§1090, 1018 alto 1 BGB).

However, for the claimant this has the consequence that she—if she does not want to let the apartment remain empty—is dependent on using the services of the defendant. The creation of the servitude served, from the view of the defendant, thus as security of future contractual obligations of the claimant. This, according to the existing Senate jurisprudence on gas stations and brewery servitudes ... and for the indirect property security of district heating obligations ... encounters no legal doubts. There is no cause to decide the case at hand differently. The claimant can use her apartment in an economically meaningful way only as a vacation home that can be rented to third parties. But this indirect actual pressure does not lead to the fact that the claimant is legally obligated to act in a certain way. The court of appeal recognises that correctly.

(c) The servitude did not limit the legal power of disposal of the claimant, but has as content—as with a housing occupation servitude ... or tourism servitude ...—a restriction in the actual use of the apartment. The power following from the ownership of the claimant to do with the object as desired and to exclude others from interference (§903 BGB) is limited in such a way that the apartment can be used only as vacation home and be leased to a changing group of persons and that the defendant for the achievement of this purpose may provide certain services. All this is directed toward a restriction of the actual use. Against such a content of the servitude no legal doubts exist. ... That is valid also from the point of view that the management and leasing of the apartment as well as the contribution of further services are exclusively for the defendant to make. These actions have a direct effect on the use of the apartment ownership; they serve as security for the use as vacation home. Doubts would exist only, if with that, the management power of the home would also be withdrawn from the claimant, to the extent that it does not serve the management and letting as vacation home. This is however not the case for the objective interpretation of the authorisation for registration of the servitude at hand. The owner is to be excluded from the management only to the extent that it concerns the use as a vacation home. In all other aspects he can dispose over the object like an owner, thus eg determine the equipment or modernisation of the object of ownership.

(d) The circumstance that the apartment can only be exclusively used as a vacation home for third parties and that only the defendant may provide the necessary services to the claimant does not exclude the claimant of all use of her apartment ownership, but entitles the defendant only to its use in specific circumstances (§§1090, 1018 alto 1 BGB). Thus the ownership powers of the claimant in respect to the co-ownership are not affected by the servitude; they remain for him without reservation. Regarding the special ownership (apartment) the possibility exists for the claimant to draw an economic advantage by obtaining payments from the leasing as a vacation home. The argumentation used in the revision, which is based on the fact that the defendant would be entitled to conclude lease contracts, is wrong in this respect. That misjudges the content of the power that was transferred to him.

The entitlement to the management and leasing of the apartment does not mean that the defendant may conclude lease contracts in his own name. Because of the remaining powers to use of the claimant it comes down to the the question raised by the court of appeal of whether a servitude different from a right of usufruct is present only if a possibility of an economically meaningful use remains with the owner of land (material demarcation), or only if in the authorisation for registration entered in the land register mentions a specific type of use or concretely specified possibilities of use (formal demarcation) is not relevant. Both conditions are currently present. Obtaining income from the lease of the apartment as vacation home is not a merely insignificant, but in a holiday village the only substantial possibility of use; also the authorisation for registration contains an enumeration of the individual powers of the defendant for the use of the apartment ownership. Therefore it can remain open whether the court of appeal rightfully departs from the presumption that for the permissible contents of a servitude the wording of the authorisation for registration is exclusively decisive, even if thereafter the owner of burdned land is left merely with a theoretical possibility of use the land.

Note

Because of the link with rights of real servitude, the restrictions on the content of real servitudes also apply to limited personal servitudes. This, in particular, includes the requirement that the servitude must rest on a piece of land and, specifically, the duty the servitude imposes must be negative in content

As in the case of real servitudes, a secondary obligation can be recognised which amounts to the imposition of a positive duty.[167] Such positive burdens could be the maintenance of a right granted as a primary obligation, eg the maintenance of a right of way over the servient land.[168] The content of these obligations will be determined by the agreement made between the parties establishing the right of servitude, but the same restrictions as in cases of real servitudes apply.[169]

(ii) Security servitudes

Introductory Note

German law recognises a very specific situation in which the law of servitudes, real and personal, is used to establish a right of servitude operating as security for the performance of an obligation. These property rights are not security rights as such, for the right does not secure the payment of a debt. They do, however, function in a similar fashion. The right is instead used to secure the performance of a certain agreement, usually the purchase of a certain product. This security element is known in German as *Sicherung*. This section provides one example of 'security' servitudes, ie the use of a limited personal right as security for the performance of a contract.

[167] See, above, BGH 25 February 1959.
[168] von Staudinger et al, above n 103, 693.
[169] See above, I.B.I.

BGH, 28 January 1988[170] **3.55 (DE)**

SECURITY SERVITUDE

The drinks contract

A limited personal servitude may be used in such a way that it acts as security for the performance of a drinks delivery contract to a restaurant.

Facts: The claimant was owner of a piece of land with a restaurant on it. The claimant had prior to acquiring ownership leased the same restaurant from a community of heirs. The lease contained an obligation to deal exclusively with a certain drinks manufacturer, the defendant in this case. This duty had been taken over from a previous lessee. In 1980 the claimant acquired ownership of the land including the restaurant.

As a part of the transfer of ownership the claimant established a limited personal servitude on behalf of the defendant, which entitled the defendant to prohibit the sale and drink of beverages on the land of the claimant.

When circumstances changed, the claimant argued for relief from the limited personal servitude. At issue was the question of validity of the agreement as well as the validity of the limited personal servitude.

Held: The court held that a limited personal servitude prohibiting the sale and use of beverages on a piece of land could be permitted. Such a property right could be connected to a contract and function in such a way as to secure the performance of that contract. However, such an agreement for an unlimited duration violated §138 BGB and could not therefore be accepted.

Judgment: (a) The servitude under consideration, according to which the right-holder can prohibit storing and serving of beverages on the burdened land (prohibition servitude), has a permissible content, also if it is to serve only the purpose of creating or securing a beverage purchase obligation, therefore materially surpassing what the parties aim at economically and contractually. ... The Senate upholds this interpretation. ...

(c) In the end, the servitude is in principle therefore not ineffective, because it is not limited. The Senate has repeatedly concerned itself with so-called security servitudes for securement of a beverage purchase obligation. It held that the obligation for the creation of such servitudes according to the principles in the jurisprudence in respect to beer supply contracts (§138 BGB) must temporarily limit the servitude ... it held the agreed minimum running time of a servitude over a maximum duration of 20 years for immoral and therefore void.

Already in the judgment of the Senate, NJW 1985, 2474 = LM §1090 BGB No 22 it remained open whether the principles of the jurisprudence on the permissible maximum duration of beer supply contracts affect the existence of the security servitude when this right is not linked to the duration of the purchase obligations by means of a resolutory condition. This question is now answered in the negative by the Senate in the present case. With the protection of a purchase obligation by security servitudes it must, similarly to the case of the so-called security [*Grundschuld*], be differentiated between the contract of sale with the purchase obligations, the contractual security arrangements and, finally, the right of servitude.

This property right is abstract and in principle independent of the underlying contractual agreements, if these have not become content of the property right itself by way of a condition (§158 BGB) or when, most rarely, a unity occurs between the

[170] V ZR 310/86, NJW 1988, 2364.

contractual and property agreements (§139 BGB). Neither one is here determined or argued. Should the causal agreement, which is the basis for creation of the servitude, be void under §138(1) BGB, then this—unlike the nullity under §138(2) BGB—would not just entail the nullity of the creation of the servitude. The property agreement (§873 BGB) would be void only if the immorality would lie in the execution of the performance, and if with the property agreement immoral purposes were pursued or the immoraility was based on it. ... These exceptions are here neither determined nor argued. The parties did not temporarily limit the creation of the servitude or connect it to a condition (§158 BGB) in respect to the existence of a contractual purchase obligation. Their agreement (§873(1) BGB) does not become immoral solely because the parties according to the statement of the court of appeal with the creation of the servitude pursued the aim of securing a still to be concluded purchase obligation. The claimant does not argue that the defendant required her to conclude an immoral purchase contract. She explicitly declared herself ready to adapt running period of the servitude to the permissible duration of a purchase obligation still to be concluded. ...

According to the present position, there are no doubts as to the effectiveness of a security arrangement, with which is, among other things, to be achieved that the claimant concludes a purchase obligation with the defendant, under §138(1) BGB. Each actual appreciation on the content of the security arrangement by the court of appeal is missing. It is therefore not ruled out that from the contract concluded in 1980 by means of direct or supplementing interpretation a temporal delimitation can be found for the case, that it comes to the conclusion of a beverage purchase contract between the parties. ... If the security arrangement should have exceeded a temporal limit, permissible under §138 (1) BGB and the jurisprudence of the BGH on beer supply contract on the matter (facts to the precise contents of the intended purchase obligations are neither determined nor put forward by the parties), then it would further be possible to change the security agreement according to the principles of the jurisprudence to a permissible length of time if this corresponds to the actual or presumed intention of the parties.

Notes

(1) This German decision shows a very specific application of the right of limited personal servitude. Because the content of these servitudes must be negative, forcing an owner to do something is not allowed. However, with a general prohibition on doing something, the right-holder of this type of limited personal servitude can impose a very serious restriction on the use of the land. For example, through a contract with the holder of the limited personal servitude, the owner of the servient land agrees to buy beverages exclusively from the right-holder and use the land as a restaurant, even though the content of the servitude prohibits the owner from having a restaurant on the land.[171] In the same contract the parties agree that the holder of the limited personal servitude will not exercise his right under certain conditions.

The limited personal servitude allows the right-holder a certain amount of control over the use of the servient land. When the owner of the servient land does not

[171] However, also case law concerning petrol stations has contributed to the development of these security servitudes. See BGH 22 September 1961, NJW 1961, 2157.

perform his duty under the contract, the right-holder of the limited personal servitude may invoke his property right and prevent the owner of the servient land from conducting his business.

(2) What a party establishing a security-servitude actually wants to achieve is a positive duty for the right-holder of the servient land. In order to secure this exclusive purchase obligation, a limited personal servitude enables the defendant to stop the claimant from conducting his business if necessary.[172] It could be stated that because of the prohibition to impose a positive duty in property law the law of contract is used to achieve a similar result, but with the same strength and almost the same effect as a property right.

Since a security servitude greatly restricts the owner of the servient land in his right to enjoy his ownership, severe burdens on the right of ownership cannot form the subject-matter of such rights. A duty to buy beverages forever would certainly restrict the owner in his right to do with his land as he wishes. Not only do the rules on competition law apply to these agreements, but the general restrictions imposed by §138 BGB, which deals with good faith, also apply.[173] The BGH has therefore restricted the maximum duration of a security servitude construction to 20 years.[174]

I.C.5 GERMAN LAW: REAL BURDENS

Introductory Note

The German real burden or *Reallast* is a type of property right which was unknown to Roman law and does not, unlike the other rights dealt with in this chapter, entitle a person to the use and enjoyment of a piece of land but instead to a certain value connected to the land. The real burden can therefore not be held on movable assets. It is known in German law as a *Verwertungsrecht*.[175] The common law concept of rentcharge also closely resembles this particular property right.[176] The right itself can be established both between a person and a person in his capacity as owner, creating a normal real burden, or between a person and another person not in a capacity as owner, creating a so-called personal real burden.[177] In each case the right will secure the payment of a certain sum of money or a certain act. However, if that act is not performed, contrary to the other property rights dealt with in this chapter, the right holder cannot force the owner or person bound by the real burden to perform. Instead the right-holder will be entitled to payment of a monetary sum.[178]

[172] Schwab and Prütting, above n 14, 416–17.
[173] von Staudinger et al, above n 103, 271; R Stürner, 'Dienstbarkeit Heute' (1994) 194 *Archiv für die civilistische Praxis* 265–94, at 284 *et seq*.
[174] BGH 13 July 1979, V ZR 122/77, NJW 1979, 2149; Baur, Baur and Stürner, above n 83, 370–71.
[175] Baur, Baur and Stürner, above n 83, 23–24; von Staudinger et al, above n 103, 820.
[176] Below, II.A.8.
[177] Subjectiv-dingliche Reallast §1110 BGB and Subjectiv-persönliche Reallast §1111 BGB; Wolf, above n 14, 396–97.
[178] H Amann, 'Durchsetzung der Reallast ohne Verlust der Reallast' [1993] DNotZ 222–32, at 222 *et seq*.

Bürgerliches Gesetzbuch **3.56 (DE)**

§1105 A piece of land can be burdened in a way that a person, to whose benefit the right is created, is entitled to returning benefits from the land. (Real Burden). The content of a real burden can also be that the burden to provide the benefits adapts itself to changing circumstances, when, on the basis of the agreement between the parties, the nature and the scope of the burden can be established.

BayObLG, 9 December 1992[179] **3.57 (DE)**

CONCEPT OF REAL BURDEN

Heat and water supply

A real burden can be established when a right to receive and not a duty to supply has been agreed upon.

Facts: The claimants were the owners of two pieces of land. They had reached agreement on the establishment of several rights of real servitude and real burdens, part of which was an obligation on one of them to receive and pay for heat and water from the other party. However, a duty to supply heat and water had not been agreed upon. When the rights were put forward for registration, the registrar claimed that without a description of the duty to supply, no real burden could be created.

Held: A real burden can be created as a property right even though no duty to supply has been expressly agreed upon.

Judgment: 2. The requested registration of real burdens is not opposed by the fact that a purchase obligation and not a delivery obligation are agreed upon. A real burden creates a burden on a piece of land to the effect that recurring performances from the land are to be made to the right-holder (§1105(1) BGB). According to general opinion the performance cannot be a simple bearing or omitting; rather the contents of a real burden can only be a positive act of giving or doing. ... Accordingly, the nature of the property right consists of the fact that the burdened land is liable for the performance that is due, and that the beneficiary is thus entitled to enforce his rights on the piece of land by means of compulsory execution; the real burden is therefore a pure value right. ... The supply of energy or water is a typical content of a real burden. ... The content of the real burden is laid down in the notarial deed of 7 August 1991 as the right to receive heating and water to the beneficiary. Thus no doubt exists to the fact that the subject of the right is the obligation of the landowner to such a supply. The real burden is frequently registered in the land register with key words like ‚the right to' the performances which must be delivered. ... In this case it is not doubtful that content of the real burden is the obligation, ‚to performe' the respective achievement, eg the providing of maintenance, catering, food and energy.

Which key word the land register office selects in the present case, is its discretionary power to decide. ... The land register office does not have to register the right as 'right to purchase of heat and water', it can also choose the key word 'the obligation to the supply of heat and water'. The notarial deed covers both; by the provided additional classification of the right as a real burden. ... [T]he land register satisfies legal certainty principle. Because of the more detailed arrangement

[179] NJW-RR 1993, 530.

of the right a reference to the authorisation for registration will be possible anyway (see §874(1) BGB).

BayObLG, 28 April 1988[180] **3.58 (DE)**

PERSONAL REAL BURDEN

Inheritance of a real burden

A personal real burden can transfer to an heir upon death of the person burdened with the real burden.

Facts: A real burden was registered obliging an owner X to provide electricity to a couple S as well as to pay a certain amount of damages to this couple. When one of the spouses S died, the real burden was changed to allow the widower S to solely benefit from the real burden. When the widower S also died, his heirs transferred the real burden to a person Y, the defendant in this case. X, the claimant, refused to supply electricity or pay damages to Y, claiming he could not be forced to do this, because Y was not entitled to the real burden, and sought cancellation of the real burden.

Held: The personal real burden, ie a real burden affecting a person instead of an owner, was valid and its burden could pass upon death of that person to the heirs. Only when parties explicitly agreed otherwise would the burden not pass. The real burden could therefore be enforced.

Judgment: ... The claimant incorrectly argues that in relation to 1), existing for the benefit of the defendant 2) real burden entered in the land register concerned a personal property right (is elaborated). Thus a subjective personal right exists.

(b) Such a right can in principle be passed on inheritance. ... The passing of the right by way of succession is neither excluded in the deed of creation nor does such exclusion result from the nature of the performances that are to be made. The content of these performances is laid down in the private contract of 1954. This contractual regulation determines the already mentioned notarial deed as a component. A creation of a real burden for the lifetime of the beneficiary results neither from the contract of 1954 nor from the notarial deed. In §10 of the contract is elaborated that by the married couple S are also always their legal successors to be understood. From the nature of the performances to be delivered a restriction to the lifetime of the beneficiaries does not result. Both the supply of electricity and the payment of damages can be made to successors of the originally registered beneficiaries.

Notes

(1) A real burden in German law is a property right entitling its holder to a certain performance from another party.[181] In this respect the real burden is different from a right of servitude, as it generally imposes a positive burden. The content of the real burden is therefore different from that of a right of real servitude. Another difference is that when the duty the real burden imposes is not performed, instead

[180] DNotZ 1989, 567.

[181] See M Wolf, 'Marketability contra freedom of parties in the law of land burdens', in JHM van Erp and B Akkermans (eds), *Towards a Unified System of Land Burdens?* (Antwerpen-Oxford, Intersentia, 2006) 11–20, at 19–20. On Austrian law, see M Hinteregger, 'Servitudes—The Austrian Concept', in van Erp and Akkermans, *ibid*, 21–30, at 27–30.

of performance of the duty, the right-holder of a real burden is entitled to the value of the object, hence the German characterisation of this right as a *Verwertungsrecht* or value right.[182] In this way the legal system remains faithful to the negative attitude towards positive burdens.

(2) As the two cases above also show, the other party can be an owner, but also a person in his capacity as a person, not an owner. In both cases a property right is created which has effect against third parties, even upon death.[183] In each case it is the owner or the person burdened with the property right who must perform the duty.

I.D *EMPHYTEUSIS*

Introductory Notes

(a) This section deals with a property right closely resembling the right of ownership, the right of *emphyteusis*, often referred to as a right of long lease. This is not strictly accurate, however, for leases in civil law systems are personal rights, not property rights. The difference between a lease and a right of *emphyteusis* is small. Generally speaking, a right of *emphyteusis* is an agreement between an owner and another person for the use and enjoyment of a specific piece of land for a long period, though in some civil law systems such right can even be established in perpetuity. Such a right is a property right with effect against the world. As an important aspect of a right of *emphyteusis* is that the rights of the holder can be assigned. A lease, on the other hand, is generally an agreement for the use and enjoyment of land, only having effect between parties. The result of this is that the lessee cannot assign his right under the lease agreement. The lease also has some characteristics of a property right, but is not recognised as such. The right of lease is dealt with in the final paragraph of this civil law section.[184]

(b) Although the concept of the right of *emphyteusis* is of long-standing, it is not recognised in every legal system. Thus, while it is used in French and in Dutch law, this is not the case in German law. Instead, German law uses a different property right, the real burden (*Reallast*), dealt with later in this chapter.[185]

I.D.1 GENERAL RULES COMMON TO FRENCH AND DUTCH LAW.

Code rural **3.59 (FR)**

Article 451-1 The right of *emphyteusis* on immovable objects gives the holder a property right that can be susceptible to a right of hypothec; the right may be transferred or seized according to the rules on the seizure of immovable objects.

[182] Baur, Baur and Stürner, above n 83, 23–24; von Staudinger et al, above n 103, 820.

[183] von Staudinger et al, above n 103, 813; *Motive zu dem Entwurfe eines bürgerlichen Gesetzbuches für das Deutsche Reich—Sachenrecht*, vol III (Berlin, Verlag von J Guttentag, 1888) 572 *et seq*; Wolff and Raiser, above n 16, 510–11; Schwab and Prütting, above n 14, 440.

[184] Below, I.I.2.

[185] On the right of real burden, above, I.C.5.

The right can be agreed upon for a minimum of 18 years and may not exceed 99 years; it may not be tacitly renewed.

Burgerlijk Wetboek **3.60 (NL)**

Article 5:89(1) Unless provided otherwise in the deed of creation, the holder of the right of *emphyteusis* will have the same power to enjoy the object as the owner.

Notes

(1) These definitions provide several basic elements of the right of *emphyteusis*. First, the right is a property right on land. A right of *emphyteusis* cannot be established on movables and is therefore unknown in personal property law. Second, the right gives its holder similar rights to the rights of an owner, in particular the rights to use and enjoy the object. The right to transfer the ownership, however, remains with the owner. This approach to the right of *emphyteusis* can in particular be seen from the Dutch definition, but should be read into the French definition as well.[186] However, the owner will remain owner and when the right comes to an end, will have the full right to use and enjoyment of the object.

The fact that the right of *emphyteusis* rests on the object, and is not connected to the holder himself, also distinguishes the right of *emphyteusis* from the right of usufruct. Both of these rights entitle the right-holder to the use and enjoyment of an immovable object, but the right of *emphyteusis* is meant to last for a longer time than a right of usufruct.

(2) Because the right-holder of a right of *emphyteusis* is entitled to the use and enjoyment and for the period of time the right exists, the owner cannot exercise his right of use and enjoyment. For this reason the French Civil Code, protecting the unitary nature and exclusivity of the right of ownership, did not originally include the right of *emphyteusis*.[187] The fear that the right of *emphyteusis* might deprive the owner of his right of use and enjoyment in perpetuity caused the French legislator to stipulate a maximum duration of 99 years.[188]

(3) In Dutch law, which had a Civil Code modelled on the French, the right of *emphyteusis* was also originally unknown. It was, however, introduced by legislation in 1824, and now forms part of the new Civil Code, enacted in 1992. One of the major differences from the French right of *emphyteusis* is that the right in the Netherlands can be perpetual.[189]

[186] Terré and Simler, above n 18, 699; Malaurie and Aynès, above n 18, 101; C Atias, *Droit Civil—Les Biens*, 8th edn (Paris, Lexis Nexis SA, 2005) 309.

[187] See Terré and Simler, above n 18, 700.

[188] *Ibid*, 702.

[189] De Jong, above n 116, 21–22.

I.D.2 OWNERSHIP OF CONSTRUCTIONS MADE BY THE HOLDER OF AN *EMPHYTEUSIS*

Hoge Raad, 22 April 1901[190] **3.61 (NL)**

BUILDINGS CONSTRUCTED BY THE RIGHT-HOLDER

Failure to notify

In Dutch law buildings constructed by the holder of an emphyteusis become part of the ownership of the owner of the land and not the emphyteuticarius.

Facts: The defendant had been given a right of *emphyteusis* on a piece of land by the municipality of Amsterdam and had constructed a building on it. Upon completion of the construction works the defendant started to use the building. Under local building regulations, the completion of building works had to be notified by the owner or holder of a right of usufruct to the municipality. The defendant had failed to make such notification and criminal proceedings were brought against him by the municipality of Amsterdam, which claimed that the defendant was an owner of those buildings and therefore should have notified the completion of the construction works. The defendant argued he was not owner but only holder of a right of *emphyteusis* and that he was not therefore obliged to make the notification.

Held: In the absence of any specific legal provision or explicit agreement between the parties in the deed establishing the right of *emphyteusis*, the owner of the land became the owner of the buildings constructed on the land. That was so even when the building was constructed using a third party's building materials. Because there was no such provision or agreement here, the defendant was not owner of the buildings and did not have to effect the notification.

Judgment: Considering in this respect that given the absence of legal provision in the Title on the right of *emphyteusis*, and especially not from Articles 767 and 772 BW, it arises that the holder of a right of *emphyteusis* becomes the owner of the buildings constructed by him; that in the last mentioned article the holder of a right of *emphyteusis* is granted, at the end of his right, the right to take away buildings and plantings constructed and made by him, to which he normally was, because of the effects of the agreement, not entitled, but that this provision is a measure of fairness to the holder of the right of *emphyteusis* to prevent that the owner of the land would unjustly enrich himself at the expense of the holder of the right. However, the law does not recognise that the *emphyteuticarius* is entitled to a right of ownership of the mentioned buildings and plantings.

That the ruling, that no explicit legal provision in respect to the right of *emphytheusis* provides that the defendant is the owner of the buildings constructed by him on a piece of land on which he had a right of *emphyteusis*, is therefore correct and the grievance against this is not unfounded.

[190] W 7600.

Cour de cassation req, 22 June 1885[191] **3.62 (FR)**

Hospices de Roubaix v Widow Descat and others

BUILDINGS CONSTRUCTED BY THE RIGHT-HOLDER

Expropriated land

A building constructed by the holder of an emphyteusis *is owned by that holder for the duration of the property right.*

Facts: In 1824 the claimants created several rights of *emphyteusis* on several plots of land for 99 years. The contract establishing the rights of *emphyteusis* stated that at the end of the 99 years the right to use the land would return to the claimants and that this right included the right to take any building or planting on the land at that time.

One Lecomte was the holder of one of the rights of *emphyteusis* and had constructed a house on one of the plots of land. In 1881, that plot was expropriated. Therefore, the question arose as to who was owner and had therefore become expropriated and would be entitled to compensation. Lecomte had died and was replaced in the procedure by the defendants.

Held: A building constructed by the holder of an *emphyteusis* is owned by that holder for the duration of the property right. When the land and the building are subsequently expropriated, compensation must be paid, not only to the owner of the land, but also to the owner of the building.

Judgment: Considering that, in law, it is certain that by the legal effect of the right of *emphyteusis* created on March 29th 1824, the hospices of Roubaix have retained the direct ownership [*domaine direct*] of the immovables and the indirect ownership [*domaine utile*] was transferred to Mr Lecomte, the holder of the lease;—But he has not got any similar rights towards the constructions under dispute;—That these constructions made by the aforementioned Lecomte, on his own free will, after his possession, belonged to him exclusively; That he had the full ownership over them and that he could therefore destroy them, during his right of *emphyteusis*, under the only condition not to damage the land;

Note

These two cases show similar approaches to the ownership of buildings constructed by the holder of an *emphyteusis*, though reach opposite results. The Dutch case formulates the general criterion to be used in these instances. (NB: This case was decided under the old Dutch Civil Code and therefore the articles mentioned are different now.) The same rule applies in French law. However, it is in the interpretation of the solution in which Dutch and French law deviate. Confusingly, the French court uses old feudal terminology (*dominium directum* and *dominium utile*) to further complicate matters.

[191] DP 1886, I, 268.

I.D.3 PAYMENT OF A SUM OF MONEY FOR AN *EMPHYTEUSIS* AND THE RIGHT IN PRACTICE

Hoge Raad, 6 November 1998[192] **3.63 (NL)**

Karting-Bouwmans and others v City of Rotterdam

PAYMENT OF A SUM OF MONEY (CANON) AFTER SEPARATION INTO APARTMENT RIGHTS

The *canon* payment

In exchange for the grant of a right of emphyteusis an agreement for payment, known as canon, can be made. When a right of emphyteusis is divided into different shares of ownership, the payment of the canon must be shared as well.

Facts: In 1980 the municipality of Rotterdam, the defendant, granted a right of *emphyteusis* on two adjacent pieces of land to private parties. As part of the transaction, the municipality stipulated that the land was to be used for residential purposes and partly for business purposes, ie a shopping area. The *canon* for the part intended for housing was around E49,000 per year and the canon for the part with a commercial purpose around E62,000 per year. The deed allowed the parties to split their right into apartments.

On a deed executed on the same day, the holders divided their rights into 20 apartments each, including a specific division of costs between these apartments. Some apartments were to be used for commercial purposes, others for residential purposes. The claimants in this proceeding each acquired one of the apartments in the group of commercial apartment rights.

The right-holders of the apartments claimed the canon should be paid according to the scheme decided when the apartment rights were created, ie when the right of *emphyteusis* was divided into apartment rights. The municipality, however, claimed that the residential canon and the commercial canon should be seen separately. At issue was whether such a separation could be made.

Held: The *canon* could not be separated and should be paid by all right-holders of the apartment rights together. When an agreement between the right-holders of the apartment rights has been made, such division of costs should be applied. However, the court held there is no agreement in this case, as the division of costs was part of the deed of division into apartment rights and not an agreement between the right holders themselves.

Judgment: 3.4.2. So far as that the parts 1 and 4 argue that the court has denied that according to both old and current law the canon must be divided in equal portions among all holders of the apartment rights unless another division is determined by regulation between the parties, they are halted by the court's decision described in 3.4.1 that exactly reflects that this is the case. Furthermore, those parts wrongfully assume that the amount of the canon indebted to the municipality by every right-holder of the apartments is determined by what is included the regulation of the 'Association of Right-holders of Apartments Shops and Residents'. After all, the regulation is not drawn up by the association of owners, but is included in the deed of of separation. That regulation contains the formation of an association of owners (Article 875(e) and (f) (old) BW and Articles 5:111 and 112 BW). Part 2, which is also based on aforementioned wrongful starting point, cannot, because of that reason, lead to cassation. Contrary to part 1, the successive holders of the *emphyteusis* are also bound to the obligation of payment of canon included in the

[192] NJ 1999, 131.

acts of creation of the rights of *emphyteusis*. The court of appeal has also correctly assumed that a differentiated canon for a future purpose for the land (shops and hotels on the one hand and residents on the other hand) is allowed according to old and current law. As far as part 1 starts from another opinion, it also fails to this respect.

Notes

(1) This case illustrates that in exchange for the granting of a right of *emphyteusis* a duty to pay money for that right can be agreed upon. The payment for a right of *emphyteusis* can be, as the case shows, substantial. The reasoning behind this payment of money is that the right-holder of a right of *emphyteusis* enjoys a right of use and enjoyment similar to that of the owner. The right-holder is entitled to transfer his right of *emphyteusis* to another person. This transfer will be effective but the existence of the property right will remain subject to the provisions under which it was established. In addition the obligation to pay the canon will pass to the transferee, even though that transferee was not part of the original agreement between the owner and the holder of the *emphyteusis* on the payment of the money.

(2) The case above shows an important purpose of the right of *emphyteusis*. In many countries, particularly the Netherlands, the right is used by local government for planning purposes.[193] Particularly in larger cities, the terms and conditions under which a right of *emphyteusis* can be established enable the local government to impose conditions and restrictions on the right-holders.

(3) The case also shows another element of the right of *emphyteusis*, that the right itself can be subject of another property right. This other property right is not only seen in the legislative possibility in French law of establishing a right of hypothec on a right of *emphyteusis*, but also the possibility of several right-holders sharing the right of *emphyteusis* among themselves.

I.D.4 FRENCH LAW: THE CONSTRUCTION LEASE

Introductory Note

The above section has shown that the right of *emphyteusis* is particularly useful in providing for the use and enjoyment by one party but with restrictions or conditions imposed at the same time. In Dutch law it is even possible to make these restrictions or conditions, although they are contractual, part of the property right itself.[194] However, when a party, usually a municipality, wants to establish a right of *emphyteusis* and impose a duty to build on the right-holder, both Dutch and French law are reluctant to accept this as a valid content for an *emphyteusis*.[195] In order

[193] De Jong, above n 116, 3 *et seq*; van Velten, above n 116, 17–88, at 17 *et seq*.

[194] HR 16 March 1977, NJ 1977, 399; WB Plantenga and WC Treurniet, *Erfpacht En Erfpachtsvoorwaarden* (Preadviezen uitgebracht ter behandeling in de algemene vergadering van de Broederschap van Candidaat-Notarissen, 1957) 177; van Velten, above n 116, 17–88, at 47; De Jong, above n 116, 17; Rank-Berenschot, above n 15, 110–11.

[195] See van Velten, above n 116, 17–88, at 49; see also GMFR Snijders, 'Agrarische Erfpacht', *Erfpacht* (Preadvies uitgebracht voor de jaarlijkse algemene ledenvergadering van de Koninklijke Notariële

to remedy any possible restriction on these positive building duties, French legislation has introduced a separate property right, though the Dutch continue to use the general right of *emphyteusis* for this. This property right is known in French as *bail à construction*, and best translates as a construction lease.

Construction and Housing Code[196] **3.64 (FR)**

Article L251-3 The construction lease confers upon the lessee an immovable property right.

This right can be burdened with a right of hypothec, just as the constructions built on the rented land; it can be seized through the prescribed forms for seizure of immovable objects.

The lessee can transfer all or part of his rights or contribute them to a company. The transferees or the company are held to the same obligations as the transferor who remains liable for them until the completion of the whole of the constructions that the lessee has undertaken to build, by application of Article L251-1.

Notes

(1) The term construction lease is slightly misleading, for it gives the impression of a personal right. However, the purpose of the construction lease is to create a right which has effect against third parties, in particular subsequent acquirers, and the legislative definition provided by Article L251-3 states that a construction lease is a property right.

The definition provided above closely resembles the right of *emphyteusis*. In fact French doctrine treats the construction lease as a specific type of *emphyteusis* rather than a distinct property right.[197] Like the right of *emphyteusis*, it can be established for only a limited period of time, not less than 18 years and no longer than 99 years. The right is capable of transfer as well as seizure by a creditor.[198]

(2) The construction lease imposes a positive duty to build on the land. This duty is part of the contract establishing the property right. If the right-holder fails to perform his duty under the contract, the owner can rescind the contract and thereby bring the property right to an end. The contract will also contain agreement on the ownership of the constructed building. As in case of the right of *emphyteusis*, the application of the principle of accession can be decided on by the parties. In the absence of any agreement, the holder of the construction lease will become owner of the building for the duration of the property right.[199] It is usual for the parties to make an agreement about compensation for the expenses and efforts of the right-holder at the end of the construction lease.

Broederschap te houden te Nijmegen op 22 september 1995; Lelystad: Koninklijke Vermande BV, 1995) 89–116, at 155; Terré and Simler, above n 18, 702.

[196] Inserted by Law no 64-1247 of 16 December 1964.

[197] Terré and Simler, above n 18, 703–05; Carbonnier, above n 17, 296–97; Atias, above n 186, 179–80.

[198] Terré and Simler, above n 18, 704–05.

[199] Art L251-2 Code de la construction et de l'habitation; Terré and Simler, above n 18, 705.

I.E *SUPERFICIES*

Another property right, and one recognised in Roman law, is the right of superficies. The right of superficies separates the ownership of a building or construction from the ownership of the land. The property right is given to someone other than the owner of the land and burdens the right of ownership.[200] By its nature the right of superficies cannot be held on movable assets.

I.E.1 RULES COMMON TO FRENCH, GERMAN AND DUTCH LAW

Code civil **3.65 (FR)**

Article 522 Ownership of the ground involves ownership of that which is above and beneath it. The owner may make above it all plantings and constructions which he deems proper, but for the exceptions established under the heading 'Of servitudes or Land Services'. He may make underneath all constructions and excavations which he deems proper, and draw from these excavations all products that they can provide, subject to the limitations resulting from the statutes and regulations relating to mines, and from policing statutes and regulations.

Regulation on Superficies (ErbbauVO) **3.66 (DE)**

§1 A piece of land can be burdened in such a way, that the person, for whose benefit the right is established, has a transferable and inheritable right to have a building up or under the surface of that land. (Right of *superficies*)

Burgerlijk Wetboek **3.67 (NL)**

Article 5:101(1) The right of *superficies* is a property right to have or acquire a right of ownership in, on or on top of buildings, constructions or plantings on an immovable object, that belongs to someone else.

Notes

(1) As a general rule, each civil law system uses the maxim *superficies solo cedit*, that the building or constructions on the land follow the ownership of the land.[201] This maxim, which can be seen in Article 552 of the French Civil Code, is the starting point of legal analysis. However, the above-mentioned legislative provisions share a common purpose: they enable parties to separate the entitlement to a building from the entitlement to the land through agreement.

(2) The holder of a superficies is entitled to ownership of the building. This ownership is connected to the existence of the property right of superficies, so that

[200] Property rights in French and Dutch law are *iura in re aliena* or property rights on the objects of another. However, in German law an owner may also establish a property right in as far as it concerns a property right on land, on his own ownership. See §889 BGB: Wolff and Raiser, above n 16, 128; Schwab and Prütting, above n 14, 10.

[201] Art 552 Cciv, Art 5:20 BW, §§93 and 94 BGB.

when the right ends, so does the ownership of the right-holder. Nevertheless, the ownership of the right-holder falls under the general provisions of ownership dealt with earlier in this chapter.[202] The right-holder may therefore use, enjoy and dispose of his ownership as an owner, including the establishment of other property rights. As a basic rule, when the right of superficies ceases to exist, so too will the rights established on the ownership of the building or, in case of personal rights, by the right-holder of the right of superficies.[203]

(3) Like the right of *emphyteusis*, the right of superficies was not originally contained in the French Civil Code.[204] Furthermore, the German Civil Code likewise did not recognise a right of superficies. Like the right of *emphyteusis*, the right of superficies was associated with a fragmented concept of ownership, awarding the right-holder of the right *dominium utile* and the owner of the land *dominium directum*.[205]

In French law the Cour de cassation continued to recognise the right of superficies, eventually regarding it as a distinct property right.[206] It is in this way that Article 552 of the French Civil Code should be read. Only by agreement between the parties will the application of the principle of accession be postponed to the end of the existence of the property right.

Nor was the right of superficies recognised by the BGB. With a Civil Code strongly against a fragmentation of the right of ownership, the right of superficies was deliberately omitted.[207] However, under pressure from practice which demanded that less wealthy people might acquire their own home, a special regulation, the Verordnung über das Erbbaurecht (ErbbauVO), was introduced by legislation in 1919 to give a right of superficies.[208] It is from this regulation that the above excerpt is taken.

Dutch law was originally the same as French law. However, the new Civil Code of 1992 included a specific article. The article excerpted above is followed by provisions making the rules on the right of *emphyteusis* applicable to the right

[202] See above, I.A.

[203] AE de Vries and AJH Pleysier, *Erfpacht en Opstal*, 2nd edn (Zwolle, WEJ Tjeenk Willink, 1995) 116–17; Asser et al, above n 21, n 255, at 283; Terré and Simler, above n 18, 716–17; von Staudinger et al, above n 103, 127–28.

[204] See above, I.D.

[205] von Staudinger et al, above n 103, 4; AM Patault, 'La propriété non exclusive au xixe siècle: Histoire de la dissociation juridique de l'immeuble' [1983] *Revue historique de droit français et étranger* 217–37, at 224–26; Terré and Simler, above n 18, 711.

[206] Civ 18 May 1858, S 58.1.661; AM Patault, 'La propriété non exclusive au xixe siècle: Histoire de la dissociation juridique de l'immeuble' [1983] *Revue historique de droit français et étranger* 217–37, at 234.

[207] AFJ Thibaut, 'Ueber *Dominium Directum* und *Utile*', *Versuche über einzelne Teile der Theorie des Rechts,* 2nd edn (Aalen, Neudruck Scientia Verlag, 1970) 67–99; FK von Savigny, *System des heutigen römischien Rechts* (Aalen, Scienta Verlag, 1981) 367; GF Puchta, *Vorlesungen über das heutige römische Recht—I*, 6th edn (Leipzig, Verlag von Bernard Tauchnitz, 1873) 324; BJH Windscheid and T Kipp, *Lehrbuch des Pandektenrechts—I*, 9th with BGB compared edn (Frankfurt am Main, Literarische Anstalt Rütten & Loenig, 1906) 856. See also Wiegand, above n 34, 136–38, von Staudinger et al, above n 103, 3–4.

[208] von Staudinger et al, above n 103, 7. For more on the development of the right of superficies see HF von Oefele and K Winkler, *Handbuch Des Erbbaurechts*, 3rd edn (München, Verlag CH Beck, 2003) 13 *et seq*.

of superficies as much as possible.[209] Finally, the Dutch definition very clearly establishes that the right of superficies not only entitles the right-holder to use or construct a building, but also any other construction than a building. This includes trees and bushes.

I.E.2 CONTENT OF THE RIGHT OF *SUPERFICIES*

BGH, 22 April 1994[210] **3.68 (DE)**

BUILDING RIGHT AS CONTENT OF RIGHT OF *SUPERFICIES*

Building rights

Content of a right of superficies may be a general right to construct buildings on a piece of land.

Facts: The claimant granted a right of superficies to the defendant for 99 years. A term of the deed provided that:

> 'The right-holder of the right of superficies may construct any building he wants on and under the surface of the land on which the right of superficies is established. The public law requirements should be taken into account.'

The agreement further provided for the payment of money by the defendant in exchange for the granting of the right of superficies. The deed contained a term enabling the claimant to increase the amount of money to be paid when certain events occurred. The claimant made use of this term and increased the amount of money to be paid for the right of superficies. The defendant contradicted the claim. In lower instance the claim was not taken into consideration because the court held that the clause could not be part of a right of superficies. At issue in appeal was whether such a clause in a deed could be part of a right of superficies, and if so whether the claimant could raise the sum of money.

Held: The BGH held that a general building right could be part of a right of superficies and that the property right was therefore not invalid because of an illegal content. Therefore, the claim was recognised. The BGH dealt with the issue itself and ordered the defendant to pay the increased amount of money.

Judgment: The court of appeal holds the complaint to be unfounded because the contract for a right of *superficies* is void. For the effective creation of a right of *superficies* it is necessary that the contract specifies the approximate condition of the building or the buildings which the beneficiary of right of *superficies* may erect. For this the agreement made here that states he may erect on the land 'buildings according to his needs' would not be sufficient. A sufficient concretisation does also not result from that the holder of a right of *superficies* must, according to the contract, keep to the applicable construction legislation. The appeal is founded on this point.

1. Already according to older jurisprudence of the Senate, the property agreement and land register entry on creation of a right of *superficies* must make clear how the development of the land should approximately be done. ... This should take into account the need to enable the creation of rights of *superficies* also for building projects which are not certain yet in detail. ... Therefore only the indication of the generic kind of the building was regarded as necessary, eg 'a house'

[209] Art. 5:104 BW. de Vries and Pleysier, above n 203, 110; HD Ploeger, *Horizontale Splitsing van Eigendom* (Deventer, Kluwer, 1997) 169.

[210] V ZR 183/93, NJW 1994, 2024.

or 'several houses'. ... But such a requirement is still too narrow, because it would exclude the creation of a right of *superficies* without difficulty if the holder of the *superficies* could not or did not want to already commit himself in the contract to the kind of the land development. Therefore the Senate held it in BGHZ 101, 143 = NJW 1987, 2674 = LM §1 ErbbauVO No 15 as sufficient, if the property agreement permits the establishment of buildings according to the conditions of a future development plan.

The property agreement has, which the court of appeal misjudges, a similar conent in the present case. It permits not only the establishment of buildings, but also of other buildings to the holder of the right of *superficies* 'according to his needs'; it determines however that the public construction regulations must be kept. Thus the contracting parties agreed that each building permissible under the building laws may be established. This is not sufficient for the court of appeal, because land presently indicated as a commercial construction area in the land use planning, provided that special permissions were given and building obligations were taken over, could be constructed on in various ways. That does not however contradict the property agreement, since it permits each legally permissible kind of building. This is not opposed, as far as at all considerable, by the complaints from which the requirement is deduced, that the in §1(1) ErbbauVO only generally described content of a right of *superficies*—the right to have a construction on or under the surface that can be transferred and passed by inheritance—must be specified in more detail in the deed of creation. Thereby it must be ascertainable whether the building, upon extension of the right of *superficies* to the for the construction not needed parts of a piece of land, remains in accordance with §1(2) ErbbauVO economically the principal part. ... In so far as this is concerned, no doubts exist here. The power is granted to the holder of the right of *superficies* to erect a multiplicity of buildings; from this it is evident that the buildings in relation to the piece of land are economically the principal part. ... On the other hand, the loan to value ratio relevant for a burdening of the right of *superficies* with immovable property security rights should be at least to some extent recognisable. ... However, no decisive meaning is attached to this criterion as the Senate referred to in BGHZ 101, 143 (147) = NJW 1987, 2674 = LM §1 ErbbauVO No 15. Because irrespective of the accuracy with which the property agreement and land register entry specify the kind of the building that the holder of a right of *superficies* may establish, only his power under private law to use land as building ground for the designated building is fixed. Whether the holder of the right of *superficies* can actually also build in this manner, however, is determined according to the public legal construction regulations. Therefore a provider of credit is able to determine the loan to value ratio of the right of *superficies* only by examination of which kind of buildings these regulations for the burdened piece of land permit.

The designation of the kind of building in the property agreement and in the land register entry is to also ensure that between the owners of the land and the holders of rights of *superficies* as well as any legal successors sufficient clarity exists over contents and scope of the authorisation to the use of the piece of land. ... That is however the case, if the holder of a right of *superficies* is authorised to erect any building permissible under the construction laws. The creation of a right of *superficies* with this content is therefore effective.

Hoge Raad, 11 March 1981[211] **3.69 (NL)**

RIGHT TO USE AND ENJOY AS CONTENT OF RIGHT OF *SUPERFICIES*

Right to enjoy

A right of superficies includes, unless provided otherwise, the right to use and enjoy the land on which the right is established.

Facts: The first claimant transferred the right of ownership of a piece of land with several buildings on it to the second claimant, though he retained a right of superficies on the land with respect to the buildings on that land. The right to use and enjoy the land by the first claimant was of importance for the conveyance taxes which had to be paid, a higher rate beying payable if ownership including the right to use and enjoy was transferred. The Dutch tax authority questioned the possibility of creating a right of superficies which would take away all the rights to use and enjoy of the owner of the land and demanded this higher rate.

Held: A right of superficies comprised a general right to use and enjoy the land on which the right is established, but that by agreement parties may make different arrangements, including a full right to use and enjoy. Therefore, the right of superficies was validly created.

Judgment: Considering as to the following:

that the court of appeal has held that it is not possible to give full enjoyment and the right of enjoyment of the fruits of the land on which that right is created by means of creating a right of *superficies*, especially not as far as there are buildings on that land;

that the grievance of cassation correctly disputes this judgment;

that indeed according to the nature of the right of *superficies*, the rigth to use and enjoy the fruits of the object on which the right is created, only arises from that right, if and as far as this is needed for full enjoyment of that right. Yet, parties are allowed to further determine the competences of the holder of the right of *superficies* in the deed of creation and give him more rights and powers which are not needed for the full enjoyment of the rights, provided that these rights and powers have such a link with the rights that the right holder has by nature of his right, that it is justified to treat these first mentioned rigths and powers as part of that right;

that the judgment of the court of appeal can therefore not be maintained and reference to another court of appeal is needed;

Note

The most important element of the right of superficies is the fact that it gives ownership of a building, construction or plants to the right-holder. However, how this ownership is acquired and what exactly the rights of the right-holder are, apart from the ownership of the building, is determined by agreement between the parties.[212] This agreement is necessary because ownership of a building alone will not help the right-holder. When the holder of the right of superficies does not have a right to access the land on which the building is situated he may not have access to his ownership. As a general principle therefore the holder of a right of superficies will

[211] NJ 1982/76.

[212] von Staudinger et al, above n 103, 42; Asser et al, above n 21, n 251, 253, at 279, 281; Terré and Simler, above n 18, 710–12; Carbonnier, above n 17, 332.

have a right to use of the land in order to reach the building, construction or plant he owns. The annotated cases illustrate how additional agreement between the owner of the land and the right-holder give further content to the right of superficies.

I.F APARTMENT RIGHTS

Introductory Note

Each of the civil law systems under discussion enables parties to divide a building in such a way that several persons can each have their own apartment. Consequently, apartment rights only concern land. This can of course be done through contract, but property law systems also provide a solution. These rights are known as apartment rights and, in German and Dutch law, are distinct property rights which allow several people to co-own a building, but entitling each to a separate exclusive area. French law uses the law on co-ownership to the same end.

I.F.1 FRENCH LAW

Introductory Note

French law recognises a separate type of co-ownership specifically intended to enable parties to share ownership of a building. Such a situation is created through the recognition of a co-ownership regime by force of law combined with an agreement between parties dealing with the exact details of their relation.[213]

Law no 65-447 of 10 July 1965[214] **3.70 (FR)**

Article 1 The present statute governs each immovable building or group of immovable buildings of which the ownership has been divided, between several persons, in parts (*lots*) each comprising a private part and a share in the common parts.

In lack of a provision to the contrary creating a different arrangement, the present statute is equally applicable to groupings of immovables which, apart from the land, the equipment and common services, consist of parcels, built on or not, being the object of the rights of private ownership.

Article 10 The co-owners are required to participate in the charges incurred for the collective services and the components of the common equipment, according to the usefulness that these services and components present with respect to each part.

They are held to participate in the charges relating to the preservation, maintenance and management of the common parts, in proportion to the relative value of the private parts which their pieces comprise, such as that value results from the arrangements of Article 5.

The regulation of co-ownership fixes the share pertaining to each piece within each of the categories of charges.

Every regulation of co-ownership published from 31 December 2002 onwards indicates

[213] On co-ownership see above, I.A.5.

[214] Law no 65-447 of 10 July 1965, modified by Law no 66-1006 of 28 December 1966.

the elements taken into consideration and the method of calculation which enables one to fix the shares in common parts and the distribution of charges.

Notes

(1) As the excerpts from the legislation show, co-ownership of apartments combines a forced co-ownership of common parts of a building with an exclusive ownership of private parts of a building.[215] This subject is not dealt with in the Civil Code, but is governed by specific legislation.[216] The co-ownership of apartments has become a complicated structure. It combines a right of co-ownership of common parts of a building with sole ownership of private parts of a building with a membership of an association and an agreement known as a regulation.[217] The building is separated into common parts and private parts and the latter parts are allocated to the various co-owners. The common parts will be held in forced co-ownership of which each of the parties will have a share. The value of the share will be determined proportionally to the contribution made for it.[218] When parties do not stipulate a certain part of a building is to be used exclusively by one of the co-owners, that part is considered to be common.[219]

The co-owners are obliged to make regulations defining their relation.[220] These constitute a special type of agreement which will also have effect against those who contract with the co-owners, eg lessees, and holders of security rights.[221] These regulations must state which parts are common and which are private and how the object under co-ownership will be used, administered and repaired.[222]

(2) The co-owners, because they are members of a special community, form an association of co-owners or *syndicat*.[223] This association is used to administer the common parts of the object under co-ownership. The co-owners appoint a manager or *syndic* who, with a mandate from the co-owners, manages the day-to-day business of the co-ownership in general.[224] It is this person who in an earlier mentioned case was defendant to a procedure in the name of the co-owners together. The manager can be one of the co-owners, but may be a third party paid by the association. Finally, in very complicated constructions a certain part of the co-owners may also form a council or *conseil syndicat* which will support the manager in the day-to-day affairs and function as an intermediary between the manager and the general association of co-owners.[225]

[215] See Cass 21 nov 1955, JCP 1955.II.9004; Terré and Simler, above n 18, 435–36.

[216] Terré and Simler, above n 18, 437; Chabas, above n 18, 53.

[217] Art 10 Law of 10 July 1965; Chabas, above n 18, 63; Malaurie and Aynès, above n 18, 211–12.

[218] Art 1 Law of 10 July 1965, the shares are not defined and can be dealt with by the regulation. In a forced co-ownership shares are known as *millièmes* or *tantièmes*: Malaurie and Aynès, above n 18, 212, 214; Chabas, above n 18, 57.

[219] Cass civ 25 March 1966, Bull civ I.195; Malaurie and Aynès, above n 18, 212; Chabas, above n 18, 61.

[220] Art 10 Law of 10 July 1965; Malaurie and Aynès, above n 18, 222.

[221] Art 13 Law of 10 July 1965; Malaurie and Aynès, above n 18, 222.

[222] Art 8 Law of 10 July 1965, Malaurie and Aynès, above n 18, 223.

[223] Art 14 Law of 10 July 1965; Malaurie and Aynès, above n 18, 223-224; Chabas, above n 18, 63.

[224] Malaurie and Aynès, above n 18, 227–28; Chabas, above n 18, 65.

[225] Art 21 Law of 10 July 1965; Malaurie and Aynès, above n 18, 228.

I.F.2 GERMAN LAW

Introductory Notes

(a) The ownership of an apartment in German law is dealt with by specific legislation, the *Wohnungseigentumgesetz* (WEG). The WEG was needed because a right to an apartment or *Wohnungseigentum* causes a deviation from the general principles of property law in the BGB. The BGB has, as its starting point, a unitary concept of objects. Thus, §93 BGB resists a division of an object into different parts each susceptible to different property rights, and §94 BGB considers the land and a building on that land as a complete object which only together can be subject of a property right.

(b) There is another possibility in German law under which a person can be entitled to a property right in a part of a building. Combining the rules on limited personal servitudes with a special paragraph in the BGB, §1093 BGB, a right to live in a building or a so-called *Wohnungsrecht* can be established.[226]

Law on Apartment Ownership (WEG) **3.71 (DE)**

§1 (1) According to this statute a right of ownership of an apartment can be created on houses, a right of co-ownership can be created on those parts of a building that are not used to live in.
(2) A right of ownership of an apartment is an exclusive right of ownership in combination with a share in a co-ownership of the object to which it is connected.

BGH, 17 January 1968[227] **3.72 (DE)**

DIVISION OF CO-OWNERSHIP OF AN APARTMENT

Nature of co-ownership

The normal right of ownership as well as the co-ownership of an apartment can be divided in further parts.

Facts: This case concerned a preliminary question from the OLG Stuttgart on the legal nature of co-ownership constructions in German law. The answer of the German court is therefore not based on facts, but is an explanation of the law.

Held: Although legislation does not deal with a further splitting up of an already-divided right of ownership, whether normal or of a house (*Wohnungseigentum*), such a division can be made.

Judgment: III. The law regulates only the first creation of apartment ownership: it is created by means of division of the ownership of land, either via contract of several co-owners in the usual civil law meaning (§§3.4 WEG) or by a one-sided declaration of the sole owner (§8 WEG). On the question of the divisibility of existing apartment

[226] On limited personal servitudes see para 1.C.4 Germany: Limited Personal Servitudes. See also BGH 21 December 1966, BGHZ 46, 253, OLG Koblenz 8 March 2000, NZM 2001, 1095.
[227] NJW 1968, 499.

ownership (sub-division) the law is silent. It is to be decided therefore according to the sense and purpose of the character of the apartment ownership.

(a) Apartment ownership departs from the notion of ownership in general private law. It is genuine ownership …, and a mixture of sole ownership (§§903 ff BGB) and co-ownership in fractions (§§1008 *et seq* BGB): it connects the sole ownership of an apartment or an other volume unit (special ownership) with the community of ownership of land by undivided shares. … The initial theoretical controversy around the construction of apartment ownership … has in the meantime made way to the probably general realisation that without prejudice to the economic first-rateness of the special ownership, it is legally the co-ownership that is at the center of attention and the special ownership is its appendix, as may be taken from §§3 and 8 WEG regulating the right …

According to general private law both the sole ownership and the co-ownership in shares are divisible: the sole ownership can be divided both actually, by the object of the right, ie land, being divided into several independent parcels (see §1026 BGB, §7 GBO), and theoretically, when on the land several, existing independently next to each other, rights of co-ownership in shares are formed. The general private law co-ownership in shares is, in its part, again divisible: however not in a real way, since there is no complete actual object (parcel of land) at the basis of it; however, theoretically it is, by splitting up the fractions of shares (of eg ½) into several smaller ratios (eg ratios of each 1/6). …

For apartment ownership follows from this first the conceptual divisibility in purely theoretical regard: since according to private law both sole ownership and the normal co-ownership are theoretically divisible, also the apartment right, which comprises sole ownership and co-ownership rights, can be divided, with remaining real undivided volume unit (apartment), into several theoretical partial rights defined according to fractions (which is practical in particular for married people …). In the present case it concerns the actual division of an apartment right in such a manner that from the former single volume unit (here: building with baker's shop areas) several parts are to be formed (here two: 1. the apartment, 2. the baker's shop area) and each is allocated its own ownership of a space. With this actual division of the ownership necessarily a further theoretical allocation of the co-ownership (joint ownership) goes hand in hand. This, strictly speaking, concerns a mixed actual–theoretical division; the designation 'actual division' can only be understood in in this sense.

Also against this divisibility no conceptual doubts exist; unlike with normal co-ownership (§§1008 BGB *et seq*), the exclusive ownership (sole ownership) provided here does not require the allocation of an actual divisible object, which is represented by the building (here: house and baker's shop area), at least then if it can itself actually be divided into several volume units by itself, as it corresponds to the requirement §3 sub 2 WEG.

Notes

(1) The owner of an apartment has normal unitary ownership on his exclusive part of a building, ie his apartment, and co-ownership of the common parts.[228] Also the claims available to the owner through §§985 and 1004 BGB are available to the holder of this right of ownership.[229] The result of this is also that a co-owner can use §1004 BGB to exclude other co-owners from his exclusive ownership of a part of the building.[230] However, the right of ownership of the exclusive part and the co-ownership of the common parts are connected.[231]

(2) The possibility of restricting any transfer without permission of the other apartment owners already shows that there is a legal relation between the owners. Because each of the apartment owners holds a share in the community, they have to deal with each other. The WEG expressly allows the co-owners to deal with their affairs by agreement.[232] However, such provisions only take effect against third parties if they are registered as part of the exclusive ownership.[233] This agreement can contain a provision on the division of costs or a rule that a majority decision concerning the common parts of the building will bind all the owners. This agreement can only affect the common ownership and not the exclusive part.[234] Normally, the co-owners form an association of owners.[235]

I.F.3 DUTCH LAW

Introductory Note

The apartment right in Dutch law follows a slightly different approach. It constitutes a property right which combines an exclusive entitlement to a certain space with co-ownership of common parts of a building.[236] Furthermore, Dutch law adds a third element to the mix: a compulsory membership of the association of owners, comprising each right-holder of a share in the community of co-owners.

Burgerlijk Wetboek **3.73 (NL)**

Article 5:106 (1) An owner, a holder of a right of *emphyteusis* or a holder of a right of *superficies* is entitled to divide his right, created on a building with appurtenances and on the land with appurtenaces belonging to it, into rights of apartment. (2) An owner, a holder of a right of *emphyteusis* or a holder of a right of *superficies* is also entitled to divide his right to a piece of land into rights of apartment. (3) A right of apartment in turn can be subject to division into rights of apartment.

[228] Baur, Baur and Stürner, above n 83, 333.
[229] Also §823 will be available to the owner, ibid, at 333. On this see above, Chapter 2.
[230] §13 WEG: Wolf, above n 14, 68.
[231] §6 WEG: Wolf, above n 14, 67; Baur, Baur and Stürner, above n 83, 337.
[232] §10 WEG: a majority decision having impact on the exclusive ownership of a part of the house will not have effect. BGHZ 145, 158 = NJW 2000, 3500: Schwab and Prütting, above n 14, 295.
[233] §10(2) WEG.
[234] See BGH 14 June 1984, NJW 1984, 2409 = BGHZ 91, 343.
[235] See §20 *et seq* WEG.
[236] Asser et al, above n 21, n 343, at 366.

A holder of a right of apartment is entitled to this division as far as it is not determined otherwise in the deed of separation.
(4) A right of apartment is understood to include: a share in the objects involved in the division, that includes the entitlement to exclusively use certain parts of the building which according to their construction are intended or are going to be intended to be used as a separate unit. The share can also include the entitlement to exclusively use certain parts of the land belonging to the building. In case of the situation mentioned in sub 2, the share includes the entitlement to exclusively use certain parts of land, which according to their construction or designation are intended or are going to be intended to be used as a separate unit.
(5) An owner of apartment is understood to mean a holder of a right of apartment.
(6) A building in this Title is also understood to mean a group of buildings which are involved in one division into rights of apartment.
(7) A holder of a right of *emphyteusis* or a holder of a right of *superficies* is only entitled to divide his right into rights of apartment after receiving permission of the landowner. If the landowner denies the permission without reasonable grounds or does not declare at all, the permission can, on the question of the person in need of the permission, be replaced by a mandate from the subdistrict court judge of the district court in which district the building or the biggest part of the building is situated.

Hoge Raad, 19 December 1986[237] **3.74 (NL)**

Gouda and others v De Jong

LEGAL DUTY TO ESTABLISH ASSOCIATION OF OWNERS

The three-part apartment building

When a building is divided into apartment rights an association of owners of which all holders of apartment rights are member is compulsory.

Facts: The claimant was a property management company responsible for the administration of an apartment building in which the defendant held an apartment right. The apartment building was constructed in such a way that there were three different parts comprising six apartments, each with their own entrance. On 31 March 1976 the building was divided into 18 apartment rights, and three associations of owners, corresponding to the three parts of the building, were established.

The defendant applied for the establishment of a general association of owners comprising all the right-holders of the apartment rights as members. At issue was whether the duty to establish an association of owners for all right-holders under Article 875f of the old BW, similar to that in the new Civil Code Article 5:112 BW, meant that three different associations did not suffice.

Held: The court held that the association as mentioned in Article 875f of the old BW should comprise all right-holders of the rights of apartments together. The three separate associations were not invalid, but were not the association of owners as specified in the code.

Judgment: The regulation mentioned in Article 875(1)(e) must contain: the formation of 'an association of owners', that aims at looking after the common interests of the 'owners of apartments'. Article 876(1) states that every owner of an apart-

[237] NJ 1987/947.

ment is a member of 'the' association of owners by operation of the law. An owner of an apartment is understood to stand for the holder of a right of apartment (Article 875a(4)), a right of apartment is understood to mean a share in the object involved in the division (Article 875a(3)). All this leads to an association of ownership mentioned in Article 875(1)(e) to which all those who are entitled to a share in the assets involved in the division are a member.

3.3 The judgment of the court must therefore be understood as following:

(a) that 'the building locally known as Thorbeckelaan numbers 53 untill 87 (odd numbers)' in Gouda must be regarded as the object or the objects which are involved in the division respectively, and

(b) that an asscociation whose members are all those who are entitled to a share in, briefly stated, the building, was not established, and that especially none of the 'three associations of owners' which were founded by act are such an association.

Taking this as starting point, the court has, whatever its relevant considerations may be, correctly held that such an association still has to be founded. The circumstance that the apartments in question, according to the grievance in appeal, are situated 'at the three separate staircases installed in the block of flats, which are not connected to each other', does not have the effect that an association as referred to in Article 875(1)(e) does not have to be established. Neither does it have the effect, if it would be correct that 'the apartments each have their own facilities including an own heating system', that the mentioned regulation does not have to be complied with.

Notes

(1) The three elements composing the right of apartment in Dutch law are compulsory as can be seen from the definition of Article 5:106 BW and the requirement of Article 5:112 BW. These elements are connected in such a way that they cannot be transferred separately.[238]

(2) In contrast to its German equivalent, in Dutch law, the right to the exclusive part of a building is not a right of ownership but a right accessory to the share in the community. Since this right is not seen as separate from the other elements of the right of apartment, it is not a limited property right.[239] However, the accessory nature allows the right to be transferred with the other elements, together forming the property right known as an apartment right.

I.F.4 A COMPARISON OF GERMAN, DUTCH AND FRENCH LAW

Each of the civil law systems adopts a similar solution to the same problem: giving one person the right to use and enjoy a certain part of a building. A person can be entitled to the exclusive use of a certain space while having to share in the general costs of the building in which that space is situated. The systems differ in the way in which they achieve the exclusive right to use and enjoy a certain space in a building. However, it is in the co-ownership regime of the common parts that

[238] Art 5:120 BW: Asser et al, above n 21, n 344, at 368.

[239] HR 9 October 1958, NJ 1959, 8: Asser et al, above n 21, n 344, at 368; RFRH Mertens, *Appartementen* (Monografieën Nieuw Bw—B29, B29; Deventer, Kluwer, 1999) 3.

the systems are very much alike. In each of these systems the common parts are those parts which are not exclusive. Mostly these will be hallways, staircases and elevators. However, the outside walls and all supporting walls of a building are also common. This has led some authors to state that the exclusive part of an apartment right is actually nothing more than an exclusive right to a defined amount of air.[240]

Membership of the association of owners is seen as an essential element of the apartment right and will transfer from the old to the new acquirers. Furthermore, the association also enables the other owners to have a say in the transfer of apartment rights to new persons. The membership connects the co-owners and forces them to deal with their affairs in a structured way.

I.G GERMAN LAW: OPTIONS TO PURCHASE

Introductory Note

When two parties make an agreement that one party will have a right to buy a piece of land, in German law this gives rise to a property right known as *dingliches Vorkaufrecht*, literally pre-emptive property right of sale. Between the parties the holder of the right will have an option to purchase the land.[241]

Bürgerliches Gesetzbuch **3.75 (DE)**

§1084 A piece of land can be burdened in a way that the person, for whose benefit the right is created, is entitled to an option to purchase in respect to the owner.

Note

The effect of the property right is that when an owner and another person agree on the sale and transfer of an immovable object, they establish the property pre-emptive right which is designed to protect the right-holder against the owner selling and transferring the object to a third party before the formalities of the transfer are dealt with.[242] The property right entitles the right-holder to resist the conclusion of a contract of sale concluded between the owner and a third party and, under certain conditions, to demand a transfer of ownership.[243] When, however, the transfer to a third party is concluded, without additional protection through pre-emptive registra-

[240] See AA van Velten, *Regels Zijn Regels. Enkele opmerkingen over het hybride karakter van het begrip Appartementsrecht in het Nederlandse Privaatrecht. Rede uitgesproken bij de aanvaarding van het ambt van bijzonder hoogleraar op de leerstoel privaatrechtelijke aspecten van onroerend goed bij de Faculteit der Rechtsgeleerdheid aan de Vrije Universiteit te Amsterdam op donderdag 14 december 1989 door Prof. Mr AA van Velten* (Ars Notariatus Xliv; Deventer, Kluwer, 1989).

[241] In English law an option to purchase is a property right as well. See below II.A.11 options to purchase.

[242] §1094 BGB, also a share in a community of co-owners can be subject of the right, §1095 BGB. Also other land-like rights, eg the right of superficies (§11 ErbbVO) can be subject, see von Staudinger et al, above n 103, 765, 772-773.

[243] §1098 BGB. The right itself does not interfere with the party autonomy of the owner and the third party to decide on the contents of their agreement: see von Staudinger et al, above n 103, 796.

tion (*Vormerkung*) the option ceases to exist.[244] This special form of registration is dealt with in Chapter 8.[245]

I.H FRENCH LAW IN REFORM: SPECIAL PROPERTY RIGHT TO USE

Introductory Notes

(a) In the last decade French private law has been subject to a reform process. In generally, all sections in the French Code Civil have been updated. For property law this includes the 2006 reforms on the law of securities, which are dealt with in Chapter 5, which added a section to the Civil Code dealing with personal and property security rights, and the 2007 introduction of the *fiducie*, a trust-like device, dealt with in Chapter 6.

(b) In November 2008 a project to reform French property law, the law of things or *droit de biens*, was also proprosed.[246] This project is a so-called *avant-projet* or preliminary project, which is likely to be, but has not yet been, taken up by the legislature. The reform mainly offers a reorganisation of the current property law but also introduces a new type of property right: the special right to use or *droit réel de jouissance spéciale*.

Preliminary project on the reform of the law of property, Chapter IV **3.76**
(FR)

Article 608 An owner may grant, without prejudice to public policy, one or more property rights that provide the holder with a special right to use and enjoy one or more of his things.
Property rights to use in the public domain are created and exercised in conformity with the general code of property of public persons and the laws that govern these.
Article 609 A property right to use and enjoy is created in the same way as a right of usufruct.
It is held in respect to the ordinary purpose of the thing.
Article 610 The holder of a special property right to use and enjoy holds the rights mentioned in Articles 582 to 585 and bears the duties of a usufructuary mentioned in Articles 586 to 590.

Notes

(1) The special right to use and enjoy is a specific type of property right, closely resembling a right of usufruct, but without the temporary restrictions of that right

[244] §1098(2) BGB: von Staudinger et al, above n 103, 797; Baur, Baur and Stürner, above n 83, 244–45.
[245] Below, Chapter 8.
[246] Association Henri Capitant des amis de la culture Française, proposition de réforme du livre II du Code civil relatif aux biens. To be consulted on the website of the Association Henri Capitant: www.henricapitant.org.

or the restriction that the holder may use the whole of the object of ownership. The special right to use can therefore be restricted to specific uses.

(2) The special right to use and enjoy is an open type of right, as the proposed rules do not provide any limitation. The proposal therefore, although the drafters state otherwise, raises questions for the already somewhat controversial *numerus clausus* of property rights in French law.[247]

I.I SECURITY RIGHTS: HYPOTHEC

Security rights are dealt with in Chapter 5.

I.J BORDERLINE CASES

Introductory Note

As was seen in Chapter 1, each of the civil law systems under discussion recognises a *numerus clausus* of property rights.[248] The *numerus clausus* means that only a limited number of property rights are recognised. Any right falling outside that list cannot be a property right. Nevertheless, each legal system recognises certain rights which, though not recognised as property rights, so closely resemble them that they deserve mention.

I.J.1 DUTCH LAW: 'QUALITATIVE DUTIES'

Introductory Note

Dutch law has a concept in its law of obligations called 'qualitative duty'. This duty enables a person not in his capacity as an owner to bind another person in his capacity of an owner to tolerate or refrain from doing something on his land. In this respect, it resembles a right of real servitude. In fact, most of the duties which can be created through a real servitude can be created by a qualitative duty as well.

In case of a qualitative duty, a person in his personal capacity is entitled to something and therefore benefits from the right. In this respect a qualitative duty is different from a right of real servitude and comes very close to a German limited personal servitude also dealt with in this chapter.[249] However, contrary to German law, the Dutch qualitative duty is not a property right but a personal right, although with some property law effects, in particular the transfer of the right to new acquirers of the land on which it is established. After such a transfer the right will burden the new owner in his capacity as owner of the land. This section will shortly deal with this borderline concept.

[247] See *Avant Projet du réforme du droit de biens*, explanation to Chapter IV. On *numerus clausus* see above Chaper 1.

[248] Above, Chapter 1.

[249] However, limited personal servitudes are recognised as full property rights in German law. Above, I.C.4.

Burgerlijk Wetboek **3.77 (NL)**

Article 6:252 (1) In an agreement it can be stipulated that the obligation of one of the parties to tolerate something or to refrain from doing something with regard to his registered object, shall pass onto those who shall receive the object under particular title, and that those who receive a right of use of the object from the right holder shall also be bound.

(2) For the functioning of the stipulation referred to in sub 1, it is required that of the agreement between parties a notarial deed is made, followed by entry of the deed in the public registers. The person on whom the obligation rests, as created by the stipulation, must choose domicile in the Netherlands in the deed for the sake of the entry.

(3) Even after the entry the stipulation does not have effect:

(a) against those who before the entry into the registers have received a right to use under particular title on the object or a right;

(b) against a seizor of the object or of a right on the object, if the entry, at the time of the entry of the seizure report, has not yet been effected(c) against those who have received their right of a person, who in accordance with the provision in a or b, was not bound to the stipulated obligation.

(4) If for the obligation a compensation has been agreed upon, the right to compensation is also transfered when the primary obligation is transfered, as far as this stands in relation with the period after the transfer and also if the stipulation concerning this compensation has been entered in the registers.

(5) This article is not applicable to obligations which limit a right holder in his competence to transfer or burden the object.

Court of appeal of 's-Hertogenbosch, 10 January 2002[250] **3.78 (NL)**

Kwantum Nederland BV v City of Heerlen

USE OF A QUALITATIVE DUTY

The furniture store

A qualitative duty can be used by municipality acting in its private law capacity and can be strengthened with a penalty clause.

Facts: A company owned two furniture stores in different cities. It planned to consolidate the stores in a 'furniture strip', a concentration of furniture stores close to the highway on the outskirts of Heerlen. To do this, the company needed a permit from the municipality of Heerlen. The local government agreed to the move on condition of the establishment of a qualitative duty in their favour containing a prohibition on opening a furniture store in the old buildings within five years of the move. The qualitative duty was strengthened with a penalty clause of around €45,000. Both the duty and the penalty clause were registered.

The following year, the company sold one of the old buildings to another furniture company, Kwantum, the claimant in this case. Was the claimant liable to pay the amount of the penalty?

Held: The qualitative duty had been validly established. Because it and the penalty clause were registered, the claimant could have discovered it and was therefore liable for its infringement.

[250] NJ 2002/633.

Judgment: Kwantum claims that, because of the letter from the municipality of Kerkrade aforementioned in 4.1.4, it could trust that it could exploit a retail trade in home furnishings at de Locht 2 in Kerkrade. Kwantum further holds that it was not required to be prepared for the qualitative duty at issue.

4.3.1 This argument is not correct and is not of benefit to Kwantum. Now that the qualitative duty is entered in the deed of conveyance, Kwantum cannot successfully appeal against the municipality that it was not required to be prepared for the qualitative duty. Kwantum has bought the building while it knew or should have known that a private law restriction on the use rested on it. With this the appeal of Kwantum on Article 6:258 BW also fails.

4.3.2 In contrast to what Kwantum states, it cannot be held that the municipality, by stipulation of the qualitative duty, has acted unreasonably, carelessly or in violation of one or more general principles of good government. Nor are there sufficient facts brought to justify the judgment that reasonableness and fairness stand in the way of an appeal by the municipality in respect to the stipulation. It is of further importance that Vegers also had an interest in establishing the duty in order to be ensured of the co-operation of the municipality for the moving of his company.

Notes

(1) A qualitative duty is a duty not to do something which rests on the owner of a piece of land, or another registered object, in his capacity as an owner.[251] As we will see below, it is what a common lawyer would call a 'restrictive covenant', though as we will also see, such restrictive covenants require both a dominant and servient tenement. The word 'qualitative', therefore, should be read as a duty binding the owner in his capacity as owner. Thus, when the owner of the piece of land transfers his ownership to another, the transferee will be bound by the qualitative duty in his capacity as owner. In order to have this effect, the qualitative duty must be registered. However, unlike property rights on land in Dutch law, registration is not a prerequisite for the existence of the right. The duty takes effect between the original parties to an agreement, though it will only bind third parties on registration. It is because of this that the concept of qualitative duty is found in the sixth section of the Dutch Civil Code, the part dealing with the law of obligations, and not in the law of property.[252]

(2) A qualitative duty resembles a right of real servitude, not only because it imposes a burden on a piece of land, but also because of the effect the burden has against subsequent acquirers of that piece of land. Not surprisingly, the qualitative duty is subject to many of the same requirements as a right of real servitude. The duty the right imposes can only be negative in nature. A positive duty is not allowed.[253] However, unlike a right of real servitude, which is restricted to factual

[251] Art 3:10 BW defines registered objects. These include, besides land, also airplanes and ships.

[252] C Asser and A Hartkamp, *Verbintenissenrecht 4—II Algemene leer der overeenkomsten*, 11th edn (Deventer, WEJ Tjeenk Willink, 2001) n 412, at 431. For a discussion, see V Sagaert, 'Kwalitatieve verbintenissen in het Belgische en Nederlandse recht' in JM Smits and S Stijns (eds), *Inhoud en werking van de overeenkomst naar Belgisch en Nederlands recht* (Antwerpen-Groningen, Intersentia, 2005) 341, 343; Asser and Hartkamp, this note, n 411, at 430; N van Oostrom-Streep 'De Kwalitatieve Verplichting als Twee-Eenheid?' (2005) 6638 *WPNR* 786-88, at 786.

[253] Art 6:252 (1) BW.

acts, a negative duty in the case of a qualitative duty can restrict an owner in his capacity to take legal acts with the limit of the last paragraph of Article 6:252 BW.[254] Such a restriction on a legal act might, for example, be a prohibition against leasing the object. As with the case of a servitude, Dutch doctrine distinguishes between primary and secondary duties. The primary duties are covered directly by Article 6:252 BW and can therefore only be negative. Secondary duties can be positive if they support the primary negative duty.[255] The penalty clause used in the above case should be seen as such a positive secondary duty.

Furthermore, the qualitative duty, even though it is a contract, will survive the insolvency of the owner of the land. If the duty has been registered before the insolvency, the Dutch insolvency act stipulates that the duty continues to exist and continues to bind third parties, including the creditors of the owner.[256] The result will be that the object cannot be sold other than with the duty still attached.

The legal nature of the qualitative duty was the subject of a vigorous debate prior to the introduction of the new Civil Code in 1992. The debate centred on the question whether this right was actually a property right and not a personal right.[257] As stated above, the right very much resembles a real servitude, or limited personal servitude in German law, both of which are recognised as property rights.[258] However, the debate was settled by the Dutch legislator, when as we have seen, the qualitative duty was placed in the sixth section, dealing with the law of obligations.[259]

The concept of qualitative duty is commonly used in the Netherlands. It enables the establishment of a real servitude-like arrangement without the need for a dominant tenement. And though theoretically the person benefiting can be far removed from the land, in practice the qualitative duty is only used in similar situations as in the case above, as a method for local governments to impose restrictions on private

[254] JLP Cahen, *Overeenkomst en Derden*, 2nd edn (Deventer, Kluwer, 2004) 34; Asser and Hartkamp, above n 252, n 407, at 427.

[255] Asser and Hartkamp, above n 252, n 407; CE du Perron, *Overeenkomst en derden; Een analyse van de relativiteit van de contractswerking* (Deventer, Kluwer, 1999) 246 *et seq*.

[256] Art 35a FW.

[257] See inter alia SN van Opstall, 'Zakelijke rechten en kwalitatieve verbintentissen' (1966) 4919–26 *WPNR* 383–473, at 471; A Pitlo, 'Na 3 Maart 1905' in PhAN Houwing (ed), *Onroerend Goed: Opstellen geschreven ter gelegenheid van het 125-Jarig bestaan van de Broederschap der Notarissen in Nederland* (Deventer, Kluwer, 1968) 231–48; JMM Maeijer, *Erfdienstbaarheden en Kwalitatieve Verbintenissen (Huidig en Wordend Recht)* (Preadviezen uitgebracht ter behandeling in de algemene vergadering van de Broederschap van Candidaat-Notarissen, 1966) 80; HJ Rijtma, 'Kwalitatieve Rechten', *Op de grenzen van komend recht. Opstellen aangeboden aan Prof Mr JH Beekhuis* (Deventer, Zwolle; Kluwer–Tjeenk Willink, 1969) 215–29, at 229; PA Stein, 'Van Kettingbeding naar Kwalitatieve Verbintenis' (1976) 5365 WPNR 644–50, at 650; in favour see JTh Smalbraak, *Erfdienstbaarheden en kwalitatieve verbintenissen (Huidig en wordend recht)* (Preadviezen uitgebracht ter behandeling in de algemene vergadering van de Broederschap van Candidaat-Notarissen, 1966) 110; Asser and Hartkamp, above n 252, n 411, at 430.

[258] For a comparison see NC van Oostrom-Streep, *De kwalitatieve verplichting* (Den Haag, Boom Juridische Uitgevers (BJu), 2006) and B Akkermans, 'The New Dutch Civil Code: The Borderline between Property and Contract', in JHM van Erp and B Akkermans (eds), *Towards a Unified System of Land Burdens?* (Antwerpen and Oxford, Intersentia, 2006) 163–83, at 175–79.

[259] CJ van Zeben and JW du Pon, *Boek 6—Algemeen Gedeelte Van Het Verbintenissenrecht, Parlementaire geschiedenis van het nieuwe Burgerlijk Wetboek* (Deventer, Kluwer, 1981b) 942 *et seq*; CE du Perron, *Overeenkomst En Derden; Een Analyse Van De Relativiteit Van De Contractswerking* (Deventer, Kluwer, 1999) 250.

owners. It can also be used to allow local government to access land in order to maintain sewers or electricity cables.

I.J.2 LEASE OF ASSETS

I.J.2.a French and German law

Introductory Note

In each of the civil law systems, a provision in the civil code protects tenants against their landlord, in particular against a landlord selling and transferring the ownership of the land to another person. In civil law systems, the lease is not a property right, and thus creates rights binding only the parties to it. Thus, when the landlord or lessor sells and transfers the object under his ownership to another person, the lessee can only enforce the lease against the old owner, not his successor. This undesired effect has been remedied by legislation.

Code civil **3.79 (FR)**

Article 1743 If the lessor sells the object under lease, the acquirer of the object may not evict the lessee, tenant of a part of the object or tenant who has an authentic lease or one of which the date can be ascertained. He may, however, evict a non-rural lessee or tenant when he has reserved a right to do so in the lease agreement.

Bürgerliches Gesetzbuch **3.80 (DE)**

§566 If the leased living space, after the lessee has taken up the lease, is transferred to a third party, the acquirer will take the place of the lessor by force of law under the obligations following from the lease for the duration of his ownership.

Notes

(1) These provisions deal with the maxim 'a sale does not break the lease', one of the fundamentals of the modern civil law of lease. Although formulated differently, they achieve the exact same result. When a lessor sells and transfers the building in which the lessee leased space, the new owner takes over the rights and obligations of the old lessor. In other words, the sale and transfer will not break the lease agreement, and the lease agreement therefore transfers to the new owner.[260] If this provision did not apply, then the new owner could evict the lessee.

(2) This strengthening of the position of the lessee has given rise to the question in each of the legal systems whether a lease does not now constitute a property right.[261] However, the dominant view in each of these systems is that a lease remains

[260] V Sagaert, 'Het goederenrecht als open systeem van verbintenissen? Poging tot een nieuwe kwalificatie van de vermogensrechten' (2005) 42/3 *Tijdschrift voor Privaatrecht* 983–1086, at 1010; W Schön, 'Zur Analogiefähigkeit des §571 BGB' [2001] *Juristen Zeitung (JZ)* 119–27, at 119-120; R Westrik, *Koop breekt geen huur* (The Hague, Vermande, 2001) 189 *et seq*.

[261] See Schön, above n 260, 120 *et seq*; Sagaert, above n 260, 1010.

a personal right. A major argument in support of this proposition is that only the lessor can assign his part of the lease agreement; the lessee has no rights capable of assignment.[262]

I.A.2.b Dutch law

Burgerlijk Wetboek **3.81 (NL)**

Article 7:226 The transfer of an object to which a lease agreement applies and creation or transfer of an independent right of usufruct, *emphyteusis* or *superficies* on the object to which the lease agreement applies, by the lessor transfers the rights and claims of the lessor ... to the acquirer

Note

This provision creates the same protection for a lessee as in French and German law. However, in Dutch law this article, and with it the rule that a 'sale does not break a lease', applies to both land and movable assets.[263]

I.A.3 GERMAN LAW: ACQUISITION RIGHTS (*ANWARTSCHAFTSRECHTE*)

BGH, 24 June 1958[264] **3.82 (DE)**

RECOGNITION OF AN ACQUISITION RIGHT

Identifying the assets

When things are delivered under a retention of title clause, the holder of the things receives an acquisition right to receive ownership. This right can be transferred with other things for security purposes.

Facts: X had transferred ownership for security purposes to Y of a number of items held in storage. However, some of these things were not owned by X but by Z as they had been delivered under retention of title. Y claimed that he was entitled to rights in all the things, as X would have an acquisition right on the things delivered under retention of title. Y, the claimant, therefore argued when the things had been transferred to him all at once, he had received rights in all of them.

Held: X holds an acquisition right on the things delivered to him under retention of title. Although the things which were already owned by X and those things which had been delivered under retention of title, ie where X had an acquisition right, are of a different legal nature, a single transfer can transfer all of these at once.

Judgment: These conclusions are in the opinion of the relevant Senate only applicable, if the transfer of ownership and the acquisition right of the ownership must take effect following different principles. If to that extent different agreements or

[262] R Westrik, *Koop breekt geen huur* (The Hague, Vermande, 2001) 189 *et seq.*

[263] MM Asbreuk-Van Os, 'De regel "koop breekt geen huur" in Wetsvoorstel 26 089 vertoont (verborgen) gebreken' (2000) 6386 WPNR 31–35, at 32 *et seq*; in reaction JHM van Erp, 'Wordt huur een verhandelbaar goed? Een reactie op het artikel "De regel 'koop breekt geen huur" in Wetsvoorstel 26 089 vertoont (verborgen) gebreken' van Mr MM Asbreuk-Van Os in WPNR (2000) 6386' (2000) 6407 *WPNR* 456–57, at 465 *et seq.*

[264] VIII ZR 205/57= NJW 1958, 1133.

execution actions would be necessary, then a clarifying of the ownership structures on the object provided for security (the security object) and an exact concretisation of the objects which at the time of the conclusion of the agreement were owned by the provider of the security and the objects under retention of title of the suppliers would become essential, in order to create the necessary specificity. It is however recognised that the transfer of the acquisition right is subject to the same rules as the transfer of ownership of movable obejcts. ... The acquisition right is a simple preliminary stage of the property; in comparison to the property it is ‚not something diffent', but rather something ‚less' of the same nature (*wesensgleiches 'minus'*) ...

Therefore, neither a notification of the supplier, who reserved the ownership, nor his consent is necessary. The transfer of the acquisition right on an object delivered under the retention of title has rather as consequence, as expressed in BGHZ 20, 88, 100 = NJW 56, 665 in conformity with the view predominantly expressed in doctrine, that with the occurrence of the condition, ie on satisfaction of the supplier by payment of the claim, for which he reserved the ownership for himself, directly transfer the full ownership of the supplier to the acquirer under avoidance of the retention of title. In this circumstance there is no apparent reason why in case of a transfer of ownership for security purposes of merchandise that comprises objects that are still held under retention of title by a supplier, as well as retention-free objects, it is possible to designate the retained and non-retained objects required to meet the specificity requirement. More than these doubts cannot be deduced against the effectiveness of the contract from this criterion. Because from it is to be taken clearly that the protection should extend to all materials, including incomplete and finished objects.

On all these objects either the ownership or the acquisition right to the ownership of the same nature of the defendant should transfer to the claimant. Westermann ... arrives at the same conclusion, also referring to the equality of content between ownership and acquisition rights ..., Pohle ..., who does not consider the difference between ownership and acquisition right so large that a separate treatment appears to be required, and Paulus ..., who elaborates, that with the application of the specificity requirements the identification of institutional differences of the form of security device as such could not be decisive, but only the appropriate differences in the allocation of property effect. This crucial criterion, the similarity of ownership and acquisition right of the right of ownership and the transfer of both rights according to the same principles, was not sufficiently considered in BGHZ 21, 52. The starting point of view must however necessarily lead to the legal question being answered in the negative of BGHZ 21, 52 ...

... The opinion of Zunft appears correct. As already explained, it is recognised that the transfer of the acquisition right to the right of ownership has to be carried out according to the provisions that apply to the transfer of ownership of movable obejcts. The delivery of the thing can therefore be replaced by a so-called anticipated fictive transfer of possession.

Baur, Baur and Stürner, Property Law, 755–56 **3.83 (DE)**

The legal order is confronted with the problem whether the special nature of this situation must be recognised or whether it should just be determined that the right has not yet been acquired. In the law itself there are only relatively weak foundations for this, so in §878 and in §§160–162 in favour of the person entitled.

However, what is really at stake here is protection against opposing behaviours of the other party or against limitations on the power to dispose, to which he was subject in the meantime. From that not much follows with which the question can be answered if the right of the acquirer can be recognised as subjective right, as property right (with which character?). Nevertheless—at least in respect to the here-discussed position of the seller—increasingly the opinion is developed that these questions should be answered positively and that we should speak of an—also not really clear—acquisition right.

Notes

(1) The acquisition right in German law arises on movable objects when these things are delivered under retention of title. In this situation the rights of the buyer are stronger than a mere personal right against the seller.[265] Retention of title is a transfer of ownership under a suspensive condition. In such a situation the BGB provides that the owner can no longer use his power of disposal to prevent the acquisition of ownership over the object by the buyer.[266] Almost all acts by the owner will be invalid.[267] Furthermore, the buyer has a claim for compensation when the object is damaged in the care of the owner, and, in case the owner tries to prevent the fulfilment of the condition under which the transfer was made, the buyer can acquire ownership by force of law.[268] In this situation the buyer has a more secured position.

This secured position has given rise to the recognition of the right of the buyer as a 'special' right. This right is considered not just a personal right for the transfer of the object, but a pre-emptive right of ownership. In this landmark decision the Bundersgerichtshof characterised the concept of acquisition right.[269]

(2) The acquisition right will come into existence when the retention of title is made and will cease to exist when the ownership is eventually transferred to the acquirer. In the meantime the right can be used as security by its holder.[270]

(3) The legal nature of the acquisition right is debated.[271] Debate centres on the question whether the closed system of property rights entitles the judiciary to recognise new property rights.[272]

[265] Baur, Baur and Stürner, above n 83, 755.

[266] Wolf, above n 14, 314–15.

[267] §161(1) BGB, but see §161(3) BGB.

[268] §§160 and 162 BGB: Wolf, above n 14, 315.

[269] BGH 24 June 1958, BGHZ 28, 16, 21, BGH 25 February 1966, BGHZ 45, 186 (192).

[270] BGH 22 February 1956, IV ZR 164/55 (KG)=NJW 1956, 665.

[271] Schwab and Prütting, above n 14, 187; Wolf, above n 14, 315–16; Wiegand, above n 15, 128–29; Baur, Baur and Stürner, above n 83, 755–56; L Raiser, *Dingliche Anwartschaften* (Tübingen: JCB Mohr (Paul Siebeck), 1961) 45 *et seq*; PO Mülbert, 'Das inexistente Anwartschaftsrecht und seine Alternativen' (2002) 202 *Archiv für die civilistische Praxis* 912–50, at 912 *et seq*.

[272] J von Staudinger *et al*, *Drittes Buch—Sachenrecht. Einleitung Zum Sachenrecht; §§8540–882* (Berlin, Sellier de Gruyter, 2000) 27–28.

II. COMMON LAW

Introductory Note

The common law, in contrast to civil systems, draws a sharp line between property rights in respect of land, on the one hand, and property rights in respect of goods, on the other. There are at least two reasons for this. The first is that land was, but goods were not, subject to the feudal system of the Middle Ages; goods were not held 'of' a feudal superior. To some extent, this division is still part of the common law system today. The second is that the physical nature of land, in particular its permanence, its immovability, and the fact that there will generally be neighbouring land, lends itself to a far more complex system of rights than exists in respect of, say, a book or a car. This section begins with an examination of the common law's treatment of land before moving on to an examination of the property rights which can exist in respect of goods. Like the civil law, the common law, both in relation to land and goods, operates a *numerus clausus* of property rights. The difference is that the list for land, for the reasons mentioned above, is far longer than that for goods.

II.A LAND

II.A.1 A *NUMERUS CLAUSUS* OF PROPERTY RIGHTS IN LAND AT COMMON LAW

Introductory Note

The common law operates a *numerus clausus* or closed list of property rights in land. As with the civil law, it is a fundamental principle that a right which is not in this closed list of property rights is incapable of binding strangers to its creation. It will be a personal right, binding only its grantor.

Court of Exchequer, 1 May 1863[273] **3.84 (E&W)**

Hill v Tupper

A CLOSED LIST OF PROPERTY RIGHTS

The pleasure boat franchise

It is not competent for individuals to add to the list of property rights recognised by the law.

Facts: The holder of a fee simple title to a canal and its banks granted a lease of a parcel of land on the banks to the plaintiff, a boat proprietor. Among the rights granted by the lease was 'the sole and exclusive right or liberty to put or use boats on the said canal, and let the same for hire for the purpose of pleasure only'. The defendant, the landlord of an inn adjoining the canal, caused an interference with

[273] (1863) 2 H & C 121.

the plaintiff's right by letting his own boats out for hire. The plaintiff unsuccessfully sought damages for interference with this right.

Held: A grantor may bind himself by covenant to allow what rights he pleases over his property, but the law will not permit him to carve out his property so as to enable the grantee of such a limited right to sue a stranger in the way here contended for.

Judgment: Pollock CB—The grant here operates simply as a licence or covenant on the part of the lessors, the canal company, and is binding on them as between themselves and their lessee, but gives no right of action to the lessee, in his own name, against a stranger for an infringement of the alleged exclusive right. ... [Counsel for the plaintiff] asks why the owner of an estate should not be able to grant such a right as that now claimed by the plaintiff. The answer is, because the law does not recognize such rights. It is an old and well-established principle of our law that new estates cannot be created. Counsel says he sees no reasons, if a man may grant a right to cut turves, or to fish, or to hunt, etc, why such a right as that here claimed, or why an exclusive right to cut cabbages in a garden, or to collect the manure and droppings from cattle, which no doubt is of some value, may not also be granted. The answer is, that the law will not allow it. So the law will not permit a man to leave land alternatively to a male heir and a female heir. New rights or incidents of property cannot be created, nor can a new species of burden be imposed upon land at the pleasure of the owners. There are no instances of such new creations. It would be a new species of incorporeal hereditament. It has been contended that this is a sort of estate, but the owner of an estate must be content to take it with the rights and incidents known to and allowed by the law. A grantor may bind himself by covenant to allow what rights he pleases over his property, but the law will not permit him to carve out his property so as to enable the grantee of such a limited right to sue a stranger in the way here contended for. For these reasons, therefore, our judgment will be for the defendant.

Martin B—I am entirely of the same opinion. This grant is no doubt valid between the canal company and their tenant, the plaintiff in this action; but in order to enable the plaintiff to maintain his action against the defendant he must establish that, by the grant, an estate vested in him so as to enable him to maintain an action on the case against a stranger for an infringement of his alleged rights, which he has failed to do. No case has been cited to show that such a right as this can be created, or that an owner can carve out his property into an indefinite number of hitherto unknown estates. To admit the right here claimed would be to open a door to the creation of such a variety of pieces and parcels of interests in land, and to such an indefinite increase of possible estates, that we ought not to do it. ...

Bramwell B—I am of the same opinion.

House of Lords, 14 February 1916[274] **3.85 (E&W)**

King v David Allen & Sons, Billposting, Ltd

A CLOSED LIST OF PROPERTY RIGHTS

The advertising contract

Personal rights to the use of land do not bind third parties who take property rights over the land even with knowledge of those rights.

Facts: The appellant, King, held a fee simple title to a plot of land on which a company were negotiating to build a cinema. He entered into a contract by which he promised to allow the respondent, a billposting company, to affix posters to the side of the proposed cinema, when built, for a period of four years at a fee of £12 per annum. The appellant later granted a lease of the land to the cinema company, who, despite having knowledge of the billposting contract, refused to allow the respondents to affix their posters. The respondents sued the appellant for breach of contract, alleging that in granting the lease to the cinema company, he had put it out of his power to perform his contract. The respondent in turn argued that he was not in breach because the billposting contract was binding on the cinema company. His argument was rejected by the Court of Appeal in Ireland, and he appealed to the House of Lords.

Held: Appeal dismissed.

Judgment: Lord Buckmaster LC—There is a contract between the appellant and the respondents which creates nothing but a personal obligation. It is a licence given for good and valuable consideration and to endure for a certain time. But I fail to see—although I have done my best to follow the many authorities which counsel for the appellant has thought it right to place before our consideration—that there is any authority for saying that any such document creates rights other than those I have described.

Earl Loreburn— … [W]e must look at the document itself, and it seems to me that it did not create any interest in land at all; it merely amounts to a promise on the part of the appellant that he would allow the other party to the contract to use the wall for advertising purposes, and there was an implied undertaking that he would not disable himself from carrying out his contract. Now the appellant has altered his legal position in respect of his control of this land. Those to whom he granted the lease have disregarded his wishes and refused to allow his bargain to be carried out, and they have been practically enabled to do so by reason of the [lease] that he executed. In these circumstances, it seems to me that the appellant has disabled himself from giving effect to it as intended by parting with his right to present possession. That is enough to establish a case for damages against the appellant.

Lord Atkinson—I concur and have nothing to add.

Notes

(1) In both *Hill v Tupper* (1863) 2 H&C 121 and *King v David Allen & Sons, Billposting, Ltd* [1916] 2 AC 54, the nearest property right to those granted was an easement (below, II.A.5). But in neither case could the right qualify as an easement since there was no land benefited by the right, no dominant tenement.

(2) Other cases supporting a *numerus clausus* rule include *Keppel v Bailey* (1834)

[274] [1916] 2 AC 54.

2 My & K 517 (promise always to buy limestone from a particular quarry not binding on promisor's successor in title), where Lord Brougham LC said:

> [I]t must not be supposed that incidents of a novel kind can be devised and attached to property at the fancy or caprice of any owner. It is clearly inconvenient both to the science of the law and to the public weal that such a latitude should be given. There can be no harm in allowing the fullest latitude to men in binding themselves to answer in damages for breach of their obligations. This tends to no mischief, and is a reasonable liberty to bestow; but great detriment would arise and much confusion of rights if parties were allowed to invent new modes of holding and enjoying real property, and to impress upon their lands and tenements a peculiar character, which should follow them into all hands, however remote.

Ackroyd v Smith (1850) 10 CB 164 (grant of right of way not for the benefit of other land not assignable)—'a right, unconnected with the enjoyment or occupation of the land, cannot be annexed as incident to it: nor can a way appendant to a house or land be granted away, or made in gross. … [I]f a way be granted in gross, it is personal only, and cannot be assigned' (per Cresswell J); *Clore v Theatrical Properties Ltd* [1936] 3 All ER 483 (grant of 'front-of-house' rights to a theatre not capable of binding a third party)—'[T]his document does not convey any interest in land but is merely a personal contract embodying a licence. … It follows from this that there is no circumstance which enables the present appellants to assert any rights against the present respondent because there is no contractual nexus between them' (per Lord Wright MR). The *numerus clausus* rule has also been endorsed by the legislature in section 4(1) of the Law of Property Act 1925.

(3) It is, however, possible to argue that in English law the list is not closed, merely difficult to enter. Thus, in *Tulk v Moxhay* (1848) 2 Ph 774, the court added a new right to the list, covenants restrictive of the user of land (below, II.A.9). And in *National Provincial Bank Ltd v Ainsworth* [1965] AC 1175, a right was held not to bind a stranger to its creation, not on the ground of novelty, but because it did not fit the criteria of a property right laid down by Lord Wilberforce in that case ('Before a right or interest can be admitted into the category of property, or a right affecting property, it must be definable, identifiable by third parties, capable in its nature of assumption by third parties, and have some degree of permanence or stability': [1965] AC 1175, 1248). Nevertheless, the weight of authority favours a *numerus clausus* in English law.[275]

[275] For theoretical discussion of the *numerus clausus* doctrine, particularly from a law and economics perspective, see B Rudden, 'Economic Theory v Property Law: The *Numerus clausus* Problem', in Eekelaar and Bell (edd), *Oxford Essays in Jurisprudence*, 3rd edn (1987); T Merrill and H Smith, 'Optimal Standardization in the Law of Property: The *Numerus Clausus* Principle' (2000) 110 *Yale Law Journal* 1; H Hansmann and R Kraakman, 'Property, Contract and Verifiability: The *Numerus Clausus* Problem and the Divisibility of Rights' (2002) Harvard Law School, Public Law Research Paper No 37; Harvard Law and Economics Discussion Paper No 388.

II.A.2 ESTATES IN LAND NOT 'OWNERSHIP'

Introductory Note

A major difference between common law and civil law is that the former has no concept of 'ownership'. Although the word is often on the lips of laymen, and sometimes even lawyers, it has no technical content in English law. One reason for this is the feudal nature of English land law, still present, though in a severely attenuated form, in the modern common law. Land was held (*tenez*) of a lord in return for services, and held for different periods, known as 'estates'. Moreover, there could be more than one rung on the feudal ladder, with those intermediate between the king and the person in possession of the land known as 'mesne lords', mesne (pronounced 'mean') meaning 'in-between'. The person at the bottom of the feudal ladder, the person with a right to physical possession of the land, was said to be 'seised' or had 'seisin of' the land. In this feudal world of kings, lords and tenants, ownership could have no place.

AD Hargreaves, An Introduction to the Principles of Land Law[276] **3.86 (E&W)**

Roman law began with a frank acceptance of the existence of absolute ownership—dominium—over both chattels and land. ... To the Roman lawyers, this conception of dominium worked so satisfactorily that they did not admit anything else but absolute ownership; Balbus either owned a thing or he did not own it, and if he owned, he owned absolutely, he owned the whole thing. There was no such thing as 'limited' ownership. Balbus could not say that he was the 'temporary' owner of a plot of land; he had either full dominium or no ownership at all. ...

When we return to English law, we are at once faced with a different set of circumstances. Any solution to the problem which the medieval lawyers could evolve must necessarily conform to the universe of tenure in which they lived. In dealing with the relation of the owner to the land, they could not ignore the relation of the tenant to his lord. John Doe holds Blackacre of Count Brian, who holds it of the King. John received the land from Brian in return for services, and if those services be neglected, Brian has a writ whereby he may recover the seisin. How, then, is it possible to say that John 'owns' Blackacre? Nor is Brian in a better case; and if we are seeking for an absolute owner in the Roman law sense of the term, we are perhaps compelled to say that the King, and the King alone, has dominium. Our medieval lawyers were essentially practical, and they did not concern themselves overmuch with the juridical position of the King as supreme landowner, but while they concentrated on John Doe, they could not begin, as did their Roman predecessors, with the conception of absolute ownership. ...

[W]e have been speaking of absolute and temporary interests, a distinction immediately obvious to a Roman lawyer. But the medieval Englishman must have considered, at least unconsciously, that all interests were temporary; even the fee, the largest interest of them all, would only last as long as the services were performed by the tenant, and there is always the possibility that escheat will give back the seisin into

[276] AD Hargreaves, *An Introduction to the Principles of Land Law*, 2nd edn (1963) 43–45.

the hands of the lord. To him, the only difference between the various interests depended on the time and manner of their determination. The fee was a larger interest than the life interest simply because it might last longer. …

We are thus driven to the conclusion that there is no difference in English law between absolute and temporary interests save only in their duration. We cannot separate them into two mutually exclusive species, as did the Romans; we cannot say that he who has a fee is the dominus, the owner, whereas he who has a life interest has a mere servitude. Neither has dominium. But each is seised, and for that reason their interests must be included in the same category of legal conceptions; whatever their nature, they are at least of the same inherent quality.

Note

The substance of feudalism has been gradually eroded by statute over the centuries. Thus, the process by which further rungs on the feudal ladder were created, subinfeudation, was prohibited by the legislature in 1290 by the statute *Quia Emptores*. In 1660, the Tenures Abolition Act simplified the various types of tenure, and from 1925 onwards, the various estates other than the fee simple absolute in possession (II.A.4) were able only to exist behind a trust. In 1996, one of those estates, the entail, was abolished by the Trusts of Land and Appointment of Trustees Act 1996, Schedule 2.

II.A.3 POSSESSION AS A ROOT OF TITLE

Introductory Note

We have seen how the feudal origins of English land law made, and still makes, it inappropriate to talk of ownership of land at common law. A second phenomenon also renders the language of ownership redundant, the existence of remedies given to those dispossessed of land of which they were once in possession. Their history is complex, but the basic point to take from them is that in none was it necessary for the person dispossessed to prove anything other than the fact of prior possession. Most importantly, there was no need to prove anything called 'ownership'. And because ownership was never put in issue, no legal conception of ownership arose. Instead of ownership, English lawyers speak of 'title', though the word simply means 'an entitlement'. And when we ask about the content of that entitlement, we find that it is one to 'exclusive possession'. And, as we will see immediately below, that entitlement can arise from the mere fact of possession. Moreover, the fact that the possessor's entitlement (title) is itself one which is adverse to some other person similarly entitled is irrelevant. He has an entitlement, a title, which is capable of transmission to and of binding third parties.

Court of Appeal, 19 December 1881[277] **3.87 (E&W)**

Rosenberg v Cook

POSSESSION AS A ROOT OF TITLE

The case of the railway arch

The mere taking of possession of land gives the possessor a fee simple estate over that land.

Facts: Under section 127 of the Land Clause Consolidation Act 1845, a railway company had a power to sell 'superfluous' land. However, in a previous case, *re Metropolitan District Rlwy Co* (1879) 13 Ch D 607, the Court of Appeal had held that land over a railway tunnel was not superfluous land, and companies had no power to sell it. Nevertheless, a railway company purported to convey title to such a plot of land to the defendant, who in turn contracted to sell it to the plaintiff. The terms of the contract of sale between plaintiff and defendant provided, inter alia, that the title should commence with the conveyance from the railway company, that the purchaser should not require the production of, or investigate or make any objection or requisition in respect of such conveyance, and that the purchaser should send his objection, if any, to the title within seven days from the delivery of the abstract. The plaintiff declined to complete after the expiration of seven days from the delivery of the abstract, and sued for the return of his deposit. The Court of Appeal held that the deposit could not be recovered.

Held: Possession is a root of title.

Judgment: Jessel MR—In this case the vendor, believing that he had acquired a title from the railway company to the strip of ground which is the subject of the action, put it up for sale upon conditions, one of which precluded objections being taken after the expiration of seven days from the delivery of the abstract of title. By the operation of these conditions the purchaser became aware of the conveyance under which the vendor held. He knew, therefore what he was buying; he knew that he was buying land capable of supporting buildings, but having a railway tunnel underneath it. But as the railway company had no power to convey this land, the purchaser from the company, when he resold it, had only bare possession, and upon this ground an objection was taken to the title. It is said that this objection was taken too late, and that is the question with which we have to deal.

Now the title of the disseisor is in this country a freehold title, and therefore, although the vendor had a very bad title, and a title liable to be defeated, he had still a title good against all the world, except against those who might be proved to have a better one. It is suggested that because the company have no statutory power to convey, therefore no title can be acquired from them. But that is not the effect of the statute. There is nothing in the statute to the effect that the land shall not be devoted to any other purpose than that of a railway, or that possession cannot be taken from a railway company. The simple fact is that the vendor had a possession in this case, so that a fair sale of that possession is perfectly good.

Brett LJ—[T]he defendant had more than an easement or a revocable licence. He had possession of all the land above the tunnel. But it is said that this was really no possession at all, on the ground that the railway company had no power to give it, because an actual possession for any number of years would not give a title against the company. I do not agree with this, because I think that such a possession would give a title, but the point is one which is not necessary to decide. The

[277] (1881) LR 8 QBD 162.

defendant had a possession of some kind, and he assumed to sell it by a right similar to that of a disseisor or a trespasser. The object taken, therefore, was an objection to title, and was taken too late.

Cotton LJ—The first question is, did the vendor propose to convey what the particulars describe. I think that if the particulars stood alone he probably did not. But looking to the reference to the conveyance from the railway company, which the purchaser was at liberty to inspect, I think that there was sufficient description, and that what the vendor proposed to convey was the physical possession of the land described in the particulars. The second question is, whether the fact that this physical possession was acquired by a void conveyance, ought to enable the purchaser to recover his deposit. ... But that is a question of title: the purchaser was bound to know the law, and might have satisfied himself by inquiry whether the company had any special powers. Both parties having assumed that the company had the power to convey, it cannot now be inquired whether the conveyance was void or not. The vendor had an actual possession, and there is nothing in the statute to say that he had not a saleable possession, nor that the land shall not be appropriated to another purpose than that of a railway. All that the legislation on the subject amounts to is, that the railway company shall not appropriate it to any other purpose. It does not seem necessary to decide whether or not the vendor had sufficient possession to ripen into a title under the Statute of Limitations, but if it were necessary, I should decide that it had.

II.A.4 ESTATES IN LAND

Introductory Note

We will see below that, unlike civil systems, the lease of land is a fully fledged property right at common law. Since 1925, leases have been classified as 'estates' in land. But this is not strictly correct, for leases never were part of the feudal system, and the word 'estate' is traditionally used to describe the length of a feudal relation. There were various types of estate, among them the life estate, which lasted for the lifetime of the original grantee, and the fee simple absolute in possession, which lasted, for all practical purposes, forever. There were also other estates in between, the best-known being the entail, which lasted only so long as there were heirs of a specified class of the original grantee and which could only descend to such heirs. The ability to have interests limited in time inevitably generated a complex set of rules, known as the law of waste, which regulated the use persons could make of land of which they had a present right to possession to the detriment of those with future entitlements. However, for various reasons, primarily of a fiscal nature, but also because of a general trend towards treating titles to land as a commercial commodity, estates less than the fee simple absolute in possession became unpopular. And though it is still possible for titles to land to be held on trust for equivalent periods, the only estate today of any significance is the fee simple absolute in possession. It should not be forgotten, however, that the lease (below, II.A.5) is a property right at common law, and it is through the device of the lease that temporary interests in land are nowadays generally created. For these various reasons, the common law knows nothing of the usufruct of the civil law.

High Court, 10 February 1977[278] **3.88 (E&W)**

Lord Bernstein v Skyviews & General Ltd

THE CONTENT OF THE FEE SIMPLE

The case of the aerial photographs

The holder of a fee simple title to land does not have a right to sue in trespass those who fly over his land but do not interfere with his use of the land.

Facts: The defendant company was in the business of taking aerial photographs of large landed estates and offering them for sale to the occupants of that land. When it offered to sell such a photograph to the plaintiff, Lord Bernstein, he sued it for trespass to land.

Held: The action failed.

Judgment: Griffiths J—The plaintiff claims that as owner of the land he is also owner of the air space above the land, or at least has the right to exclude any entry into the air space above his land. He relies upon the old Latin maxim, *cujus est solum ejus est usque ad coelum et ad inferos*,[279] a colourful phrase often upon the lips of lawyers since it was first coined by Accursius in Bologna in the 13th century. There are a number of cases in which the maxim has been used by English judges, but an examination of those cases shows that they have all been concerned with structures attached to the adjoining land, such as overhanging buildings, signs or telegraph wires, and for their solution it has not been necessary for the judge to cast his eyes towards the heavens; he has been concerned with the rights of the owner of the air space immediately adjacent to the surface of the land.

That an owner has certain rights in the air space above his land is well established by authority. He has the right to lop the branches of trees that may overhang his boundary, although this right seems to be founded in nuisance rather than trespass. ...

It may be a sound and practical rule to regard any incursion into the air space at a height which may interfere with the ordinary use of the land as a trespass rather than a nuisance. Adjoining owners then know where they stand; they have no right to erect structures overhanging or passing over their neighbour's land and there is no room for argument whether they are thereby causing damage or annoyance to their neighbours about which there may be much room for argument or uncertainty. But wholly different considerations arise when considering the passage of aircraft at a height which in no way affects the user of the land. ... There is no direct authority on this question, but as long ago as 1815 Lord *Ellenborough in Pickering v Rudd* (1815) 4 Camp 219 expressed the view that it would not be a trespass to pass over a man's land in a balloon. ...

I can find no support in authority for the view that a landowner's rights in the air space above his property extend to an unlimited height. In *Wandsworth Board of Works v United Telephone Co Ltd* (1884) 13 QBD 904 Bowen LJ described the maxim, *usque ad coelum*, as a fanciful phrase, to which I would add that if applied literally it is a fanciful notion leading to the absurdity of a trespass at common law

[278] [1978] QB 479.

[279] To whomsoever the land belongs, to him also belongs [the space] up to heaven and down to the [deepest] depths.

being committed by a satellite every time it passes over a suburban garden. The academic writers speak with one voice in rejecting the uncritical and literal application of the maxim ... I accept their collective approach as correct. The problem is to balance the rights of an owner to enjoy the use of his land against the rights of the general public to take advantage of all that science now offers in the use of air space. This balance is in my judgment best struck in our present society by restricting the rights of an owner in the air space above his land to such height as is necessary for the ordinary use and enjoyment of his land and the structures upon it, and declaring that above that height he has no greater right in the air space than any other member of the public. ... Applying this test to the facts of this case, I find that the defendants' aircraft did not infringe any rights in the plaintiff's air space, and thus no trespass was committed. It was ... flying many hundreds of feet above the ground and it is not suggested that by its mere presence in the air space it caused any interference with any use to which the plaintiff put or might wish to put his land. The plaintiff's complaint is not that the aircraft interfered with the use of his land but that a photograph was taken from it. There is, however, no law against taking a photograph, and the mere taking of a photograph cannot turn an act which is not a trespass into the plaintiff's air space into one that is a trespass.

High Court, 1 January 1987[280] **3.89 (E&W)**

Anchor Brewhouse Developments Ltd v Berkley House (Docklands Development Ltd

THE CONTENT OF THE FEE SIMPLE

The overhanging crane

The holder of a fee simple estate has the right to an injunction to restrain cranes on neighbouring land from invading his airspace.

Facts: The plaintiff held a fee simple title to a plot of land forming part of a development site in London's Docklands. The defendant had title to a neighbouring plot, and for the purposes of development erected a tower crane on its site. When not in use, it was necessary to leave the boom of the crane free to swing in the wind; otherwise, there was a danger that the crane might collapse in high winds. Both when in use and when not in use, the crane swung over the plot of land to which the plaintiff had a title. The crane was at such a height, however, that it constituted no danger to any buildings on that land, nor did it interfere in any way with the plaintiff's use of the land. The plaintiff sought an injunction to restrain what it said amounted to a trespass in respect of the land.

Held: The injunction was granted.

Judgment: Scott J—The defendant resists the plaintiff's claims on two grounds. First, the defendant contends that there is no trespass at all. It is denied that an infringement of air space at the height at which the booms of the tower cranes pass over the plaintiffs' properties represents trespass. ... If that is wrong, and if oversailing booms do constitute trespass, the defendant contends ... that it ought not to be subjected to injunctions restraining the use of the cranes in the manner I have described. The trespass, if that is what it is, does no actual damage to the

[280] [1987] 2 EGLR 173.

plaintiffs. ... [I]t is submitted [that] the plaintiffs ought not to be granted injunctive relief but should be left to damages at common law. ...

A landowner is entitled, as an attribute of his ownership of the land, to place structures on his land thereby to reduce into actual possession the air space above his land. If an adjoining owner places a structure on his (the adjoining owner's) land that overhangs his neighbour's land, he thereby takes into possession air space to which his neighbour is entitled. That, in my judgment, is trespass. It does not depend on any balancing of rights.

I do not think [counsel for the defendant's] point that the trespass is causing no harm is a sound one except in the sense that the oversailing booms are causing no physical harm or interference with present plans. One of the rights of an owner of property is the right to allow others on terms acceptable to the owner to use the property; another right is the right to prevent others from using the property. The use by the defendant of the oversailing cranes deprives the plaintiffs of these rights. It deprives the plaintiffs of the right to bargain as they wish for the grant of rights over their property. It is not, in my view, accurate to say that no harm is being done to the plaintiffs by the trespassing cranes.

Notes

(1) Care should be taken with the use by both judges of the word 'ownership'. The use is colloquial, not legal, for, as we have seen, English law has no concept of ownership. Moreover, the result in both cases would have been no different had the claimant been a lessee or even a squatter.

(2) The cases illustrate the fact that English law protects the rights of the holder of a fee simple absolute in possession through the law of torts, in particular, the torts of trespass to land and nuisance.[281] One crucial difference between the two torts is that for trespass, any direct interference with possession, no matter how reasonable, will be wrongful. Nuisance, by contrast, is concerned with balancing the rights of neighbours, and it here becomes relevant to ask whether the defendant's acts amounted to a reasonable use of his land. A typical claim in nuisance would involve some activity on the defendant's land, such as noise emanating from a manufacturing process, which interfered with the plaintiff's peaceful enjoyment of his own land. The line between trespass and nuisance is drawn at the point of physical invasion.

(3) There is no objection in theory to dividing up rights to exclusive possession on a horizontal plane. And though this is usually done through the device of the lease (below, II.A.5), where positive burdens can run with the land, there are rare cases of so-called 'flying freeholds'. As Coke (Coke on Littleton (1628) 48b) explains: 'A man may have an inheritance in an upper chamber though the lower buildings and soil be in another.'

(4) In the case where the holder of a fee simple absolute in possession has been dispossessed of land and the dispossessor is still in possession of the land, the person dispossessed can at common law obtain an order for possession, by which a court-appointed official will physically turn the dispossessor off the land.

[281] Above, Chapter 2.

(5) The Supreme Court of the United Kingdom in *Star Energy Weald Basin Ltd v Bocardo SA* [2010] UKSC 35 held that a trespass can be committed many hundreds of metres below the surface of the land, even though no interference with the title-holder's use of the surface is caused. In speaking of the *cujus est solum* maxim, Lord Hope said:

> 26. In my opinion the brocard still has value in English law as encapsulating, in simple language, a proposition of law which has commanded general acceptance. It is an imperfect guide, as it has ceased to apply to the use of airspace above a height which may interfere with the ordinary user of land: Bernstein *of Leigh (Baron) v Skyviews & General Ltd* [1978] QB 479. The position in Scotland may be different: see Stair Memorial Encyclopaedia, vol 19, Property, para 198, where the question is seen as relating to the extent of ownership rather than the balancing of rights in the airspace. But I think that the reasons for holding that the brocard has no place in the modern world as regards what goes on below the surface, even in England, are not by any means as compelling as they are in relation to the use of airspace. In *United States v Causby* 328 US 256 (1946) the US Supreme Court regarded the airspace as a public highway to which only the public had a just claim. The same cannot be said of the strata below the surface. As Aikens LJ said in the Court of Appeal [in the present case], it is not helpful to try to make analogies between the rights of an owner of land with regard to the airspace above it and his rights with regard to the strata beneath the surface. Although modern technology has found new ways of making use of it in the public interest, there is no question of it having become a public highway. The test applied in *Chance v BP Chemicals Inc* 670 NE2d 985, that some type of physical damage or interference with the use of the land must be shown, would lead to much uncertainty. It overlooks the point that, at least so far as corporeal elements such as land and the strata beneath it are concerned, the question is essentially one about ownership. As a general rule anything that can be touched or worked must be taken to belong to someone.
>
> 27. The better view, as the Court of Appeal recognised [2009] 3 WLR 1010, [2010] Ch 100, para 59, is to hold that the owner of the surface is the owner of the strata beneath it, including the minerals that are to be found there, unless there has been an alienation of them by a conveyance, at common law or by statute to someone else. That was the view which the Court of Appeal took in *Mitchell v Mosley* [1914] 1 Ch 438. Much has happened since then, as the use of technology has penetrated deeper and deeper into the earth's surface. But I see no reason why its view should not still be regarded as good law. There must obviously be some stopping point, as one reaches the point at which physical features such as pressure and temperature render the concept of the strata belonging to anybody so absurd as to be not worth arguing about. But the wells that are at issue in this case, extending from about 800 feet to 2,800 feet below the surface, are far from being so deep as to reach the point of absurdity. Indeed the fact that the strata can be worked upon at those depths points to the opposite conclusion.

The fee simple estate (and other property rights) may be held by more than one person concurrently as 'co-owners'. Co-ownership in English law is not a different type of interest in itself, ie not 'ownership', but merely a form in which recognised property rights may be held. Indeed, even personal rights, eg the right to be paid a certain sum of money, a debt, can be co-owned. Since 1925, only two forms of co-ownership are known to English law: the joint tenancy and the tenancy in common. In a joint tenancy, no individual tenant is seen as having a share, though together they own it all. An important consequence of this thinking is the right of survivorship. Where one joint tenant dies, he simply drops out of the picture; nothing will pass under his will or intestacy. By contrast, with a tenancy in common, the co-owners are seen as having distinct shares, albeit shares which have yet to be divided up. For that reason, it is sometimes known as 'undivided shares'. But the shares must remain undivided for co-ownership to continue, for once there has been a division (through a process known as 'partition'), there is no longer co-ownership but two or more lots of sole 'ownership'. And unlike a joint tenancy, where a tenant in common dies, his undivided share passes under his will or intestacy; there is no right of survivorship. Whether a joint tenancy or a tenancy in common arises depends in part of the words used by the transferor of the right.

High Court, 4 November 1953[282] **3.90 (E&W)**

re Brown

ALIENABILITY OF FEE SIMPLE ESTATE

Restraints on alienation

A restraint on alienation which renders the right to alienate illusory is void.

Facts: A testator left his fee simple title to trustees on trust for his wife for life, and the remainder to his four sons in equal shares. By clause 6 of the will it was provided that if any of the sons were to attempt to alienate his share other than to one of his brothers, that share would be forfeit. One son wanted to alienate outside the family, and sought a declaration from the court that the restraint on alienation was void.

Held: The declaration was granted.

Judgment: Harman J—This is a point on which it appears that the authorities give no certain guide, and the various editors of *Jarman on Wills* give it up, as textbook writers, therein more fortunate than judges, are entitled to do with the bland statement that the law is uncertain.

The point is a very narrow one, and it is whether a restriction on alienation appended to an absolute devise of real estate is good or no. The instinct of any equity lawyer is, to start with, to say that all restraints on absolute interests which tend to negative the rights attached to those interest are abhorred by the law and disallowed. That is the general rule cited by *Jarman* (8th ed, vol 2, p 1477): 'A power of alienation is necessarily and inseparably incidental to an estate in fee'.

The view at the outset is that anything which seeks to deprive the feoffee (so to call him) of his rights is void, but there is no doubt that some degree of restriction may be put upon him. ... One must not, in substance, prevent a person from alienating, although in form he is left with a chance so to do. One may not, therefore, restrict his right of alienation to one person or choose some undischarged bankrupt and say that he may alienate to him. That is, in substance, although not in form, an absolute bar ...

[282] [1954] Ch 39.

It seems to me that a class of this sort, which is bound to be a diminishing class, brings it about, in substance, that this is a general prohibition on alienation. ... In my view, this is the kind of restriction which the law views, or should view, with dislike. ... It is pertinent that a number of persons, as in this clause, is in essence different from a class consisting, for instance, as Sir George Jessel's did in *In re Macleay* (1875) LR 20 Eq 186, of members of the family, which he said was a large indeterminate class of people and might, of course, increase as time went on; whereas, if alienation be restricted to three or four or five persons such as brothers, the class is bound to diminish as death takes its toll of the members. I hold therefore that the restriction in clause 6 of the will is an attempt to fetter the natural qualities of the interest given, and is accordingly void and can be disregarded.

Note

Nothing turns on the fact that the case involved a trust. The reason a trust was used here is that, since 1925, it has not been possible to create successive interests in respect of land except by the use of a trust.

II.A.5 LEASES OF LAND

Introductory Notes

(a) Apart from the various estates in land, primarily the fee simple, the entail, and the life estate, the other property right giving its holder a right to exclusive possession of land is the lease. As was seen above, the lease, which is more suitable to a 'commercial' rather than a 'family' holding of land, post-dates—and therefore never was part of—the feudal structure. For a lease to exist, there must be a grant of a right of exclusive possession for a 'term', a period with an end (from the Roman god of boundaries, Terminus, and also a word in ordinary English parlance).

(b) Unlike civil systems, the interest of the lessee can be assigned, though it is possible for the parties to agree otherwise. If the lessor, the landlord, assigns his interest, known as the 'reversion', the rights of the lessee are capable of binding his successor in title. The burden of the lease, in other words, runs with the land. Moreover, covenants (promises) in that lease are also capable of binding successors in title of both the landlord and the tenant, provided only that, for leases created before 1996, they 'touch and concern' the land. For leases created since that time, the 'touch and concern' requirement has been removed, and by statute (Landlord and Tenant (Covenants) Act 1995) all covenants in a lease run unless the covenant is expressed to be personal to a particular person.

(c) A lease will come to an end on the expiry of the term (effluxion of time). It may, however, be brought to an end prematurely by the landlord where the tenant is in breach of certain terms of the lease, through a process known as forfeiture.

Court of Appeal, 11 February 1944[283] **3.91 (E&W)**

Lace v Chantler

SUBSTANTIVE REQUIREMENTS OF A LEASE

A lease 'furnished for duration'

It is a requirement of a lease that there be a certain term.

Facts: The plaintiff, who held a fee simple title to a dwelling house, purported to grant a lease of the premises to the plaintiff at a weekly rent 'furnished for duration', by which was meant the 'duration of the Second World War'. Before the war had ended, the plaintiff issued a notice seeking to determine the 'lease'. Whether she could do so turned on whether a valid lease had been created in the first place. The plaintiff argued that a lease 'for the duration' was void for uncertainty of term, that she had only granted a weekly lease, and that that lease was therefore terminable by the giving of a week's notice.

Held: The notice to quit was valid.

Judgment: Lord Greene MR—Apart from one circumstance, there could be no question that this was an ordinary weekly tenancy, duly determinable at a week's notice. But the parties in the rent-book agreed to a term which appears there expressed by the words 'furnished for duration'—which must mean the duration of the war. The question immediately arises whether a tenancy for the duration of the war creates a good leasehold interest. In my opinion, it does not. A term created by a leasehold tenancy agreement must be a term which is either expressed with certainty and specifically, or is expressed by reference to something which can, at the time when the lease takes effect, be looked to as a certain ascertainment of what the term is meant to be. In the present case, when this tenancy agreement took effect, the term was completely uncertain. It was impossible to say how long the tenancy would endure. Counsel for the tenant in his argument has maintained that such a lease would be a good lease; and that, even if the term is uncertain at the beginning of the term, when the lease takes effect, the fact that at some future time it will be made certain is sufficient to make it a good lease. In my opinion, that argument is not to be sustained.

Notes

(1) The terms 'lease' and 'tenancy' are interchangeable, though the former is commonly associated with long-term arrangements, the latter with short-term ones. Confusingly, a lease is also sometimes called a 'demise'. And because, as we have seen, it was never part of the feudal system, it is also sometimes, though nowadays rarely, confusingly classified as a 'chattel real'. The classification has had no practical significance since 1925.

(2) There is no limit as to the length of the term. Leases for 999 years are not uncommon, and the duration of the lease used for security purposes in English law is normally 3,000 years. The longest lease on record appears to be one for 10,000,000 years (*Guinness Book of Records 1993*, 186).

(3) The rule about certainty of term is in fact not that the term itself must be certain, only its maximum duration. Thus, if the lease in *Lace v Chantler* had been

[283] [1944] KB 368.

expressed to be for '999 years or until the end of the war, whichever is the sooner', it would have been valid. Indeed, this device was utilised by the legislature in the Validation of War-time Leases Act 1944, passed as a direct result of the case. Much of the population were occupying under such 'leases', and the decision caused much public consternation. It was reversed by section 1 of the Act, by which any agreement entered into before or after the passing of the Act which purported to grant a tenancy for the duration of the war was to:

> have effect as if it granted or provided for the grant or a tenancy for a term of ten years, subject to a right exercisable either by the landlord or the tenant to determine the tenancy, if the war ends before the expiration of that term, by at least one month's notice in writing given after the end of the war.

(4) The decision in *Lace v Chantler* [1944] KB 368 was approved by the House of Lords in:

House of Lords, 16 July 1992[284] **3.92 (E&W)**

Prudential Assurance Co Ltd v London Residuary Body

SUBSTANTIVE REQUIREMENTS OF A LEASE

A lease to last until land was needed for road-widening

It is a requirement of a lease that there be a certain term.

Facts: The plaintiff's predecessor in title held a fee simple absolute title to land with a street frontage on which were shop premises. In 1930, the London County Council (LCC) used compulsory purchase powers to acquire a fee simple title to a strip of land along the street frontage for future road-widening purposes and purported to grant a 'lease' of it back to the plaintiff's predecessor in title at a rent of £30 per annum 'until the said land is required by the Council for the purposes of the widening of the Walworth Road'. Although the arrangement was only meant to be temporary, over 60 years later, the land had still not been used for road-widening purposes, and the LCC's successor in title, the London Residuary Body, desired to sell the fee simple title to third parties with vacant possession. They accordingly issued a notice to the plaintiffs to determine their 'lease'. Whether that notice was effective depended on whether the original agreement had indeed created a lease, for otherwise it was not a right capable of binding the LCC's successor in title, the London Residuary Body.

Held: The notice to quit was valid.

Judgment: Lord Templeman—A demise for years is a contract for the exclusive possession and profit of land for some determinate period. Such an estate is called a 'term'. Thus Coke on Littleton said (Co Litt (19th ed, 1832) para 45b):

> '"Terminus" in the understanding of the law does not only signify the limits and limitation of time, but also the estate and interests that passes for that time.'

Blackstone in his Commentaries (2 Bl Com (1st ed, 1766) 143) said:

> 'EVERY estate which must expire at a period certain and prefixed, by whatever words created, is an estate for years. And therefore this estate is frequently called

[284] [1992] 2 AC 386.

a term, terminus, because its duration or continuance is bounded, limited, and determined: for every such estate must have a certain beginning, and certain end.'

When the agreement in the present case was made, it failed to grant an estate in the land.

Lord Browne-Wilkinson—My Lords, I agree with the speech of my noble and learned friend Lord Templeman that this appeal must be allowed for the reasons he gives. However, I reach that conclusion with no satisfaction.

Before 1930, Mr Nathan owned shop premises, 263–265 Walworth Road, with a frontage to the street. The agreement made in 1930 between the London County Council (the LCC) and Mr Nathan was part of a sale and leaseback arrangement whereby a part (the strip) of Mr Nathan's land was sold to the LCC for road widening. Mr Nathan retained the freehold of the remainder of Nos 263–265. By the agreement, the strip was leased back to Mr Nathan for continued use, with the rest of 263–265 Walworth Road. As a result of our decision, Mr Nathan's successor in title will be left with the freehold of the reminder of Nos 263–265 which, though retail premises, will have no frontage to a shopping street: the LCC's successors in title will have the freehold to a strip of land with a road frontage but probably incapable of being used save in conjunction with the land from which it was severed in 1930, ie the remainder of Nos 263–265.

It is difficult to think of a more unsatisfactory outcome or one further away from what the parties to the 1930 agreement can ever have contemplated. Certainly it was not a result which their contract, if given effect to, could ever have produced. If the 1930 agreement had taken effect fully, there could never have come a time when the freehold to the remainder of Nos 263–265 would be left without a road frontage.

This bizarre outcome results from the application of an ancient and technical rule of law which requires the maximum duration of a term of years to be ascertainable from the outset. No one has produced any satisfactory rationale for the genesis of this rule. No one has been able to point to any useful purpose that it serves at the present day. If, by overruling the existing authorities, this House were able to change the law for the future, I would have urged your Lordships to do so. But for this House to depart from a rule relating to land law which has been established for many centuries might upset long-established titles. I must therefore confine myself to expressing the hope that the Law Commission might look at the subject to see whether there is in fact any good reason now for maintaining a rule which operates to defeat contractually agreed arrangements between the parties (of which all successor in title are aware) and which is capable of producing such an extraordinary result as in the present case.

Notes

(1) Lords Griffiths and Mustill also expressed agreement with Lord Browne-Wilkinson's dislike of the rule. So far, however, no proposals for reform have been forthcoming from the Law Commission. Indeed, the issue appears not even to be on its agenda.

(2) In *Street v Mountford* [1985] AC 809, the essence of which was that the label the parties put on a right are not determinative of its nature, Lord Templeman said obiter that, apart from the need for exclusive possession for a term, a further requirement of a valid lease was that there was a 'rent', a money payment in

return. That requirement is doubtful, and a rent was held not to be necessary by the Court of Appeal in two decisions, *Ashburn Anstalt v Arnold* [1989] Ch 1 and *Skipton Building Society v Clayton* (1993) 66 P & CR 223.

II.A.6 EASEMENTS

Introductory Note

An easement is a right to use land in the possession of another. Common easements are rights of way, rights to run drains under land, rights of light, rights of storage, and the right to use chimney flues. Although it is sometimes said that the list of easements is not closed (*Dyce v Lady Hay* (1852) 1 Macq 305, 'The category of servitudes and easements must alter and expand with the changes that take place in the circumstances of mankind' per Lord St Leonard), this statement must be read in the context of the *numerus clausus* rule outlined above. Although new types of easement can be brought into being, they must at least conform to the standard model. The requirements of this model are as follows. First, there must be a dominant and a servient tenement. Second, the easement must 'accommodate' the dominant tenement. Third, the rights to possession of the dominant and servient tenements must belong to different people. Fourth, the content of the right must be certain. Fifth, no positive obligation may be imposed on the person in possession of the servient tenement. And sixth, though subject to limited exceptions, the right must not be negative in nature, but must instead entitle the holder of the easement to do something on the servient tenement. The following is the leading case on the definition of an easement.

Court of Appeal, 15 November 1955[285] **3.93 (E&W)**

re Ellenborough Park

SUBSTANTIVE REQUIREMENTS OF AN EASEMENT

A walk in the park

For a right to exist as an easement, it must benefit land in the possession of another.

Facts: In 1855, the White Cross Estate, which included Ellenborough Park, was being developed for building purposes. The houses built on the plots surrounding the park were given no gardens of their own but, in relation to the park, the conveyances granted to the purchasers 'at all times hereafter in common with other persons … full enjoyment of the pleasure grounds, subject to payment of proportion of expenses'. During the Second World War, the park was requisitioned for use by the government. Whether the surrounding title-holders were entitled to compensation depended on whether they had been deprived of a property right. The trial judge, Danckwerts J, held the right to be an easement, a property right. On appeal to the Court of Appeal—

Held: The right was an easement, so compensation was due.

Judgment: Sir Raymond Evershed MR (giving the judgment of the court)—The substantial question raised in this appeal is whether the respondents … being the owners

[285] [1956] Ch 131.

of certain houses fronting upon, or, in some few cases, adjacent to, the garden or park known as Ellenborough Park in Weston-super-Mare, have any right known to the law, and now enforceable by them against the owners of the park, to the use and enjoyment of the park to the extent and in the manner later more precisely defined. Both the premises now belonging to the respondent, or to the owners for whom he acts as champion, and also the park itself, were originally part of an estate known as the White Cross Estate. The houses in question were built and the park laid out in the middle of the last century. None of the owners of the houses is an original grantee from the proprietors of the White Cross Estate. Similarly, the present owners of the park are the successors in title of the original grantors of the premises of the house owners.

The substantial question in the case ... is one of considerable interest and importance. ... [I]f the house owners are now entitled to an enforceable right in respect of the use and enjoyment of Ellenborough Park, that right must have the character and quality of an easement as understood by, and known to, our law. It has, therefore, been necessary for us to consider carefully the qualities and characteristics of easements, and, for such purpose, to look back into the history of that category of incorporeal rights in the development of English real property law. It may be fairly assumed that, in the case of *Duncan v Louch* (1845) 6 QB 904, the Court of Queen's Bench ..., and particularly Lord Denman CJ, who delivered the first judgment in the court, was of opinion that such a right as the respondent claims was capable of fulfilling the qualifying conditions of an easement, and Buckley J, in ... *Keith v Twentieth Century Club Ltd* (1904) 73 LJ Ch 545, answered certain questions which Byrne J had ordered to be set down to be argued before the court, themselves depending upon the assumption that such a right could exist in law. On the other hand, Farwell J, a judge peculiarly experienced and learned in real property law, on two occasions, namely, in ... *International Tea Stores Co v Hobbs* [1903] Ch 165, and in ... *Attorney-General v Antrobus* [1905] 2 Ch 188, used language appearing to treat as axiomatic the proposition, that a right, which should properly be described as a *jus spatiandi*, was a right excluded by English law, as by Roman law, from the company of servitudes.

The four cases which we have mentioned must be considered hereafter at greater length. But it can be said at once that, with the possible exception of the first, none of them constitutes or involves a direct decision upon the question now before us: and although the existence of gardens surrounded by houses, the owners or occupiers of which enjoy in practice the amenities of the gardens, is a well-known feature of town development throughout the country, no other case appears to have come before the courts in which the validity of the rights in fact enjoyed in the gardens has ever been tested.

Before we proceed to ... matters of fact, it will be proper, as a foundation for all that follows in this judgment, to attempt a brief account of the emergence in the course of the history of our law, of the rights known to us as 'easements', and thereafter, so far as relevant for present purposes, to formulate what can now be taken to be the essential qualities of those rights. For the former purpose we cannot do better than cite a considerable passage from the late Sir William Holdworth's Historical Introduction to the Land Law (1927, p 265). The author states: 'Both the term "easement" and the thing itself were known to the mediaeval common law. At the latter part of the sixteenth century it was described in Kitchin's book on courts, and defined in the later editions of the "Termes de la Ley".' After stating the definition and observing its obvious defects from the point of view of modern law, Sir William proceeds:

> 'But these defects in the definition are instructive, because they indicate that the law as to easements was as yet rudimentary. It was still rudimentary when Blackstone wrote. In fact, right down to the beginning of the nineteenth century, there was but little authority on many parts of this subject. Gale, writing in 1839, said: "The difficulties which arise from the abstruseness and refinements incident to the subject have been increased by the comparatively small number of decided cases affording matter for defining and systematising this branch of the law. Upon some points indeed there is no authority at all in English law." The industrial revolution, which caused the growth of large towns and manufacturing industries, naturally brought into prominence such easements as ways, watercourses, light, and support; and so Gale's book became the starting-point of the modern law, which rests largely upon comparatively recent decisions.
>
> 'But, though the law of easements is comparatively modern, some of its rules have ancient roots. There is a basis of Roman rules introduced into English law by Bracton, and acclimatized by Coke. ... The law, as thus developed, sufficed for the needs of the country in the eighteenth century. But, as it was no longer sufficient for the new economic needs of the nineteenth century, an expansion and an elaboration of this branch of the law became necessary. It was expanded and elaborated partly on the basis of the old rules, which had been evolved by the working of the assize of nuisance, and its successor the action on the case; partly by the help of Bracton's Roman rules and partly, as Gale's book shows, by the help of the Roman rules taken from the Digest, which he frequently and continuously uses to illustrate and to supplement the existing rules of law.'

The passage which we have read from Sir William Holdsworth sufficiently serves to explain the appearance and the prominence of Roman dicta in the English law of easements, commonly called, indeed, by the Latin name of 'servitudes': and it may well be possible that Farwell J's rejection of the jus spatiandi as a legal right by English law was derived in part from its similar rejection by the law of Rome. Thus, according to the Roman jurist, Paulus (quoted by Gale at p 19), 'ut spatiari, et ut coenare in aliena possimus, servitus imponi non potest': nevertheless, apart from the opinion of Farwell J, there has been, as we have already observed, no judicial authority for adopting the Roman view in this respect into the English law. Moreover, the exact characteristics of the jus spatiandi mentioned by the Roman lawyers has to be considered. It by no means follows that the kind of right which is here in question, arising out of a method of urban development that would not have been known to Roman lawyers, can in any case be said to fall within its scope. And, in any event, its validity must depend, in our judgment, upon a consideration of the qualities which must now be attributed to all easements by the law relating to easements as it has now developed in England.

For the purposes of the argument before us Mr Cross and Mr Goff were content to adopt, as correct, the four characteristics formulated in Dr Cheshire's Modern Real Property, 7th ed, pp 456 et seq. They are (1) there must be a dominant and a servient tenement: (2) an easement must 'accommodate' the dominant tenement: (3) dominant and servient owners must be different persons, and (4) a right over land cannot amount to an easement, unless it is capable of forming the subject-matter of a grant.

The four characteristics stated by Dr Cheshire correspond with the qualities discussed by Gale in his second chapter, sections 2, 5, 3, and 6 and 8 respectively. Two of the four may be disregarded for present purposes, namely, the first and the third. If the garden or park is, as it is alleged to be, the servient tenement in the present case, then it is undoubtedly distinct from the alleged dominant tenements, namely, the freeholds of the several houses whose owners claim to exercise the rights. It is equally clear that if these lands respectively constitute the servient and dominant tenements then they are owned by different persons. The argument in the case is found, accordingly, to turn upon the meaning and application to the circumstances of the present case of the second and fourth conditions; that is, first, whether the alleged easement can be said in truth to 'accommodate' the dominant tenement—in other words, whether there exists the required 'connexion' between the one and the other: and, secondly, whether the right alleged is 'capable of forming the subject-matter of a grant'. The exact significance of this fourth and last condition is, at first sight perhaps, not entirely clear. As between the original parties to the 'grant', it is not in doubt that rights of this kind would be capable of taking effect by way of contract or licence. But for the purposes of the present case, as the arguments made clear, the cognate questions involved under this condition are: whether the rights purported to be given are expressed in terms of too wide and vague a character; whether, if and so far as effective, such rights would amount to rights of joint occupation or would substantially deprive the park owners of proprietorship or legal possession; whether, if and so far as effective, such rights constitute mere rights of recreation, possessing no quality of utility or benefit; and on such grounds cannot quality as easements. …

We pass … to a consideration of the first of Dr Cheshire's conditions—that of the accommodation of the alleged dominant tenements by the rights as we have interpreted them. For it was one of the main submissions by Mr Cross on behalf of the appellant that the right of full enjoyment of the park, granted to the purchaser by the conveyance of December 23, 1864, was insufficiently connected with the enjoyment of the property conveyed, in that it did not subserve some use which was to be made of that property; and that such a right accordingly could not exist in law as an easement. In this part of his argument Mr Cross was invoking a principle which is, in our judgment, of unchallengeable authority, expounded, in somewhat varying language, in many judicial utterances, of which the judgments in *Ackroyd v Smith* (1850) 10 CB 164 are, perhaps, most commonly cited. We think it unnecessary to review the authorities in which the principle has been applied; for the effect of the decisions is stated with accuracy in Dr Cheshire's Modern Real Property. … After pointing out that 'one of the fundamental principles concerning easements is that they must be not only appurtenant to a dominant tenement, but also connected with the normal enjoyment of the dominant tenement' and referring to certain citations in support of that proposition the author proceeded: 'We may expand the statement of the principle thus: a right enjoyed by one over the land of another does not possess the status of an easement unless it accommodates and serves the dominant tenement, and is reasonably necessary for the better enjoyment of that tenement, for if it has no necessary connexion therewith, although it confers an advantage upon the owner and renders his ownership of the land more valuable, it is not an easement at all, but a mere contractual right personal to and only enforceable between the two contracting parties'. …

Can it be said, then, of the right of full enjoyment of the park in question, which was granted by the conveyance of December 23, 1864, and which … was … intended to be annexed to the property conveyed to Mr Porter, that it accommodated and served that property? It is clear that the right did, in some degree, enhance the value of the property, and this consideration cannot be dismissed as wholly irrelevant. It is, of course, a point to be noted; but we agree with Mr Cross's submission that it is in no way decisive of the problem; it is not sufficient to show that the right increased the value of the property conveyed, unless it is also shown that it was connected with the normal enjoyment of that property. It appears to us that the question whether or not this connexion exists is primarily one of fact, and depends largely on the nature of the alleged dominant tenement and the nature of the right granted. … Mr Cross submitted that the requisite connexion between the right to use the park and the normal enjoyment of the houses which were built around it or near it had not been established. He likened the position to a right granted to the purchaser of a house to use the Zoological Gardens free of charge or to attend Lord's Cricket Ground without payment. Such a right would undoubtedly, he said, increase the value of the property conveyed but could not run with it at law as an easement, because there was no sufficient nexus between the enjoyment of the right and the use of the house. It is probably true, we think, that in neither of Mr Cross's illustrations would the supposed right constitute an easement, for it would be wholly extraneous to, and independent of, the use of a house as a house, namely, as a place in which the householder and his family live and make their home; and it is for this reason that the analogy which Mr Cross sought to establish between his illustrations and the present case cannot, in our opinion, be supported. A much closer analogy, as it seems to us, is the case of a man selling the freehold of part of his house and granting to the purchaser, his heirs and assigns, the right, appurtenant to such part, to use the garden in common with the vendor and his assigns. In such a case, the test of connexion, or accommodation, would be amply satisfied; for just as the use of a garden undoubtedly enhances, and is connected with, the normal enjoyment of the house to which it belongs, so also would the right granted, in the case supposed, be closely connected with the use and enjoyment of the part of the premises sold. Such, we think, is in substance the position in the present case. The park became a communal garden for the benefit and enjoyment of those whose houses adjoined it or were in its close proximity. Its flower beds, lawns and walks were calculated to afford all the amenities which it is the purpose of the garden of a house to provide; and, apart from the fact that these amenities extended to a number of householders, instead of being confined to one (which on this aspect of the case is immaterial), we can see no difference in principle between Ellenborough Park and a garden in the ordinary signification of that word. It is the collective garden of the neighbouring houses, to whose use it was dedicated by the owners of the estate and as such amply satisfied, in our judgment, the requirement of connexion with the dominant tenements to which it is appurtenant. The result is not affected by the circumstance that the right to the park is in this case enjoyed by some few houses which are not immediately fronting on the park. The test for present purposes, no doubt, is that the park should constitute in a real and intelligible sense the garden (albeit the communal garden) of the houses to which its enjoyment is annexed. But we think that the test is satisfied as regards these few neighbouring, though not adjacent, houses. We think that the extension of the right of enjoyment to these few houses does not negative the presence of the necessary 'nexus' between the subject-matter enjoyed and the premises to which the enjoyment is expressed to belong.

Mr Cross referred us to, and to some extent relied upon, *Hill v Tupper* (1863) 2 H & C 121 but in our opinion there is nothing in that case contrary to the view which we have expressed. In that case, the owner of land adjoining a canal was granted the exclusive right to let boats out for hire on the canal. He did so and then sought to restrain a similar activity by a neighbouring landowner. He sought to establish that his grant constituted an easement but failed. Pollock CB said in his judgment: 'It is not competent to create rights unconnected with the use and enjoyment of land, and annex them to it so as to constitute a property in the grantee.' It is clear that what the plaintiff was trying to do was to set up, under the guise of an easement, a monopoly which had no normal connexion with the ordinary use of his land, but which was merely an independent business enterprise. So far from the right claimed sub-serving or accommodating the land, the land was but a convenient incident to the exercise of the right.

For the reasons which we have stated, we are unable to accept the contention that the right to the full enjoyment of Ellenborough Park fails in limine to qualify as a legal easement for want of the necessary connexion between its enjoyment and the use of the properties comprised in the conveyance of 1864, and in the other relevant conveyances.

We turn next to Dr Cheshire's fourth condition for an easement—that the right must be capable of forming the subject-matter of a grant. As we have earlier stated, satisfaction of the condition in the present case depends on a consideration of the questions whether the right conferred is too wide and vague, whether it is inconsistent with the proprietorship or possession of the alleged servient owners, and whether it is a mere right of recreation without utility or benefit.

To the first of these questions the interpretation which we have given to the typical deed provides, in our judgment, the answer; for we have construed the right conferred as being both well defined and commonly understood. In these essential respects the right may be said to be distinct from the indefinite and unregulated privilege which, we think, would ordinarily be understood by the Latin term 'jus spatiandi', a privilege of wandering at will over all and every part of another's field or park, and which, though easily intelligible as the subject-matter of a personal licence, is something substantially different from the subject-matter of the grant in question, namely, the provision for a limited number of houses in a uniform crescent of one single large but private garden.

Our interpretation of the deed also provides, we think, the answer to the second question; for the right conferred no more amounts to a joint occupation of the park with its owners, no more excludes the proprietorship or possession of the latter, than a right of way granted through a passage, or than the use by the public of the gardens of Lincoln's Inn Fields ... amount to joint occupation of that garden with the London County Council, or involve an inconsistency with the possession or proprietorship of the council as lessees. It is conceded that, in any event, the plaintiff owners of the park are entitled to cut the timber growing on the park and to retain its proceeds. We have said that in our judgment, under the deed, the flowers and shrubs grown in the garden are equally the park owners' property. We see nothing repugnant to a man's proprietorship or possession of a piece of land that he should decide to make it and maintain it as an ornamental garden, and should grant rights to a limited number of other persons to come into it for the enjoyment of its amenities.

Mr Cross relied, upon this part of his case, on the recent decision of *Copeland v Greenhalf* [1952] Ch 488 and the ratio of Upjohn J's judgment. The relevant facts were that a claim was made to a prescriptive right to deposit and leave, for an indefinite time, vehicles upon an undefined part of a strip of land which was subject to a right of way. It appeared that the claimant was by trade a wagon repairer and that the vehicles were deposited by him on the land in the course of his business and while awaiting repairs. It further appeared that wagons were commonly repaired while remaining so deposited. On these facts the judge—very justifiably (if we may say so)—found that the claimant was occupying and seeking the right to occupy an unspecified part of the land for the purpose of his business, and carrying on such business upon the land so occupied. 'I think,' said the judge, 'that the right claimed goes wholly outside any normal idea of an easement, that is, the right of the owner or the occupier of a dominant tenement over a servient tenement. This claim (to which no closely related authority has been referred to me) really amounts to a claim to a joint user of the land by the defendant. Practically, the defendant is claiming the whole beneficial user of the strip of land on the south-east side of the track there; he can leave as many or as few lorries there as he likes for as long as he likes; he may enter on it by himself, his servants and agents to do repair work thereon. In my judgment, that is not a claim which can be established as an easement. It is virtually a claim to possession of the servient tenement, if necessary to the exclusion of the owner; or, at any rate, to a joint user, and no authority has been cited to me which would justify the conclusion that a right of this wide and undefined nature can be the proper subject-matter of an easement. It seems to me that to succeed, this claim must amount to a successful claim of possession by reason of long adverse possession. I say nothing, of course, as to the creation of such rights by deeds or by covenant; I am dealing solely with the question of a right arising by prescription.'

We do not think that the facts of *Copeland v Greenhalf* bear any real relation to the present case, and Upjohn J's judgment constitutes no authority relevant to our decision.

The third of the questions embraced in Dr Cheshire's fourth condition rests primarily on a proposition stated in Theobald's The Law of Land, 2nd ed (1929), at p 263, where it is said that an easement 'must be a right of utility and benefit and not one of mere recreation and amusement.' It does not appear that a proposition in similar terms is stated by Gale. The passage in Theobald is justified by reference to two cases: *Mounsey v Ismay* (1865) 3 H & C 486, and *Solomon v Vintners Co* (1859) 4 H & N 585. The second of these cases was concerned with a right of support, and appears only to be relevant for present purposes on account of an intervention in the course of the argument on the part of Pollock CB and Baron Bramwell, in which it was suggested that one who had for a long period played rackets against the wall of a neighbour would have a right not to have the wall pulled down. We were also referred in argument to the Scottish case in the House of Lords of *Dyce v Lady James Hay* (1852) 1 Macq 305 and to the earlier case before Lord Eldon therein referred to of *Dempster v Cleghorn* (1813) 2 Dow 40. The former of these two cases was concerned with a claim on the part of the inhabitants of Aberdeen to roam at will over a piece of land bordering upon the River Don, and for such purpose to use every part of the land to the practical exclusion of any right of user on the part of the owner. The case was therefore one involving what could strictly be called a claim by a large and ill-defined number of people to a jus spatiandi. In Lord Eldon's case (in which the only decision was to refer the matter back to the Court of Session), the dispute was between certain persons, inhabitants of the City of St Andrews and others, claiming the right of playing golf on the St Andrews' Golf Links, and a tenant whose rabbits were said to be interfering with the proper maintenance of the golf course. Lord Eldon observed that the case had excited great warmth of feeling—which indeed may sufficiently appear from the allegation that some of the rabbits on the course were English rabbits. Neither that case nor the case of *Dyce v Lady James Hay* appear to us to lend real support to the proposition stated by Theobald, at least in its application to such a case as the present.

But the observations of Martin B, who delivered the judgment of the court in *Mounsey v Ismay* ... are much more to the point. The case concerned a claim under the Prescription Act for the freemen and citizens of a town on a certain day to enter upon a close for the purpose of holding horse races thereon. The opinion of the court was that the right claimed failed, in any event, to qualify as an easement by reason of the absence of a dominant tenement. Baron Martin considered, without deciding, the question whether an easement of the kind claimed could in any case exist as an easement in gross: and proceeded as follows: 'But, however this may be, we are of opinion that to bring the right within the term "easement" in the second section (of the Prescription Act) it must be one analogous to that of a right of way which precedes it and a right of watercourse which follows it, and must be a right of utility and benefit and not one of mere recreation and amusement.'

The words which we have quoted were used in reference to a claim for a right to conduct horse races and, in our judgment, the formula adopted by Theobald should be read in the light of that circumstance. In any case, if the proposition be well-founded, we do not think that the right to use a garden of the character with which we are concerned in this case can be called one of mere recreation and amusement, as those words were used by Martin B. No doubt a garden is a pleasure—on high authority, it is the purest of pleasures—but, in our judgment, it is not a right having no quality either of utility or benefit as those words should be understood. The right here in suit is, for reasons already given, one appurtenant to the surrounding houses as such, and constitutes a beneficial attribute of residence in a house as ordinarily understood. Its use for the purposes, not only of exercise and rest but also for such domestic purposes as were suggested in argument—for example, for taking out small children in perambulators or otherwise—is not fairly to be described as one of mere recreation or amusement, and is clearly beneficial to the premises to which it is attached. If Baron Martin's test is applied, the right in suit is, in point of utility, fairly analogous to a right of way passing over fields to, say, the railway station, which would be none the less a good right, even though it provided a longer route to the objective. We think, therefore, that the statement of Baron Martin must at least be confined to exclusion of rights to indulge in such recreations as were in question in the case before him, horse racing or perhaps playing games, and has no application to the facts of the present case.

As appears from what has been stated earlier, the right to the full enjoyment of Ellenborough Park ... was, in substance, no more that a right to use the park as a garden in the way in which gardens are commonly used. In a sense, no doubt, such a right includes something of a jus spatiandi, inasmuch as it involves the principle of wandering at will round each part of the garden, except of course, such parts as comprise flower beds, or are laid out for some other purpose, which renders walking impossible or unsuitable. We doubt, nevertheless, whether the right to use and enjoy a garden in this manner can with accuracy be said to constitute a mere jus spatiandi. Wandering at large is of the essence of such a right and constitutes the main purpose for which it exists. A private garden, on the other hand, is an attribute of the ordinary enjoyment of the residence to which it is attached, and the right of wandering in it is but one method of enjoying it. On the assumption, however, that the right now in question does constitute a jus spatiandi, or that it is analogous thereto, it becomes necessary to consider whether the right, which is in question in these proceedings, is, for that reason, incapable of ranking in law as an easement. …

Duncan v Louch (1845) 6 QB 904 … is authoritative in favour of the recognition by our law as an easement of a right closely comparable to that now in question which, if it involves in some sense a jus spatiandi, is nevertheless properly annexed and appurtenant to a defined hereditament. *Duncan v Louch* was an action brought by the plaintiff as owner of premises No 15, Buckingham Gate, Adelphi, London, on account of obstruction by the defendant of what the plaintiff alleged to be a right of way from Buckingham Gate over or across Terrace Walk to a watergate on the Thames River. On the trial before Wightman J it was objected on the defendant's part that, though the plaintiff had alleged a right of way from terminus to terminus, the right which he had in fact proved under his documents of title was a right to use Terrace Walk for the purposes of pleasure, that is, to pass and repass over every part of the close. The objection was overruled by the trial judge. The plaintiff showed cause before the Queen's Bench why the rule nisi obtained by the defendant for a verdict in his favour should be discharged; and the matter, as so often was the case in like circumstances, strictly turned upon the narrow question whether the alleged variance between the allegation and the proof was fatal to the plaintiff's case. The decision in the plaintiff's favour was to the effect that, although the right proved exceeded the allegation, nevertheless the former necessarily embraced the latter.

The argument on the defendant's part thus appears from the report:

> 'If this be a right of way, it is a right only of using the way for the purpose of passing from terminus to terminus, and not of walking for pleasure between the intermediate points. But the right is in fact one of a kind altogether different. It is like the privilege which the builder of a square, who reserves the centre for a garden common to all the houses, grants to the owners and tenants of the houses of walking about the garden, on condition of keeping it in order.'

Whether Mr Peacock's argument assumed that such a right as he had cited by way of analogy was one recognized by the law, Lord Denman CJ … in terms, so held. He said:

> 'I think,' he said, 'there is no doubt in this case. Taking the right, as Mr Peacock suggests, to be like the right of the inhabitants of a square to walk in the square for their pleasure … I cannot doubt that, if a stranger were to put a padlock on the gate and exclude one of the inhabitants, he might complain of the obstruction.'

Similarly, Patteson J:

'I do not understand the distinction that has been contended for between a right to walk, pass and repass forwards and backwards over every part of a close, and a right of way from one part of the close to another. What is a right of way but a right to go forwards and backwards from one place to another?'

And Coleridge J, in his judgment, described the right proved as an 'easement.' The reasoning of the decision and the circumstances of the case, no less than the language used, particularly by Lord Denman CJ, involve acceptance as an easement of a right such as that with which, according to our interpretation of the effect of the relevant deeds, we are here concerned.

For the reasons which we have stated, Danckwerts J came, in our judgment, to a right conclusion in this case and, accordingly, the appeal must be dismissed.

Notes

(1) *Re Ellenborough Park* [1956] Ch 131 exemplifies the main requirements of an easement. The case of *King v David Allen & Sons, Billposting, Ltd* [1916] 2 AC 54 (above, 3.85(E&W)) is also useful here in illustrating the requirement of a dominant tenement, as is *Hill v Tupper* (1863) 2 H & C 121 (above, 3.84(E&W)) for the requirement that the easement 'accommodate' the dominant tenement.

(2) A difficult question of late has been whether the right to park cars on neighbouring land can amount to an easement. Two difficulties arise. First, the right is, in a sense, one to exclusive possession of the land, and a right which excludes the servient owner from the land cannot amount to an easement: *Copeland v Greenhalf* [1952] Ch 488. Second, it is not obvious that the right 'accommodates' the dominant tenement. In what way does the right to park one's car on one piece of land make the use of a neighbouring piece of land more commodious? Nevertheless, car-parking rights have been recognised by English courts as easements on a number of occasions: *London & Blenheim Estates v Ladbroke Parks* [1992] 1 WLR 1278.

(3) It should be noted, with one 'anomalous' exception, ie the burden on a landowner to fence the land for the benefit of his neighbours (*Jones v Price* [1965] 2 QB 618; *Crow v Wood* [1971] 1 QB 77), that an easement cannot cast a positive burden on the possessor of the servient tenement. Thus, a covenant to maintain a road in good repair cannot amount to an easement: *Austerberry v Oldham Corporation* (1885) LR 29 Ch D 750. Nor can a covenant to supply hot water and central heating: *Regis Property Co Ltd v Redman* [1956] 2 QB 612; *Rance v Elvin* (1983) 49 P & CR 65. For the same reason, even though there can certainly be an easement in the form of a right of way over a neighbouring plot of land, the servient 'owner' will be under no liability to keep the road or path in good repair. As Lord Wilberforce said in *Liverpool City Council v Irwin* [1977] AC 239, 256:

> A mere grant of an easement does not carry with it any obligation on the part of the servient owner to maintain the subject-matter. The dominant owner must spend the necessary money, eg in repairing a drive leading to his house.

(4) In general, for a right to qualify as an easement, the benefit of the right must allow its holder to do something on the servient land—to walk across it, to run drains underneath it, etc. A mere right to restrain activity on the servient land

cannot amount to an easement: *Phipps v Pears* [1965] 1 QB 76. Such negative rights, if they are to exist at all, can only do so as restrictive covenants (below, II.A.9), which, because of their otherwise similar features to easements, are often known as 'negative easements': *London & South Western Rlwy v Gomm* (1882) 20 Ch D 562, 583 (Jessel MR). There are, however, some limited exceptions to this rule, the best-known of which is that there can be an easement of light: *Colls v Home and Colonial Stores Ltd* [1904] AC 179. A right to light, however, is not the same as a right to a view, and there can be no easement in respect of the latter: *William Aldred's Case* (1610) 9 Co Rep 57b.

II.A.7 *PROFITS À PRENDRE*

Introductory Note

A profit or common is different from an easement in that whereas an easement is a right to do something on the land of another, a *profit à prendre*, as the name implies, is a right to take something from the land of another. And it must be literally 'from' the land. The right must be one to take either part of the land itself, eg minerals or crops, or the wild animals living on it. Profits are ancient rights, and their content reflects an agrarian rather than an industrial economy. Typical profits are the right to graze animals on the land of another (pasture), to fish (piscary), to take game, to cut turf (turbary), to take timber (estovers) or to take minerals. Although they are often appurtenant to land, unlike easements, they can exist *in gross*. There is, in other words, no need for a dominant tenement.

Sir William Blackstone, Commentaries on the Laws of England[286] **3.94 (E&W)**

COMMON, or the right of common, appears from its definition to be an incorporeal hereditament: being a profit which a man hath in the land of another; as to feed his beasts, to catch fish, to dig turf, to cut wood, or the like. And hence common is chiefly of four sorts; common of pasture, of piscary, of turbary, and of estovers.

COMMON of pasture is a right of feeding one's own beasts on another's land; for in those waste grounds, which are called commons, the property of the soil is generally in the lord of the manor; as in common fields it is in the particular tenants. This kind of common is either appendant, appurtenant, because of vicinage, or in gross.

COMMON appendant is a right, belonging to the owners or occupiers of arable land, to put commonable beasts upon the lord's waste, and upon the lands of other persons within the same manor. Commonable beasts are either beasts of the plough, or such as manure the ground. This is a matter of most universal right: and it was originally permitted, not only for the encouragement of agriculture, but for the necessity of the thing. For, when lords of manors granted out parcels of land to tenants, for services either done or to be done, these tenants could not plough or manure the land without beasts; these beasts could not be sustained without pasture; and pasture could not be had but in the lord's wastes, and on the unenclosed fallow

[286] (1766) vol II, 32–35.

grounds of themselves and other tenants. The law therefore annexed this right of common, as inseparably incident, to the grant of the lands; and in this was the origin of common appendant: which obtains in Sweden, and the other northern kingdoms, much in the same manner as in England. Common appurtenant is where the owner of land has a right to put in other beasts, besides such as are generally commonable; as hogs, goats, and the like, which neither plough nor manure the ground. This, not arising from the necessity of the thing, like common appendant, is therefore not of common right; but can only be claimed by immemorial usage and prescription, which the law esteems sufficient proof of a special grant or agreement for this purpose. Common because of vicinage, or neighbourhood, is where the inhabitants of two townships, which lie contiguous to each other, have usually intercommoned with one another; the beasts of the one straying mutually into the other's fields, without any molestation from either. This is indeed only a permissive right, intended to excuse what in strictness is a trespass in both, and to prevent a multiplicity of suits: and therefore either township may enclose and bar out the other, though they have intercommoned time out of mind. Neither hath any person of one town a right to put his beasts originally into the other's common: but if they escape and stray thither of themselves, the law winks at the trespass. Common in gross, or at large, is such as is neither appendant nor appurtenant to land, but is annexed to a man's person; being granted to him and his heirs by deed: or it may be claimed by prescriptive right, as by a parson of a church, or the like corporation sole. This is a separate inheritance, entirely distinct from any landed property, and may be vested in one who has not a foot of ground in the manor.

ALL these species, of pasturable common, may be and usually are limited as to number and time; but there are also commons without stint, and which last all the year. By the statute of Merton however, and other subsequent statutes, the lord of a manor may enclose so much of the waste as he pleases, for tillage or woodground, provided he leaves common sufficient for such as are entitled thereto. This enclosure, when justifiable, is called in law 'approving'; an ancient expression signifying the same as 'improving'. The lord hath the sole interest in the soil; but the interest of the lord and commoner, in the common, are looked upon in law as mutual. They may both bring actions for damage done, either against strangers, or each other; the lord for the public injury, and each commoner for his private damage.

COMMON of piscary is a liberty of fishing in another man's water; as common of turbary is a liberty of digging turf upon another's ground. There is also a common of digging for coals, minerals, stones, and the like. All these bear a resemblance to common of pasture in many respects; though in one point they go much farther: common of pasture being only a right of feeding on the herbage and vesture of the soil, which renews annually; but common of turbary, and the rest, are a right of carrying away the very soil itself.

COMMON of estovers (from estoffer, to furnish) is a liberty of taking necessary wood, for the use or furniture of a house or farm, from off another's estate. The Saxon word, bote, is of the same signification with the French estovers; and therefore house-bote is a sufficient allowance of wood, to repair, or to burn in, the house; which latter is sometimes called fire-bote: plough-bote and cart-bote are wood to be employed in making and repairing all instruments of husbandry: and hay-bote or hedge-bote is wood for repairing of hays, hedges, or fences. These botes or estovers must be reasonable ones; and such any tenant or lessee may take off the land let or demised to him, without waiting for any leave, assignment, or appointment of the lessor, unless he be restrained by special covenant to the contrary.

II.A.8 RENTCHARGES

A rentcharge is an annual sum of money (rent) issuing and payable out of land, the due payment of which is secured (charged) by a right of distress. A common use of rentcharges used to be for the financing of sales of titles to land. However, with the advent of modern secured financing, this has fallen away, and rentcharges are nowadays something of an anachronism. For that reason, a statutory reform in 1977, by way of the Rentcharges Act 1977, swept most of them away. They can, however, still be created in limited circumstances, the most important of which is in connection with schemes of development and are necessary to circumvent the rule that easements cannot impose positive burdens on the servient tenement.

II.A.9 RESTRICTIVE COVENANTS

Introductory Note

As we have seen, there can, with limited exceptions, be no such thing as a negative easement, a right merely to restrict the use which a possessor can make of the land. This led to the creation in the middle of the nineteenth century of a new species of property right, the restrictive covenant.

Lord Chancellor's Court, 22 December 1848[287] **3.95 (E&W)**

Tulk v Moxhay

RESTRICTIVE COVENANT PROPERTY RIGHTS

No building on Leicester Square

A covenant restrictive of the user of land is capable of binding strangers to its creation.

Facts: In 1808, the plaintiff sold a fee simple title to a plot of land, Leicester Square in London, to one Elms, the latter covenanting with the plaintiff to 'maintain the land as a garden and pleasure ground in an open state uncovered with any buildings and to allow residents, on payment of a reasonable rent, to use the gardens'. Elms's title was sold on, and eventually came into the hands of the defendant, who bought with knowledge of the covenant. He proposed to build on the land, and the plaintiff, who still retained title to several houses in the square, sought an injunction (an equitable remedy) to prevent him from so doing. Relying on the dictum of Lord Brougham in *Keppell v Bailey* (1834) 2 My & K 517 , the defendant argued that the covenant did not run with the land, with the consequence that it bound only the original covenantor. Moreover, the fact that the defendant knew about the covenant, he argued, was not enough to make him bound.

Held: The injunction claimed should be granted.

Judgment: Lord Cottenham LC—That this court has jurisdiction to enforce a contract between the owner of land and his neighbour purchasing part of it, that the latter

[287] (1848) 2 Ph 774.

shall either use or abstain from using the land purchased in a particular way, is what I never knew disputed. Here there is no question about the contract: the owner of certain houses in the square sells the land adjoining, with a covenant from the purchaser not to use it for another purpose than as a square garden. And it is now contended, not that the vendee could violate that contract, but that he might sell the piece of land, and that the purchaser from him may violate it without this Court having any power to interfere. If that were so, it would be impossible for an owner of land to sell part of it without incurring the risk of rendering what he retains worthless. It is said that, the covenant being one which does not run with the land, this Court cannot enforce it; but the question is, not whether the covenant runs with the land, but whether a party shall be permitted to use the land in a manner inconsistent with the contract entered into by his vendor, and with notice of which he purchased. Of course, the price would be affected by the covenant, and nothing would be more inequitable than that the original purchaser should be able to sell the property the next day for a greater price, in consideration of the assignee being allowed to escape from the liability which he had himself undertaken.

That the question does not depend upon whether the covenant runs with the land is evident from this, that if there was a mere agreement and no covenant, this Court would enforce it against a party purchasing with notice of it; for if an equity is attached to property by the owner, no-one purchasing with notice of that equity can stand in a different situation from the party from whom he purchased. ...

With respect to the observation of Lord Brougham in *Keppell v Bailey*, he never could have meant to lay down that this Court would not enforce an equity attached to land by the owner, unless under such circumstances as would maintain an action at law. If that be the result of his observations, I can only say that I cannot coincide with it.

Notes

(1) It is possible to see in this decision the birth of a new property right over land. It just so happens that it is an equitable rather than a legal property right because the action was brought in a court of equity, the plaintiff having sought an equitable remedy, an injunction.

(2) Although Lord Cottenham's reasoning turns on knowledge on the part of the purchaser, the right binds donees having no notice of the right. Until 1925, the only person who could take free of the right was 'equity's darling', a bona fide purchaser for value of a legal estate for value and without notice, actual or constructive, of the covenant. Since 1925, the position is governed by the various rules of registration (see Chapter 8).

(3) Although Lord Cottenham denies that he is here allowing the burden of the covenant to run with the land, this is clearly the result of his judgment.

(4) The doctrine here espoused is laid down in extremely wide terms, and, if not restricted, would have virtually destroyed the *numerus clausus* rule. Later cases, particularly *Haywood v Brunswick Permanent Benefit Building Society* (1881) 8 QBD 403 and *London County Council v Allen* [1914] 3 KB 642 severely restrict its operation and reassert the *numerus clausus* principle.

Court of Appeal, 3 December 1881[288] **3.96 (E&W)**

Haywood v Brunswick Permanent Benefit Building Society

SUBSTANTIVE REQUIREMENTS OF RESTRICTIVE COVENANTS

A duty to keep buildings in repair?

Positive burdens do not run with the land under the rule in Tulk v Moxhay.

Facts: A fee simple title to a parcel of land was conveyed by Charles Jackson to Edward Jackson, the latter promising the former to keep the buildings on it in repair. Both parties assigned their various interests, and the question arose whether an assignee from Edward, who bought with knowledge of the covenant, was liable for failure to perform it. The trial judge, Stephen J, applying *Tulk v Moxhay* (1848) 2 Ph 774, held that he was. The defendant appealed to the Court of Appeal.

Held: The appeal was allowed.

Judgment: Brett LJ—This appeal must be allowed. I am clearly of opinion, both on principle and on the authority of *Miles v Branch* 5 M & S 411, that this action could not be maintained at common law. Miles v Branch must be understood, and as Lord St Leonard's understood it, and it will be seen, on a reference to his book,[289] that he consider the effect of it to be that a covenant to build does not run with the rent in the hands of an assignee.

This being so, the question is reduced to an equitable one. Now the equitable doctrine was brought to a focus in *Tulk v Moxhay*, which is the leading case on this subject. It seem to me that that case decided that an assignee taking land subject to a certain class of covenants is bound by such covenants if he has notice of them, and that the class of covenants comprehended within the rule is that covenants restricting the mode of using land only will be enforced. It may be also, but it is not necessary to decide here, that all covenants also which impose such a burden on the land as can be enforced against the land would be enforced. Be that as it may, a covenant to repair is not restrictive and could not be enforced against the land; therefore such a covenant is within neither rule. It is admitted that there has been no case in which any Court has gone farther than this, and yet if the Court would have been prepared to go farther, such a case would have arisen. The strongest argument to the contrary is, that the reason for no Court having gone farther is that a mandatory injunction was not in former times grantable, whereas it is now; but I cannot help thinking, in spite of this, that if we enlarged the rule as it is contended, we should be making a new equity, which we cannot do. …

Cotton LJ—I am of the same opinion. … I think that a mere covenant that land shall be improved does not run with the land within the rule in *Spencer's Case* (1583) 5 Co Rep 16a so as to give the plaintiff a right to sue at law. I also think that the plaintiff has no remedy in equity. … The covenant to repair can only be enforced by making the owner put his hand into his pocket, and there is nothing which would justify us going to that length. There is … no ground for extending the equitable doctrine as we are asked to do.

Lindley LJ—I am of the same opinion. The practical question is, whether the defendants … are bound to repair under the circumstances of the case. It is said

[288] (1881) 8 QBD 403.
[289] *Sugden on Vendor and Purchaser* (14th edn) 590.

that they took a conveyance of the land with notice of the covenant, and Stephen J has thought himself bound by *Tulk v Moxhay* ....

With regard to the question of notice, *Tulk v Moxhay* shews that a restrictive covenant will be enforced, and so do *Cox v Bishop* 8 De GM & G 815 and *Wilson v Hart* (1865) LR 1 Ch 463. But I think that the result of these cases is that only such a covenant as can be complied with without expenditure of money will be enforced against the assignee on the ground of notice. ... [W]e have been asked to extend *Tulk v Moxhay* as it has never been extended before, and we decline to do so.

Notes

(1) Notice that the rule here is the same rule as already encountered for easements (above, II.A.6). Moreover, we should not forget that positive burdens can be made to run through the device of the lease (above, II.A.5).

(2) The rule laid down in Haywood was endorsed by the Court of Appeal in *Austerberry v Oldham Corporation* (1885) 29 Ch D 750 and more recently by the House of Lords in *Rhone v Stephens* [1994] 2 AC 310. It did, however, attract some criticism in the latter case.

House of Lords, 17 March 1994[290] **3.97 (E&W)**

Rhone v Stephens

SUBSTANTIVE REQUIREMENTS OF RESTRICTIVE COVENANTS

The leaking roof

Positive burdens do not run with the land under the rule in Tulk v Moxhay.

Facts: Title to two parcels of land, one on which a house was built, the other, adjoining, on which there was a cottage, was originally held by one person. When the land was partitioned, the vendor covenanted with the purchaser on behalf of himself and his successors in title to keep the common roof which covered both the house and cottage in wind and watertight condition. The roof of the cottage fell into disrepair and was leaking and the plaintiff, the successor in title of the original covenantee, sued the defendant, the successor in title of the original covenantor, for damages for breach of covenant.

Held: The claim for damages was dismissed.

Judgment: Lord Templeman—At common law a person cannot be made liable upon a contract unless he was a party to it. ... The rigours of the common law which do not allow covenants to be enforced by and against successors in title were relaxed first by the doctrines laid own in *Spencer's Case* (1583) 5 Co Rep 16a and then by statutory enactment of those doctrines introduced by the Act 32 Hen 8 c 34 (Grantees of Reversions (1540)), the Conveyancing Act 1881 and the Conveyancing Act 1911, now repealed and reproduced in ss 141 and 142 of the Law of Property Act 1925. In the result, as between landlord and tenant both the burden and the benefit of a covenant which touches or concerns the land demised and is not merely collateral run with the reversion and term at law whether the covenant be

[290] [1994] 2 AC 310.

positive or negative. As between persons interested in land other than as landlord and tenant, the benefit of a covenant may run with the land but not the burden. …

Thus cl 3 of the 1960 conveyance, despite its express terms, did not confer on the owner for the time being of Walford Cottage the right at common law to compel the owner for the time being of Walford House to repair the roof or to obtain damages for breach of covenant to repair. In this appeal, Mr Munby QC, on behalf of the plaintiffs, contends that equity will compel the owner of Walford House to comply with the covenant to repair the roof or to pay damages in lieu.

My Lords, equity supplements but does not contradict the common law. When freehold land is conveyed without restriction, the conveyance confers on the purchaser the right to do with the land as he pleases provided that he does not interfere with the rights of others or infringe statutory restrictions. The conveyance may however impose restrictions which, in favour of the covenantee, deprive the purchaser of some of the rights inherent in the ownership of unrestricted land. In *Tulk v Moxhay* (1848) 2 Ph 774, a purchaser of land covenanted that no buildings would be erected on Leicester Square. A subsequent purchaser of Leicester Square was restrained from building. The conveyance to the original purchaser deprived him and every subsequent purchaser taking with notice of the covenant of the right, otherwise part and parcel of the freehold, to develop the square by the construction of buildings. Equity does not contradict the common law by enforcing a restrictive covenant against a successor in title of the covenantor but prevents the successor from exercising a right which he never acquired. Equity did not allow the owner of Leicester Square to build because the owner never acquired the right to build without the consent of the persons (if any) from time to time entitled to the benefit of the covenant against building. In *Tulk v Moxhay* the speech of Lord Cottenham LC contained the following passage …:

> 'It is said that, the covenant being one which does not run with the land, this court cannot enforce it; but the question is, not whether the covenant runs with the land, but whether a party shall be permitted to use the land in a manner inconsistent with the contract entered into by his vendor, and with notice of which he purchased.'

Equity can thus prevent or punish the breach of a negative covenant which restricts the user of land or the exercise of other rights in connection with land. Restrictive covenants deprive an owner of a right which he could otherwise exercise. Equity cannot compel an owner to comply with a positive covenant entered into by his predecessors in title without flatly contradicting the common law rule that a person cannot be made liable upon a contract unless he was a party to it. Enforcement of a positive covenant lies in contract; a positive covenant compels an owner to exercise his rights. Enforcement of a negative covenant lies in property; a negative covenant deprives the owner of a right over property. As Lord Cottenham LC said in *Tulk v Moxhay*: 'if an equity is attached to the property by the owner, no one purchasing with notice of that equity can stand in a different situation from the party from whom he purchased.'

[His lordship then considered, inter alia, *Haywood v Brunswick Permanent Benefit Building Society* and *Austerberry v Oldham Corporation* and said] For over 100 years it has been clear and accepted law that equity will enforce negative covenants against freehold land but has no power to enforce positive covenants against successors in title of the land. To enforce a positive covenant would be to enforce a personal obligation against a person who has not covenanted. To enforce negative covenants is only to treat the land as subject to a restriction.

Mr Munby ... referred to an article by Professor Sir William Wade [1972B] CLJ 157 and other articles in which the present state of the law is subjected to severe criticism. In 1965 a report by a committee appointed by the Lord Chancellor and under the chairmanship of Lord Wilberforce, the Report of the Committee on Positive Covenants Affecting Land (1965) (Cmnd 2719), referred to difficulties caused by the decision in the *Austerberry* case and recommended legislation to provide that positive covenants which relate to the use of land and are intended to benefit specified other land should run with the land. The Law Commission published on 5 July 1971 Working Paper No 36 in which the present law on positive rights was described as being illogical, uncertain, incomplete and inflexible. The Law Commission Report on Transfer of Land (1984) (Law Com 127) (HC 201) laid before Parliament in 1965 made recommendations for the reform of the law relating to positive and restrictive obligations and submitted a draft Bill for that purpose. Nothing has been done.In these circumstances your Lordships were invited to overrule the decision of the Court of Appeal in the *Austerberry* case. To do so would destroy the distinction between law and equity and to convert the rule of equity into a rule of notice. It is plain from the articles, reports and papers to which we were referred that judicial legislation to overrule the *Austerberry* case would create a number of difficulties, anomalies and uncertainties and affect the rights and liabilities of people who have for over 100 years bought and sold land in the knowledge, imparted at an elementary stage to every student of the law of real property, that positive covenants, affecting freehold land are not directly enforceable except against the original covenantor. Parliamentary legislation to deal with the decision in the *Austerberry* case would require careful consideration of the consequences. Moreover, experience with leasehold tenure where positive covenants are enforceable by virtue of privity of estate has demonstrated that social injustice can be caused by logic. Parliament was obliged to intervene to prevent tenants losing their homes and being saddled with the costs of restoring to their original glory buildings which had languished through wars and economic depression for exactly 99 years. ...

In the result I would dismiss the appeal and make the usual order for costs against the plaintiffs subject to the usual appropriate legal aid reservations.

Notes

(1) The topic of positive covenants is on the list of things the Law Commission of England and Wales intend to review. No work, however, has yet begun on this project.

(2) The reasoning of Lord Templeman as to why restrictive but not positive covenants are enforced against strangers is unsound, for as *Tulk v Moxhay* itself shows, equity contradicts the common law rules of privity of contract even in the case of negative covenants. It is, however, the price one pays for refusing to admit that Lord Cottenham invented a new species of incorporeal hereditament in that case.

Court of Appeal, 28 May 1914[291] **3.98 (E&W)**

London County Council v Allen

SUBSTANTIVE REQUIREMENTS OF RESTRICTIVE COVENANTS

No benefit to land

The burden of covenants under the rule in Tulk v Moxhay will only run with the land where there is a dominant tenement.

Facts: The holder of a title to a plot of land applied to the London County Council (LCC) for permission to lay out a new street on the land. The LCC granted permission, though on condition that the titleholder entered into a covenant with them to the effect that neither he nor his successors in title would build on the plot. The titleholder later sold and conveyed the title to the defendant, who had notice of the covenant. She nevertheless proceeded to build on the land, and the LCC, relying on *Tulk v Moxhay*, sought an injunction to restrain her.

Held: The injunction was refused.

Judgment: Buckley LJ—By virtue of ss 7 and 9 of the London Building Act, 1894, the London County Council have certain powers of control over land which the owner proposes to form or lay out in streets. But they have no estate or interest in such land. The plaintiffs at the date of the deed of covenant had no estate or interest in any land adjoining or in any manner affected by the observance or non-observance of the covenant contained in the deed. Under these circumstances the defendants Mrs Allen and Norris, who were not covenanting parties, contend upon this appeal that as matter of law … the plaintiffs cannot as against them maintain any action upon the covenant contained in the deed. The short proposition is that as matter of law a derivative owner of land, deriving title under a person who has entered into a restrictive covenant concerning the land, is not bound by the covenant even if he took with notice of its existence if the covenantee has no land adjoining or affected by the observance or non-observance of the covenant. I proceed to examine how the law upon this point stands upon the authorities.

The respondents do not contend that the covenant here in question runs with the land. It is the better opinion, and in *Austerberry v Oldham Corporation* the Court of Appeal by way of opinion and not of decision held, that the burden of a covenant, not involving a grant, never runs with the land at law except as between landlord and tenant. Cotton LJ … said: 'In order that the benefit may run with the land, the covenant must be one which relates to or touches and concerns the land of the covenantee.' The relation of landlord and tenant did not in the present case subsist between the plaintiffs, the covenantees, and M J Allen, the covenantor. Under these circumstances the plaintiffs admit that this covenant did not run with the land at law. As between the covenantee and the owner deriving title under the covenantor there is no privity of contract, and the law is that it is only where there is privity of estate between landlord and tenant that the burden of a covenant will run with the land. Ownership of land both by covenantor and covenantee must exist in order that *Spencer's Case* shall apply, and that the covenant shall run with the land. But it does not follow that the covenantee is without remedy where the covenant does not run with the land. *Tulk v Moxhay* established that as between the grantor of

[291] [1914] 3 KB 642.

a restrictive covenant affecting certain land and the owner of adjoining land the covenantee may in equity enforce the covenant against the derivative owner taking with notice. The reasoning of Lord Cottenham's judgment in *Tulk v Moxhay* is that if an owner of land sells part of it reserving the rest, and takes from his purchaser a covenant that the purchaser shall use or abstain from using the land purchased in a particular way, that covenant (being one for the protection of the land reserved) is enforceable against a sub-purchaser with notice. The reason given is that, if that were not so, it would be impossible for an owner of land to sell part of it without incurring the risk of rendering what he retains worthless. If the vendor has retained no land which can be protected by the restrictive covenant, the basis of the reasoning of the judgment is swept away. In *Haywood v Brunswick Permanent Benefit Building Society* the Court of Appeal declined to extend the doctrine of *Tulk v Moxhay* to covenants other than restrictive covenants. They rejected the doctrine that, inasmuch as the defendants took the land with notice of the covenants, they were bound in equity to perform them. That therefore is not the principle upon which the equitable doctrine rests. In the present case we are asked to extend the doctrine of *Tulk v Moxhay* so as to affirm that a restrictive covenant can be enforced against a derivative owner taking with notice by a person who never has had or who does not retain any land to be protected by the restrictive covenant in question. In my opinion the doctrine does not extend to that case. The doctrine is that a covenant not running with the land, but being a negative covenant entered into by an owner of land with an adjoining owner, binds the land in equity and is enforceable against a derivative owner taking with notice. The doctrine ceases to be applicable when the person seeking to enforce the covenant against the derivative owner has no land to be protected by the negative covenant. The fact of notice is in that case irrelevant.

Upon the authorities … I am of opinion that the doctrine in *Tulk v Moxhay* does not extend to the case in which the covenantee has no land capable of enjoying, as against the land of the covenantor, the benefit of the restrictive covenant. The doctrine is either an extension in equity of the doctrine in *Spencer's Case* (in which ownership of land by both covenantor and covenantee is essential) or an extension in equity of the doctrine of negative easements, a doctrine applicable not to the case of easements in gross, but to an easement enjoyed by one land upon another land. Where the covenantee has no land, the derivative owner claiming under the covenantor is bound neither in contract nor by the equitable doctrine which attaches in the case where there is land capable of enjoying the restrictive covenant.

Kennedy LJ agreed and Scrutton LJ delivered a concurring judgment.

Note

The requirement of a dominant tenement for restrictive covenants, like the rule against positive burdens, once again has parallels in the law of easements (above, II.A.6). This is in contrast to its functional equivalent in Dutch law, the 'qualitative duty' (above, I.J.1 above), which has no such requirement.

I.A.7 ESTATE CONTRACTS

Introductory Note

A further right recognised as proprietary by equity, though once again not the common law, is the benefit of a contract to purchase a title to land, a right known compendiously as an 'estate contract'. The reasoning by which this right is transformed from a right to performance enforceable only against the vendor to one enforceable against his successors in title is complicated and controversial. Briefly, the position is this. The general response of an English court to a breach of contract is to order the defendant to pay to the victim a sum of money, damages. In some circumstances, however, the court, more particularly a court of equity, will order 'specific performance' of the contractual obligation itself. One of these rare instances is where the subject-matter of the contract of sale is unique, and titles to land fall under that heading. Thus, a contract for the sale of a title to land is a contract of which a court will order specific performance, ie the conveyance of the title to the purchaser. That in turn triggers the equitable rule that the court 'considers as done that which ought to be done'. By a fiction, the court of equity sees the conveyance as having taken place at the moment the contract is concluded, even though the common law still awaits the conveyance itself. To reconcile these differing views, the court of equity imposes a trust on the vendor in the purchaser's favour. One consequence of this trust is that the title will no longer be available to satisfy the vendor's debts in the event of his insolvency. Another is that the risk of destruction of the subject-matter of the right passes to the purchaser.

High Court, 20 March 1876[292] **3.99 (E&W)**

Lysaght v Edwards

ESTATE CONTRACTS ARE PROPERTY RIGHTS

Contract to sell fee simple title

A contract to sell a title to land gives to the purchaser the benefit of a trust of the title before conveyance.

Facts: A testator, who held a title to a number of parcels of land, both outright and as trustee, had before his death entered into a contract to sell one of the titles he held outright. He died, however, before the conveyance was executed. By his will, he left the titles he held outright to Hubbard and Muller jointly, and those he held on trust to Hubbard alone. For the purpose of the execution of the conveyance, it was necessary to know who now held the title contracted to be sold. Had it passed to Hubbard and Muller jointly, or to Hubbard alone? That depended on whether the vendor was a trustee of the title at the time of his death. It was argued that such a trust only arose once a decree of specific performance had been granted, which was not the case here.

Held: The vendor was a trustee at the time of his death. A contract to sell a title to land gives to the purchaser the benefit of a trust of the title before conveyance.

Judgment: Sir George Jessel MR—In this particular case the testator made his will on the 22nd of July, 1873. He was at that time owner in fee of certain freehold estates, and he was also owner of certain copyhold estates. Among his estates was a farm called Bury Farm, partly freehold and partly copyhold. By his will he charges such part of his real estates as consisted of the Bury Farm, with debts and pecuniary legacies, and he proceeds: 'Subject to the trusts hereinafter contained for sale

[292] (1876) 2 Ch D 499.

of the same hereditaments, and to the power of postponing such sale, I direct the said debts and legacies to be raised under the statutory power for that purpose.' Then he gives to two gentlemen, named Hubbard and Muller, all his real estate, with a certain exception, which it is not material to mention, and he devised all his copyhold estates to the use of such persons as they might appoint for the purpose of carrying into effect any sale which should be made under the trusts thereinafter declared, and then he gave them the net proceeds of the sale upon the trusts therein mentioned. There is, therefore, a gift of the freehold estate upon trust to sell, and of the copyhold to such uses as they shall appoint for the purpose of effecting a sale. That is the conveyancer's form of the trust for sale of freehold and copyhold estates, the difference of form being merely to avoid the necessity of a double admission to the copyholds. The trustees are to convey the copyholds to the purchaser directly in order to avoid the expense of two fines. Then there is a power to postpone the sale; and, last of all, there is this devise: 'And I devise to the said Egerton Hubbard, his heirs and assigns, all real estate which at my death may be vested in me as trustee subject to the trusts affecting the same.' After the date of his will, he entered into a contract of sale dated the 23rd of December, 1874. It was an ordinary contract of sale. A deposit of £3000 was paid, and requisitions on the title were sent in in the usual way; but eventually the title was finally accepted by the Plaintiffs on the 1st of May, 1875. The testator, the vendor, died on the 12th of June, 1875; and, under those circumstances, the question which I have to decide is, there being a difficulty in finding the heir-at-law or customary heir of the testator, whether the trustees Hubbard and Muller, or the trustee Hubbard, takes the legal estate in the freehold and copyhold lands which have been sold. ...

What is the effect of the contract? It appears to me that the effect of a contract for sale has been settled for more than two centuries; certainly it was completely settled before the time of Lord Hardwicke, who speaks of the settled doctrine of the Court as to it. What is that doctrine? It is that the moment you have a valid contract for sale the vendor becomes in equity a trustee for the purchaser of the estate sold, and the beneficial ownership passes to the purchaser, the vendor having a right to the purchase-money, a charge or lien on the estate for the security of that purchase-money, and a right to retain possession of the estate until the purchase-money is paid, in the absence of express contract as to the time of delivering possession. In other words, the position of the vendor is something between what has been called a naked or bare trustee, or a mere trustee (that is, a person without beneficial interest), and a mortgagee who is not, in equity (any more than a vendor), the owner of the estate, but is, in certain events, entitled to what the unpaid vendor is, viz, possession of the estate and a charge upon the estate for his purchase-money. Their positions are analogous in another way. The unpaid mortgagee has a right to foreclose, that is to say, he has a right to say to the mortgagor, 'Either pay me within a limited time, or you lose your estate,' and in default of payment he becomes absolute owner of it. So, although there has been a valid contract of sale, the vendor has a similar right in a Court of Equity; he has a right to say to the purchaser, 'Either pay me the purchase-money, or lose the estate.' Such a decree has sometimes been called a decree for cancellation of the contract; time is given by a decree of the Court of Equity, or now by a judgment of the High Court of Justice; and if the time expires without the money being paid, the contract is cancelled by the decree or judgment of the Court, and the vendor becomes again the owner of the estate. But that, as it appears to me, is a totally different thing from the contract being cancelled because there was some equitable ground for setting it aside. If a valid contract is cancelled for non-payment of the purchase-money after the death of the vendor, the property will still in equity be treated as having been converted into personalty, because the contract was valid at his death; while in the other case there will not be conversion, because there never was in equity a valid contract. Now, what is the meaning of the term 'valid contract?' 'Valid contract' means in every case a contract sufficient in form and in substance, so that there is no ground whatever for setting it aside as between the vendor and purchaser—a contract binding on both parties. As regards real estate, however, another element of validity is required. The vendor must be in a position to make a title according to the contract, and the contract will not be a valid contract unless he has either made out his title according to the contract or the purchaser has accepted the title, for however bad the title may be the purchaser has a right to accept it, and the moment he has accepted the title, the contract is fully binding upon the vendor. Consequently, if the title is accepted in the lifetime of the vendor, and there is no reason for setting aside the contract, then, although the purchase-money is unpaid, the contract is valid and binding; and being a valid contract, it has this remarkable effect, that it converts the estate, so to say, in equity; it makes the purchase-money a part of the personal estate of the vendor, and it makes the land a part of the real estate of the vendee; and therefore all those cases on the doctrine of constructive conversion are founded simply on this, that a valid contract actually changes the ownership of the estate in equity. That being so, is the vendor less a trustee because he has the rights which I have mentioned? I do not see how it is possible to say so. If anything happens to the estate between the time of sale and the time of completion of the purchase it is at the risk of the purchaser. If it is a house that is sold, and the house is burnt down, the purchaser loses the house. He must insure it himself if he wants to provide against such an accident. If it is a garden, and a river overflows its banks without any fault of the vendor, the garden will be ruined, but the loss will be the purchaser's. In the same way there is a correlative liability on the part of the vendor in possession. He is not entitled to treat the estate as his own. If he willfully damages or injures it, he is liable to the purchaser; and more than that, he is liable if he does not take reasonable care of it. So far he is treated in all respects as a trustee, subject of course to his right to being paid the purchase-money and his right to enforce his security against the estate. With those exceptions, and his right to rents till the day for completion, he appears to me to have no other rights.

Notes

(1) The contract here was one to convey both 'freehold' and 'copyhold' land. 'Freehold' and 'copyhold' were different forms of tenure under the tenurial system described in II.A.3. With freehold tenure, the tenant's obligations to his feudal lord were fixed. By contrast, in copyhold tenure, the nature of the services was uncertain. Copyhold tenure was abolished by statute in 1925.

(2) The proprietary effect of an estate contract is not limited to contracts to purchase freehold titles. Contracts for the purchase of other property rights in respect of land, such as leases or easements, also have this effect.

I.A.8 OPTIONS TO PURCHASE

Introductory Note

Options to purchase a property right over land, though one stage removed from contracts to purchase the right itself, are also recognised by courts of equity, though not the common law, as property rights. Its recognition as such also turns on the fact that options to purchase, again because property rights over land are unique, are specifically enforceable.

Court of Appeal, 6 March 1882[293] **3.100 (E&W)**

London and South Western Railway v Gomm

OPTIONS TO PURCHASE ARE PROPERTY RIGHTS

Promise to reconvey title to land

A covenant in a contract of sale to reconvey title to the vendor at the vendor's request is a property right and therefore subject to the rule against perpetuities.

Facts: In 1865, the plaintiffs sold a freehold title to land to one George Powell for £100, Powell covenanting on behalf of himself, his heirs and his assigns to reconvey the title at any time thereafter to the plaintiffs in return for a payment of £100. In 1879, the defendant purchased the title from Powell, with notice of the covenant to reconvey. In 1880, the plaintiffs gave notice to the defendant to reconvey the title, and upon his refusal to do so, brought this action for specific performance. The defendant argued that the covenant to reconvey was not binding on him because, as creating an interest in land, it was subject to the rule against perpetuities, and, because there was no limit in time as to the exercise of the right, that rule was here infringed. The plaintiffs argued that the covenant was only a personal contract, binding not the land but those taking with notice of the covenant and not therefore subject to the rule against perpetuities. At first instance, Kay J had held that the rule against perpetuities did not apply to options to purchase.

Held: The appeal should be allowed. A covenant in a contract of sale to reconvey title to the vendor at the vendor's request is a property right and therefore subject to the rule against perpetuities.

Judgment: Sir George Jessel MR—If the rule as to remoteness applies to a covenant of this nature, this covenant clearly is bad as extending beyond the period allowed by the rule. Whether the rule applies or not depends upon this as it appears to me, does or does not the covenant give an interest in the land? If it is a bare or mere personal contract it is of course not obnoxious to the rule, but in that case it is impossible to see how the present Appellant can be bound. He did not enter into the contract, but is only a purchaser from Powell who did. If it is a mere personal contract it cannot be enforced against the assignee. Therefore the company must admit that it somehow binds the land. But if it binds the land it creates an equitable interest in the land. The right to call for a conveyance of the land is an equitable interest or equitable estate. In the ordinary case of a contract for purchase there is no doubt about this, and an option for repurchase is not different in its nature. A person exercising the option has to do two things, he has to give notice of his intention to purchase, and to pay the purchase-money; but as far as the man who is liable to convey is concerned, his estate or interest is taken away from him without

[293] (1882) 20 Ch D 562.

his consent, and the right to take it away being vested in another, the covenant giving the option must give that other an interest in the land.

It appears to me therefore that this covenant plainly gives the company an interest in the land, and as regards remoteness there is no distinction that I know of (unless the case falls within one of the recognised exceptions, such as charities) between one kind of equitable interest and another kind of equitable interest. In all cases they must take effect as against the owners of the land within a prescribed period. …

That appears to me to dispose of the case, unless we agree with the conclusion of Mr Justice Kay on the last point considered by him. Down to that point I agree with him. I consider that he is quite right in the view he takes of the doctrine of remoteness and of the authorities cited before him. … But Mr Justice Kay, having, as I think he has, most correctly and accurately defined the law, thinks that this case is not within it, because he comes to the conclusion that 'this covenant does not create any interest in the land.' But he had forgotten that if that were so he could not make a decree against Mr Gomm. If it were a mere contract it was not Gomm's contract, and if it did not in equity run with the land so as to give an interest in the land, it could not have been enforced against him. It is clear from his Lordship's judgment that if he had been of opinion that this covenant gave the company an interest in the land (which, I think, is the correct view) he would have decided the case the other way.

With regard to the argument founded on *Tulk v Moxhay* (1848) 2 Ph 744, that case was very much considered by the Court of Appeal … in *Haywood v The Brunswick Permanent Benefit Building Society* (1881) 8 QBD 403, and the Court there decided that they would not extend the doctrine of *Tulk v Moxhay* to affirmative covenants, compelling a man to lay out money or do any other act of what I may call an active character, but that it was to be confined to restrictive covenants. Of course that authority would be binding upon us if we did not agree to it, but I most cordially accede to it. I think that we ought not to extend the doctrine of *Tulk v Moxhay* in the way suggested here. The doctrine of that case, rightly considered, appears to me to be either an extension in equity of the doctrine of *Spencer's Case* to another line of cases, or else an extension in equity of the doctrine of negative easements; such, for instance, as a right to the access of light, which prevents the owner of the servient tenement from building so as to obstruct the light. The covenant in *Tulk v Moxhay* was affirmative in its terms, but was held by the Court to imply a negative. Where there is a negative covenant expressed or implied, as, for instance, not to build so as to obstruct a view, or not to use a piece of land otherwise than as a garden, the Court interferes on one or other of the above grounds. This is an equitable doctrine, establishing an exception to the rules of Common Law which did not treat such a covenant as running with the land, and it does not matter whether it proceeds on analogy to a covenant running with the land or on analogy to an easement. The purchaser took the estate subject to the equitable burden, with the qualification that if he acquired the legal estate for value without notice he was freed from the burden. That qualification, however, did not affect the nature of the burden; the notice was required merely to avoid the effect of the legal estate, and did not create the right, and if the purchaser took only an equitable estate he took subject to the burden, whether he had notice or not. It appears to me that, rightly considered, that doctrine is not an authority for the proposition that an equitable estate or interest may be raised at any time, notwithstanding the rule against remoteness. It is, if I may say so, another exception to the rules against remoteness, exceptions which had previously been thoroughly established in many cases at law as regards easements, and in equity as regards charities. That being so, it does not appear to me that *Tulk v Moxhay* has any direct bearing on the case which we have to decide.

On these grounds it seems to me that the present appeal ought to be allowed.

Sir James Hannen—Does this covenant create an interest or estate in the property at law, or in equity. Upon that point I have nothing to add to what has been said by the Master of the Rolls. It is not a subject with which I have been frequently called upon to deal, and therefore, any opinion that I may express on the subject has not the value it would have if it came from one of my learned colleagues, but I must say that it appears to me to be a startling proposition that the power to require a conveyance of land at a future time does not create any interest in that land. If it does create such an interest, then it appears to me to be perfectly clear that the covenant in this case violates the rule against perpetuity. …

The last question is, supposing this covenant does not create any estate or interest, what is the effect of it as a covenant? It is clear that it is not a covenant which would run with the land at law. *Spencer's Case* (1583) 5 Co Rep 16a and the notes to it in Smith's Leading Cases (vol I, 8th ed, p 90) seem to me to point very clearly to that conclusion. It has been said, however, and in fact the judgment with which we are dealing lays down, that although this is only a personal covenant, yet *Tulk v Moxhay* is an authority for the proposition that such a covenant if known to the purchaser of the estate binds him. This argument is disposed of by the decision of the Court of Appeal in *Haywood v The Brunswick Permanent Benefit Building Society* (1881) 8 QBD 403, which seems to me to put a wholesome restriction upon the application of *Tulk v Moxhay* by laying down this rule, that it only applies to restrictive covenants, and does not apply to an affirmative covenant such as a covenants binding the owner of the land at some future time to convey it.

For these reasons I am of opinion that the judgment of the Court below cannot be supported, and that the appeal must be allowed.

Lindley LJ—I am of the same opinion. This is an action for specific performance of a contract entered into not by the Defendant but by somebody else. The first thing, therefore, the Plaintiffs must shew is, upon what legal principle the Defendant is bound by a contract into which he did not enter.

It is not contended that he is bound by it on the ground that the covenant entered into by Powell runs with the land and binds him at law, but it is said that though it does not bind him at law it binds him in equity.

Then upon what principle is it that he is bound in equity? It is said that he is bound in equity because he bought the land knowing of the covenant into which his predecessor in title had entered. That proposition stated generally assumes that every purchaser of land with notice of covenants into which his vendor has entered with reference to the land is bound in equity by all those covenants. That is precisely the proposition which had to be considered in *Haywood v Brunswick Permanent Benefit Building Society* (1881) 8 QBD 403, and because it was sought there to extend the doctrine of *Tulk v Moxhay* to a degree which was thought dangerous, considerable pains were taken by the Court to point out the limits of that doctrine. In that case an owner in fee had granted a rent, and in order better to secure it, he covenanted for himself, his heirs and assigns, to build some houses on the land out of which the rent issued and to keep them in repair for ever. It was sought to enforce that covenant by bringing an action for damages against the mortgagee in possession of the land, because the houses had been allowed to get out of repair. It was of course seen that an action would not lie at law; but it was contended, on the authority of *Tulk v Moxhay*, that inasmuch as the Defendants took the land with notice of the covenants they were bound by them in equity. The Court of Appeal declined so to extend the doctrine of *Tulk v Moxhay*, and their reasons will be found very carefully stated by Lord Justice Cotton in his judgment. The conclusion arrived at by the Court was that *Tulk v Moxhay*, when properly understood, did not apply to any but restrictive covenants. … . Here we are asked to extend the doctrine of *Tulk v Moxhay*, and to apply it to a covenant to sell land at any time for a specified sum of money. That this is an extension of the doctrine cannot, I think, be denied; and for the reasons which were given by the Court of Appeal in the case to which I have referred I think we ought to decline to extend that doctrine. If so, how is Gomm to be held to be bound by this covenant? He did not enter into it, he is not bound at law, and *Tulk v Moxhay* is no authority for saying that he is bound in equity. That appears to me to dispose of this case.

I agree with the observations made by the other members of the Court, that this covenant creates an interest in land and is void for remoteness.

Notes

(1) This case provides an important reaffirmation of both the *numerus clausus* rule in English law and the rule that notice of a personal right does not in itself make a third party bound by that right. Although there is a rule that equitable property rights are not binding on a bona fide purchaser of a legal estate for value without notice (see Chapter 9 on the destruction of property rights), as Sir George Jessel MR pointed out, 'That qualification, however, did not affect the nature of the burden; the notice was required merely to avoid the effect of the legal estate, and did not create the right, and if the purchaser took only an equitable estate he took subject to the burden, whether he had notice or not.'

(2) It seems that rights beyond options to purchase do not create property rights. Thus, a right of pre-emption or first refusal has been held not to create a right capable of binding third parties because the promisee in such a case has no right to force a sale: *Pritchard v Briggs* [1980] Ch 338.

I.A.9 EQUITIES OF REDEMPTION

The right of a person who has conveyed their rights away as security for the performance of an obligation is dealt with in Chapter 5.

I.A.10 LEGAL AND EQUITABLE CHARGES

These tailor-made security rights are dealt with in Chapter 5.

I.A.11 LICENCES OVER LAND: A BORDERLINE CASE

It would not be right to end the discussion of the common law's list of property rights without a brief mention of the 'licence'. The word 'licence' simply means permission, and is a catch-all used to describe any use of land which occurs with permission of a person with a right to exclusive possession of that land but which is not pursuant to a recognised property right. Thus, the personal rights in both *Hill v Tupper* and *King v David Allen & Sons, Billposting, Ltd* would both be described as licences, in this case prefixed by the word 'contractual' to signify the fact that the permission was paid for as opposed to gratuitous. The label 'licensee' would also be attached to a customer entering a shop or a guest staying in a hotel.

If a licence, contractual or otherwise, was held to amount to a property right, then the numerus clausus principle would be virtually abolished. And it is for that reason that the attempt made by Denning LJ in *Errington v Errington & Woods* [1952] 1 KB 290 to bring at least the contractual licence into the list was rejected by the Court of Appeal in *Ashburn Anstalt v Arnold* [1989] Ch 1.

II.B GOODS

II.B.1 INTRODUCTION

In contrast to property rights in respect of land, the common law recognises very few property rights over goods. A further contrast with the common law of property rights over land is that there is in land a clear principle of *numerus clausus*, both in the case law and in legislation. Although this would also seem to be the case with goods, it is difficult to find any direct statement of the rule. Moreover, the law of property rights in relation to goods is relatively impoverished when compared to its equivalent in respect to land in that, while English land law has names for the various property rights it recognises, this is not the case with goods, where a confusion is often made between property rights in respect of a thing (I have a property right in respect of that car) and the thing itself (that car is my property). This makes it especially hard to give a coherent account of the common law in this area.

We start by outlining a few basic rules of the English law of property rights over goods before moving on to an enumeration of the rights themselves. The first is that the feudal system never applied to goods, with the result that there is no doctrine of estates for goods, and therefore no facility for the division of enjoyment over time. Thus, there is no equivalent of the life estate encountered in the common law of land or the usufruct of civil law.[294] Second, and like land in this regard, there is no concept of 'ownership' in English law with regard to goods.

II.B.1.a No doctrine of estates for chattels

Brooke's Abridgement, Done et Reminder, pl 57 **3.101 (E&W)**

[T]he gift of a chattel for an hour is a gift of it forever.

[294] Similar results, however, could be achieved through a trust. Discussion in Chapter 6.

Sir William Blackstone, Commentaries on the Law of England (1768) II, 398 **3.102 (E&W)**

By the rules of ancient common law, there could be no future property, to take place in expectancy, created in personal goods and chattels; because, being things transitory, and by many accidents subject to be lost, destroyed, or otherwise impaired, and the exigencies of trade requiring also a frequent circulation thereof, it would occasion perpetual suits and quarrels, and put a stop to the freedom of commerce, if such limitations in reminder were generally tolerated and allowed.

Court of Appeal, 19 February 1897[295] **3.103 (E&W)**

Re Hill

ESTATES IN RESPECT OF CHATTELS?

Diamond necklace

A gift of a chattel for life passes the property at law.

Facts: Viscount Hill sought to recover possession of a diamond necklace and earrings from his stepmother, the defendant. He based his claim on the will of his grandmother, who had stated in a letter to her solicitor that she received the diamond necklace and earrings upon marriage for life and that they were to be left as heirlooms.

Held: The terms of the gift did not give rise to a trust, with the result that title to the jewellery passed to the grandmother completely and thence to the defendant.

Judgment: Chitty LJ ... As the common law does not recognise such a thing as an estate in a chattel, a gift of a chattel for life accompanied by delivery passes the property at law.

II.B.1.b No concept of 'ownership' of chattels

Introductory Note

As we saw above, a second reason, apart from the existence of the feudal system, why it was inappropriate to talk of the 'ownership' at common law was that the remedies available to those dispossessed of land did not require proof of something called 'ownership', merely prior possession. The same is true in relation to goods at common law, where, as was seen in Chapter 2, there is no equivalent of the civilian vindicatio, merely claims under the various torts protecting possession. The important consequence of these torts is that the mere fact of possession in English law, both of land and goods, generates a right to possession.[296] This topic is covered in Chapter 2. For this reason, it is possible for two or more titles to exist at the same time, and it is common to find English judges talking of one person having

[295] [1897] 1 QB 483

[296] We mean, of course, a proprietary right to possession as opposed to a personal right to possession, as, for example, the case of a person who enters into a contract of hire in respect of a particular chattel but who has not yet taken physical possession of it. Much confusion in this area is caused by a failure to distinguish between proprietary and personal rights to possession.

a better title than another. As *Armory v Delamirie* (1722) 1 Str 515 demonstrates, what never needs to be decided is who has the best title of all. The issues are only ever relative ones between the parties to the litigation.

II.B.2 TITLE

Content of the right

In civil law systems, as we have seen, the most extensive property right over goods is called 'ownership'. But as we have also seen, English law has no similar concept. Moreover, the most extensive right it recognises, unlike its counterpart in land law, the fee simple, has no stable name, being variously called 'property', 'title', 'the general property in the goods', or, reflecting lay usage, even 'ownership'.

Of these, the most common is 'title', with many cases and statutes talking of a person having a 'title' to goods. And we have to say 'a title' rather than 'the title' because of the fact that more than one title may exist at the same time. The reason for this, as will be seen in Chapter 7, is that a title, a right to possession, is created by the mere fact of taking possession of the thing: *Armory v Delamirie* (1722) 1 Str 515; *Costelloe v Chief Constable of Derbyshire* [2001] 1 WLR 1437. What we are concerned with here, however, is not how the right comes into existence but with its content. Unfortunately, it is difficult to find any direct statement of the rights of a person with a 'title'. Indeed, the word itself only derives from 'entitlement', thus begging the question: 'Entitlement to what?' However, working backwards from the protection given by the various wrongs, which were discussed in Chapter 2, we can say that the entitlement of someone with title to goods is a right to exclusive possession of those goods. Thus, a person with a title can, inter alia, sue someone who deprives him of possession of the thing, or who touches the thing without the title-holder's consent, or who carelessly damages the thing. That 'title' will last so long as the physical thing itself lasts, in other words, without limit of time. As will be seen in Chapter 8, it is a right which can be freely transferred, both inter vivos and post mortem. Moreover, having a right to exclusive possession, a person with title can licence others to use the thing, either gratuitously or for reward, or destroy the thing with impunity, no matter how valuable or of historical interest.

II.B.3 LIMITED DOCTRINE OF LIFE ESTATES IN TESTAMENTARY DISPOSITIONS

High Court, 23 February 1915[297] **3.104 (E&W)**

Re Swan, Witham and Swan

DOCTRINE OF TESTAMENTARY LIFE ESTATES

Jewellery

First possessor is a trustee for the remainderman.

[297] [1915] 1 Ch 829.

Facts: A testatrix bequeathed her title to some diamond jewellery and a Brussels lace wedding veil to her daughter for her life, and the remainder to the testatrix's son. On the death of the daughter, it was discovered that she had altered or lost much of the jewellery and the son sued her estate for damages. The daughter's estate defended the claim by arguing that a series of life estates was created at law, with the result that the son's claim for damage to his interest was a claim in tort, which claim was extinguished by the death of the daughter.

Held: The claim for damages was allowed..

Judgment: Sargant J—This is a claim in the administration of the estate of Florence Julia Swan by her brother, Francis Edward Lister Swan, to recover the value of certain articles of jewellery and lace which in the events which happened were left by the will of their mother to the sister for life with remainder to the brother. … I should have thought it fairly clear that, those articles having been in the possession of this lady as tenant for life and not being forthcoming at her death, her estate was liable to make good their value to her brother, especially in view of the fact that it is shown that the absence of the Brazilian diamond necklace is due to a considerable extent at any rate to the lady having broken it up in her lifetime and converted parts of it into other ornaments. But a most elaborate argument has been addressed to me on the subject and I must deal with the argument so advanced.

Practically the defence to the claim is put in this way. It is said that by virtue of the mother's will a series of legal limitations is created, a legal limitation to the daughter for life followed by a legal limitation in remainder to her brother, and that that being so and the estates being purely legal this is a claim for a tort committed by the daughter during her life, and that on the principle 'actio personalis moritur cum persona' no effectual claim can be maintained against the daughter's estate in respect of that tort. The subject whether limitations can be created in personal property is one that has been very much debated, and the law with regard to it was not settled for very many years. There were various theories with regard to the matter, the difficulty of course lying in the fact that personal property does not admit of the creation of estates similar to those which are created in land. The first suggestion was that the property might remain in the executors. The second suggestion was that the first taker might be a usufructuary only and that the remainderman was the owner. That was held to be so at first only in cases where the use as distinguished from the article itself was given to the first taker for life, but ultimately that distinction was abolished. The third theory was that the first taker might be the absolute owner with an executory gift over; and the fourth theory was that the first taker might be in the position of a trustee either with regard to the property which he had in the article, or at any rate with regard to the possession which he had of it.

The whole matter is discussed in Fearne on Contingent Remainders, where, after dealing with a large number of cases, the learned author in vol i, pp. 413, 414, says this: "In such cases, if the first taker does not acquire the whole legal interest, upon the delivery from the executors, where is the obstacle to considering him as acquiring only a right to the use or occupation, according to the limited duration of his interest therein; and that the executor should retain the absolute property in trust for him and the legatees over; so as to preserve the right of such ulterior legatees to the possession, when their interests are to commence? Or if the whole legal interest be acquired from the executors, on their assent to the possession of the first taker; why may not he be considered as taking it in trust for the ulterior legatees, subject to his own anterior beneficial interest therein?" With regard to the first of those alternative suggestions, it appears to me that that suggestion has probably been disposed of by the case of *Foley v Burnell* 4 Bro PC 34 in the House of Lords, the decision in which appears to be incompatible or at least inconsistent with the notion of the ultimate remaindermen taking anything short of some definite legal interest under the will. But I am prepared to adopt the second suggestion, with perhaps some slight modification, and to hold that either as to the property or preferably perhaps as to his possession of the property the first taker is during his life a trustee or a quasi-trustee for the remaindermen.

The present case is really simplified by the circumstance that not only was this lady the first tenant for life, but she was also co-executrix of the will with her brother, and, if it were the fact, as counsel suggested, that there is no obligation by contract binding on the first person who takes possession unless he gives some express undertaking analogous to a contract, it seems to me that in the present case this lady could not derive any advantage from her own omission in transferring the articles from herself as executrix to herself as tenant for life without taking a proper undertaking so as to create a right by contract. But I do not wish to rest my judgment upon that ground. Independently of that it is in my opinion quite clear that the ultimate taker had a definite right in the property which would be protected by a Court of Equity during the lifetime of the tenant for life by injunction if necessary; and, if it is necessary to put the obligations of the original taker into a definite legal category, I see no reason why the first taker should not be deemed as to the possession of the articles to be a trustee for the remainderman subject to her own life interest, and to be subject in that respect to the ordinary law of trust; or, if that is not a correct way of putting it, it may well be that the first taker is in the position of a bailee of the articles the possession of which on her death she is through her legal personal representative bound to deliver over to the ultimate taker. I see no reason at all for thinking that the claim of the ultimate taker is necessarily a claim for tort, and I do see a difficulty in the way of the legal personal representative of the first taker setting up the tort of his testator in answer to a claim by the remainderman to the possession of the articles.

If that is the true view, namely, that the possession taken by the first taker is subject to an obligation, whether by way of trust or by way of implied contract as a bailee, any difficulty with regard to enforcing a claim for damages against the estate of the person in question is gone: and I think also that any doubt as to the measure of damages is also gone, at least with regard to the diamond necklace, as to which it is clear that the loss is attributable primarily to the lady having caused the diamond necklace to be broken up in a way which she was not entitled to do. It seems to me that, if there is a breach of an obligation of that kind, the person who is damaged and who was entitled to receive the specific article is entitled to compensation in the shape of money sufficient to enable him to replace the article. It would not be sufficient to give him either the amount which would have been realized by selling the article or the middle price between that amount and the amount which it would require to replace the article. That principle is quite familiar in this Court. For instance in a case where a trustee sells trust property without a breach of trust and then afterwards applies the proceeds for his own purposes he is compellable only to account for the money he received with 4 per cent interest; but, if he were selling the property for the purpose of committing the breach of trust, his obligation, if the cestui que trust so requires, is not merely to account for the money that he received with 4 per cent interest, but to replace the fund that he wrongfully sold, because the right of the cestui que trust which was first violated was a right to the property itself. In the present case, when we have arrived at the conclusion that by virtue either of an implied trust or of an implied contract in the nature of a bailment the remainderman was entitled to the specific property, it follows that, if that specific property is not accounted for and has been lost through the default of the tenant for life, then the measure of damages is the larger measure of the three that have been mentioned in argument, namely, the amount that is required to replace the property. [His Lordship then examined the evidence as to what the jewellery really was and its value, and allowed the sum of £330 to restore the necklace as it was before, £55 for the smaller articles of jewellery, and £45 for the lace.]

II.B.4 POWER TO RESCIND CONTRACT OF SALE AND REVEST TITLE

High Court, 17 January 1905[298] **3.105 (E&W)**

Re Eastgate, ex p Ward

POWER TO RESCIND CONTRACTS OF SALE

Goods on credit

Despite intervening bankruptcy, title to goods acquired through a fraudulently induced sale revests on rescission of contract.

Facts: In February 1904, a bankrupt took a lease of a house, and obtained a large quantity of goods on credit from tradesmen in its neighbourhood. The respondent had supplied goods to the value of £11. On April 20 the landlord put in a distress for rent which was paid out by the tradesmen, and on the same day the respondent commenced an action in the county court to recover the amount due to him. On April 22 the bankrupt committed an act of bankruptcy by departing from his dwelling-house with intent to defeat or delay his creditors. On April 27 the respondent and some of the other tradesmen, by permission of the landlord, broke into the house by removing a pane of glass from one of the windows, and carried off what remained of the goods which they had supplied. On May 4 a creditor's petition was presented founded on the act of bankruptcy of April 22, and on May 20 the receiving order was made, which was followed by adjudication in bankruptcy and the appointment of a trustee. This was a motion by the trustee in bankruptcy to recover from the respondent the goods he had retaken or their value.

Held: The claim was allowed

Judgment: Bigham J—The question I have to determine in this case is whether at the time the respondent Bowling took possession of those goods they formed part of the bankrupt's estate. In my opinion they did not. The bankrupt appears in February 1904, to have taken a house in the neighbourhood in which Bowling carried on business. He immediately began to make purchases on credit from the tradespeople round about, and, in my opinion, he never had the least intention of paying for any of the goods he bought. In other words, he falsely pretended to the persons from whom he obtained the goods that he intended to pay for them, when in truth and in fact he did not intend to do anything of the kind—and it was in that way that the bankrupt got possession of these goods. What was the

[298] [1905] 1 KB 465.

position of the vendors? In my opinion their position was this, that as soon as they discovered that the bankrupt had bought these goods without any intention at all of paying for them, they were entitled to treat the contract as a contract induced by fraud—induced, that is to say, by a representation which the purchaser knew to be untrue—that he was going to pay for the goods; and, being entitled to treat the contract as one induced by fraud, they were entitled within a reasonable time after they discovered the fact to disarm the contract. The sales in the particular case before me extended over a period from Mar. 9 to April 15, the house, as I have said, being taken in February. On April 20, as Bowling could not get his money, he appears to have taken proceedings in the county court to recover the price of the goods he had supplied. He did not at that time know the circumstances. Very soon afterwards, however, he did know the circumstances, because on April 22, two days afterwards, the bankrupt shut up his house and absconded, and committed an act of bankruptcy. It was then that Bowling discovered that he had been defrauded, disaffirmed the contract and took back his property. Now, did the property at the time he took it back form part of the estate of the bankrupt? I do not think it did, for when & trustee in bankruptcy acquires the interest of the bankrupt in the property which he finds in the bankrupt's possession, he takes that property subject to the rights of third parties, and one of those rights in this case was the right of the vendors of the goods to disarm contracts for sale and to re-take possession. I cannot say that I approve of the way in which the possession was re-taken in this case; but, in my opinion, Bowling was only taking, though in a wrong way, what was his own property, and, that being so, this application by the trustee must be dismissed.

Court of Appeal, 19 December 1963[299] **3.106 (E&W)**

Car & Universal Finance Co Ltd v Caldwell

POWER TO RESCIND A CONTRACT OF SALE

Jaguar

In cases of fraud, rescission does not need to be communicated to other contractual party.

Facts: Caldwell advertised his Jaguar car for sale in a local paper. One evening, he was visited by two men, one of whom called himself Norris, who persuaded Caldwell to part with the car in exchange for a cheque and a car of lesser value as security. When he tried to cash the cheque the next morning, it was dishonoured. The bank advised Caldwell to go to the police, who told him that there was a warrant out for Norris in the name of Rowley. It was then discovered that the car left as security was stolen. Caldwell told the police to find his car and get it back, and said the same to the Automobile Association, a motoring organisation. Norris later sold the car to Motobella Ltd, who sold it to G & C Finance Ltd, who sold it to a dealer, who sold it to Car & Universal Finance, who bought it in good faith and for value. In interpleader proceedings, the question for Lord Denning MR, sitting at first instance, was whether Caldwell's act of informing the police and the Automobile Association of his intention to rescind the contract of sale had the effect of revesting title in him. He held that it did. This meant, said Lord Denning, that '[T]he contract of sale to these rogues was avoided and Caldwell then became the owner of the car again. It was only after he avoided it (so that it was once again his property), that these rogues purported to sell it to Motobella and Motobella purported to sell it to

[299] [1965] 1 QB 525.

G & C Finance. Those sales were ineffective to pass the property because it had already re-vested in Caldwell.' On appeal to the Court of Appeal—

Held: Appeal dismissed.

Judgment: Sellers LJ—This appeal raises a primary point in the law of contract. The question has arisen whether a contract which is voidable by one party can in any circumstances be terminated by that party without his rescission being communicated to the other party. Lord Denning MR has held in the circumstances of this case that there can be rescission without communication where the seller of a motor-car who admittedly had the right to rescind the contract of sale on the ground of fraudulent misrepresentation, terminated the contract by an unequivocal act of election which demonstrated clearly that he had elected to rescind it and to be no longer bound by it. The general rule, no doubt, is that where a party is entitled to rescind a contract and wishes to do so the contract subsists until the opposing party is informed that the contract has been terminated. The difficulty of the seller in this case was that, when he learnt of the fraud and, therefore, ascertained his right to terminate the bargain, he could not without considerable delay find either the fraudulent buyer or the car which had been sold. Such circumstances would not appear to be so rare in transactions in motor cars (or horses in earlier days) that they would not, it might be thought, have given rise to litigation and an authoritative decision, but it seems that over the years the point in issue has not been decided in any reported cases in similar or comparable circumstances.

The sole question ... is whether the defendant avoided the contract of sale and recovered his title to the car before the purported sale by Motobella to G & C Finance on January 15, 1960. If he did not do so then, subject to the other contention which arises on the appeal, G & C. Finance obtained a good title and were able to pass it on to the plaintiffs later in the same year.

The decision of Lord Denning MR that the defendant had established a rescission on January 13, 1960, was strongly attacked before us on the ground that, though interesting, it was contrary to authority and was not supported by the various cases of election which the judge found comparable and where communication was, it was said, not required as an essential prerequisite—and reference was made in the judgment to termination of a lease for forfeiture, ratification, repudiation and affirmation of a contract. Much of the argument before us was an endeavour to show that these illustrations and comparisons were either fallacious or ambiguous. I do not pursue them for, with respect, I do not find them helpful to the decision, except possibly in the case of an affirmation of a contract which is an election to the contrary effect to a disaffirmation. An affirmation of a voidable contract may be established by any conduct which unequivocally manifests an intention to affirm it by the party who has the right to affirm or disaffirm. Communication of an acceptance of a contract after knowledge of a fundamental breach of it by the other party or of fraud affecting it is, of course, evidence establishing affirmation but it is not essential evidence. A party cannot reject goods sold and delivered if he uses them after knowledge of a right to reject, and the judgment cites a case where an instruction to a broker to re-sell was sufficient affirmation of the contract in question even though that conduct was not communicated. It may be said that a contract may be more readily approved and accepted than it can be terminated where a unilateral right to affirm or disaffirm arises. The disaffirmation or election to avoid a contract changes the relationship of the parties and brings their respective obligations to an end, whereas an affirmation leaves the contract effective though subject to a claim for damages for its breach. Where a contracting party could be communicated with, and modern facilities make communication practically world-wide and almost immediate, it would be unlikely that a party could be held to have disaffirmed a contract unless he went so far as to communicate his decision so to do. It would be what the other contracting party would normally require and unless communication were made the party's intention to rescind would not have been unequivocally or clearly demonstrated or made manifest. But in circumstances such as the present case, the other contracting party, a fraudulent rogue who would know that the vendor would want his car back as soon as he knew of the fraud, would not expect to be communicated with as a matter of right or requirement, and would deliberately, as here, do all he could to evade any such communication being made to him. In such exceptional contractual circumstances, it does not seem to me appropriate to hold that a party so acting can claim any right to have a decision to rescind communicated to him before the contract is terminated. To hold that he could would involve that the defrauding party, if skilful enough to keep out of the way, could deprive the other party to the contract of his right to rescind, a right to which he was entitled and which he would wish to exercise, as the defrauding party would well know or at least confidently suspect. The position has to be viewed, as I see it, between the two contracting parties involved in the particular contract in question. That another innocent party or parties may suffer does not in my view of the matter justify imposing on a defrauded seller an impossible task. He has to establish, clearly and unequivocally, that he terminates the contract and is no longer to be bound by it. If he cannot communicate his decision he may still satisfy a judge or jury that he had made a final and irrevocable decision and ended the contract. I am in agreement with Lord Denning MR who asked

> 'How is a man in the position of Caldwell ever to be able to rescind the contract when a fraudulent person absconds as Norris did here?'

and answered that he can do so

> '... if he at once, on discovering the fraud, takes all possible steps to regain the goods even though he cannot find the rogue nor communicate with him.'

The plaintiffs contended that in *Scarf v Jardine* (1887) 7 App Cas 345 Lord Blackburn laid it down that election to avoid a contract is not completed until the decision has been communicated to the other side "in such a way as to lead the opposite party to believe that he has made that choice," and they relied on the many works of authority which state that where a right of election exists there has to be communication. *Scarf v Jardine* is a very different case from the present. It is so well known and so often cited that it does not call for analysis. In that case Lord Blackburn and the authors, in the various works referred to, had not in mind, in enunciating a general principle, the circumstances and the arguments which have arisen in the present case. Even in the light of this statement of the law it was conceded—and rightly so—that if the defendant could have found the car and had retaken it without the knowledge of the buyer, but before resale to an innocent purchaser, the contract would have been at an end and the title restored to the defendant. Such an act would have been an unequivocal act of election to disaffirm the contract.

In the case of an innocent misrepresentation, in circumstances which would permit the party misled to rescind, the other party would not deliberately avoid communication (for that would seem to negative innocence) and circumstances would be rare where communication could not be readily made in one way or another. If communication were possible, it is difficult to see how there could be rescission without communication, and the inference would be that the contracting parties required communication of termination. Special circumstances may arise and call for future consideration but I do not think the comparison made in argument on behalf of the plaintiffs between innocent and fraudulent misrepresentation invalidates the judgment of Lord Denning MR. It has to be recognised that in transactions such as this where fraud intervenes, some innocent party may have to suffer, and it may well be that legislation is overdue to do justice between the victims of fraud and to apportion in some way the loss. In the present case, however, I can see nothing unjust in the loss falling on G & C Finance (against whom the plaintiffs can claim redress), who made the minimum inquiries, who bought a car, which, apparently, they never saw and hired it out to a man, of whose existence and identity they did not know, and who may well have been fictitious, rather than that the loss should fall on the defendant, who acted immediately and did all in his power to retract the transaction.

Upjohn and Davies LJJ delivered concurring judgments.

Notes

(1) The common law power to rescind a contract of sale and thereby revest title seems to be confined to cases of fraudulently induced sales. A right to rescind for such things as negligently or innocently induced mistakes, spontaneous mistakes, undue influence and so on seems only to exist in equity. When exercised, it turns the title-holder into a trustee of his title for the person rescinding rather than sending the title back whence it came. Prior to the act of rescission, the vendor has what is unhelpfully described as a 'mere equity'.

(2) The common law power to rescind a contract of sale and thereby revest title seems to have been invented by Parke B in *Load v Green* (1846) 15 M & W 216. For an argument that his reasoning was mistaken, see WJ Swadling, 'Rescission, Property, and the Common Law' (2005) 121 *LQR* 123.

II.B.5 SERVITUDES OVER GOODS

Introductory Note

We have seen that so far as land is concerned, the common law recognises a number of different types of servitudes, the most prominent of which are the easement and the restrictive covenant. Both, however, require the presence of a dominant tenement, something which is not possible in the case of movables. It is not surprising, therefore, to find that the common law has rejected any notion of servitudes over chattels.

High Court, 11 December 1903[300] **3.107 (E&W)**

Taddy v Sterious

SERVITUDES OVER GOODS

Tobacco

Contractual restrictions do not run with goods.

Facts: The plaintiffs, Taddy & Co, manufacturers of tobacco, sold packet tobaccos subject to printed terms and conditions fixing a minimum price below which they were not to be sold, and containing the following proviso: 'Acceptance of the goods will be deemed a contract between the purchaser and Taddy that he will observe these stipulations. In the case of a purchase by a retail dealer through a wholesale dealer, the latter shall be deemed to be the agent of Taddy.' Taddy sold to Netten, who resold for his own profit to Sterious. Sterious had notice of the conditions, but sold to the public at a price below the stipulated minimum. The plaintiffs brought an action for a declaration that the defendants were not entitled to sell any packet tobacco or cigarettes manufactured by the plaintiffs except at such prices and upon such terms and conditions of supply as were specified and contained in the invoice catalogues, price lists, labels and notices. Their application was refused.

Held: The relief sought was refused.

Judgment: Swinfen Eady J—The defendants have dealt in the plaintiffs' tobaccos for some time. It is not suggested that they were ignorant of the terms and conditions issued by the plaintiffs. Complaints were made on several occasions of the defendants selling under the minimum price, and since the writ was issued the defendant Netten has agreed not to sell them any more of this tobacco, and the supply from that source has ceased. But the claim made by Taddy & Co is not confined to tobacco obtained by Sterious & Co from Netten, but is quite general. The plaintiffs put their case in two ways. First, they contended that the conditions constituted a contract made by Sterious & Co with Netten as the plaintiffs' agents, and that they are entitled to restrain Sterious & Co from acting in breach of that contract. Secondly, they contended that the goods were sold subject to certain conditions, and that even if Netten or any one else had purported to sell them free from the conditions, Sterious & Co, having notice of the conditions, could not sell the goods except according to the conditions, and the plaintiffs were entitled to restrain them from doing so.

With regard to this last contention, there is a short answer. Conditions of this kind do not run with goods, and cannot be imposed upon them. Subsequent purchasers, therefore, do not take subject to any conditions which the Court can enforce. If there was a breach of contract, the plaintiffs could no doubt sue. The question remains, therefore, whether there was any contract. There was no direct contract between Sterious & Co and Taddy & Co, and the question does not arise as to the effect of a sale by Taddy & Co direct to a retail trader subject to these terms as to minimum retail price. The part of the conditions now in question is: 'In the case of a purchase by a retail dealer through a wholesale dealer, the latter shall be deemed to be the agent of Taddy & Co.' Now it is quite clear that Taddy & Co sell to wholesale dealers out and out. The wholesale dealers are not Taddy & Co's agents to sell the goods; they buy them out and out, and sell them for their own profit. It was argued that the words in the special condition, 'purchase by a retail dealer through a wholesale dealer', can only refer to cases where the wholesale dealers really are the agents of

[300] [1904] 1 Ch 354.

Taddy & Co, and do not apply to cases where the wholesale dealers first bought and then resold. That seems to be the right construction. If, however, the condition ought to be construed as applying to a purchase from as well as through a wholesale dealer—even then, a wholesale dealer selling for his own profit would not be an agent of Taddy & Co in the ordinary sense of that term. Nor can it be said that the wholesale dealer was selling the goods for his own profit, and at the same time entered into a collateral contract with the purchaser, as to the subsequent dealing with the goods, as the agent of Taddy & Co. No such collateral contract was in fact entered into. In my opinion, when the wholesale dealer sold the goods for his own profit, he was not in any sense whatever the agent of Taddy & Co, and the mere insertion in the condition of the words that he was to be deemed to be an agent could not make him one. Whatever may be the case as between Taddy & Co and Netten, there is no contract between Taddy & Co and Sterious & Co.

Note

See also *McGruther v Pitcher* [1904] 2 Ch 306; *Dunlop Pneumatic Tyre Co v Selfridge & Co Ltd* [1915] AC 847; *Barker v Strickney* [1919] 1 KB 121.

II.B.6 LEASES OF GOODS

Introductory Note

As we saw above, a lease of land, at least at common law, is undoubtedly a property right. It is, however, a contentious question whether the same can be said for a lease of goods.

Court of Appeal, 21 December 1989[301] **3.108 (E&W)**

Bristol Airport plc v Powdrill

LEASES OF GOODS

Airline

A lease of goods was 'property' for the purposes of the Insolvency Act 1986.

Facts: An airline, Paramount Airlines Ltd, was insolvent but had been placed in administration pursuant to the Insolvency Act 1986, the purpose of which was to allow it to trade its way out of difficulty. By virtue section 11 of the Act, no proceedings could be commenced against the company or its 'property' without the leave of the court. A company running an airport was owed money by Paramount as landing fees. By statute, the company had a right to detain the aircraft of operators who had not paid landing fees. Without obtaining leave of the court, it parked a lorry loaded with concrete in front of an aircraft operated by Paramount and served the captain with a lien notice. It argued that no leave was necessary before doing this as the aircraft, being only on lease to Paramount, was not its 'property'. Harman J held that the aircraft were the property of Paramount even though held on lease so that leave of the court was required. On appeal to the Court of Appeal—

Held: The appeal was dismissed.

[301] [1990] Ch 744.

Judgment: Sir Nicolas Browne-Wilkinson V-C—Section 88(1) of the Civil Aviation Act 1982 provides:

> 'Where default is made in the payment of airport charges incurred in respect of any aircraft at an aerodrome to which this section applies, the aerodrome authority may, subject to the provisions of this section—(a) detain, pending payment, either (i) the aircraft in respect of which the charges were incurred (whether or not they were incurred by the person who is the operator of the aircraft at the time when the detention begins); or (ii) any other aircraft of which the person in default is the operator at the time when the detention begins; and (b) if the charges are not paid within 56 days of the date when the detention begins, sell the aircraft in order to satisfy the charges.'

Subsection (3) provides that the aircraft shall not be sold without the leave of the court which must first be satisfied that a sum is due for airport charges, that default has been made in payment of such charges and that the aircraft is liable for sale under the section. Subsection (4) requires notice of any application for leave to sell to be given to persons whose interests may be affected by such sale so as to afford them an opportunity of becoming parties to such application. Subsection (6) provides that the proceeds of sale are to be applied in paying any customs or excise duty chargeable, the expenses of detaining, keeping and selling the aircraft, the airport charges which are unpaid and charges due by virtue of section 73 of the Act (which relate to charges for Eurocontrol). The surplus proceeds of sale are to be paid to or among the persons whose interests in the aircraft have been divested by reason of the sale. Subsections (7) and (8) provide that the power of detention and sale is exercisable in relation to the equipment on the aircraft and any stores and aircraft documents carried on the aircraft. Under subsection (9) the power to detain is expressly made exercisable not only on the occasion on which the charges have been incurred but also on any subsequent occasion when the aircraft is on the aerodrome on which the charges were incurred or on any other aerodrome owned or managed by the same authority. ...

It is common ground that the sale of an aircraft under this section operates so as to divest all interests in the aircraft so as to vest full legal and equitable title to the aircraft in the purchaser. Even where the charges have been incurred by a person who is not the full legal and equitable owner of the aircraft (such as Paramount in this case) the effect of a sale will be to divest the ultimate owners of the aircraft of their title. Their compensation, if any, lies in the direction under subsection (6) to apply the surplus proceeds of sale 'among the person or persons whose interests in the aircraft have been divested by reason of the sale'. It follows that the powers under the section provide a strong inducement to those ultimately interested in the aircraft to discharge the debts for airport charges, even though they have not incurred them.

Administration orders were introduced by the Insolvency Act 1985 following a report by a committee on insolvency law and practice under the chairmanship of Sir Kenneth Cork. That report identified a shortcoming in the law relating to insolvent companies. In a number of cases, companies were forced into liquidation even though they were carrying on potentially viable businesses. Such businesses were destroyed for want of a procedure whereby they could be conducted with a view either to restoring the financial health of the company or of enabling the businesses to be sold as a going concern. If the business of the company could be sold as a going concern, it would normally command a substantially higher price than on break-up. The Cork Report contrasted that position with the case where a creditor holding a floating charge had appointed a receiver and manager who was able by continuing to run the company's business to achieve the desired result to the benefit of not only the secured creditors but also the unsecured creditors and shareholders.

The Cork Report also pointed to a separate mischief, viz the inability in a liquidation to sell the whole of the company's business as a going concern without the co-operation and agreement of those holding fixed charges over its assets.

It is clear that the administration procedure introduced by the Insolvency Act 1985 and now contained in Part II of the Act of 1986 was directed to remedying these mischiefs as the provisions of the Act of 1986 themselves make clear.

Section 8 of the Act of 1986 gives the court power to appoint an administrator if the court is satisfied that the company is unable to pay its debts as they fall due and considers that the making of an order would be likely to achieve one or more of the following purposes under subsection (3):

> '(a) the survival of the company and the whole or any part of its undertaking, as a going concern; (b) the approval of a voluntary arrangement under Part I; (c) the sanctioning under section 425 of the Companies Act of a compromise or arrangement between the company and such persons as are mentioned in that section; and (d) a more advantageous realisation of the company's assets than would be effected on a winding up; ...'

So long as such order is in force 'the affairs, business and property' of a company are to be managed by the administrator appointed by the court. For that purpose the administrator is given very wide powers to carry on the business of the company, as the agent of the company, including power to take possession of the property of the company. ...

Part II of the Act contains two sections designed to protect the property of the company against adverse claims. Section 10 covers the period between the presentation of the petition and the making of the administration order. Section 11 covers the period after the making of the order and is the section directly in point in this case. So far as relevant, it provides:

> '(3) During the period for which an administration order is in force—(a) no resolution may be passed or order made for the winding up of the company; (b) no administrative receiver of the company may be appointed; (c) no other steps may be taken to enforce any security over the company's property, or to repossess goods in the company's possession under any hire-purchase agreement, except with the consent of the administrator or the leave of the court and subject (where the court gives leave) to such terms as the court may impose; and (d) no other proceedings and no execution or other legal process may be commenced or continued, and no distress may be levied, against the company or its property except with the consent of the administrator or the leave of the court and subject (where the court gives leave) to such terms as aforesaid.'

'Security' is defined by section 248(b) as meaning 'any mortgage, charge, lien or other security'.

The administrators in this case contend that the exercise of the statutory right of detention under section 88 of the Act of 1982 falls within either section 11(3)(c) (as being a step taken to enforce any security) or within section 11(3)(d) (as being the levying of a distress or 'other proceedings').

Section 15 contains additional provisions relating to property subject to a charge. It distinguishes between floating charges and fixed charges. 'Floating charge' is defined as 'a charge which, as created, was a floating charge': section 251. Therefore, for the purpose of determining whether or not a charge is a floating charge, any crystallisation of a floating charge on the making of an administration order falls to be ignored. Under section 15(1) and (4) the administrator is given power to exercise all his powers (ie including presumably the right to take possession) over property which is subject to a floating charge; in the event of a sale, the chargee's rights are shifted to the proceeds of sale. The position is different as respects property subject to a fixed charge. The administrator is given no general power to exercise his rights over such property: but the court can give leave to the administrator to dispose of such property, the proceeds of sale being applied in discharge of the secured debt. …

… It may be helpful to state what, in my opinion, is the correct approach to the construction of the provisions dealing with administrators contained in Part II of the Act. The judge was very much influenced in his construction by the manifest statutory purpose of Part II of the Act. I agree with this approach. The provisions of Part II themselves, coupled with the mischief identified in the Cork Report, show that the statutory purpose is to install an administrator, as an officer of the court, to carry on the business of the company as a going concern with a view to achieving one or other of the statutory objectives mentioned in section 8(3). It is of the essence of administration under Part II of the Act that the business will continue to be carried on by the administrator. Such continuation of the business by the administrator requires that there should be available to him the right to use the property of the company, free from interference by creditors and others during the, usually short, period during which such administration continues. Hence the restrictions on the rights of creditors and others introduced by section 10 and 11 of the Act. In my judgment in construing Part II of the Act it is legitimate and necessary to bear in mind the statutory objective with a view to ensuring, if the words permit, that the administrator has the powers necessary to carry out the statutory objectives, including the power to use the company's property.

On the other hand, however desirable it may be to construe the Act in a way calculated to carry out the parliamentary purpose, it is not legitimate to distort the meaning of the words Parliament has chosen to use in order to achieve that result. Only if the words used by Parliament are fairly capable of bearing more than one meaning is it legitimate to adopt the meaning which gives effect to, rather than frustrates, the statutory purpose. …

Mr Lightman, for the airports, submits that because the aircraft were only held by Paramount under chattel-leases they are not 'property'. The aircraft, he submits, were the property of the ultimate lessor: Paramount has only contractual rights.

'Property' is defined by section 436 as follows:

> '"Property" includes money, goods, things in action, land and every description of property wherever situated and also obligations and every description of interest, whether present or future or vested or contingent, arising out of, or incidental to, property.'

It is hard to think of a wider definition of property.

In my judgment, the interest of Paramount under a lease of the aircraft is plainly property within that definition. It is true that, to date, concepts of concurrent interests in personal property have not been developed in the same way as they have over the centuries in relation to real property. But modern commercial methods have introduced chattel-leasing. The Act of 1986 refers expressly to such leases: see section 10(4). Although a chattel lease is a contract, it does not follow that no property interest is created in the chattel. The basic equitable principle is that if, under a contract, A has certain rights over property as against the legal owner, which rights are specifically enforceable in equity, A has an equitable interest in such property. I have no doubt that a court would order specific performance of a contract to lease an aircraft, since each aircraft has unique features peculiar to itself. Accordingly in my judgment the 'lessee' has at least an equitable right of some kind in that aircraft which falls within the statutory definition as being some 'description of interest … arising out of, or incidental to' that aircraft. …

Woolf and Staughton LJJ delivered concurring judgments.

Note

Although in view of the wide definition of 'property' in the Insolvency Act 1986 the decision is arguably right on its facts, Sir Nicolas Browne-Wilkinson's equation of the availability of specific performance and the existence of a property right has not gone unchallenged: W Swadling, 'The Proprietary Effect of a Hire of Goods' in NE Palmer and E McKendrick, *Interests in Goods*, 2nd edn (1998) 491, 504–08.

I.A.7 SECURITY RIGHTS OVER GOODS

The common law recognises a number of security rights over goods. These are:

(i) Mortgage;
(ii) Pledge;
(iii) Lien;
(iv) Stoppage in transitu;
(v) Charge.

These are considered, with the exception of (iv), in Chapter 5 on security interests in property law.

III. COMPARATIVE OVERVIEW

The aim of this chapter was not only to provide an overview of the property rights which can exist over land and goods, but to also show similarities between the rights in the various legal systems. A number of common themes or concerns can be detected in this account of the civil and common law lists of property rights.

III.A LEGACY OF FEUDALISM

When it comes to property rights over land, the feudal system, though long gone in civil systems and skeletally present in the common law, continues to exert influence. The abolition of the feudal system on the continent of Europe led to a return to Roman law principles of unitary ownership in civil law systems. It also spawned the notion that property rights less than ownership burden the right of ownership, though never in such a way as was the situation under the feudal system. The doctrinal consequences of that view have been noted above. By contrast, though the feudal system still nominally exists in English law, it is by and large a dead letter, and arguably plays less of a role today than in civil law systems.

III.B NO CONCEPT OF OWNERSHIP IN ENGLISH LAW

A distinguishing feature of English law, both in relation to land and goods, is that it does not recognise a concept of ownership. So far as land is concerned, English law uses a system of property rights in which a person holds various property rights in respect of land, but never owns it.[302] This holding of rights over land might be seen as a remnant of the feudal system, and certainly the ability to divide rights on a plane of time is, but it is also true of movables, where no doctrine of estates exists. A further reason, therefore, for the currency of English law being not ownership but rights to possession is that rights to possession, because they arise from the mere fact of taking possession, can be multiple. Those systems for which ownership is the currency only accept the possibility of one such right in circulation at any one time.

III.C DEBT TO ROMAN LAW

The influence of Roman law is particularly visible in relation to property rights on land. After the French Revolution, the civil law codifications all returned to the Roman law system of property rights. And though the various legal systems provide different names for the various property rights, in content they remain similar to their Roman law equivalents.

The influence of Roman law is less pronounced, at least in respect of the typology of property rights, in English law. Nevertheless, several property rights in English law resemble Roman law property rights. In particular, the learning on easements owes much to the Roman law of servitudes.

III.D THE *NUMERUS CLAUSUS* PRINCIPLE

Property rights over land are legal relations which have effect against third parties. Each of the legal systems discussed in this chapter limits the number of available

[302] See FH Lawson and B Rudden, *The Law of Property*, 3rd edn (Oxford, 2002) 77 *et seq.*

property rights for reasons of certainty and transparency.[303] Furthermore, it is not just the number of property rights, but also the content of these rights which is restricted. Together, these restrictions are known as the principle of numerus clausus.

These restrictions on the number of property rights make it possible to discuss the full set of property rights in this casebook. In civil law, the list mainly comprises property rights enumerated in the various civil codes, occasionally supplemented by legislation. In exceptional cases, civil law courts have also recognised new property rights as well. The idea of a *numerus clausus* also exists in English law. It is, however, a product of the judge-made law, though one subsequently adopted by legislation.

III.E A DISLIKE OF POSITIVE BURDENS

In both the common and civil law, courts and legislatures have, as a general rule, resisted the demarcation of positive burdens as property rights. In continental systems, the general aversion to positive burdens can be seen to be connected with ideas developed during and after the French Revolution. In a feudal system, a tenant might be bound to perform a positive duty for his feudal lord. In the new civil law codifications following the Revolution, the legislature wanted to prevent a return to such a system. A general feature of the new unitary concept of ownership was the idea that an owner could not be forced to do something, at least not without his consent. Similarly, also in case of other property rights, the legal systems resist imposing positive burdens on the holders. However, as we have seen, both systems contain a number of exceptions to this rule. At common law, positive burdens can run with a lease. In the civil law, positive burdens can in certain cases attach to servitudes.

III.F NO SERVITUDES IN GROSS

The end of the feudal system on the continent of Europe also meant the end of the idea that a person should be bound to a property right personally. In particular, in the area of servitudes, the general idea remains today. A right of real servitude only binds parties in their capacity as owners of a piece of land and not personally. English law also resists the recognition of easements in gross.

III.G STATUS OF LEASE IN DIFFERENT SYSTEMS

A final and major difference is the status of the lease in civil law and common law. In civil law systems, whether it be a lease of land or a lease of goods, the right created amounts only to a personal one between a lessor and a lessee. Because a lease is a contract, privity of contract applies and only the parties to the contract are bound by it. However, in order to protect lessees against any possible abuse

[303] Above, Chapter 1.

by a lessor, civil law systems generally include a provision in which, subject to exceptions, a transfer of ownership of the land by the lessor causes a transfer of the lease agreement to the new owner. The lessee cannot, however, transfer his right to another person, and it is for this reason that the lease in civilian systems is still considered part of the law of obligations.

The position at common law, at least in respect of land, is different, for now both lessor and lessee have rights they can assign and which may bind their respective successors in title. Although it took some time to develop, there has been no doubt over the last 500 years that the lease of land in English law is a property right.

CONCISE BIBLIOGRAPHY

Bram Akkermans, *The Principle of Numerus Clausus in European Property Law* (Antwerp, Intersentia, 2008).

Steven Bartels and Michael Milo (eds), *The Content of the Real Right* (Nijmegen, Wolf Legal Publishers, 2004).

Sjef van Erp and Bram Akkermans, 'Property Rights: A Comparative View' in B Bouckaert (ed), *International Encyclopeadia of Law and Economics* (Northampton, Edward Elgar Publishing, 2010).

William Swadling, 'Property: General Principles' in A Burrows (ed), *English Private Law*, 2nd edn (Oxford, Oxford University Press, 2007).

CHAPTER FOUR
PROPERTY RIGHTS IN RESPECT OF CLAIMS

Caroline Lebon

This chapter further deals with the second of the six essential questions: what are property rights? In some legal systems claims can be the subject matter of property rights, some other legal systems take a very careful approach on this. When a claim is the subject matter of a property right this has effect on the property right, different from when a corporeal object is the subject matter of a property right (see Chapter 3). Therefore, this chapter deals specifically with property rights that have a claim as their subject matter.

I. GENERAL INTRODUCTION

This is a chapter that deals with claims. As we have seen in the previous chapter, property rights can be held in respect of corporeal, or tangible, objects.[1] In most legal systems, property rights can, at least in theory, also be held in respect of incorporeal or intangible objects.[2] However, depending on the definitions used in the property law systems, not all property rights can be held in respect of incorporeal objects.[3] In particular, German and Dutch law restrict the system of property law almost exclusively to corporeal objects, whereas in French law and English law

[1] See Chapter 3.
[2] See Chapter 1.
[3] See Chapter 1.

property rights can be held in respect of incorporeal objects in mostly the same way as they can be held in respect of corporeal objects.[4]

Of all incorporeal objects, the claim, a right to the performance of another, is the most important. This chapter therefore deals exclusively with claims as an example of an incorporeal object of property law. It thereby enlarges the category of objects from immovable (land) and movable (goods) with claims (known in English law as 'choses in action'). Not all property rights that we have discovered in the previous chapter can also be held on claims. However, some can and actually have a very important function in modern property law.

It is not easy to understand exactly what a claim is. It is in particular difficult to understand how a claim becomes an object of property law. Perhaps the easiest example of a claim is a right to the purchase price after a contract of sale is concluded. A right to the performance of the purchase price results from the contract and is 'held' by the seller. The purchaser, in his turn, has a right to delivery of the goods the contract was about. If the purchaser does not pay immediately, but waits for an invoice of the seller before he pays, a claim of the seller on the buyer results. The buyer is the debtor and the seller the creditor of that claim. A claim is a personal right, which can only be invoked against another person (in the example at stake against the other contracting party alone). However, as such, the claim also represents a value, a value that can be used in property law. In property law, the right to performance is known as a claim. It can be transferred, or assigned, to use the terminology of property lawyers, to someone else. This assignment can be made especially for security purposes, in other words to offer security for the repayment of a loan (which is another claim), but in addition property rights can be created in respect to the assignment. For example, a right of usufruct can be created in respect to a claim, giving the usufructuary the right to the enjoyment of the claim. More likely in this situation, a right of pledge, a property security right, can be created on the claim for payment, which will serve as security for a loan obtained by the seller.

This chapter will deal with claims, what they are, how they can be objects of property law (section I), and what property rights can be held over them (sections III and IV). Because claims are sometimes a controversial issue in property law, especially in those legal systems restricting property law to corporeal objects, some points for discussion are included.

Chapters that will follow in this casebook will also be useful for this chapter. The chapter on security rights (Chapter 5) will deal with security rights in respect to claims in more detail, the chapter on creation of property rights (Chapter 7) and transfer of property rights (Chapter 8) contain the default rules. In general, the rules relating to claims follow the default property rules on creation and transfer as much as possible. However, deviations exist that will be dealt with in this chapter.

[4] See Chapter 1. Dutch law in fact knows both a stricter and a broader notion of 'property' law. Property law in a stricter sense is limited to physical objects, property law in a broader sense includes, eg, claims. With regard to claims, ownership is not possible: a person is 'entitled' to a claim, meaning that the claim can be transferred and pledged. The latter is also possible under German law. This will be further explained below.

The destruction of property rights on claims is a different matter and will, because of the similarity with the rules relating to other objects of property law, be dealt with in Chapter 9.

I.A THE NOTION OF 'CLAIM'

Introductory Notes

(a) When we deal with objects of property law, most of us will think of corporeal or tangible objects. These objects are things that exist in the physical world and which can be touched. They are generally easy to describe. Corporeal objects are usually further divided into immovables and movables in civil law, and into land and personal property in English law.

(b) In addition to corporeal or tangible objects, there are also incorporeal or intangible objects in property law. These are objects that do not physically exist, but which are created in law. They are, in other words, rights. Of these rights, the claim, a right to the performance of another, is considered the most important.

(c) One of the most difficult aspects of property law is that in many legal systems the rules of property law apply to claims, ie incorporeal objects, in mostly the same manner as to corporeal objects. In this section we will further examine what is meant by a claim, before we can deal with the question whether and how a claim can be an object of property law and even what property rights can be held on such a claim.

(d) Finally, on terminology. As will be seen, legal systems use different terms to define what this chapter names a claim. In Dutch and German the terms used are *(schuld)vordering* and *Forderung*, referring directly to the English term claim. In French law the term *droit de créance* or *créance* is used. This can be translated into English as a right to a debt or a debt. The meaning is the same as in Dutch or German law, but simply considered from the perspective of the debtor, ie the person with the debt, rather than the perspective of the creditor, ie the person with the right to the debt, ie the claim. In English law the term *chose in action* is used to describe what will be referred to as a claim in this chapter.

MA Rakotovahiny, The Development of the Concept of Claim[5] **4.1 (FR)**

There are those notions like the notion of the claim that are so familiar, so widely used, that it is useless to go back to their meaning. It is this common use, though, that generates a progressive modification of the concept. … The French civil code does not contain a definition of the concept of a claim, but deals with lawful situations which can arise for the the creditor. Nevertheless, as autonomous concept and in the theory of obligations, the claim defines itself *stricto sensu* as the right of one person (the creditor) to demand of another (the debtor) a performance (in the broad sense of the term: action of abstention)

[5] MA Rakotovahiny, *L'évolution de la notion de créance*, Diss (Toulouse, 1999) 18.

R Feltkamp, The Transfer of Claims[6] **4.2 (BE)**

[A] claim can be described as a subjective right attributed to a person (the creditor), on grounds of the law or of a legal act, on grounds whereof one person or several persons (limited in number), the creditor or creditors, may claim a certain performance (to do, to omit or to give something), and in case of non-performance may claim a compensation equal to the value of the performance with the proceeds of the realisation of the patrimony of the debtor(s).

JC Van Der Steur, Boundaries of objects[7] **4.3 (NL)**

Claims generally result from an agreement or from an unlawful act (tort). By entering into an agreement, reciprocal obligations arise. Creditor and debtor oblige themselves to certain performances. A sells his boat to B. The contract of sale between A and B gives rise to two claims: A has a right to payment of the purchase price and can 'demand performance' of this payment and B has the right to the transfer of the boat and can 'demand performance' of this transfer.

PHM Gerver, H Sorgdrager and RH Stutterheim, Pitlo. The System of Dutch Private Law[8] **4.4 (NL)**

There is an active and a passive side to obligations. The active side is the relative right, the personal right, the claim, the right to a performance; the passive side is the obligation, the debt. What is a claim for the one side is the debt for the other. Claim and debt together form the legal relationship named obligation.

The legal subject on the active side is called a creditor and the legal subject on the passive side a debtor. The word obligation indicates a certain 'bond'. The debtor is the one bound. As the old saying goes: 'The debtor is bound to his word, as an ox is bound to his horns'.

The object of the obligation, ie its content, ie the performance, that to which the debtor is obliged.

Note

Claims are *in se* obligatory concepts which can be defined as 'rights to performance by a debtor'. Therefore a claim resides at the creditor, whereas the corresponding obligation rests with the debtor. If, for example, A lends B €10,000, repayable on 1 July, A's claim of €10,000 is matched by B's obligation to make due payment of €10,000. The performance due by the debtor may, generally speaking, be to do something (*facere*), not to do something (*non facere*) or to give something (*dare*).

[6] R Feltkamp, *De overdracht van schuldvorderingen. Onderzoek naar de mogelijkheid van een meer eenvormige tegenwerpbaarheidsregeling voor overdrachten in de burgerrechtelijke en handelsrechtelijke sfeer* (Antwerp, Intersentia, 2005) no 29

[7] JC Van Der Steur, *Grenzen van rechtsobjecten. Een onderzoek naar de grenzen van objecten van eigendomsrechten en intellectuele rechten* (Leiden, Kluwer, 2003) 26

[8] PHM Gerver, H Sorgdrager and RH Stutterheim, *Pitlo. Het systeem van het Nederlands Privaatrecht naar het nieuwe burgerlijk wetboek* (Arnhem, Gouda Quint, 1990) 343–44.

Question

Is it not strange to speak about contract law (claims are personal rights) in the spheres of a casebook dealing with property law?

I.B CLAIMS AS OBJECTS OF PROPERTY LAW?

Introductory Notes

(a) Now that we have seen what a claim is—a personal right to the performance by another, called the debtor—we can turn to the question whether a claim can be an object of property law. This paragraph will deal with the question whether claims can be qualified as 'things' that can be the object of property rights.

(b) It is important to realise that among academics this is a area of intense debate. Some believe that claims are valid objects of property rights and the law of property should apply to it. Therefore, ownership of a claim is possible. However, others argue that claims as such cannot be an object of property law as property law is restricted to corporeal objects, ie those objects that directly represent only a value.

J Ghestin, M Billiau and G Loiseau, The Regime of Claims and Debts[9] **4.5 (FR)**

A claim, ie the right that a person has to insist on the fulfilment of a performance from another person, is only a personal right. Or, a personal right can rationally not be the object of a property right. In fact, since the property right can be seen as a power directly exercisable on a thing, such a right cannot be exercised on a person who cannot become the object of a property right himself. Besides, the creditor, compared to an owner, does not have the power to extinguish the right to receive payment of a debt, which, however, would correspond to the right to dispose of a thing recognised by Article 544 of the French Civil Code and considered as one of the owner's powers. We will see that a debtor can oblige a creditor to accept a payment that he no longer wants. This observation, essential in that it reveals the irreducible opposition between property rights and personal rights, does not mean that the creditor cannot exercise certain rights over his right to receive payment of a debt, which are related to the assets in his patrimony, and that these rights are similar, but only similar, to those which an owner has according to Article 544 of the French Civil Code (*usus*, *fructus* and *abusus*). For instance, we can see that the assignment of a right to receive payment of a debt is largely accepted in French law. However, the creditor does not really deliver the 'ownership' of the debt; the assignment of the debt only leads to the establishment of a direct link between the debtor and the assignee by virtue of which the second is able to claim from the first the settlement of the debt with all its related ancillaries. One could also argue that the right to receive payment of a debt may be fragmented, for even though it is discussed with skill, it is still possible to establish what appears to be a usufruct on a debt. There are no statutory provsions that prohibit fragmentation of a

[9] J Ghestin, M Billiau and G Loiseau, *Le régime des créances et des dettes* (Paris, LGDJ, 2005) no 11, 12–13.

claim because of its quality as a claim; but in fact this merely leads to an adaptation of the judicial technique without pure and simple assimilation. The usufructuary of a claim does not always hold a property right on the debtor, but he has particular rights he can point out against the same debtor, nothing more. Furthermore, it could also argued that it is possible to pledge a claim though it was already demonstrated that the nature of the pledge depends precisely on its object and it would be abusive to qualify the right to pledge a claim as a property right. Ultimately, the expression of 'ownership of a claim' (or 'usufruct of a claim') is improper because the word ownership refers to a property right and the word claim is attached to the category of personal rights, giving an incompatibility as a result. As regrettable as can be its use, it can only be understood like a simple commodity, which does not prejudice the judicial regime applicable to it.

C Lebon, The Proprietary Nature of Claims[10] **4.6 (BE)**

The (increasing) importance of claims (mainly of claims for payment of a sum of money on account of the debtor) in current business transactions does not have anything to do with the outward appearance of claims as interpersonal legal relations. In … ordinary business transactions, claims are not only conceived as a legal relation which exists between at least one creditor and one debtor, but are objectivised or depersonalised as an object that constitutes an element valuable in money of the patrimony of the creditor. Claims are, as it were, made an object of property law. This 'objectivisation' of claims seems in my opinion, nevertheless, not to have penetrated, not until now, the traditional principles of Belgian private law in general and the law of property in particular. Still too often claims and especially the assignment of claims are being discussed only in the framework of contract law, and in property law related studies there are only discussions on the burden of a usufruct or a right of pledge, whereby doubts are raised explicitly to the property law related character of both of these rights. A systematic consideration of claims in property law has not yet happened in Belgian law.

W Mincke, Property: Asset or Power?[11] **4.7 (DE)**

That an obligation is enough to enrich the creditor is admitted everywhere: one of the first things we imagine, when we hear that somebody is rich, is a high bank balance. But against the bank we have no right *in re*, the legal relationship with the bank is personal. Even economists allow us to write the claims we have arising out of contracts on the credit side of the balance sheet. There must be something more than a relationship. Power is not enough either. There must be an asset worth money.

[10] C Lebon, *Het goederenrechtelijk statuut van schuldvorderingen* (Antwerp, Intersentia, 2010) no 2

[11] W Mincke, 'Property: Asset or Power? Objects or Relations as Substrata of Property Rights' in JW Harris (ed), *Property Problems. From Genes to Pension Funds* (The Hague, Kluwer, 1997) 82.

J Eggens, On the Relation between Ownership and Claim[12] **4.8 (NL)**

And this means that also the relative right of the creditor against his debtor has an absolute side: the negative position in which the creditor—as such—stands compared to third parties. And this means as well that the claim of the creditor can be called an object—thus an object in property law [*zaak*]. This is even more obvious if we consider that the creditor—in principle—may dispose of his claim. This makes clear that a claim is not only a right to claim performance, after all it does not solely contain the authorisation to demand the concerned performance of the debtor. That the creditor may dispose of his right, implies that this right is a thing, which is at his disposal, which he can change from 'mine' to 'yours' by commercial agreement of delivery.

FEJ Beekhoven van den Boezem, Non-assignability of Claims by Party Agreement[13] **4.9 (NL)**

Claims take a particular place in patrimonial law. They find themselves on the borderline between the law of obligations and the law of property. They originate and are formed in the law of obligations; however, with regard to assignment, they are mostly treated the same as objects.

GL Gretton, Ownership and its Objects[14] **4.10 (SC)**

Do we own physical things? Or rights? Or both? In ordinary speech, not only in English but also in many other languages, the answer is 'both'. People speak of ownership of books and houses, but also of the ownership of patents and of company shares. Likewise such verbs as 'buy' and 'sell' have, both in English and in many other languages, not only things but also rights as their object. One buys a book and sells a house, but one also buys a patent and sells a company share. Ordinary speech thus suggests that ownership can be of both things and of rights. This is also the language of accountancy: a balance sheet sets out the liabilities and the 'assets', and the latter lists both things (such as land, vehicles, stock-in-trade) and rights (such as receivables, bank deposits, patent). The balance sheet set out the patrimony, so it seems that the patrimony includes both things and rights. Is ordinary speech reliable when its groups things and rights together?

FH Lawson and B Rudden, The Law of Property[15] **4.11 (E&W)**

It is natural when we think of property to look first to tangible things. But in fact a great part of the world's wealth is not tangible. At the time of this writing, this country owes some £325,000,000,000 borrowed by the issue of government

[12] J Eggens, 'Over de verhouding tussen eigendom en verbintenis' in *Mededelingen der Koninklijke Nederlandse Akademie van Wetenschappen, afdeling Letterkunde*, nos 1–16 (Amsterdam, Noord-Hollandse Uitgeversmaatschappij, 1960) 198–99.

[13] FEJ Beekhoven van den Boezem, *Onoverdraagbaarheid van vorderingen krachtens partijbeding* (Groningen, 2003) 3.

[14] GL Gretton, 'Ownership and its objects' [2007] *Rabels Zeitschrift für auslandisches und internationals Privatrecht* 802–51.

[15] FH Lawson and B Rudden, *The Law of Property* (Oxford, Clarendon Law Series, 2002) 29.

bonds. Debts, by definition, must be owed to someone, so there must be creditors (human or corporate, British, foreign, or international). Their claims are so sage that they are called 'gilt-edged' or just 'gilts', and they form part of the creditor's fortune. Even more modest savers well hold National Savings certificates. When to all this are added the billions invested in stocks and shares and the billions in bank accounts, it will be seen that intangibles are a very large segment of wealth. Indeed, at the beginning of this century, those who were said to be the richest people in the world, were thought to do so because of the market value of their holdings, not of land and other tangible objects, but of shares in cyberspace companies—the 'dot.com millionaires'.

All this means that the category of intangibles is very disparate and is difficult to characterise in general terms. It is made up of quite different kinds of assets whose nomenclature is by no means settled as that of the physical world of land and goods. Furthermore, the law seems always to lag behind commerce, so that the new types of asset which are developed and eagerly traded (such as financial derivatives) take a dynamic of their own before the legal system catches up.

FH Lawson and B Rudden, The Law of Property[16] **4.12 (E&W)**

A lender (L) makes an unsecured loan of a £100 note to a borrower (B), repayable on demand (this is the essential structure of a current bank account which is in credit). ... The effect of the loan is that B owns the banknote and owes £100. If L calls for repayment and then has to sue, L will win; but of course the action can be brought only against B—no one else owes L that £100. For this reason L's claim is often called personal, to denote that the right is good against only one person. But in fact he can do nothing to B's person. The judgment will not be enforced by imprisoning B, or by forcing B to work for L. It will be enforced, if at all, only to B's property, which public officers will take and sell. If B has other debts which are due, and if their total exceeds the value of his assets, then B is insolvent, and may be made bankrupt (or 'liquidated' is B is a company). In those proceedings, L is entitled, in competition with other unsecured creditors, to repayment in whatever proportion B's assets are to B's debts

This situation is often summed up by saying that L only has a personal right—a money claim—against B, and has no property right over any specific object, which might be enforced against an indefinite number of people. This is an accurate description of the relation between L and B (although it does not quite capture the fact that the 'personal' claim is enforceable only against B's property overall). But there is more to be said about L's rights to the receivable. One simple way of doing so is to say that L owns the receivable, just as he owned the £100 note before handing it to B; that amount of cash in his assets has been replaced by a claim for the same sum. L owns this claim because it has value and because he can do anything he likes with it, and the law provides formalities to help him. He can give it to charity, sell it, mortgage it, declare himself a trustee of it, or leave it by his will. If, say, het does the first, and B goes bankrupt, then the charity will have only the same personal claim against B that L had. But is B stays solvent and L goes bankrupt, then the charity can take out of his assets the full claim: they can say to L's

[16] *Ibid*, 36.

creditors, you cannot use our property (the claim against B) to pay your debts. The treatment of the receivable as an object of property in the hands of L does not depend at all on the fact that the loan is repayable on demand. If it were payable in, say, one year, the lender's claim would at once have a present value. This figure would, of course, be less than £100, but not much less: it would be the sum which, at current interest rates, will amount to £100 in a year (at a rate of 5 per cent, that is £95.20). And as the date for repayment grows nearer, so the value of the claim rises until on that date, it amounts to £100.

To sum up: between the creditor and debtor, the receivable is a right to be paid, not an interest in any specific asset of the debtor: all that the creditor can do is compete with others for a rateable share in the body of assets belonging to the debtor. But as between the creditor and the creditor's assignees, the receivable is an asset, the subject of property rights. And if the creditor is insolvent, that receivable may belong to his assignee and thus not between the reach of the creditor's creditors.

Notes

(1) Approaches, in other words, differ. However, the approaches also share between them the recognition that claims deserve special attention. How the system of property law treats these is a controversial matter that varies from legal system to legal system.

(2) It is important to point to the difference of the discussion dealt with in this chapter and the discussion whether it is possible to qualify a claim as a property right itself, or on whether the creditor's right to the performance due by its debtor can be qualified as a property right.

JW Wilhelm, Property Law[17] **4.13 (DE)**

It is certain that the object [*Sache*] of the right of ownership is not the claim, but the subject of the claim, ie the performance respectively the subject of the performance, at which the performance is directed. This (performance or subject of the performance) is allocated through the claim to the creditor, just as object is allocated through the right of ownership to the owner. There is no additional allocation: there is not, in addition, a right of ownership on the ownership and, accordingly, there is also not an additional 'ownership' on the claim. In other words, there does not exist the—also not so logical and unenforceable—allocation of an allocation. Accordingly, the claim cannot, like an object, be the subject of a right of pledge. The pledge of an object is, under accurate legal examination, a partial transfer of ownership; identically, the pledge of a claim is the partial transfer of the claim (separation of rights from it).

F Oditah, Legal aspects of receivables financing[18] **4.14 (E&W)**

The question whether receivables are property rights has no practical utility. Conceptually, though, the question bears on the propriety of including security interests.

[17] JW Wilhelm, *Sachenrecht* (Berlin, Walter de Gruyter, 1993) no 47.
[18] F Oditah, *Legal Aspects of Receivables Financing* (London, Sweet & Maxwell, 2011) 32.

It is perhaps convenient to start the discussion by saying that a receivable, being a mere right of payment, is not an interest in any specific assets belonging to the creditor, save where the right to payment is secured. Rather the creditor is entitled to look to the fund of assets, indeterminate though this may be, belonging to the debtor for payment. A receivable is not a sum of money belonging to the creditor but in possession of the debtor. Yet the liability of the debtor to fulfil his obligation is a thing, a valuable one at that, capable of being dealt with like any other intangible property. The problem for the legal analyst lies chiefly in the fact that the orthodox analysis describes proprietary rights as those exigible against a thing, the res. Proprietary rights are defined by reference to the existence and location of a res, for the existence of proprietary rights correlates with the liability of a res, the subject-matter of the rights. But a mere unsecured debt is a purely personal right defined by reference to the existence and location of a particular debtor. How, then, does one include a receivable in the category of proprietary rights? One solution is to distinguish between real and personal rights. Real rights are those exercisable against a res and this is not less so because the res itself is a mere right. This, however, is not very helpful. What real rights creditors of an unsecured debt have? He cannot point to any real assets over which his rights exist. The difficulty is partly the result of the duality in the conception of res. Not only are tangible objects included, but also rights as such are treated as res even where the rights are good only against this debtor. Property could mean either the res, the subject of ownership, or the rights exercisable over the res. In either sense receivables could be the subject of property rights save that this is only possible in the relation between assignees and the debtor. As between the creditor and the debtor, a debt, even where secured, is but a personal obligation. And even in such case, the creditor's property is not in the debt, but in his security.

Notes

(1) It may be clear from the excerpts that at least in legal theory it is widely discussed whether claims ('rights to performance by a debtor'), being typically contract law concepts, can be qualified as 'things' that can be the object of property rights. The object of this chapter is to raise awareness of the ongoing discussions, without wanting to force a particular view on the reader.

(2) The commercial value and therefore importance of incorporeal objects in general, and claims in particular, has increased steadily in recent decades. Even a quick glance at a person's total wealth shows that claims form an important component thereof. This growing importance of claims in commerce can be seen in different parts of private law. In this context, the question arose whether claims could be the object of property rights: can claims be owned, pledged, be the object of a right of usufruct, etc? Legal scholars do not seem to agree on the (theoretically) correct answer to this question. Furthermore, this question has been dealt with differently in the examined legal systems: where in some legal systems claims can undeniably be the object of (some specific) property rights, notwithstanding their incorporeal character and their appearance as a contractual relationship between at least one creditor and one debtor, other legal systems have until now only dealt with claims in the law of obligations.

(3) Some of the following questions keep on puzzling legal scholars. What is a

claim? Is it merely an interpersonal relationship between at least one creditor and one debtor, or is it somehow (also) possible to qualify the relationship between the creditor and his claim as a relationship of belonging? A claim resides in the creditor: is the creditor the owner of the claim or does he only have a personal right against the debtor(s) involved? Is it correct that, if someone can own land, that someone can also own a right of servitude, a right of usufruct or a claim? Is it possible to argue that '[o]ne owns a personal right. Rights are things, and things can be owned. Ownership is thus merged, not with physical things, but with titularity. To have a right is to "own" it'?[19]

I.C FURTHER DELIMITATION OF THE CONTENT OF THIS CHAPTER: 'INCORPOREAL CLAIMS'

Introductory Note

In civil law jurisdictions, claims are thought to be incorporeal or intangible objects as long as they are not included or tied into a negotiable instrument or document (to order or to bearer). In such a situation the claim becomes treated as a corporeal object, because the instrument or document representing the claim is a corporeal object. In other words, when included in such a negotiable instrument, claims are considered to adopt the corporeal character of the instrument into which they are incorporated. The document is then considered to represent the claim, which for instance becomes transferable by the transfer of the document itself.[20] This chapter will only deal with incorporeal claims.

E. Dirix, Value-papers[21] **4.15 (BE)**

Incorporation of a right in a title is not merely a metaphor. The invisible claim—an incorporeal moveable thing—is actually materialised in a corporeal object, the paper, because the debtor has bound himself, but has just only bound himself, to perform at the delivery of the paper to the legitimate owner thereof. The claim with its inherent rights and duties is converted into a title on paper, a document or an entry in a register, which embodies or lays down the original claim and its inherent rights and duties.

... the conversion of transformation referred to here has far-reaching effects. Because the paper replaces the right, the extension of the right will henceforth be determined by the paper. Except for the rights (and the duties) which emerge from the paper itself the claimant cannot let other rights (and duties) apply. Only the letter of the paper counts (the literal character of the right now in writing). Expressed negatively this means that the relation supported on paper is released or abstracted from the legal relation which originally brought into existence the rights

[19] Gretton, above n 14.

[20] In English law one speaks of 'documentary intangibles': R Goode, *Commercial Law* (London, LexisNexis 2004) 29.

[21] E Dirix, 'Waardepapieren' in *Beginselen van Belgisch privaatrecht, XIII, Handels- en economisch recht*, I.A, *Ondernemingsrecht* (Brussels, Story, 1989) no 359.

and duties now described on the paper (the abstract character of the right now in writing). In other words, all rights and duties result from and find there origin in (ie are not 'caused' outside) the paper: outside of it there are no rights and duties.

FH Lawson and B Rudden, The Law of Property[22] **4.16 (E&W)**

The most general name which the common law gives to the call of intangibles is 'things in action' or 'choses in action', using the French word for 'thing' [*chose*]. … The word 'thing' catches the idea that, whatever it is, it is an asset; it has value, it can be inherited and traded, and can be reached by its holder's creditor. The phrase 'in action' is meant to convey the idea that this asset is not tangible and can be transformed into a tangible object only (if at all) by successfully suing someone.

WS Holdsworth, The History of the Treatment of Choses in Action by the Common Law[23] **4.17 (E&W)**

All personal things are either in possession or in action. The law knows no *tertium quid* between the two. It follows from this that the category of choses in action is in English law enormously wide, and that it can only be defined in very general terms. This is clear from the terms of the definition given by Channell J in *Torkington v Magee*, which is generally accepted as correct. It runs as follows: 'Chose in action' is a known legal expression used to describe all personal rights of property which can be claimed of enforced by action, and not by taken physical possession. In fact the list of choses in action known to English law includes a number of things which differ widely from one another in their essential characteristics. In its primary sense the term 'chose in action' includes all right which are enforceable by action—rights to debts all kinds, and rights of action on a contract of a right to damages for its breach; rights arising by reason of the commission of tort or other wrong; and rights to recover the ownership or possession of property real or personal. It was extended to cover the documents, such as bonds, which evidenced or proved the existence of such rights of action. This led to the inclusion in this class of things of such instruments as bills, notes, cheques, shares in companies, stock in public funds, bills of lading, and policies of insurance. But many of these documents were in effect documents to title to what was in substance an incorporeal right of property. Hence it was not difficult to include in this category things which were even more obviously property of incorporeal type, such as patent rights and copyrights. Further accessions to this long list were made by particular division of English law into common law and equity. Uses, trusts, and other equitable interests in property, though regarded by equity as conferring proprietary rights analogous to the rights recognised by law in hereditaments of in chattels, were regarded by the common law as being merely choses in action.

[22] Lawson and Rudden, above n 15, 29.

[23] WS Holdsworth, 'The History of the Treatment of Choses in Action by the Common Law' (1920) 33 *Harvard LR* 967, 967–68. See also LJ Sealy and RJA Hooley, *Commercial Law. Text, Cases and Materials* (London, LexisNexis, 2003) 903.

Note

English law would qualify the claims that are being dealt with in this chapter, as 'choses in action'. However this typical English category of objects also refers to several objects that in civil law are not regarded as incorporeal (claims): claims that are embodied in a certain written form and that can, for instance, only be transferred by way of transfer of the document do not lose their qualification as 'choses in action'. The term 'claim' used in this chapter is therefore not interchangeable with the English term chose in action. If necessary a distinction will be made.

I.D CLAIMS AS AN OBJECT OF PROPERTY LAW? DIFFERENT APPROACHES

Now that we have described and defined what a claim is, it is time to turn to the more difficult question whether a claim can be an object of property law. Legal systems take different approaches to this issue. In traditional French and Belgian law, the question whether claims in general satisfy the criteria which identify 'things' that can be objects of private property rights is rarely being dealt with as such. The text of the Civil Code does not give any general answer to this question.

It can be argued that the definition of the concept of ownership in Article 544 Civil Code (see Chapter 3) does not expressly limit the application of this right to corporeal objects. The concept of ownership of claims is nevertheless hardly ever dealt with in French or Belgian law.

In the Civil Code one finds though—more or less—explicit rules on the usufruct of claims and the pledge of claims, but it is a matter of much discussion whether these rights, having a claim as object, can still be qualified as genuine property rights.

In the traditional German Bürgerliches Gesetzbuch claims can definitely not be the object of property rights. The German law of property only deals with corporeal objects, movable or immovable, but accepts incorporeal objects to be charged with a right of usufruct or a pledge (see Chapter 3). It is discussed, though, whether in the event that a right of usufruct or a right of pledge is created on a claim, this right can nevertheless be classified as a property right.

An original approach of the position of claims in property law can be found in the new Dutch Civil Code.

The rules on property law are dealt with in both Book 3 and Book 5 of this Code. The Code separates all provisions pertaining to property rights in corporeal objects (*zakenrecht*) from those pertaining to property rights that can exist in both corporeal objects and incorporeal objects, ie patrimonial rights or *vermogensrechten.* The latter rules are to be found in Book 3, 'Patrimonial Law in General', the former in Book 5, 'Property Rights'.

Book 3 includes rules on registered property, acquisition and loss of property (including prescription), possession and *detentio* (*cf* bailment), *bewind* (*cf* the civil law trust), community property, usufruct, pledge and mortgage, as well as security rights over property. In Book 5 the right of ownership in general—complementing the general provisions of Book 3—and ownership in movable and immovable property in particular, as well as the rights and duties of neighbours, co-ownership in adjacent premises, *emphytheusis*, superficies and apartment rights are dealt with. One could designate the rights dealt with in Book 3 as 'limited property rights': 'of this genus, the rights *in re* of Book 5 constitute a species'.[24]

Claims can only be the object of several of the rights set out in Book 3 of the Dutch Civil Code, but not those dealt with in Book 5.

English law distinguishes between real and personal property, the former are interests in respect to land, and the latter is everything else. Personal property can broadly be divided in two groups: tangible movables and intangible movables (usually termed 'choses in action'). With respect to these intangibles, a further distinction can be made between documentary intangibles and pure intangibles. Documentary intangibles are embodied in a document so that the document is considered to represent the right, whereas pure intangible rights are not locked up in a document. The incorporeal claims that form the object of this chapter are therefore dealt with by English personal property law.

II. 'OWNERSHIP' OF CLAIMS

Introductory Notes

(a) This paragraph deals with 'ownership' of claims. The term ownership is placed between quotation marks because of the controversial nature of applying the right of ownership to claims and because of the ambivalent meaning of the term 'ownership' in English.[25] Generally stated, this paragraph therefore deals with property entitlement to claims.

(b) The order of discussion of the types of property rights one might create in respect to claims is inspired by French and Belgian law. In these legal systems, claims are considered movable objects. Movables can, in these jurisdictions and in civil law in general, theoretically be the object of the right of ownership, the right of co-ownership, the right of usufruct and the right of pledge. It will first be examined whether claims, as movables, can be considered as objects of the all-embracing right of ownership. Then, the possibility to create a right of co-ownership and a right of usufruct will be discussed. Security rights over claims are dealt with in Chapter 5.

[24] PPC Haanappel and E Mackaay, *New Netherlands Civil Code: Patrimonial Law—Nouveau Code Civil Néerlandais: Le Droit Patrimonial* (Deventer, Boston, Kluwer Law and Taxation Publishers, 1990) XVIII.

[25] See Chapter 1.

II.A OWNERSHIP OF INCORPOREAL OBJECTS?

Introductory Notes

(a) The discussion in civil law whether claims can be the object of ownership, mainly concerns the question on whether it is possible to own incorporeal objects in general.

(b) The statutory definition of the concept of ownership in the civil law jurisdictions considered will hereafter be the starting point of our discussion on the 'ownership' of claims.

II.A.1 FRENCH LAW

Code civil **4.18 (FR)**

Article 544 Ownership is the right to enjoy and dispose of things in the most complete manner, provided they are not used in a way prohibited by statutes or regulations.

Notes

(1) It has been argued that the French and Belgian Civil Codes do not explicitly restrict the application of the concept of ownership and fragmentations of ownership to corporeal objects. The term '*chose*' is not defined in the Codes and is therefore not restricted to corporeal or incorporeal objects. The same is true for the use of the term '*bien*' that is also sometimes used in the context of the objects of property rights.

(2) Certain authors still tend to narrow the scope of the right of ownership to corporeal objects. It has been argued that such doctrinal limitation of the concept of ownership does not follow from the literal interpretation of the definition of ownership in Article 544 of the Civil Code and can therefore not restrict the application of this right to corporeal objects. When we follow the text of the Code, a person can be the owner of a claim.

II.A.2 GERMAN LAW

Bürgerliches Gesetzbuch **4.19 (DE)**

§90 Only corporeal things are objects within the meaning of the law.

§903 The owner of a thing has the right to dispose of the thing at will and to exclude others from any interference, legal restrictions or third party rights notwithstanding.

Munich Commentary on the Civil Code[26] **4.20 (DE)**

§903 [BGB] formulates a unitary concept for the ownership of land and of movable objects in the sense of §90, but this concept is not applicable for intellectual property and for rights. Incorporeal objects like the so-called intellectual and industrial property (copyright and patent) or property entitlements based in public law are not included; nor does the BGB recognise ownership of communities of goods, eg a company [*Unternehmen*].

Note

German property law in general only deals with corporeal objects, movable or immovable. Therefore, only corporeal, ie physical or tangible, objects can be owned. German law does accept a right of pledge in respect to incorporeal objects (§1068 BGB) or a right of usufruct in respect to claims (§1273 BGB).

II.A.3 AUSTRIAN LAW

ABGB **4.21 (AT)**

§353 Everything that belongs to person, all his corporeal and incorporeal things, are called his ownership.

A Kletečka, Foundations of Private Law[27] **4.22 (AT)**

All corporeal and incorporeal objects are, following sections 353, 285, subject to the right of ownership law. Hence ownership would also be possible in respect to claims and intellectual property rights. However, several provisions of law show that that the rules of the Austrian Civil Code (ABGB) on the right of ownership (as well as the other property norms) are not completely applicable to the rights (incorporeal objects).

One must therefore differentiate between ownership in the narrow and in the broad sense. Subject of 'ownership in the broad sense' are in this regard all rights (section 285). The concept of 'ownership a claim' and other rights refers to the entitlement of the right alone. It only means that a certain right is granted to a certain person. The property rules are intended to ensure the physical control and are therefore fitted to ownership in a narrow sense.

[26] *Münchener Kommentar zum Bürgerlichen Gesetzbuch VI* (München, Verlag CH Beck, 2004) §903', no 1–2, 626–27.

[27] A Kletečka, *Grundriss des bürgerlichen Rechts Band I, Allgemeiner Teil, Sachenrecht, Familienrecht* (Vienna, Manzsche Verlags- und Universitätsbuchhandlung, 2006) 292.

OGH 28 October 1959[28] **4.23 (AT)**

PRESCRIPTION OF CLAIMS

The business premise apartment

Claims cannot be acquired by way of prescription.

Facts: The defendant had been leasing business premises and lived in the adjoining rooms to these premises. A dispute arose over the adjoining rooms between the claimant, the owner of the premises and the defendant, lessee of the business premise. The defendant argued that he had acquired a right of lease by prescription through uninterrupted possession of the rooms.

Held: Claims cannot be acquired by prescription (*ersessen*), without regard to whether they enjoy possessory protection (*Besitzschutz*) or not.

Judgment: The court of first instance ordered the defendant to hand over to the claimant houseowner the janitor's apartment consisting of two rooms, which, facing the yard, connect to the grocery's shop and its two adjoining rooms. It came to the conclusion that the defendant only had a lease right on the actual business premises and the two adjoining rooms, so that the defendant occupied the rooms mentioned in the judgment without title and that the defendant was obliged to vacate ...

The revision of the defendant is not grounded.

That the defendant had been tenant of the business premises and all adjoining rooms already from 1 May 1947 is an assertion of the revision, which is not backed up by the statement of facts of the lower court. The remarks of the plaintiff in appeal regarding the 'acquisitive prescription [*Ersitzung*] of a right to lease' are meaningless due to the fact that claims cannot be acquired by prescription, regardless of whether they—as for example property rights—enjoy protection through possessory actions or not.

Notes

(1) As to the literal wording of the Austrian Civil Code a right of ownership can be created on corporeal as well as incorporeal objects. Austrian doctrine and jurisprudence do not follow this literal interpretation of §353 ABGB: it is thought that it is not possible to establish a genuine right of ownership on incorporeal objects, such as claims.

(2) Austrian law is familiar, though, with the concept of 'belonging' (*Berechtigung*) of claims and other incorporeal objects to someone. Ownership of claims refers to the *Rechtszuständigkeit* of a claim to the creditor(s).

The judgment shows that this right of belonging may be protected against third party intervention, but that this does not mean that one can acquire (the belonging of) a claim by acquisitive prescription.

[28] EvBl 1959/405.

II.A.4 DUTCH LAW

Burgerlijk Wetboek (BW) **4.24 (NL)**

Article 3:2 Things are corporeal objects susceptible of human control.

Article 5:1 (1) Ownership is the most extensive right which a person can have in a corporeal object.

(2) To the exclusion of everybody else, the owner is free to use the object provided that this use does not violate the rights of others and that it respects the limitations based upon statutory rules and rules of unwritten law.

(3) Without prejudice to the rights of others, the owner of the object becomes owner of the fruits the object produces once separated.

HJ Snijders and EB Rank-Berenschot, Property Law[29] **4.25 (NL)**

Entitlement of rights does not fall under the definition of ownership according to Article 5:1 ...

Entitlement of claims may be defined as the most extensive right on a right. It also concerns a direct relation with a thing that is distinguished from possession and detention of rights and from *bewind* (trust) of rights in such a way that this relation is the relation with the most important status ...

The pledgee of a claim is in a less powerful position than the person entitled to the claim. The possessor who only pretends to be the person entitled to the claim, but who is not, of course has a lesser legal status than the person with the actual entitlement, as well as the administrator (*bewindvoerder*) who may act with regard to the claim, but who will never acquire the claim itself.

Notes

(1) The cited Articles of the New Dutch Civil Code differ radically from the corresponding Articles of the former Dutch Civil Code. Under the Old Dutch Civil Code both corporeal and incorporeal objects could be the subject-matter of the right of ownership (Articles 555 and 559 of the Old Dutch Civil Code).

(2) From the text of Articles 3:2 and 5:1 of the New Dutch Civil Code it can be argued that Dutch law has the same narrow approach of the right of ownership as German law. In both legal systems the application of the right of ownership is statutorily limited to corporeal objects. However, Dutch law is familiar with a certain concept of 'entitlement' of claims to somebody [*toebehoren*]. The content of this right of *toebehoren* is very similar to the right of ownership.

II.A.5 ENGLISH LAW

Introductory Notes

(a) It is a matter of debate whether property rights can be held over *choses in action* in English law. This is first and foremost so because a right to the performance

[29] HJ Snijders and EB Rank-Berenschot, *Goederenrecht* (Deventer, Kluwer, 2001) no 207.

of another party, a *chose in action*, is not considered in the same way in English law as it is in civil law systems.

(b) Moreover, English law does generally not concern itself with the question if property rights can be held in respect to these *choses in action*, nor is the assignability or the possibility to create a property security right in respect to it a decisive indication.

(c) Of the little authority there is, the following case provides an example of how an intangible thing, in this case a beneficial interest under a trust, can be treated by the law.

High Court of Chancery, 24 December 1828[30] **4.26 (E&W)**

Dearle v Hall

NOTICE REQUIREMENT FOR ASSIGNMENT

Assignment of beneficial interest

A complete property right, title, can be held on a chose in action. The rules of personal property law apply as much as possible.

Facts: Brown, a beneficiary, assigned his interest by way of security first to Dearle and then to Sherring. The trustees were not given notice of the assignments. Some years later, Brown assigned his interest to Hall. Before purchasing the interest, Hall made enquiries with the trustees and they indicated that the interest was unburdened. Hall gave the trustees notice of his assignment. Subsequently, Dearle and Sherring gave the trustees notice of their assignment.[31]

Held: Hall had received title to the beneficial interest. This title is a full property interest to which the rules of personal property law must apply whenever possible.

Judgment: Sir Thomas Plumer MR: Is there the least doubt, that, if *Zachariah Brown* had been a trader, all that was done by *Dearle* and *Sherring* would not have been in the least effectual against his assignees; but that, according to the doctrine of *Ryall* v. *Rowles*, his assignees would have taken the fund, because there was no notice to those in whom the legal interest was vested? In that case it was the opinion of all the Judges, that he who contracts for a chose in action, and does not follow up his title by notice, gives personal credit to the individual with whom he deals. Notice, then, is necessary to perfect the title,—to give a complete right *in rem*, and not merely a right as against him who conveys his interest. If you are willing to trust the personal credit of the man, and are satisfied that he will make no improper use of the possession in which you allow him to remain, notice is not necessary; for against him the title is perfect without notice. But if he, availing himself of the possession as a means of obtaining credit, induces third persons to purchase from him as the actual owner, and they part with their money before your pocket-conveyance is notified to them, you must be postponed. In being postponed, your security is not invalidated: you had priority, but that priority has not been followed up; and you have permitted another to acquire a better title to the legal possession. What was done *by Dearle* and *Sherring* did not exhaust the thing (to borrow

[30] (1828) 3 Russ 1.

[31] Sealy and Hooley, above n 23, 966.

the principle of the civil law) but left it still open to traffic. These are the principles on which I think it to be very old law, that possession, or what is tantamount to possession, is the criterion of perfect title to personal chattels, and that he, who does not obtain such possession, must take his chance.

Notes

(1) As Sir Thomas Plumer MR makes very clear in this case, he holds that the rules of personal property law should apply as much as is possible to *choses in action*. It is impossible to hold that this is now the leading opinion in English law, as further authority is missing. It does, however, show that at least occasionally the approach is very much the same as in civil law.

(2) As an approach therefore it can be useful to ask the question first how a case would be decided when the subject matter would have been a chattel and then apply the rules of personal property law to the *chose in action* under consideration.

II.A.6 COMPARATIVE REMARKS

The overview of the legal definitions of ownership leads to some unexpected conclusions:

(1) Both the German and Dutch definition of the right of ownership limits the application of this right to corporeal objects. Nevertheless, Dutch law is familiar with the ownership-like concept of 'belonging' (*toebehoren*) of claims to somebody.

(2) The Austrian Civil Code defines ownership as the most prominent property right that can be created on both corporeal and incorporeal objects. Austrian doctrine and jurisprudence, however, do not recognise the possibility of establishing a genuine right of ownership on incorporeal objects, such as claims. A concept of 'belonging' (*Berechtigung*) is known though.

(3) The French and Belgian Civil Code do not include indications as to the limitation of the application of ownership to corporeal objects. In doctrine similar limitations have been defended, however.

(4) In English law the classification of the *chose in action* in personal property law remains difficult. This remains a point that is generally debated in English law, but textbooks on personal property law seem to have no problem including them in their treatment of the law.

Questions

(1) The question arises why the concept of ownership should be limited to corporeal objects only?

(2) Are there, next to their incorporeal character, arguments why claims should better not be the object of ownership? What to think, for instance, of the argument that owning a claim is in fact owning a person, ie the debtor, and that therefore, if one would accept that claims can be owned, one in fact reintroduces slavery into modern society?

(3) What is precisely the object of ownership if one talks about ownership of a claim? How could one accurately describe ownership of claims?

II.B ACQUISITION OF (THE OWNERSHIP OF) CLAIMS

Now that we have discussed the possibility to own claims, we may turn to the question of how to acquire the ownership of a claim. Because a claim does not exist physically, it is sometimes difficult to apply the default property rules to this type of object. For example, the default rule for delivery by handing over possession is impossible because, as we have seen already, a claim can generally not be possessed.[32] These default rules for transfer are dealt with in Chapter 8.

We will first look at ways to acquire the ownership of claims (II.B.1), after which we will deal with the assignment (transfer) of claims (II.B.2).

II.B.1 TRANSPOSITION OF THE PRINCIPLES ON THE ACQUISION OF OWNERSHIP OF CORPOREAL OBJECTS?

Introductory Notes

(a) Chapters 7 and 8 of this casebook deal with the subject of acquisition and distinguish between original and derivative acquisition of ownership. In the case of original acquisition one receives a right that did not previously exist, which originates in the hands of the new owner or holder of the right. In the case of derivative acquisition one receives a right that previously belonged to someone else.

(b) One might want to transpose the fundamental rules on the acquisition of ownership with regard to corporeal objects to the acquisition of ownership or of a certain right or the entitlement to claims.

JM Mousseron, Values, Things, Rights[33] **4.27 (FR)**

It is ... interesting to note that, as the theory of Lavoisier affirms, 'nothing is lost, nothing is created, everything is transformed', the rule does not apply to intangible objects. If the tangible objects spring from the continuous transformation of previous objects, the intangible objects are the only objets that are properly created, to appear not as a transformation of previous objects but as fully new objects, not with transformed values with or without surplus value but especially with new values. The objects that they express in the legal organisation and the rights that they have as subject-matter must, therefore, be neither of tangible objects, nor of previous rights.

A Pelissier, Possession of Movable Intangibles[34] **4.28 (FR)**

The possession of incorporeal movables is capable to carry out the same acquisitive function as the possession of corporeal movables. The same rules apply inevitably to the same needs, and it was possible for us to demonstrate that questions relating to the acquisition of privative rights in incorporeal movables are similar to those for corporeal movables.

[32] On the acquisition of ownership and ways to transfer, see Chapter 7.

[33] JM Mousseron, 'Valeurs, biens, droits' in *Mélanges en hommage à André Breton et Fernand Derrida* (Paris, Dalloz, 1991) no 13.

[34] A. Pelissier, *Possession et meubles incorporels* (Paris, Dalloz, 2001) no 474.

C Lebon, The Proprietary Nature of Claims[35] **4.29 (BE)**

Every legal fact or every legal act, from which a new claim in the person of a creditor arises, is rightly seen as a special way of an original acquisition of ownership of claims.

With the coming into existence of a claim in his person, a person not only becomes creditor, he acquires in his capacity as creditor also the immediate right of ownership on that claim. The described acquisition of ownership can, in my opinion, be considered as a manner of acquisition of ownership of a thing which belongs to nobody, modified and adapted to suit claims through taking possession or occupation.

There are numerous examples of the coming into existence of a claim and the associated acquisition of ownership in the person of the creditor. Such an acquisition clearly occurs with the conclusion of a contract, in which one of more claims may arise in favour of one or every involved party. Also, for example, the commission of a tort can give rise, in the person of the victim, of an original acquisition of a claim to repair the harm done, which is enforceable against the perpetrator.

JWA Biemans, 'Seven Questions on the Acquisitive Prescription of Claims'[36] **4.30 (NL)**

The original acquisition of a claim that does not exist before is equal to the creation of an obligation. When an obligation is created, a claim is acquired by original acquisition, and vice versa. The most important grounds of creation of obligations are to be found in Book 6 BW. Usually two persons are involved in the creation of an obligation, but this is not necessarily so. Obligations are also created through the acquisition of a claim by assuming a provision in favour of a third party (Art 6:253 BW), the acquisition of a claim by the active debtor (*novatie*) and the acquisition of a right of insurance by the insured (*verzekerde*) which is derived from an insurance, which another, the policyholder, has concluded with the insurer. An original acquisition of a claim is also at hand in case of a regress, if the paying debtor receives a right of recovery (*verhaalsrecht*) from his joint debtors, and in case of the acquisition of rights of third parties against the principal pursuant to Art. 7:421 BW.

Notes

(1) Some authors tend to adopt a progressive approach on the acquisition of claims and smoothly transpose the principles on the acquisition of corporeal objects to the acquisition of claims. This leads to very interesting, though controversial, standpoints given the specific nature and character of claims—eg how do claims come into existence? Is it possible to qualify all relationships from which an obligation arises as analogous to the acquisition of ownership or some right of belonging of that claim by the involved creditor?

(2) What if a claim does not directly come into existence into the hands of the creditor? Suppose, for instance, that B is the keeper of A's collection of Harry Potter books and that B sells these books to C (C acts in good faith, he is a bona fide

[35] Lebon, above n 10, no 176.

[36] JWA Biemans, 'Zeven vragen over de verkijgende verjaring van vorderingen' [2007] *NTBR* 96.

purchaser,[37] being unaware of the fact that B is not the owner of these books). B has a claim against C for payment of the price of the books. B becomes insolvent. What is the status of the claim for payment of the price in B's insolvency estate? Is it possible to argue that A became the owner of the claim for payment of the price of his books?

(3) Is it possible to acquire ownership of a claim through acquisitive prescription, bearing in mind that claims may also be destroyed through extinctive prescription?[38]

II.B.2 ASSIGNMENT OF CLAIMS

The most prominent example of a derivative acquisition of ownership of a claim is through assignment. Assignment is the term used for the transfer of incorporeal objects, including claims. Assignment of a claim is usually effected by a contract aimed at transferring the right of ownership.

The standard transfer rules of property law do not automatically apply to claims as many of the criteria, most notably possession, cannot be (automatically) applied with respect to claims. Therefore, an analogous 'transfer' system exists for claims. Generally stated, the rules for the assignment of claims follow the default transfer rules as much as possible, but significant differences exist. The default transfer rules are dealt with in Chapter 8 of this casebook.

Assignment of claims is one of the most relevant aspects of modern-day property law, especially because, as will be seen in Chapter 5, the assignment for security purposes, ie the transfer of claims to serve as collateral for the securing of repayment of a debt, is one of the most common forms of modern-day finance.

II.B.2.a General principles

Introductory Notes

(a) The assignment of claims can be defined as a transaction whereby a right to performance by a debtor ('claim') is transferred from the creditor ('assignor') to another person ('the assignee'). Generally, the debtor of the assigned claim ('*debitor cessus*') is not involved in the assignment; he does not have to agree with the assignment and the replacement of the original creditor by another creditor.

(b) In Roman law, claims could not be assigned. This view was based on the idea that the original creditor(s) and the original debtor(s) of a claim were the qualifying counterparts of a claim. It was thought that the replacement of one of these original subjects would mean that the original claim would cease to exist.[39] In modern-day private law, the assignment of claims is commonly accepted and regulated by law.

[37] On the rules concerning the protection of the bona fide purchaser and third party protection, see Chapter 9.

[38] The rules on prescription are dealt with in Chapter 9.

[39] G Baudry-Lacantinerie and L Barde, *Traité théorique et pratique de droit civil, XIV, Les obligations* (Paris, Sirey, 1908) no 1763, 81–82; Y. Hannequart, 'La transmission des obligations' in *Les novelles. Corpus Juris Belgici, Droit civil*, t IV, vol II (Brussels, Larcier, 1958) nos 1–4; P Jors, W Kunkel, L Wenger, H Honsell, et al, 'Römisches Recht', in *Enzyklopädie der Rechts- und Staatswissenschaft* (Berlin, Springer Verlag, 1987) 268; M Kaser, *Das Römische Privatrecht, I, Das altrömische, das vorklassische*

(c) German law offers a very good description and illustration of assignment of claims. Therefore, this paragraph will start with German law and proceed with the other legal systems after that.

(i) German law

Bürgerliches Gesetzbuch **4.31 (DE)**

§398 Assignment

A claim may be assigned by the creditor to another person by contract with that person (assignment). With conclusion of the contract, the new creditor (the assignee) takes over the position of the previous creditor.

§407 Legal acts in relation to the previous obligee

(1) The new creditor must allow performance of the claim by the debtor to the previous creditor after the assignment, as well as any legal transaction undertaken after assignment between the debtor and the previous creditor in respect of the claim, to be asserted against him, unless the debtor is aware of the assignment upon performance or upon undertaking of the legal transaction.

(2) If, in a legal dispute that became pending at court between the debtor and the previous creditor after the assignment, a final and non-appealable judgment in respect of the claim has been rendered, the new creditor must allow the judgment to be asserted against him, unless the debtor was aware of the assignment at the time when legal proceedings became pending.

§409 Notice of assignment

(1) If the creditor gives notice to the debtor that he has assigned the claim, then he must allow the notified assignment to be asserted against him in relation to the debtor, even if it does not occur or is not effective. It is equivalent to the notice if the creditor has drawn a document [*Urkunde*] about the assignment to the new creditor described in the document and the latter presents it to the debtor.

(2) The notice can only be retracted with the consent of the person who has been designated as the new creditor.

GH Roth, Munich Commentary on the Civil Code[40,41] **4.32 (DE)**

§398 permits that, in the context of a legal transaction, the person who is a creditor in an existing contractual claim is changed. ...

und klassische Recht (München, CH Beck, 1971) §112, 478, no 6; GH Maier, 'Zur Geschichte der Zession' in W Kunkel and HJ Wolf (ed), *Festschrift für Ernst Rabel, II, Geschichte der antiken Rechte und allgemeine Rechtslehre* (Tübingen, JCB Mohr, 1954) 205; JE Spruit, *Cunabula iuris. Elementen van het Romeinse privaatrecht* (Deventer, Kluwer, 2001) no 791; R Zimmermann, *The Law of Oligations. Roman Foundations of the Civilian Tradition* (Cape Town, Juta, 1990) 58.

[40] GH Roth, 'Münchener Kommentar zum Bürgerlichen Gesetzbuch' in W Krüger (red), *Münchener Kommentar zum Bürgerlichen Gesetzbuch, II, Schuldrecht. Allgemeiner Teil. §§241–432. FernAbsG* (Munich, CH Beck, 2001) §398, no 1.

[41] Also: J Busche in M Löwisch (red), *J von Staudinger Kommentar zum Bürgerlichen Gesetzbuch mit Einführungsgesetz und Nebengesetze, II, Recht der Schuldverhältnisse. §§397–432* (Berlin, Sellier, 1999) §398, nos 1–4.

The new creditor takes the place of the former creditor (§398 S2). This causes a curious 'reification' of the claim, irrespective of its nature as relative right.

The assignment of the claim is an act of disposal of the same type as the act of disposal in respect to absolute rights.

Notes

(1) Under German law the rules on the assignment of claims form part of the statutory regulation of the general law of obligations (Book 2 BGB). German doctrine generally accepts that the assignment resorts both obligatory and proprietary effect.

(2) The assignment of a claim becomes effective with the agreement between assignor and assignee to transfer the right or claim (§398 BGB). Notification is not required for the effectiveness of the assignment. The agreement between the assignor and the assignee to transfer the claim is thought to be independent of the underlying contract between the assignor and assignee wherein the assignment as such was agreed to. This is an application of the *Abstraktionsprinzip* (principle of abstraction) dealt with in more detail in Chaper 8. The *Abstraktionsprinzip* means that the invalidity of the underlying contract does not affect the validity of the transfer agreement.

(3) After informal notification of the assignment (§409 BGB) or if the debtor has acquired knowledge of the assignment otherwise (§407 BGB), the debtor of the assigned claim can only discharge its obligation by performing to the new creditor (the *assignee*).

(ii) French law

Code Civil **4.33 (FR)**

Article 1690 An assignee is vested with regard to third parties only by notice of the assignment served upon the debtor.

Nevertheless, the assignee may likewise be vested by acceptance of the assignment given by the debtor in an authentic act [*acte authentique*].

Article 1691 Where, before the debtor has been given notice by the assignor or the assignee, the debtor has paid the assignor, he is lawfully discharged.

Monetary and Financial Code, 'Loi Dailly'[42] **4.34 (FR)**

Article L313-23. Any credit which a credit institution grants to a private-law or public-law corporation, or to a natural person for use in connection with his business activities, may give rise to the assignment or pledge by the beneficiary of the credit of any claim which it may hold on a third party private-law or public-law corporation, or natural person if it relates to his business activities, for the benefit of that institution, by simply submitting an advice note.

Cash claims which are due and payable may be assigned or pledged. Claims resulting from a deed which has already been executed, or which is yet to be executed but

[42] Inserted by Order No 2000-1223 of 14 December 2000, OJ 16 December 2000.

whose amount and due date are not yet determined, may also be assigned or pledged.

The advice note must include the following elements:

1. The designation 'deed of assignment of claims' or 'deed of pledge of claims', as applicable;

2. An indication to the effect that the document is subject to the provisions of Articles L313-23 to L313-34;

3. The name of the credit institution which is the beneficiary;

4. The designation or individualisation of the claims granted or pledged, or of the elements likely to create that designation or that individualisation, particularly by indication of the debtor, the place of payment, the amount of the claims or of their valuation and, if applicable, their due date.

However, when transmission of the claims assigned or pledged is effected via a computer process which makes it possible to identify them, the advice note may merely indicate, in addition to the elements indicated in 1, 2 and 3 above, the means through which they are transmitted, the number thereof and their global amount.

In the event of a query being raised concerning the existence or transmission of one of the claims, the assignee may prove, by any means possible, that the claim to which the query relates is included in the global amount shown on the advice note.

A document from which one of the above indications is missing does not constitute a valid deed of assignment or pledge of claims within the meaning of Articles L313-23 to L313-34.

Article L313-24 Even when it is effected by way of guarantee and without stipulation of a price, the assignment of claims transfers title to the assigned claims to the assignee.

Unless otherwise agreed, the signatory of the deed of assignment or the deed of pledge is a jointly and severally liable guarantor of payment of the assigned or pledged claims.

Article L313-27 The assignment or pledge takes effect between the parties and becomes binding on third parties on the date indicated on the advice note when it is submitted, regardless of the origination date, maturity date or due date of the claims, without any other formality being necessary, and regardless of the law applicable to claims and the law of the country of domicile of the debtors.

From that date onwards, the customer of the credit institution indicated as the beneficiary on the advice note cannot alter the scope of the rights attached to the receivables represented by the advice note without that institution's consent.

Service of the notification shall automatically entail transfer of the sureties, guarantees and accessories attached to each claim, including the mortgage sureties, and its enforceability against third parties without any other formality being necessary.

In the event of the date indicated on the advice note being challenged, the credit institution may prove the accuracy thereof by any means possible.

Notes

(1) The rules on the assignment of claims contained in the French Civil Code are original provisions of the Code Napoléon of 1804. At that time, assignment was

considered a special kind of sale of goods; rules on the assignment of claims are therefore included in the section of the Code that deals with the contract of sale.

(2) Under the French Civil Code, an assignment becomes effective between the assignor and the assignee at the time of conclusion of the contract of assignment between both parties. This is an application of the general rule of the consensual system of transfer.[43] With respect to the *debitor cessus* and all other third parties, the assignment only becomes effective after formal notification to the debtor (*signification*) through service of a document by a bailiff or after acceptance of the assignment by the debtor in an authentic act.

(3) In 1981 the French legislature wanted to facilitate the extension of credit to enterprises and elaborated for that purpose, the so-called 'Loi Dailly'.[44] The new rules on the assignment of claims, laid down in Article L313-23 and following of the Code monétaire et financier (Monetary and Financial Code), greatly deviate from the strict requirements of effectiveness set forward in the Civil Code.

(4) Under the application of these new provisions, enterprises can assign a claim or large numbers of claims to a credit institution by delivering a detailed list of these claims to the credit institution (advice notice; '*bordereau*', see Article L313-23 Monetary and Financial Code) which thereupon extends credit to the enterprise. The assignment becomes effective between the assignor and the assignee and has third-party effect as from the date of the advice notice (Article L313-27 Monetary and Financial Code).

(iii) Belgian law

Code civil **4.35 (BE)**

Article 1690 The assignment can be invoked against third parties other than the assignee through formation of the contract of transfer.

The assignment can only be invoked against the assignee from the moment that it is notified to the debtor or is recognised by the latter.

If the assignor transfers the same rights to different assignees, priority is established in accordance with the date of notification of the transfer of the transferred receivable to the debtor and provided that the transferee has acted in good faith.

The assignment cannot be invoked against a good faith creditor of the assignor to whom the good faith debtor of the assigned claim has paid before the transfer was notified to him.

Article 1691 The good faith debtor who has paid before the transfer was notified to him or was acknowledged by him, will be released.

The good faith debtor can invoke the consequences of every legal act, that has been stated in regard of the assignor, towards the assignee, before the transfer was notified to him or was acknowledged by him.

[43] See Chapter 8.

[44] Loi no 81-1 of 2 January 1981.

Notes

(1) In the Belgian Civil Code, as well as in the French Civil Code, the assignment of claims has been regulated in the section of the code that deals with the contract of sale.

(2) The cited Articles 1690 and 1691 from the French Civil Code were in Belgium abolished by the law of 6 July 1994.[45] The legislature's goal was to get rid of the formal and, especially, expensive requirements for effectiveness of the assignment against third parties.

(3) The effectiveness of the assignment against third parties, under present Belgian law, no longer depends on any notification: the requirement of notification by a bailiff or the acceptance of the assignment by the debtor in an authentic deed have been neutralised by the law of 1994 (Article 1690 §1 (2) Cciv). Exceptions on this rule are laid down in Article 1690 §1 (3) and (4) Cciv.

The effectiveness of the assignment against the *debitor cessus* (against whom the assignment resorts obligatory effect) depends on an informal notification of the assignment or the informal acceptance of the assignment by the *debitor cessus*.

(iv) Dutch law

Burgerlijk Wetboek **4.36 (NL)**

Article 3:83 (1) Ownership, limited property rights and claims are transferrable, except if the law or the nature of the right precludes a transfer.

(2) The transferability of claims can be excluded by agreement between the debtor and creditor.

(3) All other rights are only transferable, where the law so provides.

Article 3:84 (1) A transfer of property requires delivery pursuant to a valid title, performed by the person entitled to dispose of the thing.

(2) Through the title, the property must be described in a sufficiently precise manner.

(3) A legal act which has as its object the transfer of property for security purpose, or which lacks the purpose of letting the property fall into the patrimony of the acquirer after delivery, is not a valid title for delivery of that property.

(4) Where delivery is made for the execution of a conditional obligation, merely a right which is subject to the same conditions as the obligation is conferred.

Article 3:94 (1) In cases other than those provided for in the preceding Article, rights to be exercised against one or more specifically determined persons are delivered by means of a deed intended for that purpose and notice thereof given to those persons by the alienator or acquirer.

(2) The delivery of a right which is to be exercised against a specifically determined, although on the day when the deed is drawn up still unknown, person and which belongs to the alienator is retroactive until that day, if notice is given with all due speed, after the person has become known.

[45] Wet van 6 juli 1994 tot wijziging van de wet van 17 juni 1991 tot organisatie van de openbare kredietsector en van het bezit van de deelnemingen van de openbare kredietsector in bepaalde privaatrechtelijke financiële vennootschappen, alsook van de wet van 22 maart 1993 op het statuut van en het toezicht op de kredietinstellingen, *Belgian Official Gazette* 15 July 1994, 18625.

(3) These rights can also be delivered by an authentic deed or registered private document for that purpose, without notice thereof given to the persons against which the rights must be exercised, provided that these rights already exist on the moment of the delivery or will be immediately acquired from an already existing legal relationship. The delivery is not enforceable against the persons against whom these rights must be exercised, then after notice thereof given to these persons by the alienator or acquirer. Art 88 sub 1 may only be applied to the acquirer of a right that is delivered in accordance with the first sentence, if he is in good faith on the moment of the notice mentioned in the second sentence.
(4) The persons against whom the rights must be exercised may require an extract of the deed authenticated by the alienator and his title. Conditions that are of no interest to these persons do not need to be included therein. If no deed is drawn up of a title, its content must be delivered in writing insofar as it is of importance to the persons.

Notes

(1) Provisions on assignment of claims are included in Book 3 of the Dutch Civil Code, which deals with property rights on both objects and rights, and in Book 6, which contains the regulation of the general law of obligations.[46]

(2) A former version of Article 3:94 of the Dutch Civil Code set forward that the validity of an assignment of a claim could only be required by delivery of the claim by means of a deed intended for that purpose and by notice thereof given by the assignor or the assignee to the *debitor cessus*.

(3) In 2004, a new paragraph 3 was added to Article 3:94. Under the present Dutch law, the validity of an assignment can also be acquired by delivery of an authentic deed or registered private document, without any notification to the *debitor cessus*.[47] This type of assignment is known as a silent assignment [*stille cessie*] in Dutch law.

[46] C Asser, FHJ Mijnssen and P De Haan, *Zakenrecht, I, Algemeen goederenrecht, in Mr C Asser's Handleiding tot de beoefening van het Nederlands burgerlijk recht* (Zwolle, Tjeenk Willink, 1992) no 271; WHM Reehuis and AHT Heisterkamp, *Goederenrecht, in Pitlo. Het Nederlands burgerlijk recht* (Deventer, Gouda Quint, 2001) no 256; HLE Verhagen and MHE Rongen, *Cessie. De overdracht van schuldvorderingen op naam, in Preadviezen uitgebracht voor de Vereniging voor Burgerlijk Recht* (Deventer, Kluwer, 2001).

[47] This new provision was heavily discussed by Dutch authors: MHE Rongen and HLE Verhagen, 'De cessie naar huidig en komend recht: de cirkel is weer rond' [2003] *WPNR* no 6546, 679–93; AF Salomons, 'Het wetsvoorstel tot aanpassing van artikel 3:94 BW: Nederland introduceert de "stille cessie"' [2003] *WPNR* no 6546, 670–75; JHM Van Erp, 'Het wetsontwerp mededelingsvereiste bij cessie: aanleiding tot een fundamentele heroverweging van ons goederenrecht?' [2003] WPNR no 6546, 675–79; AJ Verdaas, 'De stille cessie is welkom, maar kent nog één gebrek' [2003] WPNR no 6546, 669–70; WJ Zwalve, 'Art 3:94 BW. Zo moet het niet!' [2003] *WPNR* no 6546, 667–68.

(v) English law

MP Furmston, Chesfire, Fifoot and Furmston's Law of Contract[48] **4.37 (E&W)**

At common law a chose in action, such as a right arising under a contract, could not be assigned so as to entitle the assignee to sue for its recovery in his own name. The assignment gave the assignee a right against the assignor personally, but not an independent right of action against the debtor. An action for recovery had to be brought by or in the name of the assignor, and this depended upon the willingness of the assignor to lend his name to the proceedings. The assignee could enforce payment by taking a power of attorney authorising him to sue on behalf of the assignor, but in this case he recovered the debt not as assignee, but as directly representing the person of the assignor. The common law rule was subject to two exceptions, for from the earliest times it was recognised that the Crown might make or take an assignment of choses in action; and with the growth of the doctrine of negotiability rights under bills of exchange and promissory notes became freely assignable.

The notion that a contractual right is incapable of transfer represents an archaic and inconvenient view, and it is therefore not remarkable that it was soon repudiated by equity. As early as the beginning of the seventeenth century the Court of Chancery recognised and enforced the assignment of choses in action generally. …

An equitable assignment could not of course transfer the right of action at law, but it conferred upon the assignee the right to invoke the aid of equity. Equity considers that as done which ought to be done, and, since the parties have agreed that the common law right under the contract is the property of the assignee, the assignor must allow an action at law to be brought in his own name so as to make the transaction effectual. …

No particular form is required to constitute a valid equitable assignment. The transaction upon which the assignee relies need not even purport to be an assignment nor use the language of an assignment. If the intention of the assignor clearly is that the contractual right shall become the property of the assignee, then equity requires him to do all that is necessary to implement his intention. The only essential and the only difficulty is to ascertain that such is the intention.

Law of Property Act 1925, section 136(1) **4.38 (E&W)**

Any absolute assignment by writing under the hand of the assignor (not purporting to be by way of charge only) of any debt or other legal thing in action, of which express notice in writing has been given to the debtor, trustee or other person from whom the assignor would have been entitled to claim such debt or thing in action, is effectual in law (subject to equities having priority over the right of the assignee) to pass and transfer from the date of such notice—

(a) the legal right to such debt or thing in action;
(b) all legal and other remedies for the same; and

[48] MP Furmston, *Chesfire, Fifoot and Furmston's Law of Contract* (London, Butterworths, 2001) 562–63.

(c) the power to give a good discharge for the same without the concurrence of the assignor:

Provided that, if the debtor, trustee or other person liable in respect of such debt or thing in action has notice—

(a) that the assignment is disputed by the assignor or any person claiming under him; or

(b) of any other opposing or conflicting claims to such debt or thing in action;

he may, if he thinks fit, either call upon the persons making claim thereto to interplead concerning the same, or pay the debt or other thing in action into court under the provisions of the Trustee Act, 1925.

MP Furmston, Cheshire, Fifoot and Furmston's Law of Contract[49] **4.39 (E&W)**

There are three conditions that must be satisfied if an assignment is to derive validity from the statute:

it must be absolute;

it must be written; and

written notice must be given to the debtor.

It there is a failure to comply with either of the last two conditions, or if compliance with the first is impossible, as, for instance, where the assignment is conditional or by way of charge, the transaction is not void. It is void as a statutory assignment but is still stands as a perfectly good equitable assignment. This means that the assignee of the legal chose in action cannot take advantage of the new machinery set up by the Act and bring an action in his own name, but must fall back upon the rules governing equitable assignments and join the assignor as a party. It is still the law that an assignee of a legal chose in action, who for some reason or other cannot prove a good statutory assignment, must make the assignor either a co-plaintiff or a co-defendant to any action that he brings.

The statute has not altered the law in substance. It is merely machinery. It does not confer a right of action which did not exist before, but enables the right of action that has always existed to be pursued in a less roundabout fashion.

Notes

(1) At common law it was, just like in ancient Roman law, not possible to assign claims in such a way that the assignee succeeded the assignor as creditor against the debtor. The assignee could not get an independent right of action against the debtor.

(2) Gradually an equitable form of assignment was developed. However, not every equitable assignment had the effect that the assignee acquired a right of action against the debtor. The effect of an equitable assignment depended, first, upon the nature of the assigned right and, secondly, upon the nature of the assignment as such. The assignee either got a personal right to sue the debtor in his own name, or was not entitled to such right and was only able to sue the debtor by joining the assignor as a party.

[49] *Ibid*, 567.

(3) The Law of Property Act 1925 introduced a statutory form of assignment, by which the assignee of a legal *chose in action* (ie a right that can be enforced by an action at law, such as for instance a contractual claim) acquired an action to sue the debtor in his own name. This new rule was introduced by the legislature because, under the existing system of equitable assignments of legal choses in action, a claim based on the involved chose in action was very cumbersome.

In the event that the assignment does not meet the requirement of section 136 of the Law of Property Act 1925, the assignment will not be considered a statutory assignment, but might be upheld as an equitable assignment provided that the intention to assign is clear.

(4) Written notice to the debtor is necessary to complete the title of one who claims to be a statutory assignee under section 136 of the Law of Property Act. The assignment becomes effective at the date on which this written notice is received by or on behalf of the debtor. Such notice is, however, not necessary to perfect an equitable assignment. Even without notice to the debtor, the title of the assignee is complete. There are several reasons why failure to give notice may seriously prejudice the title of an equitable assignee: the assignee is firstly bound by payments which the debtor made to the assignor in ignorance of the assignment and secondly notice will protect the assignee against other assignees of the same claim (*Dearle v Hall*, 4.47 (E&W)).

(vi) Comparative remarks

Although the assignment of claims is mainly dealt with by the law of obligations, the assignment of claims has, in fact, both obligatory and proprietary effects.

First, the assignment of a claim results in the replacement of the creditor-assignor by the assignee. The assignee will succeed the assignor as creditor in the obligatory relation with his debtor. After the assignment the *debitor cessus* is confronted with a new creditor. The assignment has obligatory effects vis-à-vis the debitor cessus.

The assignment of a claim, however, also has proprietary effects, as a claim that forms part of the set of assets and debts (estate) of the assignor will become part of the set of assets and debts of the assignee. This transfer of the claim has effect *erga omnes* (against everyone). Moreover, the proprietary effects of an assignment in the relation between assignor and assignee and against third parties, other than the *debitor cessus*, are heavily debated.

II.B.2.b Priority in case of one or more subsequent assignments

Introductory Note

The default property law rules, especially the requirement to surrender possession, prevent a transferor from making multiple transfers of the same object. As a result the law must decide on who becomes owner of the object. When it comes to the rules of assignment it is sometimes possible that an assignor assigns the same claim more than once. The question arises which assignee will get priority over the other(s) and will be able to address the debtor?

J Busche, U Noack and V Rieble, J von Staudingers Commentary on the Civil Code[50] **4.40 (DE)**

When the original creditor has transferred the claim subsequently more than once, only the first acquirer has effectively acquired the claim (principle of priority). With the conclusion of the first contract of assignment the claim is separated from the patrimony of the former creditor, who has lost the power to dispose. The assignor cannot when concluding a second or further contract of assignment effectively assign the claim to another. However, the second assignment may become effective with approval of the first assignee according to paragraph 185. Protection of good faith in favour of a future purchaser of the claims does not exist in the law of assignment of claims. When a claim is assigned to different individuals at the same time none of the assignments is effective

J Ghestin, M Billiau and G Loiseau, The Regime of Claims and Debts[51] **4.41 (FR)**

The fulfilment of the formalities of the Article 1690 of the Civil Code is important, because it allows resolution of the conflicts between several assignees of a same claim. Indeed, when the same claim is assigned twice and to two different assignees, in the forms of the assignment of the Civil Code, it is not the date of the assignment that has to be taken into consideration in order to determine who gains the claim, but the date of the notification to the debtor or the debtor's acceptance of the transfer.

E. Dirix, Form-free Assignment[52] **4.42 (BE)**

It is imaginable that a creditor assigns his claims subsequently to two different persons. Taking into account the basic principle of Article 1690, paragraph 1, one would expect that this conflict would be solved on the basis of the anteriority of the respective assignments. However, Article 1690, paragraph 3, prefers the one whose transfer was firstly brought to the attention of the debtor (or was acknowledged by him). This solution deserves the approval in the light of third party protection. The intervention of a third party, namely the *debitor cessus*, offers more securities to third parties on the anteriority of the assignment. This is, however, at odds with the basic principle of the law, namely the assignment free of form which is objectable *erga omnes*. ....

So if A transfers the claim on C successively to B and D and it is D who first gives notice, then D comes before B. This priority is, however, dependent on his good faith. This good faith must, according to the law, be judged on the moment of the notice (and therefore not on the moment of the assignment).

[50] J Busche, U Noack and V Rieble, *J von Staudingers Kommentar zum Bürgerlichen Gesetzbuch mit Einführungsgesetz und Nebengesetzen Buch 2—Recht de Schuldverhältnisse* (Berlin, Sellier, 1995) '§398', no 32.

[51] Ghestin, Billiau and Loiseau, above n 9, no 321.

[52] E Dirix, 'De vormvrije cessie' in E Dirix, I Peeters, G Van Haegenborgh and A Verbeke, *Overdracht en inpandgeving van schuldvorderingen* (Antwerp, Kluwer, 1995) no 13.

HJ Snijders and EB Rank-Berenschot, Property Law[53] **4.43 (NL)**

Notification as constitutive requirement.

Under the old law the notification was not part of the constitutive requirement for the assignment. Through the deed the assignment became effective, although the assignee, who did not and could not know of the assignment, could still pay the assignor on the basis of Article 1422 (old) Dutch Civil Code. By now considering the notification as a constitutive requirement for the delivery, the legislature more adequately gives shape to the requirement of publicity for property rights. At the same time he furthers—which is also the function of the publicity requirement—the need for legal certainty: now, it is sooner clear for third parties than before whether an assignment has or has not been effected. …

In case a claim has been assigned twice then only one of the parties of the assignor can become assignee. That is not simply the one who can refer to the oldest deed of assignment, but the one in regard of whom both requirements deed of assignment and notification are first satisfied.

HLE Verhagen and MHE Rongen, Assignment[54] **4.44 (NL)**

By making notification a constitutive requirement for the delivery, fake assignments and multiple assignments (by the same assignor) would be discouraged because of the publicity involved. This argument is not convincing. The publicity involved with the notification is of restricted value. It should be questioned whether the *debitor cessus* is the appropriate person to act as the 'registrar of mortgages'. The administration of the *debitor cessus* can be unreliable, as a result of which he is no longer informed about the earlier assignment. He can even conspire with the assignor. Fixing the date of the assignment—an advantage connected to the notification—is realised more effectively by registering the deed of assignment at the Inspection of registration and succession.

WHM Reehuis, Delivery of a Claim: On Public and Silent Assignment[55] **4.45 (NL)**

For the public civil law assignment, regulated in Article 3:94 part 1 [of the Dutch Civil Code], notification is, besides the drawing up of a deed, a constitutive requirement. The law does not provide for a compelling order, so that theoretically notification can be made even before the deed is drawn up. Only when both requirements are fulfilled, the delivery will be complete and no sooner than that moment will assignment take place, provided that the remaining requirements for an assignment are also fulfilled …

Between the moment the deed is drawn up and the moment of notification the

[53] Snijders and Rank-Berenschot, above n 29, no 348.

[54] HLE Verhagen and MHE Rongen, *Cessie in Preadviezen uitgebracht voor de Vereniging voor Burgerlijk Recht* (Deventer, Kluwer, 2000) 26–27.

[55] WHM Reehuis, 'Levering van vorderingen op naam: over openbare en stille cessie' addition to AHT Heisterkamp, GE Van Maanen and GT De Jong, *Pitlo. Het Nederlands burgerlijk recht. Goederenrecht* (Deventer, Gouda Quint, 2004) nos 260 and 262.

assignor can still, as rightful holder of the claim, dispose of the claim and thus assign it to a third party or burden it on his own behalf.

A draws up a deed of assignment in which he assigns his claim on X to B. One day later he draws up another deed of assignment for the same claim, but now C is the assignee. Both deliveries are not yet complete because there has not yet been a notification to X. If X receives the notification of the assignment A–C before notification of the assignment A–B, then, even though the deed of assignment A–B was drawn up earlier, the claim is assigned by A to C. The subsequent notification of assignment A–B will not detract anything from the transfer. After all, the claim is at the moment of the completion of the delivery no longer in the set of assets and debts (patrimony) of A, so that the requirement of power to dispose is not fulfilled. Article 3:88 does not offer B protection now that the lack of the power to dispose of the assignor does not follow from the invalidity of a previous transfer, in the course of which the assignee obtained the claim. B is left only with a default claim against A for non performance.

WHM Reehuis, Delivery of a Claim: On Public and Silent Assignment[56] **4.46 (NL)**

Article 3:94 sub 3 provides an alternative way of delivery of a personal claim, without notification thereof to the *debitor cessus*. For silent assignment an authentic deed or registered private document intended for that purpose is sufficient. The requirement of an authentic deed, respectively registration of a private document, aims at establishing the point in time upon which the assignment is completed. This prevents the situation where one has to determine a date after the assignment is complete to which certain difficulties are inherently inevitable. ... In the case of third parties claiming rights to the claim, the existence of the date of delivery simplifies the solution to collision issues wherein that date plays a role. One can think of a double assignment or of collision with a silent right of lien, respectively seizure of the claim. ...

For silent assignment by means of a private deed the assignment is not established until it is registered. The consequence of the latter is that before registration all sorts of incidents can take place that can have detrimental consequences for the assignee, just as in public assignment during the period before notification. ... When using a private deed, these problems do not arise, because the delivery is completed when the notary signs the document. The fact that the notary also still has to register the authentic document under Article 3 Rw does not alter this time of completion, since this regulatory requirement is not a constitutive element. ...

A burdening or assignment for or to a third party is effected by someone that has the power to dispose.

Notes

(1) According to the original text of Article 3:94 of the Dutch Civil Code, an assignment can only be effected by delivery of the claim by means of a deed intended for that purpose and notice thereof to the *debitor cessus*. If, therefore, an assignor would assign the same claim to more than one assignee, the assignee that

[56] *Ibid*, nos 263–64.

first acquires publicity against the *debitor cessus* of the assignment in its favour will be acknowledged as new creditor.

(2) The notification of the debtor as a constitutive requirement for the assignment of claims has been criticised severely by legal scholars. A new paragraph has been added to Article 3:94 of the Dutch Civil Code, which no longer requires the notification of the debtor for the realisation of an assignment.

(3) If the assignment is laid down in an authentic deed, ie a deed drawn up by a notary, the assignment is deemed to come into existence on the date the authentic deed is made up. As there is no time gap between the date of the assignment and the actual date, this assignment acquires third party effect and therefore the assignee loses his right as creditor and 'owner' of the claim, the assignee will not be able to undertake more than one assignment of the same claim.

If the assignment is laid down in a private document, ie a document made by the parties themselves, the assignment will only come be effective after registration to ascertain the date of this document. Where there would be two or more successive assignments, the assignee who is first to acquire registration of the assignment takes priority over the others.

High Court of Chancery, 24 December 1828[57] **4.47 (E&W)**

Dearle v Hall

NOTICE REQUIREMENT FOR ASSIGNMENT

Assignment of beneficial interest

Notice is necessary to perfect title, to give a complete property right, and not merely a right as against him who conveys his interest.

Facts: Brown, a beneficiary, assigned his interest by way of security first to Dearle and then to Sherring. The trustees were not given notice of the assignments. Some years later, Brown assigned his interest to Hall. Before purchasing the interest, Hall made enquiries with the trustees and they indicated that the interest was unburdened. Hall gave the trustees notice of his assignment. Subsequently, Dearle and Sherring gave the trustees notice of their assignment.[58]

Held: Dearle and Sherring have not perfected the assignment by given notice. Therefore, the equitable interest has remained open for traffic and thus could be assigned to Hall, who took prudent measures to ensure the interest he was about to acquire was without burdens.

Judgment: Sir Thomas Plumer MR: The ground of this claim is priority of title. They [Dearle and Sherring] rely upon the known maxim, borrowed from the civil law, which in many cases regulates equities—'qui prior est in tempore, potior est in jure' ['first in time, first in right']. If, by the first contract, all the thing is given, there remains nothing to be the subject of the second contract, and priority must decide. But it cannot be contended that priority in time must decide, where the legal estate is outstanding. For the maxim, as an equitable rule, admits of exception, and gives way, when the question does not lie between bare and equal equities. If there appears

[57] (1823) 3 Russ 1.

[58] Sealy and Hooley, above n 23, 966.

to be, in respect of any circumstance independent of priority of time, a better title in the puisne purchaser to call for the legal estate, than in the purchaser who precedes him in date, the case ceases to be a balance of equal equities, and the preference, which priority of date might otherwise have given, is done away with and counteracted. The question here is—not which assignment is first in date—but whether there is not, on the part of Hall, a better title to call for the legal estate than Dearle or Sherring can set up? or rather, the question is, Shall these Plaintiffs now have equitable relief to the injury of Hall?

What title have they shown to call on a court of justice to interpose on their behalf, in order to obviate the consequences of their own misconduct? All that has happened is owing to their negligence (a negligence not accounted for) in forbearing to do what they ought to have done, what would have been attended with no difficulty, and what would have effectually prevented all the mischief which has followed. Is a Plaintiff to be heard in a court of equity, who asks its interposition on his behalf, to indemnify him against the effects of his own negligence at the expense of another who has used all due diligence, and who, if he is to suffer loss, will suffer it by any reason of the negligence of the very person who prays relief against him? The question here is not, as in *Evans v Bicknell* ((1801) 6 Ves 174), whether a court of equity is to deprive the Plaintiffs of any right—whether it is to take from them, for instance, a legal estate, or to impose any charge upon them. It is simply, whether they are entitled to relief against their own negligence. They did not perfect their securities; a third party has innocently advanced his money, and has perfected his security as far as the nature of the subject permitted him: is this Court to interfere to postpone him to them?

They say, that they were not bound to give notice to the trustees; for that notice does not form part of the necessary conveyance of an equitable interest. I admit, that, if you mean to rely on contract with the individual, you do not need to give notice; from the moment of the contract, he, with whom you are dealing, is personally bound. But if you mean to go further, and to make your right attach upon the thing which is the subject of the contract, it is necessary to give notice; and unless notice is given, you do not do that which is essential in all cases of transfer of personal property. The law of England has always been, that personal property passes by delivery of possession; and it is possession which determines the apparent ownership. If, therefore, an individual, who in the way of purchase or mortgage contracts with another for the transfer of his interest, does not divest the vendor or mortgagor of possession, but permits him to remain the ostensible owner as before, he must take the consequences which may ensue from such a mode of dealing. That doctrine was explained in *Ryall v Rowles* ((1750) 1 Ves Sen 348, 1 Atk 165), before Lord Hardwicke and three of the Judges. If you, having the right of possession, do not exercise that right, but leave another in actual possession, you enable that person to gain a false and delusive credit, and put it in his power to obtain money from innocent parties on the hypothesis of his being the owner of that which in fact belongs to you. The principle has been long recognised, even in courts of law. In Twyne's case ((1602) 3 Co Rep 80), one of the badges of fraud was, that the possession had remained in the vendor. Possession must follow right; and if you, who have the right, do not take possession, you do not follow up the title, and are responsible for the consequences.

'When a man', says Lord Bacon (Maxims of the Law, max 16), 'is author and mover to another to commit an unlawful act, then he shall not excuse himself by circumstances not pursued'. It is true that a chose in action does not admit of tangible actual possession, and that neither Zachariah Brown nor any person claiming under him were entitled to possess themselves of the fund which yielded the £93 a year. But in *Ryall v Rowles* the Judges held, that, in the case of a chose in action, you must do every thing towards having possession which the subject admits; you must do that which is tantamount to obtaining possession, by placing every person, who has an equitable or legal interest in the matter, under an obligation to treat it as your property. For this purpose, you must give notice to the legal holder of the fund; in the case of a debt, for instance, notice to the debtor is, for many purposes, tantamount to possession. If you omit to give that notice, you are guilty of the same degree and species of neglect as he who leaves a personal chattel, to which he has acquired a title, in the actual possession, and under the absolute control, of another person.

If there the least doubt, that, if Zachariah Brown had been a trader, all that was done by Dearle and Sherring would not have been in the least effectual against his assignees; but that, according to the doctrine of *Ryall v Rowles*, his assignees would have taken the fund, because there was no notice to those in whom the legal interest was created? In that case it was the opinion of all the Judges, that he who contracts for a chose in action, and does not follow up his title by notice, gives personal credit to the individual with whom he deals. Notice, then, is necessary to perfect the title—to give a complete right in rem, and not merely a right as against him who conveys his interest. If you are willing to trust the personal credit of the man, and are satisfied that he will make no improper use of the possession in which you allow him to remain, notice is not necessary; for against him the title is perfect without notice. But if he, availing himself of the possession as a means of obtaining credit, induces third persons to purchase from him as the actual owner, and they part with their money before your pocket-conveyance is notified to them, you must be postponed. In being postponed, your security is not invalidated: you had priority, but that priority has not been followed up; and you have permitted another to acquire a better title to the legal possession. What was done by Dearle and Sherring did not exhaust the thing (to borrow the principle of the civil law) but left it still open to traffic. These are the principles on which I think it of be very old law, that possession, or what is tantamount to possession, is the criterion of perfect title to personal chattels, and that he, who does not obtain such possession, must take his chance.

I do not go through the cases which constitute exceptions to the rule, that priority in time shall prevail. A man may lose that priority by actual fraud or constructive fraud; by being silent, for instance, when he ought to speak; by standing by, and keeping his own security concealed. By such conduct, even the advantage of possessing the legal estate may be lost. ...

On these grounds, I think that the plaintiffs have not shown a title to call on a court of equity to interpose in their behalf, and to take the fund from an individual who has used due diligence, in order to give it to those whose negligence has occasioned all the mischief. There is no equality of equities between the defendant Hall, and the plaintiffs...

The bill, therefore, must be dismissed, but, as against Hall, without costs. I do not make the plaintiffs pay costs to Hall, because they may have been losers without any intention to commit a fraud, and I am unwilling to add to their loss. Constructive fraud is the utmost that can be imputed to them.

Note

It is established in *Dearle v Hall* that, in the event of a subsequent assignment of the same claim, even an equitable assignee will have to give notice to the debtor in order to secure his title against other assignees. The rule of *Dearle v Hall* even applies if the interest of the person giving notice is equitable and that of the other assignee legal.

Comparative Notes

The above description clearly indicates the existence of two different models to determine the priority between subsequent assignees of the same claim:

(1) In Germany, France and the Netherlands priority between successive assignees of the same claim will be determined by the application of the general rules on the completion of an assignment.

(2) In Belgium and England, however, special rules deal with the priority between successive assignees. In both legal systems, priority is taken by the bona fide assignee who is first to acquire publicity and therefore attains third party effect of the assignment.

II.B.2.c Contractual prohibition of assignment of claims (*pactum de non cedendo*)

Introductory Notes

(a) In some situations the debtor and creditor of a claim may decide that it is undesirable that the claim is assigned to another party, eg if the claim is personal or to prevent the creditor from using the claim for security purposes. If the claim cannot be assigned, the debtor knows that he will not be confronted with a security creditor of the claim. To reach that result a debtor and a creditor will agree on insertion of a non-assignability clause in their contract. This clause prohibits or restricts the assignment of the creditor's claims against the involved debtor.

(b) There is a great variety of approach in how such clauses limiting or prohibiting assignments are qualified in European jurisdictions. The agreement between the debtor and creditor is a contract, yet a contract which has an impact on the content of the claim. Some legal systems award effect to this clause in property law, ie give it third party effect; some refuse such effect because of the contractual nature of this arrangement.[59]

(c) Here too German law offers a very good illustration of the problem. This section will therefore begin with German law, after which the other legal systems are dealt with.

(i) German law

Bürgerliches Gesetzbuch **4.48 (DE)**

§399 BGB Exclusion of assignability in case of change of content or agreement

A claim may not be assigned if the performance cannot be made to a person other

[59] See also Chapter 3.

than the original creditor without changing its content or if the assignation can be excluded through an agreement with the debtor.

Handelsgesetzbuch **4.49 (DE)**

§354a In the event that an agreement with the debtor according to paragraph 399 prohibits the assignment of an outstanding monetary claim and that the legal transaction, which gave rise to this claim, for both parties is a commercial transaction, or the debtor is a legal person under public law or a separate set of assets under public law, the assignment is nevertheless valid. However, the debtor can perform its obligation to the existing creditor so that he is relieved of his obligation. Dissenting agreements are invalid.

Bürgerliches Gesetzbuch **4.50 (DE)**

§1069 (1) The creation of the usufruct in a right is governed by the provisions applying to the transfer of the right.

(2) A right of usufruct cannot be created on a right that cannot be assigned.

§1274 (1) A pledge of a right is created in accordance with the provisions governing the transfer of the right. If the delivery of the thing is required for the transfer of the right, the provisions of sections 1205 and 1206 apply.

(2) In so far as a right cannot be assigned, a right of pledge cannot be created in respect to that right.

§851 ZPO Non-assignable claims **4.51 (DE)**

(1) In the absence of specific provisions, a claim is only subject to a right of pledge insofar as it can be assigned.

(2) An unassignable claim according to §399 of the BGB claim can be pledged and assigned for collection in so far as the owed object is subject to the pledge.

Notes

(1) The general rule of §399 BGB provides, just like Article 3:84 of the Dutch BW, for the complete ineffectiveness of an assignment that violates a contractual prohibition of the assignability of claims. Under this provision of the BGB the prohibition clause has an absolute effect, ie an effect against third parties. This means that an assignment of a claim, in breach of the non-assignability clause, does not resort any effect: the claim will not be transferred from the assignor to the assignee and the assignee will not replace the assignor as creditor in relation to the involved debtor.

The consequences of the rule of §399 BGB are very far reaching: contractors that would normally use invoice finance facilities (eg factoring) will be prevented from doing so by a non-assignability clause and will be forced to turn to other, more expensive and less appropriate forms of finance to fill the finance gap.[60]

(2) In order to remedy some of the negative consequences of §399 BGB, a deviation of this rule has been incorporated in the HGB (Commercial Code) in 1994 (§354a HGB).[61] This new provision supersedes the general rule of the BGB if the assignor and the *debitor cessus* are merchants or if the latter is a state institution.

§354a HGB provides for the general effectiveness of an assignment that violates a prohibition clause. This means that an assignment of a claim, in breach of a non-assignability clause, will be effective against third parties. There is one exception to this rule: the *debitor cessus* is always able to discharge its obligation by performing to the assignor, whereas the assignor cannot demand performance since he no longer possesses the claim. If a creditor assigns a claim in breach of a non-assignability clause agreed to between this creditor and his debtor, the latter has a claim against the creditor for non-compliance with his contractual obligations.

(ii) French law

Cour de cassation Civ 8 June 1853 **4.52 (FR)**

Worms v Auriol

VALIDITY OF NON-ASSIGNABILITY CLAUSE

Military service for payment

A non-assignability clause violates the principle of free circulation of objects, which underlies the French Civil Code.

Facts: Mr Puech and Mr Auriol agreed that Puech would enter military service on behalf of Auriol to fulfil Auriol's mandatory military duty. Auriol would pay Puech 1,400 French francs for this, which would be payable seven years after completion of the military service by Puech. There was an explicit clause in the agreement that prohibited Puech from assigning his claim on Auriol to a third party. Nevertheless, Puech assigned his claim to Godecheau, who, in his turn, assigned the claim to Worms. Auriol invoked the non-assignability clause to Worms to refuse payment of the 1,400 francs.

Held: A non-assignability clause is not valid, because such clause is in breach with the general principles of the Civil Code.

Judgment: Concerning Articles 544, 1172, 1594 and 1598 of the Code Napoléon. Whereas the right of free disposal of property is a principle of public policy and interest, deriving from the spirit and the text of the law, notably Articles 544 and 1598 Code Napoléon. Whereas this principle precedes the free will of persons; that any property can only be declared non-assignable in the situations prescribed by law, where it is believed to have to allow a formal derogation from the fundamental prin-

[60] The total amount of claims that were blocked to be used for factoring puposes was in 1992 estimated between 140 bn and 200 bn Deutschmark (K Bette, 'Vetraglicher Abtretungsausschluß im deutschen und grenzüberschreitenden Geschäftsverkehr' [1994] *WM* 1910; B Depping and F Nikolaus, 'Das rechtsgeschäftliche Abtretungsverbot auf dem Prüfstand ökonomischer Analyse des Rechts' [1994] *DB* 1203).

[61] The German 'Factoring-Verband' announced that the total factoring turnover had until 1997 increased from 18 bn Deutschemark to 30 bn Deutschmark and that 15% of this increase was due to the introduction of §354a HBG in German law: SC Saar, 'Zur Rechtsstellung des Schuldners nach §354a S 2 HGB' [1999] *ZIP* 993, footnote 74.

ciple of the right of free disposal of property, an essential quality and characteristic of property; but that none of these prescribed situations are present in the proceedings at stake. Whereas, in fact, only a clause of non-assignability, of that nature as that contained in the replacement act [*l'acte de remplacement*] at issue, tends to modify, outside of the conditions and cases prescribed by law, the free disposition of property, and thereby putting outside of business things which, according to the current state of legislation, must stay subject to it. Accordingly, this clause cannot be binding; and, in the case at hand the debtor lacks interest to invoke it, as he remains only subject to pay the price of the replacement, fully executed on his part; and that by paying the assignee on the same terms and conditions that he would have applied vis-à-vis the assignor, his position is not worsened, and gives him no reason to complain. Whereas, by judging the non-assignability clause at issue in the proceedings to be binding and by annulling the assignments made in violation of the latter, the challenged judgment has formally violated the Articles cited.

Cour de cassation Com 21 November 2000[62] **4.53 (FR)**

Banque Scalbert v Société Clemessy

VALIDITY OF NON-ASSIGNABILITY CLAUSE

Terms and Conditions I

An assignee cannot be bound by an agreement to which he was not a party himself.

Facts: In the general conditions of Société Clemessy, that apply in her relationship vis-à-vis Société Sepi, a clause was laid down stating that her co-contractors could not proceed to transfer their claim against her without a prior written permission in that regard. The Société Sepi transferred her claim on Société Clemessy, without a prior permission, to a bank. A conflict subsequently arose between the *debtor cessus* (Société Clemessy) and the assignee (the bank). The *debtor cessus* invoked the non-assignability clause contained in the general conditions and thus refused payment to the assignee. The assignee, on the other hand, claimed that he, being a third party, could not be bound by the clause in the contract from which the claim arose, considering that he was not a party to that primary contract.
Held: The assignee cannot be bound by a clause that limits the transfer of claims, which was laid down in a contract of which he was not a party.

Judgment: Whereas after deciding, rightfully, that the bank ..., assignee of the debt arising from the contract signed between the Sociétés Clemessy and Sepi, was not party to the contract, the Court of Appeal therefrom derived rightfully that the bank was not bound by the approval clause contained therein except if the bank had accepted it, which the Société Clemessy did not demonstrate, and that therefore, without reversing the burden of proof, the court dealing with the substance of the case applied the aforementioned texts correctly.

[62] 97-16874, Bulletin 2000 IV No 180, 158.

Cour de cassation Com 22 October 2002 **4.54 (FR)**

Société marseillaise de crédit v Société Clémessy
VALIDITY OF NON-ASSIGNABILITY CLAUSE

Terms and Conditions II

An assignee can only be bound by a non-assignability clause if he accepted the clause in the contract between debitor cessus and assignor.

Facts: This case also concerned the non-assignability clause in regard to a debt of Societé Clemessy which was laid down in the general conditions. Also in this case, Societé Clemessy refused to pay the assignee (a bank) that had received the claim on her, in conflict with the non-assignability clause. The Court of Appeal of Colmar decided that Societé Clemessy was indeed obligated to pay the bank, as the non-assignability clause could not be called upon against the bank, as the bank was not a party to that primary contract, and thus did not accept the non-assignability clause.

Held: A non-assignability clause has, at least in the context of the case at hand, *erga omnes* effect. One has to admit to that the motivation of the Court is extremely brief and that the underlying motives to accept third party-effect of the non-assignability clause cannot (easily) be revealed.

Judgment: Whereas, in order to convict the Société Clemessy to pay the bank, the judgment pronounces that the disputed clause making the assignment or transfer of claim subject to the prior approval of the debtor whose debt has been assigned, should only be declared effective against the bank if the latter had accepted the general terms and conditions. Whereas by ruling this way, whilst a debtor whose debt of an assigned or transferred claim who has not accepted this assignment or transfer, can oppose the assignee credit institution with the exceptions founded on the personal links with the with the assignor, the Court of Appeal has violated the aforementioned.

FX Licari, The contractually agreed non-assignability of a claim[63] **4.55 (FR)**

A clause stipulating the non-assignability of a claim is not contrary to the principle of the free circulation of the possessions because Article 537 of the Civil Code concerns the power of the holder of a right to have a definite right, while the *pactum de non cedendo* operates upstream, and determines the contents of the right.

In other words, the agreement obliges not only the creditor to refrain from an assignment, but also removes from the claim its assignability. This means that this is another matter than the simple prohibition on the fulfillment of a legal act.

It means that the claim is shielded from the legal business by the will of the parties.

As a matter of fact, by attaching it indissolubly to the person of the original creditor, the *pactum de non cedendo* has the effect that a claim cannot be the object of a contract.

[63] [2002] *Revue de Jurisprudence Commerciale* 76–77, no 10.

Article L442-6 II Code de commerce **4.56 (FR)**

Any clauses or contracts are null and void, if they provide for a producer, a trader, a manufacturer or a person who is registered in the trade register, the possibility: ... (c) to prohibit the other contracting party to dispose to third parties the outstanding debts that he holds with him.

Notes

(1) In French case law and jurisprudence for several decades the general validity of non-assignability clauses was contested. These clauses were thought to be contrary to the general principles of property law which instigated the polemic on their validity.

(2) Once this discussion died down in favour of the validity of non-assignability clauses, a new discussion commenced on the effect of the contractual provisions prohibiting the creditor from assigning.

(3) We may assume that the Court of Cassation accepted, in its judgment of 22 October 2002, the effectiveness of non-assignability clauses. The consequences of this judgment are however definitely rather limited due to Article L442-6 of the Commercial Code. According to this provision, a contractual prohibition of the assignability of claims cannot resort any effect, not even between parties, if the debtor is a producer, merchant, industrialist or craftsman.

(iii) Belgian law

C Lebon, The Proprietary Nature of Claims[64] **4.57 (BE)**

A claim can be defined as a legal connection, *vinculum iuris*, between one or more creditors and debtors, of whom the first, the creditor(s), have the right on a performance (to give, to do or to leave) by the debtor(s).

In the first place, a claim is considered as an interpersonal personal relation between creditor(s) and debtor(s). The content of this relation is marked by the principle of party autonomy. ... Usually it is ... in application of the principle of party autonomy, that parties to a contract are entirely free to handle their mutual contractual obligations and relations as well as the claims that arise out of them in the way they wish.

A claim has however, beside its elementary appearance as an interpersonal legal relation, likewise an existence apart from the creditor(s) and debtor(s). It is possible to depersonalise and to objectivate a claim and thus turn it into an object that can be the object of property rights. Or, the legal relation that exists between one or more creditors and one or more debtors can be considered as an object in itself. A (legal) prototype of the claim as thing does not exist; the content and the modalities of the legal connection which is turned into an object of property law are purely stipulated by the parties involved. Therefore it has to be determined that, in contrast to other objects of property law, claims, are created by the parties concerned and that these creations function in property law. The agreements that the creditor(s) and debtor(s) had concluded concerning their existing claims, become inherent to

[64] Lebon, above n 10, no 684.

the claims or, in other words, the claims are characterised as things and thus as objects of property law. In property law claims do not have another existence than was agreed upon through contractual obligations by the creditor(s) and debtor(s).

The principle of party autonomy therefore, is not only the basis for competence of the creditor(s) and debtor(s) to agree on their relation pursuant to contract law, but also for their competence to model the claim existing between them as an object *erga omnes*.

I Peeters, Third Parties and Contracts with Property Effects[65] **4.58 (BE)**

What about such an agreement between the titleholder, the debtor of the claim? Prominent authors assert that the prohibition to stipulate non-assignability is not applicable to claims since they do not constitute the object of a right of ownership in the strict sense. They furthermore refer to Article 1717 BW, which permits to exclude the transferability of a lease. To adduce further support to this statement it can be held that, contrary to property rights, the parties of the agreement are initially completely free to determine the content and the terms of their contractual relation, and as a result also of the claim.

The debtor could invoke the non-assignability of the claim as exception against every assignee. The non-assignability would thereby not be linked to the property, but would merely be the consequence of the *nemo-dat* rule. Against the possibility to stipulate non-assignability, it is raised that claims cannot be made non-assignable, for the same reasons as property rights.

How convincing the arguments of the first statement may be due to the fact that they are linked to the internal structure of the claims, it still is paradoxical to continually consider claims to a larger extent as full property rights and simultaneously allow without any restriction that they are rendered non-assignable by an agreement between the creditor and the debtor. All the more because in many circumstances, and certainly when it regards mere monetary claims, it is difficult to perceive the relevance of such a stipulation. It is therefore rightly arguable to test the validity and/or enforceability of such stipulations for the sake of action's interests.

Note

The general validity of the non-assignability clause (the *pactum de non cedendo*) is accepted in Belgian law. The effect of such clauses is, however, unclear. There does not exist any case law on this topic and the question is rarely dealt with by legal scholars. Authors that do write on this question do not share identical ideas on the effect of these clauses.

[65] I Peeters, 'Derden en kontrakten met "zakenrechtelijke" gevolgen betreffende schuldvorderingen en andere onlichamelijke goederen' in *Le contrat et les tiers. Les effets externes et la tierce complicité* (Brussels, CJB, 1995) 111–12, nos 146–48.

(iv) Dutch law

Burgerlijk Wetboek **4.59 (NL)**

Article 3:83 (1) Ownership, limited property rights and claims are transferable, unless the law stipulates otherwise or the nature of the right is incompatible with the transfer.

(2) The assignability of claims can however be excluded by an agreement between the debtor and the creditor.

(3) All the other rights are only transferable when the law provides so.

Parliamentary History of the New Dutch Civil Code, Book 3[66] **4.60 (NL)**

This Article [3:83 BW] deals with rights which are assignable. In principle these are all property rights and claims. These are not assignable when they have a personal character. Property rights have such a character in exceptional circumstances, whereas claims are always personal rights when the required performance is related to the personal characteristics of the creditor. Besides this there is also a difference between the assignability of claims and property rights, that the assignability of a claim can be excluded in a clause in a contract, this is not the case for property rights. This is dependent on the chosen model in the draft Code, meaning that it is unlawful to go beyond the general type by contract then is allowed by law; whereas with claims there is the freedom through contract to decide and consent on the content of the claim, within the boundaries of the law.

Hoge Raad 17 January 2003 **4.61 (NL)**

Oryx v Van Eesteren

EFFECT OF A NON-ASSIGNABILITY CLAUSE

The pledged unassignable claim

A non-assignability clause brings with it the impossibility to create a right of pledge on such a claim.

Facts: In 1995, B provided Oryx with a right of pledge on all her existing and obtainable claims as security for the repayment of a loan from Oryx. In 1996 B, through subcontracting, obtained a claim of 65,679.91 guilders on A, the company of which the defendant in the case at hand was partner in 1995 and 1996. According to Article 6 of the relevant contract, B was prohibited to 'to cede, pledge or transfer the ownership under any title whatsoever to a third party' (hereinafter 'the prohibition to pledge' (*verpandingsverbod*)) claims deriving from the contract without the approval of A. The claim of 65,679.91 guilders on A was specified on the pledge listing (*pandlijsten*) prepared by B in the framework of the aforementioned pledge for Oryx. The question was whether the prohibition of pledge impeded the validity of the pledge of the claim.

Held: A contractual clause limiting the assignability of a claim is binding upon third parties, because it affects the claim itself as the object that is to be transferred and does not affect, as such, the power to dispose. Therefore, no bona fide third-party protection rule can be applied in cases where a claim is

[66] CJ Van Zeben and JW Du Pon, *Parlementaire geschiedenis van het Nieuwe Burgerlijk Wetboek Boek 3—Vermogensrechten in het algemeen* (Deventer, Kluwer, 1981) 314.

being pledged in violation of such a clause and the pledgor did not in fact know (and could not have known) of the non-assignability clause.

Judgment: Such a prohibition of pledge admittedly does not lead to the incompetence to dispose for the person entitled to the claim, but to non-assignability of the claim itself, but this does not discount the correctness of the judgment that the prohibition of pledge impedes the validity of the pledge and neither the fact that Oryx did not know about the prohibition of pledge nor the provisions of Article 3:36 BW can lead to another judgment.

Article 3:83 para 2 BW entails after all that the assignability of claims can be excluded by means of an agreement such as that made here between A and B. Different from what this party alleges, a transfer in violation with such a agreement is not only a non-performance by the person entitled to the claim against his debtor, but the agreement also entails the invalidity of the assignment. Pursuant to Article 3:98 this also applies to the creation of a right of pledge. It follows that in this case the claim could not be pledged due to the prohibition of pledge. Whether Oryx at the time of the pledge knew about the prohibition to create a right of pledge is irrelevant. In so far as in this part the argument about the good faith of Oryx is meant to invoke Article 3:88 in conjunction with 3:239 sub 4 BW, it fails since it does not concern incompetence which results from the invalidity of an earlier assignment, as required by those provisions. Also Oryx cannot invoke Article 3:36, because it did not base itself on a declaration or conduct of the debtor of the claim, A or the defendant; the only declaration on which it based itself, as the Court of Appeal considered unchallenged in cassation, is that of B, the other party.

Note

Under Dutch law it is not possible to prohibit or to limit the assignability or transferability of the rights of ownership and limited property rights. However, it is possible to prohibit or limit the assignability of claims (Article 3:83 BW). A contractual prohibition or limitation of the assignability has third party effect. This means that an assignment of the non-assignable claim will not result in a transfer of the claim from the assignor to the assignee: the assignor will remain the creditor, without any replacement of the creditor taking place. Moreover, a non-assignability clause obstructs the possibility to pledge the involved claim.

(v) English law

R Goode, Inalienable Rights?[67] **4.62 (E&W)**

Whether, and to what extent, a contract is effective to preclude assignment of the creditor's rights under it is in the first instance a matter of construction of the contract itself. A contract term by which a party undertakes not to assign his rights is capable of at least four alternative interpretations. The first is that the term constitutes a mere personal undertaking, the breach of which does not render the assignment ineffective against the debtor but merely exposes him to a claim for damages for breach of contract. The second is that the assignment is to be ineffec-

[67] [1979] MLR 554.

tive as against the debtor (so that he is to remain free to pay the assignor, despite notice of assignment, and to set up equities against the assignor as if no assignment had taken place) but without affecting the creditor's right to enter into an agreement for the transfer of the fruits of the contract after he has received these from the debtor. The third is that the person giving the undertaking is not to be entitled to assign the fruits of the contract even as between himself and the intended assignee, that is, under a transfer intended to take place only after the assignor has himself received the fruits from the debtor. The fourth interpretation is that a purported assignment is to constitute a breach of contract entitling the debtor not merely to claim damages but to terminate the contract and thereby reduce or extinguish the assignor's own right of payment.

House of Lords 22 July 1993[68] **4.63 (E&W)**

Linden Gardens Trust Ltd v Lenesta Sludge Disposal Ltd

VALIDITY OF A NON-ASSIGNABILITY CLAUSE

Asbestos

A non-assignability clause is valid in English law and is not contrary to public policy.

Facts: A lessee of a part of a building entered into a standard contract (JCT standard form 1963) for the removal of asbestos. The standard form constrained a clause 17 that provided: 'The employer shall not without written consent of the contractor assign this contract.' After the works had been carried out more asbestos was found. In February 1985 the lessee contracted with another company on the same terms. On 1 April the lessee assigned its leasehold interest to the claimant. On 3 July 1985 the lessee issues a writ seeking damages for negligence and breach of contract. On 14 January 1987, the lessee assigned to the claimant his rights of action to the first contractor and rights incidental to the leasehold interest. The first contractor was not asked or informed about the assignment. Subsequently more asbestos was found and the claimant made repair works at his own expense, but sought recovery of his costs against the construction companies. In lower instance the court held that the costs could not be recovered. The Court of Appeal reversed this decision and held the assignment effective.

Held: A non-assignability clause is not contrary to public policy. An assignment in breach of such clause is therefore invalid against the debtor.

Judgment: Lord Browne-Wilkinson. ... In broad terms, those issues are, first, what is the effect of a contractual provision which prohibits a party from assigning the benefit of a contract and, second, can a building owner recover substantial damages for breach of a building contract if he has parted with the property. ...

The preliminary issues in this action were therefore directed to two questions. First, were Stock Conversion's rights under the contracts effectively assigned to Linden Gardens despite the fact that assignment of the building contracts by Stock Conversion was prohibited by the terms of those contracts? If so, second, could Linden Gardens as assignee recover damages for the cost of removing the asbestos after the date of the assignment, which cost was incurred not by Stock Conversion but by Linden Gardens? ...

(1) Does clause 17(1) of the building contracts prohibit the purported assignment

[68] (1993) All ER 417.

of the benefit of the building contracts? (2) Does clause 17(1) prohibit the assignment of causes, of action for breaches of contract subsisting at the date of the assignments? (3) Is a prohibition on assignment void as being contrary to public policy?

Although it is true that the phrase 'assign this contract' is not strictly accurate, lawyers frequently use those words inaccurately to describe an assignment of the benefit of a contract since every lawyer knows that the burden of a contract cannot be assigned: see, for example, *Nokes v Doncaster Amalgamated Collieries Ltd* [1940] AC 1014, 1019–1020. The prohibition in clause 17(2) against subletting 'any portion of the works' necessarily produces a prohibition against the subletting of the whole of the works: any subletting of the whole will necessarily include a subletting of a portion and is therefore prohibited. Therefore there is no ground for reading the words 'assign this contract' in clause 17(1) as referring only to subletting the whole. Decisively, both clause 17(1) and (2) clearly distinguish between 'assignment' and 'subletting': it is therefore impossible to read the word 'assign' as meaning 'sublet'. Finally, I find it difficult to comprehend the concept of an employer 'subletting' the performance of his contractual duties which consist primarily of providing access to the site and paying for the works.

Accordingly, in my view clause 17(1) of the contract prohibited the assignment by the employer of the benefit of the contract. ...

The question is to what extent does clause 17 on its true construction restrict rights of assignment which would otherwise exist? In the context of a complicated building contract, I find it impossible to construe clause 17 as prohibiting only the assignment of rights to future performance, leaving each party free to assign the fruits of the contract. The reason for including the contractual prohibition viewed from the contractor's point of view must be that the contractor wishes to ensure that he deals, and deals only, with the particular employer with whom he has chosen to enter into a contract. ... persuade me that parties who have specifically contracted to prohibit the assignment of the contract cannot have intended to draw a distinction between the right to performance of the contract and the right to the fruits of the contract. In my view they cannot have contemplated a position in which the right to future performance and the right to benefits accrued under the contract should become vested in two separate people. ... It follows that the purported assignment to Linden Gardens without the consent of the contractors constituted a breach of clause 17. The claim of Linden Gardens as assignee must therefore fail unless it can show that the prohibition in clause 17 was either void as being contrary to public policy or, notwithstanding the breach of clause 17, the D assignment was effective to assign the chose in action to Linden Gardens.

It was submitted that it is normally unlawful as being contrary to public policy to seek to render property inalienable. Since contractual rights are a species of property, it is said that a prohibition against assigning such rights is void as being illegal. ...

In the face of this authority, the House is being invited to change the law by holding that such a prohibition is void as contrary to public policy. For myself I can see no good reason for so doing. Nothing was urged in argument as showing that such a prohibition was contrary to the public interest beyond the fact that such prohibition renders the chose in action inalienable. Certainly in the context of rights over land the law does not favour restrictions on alienability. But even in relation to land law a prohibition against the assignment of a lease is valid. We were not referred to any English case in which the courts have had to consider restrictions on the alienation of tangible personal property, probably because there are few cases in which there would be any desire to restrict such alienation. In the case of real property there is a defined and limited supply of the commodity, and it has been held contrary to public policy to restrict the free market. But no such reason can apply to contractual rights: there is no public need for a market in choses in action. A party to a building contract, as I have sought to explain, can have a genuine commercial interest in seeking to ensure that he is in contractual relations only with a person whom he has selected as the other party to the contract. In the circumstances, I can see no policy reason why a contractual prohibition on assignment of contractual rights should be held contrary to public policy.

Notes

(1) Non-assignability clauses are valid in English law. Whether such a clause is effective depends, first and foremost, on the way in which it is formulated. Lord Browne-Wilkinson follows Professor Goode's classification of possibilities in Linden Gardens Trust, but the Courts are willing to interpret clauses in favour of the *debtor cessus*.

(2) The law therefore does not provide a definite solution to the validity of non-assignability clauses. It will be for the parties to decide on the effectiveness of the clause, enforced by the courts.

(vi) Comparative remarks

Legal systems deal differently with contractual restrictions on the free assignability of claims:

(1) In the Netherlands and Germany (at least in §399 BGB) as well as in England, it has been accepted that a creditor and a debtor can freely shape the former's claim and that a contractual restriction of the assignability of that claim has full third party effect. Some French and Belgian authors and case law tend to adopt the same approach. In this opinion, an assignment, in breach with this clause, will not resort any effect: the claim will not leave the assignor's set of assets and debts (patrimony).

(2) In these legal systems, non-assignability clauses thus get the broadest effect. Precisely the opposite is true in the United States, where the Uniform Commercial Code renders these clauses totally ineffective between the debtor and the creditor and therefore naturally also with regard to third parties. Economic motives gave rise to the introduction of this rule into US law. It is thought that modern economies that need credit for their good health and that need for this end the possibility to finance and trade in commercial claims, need to promote the free transferability of claims. For this reason contractual restrictions of the assignability should not resort any effect.

(3) A diversity of 'intermediate' approaches are thinkable:

According to §354a HGB, that was introduced in German law to limit the consequences of §399 BGB, the assignment of a claim, in breach of a non-assignability clause, is effective against third parties, although it remains possible for the debtor to discharge his obligation by performing to the assignor. An assignment in breach with the non-assignability clause may give rise to a claim for non-compliance with the contractual obligations.

Article 6 of the Unidroit Convention on International Factoring and Article 9 of the United Nations Convention on the Assignment of Receivables in International Trade lay down the rule that an assignment of a receivable is nonetheless effective notwithstanding any agreement between the initial or any subsequent assignor and the debtor or any subsequent assignee limiting in any way the assignor's right to assign his claims.

According to Article 18 of the Unidroit Convention on International Factoring a contracting state may at any time make a declaration in accordance with Article 6(2) that an assignment under Article 6(1) shall not be effective against the debtor when, at the time of conclusion of the contract of sale of goods, he has its place of business in that state. A non-assignability clause will in this case have third party effect, except with regard to the debtor.

III. RIGHT OF USUFRUCT IN RESPECT TO CLAIMS

The creation of a right of usufruct in respect to a claim is not immediately easy to understand. Originally, a right of usufruct was a right to use and enjoyment of a piece of land with fruit trees on it. The holder of the right, the usufructuary, was allowed to use the land and take the fruits produced by the trees. A right of usufruct on a movable object can perhaps also be conceived. A right of usufruct on an animal will give the holder of the right the right to use the animal and to take the fruits the animal produces. The concept of fruit was discussed already in Chapter 3 and does include fruits in the literal meaning only.[69] Any periodic return an object produces can be a fruit. In case of an animal, the offspring of the animal may be considered a fruit. The usufructuary of a chicken may therefore also take the eggs and, possibly, the animal's chicken.

However, a right of usufruct in respect to a claim is much more difficult to conceive. Not only does the object itself not exist in a physical sense, it does not necessarily produce any periodic returns that can be taken as fruits. Nonetheless, civil law systems (the common law does not recognise a right of usufruct) do recognise a right of usufruct in respect to claims. This paragraph will deal with these rights.

In civil law systems, a right of usufruct is regarded as a limited property right that provides the usufructuary with the right to use and enjoy the object of this right and to acquire ownership of its 'fruits'. The right of usufruct was already dealt with in Chapter 3.[70] In all civil law systems under consideration the right of usufruct can cover both corporeal and incorporeal objects.

Finally, because this part of the chapter will deal with a property right, rather that different concepts, an integrated approach, like the approach taken in Chapter 3, will be followed.

[69] See Chapter 3.
[70] See Chapter 3.

III.A GENERAL STATUTORY PROVISIONS ON USUFRUCT OF CLAIMS

Code civil **4.64 (FR)**

Article 578 The right of usufruct is the right to enjoy an object of another in the same manner as an owner himself, but on condition that the substance of the object is preserved.

Article 581 It may be created on any kind of movable and immovable property.

Bürgerliches Gesetzbuch **4.65 (DE)**

§1068 Statutory definition of usufruct in rights (1) The subject of the right of usufruct may also be a right.

(2) The provisions for the right of usufruct in things are accordingly applicable to the right of usufruct in rights, in so far as nothing different follows from §§1069 to 1084.

Burgerlijk Wetboek **4.66 (NL)**

Article 3:210(1) Unless otherwise agreed on creation of the right, the usufructuary is entitled to demand performance of the claims subject to the right of usufruct in and outside of court as well as to receive payments.

Comparative Notes

(1) According to the French and Belgian Civil Code, it is possible to create a right of usufruct on any kind of movable and immovable objects. Indirectly, the Code accepts that claims are burdened with a right of usufruct. It should be noted that the statutory provisions on the right of usufruct are mainly shaped for immovable objects and that it is not always easy to transpose the provisions to corporeal movable objects, not to mention incorporeal movable objects.

The question whether a right of usufruct that is created in respect to a claim is also a property right or a personal right is a point of discussion in legal literature. The majority of authors argue that the right of usufruct can in this case not be qualified as a property right because it is no more than a split off of the claim itself. The right of usufruct is however thought, notwithstanding its personal character, to have third party effect in specific circumstances.

(2) This interpretation of the character of the right of usufruct on claims is adopted by the majority of German authors. In Germany it is possible to create a right of usufruct on a right. The right of usufruct cannot be qualified as a genuine property right because German law of property is restricted to corporeal objects only.

(3) In the Dutch Civil Code the rules on usufruct form a part of Book 3 of the Code which deals with patrimonial rights that can rest on both corporeal and incorporeal objects.

Who has the right to collect a claim that is subject to usufruct: the usufructuary or the bare owner (ie the owner whose right is burdened by the usufruct)? A two-part question will now be addressed: (A) who has the right to collect the claim that is burdened with a right of usufruct, is it the usufructuary or the bare owner of the claim? And (B) what are the specific consequences of the collection of this claim for the bare owner and the usufructuary?

III.B RIGHT TO COLLECT THE CLAIM: FRENCH AND BELGIAN LAW

E Van Arenbergh, Usufruct[71] **4.67 (BE)**

Can the usufructuary receive, either by amicable agreement, or through legal proceedings, the repayment of a debt which has become due during the duration of the usufruct or for which no due date was set? The opinion was put forward that following Article 584 of the Civil Code, the usufructuary has no other right than the right to receive the interest of the debt and the back-payments of the annuity. Subsequently, he cannot receive the repayment of the capital, even at the time the payment was due; he can only resist this to the extent that repayment takes place outside of his presence and requires the immediate investment.

One asserts in support of this theory that the right of the usufructuary consists in the enjoyment of the object, but with the duty to preserve the matter. Yet the substance of a debt, is the debit with the payment of the sum, which the debtor owes the debtor, thus it is this right which the usufructuary must preserve and return to the owner. Hence, it follows, one says, that the usufructuary does not have the right to receive this sum, nor, consequently, to claim it or to receive repayment. Because, in receiving the capital due to the debtor, the usufructuary would extend the debt, he would subsequently consume it even though he must preserve it. The debtor, which means the owner, alone, has this right. Such is the strictness of these principles, and we must abide by them, we conclude, because it is the only possible guarantee for the debtor, owner of the debt. To give to the usufructuary the right to claim the repayment of the capital, is to allow him to ruin the bare owner; it will be reimbursed, as this was shown, of the capital located to the mortgage, even with privilege to clear them away, or, it amounts to the same thing, to place them on simple bills without any guarantee whatsoever.

Finally, we add, if the usufructuary can claim the repayment of the capital, it will depend on him transforming his right of usufruct into a quasi-usufruct. As the usufructuary, he was not the owner of the debt, he could not sell it, neither assign it, nor consent to a novation. He only had the pleasure of the interests, the sum of money, the consumable object, of which he will become the owner and with which he can, as a consequence, to do as he pleases. Does it depend on the usufructuary to change his right of enjoyment into a right of ownership?

[71] E Van Arenbergh, *Traité de l'usufruit* (Brussels, Larcier, 1936) nos 1029–31.

A Verbeke, Creative Use of Usufruct[72] **4.68 (BE)**

The right of the usufructuary to enjoy the object of its right of usufruct like the owner himself is limited by the obligation to maintain the object. This right and this duty together give a criterion by which the usufructuary can control the object on which his usufruct rests: like the owner himself, but purpose-bound, like a good *paterfamilias* who knows that he will have to give the object back. This limitation continuously hangs above the head of the usufructuary and above every action that he takes.

Has the usufructuary by the recovery of claim the right to collect the capital of the claim on due date? Seen the principle of the purpose-bound management of a good *paterfamilias,* it must be accepted that he not only has the right, but even the duty to press for the payment of the claim in order to avoid that the capital of the owner will be affected.

C Lebon, The Proprietary Nature of Claims[73] **4.69 (BE)**

From the obligation to maintain the substance (as well as the purpose) of the objects under usufruct, follows that the usufructuary is expected to, in all matters, during his usufruct, take all measures for the conservation of the objects under usufruct and the purpose thereof. The conservative measure takes place in the common interest of the usufructuary and the bare owner. The usufructuary acts in advantage, based on a silent mandate, of the bare owner. …

This vision is able, to my opinion, to be extended such, that the usufructuary is provided with a general right to receive payment of the claim. The beneficiary has the ability and is even obliged, to prevent the evaporation of the revocation and the capital value which the claim resembles from taking place, to strive after the payment of a claim in or out of court, even if it concerns a claim under hypothec.

It is not necessary to involve the bare owner in the payment. The bare owner basically has the right to set conservative deeds with respect to the object under usufruct. Yet, to my opinion, the legal security and especially the debtor do not benefit if the bare owner involves himself in the payment of the claim. After all it is, as a rule, the usufructuary who knows the debtor better. In numerous cases it will not be the owner, but his legal predecessor, who will be the original creditor. On top of that, as a rule, the debtor will be informed of the creation of the right of usufruct and it will be the usufructuary who takes care of the daily contact with the debtor and who will incite the debtor to pay by stopping the prescription.

V Sagaert, Real Subrogation[74] **4.70 (BE)**

The widespread opinion that the usufructuary has the exclusive competence to collect the claims subject to the usufruct can be more fundamentally criticised. De Page holds that for the protection of the bare owner it should be called for the usufructuary and bare owner to collect the capital of the claim together, for example

[72] A Verbeke, 'Creatief met vruchtgebruik' (1999) 530 *T Not* nos 50 and 87.
[73] Lebon, above n 10, nos 453–54.
[74] V Sagaert, *Zakelijke subrogatie* (Antwerp, Intersentia, 2003) no 146.

on a joint bank account. Such an approach is defended in French law as well. This opinion can also be supported from a legal perspective. After all, for the usufructuary the collection of the claim *de iure* constitutes an action of disposition. Where the claim belonged to the bare owner, the money is for the usufructuary. The fact that the return is still traceable in the assets of the usufructuary, does not revive the rights of the bare owner. On the basis of Article 587 BW the usufructuary is after all competent to dispose over the sums of money, which implies that he has also become owner of these. In other words: the collection of the claim goes further than making the *de facto* exercise of ownership by the bare owner impossible, but *de jure* passes the ownership over to himself. Put differently, the collection of the claim subject to usufruct constitutes an action of disposal. Considering that the usufructuary does not dispose of such a competence, one can defend that the usufructuary can only proceed to collection of the claim with the intervention of the bare owner. Only if both of them agree to this, there can be, for the duration of the usufruct, a disposal over the monies.

C Lebon, The Proprietary Nature of Claims[75] **4.71 (BE)**

As already mentioned, by collecting of the cash payment from the claim subject to a right of usufruct, this claim is replaced by a perishable object. Through the special operation of the proprietary subrogation, the right of usufruct of the claim is by law automatically converted into a right of ownership on the received monies. The original owner definitely loses his right of ownership on the claim; the obligation with the new owner is of a mere obligatory nature.

The debtor of the claim subject to usufruct can transfer the money on the account of the usufructuary. The transferred amount in this case will form part of the account balance of the usufructuary and will allow the claim that the usufructuary/account holder against his bank grow. The account balance belongs, in full ownership, to the account holder. The usufructuary no longer maintains his position as the person entitled to a limited property right. The mechanism of the proprietary subrogation does not apply to the transfer of money by the debtor of the claim under usufruct to the usufructuary. After all, the claim on the bank does not directly take the place of the claim collected by the usufructuary. Also in the case of a transfer of money to the usufructuary the relationship which existed between the usufructuary of the claim and the bare owner becomes one of a mere obligational character.

Notes

(1) The question whether it is the usufructuary or the bare owner of the claim who may collect the claim is not dealt with in the French and Belgian Civil Codes and is much discussed in legal writings. Where some authors argue that the right to collect the burdened claim should be granted to the bare owner only and others argue that co-operation between the bare owner and the usufructuary is needed, the majority of authors and (lower) courts assert that it falls within the powers of the usufructuary to collect the claim that is the object of his property right.

(2) If a claim for money is subject to the right of usufruct, the collection of

[75] Lebon, above n 10, no 457.

that claim will result in the substitution of the claim into a certain amount of money. Instead of the claim, the amount of money will now become the object of the usufructuary's right. However, in French and Belgian law it is not possible to create a genuine right of usufruct on an object which cannot be used without being consumed, such as money, grain and liquor. These objects can only be burdened with a right of quasi-usufruct, granting the usufructuary all powers of the owners of the objects concerned: the 'usufructuary' has the right to use them, but is obliged to return, at the end of the right of usufruct, either objects of the same quantity and quality or the value of these.

The collection of a claim that is burdened with a right of usufruct thus implies that the usufructuary of the claim will become the owner of the collected amount of money.

III.C RIGHT TO COLLECT THE CLAIM: GERMAN LAW

Bürgerliches Gesetzbuch **4.72 (DE)**

§1074 Usufruct in a claim; notice and collection The usufructuary of a claim is entitled to collect the claim and, if the due date is dependent on notice by the creditor, to give notice of termination. He must ensure proper collection. He is not entitled to make other dispositions of the claim.

§1075 Effect of performance (1) Upon the performance of the debtor to the usufructuary, the creditor acquires the object provided and the usufructuary acquires the usufruct in the object.

(2) If consumable things are provided, the usufructuary acquires the ownership; the provision of Article 1067 applies accordingly.

§1076 Usufruct in claim bearing interest If an outstanding claim bearing interest is the subject-matter of a right of usufruct, the provisions of sections 1077 to 1079 will apply.

§1077 Termination and payment (1) The debtor may pay the capital only to the usufructuary and the creditor jointly. Each of them may require that payment be made to them jointly; each may require, instead of payment, deposit for both of them.

(2) The usufructuary and the creditor may give notice only jointly. The notice of the debtor is effective only if it is declared to the usufructuary and the creditor.

§1078 Co-operation in collection of payment Where the claim is due, the usufructuary and the creditor are obliged to co-operate in collection. If the due date depends on notice, either party may require the co-operation of the other in the notice, if the collection of the debt is necessary by reason of danger to its security under the rules of proper management of assets.

§1079 Investment of the capital The usufructuary and the creditor are obliged to each other to co-operate in order that the capital collected is invested with interest under the provisions applying to the investment of money held in trust for a ward and at the same time the usufruct is created for the usufructuary. The nature of the investment is determined by the usufructuary.

Note

The provisions of the German BGB on the collection of claims subject to usufruct differ depending on the fruit-bearing character or not of the claims concerned.

It is believed that if the claim does not generate any interests, the usufructuary thereof does not gain any profit of the claim as long as the claim itself exists. The usufructuary is granted a right to collect the claim that is subject to its usufruct, because this is the only way he can gain any profit of its property right. Due to the application of the principle of proprietary subrogation, the right of usufruct will automatically transfer, ie subrogate, from the claim to the collected amount of money.

If the claim that is subject to usufruct does, however, generate interests, there is no need to grant the usufructuary a right to collect the claim. The usufructuary and the bare owner have to co-operate to collect the claim that is subject to usufruct and to invest the collected amount of money into a fruit-bearing object, which must then be subject to a new right of usufruct in favour of the usufructuary of the collected claim.

III.D RIGHT TO COLLECT THE CLAIM: DUTCH LAW

Burgerlijk Wetboek **4.73 (NL)**

Article 3:210 (1) Except otherwise provided at the establishment, the usufructuary is entitled to demand performance of claims subject to usufruct judicially and extra-judicially and to receive payments.

(2) Except otherwise provided at the establishment, he is only entitled to rescind and terminate contracts where this is appropriate for sound management [*tot een goed beheer dienstig*].

(3) The principal owner is only entitled to exercise the competences referred to in the foregoing paragraphs if he has been granted the permission of the usufructuary or the authorisation of the subdistrict court judge [*kantonrechter*]. Against authorisation of the subdistrict court judge pursuant to this paragraph, no appeal is permitted.

Article 3:213 (1) What takes the place of property subject to usufruct by having been duly disposed of, belongs to the holder of the principal right and is also subject to the usufruct. This is also the case with what is received through collection of claims subject to usufruct, and for claims for compensation which take the place of property subject to the usufruct, including claims with respect to depreciation of the property.

(2) The benefits which property yields during the usufruct and which are not fruits are also subject to the usufruct.

Article 3:214(1) Unless otherwise agreed on creation of the right, money that belongs to the usufruct should be, in consultation with the person holding the principal entitlement, invested or spend in accordance with the interest of the other objects under usufruct.

Note

In Dutch law, the usufructuary does not only have a right to collect the claim that is subject to his right of usufruct, but even has the obligation to do so. The principle of proprietary subrogation applies to the collected amount of money: the right of usufruct will automatically be transposed to this amount of money. The general rules on the usufruct of claims apply which does, amongst others, imply that the usufructuary must invest the collected amount.

IV. SECURITY INTERESTS IN CLAIMS

As was already mentioned in this chapter, it is possible to hold property security rights in respect to claims. This is, in some legal systems, controversial, as these systems restrict the 'true' law of property to corporeal objects only. These systems, such as German law and Dutch law, still accept a property security right created in respect to a right of pledge. Moreover, especially in German law, claims are also assigned for security purposes. This technique follows the general rules on *fiducia cum creditore* or the transfer of ownership for security purposes.

Because the importance of property security rights and the likeness between property rights in respect to movables and property rights in respect to claims, as well as the similar development of these two types of property security rights, these rights will be dealt with in Chapter 5.

V. COMPARATIVE OVERVIEW

The purpose of this chapter was to show that property rights also exist in respect to claims and what types of property rights can be held regarding claims. The chapter also shows common themes, some of which will be highlighted in this last section.

V.A PROPERTY LAW AND CLAIMS

Not all property law systems treat claims alike. Some, such as German and Dutch law, are based on the idea that property law can only concern physical objects. Therefore, the primary property right, the right of ownership, is restricted to corporeal objects only. Other systems, such as French law, take a much wider approach to property law and include incorporeal objects in the system of property law. In English law personal property law is applied to choses in action as much as is possible.

The systems restricting property law to corporeal objects come into difficulties because they do accept property rights, the right of usufruct and the right of pledge, on claims. A mixed situation therefore results in which legal scholars distinguish between real or actual property law and aspects of property law that do not belong to the core of property law.

V.B A SPECIAL TYPE OF OBJECT

Claims are special types of objects of property law. They are special because their content can be fully provided by party agreement. This content can, in several systems, have far-reaching effect on the content of the property rights that can be held in respect of these. This is best illustrated with the *pactum de non cedendo*, or the non-assignability clause. In such a case, the claim is unassignable and hence so will generally be the property rights held in respect of it.

V.C A SPECIAL TYPE OF PROPERTY RIGHT IN RESPECT TO IT

Because claims take a special position in property law, the property rights that can be held in respect to it are also special. A claim cannot be possessed and hence there are different rules dealing with possession in case of a right of usufruct or a right of pledge. If a claim also produces, this is especially relevant in the case of a right of usufruct, different fruits to those produced by a movable object. As a result, a limited property right in respect to a claim is different from a limited property right on a movable object or on land.

CONCISE BIBLIOGRAPHY

J Eggens, 'Over de verhouding tussen eigendom en verbintenis' in *Mededelingen der Koninklijke Nederlandse Akademie van Wetenschappen, afdeling Letterkunde* (nos 1–16) (Amsterdam, Noord-Hollandse Uitgeversmaatschappij, 1960) 185–204.

J Ghestin, M Billiau and G Loiseau, 'Le régime des créances et des dettes' in J Ghestin (ed), *Traité de droit civil* (Paris, LGDJ, 2005).

GL Gretton, 'Ownership and its Objects' [2007] *Rabels Zeitschrift fuer ausländisches und internationales Privatrecht* 802–51.

WS Holdsworth, 'The History of the Treatment of Choses in Action by the Common Law' (1920) 33 *Harvard Law Review* 997.

C Lebon, *Het goederenrechtelijk statuut van schuldvorderingen* (Antwerp, Intersentia, 2010).

W Mincke, 'Property: Asset or Power? Objects or Relations as Substrata of Property Rights' in JW Harris (ed), *Property Problems. From Genes to Pension Funds* (The Hague, Kluwer, 1997) 78–88.

F Oditah, *Legal Aspects of Receivables Financing* (London, Sweet & Maxwell, 1990

MA Rakotovahiny, *L'evolution de la notion de créance*, Diss (Toulouse I, 1999).

CHAPTER FIVE
SECURITY INTERESTS

Vincent Sagaert

This chapter completes the overview of the second of the six essential questions: what are property rights. Property rights cannot only be held to use an object or claim (see Chapters 3 and 4), but they can also be held for security purposes. This chapter deals with property rights as security interests, both primary (such as ownership) and limited property rights.

Introductory Remarks

The insolvency of a debtor creates a risk for payment of the creditors. In all European legal systems, the basic rule is that the value of the available assets in the insolvency proceedings must be distributed to all creditors on the basis of the *pari passu* rule. This is generally called the *paritas creditorum* rule. However, in practice, this *pari passu* rule is highly theoretical. Creditors aim to protect their claims through security interests, both personal and property security interests. In general terms, a security interest aims at securing a personal obligation, in other words to protect the creditor against the insolvency of his debtor. It allows a creditor to be paid out of the sales proceeds of an asset, without having to share with other creditors.

A *personal security interest* consists of the 'object of execution', this is the extension of the assets on which a creditor can exercise his claim: according to a personal security interest, a creditor can exercise his claim not only on the assets belonging to his debtor, but also on assets which belong to the provider of the personal security (eg a guarantor).

A *property security interest* does not extend the amount of assets on which a claim can be realised, but grants a priority right in favour of one or more secured creditors allowing them to be paid out of the proceeds of that asset before other creditors.

This chapter will only deal with property security interests, as the personal security interests fall outside the scope of property law. Moreover, this chapter will not deal with the specific rules on statutory liens, sometimes also known as priority rights or privileges, which can be found in each legal system, such as the lien of the unpaid vendor and the lien of the unpaid lessor. The analysis of these rules would require an enumeration of the specific liens in each of the analysed legal systems, an exercise that would not have a comparative value. Moreover, many legal systems have a tendency to abolish or reduce statutory liens.

I. TYPES OF SECURITY RIGHTS

Introductory Note

All European legal systems differentiate between types of property rights, possessory and non-possessory rights of pledge, right of hypothec, lien and security ownership. Security ownership includes lease, retention of title, security transfer of ownership. However, some major technical differences exist in the categorisation of the security interests.

M Cabrillac and C Mouly, Security Rights[1] **5.1 (FR)**

All security rights can be classified, according to Article 2094 of the Civil Code, as a lien or a hypothec. According to this main distinction, the pledge would not be an autonomous category because the priority it offers would be a lien, as is meant by Articles 2073 and 2074 of the Civil Code. This twofold view of securities is a legacy of the old law which, in rejecting the hypothec on movables, has ranked all movable security rights as pledges, which has contributed to the incoherent and unclear structure of movable securities.

However, a pledge is a security right with distinct features which prohibits its identification and even its similarity to a lien. It is preferable to structure the security rights in three categories.

Even if the structure of security rights is amended in that way, it remains a baroque architecture which has at first glance the advantage of simplicity, but only creates a mental structure at the expense of confusion and artificial problems which could have been spared. It is beyond doubt that the distinction between hypothec and pledge is clear, even if its criteria are still controversial. By contrast, the classification as lien covers a disparate mosaic.

If, since 1804, the structure in the three categories has not been totally in line

[1] M Cabrillac and C Mouly, *Le droit des sûretés* (Paris, Litec, 2002) 509, no 506.

with reality, the later development has even enlarged the distance between them. This is especially the case since this development has made the distinction between statutory hypothecs and liens superfluous and because it has given rise to moveable security rights without dispossession, which have to be situated between a pledge and a hypothec. This structure in three categories contains distinctions which are so uncertain and arbitrary that it is insufficient with regard to the diversity of security rights, but remains nevertheless the official conceptual tool which one is forced to use.

Burgerlijk Wetboek[2] **5.2 (NL)**

Article 3:227(1) The right of pledge and the right of hypothec are limited rights, which aim to exercise on its object a claim in order to pay money with priority to other creditors. If the right is vested on a registered object, it is a right of hypothec; if the right is vested on another object, it is a right of pledge.

Court of Appeal, 29 July 1997[3] **5.3 (E&W)**

Re Cosslett (Contractors) Ltd

THE CLASSIFICATION OF CONTRACTUAL RIGHTS AS SECURITY RIGHTS

Washing plants

The Court of Appeal distinguishes between four kinds of consensual security known to English law.

Facts: A county council agreed in 1989 with a contractor for coal-bearing shale to be separated from the coal by means of a washing plant. The contract between the parties provided that all plants, goods and material owned by the contractor were, when on site, deemed to be the property of the council. Clause 63(1) of the agreement provided that if the contractor went into liquidation or abandoned the contract the council could enter the site and expel the contractor, but without releasing it from any of its responsibilities under the contract. Moreover this clause provided that, in the event of the company being expelled, the council could retain possession of the plant and could sell the plant on completion of the works, as well as the plant not being required to complete the works, and apply the proceeds of sale towards whatever sums might be or become due from the company under the contract. In 1991 and 1992 the contractor established two washing plants on the site but by 1993 it encountered financial difficulties and abandoned the site, leaving the plants there. Pursuant to clause 63(1) of the contract the council expelled the contractor. The contractor's administrator applied for delivery up of the washing plants or payment for their use.

Held: The contractual clause did not pass legal title in the plant to the council. On the expulsion of the company from the site clause 63(1) granted the council the right to retain possession of the plant and to use it to complete the works, which, being only a possessory right not given by way of security, did not constitute an equitable charge. The failure to register the charge rendered the security created by the power of sale void as against the administrator, but did not affect any other right of the council which was not a security and which did not require registration and, in particular, did not invalidate the council's contractual right to retain possession of plant and materials and use them to complete the works.

[2] The Dutch legislation can be found at www.wetten.nl

[3] [1998] Ch 495, 508.

Judgment: Millet LJ—(3) Does the council's power of sale arise by way of equitable charge?

By contrast the council's power to sell the plant and apply the proceeds in or towards discharge of whatever sums might be or become due from the company by reason of its failure to complete the works clearly is a security interest. The council contends that its rights constitute a possessory lien with a power of sale and not an equitable charge, and cites *Great Eastern Railway Co v Lord's Trustee* [1909] AC 109 in support.

This proposition cannot be accepted. In the Great Eastern Railway case there was no dispute that the railway company's power of sale was attached to its lien. The question which divided the House of Lords was whether the lien was contractual or possessory. The majority held that its carrier's lien was not extinguished until the goods were unconditionally delivered up to the consignee and that accordingly it did not need to rely upon any contractual right of possession.

There are only four kinds of consensual security known to English law: (i) pledge; (ii) contractual lien; (iii) equitable charge and (iv) mortgage. A pledge and a contractual lien both depend on the delivery of possession to the creditor. The difference between them is that in the case of a pledge the owner delivers possession to the creditor as security, whereas in the case of a lien the creditor retains possession of goods previously delivered to him for some other purpose. Neither a mortgage nor a charge depends on the delivery of possession. The difference between them is that a mortgage involves a transfer of legal or equitable ownership to the creditor, whereas an equitable charge does not.

In the present case the council's rights in relation to the plant and materials are exclusively contractual, and are not attributable to any delivery of possession by the company. When the company brings plant and materials onto the site they remain in the possession of the company to enable it to use them in the completion of the works. There is no question of the company delivering possession at that stage, either by way of security (ie as a pledge) or otherwise (ie by way of lien). The council comes into possession of the plant and materials when it expels the company from the site leaving the plant and materials behind. But this does not amount to a voluntary delivery of possession by the company to the council. It is rather the exercise by the council of a contractual right to take possession of the plant and materials against the will of the company.

In my judgment, therefore, the council's rights are derived from contract not possession and, in so far as they are conferred by way of security, constitute an equitable charge.

Uniform Commercial Code **5.4 (US)**

§9-109 (a) [**General scope of article**] Except as otherwise provided in subsections (c) and (d), this article applies to:

(1) a transaction, regardless of its form, that creates a security interest in personal property or fixtures by contract;

(2) an agricultural lien;

(3) a sale of accounts, chattel paper, payment intangibles, or promissory notes;

(4) a consignment;

(5) a security interest arising under Section 2-401, 2-505, 2-711(3), or 2A-508(5), as provided in Section 9-110; and

(6) a security interest arising under Section 4-210 or 5-118.

(b) [Security interest in secured obligation] The application of this article to a security interest in a secured obligation is not affected by the fact that the obligation is itself secured by a transaction or interest to which this article does not apply.

(c) [Extent to which article does not apply] This article does not apply to the extent that:

(1) a statute, regulation, or treaty of the United States preempts this article;

(2) another statute of this State expressly governs the creation, perfection, priority, or enforcement of a security interest created by this State or a governmental unit of this State;

(3) a statute of another State, a foreign country, or a governmental unit of another State or a foreign country, other than a statute generally applicable to security interests, expressly governs creation, perfection, priority, or enforcement of a security interest created by the State, country, or governmental unit; or

(4) the rights of a transferee beneficiary or nominated person under a letter of credit are independent and superior under Section 5-114.

(d) [Inapplicability of article] This article does not apply to:

(1) a landlord's lien, other than an agricultural lien;

(2) a lien, other than an agricultural lien, given by statute or other rule of law for services or materials, but Section 9-333 applies with respect to priority of the lien;

(3) an assignment of a claim for wages, salary, or other compensation of an employee;

(4) a sale of accounts, chattel paper, payment intangibles, or promissory notes as part of a sale of the business out of which they arose;

(5) an assignment of accounts, chattel paper, payment intangibles, or promissory notes which is for the purpose of collection only;

(6) an assignment of a right to payment under a contract to an assignee that is also obligated to perform under the contract;

(7) an assignment of a single account, payment intangible, or promissory note to an assignee in full or partial satisfaction of a preexisting indebtedness;

(8) a transfer of an interest in or an assignment of a claim under a policy of insurance, other than an assignment by or to a health-care provider of a health-care-insurance receivable and any subsequent assignment of the right to payment, but Sections 9-315 and 9-322 apply with respect to proceeds and priorities in proceeds;

(9) an assignment of a right represented by a judgment, other than a judgment taken on a right to payment that was collateral;

(10) a right of recoupment or set-off, but:

(A) Section 9-340 applies with respect to the effectiveness of rights of recoupment or set-off against deposit accounts; and

(B) Section 9-404 applies with respect to defenses or claims of an account debtor;

(11) the creation or transfer of an interest in or lien on real property, including a lease or rents thereunder, except to the extent that provision is made for:

(A) liens on real property in Sections 9-203 and 9-308;

(B) fixtures in Section 9-334;

(C) fixture filings in Sections 9-501, 9-502, 9-512, 9-516, and 9-519; and
(D) security agreements covering personal and real property in Section 9- 604;
(12) an assignment of a claim arising in tort, other than a commercial tort claim, but Sections 9-315 and 9-322 apply with respect to proceeds and priorities in proceeds; or
(13) an assignment of a deposit account in a consumer transaction, but Sections 9-315 and 9-322 apply with respect to proceeds and priorities in proceeds.

Notes

(1) The European approach to security rights is very different from the US approach. Article 9 Uniform Commercial Code (UCC) takes a functional view: it makes no distinction with regard to the form or classification of the security agreement, but merely takes into consideration the (security) purpose of the created right. As §9-109(a)(1) states, this provision applies 'regardless of the form' of the transaction that creates a security interest.

The excerpt demonstrates that, according to US law, title-based security arrangements—such as retention of title, fiduciary transfer of ownership or leasing for security purposes—are dealt with at the same level and are subject to the same rules as the different forms of 'conceptual' security rights such as pledges and charges. The functional US system, encompassing all rights with security purpose, allows for a more straightforward and simpler rule of priority: the first one to file his security right must prevail over all others who did not file their security right before that first creditor. It has been stated that Article 9 UCC is the supreme achievement of US realist philosophy.[4]

This US approach has gained some support in European law, as it emerges from the Draft Common Frame of Reference (DCFR). It appears from Article IX-1:109 DCFR that the drafters have also taken a semi-funtional approach, covering all devices with a security purpose, but still denominating these devices:

IX—1:102: Security right in movable asset

(1) A security right in a movable asset is any limited proprietary right in the asset which entitles the secured creditor to preferential satisfaction of the secured right from the encumbered asset.
(2) The term security right includes:
(a) limited proprietary rights of a type which is generally recognised as designed to serve as proprietary security, especially the pledge;
(b) limited proprietary rights, however named, that are based upon a contract for proprietary security and that are either intended by the parties to entitle the secured creditor to preferential satisfaction of the secured right from the encumbered asset or have this effect under the contract; and
(c) other rights which are regarded as security rights under the rules of this Book, such as the right referred to in IX.—2:114 (Right of retention of possession) and the rights covered by paragraph (3).

[4] M Bridge, 'The English Law of Security: Creditor-friendly but Unreformed' in EM Kieninger (ed), *Security Rights in Moveable Property in European Private Law* (Cambridge, Cambridge University Press, 2004) 81.

(3) A transfer or purported transfer of ownership of a movable asset which is made, on the basis of a contract for proprietary security, with the intention or the effect of securing satisfaction of a secured right can create only a security right in the asset for the transferee.
(4) Paragraph (3) applies in particular to:
(a) a security transfer of ownership of corporeal assets;
(b) a security assignment;
(c) a sale and lease-back; and
(d) a sale and resale.

(2) As emerges from the *Re Coslett* case, English law also adheres in its approach to the European-continental classification rather than to the US functionalism. English law recognises fixed and floating charges, pledge and mortgage as security rights. Hence, English law currently still adheres to a more formal (European) approach, even if it takes a rather flexible position towards the content of the security rights.[5] However, a Law Commission Consultative Document on the Registration of Security Interests has been put forward for consideration of a reform of the law of security rights that would largely remodel the law along the lines of Article 9 UCC.[6] Other developments also demonstrate that the US functional approach influences the English security devices. For instance, it will be seen that the distinction between a charge (limited property right) and a mortgage (ownership) is considered as a distinction of minor importance (III.A.4.e).

(3) There is in European legal systems no unanimity in respect to the way in which the property security rights can be classified. Most continental scholars and legislatures divide between security rights on movables, security rights on immovables, and the right of ownership as a security device. However, English textbooks take the distinction between consensual and non-consensual security rights as their starting point. Within the first category they make a distinction between possessory security rights and non-possessory security rights. Continental lawyers acknowledge that both security rights on movables and security rights on immovables can be possessory or non-possessory.

In the analysis below, the distinction between movables and immovables will be taken as the starting point, and the focus will be on contractual security rights.[7]

II. COMMON FEATURES OF SECURITY RIGHTS

II.A ACCESSORY NATURE OF THE SECURITY INTERESTS

Property security rights are said to be *accessory* with regard to the claim they guarantee. This has a double meaning.

On the one hand, they are accessory in the sense that they do not grant any

[5] *Cf* H Beale, M Bridge, L Gullifer and E Lomnicka, *The Law of Personal Property Security* (Oxford, Oxford University Press, 2007) no 1.16.

[6] Registration of Security Interests: Company Charges and Property other than Land (no 164, 2002).

[7] Statutory liens are very divergent: in a lot of systems, a long list of statutory liens exists. It is useless to analyse this in the framework of this Casebook.

power to make use of the economic value of the asset except for the priority right they confer when exercising the right to fulfil the obligation. The question whether this dimension of accessority is valid for all European legal systems will be dealt with by considering that the exercise of property security rights may not entail an unjust enrichment on behalf of the secured creditor (VI.B.3).

On the other hand, accessority can have the meaning that the existence, transfer and extinction of the property security right is dependent upon the existence, transfer and extinction of the claim of which they guarantee the payment. A change in the proprietary status of the claim will automatically entail a similar change in the proprietary status of the property security right.

Code civil **5.5 (FR)**

Article 1692 The sale or assignment of a claim includes the accessories of the claim, such as the surety, lien and hypothec.

Article 2424 A hypothec is transferred with the secured debt by operation of law. The mortgagee may subrogate another creditor to the hypothec and retain his debt. He may also, by a ranking agreement, assign his rank of registration to a creditor of a lower rank, with whom he changes priority.

Bürgerliches Gesetzbuch[8] **5.6 (DE)**

§1250 Assignment of the claim (1) The assignment of the claim automatically transfers the pledge to the new creditor. The pledge cannot be transferred without the claim.

(2) If the assignment of the claim excluded the pledge from the transfer, the pledge comes to an end.

BGH, 18 March 1968[9] **5.7 (DE)**

VALIDITY OF THE PLEDGE IF THE SECURED OBLIGATION IS VOID

Pledge of carpet

A pledge is not valid if the contractual obligation is not valid, except if the pledge also aims to secure a statutory obligation.

Facts: X has a contractual claim against Y that is secured by a right of pledge. The claim is declared void because of violation of public order (§138 BGB). Before the court, an issue arises whether the voidness of the secured claim entails the voidness of the security right.

Held: The voidness of the contractual obligation in principle also entails the voidness of the pledge. However, parties can contractually agree that the pledge also aims to secure the statutory (enrichment) claim which would arise if their secured contractual obligation would be declared void. In that case and to that extent, the pledge is held to be valid.

[8] *Cf* for a hypothec: §1153 BGB.
[9] NJW 1968, 1134.

Judgment: It is correct that if a causal legal act is declared void because of contravention of §138 BGB which allows a causal legal act to be declared void which is contrary to public order, this also entails the voidness of the proprietary legal act, in this case the pledge. The Court of Appeal has not judged that this rule applied in this case, but this cannot be criticised on legal grounds. ...

According to the decision of the Appeal Court, which is binding for the Supreme Court, the contracting parties would also have entered into the pledge agreement if they had been aware of the voidness of the secured obligation. As the secured obligation has not come into existence, there is a legal ground for revision as the pledge has not come into existence either. However, the Appeal Court has analysed that, according to the intention of the parties, the pledge would also secure the enrichment claim between the parties. Contrary to the judgment of the Appeal Court, this is legally possible.

Nothing can be derived from the fact that instead of a contractual claim a statutory obligation would arise. Nor is it significant that the statutory obligation would only be an enrichment claim. One cannot argue without furter justification that ... the contracting parties have agreed that, if their agreement would be void, their intention was that an enrichment claim would come instead. However, if they aimed also to cover the enrichment claim with the right of pledge, there is no reason to deny the will of the parties. There is no legal ground to make an exception for the case that the original secured claim did not arise because of non-compliance with public order. The legislation awards, also in this case, a claim in restitution to the creditor (§812 BGB). ... It is beyond doubt that contracting parties can, afterwards, secure this claim in creating a pledge. They can also agree upon a pledge at the moment that they enter into the void agreement. But in that case, it requires a diligent investigation whether not only the creditor but also the debtor have meant to secure also the statutory obligation of §138 BGB. There is no legal impediment against such assumption.

Notes

(1) In some legal systems, property security rights are also referred to as 'accessory property rights'. They can only come into existence and continue existing to the extent that the secured claim has come into existence and continues to exist. The secured claim can be both consensual or non-consensual and the security right itself can also be consensual or non-consensual: non-consensual security rights can be accessory to consensual claims and, the other way around, consensual security rights can be accessory to non-consensual claims. The release of the claim by the debtor also releases the security for the debt. The question is much more complicated in common law.[10]

The above-cited judgment of the German Supreme Court of 18 March 1968 extends the existence of the security right to the restitutionary claim arising at the moment that the secured claim is nullified. It must, in each specific case, be determined whether this corresponds to the intention of parties.

(2) It will become clear in the following analysis that the accessory nature of the security right is subject to exceptions. For instance, the German *Grundschuld* is not

[10] *Cf* in English law: *Cowper v Green* (1841) 7 M & W 633.

accessory to the secured claim, but is rather abstract (VI.B.3.b). Moreover, recent international legal devices distanced themselves from this principle of accessority. The French *hypothèque rechargeable* is semi-autonomous, as it requires the fulfilment of the accessority principle at the moment of its creation, while it is possible to recharge the property security right with other claims during the course of its existence. We can also make reference to the international developments which are described in Chapter 10 with regard to euro-mortgages and international interests in mobile equipment of the Cape Town Convention 2001.

II.B SPECIFICITY OF THE SECURED CLAIM

Code civil **5.8 (FR)**

Article 2333 A pledge is an agreement by which the pledgor gives to a creditor the right to be paid in priority to other creditors out of a corporeal movable or a set of corporeal movables, actual or future.

The debts secured may be actual or future; in the latter case, they must be determinable.

Article 2421 A mortgage may be granted for security of one or several claims existing or future. Where they are to come they must be determined.

Their grounds shall be determined in the title.

Cour de cassation, 28 March 1974[11] **5.9 (BE)**

Bank Lambert et Banque industrielle et commercial de Charleroi v Assurances du Crédit en Bottriaux

VALIDITY OF ALL SUMS SECURITIES

Mengal

A security can be given for conditional or future claims, under the sole condition that such claims are defined or at time of securitisation be defined.

Facts: A financial institution (X) has vested a pledge on a commercial fund.[12] According to Article 3(1) of the pledge agreement, the pledge secured 'the payment of all sums which would be due by Y to X or which would become due because of transactions which Y would have done or could do in the future with this bank'. This agreement was entered into for an undetermined period. Y obtains a credit facility of X for BEF150,000 (approx. €3,382). At the moment that Y does not pay this credit, he argues that the pledge agreement is invalid because of the fact that the secured claims are not sufficiently specified.

Held: The credit opening and the pledge can legally be considered as valid as it allows one to define the claims which are secured by the pledge.

Judgment: Considering the fact that the judgment legally considers that, under Article 1130, first paragraph of the Civil Code, a security can be given as security for condi-

[11] Cour de cassation, 1974, 833, Pas 1974, I, 776.

[12] According to Belgian law, a commercial fund is for reasons of pledge considered as a universality of assets, which is object of a pledge.

tional or future claims, under the sole condition that such claims are defined or at time of securitisation be defined; that such future claims are sufficiently defined or definable if the agreement makes it possible to specify the claims and if according to the facts underlying the case, these are the claims which parties have aimed to secure; Considering, after having indicated that it here concerns securitisation of a commercial fund, ..., the judgment determines that Mengal's company manufactures insulation clothing and that the securitisation of 24 February 1959 by Crédit commercial de Mons was made so that the company could gain funds to build a weaving machine as part of the commercial venture; this is not disputed; Considering that the judgment, considering these circumstances, determines that the securitisation was permitted within the limits of the obligations of the creditor towards the borrower, such as has been stipulated in the invoice dated 17 January 1957.

Hoge Raad, 29 June 1984[13] **5.10 (NL)**

Amsterdam-Rotterdam Bank NV v Enkelaar

VALIDITY OF AN ALL SUMS HYPOTHEC

Enkelaar

A hypothec is only valid up to the amount of the estimated value, which the parties have to register in the deed.

Facts: Company X was declared insolvent by a judgment of 30 September 1980. X was the owner of an immovable which has been burdened with a hypothec in favour of a creditor (Y). The hypothec had been vested as security for 'all sums which X would owe to Y according to the bank at that moment or would owe since longer time, regardless of the reason of the debt and covering both debts in currency account and in a simple bank credit, for NLG350,000 with interest over two years and the current year'.

Held: The bank hypothec is only valid up to the amount mentioned in the hypothec deed.

Judgment: The Court rules that according to Article 1221(2) BW, in the case that the obligation is conditional or the amount cannot be determined, as with the present bank hypothec, the hypothec is only valid up to the amount of the estimated value, which the parties have to register in the deed. In such case the deed must state the maximum amount that on the ground of the hypothec can be recovered from the good. It is only for that amount that a right of hypothec exists.

6. Central to this dispute between the parties is the question what one should understand under the words 'of the subsequently owed' in Article 58(2) of the Dutch Bankruptcy Act, in fulfilment of which the liquidator has the power of discharge mentioned in that provision.

7. In case it concerns an asset burdened with a hypothec one should understand under these words: 'the security claim for which the right of hypothec serves' or 'that for which the right of hypothec serves as security', as is meant by the relevant passage of Article 58(2) of the Bankruptcy Act in the draft Act, and the amended draft law of the Act establishing Books 3–6 of the New Civil Code (first part), the editing of which—as it becomes apparent from the parliamentary documents of

[13] NJ 1985, 68.

the drafts, especially from the explanatory memorandum—was only a terminological amendment.

8. This explanation is also the one which is most in line with the wordings of Article 1248 BW, which establishes in favour of a third party possessor a similar rule for the discharge of an asset burdened with a hypothec and which refers to the 'payment of the registered debt'.

Bürgerliches Gesetzbuch[14] **5.11 (DE)**

§1204 Legal Content of the Right of Pledge on Movable Objects (1) For the purpose of securing a claim, a movable object can be burdened in such way that the creditor is entitled to pursue fulfilment of a claim from the object (lien).

(2) The pledge can also be created for a future or for a conditional claim.

Notes

(1) In Dutch law, the rule has been reformulated, but has remained intact after the introduction of the New Civil Code in 1992 (as was noted above at the end of the *Enkelaar* excerpt, para 5.10 (NL)). Article 3:231 BW provides for the rule that the claim for which the right of pledge or hypothec serves as security must be sufficiently specified.[15] The requirement that the secured claim must be specified or that parties must be able to specify the secured claim, must be fulfilled at the moment that the security right is exercised. The Dutch Civil Code—in line with other legal systems—only requires the mentioning of a maximum amount with regard to hypothecs, but not with regard to pledges, which is explained by the organisation of the publicity systems with regard to immovables.

(2) All analysed legal systems allow the creation of security rights in order to secure present or future claims, but nevertheless require an appreciation of the specific circumstances of the case whether it is possible to specify the secured claim. The amount of the secured claim must be sufficiently determined at the moment that the security right is realised.

II.C PROHIBITION OF UNJUSTIFIED ENRICHMENT

Introductory Note

A security right exists for the sole purpose of the payment of the secured claim. The realisation of the security right cannot put the holder of the security right in a more favourable position than the one in which he would have been if the secured claim had been paid in due course. In other words, the secured creditor may not have any interest in the default of his debtor. There is in all legal systems a prohibition of unjust enrichment on behalf of the secured creditor.

[14] This provision applies to pledge, but §1113 BGB provides for a similar provision with regard to hypothecs.

[15] 'de vordering waarvoor pand of hypotheek wordt gegeven, moet voldoende bepaalbaar zijn.'

Cour de cassation, 8 November 2002[16] **5.12 (BE)**

NV SFB v BVBA VTT

DAMAGE IN CASE OF TERMINATION OF FINANCIAL LEASE AGREEMENTS

Financial lease

A sentence indicating the legal proposition for which the case stands.

Facts: X and Y entered into a financial leasing agreement of 30 months with regard to a truck. X remained the owner, but Y was entitled to use the vehicle for the lease period, after which Y had an option to purchase the vehicle. Article 16 of the financial leasing agreement provided as follows: 'The non-fulfilment of any sum which becomes due automatically gives rise to a compound interest of 1.5% per month of delay. Moreover, the entire sum which is due will be increased by 10% as a penalty, notwithstanding other forms of compensation.' Y became insolvent and the agreement was rescinded at a moment that he was in default of paying €500,000. X not only claimed restitution of the truck and the payments for which Y was in default, but also the interest rate and the penalty clause of Article 16. The plaintiff argued that the value of the object could not be taken into consideration with regard to the validity of this penalty clause.

Held: The judge terminating the lease agreement must take into account takes into the sales price of leased good in determining the contractual compensation for the creditor.

Judgment: Considering that the judgment holds that the lessor exercises his restitution claim to the extent and in fulfilment of his claim towards the lessee. ...

That in recognising the effects of the agreement which they have according to their interpretation, it does not deny the binding force of the agreement. This argument can, therefore, not be approved.

That the arguments of violation of the right of ownership have been deduced from the violation of contract law, which is to be denied.

That, finally, it is not contrary to the leasing agreement that the Judge, who terminates the agreement, takes into account the sales price of leased good in determining the contractual compensation and the lease price which has not yet been paid by the lessee.

Such judgment does not harm the security purpose of the financial leasing.

High Court, Chancery Division, 15 June 1994[17] **5.13 (E&W)**

Mathew v TM Sutton Ltd

SURPLUS MONEY OF THE PLEDGED ASSETS

Jewellery pledge

Interest is payable by a pledgee on surplus moneys remaining in his hands after the discharge of the debt out of the proceeds of sale of the pawned articles.

Facts: Mathew granted a right of pledge of jewellery to Sutton. On five separate occasions Mathew delivered articles of silver and jewellery to Sutton as a pledge and as security for loans made to him. Mathew did not redeem the pledged jewellery by the agreed redemption dates and, in accordance with

[16] Arr Cass 2002, 2440, *Rechtskundig Weekblad* 2003–04, 1459, n A Van Oevelen.

[17] [1994] 1 WLR 1455.

the terms of the agreements, Sutton caused the articles to be sold at auction. Sutton withheld payment to Mathew of the surplus balance remaining in its hands after deduction of sums due under the agreements because of a third party's claim to the ownership of the pawned articles, but following the abandonment of that claim Sutton paid the surplus value in capital to Mathew. However, he did not make restitution of the interest accured in this period.

Held: A pledgee is in a fiduciary position in relation to his customer in respect of any surplus moneys remaining in his hands after the discharge of a debt out of the proceeds of sale of pledged articles. Since interest might be awarded in equity where a person in a fiduciary position had misapplied money or made use of it for his own benefit, the pledgor was entitled to a declaration that the pledgee was liable to pay him interest on the surplus value.

Judgment: When the pawned articles are sold by the pawnee—under the power now conferred by section 121(1) of the Act of 1974—the property in those articles passes to the purchaser. The proceeds of sale are paid to the pawnee; indeed, in the usual case, they will be received by the pawnee in the form of money credited to his bank account. But there is no reason why the beneficial interest of the pawnor in the pawned articles should be extinguished to any greater extent than is necessary to give effect to the pawnee's right to realise his security. In particular, there is no reason why the beneficial interest of the pawnor should not be transferred from the articles which have been sold to the proceeds of sale; and so remain attached to the surplus in the hands of the pawnee after he has discharged the debt out of the proceeds of sale.

This analysis is, I think, consistent with the decision of Atkinson J in *Jay's The Jewellers Ltd v Inland Revenue Commissioners* [1947] 2 All ER 762. The question in that case was whether a surplus remaining after the realisation of the pawned property should be treated for the purposes of excess profits tax as trade receipts of the pawnbroker in the year in which the surplus arose or in the year in which the pawnor lost his right to demand payment under section 22 of the Pawnbrokers Act 1872. Atkinson J, after referring to the judgment of Lord Greene MR in *Morley v Tattersall* [1938] 3 All ER 296, said, at p 765:

> 'As a matter of law, these moneys when received were not the [pawnbroker's] moneys at all; they belonged to their clients, and if a client came in the next day and demanded his money they would have to pay it away.' ...

It follows, therefore, that I hold that the fiduciary relationship necessary to found jurisdiction to award interest in equity does exist between pawnee and pawnor in relation to the surplus (if any) arising on the sale of the pawned articles.

Note

A secured creditor is subject to the prohibition of unjust enrichment. Of course, the powers of the secured creditor to realise his right are limited to the value of his claim: he cannot recover more by realising his security right than he would have done by voluntary payment of the debtor. It follows from the English judgment above that this also entails that the secured creditor is obliged to make restitution of the interest on the surplus value which he was due. This is also the case in other legal systems. We can refer to Articles 2347 and 2348 of the French Civil Code, reflecting the same principle (III.A.3).

II.D PUBLICITY OF PROPERTY SECURITY RIGHTS/REPUTED OWNERSHIP IN DECLINE

EM Kieninger, Evaluation: A Common Core?[18] **5.14 (EU)**

A further common tendency on a general level lies in the decline of the significance of possession and the gradual disappearance of the doctrine of ostensible or apparent ownership. This doctrine rests on provisions like Article 2279 (French and Belgian) Cciv:[19] 'En fait de meubles la possession vaut titre.' This rule is regarded not only as the foundation of the principle governing the acquisition of ownership in good faith from a non-owner but also as the cornerstone of the doctrine according to which third parties are entitled to rely on the fact of possession when trying to evaluate their business-partner's creditworthiness. This consideration lies at the heart of the principle of publicity through (direct) possession and is thus also the foundation of the requirement that a pledge can only be constituted through a transfer of possession from the pledgor to the pledgee.

Notes

(1) As exception to the principle of the *paritas creditorum* (equality between creditors), property security rights affect the position of other (potential) creditors of the debtor. The traditional rule, certainly with regard to corporeal assets, is that these creditors can rely in good faith that the assets which are possessed by their debtor will be subject to the execution rights of the creditor in case of default by the debtor. This is the principle of reputed ownership, which is based on good faith reliance by the creditors on the possession of their debtor.

As is pointed out above by EM Kieninger, the principle of publicity is in decline. This will be one of the conclusions emerging from the analysis of the retention of title. Both in Belgian and French law, retention of title was rejected as property right by case law on the argument of the appearence of solvability ('apparent ownership' or 'ostensible ownership'). However, statutory provisions in almost all European legal systems introduced an opposable retention of title without any publicity requirement (with the exception of Switzerland: *cf* IV). The same development can be found in English law. English law has applied the principle of apparent ownership during many decades to individuals. Section 72 of the Insolvency Act 1825 provided as follows:

> [I]f any bankrupt, at the time he becomes bankrupt, shall, by the consent and permission of the true owner thereof, have in his possession, order or disposition any goods or chattels, whereof he was reputed owner, or whereof he had taken upon him the sale, alteration or disposition as owner, the commissioners shall have power to sell and dispose of the same for the benefit of the creditors under the commission.

The purpose of this provision was to prevent the bankrupt obtaining credit on the faith of a fictitious air of prosperity. However, this Act only applied the principle

[18] EM Kieninger, 'Evaluation: A Common Core?' in Kieninger, above n 4, 652
[19] With regard to French law, this article is nowadays Article 2276 Cciv.

to individuals, not to companies. With the reform of the Insolvency Act 1986,[20] the principle of reputed ownership was abolished. English law has moved in the same direction as the European civil law systems.

(2) To the extent that the security right must, according to the law, still be published, two forms of publicity are used: (a) the registration in a public register and (b) dispossession of the object of the security right by the debtor or the third party granting the security right. Between these two forms, the publicity form of dispossession is in decline in favour of the registration. The dispossession has proved to be ineffective in order to grant security rights in the course of the normal business activity. Examples of this are offered by the recent developments in both Dutch and French law.

II.E DISPROPORTIONATE SECURITY RIGHTS

Introductory Note

Several legal systems have developed case law or even statutory provisions on the issue of disproportionate security rights. The question arises whether and to which extent remedies exist with regard to security rights which are manifestly exceeding the security rights which can be—from a financial perspective—complied with by the debtor. This question arises both for property securities and personal securities.

Cour de cassation, 17 June 1997[21] **5.15 (FR)**

Banque internationale pour l'Afrique occidentale v Macron

DISPROPORTIONATE SURETY

Macron

A financial institution commits a wrongful act seeking a security such as a guarantee which is 'out of all proportion' to the patrimony and the income of the guarantor.

Facts: The director of a company, Mr Macron, had secured a company debt for an amount of FRF20 million with a non-professional guarantee. At that moment, his salary was FRF37,550 a month and he had an estate of FRF4 million. As a result, the interest rate already exceeded Mr Macron's salary by five times. The agreement contained a clause according to which Macron could terminate the guarantee at any time.

Held: A guaranty which is manifestly disproportionate to the income and patrimony of the guarantor can be declared void.

Judgment: Considering that the Bank criticises the judgment for ordering payment by the Bank to Mr Macron of the sum of FRF15,000,000 by way of damages and ordering that such sum be set off against the sum of FRF20,000,000 payable by Mr Macron under his agreement as guarantor. The court of appeal contended on

[20] S 283.

[21] JCP 1997, éd E, II, 1007, n D Legeais and [1998] *Revue trimestrielle de droit civil* 100, n J Mestre and 157, n P Crocq.

behalf of the Bank, established that Mr Macron was a company director; as such he may be presumed to have full knowledge of the importance of his obligation, having regard to his income and patrimony; by ruling as it did the court of appeal deprived its decision of a legal ground under Articles 1382 and 1383 of the Civil Code. Secondly, only an unlimited undertaking may be regarded as a perpetual undertaking; an undertaking for an indefinite period, such as a guarantee without limit as to duration, has the potential to be limited owing to the right of unilateral termination available to the guarantor. By taking, first of all, the view that the Bank had fully complied with Article 48 of the law of 1 March 1984, which requires credit institutions to remind guarantors of their right of termination at any time, and thus establishing that Mr Macron had the opportunity to avail himself of his right of unilateral termination, yet, nonetheless, taking the view that his undertaking was perpetual, the court of appeal did not adhere to the legal effects from its own findings, infringed Article 2034 of the Civil Code and misapplied an alleged principle prohibiting perpetual obligations.

Yet, considering that, after having observed that Mr Macron had entered into a guarantee for FRF20,000,000 that was 'manifestly disproportionate' to his monthly income of FRF37,550, and to his patrimony of an amount less than four million francs, the court of appeal considered that Mr Macron had not committed any error vitiating his consent but was nonetheless entitled to argue that, in the actual circumstances due to the 'enormity of the sum guaranteed by a natural person' and quite apart from the good faith shown by the Bank, the latter had committed a wrongful act by seeking such a guarantee that was 'out of all proportion' to the patrimony and the income of the guarantor; thus, without it being necessary to examine any of the other grounds going to the perpetual nature of the undertaking at issue that is challenged in the second branch, the court of appeal rendered a lawful judgment; and the appeal against this judgment is therefore ungrounded in all its elements.

Hoge Raad, 25 September 1981[22] **5.16 (NL)**

Osby-Pannan A/B v Las Verkoopmaatschappij BV

DISPROPORTIONATE TRANSFER OF OWNERSHIP FOR SECURITY PURPOSES

Osby

A creditor is liable if he enters into a security agreement of which it knows or ought to foresee that it exhausts all creditworthiness of the debtor at the expense of a new creditor.

Facts: A parent company (X) granted a credit to another company of the same concern (Y), in which the former had 100% control. As security for the credit, Y agreed to transfer the ownership of all its assets—including the future assets to X.

Held: X made a wrongful act for which it is liable as it it knew, or ought to have foreseen, that new creditors of Y would be disadvantaged by the lack of recourse, and nevertheless failed to ensure that those creditors' claims were satisfied.

Judgment: When a parent company owns all shares in a subsidiary and has granted

[22] NJ 1982, 443.

credit to the subsidiary and subsequently acquires the assets, future included, of the subsidiary for security purposes completely or almost completely, so that the subsidiary to the new creditors—who grant credit after the transfer of ownership for security purposes—virtually, no longer offers recourse. There may be, when the parent company fails to take the interests of the new creditors seriously into account, under certain circumstances a wrongful act of it against these. This will particularly be the case when the parent company has such insight and control over the policy of the subsidiary that, given the size of the claim and the transfer of ownership for security purposes and the conduct of affairs in the subsidiary company, at the time of the above-mentioned conduct it knew or ought to have foreseen that new creditors would be disadvantaged by the lack of recourse, and nevertheless failed to ensure that those creditors' claims were satisfied.

BGH, 27 November 1997[23] **5.17 (DE)**

AMOUNT OF THE SECURITY RIGHT AND PUBLIC ORDER

Security limits

If the security right is disproportionate with regard to the secured claim, the creditor can be obliged to release the security right.

Facts: The defending banking institution awarded to a private person—whose professional activity was the repair of furniture—a credit facility of DM1.35 million. As security for this credit, the debtor made a transfer of stock and all existing and future claims. It was expressly provided that, in case the value of the provided securities would exceed contractual limits, the bank would release at the request and choice of the security provider. One agreement transferring the claims provided that the security provider had to guarantee that the amount of transferred claims had to be at least 100% of the standing credit and at least DM1 million. The debtor assigned her credit claims, in contravention of the security agreement. The question arises whether the security agreement is effective.

*Held:*The limit of the security right must be connected on the one hand to the secured claims and on the other hand to the value of the transferred security. It is not possible to go around this restriction by contractual arrangements with regard to the obligation to release security objects if the debtor does not comply with his obligations.

Judgment: Furthermore the determination of the limit of a security right is not to be left to one of the Parties to the security agreement. At the same time, in accordance with §315(1) BGB the power for determination of the value can be granted to any of the parties upon the determination of the conditions for the claim. However, this should only be presumed if the security agreement contains the relevant provision which, provided that the agreement was concluded according to the form, does not unreasonably prejudice the other provisions of the agreement (§9(1) AGBG).

(bb) Upon consideration of the limit of the security right one should assume that the objective of non-accessory security is to safeguard the creditor but not to excessively restrict the debtor's freedom of movement. Therefore, the limit of the secured obligation must be connected on the one hand to the secured claims and on the other hand to the value of the transferred security (value of security). As both factors can normally change, basically only a percentaged, abstract-general limit of secured obligation sufficiently takes account of a valid security interest of the creditor. Upon

[23] BGHZ 137, 212 and NJW 1998, 671.

extension of a certain credit line or when the amount of the secured claims has not changed an equivalent limit of the security right is also eligible.

Notes

(1) In the legal systems, measures have been taken in order to limit the scope of the security interest, in order to protect the debtor who is often the weaker party in the credit negotiation.[24]

Both the French and German judgments cited above give expression to the same principle, ie that the creditor has to take care not to be oversecured. In French law, it is stated that oversecurity is grounded in the wrongful act of a professional credit-lender.[25] The French case law has been sealed in Article L341-4 of the Consumer Code, which was introduced by an Act of 1 August 2003. According to the latter provision, a professional creditor is not entitled to claim any rights out of a surety agreement in which a natural person has obliged in a manifestly disproportionate manner in relation to his income and patrimony at the moment of the conclusion of the agreement, except if the surety can comply with its obligations at the moment that the creditor has recourse to the security right.

In German law, the prohibition of oversecuritisation is based on the good-faith principle, 'which excludes all good faith by the creditor'. It was held in the landmark decision of 27 November 1997 that securities exceeding the limit necessary to secure the creditor are released *ipso iure*. This is founded in §307 BGB which contains the general rule that terms and conditions in standard form contracts which impose an unreasonable disadvantage upon the party which has not provided the contract are considered as contrary to public order and thus void.

The creditor has merely the choice about the security he releases, but not whether he releases securities. Since secured debts tend to decrease in amount as time passes (because of repayment), the value of the security must accordingly decrease in order to prevent subsequent oversecurity. The German Supreme Court uses the following approach in order to determine whether the security limits have been exceeded:

(a) The relevant security interest at any time is at most 110% of the outstanding debts (credit excluding interest). The surcharge of 10% follows from the costs of realisation of the security, which have to be borne by the creditor in the event of default.

(b) The relevant value of a debt assigned in security is only 2/3 of its nominal value. The reason therefore is to be found in the inherent risks of receivables (eg late payment, partial payment, insolvency of the assigned debtor, etc).

(c) On this ground, the Bundesgerichtshof has determined the crucial line for oversecuritisation at a procentual amount of 150% of the secured obligation.

(2) In English, Austrian and Belgian law there is no case law on this point. However, the requirement of good faith and prohibition of abuse of rights plays

[24] For a larger view on protection of non-professional sureties in European private law: A Ciacchi (ed), *Professional Sureties in Europe: Formal and Substantive Disparity* (Baden-Baden, Nomos, 2007).

[25] This extra-contractual liability does not apply in the same way to non-professional creditors: Cass fr 13 November 2007, Recueil Dalloz 2007, 3066.

an important role in both Austrian and Belgian law, so that it cannot be excluded that similar case law will develop in these countries. In Belgian law, the legislator has also intervened in order to declare a surety not for value void if it is disproportionate to the estate and the income of the surety provider.[26] English law does not impose any limit on the value of the object of the security right.

III. RIGHT OF PLEDGE

III.A RIGHT OF PLEDGE OF CORPOREAL MOVABLE ASSETS

III.A.1 NATURE OF THE RIGHT OF PLEDGE

Code civil **5.18 (FR)**

Article 2333 A pledge is an agreement by which the pledgor grants to a creditor the right to be paid in priority to his other creditors out of a movable asset or a set of corporeal assets, present or future.

The claims secured may be present or future; in the latter case, they must be determinable.

Belgian Civil Code **5.19 (BE)**

Article 2071 A pledge is an agreement by which a debtor gives possession of an asset to his creditor as security for his debt. Assets which, by law, cannot be transferred cannot be pledged.

Bürgerliches Gesetzbuch **5.20 (DE)**

§1204 Statutory content of pledge on movable assets (1) In order to secure a claim, a movable asset can be burdened in such way that the creditor is entitled to payment of his claim from the object (right of pledge).

(2) The right of pledge can also be created for a future claim or for a conditional claim.

Burgerlijk Wetboek **5.21 (NL)**

Article 3:227 (1) The right of pledge and the right of hypothec are limited rights, aiming to execute on the object of the right in fulfilment of a claim for payment

[26] A similar rule has been inserted in the Belgian Civil Code in 2007 for guarantees for free. Article 2043sexies Belgian Civil Code provides as follows: 'At the penalty of voidness and when it concerns a guaranty for free in order to secure a specific claim, the amount of the guaranty is limited to the amount mentioned in the agreement, increased with the legal or conventional interest without these exceeding 50% of the capital sum. At the penalty of voidness, no guaranty for free can be agreed upon if the amount is manifestly disproportionate to the payment abilities of the guarantor, in which case these abilities must be determined in relation to the movable and immovable goods and income of the latter.'

of a sum of money in priority to other creditors. Where such right has been created on assets subject to registration, it is a right of hypothec; where it has been created on other assets, it is a right of pledge.
(2) A right of pledge or hypothec on an object attaches to everything which the ownership of the asset encompasses.

Court of Common Pleas, 26 November 1838[27] **5.22 (E&W)**

Reeves v Capper

SUBSTANCE OF A PLEDGE

Chronometer

As long as the creditor does not part with the possession, the pledge on behalf of the pledge continues to exist.

Facts: Wilson, a ship's captain, pledged his chronometer for a debt of £50. This pledge was recorded in a written agreement to Capper, who was the owner of the ship. The pledge was created by the handing over of the chronometer to the clerk of Capper. The latter subsequently rendered the chronometer in order to allow Wilson to use the chronometer on the ship for navigation purposes for a limited period of time. After the sea voyage was over, Wilson brought the chronometer to the makers for repair and pledged it in favour of another creditor, Reeves. He gave instruction to the makers of the chronometer to hold it for the account of Reeves, with which they agreed.

Held: Capper was not deprived of the possession of the chronometer, so that he could still claim the rights arising from the valid pledge of that chronometer.

Judgment: Tindal CJ—As to the second point, we agree entirely with the doctrine laid down in *Ryall v Rolle*, 1 Atk 163, that in the case of a simple pawn of a personal chattel, if the creditor parts with the possession, he loses his property in the pledge. But we think the delivery of the chronometer to Wilson under the terms of the agreement itself was not a parting with the possession, but that the possession of Captain Wilson was still the possession of Capper. The terms of the agreement were, that 'they would allow him to use it for the voyage'; words that gave him no interest in the chronometer, but only a license or permission to use it, for a limited time, whilst he continued as their servant, and employed it for the purpose of navigating their ship. During the continuance of the voyage, and when the voyage terminated, the possession of Captain Wilson was the possession of Messrs. Capper; just as the possession of plate by a butler is the possession of the master; and the delivery over to the plaintiff was, as between Captain Wilson and the defendants, a wrongful act, just as the delivery over of the plate by the butler to a stranger would have been; and could give no more right to the bailee than Captain Wilson had himself.

Notes

(1) A 'pledge'[28] is a limited property right with regard to movable (corporeal or incorporeal) assets which grants to the pledgor a right to be paid from the proceeds

[27] 5 Bing NC 136.
[28] At common law, the terms pledge and pawn are used interchangeably.

of the forced sale of the subject matter of the pledge, in discharge of the debt or obligation secured. Pledges are most frequently restricted to movable assets.[29] In French law, the term *gage* designates a pledge on a corporeal asset, while the term *nantissement* is used for a pledge on incorporeal objects.

Usually, a pledge secures payment of a monetary debt but, in principle, there is no reason why a pledge should not secure the performance by the pledgor of some other obligation. The Dutch Civil Code limits, however, the definition of the pledge and hypothec to money claims.

(2) German law recognises the notion of *Grundpfandrechte*. This concept does not fit well in the BGB. However, this concept is broader than the traditional concept of pledge. It deals with immovables and includes both hypothec, *Grundschuld* and *Rentenschuld*.[30] We will deal with the *Sicherungsgrundschuld* when analysing ownership as instrument used for security purposes (*cf* below VI.B.3.b).

III.A.2 DISPOSSESSION OF THE PLEDGOR

Code civil **5.23 (FR)**

Article 2337 A pledge is effective against third parties due to the compliance with the publicity attached to it.
That is also the case by surrendering of its object into the possession of the creditor or a third party upon which they agreed.
Where a pledge has been duly disclosed to the public, the particular successors of the pledgor may not invoke Article 2276.

Bürgerliches Gesetzbuch **5.24 (DE)**

§1205 Creation (1) In order to create the right of pledge it is necessary that the owner transfers the property to the creditor and both agree that the creditor is entitled to the pledge. If the creditor is in possession of the asset it is sufficient to reach agreement about the creation of the pledge.
(2) The transfer of an asset of which the owner merely has constructive possession can be substituted by a transfer of the constructive possession from the owner to the pledgee and the notification of the pledge to the possessor.

Burgerlijk Wetboek **5.25 (NL)**

Article 3:236(1) The right of pledge on a movable object, on a bearer right or order right, or on the usufruct of such an object or right, is created by bringing the object or the bearer certificate or order certificate into the possession of the pledgee or a

[29] We do not deal here with the 'antichrèse', which is a special form of 'pledge' on immovables, which has its origins in old Greek law. The 2006 amendment in French law has emphasised the specific nature of this device, no longer classifying it amongst the pledge rights: 'The antichresis is the affectation of an immovable in order to secure an obligation. It entails dispossession of the person creating the antichresis' (Art 2387 Cciv).

[30] All of these rights will be dealt with below.

third party, whom the parties agreed upon. The creation of a right of pledge on an order right or on the usufruct of such also requires endorsement.

Article 3:237(1) A pledge on a movable object, a claim, or on the usufruct of such an object or claim, can also be created by authentic or registered private deed, without that movable or claim being brought under the control of the secured creditor or a third party.

Privy Council (India), 15 October 1934[31] **5.26 (E&W)**

Official Assignee of Madras v Mercantile Bank of India Ltd

PUBLICITY OF THE PLEDGE

Groundnuts

A pledge of documents is not in general to be deemed a pledge of the goods.

Facts: A company of merchants purchased groundnuts and transported them by rail to Madras. For each consignment of groundnuts, the merchants obtained a railway receipt from the railway company. The receipt entitled them to delivery of the groundnuts from the railway company. The merchants then raised loans, which were secured, inter alia, by the delivery of the consignments to the respondent bank. The merchants became insolvent, and the insolvency administrator rejected the pledge which was claimed by the bank, because the bank would not have been given possession of the groundnuts.

Held: The pledgee does not release the pledge by handing the documents representing the object of the pledge to the pledgor in order that he may collect the goods from the railway company and place them in a warehouse on behalf of the pledgee.

Judgment: At common law a pledge could not be created except by a delivery of possession of the thing pledged, either actual or constructive. It involved a bailment. If the pledgor had the actual goods in his physical possession, he could effect the pledge by actual delivery; in other cases he could give possession by some symbolic act, such as handing over the key of the store in which they were. If, however, the goods were in the custody of a third person, who held for the bailor so that in law his possession was that of the bailor, the pledge could be effected by a change of the possession of the third party, that is by an order to him from the pledgor to hold for the pledgee, the change being perfected by the third party attorning to the pledgee, that is acknowledging that he thereupon held for him; there was thus a change of possession and a constructive delivery: the goods in the hands of the third party became by this process in the possession constructively of the pledgee. But where goods were represented by documents the transfer of the documents did not change the possession of the goods, save for one exception, unless the custodier (carrier, warehouseman or such) was notified of the transfer and agreed to hold in future as bailee for the pledgee. The one exception was the case of bills of lading, the transfer of which by the law merchant operated as a transfer of the possession of, as well as the property in, the goods. This exception has been explained on the ground that the goods being at sea the master could not be notified; the true explanation may be that it was a rule of the law merchant, developed in order to facilitate mercantile transactions, whereas the process of pledging goods on land

[31] [1935] AC 53.

was regulated by the narrower rule of the common law and the latter remained stereotyped in the form which it had taken before the importance of documents of title in mercantile transactions was realised. So things have remained in the English law: a pledge of documents is not in general to be deemed a pledge of the goods; a pledge of the documents (always excepting a bill of lading) is merely a pledge of the ipsa corpora of them; the common law continued to regard them as merely tokens of an authority to receive possession, though from time to time representations were made by special juries that in the ordinary practice of merchants transfers of documents were understood to pass possession, as for instance in 1815, in *Spear v Travers* (1815) 4 Camp 251. The common law rule was stated by the House of Lords in *William McEwan & Sons v Smith* (1849) 2 HLC 309. The position of the English law has been fully explained also more recently in *Inglis v Robertson* [1898] AC 616 and in *Dublin City Distillery, etc, Ltd v Doherty* [1914] AC 823.

Notes

(1) In the tradition of the Roman law, the right of pledge of corporeal assets requires the transfer of possession of the object of the pledge. A pledge agreement traditionally does not constitute a property security right as long as the dispossession of the pledgor had not been effected. The pledgee, or a third party about whom parties have agreed, has to receive the exclusive control of the pledged objects, but this delivery could be both actual, constructive or symbolic.

A symbolic delivery means, for instance, that the keys of the immovable in which the pledged objects are situated, are handed over to the creditor of the pledge. It is questioned whether this is sufficient in order to create a right of pledge. Most case law takes a favourable position in respect of the condition that the pledgee gets access to the pledged object, and the pledgor no longer does.[32] In other words: the requirement is made that the pledgor loses control over the object of the pledge. If both the pledgor and the pledgee have a key to the warehouse where the pledged objects are situated, it is most often said that no actual or symbolic delivery has taken place and, thus, that the creditor has no property right and therefore no priority right.[33]

In most legal systems a delivery *constitutum possessorium* is traditionally not accepted as a legal ground for an enforceable pledge agreement,[34] as this offers no actual protection in favour of the other creditors: they can still be mislead by the factual circumstance that their debtor is in actual possession of the objects. This is the so-called 'ostensible ownership'.

However, it emerges from the materials cited above that the requirement of dispossession is in decline (III.A.2). Dutch law has generalised the registered pledge

[32] *Cf* in English law: *Hilton v Tucker* [1888] 39 Ch D 669 (the pledgor hired a room in a building belonging to a third party and stored the pledged goods in it. The pledgor wrote to the pledgee informing him that the third party held the key to the room 'which I place entirely at your disposal. The validity of the pledge agreement is recognized').

[33] *Cf Dublin City Distillery Ltd v Doherty* [1914] AC 823 (House of Lords). On a delivery *constitutum possessorium*, see Chaper 7.

[34] In German law: §1205(2) BGB, in Dutch law: HR 25 January 1929, NJ 1929, 616.

without dispossession in 1992, French law followed this development in 2006.[35] In both influencing systems, the parties presently have the choice between the dispossession and the registration of the pledge agreement. German law has no general provisions with regard to pledge without dispossession, but only acknowledges a registered pledge with regard to specific objects which are valuable and volatile, such as cables[36] and aircrafts[37]. However, it must be noted that German law recognises a transfer for security purposes without any publicity requirement (IV.B.3), which largely diminishes the need for a non-possessory pledge.

The advantages of registration instead of dispossession are multiple. First of all, the pledgor can continue to make use of the pledged object in the course of his normal activities or business, which can be necessary for the payment of his obligations. Moreover, the pledgee most often is not organised to administer the object in an efficient way. Thirdly, it becomes possible to grant several rights of pledge on the same object, which is important if the value of the pledged object exceeds the value of the claim of the original pledgee. The ranking of the different pledgees is determined according to their registration. Finally, it becomes possible to pledge future objects.

The decrease of the weight of the dispossession as requirement for the creation of a pledge, has been emphasised in the Draft Common Frame of Reference (DCFR): Article IX–2:103 provides, under the title 'Possessory and Non-possessory Security Rights' that 'unless otherwise agreed by the parties, the creation of a security right by contract does not require possession of the encumbered asset by the secured creditor'. In the following sections of the DCFR, two alternative methods of publicity have been provided for: granting of possession (Chapter 3.II) and registration (Chapter 3.III).

(2) English law makes a general distinction between a possessory pledge and a non-possessory pledge ('charge'). This reflects an alternative approach in order to fulfil publicity measures, which was also found in Dutch and French law.

A pledge is a transaction in which the debtor (pledgor) transfers possession of a thing to the creditor (pledgee) to hold as security. When the pledgor is an individual the transaction is often called 'pawn' and the pledgee who enters into such transactions in the course of his business is called a 'pawnbroker'.

A charge is a security right which does not require that the creditor (chargee) take possession of the charged asset. The effectiveness of a charge is subject to requirements of writing and registration. A charge can have both movable and immovable assets as object.

(3) In the analysed legal systems dealing with registered pledges without dispossession, the priority ranking of these rights of pledge is inferior to the one of rights of pledge with dispossession.

[35] French law had already more extensive exceptions to the requirement of dispossession before the implementation of the Amendment of 2006. For instance, the French system had since Decree no 968 of 30 September 1953 (French Official Gazette 1 October 1953) a pledge without dispossession on cars. The Decree was abolished by the amendment of 2006.

[36] Act of 31 March 1925.

[37] Act of 26 February 1959.

In French law, the statutory rule seems at first sight favourable to the holder of a registered pledge:

> If a thing which has been the object of a non-possessory pledge is also the object of a pledge with dispossession afterwards, the priority right of the first pledgee is effective against the second pledgee if it has been duly registered, nothwithstanding the right of retention to which the second pledgee is entitled. (Article 2340 Cciv)

However, the first legal scholars commenting this provision assume that the registration does not exclude the possessory protection of the pledgee who has been put in possession of the object.[38] This possessory protection would exclude the priority of the registered pledgee in relation to the pledgee who has the good faith possession of the goods.

An identical rule is to be found in Dutch law:

> Despite the lack of power to dispose of the goods of the pledgor is the creation of the pledge on a movable object, on a bearer instrument or on the usufruct of such an object or right, valid if the pledgee is in good faith at the moment that possession of the object has been given to him to a third party pledgee. (Article 3:238(1) BW)

In comparing the different systems, there is an obvious correlation between the validity and enforcement requirements of the pledge on the one side and the admission of security rights other than the pledge on the other side. In Dutch law, the creation of a non-possessory pledge was clearly presented as the counterpart of abolition of the fiduciary transfer for security purposes (III.A.4.c). The German legal system has developed the other way around: it sticks to the requirement of dispossession, but this has given rise in legal practice to so many constraints that title retention has been interpreted very widely (III.A.2) and the fiduciary transfer of ownership has been accepted by case law (IV.B.3).

III.A.3 REALISATION OF THE PLEDGE

Code civil **5.27 (FR)**

Article 2346 In case of failure to pay the secured obligation, a creditor may obtain a court order for the sale of the asset which is object of the pledge. That sale shall take place in accordance with the rules on enforcement proceedings from which a contract of pledge may not derogate.

Article 2347 A creditor may also obtain a court order that the asset will remain with him by way of satisfaction.

Where the value of the object exceeds the amount of the secured debt, the excess value shall be paid to the debtor or, if there are other creditors with a right of pledge [*créanciers gagistes*], shall be deposited.

Article 2348 When creating the pledge or afterwards, parties may agree that in case of failure to perform the secured obligation, the creditor will become owner of the object of the pledge.

[38] R Dammann, 'La réforme des sûretés mobilières: une occasion manquée', Dalloz 2006, 1299, no 10.

The value of the object shall be determined at the day of the transfer by an expert designated by agreement or judicially, in the absence of an official quotation of that object on a regulated market in the sense of the Monetary and Financial Code [*Code monétaire et financier*]. Any clause to the contrary is deemed not written.

Where that value exceeds the amount of the secured obligation, the excess value shall be paid to the debtor or, if there are other creditors with a right of pledge, shall be deposited.

Belgian Civil Code **5.28 (BE)**

Article 2078 The creditor cannot, in case of non-payment, dispose of the object of the pledge; but he can introduce a writ to the court to be authorised to retain the object of the pledge in fulfilment of and to the extent of his obligation, according to an appraisal made by experts, or to have the pawn sold by auction.

Any covenant authorising a creditor to appropriate the object of the pledge or to dispose of it without complying with the forms as set forth above, shall be void.

Burgerlijk Wetboek **5.29 (NL)**

Article 3:235 Each contractual arrangement in which the pledgee or hypothecee is given the power to appropriate the object of the pledge or hypothec is void.

Article 3:248 (1) When the debtor is in default of what the pledge is meant to secure, the pledgee is entitled to sell the object of the pledge and satisfy the standing obligation out of the proceeds of the sale.

(2) The parties can agree that one can only proceed to a sale after a judge, at the request of the pledgee has verified that the debtor was in default.

(3) A pledgee with a lower ranking priority right or a seizing creditor can only sell the pledged object as burdened with the higher ranking priority rights.

Bürgerliches Gesetzbuch **5.30 (DE)**

§1228 Satisfaction through sale of the object of the pledge

(1) The pledgee will be paid out of the sale of the object of the pledge.

(2) The pledgee is entitled to proceed to the sale as soon as the claim is completely or partially due. If the object of the obligation does not consist of money, the sale is only permitted after the claim has been converted into a monetary claim.

§1229 Prohibition of a forfeiture agreement

An agreement concluded prior to the moment at which the pledge is entitled to proceed to the forced sale, according to which ownerhip of an asset is attributed or is transfered to the pledgee, if he is not paid or not paid in time, is void.

Privy Council, 11 November 1915[39] **5.31 (E&W)**

The Odessa v The Woolston (In Prize)

SALE OF THE OBJECT OF THE PLEDGE

Soda

A pledgee can sell the property motu proprio and without any assistance from the Court.

Facts: The appellants were J Henry Schröder & Co, who were bankers carrying on business in London. The *Odessa* was a ship, transporting a cargo consisting of nitrate of soda. This cargo had been sold by a Chilean firm to a German company. In June 1914, the appellants accepted bills of exchange for £41,153 1s 5d (the price of the cargo) drawn by the sellers, and as security received and held the bill of lading which made the cargo deliverable to them or to their assigns. On 4 August 1914, while the ship was on her voyage, war broke out between Great Britain and Germany, and on 19 August 1914, the ship was captured at sea. A writ was issued by the Procurator-General claiming that the ship and cargo belonged to enemies of the Crown and were liable to confiscation as lawful prize. The appellants claimed the cargo alleging that it was their property and/or as holders of the bill of lading for full value.[40]

Held: The appeal is dismissed.

Judgment: When the nature of the right of a pledgee to sell is examined it will be seen that the so-called 'special' property which it is said to create is in truth no property at all. …

If it were not for the somewhat unfortunate peculiarity of English terminology involved in the established use of the words 'special property' when 'special interest' would seem better, it is difficult to see how an argument could be maintained which would effectively distinguish pledge from lien for present purposes.

The very expression 'special property' seems to exclude the notion of that general property which is the badge of ownership. If the pledgee sells he does so by virtue and to the extent of the pledgor's ownership, and not with a new title of his own. He must appropriate the proceeds of the sale to the payment of the pledgor's debt, for the money resulting from the sale is the pledgor's money to be so applied. The pledgee must account to the pledgor for any surplus after paying the debt. He must take care that the sale is a provident sale, and if the goods are in bulk he must not sell more than is reasonably sufficient to pay off the debt, for he only holds possession for the purpose of securing himself the advance which he has made. He cannot use the goods as his own. These considerations show that the right of sale is exercisable by virtue of an implied authority from the pledgor and for the benefit of both parties. It creates no *jus in re* in favour of the pledgee; it gives him no more than a jus in rem such as a lienholder possesses, but with this added incident, that he can sell the property motu proprio and without any assistance from the Court.

[39] [1916] 1 AC 145.

[40] We will not deal with the facts with regard to the Woolston, which are less relevant fo this purpose.

High Court, Chancery Division, 12 Febuary 1877[41] **5.32 (E&W)**

Carter v Wake

MANNERS OF REALISATION OF THE PLEDGE

Carter

A pledgee does not have ownership at law, and his equitable rights cannot exceed his legal title.

Facts: In 1874 Wake mortgaged to Carter certain ships, and also deposited with him (without memorandum) certain bonds of the Canada Southern Railway Company, as security for a debt. These bonds are first mortgage bonds, redeemable at par in the year 1890, but at present at a considerable discount in the market.

In 1875, Carter sued Wake praying for the usual accounts, and for a sale of the ships, and foreclosure of the equity of redemption in the bonds; or, in the alternative, for a sale of the whole. The ships had since been sold and the proceeds applied in reduction of the debt, leaving a sum of upwards of £4,000 still due to Carter. It was stated that if the bonds were now sold, they would not produce enough to satisfy the debt, but that Carter had calculated that if he could foreclose the equity of redemption now, he could repay himself in full by waiting till the bonds were redeemed in due course.

Held: An order for sale of the bonds by auction is decreed, but as there seems to be a good reason why Carter should not be forced to part with them, the judge gives him the liberty to bid.

Judgment: Jessel MR—The Plaintiff is in the position of a mere pledgee at law of certain chattels, and I do not think that a person in that position has the same right of foreclosure as a mortgagee by deposit of the title deeds of land. The principle upon which the Court acts in the latter case is, that in a regular legal mortgage there has been an actual conveyance of the legal ownership, and then the Court has interfered to prevent that from having its full effect, and when the ground of interference is gone by the non-payment of the debt, the Court simply removes the stop it has itself put on. Then, when there is a deposit of title deeds, the Court treats that as an agreement to execute a legal mortgage, and therefore as carrying with it all the remedies incident to such a mortgage. None of this reasoning applies to a pledge of chattels; the pledgee never had the absolute ownership at law, and his equitable rights cannot exceed his legal title.

Notes

(1) With regard to the realisation of the right of pledge, two issues arise. The first issue is whether the pledgee is entitled to sell the object of the pledge and to be reimbursed out of the proceeds, and whether he has to be authorised by a judge to do so. The second issue is whether parties can agree that the creditor will become owner of the pledged objects on the default of the debtor, without judicial authorisation. These questions will be dealt with separately.

(2) The first issue is the issue of the prohibition of self-help, which has survived legal debates since Roman law. According to this prohibition, a pledgee is not entitled to sell the object of a pledge without prior judicial authorisation. This prohibition still applies in Belgian law (Article 2078 Cciv) and French law (Article 2346

[41] LR 4 Ch D 605.

Cciv). However, the above-cited case law clearly demonstrates that this prohibition is subject to increasing numbers of exceptions. In Dutch law, the opposite principle applies: the creditor can sell the object of the pledge in the light of the realisation of his pledge without judicial authorisation, except if the agreement has required the prior authorisation. That is also the case in German[42] and, as it emerges from the above cited judgments, English law.

(3) According to most of the civil law systems, in line with Roman law, it is not allowed that parties agree prior to the debtor's failure to pay the obligation that the secured creditor should obtain full ownership of the pledged movable. This is the so-called prohibition of *pacta commissoria*. German, Dutch and Belgian law adhere to this position. It emerges from the *Carter v Wake* case that this is also valid for the pledge in English law. However, English legal scholars defend the view that statute or contract can provide otherwise.

French law has introduced a revolutionary rule in this respect in the legislative amendment of 23 March 2006, which introduced Article 2348 Cciv (cited above). The French *pactum commissorium* applies both to fixed and floating charges. However, this provision does not apply in relation to consumers, who are protected by the French Consumer Code.[43]

III.A.4 FIXED CHARGE–FLOATING CHARGE

Introductory Notes

(a) As we have explained above, a charge in common law is a security right which does not require that the creditor (chargee) takes possession of the charged asset. The effectiveness of a charge is subject to requirements of writing.

(b) The common law makes a further distinction between fixed and floating charges. A floating charge is a security right which covers all or most present and future assets of a debtor, but does not attach to these assets until a certain specified event happens, in which case the floating charge becomes a fixed charge. In this way, a floating charge does not prevent the chargor from disposing of the assets free from the charge. Civil law systems do not distinguish along the same lines, but it will be seen in this analysis that they nevertheless have systems equivalent to the floating charge.

II.A.4.a French law

Commercial Code **5.33 (FR)**

Article L142-1 Businesses may be the object of security rights, without complying with other conditions and formalities than those mentioned by the present chapter and Chapter III below.

[42] *Cf* F Baur and R Stürner, *Sachenrecht*, 17th edn (München, CH Beck, 1999) §55, no 26.

[43] Art L311-32 French Consumers Code: '[I]n case of failure by the debtor, the pledgee can only make use of the realisation methods of the pledge authorised by Articles 2346 and 2347 of the Civil Code, without making application of the pactum commissorium provided for in Article 2348, which is deemed to be void.'

A security right on a business does not grant to the secured creditor the right to have the business allotted to him in payment up to the full amount due.

Article L142-2 The security subject to the provisions of this chapter may cover the following items only as forming part of a business: style and trademark, leasing rights, goodwill and custom, company building, equipment or materials used for the operation of the business, patents, licences, trademarks, industrial drawings and designs, and in general the intellectual property rights attached thereto.

A certificate of addition subsequent to the security, which includes the patent to which it applies shall follow the fate of this patent and, as shall it, be part of the security as constituted.

For lack of an explicit and precise designation in the instrument creating it, the security shall cover only the style and trademark, leasing rights, clientele and custom.

If the security relates to a business and its branches, then these must be designated by the precise indication of their seat.

Code civil **5.34 (FR)**

Article 2342 Where a non-possessory pledge attaches to fungible assets, the pledgor may dispose of them if the agreement provides so, on the condition that they are substituted by the same amount of equivalent assets.

Notes

(1) In French law, the economic need to make use of the economic value of the commercial fund (*fonds de commerce*) in order to obtain credit facilities was felt at an early stage of economic development. The legislator introduced a non-possessory pledge on the commercial fund of the debtor as long ago as the end of the nineteenth century. The pledgor keeps control of his commercial fund, so that he can continue to run his business activities without being impeded by the pledge agreement. In order to make other creditors of the pledgor aware of the existence of the pledge, the legislator imposed the registration of the non-possessory pledge in a public registry kept at the Commercial Court.

(2) Legal scholars observe that this security right is rarely used in French legal practice. The reasons are various. Firstly, the pledge on the commercial fund does not have a high ranking in general, and has a lower ranking than the statutory lien of tax authorities in particular.[44] Moreover, a creditor can never be certain of the subsistence of the value of his security right. This will depend upon the question of whether or not the business activities of the pledgor are beneficial.[45]

(3) If French case law and legal scholars use the term 'floating charge' (*gage flottant*), they refer to a specific legal device, dealing with the following problem: if a security is granted to a creditor during the precedent period ('suspect period')

[44] Cour de cassation, 26 October 1971, D 1972, 61, n J Derrida.
[45] Cabrillac and Mouly, above n 1, no 704.

preceeding the bankruptcy, this security is not effective against the insolvency.[46] This raises legal uncertainty if an asset is substituted to an original asset of a pledge during the suspect period, as this could render the security right unenforceable against the bankruptcy administrator. The French Cour de cassation ruled, especially with regard to fungible assets:

> The article 2076 Cciv …, according to which the security right only persists as long as its object … remains in the possession of the creditor … only applies as long as the object of the pledge is an identifiable asset, which has to be restituted in kind. The rule mentioned in these provisions can not be applied if the stock is affected, in the common intention of parties and according to their agreement, to be sold along its becoming older and to be substituted by other assets of the same kind and amount. If, pursuant to this rule, … the stock leaves the object of the pledge, real subrogation which is grounded in the fungibility of the assets, ensures that this stock is substituted by other assets which enter and remain in the estate of the debtor.[47]

Hence, the date of creation of the pledge will remain unchanged after the substitution, regardless of the change of its object, so that this substitution does not endanger the position of the creditor. French case law largely extended the scope of this construction elaborated by case law and also applied it to non-fungible assets, even to a hypothec on immovables.[48] It would be sufficient that (i) the value of the substitute assets does not exceed the value of the original assets, and (ii) that the substitution is instantaneous.

(4) This enlargement of the scope of the floating charge has come to an end by the legislative amendment of 23 March 2006. Article 2342 of the Civil Code (cited above) expressly restricts the floating charge to fungible assets. According to this provision, 'if the non-possessory pledge has fungible assets as object, the pledgor can dispose of the assets if the agreement provides so and subject to the condition that he substitutes the initial assets by the same quantity of the equivalent assets'.[49]

[46] Art L632-1 of the French Commercial Code: 'Are void, when they have been entered into since the date of suspension of payment of the debts, the following acts: 6° Each conventional hypothec, each judicial hypothec and each legal hypothec and pledge created on the assets of the debtor as security for previously contracted debts.'

[47] Cour de cassation, 10 March 1915, D 1916, I, 214, S 1916, I, 5, n C Lyon Caen, [1915] *Revue trimestrielle de droit civil* 528 and [1916] *Revue trimestrielle de droit civil* 103, n R Demogue.

[48] Cour de cassation, 20 January 1998, Bull civ, IV, no 28: 'Attendu que la cour d'appel a retenu qu'aux termes de l'acte de 'translation d'hypothèque', il n'y avait pas eu constitution d'une sûreté nouvelle mais substitution au privilège du prêteur de deniers et à l'hypothèque inscrits sur l'immeuble vendu, d'une hypothèque sur l'immeuble acquis pour garantir le remboursement du solde du prêt; qu'elle en a exactement déduit, en dehors de toute référence à la subrogation réelle, que cette sûreté, qui n'était supérieure, ni dans sa nature, ni dans son étendue, aux sûretés auxquelles elle avait été substituée, avait été valablement inscrite pendant la période suspecte; que le moyen n'est pas fondé.'

[49] Original French text: 'Lorsque le gage sans dépossession a pour objet des choses fongibles, le constituant peut les aliéner si la convention le prévoit à charge de les remplacer par la même quantité de choses équivalentes.'

III.A.4.b Belgian law

Introductory Note

Belgian law also recognises the existence of a floating security right, similar to the French floating charge. The pledge on the commercial fund (*pand op de handelszaak* or *gage sur fonds de commerce*) is a security right over a company's present and future assets which change in the ordinary course of his business and which continue to be controlled by the chargor until the chargee executes his security rights. In order to protect third parties, this pledge must be registered in a public register.

From a conceptual viewpoint, legal scholars argue that a commercial fund has become a legal universality for the purposes of a pledge. From a functional viewpoint, it leads towards the possibility for the pledgor to remain in possession of assets and to continue on an operational basis doing business.

Act of 25 October 1919 with regard to the pledge on a commercial fund[50] **5.35 (BE)**

Article 1 The commercial fund may be pledged, subject to the circumstances laid down by this Act.

Article 2 The pledge shall include the entirety of values which constitute the commercial fund, particularly the customers, the ensign, the trade furnishings and fittings, the trade marks, the right to the contract of lease, the furniture of the warehouse and the tools, except if parties have agreed otherwise.

It may contain the inventory to a maximum amount of 50% of its value.

Notes

(1) The pledge also covers inventory, though to a maximum of 50% of its value. The legislation restricts the scope of the registered pledge in order not to create too heavy a burden on the estate of the pledgor. The creditworthiness of a debtor should not be impeded by one credit agreement.

(2) Contrary to the English *Brumark* judgment cited below (5.38 (E&W)), Belgian case law does not a priori recognise the priority of the fixed charge when it enters into conflict with a floating charge. This conflict can, for instance, arise in Belgian law if a receivable is pledged as separate asset and is also part of the commercial fund which is the object of the floating charge. Belgian case law applies the principle of anteriority, comparing the date of registration of the floating charge with the date of notification of the fixed charge to the debtor of the receivable. The first security right to have been published will prevail over the other.[51]

(3) Belgian case law has adopted, in the same line as French case law, a floating charge in the sense of a pledge which allows the substitution of the original assets without putting the creditor at risk if the substitution has taken place during the

[50] Belgian Official Gazette, 5 November 1919.

[51] Cour de cassation, 19 November 1992, Pas 1992, I, 1286.

'suspect period' preceeding the bankruptcy. The Belgian Supreme Court ruled in a judgment of 12 November 1914 as follows:

> If, during the suspect period preceeding bankruptcy, the bankrupt debtor substitutes one object to another object of the pledge, this transaction is valid unless if the assets provided to the bankrupt debtor, at the moment of the substitution, did not have the same value as the original goods.[52]

If the object of the pledge is substituted by another object of equal value during the suspect period, this substitution does not affect the effectiveness and priority ranking of the pledge: the pledge is deemed to continue from its original date.

III.A.4.c Dutch law

Hoge Raad, 23 April 1999[53] **5.36 (NL)**

Tanzania National Bank of Commerce v Sisal

CONFLICT BETWEEN FLOATING CHARGE AND SPECIFIC CHARGE

Sisal case

The floating charge and the non-possessory pledge over the business are functionally equivalent.

Facts: On 17 March 1967 the Tanzania National Bank of Commerce (NBC) and Tanzania Cordage (Cordage) entered into a credit agreement, which means that NBC will grant a credit to Cordage to the amount of £2 million. As security for this debt, a floating charge was created under the law of Tanzania. The debenture was registered on 5 April 1967 at the register of the Administrator General of Dar es Salaam. In 1994 several clients of Sisal paid by the delivery of letters of credit which were all issued in the Netherlands by the Banque de Suez Nederland in the name of Cordage, according to which Cordage acquired a claim to Banque de Suisse. Sisal started proceedings for the realisation of its claim against Cordage, on the receivables which Cordage held against Banque de Suisse. The question arose during the legal proceedings whether Sisal was entitled to initiate a seizure proceeding in the priority conflict between Sisal and NBC.

Held: The Dutch Supreme Court only decided on the part of the issue at stake. It held that NBC continues to have the right to appoint an insolvency administrator who will draft the priority ranking between the creditors.

Judgment: The question arises as to whether the claimant in respect of a security right abroad lawfully created under the applicable legal system can be equated, from the point of view of justice and efficiency, with the holder under Articles 480 and 481 Rv of a Dutch security right, and thus be entitled to request settlement of the order of priority. It is noteworthy that the decisive factor in that connection is not whether in general terms the foreign and Netherlands security rights are comparable but whether for the purposes of the application of a particular provision of Dutch law ... the foreign security right can in view of its content and purpose be equated with an equivalent Dutch security right.

Part 2a of the plea argues that the court's finding in paragraph 4.24 of its judgment that a comparison between the floating charge and the non-possessory pledge

[52] Cour de cassation, 12 november 1914, Pas 1915, I, 124.
[53] NJ 2000, 30.

under Dutch law does not lead 'to any substantive difference in purpose and result' was only appreciated in the light of two criteria, namely that the foreign law pursues the same aim and leads to the same result. It is contended in that regard that the Court applied an incorrect consideration because it did not give any consideration to the substance of the foreign right, and the legal consequences thereof, and in particular took no account of the arguments by Sisal that the floating charge cannot be regarded as a limited right, as it entails no right to follow the assets, the *priori tempore* rule does not apply, the ability to make dispositions is unrestricted and it also applies to intangible assets. The legal arguments contained in this subsection cannot succeed. As may be deduced from the considerations in point 3.3, the court did not apply an incorrect consideration for its judgment. The plea disregards the fact that the judgment cannot be challenged in an appeal on a point of law by a complaint as to the statement of reasons.

Accordingly this part of the plea cannot succeed… .

Contrary to the assertion made in that part of the plea, the court in comparing the floating charge with the non-possessory pledge did not regard it as decisive that the floating charge creates a security over the whole estate of the business but saw the similarity in the fact that both the floating charge and the non-possessory pledge confer to the lender a security right over the business assets of the borrower without the borrower being impeded in the exercise of his business activities (para 4.23). That is what the court means in para 4.24 when it speaks of the 'result'. Part 2c of the plea is therefore without legal ground.

Notes

(1) The Dutch Supreme Court ruled in the above-cited case that, in order to establish the equivalence between the Dutch and the foreign security right, the common purpose of the security right in the specific case prevails on the differences in conceptual features of both devices. In this case the floating charge was held to be functionally equivalent to a non-possessory pledge resting on a claim. An application *in concreto* is therefore necessary. This complicates matters, as a security right can only reach its purpose if the security holder has legal certainty from the outset. A judgment which determines the equivalence a posteriori always gives rise to legal uncertainty, which is irreconcilable with a security right.

(2) Dutch law has not implemented in its national law a type of enterprise charge. However, it is possible in Dutch law to grant a silent (registered) pledge on the present and future trading stock of a debtor. The only limitation is that the pledged assets must be sufficiently identifiable both at the moment of the creation of the pledge and at the moment of the exercise of the pledge. If all stock is pledged, the issue of identifiability will not be raised. If only a part of the stock is pledged, care should be taken to have the 'burdened' goods stored separately. The use of a non-possessory pledge on future stock is very common in commercial practice.

III.A.4.d German law

BGH 17 January 1995[54] **5.37 (DE)**

SECURITY RIGHT ON INVENTORY

Warenlager case

A pledge of inventory is valid and effective, even if no release clause has been agreed upon.

Facts: The predecessor of the defendant, which was the insolvency administrator of the claimant, granted a DM4.5 million credit facility, on the basis of the general banking clauses 1986. Amongst other securities, the debtor transferred ownership of inventory with floating composition. It was stipulated in the security agreement that 'the inventory must value at any moment at least DM1.5 million'. If the inventory were to exceed this limit substantially and in the long term, the Bank was to discharge securities at the choice of the grantor. After non-compliance of the credit in September 1987, the defending party took possession of the inventory. At that stage, a conflict arose with regard to the validity and efficiency of the security right.

Held: The pledge is valid as the basic requirements for the pledge are met. The Civil Code does not require a clear 'discharge clause' in order to be valid and efficient.

Judgment: Under Clause 19(2)(1) of the 1986 General terms and conditions, all objects coming into the bank's possession may be used as security for all current and future claims by the bank against the customer.

This clause provides the consent for the pledging of property, as required under §1205 I of the BGB. It continued to subsist at the time when the bankrupt party conferred on the defendant sole possession of its inventory and thus gave rise to an immediate right of pledge in favour of the defendant (*cf* BGH, NJW 1988, 3260—LM §273 BGB No 45—WM 1988, 859 (862)). It is not necessary for the contracting parties to be aware of the legal consequences at the moment of the transfer of possession.

The view of the appeal court, according to which the contractual right of pledge was tacitly revoked cannot be upheld. Under the general terms and conditions of banking business the creation of an agreement to exclude the right of pledge is subject to strict conditions. ... There may be deemed to be a tacit exclusion only if if the customer makes plain that his consent to the creation of a right of pledge is not to apply to such a transaction. ... This can particularly be the case through the customer's conveying to the Bank assets earmarked for a specific purpose. ...

In the present case, on handing over the key to the inventory the bankrupt party did not conclusively express that no right of pledge in favour of the defendant was to be created. Contrary to the appeal court's view, no such intention may be inferred from the fact that the handover of the inventory occurred in performance of the agreement for transfer by way of security that was regarded by the parties as valid. That may have been intended for a specific purpose but that fact does not preclude a right of pledge and satisfaction of the defendant's claims from it. Instead the handover of the inventory was intended to enable the defendant to turn it to account and satisfy its claims. That is the significant distinction in relation to the cases mentioned by the appeal court.

[54] BGHZ 128, 295–301 and NJW 1995, 1085–87.

(c) Nor, contrary to the appeal court's view, does Clause 19(2) of the 1986 general terms and conditions unreasonably disadvantage the bankrupt party in a manner contravening the principle of good faith. The validity of the pledge clause in the terms and conditions of banks and savings banks is recognised in the case law and academic writings. ... A qualified release clause as required by the VIIIth and IXth civil senate of the BGH on the transfer by way of security of an inventory with rotating stock is not necessary in this case in order to protect the grantor of the security right from providing a disproportionate security. ... The scope of the ancillary right of pledge is determined by the situation at any time with regard to the secured claim. It is true that this does not preclude parties from granting an excessive security right, in particular in the case of the pledging of several assets. ... However, the law tolerates a greater amount of security in favour of the pledgee than is actually needed provided that the parameters set generally by §242 BGB are not exceeded. Under §1222 of the BGB each of all pledged assets covers each aspect of the claim. As long as the pledgee's claim has not been fully paid, the pledgor may not as a matter of principle request restitution of any of the pledged assets. This will be exceptionally different under §242 BG if it emerges that the debt is adequately secured by several assets and the refusal of the pledgee to release a portion of the pledged assets would constitute an abuse of rights. ... Clause 19 VI 2 of the general terms and conditions of banking business takes this in account by virtue of the obligation upon the bank in its discretion to release items of property upon request by the customer provided that they are permanently useless for the security purpose.

(d) Nor, contrary to the appeal court's view, can the defendant's right of pledge be denied through the consideration that otherwise the nullity of the agreement for transfer by way of security would be circumvented. The presumed invalidity of the transfer by way of security owing to the absence of a release clause in no way warrants denial of a pledge as a right of security in favour of the defendant where the requisite preconditions underlying such a right are present, in particular possession by the creditor. A release clause is not required by the law.

Note

German law recognises a floating charge with regard to claims. This emerges from the possibility of an anticipated general assignment (*antizipierte Globalzession*), which can be effected without any publication (*stille Abtretung*). This possibility enables a debtor to grant a security right over all present receivables of the debtor or a clearly distinguishable part of them. Contrary to English law, the assignee has a rather high priority ranking: §51 InsO grants him the same priority ranking to be satisfied out of the proceeds of the assigned debts as the holder of a fixed charge.

III.A.4.e English law

Privy Council (New Zealand), 5 June 2011[55] **5.38 (E&W)**

Agnew and Another v Commissioner of Inland Revenue

DISTINCTION BETWEEN A FIXED CHARGE AND A FLOATING CHARGE

Brumark

A fixed charge requires that the money is available to the charger as a source of its cash flow.

Facts: Brumark Investments Ltd ('Brumark') granted a charge over the uncollected book debts of a company. According to the agreement, Brumark had the right to collect these and use the proceeds in the ordinary course of its business. Brumark subsequently became insolvent. The only assets available for distribution to creditors were the proceeds of the book debts which were outstanding when the receivers were appointed and which they have since collected. The question arises whether the charge is *in casu* a fixed charge or a floating charge. If the charge is a fixed charge, as the receivers contend, the proceeds are payable to the company's bank Westpac Banking Corporation as the holder of the charge. If, however, it was a floating charge at the time it was created, they would have been payable to the employees and the Commissioner of Inland Revenue as preferential creditors.

Held: In order to create a charge on book debts as a fixed charge, it is sufficient to prohibit the company from realising the debts itself, whether by assignment or collection.

Judgment: The thinking behind the development of the floating charge was that compliance with the terms of a fixed charge on the company's circulating capital would paralyse its business. ... A fixed charge gives the holder of the charge an immediate proprietary interest in the assets subject to the charge which binds all those into whose hands the assets may come with notice of the charge. Unless it obtained the consent of the holder of the charge, therefore, the company would be unable to deal with its assets without committing a breach of the terms of the charge. It could not give its customers a good title to the goods it sold to them, or make any use of the money they paid for the goods. It could not use such money or the money in its bank account to buy more goods or meet its other commitments. It could not use borrowed money either, not even, as Sir George Jessel MR observed, the money advanced to it by the charge holder. In short, a fixed charge would deprive the company of access to its cash flow, which is the life blood of a business. Where, therefore, the parties contemplated that the company would continue to carry on business despite the existence of the charge, they must be taken to have agreed on a form of charge which did not possess the ordinary incidents of a fixed charge.

The floating charge is capable of affording the creditor, by a single instrument, an effective and comprehensive security upon the entire undertaking of the debtor company and its assets from time to time, while at the same time leaving the company free to deal with its assets and pay its trade creditors in the ordinary course of business without reference to the holder of the charge. ...

If the chargor is free to deal with the charged assets and so withdraw them from the ambit of the charge without the consent of the chargee, then the charge is a floating charge. But the test can equally well be expressed from the chargee's

[55] [2001] 3 WLR 454.

point of view. If the charged assets are not under its control so that it can prevent their dissipation without its consent, then the charge cannot be a fixed charge. …

While a debt and its proceeds are two separate assets, however, the latter are merely the traceable proceeds of the former and represent its entire value. A debt is a receivable; it is merely a right to receive payment from the debtor. Such a right cannot be enjoyed in specie; its value can be exploited only by exercising the right or by assigning it for value to a third party. An assignment or charge of a receivable which does not carry with it the right to the receipt has no value. It is worthless as a security. Any attempt in the present context to separate the ownership of the debts from the ownership of their proceeds (even if conceptually possible) makes no commercial sense.

The draftsman of the debenture in the present case recognised this. He purported to separate the book debts and their proceeds, but he did not attempt to separate their ownership. They were charged by the same chargor to the same chargee. It is a matter of personal choice whether one describes this as resulting in two different charges or a single charge (which is said to be convertible). The critical factor which is determinative of the nature of the charge in respect of the uncollected book debts is that the event which is said to convert the charge from a fixed to a floating charge (if there is only one) or to replace the one charge by the other (if there are two) is the act of the company.

To constitute a charge on book debts a fixed charge, it is sufficient to prohibit the company from realising the debts itself, whether by assignment or collection. If the company seeks permission to do so in respect of a particular debt, the charge holder can refuse permission or grant permission on terms, and can thus direct the application of the proceeds. But it is not necessary to go this far. As their Lordships have already noted, it is not inconsistent with the fixed nature of a charge on book debts for the holder of the charge to appoint the company its agent to collect the debts for its account and on its behalf. The *Siebe Gorman* case [1979] 2 Lloyd's Rep 142 and *In re Keenan Bros Ltd* [1986] BCLC 242 merely introduced an alternative mechanism for appropriating the proceeds to the security. The proceeds of the debts collected by the company were no longer to be trust moneys but they were required to be paid into a blocked account with the charge holder. The commercial effect was the same: the proceeds were not at the company's disposal. Such an arrangement is inconsistent with the charge being a floating charge, since the debts are not available to the company as a source of its cash flow. But their Lordships would wish to make it clear that it is not enough to provide in the debenture that the account is a blocked account if it is not operated as one in fact.

Notes

(1) According to English law, three distinctive features are recognised for a floating charge:

> if a charge has the three characteristics … it is a floating charge: (1) If it is a charge on a class of assets of a company present and future; (2) if that class is one which, in the ordinary course of the business of the company, would be changing from time to time; and (3) if you find that by the charge it is contemplated that, until some future step is taken

> by or on behalf of those interested in the charge, the company may carry on its business in the ordinary way as far as concerns the particular class of assets I am dealing with.[56]

Even if the floating charge is considered to be attractive for financial institutions, it has also been subject of criticism:

- First of all, it would totally exhaust the estate which must be liquidated by the insolvency administrator and would leave nothing more than an empty shell to the other creditors. The English legislator responded to this cricital observation in introducing section 107 of the Preferential Payments in Bankruptcy Amendment Act 1897, which makes the preferential debts and fixed charges payable out of the proceeds of a floating charge in priority to the debt secured by a floating charge. Nowadays, this low priority ranking of floating charges can be found in Schedule 6 of the Insolvency Act 1986.
- Moreover, the fact that the floating charge allowed a company to continue to trade and incur credit despite the existence of the charge puts the ordinary trade creditors of the company at risk, even though they would not normally know of the existence of the charge; for the holder of the charge could step in without warning at any time and obtain priority over them. That is the reason why the compulsory registration of floating charges was introduced.

(2) The *Brumark* judgment is in line with earlier decisions in which it was held that a charge over book debts must be a floating one if the debtor company remains at liberty to collect the debts and pay them into an account it has power to withdraw from.[57] Nevertheless, it is an important judgment because it clarifies the conditions under which a pledge over book debts can be considered as a floating charge. The chargor was free to collect its book debts and use the proceeds in the ordinary course of his business, but parties themselves characterised the pledge as a fixed charge. The Privy Council decided that everything comes down to control over the charged assets. If the chargee has control, it will be a fixed charge. If the chargor keeps the control, then the charge is a floating charge.

(3) It has, however, been noticed by English scholars that the only substantial category of assets for which the bank can take only a floating charge are the raw materials, work-in-progress and inventory, in view of the impracticability of banks controlling the use and consumption of these assets.[58]

Comparative Note

The traditional rules with regard to pledge, which required a dispossession, appeared to be insufficient at the end of the nineteenth century. The floating charge was created in English law, and both the Belgian and French legislature introduced a new statutory non-possessory pledge on the commercial fund. Dutch and German law have not implemented a similar instrument. However, it has emerged from the *Sisal* judg-

[56] That is the description given by Romer LJ in *re Yorkshire Woolcombers Association Ltd* [1903] 2 Ch 284, 295.

[57] *Siebe Gorman & Co Ltd v Barclays Bank* [1979] 2 Lloyd's Report 142 (Chancery Division); *Re Brightlife Ltd* [1987] Ch 200.

[58] Bridge, above n 4, 90.

ment that Dutch case law is flexible with regard to the creation of a pledge with regard to future goods. The above-cited judgment of the German Supreme Court confirms this development.

This development has been reinforced by the introduction both in French and Dutch law of the registration instead of the dispossession as object of the publicity principle (III.A.2).

III.B RIGHT OF PLEDGE IN RESPECT OF CLAIMS

Introductory Notes

(a) Specific complications arise in the case of a pledge with regard to incorporeal movables, more particularly receivables. The issues with regard to the publicity requirements and powers of the pledgor/pledgee are put forward in a different manner for pledges on incorporeal than for pledges on corporeal movables. Most (recent) statutory texts have extensive provisions with regard to the pledge of incorporeals. As will emerge, the rules with regard to the pledge on receivables have changed throughout the decades.

(b) The rules with regard to the pledge of incorporeals should be in line with the rules on their assignment, as this is necessary in order to be able to solve priority conflicts between assignees and pledges.

Code civil **5.39 (FR)**

Article 2355 A pledge of an incorporeal objects is the affectation of an incorporeal movable or of a set of incorporeal movables, actual or future, as security for an obligation.

It may be conventional or judicial.

Judicial pledge is regulated by the rules which apply to enforcement proceedings.

In the absence of specific provisions, a conventional pledge which attaches to debts is governed by this Chapter.

In the absence of specific provisions, a conventional pledge which attaches to other incorporeal movables is governed by the rules regarding the pledge of corporeal movables.

Article 2356 At penalty of voidness, the pledge of receivables shall be concluded in writing.

The secured obligations and pledged receivables shall be designated in the instrument. Where they are future, the instrument must allow their individualisation or contain elements which allow it, such as the indication of the debtor, the place of payment, the amount of the debts or their estimate and, if there is occasion, their due date.

Article 2357 Where a pledge attaches to a future receivable, the pledgee acquires a right on the debt as from the coming into existence of the latter.

Article 2361 The pledge of a debt, actual or future, takes effect as between the parties and is enforceable against third parties as from the date of the written agreement.

Article 2362 In order to be enforceable against the debtor of the pledged receivable, the pledge of the receivable must be notified to him or he must intervene in the written agreement.

In the absence thereof, the pledgor is the only one to be entitled to obtain payment of the debt.

Article 2363 After notice, the pledged creditor is the only one to be entitle to obtain payment of the pledged receivable in capital as well as in interest.

Each creditor may realise the pledge, the others being duly summoned.

Article 2364 The sums paid in fulfilment of the pledged receivable shall be appropriated to the secured debt where it is due.

Otherwise, the pledgee shall keep them as security on an account open in an institution entitled to receive them on condition to return them if the secured obligation is performed. In case of default of the debtor of the pledged debt and eight days after a formal requisition remained ineffective, the creditor shall allocate the funds to the repayment of his debt to the extent of the unpaid sums.

Article 2365 In case of default of his debtor, a pledgee may have assigned to him, by the judge or in the way provided for in the agreement, the pledged receivable as well as all the rights which attach to it.

He may also wait until the debt becomes due.

Article 2366 Where a sum in excess of the secured obligation is paid to the pledgee, the latter owes the difference to the pledgor.

Burgerlijk Wetboek **5.40 (NL)**

Article 3:94(1) Except for the cases governed by the previous provisions, the rights which have to be exercised against one or more persons are delivered by a deed in that sense, and a notification to these persons by the transferor or transferee

Article 3:236 1. A pledge on a movable, a bearer or order right, or on the usufruct burdening such object or right, is created by bringing the object or the rights into the hands of the pledgee or of a third party about whom parties agreed. The creation of a pledge on an order right, or the usufruct thereon, also requires endorsement.

2. A pledge on other goods is created in line with the normal manners to deliver the object of the pledge.

Article 3:239 1. A pledge burdening right which has to be exercised against one or more persons and which is not an order or bearer right, or burdening a usufruct on such right can be vested by authentic or registered private deed, without notifying to these persons, if this right already exists or will come into existence pursuant to a legal relationship already existing at the moment of the creation of the pledge.

2. The second paragraph of article 237 applies by analogy.

3. If the pledgor or debtor does not comply with his obligations towards the pledgee or gives him good reasons to fear that the will not comply with his obligations, the pledgee has the power to notify the pledge to the mentioned persons. The pledgor and pledgee can agree that this power will have effect at another date.

4. Article 88 only applies to a pledgee whose right is vested with respect of paragraph 1, if he is in good faith at the moment of the notification meant in paragraph 3.

Bürgerliches Gesetzbuch **5.41 (DE)**

§1273 Statutory content of the pledge on rights

(1) A right can be the object of a pledge.

(2) With regard to the pledge of rights, the rules on the pledge of corporeals apply by analogy, except if an exception follows from the §§1274 bis 1296. The application of §1208 and §1213, para 2 is excluded.

§1274 Creation

(1) The creation of a pledge on rights is possible according to the rules applying to the assignment of those rights. If, for the transfer of that right a delivery of a good is required, the §§1205, 1206 will apply.

(2) It is not be possible to create a pledge on a right which can not be transferred.

§1275 Pledge on a right to performance

If the object of a pledge is a right which entitles to claim performance of another person, the relationship between the pledgee and the debtor will be governed by the same provisions as the ones which govern the relation between an assignee and the debtor in case of an assignment and, in case of judiciary command, §1070, para 2 will apply.

§1279 Pledge on a receivable

For the pledge on a receivable the specific provisions of §§1280–1290 apply. If the receivable has a (financial) market value, §1259 will apply by analogy.

§1280 Notification to the debtor

The pledge of a receivable, of which the assignment only requires the real agreement, is only effective if the creditor gives notification to the debtor.

§1281 Performance before the debt becomes due

The debtor can only pay to the pledgor and the creditor in common. Each of them can claim that the debtor performs to them in common. Each of them can also claim that the object of the claim is given in deposit or, if the object is not capable of being given in deposit, is given to an administrator which has been judicially appointed.

Law of Property Act 1925 **5.42 (E&W)**

Section 136 Legal assignments of things in action

(1) Any absolute assignment by writing under the hand of the assignor (not purporting to be by way of charge only) of any debt or other legal thing in action, of which express notice in writing has been given to the debtor, trustee or other person from whom the assignor would have been entitled to claim such debt or thing in action, is effectual in law (subject to equities having priority over the right of the assignee) to pass and transfer from the date of such notice—

(a) the legal right to such debt or thing in action;

(b) all legal and other remedies for the same; and

(c) the power to give a good discharge for the same without the concurrence of the assignor:

Provided that, if the debtor, trustee or other person liable in respect of such debt or thing in action has notice—

(a) that the assignment is disputed by the assignor or any person claiming under him; or

(b) of any other opposing or conflicting claims to such debt or thing in action;he may, if he thinks fit, either call upon the persons making claim thereto to interplead concerning the same, or pay the debt or other thing in action into court under the provisions of the Trustee Act, 1925.

(2) This section does not affect the provisions of the Policies of Assurance Act, 1867.

(3) The county court has jurisdiction (including power to receive payment of money or securities into court) under the proviso to subsection (1) of this section where the amount or value of the debt or thing in action does not exceed £30,000.

Companies Act 2006 5.43 (E&W)

Section 860 Charges created by a company

This section has no associated Explanatory Notes

(1) A company that creates a charge to which this section applies must deliver the prescribed particulars of the charge, together with the instrument (if any) by which the charge is created or evidenced, to the registrar for registration before the end of the period allowed for registration.

(2) Registration of a charge to which this section applies may instead be effected on the application of a person interested in it.

(3) Where registration is effected on the application of some person other than the company, that person is entitled to recover from the company the amount of any fees properly paid by him to the registrar on registration.

(4) If a company fails to comply with subsection (1), an offence is committed by

(a) the company, and

(b) every officer of it who is in default.

(5) A person guilty of an offence under this section is liable—

(a) on conviction on indictment, to a fine;

(b) on summary conviction, to a fine not exceeding the statutory maximum.

(6) Subsection (4) does not apply if registration of the charge has been effected on the application of some other person.

(7) This section applies to the following charges—

(a) a charge on land or any interest in land, other than a charge for any rent or other periodical sum issuing out of land,

(b) a charge created or evidenced by an instrument which, if executed by an individual, would require registration as a bill of sale,

(c) a charge for the purposes of securing any issue of debentures,

(d) a charge on uncalled share capital of the company,

(e) a charge on calls made but not paid,

(f) a charge on book debts of the company,

(g) a floating charge on the company's property or undertaking,

(h) a charge on a ship or aircraft, or any share in a ship,

(i) a charge on goodwill or on any intellectual property.

Chancery Division 24 December 1828[59] **5.44 (E&W)**

Dearle v Hall

PRIORITY CONFLICT BETWEEN CHARGES ON A SAME RECEIVABLE

Assignment of beneficial interest

The first one to give notice to the debtor will have priority over the latter.

Facts: Peter Brown, by his will, dated 11 September 1794, made the following disposition of a part of the residue of his personal estate and of the money to arise by the sale of his real estates: 'I do hereby direct my said executrix and executors, and the survivors and survivor of them, and the executors and administrators of such survivor, to place one moiety of the said residue of my personal estate, and of the money to arise from the sale of my real estates, out at interest upon government or real security, during the life of my son Zachariah Brown, and to pay the interest and produce thereof unto him my said son Zachariah Brown during his life.'

The executors of Peter Brown had invested the clear residue of the testator's estate, amounting to £4,600, in real securities, and the share of the interest yielded by these securities, which was payable to Zachariah Brown, came to about £93 a year.

By an agreement, dated 19 December 1808, Zachariah Brown, Charles Martin Demages and William Bircham agreed to pay to William Dearle, his executors, administrators and assigns, during the natural life of Zachariah Brown, one annuity of £37, free of and clear from all taxes, charges and deductions, by equal quarterly payments, on 19 March, 19 June, 19 September and 19 December, in every year.

The indenture further witnessed, that, 'for the better and more effectually securing the payment of the aforesaid annuity, he, Zachariah Brown, granted, bargained, sold, and assigned unto William Dearle, his executors, administrators, and assigns, all and singular the yearly sum or annuity of £93, and all arrears thereof, yearly arising or growing, and to which he, Zachariah Brown, was entitled for life, under the will of Peter Brown, and all the estate, right, title, interest, trust, property, benefit, claim, and demand of him Zachariah Brown in, to, or out of the same.'

By another indenture, dated 26 September 1809, Zachariah Brown sold an annuity of £27 for his own natural life to Caleb Sherring, which, it had been agreed, should be secured by the covenant and warrant; and it was thereby further witnessed, that, for the 'better and more effectually securing the payment of the aforesaid annuity', Zachariah Brown granted, bargained, sold, and assigned to Caleb Sherring, his executors, administrators and assigns, the above-mentioned yearly sum or annuity of £93, and all arrears thereof.

Notwithstanding these assignments, Brown, early in 1812, advertised his life-interest in the £93 for sale as an unencumbered fund; and this advertisement led to a negotiation with Joseph Hall, who proposed to become the purchaser. Hall's solicitor, Mr Patten, used all due diligence in scrutinising Brown's title; no notice of the assignments to Dearle and Sherring had been given to the executors; and as Mr Unthank was in complete ignorance of the existence of such instruments, none of his letters made any mention of or allusion to any encumbrance as affecting the property. Under these circumstances, the contract between Brown and Hall was carried into effect, by an indenture dated 20 March 1812.

On 25 April, Hall served a written notice on the executors, requiring them to pay to him, as assignee of Zachariah Brown, the moiety of the dividends of the residuary fund during Brown's life; and, in July 1812, Unthank remitted to Hall £31 12s 10d on account of the yearly dividends so assigned. On 17 October, the executors, for the first time, received notice of the assignments to Dearle and Sherring; and they thenceforward declined to pay the interest to any of the claimants, until their rights should be ascertained.

Held: The priority conflict as between the plaintiff and the defendant depended on the order in which notice of their respective interests had been given to the sub-purchasers.

Judgment: 'When a man,' says Lord Bacon (Maxims of the Law, max 16), 'is author

[59] (1828) 3 Russell 1 38 ER 475.

and mover to another to commit an unlawful act, then he shall not excuse himself by circumstances not pursued.'

It is true that a chose in action does not admit of tangible actual possession, and that neither Zachariah Brown nor any person claiming under him were entitled to possess themselves of the fund which yielded the £93 a-year. But in *Ryall v Rowles* the Judges held, that, in the case of a chose in action, you must do every thing towards having possession which the subject admits; you must do that which is tantamount to obtaining possession, by placing every person, who has an equitable or legal interest in the matter, under an obligation to treat it as your property. For this purpose, you must give notice to the legal holder of the fund; in the case of a debt, for instance, notice to the debtor is, for many purposes, tantamount to possession. If you omit to give that notice, you are guilty of the same degree and species of neglect as he who leaves a personal chattel, to which he has acquired a title, in the actual possession, and under the absolute control, of another person.

Is there the least doubt, that, if Zachariah Brown had been a trader, all that was done by Dearle and Sherring would not have been in the least effectual against his [24] assignees; but that, according to the doctrine of *Ryall v Rowles*, his assignees would have taken the fund, because there was no notice to those in whom the legal interest was vested? In that case it was the opinion of all the Judges, that he who contracts for a chose in action, and does not follow up his title by notice, gives personal credit to the individual with whom he deals. Notice, then, is necessary to perfect the title,—to give a complete right in rem , and not merely a right as against him who conveys his interest. If you are willing to trust the personal credit of the man, and are satisfied that he will make no improper use of the possession in which you allow him to remain, notice is not necessary; for against him the title is perfect without notice. But if he, availing himself of the possession as a means of obtaining credit, induces third persons to purchase from him as the actual owner, and they part with their money before your pocket-conveyance is notified to them, you must be postponed. In being postponed, your security is not invalidated: you had priority, but that priority has not been followed up; and you have permitted another to acquire a better title to the legal possession. What was done by Dearle and Sherring did not exhaust the thing (to borrow the principle of the civil law) but left it still open to traffic. These are the principles on which I think it to be very old law, that possession, or what is tantamount to possession, is the criterion of perfect title to personal chattels, and that he, who does not obtain such possession, must take his chance.

Notes

(1) All legal systems struggle with the same tensions with regard to the pledge of receivables: on the one hand a silent security right on receivables makes it possible to hamper the reliance of third parties, which are ignorant of the burdening of the receivable. On the other hand, a notification of the security right to the debtors of the security provider is not always self-evident: the security provider does not always want his debtors (clients) to know that he has had to involve the claims between them as object of a financing transaction. Commercial reasons can thus entail inhibitions for notification. Parties not infrequently insert large contractual arrangements in their security agreements.

(2) However, in all legal systems, the notification to the debtor has important

legal effects: this is necessary in the relation to the debtor, in order to ensure that he can no longer discharge the debt by paying to the chargor, and in some legal systems such notification also serves as key date for the priority conflict between different pledgees or assignees of the same receivables.

(3) The Dutch Civil Code has introduced two methods of pledging incorporeal assets, one with notification to the debtor and one 'silent pledge' with authentic or registered private documents. The latter form corresponds to the non-possessory pledge of corporeal objects. The requirement of a written agreement has also been provided in French law since the 2006 Reform. The more severe position of German law must be considered against the background of the other security devices in German law: the large possibilities to transfer ownership of the receivables for security purposes give a new perspective on the statutory rules of the BGB.

(4) According to English law, it is not possible to create a pledge on receivables, as the possession requirement plays an important role in the case of a pledge and is without object in the case of receivables. Parties have to have recourse to the charge. An equitable charge can be effected without notification to the debtor of the object of the security, the mere intention of the chargor being sufficient. Notice to the debtor is not required for the validity of the equitable charge on receivables.[60] A statutory assignment, however, gives rise to a notification requirement for the validity of the transaction. In both cases, however, the notification to the debtor will be necessary in order to determine the priority conflict according to the *Dearle v Hall* doctrine.

(5) In most legal systems it is possible to pledge a large number of receivables at the same time. Dutch law offers a good example of this, where in a series of case law the Dutch Supreme Court has relaxed the principle of specificity (see Chapter 1) in favour of an efficient creation of pledges on, especially, claims. First a list of claims (a printout of a company's administration) would be attached to a single document of creation.[61] This also happens in French law by way of a *borderau.*[62] Under pressure from practice it is now possible to create a right of pledge on existing incorporeal objects, usually monetary claims, by referring to the administration of the pledger, without specifying exactly which claims are involved.[63] The criterion used by the Dutch Supreme Court is 'as long as afterwards it can be established which claims are involved'.[64] Security rights on incorporeal objects therefore force the creation of new rules or adaptation of existing provisions.

[60] *Gorringe v Irwell India Rubber Works* [1886] LR 34 Ch D 128 (16 November 1886).

[61] HR 14 October 1994, *Stichting Spaarbank Rivierenland v Gispen*, NJ 1995, 447.

[62] Or a transfer *sur bordereau*. Art 14, Ordonnance du 28 septembre 1967. Ordonnance No 67-838 du 28 septembre 1967, specifically Art 4 (the Ordonnance was later almost fully repealed by Loi No 81-1 du 2 janvier 1981 (Loi Dailly)), see Chapter 4.

[63] HR 20 September 2002, *Mulder qq v Rabobank*, NJ 2004, 182.

[64] 'Zolang achteraf met voldoende duidelijkheid kan worden vastgesteld om welke vorderingen het gaat'. *Mulder qq v Rabobank*, NJ 2004, 182.

IV. THE RIGHT OF OWNERSHIP AS SECURITY INSTRUMENT

Analysis of the pledge in comparative perspective has lead to the conclusion that, with regard to corporeal assets, the traditional right of pledge no longer meets in all respects the needs of modern commercial life. The dispossession of the pledgor, as it was traditionally required, forms in modern commerce a barrier to the attractivity of the pledge. It has been determined that recent statutes have disapplied this requirement. Earlier in this development, legal practice had already developed non-statutory forms of security, for example, by using ownership as security instrument. In the following analysis, a main distinction is being made between the *retention* or reservation of ownership for security purposes on the one hand and the *transfer* of ownership for security purposes on the other hand.

The hire-purchase and finance lease agreement will not be dealt with here. These devices are mostly financial and tax related, in such a way that it would be more appropriate to analyse these clauses in casebooks on these topics. With regard to the proprietary topics, they can most often be equated to the security devices which are dealt with under this heading.

IV.A RETENTION OF TITLE

The essence of a retention of title clause is to reserve ownership in the assets to the seller until the price is paid in full, notwithstanding that the assets are delivered to the buyer. The purpose of this clause is to confer upon the seller some degree of security in the event of insolvency of the buyer. However, it will emerge from the following that a 'simple' retention of title does not confer absolute security to the seller: if the sales agreement relates to the the manufacturing process, the buyer will transform the sold assets, if the sales agreement relates to the distribution process, the buyer will readily proceed with a sub-sale. As always with property security rights, the security ownership requires that the assets are identifiable in the estate of the buyer at the moment of its exercise. That difficulty is the reason why parties often aim to contractually extend the reservation of title (*cf* below, IV.A.6).

IV.A.1 BASIC LEGISLATION ON RESERVATION OF OWNERSHIP

Code civil **5.45 (FR)**

Article 2367 Ownership of an asset may be retained as security through a clause of retention of title (*clause de reserve de propriété*) withholding the transferring effect of a contract until payment in full of the obligation which compensates for it. Ownership so retained is the accessory of the debt the payment of which it secures.

Article 2368 A retention of title shall be agreed upon in writing.

Commercial Code 5.46 (FR)

Article L624-16 Assets held by the debtor in detention or the assets transferred to a fiduciary estate which the debtor has the use and enjoyment of, may be vindicated if they still exist in kind.

Assets sold under a retention of title clause may equally be claimed if they still exist in kind at the time proceedings are opened. This clause must have been agreed upon by the parties in writing at the latest at the time of delivery. It may be laid down in a document governing a number of commercial operations entered into by the parties.

The vindication in kind will succeed under the same conditions with respect to movable asset incorporated in another asset if they may be removed without damaging them. A vindication claim in kind will also succeed in relation to fungible assets where assets of the same nature and the same quality are in the possession of the debtor or any person keeping them for his account .

In every instance, the asset may not be recovered if, by decision of the supervisory judge of the insolvency proceeding (*juge-commissaire*), the price is paid immediately. The supervisory judge may also, with the consent of the petitioning creditor, grant a payment delay (*délai de règlement*). The payment of the price shall thus be considered equivalent to [the payment] of debts referred to under Article L622-17.

Belgian Bankruptcy Code 5.47 (BE)

Article 103 The bankruptcy does not affect the owner's right of recovery of goods that are in possession of the debtor. Nonetheless, movable goods, sold with the clause that the transfer of ownership is suspended until the full payment of the purchase price, can only be recovered from the debtor on the ground of that clause, for as far as this has been drawn up in writing at the latest at the moment of delivery of the good. Moreover, these goods must be in the possession of the debtor in kind. Hence, they may not have become immovable through accession [*natrekking*], nor may they have been mixed with another movable asset. Under penalty of extinction, the claim of recovery must be initiated before the deposit of the first report of verification of debts. In case the deposit or the restitution of the vindicated assets has caused any expenses to the detriment of the patrimony, the administrator shall demand payment of these expenses at the time the goods are being delivered. When the owner refuses to pay these expenses, the administrator will be entitled to retain these goods.

Bürgerliches Gesetzbuch 5.48 (DE)

§449 (1) If the seller of a movable object has reserved his right of ownership until payment of the purchase price, in case of doubt, it is presumed that the right of ownership is transferred under the suspensive condition of full payment of the purchase price.

(2) On the ground of the retention of title, the seller of the good can only vindicate the object if he has withdrawn from the contract.

(3) The retention of title clause is void in so far as the transfer of ownership is

made dependent upon the payment of claims of a third person, in particular an affiliated company to the seller.

Burgerlijk Wetboek **5.49 (NL)**

Article 3:92 (1) If an agreement purports to reserve ownership of a good for one person, of which the possession will be transferred to another person, until fulfilment of the performance indebted to the other person, he will be presumed to oblige himself to a transfer of the goods to the other person, subject to the condition precedent of fulfilment of this performance.

(2) A retention of title can only validly be agreed upon for claims regarding considerations for goods delivered or due to be delivered under agreement by the transferor to the assignee or under such an agreement as well as for the benefit of the works performed or due to be performed by the transferee, as well as for claims grounded in the non-compliance with such agreements. If a condition is void for this reason, this will be assumed as unwritten.

(3) A condition as referred to in paragraph 1 will be considered fulfilled when the transferor is being satisfied in any other manner than the fulfilment of the considerations, when the transferee is being relieved from his obligations according to Article 60 of Book 6, or when the statutory limitation of the civil proceedings for the consideration have been fulfilled. Except if parties have agreed otherwise, the same applies in case the right of consideration would have been waived.

Sale of Goods Act 1979 **5.50 (E&W)**

Section 17 (1) Where there is a contract for the sale of specific or ascertained goods the property in them is transferred to the buyer at such time as the parties to the contract intend it to be transferred.

(2) For the purpose of ascertaining the intention of the parties regard shall be had to the terms of the contract, the conduct of the parties and the circumstances of the case.

...

Section 19 (1) Where there is a contract for the sale of specific goods or where goods are subsequently appropriated to the contract, the seller may, by the terms of the contract or appropriation, reserve the right of disposal of the goods until certain conditions are fulfilled; and in such a case, nothwithstanding the delivery of the goods to the buyer, or to a carrier or other bailee or custodier for the purpose of transmission to the buyer, the property in the goods does not pass to the buyer until the conditions imposed by the seller are fulfilled.

(2) Where goods are shipped, and by the bill of lading the goods are deliverable to the order of the seller or his agent, the seller is prima facie to be taken to reserve the right of disposal.

(3) Where the seller of goods draws on the buyer for the price, and transmits the bill of exchange and bill of lading to the buyer together to secure acceptance or payment of the bill of exchange, the buyer is bound to return the bill of lading if he does not honour the bill of exchange, and if he wrongfull retains the bill of lading the property in the goods does not pass to him.

Notes

(1) Title retention by an owner makes the transfer of ownership of the sold assets dependent upon the fulfilment of a condition precedent, ususally one of full payment of the purchase price (unless parties have agreed on a different meaning of the suspensive condition or have made more claims subject to that condition). The seller remains owner of the assets as long as the purchase price remains unpaid. Upon fulfilment of the suspensive condition, the right of ownership will automatically pass to the buyer, who is already in possession of the assets. The ownership does not pass at the moment of consent of parties (consensual systems) or of the delivery (tradition systems), but is delayed.[65] In doing so, the seller 'functionally' retains a property security right, as the sold assets remain out of the insolvent patrimony if the buyer becomes insolvent before having paid the full purchase price.

As the seller remains the owner of the assets, he continues to bear the risk of destruction or deterioration of the assets (*res perit domino*), unless otherwise allocated by the contract of sale.

(2) Title retention clauses are only useful if they are not only valid, but have also proprietary effect in such a way that they can be invoked in case of insolvency of the debtor. The last systems to overcome the theoretical problems arising out of the recognition of these property effects were the French-based jurisdictions. German law has already recognised this function in the Civil Code of 1900, France introduced this *opposabilité* expressly in the Act of 12 May 1980, but Belgian law has only adhered to this position since the amendment of the Bankruptcy Act of 8 August 1997.[66]

It is striking that in the French-based jurisdictions title retention has been introduced through the Bankruptcy Act. In French law, title retention has only been awarded a place in the Civil Code in the 2006 amendment. In Belgian law, there is still no general concept of title retention in the Civil Code.[67]

(3) Some legal systems require the accomplishment of formal requirements in order to make the retention of title effective in insolvency proceedings or vis-à-vis third parties. Both Belgian and (recently) French law require that a written document is made by the parties. This written document must be given to and accepted by the buyer at the latest at the moment of the delivery of the assets. However, other legal systems (eg Dutch and German) adhere to the consensual nature of the agreement with regard to the retention of title clause, also in relation to third parties. In English law, there are no formal requirements: any words, if they express sufficient evidence of the intention of the seller that ownership does not pass to the buyer according to the usual presumptive rules in the Sale of Goods Act 1979, will suffice.

[65] On the difference between these systems, see Chapter 8.

[66] Before this amendment, the Cour de cassation held that the recognition of property rights of the seller, in conflict with other creditors of the buyer, was irreconcilable with the principle of Art 2279, which is the 'possession grants title' rule (Cour de cassation, 9 February 1933, Pas 1933, I, 103, concl Proc Gen Leclercq).

[67] This has lead the Belgian Cour de cassation to reject the third party effects of title retention in other insolvency proceedings than the ones in which it has been expressly recognized (Cass 7 May 2010, www.cass.be).

(4) In none of the above-mentioned legal systems does the 'simple' retention of title require registration. There is a functional equivalence between retention of title and pledge, but a conceptual difference. Although the economic purpose of the retention of title is identical to that of a property security right, it is not made visible in the same way by the implementation of publicity requirements. From a conceptual point of view, simple retention of title clauses are not considered as a charge or as a pledge which might require registration, but simply as an ordinary contractual provision deferring the passing of ownership until the payment has been effected. In several of these legal systems, the absence of publicity is criticised. A functional approach would demonstrate that the commercial purpose of the title retention is identical to the one of a charge, ie preferential treatment in the insolvency of the buyer. Other legal systems have a registration system of title retention clauses, such as Swiss law: according to Article 715 of the Swiss Civil Code, a retention of title clause becomes valid only upon registration in a public register, the Retention of Title Clause Register (RTCR), which is kept by the Debt Collection Office in each community. In Swiss law, any third party may fully rely on the absence of registration.[68]

The fact that in the current state of law most countries recognise the proprietary effects of the title retention without implementing a publicity requirement is an important illustration of the redress of the theory of reputed ownership: normally it is thought that creditors should be able to rely on the apparent credibility of their debtor, so that concealed security rights which have proprietary effects should be restricted. This is the so-called 'reputed ownership' *(apparence de solvabilité*). The fact that the buyer under title retention has the factual possession over the goods without it being published that these goods do not belong to that person, largely undermines this principle of reputed ownership.

(5) In most legal systems there is a doctrinal debate going on as to the nature of a retention of title clause. In German law, it was suggested during the reform of the German Insolvency Code that the simple title retention would qualify as a security right (*Absonderungsrecht*). However, this proposal was not adopted. A simple retention of title is still considered in current German law as a full (but functional) ownership (*Aussonderungsrecht*). The same position is taken in French law: most French legal scholars take the view that it is contradictory to see a retention of title as the source of a right of priority, as this would entail that the goods belong to the buyer: the seller does not have a right of priority on goods of the buyer, but

[68] Swiss law is, in this sense, closer to the system of Art 9 UCC, which imposes the registration of the security interest in order to perfect it.

remains owner of the goods and can vindicate them in case of rescission of the agreement.[69] In Belgian law, legal scholars do not agree on this point.[70]

IV.A.2 RESERVATION OF TITLE AS AN ACCESSORY RIGHT?

Introductory Note

One of the main aspects for which the qualification of title retention as full ownership or mere security right can be important is the effect of an assignment of the guaranteed claim on the ownership. As we have stated above, security rights are accessory to the claim they secure. That is usually not the case for a full ownership. However, the function of a reservation of title can make it desirable to tie the connection between the ownership and the claim.

Cour de cassation, 11 July 1988[71] **5.51 (FR)**

Man Roland AG v EDM

ACCESSORINESS OF TITLE RETENTION

Reservation of title—assignment of claim—nature of title retention.

Facts: A sold and supplied goods to B, and received in exchange a bill of exchange. The sales agreement included a reservation of title. A endorsed this bill to his bank, without having made any stipulation with regard to the title retention. Later B was declared bankrupt without having paid the bill. The question arises whether the bank is entitled to argue that it has become the owner of the sold goods.

Held: A title retention is accessory to the secured claim.

Judgment: Considering that the reservation of title is accessory to the vendor's claim as it secures him payment of the price; the endorsement of a bill of exchange confers title to the bearer together with all ancillary rights; considering that in rejecting that proposition the court of appeal considered that title could not be regarded as security for the debt nor accessory thereto with the result that reservation of title which was not intended to secure payment of a sum of money could not have been conveyed to the bank by virtue of the endorsement of the bills of exchange relating to the sales price of the goods; considering that the reservation of title duly

[69] P Crocq, *Propriété et garantie* (Paris, LGDJ, 1995) 253, no 301; F Derrida, case note under Cour d'appel Limoges, 5 March 1984, D 1985, IR, 8, no 39–40; J Ghestin, 'Réflexions d'un civiliste sur la clause de réserve de propriété', D 1981, p 9, no 35; C Larroumet, Droit civil, I, p 307, no 505; Defending the opposite opinion, however: C. Mouly, 'Procédures collectives: assainir le régime des sûretés', in *Etudes dédiées à René Roblot. Aspects actuels du droit commercial français* (Paris, LGDJ, 1984) 529–64, 552, n 35: 'L'idée de concours entre sûretés sur le bien, si elle est importante pour une bonne conception du crédit, ne me paraît pas être un des piliers nécessaires du concept de sûreté. Elle aide à distinguer les bonnes sûretés, celles dont le cumul est possible, des sûretés frustes et primaires qui en sont insusceptibles. Elle n'aide pas à qualifier un procédé de sûreté ou à interdire cette qualification.'

[70] In favour of the qualification as actual ownership: V Sagaert, 'Het eigendomsrecht als volwaardig zekerheidsinstrument?', in *XXXIste postuniversitaire Cyclus Willy Delva 2003-2004* (Mechelen, Kluwer, 2006) 189–230. In favour of the identification with a (non-possessory) pledge: E. Dirix, 'Eigendomsvoorbehoud', *Rechtsk Weekbl 1999–2000* (1038) 1039, no 4; ME Storme, 'Van trust gespeend? Trusts en fiduciaire figuren in het Belgisch privaatrecht' (1998) (703) *TPR*, 723, no 24.

[71] D 1988, IR, 240. In the same sense: Cour de cassation, 15 March 1988, D 1988, jur, 331, n F Perochon.

agreed between the purchaser and the vendor secured the latter's debt; and considering that by endorsing the bills of exchange accepted by the buyer the vendor had conveyed to the bank both his debt against the drawee and rights ancillary thereto; by holding as it did, notwithstanding these matters, the court of appeal misapplied and therefore infringed the provisions mentioned above.

BGH, 11 January 1990[72] **5.52 (DE)**

TRANSFER OF OWNERSHIP SECURITY

Building project financing

The assignor has an obligation in personam to transfer the non-accessory rights, unless otherwise agreed between the security provider and the creditor.

Facts: The defendant awarded in 1980 a credit of DM75,600,000 for the financing to a principal debtor for a building project. As security, the debtor provided for two 'land charges'. In 1982, an additional credit of DM18,000,000 was awarded, which is again secured by three land charges. It was agreed that the land charges secured all existing and future claims of the building project.

The claimant awarded a partial surety for the second part of the credit, for an amount of DM10 million for the capital, rent, accessory payments, expenses and costs and obtained an assignment of the partial credit claim. The defendant directed to the claimant after the opening of an insolvency proceeding against the principal debtor. The defendant paid on 22 August 1983 DM10,131,358.91 to the defendant. The claimant argued that it could appeal to the Grundschuld as surety for the recovery of its claim, which was contested by the defendant.

Held: It is presumed that the assignor has an obligation *in personam* to transfer the non-accessory rights, unless otherwise agreed between the security provider and the creditor.

Judgment: Pursuant to §774(1)(1) BGB, the claim of the creditor against the debtor is transferred to the guarantor, from the moment that he has fulfilled his surety in favour of the creditor. By means of the claim all subsidiary rights, in particular accessory securities are passed over to the guarantor in accordance with §§412, 401 BGB.

Non-accessory security rights, such as security land charges, transfer of ownership for security purposes or retention of title do not pass to the guarantor by statute. However, by analogous application of §§774, 412, 401 BGB it is presumed that the assignor has an obligation in personam to transfer the non-accessory rights to the paying guarantor, unless otherwise agreed between the security provider and the creditor.

Parliamentary History, Book 3[73] **5.53 (NL)**

The retention of title is no accessory right, as this would require that the ownership as such is so closely connected to the seller's claim that it cannot exist without this claim. This is hardly reconcilable with the nature of the right of ownership, even when it concerns ownership under extinctive condition. Nor is another notion fully reconcilable with the principle that the title retention does not perish with the sole extinction of the claim. The solution is only different when the claim extinguishes because it is paid off or the transferor is satisfied otherwise.

[72] BGHZ 110, 41–47 and NJW 1990, 903.

[73] Parlementaire Gesch BW, Boek 3 (inv 3, 5 en 6), 1241.

It is to be observed that under the regime of the new Dutch Civil Code the retention of title is no clear security right, contrary to a right of pledge or a hypothec, since it does not necessarily result in any realisation of the claim on the object of the title retention, but it can also protect the seller in interests of another nature, such as his interest to be sure in case of rescission of the contract of sale that he will regain full disposition power over the object.

Secondly, there is no big practical need to mark the retention of title as an accessory right. If parties in an assignment or a payment that leads to subrogation aim to grant the assignee of the claim also the retention of title of the good, in such way that the transferee can also exercise the powers arising out of the retention towards the debtor, then the retained object can be transferred via the delivery of movables. This will also have as effect—which is desirable from a legal certainty perspective—that the ordinary rules regarding delivery are applicable.

Notes

(1) Since the 2006 Amendment, the accessory nature of the title retention is expressly provided for in the French Civil Code: the right of ownership that is retained is accessory to the claim the payment of which it secures (Article 2367 Cciv).[74] French law applies the principle of accessority in a strict way.[75] Parties can contractually exclude the title retention from the assignment. In that case, the receivable acquired by the assignee is not secured, but neither will the assignor be able to claim his property rights, as he is no longer the creditor. The exclusion of the title retention of the assignment will thus result in the transfer of ownership to the purchaser.[76] German law is less rigid in the sense that the Bundesgerichtshof acknowledges a presumption, but this presumption can be contractually excluded.

(2) Dutch law takes a contrary position. It applies the principle of 'non-accessority' to all forms of ownership for security purposes. The Dutch Supreme Court decided similarly with regard to the transfer of assets for security purposes that 'the conception that security ownership has an accessory nature is not supported in law'.[77] This is also the case for the fiduciary transfer of ownership for security purposes, according to the strict limits within which such transfer is valid according to Dutch law (*cf* IV.B.4).

[74] 'La propriété ainsi réservée est l'accessoire de la créance dont elle garantit le paiement.'

[75] In French legal scholarship, it is argued that a retention of title is not an accessory to the secured claim in its technical sense, but rather an inherent feature of it. Therefore, Crocq argues that it is not a 'sûreté' but a 'garantie' (Crocq, above n 69, 235, no 284).

[76] Cour d'appel Bordeaux 17 December 1987; Cabrillac and Mouly, above n 1, no 734.

[77] HR 18 February 1994, NJ 1994, at 462, no 3.3, n WMK.

IV.A.3 CLAIMS WHICH CAN BE SECURED BY A RETENTION OF TITLE

Cour de cassation, 9 January 1990[78] **5.54 (FR)**

Pogic v Astral

RETENTION OF TITLE AS SECURITY FOR FUTURE CLAIMS

Astral

The seller must prove that the goods found in possession of the debtor are the ones covered by the title retention.

Facts: The claimant had sold commercial goods to the defendant under several sales agreements included in a long-standing commercial relation. An insolvency proceeding was opened against the defendant at a point when some of the supplies had not yet been paid. It was not clear whether the goods found in the possession of the insolvent buyer corresponded to the unpaid goods.

Held: The vindication claim is dismissed.

Judgment: If parties have entered into several sales agreements with regard to identical goods, the vindication claim by the seller on the ground of the title reservation will only succeed if the seller can prove that the goods found in possession of the debtor are the ones which have not yet been paid. Parties cannot contractually agree otherwise by inserting a derogating clause in their agreement, as this rule belongs to public order.

The Court of Appeal has violated Article 65 of the Act of 13 July 967 by ruling that a presumption of identity, created by agreement, between the unpaid goods and the traced goods is not contrary to the equality between the creditors.

Cour de cassation, 29 May 2001[79] **5.55 (FR)**

Bail Equipement v Ateliers de Nissan

RETENTION OF TITLE IN MANUFACTURING AGREEMENT

Metallic parts

Parties can validly include a retention of title clause in a service agreement.

Facts: X placed an order with Y for the manufacture of metallic parts, which would be sold after the manufacturing to X. X did not pay the price and Y argued that it remained owner of the parts in accordance with the title retention which was inserted in the agreement. X rejected this claim, arguing that the title retention cannot apply because the contract binding them is not a sales agreement, but an enterprise agreement.

Held: The court confirms the applicability and effectiveness of the title retention in this case.

Judgment: Considering that, on the one hand, the good handed over under a manufacturing contract may be subject to retention of title; on the other hand an action for payment of the balance of the price for the items handed over by the

[78] Bull civ, IV, no 8 and Recueil Dalloz 1991, 130, n G Virassamy.
[79] 98-21126, not published.

Bio-alternative company to the leasing equipment company in breach of the reservation of title in favour of the Ateliers de Nissan company is not subject to the provisions of the law of 25 January 1985 even if the leasing equipment company itself passed those goods on to a company in liquidation.

Burgerlijk Wetboek 5.56 (NL)

Article 3:92(2) A retention of title can only validly be agreed upon for claims regarding considerations for goods delivered or due to be delivered under agreement by the transferor to the assignee or under such an agreement as well as for the benefit of the works performed or due to be performed by the transferee, as well as for claims grounded in the non-compliance with such agreements. If a condition is void for this reason, this will be assumed as unwritten.

BGH, 14 February 1968[80] 5.57 (DE)

TITLE RETENTION AS SECURITY FOR FUTURE CLAIMS

Car delivery

Title retention only covers future claims if it expressly states so.

Facts: X sold cars to Y under title retention. The title retention clause stipulated as follows: 'The transferor remains owner of the goods which are delivered until payment of all claims which the transferor has or which will follow from the relation between them. Parties do not agree on the question whether this clause also covers the later sale of cars.'

Held: The title retention clause does not cover claims out of subsequent purchase agreements.

Judgment: Parties normally clearly express that the extended reservation of title is to apply without limitation to all claims, eg: 'goods supplied by me and already paid for but still available shall also secure all my non-fulfilled claims' (RGZ 147 321), or 'all current or future claims' (BGHZ 26, 185 = NJW 58 457) 'confers entitlement also to seek satisfaction in respect of other claims' (BGHZ 42, 53 = NJW 64, 1788). Conversely, there are agreements in which the reservation of title is laid down to secure specific claims, eg 'all claims arising in connection with the item purchased' (NJW 58, 1231). Typical examples are the general conditions regarding the sale of motor vehicles drafted by the motor vehicle industry and trade: 'the reservation of title shall continue to exist in respect of all claims arising in connection with the sold goods, in particular claims arising from repairs, spare parts, accessories, fuel supplies, costs of adjustments and insurance and contributions to professional associations', and the defendant's own conditions of sale of the S8: 'reservation of title shall also apply to all claims arising in connection with the sold good'. The version chosen by the defendant in the [current] purchase agreement is unclear. It corresponds in no way with the wordings customarily used by commercial trade to agree upon a reservation of title in order to secure all claims which may subsequently arise out of future transactions. Finally, it cannot be disregarded that the extended reservation of title leads to the faintness of ownership and cannot therefore be extended beyond the expressly agreed cases.

[80] NJW 1968, 885.

From an objective perspective a contracting partner of the defendant only had to be concerned with the fact that the defendant wished to retain title in relation to all claims in connection either with the purchase agreement entered into or with a business relationship already in existence at the time the purchase agreement was entered into. The need to secure the defendant with regard to claims arising out of subsequent purchase agreements was even smaller as the defendant also retained title to the vehicle subsequently sold until such time as all liabilities arising under the agreement had been fully met.

House of Lords, 18 October 1990[81] **5.58 (E&W)**

Armour and Another v Thyssen Edelstahlwerke AG

TITLE RETENTION AS SECURITY FOR FUTURE CLAIMS

Steel strips

A retention of title clause can validly secure debts due to the seller under other contracts.

Facts: X sold and supplied steel strips to Y under a long-standing arrangement. The steel was used in the manufacturing process of Y. The sales agreements were subject to general conditions, which provided as follows: 'All goods delivered by us remain our property (goods remaining in our ownership) until all debts owed to us including any balances existing at relevant times—due to us on any legal grounds—are settled. This also holds good if payments are made for the purpose of settlement of specially designated claims. Debts owed to companies, being members of our combine, are deemed to be such debts.' An insolvency proceeding was opened against Y, and X claimed his ownership on the steel in payment of later sales agreements which had not been paid. Scottish law applied.

Held: A provision reserving title to the seller until payment of all debts due to him by the buyer is a lawful retention of title.

Judgment: Lord Keith of Kinkel—In the present case the parties in the contract of sale clearly expressed their intention that the property in the steel strip should not pass to Carron until all debts due by it to the appellants had been paid. In my opinion there are no grounds for refusing to give effect to that intention.

Further, section 19(1) of the same Act provides:

> 'Where there is a contract for the sale of specific goods or where goods are subsequently appropriated to the contract, the seller may, by the terms of the contract or appropriation, reserve the right of disposal of the goods until certain conditions are fulfilled; and in such a case, notwithstanding the delivery of the goods to the buyer, or to a carrier or other bailee or custodier for the purpose of transmission to the buyer, the property in the goods does not pass to the buyer until the conditions imposed by the seller are fulfilled.'

Here the appellants, by the terms of the contract of sale, have in effect reserved the right of disposal of the steel strip until fulfilment of the condition that all debts due to them by Carron have been paid. By virtue of this enactment, that has the effect that the property in the goods did not pass to Carron until that condition had been fulfilled. Counsel for Carron argued that the word 'conditions' in section 19(1)

[81] [1991] 2 AC 339.

must be read as excluding any condition which has the effect of creating a right of security over the goods. I am, however, unable to regard a provision reserving title to the seller until payment of all debts due to him by the buyer as amounting to the creation by the buyer of a right of security in favour of the seller. Such a provision does in a sense give the seller security for the unpaid debts of the buyer. But it does so by way of a legitimate retention of title, not by virtue of any right over his own property conferred by the buyer.

In all cases where a right of security is conferred the debtor retains an ultimate right over the subject matter in question. The creditor, having realised out of that subject matter a sufficient sum to meet the debt, is obliged to account to the debtor for any surplus. Where, however, the seller of goods retains title until some condition has been satisfied, and on failure of such satisfaction repossesses them, then he is not obliged to account to the buyer for any part of the value of the goods. Where the condition is to the effect that the price of the goods shall have been paid and it has not been paid, then in the situation where the market price of the goods has risen, so that they are worth more than the contract price, the extra value belongs to the unpaid seller. That is clearly the position where the condition relates to payment of the price of the actual goods, and goes to show that the retention of title provision is not one creating a right of security forming an exception to the general rule requiring possession by the creditor. The same is true, in my opinion, where the provision covers not only the price of the very goods which are the subject of the particular contract of sale, but also debts due to the seller under other contracts.

Notes

(1) There is a large difference between the legal systems with regard to the scope of the title retention as far as secured claims are concerned. In some legal systems, it is common to enlarge the conditions of the title retention by requiring that all outstanding indebtedness of the buyer to the seller should be discharged before the right of ownership can pass. These are known as 'all money' title retention clauses. This is, from an economic point of view, desirable if the seller makes frequent deliveries to the buyer under contracts containing a title retention clause. The contractual extension of the secured claims then enables parties to contractually seal the indivisibility between those agreements.

(2) In the majority of civil law systems, title reservation is restricted to claims which arise directly or—in some legal systems—indirectly from the sales agreement. Title reservation is indeed a form of 'asset-based' financing. The French Cour de cassation, however, enlarges the scope of the retention of title in recognising the effectiveness of a retention of title in service agreements that do not entail the sale of a good.[82] However, the introduction of a new provision in 1994 has weakened this prohibition: according to L624-16 of the Commercial Code, a vindication claim in kind will succeed in relation to fungible assets where assets of the same nature and the same quality are in the possession of the debtor or any person keeping them for his account (*cf* below).

[82] [2001] *Revue trimestrielle de droit civil*, 930.

(3) In German law, two different forms of extended title retention clauses must be distinguished. On the one hand, German law acknowledges the 'current account' clause (*Kontokorrentvorbehalt*). According to this clause, the claims of the seller against the purchaser are not individually settled for each delivery, but rather at regular intervals on the basis of a running account; a reservation of title clause provides that the seller retains ownership in the goods until the account has been fully settled by the purchaser. The validity of these clauses has long been debated, but is now accepted by the German Supreme Court.

The second type is the 'concern-reservation' clause (*Konzernvorbehalt*). The goods are retained by the seller until the buyer has met all the obligations outstanding between him and a company belonging to the same group of companies as the seller. The prevailing view is that such clause is illegal, on the ground of §455 II BGB.

(4) In English law, an 'all monies' clause is effective with regard to the goods covered. It is clear from the case law which is cited that an 'all monies' title retention is not to be considered as a registrable charge. All monies clauses are frequently used in English commercial legal practice.

(5) What are the remedies if the retention of title secures a claim or claims which could not be secured, ie if the scope of the secured claims is too large? Partial voidness is imposed in Dutch law. This means that the title reservation remains valid with regard to the claims which fall within the scope of the restriction, but do not secure the 'outside' claims.

IV.A.4 POSITION OF THE PURCHASER UNDER TITLE RETENTION

For an extensive analysis of the position of the buyer, we refer to the paragraph on the *Anwartschaftsrecht* in Chapter 3.

IV.A.5 RESALE OF THE ASSETS UNDER RETENTION OF TITLE

If the sales agreement containing the title retention clause is situated in the distribution process of the assets, it is likely that the buyer wants to resell the assets to his own clients as soon as possible. This will be the case if the sales agreement is to be situated in the retail stage. Two questions arise subsequently: (1) is the buyer entitled to resell the assets under title retention? And (2) what are the rights of the original seller after the resale of the assets under title retention? The first question is not merely a contractual one. It determines the power to dispose of the assets which are sold under title retention and, moreover, it determines in some legal systems the proprietary position of the original seller after the resale.

IV.A.5.a Power of the buyer to resell the goods

Cour de cassation, 11 March 1997[83] **5.59 (FR)**

Constructions navales d'Acquitaine v Sofice

POSSIBILITY OF RESALE OF ASSETS UNDER TITLE RETENTION

Shipping motors

A title reservation does not render assets unavailable as long as the undertaking's business is being carried on.

Facts: X sold and supplied shipping motors to Y, and payment was secured by a title retention. Y was declared insolvent on 5 February 1991. Some of the motors had meanwhile been sold to Z. X claimed that the resale of the motors had been effected unlawfully. As far as it can be determined on the basis of the judgment, the sales agreement did not contain any provision dealing with the possibility of resale.

Held: A title reservation does not render assets unavailable as long as the undertaking's business is being carried on.

Judgment: Considering that the judgment points out that the motors claimed on 18 February 1991 were used for the carrying on of business and notes that they were sold in fraudulent disregard of the rights of X. Considering that in so deciding, although the claim does not render assets sold under reservation of title unavailable as long as the undertaking's business is being carried on, the court of appeal infringed the above mentioned provisions.

Hoge Raad, 14 February 1992[84] **5.60 (NL)**

Hinck v Van der Werff & Visser

THE POWER TO RESELL GOODS UNDER TITLE RETENTION

Love Love

The question whether and to what extent a party obliged under a title retention is authorised to transfer the object of this retention of title to third parties, in principle has to be found by interpretation of the agreement.

Facts: The defendant constructed a boat, called *Love Love*. Once this work was complete, the defendant sold this boat to a German company Classic Yard Motorsegler- und Yachtbau GmbH for a price of £76,000, payment of which was secured with a clause of title retention. After final work on the boat had been completed by C (who acted as contractor), B sold the ship back to the defendant. The latter paid part of the purchase price, and refused to pay the balance because of deficiencies in the work. The defendant claimed that he was still entitled to exercise his ownership grounded in title retention against the claimant.

Held: The appeal of the claimant is dismissed.

Judgment: The legal argument of the claimant contests the court's judgment that he

[83] Bull civ, IV, no 70.
[84] NJ 1993, 623.

would not have obtained the boat of a person entitled to dispose of the boat. The claimant argues that a title retention as here under discussion, cannot be invoked against a third party purchaser who has bought the ship for the purpose of re-extradition from a commercial use.

That argument cannot in its absoluteness be accepted as correct. It neglects that the answer to the question whether and to what extent a party obliged under a title retention is authorised to transfer the object of this retention of title to third parties, in principle has to be found by interpretation of the agreement to which the title retention is made, and that the sole circumstance that the object was intended for re-extradition does not grant power to resell the goods.

BGH, 23 May 1958[85] **5.61 (DE)**

POWER TO RESELL GOODS UNDER TITLE RETENTION

Terrazzos

A contractual clause which prohibits assignment of the resale claim cannot in good faith be interpreted as giving authorisation for resale.

Facts: X sold and supplied to Y materials to stabilise terrazzos in July and August 1953. The payment of the sales price was secured by an enlarged and prolongated title retention clause, providing that Y assigned to X the proceeds he would acquire in case of resale of the purchased goods or of the product of their manufacturing. Y resold the building materials he manufactured out of the terrazzo materials to a building company, and it was stipulated in the agreement of resale that the assignment of the claim to pay the (re)sale price was not possible without prior consent of the purchaser. Y was declared bankrupt in 1954, and the building company at that moment owed DM1,451.80 to Y.

Held: The authorisation for resale is conditional upon the effects of the resale agreement.

Judgment: The claimant erroneously criticises the court a quo for construing the authorisation for resale as being conditional upon the effects of the resale agreement. If that view were correct, criticism would arise concerning the interpretation and acceptance of a limitation on the authority to resell since it would go beyond what can reasonably be expected of a purchaser of building materials that are intended to be sold on. However, the judgment appealed against is not to be interpreted as meaning that the authorisation for resale was made dependent on the assignment agreement, that is to say, would not exist if the agreement to assign claims arising in the future were not upheld, owing, for example, to the absence of the requisite certainty as to the future claims to which it is to relate. The appeal court did not generally make the authority to sell on dependent on the validity and entry into force of the assignment agreement but rather declined to recognise that the bankrupt party had authority to sell on in the specific case in which it contractually excluded the assignment of its claim against the customer. It may remain open whether on this interpretation of the relevant provisions of the conditions of sale it is an individual contract that is being interpreted or whether these are typical contract terms reviewable by the court hearing the appeal on a point of law in accordance with the relevant principles applicable in that connection. Even in the latter case the appeal court's view would have to be upheld. The bankrupt party could not in

[85] BGHZ 27, 306 and NJW 1958, 1281.

good faith interpret the conditions as permitting it to resell even where the anticipatory assignment of future claims could not have effect because the bankrupt party was contractually bound by a restriction of the assignment of claims against its customers, that is to say making such assignment dependent on the agreement of the subsequent transferee of the goods.

Notes

(1) The buyer under title retention has no property rights on the purchased goods until he pays the full purchase price. Until then, he merely holds the assets for the account of the seller. However, most legal systems recognise that it is possible to grant to the buyer the right to resell the goods. In practice, however, most legal systems accept that a title retention clause usually does not restrict the buyer's right to resell the goods in the normal course of his business, because that is not the economic purpose behind the clause, although some legal systems (eg Dutch law) additionally pay attention to the intention of the parties. Even in the absence of express authority to resell, such an authority will often be implied from the very nature of the transaction and of the goods which are involved. Even if the reservation of title clause does impose (expressly or impliedly) restrictions on resale, they will most often not be of any effect against a purchaser (for value) without notice to the extent that the latter has acquired title through bona fide possession.[86]

In none of the analysed legal systems does such an (implicit or explicit) power to dispose affect the validity or proprietary effects of the title retention.[87]

(2) There is, however, no unanimity between the legal systems on the proprietary consequences of the resale. In Germany, England[88] and Austria, the buyer's entitlement to resell the assets gives him the power to transfer ownership directly from the original seller to the sub-purchasers (*Direkterwerb*). While in English law, this power is directly based on the statute, German law acknowledges this legal possibility through the concept of *Verfügungsbefügnis* (literally: power to dispose) which can—according to German law—be separated from the title on these assets.[89] In Dutch law, the result is quite similar: the prevailing view is that the suspensive condition to which the transfer was made subject is deemed to be fulfilled by the resale. In other words, the resale is a resolutive condition of the title retention.[90] Finally, in French and Belgian law, the sub-purchaser will only acquire ownership on the basis of bona fide purchase (Article 2279 Cciv).

Once again, it emerges that the dividing line is not between common law and

[86] We can refer to the protection of the good faith acquirer of movables, see Chapter 7.

[87] By way of exception, a clause of title retention is invalid in Swedish and Finnish law if it is coupled with a power for the buyer to resell on his own account prior to payment.

[88] For English law: s 24 Sale of Goods Act 1979.

[89] See §185 BGB: 'An act of disposition, which a non-authorised person operates with regard to an asset, is effective, if the non-authorised person had the consent of the right-holder.'

[90] For a more extensive analysis: RD Vriesendorp, 'Het eigendomsvoorbehoud: een onderzoek naar een praktische verkoperszekerheid in het huidige en komende Nederlandse recht', in *Recht en praktijk* (Deventer, Kluwer, 1985 *et seq*) 94; J Fesevur, *Goederenrechtelijke colleges*, 3rd edn (Nijmegen, Ars Aequi Libri, 2006) 107; WHM Reehuis, 'Eigendomsvoorbehoud', in *Monografieën Nieuw BW* (Deventer, Kluwer, 1998) no 38.

civil law; German law seems to be in this respect closer to the common law than to, for instance, French law.

IV.A.5.b Rights of the original seller to the proceeds of the resale

Introductory Note

The previous section was devoted to the question whether the buyer under title retention has authority to resell the goods even before he has fully paid the purchase price. Another question arises with regard to the legal effects of such (authorised or unauthorised) resale. Can the ownership of the original seller under title retention be upheld if the purchaser under title retention passes on the goods to a subsequent transferee?

If the answer is positive, the issue of priority ranking arises. It is in all legal systems a much-debated issue as to whether priority lies with the initial seller, or with a third party which has obtained property rights via resale (eg through an assignment).

Cour de cassation, 20 June 1989[91] **5.62 (FR)**

BNP v Micro-informatique et télécommunications

PROPRIETARY STATUS OF THE RESALE CLAIM

Paribas 1

The title retention continues on the resale claim after the sale of the initial goods.

Facts: Company A sold materials to company B. The latter resold these materials to C, before having paid the purchase price. At the same time, the claim out of the resale was assigned to C. B was declared insolvent after both operations. A claimed that his ownership was transferred to the sub-sale claim on the basis of real subrogation (the resale claim was substituted for the initial goods), but C argued that he was the assignee of the claim, in such way that real subrogation was neutralised.

Held: The judgment rendered by the Court of Appeal which gives priority to A, is approved.

Judgment: The price payable [to the reseller] is thereby subrogated to the goods of which the [original seller] remained the owner; the court of appeal rendered a lawful judgment by stating that the assignment of the claim relied on by [the assignee] could not defeat the vindication by the [original seller].

[91] Bull civ, IV, no 197, D 1989, jur, 431, with critical observations of F Perochon.

Cour de cassation, 15 January 1991[92] **5.63 (FR)**

Micro-informatique et telecommunications v PNB

STATUS OF THE EXCESS VALUE OUT OF THE RESALE

Paribas 2

A title retention can never cover the profit margin of the resale.

Facts: A sold goods to B under title retention. Before the latter had paid the full purchase price, he resold the goods to his own clients. B was declared bankrupt before he had received payment from his own clients. The price of repurchase exceeded the price of the original sales agreement. A debate arose with regard to the entitlement to this price difference.

Held: The seller under title retention is not entitled to the margin of resale.

Judgment: The vindication of the price was grounded in the substitution to the goods themselves whose price was fixed upon the conclusion of the contract. Hence, the price of those goods of which [the creditor] had remained the owner could not be altered either by the reservation of ownership clause or by the resale of those goods to the subsequent purchasers; the court of appeal was therefore correct and lawfully held that the price payable … to the creditor could not include the profit margin that … the purchaser had imposed upon his customers.

BGH, 16 March 1977[93] **5.64 (DE)**

STATUS OF THE RESALE CLAIM

Milk products

Title retention can continue on the resale claim, except if the buyer has lawfully resold the initial goods with consent of the initial seller.

Facts: X (defendant) sold and supplied milk products to Y (claimant) under title retention. Y was a retail company, selling the manufactured and perishable milk products to warehouses. Y was declared bankrupt, owing at that point more than DM500,000 to X. It was accepted before the German Supreme Court that the sold goods had remained identifiable at the moment that they were resold.

Held: The appeal is dismissed.

Judgment: The claimant argues that the requirements for real subrogation as protection for the property right [*Ersatzaussonderung*] under §46 of the Konkursordnung[94] were not fulfilled in the present case because the bankrupt party for its part had likewise only passed on the goods supplied by the claimant to its customers under retention of ownership, while §46 KO requires a disposition a transfer of ownership. The Court cannot adhere to the argument of the claimant.

The appeal court correctly proceeded on the starting point that a right to ring-fence under §46 KO was permitted in the event of a resale by the seller subject to

[92] Bull civ, IV, no 31, D 1993, somm comm, 297, n F Perochon.

[93] NJW 1977, 901. This solution had already been put forward before: BGH 11 June 1959, BGHZ 30, (176) 184.

[94] This was the provision on the so-called *Ersatzaussonderung*, which is now included in §48 Insolvenzordnung.

retention of ownership, which is to be presumed in the ordinary course of business. A disposal lawfully occurring with the consent of the owner of an object cannot give rise to a claim for real subrogation by the owner (§46 KO).

BGH, 30 April 1959[95] **5.65 (DE)**

VALIDITY OF A GLOBAL ASSIGNMENT OF RESALE CLAIMS

Leather

An assignment of future claims which will arise out of a resale of goods under title retention is void.

Facts: The claimant awarded a loan to a leather manufacturer, which was secured by an assignment of claims. The debtor, however, was declared bankrupt during the loan agreement. The insolvency administrator received payment of the debtor of the assigned claim on a trust account. The claimant now argued that it was entitled to that sum.

Held: The assignment of future claims which will arise out of a resale of goods under title retention is void.

Judgment: A global assignment to a bank of future receivables in order to secure a loan is *contra bonos mores* and void where it is intended by the contracting parties also to include such claims as the debtor must in future assign, and does assign, to his suppliers on the basis of an extended reservation of ownership.

Hoge Raad, 25 June 1954[96] **5.66 (NL)**

R Hoving v Rotterdamse Bank

STATUS OF THE RESALE CLAIM

Ray Fish

The original seller has a right to the purchase price owed by the second purchaser and that right cannot be undermined by an assignment of that claim.

Facts: X sold and supplied 300 kg of fish to Y, who resold and resupplied 150 kg to Z. Neither Y nor Z paid the sales price. During the proceedings, the Bank of Rotterdam intervened, arguing that Y promised to assign to it all claims which it would acquire vis-à-vis third parties, and assigned—pursuant to this promise—the claim against Z seven days later, which it notified to Z on the same date. According to the old Dutch law, X can claim a right of vindication on the sold goods, and on the proceeds of the resale (Article 1192a old Dutch BW).

Held: The original seller has a right to the purchase price owed by the second purchaser and that right cannot be undermined by an assignment of that claim.

Judgment: Considering that ... the original seller cannot be denied the right to the purchase price owed by the second purchaser and that right cannot be undermined by an assignment of the claim which the first buyer has on the second seller to the Rotterdam Bank. That is at least the case if that assignment, as in the present case,

[95] BGHZ 30, 149. See also: BGH 9 June 1960, BGHZ 32, 361; BGH 12 November 1970, BGHZ 55, 34; BGH 24 April 1968, NJW 1968, 1516, n J Werhahn.

[96] NJ 1955, no 685, concl Adv Gen Loeff and n PS.

was not yet notified to the first seller nor had the latter accepted or acknowledged it in writing at the time when the first seller brought proceedings. ...

that it is not unreasonable that a claim which the purchaser has acquired through selling the goods bought in cash but not yet paid for during thirty days after the original delivery should remain charged in favour of the original seller. This is justified given the fact that the legally recognised interests of the original seller do not rank lower than the interests of the person to whom, notwithstanding the fact that the original seller's claim remains unpaid, the claim has been assigned.

Court of Appeal, 16 January 1976[97] **5.67 (E&W)**

Aluminium Industrie Vaassen BV v Romalpa Aluminium Ltd

CONTRACTUAL EXTENSION OF TITLE RETENTION

Romalpa

On the basis of a contractual 'Romalpa clause', a seller can be entitled to trace the proceeds of the sale.

Facts: Between September 1973 and October 1974 the claimant, a Dutch company Aluminium Industrie Vaassen (AIV), sold to the defendants, an English company, aluminium foil, some of which the defendants sold on to third parties. The plaintiffs' general selling terms and conditions, which the court found applied to all transactions between the parties, stipulated by clause 13, as follows. Given its importance to the judgment, the clause (which become known as the 'Romalpa clause') is cited here in full:

> The ownership of the material to be delivered by AIV [the claimant] will only be transferred to purchaser when he has met all that is owing to AIV, no matter on what grounds. Until the date of payment, purchaser, if AIV so desires, is required to store this material in such a way that it is clearly the property of AIV AIV and purchaser agree that, if purchaser should make (a) new object(s) from the material, mixes this material with (an)other object(s) or if this material in any way whatsoever becomes a constituent of (an)other object(s) AIV will be given the ownership of this (these) new object(s) as surety of the full payment of what purchaser owes AIV To this end AIV and purchaser now agree that the ownership of the article(s) in question, whether finished or not, are to be transferred to AIV and that this transfer of ownership will be considered to have taken place through and at the moment of the single operation or event by which the material is converted into (a) new object(s), or is mixed with or becomes a constituent of (an)other object(s). Until the moment of full payment of what purchaser owes AIV, purchaser shall keep the object(s) in question for AIV in his capacity of fiduciary owner and, if required, shall store this(these) object(s) in such a way that it (they) can be recognised as such. Nevertheless, purchaser will be entitled to sell these objects to a third party within the framework of the normal carrying on of his business and to deliver them on condition that—if AIV so requires—purchaser, as long as he has not fully discharged his debt to AIV shall hand over to AIV the claims he has against his buyer emanating from this transaction.

An insolvency proceeding was opened against the defendant, owing at that moment to the plaintiffs over £122,000. The receiver found some £50,000 worth of foil still in the possession of the defendants, and he received from sub-buyers £35,000, which was held in an account in his name with the defendants' bankers. The original seller claimed an order for delivery up of the foil in possession of the defendant and a declaration that they were entitled to a charge on the money in the account of the receiver. They argued that they were entitled to the proceeds of the sale to sub-purchasers.

Held: The appeal is dismissed.

Judgment: Roskill LJ—Are the plaintiffs entitled to the proceeds of sales to sub-

[97] [1976] WLR 677.

purchasers now held by the receiver? We were told both by Mr Price and by Mr Lincoln that the receiver received these moneys after he had entered into his receivership from sales made by the defendants to sub-purchasers before that date. The receiver, properly if I may say so, kept those moneys separate; and we were told that there is no complication arising from those moneys having become mixed with other moneys, because they were always kept separate. There was no suggestion that the sub-sales in question were other than authorised by the plaintiffs or that the sub-purchasers concerned did not acquire a valid title to the several quantities of foil which each of them bought. The sole question is whether, on the facts and on the true construction of the bargain, including the general conditions, between the plaintiffs and the defendants, the plaintiffs, are entitled to trace and recover those proceeds of the sub-sales, upon the well-known principles laid down in the judgment of Sir George Jessel MR in *In re Hallett's Estate* (1880) 13 ChD 696. Those principles are so well known that it is not necessary to quote the Master of the Rolls' famous judgment or from the various restatements of principle in the several textbooks to which Mr Price has referred. The most relevant passages from that judgment will be found in Mocatta J's judgment (ante, pp 681A–B *et seq*).

The critical question is whether there was a fiduciary relationship between the plaintiffs and the defendants which entitles the plaintiffs successfully to claim these moneys in the way and upon the footing which I have just described.

...

The defendants as sellers were to retain the property in the goods until all—*and I underline 'all'*—that was owing to them had been paid. It is a curious fact that the first part of clause 13 is so short while the second part is so long and detailed. But, as Mr Lincoln said, the problems with which the second part had to deal were infinitely more complex than those with which the first part had to deal. It is obvious, to my mind, that the business purpose of the whole of this clause, read in its context in the general conditions, was to secure the plaintiffs, so far as possible, against the risks of non-payment after they had parted with possession of the goods delivered, whether or not those goods retained their identity after delivery. I unhesitatingly accept that part of Mr Lincoln's submission. In the case of unmanufactured goods this was to be achieved by the plaintiffs retaining the property until all payments due had been made, to which were added the special rights given by clause 25. In the case of mixed or manufactured goods, more elaborate provisions were made and indeed were obviously required if the avowed object of clause 13 were to be achieved in the case of the latter class of goods. The plaintiffs were to be given the ownership of these mixed or manufactured goods as 'surety' for 'full payment.' 'Surety' I think in this context must mean, as Mr Lincoln contended yesterday, 'security.' This is as between the defendants and the plaintiffs, and it is not necessary to consider how far this provision would protect the plaintiffs against adverse claims, at any rate in this country, by third parties. Further, the clause later provides that until 'full payment' is made the defendants shall keep the mixed goods for the plaintiffs as 'fiduciary owners'—not perhaps the happiest of phrases but one which suggests, at least to an English lawyer, that in relation to mixed or manufactured goods there was produced what in English law would be called a fiduciary relationship in this respect. The clause goes on to give to the defendants an express power of sale of such goods, and the right to deliver them; and adds an obligation upon the defendants, if required by the plaintiffs so to do, to assign (to use English legal language) to the plaintiffs the benefit of any claim against a sub-purchaser so long as the defendants have not fully discharged all their indebtedness to the plaintiffs.

For my part I accept that this last-mentioned provision is not itself an equitable assignment in English law. But I think that Mr Lincoln is right in his general approach to the construction of the second part of clause 13. Like the first part, it contemplates the resale by the defendants of goods which at the time of such resale were to be the property of the plaintiffs and not of the defendants. The second part of clause 13 clearly contemplates the creation of a fiduciary relationship in relation to mixed goods; and the assignment provisions are, as I think, clearly designed to give the plaintiffs, if they so require, an additional security to recover debts otherwise payable to the defendants but not paid to them by the sub-purchasers, if the defendants have failed to discharge all or any of their current indebtedness to the plaintiffs. …

Now, the crucial facts to my mind are two: first, that the defendants were selling goods which the plaintiffs owned at all material times; and secondly, that clause 13 as a whole is obviously designed to protect the plaintiffs, in the event of later insolvency. … When, therefore, one is considering what, if any, additional implication has to be made to the undoubted implied power of sale in the first part of clause 13, one must ask what, if any, additional implication is necessary to make effective the obvious purpose of giving the requisite security to the plaintiffs? One is, I think, entitled to look at the second part of clause 13 to answer this; for it would be strange if the first part were to afford no relevant security when the second part is (as I think) elaborately drawn to give such security in relation to manufactured or mixed goods.

I see no difficulty in the contractual concept that, as between the defendants and their sub-purchasers, the defendants sold as principals, but that, as between themselves and the plaintiffs, those goods which they were selling as principals within their implied authority from the plaintiffs were the plaintiffs' goods which they were selling as agents for the plaintiffs to whom they remained fully accountable. If an agent lawfully sells his principal's goods, he stands in a fiduciary relationship to his principal and remains accountable to his principal for those goods and their proceeds. A bailee is in like position in relation to his bailor's goods. What, then, is there here to relieve the defendants from their obligation to account to the plaintiffs for those goods of the plaintiffs which they lawfully sell to sub-purchasers? The fact that they so sold them as principals does not, as I think, affect their relationship with the plaintiffs; nor (as at present advised) do I think—contrary to Mr Price's argument—that the sub-purchasers could on this analysis have sued the plaintiffs upon the sub-contracts as undisclosed principals for, say, breach of warranty of quality.

It seems to me clear (and so far from helping Mr Price I think the second part of clause 13, properly construed, helps Mr Lincoln) that to give effect to what I regard as the obvious purpose of clause 13 one must imply into the first part of the clause not only the power to sell but also the obligation to account in accordance with the normal fiduciary relationship of principal and agent, bailor and bailee. Accordingly, like the judge I find no difficulty in holding that the principles in Hallett's case, 13 ChD 696 are of immediate application, and I think that the plaintiffs are entitled to trace these proceeds of sale and to recover them, as Mocatta J has held by his judgment.

Mr Price relied upon the conduct of the parties after the defendants took over from the partnership, pointing out (as was the fact) that the defendants were never required to account to the plaintiffs in the way I think, as a matter of law, the plaintiffs were entitled to require them to account. As a matter of business I would not have expected the plaintiffs so to have required the defendants to account. But, as Mr Lincoln forcefully replied on this point, clause 13 is directed to a state of insolvency, not to what he described as to the halcyon days of solvency; and it is only upon insolvency that the question of what the powers are under clause 13 comes into play.

On the view which I have formed of this case it is not necessary to discuss some of the other interesting points on which we had the benefit of argument from counsel on both sides, and I refrain from doing so.

Goff LJ—I need not repeat any general statement of the facts. They have been fully set out in the judgment just delivered by Roskill LJ.

The first question which arises for determination is whether clause 13 of the general selling terms and conditions applied to the contracts made between the plaintiffs and the defendants or only to those made whilst the business was still being carried on by the partnership. If it did apply to the defendants, then it follows that the plaintiffs are entitled to recover the unsold stock and the appeal must fail as to that item. There is, however, then a second question whether, even so, the judgment is right in allowing the plaintiffs to recover the £35,000 odd proceeds of sale. I turn to the first of these questions. [His Lordship said that there was in his view no doubt at all that, the partners having accepted and signed the translation of the general terms and conditions, the whole of those terms, including clause 13, applied to the contracts made by them and he agreed with Roskill LJ that the reasoning of Mocatta J on that part of the case was quite unchallengeable. His Lordship continued:]

In my judgment the second part of the case comes down to a short question of construction. It is common ground that a power of sale during the period that any money remains owing to the plaintiffs must be implied; but the question is upon what terms.

I do not think it is necessary to go into the cases cited before Mocatta J, since it is clear to me, and was for a long time during the argument, that the plaintiffs must, on the principle of *In re Hallett's Estate*, 13 ChD 696 , be entitled to trace their aluminium into the proceeds of sale so as to enable them to take the £35,000, and to take that sum in priority to the general body of the defendants' creditors and in priority to the secured creditor Hume, unless, as the defendants contend, one ought to imply a power to sell and apply the proceeds of sale for their own purposes, or, as they put it, to sell for their own account. In the end this was accepted by both counsel, and nothing short of that will serve the defendants' purpose.

The plaintiffs say that the power should be qualified so as to maintain for them the security which they Eave themselves by providing that property in the aluminium should not pass so long as any money remains owing to them, and accordingly it could only be exercised for their benefit in this sense, that the proceeds of sale must be held in trust for them until all the defendants' indebtedness to them on any contract be discharged.

In considering this problem, one may at the outset dispose of one point. The provisions in the latter part of clause 13 dealing with cases where there has been admixture cannot, in my judgment, as a matter of construction apply to the type of case with which we are concerned where there has been no admixture. Those provisions are, however, as Roskill LJ has said, relevant in so far as they throw light upon what the implication in the earlier part should be; and indeed in an alternative submission, introduced by amendment, to which I must return later, the defendants submit that the power of sale to be implied is the same as what expressly provided in that latter part of clause 13.

In considering what should be implied in a contract the court has to consider what is required to give it business efficacy; but I agree with Roskill LJ that there are two distinct and opposing approaches to 'business efficacy.' The one, looking at the matter from the point of view of the defendants, suggests that an unqualified power is required, because they would need to use the money in carrying on their business, and indeed, so it is suggested, anything else would largely stultify the agreement that they should have 75 days' credit. The other is, from the standpoint of the plaintiffs, that the power should not be so wide as to frustrate the whole purpose of clause 13, which it is submitted, and in my judgment rightly submitted, discloses a manifest intention to preserve the vendors from being left in the position of unsecured creditors.

In the end, in my judgment, the question is which of these ought to prevail; and I have come to a clear conclusion that the plaintiffs' contention should be preferred.

There is no doubt force in Mr. Price's argument that this as a matter of strict law destroys the benefit of the 75 days' credit. I would observe, as Roskill LJ has pointed out, that the General Selling Terms and Conditions as originally accepted by the partners provided for 14 days' credit only, and it may well be that in considering what should be implied one should disregard the later extension of time, in which case the point would be much weakened, although not altogether destroyed. I will assume, however, that the court ought to consider the matter in the light of that extension. Even so, in my judgment this is not enough to require, or entitle, the court to imply a term plainly and utterly inconsistent with the clear intention of the clause into which it is to be implied.

The difficulty arises largely because the general conditions tie the passing of the property not to the particular contract but to all indebtedness. But for that, the qualified power would not prevent the defendants from enjoying reasonable advantages from the 75 days' credit. No doubt in practice, so long as all went well the plaintiffs would allow the defendants to use the proceeds of sale in their business, as I understand they did; but things ceased to go well, and now one has to determine the strict rights of the parties, and in my judgment the difficulty so imported is not enough to drive one to imply a term defeating the whole object of clause 13.

I turn to the alternative argument which I have already mentioned. I do not myself think it is a correct approach simply to imply in the first part of clause 13 the same power as is expressed in the latter part and which as a matter of construction does not apply to the first part and which is dealing with a different state of affairs. Even, however, if one does, it does not in my view help the defThe argument is that under that clause there is no equitable assignment of the book debts until the plaintiffs require the defendants, in the words of the translation before us, to 'hand over to AIV the claims he has against his buyer,' and, further, that as no such requirement was made before the security crystallised by the appointment of the receiver any equitable assignment resulting therefrom could only be subject to the security created by the debentures.

I accept that as far as it goes, but it still leaves the question whether one should then construe the power as entitling the defendants to sell and use the proceeds as and when received for their own benefit unless and until required to assign the debt, or whether on the contrary, as the plaintiffs contend, it is implicit that the proceeds of sale when received are received on their account and the right to call for an assignment is ancillary only. In my judgment that would be the right view, even if one simply implied a power in precisely the same terms as expressed concerning mixed cases.

In short, my conclusion is that the power of sale to be implied where none has been expressed must be so qualified as not to defeat the intention clearly shown by clause 13 as a whole, including the latter part, which only emphasises this. It follows that there was, as Roskill LJ says, a sufficient fiduciary relationship between the parties, and this is indeed expressly contemplated in the reference to a fiduciary owner in the second part of clause 13. The implied power must, therefore, in my judgment be a power to sell, not for the defendants' own account, but for the account of the plaintiffs unless and until all moneys owing be paid.

Notes

(1) German and English law are rather similar in the solution they give to the issue of the rights of the original seller in the proceeds of the resale.

In German law, §48 of the Insolvency Act (*Insolvenzordnung*)[98] protects the position of the holder of a proprietary interest, which includes the seller under title retention. This provision allows the owner of an *Aussonderungsrecht* to exercise his rights on the substitute of the initial goods if the latter have been sold by the debtor (before opening of the insolvency proceedings) or by the trustee in bankruptcy (after opening of the insolvency proceedings). In that case, the traceable claim to pay the price of the sub-sale will be substituted to the initial goods as object of the *Aussonderungsrecht*, so that X remains protected against the insolvency of Y.[99] However, paragraph 48 *Insolvenzordnung* has no general scope: it only applies if the sub-sale was unlawful. An application of paragraph 48 is excluded if the original seller (X) has given his consent to the original purchaser (Y) for the resale of the things still belonging to X. This restriction can be overcome by contractually extending the claim to the claim arising out of the repurchase. A so-called extended title retention (*verlängerter Eigentumsvorbehalt*) contains an anticipatory assignment of the claims arising out of the sub-sales (*Abtretungsklausel*). Unlike French, Belgian and Dutch law, German law recognises that such contractual agreements have proprietary effects against the concurring creditors, and thus can be invoked against the trustee in bankruptcy of Y. Austrian law is similar to German law in this regard.

In English law, a simple title retention will not, of itself, impose upon the buyer an obligation to account to the seller for the proceeds of sale of the goods in which property is retained.[100] As a result of the *Romalpa* case, it has become

[98] §48 Insolvenzordnung: 'If an asset, which can be the object of a separate right ('*Aussonderungsrecht*') has been unlawfully sold before the opening of the insolvency proceedings or after the opening of the insolvency proceedings by the insolvency administrator, the holder of the separate right can claim rights in the counterprestation, as long as it has not been fulfilled. He can claim the counterprestation out of the insolvency patrimony, as long as it is identifiable in the insolvency patrimony.'

[99] For extensive comments on the application of this provision on the seller under title retention: R Moritz, *Die Rechte des Vorbehaltsverkäufers nach §46 KO im Konkurs des Käufers* (München, Thesis, 1970) 80.

[100] *Hendy Lennox (Industrial Engines) Ltd v Grahame Puttick Ltd* [1984] 1 WLR 485.

common practice for sellers to insert in their standard conditions of sale a so-called 'Romalpa clause', reinforcing the position of the seller in creating an obligation of the buyer to hold the proceeds on trust or in a fiduciary capacity for the seller. This gives to the seller the right to apply the larger rules of equitable tracing and thus to protect their property right against mixing and commingling of their object. These clauses have been challenged on two grounds: (1) it has been alleged that the sellers under title retention have acquired in this way a charge over the goods, which is void unless it has been the object of registration pursuant to section 395 of the Companies Act 1985 (this criticism only applies if granted by a company); (2) the interpretation of the clause in particular circumstances gives rise to uncertainties. The original sellers claim more extensive rights than the ones which are conferred by the clause. Staughton J described this area of law as 'presently *a maze if not a minefield*'.[101]

(2) It is no surprise that French, Belgian and Dutch law do not recognise the possibility of contractually extending the retention of title to the claim arising out of the resale. These are the legal systems which are reluctant to recognise the transfer of ownership for security purposes (see IV.B) The contractual extension of the title retention to the proceeds of resale (*verlängerte Eigentumsvorbehalt*) is mostly grounded in an anticipatory and fiduciary transfer of the claim arising out of the subsale.

This does not endanger the position of the original seller in French and Belgian law, to the extent that they can claim the proceeds of the sub-sale on the basis of real subrogation. In other words: the seller under title retention in French and Belgian law does not need a contractual clause because he is protected at law.[102] This emerges from the judgment of 20 June 1989 cited above and the later case law of the French Cour de cassation.[103]

In Dutch law, the original seller will be protected if the claim of the sub-sale is pledged in favour of the original seller, but this pledge will have to be registered or the sub-purchaser will have to be notified of the pledge agreement.

(3) If the seller is granted a property right in the proceeds pursuant to the operation of law (real subrogation) or the contractual clauses ('proceeds clause'), he will face considerable practical problems in enforcing his rights. He will have to trace the proceeds of the sale. He must comply, in passing this process, with the tracing rules which will be described in Chapter 7. In legal practice this generally means that he will only maintain his property position if the sub-purchaser has not yet paid the purchase price or has paid the price into a separate account. Only equitable tracing in English law allows more flexible rules of tracing the value in goods through commingling (see Chapter 7).

[101] *Hendy Lennox (Industrial Engines) Ltd v Grahame Puttick Ltd* [1984] 1 WLR (485) 493.

[102] For Belgian law: see V Sagaert, *Zakelijke subrogatie* (Antwerp, Intersentia, 2003) nos 152–58; E Dirix, 'Eigendomsvoorbehoud' [1997–98] *Rechtskundig Weekblad* 491, no 34; A Cuypers, *Kredieten en zekerheden bij faillissement en gerechtelijk akkoord* (Antwerp, Kluwer, 1998) no 89.

[103] Cour de cassation, 5 October 1993, Bull civ, IV, no 317; Cour de cassation, 26 April 2000, D 2000, jur, 278, n P Pisoni; Cour de cassation, 8 March 1988, Bull civ, IV, no 99 and [1989] *Revue trimestrielle de droit com* 113, no 12, n B Bouloc.

(4) What are the limits of the rights of the initial seller where the proceeds of the resale exceed the original sales price? According to the above-cited judgment of the French Cour de cassation, the property rights of the original seller are limited to the original sales price. He would not be entitled to the profit made by the original buyer.

However, the *Romalpa* judgment of the Court of Appeal involved the conclusion that all the money received by the original buyers from the resale of the goods had to be held on trust for the original sellers. This has been criticised by English scholars, and some later judgments have purported to restrict the authority of *Romalpa*.[104] First of all, it was stressed that the buyers in *Romalpa* were bailees of the aluminium foil, according to the express retention of title clause in that case. This is, however, exceptional. Later case law ruled that if a buyer was permitted to resell goods in the normal course of his business before paying the seller for them, the normal implication is that he would do so for his own account and not as a fiduciary who was obliged to account to the seller for all the proceeds of sale. Even if the parties have expressly or impliedly agreed that the buyer had to account for the proceeds of the resale, it is submitted that it concerns more an interest by way of security than an absolute interest.[105] This conclusion, in its turn, would (i) narrow the gap between the French vision and English opinion on this aspect and (ii) fortify the view that a charge over the proceeds is created, and thus requires a registration.

(5) An additional complication may occur: a supplier (X) sells certain merchandise to a client (Y), under retention of title. Before payment of the purchase price, Y resells the merchandise to a third party (Z).[106] Z assigns or pledges the claim arising out of the sub-sale to Q. If it is submitted that the title retention also extends to the proceeds of the resale by way of law or by way of operation, a priority conflict arises between X and Q.

The conflict involved is a conflict between two financing methods of a different nature: the seller under title retention provides credit on the basis of 'asset-based financing', which means that the object of the security right is also the object of the financing. In contrast, the assignee provides credit ascertained by a security right on assets which are not 'objectively' related to the credit itself. In German law, one makes the contrast between *Warenkredit* (title retention) and *Geldkredit* (security assignment, pledge).[107]

It emerges from the above-cited case law that both French and German law are inclined to give priority to asset-based financing (*Warenkredit*) to the detriment of

[104] E Pfeiffer, *Weinkellerei-Weineinkauf GmbH & Co v Arbuthnot Factors Ltd* [1987] BCLC 522.

[105] See also AG Guest, *Benjamin's Sale of Goods* (London: Sweet & Maxwell, 2002) 5-153.

[106] It is presumed that Z acted in good faith, not knowing that he bought assets from a person who was not the owner.

[107] See eg: Baur and Stürner, above n 42, §59, no 50 *et seq*. Also: V Beuthien, 'Verlängerter Eigentumsvorbehalt und Globalabtretung' [1971] BB 375–81; P Erman, 'Verlängerter Eigentumsvorbehalt und Globalzession' [1959] *BB* (1109) 1111; J Esser, 'Globalzession und verlängerter Eigentumsvorbehalt' [1968] *JZ* 281–85 at 529; W Flume, 'Zur Problematik des verlängerten Eigentumsvorbehalts' [1959] *NJW* 920; H Kaduk, 'Verlängerter Eigentumsvorbehalt und Globalzession als konkurrierende Gläubigerrechte', in *Festschrift für Karl Larenz zum 70 Geburtstag* (München, CH Beck Verlag, 1973) 695.

the creditors who financed the same debtor on the basis of receivables financing (*Geldkredit*). The line of reasoning of the Cour de cassation, the Bundesgerichtshof and the Dutch Hoge Raad is different, as the French case law reasons along the line of property law, while German case law solves the conflict on the level of the validity of the obligatory agreement.[108] However, the result they achieve is similar.

There seems to be a legal-economic argument in support of the solution provided by the Cour de cassation and the BGH: financial institutions are generally better equipped than professional sellers for investigating the proprietary status of assets belonging to their debtor. The economic loss due to his investigation is therefore smaller than the economic loss due to an investigation effected by a seller. The legal-economic argument seems to have played an important role, particularly in the judgment of the Dutch Supreme Court, which dates from the period that Dutch law admitted extended clauses of retention of title.

IV.A.6 MANUFACTURING OF THE ASSETS UNDER RETENTION OF TITLE

If the sale under retention of title is situated in the stage of production of the assets, they will be manufactured, and thus transformed, by the buyer. We deal later with the proprietary consequences of transformation (*specificatio*) (see Chapter 7). We will in this section deal with the question whether it is possible to improve the position of the seller under title retention by using a different, extended, type of retention of title clause. In German law, this is known as a *Verarbeitungsklausel* or manufacturing clause.

Hoge Raad, 5 October 1990[109] **5.68 (NL)**

Machinefabriek Breda NV v Machinefabriek Plaatwerkerij en Constructiefabriek St Antonius

RETENTION OF TITLE AND TRANSFORMATION OF THE GOODS

Ship framework

If the manufacturer of a product does not become the owner of the product at law, he will indeed not be able to reserve ownership to that product in a way which is effective against his principal.

Facts: Breda transferred ownership of steel to its bank in security of a debt. Afterwards, Breda entered into an agreement with Antonius, according to which the latter was to manufacture on behalf of Breda the framework of a ship out of the steel delivered by the latter. The manufacturing process had a big impact, and the cost of it exceeded the value of the materials. The general conditions applying to the agreement determined, in favour of Antonius, that 'all goods are supplied under retention of title until full payment has been effected of all current and future claims by the principal, including the interest and expenses. Our ownership extends to the new goods which are manufactured out of the supplied

[108] The global assignment of the (future) resale claims is even considered to be void if the bank-assignee obliges to pay the seller under title retention with priority out of the proceeds of the claims (BGH 24 April 1968, NJW 1968, 1516).

[109] NJ 1992, 226.

goods. The principal manufactures the goods for us and holds them for us under exclusion of their ownership.' An insolvency proceeding was later opened against Breda, and the question arose as to the property status of the manufactured goods.

Held: Breda has become owner of the product of the manufacturing.

Judgment: In the proceedings Antonius argued that through its manufacturing work it has become the owner under Article 661 of the hulls, curves and manufactured goods by it and that it retained ownership after delivery thereof to Breda. Conversely Breda contended that Antonius carried on its activities on the basis of a salaried employment and had therefore not manufactured the relevant objects for itself but for Breda with the result that Antonius never acquired ownership of those objects. The tribunal in first instance rejected Breda's view. The appeal court held the pleas to be unfounded. The legal arguments raise a series of complaints.

3.3. The arguments read together must succeed. Breda's assertion in the proceedings is that it had the objects in question manufactured for itself by Antonius from materials made available for that purpose by it. If that turns out in fact to be the case, Article 661 in conjunction with the more detailed provision in Article 5:16(2) of the Civil Code purports to Breda and not Antonius having become the owner of the manufactured objects. Whether that is the case will depend on the legal relationship between the parties in the light of commercial practices. In the case of an industrial manufacturing as in the present case it will turn on the question who had the decisive influence on the production method and the final form of the product and who within the legal relationship bore the risk with regard to losses owing to declining usability, marketability or profitability of the product.

In that view, it is important in the present case—save the matters mentioned under 3.1—that the Court took in the appeal judgment (point 4.7.6) as starting point that Antonius worked on the basis of detailed descriptions provided by Breda and that for Antonius itself the end product was useless. On the basis of that finding it must be presumed that the appeal court was proceeding on the assumption that the following matters were correct, or left open whether they were correct:

a. that Antonius for a fixed price for the manufactured product, which was precisely determined by Breda, manufactured the products from material made available to it by Breda on the orders and for the account of Breda;

b. that Antonius in regard to usability, marketability or profitability of the product incurred no risk but merely had to agree a commercially realistic price for its own activities;

c. that the risk in respect of damage in the course of the manufacturing process in light of the aforementioned clause 3.1 entitled 'salaried employment', however that term be interpreted, was born to a considerable extent by Breda.

In the light of the foregoing the appeal court's view that Antonius became the owner of the above-mentioned objects by its manufacturing is grounded either in a view of the law that is incompatible with the matters mentioned above and therefore incorrect or in a line of reasoning which in the absence of any further explanation is unintelligible. In that connection it is important to observe that the appeal court in paragraph 4.5.4 attributes considerable importance to the fact that the proceedings in this case involved a very high added value because the costs of the material made available by Breda were appreciably lower than the production costs made by Antonius. In that connection the appeal court took in all respect an unlawful starting point since, in derogation of the provision in Article 571 of the

Civil Code that appears neither in the current Article 661 et seq of the old or new Civil Code, as a matter of principle the low value of the materials used in relation to the work required is irrelevant to the question who becomes the owner after a manufacturing process. Moreover, the appeal court in the light of the foregoing in any event paid insufficient attention to the meaning of the wording 'for its own account and risk' in paragraphs 4.5.4 and 4.5.5. where the wording relates to the 'carrying out of the manufacturing process' or the 'wanting to take in hand and having taken in hand' by Antonius of the manufacturing of the objects. Moreover, it is clear from paragraph 4.1 that the appeal court proceeded along the findings of the lower court that, according to what is said in point 3.1, Antonius carried on the relevant activities 'on the orders and for the account' of Breda.

The question what would have been the solution if the products were not manufactured from materials supplied by Breda but by materials bought by Antonius itself, as it was raised by the appeal court itself in paragraph 4.5.6, does not arise in this case.

It should be further observed that if the actual manufacturer of a product upon application of the abovementioned criterion does not become the owner of the product by virtue of its manufacturing, he will indeed not be able to reserve ownership to that product in a way which is effective against his principal or the latter's bank to whom a security right is conferred on the product. However, he is not precluded from invoking any security for payment of remuneration of his activities since normally he can suspend the fulfilment of his obligation to deliver the products in accordance with Article 6:52(2) of the NBW until he receives satisfaction of the obligations due to him also in relation to products already manufactured and supplied under earlier contracts.

BGH, 19 October 1966[110] **5.69 (DE)**

THE EFFECTIVITY OF A TRANSORMATION CLAUSE IN TITLE RETENTION

Leather shoes

It is possible and effective to extend a retention of title to the product of manufacturing.

Facts: X sold and supplied to Y, a shoe producer, leather and similar materials. Y produced shoes out of the materials. The clause of retention of title provided that

> 'X supplies leather and similar materials and remains owner until final payment. Ownership only passes after unreserved fulfillment of all obligations by the buyer. The owenrship will not perish through the manufacturing and workmanship of the final product. The buyer can only manufacture the goods in the normal course of its business. During the manufacturing, the ownership of X will continue on the parts and the final product. X acquires ownership to the extent of the value of the raw materials it supplied toghether with the anticipatorily paid wages and operational expenses on the semi or final product.'

The buyer was declared bankrupt at 20 March 1961. The proprietary status of the shoes was debated in legal proceedings.

Held: The seller can exercise his title retention, but this title retention can not cover the wages and operational costs.

[110] BGHZ 46, 117, NJW 1967, 34. See also: BGH 3 March 1956, BGHZ 20, 159; BGH 23 October 1963, BB 1963, 1354.

Judgment: That the supplier, who supplies raw materials to a producer, can retain his title through a so-called 'transformation clause' [*Verarbeitungsklausel*] can claim title on the basis of paragraph §950 BGB in the product, is not contested. However, it is debated which legal ground is underlying this title, which are the limits of such agreement and what is the solution in case of competition between different suppliers. ...

The problem of the competition between different suppliers has been erased in legal pratice as suppliers do not claim title to the entire final product, but only to the part of the raw materials, such as in this case 'to the extent of the value of the raw materials it supplied toghether with the anticipatorily paid wages and operational expenses on the half or final product'. However, this raises a new issue.

Where, as in this case, the supplier does pretend to be entitled to the whole semi-final products on the basis of his retention of ownership, that can only occur in the form of shared ownership, that is to say, only in the form of joint ownership on the basis of fractions, as in this case the form of corporate collective ownership does not apply. It must therefore be clear from the agreement extending the retention of ownership for which fraction the supplier, on the basis of his reservation of ownership in the raw material, is to become a co-owner of the finished product. However, in the present case, the parties to the sales contract did not agree any such fraction, but, if one goes by the letter of the contractual provision, sought to give the claimant ownership for the amount of the value of the reserved goods together with the wages and operational expenses incurred by the manufacturer. Such a division according to absolutely specific portions of value does exist in German law for claims but not for ownership. Without providing further reasoning, the appeal court construed the contractual provision as conferring upon the claimant a co-ownership for a part corresponding to the proportion of the value of the reserved goods, wages and operational expenses in comparison to the total value of the shoes at the end of the manufacturing process. However, this interpretation is not self-evident, and was indeed contradicted by the claimant, represented by Counsel, at the hearing. But in the result, the interpretation by the appeal court cannot be impugned because only in this way could the reservation of ownership—which both parties intended—be lawfully extended. Even the appellant has not argued to the contrary in this regard.

High Court, Chancery Division 11 March 1983[111] **5.70 (E&W)**

In Re Peachdart Ltd

RETENTION OF TITLE—MANUFACTURING OF THE ASSETS—MANUFACTURING CLAUSE

Re Peachdart

According to the agreement, the property in the manufactured goods would vest in the seller as security.

Facts: The seller supplied leather to the buyer, a company which manufactured handbags. The sales agreement included a title retention clause which stated that until payment was received in full the seller retained ownership of the leather including the right of resale if payment was overdue, and had

[111] [1983] 3 All ER 204.

the right to trace any proceeds of sale by the buyer including any goods made with the leather, by the creation of a fiduciary relationship between buyer and seller.

In August 1981, the company's bankers appointed a receiver under a debenture granted to them by the company in January 1980, duly registered under section 95 of the Companies Act 1948, under which all the company's book debts were made subject to a fixed charge and stock to a floating charge.

Held: The language used in the terms and conditions of sale was consistent with the view that once the process of manufacture had started which resulted in goods of a distinctive character being produced, the property in those goods would vest in the seller only as security for any outstanding balance of the price of the relevant parcel of leather.

Judgment: Vinelott J—To my mind it is impossible to suppose that in the instant case, even assuming in Freudenbergs' favour that the company became a bailee of the leather when it was first delivered to it, the parties intended that until a parcel of leather had been fully paid for the company would remain a bailee of each piece of leather comprised in the parcel throughout the whole process of manufacture, that Freudenbergs should have the right until the parcel had been fully paid for, to enter the company's premises and identify and take away any partly or completely manufactured handbag derived from it, and that on the sale of a completed handbag the company would be under an obligation to pay the proceeds of sale into a separate interest bearing account and to keep them apart from their other moneys and not employ them in the trade.

It may be that … an expert in the leather trade could identify each handbag whether partly or completely manufactured as made from a skin comprised in a particular parcel of leather. But after a handbag had been sold it would be impossible to do so. There is nothing in the conditions of sale which requires the company to keep a record of handbags sold so as to identify those of which it was a bailee and agent of Freudenbergs. No such records were in fact kept and there is nothing in the evidence which suggests that the parties contemplated that they would be. Indeed on the facts of this case it would be impossible for Freudenbergs now to prove that the handbags sold by the company but not paid for when the receiver was appointed were in fact made out of leather comprised in any of the parcels to which the unpaid invoices relied on by Freudenbergs relate. It seems to me that the parties must have intended that at least after a piece of leather had been appropriated to be manufactured into a handbag and work had started on it (when the leather would cease to have any significant value as raw material) the leather would cease to be the exclusive property of Freudenbergs (whether as bailor or as unpaid vendor) and that Freudenbergs would thereafter have a charge on handbags in the course of manufacture and on the distinctive products which would come into existence at the end of the process of manufacture (the value of which would be derived for the most part from Mr Launer's reputation and skill in design and the skill in his workforce). The charge would in due course shift to the proceeds of sale. That I accept does some violence to the language of clause 11(b) in so far as that clause provides that, 'The property in the whole or such other goods shall be *and remain* with the seller' [emphasis added]. I do not think that those words compel the conclusion that the company was to be a mere bailee throughout the whole process of manufacture until the whole purchase price of the relevant parcel had been paid, and that on a sale before that time it would be no more than an agent for Freudenbergs. The language is, I think, consistent with the view that once the process of manufacture had started so that in the course of manufacture work and materials provided by the company would result in the leather being converted into (that is incorporated in or used as material for) other goods of a distinctive character the property in those other goods would vest in Freudenbergs only as security for any outstanding balance of the price of the relevant parcel of leather. What the draftsman has done is to elide and I think confuse two quite different relationships, that of bailor and bailee, with a superimposed contract of sale (or of vendor and purchaser) on the one hand and that of chargor and chargee on the other hand.

Mr Littman conceded, and I think he must concede, that if [the sellers] had no more than a charge on the partly completed and completed handbags the charge was void for non-registration. It was also void as regards the book debts against the bank, which under the debenture had a prior fixed charge ... and as regards the completed or partly completed handbags against the preferential creditors by virtue of sec 94.

Notes

(1) In German law manufacturing clauses have been constantly held valid and effective against third parties by a long line of cases. The seller acquires security ownership not only *inter partes*, but also *erga omnes*. The seller under title retention can claim his ownership to the product of the manufacturing process, and this ownership will also be effective, after the buyer has become insolvent, against the other creditors. In other words, the seller will have a proprietary claim on the product of the manufacturing against the insolvency patrimony. According to the German case law, parties' agreements should be taken into account in determining the security ownership of the manufactured goods.

(2) In most other European countries, the extension of the retention of title into products is regarded as a charge over goods otherwise not belonging to the creditor. According to Dutch law, a registered charge over future movable object, is the only legal device enabling the buyer to grant to the seller a property right into the product of the manufacturing process. This, however, does not grant an equal security to the seller as his title retention: if the product has been pledged in advance to another creditor, the latter will prevail over the seller.

In French and Belgian law, it is by the same line of reasoning not possible to cover the manufactured assets: any right of the seller in the products would amount to a non-possessory security right and therefore would violate the general principles of French and Belgian security law. The question whether the manufacturer has become owner at law through the rules on manufacturing (see Chapter 7) are the sole rules determining the ownership of the goods.

(3) In English law, the effectiveness of these clauses is a debated issue. If they are registered, they can be regarded as charges, and will therefore be valid and effective. English law leaves very little space to such clauses, as is demonstrated by the *Re Peachdart* judgment. Some case law rules that a 'manufacturing clause' is only valid if it has been registered. If it is held to be effective, it is thus considered as a charge.[112]

[112] *Specialist Plant Services Ltd v Braithwaite Ltd* [1987] BCCL 1. See also D Webb, 'Title and Transformation: Who Owns Manufactured Goods?' [2000] *Journal of Business Law* 531–39.

If a simple clause of retention is contained in the sales agreement, the ownership of the seller will not extend to the product of the manufacturing. For instance, the Court of Appeal held in *Borden (UK) Ltd v Scottish Timber Products Ltd*[113] that the seller of resin for the manufacture of chipboard by the buyer company could no longer trace the resin into the chipboard, as it had lost its identity. Moreover, Templeman LJ held that

> if the seller had any interest or share in the chipboard, any such interest or share must have been agreed to be granted and must have been created as security ..., and so require registration as a charge.

IV.B TRANSFER OF OWNERSHIP FOR SECURITY PURPOSES

Section IV.A dealt with the retention or reservation of ownership for security purposes. A retention of title is often not considered as a property security right because it is not granted but reserved. Therefore, the transfer of ownership for security purposes is even more debated. In that case, a debtor transfers to a creditor ownership of assets as security for whatever claim the transferee might have against the transferor, under the obligation for the former to make restitution of the assets if the secured claim has been fully discharged. Hence, this transfer of ownership for security purposes actually uses ownership as property security. As it will emerge, national legal systems take fundamentally different and even contrasting views with regard to this device. These differences affect the foundations of ownership as they relate to (1) the *numerus clausus* principle, (2) the essential features of ownership and (3) the structure of property security rights.

IV.B.1 FRENCH LAW

Financial and Menetary Codes **5.71 (FR)**

Article L313-23 Any credit which a credit institution grants to a private-law or public-law legal entity, or to a natural person in the exercise of his business activities, may give rise to the assignment or pledge by the beneficiary of the credit of any claim which he may have as against a third party, private-law or public-law legal entity, or natural person, if it relates to his business activities, for the benefit of that institution, by simply submitting a statement.

Claims which are due and payable may be assigned or pledged, even if they are not yet due. Claims resulting from a contract which has already been executed, or which is yet to be executed but the amount and due date of which have not yet been determined, may equally be assigned or pledged.

The statement must include the following elements:

1. the designation 'contract of assignment of receivables' or 'contract of pledge of receivables', as applicable;

[113] [1981] Ch D 25.

2. an indication that the document is subject to the provisions of Articles L313-23 to L313-34;
3. the name of the credit institution which is the beneficiary;
4. the designation or individualisation of the claims assigned or pledged, or of the elements likely to enable such designation or individualisation, particularly by indication of the debtor, the place of payment, the amount of the claims or of their valuation and, if applicable, their due date.

However, when the transfer of the claims assigned or pledged is effected via an electronic process which makes it possible to identify them, the invoice may merely indicate, in addition to the elements indicated in 1, 2 and 3 above, the means through which they are transferred, their number and their overall amount.

In the event of a dispute being raised concerning the existence or transfer of one of the claims, the assignee may prove, by any legal means, that the claim which is the object of the dispute is included in the overall amount indicated in the statement.

A document from which one of the above indications is missing does not constitute a valid act of assignment or pledge of claims within the meaning of Articles L313-23 to L313-34.

Cour de cassation, 8 January 1991[114] **5.72 (FR)**

Hottot v Banque régionale d'escompte et de dépôts

FIDUCIARY TRANSFER FOR SECURITY PURPOSES OF FUTURE CLAIMS

Hottot

A fiduciary transfer for security purposes is valid and effective under the statutory conditions and grants to the assignee all powers related to the assigned claim.

Facts: On 12 December 1986 the claimant assigned to the defendant, Banque régionale d'escompte et de dépôts (BRED), claims he has against Société des transports Sivet (Sivet), which had fallen due several months before. This was an assignment for security purposes operated under the conditions of L313-23 of the Code monétaire et financier. As counterpart, the claimant was granted by the defendant a delay in the payment of his debts. The defendant also granted a payment delay to Sivet. However, in spite of the payment delay and the assignment, the claimant assigned Sivet in bankruptcy, and also assigned BRED for guaranty. The Appeal Court rejected this claim on the basis of the fiduciary transfer of ownership. Hottot contested before Cour de cassation both the validity of the transfer for security purposes and his incapacity to assign Sivet in bankruptcy.

Held: The fiduciary assignment for security purposes is valid and effective, so that the appeal is dismissed.

Judgment: Considering that the judgment [of the Court of Appeal] rightly observes that the assignments of debts due are in principle authorised, even for security purposes, by the Act of 2 January 1981;[115] after having observed in the present case that the assignment at stake had enabled Mr Hottot to obtain from his bank a grace period for the repayment of his debt towards its bank, the Court of Appeal was entitled to infer therefrom that that assignment was based on a valuable consideration; the legal argument can therefore not succeed. …

[114] Recueil Dalloz 1991, 44.
[115] This Act was afterwards inserted as L623-13 in the Code monétaire et financier.

Considering ... that a bank to which a claim already due has been assigned under the conditions provided for in the law of 2 January 1981 and who notified that assignment to the debtor has sole authority to proceed against the latter or grant him payment grace period except for incurring liability towards the assignor if it has allowed actual possibilities of fulfilment of the claim pass by. The Court of Appeal rendered a lawful judgment in deciding that Mr Hottot although remaining the guarantor of payment of the debt could not substitute himself for the Bank in order to request judicial recovery proceedings against the debtor and that he was bound by the grace periods granted by the Bank.

Considering in the second place that the Court of Appeal likewise rendered a lawful judgment in deciding that the amount of interests payable by the assigned debtor could not before their actual receipt by the assignee bank be credited to Mr Hottot's account, as he requested.

Cour de cassation, 19 December 2006[116] **5.73 (FR)**

DIVA v Caisse Fédéral du Crédit Mutuel du Nord de Paris

CATEGORISATION OF THE TRANSFER OF OWNERSHIP FOR SECURITY PURPOSES

DIVA

The fiduciary transfer for security purposes constitutes a pledge over a claim.

Facts: A real estate company, Foncière Forum 20, acquired on 7 January 1992 a commercial complex after having obtained a credit from the bank CGER. In order to give security to the bank, the debtor assigns the claims out of the leasing agreements with the lessees of the complex. One of the lessees, and thus assigned debtors, Pills Music, assigned its contractual position to DIVA. CGER assigned its claim to the defendant bank. The latter sued the real estate company, which had become insolvent, and requested payment by DIVA. The latter argued that the assignment was merely for security purposes, so that the claims had not disappeared out of the insolvent patrimony of the real estate company.

Held: the claim of the bank is declared ungrounded and the plea of the debtor is grounded.

Judgment: Considering that, in ordering the DIVA company to pay to the bank the sum of €125,049.47 together with interest, the judgment [of the Court of Appeal] observes that since under the act of 7 January 1992 the assignment of rental claims in favour of the CGER Bank was stipulated as additional security for all sums that may be owing to it, CGER Bank had acquired ownership of that claim as from that date and that claim was capable of being conveyed to the defendant bank under the act of 30 May 1997.

Considering that, in rendering this judgment, while in cases not statutorily regulated, the act under which a debtor assigns to his creditor by way of guarantee all his rights over claims constitutes a pledge over a claim, the court of appeal infringed the above-mentioned provisions.

[116] Bull 2006, IV, no 250 and Recueil Dalloz 2007, 344.

Notes

(1) Contrary to Roman law, French law has traditionally taken a hostile position towards the fiduciary transfer of ownership for security purposes. French case law, for many decades, considered the fiduciary transfer for security purposes as a right of pledge, which was held to be void because it did not meet the requirements of dispossession and did not take into account the prohibition of the forfeiture clause (see on this prohibition: above, VI.D.1).[117]

(2) However, the internationalisation of commercial transactions has necessitated the introduction of a more modern security device.[118] This has led the legislator to introduce the fiduciary transfer in the framework of banking/financial operations. This was done through the Act of 2 January 1981 (known as the 'Loi Dailly'), which is now laid down in Article L313-23 of the Monetary and Financial Code. According to this Act, a credit institution can acquire the fiduciary ownership of professional claims to which the debtor is entitled. This transfer is effective in case of insolvency of the assignor, even if the assigned claim only becomes due after the insolvency of the assignor.[119]

The fiduciary assignment 'temporarily' grants all the powers to the assigned claim to the creditor. As emerges from the judgment of 8 October 1991, the creditor has the power to grant delay to his debtor, to sue his debtor in bankruptcy.

(3) The judgment of the grand chamber of the commercial section of the Cour de cassation of 19 December 2006 was a major surprise because it was contrary to ongoing development and resulted in a more liberal attitude towards fiduciary ownership. It has been heavily criticised by French legal scholars.[120] More recently, the French legislature has generalised the fiduciary ownership by introducing, through an Act on the *fiducie*, the following provision in Article 2011 Cciv:

> A fiduciary arrangement is the operation according to which one or more settlers transfer current or future goods, rights or securities, or a universality of current or future goods rights or securities, to one or more trustees who act with a specified purpose to the benefit of one or more beneficiaries and keep them separate from their personal patrimony.

Although this provision does not specifically mention the transfer for security purposes, it results from the parliamentary works that the fiduciary transfer for security purposes is also encompassed by this Act.[121] See Chapter 6, where the Act of 19 February 2007 introducing the *fiducie* in French law is dealt with more extensively.

[117] Cour de cassation, 13 January 1965, JCP 1965, II, no 14.469, n RDM.

[118] Cabrillac and Mouly, above n 1, no 530.

[119] Cour de cassation, 7 December 2004, D 2005, jur, 230, n C Larroumet.

[120] L Aynes, 'La cession de créance à titre de garantie: quel avenir?' [2007] *Droit & Patrimoine* 28-30.

[121] Report Senate no 11, 2006–07, p. 43: 'The legislator has made a choice to make a general Act on the introduction of the 'fiducie', without trying to regulate in view of specific usages, for security purposes or management purposes, as the parties intend to do so.'

IV.B.2 BELGIAN LAW

Cour de cassation, 17 October 1996[122] **5.74 (BE)**

ASLK v Centre régional d'action culturelle du Sart-Tilman

PROPRIETARY EFFECTS OF A TRANSFER FOR SECURITY PURPOSES

Sart Tilman

A fiduciary transfer for security purposes goes beyond the statutory ground for priority.

Facts: A banking institution (claimant) granted a credit to a cultural company Centre régional d'action culturelle du Sart-Tilman (defendant) in November 1984. The activities of the cultural company were subsidised by the government. Article VI of the credit agreement provided as follows: 'In order to secure the reimbursement of the credit and in conformity with the general conditions which are to be taken into account, Y obliges to assign irrevocably the subventions which are owed by the French-speaking community, the Department of Education and the European Social Fund.' The cultural company became the object of a winding-up proceeding in November 1988. There was no discussion about the money which had already been received by the claimant at the moment of the winding-up: parties agreed that the claimant could claim a separate right to this money, at least on the basis of set-off. The claimaint claimed that he was owner of the part of the subventions which had not yet been paid at the moment of the decision of liquidation.

Held: The claimant is dismissed in his argument that he has a separate right in the subventions, and therefore the appeal judgment is confirmed.

Judgment: Considering that the winding-up of [Y] has led to a *'concursus creditorum'*; that in accordance with the principle of equality as between creditors ... all things of the debtor form the object of security of the creditors unless as between the creditors legal grounds exist for granting priority;

Considering that in the judgment [of the Court of Appeal] it is held that the agreement between claimant and defendant seeks to give security outside the rules laid down by the statute and thus contravenes the principle of equality as between creditors; that the judgment rendered the agreement—conferring priority on the claimant without any statutory ground, thereby disadvantaging the other creditors of the defendant—of no effect after the *'concursus creditorum'*, and thus correctly applied the above-mentioned principle and provisions of law; that for this reason the judgment of the court of appeal ordering the claimant to pay back to the defendant the amounts received by it after the winding-up of the defendant is lawful.

[122] [1996] Arr Cass 930; [1996–97] *Rechtskundig Weekblad* 1395, n ME Storme.

Cour de cassation, 3 December 2010[123] **5.75 (BE)**

Vanden Avenne-Ooigem v Landbouwkrediet, Flemmish Community, Insolvency administrator of RB

CATEGORISATION OF A TRANSFER FOR SECURITY PURPOSES

Vanden Avenne

An assignment of claims for security purposes grants no more powers to the assignee than an pledge.

Facts: RB had assigned a claim to Landbouwkrediet on 14 May 1997 and 27 July 1998, which was notified to the debtor. Another creditor of RB, the claimant, on 9 October 2003 seized debts which were due by the Flemmish authorities to the debtor, which were part of the prior assignment. Not only the claims, but also a huge termination compensation was at stake. After the insolvency of the debtor, a priority conflict arises between the security assignee and the seizing creditor. The Court of appeal granted priority to the assignee for both the capital sum and the termination compensation.

Held: The appeal judgment is declared void.

Judgment: The principle of '*paritas creditorum*' and Articles 7 and 8 of the Hypothec Act deviate from Articles 1165, 1134 and 1135 of the Civil Code in such way that a security right which was not provided for by statute can not be effective to the other creditors.

An agreement in which a claim is assigned cannot grant more rights in relation to other creditors, in such way that the assignee cannot exercise more powers than the ones which a pledgee could exercise.

The appeal judges analyse that the sixth defendant has assigned her claim to the first defendant as security for her debts and judge that this assignment for security purposes has as effect that the claim has disappeared out of the patrimony of the sixth defendant and is, after the insolvency of the latter, effective in the insolvency proceedings.

In rendering this judgment, the appeal court acknowledged more rights to the first defendant than the one which would have been at the disposition of the pledgee, and rendered an unlawful judgment.

Note

Pursuant to the *Sart Tilman* judgment, the fiduciary transfer for security purposes is in Belgian law valid, but does not have any third party effect. From a theoretical perspective, this means that Belgian law takes an intermediary position between, for instance, Dutch law (where a fiduciary transfer for security purposes is held to be invald, *cf* below) and German law (where a fiduciary transfer for security purposes is valid and effective).

However, later developments have altered the perspective on the fiduciary transfer of ownership. First of all, the Belgian Cour de cassation had to deal in 2003 with the question of who was entitled to the fruits of the asset which had been

[123] This judgment can be found at www.cass.be, [2010] *Nieuw Juridisch Weekblad* 834, n V Sagaert.

transferred for security purposes.[124] The Court held that the fiduciary creditor was entitled to the fruits, 'on the basis of the ownership which had thus been vested on his behalf'.[125] The president of the Supreme Court moreover declared that the sale and leaseback operation would be effective vis-à-vis third parties. Finally, the Belgian Act of 12 December 2004 implemented the European Financial Collateral Directive[126] (see Chapter 10) into Belgian law, including the possibility to transfer validly and effectively financial instruments and cash for the sole purpose of security. These developments raised the question as to what extent the judgment of 4 April 2003 is still valid in Belgian law. This question was answered in the judgment of 3 December 2010 whereby the Belgian Supreme Court recognised that the assignment for security purposes of receivables can be converted into a pledge of receivables. In doing so, the Belgian Supreme Court adopted the same view as the French Supreme Court in its 2006 judgment (*cf* below). This judgment cannot be extended to corporeal movables as long as the requirement of dispossession comes into play.

IV.B.3 GERMAN LAW

RG, 8 November 1904[127] **5.76 (DE)**

VALIDITY AND EFFECTIVENESS OF AN ASSIGNMENT FOR SECURITY PURPOSES

Domestic goods

A pledge is not conceived by the legislature as an exclusive security device.

Facts: X entered on 23 October 1901 into an agreement with his sister (Y), providing that 'he as security for a granted credit of DM500 … transfer to her the ownership of goods listed in a separate annex (mainly domestic goods), but retained the use of it as before'. X was also obliged to use the object in a proper manner, to notify Y of any damage, to effect reparations at his own expense, to substitute objects which became useless and to cover the deterioration of the goods by paying insurance premiums.

Held: The fiduciary transfer for security purposes is valid and effective.

Judgment: What is decisive is that the intention of the contracting parties was directed to the transfer of ownership of the objects, and this intention is unambiguously expressed in the agreement of 23 October 1901, in which it is stated that X freely conveys to Y as owner the objects listed in the annex, and that Y confirms and accepts such transfer. The agreement of both parties as to the transfer of ownership could not be more clearly expressed and the delivery required by §929 BGB is replaced by the subsequent loan agreement (§930 BGB).

The only question which can arise is whether in law the intention to grant a pledge, which is underlying the actual intention to transfer ownership and is plain

[124] Cour de cassation, 4 April 2003, Bank Fin R 2003, afl 6, 375, n I Peeters, [2003–04] *Rechtskundig Weekblad* 1689, n ME Storme.

[125] *Ibid.*

[126] Directive 2002/47/EC of the European Parliament and of the Council of 6 June 2002 on financial collateral arrangements, OJ L168/43.

[127] RGZ 59, 146.

from the agreement concerning the use of the objects transferred, precludes the validity of the transaction. That would be the case only if §1205 BGB were to be accorded such scope that security can be provided by movables belonging to the debtor only by way of a pledge under that provision, and if it was the legislature's intention to exclude any other form of security. Only in this interpretation of the law would it be feasible that a transfer by way of security constituted circumvention and as such was null and void. However, such interpretation is not required either by the wording or the historical background of the law and, as long as there is no clear intention to the contrary on the part of the legislature, the parties must be allowed to choose means other than granting a pledge to secure credit. If such means cause constructive possession rather than actual delivery to apply, that does not constitute an infringement of §1205 BGB, which merely relates to the charging of an object with a right of pledge.

Notes

(1) The German Civil Code merely provides for the (possessory) pledge as security right on movables. However, the German Reichsgericht accepted the effectiveness of the fiduciary transfer for security purposes soon after the coming into existence of the Civil Code. While in French law, the Civil Code was literally interpreted and applied in the first decades after its entry into force, the German Supreme Court distanced itself from the actual text, as the judgment of 1905 demonstrates. In fact, the Supreme court had recognised the fiduciary transfer for security purposes even before the introduction of the BGB,[128] and this position was reaffirmed after the introduction of the Code, as emerges from the above-cited judgment of the Reichsgericht.

The reason why case law unanimously accepted the effectiveness of this legal institution is most frequently seen in terms of the legal-economic background: the fiduciary transfer corresponds to the economic need for a non-possessory security right. In current German law, the validity and effectiveness is undoubted and is sometimes even referred to as customary law (*Gewohnheitsrecht*).[129] However, legal scholars acknowledge that it is difficult to give legal ground to the fiduciary transfer for security purposes from a doctrinal perspective in the absence of statutory provisions.[130]

From a legal perspective, the fiduciary transfer for security purposes is based on §930 BGB, which allows parties to transfer ownership without actual delivery. A contract by which the transferor agrees to grant possession of the collateral to the transferee is substituted for actual delivery.

(2) German law makes a distinction between the *Sicherheitsübereignung* and the *Sicherheitsabtretung*. The former deals with the transfer for security purposes of corporeal goods, the latter has as object a claim of the debtor against the sub-debtor.

[128] RG 2 June 1890, RGZ 26, 180.
[129] Baur and Stürner, above n 42, §57, no 1.
[130] Baur and Stürner, above n 42, §57, no 1.

IV.B.4 DUTCH LAW

Burgerlijk Wetboek **5.77 (NL)**

Article 3:84(3) A legal act aiming at the transfer of a good for security purposes or that lacks the purpose to bring the good after the transfer into the patrimony of the transferee is no valid title for the transfer of that good.

Hoge Raad, 19 May 1995[131] **5.78 (NL)**

Mr Keereweer as the insolvency administrator of De Zaaiers BV v Sogelease BV

PROPERTY EFFECTS OF A SALE AND LEASEBACK

Sogelease

A sentence indicating the legal proposition for which the case stands.

Facts: De Zaaiers acquired on 21 May 1991 ownership of some printing presses from a supplier, and took possession of the machines. The purchase was financed on the basis of a sale-and-leaseback agreement between the claimant and the defendant (Sogelease). The conditions for the sale-and-leaseback are that (1) Sogelease would grant the right to use the printing presses to X for a period of seven years after the transfer and against a monthly rent for a monthly rent price of GLD27,147 for a period of seven years, thus in total GLD2,280,348; (2) that Sogelease would retransfer the printing presses at the expiration of that period against a sales price of NLG100; (3) that all costs of maintenance, insurance, and the risks for perishment or deterioration are to be borne by De Zaaiers; and (4) that Sogelease is entitled to terminate the agreement and keep the ownership of the printing presses, which is irrefutably presumed if De Zaaiers does not comply with any one of his obligations. The printing presses figure on the balance sheet of De Zaaiers, but not on that of Sogelease.

De Zaaiers was declared bankrupt on 20 January 1993, and the insolvency administrator of De Zaaiers argued that the printing presses could be sold and the proceedings must be distributed amongst the creditors.

Held: The rights of Z are validly vested and have proprietary effect.

Judgment: The criterion in Article 3:84(3) BW must, in regard to the phrase 'which seeks to assign a good by way of security', be sought in the answer to the question whether the legal transaction is intended to create a right of security on the good in favour of the other party in order to protect the interests of that party as a creditor in regard to other creditors. The core of such protection is by its nature the ability to have recourse to the goods in priority to other creditors which precludes the ability to appropriate the thing (cf Article 3:235). Accordingly an agreement that limits the powers of the person to whom the good is transferred in the event of default by the other party to forced sale of the good in order to fulfill his claim from the proceeds subject to the requirement to account for any surplus proceeds to the other party, does not give a legal title under Article 3:84(3): parties in that case have to make use of the right of pledge or hypothec. If conversely the transaction of the parties purports to an 'actual transfer' (in the case of a object: to transfer ownership) and if it is therefore intended that the good is conveyed without restriction to the transferee and that person acquires therefore more than merely a right

[131] NJ 1996, 119.

in the good to protect his interests as a creditor, that is not precluded by Article 3:84(3). This provision more precisely allows an agreement entailing on the one hand that a good is sold and transferred by the transferor to the transferee and on the other hand that the good is given in use by the transferee to the transferor against payment, under such conditions that the transferee in the event of default by the other party can simply terminate the agreement with regard to use in order to be able to again freely and completely dispose of the good. That is also the case where the agreement is entered into in relation to the award of any form of credit to the transferor as will be the case of a sale and leaseback agreement by its nature. It is important to observe in that perspective that it does not make a difference either if the agreement relates to goods which the person requiring financing wishes to acquire or to objects which he has owned for a long period of time, just as it is irrelevant what the purpose is for which he on the sale of the objects to the leasing company wishes to apply the monies received from it in return. Nor does any stipulation under which maintenance and risk remain for the account of the transferor preclude an assumption that the agreement amounts to an 'actual transfer' in the above-mentioned sense. …

This criterion seeks to prevent that, in contravention of the closed system of property law, rights having effect in property law can be created in a manner not provided for by the statute, but it does not preclude a contractual arrangement under which a party has full ownership and the other party only has personal rights and obligations such as a personal right of use, a personal obligation to pay the instalments under the lease and an option to acquire ownership of the objects at the end of the leasing period. That is not altered by the fact that this option is structured in such way that in practice it is invariably exercised.

Notes

(1) The use of the right of ownership as a security device is in Dutch law severely prohibited by Article 3:84(3) of the Civil Code. This is a radical change with regard to the 'old' law, which generally recognised the validity and effectiveness of the fiduciary transfer for security purposes.[132] In current law, the purpose of creating a security right is not a valid or sufficient *causa* for the transfer of ownership.[133] Not only has a transfer for security purposes no property effect, but moreover has a transfer for security purposes not a valid consideration, which leads to its voidness *inter partes*. As a counterpart, the requirements for the validity and effectiveness of a pledge agreement have become more flexible. The dispossession of the pledgor is not always a condition in order to create a right of pledge (*cf* above II.A.2).

(2) However, Dutch law has been subject to an important development since 1992.

[132] HR 21 jun 1929, NJ 1929, 1096: 'An agreement, in which ownership of a movable good is transfered for security purposes, and of which the debtor remains detentor with a regulation on the exercise of the ownership rights, is not contrary to statute and does not aim at eluding the statutory provisions with regard to the pledge agreement.'

[133] See eg for an analysis: S de Groot and AF Salomons, 'Zekerheidsoverdracht in het Nederlandse BW, de Franse Code civil en de Europese DCFR' [2011] *Ars Aequi* 383–90; JTAM van Mierlo, 'Bezitloze zekerheidsrechten op roerende goederen. Tegengestelde rechtsontwikkelingen in Nederland en Frankrijk' [1993] *Weekblad voor Privaatrecht, Notariaat en Registratie* 107–11; JW Tellegen en O Tellegen-Couperus, 'Fiducia cum creditore en ons systeem van zakelijke rechten' [2002] *Tijdschrift voor Privaatrecht* 1475–95.

Case law has weakened the *fiducia* prohibition by struggling with the distinction between a fiduciary transfer and an outright transfer. In the above-cited *Sogelease* case, the Dutch Supreme Court indicated that security ownership is held to be valid if the ownership arises within the framework of a sale-and-leaseback operation.[134] The Court held that the prohibition of Article 3:83(3) of the Dutch Civil Code forms no bar when parties intend to operate an 'actual transfer', a transfer where the buyer is to obtain ownership without restriction, such as a right only to the proceeds. The Dutch Supreme Court specified in a later judgment that there is no presumption that the transfer is 'actual'. The agreement must be interpreted in accordance with the general rules of the law of obligations. The fact that a discrepancy exists between the transferred object and the counterclaim can contribute to the analysis that parties have not aimed at creating an outright transfer.[135]

(3) It can be concluded that Dutch law takes an ambiguous position with regard to the use of ownership as security instrument: on the one hand, Dutch law fully recognises the validity and proprietary effects of a retention of title clause; on the other hand Dutch law refuses, as a matter of principle, to recognise the validity of a fiduciary transfer for security purposes, except if the ownership device is part of the financial transaction.

Given this ambiguous position, Dutch law had big difficulties in implementing the Financial Collateral Directive,[136] which is dealt with in greater detail in the comparative remarks. This Directive imposed upon the Dutch legislator the duty to introduce a title transfer financial collateral arrangement, which is defined as an arrangement, including repurchase agreements, under which a collateral provider transfers full ownership of financial collateral to a collateral taker for the purpose of securing or otherwise covering the performance of relevant financial obligations. The Dutch legislature has taken care of the question whether this could be reconciled with the prohibition of a fiduciary transfer. Article 7:55 of the Dutch Civil Code therefore currently provides that a transfer pursuant to a title transfer financial collateral arrangement 'is not a transfer for security purposes or a transfer lacking the effect that the good is part of the estate of the transferee in the sense of Article 3:84(3) BW. The rules on pledge do not apply to this agreement nor to its execution.'

[134] See for a comparative analysis: GW Mincke, 'Sale and Lease Back, Art 3:84 lid 3 BW, eigendomsvoorbehoud en de numerus clausus' [1995] *Nederlands Tijdschrift voor Burgerlijk Recht*, blz 175 t/m 179; HC Sigman, 'Keereweer v Sogelease BV Seen from an American Perspective' [1996] *Weekblad voor Privaatrecht, Notariaat en Registratie* 167–70.

[135] HR 18 November 2005, NJ 2006, 151.

[136] Dir 2002/47/EC, OJ L168/43.

IV.B.5 ENGLISH LAW: THE MORTGAGE

Court of Appeal, 4 August 1899[137] **5.79 (E&W)**
Santley v Wilde

PROPERTY EFFECTS OF A MORTGAGE

Santley

Any provision preventing redemption is void.

Facts: S, the sub-lessee of a theatre, had an option to acquire the reversion of the head-lease on paying £2,000 within a limited time. W agreed to advance the money on the terms of the loan being repaid with 6 per cent interest, and secured by a legal mortgage, which was also to provide for payment to W of one-third of the clear net profit rental of the theatre. The mortgage executed in pursuance of this agreement was for the whole of the term acquired by S minus one day, and contained a covenant by her for repayment of the £2,000 by 20 quarterly instalments of £100 each (the payment of the last of which, if all had been duly paid, would have been more than four years before the end of the mortgage term), and also a covenant to pay the one-third of the profit rental during the whole of the mortgagor's term, although the £2,000 and interest had all been paid. The property was redeemable only on payment of £2,000 and interest, and all other moneys covenanted to be paid. When some of the instalments were in arrears, W gave S three months' notice to pay off all the principal moneys and interest secured by the mortgage. S paid the instalments in arrears, and within the three months tendered the balance of the £2,000, with interest to the end of the three months and the costs, but W refused to accept the money.

Held: (1) The stipulations for a share of the profit rental were an illegal clog on the equity of redemption, and (a) did not prevent S from redeeming at the amount of her tender, and (b) did not enable W to recover the share of profit rental; (2) W's notice requiring payment could not be withdrawn without the consent of S.

Judgment: It appears to me that the true principle running through them is not very difficult to discover, and I think that it can be applied so as to do justice in this case and in all other cases on the subject that may arise. The principle is this: a mortgage is a conveyance of land or an assignment of chattels as a security for the payment of a debt or the discharge of some other obligation for which it is given. This is the idea of a mortgage: and the security is redeemable on the payment or discharge of such debt or obligation, any provision to the contrary notwithstanding. That, in my opinion, is the law. Any provision inserted to prevent redemption on payment or performance of the debt or obligation for which the security was given is what is meant by a clog or fetter on the equity of redemption and is therefore void. It follows from this, that 'once a mortgage always a mortgage'; but I do not understand that this principle involves the further proposition that the amount or nature of the further debt or obligation the payment or performance of which is to be secured is a clog or fetter within the rule: see 1 Powell on Mortgages, 6th ed pp 116 et seq: Title, 'How a Mortgage is considered in Equity.' The right to redeem is not a personal right, but an equitable estate or interest in the property mortgaged. A 'clog' or 'fetter' is something which is inconsistent with the idea of 'security': a clog or fetter is in the nature of a repugnant condition. If I convey land in fee subject to a condition forbidding alienation, that is a repugnant condition. If I give a mortgage on a condition that I shall not redeem, that is a repugnant condition.

[137] (1899) Ch 474.

Notes

(1) The concept of mortgage in English law is extremely complex. Famous are the words of Lord Macnaghten in the *Samuel v Jarrah Timber* case, in which he considered that 'no one, I am sure, by the light of nature ever understood an English mortgage of real estate'.[138]

Continental lawyers often simplify things by considering that a mortgage is, according to English law, similar to a hypothec (*hypothec, hypotheek, hypothèque*) in continental systems, eg a property security right on immovables.

This view is, however, mistaken. A mortgage is a transaction in which the mortgagor transfers to the secured creditor his entire title, on condition or subject to an undertaking, that when the debt is repaid the title will be retransferred.[139] In English law, the mortgagee becomes the owner of the good which is subject to the mortgage. The mortgagor merely retains a right of redemption, eg the right to claim the asset upon the full payment of the secured claim even after the term for repayment has expired. In that sense, a mortgage should be distinguished from a charge, which merely grants a limited property right to the chargee. On the other side, it makes clear that there are great similarities between a (common law) mortgage and a civil law fiduciary transfer of ownership.

However, English case law and legal scholars have emphasised that the practical distinction between mortgages and charges is relatively unimportant and the terms are frequently used virtually interchangeably. Moreover, the technical differences are further blurred by the Law of Property Act 1925 which has changed the legal nature of a mortgage of land and speaks of a 'charge by way of legal mortgage'. The words of Lord McNaghten cited above should therefore not come as a surprise.

(2) Under old English law,[140] the mortgage could only be created by way of transfer of possession. Since the Bills of Sale Act 1854, the delivery of possession to the mortgagee is not necessary to create a mortgage. This Act provided for the first time a public registration system for non-possessory chattel mortgages. However, another risk for the effectiveness of the mortgage was the so-called 'reputed ownership' clause,[141] which invalidated transfer of assets which remained in the possession of the debtor in such circumstances that other creditors could believe themselves to be entitled to the full value of the asset. If the mortgagor keeps the possession of the asset, the mortgagee would not be entitled to oppose his rights to the insolvency

[138] *Samuel v Jarrah Timber & Wood Paving Corp Ltd* [1904] AC 323, 326, HL.

[139] R Goode, *Commercial Law* (London, Butterworths, 2004) 586; FH Lawson and B Rudden, *The Law of Property* (Oxford, Clarendon Press, 2002) 140. However, the double meaning of mortgage is often an object of consideration in English law: 'The word "mortgage" is used throughout this chapter, and it is necessary to say exactly what it means. In its most precise sense, the word 'mortgage' refers to the transfer (but not the creation) of a proprietary interest, by way of security. In this section, "Real Security Over Land", following common legal usage, "mortgage" refers to any interest in land held as security for a debt. The "mortgagor" is the debtor who grants this interest, and the "mortgagee" is the creditor who acquires it' (LD Smith, 'Security' in A Burrows (ed), *English Private Law* (Oxford, Oxford University Press, 2007) no 5.01).

[140] Fraudulent Conveyances Act 1571.

[141] S 38 Bankruptcy Act 1914.

administrator. The Insolvency Act 1985 abolished the reputed ownership provision, so that it is no longer a barrier for the effectiveness of a non-possessory mortgage.

IV.B.6 COMPARATIVE REMARKS

Roughly speaking, legal systems take three positions in respect to the issue of a fiduciary transfer for security purposes. The first position is to hold the fiduciary transfer for security purposes invalid, as is the case for Dutch law. We have analysed how Dutch case law and statutes have had to weaken this severe starting point. The second position is taken by the legal systems that recognise the validity of the fiduciary transfer for security purposes, but do not recognise the property effects of such transfer. The result of this position towards the creditors is identical to the one of the first position: the security ownership cannot establish the security purpose it is created for, and is thus useless. The third category of legal systems are the systems that recognise the validity and effectiveness of the fiduciary transfer for security purposes. The most obvious example of such a system is German law.

It has been observed for the legal systems of both the first and second category that case law tends to interpret the restriction as to the effectiveness of the fiduciary transfer of ownership as widely as possible. For instance, in Dutch law Article 3:84(3) of the Civil Code has been narrowed. In French and Belgian law, such fiduciary transfer for security purposes was traditionally said not to have proprietary effects, but is according to recent case law effective against third parties as pledge agreement, but not as assignment.

Ownership as security instrument is developing. In analysing legal systems, emphasis has already been placed on the fact that the requirement of dispossession is harmful for credit purposes, because of economic reasons. We have seen that Dutch and (recently) French law have introduced a non-possessory pledge on movables, and that Belgian law has introduced a non-possessory pledge on commercial funds. German law provides another solution to the problem of dispossession, in accepting the effectiveness of the fiduciary transfer of ownership without actual statutory basis. It emerges from the preceeding analysis that the creation of a non-possessory pledge is not sufficient. The French legislator aims to introduce a *fiducie* with general scope, and Belgian and Dutch case law intend to reintroduce a (narrower) concept of fiduciary transfer of ownership. Apparently, the disadvantageous priority rules with regard to the non-possessory pledge are underlying the appeal for ownership as security instrument.

It is remarkable a clear interaction exists between the rules on private international law and the substantive law.[142] The legal systems that deny the validity and/or the proprietary effects of the transfer of ownership for security purposes implement flexible rules with regard to conflict of law. For instance, the Dutch Supreme court

[142] See L d'Avout, *Sur les solutions du conflits des lois en droit des biens* (Paris, Economica, 2006) 666, no 506; V Sagaert, 'Party Autonomy in French and Belgian Law. The Interconnection between Substantive Property Law and Private International Law' in R Westrik and JA Van Der Weide (eds), *Party Autonomy in International Property Law* (München, Sellier, 2011) 119–41.

ruled that rules applicable to the property aspects of a fiduciary transfer of a claim for security purposes are subject to party autonomy:

> The conflict rule in Article 12(1) applies not only to the legal relationship between assignor and assignee but also to the property law aspects of the assignment. The validity requirements for the transfer of the assigned claim to the patrimony of the assignee and the effect of that transfer on other third parties than the debtor are therefore governed by the law that as a result of the ECC-conflict rule on the assignment agreement is applicable to the assignment agreement.[143]

The harmonisation of the issue of the fiduciary transfer of ownership for security purposes is highly influenced by the European legislator. The European legislator has imposed the validity and enforceability of the fiduciary transfer of ownership with regard to financial instruments and cash. The European Directive 2002/47144 defines a 'title transfer financial collateral arrangement' as an arrangement, including repurchase agreements, under which a collateral provider transfers full ownership of financial collateral to a collateral taker for the purpose of securing or otherwise covering the performance of relevant financial obligations (Article 2(1)(b)). Member States shall ensure when an enforcement event occurs, the collateral taker shall be able to realise any financial collateral provided under, and subject to the terms agreed in, a security financial collateral arrangement (which includes title transfer financial collateral arrangements) (Article 4(1)).

V. RIGHT OF RETENTION/LIEN

Introductory Notes

(a) In the sections above, we have dealt with consensual security rights which were contractually agreed between the security provider and the security holder. All legal systems acknowledge non-conventional rights of priority, making an exception for the *paritas creditorum* rule. As we have explained above, we will not deal with the statutory privileges which are awarded to some claims due to their nature. The statutory privileges constitute a long list, which can vary from one system to another, and which lacks in most countries coherence, which makes it difficult to analyse. Typical examples of claims which are awarded a priority are tax claims and social security claims, which should improve recovery rates by public authorities.

(b) However, there is one security device which is common to most legal systems, namely the right to retain factual possession over a good until a claim connected with that good is fulfilled. The precise term is 'right of retention' in order to avoid confusion with a 'retention of title'. A right of retention is a consensual security right based on ownership, while a retention of title is not consensual and merely gives

[143] NJ 1998, 585. See for a profound analysis of this judgment: THD Struycken, 'The Proprietary Aspects of International Assignment of debts and the Rome Convention' [1998] *Lloyd's Maritime and Commercial Law Quarterly* 358.

[144] Directive 2002/47/EC of the European Parliament and of the Council of 6 June 2002 on financial collateral arrangements, OJ L168/43.

a factual possession, but not the ownership to the security holder. A right of retention is a right, awarded to a creditor, to suspend his obligation to make restitution of a good until payment has been effected of a debt connected with that good. The right of retention can be roughly considered as an application of the Roman law device *exception non adimpleti contratus*, allowing a party to suspend execution of his obligation as long as the other contracting party has not executed his obligation.

Code civil **5.80 (FR)**

Article 2286 May claim a right of retention to an asset:

(1) The person to whom the asset was handed over until payment of his debt;

(2) The person whose outstanding debt results from the contract which binds him to deliver it;

(3) The person whose outstanding debt arose at the moment that he obtained the assets in his hands. A right of retention is lost through voluntary relinquishment.

Commercial Code **5.81 (FR)**

Article L624-14 The seller may retain goods which have not been delivered or dispatched to the debtor or to a third party acting for his account.

Cour de cassation, 9 February 1988[145] **5.82 (FR)**

Huet v Banque Vernes

CONDITIONS FOR THE EXERCISE OF A RIGHT OF RETENTION

Huet

A creditor is not entitled to a right of retention if no connection between the debt to return goods and the obligation of the counterparty can be demonstrated.

Facts: Mr Huet gave two personal securities for two loans in favour of a bank called Vernes. The first one amounts up to FRF200,000, the second one to FRF400,000. Mr Huet subsequently made a deposit of financial instruments at the same bank. The principal debtor of the loans became insolvent and the bank sued Mr Huet for an amount of FRF600,000. The latter refused to pay because he was convinced that the two amounts should not be added to each other, but that it was the common intention of parties to limit the secured part of the claim to FRF400,000. Some time later, Mr Huet claimed restitution of the instruments. The bank refused to release them because it argued that it could exercise its right of retention.

Held: It is not demonstrated that the requirement for the exercise of a right of retention are fulfilled.

Judgment: Having regard to Articles 1944 and 1948 of the Civil Code;

Considering that under the former of those two provisions objects deposited must be returned to the depositor whenever the latter requests it unless the depository is in possession of a writ of execution or an objection to restitution and removal of the object deposited; there can be no exception to this rule except where under

[145] Bull civ, IV, no 32 and Dalloz 1988, 448, n E Delebecque.

the latter of the two provisions the depository is the depositor's creditor under the contract of deposit or where at least there is a connecting link between the depository's claim and the contract of deposit agreement.

Considering that on 14 January 1982 Mr Huet requested the Vernes bank to return to him securities which he had deposited with it; that the bank refused that request; that the judgment of the appeal court rejected the claim for damages made on that ground by Mr Huet on the basis that he was the bank's debtor in his capacity as guarantor and had been fruitlessly noticed that he did not comply with his obligations by documents dated 15 July and 15 September 1981; that the risk for the bank of not getting fulfilment at its detriment of a part of its claim provided the bank with a legal ground for declining to return the securities with the result that its refusal was warranted;

Considering that in ruling on those grounds, although the bank should not have been authorised to enforce execution on its own motion until 5 February 1982, subsequent on the request for return of the securities, and without establishing a connection between the debt to return the securities and the guarantor's obligation, which link might have warranted the exercise by the bank of a right of retention, the court of appeal failed to ensure that it rendered a lawful judgment.

Cour de cassation, 16 December 1998[146] **5.83 (FR)**

REQUIREMENTS FOR THE EXERCISE OF A RIGHT OF RETENTION

Pelletier de Chambure

A right of retention can be exercised on immovable goods.

Facts: A building compagny was obliged by a contract dated 20 December 1993 to sell a castle to Mr Pelletier de Chambure. The agreement provided for the immediate payment and immediate transfer of possession of the castle, but left to the purchaser a period expiring on 31 December 1996 in order to decide whether he would exercise the option of purchase. Mr Pelletier de Chambure paid the price and entered into possession of the castle. The building company was then declared insolvent on 7 December 1994. Mr Pelletier de Chambure lodged a claim amounting to the sales price and the expenses of improvement and restoration. He claimed to exercise his right of retention on the castle, which was also burdened with a hypothec in favour of Mr Serres.

Held: The exercise of the right of retention is lawful.

Judgment: Considering that the appeal court judgment is criticised for finding that Mr Pelletier de Chambure is entitled to award himself of a right of retention on the object as against the liquidator and the creditors with a right of hypothec until restitution of the price paid in advance and reimbursement of the expenditure and for declaring that that right be deducted from the sales price of the building after its sale at auction by the liquidator, whereas the claimants argue that a right of retention is a right *in rem* applicable *erga omnes*; that consequently when it relates to a building the contract creating it is subject to the requirement of publication in the hypothec and charges register, failing which such right cannot be availed of as against a third party, such as a mortgage creditor, who has acquired from the same source a property right on the same object; that by declaring applicable as against

[146] [1994] *Revue trimestrielle de droit civil* 739, n P Crocq.

Mr Serres, a creditor whose hypothec had been duly publicly notified, the right of retention recognised in Mr Pelletier de Chambure's favour on the basis of an undertaking to sell which was not publicly notified, the court of appeal infringed Articles 28-1 and 30-1 of the decree of 4 January 1955;

But considering that the enforceability of the right of retention is not subject to notification, the plea is of no avail.

Notes

(1) Article 2286 Cciv has been introduced by the Act which amended the security provisions of the Civil Code. The original French Civil Code only provided for specific applications of a right of retention.[147] However, French case law and legal scholarship has accepted for many decades the possibility for the actual possessor of a movable asset to withhold the assets until the moment that all obligations connected to these assets have been met by the debtor.

(2) The French Supreme Court decided in its judgment of 16 December 1998 that a right of retention can be exercised on an immovable, and that the right of retention is not subject to any publicity requirements. This judgment is in line with the precedent case law stating that a right of retention does not grant any property security right to the creditor.[148] For the same reason, French case law determines that a right of retention is not provided with a right to follow: in the case of involuntary deprivation of the assets, the former retentor of the assets will lose his right of retention.[149] However, things have been complicated since the French Supreme Court decided more recently that 'a right of retention is a property right, effective against everyone, also against them who are not obliged by the debt'.[150]

(3) Article L624-14 of the French Commercial Code determines that the right of retention can have effect in the case of insolvency of the debtor. The right of retention is effective both against general creditors and against creditors whose claim has a priority rank. Although a retentor does not have a priority, he is in fact considered as holder of a priority of the first rank, given the factual protection to which he can appeal.

(4) The judgment of 9 February 1988 demonstrates that, according to French law, a creditor can only exercise a right of retention if there is a connection between the secured claim and the asset that is withheld.

[147] Eg Art. 1612 Cciv: 'The seller is not obliged to deliver the thing where the buyer does not pay the price of it unless the seller has granted him time for the payment'; Art 1673 Cciv: 'A seller who makes use of a clause of redemption shall reimburse not only the purchase price, but also the expenses and fair costs of the sale, the necessary repairs and those which have increased the value of the tenement, up to the amount of that increase. He may be vested into possession only after having discharged all those obligations'; Art 1749 Cciv: 'A lessee may not be evicted unless the damages explained above have been paid to him by the lessor or, in his default, by the new purchaser'; Art 1948 Cciv: 'A depositary may retain the deposit until full payment of what is owed him by reason of the deposit.'

[148] Cour de cassation, 20 May 1997, Dalloz 1998, 479, n Keriderian.

[149] Cour de cassation, 15 January 1957, JCP 1958, II, no 10.849, n E Becque.

[150] Cour de cassation, 24 September 2009, JCP, éd E, 2009, 2088, n L Aynès.

V.A GERMAN LAW

Bürgerliches Gesetzbuch **5.84 (DE)**

§273 Right of retention (1) If the debtor has a claim that is due against the creditor under the same legal relationship as that from which his obligation arises, he may, unless another consequence follows from the obligation relationship, refuse the performance owed by him, until the performance owed to him is effected (right of retention *[Zurückbehaltungsrecht]*).

(2) A person who is obliged to return an object has the same right, if he is entitled to a claim that is due for expenditure on the object or because of damage caused to him by the object, unless he obtained the object by means of an intentionally committed wrongful act [*unerlaubte Handlung*].

(3) The creditor may avert the exercise of the right of retention by providing security. The provision of security by guarantors is excluded.

Handelsgesetzbuch **5.85 (DE)**

§369 Right of retention by merchants (1) A merchant has, on the basis of claims which have become due which have been agreed upon in relation to another merchant, a right of retention with regard to corporeal assets and securities of the debtor, if these assets and securities have voluntarily been handed over in the possession of the former in execution of their mutual consent and he still has the possession and can dispose of it through bill of lading, waybill or warrant. The right of retention is also lawful if the ownership in the assets has passed from the debtor to the creditor or from a third party to the creditor, but must be retransferred.

(2) The right of retention is effective in relation to those third parties to whom the objections against restitution of the assets can be opposed.

(3) The right of suspension is excluded if the retention of the assets contradicts the notice given by the debtor before or at the occasion of the factual delivery or the obligation taken over of the creditor.

(4) The debtor can preclude the exercise of a right of retention by granting a security. The granting of a security by the guarantors is excluded.

Insolvenzordnung **5.86 (DE)**

§51 Other secured creditors The following parties are equal to the creditors mentioned in §50:

1. Creditors to whom the debtor has transfered a movable object to secure the performance of a claim;

2. Creditors that have a right of retention on an objects, so they have something to use the object in so far as their outstanding claim does not superside the value of the advantage offered to them;

3. Creditors that have a right of retention under the commercial code [*Handelsgesetzbuch*];

4. The Federation, states, municipalities and communities, if there are duty or tax

matters in accordance with statutory provisions relating to the securement of to public duties.

Notes

(1) There is a pronounced difference between the conditions for the exercise of a right of retention set forward in the German Civil code and in the German Commercial Code. According to the Civil Code, the claim which is secured by the right of retention must be arising from the same obligatory relationship as the relationship which has granted him factual possession of the asset. This condition is not set forward by the Commercial Code. In commercial transactions, the right of retention (*Zurückbehaltungsrecht*) can be exercised in order to secure payment of any claim arising in the relation between the actual possessor of the object and its owner, even if this claim does not have any connection with the claim that is exercised by the counterparty.

(2) As in French law, the right of retention can have effect in insolvency proceedings. §51 Insolvenzordnung grants a separate right (*Aussonderungsrecht*) to the holder of a right of retention.

(3) The position of the right of retention in the German Civil Code is remarkable: §273 is situated in the second book of the German Civil Code, eg the book on the law of obligations. It can be derived that, in the view of the drafters of the Civil Code, the right of retention was rather considered as a means to postpone the compliance with an obligation than as a security device with proprietary effect. In this way, German law takes a fundamentally different position to that of French law.

V.B DUTCH LAW

Burgerlijk Wetboek **5.87 (NL)**

Article 3:290 A right of retention is the power of a creditor, in those cases mentioned by law, to suspend performance of an obligation to deliver an asset to his debtor until the claim has been satisfied.

Article 3:291 (1) The creditor can appeal to his right of retention also against third parties which have acquired a right to the asset after his claim has arisen and the asset came into his hands.

(2) He can also appeal to the right of retention against third parties with an older right, if his claim arises from a contract that the debtor was entitled to enter into with respect to the object, or if he had no reason to have any doubt with regard to the entitlement of the debtor.

(3) The creditor cannot appeal to the right of retention against the Minister of Education, Culture and Science, who, on the basis of Article 7 of the Act on the restitution of cultural goods from occupied territory, initiates a claim.

Article 6:53 A right of suspension can also be effective against the creditors of the other party.

Hoge Raad, 6 February 1998[151] **5.88 (NL)**

Winters Bouwbedrijf BV v Kantoor van de Toekomst NV

RIGHT OF RETENTION ON AN IMMOVABLE

Office of the future

A right of retention may also be exercised in respect to an immovable object.

Facts: A building company (the claimant) entered into a contracting agreement with Bolduc, in order to erect a construction for the latter. The building agreement charged the claimant with the survey, security and locking up of the plot of land. Bolduc entered in 1991 into a lease agreement with regard to the building under construction with a company, called Kantoor van de Toekomst (the defendant). In 1993 the building company finished the works and communicated this to Bolduc. However, it was mentioned in the same communication that as the price had not been fully paid by Bolduc (the remaining part being FL2.3 million), the building company was refusing to give acces to the building and would keep the keys in its possession. It also denied access to the defendant lessee of the building. After the insolvency of Bolduc, the defendant claimed that the building should be released by the building company.

Held: The building company is entitled to exercise its right of retention and make it effective to the lessee.

Judgment: To the extent relevant, a creditor may only exercise a right of retention over an asset if he is the holder of the asset, that is to say, directly or indirectly, has actual power, as determined by commercial use, law and external circumstances, over it in such way that according to the terminology of Article 3:290 'delivery' is necessary in order to bring the asset once again within the power of the debtor or his successor. The creditor's right as holder of the asset subsists, under Article 3:294 by analogy with Article 3:117(2), for as long as the asset does not come in the hands of the debtor or his successor. These rules also apply in the case of a right of retention over an immovable object subject to the provision that in such a case the delivery whereby the object is once again brought within the power of the debtor or his successor is usually effected by vacating it.

In that respect it should be noted that a right of retention over an immovable asset is by its nature not cognisable from the public registers and therefore can constitute a source of uncertainty for third parties who have consulted these registers in order to ascertain the legal situation with regard to the immovable asset. In view of that situation such right of retention over an immovable object can only be relied on against a third party who acquired its right on the object after the right of retention was established, where the creditor exercises actual power over the object in a manner which is sufficiently clear also to the third party (HR 23 June 1995, NJ 1996, 216).

A creditor, here a building contractor, who wishes to be in a position to continue to invoke his right of retention over the asset built by him also against third parties later acquiring a right over the asset must ensure, as may be inferred from the foregoing, that he continues to exercise actual power over the building constructed by him in a manner that is sufficiently clear as far as the third parties are concerned. If he allows workmen into the building in order to, on behalf of the debtor or a person who under an agreement with the debtor has the right to make use of the building, carry out works in it in preparation for taking over the building entirely

[151] NJ 1999, 303.

or partially, then there is more than a theoretical risk that it will be no longer be sufficiently clear to the third parties just mentioned that the building is still in the hands of the building contractor. That is why the building contractor, who in a case such as this does not allow the user on to the premises let, is in principle not acting contrary to what is expected from him in commercial use towards the future user.

5.3. In view of the foregoing considerations, the court proceeded on the basis of an incorrect legal view or did not underpin its view with adequate reasoning. As to the first possibility one can not make intelligible that Winters acted unlawfully when it refused the defendant, who derived his rights to use part of the building solely from his letting agreement with Bolduc BV, access to the building. If the court considered that Winters had misused the powers under its right of retention then its judgment is based on an inadequate statement of reasons since the court did not establish the circumstances on which the judgment could be supported. The appeal arguments on this point must be upheld; there is no need to examine the other claims contained in the plea.

Notes

(1) The conditions for the exercise of a right of retention are, in Dutch law, rather flexible. The Civil Code does not impose the requirement that there should be a connection between the retained object and the claim which is secured by the right of retention. Moreover, the above-cited judgment allows the exercise of a right of retention on immovables under the same conditions.[152]

(2) Dutch law attaches important legal effects to a right of retention. They can be opposed to a holder of a property right which has come into existence after the object had come into his possession. He can also invoke the right of retention against the holder of older property rights if the debtor has the power to enter into the agreement which gave rise to the claim in security of which the right of retention is exercised. An example can clarify the latter application: if the lessee of a car gives this car to his mechanic in order to make the necessary repairs, the latter will be entitled to exercise his right of retention also in relation to the lessor of the car, as the mechanic could believe in good faith that the lessee had the power to enter into the repair contract.

V.C COMMON LAW LIEN

Sale of Goods Act 1979 **5.89 (E&W)**

Section 41 Seller's lien

(1) Subject to this Act, the unpaid seller of goods who is in possession of them is entitled to retain possession of them until payment or tender of the price in the following cases—

(a) where the goods have been sold without any stipulation as to credit;

(b) where the goods have been sold on credit but the term of credit has expired;

[152] For a more extensive analysis: *cf* JE Fesevur, *Retentierecht* (Deventer, Kluwer, 1988); CJ Aarts, *Het retentierecht* (Arnhem, Gouda Quint, 1990).

(c) where the buyer becomes insolvent.

(2) The seller may exercise his lien or right of retention notwithstanding that he is in possession of the goods as agent or bailee or custodier for the buyer.

Section 42 Part delivery

Where an unpaid seller has made part delivery of the goods, he may exercise his lien or right of retention on the remainder, unless such part delivery has been made under such circumstances as to show an agreement to waive the lien or right of retention.

Section 43 Termination of lien

(1) The unpaid seller of goods loses his lien or right of retention in respect of them—

(a) when he delivers the goods to a carrier or other bailee or custodier for the purpose of transmission to the buyer without reserving the right of disposal of the goods;

(b) when the buyer or his agent lawfully obtains possession of the goods;

(c) by waiver of the lien or right of retention.

(2) An unpaid seller of goods who has a lien or right of retention in respect of them does not lose his lien or right of retention by reason only that he has obtained judgment or decree for the price of the goods.

Court of Appeal, 11 July 1963[153] **5.90 (E&W)**

Tappenden v Artus and another

CONDITIONS FOR THE EXERCISE OF A COMMON LAW LIEN

Tappenden

Where possession of the goods was originally given by a non-owner, a common law lien may be exercised against the owner if the non-owner was authorised (or the owner is estopped as against the retentor from denying that he authorised) the non-owner to give possession of the goods to the retentor.

Facts: Tappenden allowed Artus to use a van during the period of negotiation of a hire-purchase agreement between them. It was agreed between parties that Artus should pay the taxes and insurance premiums of the vehicle at his own expense. The van broke down and Artus took it to a garage for repair. Shortly afterwards, Tappenden terminated the agreement to use the van and claimed restitution of the van in relation to the garage owner. The latter refused to 'release' the van until the price for the repair had been paid.

Held: The artificer is entitled to exercise a lien on the van.

Judgment: The common law remedy of a possessory lien, like other primitive remedies such as abatement of nuisance, self-defence or ejection of trespass to land, is one of self-help. It is a remedy in rem exercisable upon the goods, and its exercise requires no intervention by the courts, for it is exercisable only by an artificer who has actual possession of the goods subject to the lien. Since, however, the remedy is the exercise of a right to continue an existing actual possession of the goods, it necessarily involves a right of possession adverse to the right of the person who, but

[153] [1964] 2 QB 185.

for the lien, would be entitled to immediate possession of the goods. A common law lien, although not enforceable by action, thus affords a defence to an action for recovery of the goods by a person who, but for the lien would be entitled to immediate possession.

Since a common law lien is a right to continue an existing actual possession of goods (that is to say, to refuse to put an end to a bailment) it can only be exercised by an artificer if his possession was lawful at the time at which the lien first attached. To entitle him to exercise a right of possession under his common law lien adverse to the owner of the goods, he must thus show that his possession under the original delivery of the goods to him was lawful—*Bowmaker Ltd v Wycombe Motors Ltd*—and continued to be lawful until some work was done by him upon the goods. Where, therefore, as in the present case, possession of the goods was originally given to the artificer not by the owner himself, but by a bailee of the owner, the test whether the artificer can rely upon his common law lien as a defence in an action for detinue brought against him by the owner is whether the owner authorised (or is estopped as against the artificer from denying that he authorised) the bailee to give possession of the goods to the artificer. This, it seems to us, is the test which, after some vacillation, is laid down by the modern authorities. It is as a result of applying this test that the cases which have been cited to us fall upon one side or other of the line. Where the owner of goods has specifically authorised his bailee to give possession of them to an artificer for the latter to do work upon them, no question arises. The cases are thus concerned with the general authority given by the owner to his bailee. It is clear that the bare fact of bailment of goods does not of itself give to the bailee any authority to give actual possession of the goods to anybody else: see *Buxton v Baughan*.

...

In the present case the purpose of the bailment of the Dormobile van was clearly for use on the roads by the bailee. Mr Forbes has submitted that it was a gratuitous bailment, made in anticipation of the bailee's entering into a hire-purchase agreement in respect of the van. We do not think this is right. It was a term of the bailment that the bailee, not the bailor, should license the van at his own expense and insure it upon comprehensive terms. This was in fact done in the bailee's own name although it does not appear whether or not this was a term of the prior agreement as to licensing and insurance. There was thus good consideration in law for the bailment, and it is unnecessary to consider what the position would have been if the bailment had been purely gratuitous.

It is a statutory offence to use a motor vehicle on the highway which is in an unroadworthy condition. If the van should become unroadworthy during the period of the bailment the bailee could not use it for the purposes of the bailment unless he were to have it repaired. In the ordinary way, save in the case of minor adjustments, a motor vehicle can be repaired only by delivering possession of it to an expert mechanic to effect the repairs; and in our view the giving of actual possession of a motor vehicle to an artificer for the purpose of effecting repairs necessary to render it roadworthy is an act reasonably incidental to the bailee's reasonable use of the vehicle. If the bailor desires to exclude the bailee's authority to do this, he must do so expressly. In the present case it is not suggested that there was any express exclusion of this right by the bailor; but Mr Forbes has argued that on the facts of the present case such authority is to be excluded by necessary implication because the bailor himself carried on business as a motor mechanic. It is contended that he can hardly have intended that if the van became unroadworthy, it should be repaired by any artificer other than himself so as to give the other artificer a remedy of lien against the van for the costs of the repairs. Even if it were possible to exclude the authority of a bailee for use by implication (which we do not think that it is), we would not be impressed by this submission. The bailee was not restricted in his use of the van; the unroadworthiness might have developed at a considerable distance from the bailor's premises. Furthermore, the bailor, as owner of the vehicle, would obtain the benefit of the repairs by whomever they were executed, and there is nothing unreasonable in his having to pay for them if his bailee makes default in doing so.

Different considerations would apply to repairs which were not necessary to make the van roadworthy, for the execution of such repairs might not be reasonably necessary to the reasonable use of the van by the bailee, which was the purpose of the bailment; but there is no suggestion in the evidence that any of the repairs in respect of which the lien was claimed were not necessary to make the van roadworthy.

We are, therefore, of opinion that the artificer was entitled to a common law lien upon the van in respect of the repairs which he effected, and he is entitled to assert that lien against the bailor because the bailor gave the the van roadworthy.

For these reasons we allow this appeal.

Court of King's Bench, 8 February 1806[154] **5.91 (E&W)**

Rushforth v Hadfield

CONDITIONS FOR THE EXERCISE OF A COMMON LAW LIEN

Rusforth

A general common law lien is only possible if both parties have agreed so.

Facts: A common carrier retained the goods of a bankrupt commercial partner, after the cost of carriage of those goods has been paid, on the ground that the price of carriage of other goods has not been paid yet. The common carrier claimed a general lien arising from a general usage of the trade.

Held: There must be a new trial in order to determine whether both parties have agreed upon the general common law lien for the common carrier.

Judgment: Lawrence J—I agree that there ought to be a new trial. Common carriers are every day attempting to alter the situation in which they have been placed by the law. At common law they are bound to receive and Carry the goods of the subject for a reasonable reward, to take due care of them in their passage, and to deliver them in the same condition as when they were received: but they are not bound to deliver them without being paid for the carriage of the particular article, and therefore they have a lien to that extent. Of late years however they have been continually attempting to alter their general character by special notices on the one hand to diminish their liability, and on the other hand by extending their lien. But what evidence have we in this case to say that their common law situation is altered?

[154] (1805) 6 East 519.

To do that it must be shown that both parties have consented to the alteration: the carrier cannot alter his situation by his own act alone. It is said that a general lien is convenient to the parties concerned: I do not say that it may not be so, but it must arise out of the contract of the parties. It may be convenient enough for the customer to say, that in consideration that you, the carrier, will give up your right to stop each particular parcel of goods for the price of the carriage, I will agree that you may stop any one parcel of my goods for the carriage price of all together. But still this must be by contrast between them; and usage of trade evidence of such a contract. And where such a usage is general, and has been long established so as to afford a presumption of its being commonly known, it is fair to conclude that the particular parties contracted with reference to it. Then, if in this case there had been evidence of a usage so uniform and frequent as to warrant an inference that the parties contracted with the reference to it, it should have been left to the jury to infer that it was part of their contract.

Court of Queen's Bench, 23 May 1849[155] **5.92 (E&W)**

Forth v Simpson

CONDITIONS FOR THE EXERCISE OF A COMMON LAW LIEN

Racehorses

A lien requires that the party claiming it has the right of continued possession.

Facts: The owner of racehorses stabled them with a trainer to be trained and kept. From time to time, the horses were used, by order of the owner, to run at horse races, where the owner selected and paid the rider. The trainer claimed a lien over the horses for the cost of training, and exercised a right of retention, against which the owner of the horse opposed.

Held: The trainer has no lien as he does not have a continued possession.

Judgment: Lord Denman CJ—I have little doubt that the care and skill employed by a trainer upon a race horse are of such a nature as would on general principles, give a right of lien. But it is essential to a lien that the party claiming it should have the right of continued possession. In the present case there was no right of continued possession. For the owner of the horses might, at his own pleasure, have sent them to any race, and to be ridden by any jockey of his own selection. The circumstances of this case, therefore make it like the case of a livery stable keeper; for it is immaterial whether the owner's possession be more or less, if he has a right to assert it at all, and to interrupt the possession of the party claiming the lien.

Notes

(1) The common law distinguishes four categories of liens: (a) common law, (b) statutory, (c) equitable and (d) maritime. The first two types are possessory liens. The functional equivalent of the civil law right of retention is the common law lien. The conditions set forward and effects of these liens are very similar.

The main statutory lien in English law is the unpaid seller's lien. The most

[155] (1849) 13 QB 680.

typical example of an equitable lien is the lien of the unpaid seller of land. The most typical example of the maritme lien is a right of action against a ship and freight for payment of the cost of salvage or for damage caused by a ship.

(2) The common law also puts forward the requirement of connectivity between the secured claim and the retained assets. A general lien is, as emerges from *Rushforth v Hadfield*, in principle not allowed. Nevertheless, the judgment leaves room for general liens, eg (1) if parties have agreed so and (2) if the general lien follows from a general usage, which has been long established so as to afford a presumption of its being commonly known. In another case of one year later, Le Blanc J ruled in another judgment between the parties that 'the party who sets up a claim for a general lien ought to make out a very strong case'.[156]

V.D COMPARATIVE NOTES

(1) A right of retention is the right deriving from the factual control of an asset to withhold that asset against the actual owner of the asset until the moment that the latter has complied with all his obligations relating to that asset. It is a right suspending the obligation of the possessor of the asset to comply with his obligations relating to that asset. Like a right of pledge, a right of retention depends on possession. However, there are major differences between a right of plege and a right of retention. First of all, a right of pledge is based on a security agreement, whereas a right of retention is non-consensual. Moreover, a right of retention depends on the holder already having possession, whereas a pledge involves a delivery of possession.

(2) Apart from the technical differences existing between the legal systems and the differences in approach, all legal systems grant the actual possessor of another's asset a right to withdraw the asset as long as the owner did not meet an obligation with regard to that asset. In all the analysed legal systems, the right of retention has effect in insolvency proceedings. The Draft Common Frame of Reference recognises the right to retain possession: Article IX—2:114 provides that 'where under a contract or rule of law a person is entitled as against the owner of an asset to retain possession of the asset as security for a right to performance, this right of retention of possession gives rise to a possessory security right'.

(3) The factual possessor of the asset must meet several conditions in order to be entitled to exercise a right of retention. These conditions are not identical in all countries, but nevertheless have large similarities:

(a) The person exercising the right of retention must have a claim which has become due by the owner or by a third person. All legal systems deal with the connectivity which has to exist between the asset that is retained and the claim which is factually secured. In none of the legal systems is this requirement absent.

(b) His possession must be lawful, eg not be obtained by force or other tortuous means, or as a result of fraud or misrepresentation.[157]

[156] *Rusforth v Hadfield* (1806) 7 East 224.
[157] *Bernal v Pim* (1835) 1 Gale 17.

(c) He must not have lost his factual possession in the meantime. This is demonstrated by the above-cited case of *Forth v Simpson*, where the trainer had lost possession at several times in the period between the compliance with his obligation and the moment at which he exercised his right of retention.

(d) Most legal systems require the existence of a legal or (at least) material connection between the secured claim and the withheld asset. This difference appears most sharply in German law, where the requirement is set out by the Civil Code, but does not apply in the Commercial Code.

(e) It is a difficult issue to determine whether a right of retention can be exercised if the assets were not entrusted by the owner of the asset. It emerges from the above-cited provisions and case law that most legal systems allow creditors to exercise a right of retention on an immovable thing. The Dutch Supreme Court emphasises in its judgment of 6 February 1998 that the condition of continued possession applies in the same way to immovables as to movables.

VI. SECURITY RIGHTS IN IMMOVABLE ASSETS

In most civil law systems, the *summa divisio* is the one between securities on movables and securities on immovables. There are other security devices with regard to movables than with regard to immovables. English law does not follow the same line, as some security devices (mortgage) can cover both movables and immovables.

The position of security rights on immovables is, in a comparative perspective, ambiguous. On the one hand, security rights on immovables are almost absent in the harmonisation debate. The analysis below will demonstrate that there is in different Member States an ongoing 'natural' and 'implicit' development towards more autonomous and flexible security rights on immovables, which makes these security rights more performing and cost-friendly than before.[158] However, it will also be analysed that these 'implicit' developments are only initial steps in a huge process.

For the registration aspects of the immovable security rights, we refer to Chapter 8.

VI.A DEFINITION OF A RIGHT OF HYPOTHEC—COMPARISON WITH THE (ENGLISH) MORTGAGE

Code civil[159] **5.93 (FR)**

Article 2393 A hypothec is a property right on immovables affected to the discharge of an obligation.

It is, by its nature, indivisible and remains in existence in its entirety on all the immovables concerned, on each one and on each part of those immovables.

[158] Cf JHM Van Erp, 'A Comparative Analysis of Mortgage Law: Searching for Principles' in MES Jordan and A Gambarro (eds), *Land Law in Comparative Perspective* (The Hague, Kluwer, 2002) 70–86.

[159] This provision is identical to Art 41 of the Belgian Mortgage Act of 16 December 1851 (Belgian Official Gazette 22 December 1851).

It follows them in whatever hands they may pass.

Bürgerliches Gesetzbuch **5.94 (DE)**

§1113—Content of a right of hypothec (1) A plot of land can be burdened in such a way that the person, for whose benefit the right is created, is entitled to be paid a specific sum of money out of the land in fulfilment of a claim to which he is entitled (Hypothec).
(2) The right of hypothec can also be created for a future claim or a conditional claim

Burgerlijk Wetboek **5.95 (NL)**

Article 3:227(1) The right of pledge and the right of hypothec are limited rights, which aim to exercise on its object a claim in order to pay money with priority to other creditors. If the right is vested on a registered good, it is a right of hypothec; if the right is vested on another good, it is a right of pledge.

L Smith, Security[160] **5.96 (E&W)**

The comprehensive reform of land law which took effect in 1926 has simplified the possibilities for the creation of legal mortgages. Since that reform, land in England and Wales is held under two systems, registered and unregistered. Most land is now registered. In unregistered land, there are now only two conceptual possibilities for creating legal mortgages: (i) a mortgage by demise and (ii) a legal charge, called in the legislation a 'charge by way of legal mortgage'. Any transaction which purports to be a conveyance of a legal fee simple by way of mortgage takes effect as a mortgage by demise with a term of 3,000 years. A transaction which purports to be an assignment of a leasehold estate by way of mortgage takes effect as a mortgage by sub-demise, with a term ten days less than the term expressed to be assigned. These provisions operate not only when the transaction's nature as a mortgage is clear from its terms, but also when an apparently absolute transfer is proved by extrinsic evidence to be, in substance, the creation of a mortgage.[161] In registered land, since the coming into force of the Land Registration Act (LRA) 2002, there is only one possibility, and that is the legal charge. A person holding a legal charge over land has the power to create a sub-charge over his charge.

Notes

(1) One of the reasons why comparative work in the field of property law, in general, and immovable security, more specifically, has been thoroughly difficult is to be found in the misconception of an English mortgage. With regard to immovable securities, continental lawyers often simplify things by considering that a mortgage is, according to English law, similar or equivalent to a hypothec ('*hypothec*', '*hypothèque*', '*hypothek*') in continental systems, eg a real security

[160] L Smith, 'Security', in *English Private Law* (Oxford, Oxford University Press, 2007) no 5.05.
[161] *Grangeside Properties Ltd v Collingwoods Securities Ltd* [1964] 1 WLR 139, CA.

right on immovables. A mortgage, in its most precise legal-technical interpretation, is a transaction in which the mortgagor transfers to the secured creditor his entire title, on condition or subject to an undertaking that when the debt is repaid the title will be transferred.

(2) Even if the words 'hypothec' and 'mortgage' are often used interchangeably in comparative legal literature, both devices are fundamentally different.[162] At least two main differences exist between the two security devices. First of all, we have already analysed that a mortgage creates a conditional ownership on behalf of the mortgagee, which is different from the holder of a right hypothec, who merely has a limited property security right (*cf* above, VI.A). Moreover, a mortgage is not restricted to immovable things, but can have as object also movable things (also shares, patents, etc). A hypothec in the civil law systems is traditionally restricted to immovables, or at least registered goods.

(3) However, it has already been pointed out that even English case law acknowledges the enormous complexity of security rights on immovables.

(4) The functional equivalent of a (civil law) hypothec is not a (common law) mortgage, but rather a charge on land. Since 1925, the system of security rights has been significantly simplified by rendering it impossible to mortgage land by way of transferring title. Since 1925, the owner of a registered land may effect a mortgage of that land by way of a registered charge. The Law of Property Act 2002 has simplified the matter, as the legal charge has become the only legal mortgage in registered land. When dealing with a mortgage in English law in the following, we will refer only to a security right other than ownership on land. In order to translate this notion into English law, the following will only deal with a legal charge on land.

(5) A right of hypothec is substantially different from a right of pledge. First of all, a hypothec has an immovable object, while a pledge has a movable object as its subject matter. Secondly, a hypothec does not require dispossession of the hypothecor. In contrast, a pledge normally requires dispossession of the pledgor. However, as was analysed above, registration is gradually coming instead of dispossession as means of publication of a right of pledge also (*cf* above, III.A.2). In English law, the difference based on the way of publicity is not applied: non-possessory security rights are known as charges, independent of whether they involve movables or immovables.

(6) Moreover, it should be observed that some legal systems still acknowledge the Roman law possessory security devices on immovables. These possessory immovable security rights are, since Roman law, termed *antichresis*. Although some legal developments demonstrate that this kind of security rights is still in force,[163] the

[162] For a more extensive analysis: V Sagaert, 'Harmonization of Security Rights on Immoveables: An Ongoing Story', in A Hartkamp, MW Hesselink, E Hondius, C Mak and CE Du Perron (eds), *Towards a European Civil Code* (Deventer, Kluwer Law International, 2010) 1046–48.

[163] The French legislator has modernised this legal institution in the French 2006 Reform. The validity and effectiveness of this operation are nowadays confirmed by Art 2390 CC (see eg G Piette, 'La nature de l'antichrèse, après l'ordonnance no 2006-346 du 23 mars 2006' [2006] *Recueil Dalloz* 1688).

importance of this security device in legal practice is far less than the impact of non-possessory security rights.

VI.B MAIN FEATURES OF A HYPOTHEC

VI.B.1 IMMOVABLE NATURE OF A HYPOTHEC

Code civil **5.97 (FR)**

Article 2397 Can only be object of a hypothec:

(1) Immovable assets which may be the subject matter of legal transactions, and their accessories deemed immovable;

(2) The usufruct on the same thing and accessories for the time of its duration.

A hypothec covers the improvements which are made to the immovable.

Article 2419 As a rule, a hypothec may be granted only with regard to existing immovables.

Article 2420 Derogating from the preceding article, a hypothec may be granted with regard to future immovables in the following circumstances and subject to the following conditions:

(1) He who does not possess existing and unburdened immovables or who does not possess a sufficient amount of them to secure the claim may agree that each one which he may subsequently acquire will be affected to the payment of the latter as the acquisitions proceed;

(2) He whose existing immovable burdened with a hypothec has perished or suffered deteriorations so that it has become insufficient for the security of the claim may likewise do so, without prejudice to the right of the creditor to enforce at once his reimbursement;

(3) He who possesses an existing right which allows him to build for his own account on another's tenement may burden with a hypothec the buildings of which the construction has been started or merely planned; in case of destruction of the latter, the hypothec will continue on the new buildings erected on the same plot of land.

Burgerlijk Wetboek **5.98 (NL)**

Article 3:227 (1) The right of pledge and the right of hypothec are limited rights, which aim to exercise on its object a claim in order to pay money with priority to other creditors. If the right is vested on a registered good, it is a right of hypothec; if the right is vested on another good, it is a right of pledge.

(2) A right of pledge or of hypothec on a thing extends to all that belongs to the ownership of that thing.

Bürgerliches Gesetzbuch **5.99 (DE)**

§1113 (1) A plot of land can be burdened in such way that the person, for whose benefit the right is created, is entitled to be paid a specific sum of money out of the land in fulfillment of a claim to which he is entitled.

(2) The right of hypothec can also be created for a future claim or a conditional claim.

§1114 A share in a piece of land can, with the exception of the cases mentioned in §3 paragraph (6) of the Land Register Code, only be burdened with a right of hypothec if it concerns a share in a co-ownership.

Notes

(1) In dealing with rights of pledge, we have established that the principle of specificity with regard to the subject matter of the pledge is in decline. The recognition of devices as the floating charge, and equivalent devices in civil law, have diminished the power of this principle with regard to the right of pledge (*cf* above, III). However, this development is not reflected in the right of hypothec. A hypothec must have a specific thing as subject matter.

(2) In most legal systems, a hypothec can only be vested on immovable assets or rights in an immovable asset. It has already been analysed in the foregoing that Dutch law no longer uses the basic movable/immovable distinction, but has replaced it by the distinction between registered things and non-registered things. According to Dutch law, the basic principle is that registered aircrafts (Article 8:1305 Dutch Civil Code) and ships (*cf* Article 8:197 *jo* Article 8:199 Dutch Civil Code) can also be the object of a hypothec. However, analysis shows that other legal systems often make exceptions with regard to those registered assets in order to enable the creation of a right of hypothec on these.

(3) In spite of the immovable nature of the hypothec, all analysed legal systems provide for a protection of the hypothec in case of destruction or deterioration of the immovable object of the hypothec. If the object is destroyed, and it was insured by the debtor, the hypothec will be transferred to the insurance sum as long as the latter is identifiable. The hypothec holder will be entitled to exercise a right of priority on this insurance sum. This is the case in French law (Articlw 121-13 Code des assurances), Belgian law (Article 10 Mortgage Act), Dutch law (Article 3:229 BW) and German law. The priority conferred to the hypothecee continues to exist in spite of the movable nature of the substituting thing (money).

(4) This feature does not apply to English law, as a charge can exist both with regard to movables and with regard to immovables.

VI.B.2 FORMAL NATURE OF A HYPOTHEC

Code civil **5.100 (FR)**

Article 2416 A consensual hypothec may only be granted by notarial deed.

Burgerlijk Wetboek **5.101 (NL)**

Article 3:260(1) A right of hypothec is created by a notarial deed between the parties in which the hypothecor grants a right of hypothec on a registered asset to the hypothecee, followed by registration of the deed in the relevant public registers. The deed must contain a reference to the claim for which the right of hypothec provides security, or to the facts on the basis allowing determination of that claim. In addition, the amount of money for which the right of hypothec is created, or, when the amount of money is not yet determined, the maximum amount of money for which the creditor can realise his claim on the basis of the hypothec, must be mentioned. The hypothecee must in the deed choose residence in the Netherlands.

Bürgerliches Gesetzbuch **5.102 (DE)**

§873 Acquisition through agreement and registration (1) In order to transfer title in an immovable, to vest a limited property right on such an immovable or in order to transfer or burden such right, an agreement between the holder and the other with regard to the change of the legal status and registration in the hypothec register is necessary, except if the statute provides otherwise.

Law of Property Act 1989 **5.103 (E&W)**

Section 2 Contracts for sale etc of land to be made by signed writing (1) A contract for the sale or other disposition of an interest in land can only be made in writing and only by incorporating all the terms which the parties have expressly agreed in one document or, where contracts are exchanged, in each.

(2) The terms may be incorporated in a document either by being set out in it or by reference to some other document.

(3) The document incorporating the terms or, where contracts are exchanged, one of the documents incorporating them (but not necessarily the same one) must be signed by or on behalf of each party to the contract.

(4) Where a contract for the sale or other disposition of an interest in land satisfies the conditions of this section by reason only of the rectification of one or more documents in pursuance of an order of a court, the contract shall come into being, or be deemed to have come into being, at such time as may be specified in the order.

(5) This section does not apply in relation to—

(a) a contract to grant such a lease as is mentioned in section 54(2) of the [1925 c 20.] Law of Property Act 1925 (short leases);

(b) a contract made in the course of a public auction; or

(c) a contract regulated under the [1986 c 60.] Financial Services Act 1986;

and nothing in this section affects the creation or operation of resulting, implied or constructive trusts.

(6) In this section—

'disposition' has the same meaning as in the Law of Property Act 1925;

'interest in land' means any estate, interest or charge in or over land or in or over the proceeds of sale of land.

Land Registration Act 2002 **5.104 (E&W)**

Section 27 Dispositions required to be registered (1) If a disposition of a registered estate or registered charge is required to be completed by registration, it does not operate at law until the relevant registration requirements are met.

Law of Property Act 1925 **5.105 (E&W)**

Section 52 Conveyances to be made by deed(1) All conveyances of land or of any interest therein are void for the purpose of conveying or creating a legal estate unless made by deed.

(2) This section does not apply to:

(a) assents by a personal representative;

(b) disclaimers made in accordance with sections 178 to 180 or sections 315 to 319 of the Insolvency Act 1986, or not required to be evidenced in writing;

(c) surrenders by operation of law, including surrenders which may, by law, be effected without writing;

(d) leases or tenancies or other assurances not required by law to be made in writing;

(e) receipts other than those falling within section 115 below;

(f) vesting orders of the court or other competent authority;

(g) conveyances taking effect by operation of law.

Notes

(1) An agreement to create a right of hypothec is a formal agreement; it requires a document in writing and, in those legal systems where the notarial office is known, even a notarial deed.

A private agreement to create a right of hypothec merely creates a promise to create a right of hypothec on a thing on behalf of the debtor. If the latter does not comply with his promise, the creditor will not be entitled to enforce the person who made the promise to sign the notarial deed. In other words: the only sanction for the non-compliance with a promise to create a right of hypothec is that the debtor has to pay damages, a sanction that does not give any protection in case of insolvency. Hence, the security granted by a private deed of hypothec is thus minimal.

It can also happen that the debtor gives an (irrevocable) mandate to vest a hypothec. These are often used as alternative, but less efficient security devices.

(2) Additionally, German and Dutch law requires the registration of this deed in a public register, in which case this registration has constitutive effects.[164] The same is true for legal charges in English law, as it 'does not operate at law' as long as it has not been registered. Equitable charges are not registered.

VI.B.3 ACCESSORY NATURE OF A HYPOTHEC

Bürgerliches Gesetzbuch **5.106 (DE)**

§1153 (1) With the assignment of the claim, the right of hypothec is transferred to the new creditor.

[164] WHM Reehuis, AHT Heisterkamp, GE van Maanen and GT de Jong, *Goederenrecht, in Pitlo. Deel 3* (Deventer, Kluwer, 2006) no 845.

(2) The claim cannot be assigned without the right of hypothec, the right of hypothec cannot be assigned without the claim.

§1162 If the hypothec-document [*Hypothekenbrief*] is lost or destroyed, it can under the cancellation proceedings [*Aufgebotverfahrens*] be declared to be without effect.

Notes

(1) A right of hypothec has, as other security rights, an accessory nature. This means that it follows the status of the secured claim: if the secured claim is extinguished or destroyed, the hypothec will also be extinguished or destroyed.[165] If the secured claim is transferred, the hypothec will automatically be assigned to the assignee of the claim. It is, in that respect, not necessary or useful to insert an express clause in the assignment agreement.

The accessory nature of immovable security rights is, however, not applied in a very strict sense. According to the European Mortgage Federation, in more than half of EU Member States (15), a hypothec may be granted in respect of 'existing and future debts' or 'for all debts'.[166] In consumer transactions, the protection of the creditworthiness and lending capacity of the debtor interferes in many legal systems with the possibility to create an all sums hypothec: the possibilities to create hypothecs securing 'all future debts' is restricted in order to protect the consumer debtor.

It has already been noted above that several developments in the legal systems and in international instruments demonstrate that the accessory nature of property security rights in general is in decline (II.A). This subsection will deal with this development particularly with regard to the right of hypothec.

(2) Also see the general remarks with regard to the accessority of security rights in general (*cf* above, II.A)

VI.B.3.a Semi-exception: rechargeable hypothec (*hypothèque rechargeable*) in French law

Code civil **5.107 (FR)**

Article 2421 A hypothec may be granted for security of one or several claims, present or future. Where they are future, they must be determinable.

Their grounds shall be determined in the title.

Article 2422 A hypothec may be subsequently affected to secure other claims than those mentioned in its title provided that the latter expressly provides for this possibility.

[165] See for a more extensive analysis: M Steven, 'Accessoriness and Security over Land' [2009] *Edinburgh Law Review* 387–426. See also M Habersack, 'Die akzessorietät—Strukturprinzip des europäischen Grundpfandrechts' [1997] *Juristenzeitung* 857; R Stürner, 'Das Grundpfandrecht zwischen Akzessorietät und Abstraktheit und die europäische Zukunft', in *Festschrift für Rolf Serick zum 70 Geburtstag* (Heidelberg, 1992) 377–88; JHM van Erp, 'Surety Agreements and the Principle of Accessoriness—Personal Security in the Light of an European Property Law Principle' [2005] *European Review of Private Law* 309–31.

[166] U Reifner, S Clerc-Renaud, EF Perez-Carillo, A Tiffe and M Knobloch, 'Study on Equity Release Schemes in the EU, Part I: General Report' (Hamburg, 2007) 117.

The hypothecor may then offer it as security, up to the amount provided for in the title and specified in Article 2423, not only to the original creditor, but also to a new creditor although the first one has not been paid.

The agreement for the coverage of new debts which he concludes, either with the original creditor or with the new creditor, shall be drawn up in notarial form.

Public notice thereof shall be given, according to the formal requirements mentioned in Article 2430, under the penalty of the lack of third party effectiveness.

Its date of registration fixes, as between them, the priority ranking of the creditors registered under the rechargeable hypothec.

The provisions of this Article are of public order and any clause violating these provisions shall be deemed to be inexistent.

Article 2423 A hypothec is always granted, as regards the capital, up to a fixed amount which the notarial instrument shall specify under penalty of annulment. Where appropriate, the parties shall estimate for that purpose the annuities, benefits and undetermined, contingent or conditional rights. Where the debt is subject to an index-linking clause, the guarantee extends to the revalued debt, provided the instrument expressly provides so.

A hypothec extends by operation of the law to interest and other accessories.

Where it is granted for security of one or several future debts for an undetermined duration, the hypothecor may at any time terminate it subject the respect of a three month's notice. Once terminated, it continues to exist only for security of pre-existing claims.

Article 2424 A hypothec is transferred with the secured debt by operation of law. The hypothecee may subrogate another creditor to the hypothec and retain his debt.

He may also, by a ranking agreement, assign his priority ranking to a creditor of a lower rank, with whom he changes his priority position.

Notes

(1) The 'rechargeable hypothec' (*hypothèque rechargeable*) of Article 2422 Cciv is one of the major innovations of the 2006 reform of French security law. Until 2006, it was possible to create a hypothec in order to secure future claims, but it was necessary that these claims could be determined at the moment the right of hypothec came into existence. In other words, the foundation and cause of the security right had to be determined in the deed of hypothec.

The rechargeable hypothec makes it possible in French law to secure (future or present) claims on which the deed of hypothec remains silent, which are unknown or cannot be determined at the moment of the creation of the hypothec. The debtor who granted the hypothec can determine, according to his party autonomy, the claims which will be secured by the hypothec in the future.

This also shows a difference in where the interest is situated between a hypothec in security of a future claim and a rechargeable hypothec: the former is created in favour of the creditor; the latter is created in favour of the debtor. The debtor has the right to 'charge' his hypothec in favour of the original creditor or in favour of another creditor (*cf* Article 2422(2) Cciv), but this *enchargement* or charging must be effected by notarial deed. It could be said that the rechargeable hypothec is accessory in its constitution, but autonomous during its course. In other words: a rechargeable hypothec is *semi-autonomous*.[167] Therefore, we can say that the French legislator has weakened, but not abolished, the principle of accessoriness of the hypothec. The 'rechargeable hypothec' in French law is a step halfway towards the *Grundschuld*.

(2) The rechargeable hypothec does not extract the object from the rights of the other creditors. If the hypothec has not been charged by the debtor, the object will be subject to execution measures by his creditors or will be part of the insolvency patrimony. In other words, the rechargeable hypothec merely grants a priority to the claims with which the right of hypothec has been 'charged'.

(3) The priority ranking of the rechargeable hypothec is determined as follows: the hypothec is perfected by the registration of the deed of hypothec. From that moment on, the creditor whose claim has charged the hypothec will gain priority over other creditors, who are the beneficiary of a 'simple' hypothec. In the internal relation between the creditors whose claim is secured by the rechargeable claim, the priority of the registration of the *enchargement* determines the ranking.

VI.B.3.b Full exception: security land charge (*Sicherungsgrundschuld*) in German law

Bürgerliches Gesetzbuch **5.108 (DE)**

§1191 Legal content of the right of *Grundschuld*

(1) A plot of land can be burdened in such way, that the person for whose benefit the right is created, is entitled to receive a specific amount of money out of the plot of land (*Grundschuld*).

(2) The right can also be created in such a way that interest from the sum of money or other secondary performances are to be paid arising from the piece of land.

§1192 Applicable provisions

(1) The provisions with regard to the right of hypothec apply *mutatis mutandis* to the *Grundschuld*, except for the fact that it does not follow from these that a *Grundschuld* must be connected to a claim.

(2) The provisions on interest on the claim arising from the right of hypothec apply to the interest on the *Grundschuld*.

§1199 Legal content of the right of *Rentenschuld*

(1) A *Grundschuld* can be created in such way, that on regular and recurrent fixed dates a certain sum of money arising from the plot of land must be paid (*Rentenschuld*).

(2) When the *Rentenschuld* is created the amount of money which has to be paid in order to release the *Rentenschuld* shall be determined. This amount shall be registered in the land registry.

[167] For a more extensive analysis: M Grimaldi, 'L'hypothèque rechargeable et le prêt viager hypothécaire', [2006] *Juris-classeurs périodiques*, études, no 9; D Legeais, 'Réforme des sûretés: crédit garanti par une hypothèque rechargeable' [2006] *Revue trimestrielle de droit commercial* 640 *et seq*; see also G Khairallah, 'Hypothèque rechargeable et prêt viager hypothécaire, aspects internationaux' [2007] *Defrénois* 929 *et seq*.

Notes

(1) The idea behind the *Grundschuld* is that a land is charged with a property right which entitles the holder of the *Grundschuld* to a certain amount of money out of the value of the burdened land.[168] This land burden can be created and continue to exist independently from a debt between the right-holder and the owner of the land. Hence, it is not necessary that the holder of the *Grundschuld* is creditor of the grantor. A subsequent agreement is necessary in order to connect the *Grundschuld* to a particular debt.

From a functional perspective the *Sicherungsgrundschuld* is similar to a right of hypothec: it secures the payment of a claim through a property security right on an immovable object. However, the distinctive feature is that a *Sicherungsgrundschuld*, unlike a right of hypothec, is not accessory to the secured obligation. It is a non-accessory right. It should therefore not be a surprise that the definition of §1191 BGB is identical to that of a hypothec, with the exception of the connection to a claim. The *Sicherungsgrundschuld* can exist independently from any secured obligation. This means that

(a) the *Sicherungsgrundschuld* can come into existence even if no secured obligation has come into existence. The security right even remains in existence if the secured obligation is destroyed afterwards. In that case, the debtor can only claim on the basis of unjust enrichment (§812 BGB).

(b) the assignment of the secured obligation does not entail the automatic transfer of the *Sicherungsgrundschuld*. If the parties have not expressly provided for the transfer of the *Grundschuld*, the assignee will not be protected in his claim against the debtor. The owner of the *Grundschuld* who is not meanwhile the creditor can in practice most frequently not exercise his *Grundschuld* because the security agreement is mostly interpreted in such a way that the splitting up of the claim and the security right is only allowed after the debt has become due.

A practical consequence of the autonomy of the *Grundschuld* is that such security right can secure obligations due by several debtors.

(2) In German legal practice, the *Grundschuld* has to a large extent replaced the hypothec as security instrument, because it offers major advantages to the creditor: he can exercise the security right in order to recover the money he has lent to the debtor, even if the secured claim is void. Moreover, it can secure claims which are not determinable at the moment of the creation of the *Grundschuld*.[169]

(3) The distinction between a *Grundschuld* and a *Rentenschuld* lies in the nature of the secured claim. The claim secured by a *Grundschuld* is the payment of a capital sum, while the claim secured by a *Rentenschuld* covers a periodic amount. The latter is similar to a *Reallast*, which is dealt with in Chapter 3, because both devices have as object the payment of a periodic amount which is secured by a land burden. However, the distinction is that a *Rentenschuld* always includes the

[168] For a more extensive analysis, see Baur and Stürner, above n 42, p. 519, §45, no 24 *et seq.* For an in-depth analysis of the Sicherungsgrundschuld, see F Wenzel, *Sicherung von Krediten durch Grundschulden* (Bank Verlag, Köln, 2001).

[169] W Brehm and C Berger, *Sachenrecht* (Tübingen, Mohr Siebeck, 2006) 309.

possibility for the owner to pay a lump sum in order to discharge the land from the burden (§1199 BGB). More importantly, a *Rentenschuld* only applies to an immovable asset, while the owner of a land burdened with a *Reallast* is personally liable with all his assets.[170]

(4) The *Grundschuld* is not an isolated legal institution particular to German law. The Swiss *Schuldbrief* resembles the *Grundschuld* to a large extent[171] and some eastern European countries, eg Estonia, Hungary and Slovenia, have introduced a similar device.[172] In most countries, the non-accessory model comes as an additional type, rather than replacing the accessory model. These models are frequently based on studies demonstrating the cost efficiency and the time gain generated by non-accessory security models.

VI.C PRIORITY RANKING OF RIGHTS OF HYPOTHEC

Code civil **5.109 (FR)**

Article 2425 As between creditors, a hypothec, either statutory, judicial, or conventional, only takes its priority ranking from the day of the registration made by the creditor at the land registry, in the form and manner prescribed by law.

Where several registrations are submitted for registration at the same day with regard to the same immovable, the registration by virtue of the oldest deed shall be deemed to have the higher priority, whatever the ranking resulting from the register provided for in Article 2453 may be.

However, the registrations of separation of patrimony provided for by Article 2283, in the case referred to in Article 2386, second paragraph, as well as those of the statutory hypothecs provided for in Article 2400, 1°, 2° and 3°, shall be deemed to have a higher priority ranking than any registration of judicial or conventional hypothecs made at the same day.

If several registrations are made on the same day with regard to the same immovable, either by virtue of deeds provided for in the second paragraph with the same date, or for the benefit of parties submitting for registration vested with the prior claim or the hypothecs referred to in the third paragraph, the registrations rank equally whatever the order of the above-mentioned register may be.

The registration of a statutory hypothec of the tax authorities or a conservatory judicial hypothec shall be deemed to have a higher priority ranking than that conferred on an agreement for the coverage of new claims where the registration of the aforesaid agreement is subsequent to the registration of that hypothec.

The provisions of the fifth paragraph apply to the registration of the statutory hypothec of administrative organs of an obligatory regime of social protection.

The priority ranking between creditors having a prior claim or hypothec and holders of warrants, insofar as the latter are secured on assets deemed immovable, is deter-

[170] KH Schwab and H Prütting, *Sachenrecht. Ein Studienbuch*, 31st edn (München, Verlag CH Beck, 2003), no 775.

[171] See §§852–74 Zivilgesetzbuch.

[172] C Schmid and C Hertel, Real Property Law and Procedure in the European Union: General Report (2005) 85 and 89 available at www.iue.it/LAW/ResearchTeaching/EuropeanPrivateLaw/ProjectRealPropertyLaw.shtml.

mined by the respective date on which the respective deeds have been registered, the publicity of warrants remaining subject to the special statutes governing them.

Burgerlijk Wetboek **5.110 (NL)**

Article 3:21 (1) The priority ranking of registrations with regard to the same registered asset is determined by the order of registration, unless another priority ranking follows by law.

(2) If two registrations are made on the same time and could lead to two competing rights being held by two different persons on the same asset, the priority ranking is determined:

(a) in case the deeds that are submitted for registration are passed on a different date, by the order of those dates.

(b) in case both deeds have been passed on the same day and the deeds are notarial deeds, including notarial statements, by the order of the time at which the deeds or statements have been passed.

Land Registration Act 2002 **5.111 (E&W)**

Section 48 Registered charges

(1) Registered charges on the same registered estate, or on the same registered charge, are to be taken to rank as between themselves in the order shown in the register.

(2) Rules may make provision about—

(a) how the priority of registered charges as between themselves is to be shown in the register, and

(b) applications for registration of the priority of registered charges as between themselves.

Section 49 Tacking and further advances

(1) The proprietor of a registered charge may make a further advance on the security of the charge ranking in priority to a subsequent charge if he has not received from the subsequent chargee notice of the creation of the subsequent charge.

(2) Notice given for the purposes of subsection (1) shall be treated as received at the time when, in accordance with rules, it ought to have been received.

(3) The proprietor of a registered charge may also make a further advance on the security of the charge ranking in priority to a subsequent charge if—

(a) the advance is made in pursuance of an obligation, and

(b) at the time of the creation of the subsequent charge the obligation was entered in the register in accordance with rules.

(4) The proprietor of a registered charge may also make a further advance on the security of the charge ranking in priority to a subsequent charge if—

(a) the parties to the prior charge have agreed a maximum amount for which the charge is security, and

(b) at the time of the creation of the subsequent charge the agreement was entered in the register in accordance with rules.

(5) Rules may—

(a) disapply subsection (4) in relation to charges of a description specified in the rules, or

(b) provide for the application of that subsection to be subject, in the case of charges of a description so specified, to compliance with such conditions as may be so specified.

(6) Except as provided by this section, tacking in relation to a charge over registered land is only possible with the agreement of the subsequent chargee.

Notes

(1) In all legal systems, the priority ranking of a hypothec is determined according to the date of its registration—or more correctly, submission for registration—in a public register.

(2) We will not deal in this chapter with the procedural aspects or effects of the registration of a right of hypothec. The registration of property rights in general, and the several manners in which the registration system can be organised, are dealt with in Chapter 8.

VI.D REALISATION OF A RIGHT OF HYPOTHEC

A final question is to determine the way in which a hypothec can be realised. If the debtor is in default, at law or as contractually agreed, the hypothecee can realise his hypothec. This realisation can be termed 'foreclosure'.[173] Prolonged proceedings of foreclosure make security rights often burdensome, and diminish their economic value.

We will not deal in this chapter with the procedural or insolvency aspects of the foreclosure procedure.

VI.D.1 FRENCH LAW

Code civil **5.112 (FR)**

Article 2458 Unless one takes action to sell the thing burdened with a hypothec under the terms provided for by the laws which apply to enforcement proceedings, from which a contract of hypothec may not derogate, an unpaid hypothecee may request the court that the immovable remains with him.

Article 2459 It may be agreed in an agreement of hypothec that the creditor shall become owner of the immovable burdened by the hypothec. However, that clause is ineffective in respect to an immovable that is the principal residence of the debtor.

[173] Foreclosure can be defined as 'the legal process by which a borrower in default under a mortgage is deprived of his or her interest in the mortgaged property. This usually involves a forced sale of the property at public auction with the proceeds of the sale being applied to the mortgage debt.' This definition has been attached by the European Mortgage Federation in Annex 3 to this Green Paper simply by way of an illustration of some technical terms used within it (http://eur-lex.europa.eu/LexUriServ/site/en/com/2005/com2005_0327en01.pdf, 25).

Cour de cassation, 25 March 1904[174] **5.113 (FR)**

Consorts Demaret v Médard

VALIDITY OF SELF-HELP CLAUSE IN HYPOTHEC DEED

Médard

A clause according to which the creditor is authorised to sell the object of his debtor without having recourse to the formalities of attachment is void, except if the debtor in order to release himself from his obligations gives his creditor instruction to sell in a joint interest.

Facts: X granted a credit to Y, secured by a hypothec. After the death of Y, his heirs (Z) signed a notarial deed stating that they assigned their rights on the burdened assets, in order to avoid a realisation of the hypothec. The act of assignment also contained a clause stating that the creditors had the power to sell the assets under the forms prescribed by Article 904 Cciv.

Held: A clause according to which the creditor is authorised to sell the object of his debtor without having recourse to the formalities of attachment is void, except if the debtor in order to release himself from his obligations gives his creditor instruction to sell in a joint interest.

Judgment: Article 742 of the Judicial Code declares null and void an agreement whereby in the absence of compliance with the obligations entered into towards him, the creditor is authorised to sell the things of his debtor without having recourse to the formalities of attachment. The wording of that provision demonstrates that the agreement sought to be prohibited by the legislature is the agreement that gives the creditor the power to sell at the time the obligation is entered into in order to ensure compliance with it.

That is a measure adopted in favour of the debtor in order to protect him from requirements becoming apparent in many cases and which the need for money could require him to accept. That provision does not apply where subsequently the debtor in order to release himself from his obligations gives his creditor instruction to sell in a joint interest.

Notes

(1) In French law, Article 2458 of the Civil Code is called the 'prohibition of self-help' (*prohibition de voie parée*). A clause in which parties agree that the creditor can sell the immovable asset if the debtor is in default to comply with his obligations is void. The reasoning behind this rule is of a legal-economic nature: such a clause would entail the risk that the creditor would sell the asset against a sales price which is sufficient to pay his claim, but which is below market value. However, French case law has for a long time accepted the right of the debtor to derogate from this prohibition, as the above-cited judgment of the French Cour de cassation of 25 March 1904 demonstrates. French legal scholars accept that this case law remains valid after the 2006 reform of French security law,[175] which is based on an *a contrario* reasoning out of Article 2458 of the Civil Code.

[174] D 1904, I, 273, n E Guenée.

[175] P Dupichot, 'La réforme du régime hypothécaire', D 2006, 1293.

(2) The right of the hypothecee to agree that the immovable asset will belong to him in payment of the obligation is a major innovation of the 2006 reform. It makes a hypothec more flexible. This means that the prohibition of forfeiture clauses (*pacta commissoria*) has been abolished in French law. We have already analysed the same development of French law with regard to the realisation of the pledge on movables: *cf* above, III.A.4.a.

VI.D.2 GERMAN LAW

Bürgerliches Gesetzbuch **5.114 (DE)**

§1147 Fulfilment through foreclosure The satisfaction of the creditor out of the land and its belongings [*Gegenständen*] to which the right of hypothec applies, occurs by way of compulsory execution.

Zivilproßesordnung **5.115 (DE)**

§869 Compulsory auction and forced administration The compulsory auction [*Zwangsversteigerung*] and the forced administration [*Zwangsverwaltung*] are regulated by special laws.

Zwangversteigerungsgesetz **5.116 (DE)**

§15 Judicial request The compulsory auction [*Zwangversteigerung*] of a piece of land is ordered by the enforcement court at the request oft he parties.

Note

German law distinguishes two forms of forced execution of the hypothec, namely the *Zwangsversteigerung*, the compulsory auction, and the *Zwangsverwaltung*, the forced administration. The procedural aspects of both forms are governed by specific regulation.[176] The *Zwangsversteigerung* determines the realisation of the hypothec on the substance of the immovable asset, whereas the *Zwangsverwaltung* determines the realisation on the 'fruits', such as the lease price or natural resources of the asset.

VI.D.3 DUTCH LAW

Burgerlijk Wetboek **5.117 (NL)**

Article 3:268 If the debtor is in default of fulfilling the obligation which is secured by the hypothec, the hypothecee has the power to order the forced sale of the affected asset in public with the intervention of a competent public notary.

The judge can, at the request of the hypothecee or hypothecor, admit that a private sale will be operated after having submitted the draft agreement for approval. If the hypothecor or hypothecee, seizing creditor or limited right-holder, who has

[176] *Gesetz über die Zwangsversteigerung und die Zwangsverwaltung* of 24 March 1897.

interest in a higher foreclosure price, can submit a better offer to the judge, the latter can rule that the asset will be sold in conformity with the offer.

The request mentioned in paragraph 2 is submitted within the term mentioned in the Judicial Code. The judgment cannot be appealed.

A realisation as mentioned in the previous paragraphs must be done with respect of the formalities prescribed by the Judicial Code.

The hypothecee cannot realise in another manner on the affected object. A clause violating this provision is void.

VI.D.4 ENGLISH LAW

Law of Property Act 1925 **5.118 (E&W)**

Section 101 A mortgagee, where the mortgage is made by deed, shall, by virtue of this Act, have the following powers, to the like extent as if they had been in terms conferred by the mortgage deed, but not further (namely):

(i) A power, when the mortgage money has become due, to sell, or to concur with any other person in selling, the mortgaged property, or any part thereof, either subject to prior charges or not, and either together or in lots, by public auction or by private contract, subject to such conditions respecting title, or evidence of title, or other matter, as the mortgagee thinks fit, with power to vary any contract for sale, and to buy in at an auction, or to rescind any contract for sale, and to re-sell, without being answerable for any loss occasioned thereby; and

(ii) A power, at any time after the date of the mortgage deed, to insure and keep insured against loss or damage by fire any building, or any effects or property of an insurable nature, whether affixed to the freehold or not, being or forming part of the property which or an estate or interest wherein is mortgaged, and the premiums paid for any such insurance shall be a charge on the mortgaged property or estate or interest, in addition to the mortgage money, and with the same priority, and with interest at the same rate, as the mortgage money; and

(iii) A power, when the mortgage money has become due, to appoint a receiver of the income of the mortgaged property, or any part thereof; or, if the mortgaged property consists of an interest in income, or of a rentcharge or an annual or other periodical sum, a receiver of that property or any part thereof; and

(iv) A power, while the mortgagee is in possession, to cut and sell timber and other trees ripe for cutting, and not planted or left standing for shelter or ornament, or to contract for any such cutting and sale, to be completed within any time not exceeding twelve months from the making of the contract.

High Court, Chancery Division, 20 March 1957[177] **5.119 (E&W)**

Four-Maids Ltd v Dudley Marshall (Properties) Ltd

FORECLOSURE OF THE IMMOVABLE SECURITY RIGHTS

Dudley Marshall

A mortgagee, unless precluded by some term expressed or implied in the mortgage, has a right at any time to go into possession of mortgaged property.

Facts: By a registered mortgage dated 17 February 1956, Dudley Marshall (Properties) Ltd charged the property known as 6 Whitechapel High Street, Stepney, London, in favour of the plaintiffs, to secure repayment of the sum of £6,000 on 17 August 1956, together with interest thereon payable half-yearly on August 17 and February 17 every year. The charge provided that if the mortgagor should pay each instalment of interest within seven days after the day on which the same should become due, and should comply with his obligations thereunder, the principal moneys should not be called in before 31 December 1958.

The mortgagor was, at and ever since the execution of the charge, in possession of the mortgaged property. On 17 July 1956, the mortgagee gave the mortgagor a written statement of the amount of the instalment of interest which would become due on 17 August 1956. The mortgagor failed to pay the said instalment or any part thereof on or before 17 August 1956, or within seven days thereafter. On 29 August 1956, the mortgagee served on the mortgagor a written notice requiring payment forthwith of the said principal sum of £6,000 and interest. On 19 September 1956, the mortgagee issued a writ in the Queen's Bench Division claiming payment of the interest due under the mortgage. On 27 September 1956, the mortgagor paid the instalment of interest which became due on August 17. The whole of the principal money remained due.

Held: A mortgagee, unless precluded by some term expressed or implied in the mortgage, has a right at any time to go into possession of mortgaged property by virtue of the legal interest he has therein, whether or not any payment under the mortgage is outstanding.

Judgment: The plaintiffs, being proprietors of a legal charge on the register, have under section 34(1) of the Land Registration Act, 1925, all the powers and rights of a legal mortgagee. This subject is one which is constantly being agitated in this court. I have had my attention called to some observations I made on it recently in *Hughes v Waite*, and even more recently in *Alliance Perpetual Building Society v Belrum Investments Ltd*, which came before me on an application to commit the editor of the 'Daily Mail' for comments on a mortgagee's action for possession of a sort exactly similar to the present. The comments and, indeed, the arguments of counsel for the newspaper showed an entire misapprehension of what an originating summons for possession is about. They all assumed that it involved some kind of default on the part of the mortgagor, but I said there, and I repeat now, that the right of the mortgagee to possession in the absence of some contract has nothing to do with default on the part of the mortgagor. The mortgagee may go into possession before the ink is dry on the mortgage unless there is something in the contract, express or by implication, whereby he has contracted himself out of that right. He has the right because he has a legal term of years in the property or its statutory equivalent. If there is an attornment clause, he must give notice. If there is a provision that, so long as certain payments are made, he will not go into possession, then he has contracted himself out of his rights. Apart from that, possession is a matter of course.

[177] [1957] Ch 317.

...

There was a provision in the mortgage that so long as interest was punctually paid the mortgage money would not be called in before December, 1958. But the mortgage interest was not punctually paid in August, 1956, and the mortgagee, as it was entitled by its contract to do, thereupon called in its mortgage money. Within three months of that it became entitled to exercise its power of sale, the mortgage money not having been paid. That is a right under section 103 of the Law of Property Act, 1925. That time having passed, the present originating summons was taken out on January 4, 1957, there being at that time no default in the payment of interest because the arrears had been paid up. There is no default at the present moment. But that has nothing to do with the matter.

The master at the hearing on February 22, 1957, held that the mortgagee was entitled to his order, but, nevertheless, deferred the effect of it for two months. Whether he had authority to go so far I have some doubt. Twenty-eight days is the ordinary time; but he made that order and the mortgagee does not greatly object. I propose to treat that order as having been made, but so far as delay in its execution is concerned, as being made with consent. I cannot, in my judgment, possibly upset the master's order. It is clear that the mortgagee is entitled to relief, and the court has no power to refuse it the relief for which it asks. There will be an order for possession within two months from February 22, 1957.

Notes

(1) In English law, the proprietor of a legal charge has the choice between four means to enforce the security right: (a) taking possession, (b) enforced sale of the immovable, (c) foreclosure and (d) the appointment of a receiver. In legal practice, the hypothecee will almost always take possession before exercising the power to sell, because it will be impossible to get the best price unless vacant possession is offered.[178] The taking of possession of the asset is therefore often the first stage in the sale of the property.

(2) Foreclosure means that the chargor is deprived of his right to redeem under the terms of the mortgage agreement. Foreclosure will terminate the hypothec and leave the hypothecee holding beneficially the rights which the chargor used to hold in the land. Foreclosure is only possible in a judicial way. It resembles to a certain extent the forfeiture clauses, which have recently been made possible in the French Civil Code (*cf* above, VI.D.1).

(3) Finally, the hypothecor, whether or not in possession, may appoint a receiver to take control of the burdened land and receive the income therefrom. The receiver will then act as the agent of the chargee.

Comparative Remarks

(1) It has emerged from the analysis above that there is a great deal of divergence between the manners in which hypothecs can be realised in the different national legal systems. The European Commission identified this problem in its Green Paper

[178] LD Smith, 'Security', in A Burrows (ed), *English Private law* (Oxford, Oxford University Press, 2007) no 5.36.

of 2005 and expressed its concern that such variety could have the effect of hindering cross-border activity and perhaps add to the price of the mortgage credit. More fundamentally, such variety could have a direct impact on funding structures, in particular by inhibiting the cross-border pooling of mortgage *collateral*.[179]

Two years later, in its White Paper on the Integration of the Mortgage Markets, the Commission formulated certain directions in which the realisation procedures had to go:

> Member States should improve the efficiency of their forced sales and land registration procedures. These factors raise the cost of doing business for mortgage lenders, increase the uncertainty for investors about the quality of the underlying security and elevate refinancing costs, reducing the efficiency of existing providers and deterring new market entrants.[180]

(2) As has emerged above, long-standing principles have been abolished in favour of more flexibility. The French developments towards more flexibility are not isolated within Europe; Spanish and Italian law shows a similar tendency.[181] An exception to this analysis is German law, in which there are two forms of forced execution of the hypothec, the *Zwangsversteigerung* and the *Zwangsverwaltung*. The procedural aspects of both forms are subject to specific statutes, which impose judicial action.[182]

(3) The development towards more flexible security rights in national legal systems is moreover in line with international developments in other fields. We can refer to the European Directive 2002/47/EC of 6 June 2002 on financial collateral agreements, and the Unidroit Convention on International Interests in Mobile Equipment can also be used as a source of inspiration with regard to registered goods. The Convention provides for flexible ways to realise international interest: Article IX of his Convention provides that 'the chargee and all the interested persons may agree that ownership of (or any other interest of the chargor in) any object covered by the security interest shall vest in the chargee in or towards satisfaction of the secured obligations'. We will deal with these instruments in Chapter 10 of this Casebook.

CONCISE BIBLIOGRAPHY

E Dirix, 'Effect of Security Rights vis à vis Third Persons' in U Drobnig, HJ Snijders, E-J Zippro (eds), *Divergences of Property Law, An Obstacle to the Internal Market?* (München, 2006) 69–93.

[179] European Commission, Green Paper, Mortgage Credit in the EU, 19 July 2005, no 40-42. This Green Paper can be found at http://eur-lex.europa.eu/LexUriServ/LexUriServ.do?uri=COM:2005:0327:FIN:EN:PDF.

[180] White Paper on the Integration of EU Mortgage Credit Markets, 18 December 2007, 8. See the White Paper on: http://ec.europa.eu/internal_market/finservices-retail/docs/home-loans/com_2007_807_en.pdf .

[181] Muniz Espada writes in her comparative analysis of the flexibility of security rights that 'la prohibition absolue du pacte commissoire ne peut désormais plus puiser ses justifications dans la volonté officielle d'éviter un mécanisme d'usure et un traitement abusive du débiteur dans le besoin, dans la mesure où les taux d'intérêts sont bas—circonstance qui peut cependant encore changer' (E Muniz Espada, 'La flexibilité attendue des systèmes hypothécaires et l'eurohypothèque', in Y Picod and P Crocq (eds), *Le droit des sûretés à l'épreuve des réformes* (Paris, 2006) no 137).

[182] *Gesetz über die Zwangsversteigerung und die Zwangsverwaltung* of 24 March 1897.

U Drobnig, 'Security Rights in Movables', in A Hartkamp, MW Hesselink, E Hondius, C Mak and CE Du Perron (eds), *Towards a European Civil Code* (Deventer, Kluwer Law International, 2010) 1025–42.

H Eidenmüller and E-M Kieninger (eds), *The Future of Secured Credit in Europe* (Berlin, De Gruyter, 2008).

JHM van Erp, 'A comparative analysis of Mortgage Law: Searching for Principles', in MES Jordan and A Gambarro (eds), *Land Law in Comparative Perspective* (The Hague, Kluwer, 2002) 70–86.

JHM van Erp, 'Surety Agreements and the Principle of Accessoriness—Personal Security in the Light of an European Property Law Principle' [2005] *Eurpean Review of Private Law* 309–31.

M Hinteregger and T Boric (eds), *Sicherungsrechte an Immobilien in Europa* (Wenen, Lit Verlag, 2009).

E-M Kieninger (eds), *Security Rights in Movable Property in European Private Law* (Cambridge, Cambridge University Press, 2004).

V Sagaert, 'Harmonization of Security Rights on Immoveables: An Ongoing Story', in A Hartkamp, MW. Hesselink, E Hondius, C Mak and CE Du Perron (eds), *Towards a European Civil Code* (Deventer, Kluwer Law International, 2010) 1043–64.

PR Wood, *Comparative Law of Security Interests and Title Finance* (London, Sweet & Maxwell, 2007).

CHAPTER SIX
MANAGEMENT: TRUST, *TREUHAND* AND *FIDUCIE*

*Alexandra Braun and William Swadling**

This chapter deals with the third of the six essential questions: how can property rights be held? Although property rights are normally held outright, they may also be held for the purpose of management. It should be noted that personal rights may also be held in the same way.

Introductory Note

It is a common demand of citizens that the legal system provide mechanisms for the management of rights on behalf of others. All legal systems respond to this demand, though in different ways, and the systems examined in this book all provide devices for the management of rights by one person on behalf of another. This chapter examines three such devices: the common law trust, the German *fiduziarische Treuhand* and the French *fiducie*. The chapter begins with an outline of each device, and then asks a number of common questions about them. Since security rights are dealt with elsewhere in this book (Chapter 5), this chapter focuses on the use of the three institutions in the management of rights on behalf of others. The subject is vast, with whole books being devoted to these various devices in their home jurisdictions. For that reason, the focus will be on what might be loosely described as the 'proprietary' aspects of these institutions, ie the ways in which the trust, the *Treuhand* and the *fiducie* impact on third party rights. Though there

* William Swadling wrote the parts concerning the Common law trust and Alexandra Braun wrote the part concerning the *Treuhand* and the *Fiducie* as well as the comparative overview.

are other management devices in the various jurisdictions, space does not permit examination of them here.[1]

I. GENERAL OVERVIEW

I.A THE COMMON LAW TRUST

Introductory Notes

(a) At its most basic, the word 'trust' describes the holding by one person of a right or rights on behalf of another or, in limited circumstances, for a purpose. The rights in question might be property rights, both in respect of land and goods, intellectual property rights (patents, trademarks, copyright), and personal rights, such as shares, the benefit of debts, and even such non-assignable rights as milk quotas under EU law. The person creating the trust is called the settlor, the person holding the rights the trustee, and the person for whom they are held the beneficiary. Where in the limited circumstances in which the law allows rights to be held for a purpose, there are no beneficiaries as a matter of law, though persons may 'benefit' in fact.

(b) Like the *Treuhand* and *Fiducie*, the trust can be utilised for a number of purposes. Although nowadays primarily a device for managing rights on behalf of others, it has in the past had other functions. So, for example, in medieval times it was standard practice for those with freehold estates in land to convey them to trusted friends to hold for the transferor. This had a number of important advantages, most prominent among them being that it was now possible to make wills of land; it also meant that various feudal dues were not payable on the death of the transferor. The trust was also a useful device for those who, for one reason or another, did not want to hold a property right themselves, one example being members of religious orders who had taken vows of poverty. Other purposes to which the trust has been put include keeping of rights out of the hands of a spendthrift, minimising the exposure of right-holders to taxation, the division of entitlement to rights on a plane of time, the avoidance of publicity, and the securitisation of rights. The trust has also proved a useful device for the legislature, for example in the reform of co-ownership and settlements of land.

(c) Most trusts arise because of a manifestation by a right-holder of an intention to create a trust. This manifestation of intent is known as a 'declaration' of trust. In England, the vast majority of trusts are 'declared'. They are sometimes called 'express' trusts to denote the fact that the declaration of trust must be pushed out (expressed). There are, however, some trusts which arise for reasons which have nothing to do with expressions of intent that they arise. We have already seen how the legislature sometimes utilises the trust device. Occasionally, courts do so

[1] The Netherlands, for instance, provides for a management device entitled *kwaliteitsrekening* which enables notaries to set up a trust account for their clients and which presents some similar features to the German *Treuhandkonto*. However, given its specific nature, it is not included in this chapter. For details, see A Steneker, *Kwaliteitsrekening en afgescheiden vermogen* (Deventer, Kluwer, 2005).

too. Such trusts are normally called 'constructive' trusts, the word 'constructive' indicating that they have been constructed or created by the court rather than by an individual right-holder. Constructive trusts, however, are hardly trusts at all, for they contain little of the content of express trusts. Indeed, in the United States they are excluded from the *Restatement of Trusts* for that very reason. To Americans, constructive trusts bear the same relationship to trusts as quasi-contracts do to contracts. They are akin to an award of damages for a wrong or an order for the giving up of an enrichment unjustly obtained, and for that reason are said to be 'remedial'. In any event, constructive trusts are not management devices, and will not therefore be considered here.

(d) Although it is common to speak of the trust as if it was something separate from the parties to it, such reification is inaccurate. Differently to a corporation, foundation or *Stiftung*, a trust is not a separate legal person. Instead, the nearest analogy is with a contract or a will, both of which also involve manifestations of intent, and where, though we once again talk of the contract or will as a thing in itself, we readily acknowledge that this is inaccurate. Trusts are no different in this regard. Thus, to speak of a trust only describes the fact that there is a certain relationship between persons in respect of a right, in the same way that a contract is merely a relationship between people, not a person in its own right. Thus, if a sole trustee were to die, the rights concerned would have to be conveyed to new trustees. It is different in the case of the death of a director of a company, where there is no need to appoint a new director. In the same way, a trustee will be personally liable for contracts made in respect of the administration of the trust, whereas this is not the case with a company director, for the company itself, as a legal person, is able to contract.

(e) However, though similar to a contract, it must be stressed that a trust is not a species of contract but an independent source of rights. Thus, while it is not possible to create a contract on death, it is possible to create a trust. Likewise, while it is not possible to contract with oneself, there is no difficulty in a right-holder making himself a trustee. And though English law had until recently no concept of contracts for the benefit of third parties, a trust has always been able to confer rights on third party beneficiaries. Finally, trustees never act as the agents of their beneficiaries, but as principals.

(f) As has already been noted, all manner of rights can be held on trust, both proprietary and personal. It is vital to notice that the vesting of a right in a person on trust in no way alters the nature of the right so held. Thus, it is axiomatic that in English law personal rights cannot be enforced against third parties, and vesting them in a trustee does not alter that fact. Suppose, for example, A lends B £10, so creating a personal right in A to the payment to him by B of £10. A might subsequently create a trust of that right in favour of C, using either himself or a third party as trustee. But it is still B alone who is obliged to perform the obligation. By vesting the right in trust, A has not given himself a right to sue third parties. By the same token, a freehold title to land gives its holder a right to exclusive possession of that land in perpetuity against all persons. That effect is not lost simply because the title is vested in persons as trustees.

(g) Just as the nature of the right remains unchanged when held on trust, so too is the identity of the person able to exercise it. That person is the person with the right, now the trustee. The beneficiary of the trust is given no rights to exercise the right held by the trustee, for the simple reason that the right is not vested in him. So, for example, if a trustee holds a right to the exclusive possession of land on trust for a beneficiary, it is the trustee, not the beneficiary, who has the right exclusively to possess. And though the trustee may, if he wishes, permit the beneficiary to possess the land, the beneficiary has no right so to do; it is for the trustee to decide how the land is used. So too where what is involved is a sum of money. The beneficiary has no right to spend it. That is the prerogative of the trustee. The same is true where the subject-matter of the trust is shares: it is the trustee, not the beneficiary, who has the right to receive dividends and to vote in the company meeting. This point is illustrated by the decision of Lightman J in *Don King Productions v Warren* [2000] Ch 291, who said that the placing of a right on trust was in no way equivalent to an assignment of the right in question to the beneficiary of the trust. For that reason, a self-declaration of trust in respect of a non-assignable contractual right was held to be perfectly valid.

(h) Because the beneficiary does not have the right vested in him, he cannot sue third parties who interfere with that right. This is once again the prerogative of the trustee—indeed, this is what it means to say that the trustee holds the right. Without the right vested in him, the beneficiary cannot complain of its violation. Though a trespasser on the land over which A holds a title on trust for B can be sued by A in trespass, no action can be brought against him by B, for the simple reason that B does not have vested in him the right to exclusive possession and cannot therefore complain of any infringement of that right. Indeed, if it was B rather than A who held the right, there would be no trust. The whole point of a trust is that the right is held *for* the beneficiary, not *by* him. The only thing B can do in such a case is to attempt to sue the trespasser using A's name, though that only reinforces the point that the right is A's, not B's. It is exactly the same with the theft of goods, title to which is held on trust. In such a case, it will be the trustee who must bring the claim in the tort of conversion against the thief, not the beneficiary.

(i) Instead of being given the right which is held on trust, the beneficiary has rights to control the exercise by the trustee of the rights he is holding on the beneficiary's behalf. So, for example, if I hold a title to a painting outright and deliberately put a match to it, no one can complain about the manner in which I have exercised my rights; for that, I am answerable only to myself. But if I now hold that title on trust, my setting fire to the painting will be a breach of trust, and will open me up to money claims by the beneficiaries. The fact that the right was held on trust means that I am answerable to them for the ways in which I have exercised the rights vested in me as trustee. A further right given to a beneficiary, although not in all common law jurisdictions which recognise the trust, most notably certain states in the United States, is in certain circumstances to collapse the trust by calling for a conveyance of the right to himself.

(j) Assuming, though, that the trust is still on foot, how should a trustee exercise the rights he holds on behalf of the beneficiary? The basic rule is that in the exercise of the rights vested in him, the trustee must use them not for his own benefit but for the good of the beneficiary. Thus, if the trustee is holding a title to land, he will not be entitled to do what a non-trustee can do and occupy the land himself, or install his family or friends. He must instead exercise his right in ways benefiting the beneficiary, usually by leasing it out and paying over the income to the beneficiary, or by selling the title and investing the proceeds of sale, or perhaps allowing the beneficiary to occupy. It is the same where company shares are held on trust. Although it is the trustee who has the right to receive dividends and to vote in the company meeting, he cannot take the dividends and buy himself a holiday, or use his voting rights in ways which benefit himself. The rights must be exercised in ways which benefit the beneficiary, not the trustee.

(k) If they are not so exercised, the trustee will be liable to a money remedy in favour of the beneficiary. A typical example is of investment. A well-drawn trust instrument (the declaration of trust) will place a primary duty on the trustee to invest the rights he holds on trust. If the trustee invests in rights which he is not permitted by the declaration to purchase, or carelessly invests in rights which he is permitted to purchase, then, if in either case the value of the substitute rights falls, he commits the wrong of breach of trust and will be liable to make good the loss from his own pocket. This secondary obligation is, however, personal to him, and cannot be enforced against third parties. Thus, if in breach of trust, the rights are transferred to a third party, that third party does not come under the same investment duties as the trustee and cannot be sued for breach of those duties. For the same reason, as regards money claims against the trustee, the beneficiaries in the event of the trustee's insolvency will fall into the class of unsecured creditors, and must be content with a proportionate share of what they are owed, which may well be nothing, once the claims of the secured creditors are satisfied.

(l) To understand the institution of the trust, it is also vital to realise that it is not simply a matter of duties being cast upon trustees and rights on beneficiaries. Trustees will often have an array of powers at their disposal to facilitate their management of the trust fund. Principal among them are the power to employ agents, to advance income for the maintenance of infant beneficiaries, and to advance capital to infant beneficiaries with contingent interests. Like the duties discussed above, these powers are personal to the trustee. If in breach of trust the rights are transferred to a third party, the third party does not thereby become entitled to exercise the trustee's powers of maintenance and advancement, for they are personal to the trustee alone. Nor can the third party transferee exercise the power in a discretionary trust to choose who will benefit from a class of potential beneficiaries.

(m) Finally, it should be noted that not only do trustees have duties and powers, but they often have rights, most particularly, rights to remuneration, conferred on them by the trust instrument, or, if there is no provision for remuneration contained therein, by statute.

Court of Appeal, 29 July 1886[2] **6.1 (E&W)**

Re Whiteley

INVESTMENT DUTIES OF TRUSTEES

Loss of legacy

A trustee must take such care as an ordinary prudent man would take if he were minded to make an investment for the benefit of other people for whom he felt morally bound to provide.

Facts: An action was brought by Elizabeth Whiteley and her infant children against the executors and trustees of the will of Benjamin Whiteley seeking to make them answerable for the loss of a legacy of £5,000, which, it was alleged, had been invested by them on insufficient securities. The will contained a power to invest the fund on certain investments, including 'real securities'. The trustees invested £3,000 upon a mortgage at 5% of a freehold brick-field, on which the business of brickmaking was being carried on, comprising about 10 acres, 'with the engine-house, sheds, brick and pipe kilns, and buildings thereon, and all fixtures and fittings thereon'. The remaining £2,000 they invested on mortgage at 5% on four small freehold houses, one used as a shop, in Manchester. The title-holders of the brickfield became bankrupt in October 1884, and the title-holder of the four houses also filed a petition for liquidation; and the rights in both cases being found insufficient for payment of the money advanced by the trustees, the present action was brought. In the court below, Bacon V-C held that the trustees were not authorised by the power of investing in 'real securities' to invest the money on the brickfield, and were consequently responsible for the failure of the investment; but that the trustees had exercised sufficient caution with respect to the mortgage of the four houses, and were not responsible for the insufficiency of that investment.

Held: That though the investment in the brickfield was authorised, it was negligent, while in relation to the four houses there had been no breach of the trustees' duty of care.

Judgment: Cotton LJ—[W]e ought to consider the question which is applicable both to this case and to the cross appeal, namely, what are the duties and liabilities of trustees. As I understand it the rule is this. They must take such care in conducting the business of the trust as a reasonably cautious man would use, having regard, not only to the interests of those who are entitled to the income, but to the interests of those who will take in future. That is to say, it is not like a man simply investing his own money where his object may be a larger present income than he can get from a safer security; but trustees are bound to preserve the money for those entitled to the *corpus* in remainder, and they are bound to invest it in such a way as will produce a reasonable income for those enjoying the income for the present. And in doing so they must use such caution as a reasonably prudent man would with reference to transactions in which he may be engaged of a similar nature.

Lindley LJ—The principle applicable to cases of this description was stated by the late Master of the Rolls in *Speight v Gaunt* to be that a trustee ought to conduct the business of the trust in the same manner that an ordinary prudent man of business would conduct his own, and that beyond that there is no liability or obligation on the trustee. I accept this principle; but in applying it care must be taken not to lose sight of the fact that the business of the trustee, and the business which the ordinary prudent man is supposed to be conducting for himself, is the business of investing money for the benefit of persons who are to enjoy it at some future time,

[2] (1886) 33 ChD 347.

and not for the sole benefit of the person entitled to the present income. The duty of a trustee is not to take such care only as a prudent man would take if he had only himself to consider; the duty rather is to take such care as an ordinary prudent man would take if he were minded to make an investment for the benefit of other people for whom he felt morally bound to provide. That is the kind of business the ordinary prudent man is supposed to be engaged in; and unless this is borne in mind the standard of a trustee's duty will be fixed too low; lower than it has ever yet been fixed, and lower certainly than the House of Lords or this Court endeavoured to fix it in *Speight v Gaunt*.

Such being the principle, we have to apply it to this case, and to consider the two investments which the trustees made. One observation applies to both of them, viz, that the trustees acted *bona fide*, and obtained and acted on the advice of a solicitor and valuer who were apparently competent men in their respective professions. It was contended on behalf of the trustees that this circumstance alone was enough to exonerate the trustees from liability. But this contention goes too far. If it were to prevail the Court would in effect decide that trustees could delegate their trust to any competent persons, and so terminate their own responsibility. This, however, trustees cannot do. They may and must seek advice on matters they do not themselves understand; but in acting on advice given to them they must act with that prudence which I have already endeavoured to describe.

Lopes LJ delivered a concurring judgment.

High Court of Justice, 27 January 1948[3] **6.2 (E&W)**

Re Brockbank, Ward v Bates

CONTROL OF TRUSTEES BY BENEFICIARIES

New trustees

Beneficiaries of a trust cannot direct trustee as to exercise of a discretion vested in him.

Facts: A testator by his will settled his residuary estate in trust for his widow for her life and after her death for his children. Ward and Bates, the defendants, were the trustees of the will. Ward wished to retire and the widow and children desired that a bank should be appointed trustee. Bates was unwilling to join in exercising the statutory power of appointment vested in himself and Ward and to appoint the bank, and the widow and children asked that Bates might be directed to concur with Ward in making the appointment.

Held: The application was refused.

Judgment: Vaisey J—This case involves a question which is said to be novel. It is possible, I think, that the reason for the novelty is that the courage required for the raising of it has hitherto been lacking.

The two alternative grounds of relief claimed are sought to be justified by the following argument: It is said that where all the beneficiaries concur, they may force a trustee to retire, compel his removal and direct the trustees, having the power to nominate their successors, to appoint as such successors such persons or person or

[3] [1948] Ch 206.

corporation as may be indicated by the beneficiaries, and it is suggested that the trustees have no option but to comply.

I do not follow this. The power of nominating a new trustee is a discretionary power, and, in my opinion is no longer exercisable and, indeed, can no longer exist if it has become one of which the exercise can be dictated by others. But then it is said that the beneficiaries could direct the trustees to transfer the trust property either to themselves absolutely, or to any other person or persons or corporation, upon trusts identical with or corresponding to the trusts of the testator's will. I agree, provided that the trustees are adequately protected against any possible claim for future death duties and are fully indemnified as regards their costs, charges and expenses. But the result of such a transaction (that is to say a transaction which involves the repetition of the former trusts) would be to establish a new settlement, with (as it seems to me) two consequences which would be to the disadvantage of the beneficiaries: First, it would probably attract an ad valorem stamp duty and, secondly, the benefit of the exemption from estate duty given by section 14 of the Finance Act 1914, on the death of the widow, as a surviving spouse, would be lost.

It seems to me that the beneficiaries must choose between two alternatives: Either they must keep the trusts of the will on foot, in which case those trusts must continue to be executed by trustees duly appointed pursuant either to the original instrument or to the powers of section 36 of the Trustee Act 1925, and not by trustees arbitrarily selected by themselves; or they must, by mutual agreement, extinguish and put an end to the trusts, with the consequences which I have just indicated.

The claim of the beneficiaries to control the exercise of the defendant's fiduciary power of making or compelling an appointment of the trustees is, in my judgment, untenable. The court itself regards such a power as deserving of the greatest respect and as one with which it will not interfere, as is shown by the case of *In re Gadd* of which it will suffice if I read the headnote:

> 'A decree for the administration of the trusts of a will directed "that some proper person be appointed" a trustee of the will in the place of a deceased trustee. The power of appointing new trustees was given by the will to the surviving trustee, who was the defendant. The plaintiff took out a summons to have AB appointed trustee, and the defendant a summons to have CD appointed. The summonses were adjourned into court and Bacon V-C appointed the nominee of the plaintiff. Held, on appeal, that the decree did not take away from the defendant the power of appointing new trustees, though after decree he could only exercise it subject to the supervision of the court; that if he nominated a fit and proper person such person must be appointed, and the court would not appoint some one else on the ground that such other person was in the opinion of the court more eligible, and that if he nominated a person whom the court did not approve the court would not itself make the choice, but would call on him to make a fresh nomination. Held, therefore, that the appointment of AB must be discharged.'

...

If the court, as a matter of practice and principle, refuses to interfere with the legal power of appointment of new trustees, it is, in my judgment, *a fortiori* not open to the beneficiaries to do so. As I have said, they can put an end to the trust if they like; nobody doubts that; but they are not entitled, in my judgment, to arrogate to themselves a power which the court itself disclaims possessing, and to change trustees whenever they think fit at their whim or fancy—for it follows from Mr Cross' argument for the present plaintiffs (as appeared from his reply to a question I put to him during the course of the hearing) that whenever the beneficiaries choose to say that they do not like their trustee, they can order him to retire and order him to appoint anyone they like to succeed him. That seems to me to show a complete disregard of the true position. As I have said, as long as the trust subsists, the trust must be executed by persons duly, properly and regularly appointed to the office. ...

Let me say at once that if the beneficiaries had called upon the defendant to transfer to them the trust property, subject, of course, to his being sufficiently protected against all possible claims, there would have been no sort of answer to the application. But he was never asked to do that. What he was asked to do was to execute what I think would have been a fictitious appointment, the appointment of a new trustee, which would purport and appear to be something done of his own volition, while all the time he was in fact being told, 'You have no option and no choice; you must do exactly what you are told'. That is, I think, a misconception of the position; but whether the plaintiffs will follow what I think is the very unwise course of setting up a new trust, which will have the general consequences to which I have alluded, I do not know, and I cannot stop them doing that if they think it is right to do it: so much the better for the exchequer. They may elect to have the property made over to them or they may think it better, having regard to the age of the tenant for life, to allow the trust to run its course under a trusteeship duly and properly constituted. ...

Note

The decision in *re Brockbank*, at least so far as it applies to the power to appoint new trustees, has since been reversed by legislation. By virtue of section 19 of the Trusts of Land and Appointment of Trustees Act 1996, beneficiaries who are all of full age and sound mind and between them absolutely entitled under the trust can require trustees to retire and appoint new trustees nominated by the beneficiaries. The statute only applies, however, in the absence of any provision to the contrary in the trust instrument.

I.B THE *FIDUZIARISCHE TREUHAND*

German law does not provide for a single institution which by itself performs the numerous functions of the common law trust.[4] However, there are a number of devices by means of which rights are held by somebody to be managed for the benefit of a beneficiary or for a specified purpose, and which satisfy certain needs catered for by the trust. Some of these devices are regulated by the German Bürgerliches Gesetzbuch (BGB) among which are the reversionary heirship (*Nacherbfolge*)[5] and the mutual will (*gemeinschaftliches Testament*),[6] which, when combined with

[4] H Kötz, 'Trusts: A Matter of Property or of Obligation?', German National Reports, 15th International Congress of Comparative Law, Bristol, 1.

[5] §§2100–46 BGB.

[6] Regulated at §§2265–73 BGB.

the executorship (*Testamentsvollstreckung*),[7] reach similar results to those achieved by an English testamentary trust. At §§80–88, the BGB also regulates the charitable foundation (*Stiftung*), while a special statute governs the relationship between investment companies (*Kapitalanlagegesellschaften*) and investors.[8]

Alongside these devices, German law also recognises another general legal instrument, the *Treuhand*. Despite the fact that this instrument is not regulated by the BGB or any other statutory provision, it is very popular in various fields of German legal practice and therefore represents the central point of our examination. According to Helmut Coing, one can speak of a *Treuhand*:

> when a person [the *Treuhänder*] is entrusted with certain rights which he can dispose of, not in his own interest, but only in the interest of another person or a specific purpose.[9]

Depending on the type of power conferred upon the *Treuhänder*, three different types of *Treuhand* are normally distinguished: the *fiduziarische Treuhand* (often also called *Vollrechtstreuhand*), where the *Treuhänder* acquires the title to the assets he is to administer;[10] the *Ermächtigungstreuhand*, where the manager is simply authorised to dispose of the assets of which the transferor remains the owner; and the *Vollmachtstreuhand*, where the manager merely receives a power to dispose of the assets.

Given its widespread practical application, this chapter deals only with the *fiduziarische* or *Vollrechtstreuhand*,[11] a device of Romanistic origin which owes its position in German law to its discussion by the jurist Ferdinand Regelsberger. It is he who, at the end of the nineteenth century, defined for the first time the *fiduziarische Rechtsgeschäft* and contrasted it with simulated and fraudulent transactions.[12] German courts promptly recognised this new type of legal relationship which, given the silence of the legislature,[13] is still governed by academic writings and judge-made law.[14] Although this has meant that the law regulating the *Treuhand* has a certain degree of flexibility, it has also meant that there is an absence of technical refinement of certain aspects.[15]

[7] §§2197–28 BGB.

[8] *Investmemtgesetz* (Investment Act) of 15 December 2003 (BGBl I S 2676) as modified in 2007 and 2011.

[9] H Coing, *Die Treuhand kraft privaten Rechtsgeschäfts* (München, CH Beck, 1973) 1.

[10] The *fiduziarisches Rechtsgeschäft* aside, another doctrine which has played a role in the development of the *Treuhand* in German law is the *deutschrechtliche Treuhand* developed by Alfred Schultze at the end of the nineteenth century. This will not be examined further. Detail in A Schultze, *Die langobardische Treuhand und ihre Umbildung zur Testamentsvollstreckung* (Breslau, Wilhelm Koebner, 1895).

[11] When use is made of the term '*Treuhand*' in this chapter, unless otherwise stated, reference is made to the *fiduziarische Treuhand*.

[12] F Regelsberger, 'Zwei Beiträge Zur Lehre von der Cession' (1880) 63 *AcP* 157–207.

[13] This does not mean that no attempts were made to regulate the *Treuhand* by statute. See S Grundmann, 'Trust and Treuhand at the End of the 20th Century. Key Problems and Shift of Interest' (1999) 47 *American Journal of Comparative Law* 401, at 406.

[14] RG 2 June 1890, RGZ 26, 180; RG 17 September 1889, RGZ 24, 161; RG 23 December 1899, RGZ 45, 80.

[15] See Kötz, above n 4, 2.

I.B.1 NATURE AND SCOPE OF THE *FIDUZIARISCHE TREUHAND*

Introductory Notes

(a) The *fiduziarische Treuhand* arises out of a contractual agreement, the so-called *Treuhandabrede* (also referred to as *Treuhandvertrag*), concluded between a transferor, the *Treugeber*, and a transferee, the *Treuhänder*, which is followed by a transfer of assets. Given the contractual nature of the *Treuhand*, and differently to the common law trust, a unilateral declaration whereby a person declares himself to be a *Treuhänder* in favour of someone else does not seem to be permitted.[16] As we will see, the same is true for France, where a unilaterally declared *fiducie* does not appear to be contemplated by the legislature. However, unlike the *fiducie* or the common law trust, which is governed by a rule against perpetual trusts, no limits seem to apply to the duration of the *Treuhand*.

As mentioned earlier, in the *fiduziarische Treuhand*, the *Treugeber* transfers to the *Treuhänder* a full and unconditional title to the assets, unlimited from the proprietary point of view, but limited from the obligational point of view because of the commitment of the *Treuhänder* to dispose of it only within the scope of the agreement. The *Treuhänder* therefore becomes full owner, so far as third parties are concerned, of the assets transferred to him (the so-called *Treugut*), but bound, as regards the *Treugeber*, by the obligations assumed through the *Treuhandabrede*. Consequently, the former has certain duties towards the *Treugeber* which differentiates the *Treuhand* from the common law trust.[17] It follows that as owner of the rights transferred to him, the *Treuhänder* is legally permitted to dispose of them in the same way as any other owner, but, on the basis of the obligations assumed when he entered the fiduciary relationship, he will only be able to do that which he has been permitted to do. There is therefore a significant difference between the legal powers which have been conferred on him and those which he is permitted to exercise under the terms of the fiduciary agreement. This situation can create problems as far as the protection of the *Treugeber* or potential beneficiaries are concerned, but, as we will see later, German courts have tried to overcome them.

(b) The *fiduziarische Treuhand* represents a security (referred to as *Sicherungstreuhand* or *eigennützige Treuhand*) as well as a management device (referred to as *Verwaltungstreuhand* or *fremdnützige Treuhand*). Since its use for security purposes is discussed elsewhere in this work,[18] we will focus on the use of the *Treuhand* for management purposes. This can occur in several situations. One speaks, for instance, of a *fiduziarische Treuhand* where investors transfer money to investment companies which invest it in shares and ownership of land and which constitutes a separate fund. While there are specific statutory provisions to regulate this relationship,[19]

[16] See Coing, above n 9, 107. The *Testamentsvollstreckung* is different, for there the source of the fiduciary relationship is a unilateral act.

[17] Under English law, the trustee is accountable to the beneficiaries, not the settlor. This is one reason why English law has difficulty with trusts for purposes rather than persons, for a purpose cannot call the trustees to account.

[18] See Chapter 5.

[19] See the Investment Act mentioned above in n 8.

there are other cases of *fiduziarische Treuhand* for administrative purposes which are not provided for by legislation. This is, for instance, the case with the so-called *Treuhandkonto*, an account opened with a bank on the understanding that the money paid into it is held by the account holder as *Treuhänder* on behalf of another. These types of accounts have been recognised by the German banking practice since the 1930s and are now used for a number of different purposes. Most commonly, they are opened by practising lawyers and notaries, in particular, in relation to the sale and transfer of ownership of land so as to prevent the purchase money being paid to the seller until ownership has been transferred to the purchaser.[20]

BGH, 5 May 1969[21] **6.3 (DE)**

MISAPPROPRIATION OF MONEY BY TREUHÄNDER

Embezzelment of money

There is no standard-form Treuhandvertrag regulated by specific rules. Instead, the legal relationship must be determined by the specific circumstances of the individual case, and, in particular, by the underlying mandate or, where remuneration has been agreed, by the contract for the management of the affairs of another.

Facts: The defendant owned 99 1/3 of the shares in the claimant company. The defendant held the shares on trust for International Corporation for A and P Inc in Panama. According to the *Treuhandvertrag*, for the duration of the contract, the business I Inc gratuitously granted the defendant the sum necessary for the purchase of the shares. Furthermore, I Inc exempted the defendant from any kind of duty, in particular duties arising towards the company (the claimant) in relation to the acquisition of the shares and statutory liabilities and undertook to cover all sorts of expenses and taxes arising in relation to the administration of the *Treuhand*. The defendant undertook to assign all rights and payments she was entitled to in relation to the shares to I Inc.

In January 1961, the claimant opened a bank account authorising several persons, including an accountant, Mrs L, to draw on the account. Mrs L embezzled money and was later (in 1964) imprisoned. In 1965, on the instruction of I Inc, the defendant sold her shares in the claimant to a Swiss trust company. The claimant sued the defendant for compensation of the amounts Mrs L had embezzled. It based its claim on the assignment of I Inc which had thereby assigned all types of claims based on the breach of the *Treuhandvertrag*.

Held: The BGH upheld the judgments by the lower courts, which had rejected the claim of the claimant.

Judgment: The appeal court whose judgment is impugned on a point of law is of the view that the claimant cannot claim damages from the defendant in respect of the amounts embezzled by Mrs L. The defendant, the court says, has not infringed the duties incumbent on it towards L or the claimant. The appeal on a point of law challenges that view. The appeal is unfounded.

...

[20] *Treuhandkonten* are, however, also used by administrators of *Wohnungseigentümergemeinschaften* or as an account into which the landlord pays the deposits of his tenants.

[21] BGH WM 1969, 935. This decision reflects the dominant opinion of the German judiciary. For earlier decisions, see RG 6 March 1930, RGZ 127, 341, 345; BGH, 25 November 1964, WM 1965, 173, 174.

(dd) A standard-form *Treuhandvertrag* determined by specific rules does not exist. Instead, the legal relationship must be determined by the specific circumstances of the individual case, in particular by the underlying mandate or, where remuneration has been agreed, by the contract for the management of the affairs of another (§675 BGB) (RG 127, 341, 345; BGH WM 1966, 445). The appeal court interpreted the agreement in light of the interests of both parties and their declared contractual intent, having regard to commercial usages. Its interpretation discloses no breaches of procedure, errors of reasoning or any infringement of recognised rules of interpretation. It is therefore binding on the court on a point of law.

Notes

(1) A typical *Treuhandvertrag* regulated by specific provisions does not exist. If the *Treuhänder* acts gratuitously, the *Treuhandvertrag* is qualified as a type of mandate (an *Auftrag* as regulated by §§662 *et seq* BGB).[22] Otherwise, if the *Treuhänder* receives remuneration, the contract is regarded as a contract for the management of the affairs of another (a *Geschäftsbesorgungsvertrag* as regulated by §§675 *et seq* BGB).[23] Correspondingly, unless otherwise stated in the contract, the provisions regulating the mandate as well as those governing the contract for the management of the affairs of another are applicable to the relationship between the *Treugeber* and the manager.

(2) Differently to the *fiducie* in France, in Germany, the contract itself does not have to be expressly defined as *Treuhandvertrag*.[24]

(3) As far the content is concerned, the *Treuhandabrede* would normally define the purpose of the *Treuhand* as well as the content of the obligations of the manager. It also establishes whether the manager has a right to receive remuneration and defines his right of withdrawal from the contract.[25] Further, the contract determines whether the *Treugeber* can demand a re-transfer of the fund at any time.[26] Finally, it sets out when and for what reasons the *Treuhand* shall terminate. The parties can, for example, provide that the contract does not terminate with the death of the *Treuhänder*. In any event, the *Treuhand* terminates should the *Treugeber* become insolvent (§115(1) of the German Insolvency Act (Insolvenzordnung, InsO))[27] in which case the manager has the duty to release (*Herausgabepflicht*) the *Treugut* to

[22] §662 BGB provides: By accepting a mandate, the mandatary agrees to carry out the transaction entrusted to him by the mandator gratuitously.

[23] §675 (1) BGB provides: The provisions of §§663, 665–70 and 672–74 apply to a service contract or a contract to produce a work dealing with the management of the affairs of another to the extent that nothing else is provided in this subtitle and, if the person obliged is entitled to terminate without complying with a notice period, the provisions of §671(2) also apply with the necessary modifications.

[24] See RG 19 February 1937, RGZ 153, 366, 368. It can also be a deed for sale, as in BGH, 25 November 1964, WM 1965, 173, and confirmed by the decision of the BGH, 1 July 1993, NJW 1993, 2622.

[25] The contract can also authorise the *Treugeber* to dispose of the *Treugut*. See eg BGH 20 March 1972, DB 1972, 2010.

[26] Such as was the case in BGH 9 February 1972, FamRZ 72, 559.

[27] §115 (1) InsO reads: Any mandate ordered by the debtor referring it to the property forming part of the assets included in the insolvency proceedings shall expire upon the opening of the insolvency proceedings

the *Treugeber*.[28] The same duty arises whenever the purpose of the *Treuhand* has been fulfilled.[29]

I.B.2 PARTIES TO THE *TREUHAND*

As far as the parties to the contract are concerned, the person setting up the *Treuhand* is defined as the *Treugeber*, and the manager as the *Treuhänder*. Anyone with legal capacity can be a *Treugeber* or *Treuhänder*, be it a natural or a legal person. By contrast, in France only *avocats* or certain corporate bodies can operate as a *fiduciaire*.[30] Depending on which interests are furthered, the *Treuhandabrede* is or is not a contract in favour of third parties.

Interestingly, the German vocabulary does not provide for a specific expression in order to identify the third party beneficiaries. This is probably due to the fact that the German *Treuhand* is largely conceived of as a relationship between two parties, the *Treugeber* and the *Treuhänder*, and not a three-party relationship. Be that as it may, anyone with legal capacity can be nominated as a beneficiary of a *Treuhand*. Both *Treugeber* and *Treuhänder* can be either the sole beneficiary or one of many (this is in marked contrast with English law where the trustee cannot be the only beneficiary). In the case of a *Treuhand* used for security purposes, the *Treuhänder* is usually the beneficiary, whereas in the case of a *Treuhand* for management purposes, the beneficiary is often the *Treugeber* himself.

I.B.3 THE SUBJECT-MATTER OF THE *TREUHAND* (THE *TREUGUT*)

Introductory Note

All manner of rights can be held by the *Treuhänder*. Moreover, the assets can be transferred from the *Treugeber* to the *Treuhänder* subsequent to the formation of the contract. Furthermore, they can also be transferred from a third party to the *Treuhänder* at the request of the *Treugeber*. Finally, and differently to the case of the French *fiducie*, it is possible for the *Treuhänder* to acquire the assets from a third party (on the basis of what is established by the *Treuhandabrede*). In each case, the transfer has to take place in accordance with the general provisions of §§929 *et seq* BGB.

[28] RG 19 February 1937, RGZ 153, 366, 369. In this regard, the *Treuhand* is completely different to the common law trust.

[29] This is true also if the contract terminates because of a gross breach of duty by the *Treuhänder*. That was the case in BGH, 22 January 1979, BGHZ 73, 294, 299; NJW 1979, 1503.

[30] See below 6.10 (FR).

BGH, 21 April 1955[31] 6.4 (DE)

MIXING OF MONEY BY THE TREUHÄNDER

Property under special administration

A manager of another person's monies is expected to keep those monies entirely separate from their own money and to make it available at all times in cash or in a special account.

Facts: The claimants were the owners of a piece of land, which had been placed under special administration (*Vermögenskontrolle*) from 1947 to 1950, as it was Jewish property. Until April 1949, an economic advisor, M, was *Treuhänder* of the property. He also managed a variety of other properties and had his own construction company. During a check carried out in October 1948, it emerged that the *Treuhänder* had only opened one bank account into which he paid the rents for several properties. That money was now missing. The regional authorities decided to retain the *Treuhänder* and advised him to pay the *Treuhandgelder* into an account that was separate from the others. When in 1949 they ordered a further check it was clear that additional *Treuhandgeld* was missing and M was therefore dismissed from his office.

The claimants filed an action for damages against the *Land*, which was granted. The appeal against the first instance decision was unsuccessful.

Held: The regional appeal court judged the defendant liable. The BGH confirms the decision.

Judgment: ... These legal and financial considerations further show that the temporary use of *Treuhand* funds for purposes unconnected with the *Treuhand* do not, contrary to the appellant's assertions, constitute 'an infringement of formal provisions governing the operation of the *Treuhandkonto* frequently committed by *Treuhänder*'. To use funds contrary to the provisions of the *Treuhand* is a serious substantive breach of the fiduciary's duties. Such a breach will, as a matter of principle, be imputed to any manager of third party monies (*Treuhänder*) as a serious infringement of substantive obligations and not merely as a formal regulatory breach because they are such fundamental duties of a manager of third party assets that they are recognised by any person, even by the least qualified manager (*Treuhänder*). However, this applies with even greater force to the *Treuhänder* M owing to his previous professional activity. If such a well-qualified *Treuhänder* commingles trust monies with private monies, then spends them for private purposes (proposals for building on various building plots owned by him in his capacity as a building contractor), and is able to pay them into a special account only 'after receipt in the next few days of large sums of money', that is no longer 'an infringement of formal provisions governing the operation of *Treuhandkonto* frequently committed by *Treuhänder*', as is asserted by the appellant. Rather he was entirely unsuited to the office of *Treuhänder* and his appointment should have been immediately revoked. Owing to the *Treuhänder*'s unsuitability in terms of either know-how or personal characteristics, the assets under management would in any event be placed at risk, were such *Treuhänder* to be retained.

Notes

(1) As mentioned above, the rights transfered to the *Treuhänder* represent the *Treugut* (the subject-matter of the *Treuhand*), which he is obliged to keep separate

[31] NJW 1955, 986, 987–88; BGHZ 17, 140, 146.

from his personal set of assets and debts (also referred to as patrimony). However, this does not mean that the rights form an autonomous and separate entity, such as is the case, for instance, in Quebec.[32] The *Treuhänder*, like his common law counterpart, the trustee, becomes fully entitled to the rights, though they are segregated from his personal patrimony and, as will be seen later, can neither be seized by his creditors nor fall within the insolvency estate. As far as the fiduciary relationship between investors and investment companies is concerned, the duty to keep the assets separate is provided for by the Investment Act.[33]

(2) The duty to keep the *Treugut* separate from his own patrimony aside, the *Treuhänder* also has a duty of care (*Sorgfaltspflicht*)[34] to administer the *Treugut* in accordance with the *Treuhandabrede* and in compliance with the standards of an orderly administration. Moreover, he must perform his duties not in his own interest, but in the interest of those indicated in the contract. The *Treuhänder* is further obliged to keep an account of his activity[35] and to provide the *Treugeber* with the necessary information,[36] as well as to act personally, unless the parties have agreed differently.[37]

I.B.4 FORMALITY REQUIREMENTS AND REGISTRATION OF THE *TREUHAND*

Introductory Note

No particular form is prescribed for the *Treuhandabrede* or *Treuhandvertrag*. However, a specific form might be necessary if the rights transferred require it. This is, for instance, the case when the subject-matter of the *Treuhand* consists of shares in a limited liability corporation.

Law on limited liability companies (GmbHG)[38] **6.5 (DE)**

§15 Transfer of company shares (3) An assignment of shares by a shareholder requires a contract entered into in notarised form.

(4) Notarised form is further required for an agreement under which a shareholder undertakes the obligation to assign a share in a company. However, an agreement entered into other than in that form shall acquire validity as a result of the assignment agreement entered into under the terms of the preceding paragraph.

[32] See Art 1261 of the Québec Civil Code. The article reads: 'The trust patrimony, consisting of the property transferred in trust, constitutes a patrimony by appropriation, autonomous and distinct from that of the settlor, trustee or beneficiary and in which none of them has any real right.'

[33] See the Investment Act cited above n 8.

[34] BGH 11 February 1960, BGHZ 32, 67, 70; NJW 1960, 958, 959.

[35] Coing, above n 9, 143.

[36] See §666 BGB: The mandatary is obliged to provide the mandator with the required reports, and on demand to provide information on the status of the transaction and after carrying out the mandate to render account for it.

[37] See §664(1) BGB: In case of doubt the mandatary may not transfer the performance of the mandate to a third party. If the transfer is permitted, then he is only liable for fault in connection with the transfer. He is liable under §278 for fault on the part of an assistant.

[38] Gesetz betreffend die Gesellschaften mit beschränkter Haftung of 20 April 1892 (RGBl I S 477).

BGH, 19 April 1999[39] **6.6 (DE)**

FORM OF A *TREUHANDVERTRAG* CONCERNING SHARES

Shares in a limited liability company

(1) A Treuhandvertrag concerning shares in a limited liability company entered into before the notarisation of the articles of incorporation is not subject to the formality requirements set out in §15(4) of the law on limited liability companies (GmbHG).

(2) When a shareholder undertakes to hold his shares in the company on behalf of a Treugeber, such agreement must be notarially attested. The same applies to the Treuhandvertrag which the shareholder enters into after incorporation but before registration of the limited liability company in respect of the future share.

Facts: In 1992, the defendant and the Kaufhaus J GmbH & Co KG set up J & L Kaufhaus GmbH (a limited liability company) in notarial form. The defendant decided to cover three deposits out of a total of seven. Half of them were to be paid in cash. The defendant and his wife took out a loan in order to finance the payment. The loan was taken out from a bank where the claimant acted as a member of the board of directors. The claimant and the defendant entered into a written *Treuhandvertrag* which established that the *Treuhänder* (the defendant) had taken on the payment of DM115,000 of the capital of the company. It further provided that after registration of the limited liability company, the defendant would become entitled to the shares which he would acquire for the *Treugeber*.

Among the duties of the *Treuhänder* was the obligation to hand over everything he had acquired through the quota and to provide the *Treugeber* with information when requested. The *Treugeber*, on the other hand, had to provide the *Treuhänder* with the means necessary for him to perform his duties.

The *Treuhänder* (the claimant) later lent the defendant and his wife money which they used in order to pay off the debit with the Bank. At the end of 1993, the parties fell out over a request for provision of information from the claimant. At that point, the defendant repaid the loan to the claimant and withdrew from the *Treuhandvertrag*. However, he refused to transfer the shares he was holding for the *Treugber*. Instead he repaid the money the claimant had transferred to him. At that point, the claimant withdrew from the contract. He demanded the assignment of the quota and that the defendant be held liable for not having provided him with the accounts.

The court of first instance rejected the claim. This decision was substantially upheld by the regional appeal court with the exception that it rejected only the claim for exhibition of the financial statements. The appeal to the BGH was successful.

Held: The second Senate of the BGH referred the decision back to the regional appeal court.

Judgment: (d) Contrary to the opinion of the court hearing the appeal on its merits, the rationale of the provision as to form also requires that a *Treuhandabrede* entered into after incorporation but before registration of the company be concluded in notarial form.

Unlike §313 BGB, which is a provision essentially affording protection against precipitateness, §15(4) of the GmbHG (law on limited liability companies) not only seeks to guarantee the matter of proof of direct share ownership that is particularly important in light of §16 of the GmbHG, but also seeks to prevent shares in limited liability companies from becoming freely marketable. This has been repeatedly reaffirmed by the BGH, which has followed the settled case law in this connection of the RG.

The aim of that provision would be frustrated if, in respect of an existing company share, a fiduciary relationship could be established without any requirement as to

[39] DStR 1999, 861; NZG 1999, 656.

form, under which the *Treugeber* could require the company share to be transferred to himself, particularly since it would be open to the *Treugeber* on his part to enter into further *Treuhandverträge* under which he would be obliged to hold that share on trust for a third party. For it to be permissible to enter into such a *Treuhandvertrag*, without any requirement as to form, would undermine the case law of the Senate under which the assignment, free of any requirement as to form, of claims to the transfer of a company share can never be recognised by the legal order and not only in a case where a deliberate intention to circumvent the requirement as to form is established. The question whether a *Treuhandvertrag* may be entered into without observance of a requirement as to form was earlier expressly left open by the Senate and has occasionally found its advocates in academic writings (*cf Hachenburg/Zutt*, GmbHG, Annex, Section 15, §52 *et seq*. Conversely, as to the prevailing opinion *cf Baumbach/Hueck*, GmbHG, 16th ed, Section 15 §55 *et seq*; *Rohwedder*, GmbHG, 3rd ed, Section 15, §28; *Lutter/Hommelhoff*, GmbHG, 14th ed, Section 15, §45; *Scholz/Winter*, GmbHG, 8th ed, Section 15, §62; *Ulmer*, WPg 1963, 120; see also *Schlegelberger/K Schmidt*, HGB, 5th ed, Section 335, §§44 and 47, cited by Zutt in support of his view).

The above-mentioned protective machinery contained in §15(3),(4) GmbHG comes into play even during the period within which the limited liability company is being incorporated. The Court has repeatedly so held in regard to assignments of the future company share to be created on registration and the attendant liability to enter into that obligation. It cannot be otherwise in the case of a *Treuhandvertrag* entered into during the limited liability company's incorporation period concerning the company share coming into existence only on registration of the company; if it were, the aim of the mandatory provision as to form would be frustrated.

Accordingly, where the reasoning of the judgment appealed against does not support the decision, the Senate is nevertheless precluded from making a definitive decision in the form sought in the appeal on a point of law. From its vantage point the appeal court consequentially did not examine whether the parties entered into a *Treuhandvertrag* even before finalisation of the notarial instrument of incorporation of J L-GmbH. It was permissible for that to be done without observance of requirements as to form: no share in the company was available, nor had the process for creating such shares been initiated, which was dependent upon registration of the company in the register of companies. The circumstances of the incorporation of J L-GmbH on which the defendant, it is not disputed, took a total of three shares, including one in the amount of DM 205,000, on behalf of his wife, as well as the manner in which the defendant acquired the requisite funds and finally the discussions conducted between the parties preceding the conclusion in writing of the *Treuhandvertrag*—especially those held on 20 March 1992 in the presence of the lawyer and auditor Dr B—are all matters that may indicate the existence of a consensus between the parties even before notarisation of the instrument of incorporation of J L-GmbH. Reference back gives the court hearing the appeal on its merits the opportunity to make the necessary findings of fact.

Note

In the first decades following the introduction of the BGB, parties frequently noted the existence of the *Treuhand* (or the fact that the transferee was a *Treuhänder*) in the Land Registry.[40] Since a decision of the *Kammergericht* in 1933, however, the judiciary has objected to this practice.[41] According to that court, 'the Treuhandrelationship cannot limit the proprietary rights of the manager'.[42] In other words, the rights of the *Treugeber* are only personal rights and registration in the Land Registry is therefore meaningless. However, as we shall see later, even though the *Treuhänder*'s rights are limited from an obligational point of view, under certain circumstances, the fiduciary nature of the relationship can be enforced against third-party creditors.[43]

I.C THE *FIDUCIE*

For a long time, France did not have a general device allowing persons to transfer rights to another to be managed for the benefit of a beneficiary or a purpose.[44] Although the *fidéicommis* and other fiduciary devices were known under the *ancien régime*, they were abolished during the codification process. Over the last 30 years or so, however, a number of transactions of a fiduciary nature (the so-called *fiducies innommées*) have been developed to satisfy needs of business and financial life.[45] Moreover, since the late 1980s, several attempts have been made to introduce into the Civil Code a general system of rules on fiduciary relationships.

A first preliminary draft, composed of eight articles, was published in 1989, though it was never turned into a proper bill. In February 1991, another more detailed proposal was drafted,[46] but it was only a year later that the French government submitted a 'real' proposal with the aim of introducing the *fiducie*.[47] Apart from legal academics expressing their interest in the study of this legal device, practitioners, notaries, bankers and lawyers all called for the introduction, along with the *fiducies innommées*, of a so-called *fiducie nommée*. There were several reasons for this. On the one hand, it was clear that this institution could have multiple applications; on the other hand, there was also a need to make French law more attractive to foreign investors and, in particular, to provide for an alternative to the common law trust. In fact, the creation of a domestic 'trust-like' device seemed to be considered a prerequisite for the ratification of the 1985 Hague Convention on the Law Applicable to Trusts and on their Recognition.[48] The fear was that the

[40] Coing, above n 9, 120.

[41] KG 3 August 1933, JFG 11, 273.

[42] '[T]atsächlich kann das Treuhandverhältnis derartige das Recht des Treuhänders dinglich beschränkende Wirkungen keinesfalls haben.'

[43] BGH 1 July 1993, NJW 1993, 2622.

[44] L Thévenoz, 'Civil Law Jurisdictions on their way to trusts? A Swiss Viewpoint', in D Hayton (ed), *Extending the Boundaries of Trusts and similar Ring-Fenced Funds* (The Hague, London, New York: Kluwer Law International, 2002) 115, 118.

[45] Among these are the *portage d'actions*, the *cession Dailly* (Arts L313-23 and following of the Code monétaire et financier) allowing fiduciary assignments of receivables, the asset securitisation through *fonds commun de créance*, the *pret* or *prise en pension de titres financieres* and the *defeasance*.

[46] For a comment of the project of 1991, see M Grimaldi, 'La *fiducie*: réflections sur l'institution et sur l'avant-projet de loi qui la consacre', Defrénois, 1991, Art 35085, 897 and Art 35094, 961.

[47] *Projet de loi instituant la fiducie*, no 2583, of 20 February 1992.

[48] France signed the Hague Convention on 26 November 1992, but has not yet ratified it.

ratification of the Convention without the provision of a domestic equivalent to the trust would cause business to flee from France. Unfortunately, the proposal, which contained a mixture of general and special provisions, left several issues unresolved. Apart from the difficulties the use of the *fiducie* was to create in the field of the *libéralités*, the major problems seemed to derive from tax considerations. According to the Ministry of Finance, a definition of the *fiducie* which was too wide could further tax evasion. Ultimately, the bill lapsed. Although towards the end of 1994 new attempts were undertaken in order to adopt the *fiducie*, these were unsuccessful.

A new proposal was finally submitted by Senator Philippe Marini in 2005. Once again, the tax authorities pointed out difficulties[49] and further changes had to be made, with the result that the final text differs substantially from the project originally presented in 1995.

Be that as it may, after nearly 20 years of discussion, France has had since February 2007 a general regime of the *fiducie*, alongside the already existing *fiducies innommées*.[50] This regime consists of 21 articles which were introduced into book III of the Civil Code (concerning the 'différentes manières dont on acquiert la propriété') under a new heading entitled 'De la fiducie'.

The *fiducie* in its final version met with strong criticisms by several French legal scholars[51] and has so far only had limited application.[52] It is thus not surprising that soon after its enactment, changes were brought about through a statute aiming at the modernisation of the French economy, passed on 4 August 2008.[53] This statute was then followed by several other legislative interventions in 2008 and 2009 which have further modified the *fiducie*.[54] Several improvements were made and special provisions introduced concerning those instances in which the *fiducie* is employed as a means of creating security.

I.C.1 NATURE, SCOPE AND VALIDITY OF THE *FIDUCIE*

Code civil **6.7 (FR)**

Article 2011 The *fiducie* is a transaction through which one or more *constituants* transfer things, rights or securities, or a collection of things, rights or securities, to one or more *fiduciaires* who, keeping them segregated from their own patrimony, act so as to further a particular purpose for the benefit of one or more beneficiaries.
Article 2012 The *fiducie* is created by statute or by contract, and must be express. If

[49] See text no 178, presented to the Senate on 8 February 2005. See the text at www.senat.fr/leg/ppl04-178.html.

[50] Loi no 2007-211 of 19 February 2007. The translation provided in this chapter is based on P Matthews, 'The French Fiducie: And Now for Something Completely Different' (2007) 21 *Trust Law International* 17, 22.

[51] See eg C Larroumet, 'La loi du 19 février 2007 sur la fiducie. Propos critiques' (2007) Recueil Dalloz, no 20, 1350 and P Crocq, Lacunes et limites de la loi au regard du droit des sûretés, *ibid*, 1354.

[52] M Gdanski and T Pichardo-Angadi, 'Recent Changes to French law Affecting Fiducie and Rights of Secured Creditors' (2009) *Journal of International Banking Law and Regulation* 262, at 263.

[53] Loi no 2008-776 of 4 August 2008, Art 18.

[54] Ordonnance no 2008-1345 of 18 December 2008, Ordonnance no 2009-112 of 30 January 2009 and Loi no 2009-526 of 12 May 2009.

the things, rights or securities transferred to the *fiduciaire* belong to spouses subject to the community property regime or are co-owned, the contract is valid only if entered into before a notary.

Notes

(1) In providing that the *fiducie* can be established by either statute or contract, the French legislature has reserved the possibility of creating new types of statutory *fiducies*.[55] While the legislature has this ability, the wording of Article 2011 prevents the courts from creating a *fiducie* (in the way that English courts sometimes create a constructive trust). In practice, however, the *fiducie* will usually arise from a contract which has to be made in conformity with Articles 2011–30 Cciv. The *fiducie* thus represents a new type of special contract concluded between the transferor, the *constituant*, and the transferee, the *fiduciaire*, which must be express.[56]

(2) Since the *fiducie* arises out of a contract and involves a transfer of assets from the *constituant* to the *fiduciaire*, it is assumed that no self-declaration is possible through which a *constitutant* declares himself *fiduciaire* of a *fiducie*.[57] Furthermore, since the transfer spoken of is one from *constituant* to *fiduciaire*, it would appear that the *fiduciaire* cannot arise by means of a transfer of rights from a third person to the *fiduciaire*.[58]

(3) According to Article 2011, the *fiduciaire* receives the assets for the benefit of one or more beneficiaries. Furthermore, Article 2018 requires the contract to specify the beneficiary or beneficiaries, or at least to provide for their ascertainment. It would therefore seem that, unlike a *Treuhand*, a *fiducie* cannot be created for the furtherance of a private or charitable purpose.

(4) The object of the transfer can be present or future things, rights or securities, immovables or movables, corporeal and incorporeal things. Correspondingly, the *patrimoine fiduciaire* (which can be defined as the entirety of the subject-matter of the *fiducie*) can also be composed of the benefit of debts, but not solely.[59] The newly introduced Article 2018-2 states that the assignment of a debt is good against third parties from the date of the stipulation of the contract of *fiducie* or that of the accessory contract that acknowledges it. It is not good against the debtor until he will be notified by the assignor or the *fiduciaire*.

(5) Article 2011 does not state whether the transfer of the asset must involve a transfer of possession. However, the newly inserted Article 2018-1 refers to the instance in which the *constituant* maintains the usage or the usufruct of a business (*fonds de commerce*) or an immovable used for professional reasons. This suggests that the *constituant* can remain in possession of the object of the transferred right,

[55] Rapp AN no 3655 (M Xavier de Roux) at 34.

[56] The case of the *Treuhand* is different as we have seen. See above at I.B.1.

[57] Interestingly, unilaterally declared trusts are common in Italian legal practice, but contrary to what sometimes happens in the international world of trusts, in Italy the settlor is the 'real' settlor.

[58] As it is, for instance, possible under German law. See above at I.B.3.

[59] Rapp Sénat no 11 (2006–07) (M Henri de Richemont) at 45: 'In effet important d'éviter que la fiducie puisse permettre à une personne de se décharger de l'intégralité de son passif, au mépris des droits de ses créanciers.'

as is the case with the German *Sicherungsübereignung*.[60] Nothing is said with regard to the mode of the transfer, which is therefore regulated by the *droit commun*.[61]

(6) The rights transferred to the *fiduciaire* do not become part of his personal patrimony. In fact, like the trustee and the *Treuhänder*, the *fiduciaire* has a duty to keep the assets received separate from his personal patrimony. And as in England and Germany, the *patrimoine fiduciaire* does not represent a separate legal person.

(7) So far as the functions of the *fiducie* are concerned, and differently to Senator Marini's proposal, law no 211 of 2007 does not distinguish between the *fiducie* for management purposes (*fiducie-gestion*) and the *fiducie* for security purposes (*fiducie-sureté*). All the provisions are therefore equally applicable to both types of transactions, and one transaction may also serve the purposes of both management and security.[62]

Code civil **6.8 (FR)**

Article 2013 As a matter of public policy, the contract of *fiducie* is void if it is made with the intention of conferring wealth upon a beneficiary.

Notes

(1) One of the most controversial provisions on the *fiducie* is Article 2013, by which the French legislature has eliminated the possibility of gratuitous transfers from the *constituant* to the beneficiary.[63] In doing so, the legislature outlawed the employment of the *fiducie* in the field of gifts, either *inter vivos* or *post mortem*. Thus, the *constituant* is not acting out of generosity, but is seeking an economic remuneration.

(2) The reasons for the introduction of these limitations are controversial. According to Senator Henry de Richemont, who wrote the report for the Commission de Loi of the Senate, the main reason for the restriction is to be found in the fact that recent reforms in the field of the law of succession[64] led to the introduction of the *mandat à effet posthume* as well as the *libéralités graduelles et résiduelles*, which, according to the Senator, fulfil similar goals.[65] This explanation is, however, doubtful, for neither the *mandate à effet posthume* nor the *libéralités graduelles et résiduelles* actually produce the same result as the *fiducie*. The real reasons behind the restriction seem to lie elsewhere. First, there was most likely the fear that the *fiducie* could be used as a means of evading the dispositions concerning forced heirship. A circumvention of these dispositions could, however, have been prevented in other ways, without requiring such a restriction. Secondly, the concern of tax avoidance seems to have played a role in the decision.

[60] See Chapter 5.

[61] The term *droit commun* is usually employed in order to refer to the general scheme of regulations. In this case, the general provisions concerning the transfer of property.

[62] This creates several problems as far as security transactions are concerned. On this point see in particular the critical comments by Crocq, above n 51.

[63] Notice, however, that the contract can itself be either gratuitous or for a consideration.

[64] Loi no 2006-728 of 23 June 2006.

[65] Rapp Sénat no 11 (2006–07) at 15.

(3) This apart, the article is criticised on the ground that it leaves open the question of the type of transactions which are covered. From the wording, it appears that some consideration has to be given by the beneficiary. It is most likely that the third party beneficiary has to confer upon the *constituant* a benefit somehow equivalent to the value of the things he receives. The consideration can probably consist of money or of the performance of a service.[66] However, when does the beneficiary have to confer the benefit, at the moment he receives his benefit or earlier? And who is to verify whether or not there is a sufficient consideration?

I.C.2 PARTIES TO THE FIDUCIE

Introductory Note

From what has been said so far, it seems that the contract is only concluded between the *constituant* and the *fiduciaire*. In other words the beneficiary is not a party to the contract. However, unless the *constituant* or the *fiduciaire* are themselves the beneficiaries,[67] the relationship is a triangular one, in which case the nature of the *fiducie* is that of a contract in favour of third parties (*stipulation pour autrui*, Article 1121 Cciv). This is similar to the situation in Germany. Interestingly though, the French legislature has also envisaged that a fourth person may be involved in the *fiducie*.

Code civil **6.9 (FR)**

Article 2017 Subject to provision to the contrary in the contract of *fiducie*, the *constituant* may at any time appoint a third party who is entrusted with the function of protecting the interests of the *constituant* in the context of carrying out the contract and who may exercise any of the powers conferred by law on the *constituant*.

When the *constituant* is a natural person he cannot abdicate this possibility.

Notes

(1) The reasoning behind this provision seems to be a desire to make the *fiducie* a more secure device. In fact, according to the report of Xavier de Roux, the function of the 'protector' is primarily to avoid conflicts of interest in those cases in which the *fiduciaire* is also the beneficiary of the *fiducie* (which is the case of the *fiducie* for security purposes).[68] Interestingly, no restrictions are imposed so far as the identity of the 'protector' is concerned, it being possible to nominate an individual as well as a corporate body.

(2) Although the practice of appointing such a 'protector' is largely foreign to

[66] Rapp AN no 3655 at 36 states that: 'Le beneficiaire désigné par le contrat de fiducie n'étant pas une partie au contrat de fiducie, la contrepartie résultera en principe d'une relation contractuelle estérieure (example: la remise de l'actif fiduciaire peut s'analyser comme le paiement par le constituant d'une prestation effectuée par le bénéficiaire en qualité de fournisseur ou de sous-traitant.'

[67] Which is explicitly foreseen by Art 2016 Cciv.

[68] Rapp AN no 3655, at 41.

English law, it has been a well-known device in offshore jurisdictions since the 1980s. The same is true for Italian legal practice, where so-called guardians or protectors are nominated, who have the function of monitoring the trustee's activity and to make sure that he is not committing a breach of trust. These guardians can give instructions to the trustee as to how to perform certain duties or even directly exercise specific powers concerning management and disposition.

Code civil **6.10 (FR)**

Article 2015 A *fiduciaire* must be a lender within the meaning of Article 511-1 of the Monetary and Financial Code, an institution or agency referred to in Article 518-1 of that code, an investment enterprise referred to in Article 531-4 of that code, or an insurance company regulated by Article L 310-1 of the Insurance Code.
Members of the legal profession of *avocats* may also act as a *fiduciaire*.

Notes

(1) At first, the French legislature introduced a number of restrictions concerning the *constituant* and the *fiduciaire*. Not only did both have to be resident in a Member State of the European Union or in a state or country which has concluded a double tax treaty with France providing for administrative assistance with regard to the battle against fraud and tax avoidance, but the legislature also limited the sorts of persons who could enter into a contract of *fiducie*.

(2) So far as the *constituant* is concerned, Article 2014 (abolished in August 2008) set out two conditions: first, the *constitutant* of a *fiducie* could only be a corporate body and second, it had to be a corporate body subject to corporation tax, whether as a matter of law or by election.[69] Differently to Germany and England, natural persons were at first prevented from setting up a *fiducie*. This restriction was controversial and was not present in Senator Marini's original draft. According to the report written by de Roux, the limitation was motivated by a desire to guarantee certain levels of transparency and deontology.[70] Furthermore, recent reforms in the field of the law of succession, the law applicable to *incapacitées* and securities have introduced several instruments of fiduciary character which perhaps justified this restriction. According to de Roux, 'It is likely that the fiducies created by natural persons will only represent a marginal part of the new legal instrument, 90% of the Anglo-American trusts pursue commercial purposes.'[71] The real reason for the limitation seems, however, to have been the fear that the *fiducie* would be used for tax avoidance or to circumvent the rules regarding inheritance as well as *incapacitées*. Be that as it may, the statute for the modernisation of the French economy passed

[69] A '*société civile*' which has opted for the payment of the corporation tax can thus make us of a *fiducie*.

[70] Rapp AN no 3655, at 38.

[71] 'Il est probable que des fiducies créées à l'initiative de personnes physiques n'auraient représenté qu'une part marginale du recours à ce nouveau mécanisme juridique, 90% des trusts anglo-saxons ayant une finalité commerciale.' Rapp AN no 3655, at 37.

on 4 August 2008 abolished Article 2014, which means that both natural and legal persons, even if they are not subject to corporation tax, can now create a *fiducie*.

(3) Restrictions still exist, however, so far as *fiduciaires* are concerned. Differently to England or Germany, only specific institutions or professions can function as a *fiduciaire*.[72] Initially, only certain lenders, institutions, agencies or investment enterprises referred to in the Monetary and Financial Code, as well as certain insurance companies, could act as such. Since August 2008, however, *avocats* are also authorised to act as *fiduciaire*, though notaries and financial advisers are still excluded.[73]

Code civil **6.11 (FR)**

Article 2016 The *constituant* or the *fiduciaire* may be the beneficiary or one of the beneficiaries of a contract of *fiducie*.

Notes

(1) While there are restrictions so far as the *fiduciaire* is concerned, no restrictions have been imposed on the identity of the beneficiary. It is possible to appoint a natural person as well as a corporate body. As in Germany, both the *constituant* and the *fiduciaire* may be one of the beneficiaries or even the sole beneficiary of a contract of *fiducie*. In cases of a *fiducie* for security purposes, the *fiduciaire* is normally the beneficiary, while in cases of a *fiducie* for management purposes, it is the *constituant*. The *fiducie* might therefore involve two persons, not three.

(2) Interestingly, no distinction is made between income beneficiaries and capital beneficiaries.

I.C.3 FORM AND CONTENT OF THE *FIDUCIE*

Code civil **6.12 (FR)**

Article 2018 A contract of *fiducie* is void unless it specifies:

(1) the things, rights or securities transferred (if they are future things, rights or securities, they must be identifiable);

(2) the period for which they have been transferred, which must not exceed 99 years dating from the execution of the contract;

(3) the identity of the *constituant* or *constituants*;

(4) the identity of the *fiduciaire* or *fiduciaires*;

[72] Similar restrictions are, however, foreseen in Luxembourg where the *fiduciaire* must be one of a limited kind of financial institution or public bodies. Art 4 of the new Law of 27 July 2003 states that: 'This title only applies to fiduciary contracts where the fiduciary is a credit institution, an investment firm, an investment company with variable or fixed share capital, a securitisation company, a fiduciary representative acting in the context of a securitisation transaction, a management company of common funds or of securitisation funds, a pension fund, an insurance or reinsurance undertaking or a national or international public body operating in the financial sector.' For an analysis of the new law on the fiducie, see A Prüm and C Witz, 'La nouvelle fiducie luxembourgeoise', in *Trust et fiducie. La Convention de La Haye et la nouvelle législation luxembourgeoise* (Paris: Montchrestien, 2005) 65.

[73] See Art 2015(2).

(5) the identity of the beneficiary or beneficiaries, or at least provides for criteria by which they are to be ascertained;

(6) the purpose which the *fiduciaire* or *fiduciaires* have undertaken, and the extent of their powers, both administrative and dispositive.

Notes

(1) Apart from being expressly defined as *fiducie*, the contract has to indicate a number of other elements. Among these are the identities of the beneficiaries or the criteria by which they are to be ascertained. This would seem to exclude the possibility of a *fiduciaire* having any discretion to determine who will benefit from a *fiducie*, though this is not certain.

(2) Unlike the original proposal presented in 1995, the law of 2007 does not expressly require the contract to be in writing. However, a requirement of writing seems to be implicit in Article 2018, which states that the contract is void if it does not contain all of the six elements indicated above. However, this does not mean that the contract has to be written by a notary or executed before him. A private document whether on paper or in electronic form will suffice, unless, as mentioned above, the subject-matter of the *fiducie* is composed of things, rights or securities which are co-owned or which belong to spouses who are subject to the community property regime. If that is the case, the contract has to be executed before a notary.

(3) Unlike the German *Treuhand*, the *fiducie* has a maximum duration, at the end of which it is extinguished. The limit was originally proposed at 99 years, in line with the rules applicable to corporations, but then reduced to 33 years by law no 2007-211 of 19 February 2007. However, the statute passed in August 2008 moved the limit back to 99 years.

I.C.4 REGISTRATION

Code civil **6.13 (FR)**

Article 2019 A contract of *fiducie* and any variation or modification of such a contract is void unless it is registered within one month of its date with the tax office of the place where the *fiduciaire* has its seat or, where the *fiduciaire* has no domicile in France, with the tax office for non-residents.

Where such a contract or other instrument deals with immovable things or immovable property rights, it is also void unless it receives the publicity required by Articles 647 and 657 of the French Tax Code.

Both the transfer of rights resulting from a contract of *fiducie*, and, if the beneficiary is not named in the contract, his subsequent designation as beneficiary, must be in writing, to be registered as set out above.

Article 2020 A national register of *fiducies* will be constituted in accordance with the requirements of a decree of the Conseil d'État.

Notes

(1) In order to make the *fiducie* transparent, it has to be registered with the local tax administration. Although Article 2020 does not specify who has the duty to register the contract—the *constituant*, the *fiduciaire* or the beneficiary—its wording leads to the conclusion that it is the *fiduciaire*'s duty to provide for a timely registration. Given the silence of the legislature on this matter, it is also difficult to establish which is the competent tax office in case of there being more than one *fiduciaire*.

(2) The function of the national register appears to be to centralise the information concerning the contracts of *fiducie*. This way, it will be easier for the courts, as well as the institutions working against money laundering and the financing of terrorism, to exercise control over these types of transactions. In fact, according to parliamentary material, access to the register is only given to those two types of public authorities.

I.C.5 MODIFICATION, REVOCATION AND TERMINATION OF THE *FIDUCIE*

Code civil **6.14 (FR)**

Article 2028 The contract of *fiducie* may be revoked by the *constituant* at any time before it has been accepted by the beneficiary.

After such acceptance, the contract may only be modified or revoked with the consent of the beneficiary or by a decision of the court.

Article 2029 A contract of *fiducie* terminates if the *constituant* who is a natural person dies, if it reaches its expiry date or if its object has been achieved before then.

If all the beneficiaries wish it to come to an end, the *fiducie* will also terminate automatically, subject to provisions to the contrary contained in the contract which envisage the circumstances in which the contract is to continue. Subject to the same reservation, the *fiducie* terminates if the *fiduciaire* becomes subject to a compulsory liquidation (*liquidation judiciaire*) or dissolution, or ceases to exist as a result of an assignment or a merger and, in case he is an *avocat*, if he is temporarily suspended, or cancelled or omitted from the 'professional register'.

Notes

(1) The French legislature gives the *constituant* the possibility of revoking the contract at any time up to the moment at which the beneficiary accepts it. After acceptance, the contract can be modified or revoked only with his consent or by order of the court.[74] This represents a noticeable difference with the common law trust, which is usually irrevocable. The Article does not indicate the possible reasons for the revocation of the contract, these being left to the *constituant*, the beneficiary and the judge to decide. It is also silent with regard to the form prescribed for the revocation.

(2) The *fiducie* terminates if it reaches its maximum period of 99 years or if its

[74] Notice that the French legislature does not make use of the expression '*resiliation*', but '*révocation*' which is typical of the vocabulary of the mandate (Art 2004 Cciv).

object has been achieved before then. Furthermore, while the death of the *Treugeber* does not usually determine the *Treuhand*, the death of the *constituant* brings the *fiducie* to an end. Interestingly, the contract of *fiducie* can also be terminated by a decision of the court if, in the absence of terms providing for the circumstances in which the contract is to continue, all the beneficiaries wish it to come to an end. A similar rule in English law exists under the doctrine in *Saunders v Vautier* (1841) 4 Beav 115. Article 2029 also states that the *fiducie* terminates when the *fiduciaire* becomes subject to compulsory liquidation (*liquidation judiciaire*) or dissolution, or ceases to exist as a result of an assignment or merger. If the *fiduciaire* is a practising lawyer, the *fiducie* will determine if he is temporarily suspended or expelled from office. Surprisingly, nothing is said as to what happens in case of death of an *avocat* who acts as a *fiduciaire*. It seems likely, however, that such an event will bring the relationship to an end.

Code civil **6.15 (FR)**

Article 2030 If the contract of *fiducie* terminates at a time when there are no beneficiaries, the rights, things or securities forming part of the *patrimoine fiduciaire* revert to the *constituant*. If the contract terminates because of the death of the *constituant*, the *patrimoine fiduciaire* automatically reverts to the residuary estate.

Notes

(1) If the contract terminates at a time when there are no beneficiaries (because they have surrendered, or have died (if it is an individual person) or have been dissolved (if it is a corporate body), the subject-matter of the *fiducie* reverts to the *constituant*. Article 2030 also states that if the contract terminates because of the death of the *constituant*, who can now be also a natural person, the subject-matter of the *fiducie* will automatically revert back to him and form part of his residuary estate.[75]

(2) What happens if the contract comes to an end at a time when there are still beneficiaries? The legislation is silent on this point, but it is likely that the *patrimoine fiduciaire* will be distributed amongst the beneficiaries.

II. MISAPPROPRIATION OF ASSETS BY THE MANAGER

II.A ENGLISH LAW

What is the effect of the trust on third party recipients of rights dissipated in breach of trust? Where the trustee conveys away the rights he holds in breach of trust, the beneficiary may have rights against third party recipients. The rights the beneficiary

[75] Given the fact that natural persons can now create a *fiducie*, Art 2031, which established that the rights of the *constituant* under a *fiducie* are not transferable, whether by gift or for consideration except to such a legal person (that is to say a corporate body subject to corporation tax), has now been abolished.

has against such persons are, however, of a limited nature. Most importantly, he will have no rights whatsoever against a transferee of a common law right received in good faith, for value, and without notice, actual, imputed or constructive, that the dissipation was made in breach of trust. If the transferee is such a person, compendiously known as 'equity's darling', then the effect of the transfer will be to destroy any rights the beneficiary would have otherwise had against him. As we have seen, the beneficiary will still have a claim in the law of obligations against the trustee, but that may be worthless, eg because of his insolvency. If the recipient is not 'equity's darling', then the first thing to notice is that the recipieint does not step into the trustee's shoes, inheriting the duties of his transferor. The only thing the recipient must do is restore the rights dissipated in breach of trust, either to the former trustee, or, more likely, to other persons nominated by the beneficiaries. In the meantime, the recipient is said to hold the rights as trustee, though this is not the same trust as before, but one created by the courts, ie a constructive trust. Its only purpose, it seems, is to safeguard the rights until they are reconveyed. This obligation, through the law of 'tracing', also extends to rights substituted for the trust right.[76] So, for example, if a recipient receives a title to money from a trustee dissipated in breach of trust and exchanges that title for a title to a painting, the recipient will hold the title to the painting on trust for the beneficiary. This too is a constructive trust.

In exactly the same way that a transferee of a right dissipated in breach of trust is bound to restore the rights to the trustee unless he is equity's darling, so too are incumbrances created by the trustee in breach of trust not binding on the beneficiary with respect to the trust rights unless the incumbrancer is once again equity's darling. Thus, if a trustee grants a security interest over a title to land he holds on trust, the holder will take free of the beneficiary's interest if he is equity's darling. But if he is not, because, for example, the security he takes is equitable rather than legal, he will take subject to the beneficiary's interest.

What of the case where the recipient no longer has the trust right dissipated in breach of trust (or a traceable substitute) vested in him? Is there any possibility of a claim against him in the law of obligations in respect of his receipt? English law does provide such a claim, though the law in this area is unsettled, the point of dispute being whether liability is triggered only by a dishonest receipt, whether a negligent receipt suffices, or whether the mere fact of receipt triggers the liability. It is equally uncertain whether this liability is subject to a defence of good faith change of position. One of the reasons this question is so difficult is that English law is undecided on whether this obligational liability is one in wrongs, unjust enrichment, or another category altogether.

Court of Chancery, 1 January 1732[77] **6.16 (E&W)**

Mansell v Mansell

[76] On tracing, see also Chapter 7.

[77] (1732) 2 P Wms 678.

THIRD PARTY EFFECT OF TRUST

Breach of trust

Trust binds all save equity's darling.

Facts: Trustees of titles to land had in breach of trust conveyed those titles to the defendants, who could not claim to be bona fide purchasers for value without notice of the estates conveyed to them.
Held: The estates were held by the defendants subject to the trusts.

Judgment: Lord Chief Baron Reynolds—That this is a breach of trust is so plain, that I know not how, by any thing I have to say, to make it more so. Indeed, had this conveyance been for valuable consideration without notice, the purchaser could not have been affected; but when any one claims by a voluntary conveyance with notice, he must take the conveyance clothed with all its trusts.

Notes

(1) Although the case talks of the conveyance being 'clothed with all its trusts', this does not mean that the defendants assumed the position of trustees vis-à-vis the beneficiaries of the trust, merely that the titles they received in breach of trust had to be returned: *Willoughby v Willoughby* (1756) 1 TR 763, 771 (Lord Hardwicke LC).

(2) Despite what Reynolds LCB says about lack of notice, a transferee without notice who gives nothing in exchange will be bound by the trust. As the following case shows, the only person who can takes free of the trust, ie free of the obligation to return the trust right, is a bona fide purchaser of a legal estate for value without notice, actual, constructive or imputed, of the fact that the disposition to him was made in breach of trust.

Court of Appeal in Chancery, 29 January 1872[78] **6.17 (E&W)**

Pilcher v Rawlins

THIRD PARTY EFFECT OF TRUST

Trust and fraud

Good faith purchase of a legal estate for value without notice is a defence to the jurisdiction of the court of equity.

Facts: A trustee, Pilcher, lent trust funds to Rawlins, taking as security a title to land held by Rawlins. As a result, Pilcher held the title on trust for the beneficiairies. Rawlins later arranged to borrow further sums from a third party, fraudulently asserting that he still held the title which had been previously conveyed to Pilcher as security. Pilcher joined in Rawlins' fraudulent scheme, and, in breach of trust, conveyed the title to Rawlins for this purpose, though without the secured debt being redeemed, and without the two conveyances, that to Pilcher as security and that from Pilcher to Rawlins, being revealed to the third party. When the fraud was discovered, the beneficiaries claimed that the third party mortgagee held his title subject to their interests under the trust.

[78] (1872) LR 7 Ch 259.

Held: The Court of Appeal held that as the third party was a good faith purchaser of a legal estate for value without notice, he took free of the beneficiaries' interests.

Judgment: Sir WM James LJ—I propose simply to apply myself to the case of a purchaser for valuable consideration, without notice, obtaining, upon the occasion of his purchase, and by means of his purchase deed, some legal estate, some legal right, some legal advantage; and, according to my view of the established law of this Court, such a purchaser's plea of a purchase for valuable consideration without notice is an absolute, unqualified, unanswerable defence, and an unanswerable plea to the jurisdiction of this Court. Such a purchaser, when he has once put in that plea, may be interrogated and tested to any extent as to the valuable consideration which he has given in order to shew the bona fides or mala fides of his purchase, and also the presence or the absence of notice; but when once he has gone through that ordeal, and has satisfied the terms of the plea of purchase for valuable consideration without notice, then, according to my judgment, this Court has no jurisdiction whatever to do anything more than to let him depart in possession of that legal estate, that legal right, that legal advantage which he has obtained, whatever it may be. In such a case a purchaser is entitled to hold that which, without breach of duty, he has had conveyed to him.

Lord Hatherley LC delivered a concurring judgment.

Sir G Mellish LJ—The general rule seems to be laid down in the clearest terms by all the great authorities in equity, and has been acted on for a great number of years, namely, that this Court will not take an estate from a purchaser who has bought for valuable consideration without notice; and I find that the Appellants in both the cases before us are very clearly purchasers for valuable consideration without notice.

Note

This rule is not peculiar to the interests of beneficiaries of a trust, but applies to all rights, proprietary or personal, recognised only by equity. It is further considered in Chapter 9.

II.B GERMAN LAW

Since the *Treuhänder* is the owner of the *Treugut*, he can dispose of it. In doing so, he encounters certain limitations set out in the *Treuhandabrede*, but these have only obligatory effect, by which is meant that dispositions made in breach of such obligations are generally valid. However, where the *Treuhänder* conveys away the rights he is holding in breach of the contract, the *Treugeber* (or the beneficiary, if the *Treuhand* is set up in favour of a third party beneficiary) has a claim to compensation against the *Treuhänder* who is liable for intentional or negligent breach of his duties in accordance with the rules concerning mandates. Differently to the common law trustee, the *Treuhänder* is not strictly liable for breach of the *Treuhandvertrag*.

If the *Treuhänder* is solvent, the interests of the *Treugeber* or the third party beneficiary are sufficiently protected by their claim to compensation. A problem arises in the case of the *Treuhänder*'s insolvency. Has the *Treugeber* or the third party beneficiary any claim against the transferee? If the transferee was merely negligent in his receipt, he will acquire the rights from the *Treuhänder* free from any obligation towards the *Treugeber* or third party beneficiary. In such case, it is not relevant that he knew or ought to have known that the assets were part of a *Treugut*. Neither actual nor constructive notice will make the transferee liable.[79] Things are, however, different where the third party transferee deliberately conspires with the *Treuhänder* in an attempt to damage the *Treugeber* or the third party beneficiary. In such a case, the *Treugeber* or beneficiary has a claim in tort on the basis of §826 BGB.[80]

BGH, 9 July 1992[81] **6.18 (DE)**

PARTICIPATION IN BREACH OF CONTRACT COMMITTED BY THE TREUHÄNDER

Misappropriation of *Treugut*

A person who is aware of a Treuhandabrede and is involved in a breach of contract by the fiduciary may be liable to pay damages under §826 of the BGB.

Facts: The claimant and defendant, who were at the time married, were co-owners of a developed parcel of land on which the defendant managed a beauty farm in the form of a limited liability company. The claimant acquired two savings certificates (*Sparkassenbriefe*) of DM40,000 and DM170,000 respectively. The certificates were issued in the name of the mother of the defendant, the mother having given the claimant a power of attorney. Both certificates were pledged in order to secure the joint obligations of the parties. Later, the mother of the defendant revoked the power of attorney and instead granted another to the defendant. The defendant used the power to transfer the savings certificates into her own name and later used the money represented by the certificates to purchase new ones in her own name, which she also pledged. The claimant demanded the defendant pay him DM210,000 with interest. He based his claim upon the allegation that the mother of the defendant held the savings certificates as a fiduciary for tax reasons and that from an economic point of view he had remained the owner of the claim. Against this the defendant opposed that her mother was the owner of the claim, who had made an outright gift to her. The lower courts rejected the claim.

Held: The judgments of the lower courts were set aside.

Judgment: 3. (a) On the basis of the alleged *Treuhandabrede* between the claimant and the defendant's mother there may be a claim for damages against the defendant under §826 of the BGB. For the purposes of an appeal on a point of law, the defendant may be presumed to have had knowledge of the *Treuhandabrede*. The appellant on a point of law correctly complains that the appeal court did not adequately elucidate the facts on this point and disregarded offers to adduce evidence. Underlying the claimant's submissions, including his requests to adduce evidence and to hear the evidence of the tax advisor and of the defendant, is the assertion that all participants, including the defendant, were aware that for tax reasons the mother was put up only as a 'nominee'.

In accordance with settled case-law, the involvement of the third party in the breach of a contract by one contracting party may in appropriate circumstances constitute an unlawful injury of the other contracting party giving rise to a claim

[79] See BGH, 4 April 1968, NJW 1968, 1471.

[80] §826 BGB reads: 'A person who, in a manner contrary to public policy, intentionally inflicts damage on another person is liable to the other person to make compensation for the damage.'

[81] NJW-RR 1993, 367. Before that see BGH, 24 February 1954, BGHZ 12, 308, 317; NJW 1954, 1159; BGH, 19 February 1979, NJW 1979, 1704; BGH, 13 March 1981, WM 1981, 624, 625; BGH, 1 April 1992, NJW 1992, 2152. See also BGH, 25 September 1990, NJW 1991, 101.

for damages by analogy with §826 BGB. However, mere involvement of a third party in a breach of contract is not sufficient; rather there must be specific circumstances occurring that characterise that person's conduct as an injurious act. That would, for instance, be the case where a contracting party is induced into a breach of contract or where there is a systematic concerted breach. A permissible indication of illegality will be found where there is a breach of duties imposed on a contracting party under a particular relationship of loyalty, for example under a deed of incorporation or, as in this case, under a *Treuhandabrede* with the *Treugeber*.

An intentional injurious act giving rise to a claim for damages under §826 of the BGB may be constituted by the fact that the defendant, although aware of her mother's fiduciary obligations, prompted her mother, who was more than eighty years of age, to revoke the claimant's authority and to transfer it to herself, thus enabling her—by assignment under the self-contracting provisions in paragraph 181 of the BGB—to have the letters transcribed into her own name and thereby incorporated into her own patrimony. There is the additional factor of the secrecy of the proceedings since, under an instruction from the mother of 17 February 1984, the LzO (Oldenburg Savings Bank) was no longer allowed to provide the claimant with information. These are matters that the appeal court will have to include in its evaluation of the case should it be established, as the claimant has alleged, that there was a *Treuhandabrede* which the defendant was aware of.

Notes

(1) According to the prevailing case law, in order to hold the third party transferee liable for his actions, it is not sufficient that he merely participated in the breach of contract. The third party transferee must have either induced the *Treuhänder* to breach the contract or systematically collaborated with him in the breach. Pursuant to §249 BGB, the claim against the third party transferee can also have as its object the transfer of the asset from the third person to the *Treugeber*.[82]

(2) Additionally, the transaction between the *Treuhänder* and the third party transferee can be considered either as against good morals, and therefore void under part 1 of §138 BGB,[83] or as in breach of a statute and thus void under §134 BGB.[84]

(3) The situation can also amount to a criminal offence (§266 of the Strafgesetzbuch (StGB = Criminal Code,[85] in connection with §823(2) BGB).[86] In fact, if the *Treuhänder* commits a breach of his fiduciary duties that is considered

[82] §249(1) BGB reads: 'A person who is liable for damages must restore the position that would exist had the circumstances obliging him to pay damages not occurred.'

[83] §138(1) BGB states: 'A legal transaction which is contrary to good morals is void.'

[84] §134 BGB states: 'A legal transaction that violates a statutory prohibition is void, unless the statute leads to a different conclusion.'

[85] §266 StGB(1) states: (1) Whoever abuses the power accorded him by statute, by commission of a public authority or legal transaction to dispose of assets of another or to obligate another, or violates the duty to safeguard the property interests of another incumbent upon him by reason of statute, commission of a public authority, legal transaction or fiduciary relationship, and thereby causes detriment to the person whose property unterest he was responsible for, shall be punished with imprisonment for no more than five years or a fine.

[86] §823(1) BGB reads: 'A person who, intentionally or negligently, unlawfully injures the life, body, health, freedom, property or another right of another person is liable to make compensation to the other party for the damage arising from this.'

culpable, and this is known to the third party transferee, the latter becomes an accomplice in a criminal offence and will be obliged to return what he has received.

BGH, 4 April 1968[87] **6.19 (DE)**

EFFECT OF DISPOSITIONS MADE IN BREACH OF A PROHIBITION TO DISPOSE

Inheritance and management of shares

The principle that no rights accrue under a legal transaction entered into by a representative manifestly in breach of his mandate does not apply to the relationship between a shareholder and a Treuhänder.

Facts: Three brothers, the two defendants and the claimant's father, were shareholders and directors in several companies. While the father was still alive, his two brothers created another company, along with the claimant's mother. This second company invested in land. The mother and her two daughters inherited the patrimony of the claimant's father. In 1953, the company acquired several pieces of land and the relations between the shareholders were, by contract, reordered. The mother was to be entitled to one fifth, and the two brothers were each to have two fifths. The mother received financial compensation for this. A representative of the children, who were minors at that time, participated in the operation.

After the death of her father, the claimant, having now attained her majority, challenged the division, claiming a higher share (that is to say, $16^2/_3$%). The claimant argued that the mother, in agreement with all parties, had participated in the land acquisition company merely as a *Treuhänderin* of the claimant's father. After the death of the father, the mother therefore automatically became *Treuhänderin* of the patrimony of the father. In her capacity as *Treuhänderin*, she could have agreed to the redivision of the shares only with the express consent of all the heirs, which was not however obtained. The claim was rejected in the lower courts.

Held: The relationship between a *Treugeber* and a *Treuhänder* is personal and has no third party effect; the present facts amounted to a case of *Treuhand* to which the principles of representation do not apply, the *Treuhänder* acting in his own name. Thus the claim of the claimant was rejected.

Judgment: The appellant seeks to transpose to the fiduciary relationship the principle that no rights may derive from a legal transaction that a representative enters into in manifest disregard of the terms of his authority (BGH, NJW 66, 1911 and further references). That cannot be accepted. The representative acts in the name of the person represented. The transaction cannot have effect against his will if his contrary intention was known or ought to have been known to the contractual partner. In a fiduciary relationship the *Treuhänder* acts in his own name and by his own right. Such prohibition on dispositions as may exist within the internal fiduciary relationship with the *Treugeber* can have no effect *in rem* (§137 BGB). Dispositions by the *Treuhänder* must therefore as a matter of principle be recognised as valid even if they have been made in breach of a prohibition to make dispositions. … Legal certainty requires nothing less (Soergel-Schultze Lasaulx, BGB, 10th Ed, §264, preliminary observation 73). Contrary to the appellant's view, that cannot be altered even by the duty of loyalty under a shareholder relationship and a situation where the persons involved are related. Aside from his entitlement to claim damages against the *Treuhänder*, the *Treugeber* can only be afforded protection under §§138, 823 (2)

[87] NJW 1968, 1471; JZ 1968, 428; WM 1968, 649. See also BGH, 4 November 1976, WM 1977, 525, 527 (with casenote written by U Huber).

(in conjunction with §266 of the Criminal Code—StGB) or 826 of the BGB. However, these provisions do not avail the claimant.

Notes

(1) Several commentators have suggested the application of the doctrine of abuse of agency (*Missbrauch der Vertretungsvollmacht*)[88] to the abuse of the power to dispose of a thing belonging to the *Treugut*. According to this doctrine, a person who concludes a contract with an agent or representative cannot derive rights from the contract if, by the exercise of reasonable care, he would have known that the agent was abusing his authority in entering the contract. Despite the fact that many legal writers favour such an application,[89] German courts have rejected the idea.[90] There are essentially three reasons for this and they are clearly outlined in the case above. First, the position of the *Treuhänder* cannot be compared to that of a person receiving an authority, since he acts in his own name and disposes of his own rights, while the representative acts in the name of the person represented.[91] Second, it is said that the application of the provisions concerning the *Vollmacht* is incompatible with §137 BGB, which forbids any exclusion or limitation of the power to dispose of alienable rights.[92] Third, it would be contrary to the principle of clarity of the law (*Rechtsklarheit*).

(2) In order to achieve a better protection for the *Treugeber* or the beneficiary, the transfer of the rights to the *Treuhänder* could be brought under the resolutory condition that the *Treuhänder* does not misappropriate the *Treugut*. These sorts of conditions are occasionally employed when a transfer is made for security purposes (see the *Sicherungsübereignung*).[93] In such cases §161 of the BGB[94] is applied and a disposition in breach of duty is considered ineffective.[95]

[88] On the doctrine of abuse of agency see BGH, 28 February 1966, *Neue Juristische Wochenschrift* (*NJW*) 1966, 1911.

[89] So eg H Kötz, 'The Modern Development of Trust Law in Germany', in D Hayton (ed), *Modern International Developments in Trust Law* (The Hague, London, Boston, Kluwer Law International, 1999) 49, at 61; id, (1968) NJW 1471 (note to BGH 4 April 1968); H Schlosser, 'Außenwirkungen verfügungshindernder Abreden bei der rechtsgeschäftlichen Treuhand' [1970] *NJW* 681; U Huber [1968] *JZ* 791 (note to BGH 4 November 1976); V Beuthien, 'Treuhand and Gesellschaftsanteilen' [1974] *ZGR* 26, at 60.

[90] BGH 4 November 1976, WM 1977, 525, 527.

[91] This argument has met with increasing criticism on the part of the legal academics. See amongst the others Kötz, above n 89, 61 and Coing, above n 9, 165 *et seq.*

[92] §137 BGB reads: 'The power to dispose of an alienable right may not be excluded or restricted by a legal transaction. This effectiveness of an obligation not to dispose of such a right is not affected by this provision.'

[93] See Chapter 5.

[94] §161 BGB states: '(1) If a person has disposed of a thing, and the disposition is subject to a condition precedent, any further disposition which he makes as regards the thing in the period of suspense is ineffective on the satisfaction of the condition to the extent that it would defeat or adversely affect the effect subject to the condition. Such a disposition is equivalent to a disposition which is effected during the period of suspense by execution or attachment or by the administrator in insolvency proceedings. (2) In the case of a condition subsequent, the same applies to the dispositions of a person whose right expires on the fulfilment of the condition.'

[95] A solution also suggested by W Siebert, *Das rechtsgeschäftliche Treuhandverhältnis* (Marburg, Elwert, 1933) 219–20.

II.C FRENCH LAW

Code civil **6.20 (FR)**

Article 2026 The *fiduciaire* is personally liable for any wrongs that he commits whilst carrying out his functions.

Notes

(1) According to Article 2026, the liability of the French *fiduciaire*, differently to the liability of the English trustee, is not strict but depends on the degree of his wrongdoing.[96] This is similar, as we have seen, to the case of the German *Treuhänder*, who is liable only for intentional or negligent breach of duty. The initial proposal for the introduction of a *fiducie* foresaw a different grading of the liability based on the gravity of the wrong committed by the *fiduciaire*. The Senate, however, came to the conclusion that such distinctions were not necessary as the role of a *fiduciaire* can only be taken up by corporate bodies in the banking, insurance or finance sectors, already subject to state control. However, this has changed given that *avocats* can now act as a *fiduciaire*. Be that as it may, it appears that the French legislature intended to give the judiciary sufficient discretion in order to evaluate each specific case.[97]

(2) Interestingly, the French legislature has not established precisely what type of liability it is referring to. Is it liability for breach of contract or liability in tort? The report drafted by Xavier de Roux tells us that this was a deliberate choice of the draftsmen.[98] It is further explained that if the victim is party to the contract (such as is the *constituant*), he will probably sue the *fiduciaire* for breach of contract (in accordance with Article 1147 Cciv). On the other hand, if the victim is a third party, the rules on liability on tort will be applicable (Article 1382 Cciv). So far as third party beneficiaries are concerned, one has to consider whether the beneficiary has accepted the *fiducie*,[99] in which case he could be considered a party to the contract and therefore sue for breach of contract. Otherwise, it is more likely that the tort rules will apply.

(3) A problem may arise if the *fiduciaire* is insolvent. What rights, if any, does the beneficiary have against third parties who receive the rights held by the *fiduciaire* or who assist him in the commission of his breach of fiduciary duties? The French legislature has not specifically addressed the question, Article 2023 Cciv merely providing that:

[96] Furthermore, according to Art 2027, in the absence of contractual terms providing for its replacement, if the *fiduciaire* fails in his duty or endagers the interests which have been entrusted to him, or if he is made object of a *procédure de sauvegarde* or *redressement judiciaire*, he can be replaced at the behest of the *constituant*, the third party beneficiaries or the third party nominated according to Art 2017.

[97] Rapp AN no 3655, at 51.

[98] *Ibid.*

[99] Art 2028 refers to the fact that the beneficiary can accept the benefit. The acceptance does not seem to constitute a condition for the validity of the contract. After such acceptance, the contract may only be modified or revoked with the consent of the beneficiary or by a decision of the court. See above at 6.14 (FR).

> In dealing with third parties, a *fiduciaire* is deemed to enjoy the widest powers over the fiduciary patrimony, except to the extent that the third party is shown to know of any limitation on those powers.

Nothing is said as to whether the transaction is void where the third party knows that the *fiduciaire* acted beyond his powers.[100]

III. THE DEATH OF THE MANAGER

III.A ENGLISH LAW

Introductory Note

It is standard practice for trust rights to be vested in two or more trustees as joint tenants. One reason for this is that on the death of one, the doctrine of survivorship (*jus accrescendi*) will ensure that the rights remain vested in the surviving trustee(s) and not pass to the estate of the deceased trustee. Where, however, the trustee was the sole trustee on his death, the rights will devolve on his personal representatives, those appointed by his will to administer his estate or, where he dies intestate, his administrator. Such persons will not, however, take the rights outright (beneficially) but subject to the trust. Nor will persons to whom the rights are distributed by the executor or administrator take outright. In this respect, the holders of such rights are treated no differently from recipients from a trustee who had dissipated the trust rights in breach of trust.

The proposition that recipients of trust rights on the death of the trustee are bound by the trust, in the sense that they cannot retain such rights for their own benefit, is so well entrenched in English law that it is difficult to find authority in support. What case law there is takes that for granted, and deals with the further question whether the recipient can exercise the powers of management as could the deceased trustee. At common law, the answer to that question was that he could not.

Court of Chancery, 25 May 1847[101] **6.21 (E&W)**

Mortimer v Ireland

WHETHER UNAUTHORISED RECIPIENT OF TRUST RIGHTS A TRUSTEE

Unauthorised receipt

Unauthorised recipient of trust rights does not have rights and duties of trustees.

Facts: The survivor of two executors and trustees bequeathed the trust property to Ireland, upon the

[100] According to Paul Matthews, if the fiduciaire acts beyond his powers, and the third party is aware of this, the contract will be void, and each party will be returned to his/her previous position. The third party will not obtain the property right he/she was bargaining for, and any money paid will have to be returned: Matthews, above n 50, 22.

[101] (1847) 16 LJ Ch 416, (1847) 6 Hare 196.

trusts declared by the original testator, the settlor, expressing by the same instrument his wish that Ireland would execute the trusts with fidelity. No direction was given by the will of the original testator as to the appointment of new trustees. A bill was filed by the *cestuis que trust* for the appointment of new trustees of the legacies, and the transfer to them of the funds and securities upon which they were invested. The claimants argued that though the trust funds and securities had, by operation of law, become vested in the defendant, Ireland, and the trust property being the property of the *cestuis que trust*, Ireland was in that sense a trustee, yet he was not a trustee in whom the settlor had reposed any confidence, nor a trustee appointed under any competent authority, and that, therefore, the claimants (in the absence of any express power to appoint new trustees) were entitled to have trustees appointed by the court. Ireland was merely the party to whom both the law and Mr Pruen, the last survivor of the two trustees, had given the custody of the trust property until new trustees should be duly constituted. The trust created by the original will contained discretionary powers of investment which the original trustees had no authority to delegate. The Vice-Chancellor, Sir James Wigram, held that the claimants were entitled to have new trustees appointed under the decree of the court. That the property should be vested in a representative of the survivor of the trustees was a consequence which the testator must be supposed to have contemplated; but such a representative could not claim to hold it as the trustee of the parties beneficially interested against their will. It was not a case in which any special confidence had been delegated. He referred it to the Master to appoint two proper persons to be trustees of the trust monies and premises, the defendant, Ireland, to be at liberty to propose himself as one of such trustees, but that to be without prejudice to any question in the cause. His decision was upheld on appeal to the Lord Chancellor.

Held: that Ireland, though legally in the possession of the trust property, was not a trustee properly constituted, and that the *cestuis que trust* were entitled to have new trustees appointed by the Court.

Judgment: Lord Lyndhurst LC: 'The property might vest in the personal representatives of the ... trustee, but they were not placed in such a position as to establish the character of trustees and cestuis que trust between themselves and the persons who were beneficially interested in the fund'.

Note

The rule in this case has been altered by statute. Although the personal representatives are not bound to act as trustees, they now have the power to do so if they wish: Trustee Act 1925, s 18(2).

Trustee Act 1925 **6.22 (E&W)**

Section 18(2) Until the appointment of new trustees, the personal representatives or representative for the time being of a sole trustee, or, where there were two or more trustees of the last surviving or continuing trustee, shall be capable of exercising or performing any power or trust which was given to, or capable of being exercised by, the sole or last surviving or continuing trustee, or other the tursteees or trustee for the time being of the trust.

III.B GERMAN LAW

Bürgerliches Gesetzbuch **6.23 (DE)**

§673 Death of the mandatary In case of doubt, the mandate is extinguished on the death of the mandatary. If the mandate is extinguished, then the heir of the mandatary must notify the mandator of the death without undue delay and, if postponement entails danger, must continue carrying out the transaction entrusted to him until the mandator can make other arrangements for the agency business; in this respect, the mandate is deemed to continue.

§667 Duty to return The mandatary is obliged to return to the mandator everything he receives to perform the mandate and that which he obtains from carrying out the transaction.

Notes

(1) Whilst a trust does not usually fail for want of a trustee, in the case of the *Treuhand*, the *Treuhandvertrag* will provide whether or not the death of the *Treuhänder* terminates the relationship.[102] If there is only one *Treuhänder* and the contract is silent on the matter, the relationship usually comes to an end. This can be deduced from the provision in §673 BGB concerning the death of the mandatary which is applicable to the *Treuhand.*[103]

(2) If the *Treuhand* terminates, the *Treugut* falls formally within the residuary estate of the *Treuhänder*.[104] As a consequence, certain follow-up obligations arise for the heir of the *Treuhänder*,[105] who has to continue managing the *Treugut* until the *Treugeber* can make other arrangements. Moreover, according to §667 BGB,[106] the heir has to release the *Treugut* and, if necessary, to account for his actions.

(3) Things are different where there is more than one *Treuhänder* and they have, for instance, founded a partnership.[107] In this case, the contract with the partnership does not terminate with the death provided that the partnership agreement says so: §736 BGB.[108]

(4) If, on the other hand, the *Treuhänder* is a corporate body, the *Treuhand* terminates with the dissolution of the corporate body, while in the case of a merger, the absorbing company takes over the duties arising out of the *Treuhand.*[109]

III.C FRENCH LAW

Until August 2008, the manager of a *fiducie* could only be a corporate body, and the problem was therefore one of dissolution of that body. As has been seen

[102] KG 12 March 1931, HRR 1931, no 1866.

[103] On the other hand, the death of the *Treugeber* does not usually determine the end of the *Treuhand* (§§672, 675 BGB) and his heir will become the *Treugeber*.

[104] KG 12 March 1931, HRR 1931, no 1866. See also, KG, 5 June 1930, JFG 7, 299, 307.

[105] Coing, above n 9, 184. The case is different where the holder of a *Treuhandkonto* or *Anderkonto*, such as a notary or a fincancial advisor, dies.

[106] In relation to the right to demand the release (*Herausgabeanspruch*) see M Martinek, §667, Rn 17, Staudinger BGB, 2006.

[107] Coing, above n 9, 188.

[108] §736 BGB reads: 'If the partnership agreement stipulates that if a partner gives notice or dies or if insolvency proceedings are opened in relation to his assets, the partnership will be carried on by the remaining partners, then upon the occurrence of such an event the partner personally so affected retires from the partnership'.

[109] KG 5 June 1930, JFG 7, 299, 307.

above,[110] Article 2029 Cciv establishes in paragraph 2 that the contract terminates if the *fiduciaire* becomes subject to *liquidation judiciaire* or dissolution, or ceases to exist as a result of a merger or an assignment. Given that practising lawyers too can now act as a *fiduciaire*, the newly formulated paragraph 1 of the same Article states that the *fiducie* comes to an end if the *fiduciaire*, who is a practising lawyer, is temporarily suspended or expelled from office. As mentioned earlier, and somewhat surprisingly, Article 2029 does not mention the death of the practising lawyer who acts as a *fiduciaire*. It seems, however, likely that, as in Germany, and differently to England, the lack of a *fiduciaire* brings the relationship to an end. As far as the impact of the dissolution of the fiduciaire on the *patrimoine fiduciaire* is concerned, reference should be made to what is said above in relation to Article 2030.[111]

IV. INSOLVENCY OF THE MANAGER (INCLUDING CASES WHERE PERSONAL CREDITORS OF THE MANAGER TRY TO SEIZE THE FUND HE IS MANAGING)

IV.A ENGLISH LAW

Statute of 13th Elizabeth I **6.24 (E&W)**

The commissioners shall have power and authority to sell and dispose of such lands which the bankrupt had in his own right, and for such use and interest right or title as such banrkrupt had in the same, and his or her money goods chattels wares merchandizes and debts.

Insolvency Act 1986 **6.25 (E&W)**

Section 283 (1) Subject as follows, a bankrupt's estate for the purposes of any of this Group of Parts comprises—

(a) all property belonging to or vested in the bankrupt at the commencement of the bankruptcy, and

(b) any property which by virtue of any of the following provisions of this Part is comprised in that estate or is treated as falling within the preceding paragraph.

(2) Subsection (1) does not apply to—

(a) such tools, books, vehicles and other items of equipment as are necessary to the bankrupt for use personally by him in his employment, business or vocation;

(b) such clothing, bedding, furniture, household equipment and provisions as are necessary for satisfying the basic domestic needs of the bankrupt and his family. …

[110] Above 6.14 (FR).
[111] Above 6.15 (FR).

(3) Subsection (1) does not apply to—

(a) property held by the bankrupt on trust for any other person, or

(b) the right of nomination to a vacant ecclesiastical benefice.

High Court of Justice, 4 October 1974[112] **6.26 (E&W)**

Re Kayford

WHETHER VENDOR OF GOOD CREATED TRUST OF PAYMENTS

Money on trust

Payment of purchase monies into customers' trust account created a trust.

Facts: Customers of a company which carried on a mail order business either paid the full price for the goods in advance or paid a deposit. By November 1972, the company's chief suppliers got into difficulties and went into liquidation. The company could not meet the orders. It was advised by its accountants to open a separate bank account (to be called a 'Customers' Trust Deposit Account') and to pay into it moneys received from customers for goods not delivered to them, withdrawing the moneys only if the goods were later delivered. The object of the arrangement was that should the company go into liquidation, the moneys in the deposit account could and would be refunded to those customers who could not be supplied with the goods they had ordered. The company accepted the advice and paid the moneys into a dormant deposit account in the company's name. One month later, the company went into voluntary liquidation. The liquidator issued a summons seeking to determine whether the moneys formed part of the general assets of the company or whether they were held on trust for the customers in proportion to the amounts paid by them.

Held: The moneys were held by the insolvent company on trust and did not therefore form part of the estate available for liquidation.

Judgment: Megarry J—The question for me is whether the money in the bank account ... is held on trust for those who paid it, or whether it forms part of the general assets of the company. Mr Heyman appears for the joint liquidators, one of whom is ... Mr Wainwright: and he has contended that there is no trust, so that the money forms part of the general assets of the company and thus will be available for the creditors generally. On the other hand, Mr Kennedy appears for a Mr Joels, who on December 12 paid the company £32.20 for goods which have not been delivered; and a representation order is sought on behalf of all others whose moneys have been paid into the bank account, some 700 or 800 in number. I make that order. Mr Kennedy, of course, argued for the existence of an effective trust. I may say at the outset that on the facts of the case Mr Heyman was unable to contend that any question of a fraudulent preference arose. If one leaves on one side any case in which an insolvent company seeks to declare a trust in favour of creditors, one is concerned here with the question not of preferring creditors but of preventing those who pay money from becoming creditors, by making them beneficiaries under a trust. I should add that I had some initial

[112] [1975] 1 WLR 279.

doubts about whether Mr Joels was the most suitable representative beneficiary, in view of the date when he paid his money, and whether Mr Heyman, in representing Mr Wainwright (as well as the other joint liquidator), was not to some degree committed to arguing against the efficacy of the course that Mr Wainwright had advised: but discussion has allayed these doubts.

Now there are clearly some loose ends in the case. Mr Kay, advised to establish a 'Customers' Trust Deposit Account', seems to have thought that it did not matter what the account was called so long as there was a separate account; and so the dormant deposit account suggested by the bank manager was used. The bank statement for this account is before me, and on the first page, for which the title is simply 'Deposit account Kayford Ltd', nearly £26,000 is credited. The second and third pages have the words 'Customer Trust Deposit Account' added after the previous title of the account; and Mr Joels' payment was made after these words had been added. Mr Kay also left matters resting on a telephone conversation with the bank manager until he wrote his letter of December 12 to the bank. That letter reads: 'We confirm our instructions regarding the opening of the deposit account for customer deposits for new orders'; and he then makes some mention of other accounts with the bank. The letter goes on: 'Please ensure the reopened deposit account is titled "Customer Trust Deposit Account"'. Then he gives the reference number and asks for confirmation that this has been done. Nevertheless, despite the loose ends, when I take as a whole the affidavits of Mr Wainwright, Mr Kay and Mr Hall (the bank manager) I feel no doubt that the intention was that there should be a trust. There are no formal difficulties. The property concerned is pure personalty, and so writing, though desirable, is not an essential. There is no doubt about the so-called 'three certainties' of a trust. The subject-matter to be held on trust is clear, and so are the beneficial interests therein, as well as the beneficiaries. As for the requisite certainty of words, it is well settled that a trust can be created without using the words 'trust' or 'confidence' or the like: the question is whether in substance a sufficient intention to create a trust has been manifested.

In *re Nanwa Gold Mines Ltd* [1955] 1 WLR 1080 the money was sent on the faith of a promise to keep it in a separate account, but there is nothing in that case or in any other authority that I know of to suggest that this is essential. I feel no doubt that here a trust was created. From the outset the advice (which was accepted) was to establish a trust account at the bank. The whole purpose of what was done was to ensure that the moneys remained in the beneficial ownership of those who sent them, and a trust is the obvious means of achieving this. No doubt the general rule is that if you send money to a company for goods which are not delivered, you are merely a creditor of the company unless a trust has been created. The sender may create a trust by using appropriate words when he sends the money (though I wonder how many do this, even if they are equity lawyers), or the company may do it by taking suitable steps on or before receiving the money. If either is done, the obligations in respect of the money are transformed from contract to property, from debt to trust. Payment into a separate bank account is a useful (though by no means conclusive) indication of an intention to create a trust, but of course there is nothing to prevent the company from binding itself by a trust even if there are no effective banking arrangements.

Accordingly, of the alternative declarations sought by the summons, the second, to the effect that the money is held in trust for those who paid it, is in my judgment the declaration that should be made. I understand that questions may be raised as to resorting to the interest on the moneys as a means of discharging the costs of the summons; on that I will, of course, hear argument. I should, however, add one thing. Different considerations may perhaps arise in relation to trade creditors; but here I am concerned only with members of the public, some of whom can ill afford to exchange their money for a claim to a dividend in the liquidation, and all of whom are likely to be anxious to avoid this. In cases concerning the public, it seems to me that where money in advance is being paid to a company in return for the future supply of goods or services, it is an entirely proper and honourable thing for a company to do what this company did, upon skilled advice, namely, to start to pay the money into a trust account as soon as there begin to be doubts as to the company's ability to fulfil its obligations to deliver the goods or provide the services. I wish that, sitting in this court, I had heard of this occurring more frequently; and I can only hope that I shall hear more of it in the future.

Notes

(1) Although Megarry J denied it, many writers argue that the act of the company in creating a trust for certain of its customers was a fraudulent preference: see eg Goodhart and Jones (1980) 43 *MLR* 489.

(2) Although not dealt with in this chapter, it should be noted that the immunity of trust rights from the insolvency of the trustee also extends to rights held on constructive trusts. Indeed, it is often for this reason that the claimant asks the court to create such a trust in his favour, which request was granted by Goulding J in *Chase Manhatten v Israel-British Bank* [1981] Ch 1–5, where US$2 million was paid by the claimant to the defendant by mistake. Given the preferential insolvency treatment such trusts give, their award is contentious in the extreme.

IV.B GERMAN LAW

Reichsgericht, 23 December 1899[113] **6.27 (DE)**

INSOLVENCY OF THE MANAGER

Separation of interests

An asset conveyed to the insolvent on the understanding that it may not be treated by him as belonging to his patrimony and that, from an economic point of view, it is to remain the property of the transferor, only belongs to the insolvent in a formal and legal sense, not substantively and economically.

Facts: The claimants demanded the separation of interests in land included in the insolvency of the businessman H. They claimed that their testator had transferred the assets to the businessman St but only as security for a loan. Once the loan had been repaid, St had transferred the interests to H on instruction of the claimants who had authorised H to hold the interests for them in order to facilitate the management of the inheritance. The trustee in bankruptcy (the defendant) refused to transfer the interests to the claimants because according to him they no longer belonged to the claimants who did not therefore have a right to demand the separation of their interest.

The judge of first instance rejected the request of separation, but on appeal the court found that the trustee in bankruptcy had to transfer the interest to the claimants.

Held: The appeal against this decision is rejected.

Judgment: This is a fiduciary transaction concerning a transfer of assets that was not intended to increase the patrimony of the beneficiary H, but was carried out in the claimants' interests so as to facilitate the disposal of the shares in the assets to third parties through the intermediary of H. Merely to instruct H to sell was not satisfactory to the claimants because they wished to avoid the difficulties which could arise in connection with completion of the sale entered into by H or completion of several sales by several heirs. That is why they chose the method of transferring the assets to their representative H, which enabled him to complete the intended sales transaction without their further involvement. The transfer of assets was therefore based on a power that required H to dispose of the assets conveyed to him only within the limits of his mandate and, in particular, not to treat it as part of his own patrimony. There was a consensus that H was only the bare owner for the claimants and, as a further consequence thereof, was obliged to transfer the assets back to the claimants if the instruction to sell were to be withdrawn before it was acted upon or otherwise cancelled, as is now the case as a result of the initiation of bankruptcy proceedings concerning H. Unless otherwise provided for by the insolvency rules, the trustee in bankruptcy must be regarded as obliged to return the shares in the assets to the claimants for, in the absence of any legal provision to the contrary, the insolvent's creditors cannot, for the purpose of satisfying their claims from the insolvent's patrimony, be entitled to more rights than the insolvent himself possessed. In particular, they may not dispose of the assets of the insolvent in a manner which was not open to the insolvent himself and would even found an allegation of fraud. ...

An item conveyed to the insolvent on the understanding that it may not be

[113] RGZ 45, 80, at 85.

treated by him as belonging to his property but, from an economic point of view, is to remain part of the property of the transferor, belongs to the insolvent in a formal and legal sense but not substantively and economically; therefore, from that latter point of view it would even be inaccurate if the legislature were to seek to apply those terms also to this relationship.

Insolvency Act[114] **6.28 (DE)**

§47 Right to separation A person who on the basis of a property right or a personal right is entitled to claim that an object does not belong to the assets involved in the insolvency proceedings [*Insolvenzmasse*], is not a creditor of the insolvency proceedings. His claim to separation of the object is governed by the laws that apply outside the insolvency proceedings.

Notes

(1) From an early stage, German courts sought to provide protection for the *Treugeber* or third party beneficiary in the case of insolvency of the *Treuhänder*, by granting them a right to request the release of the assets of the fund on the basis of §47 of the German Insolvency Act (*Insolvenzordnung*),[115] unless the *Treuhänder* was merely a nominee (*Strohmann*) of the *Treugeber*.[116]

(2) The reason usually given by the courts to justify such protection is that, from an economic point of view, the *Treugut* is considered to remain part of the patrimony of the *Treugeber*. In other words, the *Treuhänder* owns the assets only in form, not in substance.[117] This however seems to be so only when the *Treuhand* fulfils management purposes.[118] In fact, in the case of a *Treuhand* for security purposes, the right to demand the release of the asset (*Aussonderungsrecht*) is given if the debt (which has been secured) has been extinguished. As long as the debt is not extinguished, the trustee in bankruptcy of the *Treuhänder*, is entitled to keep the asset.[119]

(3) In order to avoid any difficulties and to achieve a high level of protection of the *Treugeber* or third party beneficiary, parties often agree in practice upon a resolutory condition by means of which, in case of insolvency of the *Treuhänder*, the *Treugut* returns automatically to the *Treugeber*.

(4) The *Treugeber* or third party beneficiary is not merely protected in the case of insolvency of the *Treuhänder*, but their interests are also secured from attacks from personal creditors of the manager. Whenever a creditor of the *Treuhänder* tries to seize an asset belonging to the *Treugut*, they can exercise a third party claim

[114] *Insolvenzordnung* of 5 October 1994 (BGBl I S 2866) which replaces the former *Konkursordnung*. §47 of the new Insolvency Act corresponds to §43 of the old *Konkursordnung*.

[115] See RG 10 October 1917, RGZ 91, 12, 16; RG 15 January 1930, RGZ 127, 8, 9; RG 9 June 1931, RGZ 133, 84, 87.

[116] See BGH 11 December 1963, WM 1964, 179.

[117] This view was adopted by the BGH 14 January 1969, WM 1969, 475; ZIP 1993, 213, 214. See also BGH 5 November 1953, BGHZ 11, 37, 41; NJW 1954, 190, 192; WM 1955, 372; BGH 7 April 1959, WM 1959, 686, 687; BGH 11 December 1963, WM 1964, 179.

[118] BGH 19 November 1992, ZIP 1993, 213, 214.

[119] P Bassenge, §930, Rn 31, Palandt, 66th edn, 2007.

to set aside the compulsory enforcement (*Drittwiderspruchsklage*),[120] in accordance with §771 of the Code of Civil Procedure (*Zivilprozessordnung*).[121] In a case of 10 October 1917, the Reichsgericht said that:

> The settled case-law of the Reichsgericht (Imperial Court) has been that there is a claim to the separation of things which, though formally in the ownership of the bankrupt, do not substantively and economically belong to his patrimony but were conveyed to him under a fiduciary relationship as *Treuhänder* on behalf of another person by such person; it is based on the same legal notion that, even in cases other than bankruptcy proceedings, where a fiduciary relationship of that kind exists, the *Treugeber* can oppose seizure of the property by a creditor of the *Treuhänder* by way of an application to set aside.[122]

The rationale given for such third party claims is the same used to justify the *Aussonderungsrecht* in the case of the insolvency of the *Treuhänder*, namely that from an economic standpoint the assets are still considered to be with the *Treugeber*, in whose interest the *Treuhand* for management purposes is usually set up.[123]

Reichsgericht, 19 February 1914[124] **6.29 (DE)**

THE PRINCIPLE OF IMMEDIACY

The essentials of a *Treuhand*

For a Treuhand to exist it is necessary that a person conveys assets to another person in such manner that the latter may exercise the right conveyed in his own name but not for his own benefit.

Facts: B bought land at a public auction and was registered as owner in the Land Registry (Grundbuch). Several lessees had concluded leases over dwellings on the land. The Vereinsbank had a claim against B, and in order to enforce the claims it seized B's claims against the lessees. The Westholsteinische Bank argued that B had bought the land and concluded the contracts of leases for them, that B acted as *Treuhänder*. §771 ZPO should be applied.

Held: The claim is denied. There is no *Treuhand*.

Judgment: The appellant seeks in vain to infer that the claimant (Westholsteinische Bank) has authority to act in the matter under a fiduciary relationship between B and the claimant. No such relationship exists, even if in the acquisition and management of the land B acted as the claimant's trusted collaborator and even if B and the claimant erroneously regarded the relationship existing between them as a fiduciary one. Even under general notions of commerce, and certainly from a legal point of view, such a relationship can exist only if one party (*Treugeber*) entrusts the other person (*Treuhänder*) with assets from his patrimony, that is to say conveys it to the

[120] RG 19 February 1914, RGZ 84, 214; RG 10 October 1917, RGZ 91, 12; 127, 341; BGH 11 November 1970, BGHZ 1955, 20, 26.

[121] §771(1) *Zivilprozessordnung* states that: 'Behauptet ein Dritter, dass ihm an dem Gegenstand der Zwangsvollstreckung ein die Veräußerung hinderndes Recht zustehe, so ist der Widerspruch gegen die Zwangsvollstreckung im Wege der Klage bei dem Gericht geltend zu machen, in dessen Bezirk die Zwangsvollstreckung erfolgt.'

[122] RG 10 October 1917, RGZ 91, 12.

[123] See above n 117.

[124] RGZ 84, 214.

other person in such a manner that the other person may exercise the right conveyed in his own name but not for his own benefit. From then on the asset subject to the fiduciary arrangement no longer legally forms part of the *Treugebers*'s patrimony, though it continues to do so from an economic point of view. The notion of fiduciary relationship would however be completely blurred if one were to reject the requirement of assets placed in trust and sought to find such a relationship wherever a person acts for the account of another person and on that person's behalf but in his own name.

Notes

(1) Prior to the decision of the German Imperial Court of 19 February 1914, the *Treugeber* or third party beneficiary was protected irrespective of the way in which the *Treuhänder* had acquired the *Treugut*. With this landmark decision, things changed and since then, the *Treugeber* or the third party beneficiary has had the power to raise the fiduciary nature of the relationship only in cases of direct transfers of assets from the *Treugeber* to the *Treuhänder*. The court established the so-called principle of immediacy (*Unmittelbarkeitsprinzip*), following which the *Treugeber* has a right to demand the release of the assets (*Aussonderungsrecht*) against other creditors of the *Treuhänder* only where the rights were transferred to the *Treuhänder* by the *Treugeber* himself. Anything acquired by the *Treuhänder* from a third person on behalf of the *Treugeber* or the third party beneficiary will not become part of the *Treugut*. This is so even though the *Treuhänder* may have financed the acquisition with funds provided for this purpose by the *Treugeber*.

(2) By applying the principle of immediacy, the German judiciary considerably restricted the protection of the *Treugeber* and third party beneficiaries. This was justified by the fear that the concept of the *Treuhand* would otherwise become undefined (*ins Unbestimmte zerfließen*). In fact, it appears that in this way the Imperial court intended to maintain the distinction between the *Treuhand* and the indirect agency (*indirekte Stellvertretung*).

(3) In later years, the Imperial Court recognised that a *Treuhandverhältnis* also exists when there is no direct transfer, introducing the distinction between the *Treuhand* in the 'proper sense' (*eigentliche Treuhand*) and *Treuhand* in an 'improper sense' (the *uneigentliche Treuhand*).[125] A *Treuhand* in a 'proper sense' exists when there is a direct transfer of the assets from the *Treugeber* to the *Treuhänder*, while one speaks of an 'improper' *Treuhand* in cases in which there is no direct transfer. Only in the first case does the *Treugeber* or the third party beneficiary have a right to demand the release of the assets (*Aussonderungsrecht*) as well as a third party claim to set aside the compulsory enforcement (*Drittwiderspruchsklage*).[126]

(4) Over the years, the principle of immediacy has met with widespread criticism

[125] This distinction between 'proper' and 'improper' *Treuhand* was adopted also by the Bundesgerichtshof. See BGH 30 October 1959, BGH WM 1960, 325, 326.

[126] RG 27 March 1939, RGZ 160, 52, 59.

from the academic community.[127] The courts have been accused of having developed a principle lacking any statutory basis, so contravening one of the fundamental principles of the German legal system. Be that as it may, the BGH persists in its viewpoint, though admitting certain exceptions to the principle of immediacy when it comes to the so-called *Treuhandkonto*, mentioned earlier.[128] The BGH has indeed recognised that in the case of a *Treuhandkonto*, a right to demand the release of the assets and the third party claim to set aside the compulsory enforcement is granted to the *Treugeber* or third party beneficiary even where third parties have paid directly into the bank account, either at the behest of the *Treugeber* or because they have been authorised to do so,[129] or the *Treuhänder* has invested directly received cash into the bank account.[130] In doing so, the *Bundesgerichtshof* initially specified that the protection would be granted only when it was made sufficiently clear to the bank that the account was a trust account.[131] In other words, while the fiduciary character did not have to be manifest in order to qualify the contract as a *Treuhand*, it was an important requirement in order to benefit from the right to demand the release of the assets and the third party claim to set aside the compulsory enforcement. More recently, however, the BGH has said that in order for the *Treugeber* to act on the basis of §771 ZPO or §47 InsO, the making public of the fiduciary character of the bank account is not essential. What is necessary, however, is that the account be used only in order to administer money received as a *Treuhänder*.[132]

IV.C FRENCH LAW

Code civil **6.30 (FR)**

Article 2024 The institution of any *procédure de sauvegarde, redressement judiciaire,* or compulsory liquidation [*liquidation judiciaire*] for the benefit of the *fiduciaire* has no effect on the *patrimoine fiduciaire*.

Article 2025(1) Without prejudice to the rights of any creditors of the *constituant* who have a right of recourse against a security, notice of which was given before the contract of *fiducie* [was entered into], and except in the case of fraud on the

[127] Coing, above n 9, 179; J Gernhuber, 'Die fiduziarische Treuhand' [1988] *Juristische Schulung* (*JuS*) 355, 360; H Kötz, *Trust und Treuhand, Eine rechtsvergleichende Darstellung des anglo-amerikanischen trust und funktionsverwandter Institute des deutschen Rechts* (Göttingen, Vandenhoeck and Ruprecht, 1963) 129 *et seq.*

[128] The same is true for the *Anderkonto*. An *Anderkonto* is an express trust account which only certain professional categories can open, such as, for instance, practising lawyers, patent agents or notaries. The function of such accounts is to administer money which belongs to other people and which remains separated from the personal patrimony of the *Treuhänder*.

[129] BGH 5 November 1953, BGHZ 11, 37, 41; NJW 1954, 190, 192; WM 1955, 372 and BGH 7 April 1959, NJW 1959, 1223.

[130] BGH 7 April 1959, NJW 1959, 1223. According to the BGH it was however necessary that the payment was made on the basis of a direct claim of the *Treugeber* and not the *Treuhänder*.

[131] BGH 5 November 1953, BGHZ 11, 37, 41; NJW 1954, 190, 192.

[132] BGH 25 June 1973, BGHZ 61, 72, 77; See most importantly BGH 1 July 1993, WM 1993, 1524 and BGH 8 February 1996, NJW 1996, 1543; BGH 24 July 2003, WM 2003, 1641; BGH 7 July 2005, WM 2005, 1796, 1797.

creditors of the *constituant*, the fiduciary patrimony is subject to execution only for debts arising from the keeping or the management of this patrimony.

Notes

(1) Article 2011 expressly provides that the assets of the *fiducie* form a segregated patrimony and Article 2025(1) adds that this patrimony is protected from claims by creditors in matters not connected with the management or the conservation of the *fiducie* itself.[133]

(2) According to Article 2024 the insolvency of the *fiduciaire*, though bringing the *fiducie* to an end, does not affect the *patrimoine fiduciaire*. In other words, the *patrimoine fiduciaire* does not fall into the insolvency estate, nor may personal creditors of the *fiduciaire* seize or attach things which are part of the *Treugut*.

V. INSOLVENCY OF THE SETTLOR, *TREUGEBER* AND *CONSTITUANT*, INCLUDING CASES WHERE HIS PERSONAL CREDITORS TRY TO SEIZE THE FUND

V.A ENGLISH LAW

Introductory Note

In English law, the settlor will normally drop out of the picture once a trust has been created. He cannot, therefore, revoke the trust, just as a donor cannot revoke a gift. As a consequence, should a settlor become insolvent after setting up a trust, the rights held by the trustee or by the settlor himself as trustee, will not be available to satisfy the claims of his creditors. An exception occurs where the creditors are able to attack the trust on the ground that it was a sham, ie that it was no trust at all, merely a smokescreen to deceive others. Even where the trust is not a sham, just as in the case of outright gifts, the setting up of a trust can be attacked under the general rules of the English insolvency legislation (Insolvency Act 1986, section 423), by which certain transactions at an undervalue or for no consideration can be set aside by the court.

[133] Both expressions 'management' and 'conservation' are to be interpreted in the most ample way. See Rapp. Sénat no 11 at 62: 'Il conviendra de reconnaître aux termes de 'conservation' et de 'gestion' l'acception la plus large. Ainsi, par exemple, le créancier qui aurait accordé au fiduciaire un prêt pour financer des travaux d'amélioration d'un immeuble transféré au sein du patrimoine fiduciaire serait bien entendu recevable à exercer son droit de poursuite sur le patrimoine fiduciaire'.

High Court of Justice 10 June 1994[134] **6.31 (E&W)**
Midland Bank plc v Wyatt

SHAM TRUSTS

Without effect

Declaration of trust did not intend to confer legally enforceable interest on beneficiaries and was therefore a nullity.

Facts: In December 1981, the defendant and his wife purchased a title to land which was registered in their joint names. They executed a legal charge with the claimant bank to secure a loan. The defendant decided to set up his own textile company and accordingly, as he alleged, in order to protect his family from long-term commercial risk, and acting on the advice of his solicitor, he and his wife executed a deed whereby they declared that they held the title to the house on trust for the wife as to one half and for their two daughters as to one quarter each. The trust deed was dated 17 June 1987 and was signed by the defendant and his wife, though the wife was not aware of its import or effect. Thereafter, the defendant negotiated further loans with the bank to finance his business on the security of his title to house. He separated from his wife in 1989, and in 1991 the business went into receivership. Neither the bank nor his business partners nor the solicitors acting for his wife in the separation arrangements were made aware of the declaration of trust, and all dealings were entered into on the basis that the husband and wife held the title outright. Following judgment for the claimant against the defendant for £63,134.50 plus costs, the bank obtained a charging order nisi on the defendant's interest in the property. The defendant in reliance on the declaration of trust resisted the making absolute of the charging order. The bank contended that if the declaration of trust was executed on the date named, it was either void as being a sham transaction or voidable by reason of section 423 of the Insolvency Act 1986 as a transaction to defraud creditors.

Held: The declaration of trust was both a sham and made for the purpose of the debtor putting his interest in the house out of reach of any future creditors who might make a claim with respect thereto. On both grounds, it was void and of no effect.

Judgment: DEM Young QC—*Sham Transaction*

... I do not believe Mr Wyatt had any intention when he executed the trust deed of endowing his children with his interest in Honer House, which at the time was his only real asset. I consider the trust deed was executed by him, not to be acted upon but to be put in the safe for a rainy day—as Mr Wyatt states in his affidavit, as a safeguard to protect his family from longterm commercial risk should he set up his own company. As such I consider the declaration of trust was not what it purported to be but a pretence or, as it is sometimes referred to, a 'sham'. The fact that Mr Wyatt executed the deed with the benefit of legal advice from Mr Ellis does not in my view affect the status of the transaction. It follows that even if the deed was entered into without any dishonest or fraudulent motive but was entered into on the basis of mistaken advice, in my judgment such a transaction will still be void and therefore an unenforceable transaction if it was not intended to be acted upon but was entered into for some different or ulterior motive. Accordingly, I find that the declaration of trust sought to be relied upon by Mr Wyatt is void and unenforceable.

I should add as a general matter it is clear that when it was expedient to do so Mr Wyatt was prepared to allow the bank to remain in ignorance of the true position (both with regard to the loan being unsecured and with regard to the existence

[134] [1995] 1 FLR 697.

of the trust deed and/or the fact that he no longer had any beneficial interest in Honer House) or even to mislead (as he admits was the case with Mr Howick over outstanding debts to him). From his dealings with his own solicitors, it appears that when it suited him to do so he did not disclose the full facts, in particular his failure to tell either Mr Minton or Mrs Bevis about the trust deed can only be explained on the basis of Mr Wyatt having forgotten all about it or deliberately concealing it.

Insolvency Act 1986, s 42

The section applies to transactions entered into at an undervalue or for no consideration. The declaration of trust was such a transaction in that it purported to transfer Mr Wyatt's interest in Honer House to his two daughters for no consideration. Section 423(2), (3) provides as follows:

> '(2) Where a person has entered into such a transaction, the court may, if satisfied under the next subsection, make such order as it thinks fit for—
> (a) restoring the position to what it would have been if the transaction had not been entered into, and
> (b) protecting the interests of persons who are victims of the transaction.
> (3) In the case of a person entering into such a transaction, an order shall only be made if the court is satisfied that it was entered into by him for the purpose—
> (a) of putting assets beyond the reach of a person who is making, or may at some time make, a claim against him, or
> (b) of otherwise prejudicing the interests of such a person in relation to the claim which he is making or may make.'

As I have already found, the declaration of trust was entered into not with the intention of endowing his daughters with Mr Wyatt's interest in Honer House, but as a safeguard to protect his family from long-term commercial risk should Mr Wyatt set up his own company, which by June 1987 he was contemplating. …

As of June 1987 Mr Wyatt was of sound financial standing as I have already stated … and whilst he was still employed by Whitehead Fabrics he was contemplating his own business albeit only in general terms. The question I have to decide is whether and how far the provisions of section 423 cover the voluntary disposition of assets to avoid future but unknown creditors. Setting up any new business, not yet formulated, as Mr Wyatt states was the case at the time of executing the trust deed, would no doubt to any experienced businessman involve potential risks of a personal nature such as personal guarantees even though the intention may be to operate through the limited liability of a company. Certainly such long-term risks of a personal nature were being contemplated by Mr Wyatt, as he so states in his affidavit that that was one of the reasons for transferring his assets.

I was referred to *Mackay v Douglas* (1872) 14 Eq 106 and *Re Butterworth* (1882) 18 ChD 588 as establishing under the pre-Insolvency Act position (which it is common ground is not materially different to the relevant Insolvency Act provisions) that a person who settles property at a time that he has no creditors but is planning to embark on a new business venture may have the necessary intention to keep the property safe from future creditors. Mr Farber contended that these two cases were distinguishable on the facts. In the case of *Mackay v Douglas*, the settlor six weeks after entering into the settlement went into a hazardous business partnership of jute speculation. This is to be contrasted with Mr Wyatt's contemplated fabrics business which had good prospects, set up some nine months later not as a partnership but as a limited liability company. In the case of *Re Butterworth,* the settlor one month after entering into the settlement went into a grocer's business, which he was not familiar with, at a time when he was unable to pay his debts as a result of the settlement.

Mr Farber contends that the principle to be derived from these cases is that a settlement will be voidable only where the settlor is about to enter into a business involving a high degree of risk either as a sole practitioner or as a partner.

Whilst it is true that the two cases referred to were cases of that nature, at the end of the day it is necessary to apply the words of the section, namely whether the court is satisfied that the transaction was entered into by Mr Wyatt for the purpose of putting assets beyond the reach of a person who may at some time make a claim against him.

The purpose of so doing may not be the sole purpose or intention. In *Re Butterworth* Lindley LJ, having asked the question why did he make the settlement on his family that he did, stated:

> 'Obviously not simply to benefit his wife and children but to screen and protect them against the unknown risks of the new adventure.'

In *Chohan v Saggar* [1992] BCC 306 at p 323, following *Lloyds Bank v Marcan* [1973] 1 WLR 1387 ..., Deputy Judge Evans-Lombe (as he then was) stated that section 423(3) required the dominant purpose to be the removal of assets from the reach of potential claimants or creditors. The fact that it was also his intention to benefit a third party did not affect the applicability of the section.

As I have already found that Mr Wyatt had no intention of disposing of his interest to benefit his children, it must follow that the real purpose of entering into the declaration of trust was to screen or protect them against the unknown risks of the new adventure.I consider that if the purpose of the transaction can be shown to put assets beyond the reach of future creditors, section 423 will apply whether or not the transferor was about to enter into a hazardous business or whether his business was as a sole practitioner or as a partner or as a participant in a limited liability company. It is a question of proof of intention or purpose underlying the transaction. Clearly, the more hazardous the business being contemplated is, the more readily the court will be satisfied of the intention of the settlor or transferor.

On the facts of this case, that intention and purpose was stated by Mr Wyatt at the outset in his affidavit and not resiled from in his evidence, namely to protect his family from the long-term commercial risk should he set up his own company. In hindsight whilst not in any sense conclusive, it appears that Mr Wyatt's fears in 1987 of commercial risk have been realised; Mr Wyatt's interest in Honer House has indeed been exposed to claims by his creditors, namely the plaintiff bank and Mr Howick, his partner.

Accordingly, I am also satisfied that the declaration of trust was entered into by Mr Wyatt for the purpose of putting his interest in Honer House out of reach of any future creditors who might make a claim with respect thereto and therefore cannot be relied upon by Mr Wyatt in view of section 423.

V.B GERMAN LAW

Insolvency Act **6.32 (DE)**

§115 Expiry of mandates

(1) Any mandate ordered by the debtor referring to the property forming part of the assets involved in the insolvency proceedings shall expire upon the opening of the insolvency proceedings.

(2) If suspension of such mandate would cause a risk, the mandatary shall continue to perform the mandated transaction until the insolvency administrator is able to otherwise take care of any such transaction himself. For this purpose the mandate shall be deemed to continue. The mandatary may claim reimbursement of the expenses incurred for such continuation as a creditor of the assets involved in the insolvency proceedings.

(3) As long as the mandatary is not at fault in being unaware of the opening of insolvency proceedings he shall benefit from the presumption that the mandate continues. The mandatary shall rank among the creditors of the insolvency proceedings with his reimbursement claims arising from such continuation.

§116 Expiry of management contracts

If anyone is obligated under a service or work contract with the debtor to manage a business transaction for the latter, section 115 shall apply *mutatis mutandis*. The provision governing reimbursement claims arising from a continuation of such management contract shall also apply to claims to remuneration.

Note

According to §§115 and 116 of the German Insolvency Act, the insolvency of the *Treugeber* brings the *Treuhand* to an end. The question then arises as to what happens to the *Treugut*. The answer varies according as to whether the *Treuhand* arose in the interest of the *Treugeber* or the *Treuhänder*. In the former, which is the case of the *Treuhand* for management purposes with which we are dealing with in this chapter, the *Treugut* belongs to the insolvency estate and thus the trustee in bankruptcy can request the release of the *Treugut* from the *Treuhänder*.[135] In this case, the *Treuhänder* has no right to keep the assets.[136]

[135] Liebich/Mathews, *Treuhand und Treuhänder in Recht und Wirtschaft*, 2nd edn (Herne, Berlin, 'Neue Wirtschafts-Briefe', 1983) 156.

[136] Ganter, InsO §47, Rn 371, *Münchener Kommentar. Insolvenzordnung*, vol 1, 2nd edn (München, CH Beck, 2007).

BGH, 25 April 1962[137] 6.33 (DE)

INSOLVENCY OF THE TREUGEBER

Fraudulent behaviour

Where a Treuhandvertrag for the management of the affairs of another terminates by reason of insolvency and the transfer of the Treugut to the trustee in bankruptcy does not occur under the condition subsequent of supervening insolvency, the Treugut does not automatically revert back to the Treugeber (trustee in bankruptcy). However, the Treuhänder is obliged to transfer the Treugut to the trustee in bankruptcy unless it no longer forms part of the assets of the Treugeber.

Facts: K entered into insolvency proceedings on 5 January 1954 and the claimant was appointed trustee in bankruptcy. From 1949, K had been leasing a plot of land from the mother of the originally joined defendant, Ms F, who later inherited her mother's patrimony. K began the construction of a residential and commercial building on the land, but due to a lack of funds could not complete the works. With regard to the construction of this and another building, K had committed an extensive fraud. In particular, he had leased apartments in these buildings several times over and had received construction payments for these from several lessees of the same apartments. When K stopped making payments and was put under severe pressure by his creditors, he first sold the other plot that was under construction and then sought a party interested to take over his lease and payment duties. In 1953 K assigned his claims against Ms F to the defendant, who in turn obliged himself to pay DM40,000 to K and to take the place of K in the lease contracts of the commercial and residential premises. In addition, the defendant took over the construction grants provided for in the lease contracts up to a maximum of DM4,000. Of the DM40,000, DM18,000 was due immediately, while the remaining DM22,000 was to be irrevocably transferred to a notary, Dr S, who would use this money exclusively in order to satisfy those who had provided construction payments.

The claimant argued that the compensation promised by the defendant was short of DM19,500. He challenged the contract under the provisions of the insolvency law and requested that the defendant and Ms F be held liable and ordered to give up their rights arising from the notarial contract with effect against the creditor of the bankruptcy estate and the trustee in bankruptcy. The claimant subsidiarily requested the court to grant him payment of the money paid to the notary, or in the event the defendant had not yet paid the notary, payment to the claimant directly. The lower court held against the claimant and Ms F in the main proceedings. The Court of Appeal later dismissed the judgment against Ms F. On appeal, the claimant merely demanded payment of the DM22,000, a claim which, after payment of DM11,000 by the defendant, was reduced to DM11,000 and awarded as such by the Court of Appeal. The appeal of the defendant was dismissed.

Held: Where a *Treuhandvertrag* for the management of the affairs of another terminates by reason of insolvency and the transfer of the *Treugut* to the trustee in bankruptcy does not occur under the condition subsequent of supervening insolvency, the *Treugut* does not automatically revert back to the *Treugeber* (trustee in bankruptcy). The decision of the Court of Appeal is therefore upheld.

Judgment: The appeal does not question that the notary Dr S was only to have the position of a *Treuhänder* in the relationship between K and defendant. In the case of a *Treuhandvertrag* for the management of the affairs of another the rule in §23 KO is applicable, as the appeal court rightly pointed out, with the result that the agreement ceases to exist. Contrary to the respondent's view, on termination of the *Treuhandvertrag* the *Treuhand* assets did not *ipso jure* revert to the *Treugeber*, in this case the trustee in bankruptcy. Such automatic reversion would have occurred only if the *Treuhand* assets had been transferred to the *Treuhänder*, on conclusion

[137] NJW 1962, 1200.

of the *Treuhandvertrag*, subject to a condition subsequent of supervening insolvency proceedings (*cf* RGZ 145, 253, 257). However, according to the findings of the appeal court, the *Treuhandvertrag* entered into between the parties contains no such condition subsequent; nor does the case file contain any indication that such a condition subsequent was in this connection contemplated by the parties, particularly since on conclusion of the agreement of 27 November 1957, they did not contemplate the possibility of the initiation of bankruptcy proceedings. None the less, as the appeal court correctly assumed, the *Treuhänder* is obliged to assign the claim to the insolvent estate on termination of the *Treuhandvertrag* (Jaeger, KO, 8th ed, §23, no 8). That is not precluded by the fact that the *Treuhandvertrag* in the contract of 27 November 1953 formed only part of the overall contract concerning the assets entered into at that time. It would be otherwise if the intention of the *Treuhandvertrag* entered into at that time had been that the claim to payment of DM22,000 was definitively removed from the patrimony of the vendor, that is to say the claimant, by virtue of the transfer to the *Treuhänder*. However, such an interpretation of the fiduciary clause is unsupported either by the findings contained in the judgment appealed against or any other indication in the court file. Nor is that altered by the fact that the fiduciary clause states that the transfer to the fiduciary is irrevocable. As the appeal court discernibly assumed, the irrevocability agreed in the contract was intended merely to mean that the vendor, subsequently insolvent, could not for his part freely revoke the transfer of the claim to payment of part of the purchase price. Conversely, it may not be inferred from this clause that the trustee in bankruptcy would not for his part be able, after initiation of insolvency proceedings, to demand the retransfer of the claim to the purchase price, following termination of the *Treuhandvertrag*. The assumption that the transfer of the claim to the purchase price of DM22,000 to the notary as *Treuhänder* has definitively removed this claim from the vendor's patrimony is nullified in particular by the fact that at that time those involved were not clear as to the extent to which the amount of DM22,000 would in fact be claimed by the creditors of advances paid in respect of building costs; nor, in particular, was it yet agreed between those involved which particular claims should be met by the *Treuhänder* from that fund. All these factors plainly militate against a finding that those involved viewed the *Treuhand* assets as separated from the vendor's patrimony upon its transfer to the *Treuhänder*. Accordingly, the view formed by the appeal court cannot be impugned on legal grounds.

Notes

(1) According to the BGH, the insolvency of the *Treugeber* terminates the *Treuhand*, but the *Treugut* does not automatically revert to the *Treugeber*. The trustee in bankruptcy has only a personal right against the *Treuhänder*, unless the contract contains a resolutory condition providing for the case of insolvency. Problems may consequently arise when the *Treugut* is no longer in the hands of the *Treuhänder*. If, however, the *Treuhand* has been established in the interest of the *Treuhänder*, such as is the case when it is used for security purposes, then the trustee in bankruptcy may make use of the things which are in his possession (§166 InsO)[138]

[138] §166(1) InsO reads: 'Der Insolvenzverwalter darf eine bewegliche Sache, an der ein Absonderungsrecht besteht, freihändig verwerten, wenn er die Sache in seinem Besitz hat.'

and the *Treuhänder* has a right to separate satisfaction (*Absonderungsrecht* §51(1) InsO—priority right).[139]

(2) According to the majority opinion of German scholars, the (personal) right of the trustee in bankruptcy to recover the *Treugut* from the *Treuhänder* is justified by the fact that the *Treugut* does not belong economically to the patrimony of the *Treuhänder* but to the patrimony of the *Treugeber*.[140] The same justification, as we saw earlier,[141] is used to explain the decision of the German courts to protect the *Treugeber* and third party beneficiary in case of insolvency of the *Treuhänder* as well from claims coming from the personal creditors of the latter. Some writers, however, suggest that the *Treugut* is part of the insolvency patrimony of the *Treugeber* because the contract has come to an end, or because it can be terminated by the trustee in bankruptcy.[142]

BGH, 5 November 1953[143] **6.34 (DE)**

ACTION BY CREDITORS OF THE TREUGEBER

The Treuhand account

The Treugut does not belong to the Treuhänder and therefore creditors of the Treugeber must revert to him and not the Treuhänder.

Facts: B was a master baker operating a bakery. He had fallen into financial difficulties. In the arrangement of his financial affairs, B entrusted the A GmbH with the management of his patrimony. In the course of this management, A GmbH created a bank account under the name 'JB Treuhandkonto H' at the local Savings and Loans Bank (the *Spar-* und *Darlehnskasse*). From the account pro rata payments were made to outstanding claims and running costs of the bakery. The financial arrangements were notified to the creditors and the *Amtsgericht* by letter. On 20 January 1952, B paid DM800 and on 24 January 1952 DM300 into the bank account.

The defendant, who held an enforcement order against B, obtained a decision from the *Amtsgericht* ordering the claim of B, for payment from the bank account, to be pledged and transferred to the defendant. The assignment of the pledge was notified to the third party creditor on 12 February 1952.

In the meantime, B had replaced A GmbH with the claimant in the organisation of his financial affairs. On 16 February 1952, the claim on the *Treuhandkonto* was therefore assigned. The Savings and Loan Bank refused payment from the *Treuhandkonto* to the claimant, referring to the right of pledge on the claim and the existing enforcement order. The claimant requested the court to establish that the money on the *Treuhandkonto* belonged to him. The lower court granted the request. The Court of Appeal, however, ruled in favour of the defendant.

Held: The *Treuhänder* does not own the *Treugut* and therefore creditors of the *Treugeber* must revert to him to satisfy their claims. However, the claim of the *Treugeber* against *Treuhänder* is open to them.

Judgment: Now it is indeed correct that according to case law, and with the approval of the almost overwhelming opinion expressed in academic writings, the *Treugeber*

[139] §51 InsO reads: 'Den in §50 genannten Gläubigern stehen gleich: 1. Gläubiger, denen der Schuldner zur Sicherung eines Anspruchs eine bewegliche Sache übereignet oder ein Recht übertragen hat'. P Bassenge, above n 119.

[140] See among others F Baur and R Stürner, Insolvenzrecht, Rn 14.22; Brinkmann, in W Uhlenbruck, Insolvenzordnung, 13th edn, 2010, §47 Rn 34.

[141] Above IV.B.

[142] Ganter, InsO §47, Münchener Kommentar, above n 136.

[143] BGHZ 11, 37, 41; NJW 54, 190, 192; WM 1955, 372.

is accorded a right of action to bring an application to set aside under §771 of the Rules of Civil Procedure (ZPO) where a creditor of the *Treuhänder* levies execution in regard to assets held in *Treuhand*. The permissibility of such action is substantiated by the fact that although the right against which execution is levied formally and externally belongs to the *Treuhänder*, the *Treugeber* is the owner from an economical point of view and in relation to the *Treuhänder* the *Treugeber* is the beneficiary of whose patrimony the *Treugut* continues to be a part of. However, it cannot be inferred from this that the *Treugeber*'s creditors may obtain a writ of execution against the *Treugeber* and levy execution directly on the *Treuhänder s* assets. There is only an apparent exception to the abovementioned principle in the case of mandatory enforcement over movables held as part of the *Treugut* in the possession of the *Treugeber*. In this case execution is levied on the *Treugut* on the basis of a writ obtained against the *Treugeber*; nor may the *Treuhänder* oppose enforcement by an application to set aside under §771 of the Rules of Procedure. That is owing to the fact that in the case of execution conducted in respect of movables all items in the safe keeping of the person on whom execution is levied are subject to seizure and realisation and that there is no initial verification of ownership of items on which execution is levied (§808 ZPO). Nor can the *Treuhänder* raise any opposition by way of an application to set aside under §771 ZPO. For, as regards the *Treuhänder*, the asset confiscated belongs to the *Treugeber*'s patrimony and the *Treuhänder* has to acquiesce in the *Treugeber*'s creditors having recourse to the items in his safe keeping when the writ of execution is directed against the *Treugeber*. That is in the nature of execution over moveable property. Third parties are not involved in the enforcement proceedings.

This is not the case where execution is levied over movables within the *Treugut* that are in the possession of the *Treuhänder*. In this case the *Treuhänder* may take action against execution occurring against his will based on §766 ZPO, where execution is levied only under a writ against the *Treugeber*. It is completely otherwise, however, in the case of rights against third parties belonging to the *Treugut*, in particular, rights of pledge over claims. Here the above mentioned principle must be used, that only the asset of the person against whom execution is levied is subject to execution. This is so because execution does not only involve the credit and debtor but also a third party. As such, in the case of a pledge, this is the third-party debtor. The third-party debtor is prevented from paying the debtor (§829(1) ZPO). The same is true of other rights that have to be exercised in regard to a third person (§859(1), loc cit). In this connection it cannot be overlooked that, in the case of fiduciary assets, right and title to the assets pass with full effect to the acquirer with the legal consequence that all connections that the holder of the property rights had in the *Treugut* are dissolved and the obligation on the *Treuhänder* to make only certain dispositions over the *Treuhand* asset are merely founded in the law of obligations (§137 BGB). The same applies to the *Treuhänder*'s obligation to return the *Treugut* to the *Treugeber* on termination of the fiduciary relationship in accordance with §§667, 675 BGB (RGZ 153, 366 [369]). As against the third party subject to the right (claim) only the person entitled under the fiduciary relationship is entitled to claim. Only he can enforce the claim against the debtor. Only as against the *Treugeber* can claims belonging to the *Treugut* not be enforced under a writ of execution. Nor is there any need for such enforcement. That does not leave the *Treugeber* and his creditors without rights. Any claim, whether present or future, by the *Treugeber* against the *Treuhänder* is subject to recourse by them. The third-party debtor in respect of that claim is the *Treuhänder*. This is also in line with the general view expressed in academic writings concerning third-party accounts on the question of enforcing fiduciary claims on account holders' credit balances (Siebert, loc cit p 357; Aengenheister, Treuhandkonto [fiduciary account], p 82 note 152).

Note

If a personal creditor of the *Treugeber* tries to seize assets belonging to the *Treugut*, the *Treuhänder* has no right to exercise the third party claim to set aside the compulsory execution (*Drittwiderspruchsklage*) of §771 of the German Code of Civil Procedure against the creditor, independent of the fact that the *Treuhand* fulfils management or security purposes.[144] The reason is that from an economic point of view, the *Treugut* does not belong to him.

V.C FRENCH LAW

Code civil **6.35 (FR)**

Article 2025(1) Without prejudice to the rights of any creditors of the *constituant* who have a right of recourse against a security, notice of which was given prior to the contract of *fiducie* [being entered into], and except in the case of fraud on the creditors of the *constituant*, the fiduciary patrimony is subject to execution only for debts arising from the keeping or the management of this patrimony.

Notes

(1) There is no specific provision of the *fiducie* dealing with the insolvency of the *constituant*. Article 2025(1) Cciv provides that the assets transferred to the *fiduciaire* are part of the *patrimoine fiduciaire*, and that the personal creditors of the *constituant* cannot seize the assets unless they have been defrauded or they have a right attached to a surety which has been registered before the *fiducie*. No reference is, for instance, made to the *actio pauliana*, an action given to creditors who have been defrauded.

(2) As said above, Article 2018(2) states that the assignment of a debt is good against third parties on the date of the stipulation of the contract of *fiducie* or of that of the accessory contract that acknowledges it. It is not good against the debtor until he is notified by the assignor or the *fiduciaire*.

(3) However, the legislative interventions in 2008 and 2009 have introduced specific provisions concerning the *fiducie* for security purposes which consider, among other things, the position of beneficiaries of a *fiducie* in the event of opening of either safeguard or insolvency proceedings against the debtor, the *constituant*. *Ordonance* 1345 of 2008 established that a *fiducie* stipulated during the 'suspect period', ie the period between the date on which the debtor effectively became

[144] RG 9 April 1929, RGZ 124, 73, 75; BGH 14 July 1952, NJW 1952, 1169; BGH 4 February 1954, BGHZ 12, 232, 234. Both cases decided by the BGH are cases in which the *Treuhand* is used for security purposes.

insolvent and the date of the opening judgment, is valid only if concluded in order to secure a debt contracted at the same time, and not a prior debt.[145]

VI. COMPARATIVE OVERVIEW

Although traditionally associated with the common law, the notion of the trust is universal. Indeed, it seems to be an older institution in the Roman-based civil systems, where it took forms different to that in England. [146] However, on the continent these institutions never became a general legal form and the codifications left only some traces of them. In England, by contrast, the trust developed as a uniform and general legal instrument, able to respond to a variety of different needs.

Civil lawyers have always had a certain fascination with the common law trust, but since the 1980s that interest has been renewed, and studies have been undertaken of its structures and functions.[147] Such interest increased with the signing on 1 July 1985 of the Hague Convention on the Law Applicable to Trusts and on their Recognition,[148] now ratified by several civil law countries such as the Netherlands, Italy, Malta, Luxembourg, San Marino, Liechtenstein and, more recently, Switzerland and Monaco. In some cases, it has even led to the development of a new domestic device. In fact, in view of a possible ratification of the Hague Convention, some European countries have introduced domestic devices inspired by the common law trust or which were at least meant to offer an alternative instrument. This was the case, for example, in Luxembourg, where in 1983 a decree allowed banks to enter into fiduciary transfers of property.[149] In July 2003 this decree was substituted by a law not only ratifying the Hague Convention, but also improving the status and flexibility of the 1983 *contrat fiduciaire*.[150] In September 2004, the Republic of San Marino ratified the Hague Convention and a year later, in 2005, a statute was passed introducing the trust instrument in San Marino.[151] In 2010, the trust provisions of San Marino were reformed,[152] and an additional fiduciary device, entitled *affidamento fiduciario*, introduced.[153] Finally, as has been seen, in February 2007, France passed a statute introducing the *fiducie* into the Code civil.[154]

At the same time, in Italy the Hague Trusts Convention led to a completely different development, whereby Italian courts recognise domestic trusts, all of whose

[145] For a more detailed analysis of the changes brought about by the *Ordonnance*, see Gdanski and Pichardo-Angadi, above n 52, 262.

[146] M Lupoi, 'Trust and Confidence' (2009) 125 *Law Quarterly Review* 253.

[147] D Waters, 'The Future of the Trust from a Worldwide Perspective', in D Hayton (ed), *The International Trust*, 3rd edn (Bristol, Jordans, 2011) 837, 857. See also David J Hayton, 'Trusts and their Commercial Counterparts in Continental Europe', Report for the Association of Corporate Trustees (2002) Trusts & Trustees, 22.

[148] Convention of 1 July 1985 on the Law Applicable to Trusts and on their Recognition.

[149] Royal Decree of 19 July 1983.

[150] Law of 27 July 2003 entitled '*loi sur la fiducie*'.

[151] Statute no 37 of 17 March 2007.

[152] Law no 42 of 1 March 2010.

[153] Law no 43 of 1 March 2010.

[154] See above I.C.

elements, except for the law which regulates them, are connected with Italy. In other words, since the ratification of the Convention, Italy recognises not only foreign trusts but also so-called *trust interni*, Italian trusts regulated by foreign laws. It thus seems that over the last few decades, 'trust' or 'trust-like devices' have been adopted in some European civil law jurisdictions without great difficulties, mostly through reception or transplantation.[155] The trust can therefore no longer be considered merely a common law device.

This chapter, however, has not been concerned with an analysis of the reception of the trust idea in civil law countries but rather with an attempt to analyse three legal devices which are used in order to manage rights on behalf of others: the trust, the *Treuhand* and the *fiducie*. Given that this is a book on property law, the chapter focused on the proprietary aspects of these legal devices and in particular on how they might affect third party rights. Interestingly, only one of the three devices, the *fiducie*, is the product of a statutory intervention. The German *Treuhand*, a product of legal practice, is mostly regulated by case law.

VI.A COMMUNALITIES AND DIFFERENCES IN RELATION TO THE PROPRIETARY ASPECTS INVESTIGATED

In all three devices examined in this chapter, the English trust, the German *Treuhand* and the French *fiducie*, a transfer of the title to the manager takes place. But these rights do not become part of his personal patrimony. In all three cases the manager has a duty to keep the assets he is managing separate from his own.

Differently to England, however, in France and Germany the source of the relationship is a contract between the transferor and the transferee. Consequently, unlike the English trust which can also be self-declared, the *Treuhand* and *fiducie* cannot arise from a unilateral declaration, but represent bilateral agreements in favour of one of the parties or a third person. More often, however, there is no third party beneficiary. As was said above, in a *Treuhand* for management purposes the beneficiary is usually the *Treugeber*, whereas in the case of a *Treuhand* for security purposes, it is the *Treuhänder*. The same is true for the *fiducie*, where both the *constituant* and the *fiduciaire* can be the beneficiary.

Given the contractual nature of the *fiducie* and the *Treuhand*, the transferor never drops out of the picture and this gives rise to several consequences. Firstly, the manager has a duty to account for his behaviour towards the *Treugeber* and *constituant*. Secondly, differently from the English trust, which is usually irrevocable, both the *Treuhand* and *fiducie* can be revoked by the transferor. In the case of the *Treuhand* the contract normally provides for the termination of the relationship. In France, the legislature gives the *constituant* the ability to revoke the contract at any time up to the moment at which it is accepted by the beneficiary. After acceptance, the contract can only be modified or revoked with the beneficiary's consent or by order of the court. Thirdly, as will be seen, because of the contractual nature of the

[155] This is true also for non-European countries such as China, Quebec, Israel and countries of Central and South-America.

Treuhand and the *fiducie*, the insolvency and the death of one of the contractual parties can have an effect on the relationship.

VI.A.1 MISAPPROPRIATION OF ASSETS BY THE MANAGER

In case of misappropriation of property by the manager, the strongest protection of beneficiaries seems to be given in England. The liability of the trustee is strict and if the trustee is insolvent the beneficiary may have rights against the third party transferee who must restore the rights dissipated unless he is a bona fide purchaser for value without notice. If he is such a person, the beneficiary still has a personal claim against a third party who has assisted the trustee in his breach or who has received trust property in breach of trust. It is, however, uncertain whether the liability is triggered by mere receipt or by a dishonest receipt. Current authority indicates that the liability is fault based.

In Germany the liability of the *Treuhänder* is not strict. He is liable only for intentional and negligent breach of his duties. And if the *Treuhänder* is found liable but turns out to be insolvent, the beneficiary has a claim in tort against the third party transferee, but only if he has conspired with the manager in an attempt to damage the *Treugeber* or *beneficiary*. If the third party transferee was merely negligent he will acquire the rights free from any obligation.

The liability of a *fiduciaire* is not strict either. His liability is fault based. It is however not clear whether this is a liability in contract or in tort and the degree of fault required is uncertain too. A problem may arise if the *fiduciaire* is insolvent. The French legislature does not specifically address what rights the beneficiary has against a third party transferee. It would seem that if the manager acts beyond his powers to the knowledge (and not merely notice) of the third party the contract will be void.

VI.A.2 DEATH OF THE MANAGER, SETTLOR, *TREUGEBER* OR *CONSTITUANT*

As was said earlier, the death of the trustee does not bring an English trust to an end. This is different in the case of the *Treuhand* and the *fiducie*. The *Treuhandvertrag* establishes what happens in case of death of the *Treuhänder*. If there is only one *Treuhänder* and the contract is silent, the relationship usually comes to an end. That is not the case where there is more than one *Treuhänder* and they have created a partnership. As far as the *fiducie* is concerned, the dissolution of a legal person acting as a *fiduciaire* as well as the expulsion or temporary suspension from office of the practising lawyer bring the relationship to an end. The same applies in case of death of the *constituant*. In England, however, the death of the settlor does not affect the trust. And in Germany the death of the *Treugeber* does not usually determine the *Treuhand*.

VI.A.3 INSOLVENCY OF THE MANAGER OR ATTACKS BY PERSONAL CREDITORS

The insolvency of the trustee does not affect the trust fund. As far as the *Treuhand* is concerned, since the *Treugeber* never really drops out of the picture, the rights he assigns to the manager are still considered to belong economically to his patrimony. For that reason, as we have seen earlier, the German courts have granted the *Treugeber* and third party beneficiaries certain protections. They may demand the release of the assets and oppose attacks from personal creditors of the manager. Both rights are, however, usually granted only in the case of a direct transfer of the assets from the *Treugeber* to the *Treuhänder*, an exception being made for the *Treuhandkonto*.

If the *fiduciaire* is insolvent, the relationship comes to an end, but the *patrimoine fiduciaire* does not fall into the insolvency estate nor may personal creditors of the *fiduciaire* seize assets belonging to the *patrimoine*.

VI.A.4 INSOLVENCY OF THE TRANSFEROR OR ATTACKS BY HIS PERSONAL CREDITORS

Since the settlor drops out of the picture, should he become insolvent after the setting up of a trust, the rights held by the trustee or by the settlor himself as trustee will not be available to satisfy the claims of his unsecured creditors. Exceptions exist where the trust is a sham or a transfer at an undervalue or for no consideration.

As far as the *Treuhand* is concerned, the relationship ends because of the insolvency of the *Treugeber* and the *Treugut* can be reclaimed from the *Treuhänder*. In fact, in the case of a *Treuhand* for management purposes, the *Treugut* belongs to the insolvency estate of the *Treugeber* and thus the trustee in bankruptcy can claim the release of the *Treugut* from the *Treuhänder*. This is, however, only a personal claim.

If a personal creditor of the Treugeber tries to seize assets, the *Treuhänder* has no right to exercise the third party claim against the creditor. Third party beneficiaries of a *Treuhand* for management purposes are therefore protected in case of insolvency of the manager or attacks from his personal creditors, but not in case of insolvency of the *Treugeber* or attacks from his personal creditors. The justification for hat is found in the argument that from a substantive and economic point of view the *Treugut* belongs to the patrimony of the *Treugeber*.

The French legislature does not state the effect of the insolvency of the *constituant*. Article 2025(1) Cciv makes clear, however, that personal creditors of the *constituant* may seize the assets if they have been defrauded or if they have a right of recourse against a security, notice of which was given prior to the contract of *fiducie*.

CONCISE BIBLIOGRAPHY

M Graziadei, U Mattei and L Smith (eds), *Commercial Trusts in European Private Law* (Cambridge, Cambridge University Press, 2005).

M Grimaldi, 'La *fiducie*: réflections sur l'institution et sur l'avant-projet de loi qui la consacre', Defrénois, 1991, Art 35085, 897 and Art 35094, 961.

DJ Hayton (ed), *The International Trust*, 3rd edn (Bristol, Jordans, 2011).

DJ Hayton, SCJJ Kortmann and HLE Verhagen (eds), *Principles of European Trust Law* (The Hague, Kluwer Law International 1999).

M Lupoi, *Trusts: A Comparative Study* (Cambridge, Cambridge University Press, 2001).

C Mitchell, *Hayton and Mitchell: Commentary and Cases on the Law of Trusts and Equitable Remedies*, 13th edn (London, Sweet & Maxwell, 2010).

G Moffat, *Trusts Law: Text and Materials*, 5th edn (Cambridge, Cambridge University Press, 2009).

J Oakley, *Parker & Mellows: The Modern Law of Trusts*, 9th edn (London, Sweet & Maxwell, 2008).

CHAPTER SEVEN
CREATION

Lars van Vliet

This chapter deals with the fourth of the six essential questions of property law: how are property rights created? The chapter therefore explains how property rights can originate. This is a complicated and technical part of property law, which deals with accession of movables to land, mixing (commingling), making new objects (*specificatio*), and acquisition of a property right through lapse of time (prescription).

The law distinguishes between derivative and original acquisition of property. In the case of derivative acquisition one receives a right which previously belonged to someone else. When A sells his car to B and transfers ownership to B, the latter acquires a right of ownership that previously belonged to A. The same happens where B inherits A's car. Original acquisition, on the other hand, is acquisition of a right which did not previously exist, which originates in the hands of the new owner or holder of the right. When, for example, B makes car parts from aluminium sheets belonging to A, A or B will become the owner of the newly created car parts which did not exist before. We use the term *original acquisition* also where the right of ownership of a principal thing is extended to cover a thing attached to the principal object. In these cases no new right of ownership is created. We will start off the chapter by looking at these latter cases. In practice, most cases involve the attachment of movable property to land, because these cases often involve the largest financial interests.

The standard examples of original acquisition to be found in many textbooks on property law are the following: accession of movables to movables, accession of movables to land, commingling of movables, specification of movables, and instances which are less important in practice, such as alluvion (acquisition of sediment on land), treasure trove, finding, appropriation of *bona vacantia* or *res nullius* (things belonging to no one). It would be impossible to list all instances of original acquisition. Apart from these cases there are many other examples in specific statutes and even in the general body of private law, for example an obligation which arises from a contract or a right of servitude created by deed. The following will concentrate on those instances which are most relevant in practice and give rise to a large body of case law. Original acquisition of beneficial interests is discussed in Chapter 6 on trusts.

I. ACCESSION

I.A ACCESSION OF MOVABLES TO LAND

Introductory Note

Accession involves that a thing which is united with another thing becomes an integral part (component) of that thing. It presupposes that one object can be regarded as the main object. Where land is involved the land is always treated as the main object. Any building erected on the soil is seen as a mere attachment to the ground, even if the building is worth more than the bare land. The reason is that, in contrast to buildings, land is almost indestructible and is therefore considered permanent.

In land law the foundation of the modern law of accession is the famous Roman rule *superficies solo cedit* (the building accrues to the land).[1] This principle applies in legal systems based on Roman law. It is very probable that English law has also been influenced by the rule, possibly via Bracton, who describes the rule in his *De legibus et consuetudinibus Angliae*.[2] Nevertheless, modern English law does not normally use the term accession (based on the Roman term *accessio*). In the English law of landlord and tenant the problem of accession is treated under the heading 'tenant's fixtures'.

To understand whether or not we should allow subjective intention to play any role in determining questions of accession we first have to look to the principles behind the concept of accession. Particularly in German and Swiss literature attention has been paid to the rationale of accession.[3] The argument most frequently mentioned is preservation of value, that is, preservation of the unity of things. Once different objects have been joined adding value to the individual parts the law should prevent the value thus created from being destroyed by taking the unity apart.[4]

[1] *Cf* Inst 2,1,29 and Gaius. D. 41,1,7,10.

[2] GW Woodbine, 'On the Laws and Customs of England', in *On the Laws and Customs of England*, trans SE Thorne, 4 vols (Cambridge, MA: The Belknap Press of Harvard University Press, 1968–77) vol 2, §46.

[3] But see also the Dutch thesis by HD Ploeger, *Horizontale splitsing van eigendom* (Deventer, Kluwer, 1997) ch 3.

[4] This argument was already referred to in Inst 2,1,29: '… quod ideo provisum est, ne aedificia rescindi necesse sit…' (This has been so provided to make it unnecessary to take the building apart). See also: RG 28 June 1904, RGZ 58, 338 *et seq*, 341; RG 26 June 1908, RGZ 69, 117 *et seq*, 120; BGH 8 October 1955, NJW 1955, 1793–94 quoted hereunder; D Medicus, *Allgemeiner Teil des BGB*, 8th edn (Heidelberg, Müller, 2002) 458 *et seq.*

Explanation to the draft of a Civil Code for the German Nation, Book 41 **7.1 (DE)**

It is beyond doubt that the component parts that are dealt with here fulfil their economic function and therefore have their value only in the object they make up. Their separation not only leads to the dissolution of the entirety, but it also damages and changes the nature of the component parts to be obtained, and as a consequence it reduces or eliminates the value of property, a result which is contrary to economic interests. However, allowing special rights to exist in the separate components would inevitably facilitate a separation of them. The exclusion of them [ie of special rights] is thus based on economic interests which the legislator has to take into account.

Notes

(1) This approach presupposes that the sum of all parts is worth more than all parts taken separately. If removal of an attachment were to cause physical damage to one of the things involved, the rules of accession prevent such damage and loss of value by providing that no separate property rights can exist in relation to the attachment. Where the owner of the thing attached and the owner of the main thing are two different persons, accession will cause the first owner to lose his right of ownership to the owner of the main thing. The latter's right will henceforth cover the original thing and the attachment as well. The same happens to limited property rights. If the thing to be attached is burdened with a right of pledge, this right lapses upon attachment of the thing.[5] As a result of the lapsing the former holders of property rights are no longer able to claim back the thing attached. This reduces the risk that the unity may be dismantled.[6]

We can now see that attachment of a movable thing to land has two different legal consequences. First the annexation to the land changes the status of the thing from movable into immovable. Second, as a result of original acquisition, the owner of the land acquires ownership of the attachment, or rather his right of ownership of the land henceforth covers the attachment as well. However, these effects do not necessarily go hand in hand. In many legal systems it is possible to exclude accession of a building to the land by creating a so-called right of superficies.[7] This excludes the second legal effect, accession in the strict sense of the word, that is, the original acquisition of ownership as a result of attachment. Of course it does not change the first effect: the existence of a right of superficies does not turn a building into a movable thing. It is immovable because of its attachment to the ground.

In order for accession to take place the bond between the two things need not necessarily be physical. A strong economic bond suffices where, as a result of

[5] Note that Dutch law recognises a pledge on movables in which the pledgor remains in actual control of the thing (Art 3:237 BW).

[6] As to limited property rights, this argument is naturally confined to those rights which could lead to the component being taken away.

[7] Superficies is a property right for the use of land. Buildings erected by the lessee do not become the property of the owner of the land because superficies prevents accession. Above, Chapter 3.

economic unity, the value of the unity is much more than the value of the individual objects.

(2) The second principle behind the concept of accession is the protection of third parties. If, according to common opinion, something is immovable, it should be treated as such. Third parties should be able to trust their eyes.[8] The buyer of a building should be certain, simply by inspecting the premises, what objects are included in the transfer of the land; so should acquirers of limited property rights, such as mortgagees, or hypothecees. If the outward appearance of unity is false, the correct legal situation should be reflected in the land register. If, to give an example, accession is prevented by the creation of a right of superficies, this right should be registered.

Neither of the two principles tolerates any influence of subjective factors. The parties cannot by mere agreement determine whether something is a physical or economic unity. And, as to the second principle, if subjective factors had any influence, third parties would no longer be able to rely on the factual situation.

I.A.1 DUTCH LAW[9]

Hoge Raad, 31 October 1997[10] **7.2 (NL)**

Tax authorities v Rabobank

IS THE PORTACABIN IN QUESTION IMMOVABLE?

Portacabin

The portacabin in question is immovable as it is designated, by its nature and design, to remain there for a considerable period.

Facts: Question is whether a portacabin was movable or immovable. A businessman, called Buys, needed extra office space and opted for a portacabin to be placed on his land next to an existing building. The portacabin was seamlessly attached to the land and building. It was placed on a concrete foundation with a skirting-board to close the gap between the land and the cabin. The cabin was connected to the sewerage and to gas, water, electricity and telephone. A pleasant garden surrounded both buildings. Visually the portacabin seemed to form part of the building.

When Buys needed a loan he burdened the land with a right of hypothec in favour of Rabobank.[11] Eventually the bank had to exercise its right of security: the property was sold by public auction and bought by Rabobank itself. Some weeks later the Inspector of Taxes sold in execution all movable property belonging to Buys to satisfy the latter's tax debts. To Rabobank's surprise the inspector also sold the portacabin because he regarded it as movable property. The cabin was purchased by a third party and removed from the premises.

The question whether the portacabin was movable or immovable determined the competing claims of the two creditors, the bank and the tax inspector. If it was immovable it formed part of the land and

[8] F Endemann, *Lehrbuch des bürgerlichen Rechts*, vol 1, 9th edn (Berlin, Carl Heymanns Verlag, 1903) 241, fn 19; H Rey, *Die Grundlagen des Sachenrechts und das Eigentum* (Bern, Stämpfli, 2000) 1080 *et seq*.

[9] See HW Heyman, 'Wanneer is een gebouw of werk "duurzaam met de grond verenigd"?' in SE Bartels and JM Milo, *Open normen in het goederenrecht* (The Hague: Boom Juridische Uitgevers, 2000) 91–122.

[10] NJ 1998/97.

[11] Functionally this right is comparable to the English mortgage.

was therefore subject to the hypothec burdening the land, for a property right covers the thing and all its components. If, on the other hand, the cabin was movable, it was not burdened with the hypothec and the tax inspector had the right to seize it in execution.

Held: The Dutch Supreme Court upheld the court of appeal's decision that the portacabin was immovable. According to the Supreme Court, a building may be immovable in the sense of Article 3:3 of the Dutch Civil Code (BW)[12] if according to its character and construction the object is destined to remain on its place permanently, regardless whether it is technically possible to move the building to another site. In answering this question regard shall be had to common opinion. The intention of the builder is relevant only as far as it is patent for everyone to see. As the Supreme Court pointed out, property rights should be easily recognisable for third parties (this is called the principle of publication[13]).

Judgment: 3.3 (a) A building can be permanently connected to the land within the meaning of Article 3:3 BW, when it is designated, by its nature [*aard*] and design [*inrichting*], to remain there for a considerable period. ... The technical possibility to move the building is irrelevant.

(b) in answering the question whether a building or construction is designated to stay located for a considerable period, as was mentioned in the memorandum of reply II relating to Article 3:3, attention must be paid to the intention of the builder in so far as this can externally established. The builder is he according to whose assignment the building was placed.

(c) As can be seen from the memorandum of reply II mentioned under (b), the purpose of a building or construction to remain there for a considerable period must be recognisable to third parties. The criterion follows from the importance for third parties to know about proprietary relations.

(d) Public opinion [*verkeersopvattingen*] can—unlike the question as to whether something is a component [*bestanddeel*] of an object in the meaning of article 3:4—not be used as a separate criterion to decide whether an object is movable or immovable. It can, however, be taken into account in those cases where there is uncertainty whether an object has a durable link to the land, and when for the application of that criterion in a certain case it must be established what 'durable', 'connection', 'designation' or 'recognisable for third parties' means.

Notes

(1) Article 3:3(1) BW gives a definition of what is immovable: 'Immovable are the land, ... and buildings and constructions which have been attached permanently to the land, whether directly, or indirectly by attachment to other buildings or constructions.' Article 5:20 BW uses the same criterion but indicates what is covered by the right of ownership of a parcel of land. It ensures that those objects which, according to Article 3:3 BW, are immovable belong to the owner of the parcel on or in which they are fixed. This effect can be prevented by creating a right of superficies.

(2) At first the Dutch Supreme Court uses the intention of the annexor as a criterion: the person attaching the movable object himself or who orders someone

[12] Art 3:3 subs 1 BW: Immovable are the land, ... and buildings and constructions which have been attached permanently to the land, whether directly, or indirectly by attachment to other buildings or constructions.

[13] See eg LPW van Vliet, *Transfer of Movables in German, French, English and Dutch Law* (Nijmegen, Ars Aequi Libri, 2000) 30.

to attach it for him. This misleadingly gives the impression of being a subjective element. However, the court adds that the intention can be taken into account only as far as it is recognisable to third parties. But then the criterion is incoherent: the word 'intention' should be avoided completely, as its natural meaning is subjective rather than objective.

In subsequent cases the Dutch Supreme Court was able to stress yet again that subjective intention cannot decide whether an object is movable or immovable.[14] In a tax case the owner of mobile harbour crane told the tax authority that he would relocate the crane to a different wharf within Rotterdam harbour. The Supreme Court made clear that the owner's subjective intention is not relevant and that the 'intention' can only be inferred from the 'nature and design'.[15]

Hoge Raad, 15 January 2010[16] **7.3 (NL)**

IS THE FLOATING HOUSE IN QUESTION MOVABLE OR IMMOVABLE

Floating house

The intention should only be inferred from the nature and design of the object itself and not from the surrounding area.

Facts: The owner of a floating house should pay immovables tax to the city council provided the floating house is immovable in the sense of Article 3:3 BW. The city council asserts that the floating house is immovable and the owner denies that the floating house is immovable. The house is attached with brackets to mooring posts which in turn are fastened into the bottom beneath the house, so that the house is able to move up and down while attached to mains supplies. Factors from the surrounding area play no role in assessing the immovable character of an object.

Judgment: 4.1 The Court of Appeal has rightly held that for the application of the Statute on Valuation of Immovables and for the levying of immovables tax the distinction between movables and immovables is based on the provision of Article 3:3 BW (cf Supreme Court 7 June 2002, nr 36759, LJN AE3831, BNB 2002/283). Rightly the Court has taken as a starting point that this also applies to floating houses. As far as the complaints are directed against this, they fail.

4.2 Further the Court has held, referring to the judgment of the Supreme Court of 20 September 2002, nr 37128, LJN AE7857, BNB 2002/374, that the floating house in question is attached to the land, as it is connected with brackets to mooring posts grounded into the bottom. The complaints against this assessment succeed. The case is about an object that according to its construction is designed to float and does indeed float, so that it is a ship in the sense of Article 8:1 BW. A ship is generally a movable object. A connection between a ship en the bottom underneath the ship which allows the ship to move with the water level cannot lead to the opinion that the ship is attached to the bottom in the sense of Article 3:3(1) BW. Appar-

[14] See eg HR 5 January 2000, BNB 2000/83 (maritime cargo containers): the claimant asserted that, as he intended the containers to remain in place permanently, they had to be regarded as immovable property. The Supreme Court, however, maintained that the claimant's intention could be relevant only as far as it might be inferred from the physical situation.

[15] HR 24 December 2010, LJN: BO3644.

[16] LJN: BK9136.

ently, there is such a connection in the case at hand, so that the floating house is not connected to the bottom underneath the house in the above-mentioned sense.

4.3 The Court's judgment cannot he upheld. Referral to another Court of Appeal should follow in order to investigate whether the floating house is connected to the bank in such a way that there is a connection in the sense of Article 3:3(1) BW. It should be noted that it follows from the Supreme Court's judgment of 22 July 1988, nr 25546, LJN AA7150, BNB 1988/282, NJ 1989, 257, that no such connection can be accepted only because of a connection with cables and a connection to mains and sewers.

4.4.1. If the question mentioned in 4.3 is answered positively the Court of referral should also investigate whether the connection to the bank is permanent. In this case the Court has inferred such a connection from, among other things, the following circumstances: (i) the installation of the floating house was only possible by temporarily making an opening in a dike, (ii) the floating house is situated next to a part of the bank (a parking place) belonging to the claimant and a water space belonging to the claimant, (iii) the floating house is situated in a residential area, (iv) it is situated between low bridges and consequently cannot be towed away to another location in its entirety, and (v) the entry on the upper deck of the floating house has a special connection to the promenade on the bank.

4.4.2. As far as the complaints are directed against this opinion they are successful, as the circumstances mentioned in 4.4.1 concern the surrounding area of the floating house, and cannot be regarded as visible characteristics of the nature and design of the floating house itself (cf Supreme Court 17 November 2006, nr 41434, LJN AZ2377, BNB 2007/50).

Note

The case shows that not all objective factors can play a role in assessing whether or not the object is movable or immovable. Factors from the surrounding area cannot play any role. Only the nature and design of the object itself are relevant factors.

Hoge Raad, 15 November 1991[17] **7.4 (NL)**

Dépex v curatoren Bergel

DISTILLATION EQUIPMENT BECOMES PART OF THE FACTORY BUILDING

Distillery

The distillery equipment is an integral part of the building only if the equipment and the building are specially constructed to fit each other or if the building would be incomplete without the equipment.

Facts: Dépex sold distillery equipment to Bergel Manufacturing under a reservation of ownership clause. The purchase price was never paid and Dépex went into administration and insolvency. Dépex revindicated ownership of the equipment, claiming that it still owned the equipment. Bergel and its administrator in insolvency countered that the equipment had become an integral part of Bergel's factory building and that therefore the equipment belonged to the insolvent's estate.

[17] NJ 1993/316.

Held: The distillery equipment is an integral part of the building only if the equipment and the building are specially constructed to fit each other or if the building would be incomplete without the equipment. Whether or not the equipment is important for the production process of the factory is irrelevant.

Judgment: 3.3. The question on appeal in cassation is whether the Court of Appeal has, on good grounds, held that the distillery equipment must be seen as a component part [*bestanddeel*] of the immovable of Bergel. Following the president of the lower court, the Court of Appeal has based its judgment on the physical connection between the equipment and the building. As can in particular be seen from the Court's reasoning under 6, the Court has exclusively looked whether the equipment, according to public opinion, is part of the factory.

Part 2a of the grievances correctly presumes that in order to answer this question the building that houses the factory must be the principal part. Whether the Court of Appeal has done this, or has held that not the building but the factory in the sense of a production-installation must be considered the principal part, cannot be derived with certainty from the judgment of the Court of Appeal. Because of this it is not possible for the Court on appeal in cassation to see whether the Court of Appeal used to correct approach to the law. Grievances 2a and 2d are effective in so far as that they hold that the Court of Appeal has not motivated, as is required by law, its judgment sufficiently.

3.4. Grievances 2b and 2c seek to argue that the reasoning of the Court of Appeal that the equipment belongs to the 'essence [*wezen*] of the factory', in the meaning of article 563 BW, is wrong or at least cannot be understood. These grievances also hold. When the Court of Appeal meant that the provision of Article 564 sub 1, under 1e BW, must be applied here, it has shown an incorrect approach as this provision can only be used to answer the question whether an object is immovable by its designation. If the Court of Appeal intended that the circumstance that the equipment is essential for the correct functioning of the pharmaceutical production installation in the building brings with it that the equipment is a component part of the 'factory' then it also has shown an incorrect approach to the law, either by not designating the factory building, but the production-installation in that building as the principle part (see above 3.3), or by answering the question if the equipment, according to public opinion, whether the equipment is a component part of the building primarily on the basis of the role the equipment fulfils in the production process.

In any case, it does not follow clearly from the attacked judgment of the Court of Appeal whether the incorrect criteria dealt with are applied or the Court has incorrectly applied the law. The Court of Appeal has therefore not motivated its judgment sufficiently.

3.5 Part 3 presumes that the Court of Appeal has held that the distillation equipment is immovable by its designation. This presumption is incorrect, so that the complaint contained in this part that the Court of Appeal has incorrectly applied article 563 BW, is without meaning and therefore does not need to de dealt with further.

3.6 Part 4 contradicts the holding of the Court of Appeal that the equipment is really part of the essence of the factory in the meaning of Article 563 (sub 1 under 1). From the consideration above follows that this holding cannot be part of a correct resolving of the dispute, so that this part does not need to be dealt with further.

3.7 From the above considerations under 3.3 and 3.4 follows that the judgment of the Court of Appeal cannot be maintained. Referral is necessary. In the light of the research that must be conducted after the referral of the case, the following is added. Cases as these are about answering the question whether equipment and a building should be seen together as one object. When a building and equipment in construction are made dependent on each other, a clue is provided to positively answer that question. The same applies when a building from the viewpoint of its suitablility as a factory building—a building suited to house a production installation—in the absence of the equipment must be seen as incomplete. The function the equipment fulfils is not a part of applying this criterion.

Notes

(1) The portacabin judgment and its affirmation in subsequent cases on Article 3:3 BW give an incomplete picture of the Dutch law of accession. In Dutch law there are different articles which can lead to accession of movables to land. When a certain object attached to the land should be seen as immovable under Article 3:3 BW, it is acquired by the landowner by way of accession under Article 5:20 BW. However, in addition to these articles, Article 3:4 gives a definition of the component parts of a thing:

> (1) Everything which according to public opinion forms part of a thing, is part of that thing.
>
> (2) A thing which is connected to a principal thing in such a way that it cannot be separated without considerable damage to one of the things, becomes part of the principal thing.

Article 5:3 BW then adds that ownership of a thing covers all its component parts. Therefore, if a movable thing becomes part of the land in the meaning of Article 3:4 BW it leads to accession to the land. The application of either of these two norms (Articles 3:3 + 5:20 BW or Articles 3:4 + 5:3 BW) in itself can lead to accession. Either something accedes to the land because it should be seen as immovable in the sense of Article 3:3, or it accedes because it should be regarded as a component part of the land under Article 3:4. For this reason the criteria for accession should ideally be the same whether Article 3:3 or 3:4 is applied. It seems that the legislator has not reconciled Articles 3:3, 5:20, 3:4 and 5:3 BW and has not seen the potential conflict between these norms: doctrine tries in vain to reconcile these norms.[18]

Oddly, though, it might seem that the Dutch Supreme Court does not apply uniform criteria for both norms. The portacabin criterion, which is based on Article 3:3 BW, seems to conflict with the criteria formulated in a large number of earlier judgments on Article 3:4 BW and its predecessor under the old Civil Code.[19] An object should be regarded as a component part in the sense of Article 3:4 BW if the main object would be incomplete without the component part.

[18] In HR 25 October 2002, NJ 2003/241 (gravestones) the Supreme Court seems to suggest that a gravestone is not a component part of the land but none the less belongs to the ownership of the land under Art 5:20 BW. This would lead to the gravestone being an object separate from the land but still belonging to the land. Yet, it cannot in itself be transferred or burdened with a limited property right; in short, it cannot be a separate object of rights. But that is exactly what the notion of 'component part' is meant for! Ownership of gravestones is now regulated by Art 32A Wet op Lijkbezonging.

[19] Heyman, above n 9, 101–05.

In *Dépex v curatoren Bergel*[20] a distillery installation in a pharmaceutical factory which was indispensable for the production of pharmaceuticals was not regarded as a component part of the building in question. According to the Supreme Court accession could happen only if the installation were an indispensable part of the *building itself*. This could be the case if the building and/or the installation are specially constructed to fit each other. Yet, the question whether the installation is essential for the process of production is irrelevant.

If, however, removal of the installation would cause substantial damage to the installation or the building, it has become a component part under the separate criterion in Article 3:4 (2) BW. Of course, where machines are installed into a hall using bolts and nuts this criterion of damage does not apply for obvious reasons. In such cases, therefore, the criterion of completeness is of principal importance.

(2) It seems that the criterion of completeness sets a requirement for accession which is much more severe than the criterion in the portacabin case. Under the *Dépex* criterion of completeness industrial equipment installed in a machine hall will commonly not accede to the machine hall. An important consequence is the possibility of financing expensive industrial equipment separately, ie without using the right of mortgage on the machine hall. As the machines do not accede to the building, they may be sold to the factory under a reservation of ownership clause, or they may be made the object of a non-possessory pledge or a sale-and-leaseback transaction. This significant possibility of separate financing could be jeopardised if the same equipment would nonetheless accede under the portacabin criterion of Article 3:3.[21]

I.A.2 GERMAN LAW

Introductory Note

In German law attachments which become an integral part of another thing by way of accession are called *wesentliche Bestandteile* (essential components). As these components do not have an independent legal existence and no separate property rights can exist in relation to them they are sometimes referred to as *sonderrechtsunfähiger Bestandteil* (components which cannot be the object of special property rights). Apart from specific provisions, the question of accession has been laid down in §§93–95 and 946–47 of the Bürgerliches Gesetzbuch. §§93–95 determine when something is a *wesentlicher Bestandteil*, and §§946–47 provide that the right of ownership which existed in relation to the component lapses upon attachment and that the right of ownership of the main thing henceforth covers the attachment as well. §949 BGB draws attention to the fact that limited proprietary rights over the attachment also lapse as a result of accession.

The key article is §93 which gives a general definition of components:

[20] See also HR 26 March 1936, NJ 1936/757; HR 11 December 1953, NJ 1954/115; HR 27 November 1992, NJ 1993/317; HR 28 June 1996, NJ 1997/397.

[21] See also Heyman, above n 9, 102–03.

> Components of a thing which cannot be separated without damaging or changing the nature of one of them (components) cannot be the object of separate rights.[22]

Two criteria may be derived from this paragraph: causing damage and substantial change. Case law and literature, however, acknowledge that accession may also take place where removal, though technically possible, would entail disproportionately high costs.[23] The *Motive* quoted above stress the argument of preservation of value.

The criterion of 'change in nature' refers to the economic usefulness of the principal thing and the attachments after their separation. A thing is turned into a component if without attachment to the principal thing it cannot fulfil the function it had within the entirety, not even by attaching it to another object. Accession also takes place where the principal thing cannot fulfil its economic function without the component in question, unless a similar component may be attached to the principal thing, reviving its economic function.

As this interdependence will not often exist, the criterion in §93 BGB is much narrower than might be commonly thought. The man in the street will regard the wheels and engine of a car as essential components because the car cannot function without them. In principle, however, these parts will not be regarded as components in the sense of §93 BGB. After removal the wheels and engine do not lose their economic function, as they can be used for another car. Nor does the car lose its economic function: it may be fitted with another engine and other wheels.[24]

An important example of this narrow accession rule is the sale of mass-produced engines. Such engines can be sold with a reservation of ownership clause without the seller's risk of losing ownership as a result of an engine being permanently attached in an engine hall. As we have seen before, Dutch law reaches a similar result using the completeness-test from the judgment in *Dépex*.

On the other side, a machine specially made for a particular hall or a particular ship does become a component.[25] The same applies to components of minor value, such as bolts and screws.

OLG Oldenburg, 4 July 1962[26] **7.5 (DE)**

DID A STEAM PRODUCER BECOME PART OF THE FACTORY BUILDING?

Quick steam generator Dampffix

The definition of essential component in the sense of §§93 and 94 BGB.

Facts: A quick steam generator[27] in a factory building was used in the industrial process and at the

[22] Bestandteile einer Sache, die voneinander nicht getrennt werden können, ohne daß der eine oder der andere zerstört oder in seinem Wesen verändert wird (wesentliche Bestandteile), können nicht Gegenstand besonderer Rechte sein.

[23] Staudinger-Jickeli and Stieper (2004), §93, Rn 17.

[24] Medicus, above n 4, Rn 1187.

[25] Staudinger-Jickeli and Stieper (2004), §93, Rn 18–21.

[26] Nr 2 U 59/62.

[27] These steam generators are mostly used in the clothing industry.

same time for heating the factory building. The question arose as to whether the generator was an essential component of the factory premises.

Held: The steam generator was not an essential component of the factory premises.

Judgment: According to §985 BGB the claimant is allowed to demand the return of the steam engine 'Dampffix' and any other object as stated in the petition from the defendant, since the claimant is the owner of these objects and the defendant as owner of the premises, which include the above-located factory building, in which the claimed objects are located, is the possessor of these objects. The 'Dampffix' as well as the other appertaining parts have not become essential components of the premises, neither according to §93 nor according to §94 BGB. According to §93 BGB components of a thing, which cannot be separated without damaging or changing the nature of one of them, cannot be the object of separate rights. According to §94 subs 1 BGB things which are firmly attached to the soil, especially buildings, etc, belong to the essential components of the land. The 'Dampffix' and the other objects do not appertain to them. The 'Dampffix' and the other parts delivered by the claimant can be separated and reused elsewhere without damaging or changing the nature of one of them and there is no use taking evidence in this respect. They are prefabricated parts which have been produced in bulk. Further, the fact that they can be removed from the building without being damaged can easily be seen from the submitted photos. Even if the 'Dampffix' was attached to the base on which it is situated with screws or cement, this attachment could be separated without damaging parts of the building or the installation delivered by the claimant considerably.

According to §94 subs 2 BGB things inserted for the construction of a building belong to the essential components of a building, even if they are not firmly attached to the land. The opinion of the court of first instance, according to which the 'Dampffix' and the other parts delivered by the claimant have become essential components pursuant to this provision, cannot be approved. It is unnecessary to determine here if basically a heating system also belongs to a modern manufacturing plant and if a factory building is to be treated as incomplete, as long as a heating system has not been installed. This case, after all, does not involve such a heating system. According to a letter from the proprietor of the factory to the claimant, the factory needed a fast steam engine ('Schnelldampferzeuger') in order to be able to heat their distilling balloons in the industrial process. If the factory, as may also be inferred from the letter, intended to use the produced steam also to warm the radiators in the rooms of the factory, this obviously was only a subordinate purpose. ... Therefore, it was not inserted for the construction of the building pursuant to §94 subs 2 BGB in order to be able to heat the building, but it was installed in order to have a steam producer which is necessary for the industrial process. If it was removed, the intended use as factory building would not be changed, since any other business can be set up in it. The fact that if in the present case the 'Dampffix' was removed, at the same time the rooms of the factory could not be heated centrally any more, as long as a boiler has not been installed, does not change anything. As it has already been explained, the 'Dampffix' not only or even predominantly served to heat the rooms, but it was at least to the same extent necessary to heat the distilling balloons. That is why the 'Dampffix' is legally to be treated in the same way as otherwise machinery in a factory building, which regularly is not to be considered as essential components according to the rulings of the Supreme Court.

Bürgerliches Gesetzbuch **7.6 (DE)**

§94 (1) Essential components of the land include objects which are firmly attached to the land, especially buildings, and the products of the land as long as they are united with the land. Seeds become an essential component of the land when they are sowed, plants do so when they are planted.
(2) Essential components of a building include objects inserted for the construction of the building.[28]

Notes

(1) In §94 a definition of components of land is given. This paragraph should not be seen as a *lex specialis*, a special rule having priority over the more general §93. §94 extends the notion of component by ensuring that certain things are components of the land, even if they are not components in the sense of §93.

Common opinion (*Verkehrsauffassung*, or common sense) determines when a building, a term which includes building materials, is firmly fixed to the ground. Such attachment may already exist when removal is possible only with great effort and at high costs.[29] A building may even become attached to the land in the sense of §94 simply by its own weight.[30] However, as indicated, fixing a machine to the ground will not normally lead to accession.

(2) The decisive measure for accession in the second subsection of §94, things inserted for the construction of a building, is not a firm physical bond, but rather a spatial relationship (*räumlicher Zusammenhang*) or incompleteness of the building as such. Roof tiles, to take an example, are components of a house and thus components of the land even though they are not firmly attached to the roof.[31] Unlike in the above instance of the wheels and engine of a car, the fact that the tiles have not been made especially for the house involved does not prevent accession. To our way of thinking, this difference cannot be explained satisfactorily. Central heating and toilets make the building complete and are thus essential components. Equipment used in the production process cannot be seen as essential components. This completeness test reminds us of the Dutch judgement in *Dépex* cited above.

[28] Absatz 1. Zu den wesentlichen Bestandteilen eines Grundstücks gehören die mit dem Grund und Boden festverbundenen Sachen, insbesondere Gebäude, sowie die Erzeugnisse des Grundstücks, solange sie mit dem Boden zusammenhängen. Samen wird mit dem Aussäen, eine Pflanze wird mit dem Einpflanzen wesentlicher Bestandteil des Grundstücks. Absatz 2. Zu den wesentlichen Bestandteilen eines Gebäudes gehören die zur Herstellung des Gebäudes eingefügten Sachen.

[29] Staudinger-Jickeli and Stieper (2004), §94, Rn 7; MünchKomm BGB-Holch (2006), §94, Rn 4.

[30] Staudinger-Jickeli and Stieper (2004), §94, Rn 8; MünchKomm BGB-Holch (2006), §94, Rn 4.

[31] Staudinger-Jickeli and Stieper (2004), §94, Rn 24 and 30; MünchKomm BGB-Holch (2006), §94, Rn 23.

BGH, 27 September 1978[32] 7.7 (DE)

Component of a building?

Boiler

A heating boiler is an essential component of a school building.

Facts: The claimant delivered two boilers and installed them on foundations in the cellar through a large hole in the wall. The cellar wall was then bricked up in such a way that it could later be undone should one of the boilers have to be replaced. The claimant worked as a subcontractor at the request of the principal contractor who was later declared insolvent. The owner of the school building, the local city council, defendant in the proceedings, agreed that it would pay the claimant for the two boilers if they still belonged to the claimant when the principal contractor was declared insolvent. The city council asserted that the claimant had lost ownership of the boilers as a result of accession (§946 BGB), if not already as a result of delivery.

Held: The court of first instance held in accordance with the claimant's petition that ownership of the boilers had not passed to the city council as a result of their installation. The Court of Appeal, on the other hand, held that the boilers were essential components. The Supreme Court agreed with the Court of Appeal. According to common opinion a heating boiler is an essential component of a middle European school building.

Judgment: The holding of the Court of Appeal, that each single part, of which a heating system of a school building is assembled, is an essential component of this building pursuant to §94 subs 2 BGB, is correct. According to common opinion a school building is not finished without a heating system, considering the climatic standards of Central Europe (see BGH, NJW 1953, 1180); the parts of the installation are inserted into the building 'for its construction'.

The appellant argues that in case of a dispute the definite construction of the building would not be in question; the installation of boilers ('Heizkessel') would not be necessary for the erection of an unfinished carcass. According to §94 subs 2 BGB the legal quality of the inserted thing, however, is determined by the purpose of the insertion. For that reason it suffices that the boilers served for the completion of the planned building. Having been inserted into the unfinished building, they [ie the boilers] have become essential components of the building as well as of the premises (Senate, NJW 1978, 1311), since the building was firmly attached to the land (§94 subs 1 BGB). Therefore the question is, if the boilers have been inserted into the carcass in the sense of §94 subs 2 BGB. The Court of Appeal affirms this on the ground that both boilers have already been placed at their final position, namely not only in the heating control room, but also on the foundation prepared for them. The fact that they still were to be adjusted was unimportant. It was a question of some centimeters; they just needed to be moved into place. The intention to definitely leave the boilers in the heating control room was supported by the fact that the hole in the wall needed for the setting up had been bricked up.

These circumstances justify the finding that the boilers have been inserted into the building under construction. The provision (§94 subs 2 BGB) primarily serves the establishment of secure legal relationships. That is why the facts visible to an outside observer, in particular to someone who is interested in the purchase of the premises, are of significant importance for the question of ownership. In the case of dispute it will be argued that the boilers were placed according to the architectural and

[32] NJW 1979, 712.

operational requirements and that they definitely should stay at the place where they were and that they were not only provisionally placed in the carcass or in the room designated for the heating control room. In this connection the fact that they were placed on a prepared foundation and the fact that the hole in the wall, which was necessary to bring in the boilers, was bricked up again, were of the same weight.

It is unnecessary to discuss if putting down the boilers on the foundation in a way which was apparently inconsistent with the architectural and operational requirements would conflict with the conclusion that they have already been inserted into the building under construction. It is true that the Court of Appeal does not describe the features of the foundation with respect to the intended purpose; it determines, however, that the boilers were only to be adjusted within the range of some centimeters. This deviation from their final position was meaningless for a third party, who formed an opinion about the obtained condition of the building and the question of ownership, considering the criterion emphasised by the Court of Appeal.

The appellant pleads in error that the boilers have not been linked up with cables conveying gas, power and water and with cables draining off heating water and waste gas yet. There is no use in discussing, if in borderline cases the connection with cables, which are necessary for the operation, can present the only sure criterion with respect to the insertion of a thing, which was delivered to its due location for the construction of the planned building and which does not need to be fixed to the brickwork because of its own weight, as for instance a stove, which becomes an essential component of the apartment house. In this case several significant facts have come together, which point to the definite insertion of the boilers. Contrary to the appellant's opinion, the focus must not be laid upon the fact that the bricking up of a hole in the wall, which was left open to bring in parts of the installation, is regularly ordered by the supervision of building works and not (by the landowner or) by the constructor of the installation. Experience of life does not show that this regularly happens without approval of the constructor of the installation; legal certainty with respect to the state of the construction and the question of ownership can only be granted if the person who for whatever reason has to find out who the owner is does not need to investigate if the installation was approved or not by the supplier in the individual case. It is in the interest of the transparency of the law (and of the preservation of value) that in all cases of §§946 et seq BGB the law makes the loss of ownership independent of the question who created the annexation and whether that person was entitled to do so. Finally, the appellant's remark that the boilers themselves were not complete and ready for use, because they lacked among other things operating panels, sound absorber and thermostats, cannot be accepted. The loss of ownership caused by the insertion into a building does not require the insertion of 'complete' things. According to the definition of §90 BGB as well as common opinion a boiler is a separate thing before it is inserted into a building. If the constructor of the installation needs to attach additional things in order to furnish the building with a heating system ready for use (group of assets [*Sachgesamtheit*]), then the right of ownership with respect to these separate things passes to the landowner upon their attachment according to §§94 subs 2, 946 BGB. Consequently, on November 11, 1974 both boilers belonged to the city council in P.

Note

The case below shows that §94 BGB is applied by analogy to registered ships.

BGH, 9 January 1958[33] **7.8 (DE)**

COMPONENT PART OF A REGISTERED SHIP

Ship's engine

A registered ship's engine is an essential component of the ship under §94 Abs 2, BGB.

Facts: Company U acquired a ship from a Dutch seller and it was registered at the registry in Emden under the name *M*. The engine of the ship was replaced with a new engine that U acquired from the claimant. To secure payment of a part of the purchase price (DM50,000 was paid in cash, DM40,000 remained outstanding) the claimant acquired a right of ship-hypothec and the engine was delivered under a reservation of ownership clause.

On 5 February 1954 the defendant and company CC, and the ship manufacturer, a daughter company of the defendant, asked for the opening of insolvency proceedings on ship *M* of Company U because of outstanding personal claims they held on U. On 6 February 1954 this request was granted and registered in the ship register. Additional creditors joined the proceedings, including the defendant and company CC, who held rights of ship hypothec, and company B, which held a priority claim for the payment of salaries.

The claimant argued she still owned the engine as it was delivered under a reservation of ownership clause and that U had not yet paid the sum of DM90,000 in full. Moreover, she argued that the engine was placed in a ship for the first time and was intended to serve as a backup engine, so that the connection with the ship was made temporary only. In a letter of 7 February 1954 U wrote to the claimant that the engine was not a perfect fit and made the engine available for the claimant. On this, the claimant changed her claim and demanded the release of the engine from the insolvency procedure. Awarding that claim would depend on the return of the purchase price to U to make it available to other creditors. The dispute before the court was whether the engine could be returned or whether it had become a component part of the ship.

Held: The motor of a registered motor vessel is put into the vessel to make it a motor vessel. Without the motor it would not be a motor vessel. Therefore the motor is an essential component even if the motor is mass produced.

Judgment: The fourth senate for civil matters of the BGH has held in its judgment which was prior published in the official law reports (vol 18, 226 = NJW 55, 1793) that the engine of a motor vehicle produced in quantity was not an essential component of the vehicle according to §93 BGB, at least as long as the vehicle belongs to the property of the manufacturing firm. In doing so the fourth senate discussed the judgment of the Supreme Court of the German Reich (*RG*) in RGZ 152, 91, in which the Supreme Court assumed that the engine of a motor vessel was an essential component of the vessel, even if the hull and the engine are not designed for each other and if they can be separated without damage to the individual parts. The judgment of the BGH points out, that the legal relations with respect to a marine vessel, which has already been devoted to its proper purpose, can be different compared to those with respect to a motor vehicle, which is still with the manufacturer. Since a motor vehicle can only be viewed according to the provisions valid for movable goods, the BGH dealt and could only deal with the interpretation of the term essential component in the sense of §93 BGB. In the present

[33] NJW 1958, 457, II ZR 275/56 (Oldenburg).

case the Court of Appeal as well as the Supreme Court of the German Reich in the cited judgment has accepted the nature of the ship engine as essential component of the ship as well in the sense of §93 as in the sense of §94 subs 2 BGB. There is no use in discussing, if with respect to the engineering progress the arguments of the Court of Appeal and of the Supreme Court of the German Reich must be followed. In the present case the ship engine has become an essential component of the ship according to §94 subs. 2.

According to §94 subs 2 things inserted for the construction of a building belong to the essential components of the building, even if the building itself is not an essential component of the land. In RGZ 152, 97 it is explained that ships certainly were not to be considered as land or buildings in the sense of §94 subs 1 first sentence, that the sentence expressed in §94 subs 2, however, allowed a transfer to ships, which were buildings after all. At the time of that judgment the legal situation still could appear to be doubtful, because a certain relationship between the law valid for registered ship and real property rights only existed with respect to the ship mortgage, which was regulated in §§1259 et sequ BGB old version under the general title 'pledge of movables' (§§1204 et seq). In the meantime the approximation of the law valid for registered ships and the real property rights has been largely affected by the law regarding the rights with respect to registered ships and ships under construction (*Gesetz über Rechte an eingetragenen Schiffen und Schiffsbauwerken*, SchiffsRG) of November 15, 1940 (Reich Law Gazette I 1499). The appeal also is not unaware of the fact that at present registered ships are both on the merits and with respect to the execution (see in particular §§864 et seq ZPO, §§162 et seq ZVG) subject to the principles of the law of real property, even if there exist some material differences, so that it must be examined in detail if a legal rule valid for the basic right is also to be applied to registered ships (see Krieger, DJ 41, 97). The introduction of the term essential components, which cannot be the object of separate rights, goes back to economic interests. With respect to buildings it does not only serve the preservation of values, but it also promotes the security of legal relations. The establishment of secure legal relationships is of significant importance for property dealings. The land register system with its registration principle and the provisions regarding the public faith of the land register aims at the creation of clear and secure legal relationships. This purpose would partially be endangered, if things inserted for the construction of the building could be the object of separate rights, which cannot be seen from the land register. The same aspects must count for registered ships because of their considerable economic value, which often exceeds the value of land by far. With respect to ships the register of ships largely serves the same functions as the land register with respect to property dealings does. Since in principle registered ships are legally treated like immovable goods, it is rather obvious to regard things that are firmly attached to such a ship as essential components (§94 subs 1 first sentence). It might be doubtful, though, if in the present case the prerequisite firm attachment is fulfilled as required by the law. In any case things that are inserted for the construction of such a ship belong to the essential components of the ship (§94 subs 2).

The construction of a motor vessel requires the insertion of a ship engine. Contrary to §93 (BGHZ 20, 154 [156 et seq]—NJW 56, 945) the interpretation of §94 subs 2 must not start from the separable component, but from the building (ship) as a whole, such as the building (ship) presents itself in its own extraordinary nature and in its own extraordinary purpose (RGZ 150, 22 [26]; BGH LM Nr 2 at §93 BGB).

A ship, which should run with its own driving force, is not yet a ship without a driving element, but rather the body of a ship, a hull. A ship without a ship engine is not yet a motor ship. It becomes a motor ship not before the engine is inserted, without which it could not fulfil its special purpose to serve as means of transport with its own driving force on the water. That is why the engine itself serves 'for the construction' of the motor ship. In addition it is 'inserted' into the motor ship. According to the pleading the installation of the engine happens in such a manner that the engine is attached on the foundation with a foundation bolt in the engine-room. Since according to the provision of §94 subs 2 the firmness of the attachment with the building (ship) is not important (RGZ 150, 27), the prerequisite insertion into the ship is also fulfilled. The fact, that the ship engine can be produced in quantity and be replaced by another does not change anything.

Bürgerliches Gesetzbuch **7.9 (DE)**

§95 (1) Objects attached to the land only for a temporary purpose do not belong to the components of the land. The same applies to a building or other construction attached to the land by the holder of a right over another's land in the exercise of this right.

(2) Objects inserted into a building only for a temporary purpose do not belong to the components of the building.

Notes

(1) In certain cases accession to the land is barred by §95. The paragraph clearly demonstrates that in German law the measure for accession is not purely objective and recognisable to third parties. Whereas §§93 and 94 do not allow the intention of the parties to play any role in the question of accession, §95 provides that the intention to attach a thing only temporarily prevents accession from taking place.

(2) It is true that to some extent the intention of the builder is inferred from objective factors.[34] From an attachment being short-lived it may be inferred that the annexation is meant to be temporary. To give another example, where removal of the attachment would cause damage it may be presumed that the connection is intended to be permanent. Moreover, it should be stressed that a reservation of ownership clause is of no importance for the question whether the annexation is permanent or temporary.[35]

(3) In §95 the subjective intention remains the principal measure.[36] In certain cases the intention is inferred from a lease contract: a contractual provision that the lessor may keep buildings erected by the lessee will entail that the building is seen as a permanent attachment. Of course, such a provision is unknown to third parties. Moreover some of the objective factors are unknown to them. Where a thing has

[34] Staudinger-Jickeli and Stieper (2004), §95, Rn 6; MünchKomm BGB-Holch (2006), §95, Rn 3 *et seq.*

[35] BGH NJW 1970, 895; MünchKomm BGB-Holch (2006), §95, Rn. 6.

[36] Staudinger-Jickeli and Stieper (2004), §95, Rn 6; MünchKomm-Holch (2006), §95, Rn 3.

been attached by a lessee (*Mieter* or *Pächter*) it is presumed that the connection is intended as temporary in the sense of §95(1), first sentence, or §95(2). Third parties, however, cannot see whether the things have been annexed by the lessee, the landowner or someone else. As a result §95 BGB infringes the principle of third party protection, one of the foundations of the accession rules.

(4) Even if things attached by the lessee do accede to the building, the lessee in principle has a right of removal under §539(2) BGB. However, in the lessor's insolvency this right cannot be set up against the insolvent's administrator or the insolvent's creditors. The lessee then has a mere unsecured claim.[37]

(5) In addition the principle of third party protection is also violated by §95(1), second sentence: 'The same applies to a building or other construction attached to the land by the holder of a right over another's land in the exercise of this right.' The term 'right over another's land' (*Recht an einem fremden Grundstück*) covers among other things limited property rights to the use of land which allow its holder to erect a building on another's land, such as a *Dienstbarkeit* (servitude), *Nießbrauch* (usufruct), *Recht zum Überbau*[38] and *Erbbaurecht* (right of superficies).[39] However, the term also covers some rights to the use of land based on public law.[40] Apart from the right of superficies, which is subject to different provisions, §95(1), second sentence, applies only when the building has been erected during the right of use by the holder of the right.[41] In such a case the buildings do not accede to the land. What is more, they are considered as movable things and in principle underlie the rules applying to movable property.[42] The second sentence thus bars accession just as the first sentence and the second subsection do.

(6) Now, although these property rights are entered into the land register it is not registered whether the building has been erected by the holder of the right of use during the time for which the right was granted to him. Often the building has been erected by the landowner before the right of use was granted. In that instance the building is regarded as a component of the land and belongs to the

[37] The right of removal is not regarded as an *Aussonderungsrecht* (a kind of revindication) in the sense of para 47 Insolvenzordnung. See Nerlich and Römermann/Andres, *Insolvenzordnung*, 17th loose leaf addition (Munich, CH Beck 2009) §47, nr 46 and MünchKomm InsO/Ganter, 2nd edn (2007) §47, nr 325.

[38] Comparable to a servitude to allow a building to stand partly on the servient land. Above, Chapter 3, Real Servitudes.

[39] Under §12(1) first sentence, of the *Gesetz über das Erbbaurecht* the building does not become a component of the land but rather a component of the right of superficies. Yet, the building is regarded as an immovable thing. See H Von Oefele and K Winkler, *Handbuch des Erbbaurechts*, 4th edn (Munich, CH Beck, 2008) Rn 2.38–2.39

[40] MünchKomm-Holch (2006), §95, Rn 24.

[41] The paragraph, by the way, applies also to a person to whom the holder of the right of use has given a personal right to exercise his right of use (eg *Miete* or *Pacht*). See MünchKomm BGB-Holch (2006), §95, Rn 32.

[42] Medicus, above n 4, Rn 1191; MünchKomm BGB-Holch, 5th edn (2006), §95, Rn 34–35. In the case of superficies the buildings are, however, immovable (see above n 40).

landowner.[43] The *öffentlicher Glaube* ('public faith')[44] of the German land register does not protect against this false appearance.[45]

BGH, 13 March 1970[46] **7.10 (DE)**

LAPSING OF RESERVATION OF OWNERSHIP

Unpaid oil heating

Reservation of ownership does not lead to temporary connexion.

Facts: The seller sold and installed an oil heating system into a house. He made a reservation of ownership clause and remained unpaid. The house was sold in a forced sale by the mortgagee who sold the house together with the new oil heating system.

Held: The oil heating system is an essential component of the house. This is not changed by the reservation of ownership clause. This clause does not lead to the oil heating system being installed only for temporary purposes in the sense of §95(2) BGB.

Judgment: Finally, the lower court is also right in holding that a reservation of ownership of the attached component stipulated by the supplier does not normally lead to an attachment only for a temporary purpose. Also such an object shall, according to the parties' will, pass in ownership to the home owner upon full payment; return of the object to the supplier is only intended for the abnormal case that the purchase price remains unpaid.

BGH, 21 December 1956[47] **7.11 (DE)**

THINGS ATTACHED TO THE LAND FOR A TEMPORARY PURPOSE

Wooden house

Things attached to the land for a temporary purpose do not pass to the landowner when the temporary purpose lapses.

Facts: The defendant, a tenant, erected a wooden house on the land of someone else.

Held: A thing attached to the land for a temporary purpose does not automatically become a component of the land when the purpose is later changed. For the passing of ownership of that thing it is required that the owner of the thing and the owner of the land should agree about the passing of ownership. §929 BGB applies to the passing of ownership.

[43] This is different in the case of *Erbbaurecht* (right of superficies): ownership of a pre-existing building will pass to the holder of the *Erbbaurecht* upon creation of the right of superficies (§12(1) 2nd sentence Gesetz über das Erbbaurecht). Above, Chapter 3.

[44] This term refers to a set of rules protecting *bona fide* third parties against mistakes and incompleteness of the land register.

[45] Medicus, above n 4, Rn 1191.

[46] V ZR 71/67, NJW 1970, 895.

[47] NJW 1957, 457.

Judgment: If the Court of Appeal, while looking at the facts of the case, had in view that the construction on the land of another by a tenant regularly gives rise to the assumption that the tenant has only done this in his own interest and not with the intention to surrender the building to the owner of the land after termination of the contractual relationship, and if the court of appeal has considered the presence of a positive contrary intention on the part of the constructor necessary in order to be able to exclude the applicability of §95 subs 1 first sentence BGB, it is in line with long standing opinion, which the senate also followed in several judgments. ... There is no reason to depart from this principle in the present case. ...

The senate has already discussed the question, if and under what prerequisites an ostensible component in the sense of §95 subs 1 first sentence BGB becomes an essential component of the land, when the purpose of insertion subsequently changes, in its judgment of Mai 16, 1956 (V ZR 146/54, printed LM Nr 7 at PreisstopVO). There it argued, rejecting the opposite opinion of the Reichsfinanzhof (JW 23, 790) and contrary to Staudinger-Riezler (10th edition, §95 annotation 3c marginal note 9; just as now Staudinger-Coing, 11th edition, loco citato), that §95 focuses on the moment of the attachment of the thing to the land and does not mean that the exclusion from the nature as component is only valid as long as the initial purpose persists; that the further legal proprietary regime is therefore governed by §§929 et seq BGB. This opinion is followed among others by the RGRK (BGB, 10th edition, §95 annotation 1 a E) as well as by Soergel (BGB, 8th edition, §95 annotation 2), Oertmann (BGB, 3rd edition, §95 annotation 2 ad), Planck-Strecker (BGB, 4th edition, §95 annotation 2 a) and Stillschweig (JW 23, 790), which was indicated in the cited judgment as well. In its judgment of January 26, 1933 (WarnRspr 1934 Nr 19) also the Reichsgericht—leaving out of consideration the special case of a subsequent merger of the ownership of the land and of the attached thing—did not consider the mere lapse of the initial purpose as sufficient in order to let the thing become an essential component of the land, but it required as further prerequisite that the attachment could be recognised as intended to be henceforth permanent; according to this judgment the subsequent change of the purpose of the insertion amounts to something 'similar to a disposal' and therefore it is legally to be considered in the same way as a disposal of a thing. The senate, referring to this reasoning of the Reichsgericht, stated further in the cited judgment of May 16, 1956, that such cases asked for the application of §§929 et seq BGB in a modified manner. The establishment of the component quality required the consent of the owner of the land in the sense of an agreement with respect to the transfer of ownership.

Applying these considerations, made in the judgment of May 16, 1956, ... to the present case, the opinion of the court of appeal, that the house in dispute was not automatically transferred into the ownership of the claimant because of a subsequent change of its initial purpose, is correct. There was no agreement of the parties regarding such a transfer of ownership; above all, as the attacked judgment has established pursuant to the evidence taken, the defendant never showed his will to abandon his right of ownership regarding the wooden house—neither to the claimant, nor to the owner of the land nor to a third person; anyway, it is quite obvious that he lacked any motive to undertake something in this respect.

I.A.3 ENGLISH LAW

Introductory Note

English case law gives a clear and consistent treatment of accession of movables to land. One of the recent leading cases, the House of Lords' judgment in *Elitestone Ltd v Morris and Another*,[48] upholds a line of authority which in outline has been unchanged since the beginning of the nineteenth century.

House of Lords, 1 May 1997 **7.12 (E&W)**

Elitestone Ltd v Morris and Another

ATTACHMENT OF THINGS TO LAND

Wooden bungalow

The objective intention, mainly derived from the nature of the thing attached and the way it is attached, is decisive to answer the question whether things attach to land.

Facts: Morris was the tenant of Lot No 6 in an area of land known as Holt's Field, which was owned by the claimants. On this plot of land a wooden bungalow had been placed about 50 years previously. The bungalow was not physically attached to the land. The foundations were sunk into the ground. It did not appear that there was any particular adaptation of the foundations to the structure above nor any adaptation of the structure to suit the foundations. The main structural elements of the bungalow simply rested on the concrete blocks. The bungalow and the foundations were severable from each other.

Held: The question of whether things attached to the land become part of the land or remain movable is answered by reference to the objective intention which is mainly derived from the nature of the thing attached and the way in which has been attached.

Judgment: Lord Lloyd of Berwick—My Lords, The plaintiffs, Elitestone Ltd, are the freehold owners of land known as Holt's Field, Murton, near Swansea. The land is divided into 27 lots. The defendant, Mr Morris, is the occupier of a chalet or bungalow on Lot No 6. It is not known for certain when the chalet was built. But it seems likely that it was before 1945. Mr Morris has lived there since 1971.

The plaintiffs acquired the freehold in 1989 with a view to redevelopment. On 30 April 1991 they issued proceedings in the Swansea County Court claiming possession against all 27 occupiers. Five lead actions were selected, including that in which Mr Morris was defendant. They came on for trial before Mr Assistant Recorder Bidder in November 1994. The assistant recorder had a number of issues to decide. He dealt with them in a most impressive manner. So far as Mr Morris is concerned, his defence was that he is a tenant from year-to-year, that he occupies the premises as his residence, and is therefore entitled to the protection of the Rent Act 1977. He claims a declaration to that effect.

The assistant recorder held, correctly, at the end of what was necessarily a very lengthy judgment that the question in Mr Morris's case turned on whether or not the bungalow formed part of the realty. If it did, then Mr. Morris was entitled to his declaration.

[48] [1997] 2 All ER 513. The decision was followed in *Potton Developments Ltd v Thompson and another*, 16 March 1998, [1998] NPC 49, ChD, and followed by the Court of Appeal in *Chelsea Yacht & Boat Co Ltd v Pope* [2000] 22 EG 147.

Having visited the site, the assistant recorder had this to say:

> 'While the house rested on the concrete pillars which were themselves attached to the ground, it seems to me clear that at least by 1985 and probably before, it would have been clear to anybody that this was a structure that was not meant to be enjoyed as a chattel to be picked up and moved in due course but that it should be a long-term feature of the realty albeit that, because of its construction, it would plainly need more regular maintenance.'

The Court of Appeal disagreed (unreported), 28 July 1995, Court of Appeal (Civil Division) Transcript No 1025 of 1995. Aldous LJ, who gave the leading judgment, was much influenced by the fact that the bungalow was resting by its own weight on concrete pillars, without any attachment. He was also influenced by the uncertainty of Mr Morris' tenure. Although Mr Morris had been in occupation since 1971, he was required to obtain an annual 'licence'. At first the licence fee was £3 a year. It rose to £10 in 1984, then to £52 in 1985, and finally to £85 in 1989. In 1990 the plaintiffs required a licence fee of £1,000: but Mr Morris, and the other occupiers, declined to pay.

On these facts Aldous LJ inferred that it was the common intention of the parties that the occupiers should acquire the ownership of their bungalows, but the ownership of the sites should remain in the freeholders. On that footing Mr Morris' bungalow was to be regarded as a chattel. It was never annexed to the land, so it never became part of the realty. It followed that the tenancy did not include the bungalow, and Mr Morris was not a protected tenant.

Unlike the judge, the Court of Appeal did not have the advantage of having seen the bungalow. Nor were they shown any of the photographs, some of which were put before your Lordships. These photographs were taken only very recently. Like all photographs they can be deceptive. But if the Court of Appeal had seen the photographs, it is at least possible that they would have taken a different view. For the photographs show very clearly what the bungalow is, and especially what it is not. It is not like a Portakabin, or mobile home. The nature of the structure is such that it could not be taken down and re-erected elsewhere. It could only be removed by a process of demolition. This, as will appear later, is a factor of great importance in the present case. If a structure can only be enjoyed in situ, and is such that it cannot be removed in whole or in sections to another site, there is at least a strong inference that the purpose of placing the structure on the original site was that it should form part of the realty at that site, and therefore cease to be a chattel.

There were a number of other issues in the Court of Appeal. I need only mention one. This was an argument by the plaintiffs that Mr Morris was estopped by convention from denying that the bungalow was a chattel. There was, so it was said, a common assumption that the chalets were owned separately from the land, since each occupier purchased his own chalet from the previous occupier (Mr Morris paid £250 for No 6 in 1971), and each occupier paid an annual licence fee to the freeholders. Since the Court of Appeal held that the bungalow was a chattel, they did not find it necessary to deal with the estoppel argument. The plaintiffs might have renewed the argument before your Lordships. But in the meantime the House had given judgment in *Melluish v BMI (No 3) Ltd* [1996] AC 454. In that case Lord Browne-Wilkinson said, at p 473:

> 'The terms expressly or implicitly agreed between the fixer of the chattel and the

owner of the land cannot affect the determination of the question whether, in law, the chattel has become a fixture and therefore in law belongs to the owner of the soil: . . . The terms of such agreement will regulate the contractual rights to sever the chattel from the land as between the parties to that contract and, where an equitable right is conferred by the contract, as against certain third parties. But such agreement cannot prevent the chattel, once fixed, becoming in law part of the land and as such owned by the owner of the land so long as it remains fixed.'

If an express agreement cannot prevent a chattel from becoming part of the land, so long as it is fixed to the land, it is obvious that a common assumption cannot have that effect. It is not surprising, therefore, that Mr Thom abandoned his estoppel argument.

Thus the sole remaining issue for your Lordships is whether Mr Morris' bungalow did indeed become part of the land, or whether it has remained a chattel ever since it was first constructed before 1945.

It will be noticed that in framing the issue for decision I have avoided the use of the word 'fixture'. There are two reasons for this. The first is that 'fixture', though a hallowed term in this branch of the law, does not always bear the same meaning in law as it does in everyday life. In ordinary language one thinks of a fixture as being something fixed to a building. One would not ordinarily think of the building itself as a fixture. Thus in *Boswell v Crucible Steel Co* [1925] 1 KB 119 the question was whether plate glass windows which formed part of the wall of a warehouse were landlord's fixtures within the meaning of a repairing covenant. Atkin LJ said, at p 123:

'... I am quite satisfied that they are not landlord's fixtures, and for the simple reason that they are not fixtures at all in the sense in which that term is generally understood. A fixture, as that term is used in connection with the house, means something which has been affixed to the freehold as accessory to the house. It does not include things which were made part of the house itself in the course of its construction.'

Yet in *Billing v Pill* [1954] 1 QB 70, 75 Lord Goddard CJ said:

'What is a fixture? The commonest fixture is a house which is built into the land, so that in law it is regarded as part of the land. The house and the land are one thing.'

There is another reason. The term fixture is apt to be a source of misunderstanding owing to the existence of the category of so called 'tenants' fixtures', (a term used to cover both trade fixtures and ornamental fixtures) which are fixtures in the full sense of the word (and therefore part of the realty) but which may nevertheless be removed by the tenant in the course of or at the end of his tenancy. Such fixtures are sometimes confused with chattels which have never become fixtures at all. Indeed the confusion arose in this very case. In the course of his judgment Aldous LJ quoted at length from the judgment of Scott LJ in *Webb v Frank Bevis Ltd*. The case concerned a shed which was 135 feet long and 50 feet wide. The shed was built on a concrete floor to which it was attached by iron straps. Having referred to *Webb v Frank Bevis Ltd* and a decision of Hirst J in *Deen v Andrews* [1986] 1 EGLR 262 Aldous LJ continued:

'In the present case we are concerned with a chalet which rests on concrete pillars and I believe falls to be considered as a unit which is not annexed to the land. It was no more annexed to the land than the greenhouse in *Deen v Andrews* or the large shed in *Webb v Frank Bevis Ltd*. Prima facie, the chalet is a chattel and not a fixture.'

A little later he said: 'Unit 6 was just as much a chattel as the very large shed was in the Webb case and the greenhouse in *Deen v Andrews*.'

But when one looks at Scott LJ's judgment in *Webb v Frank Bevis Ltd* it is clear that the shed in question was not a chattel. It was annexed to the land, and was held to form part of the realty. But it could be severed from the land and removed by the tenant at the end of his tenancy because it was in the nature of a tenant's fixture, having been erected by the tenant for use in his trade. It follows that *Webb v Frank Bevis Ltd* affords no parallel to the present case, as indeed Mr Thom conceded.

For my part I find it better in the present case to avoid the traditional two-fold distinction between chattels and fixtures, and to adopt the three-fold classification set out in Woodfall, Landlord and Tenants, Release 36 (1994), vol 1, pp 13/83, para 13.131:

'An object which is brought onto land may be classified under one of three broad heads. It may be (a) a chattel; (b) a fixture; or (c) part and parcel of the land itself. Objects in categories (b) and (c) are treated as being part of the land.'

So the question in the present appeal is whether, when the bungalow was built, it became part and parcel of the land itself. The materials out of which the bungalow was constructed, that is to say, the timber frame walls, the feather boarding, the suspended timber floors, the chip-board ceilings, and so on, were all, of course, chattels when they were brought onto the site. Did they cease to be chattels when they were built into the composite structure? The answer to the question, as Blackburn J pointed out in *Holland v Hodgson*, depends on the circumstances of each case, but mainly on two factors, the degree of annexation to the land, and the object of the annexation.

Degree of annexation

The importance of the degree of annexation will vary from object to object. In the case of a large object, such as a house, the question does not often arise. Annexation goes without saying. So there is little recent authority on the point, and I do not get much help from the early cases in which wooden structures have been held not to form part of the realty, such as the wooden mill in *Rex v Otley*, the wooden barn in *Wansborough v Maton* and the granary in *Wiltshear v Cottrell*. But there is a more recent decision of the High Court of Australia which is of greater assistance. In *Reid v Smith* [1905] 3 CLR 656, 659 Griffiths CJ stated the question as follows:

'The short point raised in this case is whether an ordinary dwelling-house, erected upon an ordinary town allotment in a large town, but not fastened to the soil, remains a chattel or becomes part of the freehold.'

The Supreme Court of Queensland had held that the house remained a chattel. But the High Court reversed this decision, treating the answer as being almost a matter of common sense. The house in that case was made of wood, and rested by its own weight on brick piers. The house was not attached to the brick piers in any way. It was separated by iron plates placed on top of the piers, in order to prevent an invasion of white ants. There was an extensive citation of English and American authorities. It was held that the absence of any attachment did not prevent the house forming part of the realty. …

Purpose of annexation

Many different tests have been suggested, such as whether the object which has been fixed to the property has been so fixed for the better enjoyment of the object as a chattel, or whether it has been fixed with a view to effecting a permanent improvement of the freehold. This and similar tests are useful when one is considering an object such as a tapestry, which may or may not be fixed to a house so as to become part of the freehold: see *Leigh v Taylor*. These tests are less useful when one is considering the house itself. In the case of the house the answer is as much a matter of common sense as precise analysis. A house which is constructed in such a way so as to be removable, whether as a unit, or in sections, may well remain a chattel, even though it is connected temporarily to mains services such as water and electricity. But a house which is constructed in such a way that it cannot be removed at all, save by destruction, cannot have been intended to remain as a chattel. It must have been intended to form part of the realty. I know of no better analogy than the example given by Blackburn J in *Holland v Hodgson*, LR7 CPP 328, 335:

> 'Thus blocks of stone placed one on the top of another without any mortar or cement for the purpose of forming a dry stone wall would become part of the land, though the same stones, if deposited in a builder's yard and for convenience sake stacked on the top of each other in the form of a wall, would remain chattels.'

Applying that analogy to the present case, I do not doubt that when Mr Morris' bungalow was built, and as each of the timber frame walls were placed in position, they all became part of the structure, which was itself part and parcel of the land. The object of bringing the individual bits of wood onto the site seems to be so clear that the absence of any attachment to the soil (save by gravity) becomes an irrelevance.

Finally I return to the judgment of the Court of Appeal. I need say no more about the absence of attachment, which was the first of the reasons given by the Court of Appeal for reversing the assistant recorder. The second reason was the intention which the court inferred from the previous course of dealing between the parties, and in particular the uncertainty of Mr Morris' tenure. The third reason was the analogy with the shed in *Webb v Frank Bevis Ltd*, and the greenhouse in *Deen v Andrews*.

As to the second reason the Court of Appeal may have been misled by Blackburn J's use of the word 'intention' in *Holland v Hodgson*. But as the subsequent decision of the Court of Appeal in *Hobson v Gorringe* made clear, and as the decision of the House in *Melluish v BMI (No 3)* put beyond question, the intention of the parties is only relevant to the extent that it can be derived from the degree and object of the annexation. The subjective intention of the parties cannot affect the question whether the chattel has, in law, become part of the freehold, any more than the subjective intention of the parties can prevent what they have called a licence from taking effect as a tenancy, if that is what in law it is: see *Street v Mountford*.

As for the third of the reasons, I have already pointed out that *Webb v Frank Bevis Ltd* does not support the Court of Appeal's conclusion, because the shed in that case was held to be a fixture, albeit a fixture which the tenant was entitled to remove.

In *Deen v Andrews* the question was whether a greenhouse was a building so as to pass to the purchaser under a contract for the sale of land 'together with the farmhouses and other buildings'. Hirst J held that it was not. He followed an earlier decision in *HE Dibble Ltd v Moore* in which the Court of Appeal, reversing the trial judge, held that a greenhouse was not an 'erection' within section 62(1) of the Law of Property Act 1925. I note that in the latter case Megaw LJ, at p 187G, drew attention to some evidence 'that it was customary to move such greenhouses every few years to a fresh site'. It is obvious that a greenhouse which can be moved from site to site is a long way removed from a two bedroom bungalow which cannot be moved at all without being demolished.

For the above reasons I would allow this appeal and restore the order of the assistant recorder.

Lord Clyde—My Lords, …

The question posed by the parties in their agreed statement of facts and issues is: 'Whether the bungalow erected at Unit 6, Holt's Field was a chattel or a fixture.' I entirely share the unease which has been expressed by my noble and learned friend, Lord Lloyd of Berwick on the use of the word fixture. The ambiguity is illustrated by a passage in the judgment of Rigby LJ in *In re De Falbe* where having referred to an originally unbending rule that everything affixed to the freehold was held to go with the freehold his Lordship stated:

> 'But in modern times there have come to be important exceptions to this rule, one being in favour of trade fixtures and entitling a person who has put up what are now called 'fixtures' (which means removable fixed things) for the purposes of trade to remove them.'

Later in his judgment he stated, at p 533:

> 'But the question is, whether they were not made 'fixtures,' meaning thereby objects fixed to the wall which might be removed at the will of the person who had fixed them.'

In *Boyd v Shorrock*, Page Wood V-C regarded as conclusive of the case before him a definition given in *Ex parte Barclay* (1855) 5 De G M & G 403, 410:

> 'By "fixtures" we understand such things as are ordinarily affixed to the freehold for the convenience of the occupier, and which may be removed without material injury to the freehold, such will be machinery, using a generic term; and in houses, grates, cupboards, and other like things.'

As the law has developed it has become easy to neglect the original principle from which the consequences of attachment of a chattel to realty derive. That is the principle of accession, from which the more particular example has been formulated, inaedificatum solo cedit. A clear distinction has to be draw between the principle of accession and the rules of removability.

My Lords, the distinction between these two matters was pointed out long ago by Lord Cairns LC in *Bain v Brand* (1876) 1 AppCas 762. In that case it was declared that the law as to fixtures is the same in Scotland as in England. His Lordship stated, at p 767, that there were two general rules under the comprehensive term of fixtures:

> 'One of these rules is the general well-known rule that whatever is fixed to the freehold of land becomes part of the freehold or inheritance. The other is quite a different and separate rule;—whatever once becomes part of the inheritance cannot be severed by a limited owner, whether he be owner for life or for years, without the commission of that which, in the law of England, is called waste, and which, according to the law of both England and Scotland, is undoubtedly an offence which can be restrained. Those, my Lords, are two rules, not one by way of exception to the other, but two rules standing consistently together. My Lords, an exception indeed, and a very important exception, has been made, not to the first of these rules, but to the second. To the first rule which I have stated to your Lordships there is, so far as I am aware, no exception whatever. That which is fixed to the inheritance becomes a part of the inheritance at the present day as much as it did in the earliest times. But to the second rule, namely, the irremovability of things fixed to the inheritance, there is undoubtedly ground for a very important exception. That exception has been established in favour of fixtures which have been attached to the inheritance for the purposes of trade, and perhaps in a minor degree for the purpose of agriculture. Under that exception a tenant who has fixed to the inheritance things for the purpose of trade has a certain power of severance and removal during the tenancy.'

It would be right to add that the exception has been developed so as to extend beyond the purposes of trade. By the end of the 19th century it was clearly established that the exception included objects which had been affixed to the freehold by way of ornament: *In re De Falbe*. This reflected not a change in the law but, as Lord Macnaghten put it in *Leigh v Taylor* a change 'in our habits and mode of life'. No doubt the category of exceptions may continue to change.

The present case, however, is concerned with the first of the two rules and not the second. But it is not altogether clear that the distinction between the two rules was clearly put before the Court of Appeal in the present case. If the distinction is not noticed there is a danger that the true issue may become confused by questions truly relating to removability. The Court of Appeal found assistance in the decision in *Webb v Frank Bevis*, regarding the bungalow as no more annexed to the land and just as much a chattel as the large shed in that case. But the court in the Webb case held that the large shed was a fixture but was removable by the tenant. I should add that the second rule may involve particular consideration of the various relationships between the interested parties which may play a part in the matter of removability, such as landlord and tenant, or mortgagor and mortgagee. But those differences play only a subordinate role in relation to the first rule. ...

The first of these factors may serve both to identify an item as being real property in its own right and to indicate a case of accession. But account has also to be taken of the degree of physical attachment and the possibility or impossibility of restoring the article from its constituent parts after dissolution. In one early Scottish case large leaden vessels which were not fastened to the building in any way but simply rested by their own weight were held to be heritable since they had had to be taken to pieces in order to be removed and had then been sold as old lead: *Niven v Pitcairn*. In *Hellawell v Eastwood*, Parke B, in considering the mode and extent of annexation of the articles in that case, referred to the consideration whether the object in question 'can easily be removed, integré, salvé, et commodé, or not, without injury to itself or the fabric of the building'. It is agreed in the present case that as matter of fact that 'the bungalow is not removable in one piece; nor is it demountable for re-erection elsewhere'. That agreed finding is in my view one powerful indication that it is not of the nature of a chattel.

In many cases the problem of accession arises in relation to some article or articles which have been placed in or affixed to a building. An unusual, although by no means unique, feature of the present case is that the alleged chattel is the building itself. This invites the approach of simply asking whether it is real property in its own right. Apart from the considerations which I already mentioned it seems to me that it is proper to have regard to the genus of the alleged chattel. That approach was adopted in the Australian case, *Reid v Smith* (1905) 3 CLR 656. At p 668 Griffith CJ said under reference to the decision in the lower court:

> 'I differ from the learned judge in thinking that it is not sufficient to show that the thing in question is a dwelling-house—an ordinary dwelling-house, on a town allotment, in an inhabited town. In the case of a similar building in another part of the country, erected under entirely different circumstances, a different conclusion might be drawn.'

O'Connor J put the point more strongly, at p 679:

> 'It would I think be stretching the rules of the common law to a point at which they cease to be rules of common sense, if it were to be laid down as a general rule that, except in very exceptional cases, wooden houses, resting by their own weight on land, could ever be regarded as mere chattels, removable at the will of the owner of the timber of which they are built.'

… Beyond question Mr Morris' bungalow is of the genus 'dwelling-house' and dwelling houses are generally of the nature of real property. While it is situated in a rural setting it evidently forms part of a development of a number of other houses whose positions are even noted on the ordnance survey map. I find no factors which would justify taking it out of the category of dwelling-houses. On the contrary there are powerful indications that it and its constituent parts do not possess the character of a chattel. It seems to me to be real property.

If the problem is approached as one of accession it has to be noted that in the present case the bungalow is not attached or secured to any realty. It is not joined by any physical link which would require to be severed for it to be detached. But accession can operate even where there is only a juxtaposition without any physical bond between the article and the freehold. Thus the sculptures in *D'Eyncourt v Gregory* which simply rested by their own weight were held to form part of the architectural design for the hall in which they were placed and so fell to be treated as part of the freehold. The reasoning in such a case where there is no physical attachment was identified by Blackburn J in *Holland v Hodgson* (1872) LR 7 CP 328, 335: 'But even in such a case, if the intention is apparent to make the articles part of the land, they do become part of the land.' He continued with the following instructive observations:

> 'Thus blocks of stone placed one on the top of another without any mortar or cement for the purpose of forming a dry stone wall would become part of the land, though the same stones, if deposited in a builder's yard and for convenience sake stacked on the top of each other in the form of a wall, would remain chattels. On the other hand, an article may be very firmly fixed to the land, and

yet the circumstances may be such as to show that it was never intended to be part of the land, and then it does not become part of the land. The anchor of a large ship must be very firmly fixed in the ground in order to bear the strain of the cable, yet no one could suppose that it became part of the land, even though it should chance that shipowner was also the owner of the fee of the spot where the anchor was dropped. An anchor similarly fixed in the soil for the purpose of bearing the strain of the chain of a suspension bridge would be part of the land. Perhaps the true rule is, that articles not otherwise attached to the land than by their own weight are not to be considered as part of the land, unless the circumstances are such as to shew that they were intended to be part of the land, the onus of shewing that they were so intended lying on those who assert that they have ceased to be chattels, and that, on the contrary, an article which is affixed to the land even slightly is to be considered as part of the land, unless the circumstances are such as to shew that it was intended all along to continue a chattel, the onus lying on those who contend that it is a chattel.'

It is important to observe that intention in this context is to be assessed objectively and not subjectively. Indeed it may be that the use of the word intention is misleading. It is the purpose which the object is serving which has to be regarded, not the purpose of the person who put it there. The question is whether the object is designed for the use or enjoyment of the land or for the more complete or convenient use or enjoyment of the thing itself. As the foregoing passage from the judgment of Blackburn J makes clear, the intention has to be shown from the circumstances. That point was taken up by AL Smith LJ in *Hobson v Goringe* [1897] 1 Ch 182, 193, a decision approved by this House in *Reynolds v Ashby & Son* [1904] AC 466, where he observes that Blackburn J,

'was contemplating and referring to circumstances which shewed the degree of annexation and the object of such annexation which were patent for all to see, and not to the circumstances of a chance agreement that might or might not exist between the owner of a chattel and a hirer thereof.'

Regard may not be paid to the actual intention of the person who has caused the annexation to be made. In *In re De Falbe* [1901] 1 Ch 523, 535, Vaughan Williams LJ said that there was not to be an inquiry into the motive of the person who annexed the articles, 'but a consideration of the object and purpose of the annexation as it is to be inferred from the circumstances of the case.' As Lord Cockburn put it in *Dixon v Fisher* (1843) 5 D 775, 793 'no man can make his property real or personal by merely thinking it so'. The matter has to be viewed objectively.

If one considers the object or purpose which the structure serves by being placed where it is, it was clearly placed there to enable the amenity of Holt's Field to be enjoyed through the establishment of a residence. The bungalow was built there in order that people could live in what is represented as being an idyllic rural environment. The Court of Appeal, however, had regard to the belief of Mr Morris that he owned the bungalow as evidence of his intention. But his belief cannot control the operation of the law in relation to accession and the matter of intention has to be judged objectively. Indeed the fact that the freeholders may have believed and reminded the occupants that their rights to remain could be terminated, which was also a factor on which the Court of Appeal relied, cannot affect the operation of the law.

Accession also involves a degree of permanence, as opposed to some merely temporary provision. This is not simply a matter of counting the years for which the structure has stood where it is, but again of appraising the whole circumstances. The bungalow has been standing on its site for about half a century and has been used for many years as the residence of Mr Morris and his family. That the bungalow was constructed where it is for the purpose of a residence and that it cannot be removed and re-erected elsewhere point in my view to the conclusion that it is intended to serve a permanent purpose. If it was designed and constructed in a way that would enable it to be taken down and rebuilt elsewhere, that might well point to the possibility that it still retained its character of a chattel. That the integrity of this chalet depends upon it remaining where it is provides that element of permanence which points to its having acceded to the ground. The Court of Appeal took the view that the bungalow was no more annexed to the land and just as much a chattel as the greenhouse in *Deen v Andrews* [1986] 1 EGLR 262 (or, as I have already mentioned, the large shed in *Webb v Frank Bevis Ltd*). But there is a critical distinction between *Deen v Andrews* and the present case in the fact that the greenhouse was demountable while the bungalow is not. I prefer the conclusion reached by the learned assistant recorder after hearing the evidence and visiting the site to form his own impression of the situation. As he observed towards the end of his judgment, a judgment which deserves commendation for the detail and care which has gone into it:

> '…it seems to me clear that at least by 1985 and probably before, it would have been clear to anybody that this was a structure which was not meant to be enjoyed as a chattel to be picked up and moved in due course but that it should be a long-term feature of the realty albeit that, because of its construction, it would plainly need more regular maintenance.'

In my view the conclusion reached on this matter by the assistant recorder was correct. The appeal should be allowed and the order made by him relating to Unit 6 should be restored.

Notes

(1) The proceedings concentrate on whether or not the occupiers are entitled to protection under the Rent Act 1977. As the Act gives protection only to the rent of a dwelling-house,[49] the answer depends on whether the bungalow is included in the licence given to an occupier. In the contracts giving the licences no mention is made of the bungalows: the licences were given for the use of the land. However, if, as a result of accession, the bungalow forms an integral part of the land it is automatically included in the contract and the occupier enjoys protection under the Rent Act 1977.

(2) Lord Lloyd of Berwick draws attention to the fact that the term 'tenant's fixtures', often used in cases of accession, is unclear. The term denotes additions attached to the land or building by a tenant and which the tenant may remove during or at the end of the lease, even though they have become part of the land as a result of accession. According to Lord Lloyd it would be clearer in such cases to

[49] See s 1 of the Act.

distinguish between three categories: either (a) something has remained a movable thing, or (b) it has become a tenant's fixture, or (c) it has become an integral part of the land.[50] Both in cases (b) and (c) accession has taken place. The difference is that in the second case the tenant has the right to remove the fixture, or to use a Roman term, he has the *ius tollendi*.

To set out the rules of accession Lord Lloyd refers to the decision in *Holland v Hodgson*[51] in which Blackburn J held that the question whether there is accession depends on the circumstances of the case, and in particular on the degree of fastening and the object attached. Despite the large number of examples given by Blackburn J his decision does not provide a general criterion for accession. On the other hand, the judgments of Lords Lloyd and Clyde in *Elitestone* give fairly distinct answers to the question.

(3) Where the degree of attachment is such that severance of the physical bond will damage the attachment or the thing to which it has been attached, there will undoubtedly be accession. Yet the judgments in *Hobson v Gorringe*[52] and *Reynolds v Ashby & Son*[53] show that there may be accession to the land even where things have been attached with screws or bolts so that the object may be easily removed. Both cases involved machines which were screwed into concrete foundations. The machines were regarded as part of the land. Moreover, in *Elitestone* Lord Lloyd and Lord Clyde explain that a building may be firmly attached to the foundation merely by its own weight.[54]

(4) In addition to this purely physical criterion, Lord Lloyd and Lord Clyde mention the purpose of the annexation as a measure for accession. Yet, they both stress that the subjective intention of the person who attached the thing is irrelevant. The intention is relevant only as far as it can be recognised by third parties.[55] So, the terms 'intention' and 'purpose' are regarded objectively, that is to say, intention and purpose should be inferred from objective factors such as the nature of the things attached and the way of attachment.

(5) In *Melluish (Inspector of Taxes) v BMI*,[56] a case affirmed by Lord Lloyd,[57] it is decided unequivocally that a contract or an agreement has no influence whatever on accession. As expressed by Lord Clyde:

> It is important to observe that intention in this context is to be assessed objectively and not subjectively. Indeed it may be that the use of the word intention is misleading. It is the purpose which the object is serving which has to be regarded, not the purpose of the person who put it there.[58]

[50] [1997] 2 All ER 513 at 517(j).
[51] [1872] LR 7 CP 328.
[52] [1897] 1 Ch 182.
[53] [1904] AC 466.
[54] See [1997] 2 All ER, 518(c)–(j) per Lord Lloyd and 523(j)–524(a) per Lord Clyde.
[55] [1997] 2 All ER 519(g)–(h) (per Lord Lloyd) and 524(f) (per Lord Clyde). Followed in *Chelsea Yacht & Boat Co Ltd v Pope* (Court of Appeal, 6 April 2000) [2000] 22 EG 147, at 149–50 (per Morrit LJ).
[56] [1996] AC 454.
[57] [1997] 2 All ER, 519(g).
[58] [1997] 2 All ER 524(f).

A further requirement for accession, Lord Clyde observes, is that the circumstances of the case make clear that the annexation is intended as permanent. In his view the bungalow involved has been 'constructed where it is for the purpose of a residence and that it cannot be removed and re-erected elsewhere point in my view to the conclusion that it is intended to serve a permanent purpose'.[59]

In *Melluish (Inspector of Taxes) v BMI (No 3) Ltd*[60] a financing company sold a central heating system to a local authority on hire-purchase. The contract between the financing company, BMI, and the local authority stipulated that the heating system would remain the property of BMI even if the system were installed into a building, and that the financing company would have the right to remove the system in case of non-payment. BMI claimed certain tax allowances in regard to the goods delivered. To acquire these allowances it was necessary that the goods had indeed remained the property of BMI. However, according to the tax inspector, BMI had lost ownership as a result of the heating system being installed.

(6) Could the parties stipulate in the hire-purchase contract that despite installation the heating system would remain the property of the seller? Or, more precisely, could they postpone accession of the thing by mere agreement? To support its view that accession may indeed be postponed in this way BMI referred to the judgment in *Simmons v Midford*.[61] Lord Browne-Wilkinson, however, does not follow this decision and instead follows the judgments in *Hobson v Gorringe* and *Reynolds v Ashby & Son*.[62] Lord Browne-Wilkinson shows that according to the last two judgments the intention of the parties can be relevant only as far as it may be inferred from the degree and the object of annexation:

> I agree with the conclusion and reasoning of the Court of Appeal. The equipment in these cases was attached to the land in such a manner that, to all outward appearance, it formed part of the land and was intended so to do. Such fixtures are, in law, owned by the owner of the land. It was suggested in argument that this result did not follow if it could be demonstrated that, as between the owner of the land and the person fixing the chattel to it, there was a common intention that the chattel should not belong to the owner of the land. It was said that clause 3.10 of the master lease disclosed such an intention in the present cases. In support of this argument reliance was placed on the decision in *Simmons v Midford* [1969] 2 Ch 415 where Buckley J. held that even where the outward and visible signs were only consistent with the chattels (in that case an underground drain) having become part of the land, the circumstances and language used in the grant of the

[59] [1997] 2 All ER, 525(d).

[60] [1996] AC 454.

[61] [1969] 2 All ER 1269.

[62] *Hobson v Gorringe*, [1897] 1 Ch 182, and *Reynolds v Ashby & Son* [1904] AC 466, are both about a machine bought under a hire-purchase contract which has been screwed onto a foundation in the ground. The land is mortgaged and after insolvency of the buyer a conflict arises between the seller, who has not been fully paid, and the mortgagee. According to the seller, the contract of hire-purchase entails that despite the physical attachment to the ground the machine is still his property. See [1897] 1 Ch 182, 193 (per Smith LJ): 'Now, in *Holland v Hodgson*, Lord Blackburn, when dealing with the "circumstances to shew intention", was contemplating and referring to circumstances which shewed the degree of annexation and the object of such annexation which were patent for all to see, and not to the circumstance of a chance agreement that might or might not exist between an owner of a chattel and a hirer thereof. … In each of these instances it will be seen that the circumstance to shew intention is the degree and object of the annexation which is itself apparent, and thus manifested the intention.'

> right to lay the drain showed an intention that the ownership of the drain should not be vested in the owner of the soil. He held that in consequence the drain was not owned by the owner of the soil in which it had been laid.
>
> Unfortunately, the decision in *Hobson v Gorringe* [1897] 1 Ch 182 was not cited to Buckley J. That case (which was approved by this House in *Reynolds v Ashby & Son* [1904] AC 466) demonstrates that the intention of the parties as to the ownership of the chattel fixed to the land is only material so far as such intention can be presumed from the degree and object of the annexation. The terms expressly or implicitly agreed between the fixer of the chattel and the owner of the land cannot affect the determination of the question whether, in law, the chattel has become a fixture and therefore in law belongs to the owner of the soil: see pp 192–193. The terms of such agreement will regulate the contractual rights to sever the chattel from the land as between the parties to that contract and, where an equitable right is conferred by the contract, as against certain third parties. But such agreement cannot prevent the chattel, once fixed, becoming in law part of the land and as such owned by the owner of the land so long as it remains fixed. To the extent that Simmons v Midford decides otherwise it was wrongly decided.

It may be noted that if the seller who sold under a retention of title clause stipulated a right of removal (*ius tollendi*) this right will not be thwarted by accession. Despite accession it may be invoked against the buyer/owner of the thing. It may even be invoked as against third parties because it is not a purely contractual right. The stipulation in the contract gives the seller an equitable interest which works against third parties provided that it has been entered onto the Land Register.[63] Because of the requirement of registration third parties are sufficiently protected.[64]

(7) In the case of a lease the right of removal should be seen as an incident of the lease rather than a separate right. As such it works against all third parties who are bound by the lease itself. The tenant's right of removal is recognised at common law. No separate registration is needed apart from the registration requirement of the lease. In principle mortgagees are bound by subsequent leases. Section 99 Law of Property Act 1925 gives the mortgagor the right to lease the property, but this right is commonly excluded in a written agreement between the mortgagee and the mortgagor under section 99(13) Law of Property Act 1925, unless the property is destined for leasing. If the right to lease is so excluded, the mortgagee is not bound by the lessee's right of removal. Note that this is different in Dutch law where the right of removal can be set up against the mortgagee even if the lease itself cannot be invoked against the mortgagee. See Hoge Raad 2 June 1989, NJ 1990/253 (*Christenhusz v Brunsveld*).

[63] RJ Smith, *Property Law*, 3rd edn (Harlow, Longman, 2000) 77; G McCormack, 'Hire-purchase, Reservation of Title and Fixtures' [1990] *Conveyancer and Property Lawyer* 275–87; K Gray and SF Gray, *Elements of Land Law*, 5th edn (Oxford, Oxford University Press, 2009) 1.2.68. Naturally this applies only to registered land.

[64] A small exception to the rules of accession is the tenant's right of removal under an agricultural holding or farm business tenancy. In principle movables attached by the tenant and even a building erected by him do not accede to the land and may be removed during or at the end of the tenancy: s 10 Agricultural Holdings Act 1986 and s 8 Agricultural Tenancies Act 1995.

I.A.4 FRENCH LAW

Introductory Note

The French law of accession to land is very opaque and confusing. Unfortunately, the legal literature fails to shed any light on the matter. According to Article 551 Cciv, ownership of a thing comprises everything which is united with the thing: 'Everything which is united with or incorporated into the thing belongs to the owner, according to the provisions hereafter mentioned.'[65] The requirement for accession is often referred to as incorporation.[66]

In the case of accession to land the traditional interpretation of the criterion of incorporation is attachment of a thing to immovable property in such a way that it cannot be removed without causing damage to the thing itself or to the immovable property. Esmein, however, asserts that in certain cases accession may take place even if removal would not cause damage. Equipment without which the building would be incomplete is immovable by nature and thus accedes to the building, even if it may be removed easily. A typical example would be roof tiles which can be taken off the roof without causing any damage to them or to the roof, the keys of the house, or the doors. On the other hand, equipment which is not necessary to make the building complete will accede only if it is firmly attached so that removal would cause damage.[67]

Nevertheless, the view that these objects should be considered as immovables is not generally accepted. The problem is not often treated explicitly in the literature, but some authors regard these objects as auxiliaries of the building which do not accede to the building (*immeubles par destination*), thus giving the impression that ownership of these objects cannot be acquired by way of accession. After all, a movable thing can be made an auxiliary thing of a building only if the auxiliary and the principal object are already owned by the same person.[68]

Although the doctrine is divided and unclear, it is to our way of thinking tenable to say that there are two different criteria for accession to immovable property: next to the physical criterion of removal causing damage there is a second criterion of incompleteness, which accords with the criterion of common opinion. Roof tiles, the keys to the doors, the doors themselves, are component parts of the house, even though they do not meet the first physical criterion.

In the following judgment the Cour de cassation has held that the rules of accession in the Civil Code are not mandatory law: the parties are able to post-

[65] 'Tout ce qui s'unit et s'incorpore à la chose appartient au propriétaire, suivant les règles qui seront ci-après établies.' See also the more general Art 546 Cciv.

[66] J-L Bergel, M Bruschi and S Cimamonti, *Les biens*, 2nd edn (Paris: LGDJ , 2010) no 185.

[67] Ch Aubry and Ch Rau, *Droit civil*, vol 2: *Biens*, 7th edn (by P Esmein) (Paris, Librairies techniques, 1961) 13 and 211. A similar view, yet expressed less clearly, can be found in C Demolombe, *Cours de Code Napoléon,* vol IX: *Traité de la distinction des biens*, vol. 1, 4th edn (Paris, Auguste Durand/Hachette, 1870) 291 *et seq*.

[68] Oddly, some authors even hold that things firmly attached to a building so that removal would cause damage are mere auxiliaries (immovable by their owner's destination, *immeubles par destination*). Others rightly reject this view saying that whenever such a physical bond exists the objects are immovable by their nature (*immeubles par nature*). See Bergel, Bruschi and Cimamonti, above n 67, nos 19–20.

pone or even opt out of accession.[69] The same rule applies to the Civil Code's rules on commingling and *specificatio*: they are *dispositive law*. It should be noted that in French law the term accession is often used as an umbrella term to cover commingling and *specificatio* as well. The section of the Civil Code treating accession, commingling and *specificatio* (Articles 565–77) is titled 'Du droit d'accession relativement aux choses mobilières' ('About the Right of Accession Relating to Movable Objects').

Cour de cassation Civ 3, 6 November 1970[70] **7.13 (FR)**

David v Ruhl

PARTIES' INTENTION TOWARDS ACCESSION

Opting out of accession

The landowner may opt out of the automatic accession of buildings.

Facts: In 1953 Mr and Mrs David, who are tenants, and Mrs Lemaignon, the owner of the land, made a deed indicating that buildings erected by the Davids at their own costs would remain their property. Mrs Ruhl is Mrs Lemaigon's successor in title. The question was whether at the end of the lease Mrs Ruhl could indicate which buildings she wanted to preserve against payment of an indemnity to the Davids.

Held: The owner of the land is able to opt out of accession by express agreement. The Court of Appeal should have checked whether it was the intention of the parties to waive the right of accession in which last case Article 555 Cciv does not apply.

Judgment: On the only argument: in view of the Articles 551 and 555 of the Civil Code;

Considering that the provisions of the first of these texts, according to which all that is united with and incorporated in the object belongs to the owner, are not mandatory law and can be discarded by his express renunciation;

That the provisions of the second regulate exclusively the case in which the constructor does not have, with the owner of the ground, any agreement referring to the erected buildings.

Considering that it results from the statements of the judges in the main proceedings, that by a mutually agreed private act of March 31 1953, the spouses David, lessees, and widow Lemaignon, owner, whose rights are exercised by Madame Ruhl, have erected a range of buildings, realised on the premises by the spouses David, and have agreed that the latter would remain owners of these buildings.

Considering that the nullifying judgment as attacked accedes to Madame Ruhl the right to exercise, by way of lease, an option to indicate those of the buildings that she means to conserve with the burden on her to pay the damages provided in Article 555 of the Civil Code, for the reason that, not presuming the renunciation, the fact that the lessor has stipulated that the realised buildings on the immovable property have been paid by the lessees, of which they remain owners, does not imply that said lessor has renunciated to presume on the legal provisions

[69] Cass civ 3, 6 November 1970, no 69-11.900, D 1971.J.395. See also Ph Malaurie and L Aynès, *Droit civil, Les biens*, 4th edn (Paris, Defrénois, 2010) no 451.
[70] No 69-11900; D 1971.J.395.

that permit him either to demand the removal of the buildings or to keep them in exchange for compensation.

Considering that the Court of Appeal, by stating for these reasons, that when the owner was supposed to investigate if, by interpretation of the disputed agreement, in the common intention of the parties, the owner had not renounced the prerogative of accession for the group of buildings that were immovable, it would render, in this case, inapplicable, because of their fate, the provisions of Article 555 of the Civil Code, the Court has not given a legal basis to its decision;

For these reasons: nullifies the judgment rendered between the parties, by the Court of Appeal of Rouen, 12 December 1968.

Notes

(1) Where land is leased the lessor and lessee can agree that any buildings which the lessee may erect on the land will remain his property or the property of a third person, and will not become part of the land. Such exclusion or postponement, often called *renonciation à l'accession* (renunciation of accession), may in certain cases be implicit, eg where the lessor has given authorisation to the lessee to build on the land.[71]

With certain kinds of lease, accession is by statute excluded, or at least postponed, until the end of the lease. These kinds of lease include the *bail emphytéotique*,[72] the *bail à construction*,[73] the *bail à réhabilitation*,[74] the *concession immobilière*,[75] the *bail à domaine congéables*, also called *bail à convention*, and the contract to exploit a mine.[76]

(2) If in the case of a normal *bail* (lease) the lessor/owner made an explicit or implicit *renonciation à l'accession*, the buildings attached by the lessee remain the lessee's property until the end of the lease. When the lease has elapsed, ownership of the building passes to the landowner. However, there has been much controversy in legal doctrine and case law how the question of accession should be answered if such a *renonciation à l'accession*, even an implicit one, did not take place.[77] The two opposing viewpoints were postponement of accession until the end of the lease and immediate accession at the moment of building. From at least 1964 the Cour

[71] Juris-classeur civil, Arts 551 and 552 (Ph Kaigl) no 13; P Jourdain, *Les biens* (Paris: Dalloz, 1995) 186.

[72] Art L451-1 *et seq.* Code rural, Art L451-10: 'L'emphytéote profite du droit d'accession pendant la durée de l'emphytéose' (Any accession during the right of *emphyteusis* are for the benefit of the holder of this right).

[73] Art L251-1 to L251-9 Code de la construction et de l'habitation, see Art L251-2. Note, however, that here the lessee is not entitled to demolish the buildings erected by him. He is even obliged to maintain these buildings in good condition. Thus, there is no right of removal in whatever form.

[74] Art L252-1 to L252-4 Code de la construction et de l'habitation.

[75] Loi no 67-1253 of 30 December 1967, Art 48 *et seq.* Although the statute itself does not provide this, some authors accept that the buildings erected during the lease are owned by the lessee until the end of the lease. See R Saint-Alary and C Saint-Alary–Houin, Dalloz, *Répertoire de droit immobilier, concession immobilière* (January 2009), nr 50-51 and the authors mentioned there; Bergel, Bruschi and Cimamonti, above n 67, no 290.

[76] Art 36 Code minier.

[77] J-P Bertrel, 'L'accession artificielle immobilière. Contribution à la définition de la nature juridique du droit de superficie' (1994) 4 *Revue trimestrielle de droit civil* 737–75, at 758–63; F Terré and Ph Simler, *Les biens*, 5th edn (Paris, Dalloz, 1998) 252 and 877.

de cassation changed its viewpoint from the theory of immediate accession into the theory of deferred accession.

Cour de cassation civ, 1 December 1964[78] 7.14 (FR)

Pocchiola v Ferouillet

PARTIES' INTENTION TOWARDS ACCESSION IN THE CASE OF LEASE

Destruction by acts of war

Tenant remains owner of building during lease.

Facts: Mr and Mrs Pocchiola had leased an undeveloped piece of land to Ferouillet. The buildings erected by Ferouillet were then destroyed by acts of war. The conflict between the parties concerned to whom the indemnity for war damage should be paid. The answer depended on whether or not the buildings had become part of the land belonging to Pocchiola.

Held: During the lease the tenant remains the owner of any buildings erected by him.

Judgment: On the only argument: considering that it results from the statements of the confirmative judgment as challenged that the partners Pocchiola have leased to Ferouillet a bare terrain on which the lessee has built constructions that have been destroyed by war;

That, a conflict having risen between the contracting parties concerning the attribution of the compensation for the damages caused by war, the Court of Appeal has attributed this compensation to the assignees of the lessee, the partners Ferouillet;

Considering that the judges of appeal are being reproached with having decided this way, for the reason that the pretension of the lessors to presume on the accession immediately after building the constructions, is contrary to the interpretation currently held in the case law on Article 555 of the Civil Code;

That when there was no particular provision in the lease contract, the general law needed to be applied, and that the right of accession of the lessors needed to be acknowledged from the moment of building the constructions.

But considering that if, in the absence of any agreement between parties, the destination of the constructions erected by the lessee is regulated, from the moment of expiration of the lease on, by Article 555 of the Civil Code, paragraphs 1 and 2, the lessee remains owner, during the duration of the lease, of the constructions that he has built on the terrain of the lessor;

That therefore the argument must be discarded;

For these reasons: rejects the appeal formed against the judgement rendered March 18, 1958 by the Court of Appeal of Aix-en-Provence.

[78] Cass civ 1 December 1964, JCP 1965.II.14213; followed eg in Cass civ 23 October 1990, D 1990. IR.266; Jourdain, above n 72, 178.

Cour de cassation civ 3, 20 April 2005[79] **7.15 (FR)**

SCI de Gestion Saussaie République and Mr X v Axa France

INDEMNITY FOR IMPROVEMENTS

Compensation for loss

The improvements in question belonged to the tenants during the lease and therefore the lessor cannot claim under the insurance policy.

Facts: Several business premises were given under a commercial lease. The premises were destroyed by fire. After the fire the lease contract was terminated by the landlords. The owners received an indemnity from their insurance company, Axa France. They sued Axa France for payment of an additional indemnity to compensate the loss of several improvements added by the tenants.

Held: During the lease the improvements in question still belonged to the tenants. Therefore the landlords have no right to indemnity from Axa France.

Judgment: Considering, according to the challenged judgment (Paris, October 7 2003) that on 6 January 1997, the premises for commercial use, belonging in part to the civil law partnership in real estate of Gestion Saussaie République and in part to Mr X, given in lease to the savings bank Île-de-France Paris and to Mr Y, exploiting a toy shop, were destroyed by a fire, that the premises were insured with the company Axa Courtage IARD, in whose name has appeared the company Axa France IARD;

That, after having obtained from the Axa Company a partial compensation based on different expertises, of which one was judicial, Gestion Saussaie République and Mr X have summoned this insurance company to pay complementary compensation.

On the first argument:

But considering, having put forward, for adopted reasons, that the lease, provided to the savings bank on 1 September 1978 and constantly renewed with periods of twelve years since 1 November 1982, contained a clause according to which the lessee has taken upon him to leave, at the end of the lease, all improvements, furnishing and decoration to the property, without compensation, and having held, interpreting the meaning of this clause within its competence to judge the facts of the case, that the decorations destroyed by the fire were solely meant to become ownership of the lessor at the end of the lease, the Court of Appeal has precisely deducted from it that the lessor, which had served the termination of the lease to the lessee because of the total loss of the leased object, could not compensate of the objects that no longer existed on the day of termination and that, on that catastrophic day, belonged to the lessee.

From which it follows that the argument is not founded;

And, considering that there is no reason to comment on the second argument, which would not be as such to permit the admission of the appeal;

For these reasons: rejects the appeal.

Notes

(1) The three cases above clearly show that during the lease buildings or things attached by the tenant in principle remain his property and do not accede to the

[79] No 03-20927.

land. Moreover, the Cour de cassation holds that all buildings erected by the lessee under a normal lease may be removed by the lessee during the contract of lease.[80] Thus the tenant has a so-called *ius tollendi*. Using this right, he is entitled to remove even an entire building.

(2) A large number of authors assert that in all cases mentioned above in which a temporary or permanent separation is made between ownership of the buildings and ownership of the land a right of superficies (*droit de superficie*) is created.[81] See Chapter 3. The right of superficies should be regarded as dependent on the right of lease. And, in turn, ownership of any building erected by the tenant is dependent on the right of superficies. As a result of this second relationship the tenant's ownership of the building and any limited property rights granted on the building by him will lapse when the right of superficies ends. Because of the first relationship the right of superficies will in principle come to an end at the moment the right of lease ends. The dependence entails that when the lease is transferred to a third party the latter will automatically acquire the right of superficies, and consequently ownership of the building, if any building is in existence at that time.

(3) However, unlike the above-mentioned kinds of lease a reservation of ownership clause is unable to postpone accession totally. The statement that accession of movables to land is not mandatory law (not *d'ordre public*) is slightly misleading. It applies only to the rules on accession in the civil code (551 *et seq*). Once the buyer is declared insolvent, mandatory rules in the Commercial Code apply (Article L624-16).[82]

(4) Whatever the answer to the above questions may be, it is plain that where a legal system allows parties to postpone or even exclude accession (here, in the case of leases) the question arises whether such an agreement works against third parties without entry onto the land register. Although a lucid answer cannot be found in the French literature, it would appear that the answer depends on whether the contract of bail works against third parties without registration. The postponement or exclusion of accession, which creates a right of removal (*ius tollendi*), is part of the right of lease. To the extent that the lease works against third parties the right of removal works against them.

(5) Under Article 1743 Cciv the lease works against the buyer of the immovable

[80] Cass req 22 November 1864, S 65.1.41; Jourdain, above n 72, 130; Malaurie and Aynès, above n 70, no 453.

[81] Jourdain, above n 72, 176-2; J Carbonnier, *Droit civil*, vol 3: *Les Biens*, 19th edn (Paris, PUF, 2000) 215; Bergel, Bruschi and Cimamonti, above n 67, no 289; Terré and Simler, above n 79, no 877; C Larroumet, *Droit civil*, vol 2: *Les biens. Droits réels principaux* (Paris, Economica, 1997) 672. Malaurie and Aynès, above n 70, no 453. The character of the right of superficies is controversial in French literature. See P Walet, Dalloz Répertoire de droit civil, Superficie (2000), no 24-31.

[82] On 21 September 2000 the former Insolvency Act, Loi no 85-98 of 25 January 1985, was incorporated into the Commercial Code. Art 121, as amended by Loi no 94-475 of 10 June 1994, was renumbered Art L621-122. The newest version is numbered Art L624-16 Ccomm and came into force on 24 March 2006. The scope of the article is confined in two important respects: it is limited to contracts of sale, and it is limited to the question of whether the thing may be revindicated from the insolvent buyer's estate.

property.[83] A lease also works against a mortgagee and the buyer in the case of a forced sale (enforcement of the mortgage).[84]

(6) To the extent that non-registration of the right of superficies is sanctioned with third party protection of the land register, we should bear in mind that this protection is available only to a very limited group of persons: the transfer of land or the creation of a limited property right in land French law does not require entry into the land register.[85] A right of superficies is created by contract[86] and is immediately effective not only between the contracting parties but also against many third parties, such as the landowner's unsecured creditors.[87] This effect against third parties applies irrespective of the question whether the creditor's claim has come into being before or after the creation of the right of superficies. Broadly speaking the protection of third parties against unregistered rights in land is restricted to third parties in good faith who received a property right which has been entered into the register prior to the registration of the right against which they claim protection. If protection is available to them the right, although validly created, does not work against them, even though it is effective against others.[88]

Commercial Code **7.16 (FR)**

Article L624-16 Goods held by the debtor, either on consignment or for sale on behalf of the owner, may be claimed if they still exist in kind.

Things [*biens*] sold under a retention of title clause may equally be claimed if they still exist in kind at the time proceedings are opened. This clause must have been agreed upon by the parties in writing at the latest at the time of delivery. It may be laid down in a document governing a number of commercial operations entered into by the parties.

The recovery claim in kind may be brought under the same conditions with respect to movable things incorporated in another thing where they may be removed without damaging them. A recovery claim in kind may also be made in relation to fungible things where things of the same nature and the same quality are in the possession of the debtor or any person keeping them on his behalf has.

In every instance, the thing may not be recovered if, by decision of the supervisory judge [*juge-commissaire*], the price is paid immediately. The supervisory judge may also, with the consent of the petitioning creditor, grant a moratorium [*délai*

[83] J Huet, *Traité de droit civil, Les principaux contrats spéciaux*, 2nd edn (Paris, LGDJ, 2001) 21206 ; Ph Malaurie, L Aynès and P-Y Gautier, *Droit civil, Les contrats spéciaux*, 4th edn (Paris, Defrénois 2009) no 671.

[84] L Aynès and P Crocq, *Les sûretés, La publicité foncière*, 4th edn (Paris, Defrénois 2009) no 686.

[85] As shown before, French doctrine is divided about the nature of superficies, some authors claiming that it is a special form of ownership, others claiming that it is a limited property right, or a combination of the two, or that it is no property right at all. The answer to the question has no influence on the third party effect. Decisive is the fact that superficies is generally regarded as a property right. It is subject to compulsory registration. This may be inferred indirectly from Art 7(2) of the Décret no 55-22 of 4 January 1955. See also Carbonnier, above n 83, 212.

[86] Jourdain, above n 72, 176-2.

[87] See Ph Simler and Ph Delebecque, *Droit civil, Les sûretés, La publicité foncière*, 3rd edn (Paris, Dalloz, 2000), 744.

[88] See Art 28(1) and 30(1) *Décret* no 55-22 of 4 January 1955.

de règlement]. The payment of the price shall thus be considered equivalent to [the payment] of debts referred to under Article L622-17(1).

Note

Under Article L624-16 Code de commerce the retention of title is able to subsist as long as the object exists *en nature* (in its natural state) and may be removed without causing damage to the thing itself or the thing to which it is attached.[89]

Cour de cassation com, 11 March 1997[90] **7.17 (FR)**

Liquidateur judiciaire Constructions navales d'Aquitaine v Sofice

OWNERSHIP OF ENGINE FITTED INTO A SHIP

Ship engines

As the engines could be easily removed they can be subject to an action for revindication.

Facts: Iveco sold and delivered ship engines to Constructions navales d'Aquitaine under a reservation of ownership clause. After the buyer was declared insolvent, Sofice, who was subrogated into the seller's rights, tried to revindicate the engines already built into the ships.

Held: As the Court of Appeal held that the engines could easily be removed from the ships without causing damage either to the engines or to the boats, the judges rightly held that the engines could be revindicated.

Judgment: Considering, according to the confirmative judgment as attacked, that the company Naval Constructions of Aquitaine has been admitted to suspension of payment on February 5th 1991 and consequently to bankruptcy, without having paid the ship engines that the company Iveco, with a clause of retention of ownership, had sold to it; that, subrogated in the rights and actions of Iveco, the company Sofice has claimed these motors, inventorised on February 21th 1991; that the court of appeal has condemned the insolvency administrator to return the motors to the Sofice company or to pay it the price, based on Article 121 of the law of January 25th 1985;

And on the second argument:

Considering that the insolvency administrator objects as well to the judgment having acceded the request of the Sofice company, while, according to the appeal (of the insolvency administrator), the objects that have been incorporated into fabricated goods cannot be the object of revindication; that, in this case, from the moment that the Sofice company established that the claimed motors were part of ships in the course of being finished or finished, in which the motors were inserted, the Court of Appeal could not confirm that they were found in their natural state, for their

[89] Cf Cass com 10 July 1990, D 1990.IR.192; Cass com 12 February 1991, Bull Civ IV, no 69; CA Paris 30 April 1993, D 1993.IR.158; Cass com 15 March 1994, JCP 1994 II 22277; Cass com 2 March 1999, D 1999.IR.98 and D. 2000.J.72.

[90] No 94-20069.

incorporation was not irreversible, and therefore nor condemn the insolvency administrator to return them without violating Article 121 of the law of January 25th 1985;

But, considering that, for adopted reasons, having put forward that the removal of the motors needed only a simple dismantling, from which follows that the motors still existed in their natural state, the Court of Appeal has legally justified her decision; that the argument has no foundation;

For these reasons:

Nullifies and annuls, in all its dispositions, the judgment rendered September 27th 1994, between the parties, by the court of appeal of Bordeaux.

Notes

(1) When the thing is transformed into another thing (*specificatio*) or if it is incorporated into another thing (*accessio*) it no longer exists in its natural state. The criterion for accession in Article 551 Cciv, incorporation, is different from the criterion mentioned in Article L624-16 Code de commerce. The latter article states that despite incorporation revindication is possible provided that the thing can be separated without causing damage.

(2) If accession and its criterion, incorporation, always needed a strong physical bond so that removal were to cause damage, it would be difficult to see any difference with the criterion of existence in its natural state of Article L624-16 Code de commerce. However, we have seen previously that there is a second criterion for accession, namely incompleteness: the roof tiles and doors are considered as parts of the house. In the above case the ship's engine could be seen as making the ship complete. Nevertheless, the engine can be revindicated because it can be removed from the ship without causing damage to the ship or the engine.

I.A.5 COMPARATIVE OVERVIEW

The comparative survey shows that Dutch and English law apply purely objective criteria for accession, such as the degree of annexation and the character of the objects attached. These objective factors are recognisable to everyone by looking at the factual situation and thus meet the principle of publication.[91] Although these legal systems use the 'purpose of annexation' as one of their criteria for accession, the intention of the annexor is relevant only as far as it can be inferred from the facts, such as the nature of the things and the manner of annexation. In this regard the term 'intention' could be called misleading. In using objective criteria these legal systems meet both principles underlying accession: the protection of value and the principle that all legal relations that work against everyone should be recognisable to everyone (principle of publication).

However, at the same time Dutch, English and German law allow a tenant who attached fixtures to the landlord's land to remove these fixtures. Commonly, third

[91] With the exception of English agricultural leases. Here outsiders cannot see which things do not accede to the land and still belong to the tenant.

parties do not know which fixtures have been attached by the tenant. This right of removal thus contravenes the principle of publication.

In German law the intention of the annexor is not purely objective and recognisable to outsiders. Under §95 BGB things attached for temporary use do not accede. This intention is in principle seen as a subjective element, although there is a certain amount of controversy and inconsistency as regards its meaning. Under this paragraph buildings and other objects annexed by the holder of a proprietary right of use do not accede either. Although the existence of such a right is an objective factor third parties are unable to rely on what they see: even if the right of use is registered they cannot see whether the thing has been attached by the holder of this right during the right of use. §95 thus violates the publication principle.

In French law certain types of lease entail that things attached by the tenant do not accede to the building. In the case of a normal contract of lease lessor and lessee may agree that things attached by the lessee do not accede during the lease. For the same reasons as in German law this conflicts with the publication principle. Outside the field of leases a contract or the intention of one of the parties has no relevance, according to many authors. A thing may either accede to a building if removal would cause damage or if removal would render the building incomplete. However, it might seem that under the special insolvency provisions a reservation of ownership clause does have some influence.

I.B RIGHT OF REMOVAL

Introductory Note

As we have seen, the subject of accession cannot be treated without taking into consideration the right of removal, the *ius tollendi*, given to a lessee or other person entitled to the use of the land. It forms an important exception to the rules of accession. To a certain extent it is recognised in all the legal systems described. The right of removal may take either of two forms. In its first form it prevents the attachment from acceding to the land. The tenant or any other person holding a personal of limited property right to use the land will remain owner of the objects he attached to the land, and because of his ownership he is entitled to remove the objects. In its second form objects annexed will immediately become part of the land but the tenant or user is given the right to remove these objects *despite* accession. Here the right of removal entitles its holder to remove objects which have become the landlord's property.[92]

Dutch[93] and English law[94] recognise the right of removal in its second form.

[92] Ch Petit, 'Het wegbrekingsrecht van den huurder' (1954) 4341 *Weekblad voor Privaatrecht, Notariaat en Registratie* (*WPNR*) 157 *et seq*, 160.

[93] *Ibid.*

[94] RJ Smith, *Property Law*, 7th edn (Harlow, Longman, 2011) 93. There is an exception for agricultural fixtures: they are removable by the tenant and do not accede to the land. S 10 Agricultural Holdings Act 1986 or within s 8 Agricultural Tenancies Act 1995.

Since 1964 French law has recognised the tenant's right of removal in its first form postponing accession until the end of the lease.

German law has opted for a combination of both forms: postponement of accession in §95 BGB and, in the case that objects attached by a tenant have become the landlord's property by way of accession, a right of removal in its second form (§539(2) BGB).[95] German law accepts that buildings erected by the lessee during his right of lease do not accede to the land. Under §95 BGB entire buildings may be removed.[96]

On a more limited scale English law recognises a similar exception to the rules of accession. Where a tenant under an agricultural lease attaches movables or erects a building, these remain his property and may be removed by him during or at the end of the lease. It seems that the normal right of removal in English law would not allow the removal of an entire building.

Legal systems which use objective standards for accession recognise that the rules of accession ought to protect third parties. They do not allow a reservation of ownership clause to bar or even postpone accession. Allowing a lease unknown to outsiders to influence accession would be inconsistent with this approach.

Does the right of removal work against third parties? In principle the answer would be as follows. If a certain right to use land gives its holder a right of removal it forms part of the right of use. It should be seen as a natural element of this right.[97] From this we can draw the following conclusion. If and so far as the right of use works against third parties, the right of removal works against them as well.[98] So, normally the tenant will be able to exercise his right of removal not only against the original landlord but also against a new owner or certain other third parties, such as mortgagees. This may seem inappropriate since the new owner is unable to see which things have been added by the tenant.

The solution may be different where the right of removal automatically creates a right of superficies which is subject to compulsory registration onto the land register. Third party protection will then normally follow the general rules on the protection against unregistered property rights. As we have seen previously, French law, which follows this approach, most probably acknowledges that the right of removal works against a large category of third parties (eg unsecured creditors) even if the right of superficies has not been registered.

The right of removal takes into account only the interests of the landowner and the person attaching the movable object. The rationale of the right of removal is to prevent unjust enrichment of the landlord. Fairness in the relationship of landlord

[95] Since the amendment of the law of lease (1 September 2001) this subsection replaces the former §547a BGB.

[96] MünchKomm BGB/Holch, 5th edn (2006), §95, no 14.

[97] Many legal systems distinguish between provisions which are considered an essential part of the property right and which therefore work against third parties, and, on the other hand, provisions which work only between the original parties. It is an essential part if the provision is *inter naturalia*, that is to say, in accordance with the nature of the property right in question.

[98] It does not matter whether the right of use is a property right, as in the case of an English lease, or *locatio conductio*, a right which is in principle a personal right, but works against certain third parties as a result of special legislative provisions.

and tenant demands that either the tenant receives just compensation for valuable additions or that he has the right to remove all objects annexed by him. However, as the law would not permit the owner to be saddled against his will with objects annexed by the tenant, the latter will normally not be entitled to compensation. What is more, the landlord will often have the right to demand removal of the attachments and restoration of the original situation.

Nevertheless, where the tenant is entitled to remove objects which have become part of the leased land, this right of removal infringes the principles underlying accession: the preservation of value and the protection of third parties.[99]

The importance of the infringement depends on the scope of the right of removal in the various legal systems. In English law the tenant has the right to take away so-called trade fixtures and ornamental or domestic fixtures. The right to remove trade fixtures was developed during the Industrial Revolution and in principle covers all industrial or trade equipment attached by the tenant to the land to exercise his business. Ornamental or domestic fixtures is a much more limited concept that covers, for example, an ornamental chimney-piece, a water-tub or an oven.[100] In German law the right of removal is confined to so-called *Einrichtungen* (improvements). These are movable objects which are attached to enhance the use of the leased object. The definition is rather narrow and certainly does not cover buildings or building materials. In general, as the objects have been attached only for a temporary purpose they do not accede to the object leased. However, the right of removal may be exercised even when the objects involved did accede.[101]

In Dutch and French law, on the other hand, even entire buildings may be removed. In Dutch law this does not only apply to the contract of lease (*huur*)[102] but also to the property rights of *emphyteusis* (*erfpacht*),[103]superficies (*opstal*)[104] and usufruct (*vruchtgebruik*).[105]

Thus, from a common background, Roman law, rules of accession have developed which vary considerably from country to country. In addition, the rules on the right of removal are wholly different in the legal systems described. We should keep in mind that any attempt in European private law at harmonising security rights, such as reservation of ownership, mortgage on immovables, and, to a lesser degree, secu-

[99] Perhaps the problem could be avoided by confining the right of removal to those things which a lessee will normally take away at the end of the lease.

[100] See eg of trade and ornamental fixtures, R Megarry and W Wade, *The Law of Real Property*, 7th edn (ed C Harpum et al) (London, Sweet & Maxwell, 2008) 23-012 and 23-013. As noted above, fixtures within s 10 Agricultural Holdings Act 1986 or within s 8 Agricultural Tenancies Act 1995 are removable because they do not accede to the land.

[101] MünchKomm BGB-Bieber (2008) §539, Rn 15 *et seq.*

[102] Art 7:216 BW.

[103] Art 5:89 (3) BW.

[104] Before the expiry of the right of superficies the holder of this right is entitled to remove buildings and other improvements as a result of his right of ownership. After the expiry of the right of superficies ownership of the buildings passes to the landowner. The exclusion of accession comes to an end. Therefore the Civil Code had to provide expressly that the former holder of the right may remove buildings and other improvements directly after expiry of his right: Art 5:105(2) BW. See WHM Reehuis et al, *Goederenrecht*, 12th edn (Deventer, Kluwer 2006) no 672.

[105] Art. 3:208(2) BW. On these rights, see above, Chapter 3.

rity on movables, will fail unless the rules on accession and the right of removal are harmonised at the same time.

Hoge Raad, 2 June 1989[106] **7.18 (Nl)**

Christenhusz v Brunsveld

ERGA OMNES EFFECT OF TENANT'S RIGHT OF REMOVAL

Oak kitchen

Right of removal works against third parties.

Facts: The owner of a house, Christenhusz, had created a mortgage on his house in favour of a bank. Under the terms of the mortgage he was not allowed to let the property to a tenant. He nonetheless let the upper floor to his son. When the bank exercised its mortgage by forced sale the property for sale was described to have an oak kitchen on the upper floor. After the property had been vacated, the kitchen had disappeared. The kitchen turned out to have been built by the tenant and had been removed by him under his right of removal. The buyer of the property, Brunsveld, claimed damages from Christenhusz, the former owner of the house. Christenhusz argued, among other things, that the kitchen had been installed by the tenant and had been removed by the tenant under the tenant's right of removal. The Court of Appeal held, among other things, that the lease did not work against the mortgagee and the buyer, and that nor did the tenant's right of removal work against them.

Held: If under the mortgage conditions the lease does not work against the mortgagee and the buyer on the forced sale, there is no good reason why the tenant should be unable to invoke against the mortgagee and the buyer his right of removal.

Judgment: 3.1 This dispute deals with the question whether the owner of an immovable object ('the owner') leased without permission of the holder of a right of hypothec who has made the stipulation of Article 1230 BW, is bound to repay damages to the person who has acquired that object from the holder of the hypothec during the realisation of that right 'free from lease' and 'in the state it was in at the moment of auction' arising because between the sale at auction and the eviction of the owner the lessee invoking Article 1603 BW has taken away that what he installed during the lease. ...

3.4 The ground mentioned above on which the Court of Appeal set aside the right of the lessee on which the owner based his arguments, shows an incorrect application of the law. In so far as parts 3 and 4 complain about this, they stand.

It is correct that the owner must provide possession of the object to the buyer in the state in which it is in at the moment of auction, but when the object was subject to a lease, that 'state' is the leased state including the right to remove that may, in principle, be exercised by the lessee also against the holder of the right of hypothec.

This does not change now that the lease was made in violation of the stipulation as mentioned in Article 1230 BW. This stipulation can bring with it that the buyer is authorised to invoke the invalidity of the lease contract and seek the eviction of the lessee (cf HR 3 febr 1989, RvdW 1989, 62), but there is no reason why a lessee to whom in violation of the stipulation an immovable object was leased, would not be allowed to use his right of removal in the same way and to the same

[106] NJ 1990/253.

extent as other lessees to whom the holder of the right of hypothec cannot object. The protected interest of the holder of the right of hypothec under Article 1230 BW does not justify such a distinction.

Note

The above judgment shows that the tenant's right of removal works against third parties, such as the mortgagee and the buyer at the forced sale. The main point of the procedure was about the mortgagor's liability against the buyer for not having informed the mortgagee and the buyer of the tenant's right of removal. These points have been removed from the excerpt in order to focus on the point which is important to our discussion: the *erga omnes* effect of the right of removal. Oddly, in this case the contract of lease itself could not be set up against the mortgagee since the mortgage deed pre-dated the lease and excluded the mortgagor's right to lease the property. Nevertheless, the right of removal, which is an incident of the lease contract, could be invoked against the mortgagee.

I.C ACCESSION OF MOVABLES TO MOVABLES

I.C.1 GERMAN LAW

BGH, 8 October 1955[107] **7.19 (DE)**

OWNERSHIP OF ENGINE FITTED INTO TRACTOR

Tractor engine

No accession or specification arises by fitting an engine into a tractor.

Facts: The defendant built an engine into a tractor. The defendant paid a sum of money to the claimant but agreed with him that the claimant should pay back this sum if as a result of the fitting the defendant acquired ownership of the engine.

Held: The engine of a tractor is not an essential component of the tractor, at least as long as the tractor still belongs to the manufacturer. Nor does the manufacturer become owner of the engine through *specificatio* under §950 BGB.

Judgment: On the grounds: According to the agreement made between the parties, the claimant should reimburse the amount paid of DM962 to the defendant, when the latter through fitting the engine into the tractor obtains ownership of the engine. The decision on the action for a negative declaratory judgment is therefore dependent on whether the defendant has become owner through building in the engine into the tractor.

1. The Court of Appeal correctly states that the defendant did not obtain ownership according to §950 BGB through manufacturing. The manufacturing of multiple substances to a new thing within the meaning of this provision, however, may also consist of the manufacturer joining several independent things to a new unitary thing. As a general rule he will become owner of the new thing, and the old ownership

[107] IV ZR 116/55 (Karlsruhe), NJW 1955, 1793.

on the joined things ceases. This legal consequence does not materialise according to §950, when the value of the manufacturing of the transformation is substantially lower than the value of the substances. The value of the manufacturing is not only the expenses for the manpower, but also the value of the performed work, as reflected in the real value. It results when the value of the substance, of which the tractor is made, not only the value of the engine delivered by the claimant, is subtracted from the value of the whole tractor. This value is, according to the observations of the Court of Appeal, considerably lower than the value of the different substances, of which the whole tractor consists.

2. Neither did the defendant become, as the Court of Appeal has correctly stated, owner or co-owner of the engine according to §947 BGB. This would only have been the case if the engine, through installation, would have become an essential component of the tractor. This is not the case, as the Court of Appeal has observed without erring in law.

However, the tractor is not a single entity composed of several independent things, but, like any other mass-produced motor vehicle, a composed unitary thing. This point of view is the natural approach. A tractor is, just like a motor vehicle, considered to be a unitary thing and not only a composition of several independent things, which are assembled to attain an economic purpose. The chassis frame, carriage and engine of a motor vehicle are only parts of a unitary whole, which, in so far as they were independent things before their composition, have lost their corporeal independence and have been absorbed by the whole as parts. Also in the legal sense, the engine built into the tractor has, through fixing, lost its former characteristic of an independent thing. The connection with the chassis frame is according to the Court of Appeal loose indeed. The engine can be dismantled by loosening several screws within a short period of time without problems. Nevertheless it has become a component part of a unitary thing. This is due to the fact that the engine, through fixing it in the tractor, has acquired its proper purpose, a purpose which it admittedly could have found in other ways, and especially due to the fact that the conventional use of the thing has become possible only through the connection with the engine.

Through fixing, the engine has only become a simple and not an essential component part of the tractor. Simple parts of a thing are all those parts that are not essential. Essential parts of a movable are according to §93 BGB only those parts that cannot be separated from one another, without one or the other being destroyed or changed in its nature. It is undisputed that neither the engine nor the other parts of the tractor are damaged by dismantling the engine. It is only questionable whether the separate parts are changed in their nature. It is immaterial whether the nature of the whole thing, the tractor, is being changed by dismantling the engine. In fact, it depends only on whether after separation the different parts can be used economically in the same manner, be it only after they have been connected to another thing for this purpose (BGB RGRK 10 Aufl §93 Anm 3 S 151). This applies in the case at hand. After being dismantled from the tractor, the engine retains its nature. It can be used as a main engine for other vehicles or also stationary any time. Also the other parts of the tractor, after having been dismantled, can still be used. This applies in any case as long as the tractor is still, as in the case to be decided, the property of the manufacturing company. From the economic point of view to be applied here, it is decisive whether the parts can be used economically in the same manner. The economic utilisation of the separate parts of the tractor can vary with different owners. For the manufacturing company, it consisted of them being used for the production of the tractors, which were designated for sale. So, the parts remaining after the dismantling of the engine can still be used by the manufacturing company. It is immaterial that as a result of applying the engine the nature of the separate parts, as long as the connection is continued, no longer materialises economically, but that the nature of the whole thing is important for the various parts. It can be left undecided whether it would have been different had the tractor already been transferred.

In RGZ 152, 91f [98f] the Reichsgericht held that the engine of a motor ship is an essential part of the ship, even if the hull and engine are not adapted to each other and if the parts can be separated from each other without damage. It considered that through the separation a change in nature would materialise, as the ship would become an unfinished piece and could not be used for seafaring on its own. The Reichsgericht did not base itself on the nature of the hull and the engine as such, but considered the economic purpose of the whole to be equal to the economic purpose of the hull, as this is the main part of the ship. It can be left unanswered whether this legal opinion of the Reichsgericht should be supported or not. The case decided by the Reichsgericht can be distinguished on decisive points from the legal dispute to be decided in the case at hand. The legal relationships in the case of a seagoing vessel, which has already been given its purpose can be different from those of a serialised motor vehicle which is still owned by the manufacturing company and is designated for sale. Likewise, the case at hand can be distinguished from cases which concern the mounting of engines into factory buildings. The opposite views to be found in RGZ 50, 240f [243]; 58, 338f [341]; 62, 406f [409]; 69, 150f [158]; JW 05, 3872 and JW 11, 573 do not conflict with the decision at hand.

In the judgment published in RGZ 152, 91f [98] the Reichsgericht has, referred to the fact that today's technology has made huge progress in such a way that things which according to the natural point of view and common opinion seem to be unitary things, a seagoing vessel, an organ, a motor vehicle, can be designed so that things which are especially subject to wear, can be taken out and replaced with other pieces without damage. Therefore [according to this judgment] when separating parts the aspect of the change of nature must be weighed heavily, because otherwise a thing which is seen as a unitary thing according to common opinion and is regarded as such in business contracts, very often proves, on closer examination, to be a composition of pieces of different owners, and the assumed unity would dissolve legally.

This deliberation of the Reichsgericht cannot in general lead to an equation of the nature of a chassis frame and chassis of a motor vehicle, or the nature of a chassis frame of a tractor, with the nature of the whole vehicle, in order to prevent that something which form a unity from a natural point of view does not hold in a legal sense. Neither legal certainty nor the general economic interest of the preservation of unities, circumstances to which the Reichsgericht points, call for such an opinion. However, the legislative rationale of the §§93, 947 BGB is based, among other things, on these two aspects. The distinction between essential and non-essential parts is not based on a legal but on economic reasons. It aims at preventing any unnecessary destruction of economic values. In the interpretation this purpose must be taken into account (see also RGZ 58, 341). Since enactment of the BGB the technological developments have made substantial progress, and the economic circumstances have changed considerably. These circumstances must be taken into account decisively. They entail that §§93, 947 BGB do not have the same meaning as in former times. In many cases, in which for things which have been manufactured according to the state of technology of 1900, essential parts were to be assumed, this is not the case if they are produced on the basis of contemporary technology. The economic circumstances of the present time would not be respected adequately, if case law, in order to continue to consider them as essential parts, would interpret the notion of the change of nature in §93 BGB differently and wider than has mostly happened until now. The economic interest of the preservation of a unity is not very significant if the separation and assembly of the parts can be done without any damage and without significant manpower. It stands back, if from an economic point of view justified private-economic interests demand the separation. That is, however, the case if suppliers of individual components reclaim their property from the manufacturing company for the reason that their claim for the purchase price of these articles is not satisfied. It may not be neglected that under present economic conditions the supply to manufacturing companies very frequently takes place under retention of title on credit. It would be economically unjustified, if the suppliers lost their rights due to the fact that the acquirer joins the supplied thing with other things to a uniform thing, although the separation can be made at any time without difficulties and without damage to the individual parts. Nor does the principle of legal certainty demand that only a uniform legal relationship exists in regard to compound uniform things. Especially if in trade the thought that the uniform thing consists of different non-essential components does not arise in practice, legal certainty enjoys the necessary protection. For, the person which acquires such a thing under these conditions becomes owner of the whole thing including all its components according to §§932 et seq BGB, or §366 HGB. For the purchaser cannot generally be required to inquire whether the sellers are also owners of all individual components of the thing. Should he exceptionally know that the seller is not the owner, he does not require special protection.

Since in the case at hand there is no other possibility on the basis of which the defendant could have become owner of the tractor through the installation of the engine, the claimant did not lose ownership of the engine as a result of the installation.

Note

German law distinguishes between essential and non-essential parts. In the above case the engine is regarded as a non-essential part. Essential parts are those objects that cannot be removed without causing damage or changing the character of one or more of the objects involved. This does not hold for the engine. Nevertheless, it is a part because it enables the tractor to exercise its function. Therefore, it is a non-essential part. Under §947 BGB accession takes place only in regard to essential parts. For that reason no accession takes place even though the engine is a component part.

BGH, 3 March 1956[108] 7.20 (DE)

ACCESSION BETWEEN A MACHINE AND ITS COVER

Aluminium covers

If covers are needed to protect machines and operators, the covers are essential components.

Facts: The claimant delivered aluminium plates to company S which used the materials to make aluminium covers for machines. Machines with these aluminium covers were then delivered to the defendant. The claimant asserted that, because it delivered the aluminium under a reservation of ownership clause, it remained owner of the covers and, accordingly, he tried to revindicate the covers from the defendant. The first question was whether or not the covers were essential components of the machines so that the claimant lost ownership as a result of *accessio*. The second question was whether the claimant lost ownership as a result of *specificatio* when company S used the material to make the covers.

Held: if the covers are needed to protect the machines and the persons operating these, the covers are essential components, and the machines cannot be seen as the principal objects. Where the contract stipulates that the delivery of aluminium took place under a reservation of ownership clause and that the production of the covers was to take place for the benefit of the supplier, the manufacturer should be seen as the manufacturer in the sense of §950.

Judgment: The Court of Appeal concurs with the court of first instance, that the semi-finished materials supplied by the claimant became an essential component of the finished machines due to the fact that the devices were built into the housings manufactured by them [the semi-finished materials]. The Court of Appeal followed the opinion of law of the court of first instance to the extent that the economic purpose and the nature of the main part are to be equated with the economic purpose and the nature of the whole machine. Through the displacement of the housing the equipment would become an incomplete piece, which could no longer function by itself in accordance with its purpose. The remaining machine would thereby change in its economic function. …

Contrary to the opinion of the Court of Appeal, it also depends on whether material of the applicant was used for the machines that were transferred to the defendant. For the remarks of the Court of Appeal that by the installation of the equipment into the housings the property of the housing passed to S are legally unfounded.

The applicant states that the devices, by releasing a few screws, could be removed from the housings without destroying these or the remaining machines. If this statement is true, then the housings would only be an essential component according to §93 BGB, if they or the remaining components were changed in their nature by the separation. It is in principle insignificant whether the whole machine is changed in its nature by the removal of the housing, especially whether the remaining equipment after the removal of the housing can be used as before. In principle it is important only whether the different components are changed in their nature by the separation. That depends on whether they can still, after the separation, be used economically as they have been before, be it only after they are connected again with other things for this purpose.

It can be assumed that all machines manufactured by S are unitary objects

[108] BGHZ 20, 159, NJW 1956, 788.

consisting of several components. In such cases it cannot be maintained without reservation that, contrary to the general rule just mentioned, the economic purpose or the nature of the main part is equal to the economic purpose and nature of the whole thing.

The Reichsgericht may have defended this point of view in different judgments. ... The Senate has already left open in its decision published in BGHZ 18, 226f = NJW 55, 1793, whether one should concur with this legal opinion, as it does not do justice to modern economic and technical relations. It cannot be applied as a general rule.

The question about the nature and purpose of things and components of a thing is to be judged from a technical-economic point of view. According to the spirit and purpose of §93 BGB, it should be prevented that economic values are destroyed without justifying reasons and that the national economy is thereby damaged.

According to its spirit and purpose the question as to when separation of components changes their nature must also be decided primarily on the basis of economic criteria. The different components of a thing vary in their nature. They serve different purposes. From an economic-technical point of view, these purposes differ not only according to their special nature, but are also of varying significance. In the case of a compound uniform thing the main feature of the different components, of which the thing consists, is that these components should serve to make the practical use of the uniform thing more or less possible. There are components whose nature is determined by this purpose in such way that, after they are inserted into the whole, they have, from a general point of view, no longer their own nature at all. Upon installation, their purpose merges completely with the whole. It gives itself to this. Therefore it can be correct, economically seen, after the separation of such components, to equate the nature of the remaining main part with the nature of the whole thing. That could apply, for example, to the relationship of individual screws and lever of a machine or of an individual wheel in a transmission to the remaining machine or the remaining transmission.

However, there are also components, which are to serve also the operation of the whole thing, but the own nature of which, due to its special nature and meaning, generally economically seen, adheres to the component in a way that this nature is further maintained for this component also after the installation, which do not merge with the whole object and do not give themselves to the latter. That will be usually the case if the component concerns technically independent devices or machines, which are to enable the operation of the whole as auxiliary devices. The same can also apply to the housing, which is to serve to take up and protect the equipment during operation. In such cases, where the separation of these components is concerned, it is impossible to equate the purpose and the nature of the remaining special components with the purpose and the nature of the whole thing. Should this happen, then with consideration of today's economic and technical developments, results would be obtained which are not justified. As a result, provision §94(2) BGB, which for special reasons is made for the component parts of a building, according to which also the things attached for the construction of the building are essential components, would practically, by means of interpretation of §93 BGB, be expanded at least partly to other things as well.

If it is true that the equipment can be removed from the housing by loosening of the connecting bolts, without the equipment or the housing being damaged, the housing would generally, in economic terms, keep its nature even after the equipment is built into the housing. This nature does not merge with the whole, and therefore the nature and purpose of the remaining equipment cannot be equated with the nature and purpose of the whole machine after a separation. A change of ownership relationships due to the installation of the equipment into the housing would therefore only have occurred if the housing were changed in its nature by the separation. A change in the ownership relationships by the installation of the equipment into the housing would have occurred therefore only if the housing were changed in its nature by the separation. That could be the case if the housing could only be used for the manufactured devices of S, so that it would become economically worthless by the separation and have only scrap value. In this case the housing would be an essential component of the whole machine. The applicant would have become co-owner according to §947(1) BGB, unless according to §947(2) BGB the one part should be regarded as the main thing in relation to the other one. The Court of Appeal must still examine whether the actual device is the main thing in relation to the housing. The question as to which is to be regarded as the main thing, and which the secondary thing, of a uniform object consisting of several things, depends on common opinion. Neither the value ratio nor the relationship of the spatial scale is decisive by itself. One can speak of a main thing according to common opinion only if the remaining components could be missed without the nature of the thing thereby being impaired.

Such a relationship between main thing and secondary thing could be assumed if the housing would essentially serve to give the device a better appearance, if the device could fulfil its actual and principal purpose without the housing. On the contrary, if the housing fulfils other tasks as well, especially if it protects the device and the persons who use the device, or if the installation of the device into the housing enables its practical operation, after installation one cannot consider the housing in relation to the remaining components to be only a secondary thing, according to common opinion. In such a case it would be irrelevant that the device could technically be put into operation without the housing. It rather depends on whether it can be put to practical use without the housing.

Note

If the aluminium covers should be seen as essential components of the machines, this does not mean that the owner of the engines becomes owner of the covers as well. It is yet to be seen whether or not any of the constituent parts should be regarded as the main thing. Only where there is a principal object do the 'other' parts, the so-called accessory things, accede to the ownership of the principal thing. Whether or not there is a principal object depends on common opinion. If none of the parts can be seen as the principal object, the owners of the parts become co-owners of the composed object under §947(1) BGB. The co-ownership shares are then determined by the value of the parts at the time of accession.

II. COMMINGLING

II.A DUTCH LAW

Introductory Note

Dutch law treats the commingling of oil or grains differently from the commingling of a pile of steel plates. In the first case the oil in the tank or grain in the silo is seen as one thing, whereas in the second example the steel plates are still seen as separate objects. Common opinion dictates what has to be regarded as one thing and what has to be regarded as a number of separate items. The difference is important because the provision in the Dutch civil code about commingling applies only to the first case where coal, grains, fluids or gases, etc, are mixed. The legislator expressly left the other category to case law. This second category is called quasi-commingling. In the first category (genuine commingling) as a rule the different owners of the quantities mixed will become co-owners of the entire bulk. In the case of quasi-commingling, however, co-ownership seems impossible and the holder of the things should be regarded as the owner of all objects.

The distinction between commingling and quasi-commingling is made in many civil law jurisdictions. Genuine commingling creating one inseparable thing is called *confusio* and quasi-commingling is called *commixtio*. The terms are based on Roman law but the distinction is not of Roman origin.

Hoge Raad, 12 January 1968[109] **7.21 (NL)**

Mulder, Peijnenburg and Drucker v Teixeira de Mattos

REVINDICATION OF UNSPECIFIED GOODS

Teixeira de Mattos

No revindication of unspecified goods.

Facts: The commercial bank Teixeira de Mattos held certificates of shares in the company Nillmij. It held these shares on behalf of two clients but also on its own behalf. The bank regularly traded in these shares on its own account. The contract of deposit between the bank and its clients obliged the bank to register the individual numbers of the certificates held on behalf of its clients, but the bank failed to do so. All certificates, including those held by the bank on its own behalf, were held in the vault. Mulder and Peijnenburg had deposited with the bank one and three certificates, respectively. The bank was subsequently given an administration order. At that moment there happened to be exactly four of these certificates held by the bank. There were no other clients who had deposited these certificates with the bank at the time of the administration order. The two clients tried to revindicate 'their' certificates.

Held: It is essential for a revindication that the numbers of the certificates be known. As the numbers are unknown to Mulder and Peijnenburg and unknown to the bank it cannot be proven that the certificates in the bank's deposit are the same certificates once deposited by Mulder and Peijnenburg. As a result they cannot revindicate the certificates. The bank owns the certificates.

Judgment: Considering that in part 2 it is agued in the first place that the Court

[109] NJ 1968/274.

of Appeal would have misunderstood that Teixeira on the bases of the agreement of open deposit was obliged to return one Nillmij certificate to Peijnenburg.

That the Court in its seventh consideration has held that the numbers of the Nillmij certificates which have been given in deposit, to Teixeira are unknown to Mulder and Peijnenburg, and that they became part of Teixeira's general stock of certificates without any number specification, so that it could no longer be determined whether the four Nillmij certificates now present in the general stock are the ones that were provided by Mulder and Peijnenburg, or that they are other certificates;

That the Court has expressed with this that Mulder and Peijnenburg were incorrect in there claims in so far as—one of two alternative possibilities—they claimed that the present certificates Nillmij were the same as were provided by Mulder and Peijnenburg to Teixeira;

That, now that the last-mentioned circumstance which, leaving apart the second alternative to be discussed hereunder, is essential for allowing the revindication has not been proven, it is not essential that Teixeira was obliged under the contract to return one certificate to Mulder and three to Peijnenburg;

That in part 2, relating to the alternative possibility, it is argued that the Court would have misunderstood that on the basis of the agreements of open deposit of Teixeira shares was, in the case of transfer of one or more of them, obliged to replace the certificates with others and to hold these for Mulder (one) and for Peijnenburg (three) and further that since 1 January 1966 Teixeira was obliged to ensure that the numbers of the certificates it held for its clients were registered separately.

That the Court in its seventh consideration has added to its factual assessment already mentioned, that, now that it has been established that at the opening of the deferment of payments procedure Teixeira had not yet registered the numbers of individual certificates of this class in relation to individual clients, Teixeira did not, of these four certificates, hold a certain certificate for Mulder and the other three for Peijnenburg.

That the Court expressed with this that the claims of Mulder and Peijnenburg are incorrect, in so far as they argue that Teixeira held the present Nillmij certificates for them;

That, now that in the second alternative in discussion here, this last element is essential for awarding the revindication claim, it is of no concern that Teixeira was obliged under the contracts to replace the certificates Nillmij it transferred to third parties and hold these new certificates on behalf of Mulder and Peijnenburg;

That the second part cannot lead to cassation;

Considering, that part 3 relates to the claim that the four Nillmij certificates have become owned by Mulder and Peijnenburg together.

That it is shown in the eighth consideration of the judgment on appeal that the Court of Appeal is of the opinion that the legal relations between Teixeira and its clients, such as Mulder and Peijnenburg, based on the contracts of deposit or orders given to it and performed by it, did not oblige Teixeira, if it did not keep certain certificates separately for each client, to hold certificates collectively for the relevant clients, between whom there was no legal relationship, so as to make them co-owners of the certificates.

That the part assumes that the Court, in judging so, applied the general rules of law to the case;

That this is, however, not the case, as the Court of Appeal has interpreted the contracts concluded between the parties, which interpretation, as it is of a factual nature, cannot be examined for its correctness on appeal in cassation;

That the part furthermore challenges the decision of the Court of Appeal that the four Nillmij certificates present are owned by Teixeira;

That the decision of the Court of Appeal is correct, as these certificates, that are part of the general stock of certificates of Teixeira, which was subject, also in regard to the certificates in question, to constant change and substitution, and in relation to which certificates it could not be determined that these are the same as those provided by Mulder and Peijnenburg, and neither that Teixeira held these for Mulder and Peijenenburg, either separately or together, must be considered to be in the ownership of Teixeira; that the third part therefore was made unsuccessfully.

Notes

(1) The principle of specificity requires that it be known which exact things are the objects of a property right. As the numbers of the certificates were unknown the clients could not revindicate the certificates. The certificates were owned by the bank. Commingling thus results in original acquisition of the things. The clients also asserted that the bank on acquiring the certificates in question acted on behalf of the clients, each of them separately or both collectively, in such a way that the clients would become owners and the bank a mere detentor of the shares. Although this would have been possible in theory, there was no indication that this had actually happened.

(2) The solution which Dutch law gives is comparable to the special rule which Roman law had for money: if in Roman law coins of different owners had been mixed, the possessor became owner of the coins.[110]

Under Dutch law the problem is now solved by a special statute.[111] Most publicly traded shares are now deposited in a central depository and all dealings take place electronically. The statute gives the clients a co-ownership share in the collective deposit for the amount of shares deposited in their name.

II.B GERMAN LAW

Introductory Note

In the German civil code the distinction between *confusio* and *commixtio*, which was still relevant in nineteenth century *Pandektenrecht* was made irrelevant: both are now united and covered by §948 BGB.[112]

The German *Motive* stress that in the case of commingling, co-ownership as a solution can be awarded only if there is a specific bulk in which the goods of the different owners have been mixed. If no specific bulk can be identified, it cannot be ascertained which specific goods are held in co-ownership.

[110] Iav D 46,3,78.

[111] Wet Giraal Effectenverkeer 1977.

[112] See Motive III, 359.

Explanations to the draft of a Civil Code for the German Nation, Book III, 60 **7.22 (DE)**

The provisions §892 [948] presuppose that there is a specified quantity, to which different parties have contributed and which legal destiny has to be decided.
If there is no specified quantity but it is only proven that quantities of money, grain etc have been mixed with another person's unspecified stock, the premisses of the legal rule do not apply. That the former holder of the mixed quantity cannot revindicate is a consequence of the fact that the object of revindication cannot be described or established.

Note

It should be noted, however, that in almost all cases money that has been paid to another person has so been mixed with the other person's own money that no specific bulk can be identified. As a consequence, the payor will never be able to revindicate the money he paid. He will have no more than an unsecured claim against the payee. Co-ownership will come into being, for example, in the rare case that physical money has been mixed, say in a box.

OGH, 15 December 1981[113] **7.23 (AT)**

REVINDICATION OF A CERTAIN SUM OF MONEY

Stolen money

Commingling of money leads to co-ownership.

Facts: Walter P received money from Leopold H. (a sum not exceeding 1,000 schilling) which he knew had been stolen by Leopold H. The thief, Leopold, had stolen 4,000 schilling and he had put the money into his wallet in which it was mixed with his own money. It is unknown how much of his own money was in his wallet, but it could not have been much. After the theft Leopold paid off a debt to Walter, the current accused, using mainly the stolen money. Walter appealed a judgment sentencing him for receipt of unlawfully acquired property, claiming that the money he received had become Leopold's by way of commingling.

Held: The mere fact that Leopold acquired ownership of the money did not exclude that the acquisition by Walter was a receipt of unlawfully acquired property. In addition, the commingling did not give Leopold ownership of the money, as the amount stolen was known. The person from whom it was stolen had co-ownership of the money. The appeal was dismissed.

Judgment: On the other hand it cannot be held that Leopold H, who according to the information on which the decision is based, had 'once again' gambled away his money, obtained ownership of the stolen amount in accordance with §371 ABGB by commingling the clearly ascertainable specific amount of the loot (consisting of a certain sum of paper money and an exactly ascertainable amount of coined money) with his loose change (which according to the assumptions in the judgment amounted in any case only to some schillings).

According to current doctrine and case law (Klang in Klang, 2 Auflage, II 232; Koziol-Welser, Grundriß, 4 Auflage, II 59; SZ 46/50 and 50/42; 6 Ob 731/78 ua)

[113] 9Os83/81.

§415 ABGB grants, in the case of commingling of clearly distinguishable quantities of homogenous things, eg money of different owners, to each owner a claim of ownership on the specifiable quantity that derives from him (quantity revindication or Quantitätsvindikation), which is directed at separating a corresponding part of the commingled property, while §371 ABGB excludes an action of revindication in the case of commingling after which such a demarcation and clear distinction are no longer possible, and the things are lost in the other person's patrimonium.

The amount deriving from the theft and therefore the theft victim's portion of the total sum originating from the commingling, could be ascertained clearly according to the judgment assumptions in the case at hand.

According to the facts ascertained in the first instance, it cannot be maintained that the stolen money, through commingling with the (small) own cash amount in the thief's wallet was 'lost' into the latter's patrimonium.

Thus the stolen money had not passed into the (sole) property of the thief; rather it remained co-ownership, subject to revindication, of the victim of the theft, who had an action for separation of the corresponding portion of the (money) amount. ...

Note

In contrast to the Roman rule that the possessor of the money becomes owner of all the money,[114] Austrian law takes the position that the owner from whom the money was taken becomes co-owner of the money and thus has a real action against the possessor.

This judgment is in line with, for example, OHG 23 November 1978, 6 Ob 731/78. Surprisingly, the rule is also applied to money on a bank account. See OGH 10 April 1997, 6Ob2352/96t:

> Money from different owners can be separated and clearly distinguishable from their other patrimonium and give rise to quantity co-ownership as a subcategory of co-ownership not only if they are stored in a cashbox or wallet, but also if they have been paid into a current account or savings account.

II.C ENGLISH LAW

High Court, Queen's Bench Division, 18 March 1987[115] **7.24 (E&W)**

Indian Oil Corporation Ltd v Greenstone Shippings SA (Panama)

CO-OWNERSHIP THROUGH MIXING

Mixture of oil

Co-ownership of mixture.

Facts: The defendant, the owner of a ship chartered to transport Russian crude oil, owned by the claimant, mixed the Russian oil with its own crude oil already on board the vessel. The mixture of

[114] Iav D 46,3,78.
[115] [1988] QB 345.

oils could not be separated. At the port of destination the claimant received less oil than the amount indicated on the bill of lading. In arbitration the claimant asserted that it was entitled to the whole of the pumpable oil on board the ship at the port of destination and to damages of $388,000. The arbitrators awarded only damages for short delivery ($46,014.90). The case was decided applying English law.

Held: The claimant and defendant became co-owners of the mixture.

Judgment: Staughton J—Seeing that none of the authorities is binding on me, although many are certainly persuasive, I consider that I am free to apply the rule which justice requires. This is that, where B wrongfully mixes the goods of A with goods of his own, which are substantially of the same nature and quality, and they cannot in practice be separated, the mixture is held in common and A is entitled to receive out of it a quantity equal to that of his goods which went into the mixture, any doubt as to that quantity being resolved in favour of A. He is also entitled to claim damages from B in respect of any loss he may have suffered, in respect of quality or otherwise, by reason of the admixture. ...

The answer to this point is ... that the mixture was held in common by the receivers and the owners. The receivers were entitled to an amount equal to their contribution to the mixture. That has been delivered to them, except for the small shortage in respect of which the arbitrators awarded them damages. What remained in the vessel became the property of the owners alone.

Court of Common Pleas, 18 April 1868 **7.25 (E&W)**

Spence and Another v The Union Marine Insurance Company Ltd

CO-OWNERSHIP THROUGH COMMINGLING

Cotton bales

Commingling leads to co-ownership.

Facts: A ship transporting bales of cotton of different owners to Liverpool was wrecked near Key West: 43 bales belonged to the claimants, and were insured by the defendants. Some of the cotton was lost, and some was so damaged that it had to be sold at Key West. The rest of the cotton was transported to Liverpool in another ship. The marks on a large number of the bales were so obliterated by seawater that none of the cotton lost or sold at Key West, and a portion only of that carried to Liverpool, could be identified as belonging to any particular owner. Only two of the claimants' 43 bales were identified. The claimant asserted that the rest of his bales, 41 bales, were lost completely and claimed the insurance cover from the defendant.

Held: There was no total loss of the claimant's cotton. As regards the cotton lost, and the cotton sold at Key West, there was a total loss of a part of each owner's cotton. All the owners became co-owners of the cotton which arrived at Liverpool without marks. The share of each owner's loss in the cotton totally lost or sold at Key West, and his share in the cotton which arrived at Liverpool was the proportion that the quantity shipped by him bore to the whole quantity shipped.

Judgment: Bovill CJ—It is manifest that the plaintiffs' argument would equally apply if not a single bale of cotton had been lost or damaged out of the whole cargo, and if the marks only had been obliterated from this and other cotton by the same vessel; and it would lead to the strange anomaly that, although all the goods which had been put on board arrived safely at their destination, there would, according to the plaintiffs' contention, be a total loss, for the purpose of insurance law, of the whole of them. ...

In our own law there are not many authorities to be found upon this subject; but, as far as they go, they are in favour of the view, that, when goods of different owners become by accident so mixed together as to be undistinguishable, the owners of the goods so mixed become tenants in common of the whole, in the proportions which they have severally contributed to it. The passage cited from the judgment of Blackburn J, in the case of the tallow which was melted and flowed into the sewers, is to that effect: *Buckley v Gross*. And a similar view was adopted by Lord Abinger in the case of the mixture of oil by leakage on board ship, in *Jones v Moore*.

It has been long settled in our law, that, where goods are mixed so as to become undistinguishable, by the wrongful act or default of one owner, he cannot recover, and will not be entitled to his proportion, or any part of the property, from the other owner: but no authority has been cited to shew that any such principle has ever been applied, nor indeed could it be applied, to the case of an accidental mixing of the goods of two owners; and there is no authority nor sound reason for saying that the goods of several persons which are accidentally mixed together thereby absolutely cease to be the property of their several owners, and become bona vacantia. The goods being before they are mixed the separate property of the several owners, unless, which is absurd, they cease to be property by reason of the accidental mixture, when they would not so cease if the mixture were designed, must continue to be the property of the original owners; and, as there would be no means of distinguishing the goods of each, the several owners seem necessarily to become jointly interested, as tenants in common, in the bulk.

This is the rule of the Roman Law as stated in Mackeldey's Modern Civil Law, under the title Commixtio et Confusio, in the special part, Book 1, s 270. In the English edition of 1845, at p 285, the passage is as follows: 'The mixing together of things solid or dry (commixtio) or of things liquid (confusio) which belong to different owners, has no effect upon their rights in the things, if the latter can be separated. If, on the other hand, such separation, is not practicable, then the former proprietors of the things now connected will be joint owners of the whole, whenever the mixture has been made with the consent of both parties, or by accident.'

We need not discuss the distinction sometimes made between commixtio and confusio, apparently upon the ground that it is possible to separate the individual solid particles, but not the liquid; because, in cases like the present, it is impracticable, and for all business purposes therefore impossible, to distinguish the particles, in respect of ownership.

The passages in Mr Justice Story's work on Bailments, s 40, and in the 9th volume of Pothier, 'De La Confusion', as well as the French and various other codes, are to the same effect.

We are thus, by authorities in our own law, by the reason of the thing, and by the concurrence of foreign writers, justified in adopting the conclusion that, by our own law, the property in the cotton of which the marks were obliterated did not cease to belongto the respective owners; and that, by the mixture of the bales, and their becoming undistinguishable by reason of the action of the sea, and without the fault of the respective owners, these parties became tenants in common of the cotton, in proportion to their respective interests. This result would follow only in those cases where, after the adoption of all reasonable means and exertions to identify or separate the goods, it was found impracticable to do so.

We cannot assume that the whole of the plaintiffs' forty-one bales were amongst those that were destroyed, any more than we can assume that they all formed part of the 1,645 which were brought home; and we see no means of determining the extent of the interest of the several owners, except by adopting a principle of proportion, and which would, we think, be equally applicable in determining the plaintiffs' portion of the 231 bales that were totally lost as of the 1,645 which arrived in this country, though without the marks. ...

Upon the main question, therefore, that was argued before us, we think that there was not an actual total loss of the plaintiffs' forty-one bales of cotton. We think also there was not a constructive total loss of those bales.

II.D FRENCH LAW

Commercial Code **7.26 (FR)**

Article L624-16 (2) Things sold under a reservation of ownership clause may equally be revindicated if they still exist in their natural state at the time the insolvency proceedings are opened. This clause must have been agreed upon by the parties in writing at the latest at the time of delivery. It may be laid down in a document governing a number of commercial operations entered into by the parties.

(3) The revindication of the things in their natural state may be brought under the same conditions with respect to movable things incorporated in another thing provided they can be removed without damaging the things. A revindication of the things in their natural state may also be made in relation to fungible things where things of the same nature and the same quality are in the possession of the debtor or any person keeping them on his behalf.

Article L624-18 The price or a part of the price of the things as referred to in Article L624-16, which was not paid nor settled in value or set off in the form of credit on a current account between the debtor and the purchaser at the date of the order opening the proceedings, may be claimed. Insurance payouts subrogated for the property may be claimed under the same conditions.

Code civil **7.27 (FR)**

Article 2369 The reservation of ownership of a fungible object, up to the amount of the debt remaining due, extends to things of the same nature and quality detained by the debtor or on his behalf.

P Crocq, Reservation of ownership clauses[116] **7.28 (FR)**

94. ... The exception thus made here to the requirement of identification is, in effect, all the more surprising as this condition is inherent to the very notion of the proprietary right and has led case law in the past to affirm that it was impossible for the parties to derogate from this condition of identification and to deny all effect to clauses presuming that the merchandise found in stock were those that were object of the retention of ownership clause and were not fully paid for (Cass

[116] P Crocq, JurisClasseur *Procédures collectives*, fasc 2545 (2007), Sauvegarde, redressement et liquidation judiciaires—Situation du vendeur de meubles—Clause de réserve de propriété.

Comm January 9 1990, Bull Civ IV, no. 8). ... Two different explanations could be given for this. One consists in confirming that the exception is justified because of the specific nature of the object of the reservation of ownership clause: the right of ownership of the seller with reservation of ownership is not changed but this ownership is simply 'floating' because of the fungibility of its object. ... The other explanation is based on the acknowledgement of a change in insolvency law to the effect that a reservation of ownership clause is put on a par with a traditional proprietary security right ... and states that the exception made by the legislator in 1994 is just an element, among others, of that change, that the legislator has not decided that upon commingling the seller's ownership will totally disappear but that it will be transformed in a sort of first-ranking privilege on the stock of goods of the same nature as the goods that had been sold and that belong to the buyer ..., and coupled with a legal power to grant [to its holder] ownership of part of its object. ...

95. Unimportance of the rotation of stock. The Paris Court of Appeal has confirmed that the argument according to which the quick rotation of the stock would exclude that the goods found in its original state at the buyer's premises were the same as sold under reservation of ownership, was unfounded (CA Paris, 3 April 1998: D Affaires 1998, p 845. ... The commercial chamber of the Supreme Court upheld this judgment.on 5 March 2002 ... (Cass Com, 5 March 2002, nr 98-17.585) ...

96. Unimportance of manufacturing numbers. It is also unimportant, in regard to this text, that the revindicated goods can be individualised by manufacturing numbers. As demonstrated by Mrs Anne Laude, the criterion of fungibility means that the goods are interchangeable and may be replaced with others, which has the consequence that individualisation does not exclude fungibility. ... Thus it is possible for the seller to revindicate goods identical to the goods delivered even if those goods have numbers and the numbers do not correspond to the goods delivered by him (CA Paris, 3e ch, sect B, 26 June 1998: D Affaires 1998, p 1401. ...

97. Problem of plurality of revindicating parties. The law of 10 June 1994 has not foreseen the case where several sellers revindicate the same generic goods, without any of them being able to identify precisely the goods that he has delivered. In this case, it would be just that the goods are distributed among them 'pro rata' according to the sum remaining due to each of them, which fits into the reasoning of an analysis of the right of the seller as a variety of privilege ...

III. *SPECIFICATIO*

Introductory Note

In the case of *specificatio* materials are used to make a new thing with an identity different from the identity of the materials used. The things used disappear and with them the right of ownership falls away. A new right of ownership originates. The crucial question is: who owns this new object? Another vital question is whether or not the rules deciding who owns the new thing can be opted out of; in other words, whether the rules are dispositive law or rather mandatory law.

If the person making the new thing is different from the owner of the original materials, then there is a clear conflict of interests over ownership of the new object. In industrial processes this typically occurs where goods delivered under a reservation of ownership clause are used in a manufacturing process. At the same time the second question should be answered in these cases: whether the reservation of ownership clause or any other special contract term is able to set aside the rules on *specificatio* in such a way that the object manufactured belongs to the seller rather than to the manufacturer. In answering these questions the various legal systems shown below offer quite different solutions.

Similar questions arise in other instances of original acquisition, such as accession or commingling. Often legal systems apply similar rules to all cases of original acquisition.

III.A DUTCH LAW

Hoge Raad, 5 October 1990[117] **7.29 (NL)**

Machinefabriek Breda NV v BV Machinefabriek Plaatwerkerij en Constructiefabriek St Antonius

FOR WHOM DOES *SPECIFICATIO* TAKE PLACE

Metal parts

Influence on production and risk are decisive.

Facts: Antonius produced metal parts for Breda. The materials needed for the production had been supplied by Breda. Antonius had to follow strict instructions, provided by Breda, for the production. After production the products were 'delivered' by Antonius to Breda. Antonius sent three invoices for these orders. The invoices remained unpaid, despite repeated reminders. The district court gave a provisional administration order to Breda. The general conditions which applied to the contract contain a reservation of ownership clause for the benefit of Antonius. Before the materials were given to Antonius, Breda had transferred ownership of the materials for security purposes to the bank financing Breda. Antonius claims to have become owner of the products made by him through specification. Breda, however, asserts that Antonius worked on behalf of Breda so that Antonius never acquired ownership.

Held: The answer to the question for whom the new things are made and who therefore becomes owner, depends, in the case of industrial production, on who has decisive influence on the production process and who bears the risk of disappointing usefulness, sales and profits.

Judgment: 3.3. The parts, read in connection to each other, are successful. The argument of Breda in this dispute is that Breda has ordered Antonius to manufacture certain objects for himself from materials he made available himself. When it is established that this is the case, Article 661 to its meaning—similar to the further developed Article 5:16 sub 2 New BW—brings with it that Breda and not Antonius became owner of the manufactured objects. Whether this is the case will depend of what follows, based on common opinion, from the legal relationship between the parties. In the case of industrial manufacturing—as is the case here—it will come down to the question who had decisive influence on the way of production and the definitive form of the product and who, with regard to the legal relationship, bore the risk of loss in case of disappointing usability, marketability or profitability of the product.

[117] NJ 1992/226.

In relation to this it is—besides from the circumstances just remarked on under 3.1—also of relevance to the Court's starting point in reasoning 4.7.6 that Antonius worked on the basis of detailed descriptions of Breda and that the end product was unusable for Antonius himself.

Following this it must be assumed that the Court accepted the following circumstances as correct or left the correctness of these undecided:

(a) that Antonius manufactured, for a set price and carefully drafted manufacturing per product, products from materials provided to him by Breda by order and on the account of Breda.

(b) that Antonius regarding the usability, marketability and profitability of the products did not run any risk, and only had to make a commercially reasonable price for her own activities.

(c) that the risk for damages during manufacturing according to the clause mentioned above under 3.1 bearing the title 'contract work', in whatever way this is interpreted, was largely allocated to Breda.

In the light of this the Court's judgment that Antonius has become owner of the objects by specificatio is either based on a different and therefore incorrect application of the law, or on reasoning that cannot, without further arguments, be followed. It deserves to be noted that the Court gives great importance in its paragraph 4.5.4 to the circumstance that there was substantial additional value, as the costs of the materials provided by Breda were substantially lower than the production costs incurred by Antonius in the manufacturing of the objects. In so far as the Court has applied the law incorrectly, now that—in deviation of the provision in Article 571 of the Civil Code, that was not adopted in Article 661 and onwards, nor in the new Civil Code—for the question who has become owner through specificatio the limited value of the materials used in relation to the labour invested to make new objects is in principle of no relevance. ...

It does deserve attention that, if the actual manufacturer of a product on the basis of the application of the criterion developed here, does not become owner of that product by specificatio, he may not reserve his right of ownership with effect against the person making the order or that person's bank to which the product was provided as security, but that he is not as a result deprived of all security for the agreed payment of the labour made by him, as he normally could postpone the delivery of the products, following the provision in Article 6:52 sub 2 New BW, until the performance of the obligation to which is he is entitled under the contract, also in relation to former orders and former manufactured products.

3.4. The above brings with it that the judgment of the Court of Appeal cannot be maintained. ...

Note

The judgment makes clear that under Dutch law the parties to the contract cannot opt out of the rules on *specificatio*. These are mandatory law. Objective standards decide who becomes owner of the manufactured product. A reservation of ownership clause or any other contractual clause cannot alter the outcome. This makes the reservation of ownership clause much weaker than in legal systems that do allow parties to opt out of the rules on specification, such as German law.

III.B GERMAN LAW

BGH, 3 March 1956[118] **7.30 (DE)**

SPECIFICATIO WHERE ALUMINIUM PLATES WERE FORMED INTO COVERS?

Aluminium covers

If covers are needed to protect machines and operators, the covers are essential components.

Facts: The claimant delivered aluminium plates to company S which used the materials to make aluminium covers for machines. Machines with these aluminium covers were then delivered to the defendant. The claimant asserts that, because it delivered the aluminium under a reservation of ownership clause, it remained owner of the covers and tried to revindicate the covers from the defendant. The first question is whether or not the covers were essential components of the machines so that the claimant lost ownership as a result of *accessio*. The second question, the question that is relevant here, is whether the claimant lost ownership as a result of *specificatio* when company S used the aluminium sheets to make the covers.

Held: Where the contract stipulates that the delivery of aluminium took place under a reservation of ownership clause and that the production of the covers was to take place for the benefit of the supplier, the supplier should be seen as the manufacturer in the sense of §950.

Judgment: The claimant has not lost ownership of the aluminium plates supplied by him merely because these were turned into machine covers. The question who was the manufacturer in the sense of §950 BGB should also here be answered according to common opinion. It would be possible that employees of S were not aware of the reservation of ownership clause when they processed the aluminium plates and that they even thought that the reservation of ownership would disappear as a result of the processing. They do not thus become manufacturer in the sense of §950 BGB. When raw materials are supplied under reservation of ownership with the stipulation that the manufacturing will take place for the benefit of the supplier, then from the standpoint of an objective observer this company is normally the manufacturer in the sense of §950 BGB. The supplier of the materials loses its status of manufacturer only if the situation regarding the stocking and processing of the materials created by contract has changed in such a way that form the mentioned standpoint another person should be seen as the manufacturer. In this case the aluminium plates were processed by the buyer in a way that was to be expected and planned when making the reservation of ownership clause. In these circumstances even the will of S to process the aluminium plates for his own benefit, in breach of the agreement, would not change the situation in such a way that therefore generally S could be regarded as manufacturer. This intention would be as irrelevant as the intention of the company's employees to execute their orders not for the benefit of the employer but for their own benefit. ...

Notes

(1) This excerpt is the continuation of a case which we have already seen above in excerpt 7.20 (DE). The first part of the case is about accession, the second is about

[118] BGHZ 20, 159, NJW 1956, 788

specification. Here the *Bundesgerichtshof* gives effect to a so-called manufacturing clause (*Verarbeitungsklausel*). Although it is mandatory law that under §950 the manufacturer will become owner of the new product, parties to the supply contract can decide themselves who will be regarded as the manufacturer. According to long-standing case law of the BGH the question who is to be seen as manufacturer of the product should be answered with reference to public opinion (*Verkehrsauffassung*). This gives the false impression that a purely objective standard is used. The BGH does not focus on the perspective of an outsider unknown to the contract terms, but rather on the perspective of an insider who knows the contract terms between seller and buyer. The reasoning is as follows: if under the contract between supplier and buyer the goods will be manufactured for the benefit of the supplier, then from an objective perspective it is the supplier who should be regarded as manufacturer in the sense of §950 BGB. Only where the factual situation is clearly in contradiction with the contract terms, ie where it is clear that the buyer manufactures the goods for his own benefit, will the buyer himself become owner under §950 BGB.[119]

In modern academic writing this case law of the BGH is heavily criticised. Almost all academics stress that the rules of original acquisition should be mandatory law and that it should not be possible for the parties to opt out these rules by deciding who will be seen as the manufacturer.[120]

BGH, 22 May 1995[121] **7.31 (DE)**

REQUIREMENTS FOR *SPECIFICATIO*

BMW M3

New function of an object is relevant; no specificatio if value of manufacturing is 60% or less of value of objects.

Facts: K sold a BMW M3 car to the defendant who sold the car on to the claimant. Afterwards it was discovered that the engine block, the version made for the BMW M5 version, was stolen from BMW AG. The motor block came from a complete engine stolen from BMW AG. The block had been completed into a functioning engine and built into the car. The claimant avoided the contract for fraud and, for safety's sake, terminated the contract for the reason of not having provided ownership of the engine block. The Landgericht condemned the defendant to pay back the purchase price, provided the claimant returned the car. The court of appeal dismissed the defendant's appeal. It held that, by transforming the engine block into a complete engine, K did not acquire ownership of the engine block.

Held: K acquired ownership of the complete engine as a result of *specificatio*. A thing can be considered as new in the sense of §950 BGB if it has a function which goes beyond the function of the component parts, in this case a complete engine as against the engine block. In answering the question whether the value of the manufacturing process is considerably less than the value of the materials used, the relevant ratio is 60 (manufacturing) to 100 (materials). The burden of proof lies on the owner of the materials or the person denying the manufacturer's acquisition through *specificatio*.

Judgment: I. The Court of Appeal alleges that from the complete engine which was stolen from BMW AG—an engine with all mounted parts and auxiliaries

[119] Staudinger/Wiegand (2004), §950, Rn 23.
[120] Staudinger/Wiegand (2004), §950, Rn 25.
[121] II ZR 260/94, NJW 1995, 2633.

such as exhaust manifold, intake manifold, ignition cable harness, generator, belt pulleys, flywheel and clutch—only the engine block can be found in the car sold by the defendant. Witness K, had bought this engine from company S in Munich, completed it into a functioning engine and built it into the car. During the further appeal proceedings the above is regarded as established facts for the benefit of the defendant.

II. The Court of Appeal negated that witness K, from whom the defendant bought the BMW M3, acquired ownership of the engine, including the engine block, by completing the engine block to a complete engine. ... The appeal against the decision is successful.

1. It can be left unanswered whether the complete engine through the assembly into the car became its essential component. As a processing in terms of §950 BGB is present, §947 BGB can be dismissed as a rule for testing, if the qualifications of §950 are fulfilled (cf Quack, in: MünchKomm, 2 Edition, §950 mn 20; Staudinger/Wiegand, BGB, 12 Edition, §950 mn 15). Witness K produced a new object in the terms of §950 BGB by completing the engine block into a functioning engine. What can be regarded as a new object derives from prevailing common opinion. Regardless of the discussion in literature about what in particular can imply a new object—new name, higher production stage, change of character (cf Quack, in: MünchKomm, §950 mn 7 ff; Staudinger/Wiegand, §950 mn 9; Westermann, p 393)—a new object is present, if it fulfils an independent function, which is advanced compared to the single objects used in the manufacturing process. This is the case here. The complete engine is—unlike the mere engine block—capable of powering a car. Its advanced function is therefore obvious.

2. The Court of Appeal took for granted that the additional requirement of §950 I BGB, that the value of the manufacturing is not substantially lower than the value of the substance, was fulfilled, without providing the necessary explanation for this. The value of the manufacturing is the difference between the value of the new thing and the value of all processed substances. Starting point is that in any case a substantially smaller processing value in relation to the value of finished materials is to be assumed if the value of the used materials is to the value of the manufacturing process as approximately 100 is to 60. Whether this or a similar case is present cannot be inferred from the circumstances as determined by the Court of Appeal. This cannot be borne by the defendant. The obligation of statement and proof that the processing value is substantially smaller than the value of the materials lies not with the defendant but the claimant, since the latter takes the position of the materials owner here, who denies the acquisition of property by processing. ...

Note

This case illustrates two things. First, it shows that §950 BGB takes priority over §947 BGB, the paragraph on accession of movables to movables. If the conditions of *specificatio* are met, the case should be solved according to the rules on *specificatio*, even if the conditions of *accessio* are also met.

Secondly, it demonstrates that no *specificatio* is accepted if the value of the work added to the materials is considerably lower than the value of the materials used. The Bundesgerichtshof even specifies that the value of the work is considerably lower than the value of the materials if the ratio is 60 (work) to 100 (materials).

BGH, 19 October 1966[122] **7.32 (DE)**

DETERMINATION OF CO-OWNERSHIP SHARE OF SUPPLIER UNDER MANUFACTURING CLAUSE

Shoes

Co-ownership share can be determined by manufacturing clause but should comply with principle of specificity.

Facts: A supplier sold and delivered leather skins to a shoe manufacturer under a reservation of ownership clause. The clause stipulated that the supplier would become co-owner of the final products.

Held: A manufacturing clause in a reservation of ownership clause may stipulate that the owner of the materials supplied will only become co-owner to the proportion that the value of his materials bear to the value of the final product. Another possibility is for the manufacturing clause to stipulate that the owner of the materials supplied will become co-owner to the proportion that the value of his materials and the value added by the manufacturer bear to the value of the final product. However, it is impossible for a manufacturing clause to stipulate that the supplier's co-ownership share depends on the value of the goods supplied and the manufacturer's labour and overhead costs. Third parties cannot easily assess the manufacturer's production costs, whereas it is easy for them to assess the added value. When the co-ownership share is difficult for third parties to assess, the principle of specificity would be violated.

Judgment: On those grounds:

1. (a) The fact that a supplier, delivering raw materials to a manufacturer under a retention of ownership clause, can, by agreement on a so-called processing clause, despite §950 BGB, extend his retention of ownership into the finished product is to be regarded as undisputed, according to legal doctrine and case law. Yet it is disputed by which legal-constructive means this result can be achieved, which limitations are set for such an agreement and how the competition of various suppliers, which have supplied under retention of ownership clause, is to be treated. ...

For the decision in the case at hand, only a fragment of the entire issue has to be considered.

The parties have attempted to sidestep the issue of competition amongst various suppliers by stipulating that under the 'delivery-contract' the claimant's retention of ownership for the leather did not extend to the entire finished product, including the other suppliers' shares, but rather that the claimant would only acquire the 'ownership rights for the value of ... the raw materials and for the value of the full employees' wages and overhead costs invested into the semi-finished or finished product by S'. However, this creates a problem at first. If, as in this case, the supplier does not claim the entire (semi- or) finished product for his retention of ownership clause, the retention of ownership can, by means of a fragmentation of ownership, only be effectuated by co-ownership in the form of a community by fractions. ... The agreement on the extension of the retention of ownership must therefore disclose the supplier's share as a co-owner in the finished product, based on his retention of ownership of the raw material. In the present case the parties did not agree on such a share in the 'supply-contract', but rather, taking the provisions of the agreement literally, intended to attribute to the claimant ownership 'for the value' of the retained goods, the employees wages and overhead costs invested by the manufac-

[122] BGHZ 46, 117, NJW 1967, 34.

turer. Such a division determined by an absolute share of components does indeed exist in German law for claims, but not for ownership.

The Court of Appeal has understood the provisions of the contract to mean that the claimant was to become co-owner for the share that corresponds to the ration of the value of the retained products as well as the wage- and overhead costs to the total value of the shoes at the time of the manufacturing. ...

(b) A processing clause interpreted in this way does not raise any objection insofar as the co-ownership share of the claimant should be determined by the ratio of the value of the retained product to the value of the finished product. Through such an agreement the supplier receives exactly what is intended by the extension of the retention of ownership: instead of the ownership of the raw materials, which no longer legally exist, the share of the finished product to the value of which he has contributed by the delivery of the raw material. In this way the retention of ownership of the raw material will be extended into the finished product. A collision (of interests) with the other suppliers is out of the question, if they also restricted themselves to the extension of the retention of ownership for the raw materials supplied by them.

(c) The motivation of the judgment on appeal does not make clear with certainty whether according to the wording of the supply contract the Court of Appeal in calculating the co-ownership portion of the claimant only wanted to consider the raw material value, wages and overhead cost or whether it did rather—ignoring the profit—equate the wages and overhead costs to the processing value, that is the difference between the value of the finished article and the value of the processed substances. In any case, during a renewed interpretation the question arises to the Court of Appeal, to which the procedure must in any case be referred back, whether the processing clause is to be interpreted here in such a way. The clause would then mean that the supplier, who agrees upon it, claims ownership of the finished product to the extent that the value of the finished product does not also contain the value of the raw materials supplied from by other suppliers. Also a processing clause interpreted in such a way does not raise any objections.

It has in common with the clause under (b) that it gives consideration to the potential retention of ownership of other raw material suppliers. On the other hand, it does, however, extend the portion of the supplier, who agrees upon it, to a portion corresponding to the processing value. In that respect there is no longer an extension of the retention of ownership. Rather, a supplier who agrees upon this clause wants to receive additional security in the value created by the manufacturer through the processing. However, the manufacturer is just as able and authorised to conclude such an agreement, as he is to provide the supplier with an appropriate portion of co-ownership by way of transfer for security purposes. How the legal conflict would have to be solved if also another supplier had agreed upon a processing clause just as extensive, so that the legal effects of the processing clauses would thus overlap in the processing value, does not need to be decided here; such a case is not given here.

(d) The processing clause in supply contract, however, raises severe objections, if and in so far as it its wording is interpreted in a way that the co-ownership portion of the claimant should be determined according to the ratio of raw materials value, wages and overhead cost to the value of the finished product. In the interest of legal certainty in general and as a legal transaction concerning the allocation of property rights specifically, a processing clause requires a certain degree of specificity and clarity, just like a transfer by way of security does.

For the latter transfer the BGH has, regarding transfers by way of security of a collection of constantly changing objects, in steady case law demanded that at the point of time of the transfer of ownership it should be apparent to everybody knowing the agreement of the parties, which individually ascertained objects are included in the transfer. It did not regard this condition as given, where the question requires an investigation of circumstances outside the contract and where it can be answered only after further investigations. Similarly, borders must be drawn also where a processing clause gives rise to the question to which extent half-finished or finished products of the manufacturer are subject to a co-ownership share of the supplier.

As far as the processing clause is limited to the extension of ownership of the raw materials so that it only provides the suppliers with co-ownership according to the ratio of the value of the raw materials to the value of the finished product, it is for a—presupposedly competent—third party relatively easy to answer the question about the co-ownership portion. …

The determination of the co-ownership portion of the supplier is no more difficult if by the processing clause he secures himself a portion which corresponds to the value of the raw materials supplied by him plus the processing value, thus excluding for other suppliers only a portion corresponding to the value of the raw materials supplied by them. …

This is, however, totally different if supplier and manufacturer decide the co-ownership portions according to the wages spent on the manufacturing and the overhead costs of the manufacturer. A third party, if he has the commodity and the contract in front of him, cannot so easily determine these on the basis of experience. … The processing clause lacks therefore in the part which includes wages and overhead cost into the assessment of the co-ownership ratios, the necessary specificity and is therefore in this respect legally ineffective. …

Notes

(1) If the seller of materials can reserve his ownership in such a way as to become owner of the end-product made from his materials, it is logical to say, as the German Bundesgerichtshof does, that a less far-reaching contract term is also valid: parties may agree that as a result of the manufacturing the seller does not become the full owner of the end-product but merely a co-owner of it.

(2) It is very interesting to see that the BGH stresses that co-ownership of things is possible only for a certain proportion, not for an absolute quantity in contrast to claims where such an absolute share is possible. There are, however, more exceptions, even in the case of things. It would thus have been better for the BGH to say that this rule is a principle rather than to suggest that there are no exceptions. In the case of movable property co-ownership of an absolute quantity is created by statute when someone deposits goods in a warehouse where the goods are mixed with similar goods from other clients (*Sammellagerung*: collective depositing).[123]

[123] See §469 HGB and Staub/Koller, *Handelsgesetzbuch, Großkommentar*, 4th edn (Berlin/New York, De Gruyter, 2004) §419, Rn 8; MünchKomm HGB/Frantzioch, 2nd edn (Munich, CH Beck 2009) §469,

Another example of co-ownership for an absolute quantity is to be found in the German *Depotgesetz*,[124] which gives the client on the account of whom shares or bonds have been deposited in a central depository a co-ownership share for the exact amount of shares registered in his name.

(3) Another interesting point is that according to the judgment the principle of specificity is violated when third parties, known to the reservation of ownership clause, cannot easily calculate the supplier's exact co-ownership share in the final products.

III.C ENGLISH LAW

Court of Appeal, 10 July 1979[125] **7.33 (E&W)**

Borden (UK) Ltd v Scottish Timber Products Ltd and Another

SPECIFICATION AND RESERVATION OF TITLE

Chipboard

Specificatio destroys reservation of title.

Facts: The claimants sold resin to the defendants, which was to be used by them to make chipboard. The contract contained a retention of title clause, to the effect that property in the resin should pass when all goods supplied by the claimants had been fully paid for. The parties knew that the resin would be used before it had been paid for. When mixed with certain other substances, the resin as such could no longer be recovered. The defendants were declared insolvent and the claimants sued for the unpaid purchase price, asserting that any chipboard manufactured with such resin or any money or property representing the proceeds of sale of such chipboard was charged with the unpaid sum and, further, that any such charge was not void by reason of section 95 of the Companies Act 1948.

Held: A simple reservation of title clause lapses as a result of *specificatio.*

Judgment: Bridge LJ—The lesson to be learned from these conclusions is a simple one. If a seller of goods to a manufacturer, who knows that his goods are to be used in the manufacturing process before they are paid for, wishes to reserve to himself an effective security for the payment of the price, he cannot rely on a simple reservation of title clause such as that relied upon by the plaintiffs. If he wishes to acquire rights over the finished product, he can only do so by express contractual stipulation. We have seen an elaborate, and presumably effective, example of such a stipulation in *Aluminium Industrie Vaassen BV v Romalpa Aluminium Ltd* [1976] 1 WLR 676. An attempt to acquire rights over the finished product by a stipulation which proved ineffective for want of registration under section 95 of the Companies Act 1948 is to be seen in the decision of Slade J in *In re Bond Worth Ltd* [1980] Ch 228 to which in the course of argument we were helpfully referred.

Buckley LJ—It is common ground that it was the common intention of the parties that the defendants should be at liberty to use the resin in the manufacture of

Rn 27. See also §§23 and 30 Verordnung über die Orderlagerscheine.

[124] Gesetz über die Verwahrung und Anschaffung von Wertpapieren, 4 February 1937 (Reichsgesetzblatt I 171), in the version of 1 August 1994 (BGBl. I 34); for the co-ownership regime, see §6.

[125] Court of Appeal [1981] Ch 25.

chipboard. After they had so used the resin there could, in my opinion, be no property in the resin distinct from the property in the chipboard produced by the process. The manufacture had amalgamated the resin and the other ingredients into a new product by an irreversible process and the resin, as resin, could not be recovered for any purpose; for all practical purposes it had ceased to exist and the ownership in that resin must also have ceased to exist. …

It was impossible for the plaintiffs to reserve any property in the manufactured chipboard, because they never had any property in it; the property in that product originates in the defendants when the chipboard is manufactured. Any interest which the plaintiffs might have had in the chipboard must have arisen either by transfer of ownership or by some constructive trust or equitable charge, and, as I say, I find it impossible to spell out of this condition anything of that nature.

Note

In the above case the contract between seller and buyer did not contain a clause stipulating that the products made from the goods delivered would equally be subject to the retention of title clause. The question therefore arises what the effect would be if such a clause had been made. The answer can be found in the following judgment. The judge's reference to *Aluminium Industrie Vaassen v Romalpa Aluminium*, by the way, is no longer correct, as the scope of this case has so been reduced by subsequent judgments as to deprive it of any practical meaning.[126]

High Court, Chancery Division, 22 September 1992[127] **7.34 (E&W)**

Modelboard Ltd v Outer Box Ltd (in liquidation)

RESERVATION OF TITLE EXTENDED TO NEW PRODUCTS

Cardboard

Extended reservation of title constitutes a charge.

Facts: The claimant sold to the defendant cardboard sheet boards under a reservation of title clause which provided among other things that the end products belonged to the claimant until full payment of the price. The defendant did not pay the purchase price and was declared insolvent. The question was whether or not the contractual clause created a charge on the new products in favour of the claimant which was void for non-registration.

Held: The contractual clause created a charge which was void for non-registration.

Judgment: Sir Michael Hart QC—That analysis still leaves open the question of the nature of the plaintiff's rights under cl 11.8 in the finished product. Is it absolute ownership (as implied by the words 'sole and exclusive property') or an interest by way of mortgage or charge? As in the case of the proceeds of sale, I am helped to answer that question by focusing on the nature of the defendant's continuing obligation to pay the price for the original 'goods'. The obligation to pay that price clearly remains, and it is equally clearly not a price payable in connection with a

[126] E McKendrick, *Goode on Commercial Law*, 4th edn (London, Penguin Books, 2010) 495 and 648.
[127] [1992] BCC 945.

sale by the plaintiff to the defendant of the new product. Payment of the price of the original board must, as a matter of necessary implication, have the effect of vesting (or revesting) property in the new product in the defendant: otherwise the plaintiff would be entitled to the product and to the price. On the analysis adopted above the property in the new product originates with the defendant but becomes or is deemed to be the property of the plaintiff pending the discharge by the defendant of its obligation to pay the purchase price of the original board. Accordingly, I conclude that the plaintiff's interest in the new product was created simply by way of security for the satisfaction of the defendant's obligation to pay the price of the original board, and was therefore a charge which ought to have been, but was not, registered.

Note

The retention of title clause can be extended to the end product made from the materials delivered by the seller. Not that the seller becomes owner of the new products, but rather he receives a charge on the newly created products. The problem, however, is that such a charge is void under section 395 Companies Act 1985 if unregistered.[128]

III.D FRENCH LAW

Cour de cassation com, 24 March 2004[129] **7.35 (FR)**

Jacques Moyrand v Siemens

SPECIFICATIO OF INSTALLED EQUIPMENT

Installed equipment

The installed equipment cannot be easily taken out and therefore forms a part of a new thing and can no longer be revindicated.

Facts: Siemens sold and delivered numerical control devices to Prorectif under a reservation of ownership clause. The materials remained unpaid and Prorectif was declared insolvent. Siemens tried to revindicate not only the unused materials but also the equipment already installed into the end products (computer-controlled machines). The Court of Appeal had held that the installed equipment could not easily be taken out and that the whole formed a new thing, and that, as a consequence, Siemens' installed equipment no longer existed in its natural state at the start of the insolvency procedure.

Held: The Court of appeal could draw this conclusion and has justified its decision correctly.

Judgment: Considering that, according to the contested judgment ... that the company Prorectif has been declared insolvent on 11 January 1993; that, by means of a writ of a bailiff of 18 January 1993, the company Siemens has claimed the revindication of various materials sold to the company Prorectif under a reservation of ownership clause; that, by order of 28 April 1993, the official receiver has rejected the request of revindication of the materials delivered by the company Siemens; ...

[128] McKendrick, above n 128, 649.
[129] N 01-10.280.

That it has, however, been demonstrated that the dismantling, involving the disconnection of cables, the removal of cards, control panel, the electric motors and the storage of the program, is complex and that the installation of the numerical control devices was not merely putting an accessory in, but was the installation of a vital element that resulted in the creation of a new thing. The Court of Appeal could hold that the numerical control devices did no longer exist in their natural state at the start of the insolvency procedure. The Court has legally justified its judgment.

Note

In the following case, which looks quite similar to the previous, neither *specificatio* nor *accessio* was accepted.

Cour de cassation com, 4 January 2005[130] **7.36 (FR)**

Philippe Jeannerot v Num

REQUIREMENTS FOR *SPECIFICATIO*

Computer parts

No specificatio when objects can be disassembled without change of nature or damage.

Facts: Under a contract of deposit Num delivered to René Clément computer equipment destined to be installed in computer-controlled machines sold by René Clément. The latter was declared insolvent and Num tried to revindicate the numerical control divices delivered by him under a reservation of ownership clause and installed into machines by René Clément. The Court of Appeal allowed the revindication, because, even though the computer equipment had been adapted specifically to the machine and connected with cables which would lose their value if the machine were dismantled, the dismantling would not cause damage to the equipment and the machine itself.

Held: The Court of Appeal held that the parts of the machine can be disassembled without changing the nature of the parts or causing damage to any of the parts, even though the cables and connectors could not be reused. The Court of Appeal has the sovereign power to judge these questions and it justified its decision correctly.

Judgment: About the only legal argument, taken in its two parts: ...

But considering that it is in the exercise of its power of judging the facts which were submitted to it and without misunderstanding the subject of the dispute that the Court of Appeal has held that the numerical control devices could effortlessly be removed from the tool-machines in which they had been installed, without alteration or damage to any of the elements thus separated, and that the impossibility of reusing the cables and connectors did not result from their deterioration but from the necessity of adapting them to every tool-machine;

That it has thus legally justified its decision; that the argument is unfounded in all its parts.

For these reasons: rejects the appeal.

[130] N 02-10.539.

Note

These two judgments illustrate the limited power of many supreme courts to judge the facts of the case. Many supreme courts, not only the French, in principle do not judge the facts of the case and therefore leave the lower courts a large freedom to judge the facts. Here the relevant fact is whether or not the computer equipment can be easily dismantled from the machine without changing the nature of the parts and without damaging any of the parts.

Cour de cassation com, 11 July 2006[131] **7.37 (FR)**

Clément v Bac and others

DOES THE END PRODUCT HAVE THE SAME NATURE AS THE ORIGINAL PRODUCT

Wine co-operative

Must turned into wine did not lose its original state.

Facts: Wine growers brought the must of their grapes to their co-operative for the production of wine. When the co-operative was declared insolvent they tried to revindicate the wine produced from their must.

Held: The wine growers never intended to transfer ownership of the must to their co-operative. They remained owners of their must. Even though the must of different owners had been mixed and had been turned into wine, the must had not been transformed in such a way as to lose its natural state. Therefore the growers are able to revindicate their wine as co-owners in accordance with their contribution.

Judgment: And about the second legal remedy: …

But considering that after having stated that it is for the revindicating owner to bring the proof that the revindicated goods were, at the moment of the opening of the insolvency procedure, present in the hands the debtor in their original state and that there should be identity between the delivered goods and the revindicated goods, any transformation or attachment not being important as long as it does not modify the characteristics, nor the ownership, the decision holds that each of the members of the co-operative proved its declarations of the yearly harvest which mention clearly and individually the different produced goods which are therefore identifiable, and that the stock of the wine-cellar of the co-operative is composed of hectolitres originating from the harvests 1999, 2000 and 2001 divided in diverse clear appellations; that in the light of these facts and opinions, the Court of Appeal … has only used its power of judging the facts when it held that the revindicated goods were still present in their original state in the wine-cellars of the co-operative, since the mixing of the musts one with the other and the development process and the wine production out of the contributed harvests had not transformed their substance; that the argument is not founded;

For these reasons: rejects the appeal;

[131] No 05-13.103, Bulletin 2006 IV No 181, 199.

Notes

(1) Article 571 Cciv stipulates that the manufacturer becomes owner of the new thing made by him provided that the cost of his work clearly exceeds the value of the materials used.

In practice the provisions of the French Civil Code on *specificatio* are hardly relevant because they are dispositive law. A seller of raw materials is able to stipulate that his reservation of ownership extends to the product made from the raw materials, so that the seller becomes owner of the final product. This extended reservation of ownership works not only against the buyer but also against third parties, such as the buyer's creditors. However, in insolvency, special provisions apply which are mandatory law. The reservation of ownership does work against the insolvent's liquidator and his creditors but under certain restrictions which cannot be set aside by contract. It is a peculiar characteristic of French law, different from the other systems reviewed, that original acquisition, such as *specificatio*, underlies rules of dispositive law as long as the buyer is not declared insolvent (the rules in the civil code then apply), but that it suddenly underlies rules of mandatory law once the buyer has been declared insolvent. The rule which applies in insolvency is Article L624-16 Commercial Code.

In the above-cited case the French Supreme Court does not expressly deal with the question whether or not the process of wine-making amounts to *specificatio*. The relevant question in the case is whether or not the goods given to the co-operative can be revindicated, and they can if the goods still exist *en nature*, that is to say, in their original state. Nevertheless, the conclusion is justified that there is no *specificatio* as long as the goods can still be found in their original state.

(2) The above case about the must of grapes and wine shows that what is seen in the other legal systems as *specificatio*, the making of a new thing, namely turning must into wine, is not regarded as *specificatio* in French law. Making wine from grapes is a standard Roman law example of *specificatio*.[132] The notion of *specificatio* looks the same in all legal systems reviewed, but it may be interpreted and applied very differently in practice.

(3) The outcome of the wine co-operative case in itself is fair, but the reasoning is, to our way of thinking, incorrect. No transfer of ownership of the must was intended and the wine had been made for the benefit of the wine farmers. This is sufficient ground to conclude that *specificatio* took place for the benefit of the wine farmers so that the farmers and not the co-operative should be seen as the manufacturers of the wine, rendering them owners of the end product rather than the cooperative itself.

It should also be remembered that the French Supreme Court, as many other supreme courts, in principle does not judge the facts of the case. It allows the Court of Appeal a large freedom to judge whether or not some connection or process amounts to accession or specification.

(4) Another point worth noting is that the mixing of must from different wine-growers leads to co-ownership between these growers. They do not lose ownership,

[132] D 41.1.7.7 (Gai) and Inst 2.1.25.

and apparently the provision of Article 573 Cciv is applied in this case. Although the present case did not involve a sale and delivery under a reservation of ownership clause, the same reasoning can be applied to reservation of ownership clauses. Where materials from different suppliers are used in a manufacturing process, the suppliers will not lose their ownership because of commingling. Those suppliers which retained their ownership will be able to revindicate a co-ownership share in the commingled mass.[133]

P Crocq, Reservation of Ownership Clauses[134] **7.38 (FR)**

78. Essential criterion: the maintenance of the identity of the good—The only criterion taken into consideration by case law in deciding whether or not to allow the revindication of a transformed thing or a thing incorporated into another movable was whether or not, despite its transformation or its incorporation, the thing kept its identity. After all, after having had a rather strict interpretation of the requirement of existence in its original state, since 1985 case law has shown to be a lot more lenient and has held with relative ease that the requirement has been fulfilled even if the thing had been modified, as long as the substance of the thing itself had not changed. ...

80. Application of the criterion in case of processing of the good—Likewise, it is accepted that a thing which has been subjected to improvements can also be considered as still existing in its original state provided that the substance of the thing has not been changed, and case law does not easily accept that such a change has taken place. ...

Cour d'appel de Lyon, 22 January 2004[135] **7.39 (FR)**

Eisen Schmid v Scarfogliero

REVINDICATION OF PURCHASE PRICE

Les Forges de la Becque

Revindication of purchase price possible only under strict conditions.

Facts: Eisen Schmid sold and delivered under a reservation of ownership clause pieces of iron to the ironworks Les Forges de la Becque, a company which sold steel sheet to the automobile industry. When Les Forges de la Becque was declared insolvent, Eisen Schmid tried to revindicate its steel from the buyer's insolvent estate. Part of the steel had already been processed into steel sheet and sold on to the ironworks' customers. For that reason Eisen Schmid also tried to revindicate the purchase price of this steel sheet from the insolvent's estate.

Held: The seller under reservation of ownership is able to revindicate from the insolvent's estate the purchase price paid by a sub-buyer to the insolvent first buyer. This revindication is allowed only if the following conditions have been met: the purchase price was still unpaid by the sub-buyer when the first buyer was declared insolvent and the materials still existed in their original state at the time of

[133] An example of specification is the making of garments from cloth: Cour d'Appel de Douai, 23 January 2003, no de pourvoi 98/06234.

[134] Crocq, above n 116.

[135] No de pourvoi: 2002/05630.

delivery to the sub-buyer. Steel which at that date had already been processed into sheet steel so that the original material is transformed irretrievably does not meet this requirement. As a consequence, the purchase price of these materials cannot be revindicated and the seller cannot invoke priority of payment.

Judgment: Considering that by application of Article L621-124 of the Commercial Code, it is possible to revindicate the price or part of the price of the goods referred to in Article L621-122 that have not been paid nor settled in value nor compensated on a current account between the debtor and the buyer at the date of the opening judgement of the insolvency procedure; and that the merchandises of which the price is revindicated has to exist in its original state on the date of the delivery to the second buyer; ...

Considering that the stock of raw steel delivered by the company Eisen Schmid has been inventoried at 242,369 tons at the moment of the opening of the insolvency procedure and that, for the remainder, Les Forges de la Becque have provided their clients of the manufactured pieces in which the steel had been treated and mixed in an indissoluble way;

Considering that, therefore, the company Eisen Schmid does not meet the legal requirements for exercising a right of revindication over the price of resale and that, consequently, the company is not entitled to seek the priority of payment under Article L621-32 of the Commercial Code;

Considering that, nonetheless, the company Eisen Schmid argues that it is entitled to rely on the fungible nature of the delivered goods; furthermore, the appellant produces some pictures of the premises of 'Les Forges de la Becque', taken at the end of January 2002 to establish that the delivered goods had remained in their original state and were perfectly individualised and interchangeable in their provenance, quality or nature, despite the turnover rate of stocks of Les Forges de la Becque;

Considering, however, that Me Scarfogliero has stated that the steels used by the company 'Les forges de la Becque' were composed of very special raw materials having an unique chemical and dynamic consistency and that each of the different suppliers of 'Les Forges de la Becque' were producing steel of particular and precise nature characterised by the absence of fungibility of the products, the pictures that had been produced by the appellant were not sufficient to bring evidence of the adduced fungibility;

That the ground has been rightly rejected by the Court of Appeal.

Notes

(1) The fact that the seller under a reservation of ownership clause is unable to pinpoint the exact materials delivered by him is normally seen as a problem for the seller in the buyer's insolvency. However, Article L624-16 of the Commercial Code solves this problem partly in that it allows a revindication if generic goods, fungible things, of the same sort can be found in the insolvent's estate. In the above case Eisen Schmid cunningly tried to claim that the materials delivered were fungible goods. If the court were to hold that the purchase price of the steel sheets cannot be revindicated, Eisen Schmid would still be able to revindicate some of the steel from other suppliers. However, the trick does not work: the court holds that the steel is not fungible because it is special steel with particular chemical and dynamic properties. Every supplier delivered steel with different properties specified on the delivery slips and marked on the steel itself.

As the judgment shows, apart for the possibility of revindicating *the goods* delivered, French law in some cases offers the possibility to revindicate the *purchase price* from a sub-sale (Article 2372 Cciv and Article L624-18 Commercial Code).[136] However, it is a highly complex instrument and dogmatically difficult to explain.[137] The Court of Appeal spelled out the requirements for revindication of the purchase price. The seller under retention of ownership is able to revindicate from the insolvent's estate the purchase price paid by a sub-buyer to the insolvent first buyer. This revindication is allowed only if the following conditions have been met: the purchase price was still unpaid by the sub-buyer when the first buyer was declared insolvent and the materials still existed in their original state at the time of delivery to the sub-buyer. Steel which at that date had already been processed into sheet steel so that the original material is transformed irretrievably, does not meet this requirement. As a consequence, the purchase price of these materials could not be revindicated and the seller could not invoke priority of payment.[138]

(2) If at the moment of such revindication the price was not yet paid to the first buyer or his liquidator, the revindication is directed towards the second buyer. If during the interval between opening of the insolvency proceedings and the moment of revindication the purchase price has been paid to the first buyer or his liquidator, the revindication is directed towards the liquidator. Where, during this interval, the purchase price is paid to a third party, eg the assignee of the claim, the revindication is directed towards this third party.[139] If the purchase price due by the sub-buyer is higher than the price due by the first buyer the sum due by the first buyer will be the maximum which the seller may revindicate,[140] as no creditor is allowed to receive with his security device more than is due to him under the secured claim.

(3) The term 'revindication' may render the false impression that the seller has a proprietary right, whereas he merely has a personal claim against the sub-buyer. It may look like a proprietary right because it entitles the seller to full payment despite the first buyer's insolvency. If after opening of the insolvency procedure the sub-buyer pays to the first buyer, this money is not treated as part of the insolvent's estate, because the claim belongs to the seller. If the money remains unpaid by the sub-buyer, the seller simply has to collect payment of his claim. However, if his debtor (the sub-buyer) is also declared insolvent before having paid, it becomes painfully clear that his claim is a mere personal right. In Cour de cassation com 6 October 2009 (*Emtec v Ricoh Europe*),[141] the Supreme Court held that the seller's claim against the sub-buyer is a personal right acquired at the time of resale and

[136] Cass com 5 Nov 2003 (no de pourvoi 00-21.357, Bulletin 2003 IV no 162, 180) shows that Art L624-18 C comm equally applies to a contract for the sale and supply of goods (*contrat d'entreprise*).

[137] See T Revet, 'La singulière présentation, par la chambre commerciale, de la subrogation, en cas de procédure collective, de la créance du prix de sous-acquisition à la chose objet d'un droit de propriété réservé' [2009] *RTD Civ* 751.

[138] See also P Ancel, *Droit des sûretés*, 4th edn (Paris, 2006) no 458.

[139] Crocq, above n 116, nos 120–21.

[140] Cass com 16 June 2009, no de pourvoi 08-10.241. See P Crocq, 'Revendication du prix de revente et plus-value de l'objet de la réserve de propriété' [2009] *Revue Trimestrielle de Droit Civil* (*RTD Civ*) 760.

[141] No de pourvoi 08-15048.

that the sub-buyer's administrator in insolvency was thus not obliged to pay the purchase price. The seller thus lost his security.

III.E THE BORDERLINE BETWEEN *SPECIFICATIO* AND FRUITS

Introductory Note

The owner of an apple tree becomes owner of the apples; similarly the owner of a cow becomes owner of the newborn calf. The apples and the calf are called fruits. And the fruits are for the owner of the thing which produces these fruits. What if a lot of effort and costs are needed to bring about these fruits? Let us say that in an industrial process eggs delivered under a reservation of ownership clause are incubated by the buyer. Who is then owner of the chicks? Was so much effort involved to call this process *specificatio*?

Hoge Raad, 24 March 1995[142] **7.40 (NL)**

Stichting Crediteurenbelangen Hollander's v Coöperatieve Raiffeissenbank 'Domburg'

FRUITS OR *SPECIFICATIO*?

Egg and chicken case

Chickens were the result of specificatio.

Facts: On 29 May 1985 Hollander's Kuikenbroederij en Opfokbedrijven BV (hereafter Hollander's Kuikenbroederij) and Hollander's Pluimvee BV were declared insolvent. The activities of Hollander's Kuikenbroederij were incubating hatching eggs (which takes about three weeks). Moreover, various poultry farms raised day-old chicks to laying-hens for the account and risk of Hollander's Kuikenbroederij.

Hollander's Kuikenbroederij had borrowed money from the Raiffeissenbank 'Domburg' (hereafter: the bank) and had transferred the ownership of all the poultry to the bank for security reasons (*fiducia cum creditore*). Moreover Hollander's Kuikenbroederij had the duty to transfer all new poultry to the bank so that all new poultry is automatically transferred to the bank. Euribrid delivered hatching eggs to Hollander's Kuikenbroederij under a reservation of ownership clause. Euribrid now claimed to have become owner of the poultry. As the poultry had been sold by the bank, with the liquidators' permission, Euribrid sued the bank for damages. Euribrid together with other creditors had set up a foundation to claim against the bank: the Stichting Crediteurenbelangen Hollander's (litt.: foundation creditor interests Hollander's).

Held: According to the Court of Appeal the chickens were not the fruits of the hens belonging to Euribrid. They were the result of *specificatio* and therefore belonged to Hollander's Kuikenbroederij. This decision is not incorrect nor unintelligible.

Judgment:

3.4.1 Part to of the argument relates to ground H, the reservation of ownership of Euribrid.

The subparts 2.1 and 2.2, which can be treated together, oppose the decision

[142] NJ 1996/158.

of the Court ... that eggs and chicks/hens are different objects because a chick by leaving the egg undergoes such a change of identity that an object comes into existence that according to common opinion has a separate identity, distinguishable from the original object. This decision does not show an incorrect application of the law. The part is unsuccessful. ...

3.4.3 Part 2.3 further complains, in short, that it does not follow from the decision of the Court of Appeal why and how Euribrid, to whom the eggs belonged according to a reservation of ownership clause, lost the ownership of the chicks. Also this complaint fails. This case is concerned with hatching-eggs that have been delivered to Hollander's Kuikenbroederij by Euribrid. For the development of the embryos in the eggs to chicks a breeding-process was necessary. By delivering the eggs, Euribrid has enabled Hollander's Kuikenbroederij to breed, in a mechanical process, the hatching-eggs. The Court has apparently accepted that the treatment of the eggs by Hollander's Kuikenbroederij must be considered as a making of new objects, ie chicks, for its own benefit, and that Hollander's Kuikenbroederij therefore has become owner of the chicks. This decision does not show an incorrect application of the law. It is also not impossible to understand, in the light of the procedure documents that show that for the artificial breeding of eggs during a period of three weeks a sequence of acts is required, such as—amongst other things—the placing of the eggs in a breeding installation and the imitation of the natural breeding process by regularly changing the position of the eggs and further by carefully managing the correct temperature and humidity in the breeding installation.

3.4.4 The first complaint contained in sub-part 2.4 can be explained as such that the Court of Appeal has not decided on the argument of the foundation [the claimant] that Euribrid was owner of the hens that had laid the eggs that were delivered to Hollander's Kuikenbroederij, so that Euribrid also became owner of the chicks that hatched from the eggs, that are, after all, natural fruits of those hens.

In the absence of factual ground this complaint cannot lead to cassation. Also under the law that applied before 1 January 1992 it must be, in so far in alignment with Article 3:9 BW, determined according to public opinion which objects can be designated as natural fruits of other objects. The decision of the Court of Appeal as dealt with above under 3.4.1 means that the chicks that were born from the eggs that have been delivered to Hollander's Kuikenbroederij and have been artificially bred there in the course of business, are not according to common opinion natural fruits of the hens that laid the eggs. From that decision—that does not show an incorrect application of the law—follows that the Court did not leave this matter undecided, but that it rejected the argument.

3.4.5 Part 2.4 complains in the second place that the Court has not decided on the claim of the foundation, shortly stated, that a chick before it left the egg is a component part of that egg and therefore belongs to the owner of the egg, also after it has left the egg.

Also this complaint cannot lead to cassation due to a lack of factual ground. The decision of the Court as dealt with under 3.4.1 means that the Court of Appeal rejected this claim.

4. Decision. The Supreme Court rejects the appeal.

Note

The Dutch Supreme Court shows that the question of whether a process amounts to *specificatio* or whether the new product should be seen as the fruit of another thing should be answered according to common opinion (*verkeersopvatting*). The Supreme Court observes that the Court of Appeal regards the process as *specificatio* and that it did reject the view that the chickens had to be regarded as fruits of the hens. It adds that the Court of Appeal's judgment does not show a wrong view of the law and that the Court of Appeal has properly explained its judgment.

Outer House, 30 June 1999 **7.41 (SC)**

Kinloch Damph Ltd v Nordvik Salmon Farms Ltd and Others

GROWING ANIMALS *SPECIFICATIO*?

Salmon smolts

Mature salmon is the same thing as the smolts.

Facts: The seller sold and delivered salmon smolts to the buyer. The two contracts contained a reservation of ownership clause. The buyer did not pay the full purchase price. The seller sought a declaration that he owned the salmon fish which have grown out of the smolts. The question raised and answered in the following excerpt is the question of whether or not the salmon are new things which became the property of the buyers by way of *specificatio*.

Held: Growing mature salmon from smolts does not amount to *specificatio*. The mature salmon is the same thing as the smolt from which it developed.

Judgment: Lord Macfayden: By contracts dated 15 January and 8 April 1998 the pursuers, Kinloch Damph Limited, supplied to the first defenders, Nordvik Salmon Farms Limited, two quantities of salmon smolts. Under the first contract the first defenders agreed to purchase and were supplied with one million smolts, at a price of £1.10 per smolt. The total contract price was thus £1,100,000. Under the second contract, the quantity of smolts which the first defenders agreed to purchase and the pursuers supplied was 250,000, the price per smolt was 80p, and the total contract price was thus £200,000. The contracts made provision for the dates on which payment was to be made by the first defenders. The payment terms were subsequently re-negotiated. Some payments to account were made. The sum which remained due by the first defenders to the pursuers when this action was raised was £712,142.41.

After the smolts were supplied by the pursuers to the first defenders they were placed in sea water in cages, and were fed and husbanded by the first defenders. They have developed from smolts into salmon, and are now thirty times their original size.

In this action the pursuers conclude (1) for declarator that 'the one million two hundred and fifty thousand salmon smolts (sic) currently in the control of the defenders' which were supplied under the two contracts are the property of the pursuers. …

In the present case, the goods that had been sold, the smolts, had ceased to exist as such. As a result of the first defenders' actings in feeding and husbanding the fish, something new—the salmon—had come into existence. Since the process could not be reversed, the new thing belonged to the first defenders. Mrs Swanson submitted further that the operation of the doctrine of specificatio could not be excluded by contract, and relied in support of that proposition on *Zahnrad Fabrik Passau GmbH v Terex Ltd* 1986 SLT 84, per Lord Davidson at 88K–L. The contractual provisions regulating the relationship between the pursuers and the first defenders as a matter of contract could not alter the fact that by virtue of the doctrine of specificatio property in the new things, the mature salmon, was vested in the first defenders. …

Mr Cowie and Mr McNeill for the pursuers responded to the first branch of the defenders' argument by analysing the terms of the retention of title clause in the contracts. It was plain, they said, from Clause 11, that the intention of the parties to the contracts was that the fish supplied by the pursuers to the first defenders would remain the property of the pursuers until the price was paid in full, and that that would be so notwithstanding the growth of the fish in the meantime. The contract, however, recognised that a pure retention of title clause could operate unfairly when the goods gained in value with the passage of time. …

The pursuers did not dispute that the doctrine of specificatio was part of the law of Scotland. Their response to the defenders' reliance on that doctrine came in two parts. In the first place, they denied that there had been in the circumstances the creation of a nova species. Secondly, they disputed the proposition that the doctrine of specificatio could not be displaced by contract. …

It is sufficient for the decision of this case that I am not satisfied that in the event there has been created a nova species in respect of which the doctrine of specificatio can operate. There was, in the end, no dispute between the parties that the doctrine of specificatio, as formulated in the media sententia referred to in the Institutes of Justinian, forms part of the law of Scotland. What was disputed was the applicability of that doctrine to the natural growth (albeit aided by nourishment and husbandry provided by man) of a living creature. There is, no doubt, a sense in which the smolts can be said no longer to exist. Certainly the process of their development into mature salmon is irreversible. But in my opinion the proper scope of the doctrine is in relation to inanimate objects or substances created by human effort out of materials which are used up and cease to exist in the process of creation. There is nothing in the authorities to suggest that the doctrine is applicable to the process of growth of living creatures. I find it instructive that the defenders were unable to refer me to any authority on such application. The examples in the writings on the subject contain no references to specificatio of growing animals. I consider that there is force in the submission that, having regard to the much greater importance of animals in daily life in former times (whether the times of the Roman writers or those of the Scottish institutional writers), the absence of such reference is a strong indication that the doctrine had no such application. There seems to me to be nothing peculiar to the development of salmon to make the doctrine more applicable to them than to other species. I am in the circumstances satisfied that it would be an unwarranted extension of the doctrine of specificatio to hold that a fish farmer who feeds and husbands large numbers of salmo salar while they develop from smolts into mature salmon creates a nova species ownership of which vests in him. On the contrary, I am satisfied that the mature salmon in the first defenders' cages are, as objects of ownership, the same things as the smolts which the pursuers supplied. …

In my opinion, the retention of title clause is valid and effective and yields the result that the salmon presently (if the Ministry has not yet intervened) in the possession of the defenders remain the property of the pursuers.

Note

In the above case the salmon were not regarded as *specificatio*, nor as fruits of the salmon smolts. There were seen as the same things as the smolts. They had simply grown. The case contrasts with the egg and chicken case cited above.

BGH, 26 October 1977[143] **7.42 (DE)**

SPECIFICATIO BY FATTENING CALVES?

Fattening calves

Fattening calves does not amount to specificatio.

Facts: From 18 January 1972 until 6 July 1972 the claimant sold 439 young calves to farmer S and delivered the calves to him under a reservation of ownership clause, retaining ownership of the calves and their offspring. Some time later, on 27 July 1972, the farmer pledged 596 calves in his stables to the defendant. In the autumn of 1972 the farmer sold some of the calves and deposited part of the money at the district court. The claimant and defendant both asserted they were entitled to the money in deposit.

Held: The fattening of calves does not amount to *specificatio*, because according to common opinion the fattened calf is not a different thing from the calf in its original state.

Judgment: ... II.1. The claimant's argument is correct that the Court of Appeal has wrongly held that the requirements for the application of §950 BGB were fulfilled. If the claimant's assertion that she still had claims against S at the time the calves reached maturity for slaughter and that the defendant seized and sold the calves, delivered by the claimant, by way of enforcement, the defendant through the enforcement disposed of the claimant's ownership as an unauthorised person.

2. An acquisition of ownership according to §950 I BGB requires, that a 'new movable object' has been created. Apparently the Court of Appeal also presumes this. When considering whether this matter of fact is present, the Court of Appeal however relied on an exclusively economic approach. A new object, it holds, came into existence here because S fed the calves a special type of food, whereby the animals became anaemic and therefore put on extra 'white meat' much valued in trade. With the reaching of maturity for slaughter a 'higher level of production' had been achieved, which in the literature and case law suffices for the acceptance of a new object within the meaning of §950 I BGB.

This cannot be agreed to in general. Admittedly, economic aspects can often be of importance, for instance in the development of an object from raw materials via semi-finished products to finished products (see also Hoffmann, NJW 1961, 1246). This is, however, based on the fact that in this kind of case an economic approach already imposes itself or—due to lack of other indications—is often solely appropriate to the matter.

There is no room for economic aspects if already from a natural viewpoint—if necessary taking into consideration common opinion—the assumption that the

[143] NJW 1978, 697.

changed object is a new object is unacceptable. From this perspective it appears unreasonable to regard an animal, that develops through mere growth—even if influenced by special feeding, which accelerates this growth and leads to increase and 'improvement' of its meat—as a new object at the moment in which it is pending for slaughter. This applies also when, as a result of the character of the feeding, another use (eg as dairy cow, draught cattle or similar) than for slaughter is to be excluded. From a natural approach a living animal is in its different stages of physical development (here: calf, veal, slaughter calf, cattle, dairy cow, draught cattle and so forth) always identical to itself and will therefore also according to common opinion never be considered a new object dependent on the state of life or growth reached. It requires no decision as to how a case should be judged, in which an animal gains by special training new characteristics that are considered commercially valuable (guide dog, show horse). If nothing more than a biological development of the animal, even though controlled and influenced by man, is present, an exclusively economic approach cannot lead to the result, that from one stage of the physical development forth, a new object in terms of §950 I BGB exists.

If it is then to be denied that the calves purchased and fattened by S became new movable objects when reaching maturity for slaughter, the additional question, whether 'processing' or 'alteration' in terms of the law was at all performed, does not matter.

Note

According to the Bundesgerichtshof, fatting calves does not create new things. The judgment is in line with the judgment in *Kinloch Damph v Nordvik Salmon Farms*. However, the *Kinloch* case in particular seems to contrast with the Dutch Supreme Court's judgment in *Stichting Crediteurenbelangen Hollander's v Coöperatieve Raiffeissenbank 'Domburg'* (the egg and chicken case).

IV. ACQUISITIVE PRESCRIPTION

IV.A ACQUISITION OF OWNERSHIP BY PRESCRIPTION

Introductory Note

Prescription may have different effects: it may lead to the acquisition of a right, or alternatively, to the loss of a right or action. Where prescription leads to the acquisition of a right it is called acquisitive prescription. The loss of a right or action through lapse of time is called extinctive prescription, as it leads to the extinction of a right or action. Many legal systems further distinguish between extinction with strong effect, in which case the right itself lapses, and extinction with weak effect, where only the action lapses but not the right itself. The terminology of English law is different in that extinctive prescription is called limitation of actions. The term 'limitation of actions' in English law is, however, misleading in that not only the action but also the underlying right itself extinguishes.[144] English law uses various terms for the positive effect of acquiring a right through long use. It is called acquisitive prescription only in relation to the acquisition of easements and profits; the acquisition of a freehold or leasehold estate in land is called adverse possession. As will be seen below, there is no acquisitive prescription of movable property in English law, although English law has rules which have the same practical effect. To denote acquisitive prescription French law often uses the term *usucapion* based on the Roman law term *usucapio*.

In the first part of this section we will focus on the acquisition of the right of ownership in land through lapse of time. The second part will cover the acquisition of movable property whereas the third part will treat the acquisition of limited property rights, notably the right of servitude, through lapse of time.

IV.A.1 FRENCH LAW

IV.A.1.a The General Provision on Prescription

Article 2258 Cciv gives a definition of acquisitive prescription.

Code civil[145] **7.43 (FR)**

Article 2258 Acquisitive prescription is a way to acquire a thing or a right through possession without requiring him, who invokes it, to show a title for acquisition and without the possibility to invoke against him the exception based on bad faith.

Cour de cassation, 2 June 1993[146] **7.44 (FR)**

Goldfinger, Sébastien and others v Slomovic and others

EXTINCTIVE PRESCRIPTION OF REVINDICATION

Goldfinger

Ownership does not lapse through non-use; revindication does not underlie extinctive prescription.

Facts: In 1939 Slomovic had a large art collection in his possession which came from the gallery of Vollard. After Vollard's death the objects were deposited with Société Générale. After Slomovic had disappeared during the Second World War, Société Générale advertised that the objects were to be auctioned publicly. As a successor in title Bertozzi revindicated the objects. Her nephew Sébastien was her heir. In addition, Slomovic's relatives, the Goldfingers and Zdenka Slomovic, claimed to be owners. The Court of Appeal held that certain objects belonged to Sébastien and that his action of revindication had not been extinguished by prescription. Before the Supreme Court the claimants asserted that the revindication had prescribed.

[144] Limitation Act 1980, ss 3 (movables) and 17 (immovables).
[145] Original number: 2262.
[146] No de pourvoi: 91-10971, no de pourvoi: 91-12013, no de pourvoi: 91-10429, no de pourvoi: 90-21982.

Held: Ownership does not lapse through non-use and the action of revindication does not underlie extinctive prescription.

Judgment: Considering that Erich Slomovic, a student with Yugoslavian nationality, found himself, during the year 1939, in possession of a important collection of objects and paintings of value, originating from the gallery of Ambroise Vollard; that after the death of the latter, suddenly on 22 July 1939, he has entrusted a part of that collection in a suitcase to the Société Générale, and transported the other part to Yugoslavia where it was exhibited in Zagreb in November 1940; that Erich Slomovic has disappeared during the Second World War; that the Société Générale has opened the suitcase on 24 October 1946, then preserved its content in a vault in Nantes until 1977; that the Société Générale had the enclosed objects in that vault described by an auctioneer, then obtained by a judgment of summary proceedings the appointment of a seizure with the purpose of having these objects auctioned; that two auctioneers, authorised by the seizure for organising that auction, have created significant publicity for the auction fixed at 19 and 20 March 1981; that informed by this publicity, Mrs Assunta Bertozzi widow of Jonas, now succeeded in her rights by her nephew and heir Mr Louis Sébastien, has revindicated, in her capacity as assignee of Ambroise Vollard, the property of the major part of the subjects found in the suitcase of the Société Générale; that at that point intervened in their capacity as heirs of Erich Slomovic, on the one hand the parties Goldfinger-Eshel ... and on the other hand, Mrs Zdenka Slomovic, ...; that a first judgment of the Court of Appeal of Paris dated 26 February 1987 has recognised the widow Mrs Jonas as having authority to act, declared the action of revindication admissible as it was not prescribed and ordered an expert's assessment; that upon the submission of the statement of the expert, the court of appeal of Paris has, by a second judgment of 3 October 1990, declared Mr Sébastien owner of certain objects, said that the other objects are part of the inheritance of Erich Slomovic, which is divided, in accordance with French law, in halves between, on one hand, the parties Goldfinger-Eshel, on the other hand, and Mrs Zendka Slomovic on the other hand; that the court has sentenced, in proportion to their inheritance share, the parties Goldfinger-Eshel and Mrs. Zdenka Slomovic to pay to the Société Générale a sum of 30,894 francs and 400,216.64 francs, and dismissed all the parts of their requests of compensation;

On the sole legal argument, taken in its two parts ... directed by the parties Goldfinger against the decision of 26 February 1987:

Considering that the parties Goldfinger accused the contested decision of having allowed the action of revindication started by Mrs Jonas and continued by Mr Sébastien, for the reason that the prescription against him only started running after the auction of 1981, whereas, on one hand, the Court did not establish that the ignorance of the existence of the disputed goods in which Mrs Jonas found herself until in 1981 was inevitable, and secondly, that it results from the judgment's own observations that Lucien Vollard, brother of Ambroise Vollard and legal predecessor of Mrs Jonas, knew the existence of the objects in possession of Erich Slomovic, who had displayed them in Zagreb in 1940, without Lucien Vollard ever attempting to regain possession of these objects;

But considering that the right of ownership cannot come to an end by non-user, the action of revindication is not susceptible to extinctive prescription; that since the Court of Appeal's judgment is based on this legal reasoning, the decision is legally justified; ...

Rejects the appeal no. 91-10971. ...

Note

The Court of Appeal's judgment was reversed by the Supreme Court on different grounds (in a different appeal) which are relevant only later in this chapter, namely the problem of equivocal possession.

Cour de cassation, civ 1, 7 October 1964[147] **7.45 (FR)**

Delaye v Sourdon

RELATIONSHIP BETWEEN EXTINCTIVE AND ACQUISITIVE PRESCRIPTION

Ownership through prescription

Acquisitive prescription despite impossibility of extinctive prescription.

Facts: The claimants revindicated a piece of land occupied by the defendants. The defendants claimed to have acquired ownership through prescription. The claimants countered that their action of revindication does not underlie extinctive prescription.

Held: Even though ownership and its action of revindication cannot prescribe, ownership lapses if a possessor meets all requirements of acquisitive prescription.

Judgment: About the sole legal argument: Considering that the confirmed decision is objected for having allowed, in an action of revindication of the ownership of a parcel of land by the married couple Delaye, the opposite party, the married couple Sourdon, to prove that they have acquired the disputed land by thirty years' prescription prior to the acquisition by the married couple Delaye, which latter acquisition was based on a deed, while the right of ownership of an immovable cannot come to an end by non-user; to be preferred over the deed of acquisition the claimed possession should have been older than the deed;

But considering that, although the action of revindication instituted by the owner deprived of the possession of his immovable is imprescriptable, the revindication cannot succeed against a defendant who proves that he has himself become owner of the revindicated immovable, by an adverse possession which meets all the requirements for acquisitive prescription; ...

That therefore the legal remedy is not founded;

For these reasons: rejects: the appeal against the judgment pronounced on 15 June 1961 by the Court of Appeal of Aix-en-Provence.

Note

The right of ownership and its action of revindication do not extinguish as a result of non-use (*non usus* in Latin). The action of revindication does not underlie extinctive prescription. However, if someone other than the owner possesses the thing and meets the requirements of acquisitive prescription, he will become owner and the dispossessed owner will lose his right of ownership.

[147] Bull I no 430.

IV.A.1.b The prescription periods

Introductory Note

A property right, ownership or any limited proprietary right, can be acquired after 30 years of continued possession, even if the possession started in bad faith. The period for acquisitive prescription is shortened to ten years if the possessor has acquired in good faith on the basis of a valid legal ground, such as a contract of sale or a contract creating a servitude.

Code civil[148] **7.46 (FR)**

Article 2272 The period required to acquire the ownership in respect to immovables through acquisitive prescription is thirty years. However, he who acquires an immovable in good faith and with a legal title acquires ownership in ten years.

IV.A.1.c The requirement of possession

Code civil[149] **7.47 (FR)**

Article 2255 Possession is the holding or the enjoyment of an object or of a right that we have or hold for ourselves, or by another that has or holds it for us.

Note

Possession is holding a thing for one's own benefit, but the article shows that possession can also be exercised by for example a tenant who holds the thing for the possessor's benefit. If the tenant occupies a strip of land belonging to his neighbour, this may amount to possession of his landlord, which may ultimately lead to the landlord acquiring ownership by way of prescription.

Cour de cassation, civ 3e, 24 January 1990[150] **7.48 (FR)**

Alfred Pirault v Pièrre Pirault

ACTS OF POSSESSION BY TENANTS

Acts of possession

Acts of possession by a tenant can be relied on by landlord.

Facts: Alfred Pirault claimed to have acquired part of the adjoining land belonging to Pièrre Pirault. He relied on acts of possession by his successive tenants. The Court of Appeal held that Alfred could not rely on acts of possession performed by his tenants.

Held: The Court of Appeal has violated article 2228 Cciv in holding that the landlord cannot rely on acts of possession performed by his tenants.

[148] Original number: 2265.

[149] Original number: 2228.

[150] No de pourvoi: 87-18747. *Cf* Cour de Cassation, Chambre civile 3, 21 March 1984, Bull 1984 III no 78.

Judgment: on the only argument: In view of Article 2228 of the Civil Code; Considering that possession is the detention or the use of an object or a right that we hold or exercise for ourselves, or by another who holds or who exercises it in our name;

Considering that, stating in a conflict concerning the delimitation of their adjacent properties, brought before the court by Mr Alfred Pirault against Mr Pierre Pirault, the attacked judgment, that has set the borderline of the properties according to the indications of the expert, has discarded the exception of acquisitive prescription presented by Mr Alfred Pirault with the reasoning that he could not invoke the acts of possession allegedly accomplished on a slope by agricultural tenants who have succeeded one another on the rented premises and that have only exercised detention.

That, in stating thus, whereas the owner of a piece of land can invoke acts of possession accomplished in his name by the tenant, the court of appeal has infringed the above-mentioned text;

For these reasons: nullifies and annuls, in all its dispositions, the judgment rendered June 24th 1987, between parties, by the court of appeal of Rennes ...;.

Note

Possession only starts when material acts have been done which amount to possession for one's own benefit.

Cour de cassation, civ 3e, 15 March 1978[151] **7.49 (FR)**

Auvray v Dessaint

MATERIAL ACTS AMOUNTING TO POSSESSION

Pavilion

There should be sufficient evidence of acts of possession.

Facts: Auvray claimed that Dessaint had built a hedge and a wall of a pavilion on Auvray's land, thus crossing the borderline between the two plots of land. Auvray claimed that Dessaint had not performed any acts of possession which could have led to acquisitive prescription.

Held: Where the owners of the land deny that the persons claiming acquisitive prescription have ever performed any material acts amounting to possession, the Court of Appeal cannot hold that ownership has been acquired by way of prescription without ascertaining that material acts amounting to possession have taken place.

Judgment: But concerning the second argument: Considering Article 2229 of the Civil Code; Considering that, the Court of Appeal based its decision that the married couple Dessaint acquired by prescription of thirty years the piece of land behind the fence separating the two properties, which piece is revindicated by the married couple Auvray, on the sole arguments that the fence in question, which was constructed long before 1939, has never been the object of whatever dispute or revindication of property on behalf of Auvray or of their predecessors in title before the year 1970, that it has not been proven that the married couple Dessaint and their predecessors knew of the exact situation before the repairs undertaken in 1970, the error of

[151] No 76-14.029.

delimitation committed being minimal and not visible and 'that it results from these circumstances that since more than thirty years before the year 1970, the moment when the dispute about the borderline of the plots emerged, the married couple Dessaint and, before them their predecessors, had possessed the narrow strip underneath the fence, as owners, continuously, not interrupted, peacefully, visibly and in an unequivocal manner.'

Considering that in deciding thus, without showing material acts likely to characterize the possession, whereas the married couple Auvray contested the existence of any act of this nature prior to the repairs undertaken by Dessaint in 1970, the court of appeal has not given a legal base to its decision.

Cour de cassation, civ 1, 3 May 1960[152] **7.50(FR)**

Millet v Chatelain

ACTS OF POSSESSION AND CONTINUITY OF POSSESSION

Manure

Once possession is established it continues without new acts.

Facts: Chatelain revindicated part of a court from Decoux and Millet. Millet countered that he had acquired ownership through 30 years' prescription. The Court of Appeal rejected Millet's claim, as his acts of possession were not continuous.

Held: Although the acts of possession were interrupted regularly, the court of appeal should have checked whether or not the acts of possession had been interrupted for an abnormally long period of time so as to render the possession discontinuous.

Judgment: Considering that possession is continuous if is exercised on every possible occasion and at every possible moment having regard to the nature of the object possessed and without abnormal interruptions long enough to amount to a lacuna;

Considering that Chatelain sued Decoux and Millet in order to revindicate part of a court adjacent to their respective plots of land, that Millet invoked as a defence thirty years' acquisitive prescription in regard to the revindicated land, that the judgment appealed against rejected the defence with the argument that the acts of possession invoked by Millet were based on the presence on the land of a dung hill and wood and could not be regarded as continuous because in the case of the dung hill 'it concerned obviously a storage which was interrupted for a large part of the year after spreading the dung on the fields' and, as to the wood, it concerned storage from time to time;

Considering that in so deciding, without indicating whether the acts of possession, invoked by Millet and the existence and frequency of which the court recognised, were performed with abnormal interruptions long enough to amount to lacunas, and thus render the possession discontinuous, the Court of Appeal has not lawfully justified its decision.

[152] Bull I, no 230.

Note

Once possession has been established, it normally continues to exist even if no material acts of power over the object are currently exercised by the possessor. Without such a rule it would be almost impossible to claim continuous possession over the period required for acquisitive prescription. In Dutch law the rule has been codified in Article 3:117 BW. This changes only when the interruptions are abnormally long.

IV.A.1.d Special requirements for the ten-year prescription period

(i) Requirement of good faith

Introductory Note

In most cases acquisition of ownership of immovable property by way of prescription will not involve an entire parcel but will be limited to the acquisition of a small strip of land. The possession of a large piece of land belonging to someone else will normally not remain unnoticed by the owner for a long time. The possession of a small strip of land, on the other hand, is very common, because it is often difficult to ascertain the exact borderline between two plots of land.

For the 30-year prescription period no good faith is needed. Following Roman law[153] the shorter prescription period of 10 years, however, demands that the possessor should be in good faith and that he should have acquired possession on the basis of a valid legal ground (*iusta causa usucapionis*). That is to say, the possessor should believe in good faith that he acquired ownership or a limited proprietary right from its owner or at least from someone authorised to dispose of the object. He is in good faith if he did not know or should have known that the transferor was not the owner of the object. His good faith should be present when the legal ground, eg the contract of sale, is made. It is irrelevant whether the possessor remains in good faith afterwards. If later on he finds out that he acquired from a non-owner, this does not stop the prescription period running in his favour: *mala fides superveniens non nocet* (bad faith coming afterwards does not harm).

Cour de cassation, civ 3e, 7 April 1994[154] **7.51 (FR)**

Menut v Roche

MOMENT WHEN POSSESSOR SHOULD BE IN GOOD FAITH

Wall on the neighbours' land

Possessor should be in good faith at the start of his possession.

Facts: Roche had built a wall on the land belonging to a couple, the Menuts. The Menuts had demanded demolition of the wall. Roche in turn claimed to have become owner of the relevant strip of land through abridged prescription (now Article 2272 Cciv). The Court of Appeal held that Roche's deed of acquisition formed a valid legal ground and that he had been in possession for 10 years so that he had acquired ownership through prescription.

[153] Mod D 50,16,109.

[154] Bull civ III no 80, D 1995 somm 192.

Held: The Court of Appeal should have stated that Roche did not acquire from the true owner and that he was in good faith when he started his possession.

Judgment: Considering that the judgment rejected the action and declared Mr Roche to be the owner of the strip of land in question with the argument that the notarial deed of 23 July 1968 formed for Mr Roche a 'legal ground' and that Mr Roche, having been in possession for 10 years, can invoke Article 2265 of the Civil Code;

In deciding thus, without holding that Mr Roche did not acquire from the true owner and without holding that Mr Roche was in good faith at the moment of his acquisition, the court of appeal violated the above-mentioned text;

For these reasons;

Quashes and annuls the judgment.

Notes

(1) The rule *mala fides superveniens non nocet*, which is of Roman origin,[155] applies also in Dutch law (Article 3:118(2) BW). Unlike Roman law, canon law required good faith during the entire prescription period.[156] German law takes a middle road between the Roman law and the canon law position in that good faith may lapse after the moment of acquisition of possession, but only as a result of *actual* knowledge. If the possessor, who started his possession in good faith, *should have* learned afterwards that he acquired from a non-owner, this does not prevent him from acquiring ownership through prescription under German law (§937(2) BGB).

(2) Let us say that A and B are two owners of neighbouring plots of land. A has erected a fence between the two properties, but after a long time it appears that the fence was 1 meter on to B's territory, so that A has used a small strip of B's land for a long time. He has been a possessor of this land for a certain time. A more difficult question, however, is whether he can be regarded as a possessor in good faith. Could and should he have known the true borderline between the two properties? Was he able and was he required to verify this? Does the registration system or any other source accessible to A show the exact boundaries of A's and B's parcels, for example on a detailed map?

(3) In French law the registration system does not contain any map or any other document indicating the exact boundaries of the parcels. This cartographic information is available only to a land surveyor (*géomètre expert*). It is collected in a national computer system called Aurige.[157] The land surveyor feeds the system with new information and is able to consult the system. The information is not freely accessible to a private person.[158] If a private person needs the information, he needs to contact a land surveyor in his region who is able to access the information on his behalf. Yet, in order for A to be a possessor in good faith it is not required that he should have obtained the relevant information from a land surveyor first.

[155] Ulp D 41,3,10 pr and Paul D 41,4,2 pr.

[156] Liber Extra 2,26,20: 'Unde oportet, ut qui praescribit in nulla temporis parte rei habeat conscientiam alienae' (As a result, it is necessary that a person who prescribes should at no point in time have known that the thing belonged to some else.)

[157] *Archives Unifiées des Répertoires Informatiques des Géomètres-Experts*. See www2.geometre-expert.fr.

[158] Art 56 Décret no 96-478 of 31 May 1996.

For that reason he is able to claim that he is in good faith even though the exact boundaries can be found in the computer system Aurige.

(ii) Requirement of a legal ground

Introductory Note

In the case of abridged prescription (10 years) the possessor's good faith and the prescription period replace the transferor's lack of ownership. Therefore the legal ground required for abridged prescription should be a legal act which would have passed ownership to the acquirer, were it not for the transferor's lack of ownership. The only problem that can be repaired is the lack of ownership. A notarial certificate of rights of succession cannot serve as a legal ground for prescription, because it is not a document which passes ownership; it is a mere declaration that ownership has passed.[159] The most common example of such a legal act which can serve as a legal ground for prescription is a contract of sale. The contract should be valid.[160]A void contract, as in the following judgment, cannot serve as a basis for abridged prescription.

Cour de cassation, civ 3, 30 November 1982[161] **7.52 (FR)**

Martin v Franco-Rondisson

JUSTE TITRE

Falsified signature

A void contract cannot be a legal ground.

Facts: Martin acquired an immovable from a non-owner on the basis of a sales contract with a falsified signature. Martin did not know that the seller's signature had been falsified and claimed to have acquired ownership through prescription on the basis of a legal ground. The Court of Appeal did not accept the sales contract as a legal ground for prescription.

Held: The Court of Appeal was right in holding that the sales contract with the falsified signature could not be regarded as a legal ground for prescription.

Judgment: On the sole argument: considering that Mr Martin complains that the judgment attacked has held, on a claim by the ladies Franco-Rondisson, that he does not profit from the abridged prescription of Articles 2265 and following of the Civil Code, with the argument that, as he based his claim on a deed with a falsified signature, he did not have a valid legal ground. According to the claimant's argument 'the legal ground is a ground of which the acquirer did not now the defects, and which, if it had come from the owner, would have transferred ownership' and since the court of appeal has not examined whether the acquirer was aware of the false signature on the deed, the court did not found its decision on a legal basis in regard to Article 2265 of the Civil Code.

[159] Cass civ 3, 25 June 2008, Pourvoi no T 07-14.649.

[160] Note that Art 1599 Cciv does not render the contract of sale void but merely voidable at the option of the buyer.

[161] No de pourvoi: 81-10148.

However, considering that the judgment, which held that the deed relied on by Mr Martin had a false signature, has rightly drawn the conclusion that a legal ground in the sense of Article 2265 of the Civil Code lacked. From this it follows that the argument is unfounded.

For these reasons: rejects the appeal …

Cour de cassation, civ 3, 31 January 1984[162] **7.53 (FR)**

Benjamin v Peramin

ACQUISITIVE PRESCRIPTION OF LAND

Based on a contract

A contract may serve as a legal ground for prescription if the contract is able to pass ownership.

Facts: Benjamin had acquired a plot of land from Baron in 1930. In 1968 Baron sold the same plot of land to Peramin. The latter claimed 10 years later to have acquired ownership. As a legal ground for prescription he relied on a sales contract that had never been entered into the land register.

Held: Despite non-registration of the sales contract the contract may serve as a legal ground for prescription if the contract is able to pass ownership.

Judgment: On the only argument: considering that the Benjamins, who in 1930 had acquired from Mrs Baron the parcel of land in question have complained that the judgment attacked (Basse-Terre, December 21st 1981) held that the spouses Peramin, to whom Mrs Baron had sold that same parcel, had acquired the land through prescription with the argument that they had a legal ground and that their good faith had not been denied effectively, whereas, according to the claimant's argument, 'on the one hand, the legal ground that serves as the base of the acquisitive prescription can only consist in an act susceptible of transferring the ownership to him who invokes it vis-à-vis him against whom it is invoked and that therefore the act of sale of 1968, unable to be invoked against the Benjamins, for lack of registration, could not serve as a base for the ten-year prescription invoked against the latter, who were third parties and who were already owners and that, secondly, the Court of Appeal could not declare the spouses Peramin acquirers in good faith without taking into account that, according to the observations of the challenged judgment itself, the act of sale of 1930 had been registered and that therefore they had acquired an object of which the prior sale to a third party had been made public and was therefore known to them;

That under these conditions, the challenged judgment has failed to observe the dispositions of Article 2265 of the Civil Code:

But considering that, on the one hand, even in the absence of registration, the acts by which the party who invokes the abridged acquisitive prescription has been put into possession of the land, constitutes a legal ground, from the moment that this act was susceptible of transferring the ownership;

Considering, on the other hand, that the power of the judges in appeal to judge

[162] No de pourvoi: 82-12156.

the facts concerning good faith of the spouses Peramin cannot be submitted to review before the Court of Cassation;

For these reasons: rejects the appeal formed against the judgment rendered December 21st 1981 by the Court of Appeal of Basse-Terre.

Note

It is surprising to see that despite registration of an earlier transfer the Court of Appeal held that the second buyers were in good faith. The case does not concern the acquisition of a small strip of land belonging to another, but the entire parcel that has previously been sold to the first buyers.

(iii) Additional requirements for acquisitive prescription

Introductory Note

The French Civil Code lays down more detailed requirements in order for possession to lead to acquisitive prescription. Some of the requirements are to be found in Article 2261 Cciv.

Code civil[163] **7.54 (FR)**

Article 2261 In order to complete the prescription uninterrupted and continuous possession, peaceful, visible, unequivocal, and as an owner is needed.

Note

Some of the requirements, namely the fact that possession should be continuous and uninterrupted and the fact that possession should be exercised as an owner, are in fact part of the very definition of possession, and should, strictly speaking, not be regarded as additional requirements. In the case of a servitude, possession as an owner should be understood as possession as holder of a right of servitude. Whether possession may exist when it is invisible or equivocal is open to debate, but French law normally treats these requirements as defects of possession, not as prerequisites of possession. The result, however, is the same: no acquisitive prescription takes place where one of these defects is present.

(iv) Peaceful possession

Cour de cassation, civ 3e, 30 April 1969[164] **7.55 (FR)**

Fauré v Payan

PEACEFUL POSSESSION OF LAND

Peaceful possession

Protests do not render possession unpeaceful.

[163] Original number: 2229.
[164] Bull civ III, no 348.

Facts: In 1957 Fauré wanted to register certain parcels of land in her name in the land register. Payan objected to this and had already previously objected to Fauré's possession of the land. The question was whether or not Fauré's possession was peaceful and could thus lead to acquisitive prescription.

Held: Repeated protests by the genuine owner do not render possession of the neighbour unpeaceful. Possession is unpeaceful only when possession has been taken or held with physical force or threats.

Judgment: ... And concerning the second subsection: In view of Article 2229 of the Civil Code;

Considering that in order to reject the exception of a thirty-year prescription invoked by Ms Fauré, the contested judgment states 'that, at the time of the preparatory works at the verification of the land registry [*cadastre*] in 1957, she had asked the registration in her name of parcels 46 and 49 ... but was faced with the claims of Payan;

... that the claims of Payan had been expressed earlier, according to the witness François Bouvier who has declared that for 15 or 20 years François Payan and thereafter his son Eugène Payan had always claimed the contested land; ... that this manner of repeated protest by Payan does not permit the widow Fauré to invoke peaceful possession, needed for prescription';

Considering that by stating this, whereas it has neither been demonstrated nor even been alleged that Ms Fauré had acquired or kept possession of the claimed parcels, by means of battery accompanied by physical violence or threats which are the only factors which could render the invoked possession unpeaceful in regard to prescription, the Court of Appeal has not founded its decision on a legal basis;

for these reasons:

Quashes and annuls the judgment delivered between the parties by the Court of Appeal of Grenoble on 5 June 1967. ...

(v) Publicly visible possession

Cour de cassation, civ 1, 7 July 1965[165] **7.56 (FR)**

Mrs Gracient v André Courbe

VISIBILITY OF POSSESSION

Subterranean cellar

Possession should have been known to person against whom it is invoked.

Facts: Underneath Mrs Gracient's house there was cellar accessible only from her neighbour's house, which belonged to Joseph Courbe. Mrs Gracient claimed that under the sales contract which passed ownership of the house to her, she had acquired ownership of the cellar as well. Her neighbour claimed to have acquired the cellar through acquisitive prescription. Mrs Gracient asserted that her neighbour's possession was not publicly visible (clandestine).

Held: Possession is not clandestine if the possession is known to the person against whom it is invoked.

Judgment: Concerning the first part of the first argument: considering that it follows from the statements of the contested judgment that, by authentic act of 4 March 1954, André Courbe has sold to Mrs Gracient the building of which he was the owner, at Poitiers, nr 15 bis, Rue Sainte-Opportune, with the adjoining outbuildings,

[165] Bull 1965 I, 459.

as well as the right to a cellar located under a building number 13 at the same street and belonging to Joseph Courbe, that Mrs Gracient, after having discovered that, on the one hand, she had no access to the cellar and, on the other hand, that there was a cellar under her building of which the only exit led to the adjacent building nr 13, which was rented to a third party by the owner of that building, has summoned André Courbe in his quality as guardian of Joseph Courbe;

Considering that the Court of Appeal, after having said that Mrs Gracient's legal ground of acquisition validates her right of ownership to the contested subterranean property as well as her right to access to the cellar, if no acquisitive prescription has taken place to the benefit of André Courbe, ..., has authorised the latter to prove that the owners of the building with number 13 had acquired said subterranean property through a thirty-year prescription;

Considering that the contested judgment is criticised for having thus stated, whereas Mrs Gracient has established that, either she herself or her predecessors in title, have exercised legal acts of possession concerning that cellar, in that she alone paid the land taxes for the entirety of the building, since the register did not indicate any division of land, that the fact itself that the building had been sold to her constituted an act of possession and that, consequently, the possession by the owner of the neighbouring building was necessarily faulty, precarious, equivocal and not publicly visible;

However, considering that the contested judgment, by responding to the argument that by reason of the situation of the premises the material acts of possession were concealed, holds rightly that, in order for the defect of public visibility to be discarded, it suffices for the possession to be known to the opposing party; ...

(vi) Unequivocal possession

Introductory Note

In order to acquire ownership by way of prescription the possession should be unequivocal. If, for example, a piece of land is co-owned by several owners and the land is used by one of them only, the latter cannot claim to have acquired full ownership of the land after a certain lapse of time, because his possession as sole possessor was equivocal. That is to say, the fact that he was the only person to use the land did not alarm the other co-owners that the user of the land behaved as a sole possessor and that a prescription period had started to run against them. Since the law does not allow a prescription period to run against an unsuspecting owner, it prevents acquisitive prescription saying that the possession is equivocal.

Cour de cassation, civ 1, 27 October 1993[166] 7.57 (FR)

Filippi v Azzena and others

EQUIVOCAL POSSESSION

Undivided inheritance

Normal exploitation of an undivided plot of land by one of the co-heirs leads to equivocal possession.

Facts: A number of heirs co-owned an undivided inheritance. When some of them demanded separation of the inheritance, Filippi, one of the heirs, claimed to have acquired sole ownership of several immovables by way of 30 years' prescription. Azzena and Quilichini challenged this view, saying that the acts performed by Filipi amount to no more than a normal exploitation of undivided property, that Filippi had not given proof of any act which demonstrated to his co-heirs his intention to possess the immovables as sole owner, and that Filipi's possession was therefore equivocal.

Held: The Court of Appeal acted contrary to the procedure prescribed by Article 455 of the Civil Code because it did not answer this argument. The Court of Appeal should have checked whether or not the exploitation of the undivided plot of land amounted to equivocal possession.

Judgment: Considering that at their deaths, the spouses Jean Joseph Finidori left two children, Jérôme and Jeannette, wife of Filippi; that she, deceased in 1912, has left six children to succeed her, of which Marie Milleliri, deceased without children on 2 May 1924, Joséphine, in whose rights the partners Azzena succeeded, Quilicus, in whose rights his son Mr Jean Jacques Filippi succeeded, and Marc, in whose rights Mr François Filippi, Mrs Géromine Filippi and Mrs Paulette Canonicci succeeded; that Jérôme Finidori deceased on 20 December 1918, leaving his two nephews, Quilicus and Marc, to succeed him, that he has indicated his sole legatees by will; that on 30 September 1974 the partners Azzena have made a judicial request to have the assets divided which made up the inheritance of the spouses Jean Joseph Finidori, and the undivided property collected through their inheritances by Jérôme Finidori and Marie Milleliri; ...

And regarding the sole argument of the incidental appeal brought by the partners Azzena and Mrs Quilichini:

Given Article 455 of the new Code of Civil Procedure; Considering that, by adopting the reasonings of the judges at first instance, the Court of Appeal has based its decision that the partners Filippi have acquired through prescription several immovables of which the division was requested, on the sole argument that the partners Filippi 'have executed continued acts of possession in relation to their assets for more than 30 years up to the day of the introductory summons to the proceedings, uninterrupted, peacefully, visibly and in an unequivocal manner';

For these reasons:

Rejects, in all its considerations, the judgment of 22 January 1991, between the parties, of the Court of Appeal of Bastia.

[166] No de pourvoi: 91-13286.

Cour de cassation, civ 3, 26 May 1993[167] **7.58 (FR)**

Severin v Perfetta

EQUIVOCAL POSSESSION

Co-owned shed

Unequivocal possession as the possessor had exclusive use and was regarded by co-owners as sole owner.

Facts: Camille and Jules Perfetta respectively owned flats 16 and 15 of an apartment building. According to the apartment regulations the owners of flats 15 and 16 had the exclusive use of a shed on the courtyard. Jules sold his part to Mrs Severin. The latter started an action of revindication against Camille, who occupied the shed.

Held: The Court of Appeal stated that Mr Camille Perfetta had the exclusive use and possession of the shed and that he was regarded by the general assembly of apartment co-owners as sole owner of the shed. Therefore, the Court of Appeal could hold that Camille Perfetta unequivocally showed his intention to behave as sole owner of the shed of which he was the exclusive possessor.

Judgment: Regarding the only argument: … However, considering that by having stated that Mr Camille Perfetta, sole user of the shed since 1947 for his professional activities, was exclusively in charge of the maintenance of the building, had been authorised by the general assembly of co-owners to restore it and was considered by all to be the sole owner already before 1958, even if Mr Jules Perfetta, who was his employee, occasionally stored his things and personal property there, the Court of Appeal has, without having any duty to establish an inversion of title or a notification to the general assembly of co-owners of his acquisition of the property through prescription, legally justified its decision, by holding that Mr Camille Perfetta had, through his acts of possession, manifested unequivocally his intention to behave as sole owner of the shed of which he had exclusive possession;

For these reasons: rejects the appeal.

Note

The fact that a person has a right to use the neighbouring land on the basis of a servitude does not necessarily prevent him from acquiring ownership by way of prescription. In the following case a person having a servitude of way erected a wall on his neighbour's land, on that part of the land on which he could exercise his right of way. Such possession, resulting from erecting the wall, is not equivocal since the servitude does not allow the holder of the servitude to erect a wall. It is thus a clear sign of a different kind of possession. As a consequence, the act of building a wall should have warned the owner of the land; it is a violation of his right of ownership which was unequivocal.

[167] No de pourvoi: 91-11185.

Cour de cassation, civ 3, 4 October 2000[168] 7.59 (FR)

Burst v Geny-Lave

EQUIVOCAL POSSESSION

Building a wall on the servient land

A right of servitude does not exclude the possibility of acquiring ownership through prescription.

Facts: Burst had acquired a servitude, a right of way, over the land that now belongs to Geny-Lave. Burst had built a low wall on the land where she exercised her servitude and claimed to have acquired part of the land as a result of prescription. The Court of Appeal held that no prescription could have taken place because Burst had a right of servitude on that part of the land.

Held: The fact that Burst had a right of servitude does not exclude the possibility of her acquiring ownership of part of the land through prescription.

Judgment: Given Article 2229 of the Civil Code, together with Article 809 of the new Code of Civil Procedure;

Considering, according to the first of those texts, that for prescription one needs continued and uninterrupted, peaceful, visible, unequivocal possession as an owner;

Considering that, according to the contested judgment ... the partners Geny-Lave who had ... each acquired half of a building comprising a yard burdened with a right of way to the benefit of Mrs Burst's land, accuse the latter of having built ... a low wall encroaching upon their yard, and have approached the interim judge in order to obtain the demolition of that construction;

Considering that in order to meet this request the judgment states that the argument invoked by Mrs Burst, which asserts that she had acquired that part of the yard bordering the contested low wall through prescription, appears to be without merit, since it results from the deed of 22 August 1949 that Mrs Burst benefits from a right of passage at that place;

That by ruling thus, whereas the existence of a right of way was not of a nature to exclude acquisition by prescription of the ground of the servient land, the Court of Appeal, which has not demonstrated the existence of a manifestly illicit disturbance, has contravened the above-mentioned texts;

For those reasons:

Rejects, in all its provisions, the judgment of 14 September 1998, between the parties, of the court of appeal of Nancy; ....

(vii) Permission

Introductory Note

As we have just seen, the requirement of unequivocal possession protects the unsuspecting owner against prescription running against him. The same reason of protecting the unsuspecting owner against prescription arises where someone who has the owner's permission to use the land, eg a tenant, claims to have acquired the land by way of prescription. These two defects, equivocal possession and permission,

[168] No de pourvoi: 98-23150.

overlap. Where a person uses land on the basis of the owner's permission, eg on the basis of a lease or usufruct or servitude, his possession may be called equivocal. At the same time, however, one could say that prescription is blocked by the owner's permission to use the thing. Where, for example, the owner's spouse, concubine or his family members use the thing, French law calls this equivocal possession,[169] but one could also say that the use is based on permission so that these persons have precarious possession or *detentio*, which can never lead to acquisitive prescription.

In some legal systems, such as Dutch law, prescription is blocked by saying that the tenant has no possession but mere *detentio*, and that the tenant cannot change his *detentio* into possession without notifying the owner, who is then able to start proceedings against the possessor to revindicate his property. The French solution is slightly ambiguous. Although the tenant or other user is said to have possession, this is a kind of possession that cannot give rise to acquisitive prescription; it is *possession précaire*, precarious possession.[170] Sometimes, to distinguish precarious possession from possession as an owner, it is called *détention*. Strictly speaking, permission does not lead to a defect of possession but permission prevents possession from arising in the first place. The rule that precarious possession cannot lead to acquisitive prescription is expressly laid down in Article 2266 Cciv, but is also based on Article 2270 Cciv.

Mere tolerance has the same effect on prescription as express permission. Possession does not arise and prescription is therefore blocked. The influence of tolerance is often discussed in cases about servitudes and will be treated below in the part on servitudes.

Code civil **7.60 (FR)**

Article 2262 Acts which are merely allowed or simply tolerated cannot give rise to possession or prescription.

Article 2266 Those who possess for another can never acquire ownership through prescription, whatever be the lapse of time. Consequently, the farm tenant, the depositary, the usufructuary, and all the others who hold precarious possession of the object of the owner cannot acquire ownership through prescription.

Article 2267 The heirs of those who hold the thing or the right on any of the bases indicated by the preceding article, cannot acquire ownership through prescription either.

Article 2270 One cannot prescribe against one's title, in the sense that one cannot oneself change the ground of and the principle underlying one's possession.

Note

However, as the following articles show, the detentor is able to change his detention into possession under certain conditions.

[169] Cass civ 1st, 7 December 1977, Bull civ I, no 469.

[170] The term is derived from the Roman term *precarium*: Ulpian, D 43,26,1 pr.

Code civil **7.61 (FR)**

Article 2257 Once one has started to possess for another, one is always presumed to possess on the same title, unless there is proof of the contrary.

Article 2268 Nevertheless, the persons mentioned in Articles 2236 and 2237 may prescribe, if the title of their possession has been inversed, either caused by a third person or because they have contradicted the right of the owner.

Note

The change from detention into possession is called *interversion* (inversion). If the inversion is valid, a prescription period starts to run from that moment. As a prescription period cannot run against an unknowing owner, the inversion is valid only if it can be known to the owner. If the inversion is the result of a contradiction of the owner's right of ownership, the contradiction should therefore have been addressed to the owner.[171] This will enable him to assert his right of ownership by revindicating the thing.

Cour de cassation, civ 1e, 25 January 1965[172] **7.62 (FR)**

Rey v Commune de la Chapelle-en-Vercors

INTERVERSION BY CONTRADICTION

Sheep barn

In order to contradict the owner's rights the detentor should make clear that in the future he will behave like an owner.

Facts: Rey occupied a piece of land belonging to the town of Chapelle-en-Vercors. He or his predecessors in title built a sheep barn on the land and also planted trees there. Rey claimed that these facts amounted to an interversion of his detention into possession and consequently claimed to have become owner of the land. His revindication was dismissed by the Court of first instance and the Court of Appeal.

Held: The lower courts have stated that Rey acknowledged that he held the land as a detentor. In order to contradict the owner's rights the detentor should make clear that in future he will behave like an owner. Building a sheep barn and planting trees cannot be regarded as a contradiction of the owner's rights sufficient to turn his detention into possession.

Judgment: Considering that the judgment appealed against is criticised for having rejected Rey's action of revindication of a parcel of land directed against the municipality of Chapelle-en-Vercors based on the long term prescription of thirty years, with the argument that the facts brought forward by the claimant do not constitute a sufficient contradiction of the rights of the municipality to amount to an inversion of possession, without responding to the claimant's assertion that neither he nor his predecessor in title had ever signed the municipal register confirming that they are detentors, and to the claimant's assertion that, in any case, the building of a sheep barn and the planting of trees on the parcel in question amounted to an inversion

[171] B Mallet-Bricout and N Reboul-Maupin, *Droit des biens, septembre 2007–juillet 2008* (Recueil Dalloz 2008) 2458.

[172] No de pourvoi 62-13.773.

of possession; the appeal criticises that the Court of Appeal did not legally justify its judgment, as it simply adopted the arguments of the judges in first instance.

However, considering that not only according to the Court of Appeal but also according to the court of first instance Rey recognised that the land in question had been granted by the municipality to his predecessors in title in detentorship;

that the Municipal Register signed by the detentors of the parcels was destroyed in a fire in Chapelle-en-Vercors during the war;

that the 'construction of a wooden sheep barn on the parcel and even planting the trees in 1890' cannot be regarded as a 'sufficient contradiction of the rights of the municipality'.

Considering, on the other hand, that the judges at lower instance rightfully stated that 'the inversion should result from the contradiction by the detentor of the owner's rights, demonstrating the detentor's intention to hold henceforth as an owner', and held that the circumstances brought forward by the claimant did not constitute a contradiction of the rights of the municipality of Chapelle-en-Vercors strong enough to lead to an inversion of title to the benefit of the occupant of the land..

That thus the Court of Appeal responded to the arguments and provided a legal basis for its decision and that the arguments in question should be dismissed.

For the reasons stated above:

The Court dismisses the appeal.

Cour de cassation, civ 3, 28 March 1969[173] **7.63 (FR)**

Paouro and Doumai Ulm v Albert Ulm

REQUIREMENTS OF POSSESSION: CONTINUITY AND LACK OF PERMISSION

Coconut palms and fruit trees

Planting of trees on land does not constitute possession, neither does walking over land only several times per year amount to continuous possession.

Facts: Paouro and Doumai Ulm among other things planted trees on a plot of land belonging to Albert Ulm. They walked over the land several days per year. Albert had given them permission to do so. They claimed to have acquired part of the land by way of prescription.

Held: The lower courts held that planting several trees on the land did not constitute possession. They also held that walking over the land a few days per year does not amount to continuous possession. Moreover, they held that the fact that the owner of the land has given permission to use the land excludes possession and thus prescription. They had the freedom to come to this conclusion.

Judgment: On the second argument taken in its two parts: ... But whereas, as much by its own reasoning as by the adoption of the reasoning of the judges in first instance, the appellate court held that 'neither the existence of some coconut palms and some fruit trees, nor the existence of four graves on the land in question can be considered as facts of possession which are able to lead to prescription ...

That Paouro's presence, only for a few days a year, to take care of the cultivation, which presence was of really low importance in relation to the surface of the

[173] No 67-14.270.

land, cannot render the possession its character of continuity required by Article 2229 of the Civil Code either ... ;

That the occupation of the parcel by Paouro himself, from 1930 onwards, with the assent of the owner, as he admits himself, amounts to detention that forms an obstacle to the thirty year prescription by application of Article 2240 of the Civil Code;

That the judges in lower instance, who, exercising in this way their power to judge the character and the vices of the claimed possession, have refused to Paouro and Doumai Ulm to invoke prescription of the land in question, have legally justified their decision;

From which it follows that the second argument is unfounded;

For this reason: rejects the appeal formed against the decision given on the 11th April 1967 by the appellate court of Noumea (New Caledonia).

Notes

(1) The above case shows that the planting of trees and walking over the land a few days per year does not suffice to constitute possession.

(2) The fact that the owner of the land has given permission to use the land excludes possession and acquisitive prescription (Article 2266 Cciv).

Cour de cassation, civ 3, 2 December 1975[174] **7.64 (FR)**

Rosset v Michalet

INTERVERSION OF POSSESSION

Rosset's inheritance

The prohibition of interversion applies only to precarious possession.

Facts: Pièrre Rosset's inheritance consisted, among other things, of various plots of land. In 1903 these lands were divided between two parties. The successors of these two parties are Michalet and Rosset, respectively. Michalet's widow tried to revindicate the lands attributed to her predecessor from Rosset, who claimed to have acquired these lands by way of prescription. The Court of Appeal rejected Rosset's offer to prove their acquisition by way of prescription, stating that Rosset possessed on the basis of the deed of division and that Rosset cannot change the ground of his possession.

Held: The rule that one cannot change the ground of one's possession applies only to cases in which a person has precarious possession. As a result, it does not apply to Rosset's possession which is based on the deed of division.

Judgment: On the only argument: Considering Article 2240 of the Civil Code;

Considering that, if in the terms of this text, someone who possesses by virtue of a title cannot oneself change the ground of and the principle underlying one's possession, this rule is inapplicable to the person who possesses an object to which the title did not give him any right; Considering that it results from the challenged judgment that the various plots of land comprised in the succession of the common predecessor, Pièrre Joseph Rosset, have been attributed, divided in halves, to his heirs by a deed of division of 10 March 1903, the first part having been attributed to the predecessors of Michalet, the second part to the predecessors of the parties Rosset.

[174] No de pourvoi: 74-10481.

That Michalet, who is now succeeded by his widow, has revindicated the ownership of the plots of the first half attributed by the division to his predecessors from the parties Rosset who claimed to have acquired them by prescription.

Considering that, in order to reject the offer of the consorts Rosset to prove that they had acquired by thirty years' prescription the plots in question, the court of appeal stated that the parties Rosset could not prescribe by way of possession exercised by virtue of the deed of division because of the impossibility 'of prescribing against one's title, in the sense that one cannot change by oneself the ground and principle of one's possession';

Considering that by ruling thus, whereas the impossibility relates only to the title by virtue of which the possession is exercised under precarious title for the benefit of others and the deed of division common to both parties did not prohibit the parties Rosset from possessing, for their own benefit the plots in question originally attributed to the predecessors of Michalet, the court of appeal has violated, by wrong application, the text referred to above;

For these reasons: Quashes and annuls the judgment rendered between the parties on 17 October 1972 by the court of appeal of Besancon.

Note

Article 2270 Cciv prevents a detentor from becoming a possessor through inversion of the cause of his possession changing his precarious possession (dententorship) into possession as an owner. The two parties in this conflict both possessed as owners on the basis of the deed of division. As Rosset was not a precarious possessor of Michalet's lands, Article 2270 Cciv does not stand in the way of acquisitive prescription.

(viii) Succession of the predecessor's possession

Introductory Note

To acquire ownership or any other property right by way of prescription it is not necessary that one single person has been in possession for the required period of 10 or 30 years. In some cases the present possessor is allowed to add to his prescription period the duration of his predecessor's possession. He may have succeeded his predecessor in two different ways: as a universal successor or as a singular successor. A universal successor, eg an heir or the acquiring company in the case of a merger, succeeds in the predecessor's entire estate or a proportionate part of it. A singular successor succeeds only in one or more particular things or rights. The buyer who acquires ownership of the thing bought is a singular successor.

Code civil **7.65 (FR)**

Article 2265 To complete a prescription, one may join to one's possession that of one's predecessor, in whatever manner one may have succeeded him, whether by virtue of a universal or specific title, whether for value or gratuitously.

Notes

(1) Both types of successors (singular and universal) are able to add the duration of their predecessor's possession. However, the universal successor automatically

takes over all qualities attached to the possession. If the first possessor was not in good faith, the universal successor continuing his possession is also deemed not to be in good faith, even though he actually is in good faith. Conversely, if he is in bad faith but his predecessor was in good faith, he will be deemed to be in good faith. The reason is that the universal successor is deemed to continue the person of the predecessor. The singular successor, on the other hand, does not automatically take over the quality of good faith or the lack of good faith.

(2) The new possessor should have acquired possession from his predecessor, eg by way of transfer. Where, however, a certain object was not included in a sales contract, there has been no transfer of possession. In that case a new prescription period starts to run.

Cour de cassation, civ 3, 17 April 1996[175] **7.66 (FR)**

Mateu v Julien

CONTINUATION OF PRESCRIPTION PERIOD

Alleyway

Continuing a prescription periods demands a transfer of possession.

Facts: Mateu claimed to have acquired ownership of an alleyway alongside the front of his house. The alleyway had been closed by his neighbour Julien with a gate. Mateu sued Julien to have the gate removed. The Court of Appeal dismissed the claim for the following reason. The alleyway was not included in the sale to Mateu. As a result, he could not continue the prescription period running in favour of his predecessor (the seller). Consequently, Mateu did not acquire ownership by way of prescription.

Held: The Court of Appeal's judgment is correct.

Judgment: On the only argument: Considering, according to the judgment on appeal (Montpellier, March 29, 1994), that Mr Mateu, who invoked the acquisitive prescription of the ownership of a alleyway alongside the front of his house, summoned his neighbour, Mr Julien, who had placed a metal gate at the entry of the alleyway, to obtain the removal of this gate;

However, considering that having correctly stated that an acquirer cannot join to his possession that of its seller in order to prescribe a thing that was left out of the sale and having noted that Mr Mateu did not deliver proof that the act by which he had become owner of his land also contained a transfer to him of rights which could have been created through the prescription invoked, the condition of the 30 years' delay not being fulfilled, the court of appeal has, solely on these grounds, legally justified its decision;

For these reason's: rejects the appeal.

Note

The above case shows clearly how difficult it is to claim a continuation of possession after sale. If an owner possesses a piece of land which does not belong to his property (an adjacent alleyway), and, after sale of his property the new owner also

[175] No 94-15.748; Bull III no 107.

uses the alleyway, the second user cannot claim a continuation of possession, unless the alleyway was included in the contract of sale. Continuous use by successive possessors does not necessarily amount to a transfer of possession from one to the other possessor, ie a succession in possession. The requirement that the use of the alleyway should be covered by the contract of sale is different from the requirement of a valid legal ground. It applies also in the case of 30-year prescription, where no valid legal ground is needed.

IV.A.2 DUTCH LAW

It is a common problem that the physical borderline between two properties, a fence, wall or hedge, does not coincide with the border as registered in the cadastre, the so-called cadastral border, or that in the long run these two no longer coincide. The cadastre, which is part of the land register, contains detailed maps showing the exact borderline of every parcel. As a result of acquisitive prescription the actual, physical, borderline may become the legal borderline between the parcels. At the outset the cadastral borderline coincides with the legal borderline, but acquisitive prescription may cause the legal borderline to differ from the cadastral borderline. It is therefore very important to distinguish these two terms.

The old Dutch Civil Code from 1838 contained provisions about acquisitive prescription which were to a large extent a literal translation of the French equivalents, which in their turn were based on the Roman requirements for acquisitive prescription. The text of the prescription provisions of the new 1992 Civil Code differs considerably from the old provisions and the French provisions, but there is not much material change from the old provisions and the French provisions.

IV.A.2.a Prescription periods

Acquisitive prescription of a piece of land requires, first of all, possession of the land. Article 3:99 BW provides that possession in good faith of registered property such as land leads to acquisition of ownership after 10 years. If the possessor cannot be regarded as being in good faith, he acquires ownership after 20 years. Article 3:105 BW provides that the person who possesses a thing (here the piece of land) at the moment when the action of revindication lapses through extinctive prescription, acquires ownership of the thing. According to Article 3:306 BW, the action of revindication is extinguished after 20 years.

In the 20-year prescription period we see a combination of extinctive and acquisitive prescription, extinctive prescription of the action of revindication leading to acquisition by the then possessor of the object. It should be noted, however, that unlike in French law, the action of revindication extinguishes 20 years after the owner has lost possession, even if acquisitive prescription does not take place because currently there is no possessor. When in such a case the revindication lapses, the right of ownership remains and does not lapse.

IV.A.2.b Possession

Below we will focus on the different requirements for acquisitive prescription in the same order as in the section on French law. It should be noted that many requirements we have seen in French law and which are described as additional requirements, ie as requirements in addition to the central requirement of possession, are no longer expressly mentioned in the 1992 Civil Code, although these requirements still apply in modern Dutch law (the requirements of Articles 2261, 2262 and 2263). The reason is that the main draftsman of the 1992 Civil Code, Meijers, considered these elements as key elements of the notion of possession, without which possession cannot exist. No material change was intended.

In Dutch law the meaning of the term possession is confined to possessing for oneself, that is to say, possessing as an owner (Article 3:107 BW, *cf* Article 2255 Cciv). Possession for another is called *houderschap*, or *detentio* in *ius commune* terminology. Once possession has been established, it continues to exist even if no material acts of power over the object are currently exercised by the possessor (Article 3:117 BW).

IV.A.2.c Good faith

Introductory Notes

(a) For the short prescription of 10 years the possessor should be in good faith. The norm of good faith means that the possessor did not know nor should have known that he did not own the thing in question (Article 3:11 and 3:118 BW). In principle the possessor of land can claim good faith in the sense of Article 3:118 BW only if he can rely on a deed entered in the public land register.[176] An example would be a deed which did not pass ownership because of a defect which the possessor did not know nor should have known. Another example is a small difference between the boundaries mentioned in the deed and the physical boundaries present on the land.[177] In the case of immovable property this requirement of good faith is especially difficult because of the influence on good faith of the public land register. Article 3:23 BW provides that one cannot claim to be in good faith in relation to rights or facts which were entered into the public land register.

(b) To understand the exact influence of this provision we should briefly describe how the registration system works and which information is available in which part of the system. The land registration system consists of two different but closely related parts: the cadastre and the public register. When a piece of land is sold and transferred, the deed of transfer should be registered into the public register. This is in fact a deeds registration: a compilation per parcel of all the deeds that are or have been relevant for the parcel in question. Each time a new deed is entered, civil servants update the cadastre which gives the current legal status of every parcel, indicating its owner and any limited property rights. The cadastre also contains the cadastral maps giving the exact borderlines of every parcel. Since the cadastre and its cadastral maps are not part of the public land register, the information of the cadastral maps does not belong to the information intended in Article 3:23 BW.

[176] See, however, HR 5 February 2010 NJ2010/294.
[177] MvA II at Art 3:99, Parl Gesch Boek 3, 409 *et seq*, at 410.

(c) As a result, if A has bought and acquired a certain parcel and the deed of conveyance has been entered into the public land register, B cannot claim to possess the same parcel in good faith, as he should have seen this deed. On the other hand, possession in good faith of a small strip of A's land is possible, because the exact borderlines of parcels do not normally appear from the conveyancing deeds in the public register. In most cases these can be known only by consulting the cadastral maps. Of course, the relevant strip of land should be relatively small in relation to the piece of land owned by B. If he bought and acquired a parcel of 10 hectares and starts using a parcel which is 15 hectares, he should know that the physical borderlines are wrong and that he is taking possession of another person's land. As a matter of course, the possessor is in bad faith if he consulted the cadastral maps and found out the exact legal boundaries of his land, despite not being obliged to consult these maps.

Hoge Raad, 20 February 1987[178] **7.67 (NL)**

Goedhart v Van den Berg

ROLE OF CADASTRAL MAPS

Spit

In order to be in good faith the possessor need not check the cadastral maps.

Facts: Goedhart acquired ownership of a piece of land called parcel no D 1706. Van den Berg owned the adjacent parcel no 2050. Van den Berg and the former owners of her land used a spit with a landing. After measurements taken by a civil servant of the cadastre and public registers it appeared that the spit and the landing formed part of parcel no D 1706. Van den Berg claims to have acquired ownership of this land by prescription. The Court of Appeal held that Van den Bergh indeed acquired ownership by prescription. Goedhart claims that the Court of Appeal wrongly decided that Van den Berg acquired possession in good faith.

Held: The Court of Appeal did not violate the law by deciding that Van den Berg was in good faith.

Judgment: 3.1 In cassation the following facts are established:
'—Goedhart has by registration of three deeds of conveyance ... of 21 August 1972, 3 September 1975 and 27 September 1976 respectively ... acquired ownership of a parcel of land and water ... (hereafter parcel D 1706);

—Van den Berg has by registration of a deed of conveyance of 20 May 1952 ... become owner of a mansion with garage, courtyard, garden and water ... (hereafter parcel D 2050);

—This parcel was sold and conveyed to Van den Berg by JW Volk, wife of HJ Vermey, who held, until the registration of the deed of 27 September 1976 mentioned above a 1/16th co-ownership share in parcel D 1706;

—At a measuring of the land ... by a civil servant of the Cadastre in the province of North-Holland, it was determined that the contested spit with a landing which are used by Van den Berg and others forms part of Parcel D 1706;

—During the period preceding the moment that Van den Berg and others took possession of the mansion with garden mentioned above Mrs Vermey-Volk used

[178] NJ 1987/1002.

the spit and the landing, and from that moment Van den Berg and others started making use of the spit and landing without anyone, either from the side of Mrs Vermey-Volk or anyone else objecting to this.'

3.2 In this dispute the parties argue over the ownership of the spit and landing, located on parcel D 1706 and bordering the parcel of Van den Berg D 2050. The Court held … that Van den Berg has become owner of the spit by prescription as mentioned in Article 2000 sub 1 BW, because she acquired the spit in good faith and on the basis of a valid legal title and has had possession of it for more than 20 years.

The first argument criticises the judgment of the Court for having decided that Van den Berg acquired the spit in good faith in the meaning of the aforementioned article. The second is aimed against the Court's judgment that Van der Berg acquired the spit on the basis of a valid legal title in the meaning of that article.

3.3 It must be stated that the Court apparently assumed that the registered deed of 20 May 1952 of the conveyance of Parcel D 2050 did not in any way make clear that the conveyance of the immovable object laid down in the deed, apart from parcel D 2050, also covered the spit and landing, which were a part of parcel D 1706. This has the consequence that, in relation to this spit and landing, the requirements for delivery of an immovable object, as set by Articles 671 and 671a BW (HR 6 June 1986, NJ 1986, 750), were not fulfilled. As will be seen further on, this does not exclude the possibility that Van den Berg acquired the spit in good faith if she assumed and could assume that this was included in the conveyance, nor that Van den Berg acquired on the basis of a valid legal ground in the above-mentioned sense.

3.4 In so far as is relevant here, the Court has based its decision that Van den Berg was in good faith on—shortly summarised—the fact that she did not have any reason to suspect that the spit, that, so the Court determined, was used by Mrs. Vermey-Volk and afterwards was brought into use by Van den Berg and others, did not belong to parcel D 2050 and that also the size of the parcel as described in the deed does not bring with it 'that she could have been required to consult the relevant registries'. With this last remark the Court apparently means that it sees no reason to assume that Van den Berg at the moment of acquisition on which she invokes her good faith, could be required to check the description of the parcel on the cadastral maps available for consultation at the Cadastre, which do not belong to the public registers under Article 671 BW, and on which she could have seen that the spit and landing did not belong to parcel D 2050 but to parcel D 1706, of which Mrs Vermey-Volk, as she could have seen, did not have the power of disposal. In reasoning like this the Court of Appeal has not violated any rule of law, nor failed to support its judgment with reasons. …

Hoge Raad, 20 June 1997[179] **7.68 (NL)**

Luidens v the country Aruba

GOOD FAITH

Aruba farm

[179] NJ 1999/301.

Good faith may supersede bad faith.

Facts: Richard Luidens acquired a concession to use two parcels on the island of Aruba in 1841 and 1867, respectively. The 1841 land was 5000 m^2; the 1867 parcel was only 52 m^2. He also took possession of a large area of 380,000 m^2 adjacent to the 1867 land. Ownership of the adjacent land became a matter of dispute between the island of Aruba and the heirs of Richard Luidens. Richard exploited a farm on the disputed land. The heirs claimed that Richard had possession for more than 30 years before his death in 1915 and that his son Quirino continued the farm and possession of the land. In a regulation from 1924 the government acknowledged that the land held in concession by the heirs of Luidens was owned by them. The heirs claimed to have acquired ownership of the disputed parcel by way of prescription. The Court of Appeal of Aruba and the Netherlands Antilles rejected this claim on the ground that acquisitive prescription requires that possession started in good faith and that Richard Luidens was not in good faith when he started possession.

Held: It is possible for a possessor who started his possession in bad faith to become a good faith possessor afterwards. If so, the legal consequences of good faith possession start to run at that later moment. No good faith is accepted in this case. Therefore the heirs Luidens did not acquire ownership.

Judgment: 3.4 Part II is aimed at the Court's judgment in reasoning 3.2 that possession can only lead to acquisition of ownership if it started in good faith. The part is founded in that it cannot be excluded that a possessor, who at the moment when he acquired possession was not in good faith, gains good faith after all at a later moment in relation to that possession with the consequence that from this moment the consequences apply that the law attaches to possession in good faith.

3.5 The part, however, cannot lead to cassation.

In order to acquire ownership of an immovable object through prescription in a case like this according to Article 1982 sub 2 BWNA/BWAr the acquirer is required to be in possession in good faith for a period of thirty years. This means that the possessor must consider himself as owner and could reasonably have considered himself as such.

Richard Luidens has acquired possession of the lands by taking possession. Possession obtained in such a way could only be in good faith and thus lead to acquisition of ownership through prescription if the possessor thought and reasonably could have thought that the land did not belong to someone else. This could only have been the case if Richard Luidens or his successors in title thought that the owner of the immovable object, in this case the state, had abandoned its ownership.

However, an owner cannot abandon his right of ownership (cf HR 11 March 1966, NJ 1966, 330), leaving aside that according to Article 572 immovable objects that have no—other—owner belong to the state.

4. Decision. The Supreme Court: rejects the appeal.

Note

The judgment, although based on the old Civil Code for Aruba and the Netherlands Antilles, is valid for contemporary Dutch law on the point that bad faith possession may subsequently turn into good faith possession. In modern Dutch law this entails that if good faith supersedes bad faith, a shorter prescription period starts to run at that later moment.[180] In the present case, however, good faith was impossible. As a matter of course, good faith could not be based on the obscurity of the boundaries, because the disputed land was much bigger than the land owned by Richard

[180] MvA II at Art 3:118, Parliamentary History, Book 3, 444.

Luidens. The land owned was 52 centiare (52 m^2), whereas the adjacent disputed land was 38 hectares (380,000 m^2). For that reason the claim was not based on this argument. One of the reasons why Supreme Court rejected good faith was that Luidens cannot in good faith have believed that the owner, the government of Aruba, had given up ownership of the land, because an owner of land cannot give up his right of ownership. See also Chapter 9.

IV.A.2.D Unequivocal possession

Hoge Raad, 7 March 1980[181] **7.69 (NL)**

Schellekens v Braam

UNEQUIVOCAL POSSESSION

Parcels of land in a row

Possession should be unequivocal as against the owner.

Facts: Mrs De Smet owned a large number of parcels of agricultural land in a row. She sold and transferred some of the parcels to Braam and the other parcels to Schellekens. The boundaries of the parcels were not clear. The parties came into dispute over the ownership of one of these parcels. When Mrs De Smet owned the parcels she had given them in lease to Van den Besselaar (the parcels to the west including the disputed parcel) and to Schellekens (the parcels to the east of the disputed parcel). Braam bought the parcels which had been leased to Van den Besselaar, including the disputed land, and Schellekens bought the land he had in lease. Although the disputed parcel was part of Van den Besselaar's lease, Schellekens had been using this land for a long time. Schellekens then claimed to have acquired ownership of this parcel by way of prescription. Braam opposed by claiming that Schellekens' possession was equivocal.

Held: Witnesses, among which was the person collecting the rent from Schellekens and the other tenants, declared that they had always regarded Schellekens as a tenant of the disputed parcel. The Court of Appeal had rightly meant to say that Schellekens has not acted in such a way that the owner of the parcel should have realised that Schellekens behaved as an owner of this parcel. Thus he cannot have had unequivocal possession.

Judgment: 2.1. Considerations 3 and 4 of the Court of Appeal's judgment must be understood as such that the Court does not consider the evidence for the acquisitive prescription provided by Schellekens conclusive because, according to the Court's judgment, the possession of Schellekens cannot be considered as unequivocal, and that the Court leaves undecided whether the other requirements for acquisitive prescription have been fulfilled.

2. In consideration 4 the Court of Appeal states that witnesses from 'the surroundings of Schellekens' whose declarations have been cited by the Court of first instance, were convinced that Schellenkens had a lease of the land. Having seen the content of the declaration by the witnesses it must be assumed that the Court intends to express that there are no external circumstances have been proven from which the owner of the parcel in question, in the given circumstances, should have inferred that Schellekens considered himself as owner, and that therefore the possession as owner alleged by him cannot be considered as unequivocal. Unlike part 1 of the

[181] NJ 1980/549.

arguments assumes, the Court does not show an incorrect application of the law. Part 1 therefore fails.

Note

Unequivocal possession means that the possession should be unequivocal *as against the owner* against whom a prescription period runs. It is therefore a relative notion. The French Supreme Court used a similar reasoning in answering the question whether or not possession of an underground cellar was publicly visible. It should have been visible to the owner of the land in which the cellar was built (see 'subterranean cellar' 7.56 (FR)).

IV.A.2.e Permission

Hoge Raad, 18 november 2005[182] **7.70 (NL)**

Van Donselaar and Cornelisse v Sterenborg

INTERVERSION OF POSSESSION

Drive

Interversion of possession is possible only by the owner or by denying the owner's right of ownership.

Facts: Werktuigencombinatie, the former owner of the land now owned by Van Donselaar and Cornelisse, gave permission to Sterenborg to use part of his drive. Almost 20 years later Sterenborg then claimed to have acquired ownership of this part of the drive by way of prescription.

Held: Acquisitive prescription demands possession. In this case, where Sterenborg started using the drive as a tenant, he may have acquired by way of prescription only if more than 20 years ago his right of lease has ended or if more than 20 years ago his detention changed into possession, either by an act committed by the then owner of the disputed land or by Sterenborg denying the owner's right of ownership.

Judgment: 3.4 ... The Court of Appeal has held that the use of land by Sterenborg was, in any case on 18 February 1981, by way of lease and that Sterenborg could have been a possessor, at least until that date, so that the required prescription period cannot have started before that moment. Now that the writ of summons in this debate dates from 13 August 2001, the right of action initiated by Van Donselaar and others to evict the premises, for which Article 3:306 BW sets a prescription period of twenty years, can only have prescribed when it emerged in the timeframe between 18 February 1981 to 13 August 1981. This requires that in this timeframe either Sterenborg's right of usage ended, or he became possessor instead of detentor. The latter (Article 3:111 BW) should have been apparent from an act by the then owner, or from a contradiction of that the latter's right. The documents of proceedings leave no other conclusion than that Sterenborg has failed to offer evidence from which it may be derived that the right of usage of Sterenborg has ended in the timeframe mentioned or that an act or contradiction as mentioned above has taken place. The claim for eviction of Van Donselaar and others has therefore not

[182] Nr C04/118HR, NJ 2006/150.

prescribed and the reliance of Sterenborg on acquisition of ownership of the disputed piece of land under Article 3:105 BW therefore fails.

Note

Dutch law distinguishes between someone who holds property for himself and someone who holds for another person. The tenant is said to hold for another, namely the owner of the thing. Only the person holding for himself is called possessor; the person holding for someone else is called detentor. As in French law, no prescription is allowed to run against an unsuspecting owner. Therefore permission cannot lead to acquisitive prescription. This result is achieved by regarding the person who gets permission to use someone's property as a detentor rather than a possessor, taking away the vital requirement of possession. Mere tolerance rather than a right to use has the same effect.

IV.A.3 GERMAN LAW

Introductory Note

Under German law the acquisition of immovable objects or property rights over immovable objects by way of prescription is possible only if the person claiming prescription has been registered in the land register as the owner of the land in question or the holder of the right in question for at least 30 years and has been in possession during this period (§900 BGB).

Ownership of movable property can be acquired by way of prescription under §937 BGB, which demands possession for one's own benefit, good faith and a prescription period of 10 years.

Bürgerliches Gesetzbuch **7.71 (DE)**

§900 (1) A person who has been registered in the land register as owner of a piece of land, without having acquired the right of ownership, acquires the right of ownership when the registration has existed for 30 years and he has been in possession of the land for his own benefit for that time. The 30-year period is calculated in the same way as the period for prescription of a movable object. The running of the prescription period is interrupted as long as an objection to the accuracy of the registration in the land register is entered.
(2) These provisions are applicable mutatis mutandis when a different right has been registered in the land register for a person who is not entitled to it, that gives a right to possession or the exercise of which is protected by the provisions on possession. The registration is decisive for the priority of the right.
§937 (1) A person who possesses a movable object for ten years for his own benefit, acquires the ownership of that object (acquisitive possession) [*Ersitzung*].
(2) Acquisitive possession is excluded if, at the moment he acquires possession for his own benefit, the acquirer is not in good faith or if he later discovers the right of ownership does not belong to him.

Note

The scope of acquisitive prescription in the field of land law is therefore much narrower than in French and Dutch law. As noted previously, the possession by a non-owner of an entire parcel is quite rare. Nevertheless, German reunification has given rise to a considerable number of cases in which owners of immovable property situated in the former German Democratic Republic revindicated their land from possessors invoking acquisitive prescription. A specific provision has been made for these situations (§937(2) EGBGB). This provision will not be discussed here.

OLG Brandenburg, 18 April 2006[183] **7.72 (DE)**

Mrs R v City Council H

ACQUISITIVE PRESCRIPTION AND REGISTRATION

Front garden

Acquisitive prescription against the public land register is impossible.

Facts: The claimant was in possession of part of a parcel of land belonging to the City Council H. The City Council had been registered in the public land register as owner of the parcel. The claimant used part of the parcel as a front garden to his house and claimed to have acquired ownership through prescription.

Held: Acquisitive prescription against the public land register is impossible.

Judgment: Nr 6 U 26/04 ...The appeal of the claimant against the judgment of 2 October 2003 by the 3rd Civil Court of the regional court Neuruppin—3 O 537/00—is rejected.

The parties argue about the revindication of a section of the parcel 773, part 1, registered in the land register of H ..., sheet 5814. This land parcel represents ... the road in H. ... In the land register the defendant is registered as its owner. The claimant uses this section as front garden in connection with her adjacent house property '... Road 9', registered in the land register as parcel 774, part 1...

II. The appeal is unsuccessful.

The regional court Neuruppin rightfully condemned the claimant to evacuation and restitution of the disputed patch of the land parcel 773 under the counteraction of the defendant.

1. The defendant has the right to return of the land according to §985 BGB against the claimant.

(a) The claimant is owner of the patch of land parcel 773, which she uses in connection with her house property as front garden. The defendant is registered as owner of the land parcel 773 in the land register, the presumption of §891 BGB is already in its favour. According to this provision the beneficiary registered in the land register is considered to be the present owner of the right. The claimant could not bring proof, which is incumbent on her, for the refutation of this presumption. The refutation of the presumption of §891 BGB takes place not already by raising

[183] Similar judgment of the same court and date, no 6 U 24/04.

serious doubts to this presumption, but through full proof of the opposite (Palandt/ Bassenge, BGB, 65th edn, §891 Rn 8).

(b) The claimant did not prove the incorrectness of the land register (§894 BGB). The incorrectness can be asserted by way of objection against the revindication under §985 BGB. The claimant raises such an objection, by asserting with reference to the decision of the OLG Hamm (judgment of 13.06.1991; NJW-RR 1992, 152) to have acquired the land on which his house stands (land parcel 772) extending to the borders which are visible today at the location, therefore including the patch of parcel 773 which is fenced off and used as front garden.

In the cited judgment, the OLG Hamm has decided that if the parties to a contract for the purchase of land visited the property beforehand and agreed on the extent of the property along the borders evident from nature (in that case: agriculturally used property), the object of the conveyance is in principle determined not by the borders drawn on the land register plan, but by the borders evident in nature. It does not matter that the parties do not describe the object of the conveyance correctly in the contract. The real intention of the parties overrides the literal wording and every other interpretation. At hand is an—innocuous—*falsa demonstratio*.

Relying on these principles, an acquirer of parcel 774/1, provided that the other conditions have been met, can by conveyance only have acquired at the same time the adjacent patch in question, if the seller was at the time of the conveyance owner of the adjacent parcels 774/1 and 773. ...

Even if in favour of the claimant it were to be assumed that at least the first acquirer of land parcel 774/1, after its emergence from the parcel 1377/109, acquired ownership of it through conveyance with the seller, who was at the same time owner of the adjacent parcel 773, ie the 'E... S... Landgesellschaft mbH', this does not alter the result. The first acquirer could have acquired ownership of part of parcel 773 only if in the end he had been registered in the land register as owner (§§873, 925 BGB). This has not happened. The registered owner has always been the Community or 'property of the people.'

Subsequent acquirers of land cannot in good faith have acquired at the time of acquisition of parcel 774/1 ownership of the adjacent part of parcel 773 at the same time, because in this respect a pre-registration of the seller is lacking. An acquisition in good faith of immovable property cannot take place 'against the land register' (§§891, 892 BGB).

IV.A.4 ENGLISH LAW

Introductory Note

Before we start discussing the acquisition of land by lapse of time, we should warn that the use of terminology in English law is misleadingly different from the use in the other jurisdictions analysed above. The term prescription is not used for the acquisition of ownership of land, ie the fee simple estate, but is confined to the acquisition of limited property rights such as easements and *profits à prendre*. The acquisition of the fee simple estate and the leasehold estate is covered by the concept of 'adverse possession'. It underlies different legislation and case law. Originally, in the system of unregistered land, adverse possession did not give rights to the adverse possessor, but merely operated to extinguish the owner's title. Losing a right through lapse of time is called limitation and hence the applicable statute is the Limitation Act 1980. However, in the new system of registered land, the adverse possessor does get a right. Here adverse possession operates as a statutory transfer of the estate in question. This positive effect is not called prescription, although it fits the description of the term prescription as used in the other legal systems described above. The Prescription Act 1832, to be discussed below in the context of acquisition of easements and *profits à prendre*, does not apply here. Despite this fragmentation, both concepts—adverse possession of a fee simple or leasehold estate and prescription of easements and profits—do share many requirements, although this has again been obscured by differences in terminology.

The rules on adverse possession differ depending on whether we are dealing with unregistered or registered land. As in the future almost all land will be registered we shall here focus on the rules applicable to registered land. The relevant statutory rules are to be found in the Limitation Act 1980 and in the Land Registration Act 2002.

Law Commission and HM Land Registry, Land Registration for the Twenty-First Century, A Consultative Document (Law Com no 254 (1998)) 205–06 **7.73 (E&W)**

What is the justification for adverse possession? ...

10.9 Fourthly, title to unregistered land is relative and depends ultimately upon possession. The person best entitled to land is the person with the best right to possession of it. The fact that adverse possession can extinguish earlier rights to possess facilitates and cheapens the investigation of title to unregistered land. The length of title that a vendor is required to deduce is and always has been closely linked to the limitation period. Indeed, the principal reason for having limitation statutes in relation to real property appears to have been to facilitate conveyancing.

10.10 This fourth reason is undoubtedly the strongest justification for adverse possession. However, it can normally have no application to registered land. Where title is registered, adverse possession facilitates deduction of title only in relation to those matters on which the register is not conclusive. These are explained below.

In what circumstances can adverse possession be justified in relation to registered land?

10.11 Where title is registered, the basis of title is primarily the fact of registration rather than possession. Registration confers title because the registration of a person as proprietor of land of itself vests in him or her the relevant legal estate (whether freehold or leasehold). The ownership of the land is therefore apparent from the register. Only a change in the register can take that title away, and the circumstances in which that can happen are significantly limited by the principle of qualified indefeasibility that we have explained in Part VIII of this Report. The main weakness of the present law is that the principles which determine whether a registered proprietor will lose his or her title by adverse possession were developed for a possession-based system of title and not one founded on registration. If a system of registered title is to be effective, those who register their titles should be able to rely upon the fact of registration to protect their ownership except where there are compelling reasons to the contrary. All that should be required of them is to keep the Registry informed of their address for service. As we explain below, the land registration system enables registered proprietors to be protected against adverse possession in ways that would be very much harder to achieve where title is unregistered. …

Land Registration Act 2002, Schedule 6, Registration of adverse possessor **7.74 (E&W)**

Right to apply for registration

1(1) A person may apply to the registrar to be registered as the proprietor of a registered estate in land if he has been in adverse possession of the estate for the period of ten years ending on the date of the application. …

Notification of application

2(1) The registrar must give notice of an application under paragraph 1 to—

(a) the proprietor of the estate to which the application relates,

(b) the proprietor of any registered charge on the estate,

(c) where the estate is leasehold, the proprietor of any superior registered estate, …

Treatment of application

3(1) A person given notice under paragraph 2 may require that the application to which the notice relates be dealt with under paragraph 5.

(2) The right under this paragraph is exercisable by notice to the registrar given before the end of such period as rules may provide [65 business days, Land Registration Rules 2003, r 189].

4 If an application under paragraph 1 is not required to be dealt with under paragraph 5, the applicant is entitled to be entered in the register as the new proprietor of the estate.

5(1) If an application under paragraph 1 is required to be dealt with under this paragraph, the applicant is only entitled to be registered as the new proprietor of the estate if any of the following conditions is met.

(2) The first condition is that—

(a) it would be unconscionable because of an equity by estoppel for the registered proprietor to seek to dispossess the applicant, and

(b) the circumstances are such that the applicant ought to be registered as the proprietor.

(3) The second condition is that the applicant is for some other reason entitled to be registered as the proprietor of the estate.

(4) The third condition is that—

(a) the land to which the application relates is adjacent to land belonging to the applicant,

(b) the exact line of the boundary between the two has not been determined under rules under section 60,

(c) for at least ten years of the period of adverse possession ending on the date of the application, the applicant (or any predecessor in title) reasonably believed that the land to which the application relates belonged to him, and

(d) the estate to which the application relates was registered more than one year prior to the date of the application.

(5) In relation to an application under paragraph 1(2), this paragraph has effect as if the reference in sub-paragraph (4)(c) to the date of the application were to the day before the date of the applicant's eviction.

Right to make further application for registration

6(1) Where a person's application under paragraph 1 is rejected, he may make a further application to be registered as the proprietor of the estate if he is in adverse possession of the estate from the date of the application until the last day of the period of two years beginning with the date of its rejection.

(2) However, a person may not make an application under this paragraph if—

(a) he is a defendant in proceedings which involve asserting a right to possession of the land,

(b) judgment for possession of the land has been given against him in the last two years, or

(c) he has been evicted from the land pursuant to a judgment for possession.

7 If a person makes an application under paragraph 6, he is entitled to be entered in the register as the new proprietor of the estate.

Land Registration Act 2002, Explanatory Notes[184] **7.75 (E&W)**

157 The Act provides a new scheme for adverse possession in relation to a registered estate in land. The essence of the scheme is that:

Adverse possession of itself, for however long, will not bar the owner's title to a registered estate in land or a registered rentcharge.

A squatter will be entitled to apply to be registered as proprietor after ten years' adverse possession and the registered proprietor, any registered chargee, and certain other persons interested in the land will be notified of the application.

If the application is not opposed by any of those notified, the squatter will be registered as proprietor of the land.

If any of those notified oppose the application it will be rejected, unless the adverse possessor can bring him or herself within one or more of three conditions.

If the squatter's application for registration is refused but the squatter remains in adverse possession for a further two years, he or she will be entitled to apply once again to be registered and will this time be registered as proprietor whether or not the registered proprietor objects.

Where the registered proprietor brings proceedings to recover possession from a squatter, the Act allows the squatter to establish certain limited defences which are consistent with the three conditions mentioned above.

Section 96: Disapplication of periods of limitation

158 Section 96 provides that, in relation to a registered estate in land or a registered rentcharge, no period of limitation runs in relation to:

actions for the recovery of land except in favour of a chargee, or

actions for redemption

and so the title to such an estate or rentcharge cannot be extinguished. The excep-

[184] Land Registration Act 2002, Explanatory Notes, Part 9: Adverse Possession.

tion in favour of chargees means that section 15 of the Limitation Act 1980 will continue to apply to an action by a chargee for possession or foreclosure, to enforce its security. As regards actions for redemption, at present, once a mortgagee has been in possession for twelve years, the mortgagor loses his or her right to redeem the mortgage and his or her title is extinguished. This will no longer be the case.

Section 97: Registration of adverse possessor

159 Even though no period of limitation runs in relation to a registered estate in land or a registered rentcharge, it will still be possible for a person in adverse possession to be registered in place of the proprietor of a registered estate or rentcharge. This section introduces Schedule 6 which makes provision for such registration.

Notes

(1) Unlike under the old law, mere lapse of time no longer leads to loss of title or acquisitive prescription. In order to acquire title the possessor, the squatter, must apply to the Land Registry for registration of his title. Such application is possible if the squatter has been in possession for at least 10 years. The new provisions reduce substantially the importance of adverse possession. It is seen as one of the most important changes in land law in the twentieth century.

(2) The squatter's application will be notified to the registered owner of the land and registered holders of some other limited property rights. If the registered owner or any of these registered holders of limited property rights object to the squatter's application, the application will be rejected.

(3) There are three instances in which objection to the squatter's application must be rejected. These are stated in Land Registration Act 2002, Schedule 6, paragraph 5. The most important one is good faith possession of a strip of land next to the borderline between two plots of land.

(4) However, if after objection the squatter remains in possession for a further two years, the squatter will be registered as the new owner of the land.

Original or derivative acquisition?

In French, Dutch and German law the acquisition of rights through adverse possession is called original acquisition, as the right acquired by the adverse possessor does not derive from the former owner: there is no transfer from the former owner to the new owner, not even by operation of law. The former owner's right is extinguished and a new right of ownership is created by law in the hands of the adverse possessor. Hence adverse possession is an instance of original acquisition in contract to a transfer which is an instance of derivative acquisition.

However, under the Land Registration Act 2002 adverse possession is held to lead to a transfer by operation of law. The adverse possessor is successor in title of the former owner:

Law Commission Report on Land Registration for the Twenty-first Century[185] **7.76 (E&W)**

The squatter is successor in title to the previous proprietor

14.71 When a squatter's application for registration is successful for any of the reasons explained above, the registrar will register him or her as the new proprietor of the estate against which he or she adversely possessed. The squatter will, therefore, be the successor in title to the previous registered proprietor. The fee simple absolute in possession which the squatter has hitherto had by virtue of his or her adverse possession will be expressly extinguished.

14.72 Registration of the squatter as proprietor will carry with it the extinction of any claims that the former registered proprietor might have had against the squatter for damages for trespass or to recover rent. This is by analogy with the rule applicable to cases where title to land is extinguished by adverse possession under section 17 of the Limitation Act 1980—

When title to land is extinguished by the statute, the rights which that title carried must also be extinguished.

The claim to mesne profits or rent is dependent on the claimant showing that he or she was entitled to possession as against the squatter. Once the squatter has been registered, the former registered proprietor is unable to do that.

14.73 As a general principle, the registration of the squatter as proprietor will not affect the priority of any interest affecting the registered estate. He or she will, therefore, take the land subject to the same estates, rights and interests that bound the previous proprietor.

Registration of the squatter and the effect on registered charges

14.74 To this general principle there is one significant exception. We have explained above that, where a squatter applies to be registered, not only the registered proprietor but also any registered chargee will be given the opportunity to object. Furthermore, if objection is made, a registered chargee is entitled to take possession proceedings against the squatter to recover the land (even if the proprietor of the registered estate does not) because, as mortgagee, it has a right to possession of the land.

House of Lords, 4 July 2002[186] **7.77 (E&W)**

JA Pye (Oxford) Ltd v Graham

ADVERSE POSSESSION OF FEE SIMPLE

Pye

Visible and unequivocal possession with the intention to possess leads to acquisition of the fee simple after the requisite period of time.

Facts: In 1977 Pye sold part of his land, Manor Farm, a farm with farmland, and retained a large

[185] Law Commission Report no 271, 'Land Registration for the Twenty-first Century, A Conveyancing Revolution' (2001) 341–42.

[186] [2002] UKHL 30, [2003] 1 AC 419.

area of adjoining agricultural land (the disputed land) as it had development potential. In 1983 the Grahams bought Manor Farm. The farm itself was run by their son Michael Graham until his death in 1998. At first Michael Graham used the disputed land under a grazing agreement with Pye. When the agreement had expired (31 December 1983) he remained using the land in the hope of getting a new license. Pye refused renewal of the license but he did not insist on Graham vacating the land. Michael Graham, without Pye's permission, used the land until his death. In 1997 he registered cautions at the Land Registry against Pye's ownership, claiming to have acquired the fee simple as a result of adverse possession. Now his widow claims ownership of the land on the same grounds.

Held: Michael Graham fulfilled the requirements for adverse possession and therefore acquired the fee simple of the disputed land.

Judgment: Lord Browne-Wilkinson

The law

31 The apparently straight forward statutory provisions have given rise to considerable difficulties, most of which flow from the remarks of the Court of Appeal in *Leigh v Jack* (1879) 5 Ex D 264 and *Littledale v Liverpool College* [1900] 1 Ch 19. In a remarkable judgment at first instance, *Powell v McFarlane* (1977) 38 P & CR 452, Slade J traced his way successfully through a number of Court of Appeal judgments which were binding on him so as to restore a degree of order to the subject and to state clearly the relevant principles. Although there are one or two minor points on which (unlike Slade J) your Lordships are not bound by authority and can therefore make necessary adjustments, for the most part the principles set out by Slade J as subsequently approved by the Court of Appeal in *Buckinghamshire County Council v Moran* [1990] Ch 623 cannot be improved upon. Hereafter I adopt them without specific recognition beyond marking with inverted commas those passages which I have quoted verbatim.

Possession, dispossession, ouster and adverse possession

32 In Powell's case Slade J was considering the Limitation Act 1939. However, apart from paragraph 8(4) of Schedule 1 to the 1980 Act the statutory provisions applicable in the present case are identical in the 1939 Act and the 1980 Act. Slade J first addressed himself to the question what was the meaning of possession and dispossession in the statutory provisions. After noticing that possession and dispossession were not defined in the 1939 Act he continued, at p 469:

> 'Possession of land, however, is a concept which has long been familiar and of importance to English lawyers, because (inter alia) it entitles the person in possession, whether rightfully or wrongfully, to maintain an action of trespass against any other person who enters the land without his consent, unless such other person has himself a better right to possession. In the absence of authority, therefore, I would for my own part have regarded the word 'possession' in the 1939 Act as bearing the traditional sense of that degree of occupation or physical control, coupled with the requisite intention commonly referred to as animus possidendi, that would entitle a person to maintain an action of trespass in relation to the relevant land; likewise I would have regarded the word 'dispossession' in the Act as denoting simply the taking of possession in such sense from another without the other's licence or consent; likewise I would have regarded a person who has 'dispossessed' another in the sense just stated as being in 'adverse possession' for the purposes of the Act.'

Save as to the last sentence I have quoted (as to which I will make certain further comments below), I entirely agree with that statement of the law. ...

35 From 1833 onwards, therefore, old notions of adverse possession, disseisin or ouster from possession should not have formed part of judicial decisions. From 1833 onwards the only question was whether the squatter had been in possession in the ordinary sense of the word. That is still the law, as Slade J rightly said. After 1833 the phrase 'adverse possession' did not appear in the statutes until, to my mind unfortunately, it was reintroduced by the Limitation Act 1939, section 10 of which is in virtually the same words as para 8(1) of Schedule 1 to the 1980 Act. In my judgment the references to 'adverse possession' in the 1939 and 1980 Acts did not reintroduce by a side wind after over 100 years the old notions of adverse possession in force before 1833. ... Although it is convenient to refer to possession by a squatter without the consent of the true owner as being 'adverse possession' the convenience of this must not be allowed to reintroduce by the back door that which for so long has not formed part of the law.

36 Many of the difficulties with these sections which I will have to consider are due to a conscious or subconscious feeling that in order for a squatter to gain title by lapse of time he has to act adversely to the paper title owner. It is said that he has to 'oust' the true owner in order to dispossess him; that he has to intend to exclude the whole world including the true owner; that the squatter's use of the land has to be inconsistent with any present or future use by the true owner. In my judgment much confusion and complication would be avoided if reference to adverse possession were to be avoided so far as possible and effect given to the clear words of the Acts. The question is simply whether the defendant squatter has dispossessed the paper owner by going into ordinary possession of the land for the requisite period without the consent of the owner.

37 It is clearly established that the taking or continuation of possession by a squatter with the actual consent of the paper title owner does not constitute dispossession or possession by the squatter for the purposes of the Act. Beyond that, as Slade J said, the words possess and dispossess are to be given their ordinary meaning. ...

39 What then constitutes 'possession' in the ordinary sense of the word?

Possession

40 In Powell's case 38 P & CR 470 Slade J said, at p 470:

> '(1) In the absence of evidence to the contrary, the owner of land with the paper title is deemed to be in possession of the land, as being the person with the prime facie right to possession. The law will thus, without reluctance, ascribe possession either to the paper owner or to persons who can establish a title as claiming through the paper owner. (2) If the law is to attribute possession of land to a person who can establish no paper title to possession, he must be shown to have both factual possession and the requisite intention to possess ('animus possidendi').'

Counsel for both parties criticised this definition as being unhelpful since it used the word being defined-possession-in the definition itself. This is true: but Slade J was only adopting a definition used by Roman law and by all judges and writers in the past. To be pedantic the problem could be avoided by saying there are two elements necessary for legal possession: (1) a sufficient degree of physical custody and control ('factual possession'); (2) an intention to exercise such custody and control on one's own behalf and for one's own benefit ('intention to possess'). ... Such intention may be, and frequently is, deduced from the physical acts themselves. But there is no doubt in my judgment that there are two separate elements in legal possession. So far as English law is concerned intention as a separate element is obviously necessary. Suppose a case where A is found to be in occupation of a locked house. He may be there as a squatter, as an overnight trespasser, or as a friend looking after the house of the paper owner during his absence on holiday. The acts done by A in any given period do not tell you whether there is legal possession. If A is there as a squatter he intends to stay as long as he can for his own benefit: his intention is an intention to possess. But if he only intends to trespass for the night or has expressly agreed to look after the house for his friend he does not have possession. It is not the nature of the acts which A does but the intention with which he does them which determines whether or not he is in possession.

Intention to possess

(a) To own or to possess?

42 ...Slade J reformulated the requirement (to my mind correctly) as requiring an 'intention, in one's own name and on one's own behalf, to exclude the world at large, including the owner with the paper title if he be not himself the possessor, so far as is reasonably practicable and so far as the processes of the law will allow'.

(b) Must the acts of the squatter be inconsistent with the intentions of the paper owner?

...The suggestion that the sufficiency of the possession can depend on the intention not of the squatter but of the true owner is heretical and wrong. It reflects an attempt to revive the pre-1833 concept of adverse possession requiring inconsistent user. ...

An admission of title by the squatter is not inconsistent with the squatter being in possession in the meantime. ...

61 ... For all practical purposes the Grahams used the land as their own and in a way normal for an owner to use it throughout the period from August 1984 onwards. During that whole period Pye did nothing on the disputed land from which they were wholly excluded save on foot ...

Lord Hutton

75 In the present case from August 1984 onwards the Grahams made full use of the disputed land as if they were the owners-they did everything which an owner of the land would have done and when an experienced chartered surveyor, called on behalf of the plaintiffs, was asked in cross-examination what an occupying owner of the disputed land might have done over and above what was done by the Grahams between 1984 and 1997, he was unable to think of anything.

76 I consider that such use of land by a person who is occupying it will normally make it clear that he has the requisite intention to possess and that such conduct should be viewed by a court as establishing that intention, unless the claimant with the paper title can adduce other evidence which points to a contrary conclusion. Where the evidence establishes that the person claiming title under the Limitation Act 1980 has occupied the land and made full use of it in the way in which an owner would, I consider that in the normal case he will not have to adduce additional evidence to establish that he had the intention to possess. It is in cases where

the acts in relation to the land of a person claiming title by adverse possession are equivocal and are open to more than one interpretation that those acts will be insufficient to establish the intention to possess. But it is different if the actions of the occupier make it clear that he is using the land in the way in which a full owner would and in such a way that the owner is excluded.

77 The conclusion to be drawn from such acts by an occupier is recognised by Slade J in *Powell v McFarlane*, at p 472:

> 'If his acts are open to more than one interpretation and he has not made it perfectly plain to the world at large by his actions or words that he has intended to exclude the owner as best he can, the courts will treat him as not having had the requisite animus possidendi and consequently as not having dispossessed the owner.'

And, at p 476:

> 'In my judgment it is consistent with principle as well as authority that a person who originally entered another's land as a trespasser, but later seeks to show that he has dispossessed the owner, should be required to adduce compelling evidence that he had the requisite animus possidendi in any case where his use of the land was equivocal, in the sense that it did not necessarily, by itself, betoken an intention on his part to claim the land as his own and exclude the true owner.'

In another passage of his judgment at pp 471–472 Slade J explains what is meant by 'an intention on his part to … exclude the true owner':

> 'What is really meant, in my judgment, is that the animus possidendi involves the intention, in one's own name and on one's own behalf, to exclude the world at large, including the owner with the paper title if he be not himself the possessor, so far as is reasonably practicable and so far as the processes of the law will allow.'

78 It is clear that the fact that the Grahams would have given up occupation to the plaintiffs or would have made payment for their occupation to the plaintiffs, if requested to do so, does not prevent the existence of the intention to possess: see the judgment of the Privy Council delivered by Lord Diplock in *Ocean Estates Ltd v Pinder* [1969] 2 AC 19, 24.

79 Therefore I consider that Clarke LJ was right to state in *Lambeth London Borough Council v Blackburn* (2001) 82 P & CR 494, 504:

> 'I would not for my part think it appropriate to strain to hold that a trespasser who had established factual possession of the property for the necessary 12 years did not have the animus possidendi identified in the cases. I express that view for two reasons. The first is that the requirement that there be a sufficient manifestation of the intention provides protection for landowners and the second is that once it is held that the trespasser has factual possession it will very often be the case that he can establish the manifested intention. Indeed it is difficult to find a case in which there has been a clear finding of factual possession in which the claim to adverse possession has failed for lack of intention.'

80 In the present case I am of the opinion that the manner in which the Grahams occupied and used the land points unequivocally to the intention to possess and I further consider, for the reasons given by Lord Browne-Wilkinson, that the witness

statement of the late Mr Michael Graham, when it is considered as a whole and together with the other evidence, does not lead to a different conclusion.

Notes

(1) It should first of all be noted that the *Pye* case was not decided under the Land Registration Act 2002.[187] The old rules on adverse possession still applied. The case, however, is still relevant to us as far as it lays down the notion of adverse possession, ie the requirements of adverse possession. However, under the new law adverse possession will no longer automatically lead to loss of title by the owner and corresponding acquisition of title by the squatter.

(2) From the *Pye* case we can already infer most of the requirements for adverse possession. The first requirement is factual possession (the factum of possession) with the intention to hold and use the land for one's own benefit (*animus possidendi*). The intention is normally inferred from the factual possession. Hence, in the *Pye* case Lord Hutton held that normally if the facts point to possession the adverse possessor will not be required to give further evidence of an intention to possess (see his citation of Clarke LJ in *Lambeth London Borough Council v Blackburn* (2001) 82 P&CR 494).

(3) Second, the possession should be visible to the outside world or at least to the owner of the land. In *Powell v McFarlane* (1979) 38 P&CR 452 at 480 (adopted in *Lambeth LBC v Blackburn* [2001] EWCA Civ 912) Slade J held that the adverse possession should be sufficiently clear to the owner of the fee simple that the owner, 'if present at the land, would clearly appreciate that the claimant is not merely a persistent trespasser, but is actually seeking to dispossess him'. In the case of fraud or concealment no limitation period will run against the owner until the owner should, with reasonable diligence, have discovered the fraud or concealment (Limitation Act 1980, section 32(1)).

(4) This requirement of visibility demands that the possession exercised on the land should be unequivocal, that is to say, that the persons against whom a limitation period runs should reasonably understand that the adverse possessor claims possession and wishes to exclude them from possession. Behaviour that could also point to the exercise of an easement and does not necessarily point to exclusive possession cannot lead to adverse possession of the land. See for recent examples *Topplan Estates Ltd v Townley* [2004] EWCA Civ 1369 and *SS Global Ltd v Sava* [2007] EWHC2087 (Ch).

(5) Third, adverse possession cannot arise where the owner has given the occupier of the land a legal right to use the land, such as a lease or contract, or permission to use the land. However, if the right or permission is given for a certain time, the possession can become adverse after the expiration of the right or permission.

(6) Fourth, the adverse possession should have been for at least 10 years immediately preceding the adverse possessor's claim (Land Registration Act 2002, section 97, Schedule 6, paragaph 1(1)). It is irrelevant whether or not the adverse possessor is in good faith: even a possessor in bad faith will acquire the estate by adverse

[187] See also below, Chapter 10.

possession, such as the Grahams in the *Pye* case. Possession in good faith and possession in bad faith are treated the same: the requirements for adverse possession and the time needed are identical.

IV.B ACQUISITION OF A SERVITUDE BY PRESCRIPTION

In many legal systems acquisitive prescription of servitudes plays a very important role in 'neighbour law'. The rules as to how neighbours should behave are partly mandatory law and can partly be laid down by the neighbours themselves, eg by creating servitudes. In French and Dutch law the main mandatory rules of neighbour law, are to be found in the respective civil codes. In addition there are rules of public law which are outside the scope of this book.

The infringement of these mandatory rules normally gives the victim a right of action to make an end to the infringement. However, after a certain time the infringement might become legalised by prescription. This may take two different forms, acquisitive prescription of a servitude, or extinctive prescription of the right of action. The servitude, once acquired, runs with the land, both the dominant tenement and the servient tenement. Depending on the legal system, the same may be true for the extinctive prescription. If the latter prescription runs with both tenements, is does not lead to a servitude but to a situation which very much resembles a servitude. In reality this is more than just the disappearance of a right of action. The fact that the prescription runs with both tenements creates a *right* to maintain the current situation and a corresponding *duty* to tolerate the infringement, and, what is more, the right works against subsequent owners and users of the 'servient tenement'. German law, as we will see, makes use only of the technique of extinctive prescription to legalise infringements of neighbour law.

IV.B.1 FRENCH LAW

In French law servitudes may come into being as a result of a legal act of creation, acquisitive prescription, destination by the owner or a statutory provision.
In the case of acquisition of ownership by way of prescription two different prescription periods may apply, 10 or 30 years. However, acquisitive prescription of a right of servitude always demands possession for a period of 30 years (Article 690 Cciv). Article 2272 Cciv, which poses the requirements of a good legal ground and good faith, does not apply to servitudes.[188]

IV.B.1a Possession

All requirements applicable to acquisitive prescription of the right of ownership apply also to the acquisition by prescription of a right of servitude. Below we will look to these requirements only where the application to servitudes poses special problems. We will also see that the French Civil Code sets up additional requirements for acquisitive prescription of servitudes.

[188] Cass civ 3, 21 May 1979, no de pourvoi 77-14873.

IV.B.1.b Visibility and permanence

Introductory Note

Apart from the requirements of possession, additional requirements apply, namely that the servitude should be visible and permanent. Many cases on acquisitive prescription of servitudes are about having trees or windows in the so-called forbidden zone. According to Article 678 Cciv, the forbidden zone for windows, balconies and the like is 1.9 metres from the border between the two neighbouring pieces of land.

Another common example is a person claiming a right of way over his neighbour's land.

The requirement of permanence will not be fulfilled where someone claims possession of a right of way. There is no permanence if the exercise of a servitude demands human intervention. Moreover, according to French law, a right of way always requires such human intervention. Possession of the servitude starts when the possessor starts walking over his neighbour's land and equally ends when he has left his neighbour's land.

Cour de cassation, civ 3, 19 May 2004[189] **7.78 (FR)**

Nonde v Sassonia

PERMANENCE OF POSSESSION

Water channel

A servitude which needs continuous human intervention does not become permanent by an installation.

Facts: Ms Nonde claimed to have acquired through prescription a servitude to draw water from Sassonia's land. There was a water channel, pump and other equipment to exercise the right. The Court of Appeal dismissed her claim holding that the servitude was not permanent.

Held: A servitude is not permanent if it needs renewed human intervention, even if there is a permanent installation specially made to exercise the servitude.

Judgment: On the only argument: Considering, that according to the judgment on appeal (Lyon, January 9, 2003), Miss Nonde, started against the married couple Sassonia an action of revindication of a servitude to draw water and a right of way to exercise it;

Considering that Miss Nonde objects to the judgment refusing her requests with the following argument:

1 that a servitude is discontinuous only when its exercise lies in human intervention; that, when it is exercised by means of permanent installations built for this purpose, although the use is only discontinuous and requires for its suspension or its start the intervention of man, it is continuous; that the judges in lower instance, who noted the existence of a permanent installation built for this exercise and consisting

[189] No de pourvoi: 03-12451.

of an inlet filter and a pipe starting from the well and leading to a pump in Miss Nonde's house, violated Articles 688 and 691 of the Civil Code by their decision ...;

2 that the existence of permanent installations for the exercise of a right of way confers on the latter the character of a continuous servitude and, therefore, of a possession as owner which is able to lead to acquisition of the installation by thirty year prescription; that thus, the judgment violated Article 2229 of the Civil Code;

But considering that a servitude is discontinuous when it can be exercised only with renewed human intervention and that it remains such even if it would be made artificially permanent by means of adapted installations since these installations can function only under the control of man; that the Court of Appeal, which noted that the asserted servitude of drawing water did not base on any title related to the servient tenement, correctly deduced that Miss Nonde was to be refused her request;

It therefore follows that the argument is unfounded;

Cour de cassation, civ 3, 4 July 2001[190] **7.79 (FR)**

Galy v Carbonne

PERMANENCE OF POSSESSION

Servitude by prescription

A servitude is non-permanent if it needs human intervention; it can be acquired only by creation.

Facts: The border between Galy's land and the properties belonging to Carbonne had had large openings for more than 30 years. Carbonne claimed to have acquired a right of servitude of way over Galy's land by way of prescription.

Held: Even though the openings are permanent signs pointing towards a servitude, they do not render the servitude permanent. As a result, the servitude of way can come into being only by creation, not by prescription.

Judgment: On the claim formed by Mr Jean Galy, ..., on appeal in cassation of a judgment of the Court of Appeal of Toulouse (1st chamber in civil matters, 1st section), to the benefit of Mr Robert Carbonne ..., defendant on appeal in cassation;

The claimant invokes, to his benefit, an argument of cassation annexed to the present judgment; ...

Considering that in support of its decision that parcel no 74 section B, belonging to Mr Galy, is subject to a right of servitude of way for the benefit of parcels no 80 and no 95 section B, owned by Mr Carbonne, the judgment under attack (Toulouse, 7 December 1998) holds that the existence for more than thirty years of large openings to the parcel in connection with the purpose for which the parcel was leased and the position of the sheds show the existence of a continuous servitude with the effect that the discontinuous servitude, unable to be acquired by prescription, has received a continuous character making it possible to be acquired by prescription by the existence of the permanent large openings created by the owners with the intention to use the parcel under litigation to get access to their parcel.

With this reasoning the Court of Appeal violated the above-mentioned provisions.

[190] No de pourvoi: 99-12.425.

For these reasons, quashes and annuls.

Note

A non-permanent servitude cannot be acquired by prescription, however long it may have been exercised:

> [T]his article [691 Cciv] entails that facts of possession, even those from time immemorial, can be taken into consideration only as far as they do not apply to a discontinuous servitude, which can be acquired only by legal act.[191]

Where a drive, half of which covers one neighbour's land and the other half of which covers the other neighbour's land, has been used by both neighbours for a long time, this obstacle is often circumvented by judges by accepting that co-ownership has been acquired by way of prescription, rather than a servitude of passage:

Cour de cassation Req, 7 Feb 1883[192] **7.80 (FR)**

Roullier v Forêt

ACQUISITIVE PRESCRIPTION OF CO-OWNERSHIP

Co-owned drive

Rules on acquisitive prescription do not apply to acquisitive prescription of co-ownership.

Facts: A drive, half of which covered one neighbour's land and the other half of which covered the other neighbour's land, had been used by both neighbours for a long time. Roullier claimed that, because of Article 690 Cciv Forêt cannot have acquired a servitude of way through prescription. The Court of Appeal held that the drive is co-owned by both neighbours. Roullier asserted that the Court of Appeal had violated Article 690 Cciv.

Held: The Court of Appeal has not violated Article 690 Cciv.

Judgment: Considering that the rules on prescription of servitudes do not apply to co-ownership; that it follows that by holding that the drive in question existed since time immemorial, the judgment could validly decide that it should be maintained for the exploitation of both properties; that rather than violating Article 690 it has rightly applied the principles in this matter.

Note

Having windows within the forbidden zone gives rise to possession of a servitude to maintain the windows, which after 30 years leads to the acquisition of that servitude. In several French judgments the servitude is called a servitude of view. This awkward term gives the impression that the possession involved a servitude not only to maintain the window but also to have a free view from that window. The latter is, however, impossible since the possession of a servitude of view, although permanent,

[191] Cass civ 1, 26 January 1965, D.1965.372.
[192] DP 1884.1.128.

is invisible. The following judgment makes clear that the French Supreme Court indeed does not allow the acquisition by way of prescription of a servitude of view.

Cour de cassation, civ 3, 13 July 2005[193] **7.81 (FR)**

Sanz v Albanèse and another

SERVITUDE OF VIEW

Car parked in front of window

Servitude of view does not allow its holder to demand removal of parked car.

Facts: The Court of Appeal held that the spouses Albanèse had acquired a servitude of view by prescription, having had a window within the forbidden zone for more than 30 years. The court also held that, as a result, the spouses Sanz were not allowed to park a car in front of the window.

Held: A servitude of view gives the owner of the servient land the duty not to erect any construction within 1.90 metres of the window, but it does not restrict his right of ownership in any other form. Appeal allowed insofar as it forbids the spouses Sanz to park their car in front of the window.

Judgment: On the second argument : ...

Considering that the judgment under attack ..., held that the spouses Albanèse ... sued the spouses Sanz, in a possessory action to demand that they abstain from parking their vehicle within 1.90 metres of the view from which parcel no 504 benefits ;

Considering that, in prohibiting the spouses Sanz to park their vehicles within a distance of 1.90 metres from the window of spouses Albanèse the judgment holds that the spouses Albanèse have a right acquired by thirty-year prescription to maintain a window overlooking parcel no 123 belonging to spouses Sanz; that the debtor of a right of servitude of view cannot erect a building or construction within 19 decimetres from the outside of the wall in which the opening has been made, that in addition they cannot park their vehicles because that act should be equated with the creation of a window; that the parking of vehicles within a distance less then 19 decimetres therefore constitutes an interference with possession;

That in deciding thus, whereas the owner of the servient tenement burdened with a right of servitude of view is only under a duty not to erect a construction within 19 decimetres from the wall where the opening is situated and does not underlie any other restriction to his right of ownership, the Court of Appeal has violated the texts mentioned above ;...

For these reasons. Quashed and annuls, but only in so far as it prohibits the spouses Sanz from parking their vehicles within a distance of 1.90 metres from the window. ...

IV.B.1.c Unequivocal possession

Where a person is in possession of a thing together with another possessor, eg where a piece of land is co-owned, both owners will have the right to use the thing. If in fact only one of them uses the thing for a long time, in principle this possession cannot be regarded as exclusive possession, that is, excluding the other co-possessor.

[193] No de pourvoi: 04-13137.

Since the co-possessor is allowed to make use of the thing as a co-possessor, the other co-possessor will not be aware that the use is intended as exclusive. Such possession is called equivocal and cannot for that reason lead to the acquisition of exclusive ownership of the land.[194] Similarly, possession of a servitude exercised by a co-owner is often equivocal.

IV.B.1.d No prescription beyond your possession

If all conditions for acquisitive prescription of a servitude are met, the possessor will acquire a servitude which mirrors his possession. He cannot acquire more than he possessed. If the right which he possessed was a servitude to maintain a window in a wall within the forbidden zone, he will acquire a servitude to maintain that window, but not a servitude of a free view from the window. The above case about a servitude of view, Cour de cassation 13 July 2005, may give the impression, at first sight, that a servitude of view can be acquired by way of prescription but the judgment makes clear that the term servitude of view only means a servitude to maintain the window, not a genuine servitude of free view (*servitus prospectus*). The terminology is quite misleading. Another reason why a servitude of view cannot be acquired by prescription is invisibility. The presence of a window is visible, but the possession of a free view is not.

IV.B.1.e No possession in the case of permission or tolerance

Introductory Note

Where the use of another's land, which would otherwise amount to possession of a servitude, is based on the owner's permission no servitude can be acquired by way of prescription. The reason is that permission turns its beneficiary into a detentor or precarious possessor rather than a genuine possessor, thus excluding one of the requirements for acquisitive prescription.[195] The same happens in the case of mere tolerance: tolerance prevents possession from arising and blocks any prescription. Note that even express permission is often called tolerance in French law.

Cour de cassation, civ 3e, 17 June 1992[196] **7.82 (FR)**

Castellane v Vérand

TOLERANCE

Tolerated windows

Tolerance prevents prescription.

[194] Cass civ 1, 10 December 1968, Bull civ I, no 320.

[195] In the case of tolerance there will be no possession of a servitude in French law. See Jourdain, above n 72, 187; G. Baudry-Lacantinerie, *Traité théorique et pratique de droit civil*, vol 28: *De la prescription*, ed A Tissier, 3rd edn (Paris, Librairie de la société du recueil général des lois et des arrêts, 1905) 282.

[196] No de pourvoi: 90-14434; Bull 1992 III no 212.

Facts: By deed of 10 March 1950 Vérand, the owner of a parcel of land, no 199, gave permission to the predecessor of his neighbour Castellane to have windows within the forbidden zone, but added that the permission could be withdrawn by the owner of parcel 199 should the latter decide to erect a building on the parcel. Castellane later claimed to have acquired a right of servitude to maintain the windows.

Held: The prescription period of 30 years to acquire a servitude started running when in 1960 the building was erected on parcel 199. The prescription period was stopped by the writ of summons in 1982. The prescription therefore could not be completed.

Judgment: Considering that the judgment under attack (Grenoble, 21 February 1990), that Vérand, owner of parcel no 199, on which between 1960 and 1964 residential buildings were erected, demanded from Castellane the removal of the windows overlooking the neigbouring land, the right to which had been given by a deed of 10 March 1950, authorising them, by simple tolerance, to have in the house constructed in 1952 windows that did not meet the legal distance requirement, but with the obligation to remove them on first demand by the owners of parcel 199 after they had erected a building or construction;

Considering that Castellane claims that, according to the argument, it follows from the judgment itself that, by act of 10 March 1950, the owner of parcel 199 authorised the predecessor of Castellane to windows in question, that the authorisation was revocable on the condition that that owner has a building erected and that the revocation, subject to a date, must be exercised at the moment the building is finished and should be contemporeneous with the building process; that it follows that, since the revocation of the right has been exercised more than 20 years after the construction, Castellane has a permament and irrevocable right; that this autorisation created their right to maintain the wndows; that in holding, after having interpreted the deed of 1950 and the aforementioned power of revocation, that in addition they have not acquired a servitude by prescription, the judgment under attack has not drawn the correct conclusions from the facts it found and has misinterpreted the articles 637 and following and 1134 of the Civil Code;

But considering that Castellane on the basis of the act of 10 March 1950 benefited from a simple tolerance, revocable on first demand if Mrs Roux or her predecessors had erected a building, the Court of Appeal has legally justified its decision and rightly concluded that according to the provisions in Article 2232 of the Civil Code the acquisitive prescription of thirty years, invoked by Castellane, and interrupted by issuing the claim of 12 September 1982, started from the erection of Vérand's building in 1960 on parcel no 199. For these reasons, rejects the appeal.

Note

It is difficult to understand why the Cour de cassation holds that despite the deed of 10 March 1950 giving tolerance, a prescription period starts to run in 1960, when the building is erected. One could object that the tolerance still runs because it can be revoked at first demand, which has never happened. It seems that the Cour de cassation has accepted that erecting the building ended the toleration and that at the same moment possession of a servitude started, which after 30 years leads to acquisition of a servitude.

IV.B.1.f Compulsory right of way (enclave)

Code civil **7.83 (FR)**

Article 682 An owner whose land is enclosed and who has no way out to the public road, or only one which is insufficient either due to an agricultural, industrial or commercial exploitation of his land, or due to operations of construction or development that are being carried out, is entitled to claim on his neighbours' land a right of way sufficient for complete access to his own land, provided he pays a compensation in proportion to the damage he may cause.

Cour de cassation, civ 3, 19 May 1993[197] **7.84 (FR)**

Dury v Guillet and others

COMPULSORY RIGHT OF WAY

Access by car

Access by car is normal access to a piece of land with a dwelling house.

Facts: The Court of Appeal held that the Durys, the owners of the landlocked piece of land, had a compulsory right of way over land belonging to the Guillets, and that a modern access to the landlocked property with a dwelling house demanded access by car.

Held: The Court of Appeal has legally justified its decision.

Judgment: On the only argument: Considering that the spouses Guillet complain that the judgment under attack (Chambéry, 26 February 1991), recognising on a piece of land belonging to them the existence of a right of way for a landlocked piece of land held by Mr Dury enabling access to the land by cars, with the argument that, firstly, in basing its decision that the land of the spouses Guillet is subject to a right of way for cars, and not just for persons walking on the land on the sole reasoning that 'the normal requirements to reach a house in these times includes the access to the land by car' the Court of Appeal reasoned in too general terms (in violation of Article 455 of the new Code of Civil Procedure), and that, secondly, by leaving aside any investigation whether, due to the use of the land and the distance that separates it from the public road, a right footpath suffices for the land of Mr Dury, the Court of Appeal has not provided a sufficient legal basis to its decision (lack of legal basis in the light of Article 682 of the Civil Code);

But considering that Article 682 of the Code Civil recognises the right of the owner to reach landlocked land via the land of his neighbours in a way necessary for the complete access to his land, the Court of Appeal, which has stated that the access with a car corresponds to the normal use of a piece of land used for residential purposes, has legally justified its decision and, using its power to judge the facts, forming the right of way in the light of that the current needs of the landlocked land of Mr Dury.

For these reasons. Rejects the appeal.

[197] No de pourvoi: 91-14.819; Bull 1993 III no 71, 45.

IV.B.2 DUTCH LAW

According to Article 5:72 BW a servitude may come into being as a result of creation by legal act or as a result of prescription. There are two different ways to acquire a servitude by prescription. First, after 10 years the possessor of a right of servitude may acquire the right of servitude under Article 3:99 BW, provided he is in good faith. Second, the possessor of a servitude may even acquire a servitude if he is not in good faith, but in the latter case the prescription period is 20 years (Articles 3:105 and 3:306 BW). At first sight it seems relatively easy to acquire a right of servitude by prescription. The Dutch Civil Code requires possession of a right of servitude and a certain lapse of time, and for the 10-year prescription period, in addition, good faith is needed. Below it will be seen that it is quite difficult to meet all these requirements and acquire a servitude by prescription. Due to the principle that permission or toleration should not lead to a loss of right (like in French law), possession of a right of servitude should not readily be accepted. It is surprising to see how much uncertainty is left by the Dutch Supreme Court in these matters. Some important questions have never been answered in case law.

Many of the cases are about trees or windows in the so-called forbidden zone. Under Article 5:42 BW is it in principle forbidden to have trees or high shrubs within 2 metres of the border to another's land, unless the owner of the neighbouring land agrees. Similarly, for privacy reasons, it is not allowed to have windows within 2 metres of another's land that give a view on the neighbouring land, unless the owner of the neighbouring land agrees (Article 5:50 BW).

IV.B.2.a The ten-year period and the difficult requirement of good faith

Although in theory it is possible to acquire a servitude by prescription in 10 years' time, in practice this is almost impossible as a result of the stern requirements that apply. In *Huizing v NSAW*,[198] a case about trees within the forbidden zone, the Supreme Court stressed that Article 3:99 BW requires possession in good faith, ie possession in good faith of the right of servitude.[199] Article 3:99 BW requires possession in good faith of the right to be acquired, and in our case that is the right of servitude.[200]

In principle the possessor of a servitude can be in good faith only if a notarial deed has been made to create a right of servitude. It is difficult to imagine that someone thinks in good faith that he has a right of servitude if a notarial deed creating a right of servitude has never been made. The standard example of acquisition of a servitude by prescription in good faith will be the case in which a notarial deed was made but did not result in the creation of a valid right of servitude, for example because the deed was invalid or because the contract underlying

[198] HR 3 May 1996, NJ 1996/501.

[199] See already HR 16 December 1942, NJ 1943/61. See also the judgment of the appeal court in HR 16 November 1934, NJ 1935, 446.

[200] Art 3:99(1) BW reads: 'Rights in movable non-registered things and bearer or order rights are acquired by a possessor in good faith as a result of a continuous possession of three years, other assets as a result of a continuous possession of ten years.'

the creation was void or has been avoided with retroactive effect. Another, though very rare, case in which someone may believe in good faith that he has a right of servitude is the case in which he thinks his predecessor in title had acquired a right of servitude by prescription. In this instance as a matter of course no notarial deed has even been made.

Burgerlijk Wetboek **7.85 (NL)**

Article 3:99(1) Rights on movable objects which are not registered objects, and rights to bearer and order are acquired by a bona fide possessor by a continuous possession of three years, other objects and rights by a continuous possession of ten years.

IV.B.2.b The twenty-year period of Article 3:105 BW

The 20-year prescription period of Article 3:105 BW does not require good faith. As a result, in practice this article offers a much better opportunity to acquire a servitude by prescription. Planting trees within the forbidden 2-metre zone amounts to an infringement of the neighbour's right of ownership in the same way as adverse possession of the land itself does (trespassing). As a consequence, the neighbour has an action to have the infringement undone. This is an action of revindication: revindication means asserting your right of ownership. It is not confined to cases in which a stolen movable object is claimed back. After the action of stopping the infringement, the revindication, has been barred by limitation, the person who has the trees within the 2-metre zone acquires a right of servitude allowing him to have these trees on that spot, provided he can show that on this moment he actually has possession of a servitude.

Burgerlijk Wetboek **7.86 (NL)**

Article 3:105(1) The person who possesses an object or right at the moment that the action to end the possession lapses as a result of limitation acquires the object or right, even if his possession was not bona fide.

IV.B.2.c Possession of a servitude

(i) Recognisability

Possession of a right consists in the factual exercise of the right as if one owns the right in question.[201] This intention should be recognisable to third parties. In the case of a servitude the requirement of recognisability is met if the circumstances of the case clearly show that the person infringing another's right of ownership has the intention of exercising a right of servitude.[202]

[201] See in relation to servitudes HR 20 December 1901, W 7701.

[202] In the case of a servitude of view (*servitus prospectus*) the exercise does not consist in an infringement but in summoning the owner of the servient land not to block the view.

(ii) Visibility and permanence

The factual exercise of a right of servitude should appear from outward facts (Article 3:108 BW). Therefore, possession of a servitude can in principle exist only where there is a visible infringement of the ownership of a neighbouring land. And this is indeed what is present in our example of the trees. True, in a judgment from 1901[203] the Dutch Supreme Court held that possession of a servitude to have trees within the forbidden zone can exist only if the trees are held there with the intention to exercise a servitude, but from the presence of these trees, or windows, as the case may be, the possession of a servitude can easily be inferred.[204] The subjective intention of the person having trees or windows in the forbidden zone cannot be relevant to the question of possession because this intention is invisible. Relevant is therefore the objective intention which is apparent form the mere presence of the trees or windows in the forbidden zone.

An example of possession of a servitude which is invisible to others is the case in which someone claims to possess a servitude of view (*servitus prospectus*). If the person has enjoyed an undisturbed view over the undeveloped land of his neighbour there are no visible facts from which possession of this servitude can be inferred. Possession of such a servitude is conceivable only where the servitude was created by deed and entered into the public land register but did not come into being as a result of some defect. In this instance entry into the land register is vital as without such an entry possession would not be recognisable to others and would therefore be impossible (Article 3:108 BW). The mere fact that someone for a long time did not develop his land or part of his land cannot lead to the conclusion that his neighbour possesses a servitude of view. Similarly, the presence of windows within the forbidden zone points at possession of a servitude to maintain these windows, but it does not point at a servitude of an undisturbed view from these windows, because the first servitude does not encompass the second servitude and the second, the servitude of view, is invisible. Thus, possession of the servitude of view, which can lead to acquisition by prescription, cannot be accepted, apart from the above-mentioned case in which the right has been entered into the land register.

Hoge Raad, 30 December 1904[205] **7.87 (NL)**

Kieselbach v de Vetten

VISIBILITY OF SERVITUDE OF VIEW

Eight windows

Windows do not lead to continuous and visible possession of a servitude of view.

Facts: De Vetten had eight windows in a wall adjoining and overlooking the land of Kieselbach. The latter erected boards on his own land but in front of the windows. De Vetten claimed to have acquired

[203] HR 20 December 1901, W 7701.

[204] Asser/Scholten, *Zakenrecht*, 8th edn (Zwolle, Tjeenk Willink, 1945) 253; JPh Suijling, *Zakenrecht* (Haarlem, De Erven F Bohn, 1940) 201.

[205] *Weekblad van het recht* (*W*) 8165.

through prescription a servitude of light, air and view from these windows and demanded removal of the boards. The Court of Appeal held that De Vetten had acquired a servitude of light, air and view. Kieselbach appealed, claiming that such a servitude cannot be acquired by prescription because it is invisible. Only a servitude to maintain the windows could have been acquired by De Vetten.

Held: The presence of the windows leads to possession of a servitude to maintain these windows, but it does not lead to continuous and visible possession of a servitude to have a free view from these windows.

Judgment: Considering that, just as the neighbour should tolerate windows built in accordance with Articles 693–697 of the Civil Code, the claimant should always tolerate the eight windows built in violation of these articles in the defendant's wall next to the claimant's open yard, provided the defendant delivers the evidence, to which he is given the opportunity, that these windows have been present there for more than 30 years.

Considering, however, that this evidence could not lead to allowing the claim issued.

Considering namely that the said windows can be regarded as visible signs of the defendant's possession of the right to maintain these windows there and to have a view out of them over the neighbour's land as long as the opportunity lasts, but not as possession of a visible and continuous right of the defendant to that effect, which would amount to the defendant's right to prevent the claimant from building on his own land, also in front of the defendant's windows, and to erect board, as he has done.

Considering namely that the opposite side of such a right of the defendant would be the claimant's duty not to act, which would require a servitude in the sense of the last subsection of Article 725 of the Civil Code, that is an invisible servitude, which according to Article 746 of the Civil Code can only be created by deed. ... Quashes the judgment appealed against.

Note

Following French law, the old Dutch Civil Code of 1838 provided that a servitude could be acquired by prescription only if the servitude is visible and permanent. Moreover, it provided that possession of an invisible or non-permanent servitude was impossible.[206] The old Civil Code considered a right of way as a non-permanent servitude which could not be acquired by prescription.[207] An exception to this rule applied where the possession of a right of way was visible from the presence of, for example, a door leading to the neighbour's land or a path on the neighbour's land which can serve only the possessor of the servitude. In these instances the possession of the servitude is permanently visible to others.[208] Possession of a servitude of waterway was accepted where the waterway could only be used for the benefit of the possessor of the servitude and could not be of any benefit to the owner of the 'servient' land.

[206] Art 744, 746 and 593(2) BW 1838.

[207] Art 724(3) BW 1838.

[208] See HR 27 September 1996, NJ 1997/496 and HR 24 September 1999, NJ 2000/18. See also HR 27 May 1950, NJ 1951/197 (a toilet that was accessible only from the 'dominant' land) and HR 30 June 1978, NJ 1979/117 (right of waterway) and the comment by Kleijn to the judgment of 1978 (in NJ 1979).

Hoge Raad, 24 September 1999[209] **7.88 (NL)**

Damen v Giesbers

PERMANENCE OF POSSESSION

Split parcels

Possession of right of way can be permanent when a door is present.

Facts: Two houses had been built on a parcel of land. In the backyard there was a path to reach another path which is situated next to the parcel. The parcel had been split into two new parcels (nos 49 and 51). For a long time the owner of no 51, Damen, had used the path over no 49 to reach the side path. When the owner of no 49, Giesbers, blocked access to his path, the owner of no 51 claimed to have acquired a servitude of way over no 49 by way of destination by the common owner of both properties.

Held: The permanent presence of doors giving way to the servient land lead to permanent possession of a servitude. This, however, cannot be accepted in this case where it is only a path that is being used.

Judgment: ... 3.3.2. In the assessment of the argument the starting point should be that, according to the law in force of before 1 January 1992, a servitude of way or footpath is not continuous within the meaning of Article 744 and 747 (old) Civil Code, because it can only be exercised by human intervention. As the Supreme Court has accepted in its judgment of 27 September 1996, Nr 15 984, NJ 1997, 496, the circumstances of the case can, however, result to an exception to this rule. The Court of Appeal has misjudged this so that the argument is well-founded in this regards. Nevertheless, it cannot lead to an annulment of the judgment. In the concerned judgment the situation under discussion was rather characterised by having to tolerate the permanent presence of doors giving access to the servient tenement than by the circumstance that the actual use of both doors necessarily involved walking over the servient tenement.

Yet the ascertained facts that are being presented in part II of the argument do not allow another conclusion than that in the given circumstances there was not such a special situation as was present in the above-mentioned judgment. The Court of Appeal has therefore correctly judged that the servitude claimed by Damen and others cannot have been created by destination.

Notes

(1) The old Dutch Civil Code of 1838 required permanence of possession for the acquisition of a servitude by way of destination and prescription. As a result, the above citation is not only relevant for acquisition by destination but also for acquisition by prescription. The claimant asserted that he had acquired a servitude on the basis of either destination or prescription. In the proceedings that followed only the first ground, creation by destination, is at issue. This ground, which under the old Civil Code was based on the French parallel provision of Article 692 Cciv, has been abolished in Dutch law in 1992. Servitudes thus created under the old regime remain in force, but no new servitudes can be created in this manner.

(2) Although the requirement of permanence in the 1838 Dutch Civil Code derives from the similar French requirements, it seems that the Dutch Supreme Court inter-

[209] NJ 2000/18.

prets this requirement in a different way, in that it does not require a permanent exercise of the right of way. The mere presence of a door or path may turn the possession of the servitude permanent. If the door or path can be used only by the possessor of the servitude it is a visible sign of his possession. In French law, however, a servitude of way cannot be acquired by prescription, not even if there is a door, opening, or other visible sign.

(3) Meijers, when drafting the text of the new Civil Code, deleted the requirements of visibility and permanence because these requirements are already included in the requirement of possession.[210] Possession is of consequence only if it is visible and not secret, because if invisible and secret, possession, which is really a contradiction in terms, could lead to acquisitive prescription, and the owner of the 'servient' land would be taken by surprise by this prescription. He would not have had a chance to prevent the prescription by exercising his right of revindication. Such a prescription is not allowed in Dutch land law.[211] Although Meijers is less clear about the requirement of permanence, it seems that to his opinion this requirement is also included in the notion of possession. It is true that because the requirement of visibility and permanence are deleted in the text of the civil code, it is in theory possible to acquire a servitude which does not meet these two requirements, but in practice it will be extremely difficult to meet the requirement of possession over a certain period of time if the exercise of the servitude is invisible or not continuous. In this respect, therefore, the new Civil Code hardly deviates from the old one. As an example of a servitude that can be acquired by prescription under the new Civil Code but which could not be so acquired under the old one, Meijers mentioned the servitude of way. Where a right of way is exercised regularly possession of a servitude may be present.

(4) However, we should still conclude that possession of a servitude can hardly ever be accepted without visibility. If the possession is invisible it will almost always be secret and thus irrelevant, even non-existent. In addition, it is also difficult to conclude possession if the possession is not permanent. Furthermore, in the case of many servitudes of way visibility and permanence are intertwined. If the exercise of a right of way does not continue, it is often invisible to others. There are, however, cases in which the two requirements are clearly separated. In the case of a drainpipe hidden under a meadow there is permanence but no visibility.[212]

(5) Under the new Civil Code acquisition by prescription of a right of way seems possible only in two instances: first, where possession is visible from the presence of a path, door, etc, that can be of use only for the possessor of the right of way,

[210] Meijers' official comment on Arts 3.4.3.1 and 5.6.3 of the draft Civil Code.

[211] In the case of stolen movable property, on the other hand, it is held that a prescription period starts to run even though the owner is unable to exercise his action of revindication as he does not know who possesses the thing. Dutch property law seems inconsistent in this respect. See HR 8 May 1998, NJ 1999/44 ('Klooster in een landschap'). The solution in these cases seems to be based on the interest of certainty. In land law, however, it is always known against whom the action of revindication should be exercised.

[212] Different: comment on Art 1538 old Civil Code, in JC Voorduin, *Geschiedenis en beginselen der Nederlandsche Wetboeken*, vol V (Utrecht, Robert Natan, akademie-boekhandelaar, 1838) 183 and HR 26 January 1883, *Ned Regtspraak*, vol 133, 60 and HR 20 February 1890, *Ned Regtspraak*, vol 154, 133.

and, second, where the use of the way is so frequent that it can no longer be seen as a series of separate infringements but should be seen as a continuing and visible unlawful situation.

IV.B.2.d Unequivocal possession

Introductory Note

Possession should be unequivocal. This requirement was also deleted in the new Civil Code because the requirement is already included in the concept of possession.[213] The requirement is closely linked to the requirement of visibility in that both requirements stem from the general principle of property law that property relationships, including possession, should be recognisable.

Hoge Raad, 31 oktober 2003[214] **7.89 (NL)**

Keesmeekers v Driessen

EQUIVOCAL POSSESSION

Butcher's shop

Possession of servitude by owner of servient land is equivocal and therefore impossible.

Facts: The owners of a parcel of land, no 35, were at the same time users, but not owners, of the adjacent parcel, no 33. They erected buildings partly on parcel no 35 and partly on parcel no 33 for the benefit of the butcher's shop which they ran on parcel no 33. Parcel no 33 had been sold and transferred to Keesmeekers and parcel no 35 had been sold and transferred to Driessen. Driessen demolished the buildings on his land. Keesmeekers then sued Driessen, claiming to have acquired a servitude to maintain these buildings on parcel no 35 by prescription. In order to do so, he had to rely on his predecessor's possession of a right of servitude.

Held: As the owner of parcel no 35 erected the buildings himself he cannot, as user of parcel no 33, have behaved as possessor of a servitude over his own land. Since such possession would be equivocal, no possession can be accepted. For the same reason the former owner of parcel no 33 cannot have had possession of a servitude over parcel no 35.

Judgment: The owner of a parcel cannot simultaneously act as a holder of a limited property right over that same parcel. Moreover, the combination of these qualities—owner of the servient tenement and user of the dominant tenement—excludes the application of prescription because in such a case there cannot be unequivocal possession of a servitude. This judgment also means that there cannot in such a case be any mediate possession of a servitude on the side of the owner of the dominant tenement. ...

The Supreme Court of the Netherlands: rejects the appeal.

IV.B.2.e No possession in the case of permission or tolerance

Where the infringement of the right of ownership is based on express permission or mere tolerance (implicit permission), possession of a servitude can never be

[213] Comment of Meijers on Art 3.4.3.1.
[214] No C01/252HR NJ 2004/38.

accepted, not even possession in bad faith. No period of prescription or limitation will run against a person who gave permission for the infringement or tolerated it. The reason is that since the owner gave his permission he cannot and should not expect a loss of his right. No prescription or limitation period shall run against an unsuspecting owner. In order to live together as good neighbours it should safely be possible to tolerate minor violations of the right of ownership without the risk that it will lead to a right or duty.[215]

This changes only from the moment that the person who was given permission (the user) claims to have more than just a personal right of use based on permission, for example a right of servitude or even a right of ownership. Moreover, he should inform the owner about this claim because otherwise the owner still thinks that the continuing use of his land is based on the permission he has given. A prescription and limitation period will only start to run from the moment that the user informed the owner about his claim. The owner will then have plenty of time to assert his rights and prevent any prescription or limitation.

Hoge Raad, 20 December 1901[216] **7.90 (NL)**

Albers v Colenbrander

REPLANTING TREES IN THE FORBIDDEN ZONE

The six poplars

Extinctive prescription of the action to remove trees does not give the right to plant new trees.

Facts: Colenbrander had a row of poplars on his land in the neighbourhood of Albers' land. He cut six of these poplars and replanted new poplars on the same spot, within the forbidden zone. Albers demanded that Colenbrander should remove these trees. Colenbrander claimed that he has acquired by way of prescription a servitude to have trees within the forbidden zone. The Court of Appeal accepted that a servitude has been created by way of prescription.

Held: The mere planting of trees within the forbidden zone cannot lead to a servitude by way of prescription. Even if the action to have the trees removed would underlie extinctive prescription, such prescription only entails that no claim for the removal of the trees can be issued. It does not, however, entail that the neighbour lacks the right to issue a claim for the removal of new trees planted to replace the old ones.

Judgment: [T]hat the acquisition by way of prescription of a servitude requires that he who relies on it, or his predecessors in title, have exercised the powers [of that servitude] during the period set by law as if they had the right of servitude, that is, with the intention of the rightful holder of that right;

That the mere having of trees within the forbidden distance does not qualify as such, if it is unclear in which circumstances and with which intention this has been done;

That such an entirely factual situation, irrespective of its duration, can never develop into a property right of servitude …

[215] G Diephuis, *Het Nederlandsch burgerlijk regt*, vol 6 (Groningen, JB Wolters, 1880) 443–44.
[216] HR 20 December 1901, W 7701. See also Suijling, above n 205, 201; Pitlo/Reehuis, no 631.

That … even if one accepts that the claim given by Article 714 of the Civil Code to the neighbour lapses as a result of non-user during 30 years, this can only (since no servitude has been created) have as a consequence that the removal of the old trees can no longer be claimed; that, however, the neighbour has the right to claim removal of the trees that have been planted to replace the old ones. …

Note

Here the Supreme Court seems to hold that having trees within the forbidden zone cannot lead to the acquisition by way of prescription of a servitude to maintain the trees. If this is the true meaning of the judgment, it is outdated on this point. The difference with modern law, in which it is accepted that this having of trees suffices for acquisitive prescription, need not be large, if it is accepted that the extinctive prescription of the action of removal runs with both properties.[217] When possession of a servitude to maintain a tree within the forbidden zone has led to acquisition of the servitude in question, the servitude is confined to maintaining that specific tree. The possessor does not acquire a servitude to plant and maintain other trees within the forbidden zone. So, he is not allowed to plant extra trees in the zone. What is more, if the original tree dies or if it is blown over, he is not allowed to plant a new tree on the same spot as a substitute. Acquisitive prescription is limited to what the acquirer possesses. Sometimes this thought is expressed by the adage *tantum praescriptum quantum possessum* (as much has prescribed as was held in possession). To give another example, from the presence of a window within the forbidden zone we may infer possession of a servitude to maintain the window, but not more than that. We cannot infer from these facts the possession of a servitude of view or a servitude that the neighbour shall not erect a building over a certain height. As said previously, in principle a servitude of view cannot be possessed as possession of such a right is invisible.[218]

IV.B.2.f The consequence of permission (other than toleration)

Introductory Note

Permission given to the owner of a neighbouring piece of land to deviate from the rules of neighbour law creates a personal right of use. Where, however, someone has a right to claim a compulsory right of way, and permission is given to him to walk or drive over his neighbour's land, his right should really be seen as a property right rather than a mere personal right. Less clear is the legal status of permission to have trees or windows in the forbidden zone.

[217] That the extinctive prescription runs with both tenements has been defended for Dutch law by LPW van Vliet in *Verjaring en erfdienstbaarheid*, Nederlands Tijdschrift voor Burgerlijk Recht (2004/5) 206–25, at 222.

[218] Unless such a right has been created by notarial deed and entered into the land register.

Burgerlijk Wetboek **7.91 (NL)**

Article 5:42 (1) It is not allowed to have trees, shrubs or hedges within the distance from another's land indicated in paragraph 2, unless the owner has given his permission or unless the land is a public road or public water.

(2) The distance indicated in paragraph 1 is two meters for trees measured from the middle of the base of the tree and for shrubs and hedges half a metre, unless a smaller distance is allowed under a municipal byelaw or a local custom. …

Article 5:50 (1) Unless the owner of the neighbouring land has given his permission, it is not allowed to have within a distance of two meters from the boundary of the neighbour's land windows or other openings in a wall or balconies and other similar buildings giving a view on the neighbouring land.

Note

Articles 5:42 and 5:50 BW both state that having trees or windows in this zone is allowed if the neighbour whose right of ownership is thus violated gives his permission to have or maintain these trees or windows. It is unclear whether this permission creates a mere personal right or rather a proprietary right. In any case, the permission can be entered into the public land register and, if so entered, it works against subsequent owners of the 'burdened' property. Therefore, the right so acquired shares an important feature of property rights: it has absolute effect, ie it works against third parties.

IV.B.2.g Compulsory right of way

When answering the question whether the owner of a piece of land has acquired a right of way by prescription we should note that in some cases a person is under a duty to allow his neighbour to walk or drive over his land even if there is no servitude to that effect. This is called a compulsory right of way (*noodweg* in Dutch) (Article 5:57 BW). The owner has the right to require a compulsory right of way if his plot of land has no (adequate) entry to a public road or public waterway. The owner of the neighbouring piece of land over which the public road or waterway would be accessible has to give a right of way to the owner of the landlocked plot of land. If access is possible over different pieces of land from different owners, the owners of these lands should negotiate who is to give a right of way. If they cannot reach agreement the judge will determine who is to give a right of way. The neighbour acquiring the compulsory right of way has to pay a fair compensation. Dutch law does not share the French view that permission to cross the neighbour's land to leave the enclave prevents the acquisition of a compulsory right of way. Moreover, unlike French law, Dutch law does not call the compulsory right a servitude. In French law it is called a legal servitude, as the law confers this right automatically to the owner of closed off land. See also Chapter 3.

IV.B.3 GERMAN LAW

Introductory Note

Under German law acquisitive prescription of servitudes is possible only under very strict conditions in the form of 'land register prescription' (§900 BGB). It therefore presupposes an entry in the land register. The mere exercise of a servitude of way or the mere presence of windows or trees in the forbidden zone can never lead to the acquisition of a right of servitude. As a result, acquisitive prescription of servitudes is much less important in German law and gives rise to a lot less case law than in French and Dutch law.

Many infringements of neighbour law are solved in a different way, namely by extinctive prescription of the right of action to stop the infringement. Unlike French and Dutch law, German law has only part of its rules on neighbour law in its Civil Code. Many others are to be found in special legislation. Most of the *Bundesländer* have a neighbour statute (*Nachbarrechtsgesetz*) or a number of specific statutes on neighbour law issues. Rules on having trees or windows in the neighbourhood of the borderline and many other rules are to be found in these statutes.

Many of the neighbour law actions based on the German Civil Code do not underlie prescription, but some of the special statutes do subject some of the neighbour law actions to extinctive prescription, see eg Article 52(1) of the Bavarian Gesetz zur Ausführung des Bürgerlichen Gesetzbuchs und anderer Gesetze (AGBGB). This particular extinctive prescription runs with the land both on the positive side (the holder of the action) and on the negative side, the person infringing the neighbour law rules.[219]

Bürgerliches Gesetzbuch **7.92 (DE)**

§917 Notweg—Compulsory right of way (1) If a plot of land does not have access to a public road necessary for ordinary use, the owner may demand from his neighbours that they allow the use of their land for making the necessary connection to correct the fault. If necessary the direction of the compulsory way and the extent of the right of use will be decided by the court.

(2) The neighbours on whose land the compulsory way runs have to be compensated in money. ...

IV.B.4 ENGLISH LAW[220]

Introductory Note

In English law only easements and *profits à prendre* can be acquired by way of prescription. The English law of acquisitive prescription is obscured by the facts that prescription may be based on three different bases. The first two, common law

[219] H Grziwotz and RR Saller, *Bayerisches Nachbarrecht*, 2nd edn (Munich, CH Beck, 2010) 71.

[220] In June 2011 the English Law Commission presented a report ('Making Land Work: Easements, Covenants and *Profits à Prendre*', Law Com no 327), which proposes, among other things, to simplify the rules on acquisition of easements by prescription.

prescription and lost modern grant, are based on the common law, the third basis is the Prescription Act 1832.

It seems as if English law felt uneasy about acquisition of easements and profits by mere lapse of time. It uses a presumption that in the past a grant has taken place.[221] In the doctrine of common law prescription, long use was seen as pointing to a usage that started before remembered time, a moment in time that was defined as the year 1189, the beginning of the reign of Richard I.[222] If usage from before 1189 could be established the use had become unimpeachable. The user of the easement or profit was helped in giving the required evidence by a presumption that 20 years' usage was evidence of usage since 1189. This presumption was, however, open to rebuttal.[223] It can often be proved that user of the easement or profit could never have existed since 1189, for example if an easement is exercised for the benefit of a building which was erected only after 1189 (*Duke of Norfolk v Arbuthnot* (1880) 5 CPD 390), or when the dominant and servient land have been in the hands of the same owner after 1189. For this reason common law prescription is not very important in modern law.

To solve this problem another doctrine was developed. Where it was obvious that no easement or profit could have been exercised since 1189, the law was willing to accept that 20 years' usage gives rise to a presumption that there has been a grant after 1189, called a 'modern' grant, which was subsequently lost: the doctrine of lost modern grant. However, even this presumption could be rebutted, namely by evidence showing that no such grant could have taken place, for example because the party who could have granted the easement or profit during the period prior to the 20 years' usage was incapable of doing so (*Dalton v Angus* (1881) App Cas 740).

A third basis for acquisitive prescription of easements and profits is the Prescription Act 1832. The Act is not self-containing, but rather presupposes the existence of the first two grounds described above. The required prescription period varies according to the type of right claimed and is either 20 or 40 (for easements) or 60 years (for profits) (sections 1–3). The existence of three different bases for acquisitive prescription is very confusing and has received judicial disapproval the Court of Appeal's judgment in *Tehidy Minerals v Norman* [1971] 2 QB 528 per curiam, at 543:

> The co-existence of three separate methods of prescribing is, in our view, anomalous and undesirable, for it results in much unnecessary complication and confusion. We hope that it may be possible for the Legislature to effect a long-overdue simplification in this branch of the law.

Acquisitive prescription of easements and profits requires, apart from the lapse of time, the following: usage as of right, which means: usage without force (*nec*

[221] EH Burn and J Cartwright, *Cheshire and Burn's Modern Law of Real Property*, 17th edn (Oxford, Oxford University Press, 2006) 613.

[222] See eg *The Earl of Stamford v Dunbar* (1845), 13 M & W 822, at 826 and *Jenkins v Harvey* (1835), 2 CM & R 393, at 400. See also introductory text to the Prescription Act 1832.

[223] *The Earl of Stamford v Dunbar* (1845), 13 M & W 822, at 826; WS Holdsworth, *Historical Introduction to the Land Law* (Oxford, Oxford University Press, 1927) 282.

vi), without concealment (*nec clam*), ie visible usage, and without permission (*nec precario*) (the famous Roman law requirements of *nec vi*, *nec clam*, *nec precario*). Tolerance may have the same effect as permission rendering acquisitive prescription impossible. However, it is not used as a technical term; in similar cases it is treated as amounting to some sort of implied permission, in other cases it is seen as acquiescence (see eg *Smith v Brudenell-Bruce* [2002] 2 P&CR 51). The latter term, which is used as a technical term, means not stopping the intrusion on your rights in a situation where you knew or could reasonably have known about the intrusion and where you were able to and expected to stop such user. It forms the basis of every acquisitive prescription in land law (*Dalton v Angus* (1881) App Cas 740).

House of Lords, 13 November 2003[224] **7.93 (E&W)**

R (ex parte Beresford) v Sunderland City Council

CONCEPT OF PERMISSION OR PRECARIO; VIOLENCE AND VISIBILITY

Sports arena

If there is no permission or implied permission the use is as of right so that prescription runs.

Facts: Sunderland City Council was the owner of a sports arena. The arena, which was open to the public, had been used by the general public for recreational purposes for more than 20 years. When the City Council planned to develop the ground, the appellant applied to the City Council for registration of the land as a town or village green under section 13 of the Commons Registration Act 1965. The City Council refused the application, contending that the use had not been 'as of right' within the meaning of section 22 of the Act, since the use was based on implied permission by the City Council. Both at first instance and at the Court of Appeal the applicant's claim was rejected with the same argument.

Held: The sports arena should be registered as a town or village green, because the user was as of right within the meaning of section 22(1) of the Commons Registration Act 1965. There was no implied permission.

Judgment: Agreeing, Lord Rodger of Earlsferry said: My lords,

[53] The town of Washington lies within the jurisdiction of the Sunderland City Council (the council). From at least 1977, members of the public have used an area near the town centre—referred to as 'the sports arena'—for recreation. In truth, it is just an open, flat area of grass of some 13 acres that Washington Development Corporation had laid out in Page 13 [2003] UKHL 60, [2004] 1 EGLR 94 around 1974. In the Washington New Town Plan 1973, the land was identified as 'parkland/open space/playing field'. In 1977, around the time of the Queen's silver jubilee visit to the ground, the development corporation constructed wooden seats along much of the perimeter. A hard-surface cricket pitch was laid out in 1979. For the rest, the public bodies that have owned the land—most recently, the council—have done little except to keep the grass cut. Local people have used the ground in their different ways. Toddlers have played there, children of all ages have kicked a ball around or played cricket and other games, a Sunday league football team has used it for its

[224] [2003] UKHL 60, [2004] 1 EGLR 94.

matches. Many have simply treated it as a place to picnic, socialise, take their ease in the sunshine or walk the dog.

[54] In 1999, the appellant, Mrs Pamela Beresford, sought to register the area as a town or village green under the Commons Registration Act 1965. In terms of the relevant part of the definition in section 22(1), as it then stood, a town or village green means land upon which the inhabitants of any locality have indulged in lawful sports and pastimes as of right for not less than 20 years. Having considered a well-reasoned and objective submission by their director of administration, the council, acting as the registration authority, refused Mrs Beresford's application, but only on the ground that although the land had indeed been used for lawful sports and pastimes for more than 20 years, the use had not been as of right but by virtue of an implied licence from the owners.

[55] In *R v Oxfordshire County Council, ex parte Sunningwell Parish Council* [2000] 1 AC 335, Lord Hoffmann explained, in illuminating detail, why the words as of right are to be interpreted in the same way in section 22(1) of the 1965 Act as in section 5 of the Prescription Act 1832 (as amended) and section 1(1) of the Rights of Way Act 1932. Long before, in *Gardner v Hodgson's Kingston Brewery Co Ltd* [1903] AC 229, at pp 238 and 239, both Lord Davey, impliedly, and Lord Lindley, expressly, had held that these words in the 1832 Act were intended to have the same meaning as the older expression *nec vi, nec clam, nec precario*. Lord Hoffmann adopted that interpretation and translated the phrase as 'not by force, nor stealth, nor the licence of the owner': see p 350H. So, if the inhabitants of any locality have engaged in lawful sports and pastimes *nec vi, nec clam, nec precario* for at least 20 years, they have engaged in them as of right and the land can be registered as a town or village green in terms of the 1965 Act.

[56] It is not suggested that members of the public used the sports arena vi—by force: the owners did not try to stop them and so there was no question of them overcoming any resistance on the owners' part. Equally, the public was not enjoying itself clam—by stealth: on the contrary, they used the land openly and the owners knew what was going on. The council concluded, however, that the local residents and others enjoying the land had been doing so precario, by virtue of the licence of the owners of the land. Admittedly, there was nothing to show that the owners had given any express permission or licence to the public. But the facts as a whole, and the cutting of the grass, and the construction of the seating in particular, showed that the owners had actively encouraged the use of the area for recreation and so had impliedly granted a licence, or given permission, for it to be used in that way. Use of the land by virtue of this licence or permission could not constitute use as of right for purposes of section 22(1) of the 1965 Act. Smith J at [2001] 1 WLR 1327 dismissed Mrs Beresford's application for certiorari to quash the council's decision, and the Court of Appeal dismissed her appeal: see [2001] EWCA 1218; [2002] QB 874.

[57] In Roman law, 'precarium' is the name given to a gratuitous grant of enjoyment of land or goods that is revocable at will. The arrangement is informal, and is based upon the grantor's goodwill, whether more or less enthusiastic. But however informal, the arrangement does involve a positive act of granting the use of the property, as opposed to mere acquiescence in its use. The name suggests, and the digest texts indicate, that, in Roman law, the paradigm case is of a grant in response to a request. The arrangement lasts for only so long as the grantor allows, *tamdiu quamdiu is qui concessit patitur*: D43.26.1 pr, Ulpian 1 *institutionum*. The concept

of *precarium* crops up in different areas of Roman law, but, importantly, in connection with interdicts. The praetor protects someone from interference if he has taken possession of land, or has begun carrying out work *nec vi, nec clam, nec precario*.

[58] In *De legibus et consuetudinibus Angliae*, Bracton took over the noun precarium and its congeners from the vocabulary of Roman law and used them in a number of contexts, but always with reference to a gratuitous grant that is revocable at any time at the grantor's pleasure. See, for instance, lib 2 ff52 and 52b. In lib 4 f221, Bracton discusses the acquisition of easements by use for some time *nec vi, nec clam, nec precario*—the last being, he says, the same as *de gratia*, of grace. Under reference to the second of these passages, in speaking of the use of a watercourse in *Burrows v Lang* [1901] 2 Ch 502, at p 510, Farwell J asked 'What is precarious?' and answered his own question: 'That which depends, not on right, but on the will of another person.' Some years before, in Sturges v Bridgman [1879] 11 Ch D 852, at p 863, Thesiger LJ had indicated that if a man 'temporarily licenses' his neighbour's enjoyment, that enjoyment is precario in terms of the civil law phrase nec vi, nec clam, nec precario. It is important to notice that, in this regard, English law distinguishes between an owner who grants such a temporary licence or permission for an activity and an owner who merely acquiesces in it: see Gale on Easements (17th ed) 2002, para 4-83. Someone who acts with the mere acquiescence of the owner does so nec precario.

[59] The council were, accordingly, entitled to refuse Mrs Beresford's application for registration of the area as a town or village green only if those who used the sports arena did so by the revocable will of the owners of the land, that is to say, by virtue of a licence that the owners had granted in their favour and could have withdrawn at any time. The grant of such a licence to those using the ground must have comprised a positive act by the owners, as opposed to their mere acquiescence in the use being made of the land. Prudent landowners will often indicate expressly, by a notice in appropriate terms or in some other way, when they are licensing or permitting the public to use their land during their pleasure only. But I see no reason, in principle, why, in an appropriate case, the implied grant of such a revocable licence or permission could not be established by inference from the relevant circumstances.

[60] In the present case, the owners did not expressly license the use of the land by the public. The council rely upon two circumstances, however, as justifying the inference that those who used the sports arena did so *precario*, merely by licence from the owners of the land. The first is that the owners cut the grass. But that is at least equally explicable on the basis that the owners were concerned, as many owners would be, for the appearance of such a large and prominent area of open land in the heart of the town. Like charity, care of amenities begins at home. The second matter relied upon is the now rather dilapidated wooden seating along the perimeter. Whatever may have been its original purpose, the continued existence of the seating is consistent with the owners of the land having acquiesced, perhaps quite happily, in people using the area for football or other games that their friends or relatives would wish, or feel obliged, to watch. To an extent, the owners may thus have encouraged these activities. The mere fact that a landowner encourages an activity on his land does not indicate, however, that it takes place only by virtue of his revocable permission. In brief, neither cutting the grass nor constructing and leaving the seating in place justifies an inference that the owners of the sports arena positively granted a licence to local residents and others, who were then to

be regarded as using the land by virtue of that licence, which the owners could withdraw at any time.

[61] In these circumstances, I would conclude that local people used the land *nec precario*.

[62] After the first hearing of the appeal, however, your lordships invited further written and oral submissions from counsel upon whether any of the statutes that might apply to local authority land had conferred on the local residents and others a right to use the sports arena, with the result that their use would be 'of right', as opposed to being 'as of right' in terms of section 22(1) of the 1965 Act. Having considered those submissions, for the reasons given by my noble and learned friend Lord Walker of Gestingthorpe, I am satisfied that, on the agreed facts, neither the designation of the land as 'open space' in the new town plan nor any of the statutes conferred any such right in this case.

[63] It follows that the local residents and others indulged in their sports and pastimes on the sports arena 'as of right' in terms of section 22(1). Mrs Beresford is accordingly entitled to have the land registered under the 1965 Act as a town or village green. ...

[65] The phrase 'nec vi, nec clam, nec precario', taken over from Roman law, has resounded just as powerfully among Scottish lawyers and judges as among their brethren south of the border. But in reading the Scottish cases, a linguistic point must be noted. English judges have tended to use 'tolerance' as a synonym for 'acquiescence': see, for instance, *Mills v Silver* [1991] Ch 271. Scottish judges, on the other hand, have tended to use the term 'tolerance' as a synonym for 'permission' and as a translation of 'precarium'. This is perfectly understandable, since an owner who, perhaps somewhat reluctantly, decides to permit the public to walk across his land until further notice may be said to 'tolerate' them doing so. That is what Lord Cockburn had in mind when he said, in Napier's Trustees, at p 1408, that the defenders have possessed the road 'by no trespass or tolerance, but as a public road'. Similarly, in a different context, in *Scottish Property Investment Co Building Society v Horne* (1881) 8 R 737, at p 740, Lord President Inglis said that to warrant the remedy of summary ejection, the defender's possession of premises had to be vicious, that is, obtained by fraud or force, or precarious possession. He added: 'A precarious possession is a possession by tolerance merely.' It is in this sense that Lord Kinnear, a recognised authority on Scottish land law, uses the phrase 'tolerance or permission' in Folkestone Corporation v Brockman [1914] AC 338, at p 356.

[66] In *Marquis of Bute v McKirdy & McMillan Ltd* 1937 SC 93, for some 70 years the public on the Isle of Bute had used a track to pass from a public road to part of the foreshore for purposes of bathing and recreation. The Marquis of Bute, who owned the relevant land, contended that the use of the track by the public should be attributed to the tolerance of himself and his predecessors in title. He therefore sought an interdict against a bus company that had been bringing large numbers of trippers to the point on the public road from which they could use the track to get to the beach. Rejecting the pursuer's contention, Lord President Normand held, at pp 119–120, that the proper question was whether: having regard to the sparseness or density of the population, the user over the prescriptive period was in degree and quality such as might have been expected if the road had been an undisputed right of way. If the public user is of that degree and quality, the proprietor, who fails for the prescriptive period to assert or to put on record his right to exclude the public, must be taken to have remained inactive, not from tolerance,

but because the public right could not have been successfully disputed or because he acquiesced in it. The First Division of the Court of Session, having concluded that the bus company had proved the existence of a public right of way for pedestrians, pronounced decree of absolvitor in their favour.

[67] In *Cumbernauld and Kilsyth Council v Dollar Land (Cumbernauld) Ltd* 1992 1035, the council raised an action of declarator that a public right of way existed over a raised walkway crossing the centre of Cumbernauld. The walkway, which the defenders had bought, along with other properties, from Cumbernauld Development Corporation, was extensively used by the public to get from one part of the town to another. Holding that a public right of way had been established, Lord President Hope observed, at p 1042I: the occasional or irregular use of a path by hillwalkers or by others who resort to the countryside can readily be distinguished from the continuous use of it by members of the public as a route from one public place to another. It seems to me to be clear, on an examination of all the later authorities, that a proprietor who allows a way over his land to be used by the public in the way the public would be expected to use it if there was a public right of way cannot claim that that use must be ascribed to tolerance, if he did nothing to limit or regulate that use at any time during the prescriptive period. In dismissing the appeal to this House from the decision of the First Division (1993 SC (HL) 44, at p 47A–D), Lord Jauncey adopted and approved both this passage from the opinion of Lord President Hope and the passage that I have quoted from the opinion of Lord President Normand in Marquis of Bute. Lord Jauncey went on to note, at pp 47H–48A, that there is no principle of law that requires that there be conflict between the interest of the users of the right of way and those of a proprietor. If acquiescence could lead to a public right of way being established, 'encouragement can even more readily be said to have the same consequences'.

[68] Similarly, in the present case, for at least 20 years before Mrs Beresford made her application, the inhabitants of Washington had played and passed the time on the sports arena in the way in which they could have been expected to do as of right on a town or village green. Therefore, in the absence of any act on the owners' part to regulate the activities on the land or otherwise to show that the inhabitants were disporting themselves only by the owners' revocable leave or licence, it is proper to infer that the owners had acquiesced in the inhabitants' use of the land as of right. The same result follows if the owners are thought to have encouraged the activities.

[69] For these reasons, as well as those given by my noble and learned friends Lord Bingham of Cornhill and Lord Walker of Gestingthorpe, I would allow the appeal.

Agreeing, Lord Walker of Gestingthorpe said: …

[72] It has often been pointed out that 'as of right' does not mean 'of right'. It has sometimes been suggested that its meaning is closer to 'as if of right': see, for instance, Lord Cowie in Cumbernauld and *Kilsyth District Council v Dollar Land (Cumbernauld) Ltd* 1992 SLT 1035, at p 1043, approving counsel's formulation. This leads at once to the paradox that a trespasser (so long as he acts peaceably and openly) is in a position to acquire rights by prescription, whereas a licensee, who enters the land with the owner's permission, is unlikely to acquire such rights. Conversely, a landowner who puts up a notice stating 'Private Land—Keep Out' is in a less strong position, if his notice is ignored by the public, than a landowner whose notice is in friendlier terms: 'The public have permission to enter this land on foot for recreation, but this permission may be withdrawn at any time.'

Notes

(1) The above case shows that in English law a difference should be made between permission, implied permission and acquiescence. Implied permission is comparable to the French and Dutch term 'tolerance'. It renders the possession precarious, or, in Dutch and French law, it leads to *detentio* rather than possession, thus excluding prescription. The term acquiescence means that the owner does nothing to stop prescription running against him: he does not prevent the use by the possessor nor grants permission to the user. Both actions, ending the use or granting permission, would stop prescription.

(2) Although the case is about permission only the judgment also treats the influence of violence and invisibility. As in French and Dutch law, both prevent prescription from running against the owner of the land.

IV.B.4.a Continuous use

Introductory Note

In order to lead to acquisitive prescription the use should also be continuous. Note, however, that in English law the requirement of continuity is interpreted differently from French law: unlike French law, English law does not regard a right of way as non-continuous by definition. It is a striking example of how seemingly similar requirements are interpreted in such a way as to make them very different in content.

High Court, Chancery Division, 6 February 1974[225] **7.94 (E&W)**

Diment v NH Foot Ltd

CONTINUITY OF RIGHT OF WAY

Panhandle

Infrequent but regular use may be continuous.

Facts: The predecessors in title of NH Foot Ltd had owned Bookham Farm since 1920. The adjoining farm to the west, Sanctions Farm, was owned by Mrs Diment. West of Sanctions Farm there was a public road. Between 1936 and 1967 Mrs Diment gave the farm in agricultural lease. In order to reach the public road from the west part of Bookham Farm, the so-called panhandle, the predecessors of the defendant used the field belonging to the claimant. There was a gateway to Sanctions Farm that was used to that effect. Mrs Diment found out about the use of her field only after she returned to Sanctions Farm. She sought to end the use. The defendant claimed to have acquired a right of way by prescription.

Held: The infrequent but regular use of the field, between six and ten times per year, makes the use continuous so that a right of way may be acquired through prescription. However, Mrs Diment did not have knowledge of the use, nor did anyone whose knowledge could be imputed to her. As a result, no prescription ran against her. The defendant should stop using the path over Sanctions Farm.

Judgment: Pennycuick V-C—I turn now to the use which the defendant company or its individual predecessors have made of field 415. According to the evidence of Mr NH Foot, the earliest date within his recollection at which his father was using field 415 as a method of access to his own land was 1936. That, it will be remembered,

[225] 28 P&CR 163.

was the selfsame year in which the plaintiff acquired Sanctions Farm and in which she made the first of the lettings which I have mentioned—there had been previous lettings. There is no evidence of any user of field 415 for access before 1936. There may have been such user, but there is no evidence of it. Since that date there has been a user and a continuous user of field 415. User has been limited to quite a few occasions in each year and particulars of this user were given in evidence both by Mr NH Foot himself and by Mr Mitchell, his tractor driver. The occasions of user were these. In the early summer there was a check on the fences around the 'panhandle', and where necessary fencing gear was taken to the 'panhandle'. In midsummer, perhaps about June, there was hedge trimming and cutting of thistles. Again, from time to time, the drinking pool was cleared out and whatever drainage work was necessary was done. It appears that field 415 was not used more than on perhaps six to ten occasions in each year. To get the point out of the way, I have no doubt that the user was sufficient in extent and regularity to be capable of creating a right of way. On the other hand, obviously it would only be apparent to anybody who happened to be there on one of those ten or so days in the year, apart from whatever traces were left on field 415 by vehicles passing across it. …

I turn now to the law and I will read first the statement of principle made by Fry J in *Dalton v Henry Angus & Co*, I should perhaps mention that this was not a decision of the court, but was advice given by a number of judges to the House of Lords under the procedure which was then sometimes adopted. Fry J's statement has been repeatedly confirmed since then and I think may be taken as an authoritative statement of the law. He says:

> 'But leaving such technical questions aside, I prefer to observe that, in my opinion, the whole law of prescription and the whole law which governs the presumption or inference of a grant or covenant rest upon acquiescence. The Courts and the Judges have had recourse to various expedients for quieting the possession of persons in the exercise of rights which have not been resisted by the persons against whom they are exercised, but in all cases it appears to me that acquiescence and nothing else is the principle upon which these expedients rest. It becomes then of the highest importance to consider of what ingredients acquiescence consists. In many cases, as, for instance, in the case of that acquiescence which creates a right of way, it will be found to involve, 1st, the doing of some act by one man upon the land of another; 2ndly, the absence of right to do that act in the person doing it; 3rdly, the knowledge of the person affected by it that the act is done; 4thly, the power of the person affected by the act to prevent such act either by act on his part or by action in the Courts; and lastly, the abstinence by him from any such interference for such a length of time as renders it reasonable for the Courts to say that he shall not afterwards interfere to stop the act being done.'

So, the third requirement is knowledge of the person that the act is done and the fourth requirement is the power of that person to prevent such act. The requirement of knowledge has subsequently been expanded so as to include imputed knowledge. I will refer to *Union Lighterage Co v London Graving Dock Co*, where Romer LJ says this:

> '… on principle, it appears to me that a prescriptive right to an easement over a man's land should only be acquired when the enjoyment has been open—that

> is to say, of such a character that an ordinary owner of the land, diligent in the protection of his interests, would have, or must be taken to have, a reasonable opportunity of becoming aware of that enjoyment.'

Then Romer LJ goes on to cite *Dalton v Henry Angus & Co* n 1. Stirling LJ says n 4: 'I think that *Dalton v Angus* establishes that there must be some knowledge or means of knowledge on the part of the person against whom the right is claimed'. Vaughan Williams LJ in his judgment dissented from the others, but expressed the same view on mean of knowledge. So in order that there may be the necessary acquiescence the owner of the servient tenement must have knowledge or the means of knowledge that the act is done—the act being here user of these lands for passage to create a right of way. I will refer in a moment to the way in which the point was put—I think rather differently—in a recent case in the Court of Appeal.

Coming to the facts of the present case, I have already held that the plaintiff had never heard that the predecessors of the defendant had been using field 415 for access to their own land until Mr Billen told her something in 1967. I have already made clear that I accept that evidence, so that she did not have actual knowledge at any time before 1967. Were the circumstances such that if she had followed up any clues she would have ascertained that the relevant acts were being done? I have reached the clear conclusion that the plaintiff did not possess any such means of knowledge.

Counsel for the defendant company contended that the plaintiff must be treated as having such means of knowledge by reason of the existence of the gateway at point B, when considered in connection with the lie of the land which made the extreme north-west tip of the 'panhandle' virtually inaccessible to vehicles except through that gate. I am not at all certain that the plaintiff, doing all the acts which a diligent landowner could have done, would have even seen gate B when she made her inspections of Sanctions Farm during this period from 1936 to 1967. During this period the plaintiff came down to Buckland Newton perhaps once a year to look over Sanctions Farm. Field 415 was an outlying part of a large farm and there is no reason I can see why one should infer that the plaintiff, looking over the farm as a whole, should have walked along the boundary of this outlying field. Even if she had done so, I am not persuaded that the mere sight of a gate at point B leading to the 'panhandle' would have put her on any further enquiry as to why that gate was there. There can be all sorts of reasons why a gate stands between two pieces of land which are not at present in common ownership and I should not have thought that the mere sight of the gate would have put her on enquiry whether the gate was in current use by the owner or occupier for the time being of Bookham Farm for the purposes of access over field 415. I conclude that it is not possible to impute to the plaintiff personally any means of knowledge.

Counsel for the defendant company put his contention of knowledge in one rather different way. I mention now the case to which I alluded previously in this judgment, namely, *Pugh v Savage*, in which Cross LJ said:

> 'When long user—here user for 36 years—of a way has been shown, I think that the law should support it if it can, and that we ought to presume, in the absence of any evidence to the contrary, that the owners of 457 in the period 1932to 1940 knew of the user and that Mr Ralphs knew of it.'

There Cross LJ—and both Harman and Salmon LJJ agreed—was stating that there is a presumption that the owner concerned knows of the relevant user of a way but, as Cross LJ said, it is obvious that the presumption can be rebutted by evidence that the owner did not have such knowledge. The effect of that statement is to throw the burden of proof on the owner concerned, that is to say instead of the other party having to establish affirmatively that he did have knowledge, the owner must establish that he did not have knowledge.

Accepting that as a correct statement of the law, it is I think an enlargement of the principle stated in *Dalton v Henry Angus & Co*. The plaintiff herself did not have such knowledge and so, as far as she is concerned, she has rebutted the presumption. But what was said by counsel for the defendant company was this: this during these years the

plaintiff employed a firm of chartered surveyors known as Henry Duke & Son of Dorchester to act for her in connection with Sanctions Farm including the making of agreements with the successive tenants in occupation of field 415. That is undoubtedly so. Then he said that any knowledge or imputed knowledge on the part of the plaintiff's agent must be treated for this purpose as her own knowledge as principal and went on to contend that this presumption applies as regards Henry Duke & Son, with the consequence that it could only be rebutted by showing that Henry Duke & Son did not in fact have knowledge of the user of the way, or means of such knowledge. I do not think the presumption can legitimately be carried so far where a landowner employs an agent in connection with his property. There cannot, I think, be a presumption, merely by reason of that relation and without reference to the particular circumstances, that the agent has knowledge or means of knowledge of any particular act on the land. That would be carrying this presumption altogether beyond anything that was said in *Pugh v Savage n 1* and would, I venture to think, lead to some very odd consequences. It seems to me that where one is concerned with an agent the role of establishing knowledge or means of knowledge must rest on the other party concerned who may discharge that burden by positive evidence or inference—the inference depending on all the particular circumstances. There is no evidence here as to the precise activities carried on by Henry Duke & Son apart from the fact that they were responsible for making the tenancies and dealing with matters of rents and so forth. There is no evidence as to what members or representatives of that firm did physically on Sanctions Farm or field 415 by way of inspection and I see no ground on which I would be entitled to hold that Henry Duke & Son had knowledge or means of knowledge of the user of this way by Mr Foot or the defendant company.

That is sufficient to decide this case because the defendant company has failed to establish that the plaintiff either had knowledge of the use of this way or the means of such knowledge and that is the third of Fry LJ's requirements.

Notes

(1) Apart from these classic requirements, which are also to be found in, for example, French, Belgian and Dutch law, English law requires that the right in question should be exercised by a fee simple owner against another fee simple owner. Use against a limited owner, eg a leasehold owner, does not give rise to prescription for the reason that the fee simple owner may have been unaware of the pretended right and may, as a consequence, have been unable to prevent the prescription running against him. It is an example of the classic rule that no prescription period

should run against an owner who could not have been aware of any prescription running against him. *Pugh v Savage* [1970] 2 QB 373, per Cross LJ. These requirements are similar to the requirement for adverse possession. There is, however, one technical difference in that adverse possession requires possession, whereas prescription, it seems, does not. French and Dutch law reviewed above, require for acquisitive prescription of a servitude possession of the servitude. This simply means use of the right as if one had this right. It seems that English law developed two different but quite similar doctrines, adverse possession and acquisitive prescription, only because use as of right in modern law is not seen as possession of the easement in question.

(2) *Diment v NH Foot Ltd* shows that knowledge on the part of the owner of the servient land is necessary in order for prescription to run against him. This is notably different from French and Dutch law where it is sufficient for prescription that the owner could have seen the user. If the user is visible, continuous and non-equivocal prescription will run against the owner because he could have been aware of the user had he been present on the land. In French and Dutch law the fact that the owner hardly ever visited the land is no excuse.

IV.B.4.b *Tantum praescriptum quantum possessum*

The adage *tantum praescriptum quantum possessum* (as much has prescribed as was held in possession) applies also in English law. When an easement or profit is acquired by prescription the content of the right is interpreted very strictly. The same strict interpretation applies in the case of implied easements, which we consider below. The typical test is a right of light acquired by prescription: does it include the right to all the light and an unobstructed view (*servitus prospectus*)? There is no clear answer to this. Generally, it seems that the dominant tenement has a right only to so much light as is reasonably necessary for the ordinary purpose of habitation or business (*Colls v Home & Colonial Stores Ltd* [1904] AC 179 at 204). However, in *Allen v Greenwood* [1980] Ch 119 the Court of Appeal seems to have been more generous towards the owner of the dominant tenement. It held that the greenhouse on the dominant tenement could not be deprived of the light necessary for growing plants.

IV.B.4.c Easement of necessity and other implied easements

Introductory Note

In some instances English law implies the grant of an easement where a fee simple owner transfers part of his land to another party. If after the partial transfer the transferor's land or the transferee's land has no access to a public road, the law creates an easement of way in favour of one or the other party. Rather than creating a statutory easement, English law uses the fiction that the parties must have intended the grant of an easement. Such an intention is easily used in favour of the transferee, as a grant (the transfer of land) should be interpreted in the broadest manner possible. However, only in rare cases is it implied that the transferor had the intention to reserve in his own favour an easement over the transferee's land, under the rule that one should not derogate from one's own grant.

Court of Appeal, 12 April 2006[226] **7.95 (E&W)**

Adealon International Proprietary Ltd v Merton London Borough Council

COMPULSORY RIGHT OF WAY; EASEMENT BY NECESSITY

High path

In principle there is no implied reservation of easement in favour of transferor if his landlocked property is surrounded also by land belonging to third parties.

Facts: A landowner, the company Boastdean, sold off the north part of its land to another company, Kempstone. To the west and the east Boastdean's property adjoined the property of third parties. To the south its property bordered a public highway (A24). Boastdean expected to be able to obtain permission to access its land from the A24, but failed to obtaining this permission. Kempstone sold its land to Merton City Council. Some time later Boastdean sold its land to Adealon, the claimant. Adealon now seeks access to another road, High Path, which is accessible from Adealon's property only by crossing the City Council's property. It runs to the north of the City Council's land. Adealon claimed that at the time of the sale its predecessor in title became entitled to an easement of necessity over the City Council's land in favour of its property. The judge at first instance dismissed its claim.

Held: An easement of necessity is created by implied intention, not by public policy. Where the landlocked property is wholly surrounded by property of the other party to the transaction, it can be readily accepted that an easement has been created by implied grant in favour of the transferee or implied reservation in favour of the transferor. If, however, the landlocked property is surrounded also by land belonging to third parties, there is a presumption that any reservation of an easement in favour of the transferor who retains the landlocked property should have been made expressly. The presumption has not been rebutted. As a result, Adealon did not acquire a right of way.

Judgment: Carnwath LJ—Easements of necessity

[10] A good starting point is Lord Oliver's succinct statement of the principle in the Privy Council in *Manjang v Drammeh* (1990) 61 P & CR 194, 196–7:

> 'It seems hardly necessary to state the essentials for the implication of such an easement. There has to be found, first, a common owner of a legal estate in two plots of land. It has, secondly, to be established that access between one of those plots and the public highway can be obtained only over the other plot. Thirdly, there has to be found a disposition of one of the plots without any specific grant or reservation of a right of access. Given these conditions, it may be possible as a matter of construction of the relevant grant (see Nickerson v Barraclough) to imply the reservation of an easement of necessity.'

[11] As that passage confirms, the principle is one of implication from the circumstances of a grant of land, not (as suggested in some of the earlier cases and in academic writings (see eg AJ Bradbrook Access to Landlocked Land: A Comparative Study of Legal Solutions 10 Sydney L Rev 39 (1983–5).)) a free-standing rule of public policy. This was settled by this court in *Nickerson v Barraclough* [1981]

[226] [2007] EWCA Civ 362, [2007] 1 WLR 1898.

Ch 426, [1981] 2 All ER 369, [1981] 2 WLR 773, where Buckley LJ summarised the correct approach:

> '… in my judgment the law relating to ways of necessity rests not upon a basis of public policy but upon the implication to be drawn from the fact that unless some way is implied, a parcel of land will be inaccessible. From that fact the implication arises that the parties must have intended that some way giving access to the land should have been granted.
>
> Public policy may inhibit the parties from carrying their intention into effect, but I cannot see how public policy can have a bearing upon what their intention was. In my judgment, that must be ascertained in accordance with the ordinary principles of construction, the language used and relevant admissible evidence of surrounding circumstances.' (p 447)

[12] The classic case of an easement of necessity is where the land of one party to a grant is entirely surrounded by that of the other. As between the two of them, it is not difficult to infer that the landlocked property, whether of the grantor or the grantee, was intended to have some form of access over the surrounding land. That was explained by Sir George Jessel MR *Corporation of London v Riggs* (1880) 13 Ch D 798, 44 JP 345, 49 LJ Ch 297:

> 'It seems to me to have been laid down in very early times—and I have looked into a great number of cases, and among others several black-letter cases … that the right to a way of necessity is an exception to the ordinary rule that a man shall not derogate from his own grant, and that the man who grants the surrounding land is in very much the same position as regards the right of way to the reserved close as if he had granted the close, retaining the surrounding land. In both cases there is what is called a way of necessity; and the way of necessity, according to the old rules of pleading, must have been pleaded as a grant, or, where the close is reserved, as it is here, as a re-grant.' (p 806)

[13] So much is uncontroversial. But as one moves away from that simple, bipartite model, to one in which the surrounding land is shared with strangers to the grant, the issues become more complex. Where there is a realistic possibility of alternative access over the land of third parties, the case for an easement of necessity is much less clear.

[14] In particular, in that situation there is no reason in my view to assume that the same rule should apply to grantor and the grantee. In this context, the presumption of non-derogation from grant works in favour of the grantee, but against the grantor. Further, the grantee may also be able to rely on other forms of implied right, not available to the grantor: see generally Megarry & Wade 6th ed para 18-097ff. As is said there:

> 'The general rule . . . is that a grant is construed in favour of the grantee. Therefore normally no easements will be implied in favour of a grantor; if he wishes to reserve any easements he must do so expressly.' (para 18-097)

Conversely:

> 'In favour of a grantee easements are implied much more readily, on the principle that a grant must be construed in the amplest rather than in the narrowest way.' (para 18-102).

[15] This contrast can be seen clearly in the leading statement of the applicable law by Thesiger LJ in *Wheeldon v Burrows* (1879) 12 Ch D 31, 48 LJ Ch 853, 28 WR 196, 49:

> '... two propositions may be stated as that I call general rules governing cases of this kind. The first of these rules is, that on the grant by the owner of a tenement of part of that tenement as it is then used and enjoyed, there will pass to the grantee all those continuous and apparent easements (by which, of course, I mean quasi easements), or, in other words, all those easements which are necessary to the reasonable enjoyment of the property granted, and which have been and are at the time of the grant used by the owners of the entirety for the benefit of the part granted. The second proposition is that, if the grantor intends to reserve any right over the tenement granted, it is his duty to reserve it expressly in the grant. Those are the general rules governing cases of this kind, but the second of those rules is subject to certain exceptions. One of those exceptions is the well-known exception which attaches to cases of what are called ways of necessity;
>
> Both of the general rules which I have mentioned are founded upon a maxim which is as well established by authority as it is consonant to reason and common sense, viz, that a grantor shall not derogate from his grant.'

[16] This distinction becomes particularly relevant when considering the possibilities of alternative access over land of third parties. In the case of the grantee, the application of the presumption should in principle be unaffected by such possibilities. The grantee's normal expectation is that access, if not otherwise available will be allowed as an incident to the grant, and thus that it will be provided by the grantor over land within his control. Where the roles are reversed, the grantor has no equivalent expectation. On the contrary, the presumption is that any rights he requires over the land transferred will have been expressly reserved in the grant, and the burden lies on the grantor to establish an exception. To that issue the existence of other realistic possibilities of access, even if not legally enforceable at the time of the grant, is clearly relevant.

[17] I have already referred to the judge's resolution of the apparent conflict between *Titchmarsh v Royston Water Co Ltd* (1899) 81 LT 673 and *Barry v Hasseldine* [1952] Ch 835. I do not see either as directly relevant to the present case, since neither concerned a claim by a grantor over land of the grantee. Neither is in any event binding on this court. However, since the judge based her decision in part on the earlier case, it may be helpful to offer some comment.

[18] Titchmarch was a decision of Kekewich J. The purchaser's land was bounded on three sides by land of the vendor, (Although the Plaintiff was a tenant of the farm, the judge felt able to treat it as a simple case 'between vendor and purchaser' (p 675).) and on the fourth side by a public road which ran in a steep cutting. The purchaser claimed a right of access to the highway over a private way across the farm, either under the general words of the conveyance, or as an easement of necessity. Both claims failed, the latter on the grounds (in the words of the headnote) that: '... the way was not a way of necessity because the Defendants could, though at some expense, cut a way from the public road.'

So understood, the case is unremarkable. However, the judge seemed to go further, apparently holding that there could never be an easement of necessity where the surrounding land was partly owned by strangers to the grant. He referred to a statement in *Pomfret v Ricroft* (1669) 2 Keb 505, 543, 569, 1 Sid 429, 1 Wms Saund 323, in which the rule was treated as applicable where someone 'having a close surrounded with his own land' grants the close to another. He thought that those words were apt to exclude a case where the granted premises are 'not surrounded by land of the vendor, but abut on one side on land of a stranger'. He added:

> 'There is no authority for extending the doctrine to such a case as that. In Gale on Easements, 5th edition, the doctrine is stated in almost precisely the same language with this addition: "So, too, if the close be not entirely enclosed by my land, but partly by the land of strangers, for he cannot go over the land of strangers, quaere." For this reference is made to Rolle's Abridgement and Viner's Abridgment. I have referred to these volumes, and have ascertained that the quotation is accurate including the quaere, which is to be found in both works, but I have not come across any comment on either the statement or the quaere. It seems to me that the statement is inconsistent with the doctrine as above explained and with the principle on which it has founded.'

[19] In *Barry v Hesseldine* Danckwerts J took a different approach. The facts were somewhat complex. The grantee's land was surrounded partly by land of the vendor, and partly by that of other parties, including a disused airfield owned by a third party. For some time following the grant they had been able to obtain access over the airfield by permission of the owner. There was an argument, rejected by the judge, that he had agreed to abandon any claim to access over the vendor's land. The issue therefore arose as to his legal rights in the event of the permissive right being unavailable. The judge held that he was entitled to an easement of necessity over the vendor's land, even though his property was not completely surrounded it.

[20] Having referred to the uncertainty on the point expressed in the then current edition of Gale on Easements and in other authorities, including *Pomfret v Ricroft*, he said:

> 'There is therefore no express authority on the point. In my opinion, however, if the grantee has no access to the property which is sold and conveyed to him except over the grantor's land or over the land of some other person or persons whom he cannot compel to give him any legal right of way, common-sense demands that a way of necessity should be implied, so as to confer on the grantee a right of way, for the purposes for which the land is conveyed, over the land of the grantor; and it is no answer to say that a permissive method of approach was in fact enjoyed, at the time of the grant, over the land of some person other than the grantor because that permissive method of approach may be determined on the following day, thereby leaving the grantee with no lawful method of approaching the land which he has purchased.' (p 339)

[21] Although there was no mention of Titchmarch in the judgment, it had been referred to in the course of argument, where it was suggested that Kekewich J's comments on the law were obiter. Danckwerts J interposed: 'If the matter depends on implied grant from which the grantor cannot derogate, it seems immaterial that there is adjoining land owned by a third party' (p 837). For reasons discussed earlier, I would respectfully agree with that observation, particularly now that it is clear that the issue is one of implication, not public policy. In so far as Titchmarch is to contrary effect, I would not follow it, although as I have said the decision can be supported on the narrower ground stated in the headnote. However, as already

explained, neither case has any relevance to the present case, which concerns implied reservation, not implied grant.

[22] For the same reason, I find no assistance in *Bolton v Bolton* (1879) 11 Ch D 968, 43 JP 764, 48 LJ Ch 467. That was another case relied on by Mr Partridge [counsel for claimant] before us, though not cited to the judge, as showing that there could be an easement of necessity, even though there were prospects of an alternative access over land of a third party. However, that again was a right claimed by the grantee, not the grantor.

[23] Of more direct relevance is *Pinnington v Gallard* (1853) 22 LJ Ex 348, 9 Exch 1, 1 CLR 819, 22 LTOS 41. A Mr Dickinson had sold, on the same day in 1839, a piece of land in three separate lots, one to a Mr Dearle, and another to a Mr Moss. An existing track through Mr Dearle's lot gave access to Mr Moss' lot and was used for that purpose for several years after the sale, but there had been no express grant or reservation of a right of way. The use was later disputed by the Defendant, Mr Dearle's successor, but was confirmed by the court. Since it could not be ascertained which grant had come first, Baron Martin considered both alternatives. Assuming the grant to Mr Moss had come first, the right over the retained land of Mr Dickinson was covered by well-established principles of implied grant, explained by Sergeant Williams in his notes to *Pomfret v Ricroft* (above). He continued:

> 'Secondly, assume that the conveyance to Mr Dearle was executed the first. In this case the Rye Holme closes were for a short period of time the property of Mr Dickinson after the property in the land conveyed to Mr Dearle had passed out of him. There is no doubt apparently a greater difficulty in holding the right of way to exist in this case than in the other; but according to the same very great authority the law is the same, for (Sergeant Williams') note proceeds thus: "So it is when he grants the land and reserves the close to himself"; and he cites several authorities which fully bear him out. ... It no doubt seems extraordinary that a man should have a right which certainly derogates from his own grant; but the law is distinctly laid down to be so, and probably for the reason given in Dutton v Taylor 2 Lutw 1487, that it was for the public good, as otherwise the close surrounded would not be capable of cultivation.'

[24] This passage is of assistance to the Appellant to the extent that that same rule was treated as applicable, whether the transaction was treated as a grant or a reservation, and even though (as appears from the plan printed with the report) there were adjoining areas belonging to third parties. However, the facts were very different to the present; and the two-stage analysis of what were essentially simultaneous transactions seems somewhat artificial to modern eyes (cf *Hansford v Jago* [1921] 1 Ch 322, 335, 90 LJ Ch 129, [1920] All ER Rep 580). In any event, there was no discussion of the significance of alternative possibilities of access over land of third parties. The case cannot therefore be regarded as authoritative on that aspect. It is true that the passage from Baron Martin's judgment was quoted by Thesiger LJ without adverse comment in *Wheeldon v Burrows* (above, at p 58). But that, as I read it, was not by way of specific endorsement of the reasoning, but simply by way of confirmation of his earlier analysis, to show—'... that the whole foundation of the judgment ... was that the way claimed in the case was a way of necessity, and ... that Baron Martin and the court whose judgment he delivered in no way disputed the general maxims to which I have referred.' In so far as Baron Martin there treated 'public policy' as the basis of the principle, later authority, as I have

said, does not support him. Thus, while I do not doubt the correctness of the decision in Pinnington, it provides no support for the present appeal.

[25] For completeness I should refer to an Australian case which was not cited to us, but which seems closer to the present on the facts, relating as it does to a claim by a vendor: *North Sydney Printing Property Ltd v Sobemo Investment Co Ltd* [1971] NSWLR 150. This also appears to be the fullest judicial discussion of the authorities in the modern cases. It was considered by Sir Robert Megarry VC in *Nickerson v Barraclough* at first instance ([1981] Ch 325, 333–4). I gratefully adopt his summary of the facts:

> 'The North Sydney case was decided in the Supreme Court of New South Wales by Hope J, sitting in Equity. Put very shortly, the facts were that a company sold part of its land, which abutted on to a street. The retained land had no access to a highway, but the company intended subsequently to sell it to the local authority as an addition to a contiguous car park owned by that authority. The proposed sale to the local authority went off, and the company was left with its retained land, which was landlocked. The company then sought a declaration that its retained land had a way of necessity over the land sold; and this claim failed. Over twenty authorities (half of them English) were cited in argument, including Packer v Wellstead, 2 Sid 111 and Dutton v Tayler, 2 Lutw 1487. ... The company contended that it was entitled to a way of necessity by virtue of public policy, and that the intention of the parties was irrelevant. The purchaser contended that public policy was irrelevant, and that the company was entitled to no right of way, since the intention of the parties was that the company should have no such right...'

[26] The claim failed. The court held that a way of necessity arises to give effect to an actual or presumed intention. On the facts the company's intention was the contrary: its intention was that the land retained should have no access over the land conveyed, but instead should have access over the car park. I note in particular the Vice-Chancellor's comment on the differences from the case before him:

> '... the claim to a way of necessity was made by the vendor, and not, as in the present case, by successors in title of the purchaser; and although ways of necessity are in a special position, the law is far more ready to imply the grant of easements than it is to imply their reservation. There is a doctrine against derogating from a grant, but not against derogating from a reservation...' (p 334)

The case was not referred to in the Court of Appeal, which differed from the Vice-Chancellor on the facts of *Nickerson v Barraclough* itself. However, I see nothing to throw any doubt on this aspect of his analysis, which is consistent with the view I have already expressed.

Conclusion

[27] For these reasons, I would reject Mr Partridge's principal submission, which is that Adealon is entitled to an easement of necessity, by operation of law, and regardless of the existence of possible alternatives over land of third parties. ....

[29] I would therefore uphold the judge's conclusion that Adealon does not have a right of way over the council's land.

Notes

(1) The other legal systems analysed, French, Dutch and German law, solve the problem of landlocked property with a statutory right of access. French law uses the term legal servitude, indicating that the servitude is created by statute rather than by the parties; Dutch and German law use another term (*noodweg* respectively *Notweg*) taking this case out of the umbrella term 'servitudes'.[227]

(2) Apart from easements of necessity which may be implied in a transfer of land, English law also recognises as a special category quasi-easements under the rule in *Wheeldon v Burrows*.[228] Where an owner transfers part of his land and during unity of possession the transferred part enjoyed, for example, support, light or a pathway from the part retained by the transferor, the owner of the transferred part acquires an easement. The factual use by the common owner of both parts before the partial transfer, which could not give rise to an easement since the parts were in common ownership, now becomes an easement. French law recognises a similar concept where the factual use by the owner leads to a servitude at the time of transfer of part of his land (servitude by destination). This technique is strikingly similar to the English quasi-easements, or to use another term, easements under the rule in *Wheeldon v Burrows*. As we have seen above, the destination should not have been made explicit; it is often implied from the circumstances of the case, obscuring the difference between servitudes created by the parties and servitudes created by law in the case of necessity. Some of the requirements for a quasi-easement are very similar to the French requirements for creation by destination as stated in the Civil Code: as in French law (Article 692 Cciv) the English quasi-easement should be continuous and apparent.[229] In French law, however, it is not required that the servitude should be reasonably necessary for the use of the dominant tenement.

Law of Property Act **7.96 (E&W)**

Section 62 General words implied in conveyances

(1) A conveyance of land shall be deemed to include and shall by virtue of this Act operate to convey, with the land, all buildings, erections, fixtures, commons, hedges, ditches, fences, ways, waters, water-courses, liberties, privileges, easements, rights, and advantages whatsoever, appertaining or reputed to appertain to the land, or any part thereof, or, at the time of conveyance, demised, occupied, or enjoyed with, or reputed or known as part or parcel of or appurtenant to the land or any part thereof.

(2) A conveyance of land, having houses or other buildings thereon, shall be deemed to include and shall by virtue of this Act operate to convey, with the land, houses, or other buildings, all outhouses, erections, fixtures, cellars, areas, courts, courtyards, cisterns, sewers, gutters, drains, ways, passages, lights, watercourses, liberties, privileges, easements, rights, and advantages whatsoever, appertaining or reputed

[227] Above, Chapter 3.

[228] (1879) 12 Ch D 31, CA.

[229] Note, however, that nowadays in French law creation by destination is also possible for non-continuous servitudes.

to appertain to the land, houses, or other buildings conveyed, or any of them, or any part thereof, or, at the time of conveyance, demised, occupied, or enjoyed with, or reputed or known as part or parcel of or appurtenant to, the land, houses, or other buildings conveyed, or any of them, or any part thereof.

(3) A conveyance of a manor shall be deemed to include and shall by virtue of this Act operate to convey, with the manor, all pastures, feedings, wastes, warrens, commons, mines, minerals, quarries, furzes, trees, woods, underwoods, coppices, and the ground and soil thereof, fishings, fisheries, fowlings, courts leet, courts baron, and other courts, view of frankpledge and all that to view of frankpledge doth belong, mills, mulctures, customs, tolls, duties, reliefs, heriots, fines, sums of money, amerciaments, waifs, estrays, chief-rents, quitrents, rentscharge, rents seck, rents of assize, fee farm rents, services, royalties jurisdictions, franchises, liberties, privileges, easements, profits, advantages, rights, emoluments, and hereditaments whatsoever, to the manor appertaining or reputed to appertain, or, at the time of conveyance, demised, occupied, or enjoyed with the same, or reputed or known as part, parcel, or member thereof.

For the purposes of this subsection the right to compensation for manorial incidents on the extinguishment thereof shall be deemed to be a right appertaining to the manor.

(4) This section applies only if and as far as a contrary intention is not expressed in the conveyance, and has effect subject to the terms of the conveyance and to the provisions therein contained.

(5) This section shall not be construed as giving to any person a better title to any property, right, or thing in this section mentioned than the title which the conveyance gives to him to the land or manor expressed to be conveyed, or as conveying to him any property, right, or thing in this section mentioned, further or otherwise than as the same could have been conveyed to him by the conveying parties.

(6) This section applies to conveyances made after the thirty-first day of December, eighteen hundred and eighty-one.

Note

The importance of the unabridged text lies in the words 'liberties, privileges, easements, rights, and advantages' to be found in subsections 1–3. Subsection 4 shows that the effect of section 62 can be excluded in the conveyance deed. Section 62 does not apply to temporary or precarious advantages. See eg *P & S Platt Ltd v Crouch* [2003] EWCA Civ 1110 and *Green v Ashco Horticulturist Ltd* [1966] 1 WLR 889, ChD.

CONCISE BIBLIOGRAPHY

LPW van Vliet, 'Accession of movables to land (I)' (2002) 6 *Edinburgh Law Review* 67–84.

LPW van Vliet, 'Accession of movables to land (II)' (2002) 6 *Edinburgh Law Review* 199–216.

LPW van Vliet, 'Acquisition and Loss of Ownership of Goods—Book VIII of the Draft Common Frame of Reference' [2/2011] *Zeitschrift für Europäisches Privatrecht* 292–334.

CHAPTER EIGHT
TRANSFER

*Monika Hinteregger and Lars van Vliet**

This chapter deals with the fifth of the six essential questions of property law: how are property rights transferred? Once someone holds a property right he or she may transfer this entitlement to another. This chapter offers an overview of transfer systems for both movable objects (goods) and immovable objects (land). When land is transferred, this usually includes recordation of the transfer in a Land Registry. This chapter therefore also deals with land registry systems and how they operate.

GENERAL INTRODUCTION

This chapter is about the voluntary transfer of assets by a legal act aimed at transferring the asset, thus leaving out transfer by operation of law, such as succession on death, or transfer by a court order in the case of expropriation. At the end, in part III, the creation of limited property rights is treated, which, traditionally, follows the rules on transfer. Part I concentrates on movables and explains the various transfer systems and their distinctions, the causal consensual system, the causal tradition system and the abstract transfer system. Part II is about the transfer of immovables and land registration systems. As will be seen, in German, Austrian and French law both the transfer of movables and immovables are based on the same transfer system. English law forms the exception in that it does not have a uniform transfer system. The transfer of immovables underlies special rules and even

* Parts I and III have been written by Lars van Vliet; parts II and IV have been written by Monika Hinteregger.

for the transfer of movables there is no uniform system: a special regime applies to the sale of movables.

I. TRANSFER SYSTEMS

Two distinctions commonly made to characterise transfer systems are the distinction between *tradition* systems and *consensual* systems, and the one between *causal* and *abstract* systems. In the course of the chapter we will see that both distinctions and the various transfer systems they entail are in fact no more than different starting points. As a result of far-reaching exceptions to the principles involved, the differences between the various transfer systems are much smaller than the opposing starting-points would make one believe at first glance.

I.A PAYMENT OF MONEY: TRANSFER?

This chapter will not deal with the transfer of money in a bank account, as this does not amount to a transfer of ownership and is thus outside the scope of the property law concept of transfer of ownership. Ownership of money can exist, but only in relation to banknotes and coins. These are treated as movable, tangible, objects the ownership of which can be transferred in the property law sense of the word.[1] Money in a bank account, on the other hand, forms an obligation between the bank, who is the debtor, and the client, who is the creditor. When the client orders his bank to 'transfer' €1,000 to the account of the client's creditor, the client's account will be debited and the payee's account will be credited with the sum of €1,000.[2] This should not be seen as a transfer or the assignment of part of the client's claim on the bank.

PW Heermann, Money and Money-Related Issues[3] **8.1 (DE)**

In the case of payment with physical money the debtor provides the creditor with title to the tokens of money, whereas in the case of payment with intangible money the debtor provides the creditor with a claim against a so-called payment intermediary (eg a financial institution or credit card company). Thus, the granting of a personal right is substituted for the granting of absolute control, which is characteristic of payment with physical money.

[1] M Wolff and L Raiser, *Sachenrecht, Ein Lehrbuch* (Tübingen, Mohr (Paul Siebeck), 1957) 233; FHJ Mijnssen, *Geld in het vermogensrecht* (Deventer, WEJ Tjeenk Willink, 1984) 5.

[2] There are one or more intermediary banks involved if the payor and the payee do not have their bank accounts with the same bank.

[3] PW Heermann, *Geld und Geldgeschäfte* (Tübingen 2003) 167.

Queens Bench Division, 2 September 1987[4] **8.2 (E&W)**

Libyan Arab Foreign Bank v Bankers Trust Co

BANK ACCOUNT AND ACCOUNT TRANSFER

Libyan bank

Money on a bank account is a personal right of the client against his bank; the bank transfer does not involve assignment of this right nor any other transfer.

Facts: The claimant held two deposits with the defendants, Bankers Trust Co, one at their New York branch and one with their London branch. Both accounts were in US dollars. A US Executive Order from President Reagan froze all assets of the Libyan government in the US. The claimant bank was owned by the Central Bank of Libya. The claimant demanded repayment in cash from the London branch, arguing that the regulation had no effect outside the US. It had also given an order to transfer part of the New York balance to the London account. It now demanded payment of the balance on the London account and payment from part of the New York balance. The defendants refused, saying that within the system of Eurodollar deposits (account in dollars held outside the US) the relevant transfer could be made only through a US clearing system (CHIPS or Fedwire) and that the transfer was thus forbidden under the executive order.

Held: Although it is customary that Eurodollars are transferred through CHIPS or Fedwire, the claimant was entitled to payment in cash or by some other means not involving CHIPS or Fedwire.

Judgment: Staughton J—... (c) The nature of a bank's obligations

It is elementary, or hornbook law to use an American expression, that the customer does not own any money in a bank. He has a personal and not a real right. Students are taught at an early stage of their studies in the law that it is incorrect to speak of 'all my money in the bank'. See *Foley v Hill*, (1848) 2 HLC 28 at p 36, where Lord Cottenham said:

> '... Money, when paid into a bank, ceases altogether to be the money of the principal ... It is then the money of the banker who is bound to return an equivalent by paying a similar sum to that deposited with him when he is asked for it. ... The money placed in the custody of a banker is, to all intents and purposes, the money of the banker, to do with as he pleases.'

Naturally the bank does not retain all the money it receives as cash in its vaults; it if did, there would be no point or profit in being a banker. What the bank does is to have available a sufficient sum in cash to meet all demands that are expected to be made on any particular day.

I mention these simple points in order to clarify the real problem, which is what the obligation of a bank is.

(d) Means of transfer

The credit balance of the Libyan bank with Bankers Trust constituted a personal right, a chose in action. At bottom there are only two means by which the fruits of that right could have been made available to the Libyan bank. The first is by delivery of cash, whether dollar bills or any other currency, to or to the order of the Libyan bank. The second is the procuring of an account transfer. (I leave out of account the delivery of chattels, such as gold, silver or works of art, since nobody has suggested

[4] [1989] 1 QB 728.

that Bankers Trust were obliged to adopt that method. The same applies to other kinds of property, such as land.)

An account transfer means the process by which some other person or institution comes to owe money to the Libyan bank or their nominee, and the obligation of Bankers Trust is extinguished or reduced pro tanto. 'Transfer' may be a somewhat misleading word, since the original obligation is not assigned (notwithstanding dicta in one American case which speak of assignment); a new obligation by a new debtor is created.

Any account transfer must ultimately be achieved by means of two accounts held by different beneficiaries with the same institution. In a simple case the beneficiaries can be the immediate parties to the transfer. If Bankers' Trust held an account with the A bank which was in credit to the extent of at least $131m, and the Libyan bank also held an account at the A bank, it would require only book entries to achieve an account transfer. But still no property is actually transferred. The obligation of Bankers Trust is extinguished, and the obligation of A bank to Bankers Trust extinguished or reduced; the obligation of A bank to the Libyan bank is increased by the like amount.

On occasion a method of account transfer which is even simpler may be used. If X Ltd also hold an account with Bankers Trust London, and the Libyan bank desire to benefit X Ltd, they instruct Bankers Trust to transfer $131m to the account of X Ltd. The obligation of Bankers Trust to the Libyan bank is extinguished once they decide to comply with the instruction, and their obligation of X Ltd is increased by the like amount. That method of account transfer featured in the case of *Momm v Barclays Bank International Ltd*, [1977] QB 790.

In a complex transaction at the other end of the scale there may be more than one tier of intermediaries, ending with a Federal Reserve Bank in the United States. Thus the payer may have an account with B bank in London, which has an account with C bank in New York; the payee has an account with E bank in London, which has an account with D bank in New York. Both C bank and D bank have accounts with the Federal Reserve Bank in New York. When an account transfer is effected the obligations of the New York Fed to C bank, of C bank to B bank, and of B bank to the payer are reduced; the obligations of the New York Fed to D bank, of D bank to E bank, and of E bank to the payee are increased. That is, in essence, how the CHIPS system works, by which a large proportion of transfers of substantial dollar amounts are made.

I shall call the three methods which I have described a correspondent bank transfer, an in-house transfer and a complex account transfer. There are variations which do not precisely fit any of the three, but the principle is the same in all cases. Sooner or later, if cash is not used, there must be an in-house transfer at an institution which holds accounts for two beneficiaries, so that the credit balance of one can be increased and that of the other reduced. In the example of a complex account transfer which I have given that institution is the New York Fed, which holds accounts for C bank and D bank.

Notes

(1) This point has been stressed also by Millet LJ in the House of Lords' judgment in *Foskett v McKeown* [2001] 1 AC 102, a case about tracing of trust assets. Millet LJ stated:

> We speak of money at the bank, and of money passing into and out of a bank account. But of course the account holder has no money at the bank. Money paid into a bank account belongs legally and beneficially to the bank and not to the account holder. The bank gives value for it, and it is accordingly not usually possible to make the money itself the subject of an adverse claim. Instead a claimant normally sues the account holder rather than the bank and lays claim to the proceeds of the money in his hands. These consist of the debt or part of the debt due to him from the bank. We speak of tracing money into and out of the account, but there is no money in the account. There is merely a single debt of an amount equal to the final balance standing to the credit of the account holder. No money passes from paying bank to receiving bank or through the clearing system (where the money flows may be in the opposite direction). There is simply a series of debits and credits which are causally and transactionally linked.

(2) When the contract obliging one party to make a payment is void or has been avoided and the payment was in cash, the payment itself, ie the transfer of the banknotes or coins, may be void as well, depending on the transfer system. The payment is regarded as a legal act of transfer. As a result, the coins and banknotes may be revindicated, provided they have not been mixed with other monies so as to make them unidentifiable.[5] The problem for the payor in these cases is that usually the monies will be so mixed: only in rare exceptions will the money be kept separate or will the numbers of the banknotes be registered. Normally the buyer will have lost ownership of the money because of the principle of specificity.[6] He has to rely on a personal claim of unjustified enrichment.

(3) What is more, nowadays payments are often made by transferring money from one bank account to the other. Here Dutch,[7] German, French[8] and English law do not regard the payment as a transfer of ownership: money in a bank account is not regarded as an asset capable of being owned. Strictly speaking no one owns the money in his bank account: it is merely a personal claim of the client against his bank. This becomes painfully evident when the bank is declared insolvent. A payment of money via bank transfer can never be revindicated.

I.B THE FIRST DIVIDING LINE: THE TRADITION SYSTEM AND THE CONSENSUAL SYSTEM

I.B.1 INTRODUCTION

If I sell my bicycle to a friend, does he become owner of the bicycle immediately,

[5] Mijnssen, above n 1, 20–23; WAK Rank, *Geld, geldschuld en betaling*, thesis Leiden (Deventer, Kluwer, 1996) 97; HR 9 September 1949, NJ 1950, 595 (Houtappel/De Hoofdgroep Verzekering et al).

[6] Sometimes co-ownership of the money may be a solution, but such a co-ownership can arise only if it is known exactly which banknotes and coins have been mixed. As the principle of specificity applies also to co-ownership all banknotes and coins that are co-owned should be identified. Only in rare cases will the principle of specificity be complied with, for example where monies have been put together in a cashbox. See for this principle: Chapter 1 and Chapter 7.

[7] *Cf* BFLM Schim, *Giraal effectenverkeer en goederenrecht* (Deventer, Kluwer, 2006) 133–43.

[8] In French law the exact nature is disputed. See G Ripert and R Roblot, *Traité de droit commercial*, vol 2 by Ph Delebecque and M Germain, 17th edn (Paris, LGDJ, 2004) 2303–12 and R Bonhomme, *Répertoire de Droit Commercial* (Paris, Dalloz, 2010), Virement, no 43.

or does he become owner only after delivery of possession? In a consensual transfer system he becomes owner without delivery of possession being needed: ownership in principle passes the moment the contract of sale is made. It is therefore often said that in a consensual system the contract itself transfers ownership of the object to the buyer. The principle that consensus about the contract suffices to pass ownership is called the *solo consensu* rule.

I.B.2 FRENCH LAW

This *solo consensu* system is the approach taken in the French Civil Code. It can be found in different articles of the Code. The general article expressing this thought is Article 1138 Cciv:

Code civil **8.3 (FR)**

Article 1138 The obligation to transfer an object is performed by the sole consensus between the contracting parties. It makes its creditor owner and places the object at the latter's risk the moment it ought to have been transferred, even if a transfer of possession has not taken place.

Note

The principle can also be found in Article 711 Cciv. For specific types of contract the principle is restated in Articles 938 (gift), 1583 (sale) and 1703 (barter). In Article 1583 Cciv the principle is concentrated on the contract of sale.

Code civil **8.4 (FR)**

Article 1583 It [the contract of sale] is performed between the parties, and ownership is acquired by the buyer as against the seller the moment they have agreed about the object and the price, even if the object has not yet been delivered or the price not yet been paid.

Portalis, Explanation of Motives[9] **8.5 (FR)**

We decide in this Bill that the sale in general is performed even if the object sold has not yet been delivered and the price has not yet been paid.

In the beginning the transfer of ownership required delivery and corporeal occupation. In Roman legal texts we find a multitude of rules and subtleties deriving from this early idea. ...

The system of French law is thus more sensible than the Roman system; it is based on the moral relations which ought to exist between persons.

This system is even more favourable to commerce. It enables that which would often be impossible if corporeal delivery of the object sold were needed to execute the sale.

[9] Portalis, 'Exposé des motif, Titre de la vente', ch 1, in *Locré, Législation civile, commerciale et criminelle, ou commentaire et complément des codes français*, vol 7 (Brussels 1836).

Through the mere expression of our intention we acquire and we transfer to another the objects which can be the object of our contracts.

Note

Portalis was one of the draftsmen of the French Civil Code.

Cour de cassation, 24 June 1845[10] **8.6 (FR)**

Catros v Blaise

TRANSFER OF MOVABLE OBJECTS

Transfer of furniture

The transfer of objects does not require corporeal delivery.

Facts: The spouses Flinn owed money to Blaise. In order to redeem their debt they sold some of their furniture to Blaise, who afterwards leased the furniture back to the spouses Flinn. Some time later Catros, another creditor of the Flinns, seized the furniture in execution. Blaise opposed the execution, asserting that the furniture belonged to him. Catros countered that no corporeal delivery of the furniture had taken place and that therefore the furniture still belonged to the Flinns and that he could seize the furniture in execution.

Held: The transfer of property does not require corporeal delivery.

Judgment: Considering that in deciding in such a case, contrary to what the judgment subject to appeal held, that the ownership of the movables sold to the defendant by the spouses Flinn had been transferred to him without there having been need for transfer of possession; By cancelling thereafter the seizure of the movables sold at the request of the claimant as affecting movables that did not belong to the spouses Flinn, the judgment challenged has in the circumstances of the case given nothing more than a just application of the articles of law invoked in support of the Cassation appeal, and has not violated any other law; Rejects.

I.B.3 ENGLISH LAW

Introductory Notes

(a) English law does not have a unified transfer system. Originally, the requirement of delivery applied to all transfers of movables. It accorded with the requirement of 'livery of seisin'[11] (transfer of possession) applicable in land law.[12] Later, already centuries before the promulgation of the Sale of Goods Act 1893, two important exceptions to the delivery rule had developed: delivery was held unnecessary where

[10] D 1845,1,309.

[11] Like the verb 'deliver' the noun 'livery' derives from the French livrer and the Latin liberare (to deliver up, to hand over). The word 'seisin/seizin' or the alternative 'sasine' derives from the old-French seisine or saisine. *Cf* the English 'seize' and the French saisir (to get hold of, to take possession of, etc).

[12] F Pollock and FW Maitland, *The History of English Law*, vol 2, 2nd edn (Cambridge, Cambridge University Press 1899) 180–81 and 210; F Pollock, 'Gifts of Chattels without Delivery' (1890) 4 *Law Quarterly Review* (*LQR*) 446 at 448. The requirement applied for example to the transfer of a freehold interest (an estate in fee simple or in fee tail).

either the transfer was based on *sale* or the transfer took place by *deed* (a sealed document). These two exceptions still exist. The rule on sale has been codified in the Sale of Goods Act 1893 and the Sale of Goods Act 1979. English common law therefore had three different ways of transferring title in movables: the original rule of delivery, and the newer rules on sale and transfer by deed.

(b) One of the most common examples of transfer of movables outside the scope of sale is a gift. Originally any gift, whether made orally or in writing, needed delivery. Yet, from the end of the fourteenth century a gift could validly be made by deed without delivery being required.[13] In the Court of Appeal's decision in *Cochrane v Moore*[14] Fry LJ analysed thoroughly the old authorities and showed that the common law has always required delivery for an oral gift to be valid.

Court of Appeal, Queens Bench Division, 28 April 1890[15] **8.7 (E&W)**

Cochrane v Moore

ORAL GIFT NEEDS DELIVERY

Donated horse

An oral gift of a movable object does not pass property to the donee without delivery.

Facts: In a conversation with Moore, Benzon, the owner of a horse named Kilworth, made an oral gift of a one-quarter share in this horse to Moore, who had just ridden the horse in a race. Moore orally accepted the gift. A few days later Benzon told Yates, in whose stables the horse was kept, of this gift. Benzon did not inform Moore of this communication to Yates, nor did Moore know of this. On several occasions afterwards Benzon borrowed money from Cochrane. As a security for these loans Benzon transferred the property of various horses to Cochrane in a bill of sale, including the horse Kilworth. The security was realised and the horses were sold under the bill of sale. Moore claimed one-quarter of the proceeds of sale on the basis of the gift to him. Cochrane claimed the money on the basis of the bill of sale. Cochrane asserted that the gift to Moore was invalid and did not pass property to Moore because no delivery had taken place.

Held: A gift of a movable made orally by the donor to the donee and accepted by the donee in the presence of the donor does not pass the property in the movable without delivery.

Judgment: Fry LJ—... Holroyd, J, [in *Irons v Smallpiece*] was equally clear on the principal point: 'In order to change the property by a gift of this description'' (by which we understand him to mean, a gift inter vivos) 'there must be a change of possession'.

The correctness of the proposition thus laid down has been asserted in many subsequent cases of high authority.

Thus in *Reeves v Caper* the Court of Common Pleas under Tindal, CJ, referred to *Irons v Smallpiece*, and the proposition 'that a verbal gift of chattels, unaccompanied with delivery of possession, passes no property to the donee' as being good law and without the expression of any doubt. ...

This review of the authorities leads us to conclude that according to the old law

[13] JH Baker, *An Introduction to English Legal History*, 3rd edn (London, Butterworth 1990) 433, where Baker refers to *Pynchoun v Geldeford* (1385) Year Book Hilary 8 Richard II: see fn 27 there.
[14] (1890) 25 QBD 57.
[15] 25 QBD 57.

no gift or grant of a chattel was effectual to pass it whether by parol or by deed, and whether with or without consideration unless accompanied by delivery: that on that law two exceptions have been grafted, one in the case of deeds, and the other in that of contracts of sale where the intention of the parties is that the property shall pass before delivery: but that as regards gifts by parol, the old law was in force when *Irons v Smallpiece* was decided: that that case therefore correctly declared the existing law: and that it has not been overruled by the decision of Pollock, B, in 1883, or the subsequent case before Cave, J. ...But assuming delivery to be necessary in the case of the gift of an ordinary chattel, two questions would remain for consideration in the present case—the first, whether the undivided fourth part of the horse admits of delivery, or whether on the other hand it is to be regarded as incorporeal and incapable of tradition; the other, whether the letter written by Benzon to Yates was either a constructive delivery of this undivided fourth part of the horse, or an act perfecting the gift of this incorporeal part so far as the nature of the subject-matter of the gift admits. On these points we do not think it needful to express any decided opinion, because in our judgment what took place between Benzon and Cochrane before Benzon executed the bill of sale to Cochrane, constituted the latter a trustee for Moore of one-fourth of the horse Kilworth.

Another objection to Cochrane's title was based on the bill of sale, which bore date July 26, 1888, and stated the consideration as a sum of £7,575 then owing by Benzon to Cochrane, and of the further sum of £2,425, then paid by Cochrane to Benzon, making together a sum of £10,000; whereas in fact at the date of the bill of sale Benzon was only indebted to Cochrane on two promissory notes then current and payable respectively in August and September, and for sums amounting together to £8,300 It is said that by an agreement arrived at at the time, this £8,300 due in futuro was to be taken as between the parties as represented by the sum of £7,575; but if so, this agreement should in our opinion have been stated in the bill of sale, and we are therefore of opinion that the document was void as not truly stating the consideration for which it was given.

For these reasons we are of opinion that this appeal should be dismissed with costs.

Court of Appeal, 27 March 1991[16] **8.8 (E&W)**

Balding v Ashley

GIFT AND DELIVERY

Donated Ferrari

The oral gift of a car is valid only when delivery takes place, for example by handing over the keys of the car.

Facts: Mr Ashley, who was married with a family, started an affair with Mrs Balding, the claimant. After Mr Ashley's wife and children had left him, he lived together with the claimant for a few years. Eventually the association ended and Mrs Balding had to leave Mr Ashley's house. She claimed that during their cohabitation Mr Ashley had made a valid gift of a Ferrari motor car to her. The judge at

[16] *Balding v Ashley*, 27 March 1991, Court of Appeal (unreported).

first instance held that Mr Ashley intended the Ferrari to be a gift to Mrs Balding. The car was registered in the claimant's name and she became a member of the Ferrari Owners' Club. In the judge's opinion, however, no sufficient act of delivery had taken place to perfect the gift.

Held: The Court of Appeal agrees that the registration process does not amount to an act of delivery, but, at the same time, it held that a handing over of the keys would have sufficed to complete the gift.

Judgment: Antony Lincoln LJ—... With regard to the Ferrari car the issue was whether, on the facts as found by the court, the respondent had in law made a gift of the car to the appellant. ...

It has to be accepted that under the existing law mere words or writing less than in deed form will not perfect a gift. There has to be an act of delivery. But it is said that the act of processing the registration of the Ferrari in the appellant's name, conjoined with all the other circumstances—the words spoken, the Ferrari Owners membership—constitutes a sufficient change of possession as to amount to constructive delivery. But what is the registration process other than putting to paper through a third party—the registration officer—a record of the respondent's verbal but unperfected gift? It falls short of the required act of ownership, or change of possession, or delivery, actual or constructive. If the facts are as they appear in the judgment below, the appellant must fail in her appeal. But it is by no means clear that these are the whole of the facts.

It is indisputable that if the respondent had handed the appellant the keys to the Ferrari, these circumstances could well constitute the basis for holding that there had been a constructive delivery. ...

I would therefore order that the case be remitted to Judge Kellock to determine the single issue of fact whether there was a transfer of possession.

Fox LJ: I agree. As regards the Ferrari the judge found as a fact that a gift was intended by the respondent to the appellant. The common law rules as to effective gifts are, however, very strict, as *In re Cole* [1964] Ch 175, [1963] 3 All ER 433, to which my Lord has referred, amply demonstrates. A gift of chattels, unless it is accompanied by something which constitutes delivery of possession, is ineffective. Mere writing is not enough unless there is an actual deed of gift, and there is no deed of gift in the present case. There was the registration in the records at Cardiff of the appellant as a keeper, and that was done with the consent of the respondent, but that registration is only a piece of written evidence indicating that a gift was intended. It does not by itself come anywhere near establishing that there was an effective transfer of possession of the chattel. It seems that the delivery may be constructive delivery (see *In re Cole* (supra) at p 186–7).

As to that, the affidavit of the appellant which was sworn initially in support of the present application does state that the keys were handed over. It does not appear from the judgment that anything was said at the trial relating to the keys. Mrs Bickford-Smith, who has appeared for the appellant upon this appeal but who did not appear below, has consulted counsel who did appear, and he has informed her that his recollection is that at the hearing he took the appellant through the affidavit and she verified her statements. However, Mr Smith, who appears for the respondent, says that he has no recollection of that at all. That is, as my Lord has observed, not surprising. The details of a trial can be easily forgotten after this length of time.

We are therefore left in the position where it is unclear precisely what evidence was before Judge Kellock at the trial.

As to the delivery of the keys by the respondent to the appellant, it is, however, a vital issue. It is accepted (quite rightly, I think) by Mr Smith for the respondent that if the keys were handed over there would then be a basis upon which the court could conclude that there was a delivery of the car, but we do not know precisely what evidence was before the judge relating to delivery. I therefore entirely agree with my Lord that it is necessary that there should be a new trial upon this point and I agree with the order which he proposes.

Note

Delivery of goods by handing over the key of a trunk or warehouse, or other means of access to the goods, has been recognised for centuries.[17] However, there was uncertainty over whether or not Mr Ashley's words of gift had indeed been followed by his handing over the keys of the car to the appellant. As the Court of Appeal had no access to all the evidence brought before the judge in first instance, it ordered the case to be remitted to the latter judge to examine if there had been such handing over of the keys.

Movable objects

Introductory Note

English law has a special transfer system for the sale of 'goods', ie movable tangible objects. It is a consensual system much like the French system. This transfer system has developed in English common law from the sixteenth century.[18]

Court of King's Bench 1827[19] **8.9 (E&W)**

Tarling v Baxter

PASSING OF PROPERTY

Burned hay

Property in the goods passes at the moment the contract is made.

Facts: Tarling bought a stack of hay from Baxter. The hay stood and remained on a field belonging to Baxter's brother. Tarling paid the purchase price. After payment the hay was accidentally lost by fire, without any fault or neglect of either party. Tarling claimed the money back from Baxter, saying that the risk of accidental loss fell on Baxter.

Held: As the property has passed to Tarling the risk has fallen on him.

Judgment: Bayley J—It is quite clear that the loss must fall upon him in whom the property was vested at the time when it was destroyed by fire. … The rule of law is, that where there is an immediate sale, and nothing remains to be done by the vendor as between him and the vendee, the property in the thing sold vests

[17] See eg *Ryall v Rowles* (1750) 1 Ves Sen 348, at 362 and *Ward v Turner* (1751) 2 Ves Sen 431, at 443. The second case is about *donatio causa mortis*.

[18] J Baker, *The Oxford History of the Laws of England*, vol VI: 1483–1558 (Oxford, Oxford University Press 2003) 740–44.

[19] 1827 6 B&C 360.

in the vendee, and then all the consequences resulting from the vesting of property follow, one of which is, that if it be destroyed, the loss falls upon the vendee. The note of the buyer imports also an immediate, perfect, absolute agreement of sale. It seems to me that the true construction of the contract is, that the parties intended an immediate sale, and if that be so, the property vested in the vendee, and the loss must fall upon him.

Note

In the text of the Sale of Goods Act 1979 the first and principal rule on the passing of property is section 17(1):

Sale of Goods Act 1979 **8.10 (E&W)**

Section 17(1) Where there is a contract for the sale of specific of ascertained goods the property in them is transferred to the buyer at such time as the parties to the contract intend it to be transferred.

Note

As the parties' intention or consensus suffices to let property pass and no transfer of possession is needed, this section 17(1) accords with the preceding cases and codifies the consensual transfer system for the sale of goods. The section may give the impression of deviating from the French system. However, in order to categorise the transfer system of the Sale of Goods Act from a comparative law perspective, we need to focus on the default rule, rather than the rule which the Sale of Goods Act itself happens to set up as the primary rule. The default rule, the rule which applies in the absence of the parties' express or implicit intention, is to be found in section 18, rule 1 and in rule 5(1):

Sale of Goods Act 1979 **8.11 (E&W)**

Section 18 Rule 1 Where there is an unconditional contract for the sale of specific goods in a deliverable state the property in the goods passes to the buyer when the contract is made, and it is immaterial whether the time of payment or the time of delivery, or both, be postponed. …

Rule 5(1) Where there is a contract for the sale of unascertained or future goods by description, and goods of that description and in a deliverable state are unconditionally appropriated to the contract, either by the seller with the assent of the buyer or by the buyer with the assent of the seller, the property in the goods then passes to the buyer; and the assent may be express or implied, and may be given either before or after the appropriation is made.

Note

This rule accords with the approach taken by French law. Note, however, that English law does not have a uniform transfer system. The rules applying to immovables differ from the rules applying to movables, and, as we have seen above, within the category of movables case law and the Sale of Goods Act have developed rules which deviate from the ancient common law. If we read that the Sale of Goods Act purported to codify English common law, we should realise that the old common law had developed special rules on the passing of property in the case of sale, which did not apply outside the area of sales contracts.

I.B.4 DUTCH LAW

Introductory Note

As we have seen above, French law deliberately deviated from the Roman transfer system which required *traditio*, that is to say, transfer of the possession of the object. Transfer systems following this approach are called tradition systems. When in the beginning of the nineteenth century the Dutch Civil Code was drafted to replace the French Civil Code, which had been in force in the Netherlands since 1811, the drafters fiercely criticised the French consensual system and opted for a return to the Roman *traditio* requirement:

JC Voorduin, History and Principles of the Dutch Codes[20] **8.12 (NL)**

The question whether one should take the French code as a basis for the new revision soon transformed itself into a different question whether it would be preferable if, according to the system of French law, ownership is acquired and transferred by contract, or whether it would be better to restore the old rule, according to the principles of Roman law, that between contracting parties, from contracts, merely rights are born, but that ownership, especially as against third parties, is acquired only through *traditio* or conveyance.

The public interest, the certainty of possessions and the security of moneylenders soon led the drafters to restore the Roman distinction between a right against persons and a right on an object (*ius in re* and *ius ad rem*). The ancient customs and preference of all Dutch provinces backed this choice; and after the adoption of this principle, the possibility to follow closely the French code necessarily fell away, as it is known to all jurists that the division of this code is based solely on the rejection of this distinction.

By restoring this distinction the drafters returned to the order of the Roman Institutes; and they hesitated a little to accept this division again on a large scale because this division stands out from all later ones by its clarity and simplicity, because it has been proven by centuries of use and because it has been, as it were, sanctified by the authority of almost all of the greatest jurists and philosophers.

[20] JC Voorduin, *Geschiedenis en beginselen der Nederlandsche Wetboeken, Deel I, eerste stuk (algemene inleiding)* (Utrecht, 1837) 195–96.

Parliamentary History of the Dutch Civil Code, Book 3, 375 and 381–82 (Explanation of Meijers to Art 3:89 Burgerlijk Wetboek and Art 3:90) **8.13 (NL)**

(A) In accordance with the case law of the HR (judgment of 10 Dec 1937, NJ 1938 no 335) for the transfer [of immovable objects], not only a deed, but also its registration is required. The system which applies to patents and which was based on the 1898 draft and which was defended by Scholten also for the transfer of immovable property was relinquished, the system that registration serves only to render the transfer effective against third parties. It is, after all, undesirable that after insolvency of a seller, registration of a sales deed to the disadvantage of the insolvent's estate can still occur. It is equally undesirable to give the buyer an action of revindication (*rei vindicatio*) against third-party possessors already before registration. One excessively weakens the significance of the registration and would induce many purchasers to neglect registration when, before such registration, they might have a title, albeit a still incomplete title.

(B) As in current law it is accepted that the delivery of title in movable objects takes place by transfer of possession. There is no reason to relinquish this system, which the legislature of 1838 preferred above that of the French Code—transfer of ownership already as a result of the legal ground, for example the contract of sale.* Even if the difference is for the most part one of construction, in those cases in which the difference in system leads to a difference in legal consequences—particularly the case of insolvency of the seller, who has not yet transferred possession—the Dutch system has worked satisfactorily.

*Also in France and Belgium the system of the Code is criticised See de Page VI p 86: 'One should abandon the translative effect of contracts, which is but a nonsense, a nest of difficulties and which the majority of contemporary legislations had the wisdom not to borrow from the French Civil Code.'

Note

Meijers, the most influential drafter of the 1992 Dutch Civil Code, maintained the distinction of the 1838 Civil Code, again criticising the French model.

Burgerlijk Wetboek **8.14 (NL)**

Article 3:84(1) The transfer of an object requires an act of transfer based on a valid legal ground performed by a person who has the right to dispose of the object.

Article 3:90(1) The transfer required for the transfer of movable objects, non-registered things, which are in the power of the transferor takes place by providing the acquirer with possession of the object.

Article 3:89(1) The transfer required for the transfer of immovable objects takes place by a notarial deed made between the parties for this purpose, followed by registration of the deed in the public land register. Both the transfer and the transferee are able to have the deed registered.

Note

In addition to the transfer of possession, it is commonly said, a tradition system requires a separate legal act aimed specially at transferring ownership: the *real agreement*. This is clearly expressed by the drafters of the German Civil Code. It is said that, unlike a consensual system, a tradition system distinguishes between, on the one hand, the underlying legal act that obliges transfer of ownership and, on the other hand, the subsequent legal act which effectuates the transfer. Whereas in a consensual system the contract, ie consensus between the parties, suffices (hence its name), in a tradition system the contract merely calls into being an obligation to transfer the object sold. In the latter system ownership will pass only after the legal act of transfer and *traditio* have taken place.[21] Making this distinction between contract and transfer is in Germany referred to as the *Trennungsprinzip* (the principle of separation).

I.B.5 GERMAN LAW

Motives for the Draft of a Civil Code for the German Nation, Book III[22] **8.15 (DE)**

If the intention of the parties, the present owner and the acquirer, is the transfer of ownership, the occurrence of the intended legal effect requires an agreement to attain this result. In this respect, the *gemeine Recht* and the modern legislations, as interpreted by the majority view in doctrine, consistently agree, even though the express characterisation of the transfer of ownership as a real agreement is missing in the modern legislations. …

French law, and the codifications which follow French law, deviate from the *gemeine Recht* and the legislations which follow the *gemeine Recht*, in that the simple formless contract should suffice for the transfer, whereas the *gemeine Recht* sets the requirement of delivery.

The draft proceeds (§91) on the principle of a lack of forms. Therefore, however, a need will have to be proved, in order to deny, in the case of the transfer of ownership through a legal transaction, effect to the mere expressions of intention and link occurrence of the intended effect to fulfilment of a further requirement. Such a need can be demonstrated by the following grounds:

As in the law of real property the principle of registration serves maintenance of the correctness of the land register and hence publicity of the current legal status, in the law of movable property the principle of delivery serves similar purposes, by precluding, if at all possible, a divergence of possession and ownership and it contributes to publicity of the current legal status. Although in comparison with the land register it works imperfectly, it is nevertheless still of great practical value. …

From the outset French law suffers from the defect that indebtedness and the belonging of the movable thing and also the promise and the disposition are not separated from one another. If one duly keeps these various things separate, it

[21] In English law the separate legal act of transfer may be called conveyance. It is a legal term mainly used in English land law.

[22] *Motive zu dem Entwurfe eines Bürgerlichen Gesetzbuches für das Deutsche Reich*, vol III, *Sachenrecht* (Berlin and Leipzig, 1888) 333–34.

becomes apparent, that the Code Civil is not fully serious about the transfer of ownership by mere contract. The thrust of the effect of this contract is curbed by Art 2279: 'in the case of movables, possession equals title'; the acquirer receives only a relative ownership vis-à-vis the seller. Should one wish to follow French law, then one would have to accept the same in its entirety. If one takes this route, this results in a strengthening of the obligation to transfer a movable thing, which does not align with the concept of obligation underlying the draft, and a linkage of the passing of ownership with the passing of possession, which does not align with the concept of ownership. That this artificial construction corresponds to a practical need, especially in the case of the insolvency of the obligor, and that therefore one must override all reservations surrounding the construction, is doubted even by by French scholarly writers.

I.B.6 AUSTRIAN LAW

Introductory Note

Austrian law on transfer of ownership is based on the seventeenth- and eighteenth-century theory of *titulus* and *modus*, requiring for every transfer of ownership a legal ground (*titulus*) and an additional formality (*modus*) such as delivery in the case of movable property. A contract of sale, for example, does not itself pass ownership to the buyer.

Algemeines Bürgerliches Gesetzbuch **8.16 (AT)**

§380 Without legal ground and without a legal way to acquire ownership, no ownership can be acquired.

F von Zeiller, Commentary to §380[23] **8.17 (AT)**

(1) In order to acquire ownership, as well as other property rights …, the acquisition must first of all be legally feasible. … This legal feasibility, or rather the ground, on which the acquisition can be justified, is called the legal ground or title.

(2) For a true acquisition, however, a fact, an act, or circumstance, must be added thereto, because otherwise the absolute, original situation, in which the extraneous objects are available for use, would continue. First of all, someone must at least have the intention to appropriate an object; for without this intention, the free use of this object would not cause a restriction on anybody's free will, and it would not injure anyone's right. However, in order to be a binding rule for others that they may not intervene with those objects, the intention must also be rendered recognisable by an external act, by a permanent sign. This act, by which one brings an object within one's custody and declares to hold it as one's own is called the mode of acquisition. In this regard, for the acquisition of ownership, in addition to the legal ground a mode of acquisition is also necessary.

[23] F von Zeiller, *Commentar über das allgemeine bürgerliche Gesetzbuch für die gesammten Deutschen Erbländer der Oesterreichischen Monarchie*, vol 2, first part (Vienna and Triest 1812) 156/157 (commentary to §380).

Algemeines Bürgerliches Gesetzbuch **8.18 (AT)**

§424 The legal ground for a derivative acquisition is found in a contract, in a disposition, in a last will of a deceased person, in a court decision, or, in statute.

§425 The mere legal ground does not give ownership. The right of ownership and all other property rights can, except for those cases dealt with by statute, only be acquired by legal transfer and acceptance.

Note

Modern tradition systems such as German, Dutch and Austrian law deviate from Roman law in that the transfer of immovable property does not require a transfer of possession but rather entry into a land register. In part II of this chapter the various systems of land registration will be dealt with.

I.C EXCEPTIONS TO THE CONSENSUAL TRANSFER SYSTEM

In consensual transfer systems there are many cases in which the contract itself does not suffice to pass ownership to the acquirer. The principle of consensualism, the *solo consensu* rule, is confined to *specific existing* objects. Where the goods sold are *generic* or *future* goods, ownership cannot pass the moment the contract is made.

I.C.1 GENERIC GOODS[24]

Cour de cassation, com, 12 April 2005[25] **8.19 (FR)**

Reza Gem v Lafont (administrator for Chaumet et cie)

PASSING OF OWNERSHIP IN SALE ON APPROVAL

Gems

The sale on approval passed ownership of the elected objects at the moment of approval.

Facts: Reza Gem regularly sold and delivered precious stones to Chaumet on approval, or deposited with an option to buy. Chaumet had the right to inspect the stones and decide afterwards which ones to buy. When the company was declared insolvent, Reza Gem tried to revindicate some of the stones which remained unpaid. The central question was whether ownership in the relevant stones had passed to Chaumet.

Held: Ownership of the elected stones passed to Chaumet at the moment it decided which ones to keep.

Judgment: But considering, in the first place, that after having raised the issue, by adopted reasons, that the contract in dispute derogated from the Code of Customs for the Jewellery-Gemstone-Goldsmith-Fancy Goods trades, the court of appeal, which at its entire discretion conducted an analysis of the contractual documents and correspondence exchanged between the parties that their connection rendered necessary,

[24] See further on movables Chapter 7.
[25] No de pourvoi: 00–19939.

found, by reasons both of its own and adopted, that the company Reza Gem recognised, on the one side, that the monthly payments made by the company, from 30 September 1986 to 28 February 1988, corresponded to definitive purchases in an amount of 7,700,000 francs, on the other side, that the company had the power to sell the jewels by virtue of a definitive purchase contract independently from the cashing of the monthly deposit slips; that the court of appeal deduced therefrom that the common intention of the parties was, as from the time at which the stones were handed over, to conclude a definitive purchase contract relating to a portion of them, with individualisation of the thing sold occurring subsequently, at the moment when the company made its election, the price being known upon delivery of the stones;

that, having found that the sale was of effect and having effected a transfer of ownership at the moment when the company made its choice, the court of appeal decided that the company Reza Gem was on the day of the commencement of the collective procedure no longer the owner of the stones forming the object of deposits nos 23, 27, 46, 53, part of deposit no 26, for which the company had requested invoicing on 7 May 1987 and whose value was included in the sum of 7,700,000 francs, it making no difference that the invoicing had not been done and the price had not been paid;

Considering, in the second place, that, after having found, by adopted reasons, that it has not produced in the proceedings any document showing that the company had, expressly or impliedly, accepted a reservation of ownership clause, the judgment finds, by its own reasons, that this clause, stipulated for the first time between the parties subsequently to delivery of the stones, is of no effect vis-à-vis the company by application of Article 121, paragraph 2, of the law of 25 January 1985; that the judgment deduces therefrom that the revindication relating to the two pear-shaped diamonds and the round emerald of 4.90 carats is not founded; that such as its findings and appreciation in the case is, disregarding the overabundant arguments criticised by the first and second branches, the court of appeal, which has not disregarded the terms of the agreement binding the parties, has legally justified its decision;

It therefore follows that the argument cannot be admitted.

Cour de cassation, civ 1e, 19 February 2002[26] **8.20 (FR)**

Balat and Lauzeral v Pépinières Boissay and Vinceneux

MOMENT OF PASSING OF OWNERSHIP

Horticultural nurseries

Ownership of movables passes when the contract is made and the objects have been individualised.

Facts: Horticultural nursery Boissay sold and delivered a number of plants to horticultural nursery Lauzeral. The claimants assert that ownership and hence risk in the goods would pass to them only after counting and weighing of the goods and not at the moment the contract of sale was made.

Held: Ownership and risk passes to the when the goods were received by the buyer.

[26] No de pourvoi: 99-12585.

Judgment: ... On the sole argument, taken in its four parts:

Considering that the judgment challenged (Orléans, 19 March 1998) is complained of for having jointly and severally ordered M Jacques Lauzeral, in his capacity as heir to Yves Lauzeral, and Mrs Lauzeral, born Balat, inheriting the rights of her husband, to pay to Earl Les Pépinières Boissay the sum of an invoice for delivery of plants to the Pépinières Lauzeral, whereas, according to the argumentation:

(1) as the sale relates to a certain number of plants and of different sizes, the transfer of risks and of ownership could only be effected after the counting and measuring operations and not by the sole meeting of offer and acceptance; from which it follows that, by stating that only Article 1583 of the Civil Code was susceptible of governing the sale in dispute and deducing therefrom that same was perfected between the parties and ownership acquired by the purchaser vis-à-vis the seller from the moment that the parties agreed on the thing and the price, even though the thing had not yet been delivered nor the price paid, the court of appeal has violated Article 1585 of the Civil Code by refusing to apply the article; ...

But considering, on the first branch, that the court of appeal found that the plants ordered from Earl Les Pépinières Boissay had been delivered and received by Pépinières Lauzeral, from which it resulted that there had been individualisation of the plants sold and, hence, transfer of the ownership and risks; that, therefore, the judgment is legally justified, without regard to the erroneous but superfluous argument relative to the application, in this case, of Article 1583 of the Civil Code.

Privy Council, 25 May 1994[27] **8.21 (E&W)**

re Goldcorp Exchange Ltd (in receivership)

APPROPRIATION

Goldcorp

No passing of property without appropriation.

Facts: In this New Zealand case a company dealing in gold and other precious metals had sold bullion for future delivery to numerous purchasers. The bullion was not appropriated to the individual contracts, but was instead stored en masse as part of the company's overall stock of bullion. Subsequently the company became insolvent and a bank holding a debenture secured by a floating charge appointed receivers. The purchasers contended inter alia that under the contracts of sale ownership of the bullion had passed to them, so that the bullion purchased was not subject to the bank's charge.

Held: The purchasers have not acquired ownership of the bullion, since no bullion has been appropriated to their individual contracts.

Judgment: Their Lordships begin with the question whether the customer obtained any form of proprietary interest, legal or equitable, simply by virtue of the contract of sale, independently of the collateral promises. In the opinion of their Lordships the answer is so clearly that he did not that it would be possible simply to quote s 18 of the Sale of Goods Act 1908 (New Zealand) (corresponding to s 16 of the Sale of Goods Act 1893 (UK)) and one reported case, and turn to more difficult issues. It is, however, convenient to pause for a moment to consider why the answer must

[27] [1995] 1 AC 74, [1994] 2 All ER 806, [1994] 3 WLR 199, 13 Tr L 434.

inevitably be negative, because the reasons for this answer are the same as those which stand in the way of the customers at every point of the case.

It is common ground that the contracts in question were for the sale of unascertained goods. For present purposes, two species of unascertained goods may be distinguished. First, there are 'generic goods'. These are sold on terms which preserve the seller's freedom to decide for himself how and from what source he will obtain goods answering the contractual description. Secondly, there are 'goods sold ex-bulk'. By this expression their Lordships denote goods which are by express stipulation to be supplied from a fixed and a pre-determined source, from within which the seller may make his own choice (unless the contract requires it to be made in some other way) but outside which he may not go. For example, 'I sell you 60 of the 100 sheep now on my farm'.

Approaching these situations a priori common sense dictates that the buyer cannot acquire title until it is known to what goods the title relates. Whether the property then passes will depend upon the intention of the parties and in particular on whether there has been a consensual appropriation of particular goods to the contract. On the latter question the law is not straightforward, and if it had been decisive of the present appeal it would have been necessary to examine cases such as *Carlos Federspiel & Co SA v Charles Twigg & Co Ltd* [1957] 1 Lloyd's Rep 240 and other cases cited in argument. In fact, however, the case turns not on appropriation but on ascertainment, and on the latter the law has never been in doubt. It makes no difference what the parties intended if what they intend is impossible: as is the case with an immediate transfer of title to goods whose identity is not yet known. As Lord Blackburn wrote in his Treatise on the Effect of the Contract of Sale (1st edn, 1845), pp 122–123, a principal inspiration of the Sale of Goods Act 1893:

> 'The first of [the rules] that the parties must be agreed as to the specific goods on which the contract is to attach before there can be a bargain and sale, is one that is founded on the very nature of things. Till the parties are agreed on the specific individual goods, the contract can be no more than a contract to supply goods answering a particular description, and since the vendor would fulfil his part of the contract by furnishing any parcel of goods answering that description, and the purchaser could not object to them if they did answer the description, it is clear there can be no intention to transfer the property in any particular lot of goods more than another, till it is ascertained which are the very goods sold. This rule has existed at all times; it is to be found in the earliest English law books ... It makes no difference, although the goods are so far ascertained that the parties have agreed that they shall be taken from some specified larger stock. In such a case the reason still applies: the parties did not intend to transfer the property in one portion of the stock more than in another, and the law which only gives effect to their intention, does not transfer the property in any individual portion.'

Their Lordships have laboured this point, about which there has been no dispute, simply to show that any attempt by the non-allocated claimants to assert that a legal title passed by virtue of the sale would have been defeated, not by some arid legal technicality but by what Lord Blackburn called 'the very nature of things'.

Sale of Goods Act 1979 **8.22 (E&W)**

Section 16 Subject to section 20A below where there is a contract for the sale of unascertained goods no property in the goods is transferred to the buyer unless and until the goods are ascertained.

Note

The requirement of identification is a consequence of one of the most important principles of property law, namely the principle of specificity, the principle that ownership, or more correctly, property rights in general, can exist in relation to specific objects only. This is also the reason why section 16 of the Sale of Goods Act provides that property of unascertained goods cannot pass to a buyer. The character of the property right makes it impossible to be owner of unascertained goods: if ownership forms a relationship between a person and a certain object, it must be known to which specific object the right relates.

I.C.2 SALE *EX BULK* UNDER THE SALE OF GOODS ACT[28]

In 1995 a reform of the Sale of Goods Act gave fresh attention to one of the most fundamental problems of property law: the problem of identity of objects. Where unascertained generic goods have been sold, property cannot pass to the buyer until goods have been earmarked as the objects to be transferred to that buyer (appropriation). This rule, which can be found in section 16 of the Sale of Goods Act 1979, is still in force, though in 1995 it has been modified for the sale *ex bulk*, as the requirement of identification was considered to be too restrictive in such instances. The identity problem is not unique to English law: Dutch, French and German law as well as many other continental legal systems know a similar identification requirement within their law of property. Dutch, German, French and Austrian law, for example, founded their property law systems on this requirement. Accordingly they all had to make special statutory regimes to cope with cases in which goods lose their identity as a result of being mixed with other identical goods.

Sale of Goods Act 1979 **8.23 (E&W)**

Section 20A Undivided shares in goods forming part of a bulk

(1) This section applies to a contract for the sale of a specified quantity of unascertained goods if the following conditions are met—

(a) the goods or some of them form part of a bulk which is identified either in the contract or by subsequent agreement between the parties; and

(b) the buyer has paid the price for some or all of the goods which are the subject of the contract and which form part of the bulk.

(2) Where this section applies, then (unless the parties agree otherwise), as soon as

[28] See more detailed: LPW van Vliet, *Transfer of Movables in German, French, English and Dutch Law* (Nijmegen, Ars Aequi Libri 2000) 93–105.

the conditions specified in paragraphs (a) and (b) of subsection (1) above are met or at such later time as the parties may agree—

(a) property in an undivided share in the bulk is transferred to the buyer, and

(b) the buyer becomes an owner in common of the bulk.

(3) Subject to subsection (4) below, for the purposes of this section, the undivided share of a buyer in a bulk at any time shall be such share as the quantity of goods paid for and due to the buyer out of the bulk bears to the quantity of goods in the bulk at that time.

(4) Where the aggregate of the undivided shares of buyers in a bulk determined under subsection (3) above would at any time exceed the whole of the bulk at that time, the undivided share in the bulk of each buyer shall be reduced proportionately so that the aggregate of the undivided shares is equal to the whole bulk.

(5) Where a buyer has paid the price for only some of the goods due to him out of a bulk, any delivery to the buyer out of the bulk shall, for the purposes of this section, be ascribed in the first place to the goods in respect of which payment has been made.

(6) For the purposes of this section payment of part of the price for any goods shall be treated as payment for a corresponding part of the goods.

Section 20B Deemed consent by co-owner to dealings in bulk goods

(1) A person who has become an owner in common of a bulk by virtue of section 20A above shall be deemed to have consented to—

(a) any delivery of goods out of the bulk to any other owner in common of the bulk, being goods which are due to him under his contract;

(b) any dealing with or removal, delivery or disposal of goods in the bulk by any other person who is an owner in common of the bulk in so far as the goods fall within that co-owner's undivided share in the bulk at the time of the dealing, removal, delivery or disposal.

(2) No cause of action shall accrue to anyone against a person by reason of that person having acted in accordance with paragraph (a) or (b) of subsection (1) above in reliance on any consent deemed to have been given under that subsection.

(3) Nothing in this section or section 20A above shall—

(a) impose an obligation on a buyer of goods out of a bulk to compensate any other buyer of goods out of that bulk for any shortfall in the goods received by that other buyer;

(b) affect any contractual arrangement between buyers of goods out of a bulk for adjustments between themselves; or

(c) affect the rights of any buyer under his contract.

Notes

(1) The Sale of Goods (Amendment) Act 1995 has created a special statutory regime in sections 20A and 20B giving buyers ex bulk under certain conditions a

proprietary interest in the bulk goods.[29] The proprietary interest takes the form of a right of co-ownership in the bulk.

(2) We should bear in mind, however, that the amendment of the Sale of Goods Act is confined to sales *ex bulk* (see section 20A(1)). Thus, if there is no sale ex bulk, section 16 will apply and accordingly property will not pass before appropriation of the goods. Hence, two elements will now play a pivotal role: the definition of the word 'bulk' and, if there is indeed a bulk in the sense of section 20A, the question whether the parties to the contract of sale intended that the goods should be taken from that bulk only. These two elements will determine whether or not the co-ownership regime will apply. The definition of 'bulk', which is now to be found in section 61 (1) of the Sale of Goods Act, is not exactly unambiguous, but from the Law Commission's report we can at least understand that it was intended to exclude the seller's general stock.[30] Apparently in cases like *Re Goldcorp* the co-ownership regime will not apply and the buyers will still have to content themselves with a personal right against the seller. There is an obvious reason for this: for co-ownership to exist, it should be known which specific assets are co-owned. The principle of specification still applies, but here it applies to the entire bulk.

(3) As regards sales ex bulk the principle of specificity, as applied before the 1995 amendment, gave rise to some odd and arbitrary results. Let us take an example. Where the owner of a cargo has sold 500 tons out of a total bulk of 1,000 tons, property does not pass to the buyer before goods have been appropriated as the objects to be transferred to that particular buyer. This is, as we have seen, the result of the specificity principle. Nevertheless, it is possible for the seller to sell a 50% share in the bulk. In that case ownership of the share passes to the buyer immediately after the contract of sale is made. No appropriation is needed because the share relates to the whole of the bulk and consequently to every item within the bulk. Since the amount of goods is exactly the same, it is hard to see any practical difference. Yet the buyer of a share acquires a proprietary interest whereas the buyer of a certain amount merely has a personal right to delivery of the goods.

(4) If, to give another example, in the first case appropriation has taken place and subsequently the 500 tons, that have now passed to the buyer, are mixed with the remaining bulk, the seller and buyer will become co-owners of the bulk. The buyer does not lose his proprietary interest, even though the goods have lost their identity: his right of property is converted into a right of co-ownership (a 50% share) of the bulk. As regards identity of the goods the situation is the same as before appropriation: the goods form part of a larger bulk. Nonetheless, the buyer whose goods have been appropriated and then mixed again, has a proprietary interest, whereas

[29] Not long before the amendment of the Sale of Goods Act, in *Re Stapylton Fletcher Ltd* [1995] 1 All ER 192, buyers of unascertained goods were given co-ownership of a collection of goods. It was decided that, if the seller has segregated goods from his general stock and appropriated them unconditionally to the buyers collectively, the buyers become co-owners (tenants in common) of those goods. Appropriation to the individual buyers was held not to be necessary.

[30] Law Com Report no 215/Scot Law Com Report no 145, 18.

the buyer, whose goods have never been appropriated, has to content himself with a personal right.[31]

(5) By using this method of calculation section 20A creates a special form of co-ownership, namely co-ownership of a certain amount of goods: the buyer will become co-owner of such number of goods as corresponds with the amount bought and paid for. The normal form of co-ownership, on the other hand, is for a certain percentage rather than a certain amount. If the prepaying buyer were given the normal form of co-ownership, he would profit from an increase[32] in the bulk and lose in case of a reduction[33] of the bulk. Where there is normal co-ownership the relative proportion of the share is fixed, ie the percentage remains the same, but the absolute amount it represents fluctuates when the bulk increases or decreases. We can therefore say that the standard form of co-ownership entails a fixed percentage and a variable amount of goods.

(6) If the requirements in section 20A are met, the buyer will become a co-owner of the bulk.[34] Even so, when the contract is for the sale of a certain number of goods the seller is obliged to pass property of these goods to the buyer. That the buyer has already received a share in the bulk does not suffice. The seller is obliged to transfer individual property[35] of a certain number of identified assets. In order to do this appropriation of the goods is needed. As to that nothing has changed. The co-ownership regime is merely a transitional phase designed to protect the buyer in the event of the seller's insolvency. We could see it as a security interest or a peculiar sort of 'buyer's lien' in the form of co-ownership. The moment of appropriation should still be considered as the moment when property of the contract goods passes. Accordingly we can assume that this is also the time when the risk passes to the buyer under section 20 of the Sale of Goods Act.

(7) The reform was induced by the decision in *The Gosforth*, a case decided by the Dutch District Court of Rotterdam in 1985. It was a case in which goods that were on board a vessel called *The Gosforth* had been sold to several buyers. The goods, citrus pulp pellets, had not been appropriated to the individual contracts. Now, although the case was decided on other grounds, which are not relevant here, the president of the court stated, in an *obiter dictum*, that under English law property of generic goods cannot pass until they are identified.[36]

[31] Both examples are mentioned in the Law Com Report on 4 and 5.
[32] For example, an increase as a result of the avoidance of a contract of sale or as a result of original acquisition.
[33] For instance, when part of the goods perish.
[34] Although, it should be noted that the new co-ownership regime is ius dispositivum: the parties can agree that co-ownership will pass at a later time or they can opt out of the new provisions altogether. See s 20A(2) and the Law Commission's report, 20 and 39.
[35] As distinct from co-ownership.
[36] S&S 1985/91.

President Rechtbank Rotterdam, 20 February 1985[37] **8.24 (NL)**

Palte en Haentjes BV and others v Comodity SA

PASSING OF PROPERTY OF BULK GOODS

The Gosforth

No property in the bulk goods passes to the buyers before appropriation.

Facts: Comodity sold an amount of citrus pulp to Josco USA, who in turn sold the bulk on to various sub-buyers via ICM, who split the bill of lading into 13 merchant delivery orders given to the sub-buyers. Josco USA did not pay the purchase price. Right after the goods had arrived in the harbour of Rotterdam, but before delivery had taken place to the sub-buyers, Comodity seized the goods. The sub-buyers opposed the seizure, claiming that at the moment of seizure the property in the cargo belonged to ICM, a company holding the bill of lading.

Held: ICM has not received property in the goods because the property in generic bulk goods does not pass until the goods are appropriated to the buyer in question. At the moment of seizure Josco USA still owns the goods.

Judgment: The purchase contracts between Josco USA and the European buyers are governed by English law. ...

The question, therefore, whether as a result of the issuance of the delivery orders ownership has passed to the holders of those delivery orders, the European buyers, therefore requires to be answered according to applicable English law and not according to the *lex rei sitae*, as the European buyers have argued.

Firstly, it is maintained that neither under English nor under Dutch law could ICM, which—as we have accepted under I—was merely the holder of the bill of lading, by the issuance of the delivery orders to the European buyers turn itself from a holder for Josco USA into a holder for the European holders and thereby deprive Josco USA of ownership of the goods.

With that, the question posed at the beginning of this ground is actually already answered.

However, even disregarding that, a 'merchant' delivery order, as is referred to in this case, does not confer any possession and ownership on the holder of such an order under the prevailing opinions both under English and under Dutch law, but solely a claim for delivery against him who has issued that order, hence ICM in the present case. Put differently: the issuance of delivery orders such as the present ones has no property law effect.

Furthermore, it occurs to us that, under English law, the holder of a 'merchant' delivery order only receives ownership of the goods embodied in the order upon delivery by him who has factual (physical) possession of the goods and who also holds those goods for the holder of the delivery order. Those conditions were not and are not fulfilled by ICM in any respect.

The contention by Comodity that, according to English law, no delivery and transfer of ownership of the goods embodied in the 'merchant' delivery orders takes place until those goods are individualised also seems to us for the time being correct but, alongside that considered in the foregoing, is no longer of importance.

[37] S&S 1985/91.

Note

Of course, there was nothing remarkable about this statement. Nonetheless it once more drew attention to the identification issue in section 16 Sale of Goods Act and led to the Law Commission examining the legal position of buyers ex bulk. In 1989 the English and Scottish Law Commissions issued a consultation paper about the subject.[38] Subsequently, in 1993 they released their final reports,[39] which, among other things, contained a list of recommendations to change the law regarding sales ex bulk and a draft bill embodying the changes recommended.

I.C.3 GOODS THAT HAVE YET TO BE MANUFACTURED

Introductory Note

Where an object is sold that has yet to be manufactured, ownership cannot pass at the moment the contract is made. The *solo consensu* principle of Article 1138 of the French Civil Code does not apply here. In principle, ownership and risk pass to the buyer when the object is finished. And, according to the Cour de cassation,[40] it is finished when it is in such a state that it can be delivered by the seller and accepted by the buyer. The object should be in the state agreed upon by the parties.[41] In the case of a specific object ownership can already pass before the object has been finished. The parties may validly agree that ownership of a ship's keel passes before the ship has been finished and this agreement passes ownership directly.[42] However, in the case of a sale of future generic objects ownership cannot pass before the objects which have to pass to the buyer have been appropriated. In the latter instance it does not suffice for the goods to have been finished.

Cour de cassation, 1 August 1950[43] **8.25 (FR)**

Coder v Ossude

PASSING OF PROPERTY IN FUTURE OBJECT

Trailer

The sale of a future object passes ownership when the object is in a deliverable state.

Facts: In 1939 the company Ossude ordered from the company Coder a trailer to be built according to Ossude's specifications. Part of the price was paid immediately. After the trailer had been finished, but before it had been delivered to the buyer, the German occupying forces seized the trailer in 1941. Coder was compensated for the loss. Ossude claims that it had become owner of the trailer at the time of the seizure and that Coder should hand over the compensation to Ossude. The Paris Court of Appeal

[38] Law Com Working Paper No 112, 'Rights to Goods in Bulk' (April 1989); Scot Law Com Discussion Paper No 83, 'Bulk Goods: Section 16 of the Sale of Goods Act 1979 and Section 1 of the Bills of Lading Act 1855' (August 1989).

[39] Sale of goods forming part of a bulk, Law Com no 215, Scot Law Com no 145.

[40] Cass civ 3, 12 July 1976, no 75–11.252

[41] See Mazeaud/Chabas, *Vente et échange* (Paris, Montchrestien, 1987) 187 and 215–16.

[42] Cass civ 20 mars 1872, DP 1872.1.140.

[43] Cass civ 1 August 1950, S 1951.1.100.

held that ownership had passed to Ossude and that the money should be handed over to Ossude. Coder appealed and in his first complaint claimed that ownership cannot have passed without delivery to and acceptance by the buyer.

Held: In the case of a sale of a future object the right of ownership passes to the buyer when the object is in a deliverable state. The first complaint is therefore dismissed. The judgment of the Court of Appeal is nonetheless reversed on different grounds.

Judgment: Considering, on the other hand, that in the case of sale of a future object, there is passing of ownership immediately when the object one has undertaken to deliver is effectively able to be delivered by the seller and received by the purchaser;

That it is constant, in this case, that on the day when the requisition order was notified to the manufacturer, the construction of the trailer as stipulated was complete; that, without doubt, the constituent elements were in the ownership of the manufacturer as long as the object had not become individualised merchandise, but that as from the moment when the manufacturing operations had made of them a certain corpus, susceptible to delivery, the trailer was located in the patrimony of the purchaser by application of Article 1583 Cciv, even though physical delivery had not been effected, given that the obligor had not been served with notice requiring him to deliver it (Art 1138 Cciv).

Cour de cassation, civ 3e, 12 July 1976[44] **8.26 (FR)**

Guibert v SMCTP

PASSING OF FUTURE IMMOVABLE OBJECT

Apartment

The sale of a future apartment passes ownership only when the apartment is in a deliverable state.

Facts: Mr and Mrs Guibert sold a plot of land to a building society. The building society developed the land by erecting an apartment building. The purchase price was to be paid in kind by transferring to the Guiberts a number of apartments to be chosen by them. The notarial deed of transfer of the apartments should have been made at 31 December 1970 at the latest. However, the act was never made, because the building society was declared insolvent after finishing the building but before making the deed. The Guiberts claimed to be owners of the promised apartments, saying that the obligation to transfer is self-executory and therefore has passed the right of ownership to them before the insolvency.

Held: In the case of payment in kind of a future object, as in the case of sale of a future object, ownership passes to the payee only when the object is effectively in such a state that it can be delivered by the transferor and can be received by the transferee. Here, the right of ownership did not pass, because no individualisation had taken place yet at the relevant moment.

Judgment: But considering that in the case of accord and satisfaction as in the case of sale of a future thing, the passing of ownership is only effected in favour of the beneficiary of this satisfaction where the object is effectively deliverable by him who must give it and received by him to whom it is given;

that after having pointed out that in terms of the act of 25 July 1969, the transfer of ownership of the apartments which were only described as to their consistency

[44] No de pourvoi: 75-11252. See also Cass civ 1er 15 November 1989, No de pourvoi: 87-19699 (*Guigou v Antoine and others*).

was to form the object of an act to be drawn up no later than 31 December 1970, that Mr and Mrs Guibert had not, in the time provided for, drawn up this act, and that although the act of separation of the building into 78 apartments had been created on 16 January 1970, it did not fix any attribution of the said apartments, the Court of Appeal states that, the building being non-existent and the apartments non-individualised upon the signature of the act of 1969, no transfer of ownership of these apartments enforceable against third parties has been effected; ...

that on these grounds, the Court of Appeal ... has, without incurring the grounds for the appeal argument, justified its decision;

on these grounds: rejects the appeal formulated against the judgment rendered on 10 July 1974 by the Court of Appeal of Montpellier.

Note

It is not always easy to tell if an object has reached the point of completion. The criterion is far from clear. Of course the object should answer to the description in the contract. But even this is too vague. How do we know whether the object meets the contract requirements? Should the manufacturer decide, or the commissioner?

Cour de cassation, 14 March 1900[45] **8.27 (FR)**

Eden v Whistler

WHEN IS A PAINTING FINISHED?

Whistler

Ownership of a commissioned painting passes only when the artist hands the painting over to the client and the latter gives his approval.

Facts: Lord William Eden had commissioned James Whistler to make a portrait of Lady Eden. Whistler started working and made a painting that fully met Lord Eden's expectations. However, ultimately Whistler refused to deliver the painting, changed it and exhibited it at Champ de Mars, Paris. Lord Eden demanded delivery.

Held: Where a painting has been commissioned, the right of ownership passes only when the artist hands the painting over to the client and the latter approves of the painting. Until that moment the artist remains the 'master of his work'.

Judgment: Considering that the agreement by which a painter undertakes to execute a portrait, in exchange for a fixed price, constitutes a contract of a special nature, by virtue of which ownership of the painting is not definitively acquired by the party that has ordered it until the artist has placed the painting at the latter's disposal and it has been approved by the latter;

Until this moment the painter remains the master of his work, although he may not retain it for himself or dispose of it in favour of a third party, in the state of a portrait, the right to reproduce the features of the model only being conferred upon him conditionally for the purpose of complete performance of the contract; and that, if the artist fails to fulfil his undertakings, he renders himself liable to damages;

Considering that it results from the findings of the judgment appealed against that

[45] D 1900.1.497; S 1900.1.489.

Whistler undertook to make the portrait of Lady Eden, but that he always refused to place the said portrait at the disposal of the claimant before the Court of Cassation who had ordered it; and that after having exhibited the painting at the Champ de Mars salon, he radically modified the painting, replacing the head of Lady Eden with that of another person;

Considering, in this state of affairs, that by deciding, on the one hand, that the claimant to the Court of Cassation, not having become the owner of the painting, could not demand its delivery in its current state, on the other hand, that Whistler would be bound to repay with damages the price received in advance, and by prohibiting, furthermore, the latter from making any use whatsoever of the canvas before having modified aspects of it, so as to render it unrecognisable, the judgment appealed against, which is motivated, far from violating the law texts referred to in the appeal, has made, on the contrary, a just application of them;

For these reasons: rejects the appeal.

I.C.4 REJECTION OF DEFECTIVE GOODS

High Court, Queen's Bench Division, 17 October 1958[46] **8.28 (E&W)**

McDougall v Aeromarine of Emsworth

PASSING OF PROPERTY AND REJECTION OF DELIVERY

Rejected yacht

Lawful rejection revests property in the seller.

Facts: McDougall entered into a contract with Aeromarine of Emsworth for the construction of a yacht. After payment of several instalments a trial run showed that the yacht had defective seams and the buyer refused to take delivery. After some additional resplining work the yacht was still not fit for delivery. It would take a lot of time to make the yacht fit for delivery. The buyer disclaimed any property in the yacht and sued the defendant for repayment of the instalments. Section 8 of the contract provided: 'The said craft together with all materials equipment fittings and machinery purchased by the builders specifically for the construction thereof whether in their building yard workshops water or elsewhere shall become the absolute property of the purchaser upon the first instalment being paid hereunder provided that the builders shall have a lien upon the craft materials equipment fittings and machinery for recovery of all sums due whether invoiced or not under the terms of this agreement or any variation or modification thereof.' The question before the court was whether this clause prevented the buyer from rejecting property in the yacht.

Held: Clause 8 of the contract does not deprive the claimant of the right to reject the yacht and if, under the contract, property has passed to the buyer, lawful rejection would revest property in the seller.

Judgment: Diplock J—The defendants' failure to tender the yacht for delivery in accordance with the contract by Sept 5 was itself a breach of condition which the plaintiff was entitled to treat as rescinding the contract. ... Such part of the property, if any, in the vessel or any portion thereof as had previously vested in him under cl 8 of the contract accordingly re-vested then in the defendants.

I hold, therefore, that by Sept 5, 1957, on the grounds that I have indicated, the plaintiff was entitled to treat the contract as rescinded by the defendants and elected to do so on Sept 19. ... The plaintiff is, accordingly, entitled to judgment for

[46] [1958] 3 All ER 431, [1958] 1 WLR 1126, [1958] 2 Lloyd's Rep.

the sum of £1,736 15s 6d as money paid for a consideration that has wholly failed. He is also entitled to recover £88 4s 7d for surveyor's fees and other expenses and damages for the loss of use of the yacht during part at least of the 1957 season.

Note

The parties to the contract may agree that property will pass before the object commissioned is finished: according to section 17 of the Sale of Goods Act property passes when the parties intend it to pass. Sometimes in ship-building contracts the parties agree that property in the future ship (the keel and everything attached to it) should pass when certain instalments have been paid.[47] Such an agreement had been made in the above case of *McDougall v Aeromarine of Emsworth Ltd*. By doing so the buyer excludes the risk of the builder's insolvency, accepting at the same time, though, the risk of accidental loss or damage, since in English law risk passes at the same time as property, unless otherwise agreed. Once the property of the keel has passed to the buyer materials used in the building process and fixed onto the future ship automatically pass to the buyer as a result of *accessio*.

House of Lords, 15 December 1983[48] **8.29 (E&W)**

Berger & Co Inc v Gill & Duffus SA

RIGHT TO REJECT

Beans

When the buyer rightfully rejects the goods property revests in the seller.

Facts: Berger & Co sold a quantity of 500 tonnes of beans to Gill & Duffus cost, insurance and freight (cif) Le Havre. Payment should have taken place against shipping documents and a specified certificate of quality. Only 445 tonnes were unloaded in Le Havre; the remaining 55 tonnes was overcarried to Rotterdam. The quality certificate was in order but related only to the 455 tonnes. The buyers rejected the entire bulk and refused to pay. When the remaining 55 tonnes arrived, the buyers again rejected these goods because the quality certificate did not cover these goods. The sellers sued the buyers for damage for non-payment and the buyers sued the sellers for non-delivery. In arbitration the umpire decided in favour of the sellers. The Board of Appeal found in favour of the sellers as to the 445 tonnes and in favour of the buyers in relation to the 55 tonnes. The Court of Appeal decided in favour of the buyers for the entire quantity. The sellers approached the House of Lords to reverse the judgment of the Court of Appeal.

Held: The buyers' refusal to pay is a fundamental breach of the contract. The buyers have to pay the contract price for the 500 tonnes unless they can prove that they would have been able to reject the goods on delivery at Le Havre. The quality certificate related only to the 445 tonnes, but, as there is no suggestion that the quality between the two loads of beans differed. The buyers have failed to show that a quality certificate would not have been issued for the remaining 55 tonnes.

Judgment: Lord Diplock—My Lords, it is trite law for which I do not find it necessary to refer to any other authority than the judgment of Devlin J in *Kwei Tek Chao v British Traders and Shippers Ltd* [1954] 2 QB 459, 487–488, that when a buyer

[47] Benjamin's Sale of Goods, §5-091.
[48] [1984] AC 382.

under a cif contract accepts shipping documents which transfer the property in the goods to him, the property in the goods that he obtains is subject to the condition subsequent that it will revest in the seller if upon examination of the goods themselves upon arrival the buyer finds them to be not in accordance with the contract in some respect which would entitle him to reject them, and he does in fact reject them. But this is because the cif contract remains on foot; and being a contract for the sale of goods, the buyer has the right under section 34 of the Sale of Goods Act 1893 to reject the goods themselves for non-conformity with the contract and retains this right until he has had a reasonable opportunity of examining the goods after they have been delivered.[49]

E McKendrick, Goode on Commercial Law[50] **8.30 (E&W)**

It is generally considered that where defective goods are tendered, the buyer has but two alternatives: to adopt the contract or to reject the goods and thereby treat the contract as discharged. Such an assumption, though deriving some support from s 11(4) of the Sale of Goods Act, is neither consonant with legal principle nor in accord with commercial practice. The typical buyer, confronted with defective goods, does not do either of these things. He tells the seller that the goods are not accepted in the condition in which they are tendered and asks that they be repaired or replaced. The tender is rejected but the buyer holds the contract open for performance by a fresh tender. Even if the buyer does not request or desire repair or replacement of the defective goods, the seller is as a rule entitled to do this if he still has time under the contract. The sole effect of rejection as such is to nullify delivery. The seller is treated as if he had not tendered delivery at all. …

Unless otherwise agreed, where the buyer exercises a right to reject, the property in the goods revests in the seller and the goods are again at his risk. …

Note

When Goode and McKendrick say '[t]he sole effect of rejection as such is to nullify delivery' he must refer to a legal act transferring property to the buyer. Delivery as a mere factual act of bringing the goods in the possession of the buyer cannot be nullified. Facts cannot be nullified; legal acts can.[51]

I.D TRANSFER OF POSSESSION: *TRADITIO VERA* AND *TRADITIO FICTA*

The most primitive way of transferring possession of a physical object is handing over the object or, in the case of bulky goods or land, giving the transferee access to the object. The *traditio* requirement was considerably mitigated already in classical Roman law (the first two and a half centuries AD). In this period forms of

[49] See also *J & H Ritchie Ltd v Lloyd Ltd* [2007] UKHL 9 and *Clegg and another v Olle Andersson* [2003] EWCA Civ 320.

[50] E McKendrick, *Goode on Commercial Law* (London, Penguin, 2010), 371.

[51] Van Vliet, above n 28, 109–10.

tradition were acknowledged in which no transfer of direct possession[52] took place: *constitutum possessorium* and *traditio brevi manu*, as they were later to be named.[53] From the period of the glossators these forms of fictitious transfer of possession or *traditio ficta* have been disseminated across the continent alongside the Roman law requirement of *traditio*.

The tradition systems of the jurisdictions considered in this case book, English, Dutch, German and Austrian law, all recognise fictitious ways of transferring possession (*traditio ficta*) in addition to the real transfer of possession (*traditio vera*). Sometimes the term *traditio symbolica* is used to denote the transfer of possession by, for examplem handing over of keys. It is doubtful whether this should be regarded as a separate way of transferring possession.

I.D.1 *TRADITIO SYMBOLICA*

A clear explanation of *traditio symbolica* was given by Lord Hardwicke in *Ward v Turner*:[54]

> It is argued, that though some delivery is necessary yet delivery of the thing is not necessary, but delivery of anything by way of symbol is sufficient: but I cannot agree to that; nor do I find any authority for that in the civil law. ... Delivery of the key of bulky goods, where wines &c are, has been allowed as delivery of the possession, because it is the way of coming at the possession or to make use of the thing, and therefore the key is not a symbol, which would not do.

Of course, the keys are not, as the term *traditio symbolica* suggests, a mere symbol representing the goods locked away. On the contrary, they are the means of access, of control, over them. Consequently, handing over of the keys is a *traditio vera*: the direct possession of the goods is transferred to the acquirer.[55] The term *traditio ficta*, on the other hand, is confined to instances in which there is a transfer of possession but no transfer of direct possession from transferor to acquirer (ie actual power over the object). Handing over of a key to transfer possession of the goods was accepted in *Wrightson v McArthur and Hutchisons Ltd.*

High Court, King's Bench Division, 21 March 1921[56] **8.31 (E&W)**

Wrightson v McArthur and Hutchisons Ltd

[52] Later the commentators (13th–15th century) called such a form of *traditio* 'fictitious' (*traditio ficta*). See J Biermann, *Traditio ficta* (Stuttgart, Ferdinand Enke 1891) 71.

[53] WM Gordon, *Studies in the Transfer of Property by Traditio* (Aberdeen, 1970) ch 1 (*constitutum possessorium*), ch 2 (*brevi manu*) and ch 3 (*longa manu*). Note, however that it is controversial whether or not Roman law recognised *constitutum possessorium* already in its classical period (ch 1 of Gordon's book). At any rate, there is no doubt that *constitutum possessorium* was acknowledged in Justinian law (6th century AD).

[54] (1751) 2 Ves Sen 431, at 442–43. The passage is cited by Pollock with approval. See Pollock and Wright, *An Essay on Possession in the Common Law* (Oxford, Clarendon Press 1888) 62 *et seq*, particularly 68. Here *Ward v Turner* and other cases concerning *traditio symbolica* are treated in great detail.

[55] Pollock and Wright, above n 54, 68; LC Hofmann, *Het Nederlandsch zakenrecht*, 3rd edn (Groningen/Batavia, JB Wolters 1944) 235.

[56] [1921] 2 KB 807.

HANDING OVER OF KEY

Warehouse key

Handing over of a key amounts to transfer of possession of locked up goods.

Facts: The defendant company created a charge on specific goods stored in a locked room in their premises. The key of the room was given to the claimant, the chargee. The chargor, in a letter, gave the chargee a license to have free access to the room and the goods. Afterwards the defendant went into liquidation and the liquidator contended that the security interest should be considered as a charge and not a pledge, and that the charge was invalid for want of registration under section 93, subsection 1(c) Companies (Consolidation) Act 1908.

Held: Possession of the goods was transferred to the claimant by the delivery of the keys of the rooms in which the goods were locked up. As a result, the charge is valid as a pledge.

Judgment: Rowlatt J—For the above reasons it seems to me that if the delivery of the keys of the rooms in which the goods now in question were locked up is to be regarded as passing the possession the security intended to be created is valid, and the question in the case is whether possession did pass.

... The point to which this case is now reduced is whether the circumstance that the rooms, the keys of which were delivered, were within the defendants' premises, prevents the delivery of the keys conferring possession of the contents of the rooms. If the keys delivered had been the outside key of the whole warehouse containing these goods I should have felt no difficulty, nor should I have felt any difficulty had the key been of an apartment or receptacle in the premises of a third party as was the case in *Hilton v Tucker*. On the other hand if, the rooms being in the defendants' premises, the keys had been given without the licence to go and remove the goods at any time I should have thought it clear that possession of the goods did not pass. It would be merely a case of the goods remaining in the defendants' possession with the security that they should not be interfered with, but without any power of affirmative control at the free will of the plaintiff. It would be like the case of furniture left in a locked room in a house that is let furnished, where the lessor has no right to enter except upon reasonable notice and at reasonable times. The actual question has to be considered in the light of the principle that delivery of a key has effect not as symbolic delivery, but as giving the actual control. This was the view expressed by Lord Hardwicke in *Ward v Turner*, where he says the key is the means of coming at the possession. The matter was fully discussed in the light of all the cases in Pollock and Wright on Possession in the Common Law, p 61 and following pages. In *Hilton v Tucker*, already referred to, in a judgment delivered since the date of that work, Kekewich J observes 'that the delivery of the key in order to make constructive possession must be under such circumstances that it really does pass the full control of the place to which admission is to be gained by means of the key'. If I might criticise that statement my criticism would only be as to the propriety of the use of the word 'constructive' in the connection in question.

I think therefore there can be no doubt as to the true principle, and the difficulty is in its application. There are two cases in which delivery of the key of a box in a house has been held to confer possession of the contents. The first was *Jones v Selby*, referred to by Lord Hardwicke in *Ward v Turner* above mentioned, the other was *Mustapha v Wedlake*, but in both those cases both parties were living in the house and therefore the person receiving the delivery could not be expected to take away the box, but could hold possession of it in the house. It has never been held, so far as I know, that delivery of the key of a box which the deliverer retains in his own house, where the other party does not live, passes possession of the contents. Upon the whole, however, I think that in the case before me the possession was transferred, having regard to the fact that a licence to come and make the necessary entry to use the key was also conferred, a licence which it seems to me could not be revoked. The door into the building would be open in business hours, and the mere fact that the plaintiff might wrongfully be excluded from the whole building does not, I think, affect the matter. If the key had been given him with the intention to pass to him the possession of the room itself upon a demise of it, I cannot doubt that possession would pass. I see no difference when the key is given to pass possession not of the room, but of the chattels. The key guards both in the same way.

Note

Confusingly, in English law the term 'symbolical delivery' is often used to denote a transfer of possession through endorsement of a bill of lading, a form of delivery which is in reality a form of attornment by a third party in possession, a form of delivery to be discussed below.[57]

Burgerlijk Wetboek **8.32 (NL)**

Article 3:114 A possessor transfers his possession by enabling the acquirer to exercise such power over the object as he himself could exercise.

Note

This article from the Dutch Civil Code makes clear that a *traditio vera*, a transfer of actual possession, does not necessarily consist in handing over of the object. Handing over of keys which give access to the goods enables the acquirer to exercise power over the goods and is therefore a genuine transfer of possession.

Burgerlijk Wetboek **8.33 (NL)**

Article 3:115 For the transfer of possession a bilateral declaration without factual act suffices:

a. where the transferor possesses the object and henceforth holds the object for the acquirer under a condition made at the moment of transfer;

b. where the acquirer held the object for the transferor;

c. where a third party held the object for the transferor and, after the transfer, holds the object for the acquirer. In this instance possession does not pass before the third party has recognised the transfer or before either the transferor or the acquirer has notified the transfer to him.

[57] An example of the use of this term is to be found in *Sanders Bros v Maclean & Co* (1883) 11 QBD 327, per Bowen LJ (341).

Note

Article 3:115 BW shows three methods of *traditio ficta*: the first method described in sub a is *constitutum possessorium* in which the possessor turns himself into a detentor, ie holder, for the acquirer. The second (sub b) is *traditio brevi manu*, literally delivery with the short hand, and the third (sub c) is attornment by a third party who attorns from the transferor to the transferee, first holding as a detentor for the transferor and afterwards holding as a detentor for the transferee. In Dutch law this is called *traditio longa manu*, literally delivery with the long hand. In Roman law the term had a totally different meaning.[58]

I.D.2 *TRADITIO BREVI MANU*

Court of Queen's Bench, 20 June 1861[59] **8.34 (E&W)**

Winter v Winter

TRADITIO BREVI MANU PERFECTS A GIFT

Donated barge

Traditio brevi manu *suffices to perfect a gift.*

Facts: A son was in the possession of a barge belonging to his father. He worked on it as a servant to his father. When the father fell ill he made a gift of the barge to the son.[60] From that moment the son used the barge as his own and paid the crew's wages. After the father had died another of his sons, acting as the deceased father's executor, challengds the validity of the gift, contending there had been no delivery of the barge.

Held: The facts amount to a valid delivery and therefore perfected the gift.

Judgment: Wightman, J—But on an examination of the evidence, it turns out that there was a change in the possession of the barge consequent upon the gift. The deft used the barge as servant to his father previously to the gift, and afterwards he possessed it and worked it as owner.

Note

Traditio brevi manu turns the acquirer who first possessed as a bailee/detentor for the transferor into a possessor who holds the object as an owner. Although English law does not know any terminological distinction equivalent to the distinction between *possessio* and *detentio*, it does recognise a similar difference. In the above case the judge clearly distinguishes between using the barge as a servant and using it as an owner. Dutch or French law would use the terms *detentio* respectively *possessio* to indicate the difference.[61] A similar terminological difficulty can be found in Roman law which did not make a clear distinction in terminology between possession for one's own benefit and holding an object for someone else. The term *detentio* was

[58] See eg Jav D 46,3,79.
[59] (1861) 4 LT 639.
[60] This was a gift *inter vivos*, not a *donatio causa mortis*.
[61] In German law *detentio* is called *Fremdbesitz* whereas *possessio* is called *Eigenbesitz*.

developed only much later. Celsus, however, in explaining what we now call *constitutum possessorium*, makes a clear distinction between the two concepts saying: 'Possessing for yourself and possessing in another's name is not the same: because possessor is the person for whom is possessed …'.[62]

I.D.3 *CONSTITUTUM POSSESSORIUM* (ATTORNMENT OF TRANSFEROR TO TRANSFEREE)

Court of Common Pleas 9 February 1809[63] **8.35 (E&W)**

Elmore v Stone

ATTORNMENT TO BUYER

Stable keeper

Constitutum possessorium amounts to a valid delivery.

Facts: The claimant sold two horses to the defendant. Seller and buyer agreed that after the sale the seller, a horse dealer and livery stable keeper, would keep the horses at livery for the buyer. The latter paid for the keeping of the horse. The defendant refused to pay for the horses and claimed that the sale was unenforceable under section 17 of the Statute of Frauds 1677, as the purchase price was more than £10, the contract was not in writing and no delivery had taken place.

Held: The character of the seller's possession has changed from that of an owner into possession as a bailee. As a result, there is sufficient delivery and the sanction of section 17 Statute of Frauds does not apply.

Judgment: Mansfield CJ now delivered judgment.

The objection made to this verdict was the want of a memorandum in writing of the sale, and of a delivery. I thought at the trial that there was no need of a memorandum in writing, because of the direction given, that the horses should stand at livery. They were in fact put into another stable, but that is wholly immaterial. It was afterwards argued that this was not a sufficient delivery, but upon consideration we think that the horses were completely the horses of the Defendant, and that when they stood at the Plaintiff's stables, they were in effect in the Defendant's possession. There are many cases of constructive delivery, where the price of goods may be recovered on a count for goods sold and delivered, instead of a count for goods bargained and sold. A common case is that of goods at a wharf, or in a warehouse, where the usual practice is, that the key of the warehouse is delivered, or a note is given addressed to the wharfinger, who in consequence makes a new entry of the goods in the name of the vendee, although no transfer of the local situation or actual possession takes place. Thus in the present case, after the Defendant had said that the horses must stand at livery, and the Plaintiff had accepted the order, it made no difference whether they stood at livery at the vendor's stable, or whether they had been taken away and put in some other stable. The Plaintiff possessed them from that time, not as owner of the horses, but as any other livery stable keeper might have them to keep. Under many events it might appear hard,

[62] Celsus, D 41,2,18 pr (*Nec idem est possidere et alieno nomine possidere: nam possidet, cuius nomine possidetur, …*).

[63] (1809) 1 Taunt 458.

if the Plaintiff should not continue to have a lien upon the horses which were in his own possession, so long as the price remained unpaid; but it was for him to consider that, before he made his agreement. After he had assented to keep the horses at livery, they would, on the decease of the Plaintiff, have become general assets: and so, if he had become bankrupt, they would have gone to his assignees. The Defendant could not have retained them, although he had not received the price. Consequently the rule must be discharged.

Note

Constitutum possessorium could be seen as the mirror image of *traditio brevi manu* in that it turns the possessor who first possessed as an owner into a bailee for the acquirer, holding the object for the bailor.

House of Lords 27 February 1914[64] **8.36 (E&W)**

Dublin City Distillery v Doherty

ATTORNMENT TO CREATE PLEDGE

Pledged whiskey

Constitutum possessorium *amounts to a valid delivery.*

Facts: Doherty, one of the directors of Dublin City Distillery, lent money to his company. The company pledged certain whiskies to Doherty as a security for the loan. This whiskey was in a warehouse of Dublin City Distillery. Access to it was possible only by Dublin City Distillery and the Excise Officer operating together, both having a key. Doherty received a warrant evidencing his pledge on the whiskies and an invoice as if the goods had been sold to him. The company entered the pledge in their books. The company became insolvent. The liquidators claim that no valid delivery, actual or constructive, had taken place, so that the right of pledge had not been validly created.

Held: The warrant, invoice and entry into the company's books do not constitute a constructive delivery of the whiskey. Therefore no right of pledge has been created.

Judgment: Lord Atkinson—As to the second question, it was not disputed that, according to the law of England, and indeed of Scotland, a contract to pledge a specific chattel, even though money be advanced on the faith of it, is not in itself sufficient to pass any special property in the chattel to the pledgee. Delivery is, in addition, absolutely necessary to complete the pledge; but of course it is enough if the delivery be constructive, or symbolical, as it is called, instead of actual.

The example of constructive delivery frequently given is the delivery of the key of the store or house in which the goods have been placed; but that is because, in the words of Lord Hardwicke, 'it is the way of coming at the possession, or to make use of the thing': *Ward v Turner*. I doubt whether, owing to the dual control over this whiskey exercised by the distillers and the Revenue officer, it would not be necessary in the present case that both keys should be delivered.

Again, it is not disputed that if a vendor who has sold goods should, after the sale has been completed, agree with the vendee to retain the physical possession of the goods, but on such terms that the nature and character of his former

[64] [1914] AC 823.

possession is changed from that of owner to that of bailee for the purchaser, that transaction will amount to an acceptance and actual receipt of the goods within the 17th section of the Statute of Frauds, and necessarily to a good constructive delivery sufficient to create a pledge. The case of *Elmore v Stone* is an example of this. There the vendee, after the sale, asked the vendor, who was a horse dealer and livery stable keeper, to keep the horse for him at livery. The right to charge for the keep of the horse obviously shewed that the character of the vendor's possession had been changed, and that he thenceforward kept possession of the horse as the bailee for the purchaser.

In *Marvin v Wallis* the vendor, after the sale of a horse for more than 10*l*, requested the vendee to lend him the horse, which the latter consented to do. The jury found that the vendee gave this consent 'as owner'. On that finding it was held that there had been an acceptance and receipt of the horse to satisfy the statute, Coleridge J. stating, however, that had the plaintiff retained possession of the horse in his character of unpaid vendor the result would have been different. In *Carter v Toussaint* the plaintiff, a farrier, sold by parol to the defendant for 30*l* a horse which required to be fired. The plaintiff subsequently, at the request and in the presence of the purchaser, fired the horse. It was arranged between them that the horse should be kept by the plaintiff without charge, and it then was, by the defendant's directions, taken by the plaintiff's servant to Kempton Park and put to grass there. The horse was not entered at Kempton Park in the books of those who took it to graze in the name of the defendant. A Court composed of Abbott CJ, Bayley and Holroyd JJ, distinguished this case from *Elmore v Stone*, and held that there had been no acceptance and actual receipt of the horse to satisfy the statute. It is said that the authority of this case, which resembles the present case more than either of the two preceding, has been questioned. I cannot find, however, that it has been overruled. It certainly was decided by three very able and distinguished judges, and was apparently approved of in *Marvin v Wallis*. The distinguishing feature in *Reeves v Capper*, the chronometer case, as it was styled in argument, is that in that case there was, in fact, a delivery of the chronometer (the chattel to be pledged) by the pledgor to the clerk or agent of the pledgee, and that after a momentary possession by the latter there was by him a redelivery, duly authorized, of the chronometer to the original pledgor, the captain of the ship, on loan. The fact that the possession of the pledgee's agent, acting for his principals, was only momentary could make no difference. The case is wholly distinguishable from the present.

... Turning to the warrant itself, it states that the goods are deliverable to the respondent or his assigns, which can only mean, I think, at most, that he or his assigns were entitled to obtain delivery of them if he or they should demand it.

... I am, therefore, of opinion that the evidence, documentary and oral, such as it is, does not establish that there was a constructive delivery to the respondent of the whiskey with which this case is conversant.

Notes

(1) At first sight it may surprise that transfer of possession is relevant at all in a sales contract. Surely, under English law it is not a requirement for the passing of property. However, in these old cases, such as *Elmore v Stone* and *Dublin City Distillery v Doherty*, delivery was still important because of section 17 of the Statute of Frauds 1677. Under this section a contract of sale with a value of £10 or more

was unenforceable unless the goods had been delivered to the buyer or the buyer had partly paid for the goods or given something in earnest. The provision did not apply, however, where the contract had been made or evidenced in writing and signed by the parties or their agents. The reason for the provision was that practice had showed that juries too easily accepted that the parties had entered into a binding contract.[65] The provision was later adopted in the Sale of Goods Act 1893 as section 4 and was repealed in 1954.

(2) A modern example of delivery by way of *constitutum possessorium* is to be found in *Michael Gerson (Leasing) Ltd v Wilkinson* [2001] QB 514, a case about sale and leaseback.[66] See for this case Chaper 9 (third party protection). Sale and leaseback with *constitutum possessorium* is also accepted in Dutch law (HR 19 May 1995, NJ 1996/119 (*Keereweer qq v Sogelease*).[67] In German law *constitutum possessorium* is very frequent in financing of movable property. As a non-possessory pledge is not accepted, practice found a way around by using the transfer of ownership by way of security (*fiducia cum creditore*). The requisite transfer of possession takes place by way of *constitutum possessorium*. For this, see Chapter 5.

I.D.4 ATTORNMENT BY A THIRD PARTY IN POSSESSION

A frequent example of attornment by a third party in possession is the warehouser or carrier attorning to the buyer of the goods. Such attornment may take place in advance by issuing a bill of lading, warehouse warrant or other document promising to surrender the goods represented by the document to the holder in due course of the document. See, for instance, for English law *Borealis AB v Stargas Ltd* [2002] 2 AC 205, *Yemen Bank for Reconstruction and Development v owners of the 'Future Express'* [1993] 2 Lloyd's Rep 542 and for Dutch law Hoge Raad 10 February 1978, NJ 1979/338 (*First National City Bank v Easco*).

The Law Commission and The Scottish Law Commission, 'Rights of Suit in Respect of Carriage'[68] **8.37 (E&W)**

(b) Documents giving a right of delivery against the carrier

5.4 At common law a document of title is a document, relating to goods, the transfer of which operates as a transfer of constructive possession of the goods. The document operates, in effect, as an attornment in advance to all holders: a recognition that the goods are being held for each holder and giving the holder a right to call for delivery of the goods. There is for certain only one document of title at common law, namely the bill of lading representing goods to have been shipped. While it is possible for other documents to become documents of title by proof of

[65] D Ibbetson, *A Historical Introduction to the Law of Obligations* (Oxford, Oxford University Press 1999) 203.

[66] Other English examples of *constitutum possessorium* are *Marvin v Wallis* (1856) 6 El&Bl 726 (sale and loan back to seller of a horse) and *Castle v Sworder* (1861) 6 H&N 828).

[67] This case is dealt with in Chapter 5.

[68] The Law Commission and The Scottish Law Commission (Law Com No 196 and Scot Law Com No 130), Rights of suit in respect of carriage of goods by sea, 1991, 40, 47.

a mercantile custom to that effect, the courts have not been eager to extend the number of such documents. ...

5.27 ... The bill of lading essentially gives to the buyer three entitlements:

(i) The transfer of constructive possession of the goods by reason of the transfer of the bill itself, the carrier undertaking to keep the goods for the holder and deliver them to him.

(ii) The right to demand delivery from the carrier on presentation of the bill.

(iii) The right to sue the carrier under section 1 of the Bills of Lading Act 1855.

5.28 A ship's delivery order is not a transferable document of title at common law and the holder of a ship's delivery order has no rights of suit under the 1855 Act. However, in many situations the tender of a ship's delivery order may put the holder in as good a position as he would have been had he received a bill of lading. A shipowner can give the buyer a right to possession of the goods, and a right of delivery on presentation of the document, in the following ways. First, the carrier may be instructed by the seller to deliver the goods to the buyer, with the carrier thereupon attorning to the buyer, that is, acknowledging that he holds the goods for his benefit. Secondly, the carrier can directly undertake to deliver the goods to the buyer or his order.

Law Commission, 'Electronic Commerce, Formal Requirements in Commercial Transactions'[69] **8.38 (E&W)**

Functions and status of a bill of lading

4.5 A bill of lading evidences the terms of the contract for carriage, is a receipt for the goods, and is a document of title. Delivery of the bill of lading effects a transfer of constructive possession of the goods; possession of the bill evidences the entitlement to delivery of the goods. The essence of the bill of lading is that the rights and obligations which it embodies are transferable without reference to the carrier or any independent registrar.

4.6 The bill of lading effectively operates as an attornment in advance to all subsequent holders. It allowed goods to be traded whilst at sea at a time when ships were not in instantaneous contact with the rest of the world. ...

Pledge

9.8 A pledge of the documents provides security to a bank making a payment under a documentary credit. A pledge is a security based upon possession. It amounts to a transfer of the possession of goods by way of security, but with the ownership of the goods remaining with the pledgor. A pledge may be created by:—

(1) Delivery of physical possession of the goods.

(2) Constructive delivery of the goods by delivery of a bill of lading.

(3) Constructive delivery of the goods by way of attornment.

9.9 The first method will be unaffected by electronic communications. As there is no

[69] Law Commission, Electronic Commerce, Formal requirements in commercial transactions, Advice from the Law Commission, December 2001, 23 and 39.

foreseeable prospect of an electronic bill of lading being developed, this will preclude the creation of an electronic pledge by the second method.

9.10 Electronic trading will be conducted through multilateral contractual systems, such as Bolero, for the foreseeable future. Contractual systems are capable of providing protection to participating banks through their terms, the use of a central registry, and the ability of carriers to create a pledge by attorning. The creation of a pledge by attornment may therefore become increasingly significant.

Page 39, footnote 9: The fact that many ships are now in instantaneous electronic contact with the outside world makes it much easier for pledges to be created by an attornment of the carrier.

I.E THE SECOND DIVIDING LINE: ABSTRACT AND CAUSAL TRANSFER SYSTEMS

In our example of me selling my bicycle, the contract of sale is said to be the *causa traditionis*, the legal ground for the transfer. The *causa traditionis* makes clear what the legal reason for the transfer of ownership is, eg sale, barter or a gift. Suppose now that one of the parties has entered into a sales contract under the influence of a mistake. According to Dutch, German, English, French and Austrian law the party influenced by the mistake has, under certain circumstances, the power to annul or avoid the contract, that is to say, to render the contract void. Avoidance of the contract has retroactive effect: having been avoided, the contract is deemed never to have existed. In a consensual system, where the contract of sale itself is held to pass ownership, it is obvious to assert that avoiding of the contract will inevitably lead to ownership reverting to the seller with retroactive effect. Moreover, if the contract is void from the outset, it has never been able to transfer ownership. So, in a consensual system, such as French law and the English Sale of Goods Act, it seems as if the transfer of ownership necessarily depends on the validity of the contract. Such a transfer system that needs a valid *causa traditionis* is called a causal system.

I.E.1 FRENCH LAW

Introductory Note

The question whether or not the French transfer system is causal is not discussed in French law. Nevertheless, it is not difficult to see that the French transfer system is causal. As in the traditional French view the contract itself transfers ownership, it follows that the contract must be valid in order to be able to pass ownership, for a void contract is unable to pass ownership. And, if a voidable contract is avoided, ownership of the object, which has passed to the acquirer, reverts to the transferor. Since avoidance has retroactive effect the contract is deemed never to have been valid. Consequently, it is taken that ownership and, because of the *res perit domino* rule,[70] risk of accidental loss or damage, has never passed to the acquirer.

Cour de cassation, civ 1er, 6 December 1967[71] **8.39 (FR)**

Crohas v Pigeon and another

REVERTING OF OWNERSHIP AND RISK

Sheep

Upon annulment of the contract ownership and risk in the goods revests in the seller with retroactive effect.

Facts: Pigeon sold sheep to Crohas. Some of the animals had a contageous illness at the time of the sale and died after the sale. The Lyon Court of Appeal declared the contract void under Article 240 of the Rural Code. It further held that Crohas was not entitled to repayment of the purchase price of those sheep that had died in between the sale and the annulment, as Crohas had not proven that these sheep had died as a result of the illness.

Held: As a result of the annulment ownership of the sheep and the risk in them revested in the seller with retroactive effect. The risk of the sheep dying has therefore always been the seller's, unless he can prove that the buyer is responsible for the loss.

Judgment: On the second branch: having seen Article 1315 of the Civil Code; considering that, to refuse Crohas reimbursement of the part of the price representing the value of the animals that had perished in his hands before cancellation of the sale, the judges of the second instance state that Crohas does not give evidence that the loss of these beasts has been due to brucellosis, whereas he has the burden of proof; that in ruling thus, whereas as an effect of cancellation of the sale Pigeon was deemed to have never ceased to be the owner of the ewes and that he bore the risks of their loss, unless he proves a fault of Crohas, the court of appeal violated the aforementioned text;

For these reasons: quashes and cancels the judgment rendered between the parties by the court of appeal …, on 28 June 1965: returns, accordingly the cause and the parties to the same and comparable state where they were before the said judgment and, for right to be done, remits them before the court of appeal of Lyon.

Cour de cassation, civ 1e, 13 October 1983[72] **8.40 (FR)**

Dufour v Compagnie d'assurances L'Union des assurances de Paris (UAP) and others

EFFECT OF TERMINATION ON TRANSFER OF OWNERSHIP

[70] The rule means that the owner of an object bears the risk of accidental damage or loss. See for this rule Ph Malaurie and L Aynès, *Cours de droit civil, Les contrats spéciaux*, 10th edn (Paris, Défrenois, 1997) 185–87. Although the wording of the rule is based on Roman law (*cf* C 4,24,9) the French application of the adage does not accord with Roman law, in which risk normally passed the moment the contract of sale was made.

[71] Bull civ, I, no 358.

[72] No de pourvoi: 82-14273, Bull civ 233.

Bakery oven

Upon termination of the contract ownership reverts to the seller with retroactive effect.

Facts: Mr and Mrs Dufour exploited a bakery in premises belonging to Mr and Mrs Boerez. Under an insurance contract with UAP the Dufours had insured the bakery against fire. The Dufours sold the bakery to the spouses Bourgy. After the sale the bakery oven was destroyed by fire. As the Bourgys had not yet paid the purchase price, the Dufours terminated the contract. The Dufours claimed payment from UAP under the insurance policy. The Douai Court of Appeal held that the Dufours were not entitled to indemnity under the insurance policy because the Dufours could not be considered as parties to the insurance policy during the fire. The claimant challenged the Court of Appeal's view.

Held: Like the sales contract itself its termination works against third parties such as the insurance company. As a consequence, the seller, who retroactively regained ownership of the insured property, has to be considered as having had the quality of insured party at the time of the accident.

Judgment: On the sole argument, taken in its second branch: seen Article L121-10 of the Code des assurances;

That the court of appeal rejected the application by Mr Dufour seeking to obtain from the company UAP payment of compensation, for the reason that, when the oven was burned, Mr Dufour had sold his business and had therefore lost the status of insured;

Considering, however, that, as an effect of the rescission of the sale of the business, which rescission is enforceable, as is the sale itself, against the insurance company, mr. Dufour, having again retroactively become the owner of this business, must be considered as having had the status of an insured at the moment of the damage;

That, hence, by ruling as they have, the judges in second instance have violated the aforementioned text: for these reasons and without there being need to rule on the first branch of the argument: quashes and cancels the judgment rendered on 21 April 1983, between the parties, by the court of appeal of Douai.

Note

The above judgment has been approved in Cour de cassation civ 1e, 11 March 1986, Bull 58. It should be noted that in French law termination of a contract for breach of contract has retroactive effect.

I.E.2 ENGLISH LAW[73]

The question whether the transfer system in the Sale of Goods Act is causal or abstract or something different is not debated in English case law and hardly debated in English legal literature.[74] The terms 'abstract' and 'causal' are not used to denote different transfer systems. What is more, the question behind these terms is unknown as well. It seems to fascinate mainly civil lawyers. This may be explained to a certain extent by English law not having originated in the continental legal tradi-

[73] See LPW van Vliet, 'The Transfer of Moveables in Scotland and England' (2008) *Edinburgh Law Review* 173–99.

[74] Only sporadically has it been discussed. See eg T Weir, 'Taking for Granted—the Ramifications of Nemo Dat' in MDA Freeman (ed), *Current Legal Problems*, vol. 49(II) (Oxford, Oxford University Press, 1996) 325 and W Swadling, 'Rescission, Property, and the Common Law' (2005) 121 *LQR* 123–53.

tion. The terms 'causal' and 'abstract' are used to indicate the influence which, for example, voidness and avoidance of a contract have on the passing of property.

In continental law the debate about our question was based on different texts in Justinian's *Corpus Iuris Civilis*.[75] This collection of texts as interpreted by the learned jurists had an enormous influence on the development of continental law. Since English law has been developed independently of continental learned law, the texts of the *Corpus Iuris Civilis* did not give rise to a discussion in English law about our problem. On the other hand, if the transfer system of the Sale of Goods Act is a consensual system, the contract itself passing property to the acquirer, it seems an inevitable conclusion that property cannot pass where the contract is void or has previously been avoided.[76]

In order to ascertain whether a transfer system is causal or abstract (or something in between) the law's treatment of defects of will, such as error and fraud, offers good evidence. For categorising the transfer system it is essential that in an abstract transfer system a transfer can be valid even though the underlying transaction is defective. The core element of an abstract transfer system is that the effectiveness of the conveyance is judged independently from the effectiveness of the underlying transaction which formed the basis of the conveyance. Many legal systems give the party who acted under the influence of a defect of will an action to annul the transaction. In its original nineteenth-century German form the abstract system gives this party an action to annul the contract, but this remedy does not have any effect on the passing of property. Property does not automatically revest in the seller. The avoidance of the contract has no proprietary effect. As a result, a transfer by the buyer to a sub-buyer is always valid, even if the sub-buyer knew of the defect of will. We shall refer to this abstract system as the Savigny-style system, since it was developed by the German scholar Friedrich Carl von Savigny and his followers in the nineteenth century. As it is the archetype of an extremely abstract system, this system is used in comparative law as the standard example of the abstract model.

Court of Appeal, 28 July 1960[77] **8.41 (E&W)**

Ingram v Little

PASSING OF PROPERTY UNDER VOIDABLE AND VOID CONTRACT

Rogue buyer

Property does not pass under a void contract.

Facts: The claimants, the sisters Ingram, advertised their car for sale. The buyer was a rogue acting under a false name. He wanted to take the car with him at once and proposed to pay by cheque. Using the name of a respectable businessman, the buyer persuaded them to accept the cheque. The cheque

[75] LPW van Vliet, '*Iusta Causa Traditionis* and its History in European Private Law' (2003) 3 *European Review of Private Law* (*ERPL*) 342–78.

[76] See DL Carey Miller, with D Irvine, *Corporeal Moveables on Scots Law*, 2nd edn (Edinburgh, W Green & Son 2005) 9.17; KGC Reid, *The Law of Property in Scotland* (Edinburgh, Law Society of Scotland/Lexis Nexis, 1996) 610; van Vliet, above n 28, 111–14.

[77] [1961] 1 QB 31.

was dishonoured and the rogue disappeared. In the meantime he had sold the car to a bona fide third party, Mr Little. The claimants started proceedings against Little for the return of the car or, alternatively, damages for its conversion.

Held: The contract between the claimants and the rogue is void and, as a consequence, property of the car has never passed to the rogue. Under the *nemo plus* rule the rogue has never been able to transfer property of the car to the bona fide purchaser. The third party must return the car to the claimants or pay damages.

Judgment: Per Pearce LJ: The real problem in the present case is whether the plaintiffs were in fact intending to deal with the person physically present, who had fraudulently endowed himself with the attributes of some other identity, or whether they were intending only to deal with that other identity. If the former, there was a valid but voidable contract and the property passed. If the latter, there was no contract and the property did not pass.

Court of Exchequer, 21 February 1846[78] **8.42 (E&W)**

Load v Green

REVERTING OF PROPERTY UPON AVOIDANCE OF CONTRACT

Handkerchiefs

Annulment of the sale before the buyer's bankruptcy revests property in the seller.

Facts: The claimant had sold cloth (handkerchiefs, silk, muslin, etc) to a buyer who never paid for the goods. The buyer was declared insolvent and the sellers sued the defendants, assignees of the insolvent (the trustees in bankruptcy) for trover of the goods. The case is about the question whether the insolvent was an apparent owner of the goods.

Held: It is accepted that the sale was fraudulent, since the buyer never intended to pay for the goods. The insolvent was not a mere apparent owner at the time of the act of bankruptcy, but was the real owner. The seller has the right to annul the contract and regain property.

Judgment: Parke, B—[a]s the goods were obtained by a fraudulent purchase, the plaintiff had a right to disaffirm it, to revest the property in them, and recover their value in an action of trover against the bankrupt; and as the assignees take, by virtue of the assignment, such interest only as the bankrupt has, the plaintiffs had a right to recover the value of the goods in the hands of the assignees, in the same form of action, on a conversion by them, …[The plaintiffs] intended to part with the property itself, and to divest themselves altogether of all right to it; and although, in consequence of the bankrupt's fraud upon them, they had a right to annul the contract, and be again the real owners, that right they did not exercise until after the bankruptcy.

[78] 15 M & W 216 (1846).

Court of Common Pleas, 1 May 1851[79] **8.43 (E&W)**
White v Garden

REVESTING OF PROPERTY AFTER AVOIDANCE

Unpaid iron

Avoidance of the contract of sale revests property in the seller.

Facts: The defendants sold iron to Parker. Most of the purchase price was never paid. Parker sold the iron on to the claimant and ordered the defendants' lighterman to deliver the goods to the claimant. The barge containing the iron was left alongside the claimant's wharf. When the defendants discovered the fraud, they ordered the lighterman to take away the barge and the iron. The claimant claims to have purchased the iron in good faith and sue the defendants for trover.

Held: Avoidance of the contract of sale revests property in the seller, but the avoidance is no longer possible after the buyer has resold the goods to a third party.

Judgment: Cresswell, J—Parke, B, there says that that case [*Load v Green*] may be supported on the ground that the transaction is not absolutely void, except at the option of the seller; that he may elect to treat it as a contract, and he must do the contrary before the buyer has acted as if it were such, and re-sold the goods to a third party; ...

Talfourd, J—It appears to me that the defendants here intentionally parted with their property in the iron when they caused it to be delivered to the plaintiff; and it is not competent to them, after a third party has by their act been induced to part with his money, to turn round and say that the contract as between them and Parker was null and void, and that Parker had no property, and therefore could pass none to the plaintiff. It appears to me that the doctrine of Parke, B, in *Load v Green* is well warranted by the authorities.

Notes

(1) As we can learn from *White v Garden*, it was accepted in nineteenth-century case law that a seller who was defrauded by the buyer had the right to avoid the transaction and that property in the goods reverted to the seller upon avoidance. This effect, however, did not take place when, before the moment of avoidance the buyer in possession of the goods had sold these goods to a bona fide purchaser for value. This rule on third party protection was to be codified at the end of the 19th century in section 23 of the Sale of Goods Act 1893 and later in the identical section 23 of the Sale of Goods Act 1979. However, where the goods have not been sold on, or where they have been sold on to a mala fide purchaser or have been disposed of without recompense, property in the goods reverts from the third party to the seller upon the avoidance of the contract between the defrauded seller and his buyer.

(2) The above rule created a difference in treatment between mistake cases and fraud cases which is difficult to justify, as the material facts in mistake cases and fraud cases are, from a *practical* perspective, almost identical when a buyer tries

[79] 10 CB 918 (1851).

to receive goods without paying for them.[80] In the case of mistake the contract is void and the bona fide third party will never be protected. In the case of fraud the third party will be protected unless the contract had been avoided before the buyer sold the object on to the third party. Moreover, it also created an odd difference in third party protection according to the time when the voidable contract is avoided: before or after the transfer to the bona fide third party.[81]

I.E.2.a Illegal contracts

Introductory Note

The clear picture given by the above cases on defects of will is to some degree disturbed by cases on transfer of property under an illegal contract. The law allows property to pass on the basis of an illegal contract. Some authors claim that because the illegal contract does have some legal consequences, among which the passing of property, illegal contracts are normally not void but merely unenforceable.[82] Others take the viewpoint that illegal contracts are void and that property can pass despite voidness of the contract.[83] Case law does not analyse this question sharply, but seems to support the latter view.

Privy Council, 16 December 1959[84] **8.44 (E&W)**

Singh v Ali

TRANSFER UNDER ILLEGAL CONTRACT

Indian haulier's permit

Property may pass under an illegal contract of sale.

Facts: As Singh could not obtain a haulier's permit he made an agreement with another haulier, Ali, who could obtain such a permit. Ali would buy a lorry and register it in his own name, and sell it on to Singh. The second sale was illegal. According to plan, Ali bought the lorry, had it registered in his own name and sold and delivered it to Singh. A conflict between the parties led Ali to seize the truck from Singh. When Singh sued Ali in detinue (an action for the return of the truck or its value), Ali defends himself setting up the illegality of the second sale.

Held: Property in the truck passed to the claimant under the illegal contract. As a result, the claimant has an action in detinue.

Judgment: Lord Denning—Although the transaction between the plaintiff and the defendant was illegal, nevertheless it was fully executed and carried out: and on that account it was effective to pass the property in the lorry to the plaintiff. There are many cases which show that when two persons agree together in a conspiracy

[80] See *Shogun Finance Ltd v Hudson* [2004] 1 AC 919, para 35 (per Lord Nicholls); see also C MacMillan, 'Rogues, Swindlers and Cheats: The Development of Mistake of Identity in English Contract Law' (2005) 64(3) *Cambridge Law Journal* 711–44, at 712.

[81] Swadling, above n 74, 131.

[82] RM Goode, *Commercial Law*, 3rd edn (2004) 78–79 and 130–35.

[83] W Swadling, 'The Role of Illegality in the English Law of Unjust Enrichment' (2000) Oxford University Comparative Law Forum, 5, http://ouclf.iuscomp.org.

[84] [1960] AC 167.

to effect a fraudulent or illegal purpose—and one of them transfers property to the other in pursuance of the conspiracy—then, so soon as the contract is executed and the fraudulent or illegal purpose is achieved, the property (be it absolute or special) which has been transferred by the one to the other remains vested in the transferee, notwithstanding its illegal origin: see *Scarfe v Morgan*, per Parke B. The reason is because the transferor, having fully achieved his unworthy end, cannot be allowed to turn round and repudiate the means by which he did it—he cannot throw over the transfer. And the transferee, having obtained the property, can assert his title to it against all the world, not because he has any merit of his own, but because there is no one who can assert a better title to it. The court does not confiscate the property because of the illegality—it has no power to do so—so it says, in the words of Lord Eldon: 'Let the estate lie where it falls'; see *Muckleston v Brown*. This principle was applied by the Court of Appeal recently in *Bowmakers Ltd v Barnet Instruments Ltd*. The parties to the fraud are, of course, liable to be punished for the part they played in the illegal transaction, but nevertheless the property passes to the transferee. ...

In this case, on the facts pleaded and the findings of the trial judge, the plaintiff had a clear cause of action. He had actual possession of the lorry at the moment when the defendant seized it. Despite the illegality of the contract, the property had passed to him by the sale and delivery of the lorry: compare *Bowmakers Ltd v Barnet Instruments Ltd* referred to above. When he commenced this action, he had the right to immediate possession. Their Lordships think that in these circumstances he had a claim in detinue.

Note

Sometimes this judgment is used as evidence that a transfer under the Sale of Goods Act is abstract, that property may pass under a void contract. However, it should be noted that Lord Denning, tendering the Privy Council's advice, did not say that the illegal contract was *void*. Although the judgment shows that property may pass under an illegal contract, the judgment cannot be used to support either a causal or an abstract transfer system.

I.E.3 THE ABSTRACT GERMAN AND THE CAUSAL DUTCH AND AUSTRIAN TRANSFER SYSTEM

Introductory Note

In a tradition system the act of transfer is considered as a distinct legal act. Having made the distinction between the underlying contract, which serves as *causa traditionis*, and the transfer, a legal system is confronted with the question how the latter act relates to the former one. Does invalidity of the underlying contract affect the validity of the transfer? Legal systems in which the validity of the transfer does depend on a valid *causa traditionis*, the Dutch system for example, are called causal tradition systems. If in such systems the obligatory contract is void or has been avoided with retroactive effect, the transfer is invalid and either ownership has never passed (in the case of a void contract) or it is deemed never to have passed to the buyer (where the contract has been avoided). The seller is then able to claim back the object sold and delivered on the basis of his ownership. In legal systems based on Roman law he would be said to have an action of revindication (*rei vindicatio*).

In German law, on the other hand, the act of transfer is in principle independent of the validity of the obligatory contract. Systems like the German are called abstract transfer systems because the validity of the transfer is judged abstractly of, that is, independently of the contract. The invalidity of the obligatory contract has no effect on the validity of the transfer; the transfer will stay valid even if the legal act that obliged to make the transfer is void or has been avoided. Yet, where there is no valid *causa traditionis* the transfer, though valid, leads to an unjustified enrichment of the buyer. It obliges him to undo his enrichment by *re*transferring the object to the seller. It is a transfer similar to the first transfer and it should accordingly fulfil all requirements every transfer should meet. The *causa traditionis* of the retransfer is the buyer's obligation on the basis of unjustified enrichment. The extreme abstract approach developed in the second half of the 19th century by Savigny and his followers has been adopted by the German legislator in the *Motive*.

Explanations for the Draft of a Civil Code for the German Nation, Book III[85] **8.45 (DE)**

The real agreement is independent of the obligations between the parties. The legal ground, on which it rests, is without influence on the legal change, which it effects with the help of the registration. If absolutely no legal ground for making the contract existed or if the ground, which the parties presupposed, were invalid or voidable, this can, without exception, only give rise to a personal claim by the one against the other.

As the motives of §828(2) show, these are consequences from the abstract nature of the real agreement, which accord with the applicable law, so far as it governs acquisition on the basis of the principle of consensus. However, in contrast with the numerous legislations which link the change in property rights to the obligationary legal ground (the title), it seems advisable to lay down those consequences expressly in the Civil Code. Such a provision is the more important here as also the abstract nature of the release contract and of the assignment is distinctly emphasised in §290(2) and §294(2) sentence 1. Taking into consideration the foundation for these paragraphs only few remarks are required for the justification of §829.

1. Where sentence 1 of the first paragraph declares that an indication of the legal ground is unnecessary for the effectiveness of the real agreement, it has the particular advantage for the law of land registration that the legal ground can be excluded from examination by the land register office. …

Notes

(1) If the contract of sale is avoided the entire transaction should be reversed: the money, if already paid, should be paid back to the buyer, and the object sold should return to the seller. This applies to a causal system as well as to an

[85] *Motive zu dem Entwurfe eines Bürgerlichen Gesetzbuches für das Deutsche Reich*, vol III, *Sachenrecht* (Berlin and Leipzig, 1888) 187–88.

abstract system. However, as we can see, the way in which the transfer of ownership is reversed differs. Whereas in a causal system ownership of the object sold and transferred reverts automatically to the seller when the contract is avoided, in an abstract system the validity of the transfer will not be affected. Here the buyer has an obligation on the basis of unjustified enrichment and the seller a correlative personal right to the retransfer of the right of ownership.

(2) The difference will normally be limited to the transfer of the object. As to the money paid to the seller, all three systems, the causal tradition system, the abstract tradition system and the consensual tradition system, cope with a similar problem: in most cases the money has been paid by a bank transfer which, as we have seen, does not involve a transfer of property at all. Moreover, where the purchase price has been paid by transferring ownership of banknotes and coins, the money will almost always have been mixed with the rest of the buyer's money rendering the money paid unidentifiable. As a result, the money cannot automatically revert to the buyer after avoidance of the contract.

(3) In opting for a causal transfer system for the 1992 Dutch Civil Code Meijers considered both the effect on third parties and the effect in insolvency.

Parliamentary History of the new Dutch Civil Code, Book 3, p 316 **8.46 (NL)**

It is immediately apparent from the wording of the article that, for the transfer of each thing, the so-called causal system is followed; accepting a valid act of delivery and the power to dispose of him, who engages in the act, to transfer the right, a valid title is stated as a third requirement, ie a fact that creates an obligation of delivery. …

The objections, that exist under the present code against the causal system, are overcome by the following article [Art 3:86]. Those who, unaware of the defects of a title from a previous acquisition have had a thing delivered to them, are protected as bona fide acquirers. The same is the case with a title presumed by the parties, which never existed. Virtually the same result is also to be achieved according to the other system, which does not demand any valid title—the so-called abstract system. Indeed this system need only be supplemented with a provision, that gives the transferor the right in the absence of a title or in the case of a defective title to demand restitution of the delivered thing not only from the acquirer, but also from third parties, who knew of the defect or the lack of a title; the right to demand restitution need not even be expressly mentioned in the present law, since one assumes that a claim arising from an illegal act can also be laid against him, whose fault may be cited for an obligation to give not being capable of being complied with.

In this manner, the choice between the causal and the abstract system is determined less by legal consequences of principle than by subordinate legal consequences and by the most efficient system. The same choice with the same motives arises each time restitution is possible from subsequent acquirers in bad faith (ie those who are aware of the facts) but not from those in good faith. … In the case now, that a delivery lacks a lawful legal ground and the acquirer is declared insolvent, the draft implies that a revindication must be accorded to the transferor.

Note

The old Dutch Civil Code of 1838 had not made a choice between a causal and an abstract system. At the time these concepts had not yet developed in Dutch law. Under the old Civil Code a definite choice for a causal system was eventually made by the Dutch Supreme Court in its landmark decision in *Damhof v De Staat.*[86]

Hoge Raad, 3 May 1950[87] **8.47 (NL)**

Damhof v De Staat

CAUSAL TRANSFER SYSTEM

German furniture

A transfer of property requires a valid legal ground.

Facts: In 1944 Damhof bought a collection of furniture from a German company. The furniture had been stored in a Rotterdam warehouse. Delivery took place by the warehousekeeper declaring to hold the goods henceforth for the buyer (attornment). After the liberation of the Netherlands the furniture was seized by a special police force because it was regarded as property of the enemy. The furniture was given away. Damhof claimed damages from the state. The state asserted that Damhof has never acquired ownership of the furniture because the sale is void under the London decree no A6.[88] Damhof opposes that he did not know nor could have known this decree, since the London decrees have never been published in the Netherlands during the occupation, and that he therefore acquired ownership as a bona fide purchaser. Damhof's claim was dismissed by the district court and by the court of appeal. Damhof nonetheless appeals in cassation.

Held: The third party protection of Article 2014 BW requires a transfer based on a valid legal ground.

Judgment: Considering that the provision of the first paragraph of Article 2014 BW only makes an exception to the general rules concerning the acquisition of ownership of moveable objects by means of delivery in so far as the lack of power to dispose of him, who transfers cannot be held against the acquirer in good faith; that, hence, also for the acquisition of ownership of a moveable object it applies unabated that the requirement made in Article 639 BW, that the delivery must rest on a legal title of ownership transfer, wherefore the delivery only then makes the acquirer owner if its takes place by virtue of valid title;

that already on these grounds the argument made by Damhof and rejected by the Court is unacceptable, that, even if the agreement, whereby he purchased the furniture, might be void, as falling under the prohibition of decree A 6, he has nevertheless become owner of the purchased objects, since he, ignorant of said decree, acquired the objects in good faith;

that therefore the Court rightfully rejected this argument, and, considering that this decision is in any case just, a reply to the question, raised for consideration by the argument, whether the Court has adduced a just ground for this decision, can remain unforthcoming;

Rejects the appeal.

[86] HR 5 May 1950, NJ 1950/1.

[87] NJ 1951/1.

[88] During the German occupation of the Netherlands, the Dutch government in exile in London issued a number of decrees. The decree in question was one of them.

Note

As said before, the seventeenth- and eighteenth-century *titulus* and *modus* theory required a legal ground and a formality in order to pass ownership. In the case of transfer of movables the formality is in principle transfer of possession. Austrian law codified this requirement in its 1811 Civil Code. Later, it drew the conclusion that this legal ground, often a contract, should be valid in order to pass ownership, thus creating a causal transfer system.

Oberster Gerichtshof (OGH), 30 August 2000[89] **8.48 (AT)**

ACQUISITION OF LAND UNDER A VOID CONTRACT

Parcel in Tirol

As the first sale to the trustee was intended to circumvent legislation on the basis of which the defendant was not allowed to buy the land, the contract is void.

Facts: In 1986 the Austrian claimant (the woman) married the German defendant (the man). In 1980 the defendant sought to buy land in Tirol. Being a foreigner he could not validly buy this land himself. Consequently, the land was bought on his account by an Austrian citizen acting as a trustee for him. After the claimant and the defendant got married, the land was sold and transferred to the claimant and registered in her name. No purchase price was paid because the seller acted as the man's trustee. After the claimant and defendant got divorced in 1998, the claimant demanded that the man leave the land.[90]

Held: As the first sale to the trustee was intended to circumvent legislation on the basis of which the defendant was not allowed to buy the land, the contract is void. As a consequence, the transfer of ownership is void and the second sale and transfer to the claimant did not pass ownership to her.

Judgment: According to now consistent case law, a transaction, whereby the requirement for official permission for an acquisition of land is circumvented by a foreigner, is subject to the legal norm that is applicable to the legal transaction that is intended in reality. …

If contract parties do not even want to apply for permission from the land transactions authority for their contracts that are subject to a requirement for permission, because they assume, that permission would be refused, then the contracts are not voidable but are void from the outset. … The thus invalid contracts entered into between the seller, the trustee and the defendant were therefore unable to procure ownership of the land for either the trustee or the defendant. … It follows therefrom, that neither the trustee nor the defendant was able to transfer ownership in the land to the claimant. A non-existent right cannot be disposed of. A purchaser, whose purchase contract is void owing to contradiction with the land transaction laws does not have any object susceptible to being disposed of. …

According to the principles applying in Austrian property law—which is applicable at least here (§31 IPRG)—for the derivative acquisition of ownership of land both a valid legal ground for acquisition and registration in the land register are necessary (§§425, 431 ABGB). Hence, neither a mere legal ground nor mere registration—as here—can on its own procure ownership. The lack of a valid legal ground

[89] 6 Ob 325/99h, Immolex 2001/11.

[90] Although it is very likely that the case was not about an undeveloped piece of land but about a house, the judgment does not mention this.

hinders the transfer of rights, so that any person can invoke the unlawfulness of the register entry. With the second purchase contract, the claimant did not have a valid legal ground for the acquisition of ownership, because neither the trustee nor the defendant as settlor was owner of the land, of which the claimant furthermore was also aware, and a sale was also not intended at all. Even if the second purchase contract were to be interpreted in reality as a gift or mixed gift, as the claimant contends, this would be ineffective, since the defendant could not even effectively dispose of the land for want on his part of validly acquired rights over it. Since, therefore, the claimant would not even then qualify as the owner of the land, if her procedural argument, that the defendant wanted ownership of the land to be transferred to her, should be proven as correct, it is at this stage already certain that the petition to leave the land lacks any success.

I.E.4 PRACTICAL DIFFERENCES BETWEEN CAUSAL AND ABSTRACT TRANSFER SYSTEMS

In a causal transfer system such as the Dutch and the Austrian system, a valid transfer always demands a valid *causa traditionis*. As a result, ownership cannot pass under a void contract, and, if at the outset ownership has passed under a voidable contract, it automatically reverts to the transferor when the contract is avoided. In Dutch and Austrian law avoidance of a contract has retroactive effect, so that when the contract is avoided after the transfer has taken place, the *causa traditionis* is deemed never to have existed and accordingly the transferee is considered never to have been owner of the thing.

In consequence, where the contract is void or has been avoided, the transferee will in principle not be able to transfer the thing to a second transferee, as he is not the owner of the object (*nemo plus* rule). Let us have a look at an example to explain the causal system. A sells and transfers an object to B who in turn sells and transfers it to C. After C has become owner of the object A finds out that he has acted under the influence of a defect of will and he accordingly avoids the contract. As a result, ownership will revert to A. The first transferee, A, is deemed never to have lost his right of ownership and C is deemed never to have become owner of the object. So, in a causal system defects in the *causa traditionis* may have wide implications on third parties: it makes the first acquirer (here: B) in principle unable to transfer ownership to a second acquirer.

Without third party protection the causal system poses a danger to third party acquirers. If a legal system finds good reason to protect C it should supplement the causal transfer system with provisions protecting third parties. As we have seen above, Dutch and French law both protect the buyer in good faith.

By deciding in favour of an abstract system instead of a causal system the German civil code intended to limit the consequences of defects in the underlying legal act, the *Verpflichtungsgeschäft*, to the parties to this legal act, with the result that these defects in principle do not affect a second acquirer. Even though the underlying contract is invalid (ie void *ab initio* or avoided) the transfer passes ownership to the first transferee (B in the above example) and thus enables him to transfer ownership of the object to a third party (C).

Offering this protection to subsequent acquirers, the abstract system in itself protects third parties in that it prevents defects in the *causa traditionis* from automatically affecting a subsequent transfer.

Meijers, the most important draftsman of the Dutch Civil Code, points out that the difference between a causal and an abstract system need not be very large. The difference is reduced even further if the abstract system is supplemented with a rule providing that, where the contract between A and B is void or has been avoided, A may claim back the object not only from B but also from C unless the latter is in good faith.

However, even if the abstract system were so extended, one essential difference remains: the difference between having a property right or rather a personal right against B and/or C. The difference is important especially in the case of insolvency. Let us take the example of the sale of a movable. The seller has entered into the contract under the influence of a defect of will, for example duress. As the transaction does not correspond to his true will the seller has the power to avoid the contract of sale. Where the object has already been delivered avoidance will oblige the buyer to return the object to the seller.

In an abstract transfer system the seller merely has a personal right to the retransfer of the object. As a result, the seller does not have any priority in the buyer's insolvency: he is an ordinary, unsecured, creditor. In a causal system, on the other hand, the seller will in principle be able to claim back the object relying on his right of ownership, which will normally revert to him as a result of the avoidance. When ownership reverts to the seller the object does not form part of the buyer's goods available for realisation and satisfaction of the buyer's debts. It should be returned to its owner by the liquidator or administrator in insolvency. For that reason it is often said that a causal system gives a better protection against insolvency of the other party.

We should bear in mind, however, that the protection against insolvency of the other party is rather imperfect. Firstly, the seller's protection against the buyer's insolvency is limited by a few exceptions: as the protection depends on the transferor's ownership, the protection is no longer available when for some reason it is impossible for ownership to revert automatically to the transferor. To give an example, the transferor's action of revindication may be frustrated when the transferee has sold the object to a bona fide third party: if available third party protection will deprive the original owner of his right of ownership. The reverting of ownership to the transferor may also be barred as a result of original acquisition, for example when the object has been mixed with identical things in the hands of the transferee (*confusio* and *commixtio*), or if the object has been used to make a new object (*specificatio*) or if it has been attached to another object (*accessio*).

Secondly, in German, Dutch and French law the protection is in principle offered only to the transferor of the *object*. The buyer, who has a duty to pay for the goods, is not given a similar protection against the *seller's* insolvency. The reason is the different nature of the things both parties have to transfer: an object and money.

We shall see below, however, that the sharp divide between causal and abstract systems and the practical differences as shown above, are mitigated as a result of a number of exceptions to the principle of abstractness. The modern German transfer system is a lot less abstract than the Savigny-style model codified in the Civil Code.

I.E.5 MITIGATION OF THE ABSTRACT SYSTEM IN GERMAN LAW

Introductory Note

In modern German law a number of exceptions to the abstract transfer system are acknowledged. First of all, the conveyance may be subject to a suspensive or resolutive condition that the conveyance will be valid only if and as long as the underlying contract is valid. This renders the abstract transfer a mere default system: the parties to the transaction may opt out of this system. The only conveyance which cannot be made subject to a condition is the conveyance of immovable objects (§925(2) BGB). This exclusion enhances the clarity and certainty of the registration system. A second exception to abstractness is that a defect of the underlying contract rendering the contract void or voidable may affect the transfer in the same way. This is called identity of defect (*Fehleridentität*). Minority affects both the contract and the transfer. Defects of will, such as fraud and duress, will normally render both the contract and the transfer voidable. Moreover, in the case of a transaction against good morals, the conveyance may be void as well.[91] A very important application of the latter exception is the doctrine of excessive security (*Übersicherung*) where both the duty to give excessive security to the creditor and the transfer made to fulfil this duty are held to be void. Often the duty to give excessive security is laid down in standard contract, in which case the legislation on unfair general conditions applies (§§305–10 BGB). The purpose of this legislation can be achieved fully only if both the duty to give security and the transfer of the security objects can be declared void. In the case of error, however, identity of defect is rarely accepted. Where the underlying contract infringes upon a legal prohibition, the transfer may be void if the prohibition is specifically aimed at the transfer itself.[92]

W Wiegand, Staudinger Commentary[93] **8.49 (DE)**

Whereas the principle of separation, ie the separation between legal ground and execution of the legal ground by disposal, to be found in many European systems of private law, has hardly met any criticism and creates hardly any problems in legal practice, the principle of abstraction has caused quite a stir before and since promulgation of the BGB.

The **abstraction of the disposal transaction** ... belongs to the typical characteristics of the German legal system and constitutes an essential element of patrimonial law of the Civil Code. ... In so far as the *criticism is directed against this decision of principle made by the legislature*, account could only be taken of this criticism by means of a **comprehensive revision** of the entire patrimonial law and an alter-

[91] In BGH 20 June 2000, XI ZR 237/99, the court held that although a clause in the loan contract was against good morals and thus void it held that the security right created on the basis of the contract was not void.

[92] RGZ 109, 201.

[93] W Wiegand, *Staudinger Kommentar zum BGB* (2004) Vorbem zu §929 et seq at 171, no 16.

ation of the above-mentioned fundamental principle which includes an adjustment of the principle of delivery and of the rules on good faith acquisition.

That does not fundamentally rule out corrections to the abstraction principle. Rather, for a long time, the courts and the literature have made occasional attempts at rectification and at avoiding insupportable consequences of the principle of abstraction or of its excessive application. ... As always in the situation of case-related judicial development of the law, it admittedly appears to be necessary and about time to develop generalised rules that codify the essential results of this legal development.[94]

W Wiegand, Staudinger Commentary[95] **8.50 (DE)**

However, from the concept of transfer of ownership as an abstract legal property transaction it follows that any defects or mistakes must affect the real agreement [*Einigung*] itself. It should therefore be specifically verified in each case whether the mistake in the underlying transaction has been repeated in the property legal act (for instance in cases of mistake) or whether the ineffectiveness of the underlying transaction affects the real agreement in the same manner. In this regard, the following is to be borne in mind: regardless of the clear, unequivocal concept of the legislator the abstractness of the property legal act may not be exaggerated and be judged purely formalistically. On the other hand, one may not fall into the temptation of undermining the principle of abstraction by a practically automatic encroachment of mistake in the causal transaction onto the disposal transaction.

BGH, 12 March 1998[96] **8.51 (DE)**

Insolvency administrator of R v X Bank

EXCESSIVE SECURITY FROM THE OUTSET

Transfer of stock and claims

Excessive security may render the obligation to give security partly void. If so, the transfer for security purposes is void as well.

Facts: The company R received a loan of DM1,350,000 from the defendant, a bank. To secure the repayment of this loan R created five rights of land charge in favour of the bank. Later it gave the bank even more security by transferring all stock and claims against customers. Afterwards R was declared insolvent. The Bank sold and transferred its claim against R and the security interests to a newly founded company M for DM700,000. The administrator in insolvency claimed that the two additional security transfers (the stock and the claims) were both void as they amount to excessive security, and that consequently the Bank had sold and transferred property that did not belong to it. He claimed payment to the insolvency patrimony of the proceeds of sale of the void security interests (the stock and R's claims).

Held: At the time of the security, transfer of the stock and claims the bank already had an excessive amount of security (70% more than its claim on R). Any additional security could therefore be excessive and immoral. This has to be determined by the Court of Appeal. If that court finds that the obligation to

[94] The ellipsis indicates the places where Wiegand refers to literature.
[95] Wiegand, above n 93, at 172, no 18.
[96] IX ZR 74/95, NJW 1998, 2047.

provide this additional security is excessive, the transfer of the stock and the assignment of the claims are void as well. The Bank should then surrender the proceeds of sale to the administrator in insolvency.

Judgment: B. On important points these considerations cannot stand up to appeal. At present, it cannot be ruled out that the claimant has a claim against the defendant for surrender of that which the defendant has received by transferring its—supposed—rights based on the transfers for security purposes (§816 (1) 1st sentence BGB). ...

II. Possibly, however, the security transfer and the security assignment had led to excessive security from the outset.

1. In the case of excessive security from the outset the contracts to provide security may be void under §138(1) BGB. ... There is excessive security from the outset if already at the moment the contract is made it is certain that in the case of execution, if needed, there will be a notable disproportion between the value of the security objects which can be realised and the value of the secured claim. ...

On the contrary, decisive is the value which can be realised according to uncertain market conditions in the case of the debtor's insolvency. This value can be ascertained by the lower courts only by taking into consideration the peculiarities of the concrete case, if necessary with expert advice. The risk of wrong or vague ascertainment must be taken into account. Excessive security from the outset entails that the transaction is contrary to good morals, if at the moment of its conclusion the transaction, according to its overall character—to be inferred from the totality of content, motive and purpose—is contrary to good morals. Above all, the excessive security should be the result of an abject intention of the security taker. This intention can be held to exist where the security taker, out of selfish motives, shows a degree of ruthlessness as to the justified interests of the security provider which is unacceptable according to moral standards.

2. ... In the case of such an accumulation of security objects it may be that already when the parties agree to provide security there is an immoral disproportion between the value of the security objects and the value of the claims to be secured. ...

3. When the contracts to provide security are void as providing excessive security from the outset, the defendant cannot—contrary to the Court of Appeal's opinion—be regarded as owner because the security objects are transferred to the special purpose company with the consent of the debtor and the claimant in his role of administrator of the insolvent company.

Notes

(1) Excessive security is the situation in which a creditor has an excessive amount of security interests in relation to his claim on the debtor, eg security rights on property worth €150,000 to secure a loan of only €100,000. German case law distinguishes between the situation in which the excess was present from the outset and the situation in which the excess comes into being later as a result of part repayments of the loan. In the latter case the debtor has a claim against the creditor that the creditor should release some of the security objects.[97]

(2) The above case is an illustration of the first instance (excessive security from the outset). In these cases the sanction of voidness is used only if the difference in

[97] See also Chapter 5.

value is excessive. In most cases the value of the burdened property will exceed the amount of the claim in order to protect the creditor against the danger that upon execution the security objects turn out to have a much lower value or market prices have gone down. If, because of excessive security, part of the contract is void, the sanction of voidness renders the transfer void as well. Thus, the entire transaction is void and the security interest did not come into being. It is another example of an exception to the abstract system.[98]

BGH, 8 December 1998[99] **8.52 (DE)**

IDENTITY OF DEFECT: BULK ASSIGNMENT AGAINST GOOD MORALS

Tea merchant

If bulk assignment is partly void for infringing upon good morals the assignment itself is partly void as well.

Facts: A tea merchant, H, who received a loan from an Austrian bank, assigned all his claims on foreign customers to the bank for security purposes. The company H was also financed by a German bank, to which H transferred tea for security purposes. H had the right to sell the tea provided it would assign the claim against the buyer to the German bank. When one of H's customers, M, received a message from the Austrian bank that he should pay to the Austrian bank, M ignored this and paid to the German bank, thus following H's instructions. The Austrian bank then sued the German bank for the amount paid by M, asserting that their assignment of the claim was from an earlier date and would therefore have priority.

Held: A bulk assignment of future claims to a bank without a release clause which works against third parties is in principle void if and as far as it also covers claims which the assignor has to assign and does assign to his supplier on the basis of an extended retention of ownership clause.

Judgment: 2. The bulk assignment to the claimant breaches good morals under German law and is therefore void (§138 I Civil Code).

(a) According to consistent case law from the Federal Supreme Court of Justice, a bulk assignment to a bank contracted in security of a credit for future customer receivables is as a rule contrary to good morals in so far as according to the intention of the contract partners it is also supposed to encompass receivables that the debtor must in future assign, and does assign, to his suppliers on the ground of extended retention of ownership provisions. To secure such interests of the borrower and his suppliers as are worthy of protection, claims under the extended retention of ownership provision must in any event precede the bulk assignment and affect property rights and not just rights based on the law of obligations. A clause that imposes on the assignor merely the obligation of satisfying the seller under a reservation of ownership is not sufficient. A bulk assignment without a part waiver clause of property rights is only not contrary to good morals when, owing to special circumstances, in exceptional circumstances a reprehensible state of mind on the part of the participating bank is absent. Such a case can occur when, in the circumstances of an individual case—especially due to the unusual nature of the extended reten-

[98] See in general D Reinicke and K Tiedtke, *Kreditsicherungsrecht*, 5th edn (Neuwied, Luchterhand 2006) Rn 732–54.

[99] XI ZR 302/97, NJW 1999, 940.

tion of ownership in the relevant economic sector—it should consider a conflict of the security rights to be excluded. …

(b) The bulk assignment takes no account of these principles.

(aa) It encompasses all receivables of H against foreign customers, hence also such claims that the assignor had to assign to its suppliers on the basis of an extended retention of ownership. A part waiver clause of property rights that from the outset ensures suppliers under a reservation of ownership a preference over the bulk assignment is not contained in the bulk assignment contract. No 4 of the bulk assignment contract is also not comparable to a part waiver affecting property rights. In terms thereof, the removal of a receivable from the bulk assignment does not happen automatically but is dependent on being identified by H in each list of outstanding amounts. Thus, contrary to the intention of the said case law on the preferential securing of lenders on goods, its suppliers under retention of ownership were reliant on the assignor identifying the receivables assigned to them. …

(c) The bulk assignment contract is in those terms contrary to good morals and void (§138 I Civil Code) with the consequence that the claimant has not acquired the receivables collected by the defendant. That the defendant is not a supplier under a reservation of ownership is of no importance. The fact that the bulk assignment is void as a result of its being contrary to good morals is of effect for and against all parties.

Note

The judgment shows that the infringement on good morals not only affects the contract between the Austrian bank and H, but also the assignment which took place on the basis of the contract. Both were held void. It is an example of identity of defect, where the same defect, an infringement of good morals, affects both the contract and the transfer. The result is that in effect the abstract transfer system is set aside.

BGH, 26 April 2005[100] **8.53 (DE)**

VOID OBLIGATION IN GENERAL CONDITIONS TO ASSIGN CLAIM

Assigned salary claim

If the general condition obliging to make the assignment is void, the assignment itself is void as well.

Facts: The claimant, bank (B) which had granted a loan to a customer X, seizes in execution X's claims on her employer for her salary. B finds out that X had previously assigned these claims to another bank (A), the defendant, for security purposes and had already notified her employer of the assignment. A's general conditions gave A the right to notify the debtor of the assigned claim without first warning X, who is the assignor and A's debtor. The claimant asserts that the assignment to B was void for infringement of §6(3) and §9 Statute on General Conditions.

Held: The general conditions applying to the contract contain a clause giving the creditor and assignee the right to collect the money from the debtor of the claim without the duty to warn the assignor first.

[100] XI ZR 289/04, BKR 2005, 320.

This clause is void under §6(3) and §9 Statute on General Conditions and renders the assignment itself void as well.

Judgment: (cc) However, the ineffective realisation rules have the consequence, contrary to what the appeal court thinks, according to §6 Abs 3 AGBG, Art 229 §5 sentence 1 EGBGB that the entire assignment is ineffective.

(1) The appeal court has without committing an error of law proceeded in its approach on the basis, that the enforcement rules in No 3 Abs 2 of the contract of assignment … is ineffective according to §9 Abs 1 AGBG. The debtor's interests are adequately protected if and only if the creditor is fundamentally obliged to announce intended enforcement of the assigned claim sufficiently in advance, that the debtor is able to lodge objections to the enforcement and can at least make efforts to prevent the far-reaching consequences of notification that threaten him. No 3 Abs 2 of the contract of assignment and No 20 Abs 2 AGB-Banken old version, which do not provide for a threat of realisation or expressly declare that to be indispensable, do not satisfy these requirements.

(2) The ineffectiveness of the enforcement rules according to the case law of the Bundesgerichtshof have the effect that the assignment as such is ineffective.

W Wiegand, Staudinger Commentary to §929[101] **8.54 (DE)**

The summary of the various defects in the underlying transaction and their effect on the transfer of ownership shows a diffuse picture. Although the approach sketched out above can be recognised as a fundamental concept, that in each case the defectiveness of the disposal transaction has to be verified on its own individual basis and separately, the various, often haphazard, results … nonetheless raise the question of the sustainability of the criteria used hitherto. The oft-appearing arbitrary differentiation is above all attributable to the varying evaluation of the abstraction principle. With regard to the differentiated interpretation the legislative decision represented here …, a standardisation would appear sensible and feasible: It is to be assumed, that defects in the formation of the underlying transaction generally also affect the transfer of ownership. Crucial in this regard is the fact that, in a correct approach, a complete isolation or neutrality of the disposal transaction cannot exist. Furthermore, the principle of abstraction must stand back behind the will of the parties, in so far as for the parties intend a connection between the two transactions …, especially since third-party interests, worthy of protection, are not at risk.

Notes

(1) As a result of this development in which more and more exceptions to the abstract transfer system are allowed, the question arises what makes a transfer system 'abstract'. The term 'causal', on the other hand, is more defined in that it does not vary from one causal system to the other. In a causal system, voidness or avoidance of the underlying contract always results in the transfer being void or avoided, respectively. However, the term 'abstract' lacks sharpness as the character of the transfer system is more determined by the exceptions to the principle of abstrac-

[101] Wiegand, above n 93, at 186, no 28.

tion. Consequently, the degree of abstractness of the German transfer system differs from other abstract systems, such as the Scottish or South African transfer system.

(2) Abstractness of the transfer does not mean that the transfer is always valid even if the underlying contract is void or has been avoided. It simply means that the validity of the transfer is judged separately from the validity of the contract. A defect in the underlying contract does not automatically affect the validity of the transfer. Hence, the definition of abstractness allows that in some or many cases the defect does affect both the contract and the transfer.

(3) Although the principle of abstractness still stands in modern German law, the exceptions have brought the German transfer system a long way from the abstract system devised by Von Savigny and his followers in the nineteenth century, the system which was captured and codified in the German Civil Code.[102]

I.E.6 ENGLISH LAW: TRANSFERS OUTSIDE SALE OF GOODS ACT

Previously, we have seen that the transfer system of the Sale of Goods Act 1979 is a consensual and causal system. The English definition of 'goods' comprises all movable tangible property. The sale and transfer of other property, eg land or claims, is therefore outside the scope of this Act. In addition, the Act does not apply to transfers which are not based on a sales contract, eg the gift of a movable.

As far as gifts are concerned, we have already seen that a gift is valid only if it is effected by deed or if delivery of possession has taken place. An oral gift is invalid. The formalities required in order to make a gift (deed or, alternatively, delivery) point to a *traditio* system. Yet, we do not know whether this *traditio* system is causal or abstract. In English law the gift is not seen as a contract which has to be fulfilled by transfer of property. The reason is that the gift does not create any duty to deliver. So, for obvious reasons the gift cannot be an obligatory contract, ie a contract creating an obligation. Of course, the gift needs the donor's will to give and also the donee's acceptance of the gift. The gift must be an agreement between the parties. The gift thus seems to be a transfer *causa donandi*, a transfer of property by way of gift. However, as there is only one legal act and no distinction between transfer and an underlying legal act, which forms the legal ground of the transfer, the gift cannot be analysed in terms of causal or abstract. These terms have no use in this matter.

The question whether or not the transfer is causal or abstract does, however, have relevancy in the case of a transfer for security reasons or the creation of a charge or pledge. Is the security interest valid if the underlying contract creating the duty to give security is invalid?

[102] JTh Füller, *Eigenständiges Sachenrecht* (Tübingen, Mohr Siebeck, 2006) para 3; van Vliet, above n 73, 194–96.

I.F COMPARATIVE OVERVIEW

In the above we have seen two dividing lines, the one between *traditio* systems and consensual systems and the one between causal and abstract systems. We have also seen that these distinctions are not as strict as they might appear at first glance. In a consensual system ownership cannot pass if generic goods have not yet been appropriated to the contract and if the goods are still future goods. Moreover, the parties to the contract are able to stipulate that ownership will pass only at a later moment, eg after payment of the purchase price. Parties in a *traditio* system are able to let ownership pass before physical delivery by agreeing on a *constitutum possessorium*. However, all transfer systems have in common that no ownership of future goods and generic goods can pass. They all adhere to the principle of specificity.

As to the second dividing line: although there are no mitigations to the causal system, there are various degrees of abstraction in the so-called abstract systems. Modern German law recognises quite a number of exceptions in which a defect in the transaction renders both the underlying contract and the subsequent transfer void or voidable.

II. TRANSFER OF PROPERTY RIGHTS IN LAND AND LAND REGISTER

The second part of the chapter deals with the creation and transfer of interests in land and the role of the land register in this process. It starts with the description of the law in Germany and Austria, where the land register (*Grundbuch*) traditionally plays a fundamental role in the transfer process. The analysis of these two countries gains special interest from the fact that Germany is a representative of the abstract transfer system while Austria follows the system of the causal tradition.[103] The first subsection concentrates primarily on Germany, indicating Austrian law only when this deviates from German solutions. The second part of this subsection explains the English system of transfer of property rights in land, which was fundamentally reshaped by the Land Registration Act 2002. The final part is dedicated to French law, where the land register is of comparatively minor relevance for the transfer procedure, but has primarily publicity effects.

[103] See part I.

II.A GERMANY AND AUSTRIA

II.A.1 THE TRANSFER OF PROPERTY RIGHTS IN LAND

II.A.1.a Germany

Introductory Note

The German BGB has specific rules for the transfer of property rights in movables (§§929 *et seq*) and land (§§873 and 925). According to the German transfer system,[104] the transfer of property rights in land requires two acts: the real agreement (*dingliche Einigung*) and the registration of the property right in the land register as a specific form of *modus*. The land register is regulated by special acts, the *Grundbuchordnung* (GBO)[105] and the *Grundbuchverfügung* (GBV).[106] Contrary to the transfer of movable property, the transfer of ownership to land is subject to several formal requirements.

Bürgerliches Gesetzbuch **8.55 (DE)**

§873 Acquisition by agreement and registration

(1) The transfer of the ownership of a piece of land, the burdening of a piece of land with a right, as well as the transfer or burdening of such a right requires, in so far as the law does not otherwise provide, the agreement [*Einigung*] of the person entitled and the other party on the occurrence of the change of title and the registration of the change of title in the Land Register.

(2) Before the registration, the parties are bound by the agreement only if the declarations are notarially authenticated or made before the Land Register Office or filed with the same, or if the person entitled has handed over to the other party an authorisation for registration [*Eintragungsbewilligung*] that is in accordance with the provisions of the Land Register Code.

§875 Destruction of a right

(1) The destruction of a right over a piece of land requires, in so far as the law does not otherwise provide, the declaration of the person entitled that he destroys the right, and the cancellation of the right in the Land Register. The declaration must be made to the Land Register Office or to the person for whose benefit it is made.

§925 Conveyance agreement [*Auflassung*]

(1) The agreement between the transferor and the acquirer required for the transfer of ownership of a piece of land under §873 (conveyance agreement) must be declared in the simultaneous presence of both parties before a competent authority. For the

[104] See part I (cross reference).

[105] Land Register Code of 24 March 1897, RGBl 1897 p 139, version promulgated on 26 May 1994, BGBl I p 1114.

[106] Regulation on the management of the land register (*Verordnung zur Durchführung der Grundbuchordnung—Grundbuchverfügung*) of 8 August 1935, version promulgated on 24 January 1995, BGBl I p 114. For further regulations providing for procedural rules concerning the operation of the land register, see KH Gursky in E Bund et al (eds), *J von Staudingers Kommentar zum Bürgerlichen Gesetzbuch: Einleitung zum Sachenrecht, §§854–882*, vol III (Berlin, Sellier de Gruyter, 2007) before §§873 *et seq* at 263, para 28 *et seq.*

reception of the declaration of conveyance, any notary, without prejudice to the competence of other authorities, is competent. A declaration of conveyance may also be stipulated in a judicial settlement or in a finally confirmed insolvency plan.

(2) A declaration of conveyance subjected to a condition or time stipulation is ineffective.

§925a Document of the contract

The conveyance agreement shall be accepted only if the document of the contract required under §311 b (1) sentence 1 is submitted or drawn up at the same time.

§928 Abandonment of ownership

(1) The ownership of a piece of land may be abandoned by a declaration of abandonment rendered by the owner to the Land Registry Office and by registration of the relinquishment in the Land Register.

Notes

(1) According to §873(1) BGB, the transfer and encumbrance of property rights to land requires both the real agreement (*dingliche Einigung*) between the parties[107] and the registration of the right in the land register. Registration in the land register, thus, has *constitutive effect*. This also applies to the destruction of a property right over land (§875 BGB) or the abandonment of the right of ownership in respect to land (§928 BGB). In this regard, §§875 and 928 BGB require for simplicity reasons, instead of the conclusion of a real agreement, only the unilateral declaration of the person entitled that he abandons his right. If the right is burdened with the right of a third person (eg a right of pledge or usufruct), the destruction of the burdened right also requires the approval of the third party (§876 BGB).[108]

(2) The constitutive effect of registration only applies to the acquisition or destruction of a property right by legal act, not if the acquisition or destruction is effected directly by the law itself or by judicial or administrative act, such as acquisition by universal succession (eg inheritance), judicial sale by way of execution (*Zuschlag*) or expropriation order. In these cases, the registration of the owner in the land register has only *declaratory effect*.

(3) In general, the real agreement does not need a specific form. For the acquisition and abandonment of ownership to land, however, §925 BGB prescribes that the real agreement must be declared before a competent authority, primarily a notary public, in the simultaneous (though not personal) presence of both parties. Representation is possible. This specific type of real agreement is called *Auflassung*. The same formal requirements apply to the transfer of co-ownership and, according to §4 WEG[109] that refers to §925 BGB, to the creation of an apartment right. Contrary to other real agreements, the *Auflassung* cannot be subjected to a condition or a time stipulation (§925 (2) BGB).

(4) The *Auflassung* need only be declared to the notary (or another competent

[107] See the explanation of the real agreement and the abstraction principle under II (cross reference).
[108] See also Chapter 9.
[109] *Wohnungseigentumsgesetz* (Apartment ownership Act).

authority). *Notarial recordation*[110] is not necessary for the legal effectiveness of the *Auflassung*, but, if it is carried out, it gives the *Auflassung* binding effect (§873(2) BGB). In this regard it must be noted that §311b(1) BGB[111] prescribes notarial recordation for the validity of the contract providing for the transfer or acquisition of ownership to land. In order to ensure compliance with this formal requirement, §925a BGB states that the notarially recorded contract must either be presented to the competent authority (usually the notary) upon declaration of the conveyance agreement (*Auflassung*) or must be drawn up at the same time. Notaries thus play an important role in the German law of land transaction.

(5) For the registration process the *Auflassung* requires *notarial authentication* as a formal prerequisite for the registration of the right in the land register (§29 GBO). For notarial authentication the *Auflassung* must be made in writing, and the notary must certify the signature of the parties (§129(1) BGB). If the *Auflassung* is already notarially recorded, notarial authentication is no more required, as §129(2) BGB provides that notarial recordation substitutes notarial authentication. Notarial authentication of the *Auflassung* has the further effect that it spares the applicant the additional presentation of the formal authorisation of registration (*Eintragungsbewilligung*, §19 GBO) in the registration procedure.[112]

(6) Before registration the acquirer of a property right to land only has an obligatory right towards the other contracting party to the performance of the transfer of the property right. The real agreement (including the *Auflassung*) is freely revocable by each party. It only receives binding effect if the parties renounce their right to revocation or if it fulfills one of the conditions prescribed by §873(2) BGB, *in concreto* if (i) the declarations are notarially recorded or (ii) stipulated before the Land Register Office or (iii) filed with the same, or (iv) if the person entitled has handed over to the other party a notarially authenticated authorisation for registration (§29 GBO, *Eintragungsbewilligung*).[113] The binding effect also extends to the heirs, if one party dies, and, in case of subsequent incapacity of one party, to the custodian (§130(2) BGB).

(7) That the real agreement has binding effect only excludes its revocation by the contracting parties, but does not yet secure that the acquirer will actually receive the right, as the other party is still legally entitled to dispose of the right (eg to sell the parcel to another). The acquirer further runs the risk that the other party subsequently, between conclusion of the contract and registration, becomes restricted in his right of disposal, eg by the opening of insolvency proceedings or an order of seizure. In order to protect the acquirer against such risk, §878 BGB provides that subsequent restrictions on the right of disposal are irrelevant, if two conditions are fulfilled: (i) the real agreement is binding according to §873(2) BGB and (ii) the

[110] Notarial recordation (*notarielle Beurkundung*) means that the notary records the whole content of the document, which thus acquires the legal quality of a public document. Notarial authentication (*notarielle Beglaubigung*) only certifies that a fact (copy, signature) is correct. See §§128 and 129 BGB.

[111] §311b(1) BGB: 'A contract whereby one party obliges himself to transfer or acquire ownership of a piece of land requires recordation by a notary. A contract not concluded in that form becomes valid in its entirety, if the conveyance agreement and the registration in the land register take place.'

[112] See the description of the registration procedure under II.A.2.c.

[113] See BGH, 25 January 1967, BGHZ 46, 398, NJW 1967, 771.

application for registration (§13 GBO) has been made. In this case, the acquirer receives a strong acquisition right (*Anwartschaftsrecht*). Contents and theoretical structure of this *Anwartschaft* are, however, very much contested.[114]

OLG Frankfurt, 3 March 1980[115] **8.56 (DE)**

PRINCIPLE OF ABSTRACTION AND COMPETENCE OF THE REGISTRAR

Void sales contract

The registrar is not entitled to check the validity of the contract (defect of form).

Facts: X sold parts of a parcel of land to Y and Z. The contract violated the formal requirement as provided by §313 (now §311b(1)) BGB as the notarial recordation of the contract did not encompass the building specification which was part of the contract. The registrar refused the registration of the new owners. The contracting parties appealed.

Held: The court grants the appeal on the reason that the registrar is not entitled to check the validity of the contract.

Judgment: In principle the land register is based upon principle of formal authorisation [*formelles Konsensprinzip*], the rule that the unilateral authorisation of the affected person is usually sufficient for the registration in the land register (§19 GBO). It saves the land registry particularly the examination, if the prerequisites of substantive law and the declarations of the parties, which are required for the change of the right, are present. Only in the cases of §20 GBO, particularly with regard to the conveyance agreement [*Auflassung*], the principle of substantive authorisation [*materielles Konsensprinzip*] is applicable, which means that the registration of the new owner may only be executed if the required substantive declarations have been established. According to the BGB, however, the acquisition of ownership is totally isolated from the underlying contractual agreement. It independently takes place from the fact, whether the underlying contractual agreement is valid or not, and only depends on the conveyance agreement between the seller and buyer [*Auflassung*] in the legal form as required by §925 BGB as well as on the registration of the purchaser in the land register (see §873(1) BGB). Consequently the land registrar, when registering a transfer of ownership based on a conveyance agreement, must in principle verify the validity of the real agreement independently from the underlying contractual agreement. The validity of the filed contract is regularly not subject to the examination of the land registry, even in the case of the transfer of ownership of a parcel [*Auflassung*]. It is, in general, not allowed to refuse the registration of the purchaser as owner, even if it should consider the underlying transaction to be invalid. Under present law the real agreement is considered to be an independent legal act, which therefore must be assessed independently, even if it and the underlying contractual agreement are contained in one single document. The effectiveness of the real agreement is basically independent from the fact of whether the underlying transaction rightfully exists or not.

[114] See J Kohler in FJ Säcker and R Rixecker (eds), *Münchener Kommentar zum Bürgerlichen Gesetzbuch*, vol VI, 5th edn (München, Beck, 2009) §873 at 148 *et seq*, para 85; JF Baur and R Stürner, *Sachenrecht*, 18th edn (München, Beck, 2009) §19 at 238 *et seq*, paras 15–20; M Wolf and M Wellenhofer, *Sachenrecht*, 26th edn (München, Beck, 2011) §17 at 257 *et seq*, paras 51 *et seq*.

[115] NJW 1981, 876.

In the present case, the courts of lower instance, upon verification whether the conveyance agreement as required by §20 GBO is provided, have entered into the legal examination of the sales contract of 23 December 1997. According to the preceding explanations, the validity of the underlying contractual transaction, however, is in principle no prerequisite for the registration. Accordingly, the courts of lower instance had to check the sales contract for any defects only if they overlapped to the real agreement and if they were able to influence its validity, as, for instance, it might be the case with the violation of §138 BGB because of violation of *bonos mores* ... or with the violation of a statutory prohibition. ... In the present case there obviously was no reason to check in this sense. Consequently the courts of lower instance should have acted on the assumption, that the possible defect of form of the sales contract does not affect the conveyance agreement which was notarially recorded at the same time.

BGH, 18 December 1967[116] **8.57 (DE)**

ACQUISITION RIGHT OF THE RECIPIENT OF A CONVEYANCE AGREEMENT (*AUFLASSUNGSANWARTSCHAFT*)

Seizure by tax office

The acquisition right of the recipient of a conveyance agreement is transferable, pledgeable and seizable.

Facts: The tax office of the *Land Hessen* ordered seizure of Xs' (several buyers of a parcel of land) acquisition rights to a parcel. At the time of the order, the buyers had already applied to the land register for the registration of their ownership, and a creditor (the *Landeskreditkasse*) had already applied for registration of a land charge. The tax office then applied for the registration of two hypothecs, which were registered and granted priority over the land charge. The *Landeskreditkasse* then objected to the registration of the two hypothecs.

Held: The registration of the two hypothecs was against the law. The recipient of a conveyance agreement who applies for the registration of his ownership at the land register has an acquisition right to ownership which is transferable, pledgeable and seizable.

Judgment: The claimant as land charge creditor as well as the tax office as executive creditor of the acquisition right derive their rights from the legal status of the plaintiff as former recipient of a conveyance agreement. That is why their legal status must be examined at first. It is the legal status of a recipient of a conveyance agreement, whose application for registration of ownership is impending at the land registry.

The mere conveyance agreement already has a binding effect for the seller in the sense, that he cannot revoke it (§925, see §873 (2) BGB); but it does not bring about a limitation of the right to dispose, in fact the seller is still able to sell and burden the parcel otherwise and to withdraw the application for registration of the recipient of a conveyance agreement as owner, which was filed by himself .... The legal status of the recipient of a conveyance agreement is considerably strengthened, if he himself files the application for registration as owner; because, pursuant to §17 GBO, the land registry must effect his application prior to subsequent applications for

[116] BGHZ 49, 197, NJW 1968, 493.

registration, as long as he upholds it, and this usually renders subsequent applications for registration pointless, which contain dispositions by the seller, which contradict the conveyance agreement. *Accordingly, today the prevalent opinion appropriately grants the recipient of a conveyance agreement whose application for registration, filed by himself, is pending a property right, which is transferable, can be pledged and can be seized* [emphasis added]. ... *According to the prevailing opinion this right is to be considered as an acquisition right.*

The fact that acquisition rights exist has been recognised by the judicature for a long time. ... An acquisition right requires that, of the several stages for the development of a right, already so many prerequisites are fulfilled, that one can speak of a secure legal position of the acquirer, which the other party involved in the development of the right, cannot destroy any more by an unilateral declaration. ... For the affirmation of these requirements one must not require low standards. The adjudicating Senate, for instance, denied an acquisition right of the recipient of a conveyance agreement ... not only in case that the application for registration was not at all or only filed by the seller, but also in case that the application for registration was filed by the recipient of a conveyance agreement himself, but rejected by the land registry (even if only in the first instance), because in this case the track was open for dispositions of the seller which contradict the registration of the right of the recipient in the land register as well. ... The question, if the recipient of a conveyance agreement holds an acquisition right, in case his application for registration was filed but not yet effected, was explicitly left open in that judgement. Now it is affirmed by the Senate.

In this case the legal position of the recipient of a conveyance agreement is sufficiently secured by the above described possibility of the recipient to render the subsequently filed application of the seller which contains impairing dispositions pointless by sustaining his own application for registration. The relevant §17 GBO is just a regulatory provision and its violation does not prevent the acquisition of a right by a third party which impairs the right of the recipient of a conveyance agreement. But this, however, does not conflict with the assumption of an acquisition right: the requirement of a secured legal position does not mean that its destruction must be prevented by all means—not even the ownership itself is secured in this sense, since it can be destroyed by good faith acquisition of a third party—it is sufficient for an acquisition right as well, if the impairment of the legal position is excluded according to the normal course of things. Because of §17 GBO this applies to the position of the recipient of a conveyance agreement in case of a pending application for registration filed by himself.

(Further explanations with respect to the mode of transfer, pledge and seizure of the acquisition right). ...

BGH, 30 April 1982[117] **8.58 (DE)**

FORMAL REQUIREMENTS FOR THE CONCLUSION AND THE RESCISSION OF THE SALES CONTRACT OF A PARCEL

Inherited parcel

The mutual termination of the contract concerning the sale of a parcel by the parties needs notarial recordation, if the acquirer has already filed for registration or if he is protected by a priority notice.

Facts: In 1972 X sold a parcel to Y and registered a priority notice in Y's favour. In 1974, after the conclusion of the conveyance agreement but before registration, both parties terminated the contract by an informal agreement. Y informed the land register of this agreement. In 1976 X died and her daughter Z, the sole heir and registered owner of the parcel, claimed from Y the formal authorisation of the cancellation of the priority notice.

Held: The BGH rejects the claim on the ground that the informal termination agreement is void. It does not fulfil the formal requirement of notarial recordation according to §313 (now: §311b(1)) BGB.

Judgment: (1) If after a sales contract of a parcel the conveyance agreement pursuant to §925 BGB has been declared, without registration of a priority notice regarding the conveyance agreement or application for registration of ownership, the parcel of land essentially belongs to the assets of the seller. Although the seller is bound by the real agreement in relation to the acquirer pursuant to §873(2) BGB; this binding effect does not result in a limitation of the right to dispose. The seller is still able to sell and burden the parcel otherwise. The same is true if the seller has filed an application for registration in favour of the recipient of the conveyance agreement, which he can withdraw at any time. ... But if the parcel of land is still at the free disposal of the seller, the termination of the contract, which was agreed upon at this stage of the performance of the sales contract, does not result in a duty of the acquirer, to which the spirit and purpose of §313 sentence 1 BGB[118] might apply. Consequently the termination of the contract can be carried out by an informal agreement.

(2) There is, however, a necessity of notarial recordation, if the recipient of a conveyance agreement has already obtained an acquisition right with respect to the parcel. A—nowadays generally recognised—acquisition right is existent, if, of the several stages for the development of a right, already so many prerequisites are fulfilled, that one can speak of a secure legal position of the acquirer, which the other party involved in the development of the right, cannot destroy anymore by an unilateral declaration. ... Such an acquisition right of the recipient of a conveyance agreement is to be accepted, if he has filed the application for registration as owner by himself; because pursuant to §17 GBO the land registry is obliged to deal with this application prior to subsequent applications for registration, so that the acquirer is secured against other dispositions of the seller. ... A unilateral destruction of the legal position of the recipient of a conveyance agreement by the seller is also not possible anymore, if a priority notice is registered in the land register in favour of the recipient of a conveyance agreement, which protects him against other dispositions of the seller according to §§883(2), 888 BGB.

[117] BGHZ 83, 395, NJW 1982, 1639.
[118] Now §311b(1) BGB.

The nature of the acquisition right is similar to the right of full ownership ..., an independently negotiable preliminary stage of ownership in land, whose development to a full right can no longer be prevented by the seller. Its nature, which is similar to ownership in land, results in the fact, that the acquisition right is not transferred by assignment pursuant to §§398, 413 BGB, but by a conveyance agreement according to §925 BGB. ... The acquisition right, closely approximated to full ownership, normally effects a change of legal competence with respect to the parcel. This legal situation demands to put not only the transfer of the acquisition right under the form, which is required for the full ownership under §925 BGB, but also—as with respect to the full right—the obligation to transfer under the form as prescribed by §313 sentence 1 BGB. The scope of the last-mentioned rule, which is to prevent the seller and the acquirer of a parcel from making an overhasty agreement and to grant them due and free consideration as well as competent and impartial advice by the notary (warning and protective function), entirely, together with the evidence and warranty function, applies to the obligation to transfer an acquisition right. ... This decision is virtually the decision concerning the transfer of the full ownership. That is why the contractual agreement concerning the obligation to sell or acquire an acquisition right with respect to a parcel is subject to notarial authentication, applying §313 sentence 1 BGB accordingly. From the equal treatment of the acquisition right and the ownership follows that the same formal requirements apply for the termination as for the full right which has already been transferred. The holder of the acquisition right is forced by the termination agreement, to give up his secured legal position with respect to the parcel in favour of the seller. That is why he must be protected like a owner of land from overhasty agreements, which result in the loss of his acquisition right with regard to a parcel. Therefore the termination agreement requires a special form, applying §313 sentence 1 BGB accordingly. ... If the termination agreement, which causes the loss of the acquisition right, would not be put under the formal requirement, the application of §313 sentence 1 BGB, would, for instance, depend on the fact, whether in case of a declared conveyance agreement the land registry has already registered the application for registration or not at the time when the contract was terminated. In the first case the ownership would have already been transferred to the acquirer, in the second case the only missing thing for the transfer of ownership would be the granting of the application, which is performed independently from the intention of the parties. Whether or not the application for registration is already granted even need not be known to the parties at the time of the conclusion of the termination agreement. The requirement of a special form would accordingly be dependent from the promptness or slowness of the land registry when handling an application for registration. Such a result, which does not allow the parties to reliably rate a requirement of form, lacks any justification, which could be supported by the spirit and purpose of §313 sentence 1 BGB.

Consequently, the termination agreement of 6 June 1974 was subject to notarial authentication in accordance with the holding of the court of appeal. Without observation of the required form it is void according to §§313 sentence 1, 125 BGB.

II.A.1.b Austria

Introductory Note

According to the Austrian transfer system,[119] the transfer of property rights to land requires a valid contract and the registration of the right in the land register. The rules on the transfer of property rights in land are provided by the Allgemeines Bürgerliches Gesetzbuch (ABGB) and the Grundbuchsgesetz (GBG, Land Register Law).

Allgemeines Bürgerliches Gesetzbuch (ABGB) **8.59 (AT)**

§431 For the transfer of ownership of immovable objects the deed of acquisition must be entered in the public registers designed for this purpose. This entry is called registration [*Intabulation*].

§432 For this purpose a document evidencing the transfer must be certified and must be prepared in the form prescribed by law or in the form of a public instrument.

§433 The document must include the exact designation of the persons who transfer and who accept the ownership; the parcel to be transferred; the legal basis of the transfer; further the place and the date of the conclusion of the contract; and the transferor must, in this or a separate document, give the express declaration that he consents to the registration.

Grundbuchsgesetz (GBG) **8.60 (AT)**

§26 (1) Registrations and prenotations can only be granted on the basis of documents, which are executed in the form as prescribed with respect to their validity.

(2) These documents, if they concern the acquisition or alteration of a property right, must contain a valid legal ground.

§27 (1) The documents, on the basis of which a registration shall be carried out, must be free from such visible defects, which impair their credibility and, if they consist of several sheets, bound in a way that no sheet can be foisted.

(2) They must also contain such a description of the persons involved in the legal act, that they cannot be mistaken for another person; with respect to physical persons the date of birth must be stated, with respect to legal persons who are registered in the commercial register the registration number of the commercial register, and with respect to domestic associations [*inländische Vereine*] the registration number of the association register.

(3) The documents must contain the declaration of the place, day, month and year of the execution of the document.

§31 (1) The registration ... can only be executed on the basis of public documents or such private documents, on which the signatures of the parties are authenticated by a court or by a notary and on which the authentication clause with respect to physical persons also contains the date of birth.

(6) On the basis of documents of an agent a registration against the principal can

[119] See above I.

moreover only be granted if the power of attorney issued by him is either granted for the particular legal act or has been issued not earlier than three years before the application for registration or constitutes a health care power of attorney [*Vorsorgevollmacht*] within §§284 *et seq* ABGB .

§32 (1) Private documents, on the basis of which a registration shall be executed, must contain apart from the requirements of §§26, 27:

(a) the exact declaration of the parcel or the right, in relation to which the registration shall be executed;

(b) the explicit statement of the person, whose right shall be restricted, burdened, destroyed or conferred to an other person, that he agrees with the registration.

(2) This statement can also be stipulated in a special document or in the land register application. In such cases, however, the document or the application, which contains the statement, must be fulfil the formal requirements for the registration.

§94 (1) The land register court must strictly examine the application and its attachments and is entitled to grant a registration only if

1. no obstacle against the requested registration arises from the land register with respect to the parcel or the right;

2. there is no founded doubt against the personal capability of the persons involved with the registration to dispose of the object, which is subject to the registration, or against the capacity of the applicants to apply for the registration;

3. the application seems to be justified by the content of the presented documents and

4. the documents are presented in the form, which is required for the granting of a registration, prenotation or notice.

Notes

(1) Like in Germany, registration has *constitutive effect*, but, contrary to German law, the acquisition of a property right depends on the validity of the contract (*principle of causal tradition*). This is provided by §431 ABGB for the transfer of ownership and extends also to the transfer of the other property rights.[120] Austrian law does not provide for any formal requirements for the validity of contracts for the transfer of land.[121] However, in order to serve as the basis of a registration, the contract must meet certain formal requirements, as laid down in §§432 and 433 ABGB and §§26, 27 and §§31, 32 GBG, including the notarial authentication (§31(1) GBG) certifying the authenticity of the signatures of the parties and the correctness of their date of birth. Like in Germany (see §19 German GBO), the entry of a property right in the land register requires the formal authorisation for registration of the entitled person (§32(1) lit b GBG; *Eintragungsbewilligung*[122]). This declaration usually forms part of the contract. If it is stipulated in a different document, this document must meet the formal requirements for registration, espe-

[120] §445 ABGB, §451 ABGB: hypothec, §481 ABGB: servitude, §530: real charge, §§1, 5 BauRG: building right, §5 WEG: apartment right.

[121] §1 NotAktsG provides for formal requirements with regard to specific sorts of contracts, such as gifts and certain contracts between spouses.

[122] This declaration is also called *Aufsandungserklärung*.

cially the notarial authentication (§32(2) GBG). Specific provisions apply for the registration on the basis of public documents (§436 ABGB, §33 GBG).

(2) The Austrian registrar is, like his German counterpart, only obliged to check whether the application meets the formal requirements of the law, but unlike in Germany this also includes the control of certain aspects of the validity of the contract. According to §94 GBG, registration must be denied, if the registrar has reasonable doubts concerning the personal ability of the entitled person to dispose of the right (eg doubts about the legal capacity of one contracting party) or if the documents, including the contract, do not meet the formal requirements prescribed by law. The registrar, however, only acts upon the application of the party and the presented documents and is not entitled to carry out any investigative steps.

OGH, 14 October 1975[123] **8.61 (AT)**

LEGAL POSITION OF THE PURCHASER OF A PARCEL BEFORE REGISTRATION

Insolvent seller

No ownership before registration.

Facts: By a sales contract of 30 April 1974 Max S sold his parcel of land to the purchasers who, on 27 June 1975, applied for registration of ownership at the land register which was granted on the same day. Against this decision an appeal was brought by the administrator in Max S's insolvency proceedings who claimed that Max S had become insolvent on 5 May 1975. According to paragraph 13 Insolvency Act, the opening of bankruptcy proceedings hinders the entry of the purchasers in the land register.

Held: The purchaser of a parcel acquires ownership only with the registration of his right in the land register.

Judgment: The claimants ignore the governance of the registration principle in the sense of §431 ABGB, when they hold the view that they have already acquired ownership upon transfer of the parcel by the seller. The law ..., has regulated the exceptions to the registration principle (§425 ABGB), for which reason there can be no room for a so-called unregistered ownership beyond this range.

II.A.2 THE LAND REGISTER

II.A.2.a Organisation and structure of the land register

In Germany the general substantive law of land registration is gathered in the BGB. The most important provisions are §§873–902 BGB, which contain the general rules on rights over land, and §925 BGB, the provision specifying the conveyance agreement (*Auflassung*). §§1113–1203 BGB deal with registration requirements applicable to the right of hypothec and the right of the land charge (*Grundschuld*). The formal rules on the land register are mainly provided by the Grundbuchordnung (GBO),[124] a

[123] 5 Ob 183/75 SZ 48/104.

[124] Land Register Code of 24 March 1897, RGBl 1897 p 139, version promulgated on 26 May 1994, BGBl I p 1114.

federal act regulating the organisation and the procedural matters of the land register, and the Grundbuchverfügung (GBV),[125] a decree implementing the GBO. §§14–17 of the Law on the right of superficies (Güber das Erbbaurecht) of 15 January 1919, RGBl p 72 and §§7–9 WEG (Law on apartment ownership) contain specific rules concerning the registration of the right of superficies (*Erbbaurecht*) and apartment ownership (*Wohnungseigentum*).

Grundbuchordnung (GBO) **8.62 (DE)**

§2 (1) The land registers must be organised by districts.

(2) The parcels are named in the land register after the official registers as established in the states (cadastral maps).

(3) One part of a parcel shall be divided from the whole parcel only if an authenticated excerpt from the descriptive part of the official register, issued by the competent authority, is submitted, from which follow the identification of the part of the parcel and the other details, which shall be transferred from the official register to the land register, as well as the alterations, which insofar occur with respect to the remaining part of the parcel. The part of the parcel must be recorded in the official register under a specific number, unless the authority competent for the administration of the official register refrains from doing so, because it is united with a neighbouring parcel or a part of it, and it certifies this to the Land Register Office. ...

§3 (1) Each parcel receives a specific location in the land register (land register folio). The land register folio is to be considered as the land register for the parcel in the sense of the Civil Code.

(2) The parcels of the Federal state, the states, the communities and other municipal organisations [*Kommunalverbände*], churches, convents and schools, the watercourses, public roads as well as the parcels, which are dedicated to a railway enterprise, which serves public traffic, receive a land register folio only upon request of the owner or of the entitled person.

(3) A parcel must be taken out from the land register upon request of the owner, if the owner is released from the duty of registration pursuant to paragraph 2 and a registration, which affects the right of the owner, is not existent.

(4) The Land Register Office may, provided that there is no confusion or an essential aggravation of the legal relations or of the administration of the land register to fear, refrain from providing a land register folio for a parcel, if the parcel is destined to serve the economic purposes of several other parcels, stands in a spatial relation to them corresponding to this provision and is in the co-ownership of the owners of these parcels (servient parcel).

§4 (1) A joint land register folio can be provided with respect to several parcels of the same owner, the land registers of which are administered by the same Land Register Office, as long as there is no confusion to fear thereof.

[125] Regulation on the management of the land register (*Verordnung zur Durchführung der Grundbuchordnung—Grundbuchverfügung*) of 8 August 1935, version promulgated on 24 January 1995, BGBl I p 114.

Grundbuchverfügung (GBV) **8.63 (DE)**

§1 (1) The land register districts are the municipal districts. As far as several districts are united in one administrative district ..., they form a land register district. But a municipal district may be divided into several land register districts on the order of the State Department of Justice or the body appointed by it.

(2) If a municipal district is united with another municipal district or a municipal district or an administrative district as laid down in paragraph 1 sentence 3 is separated into several independent administrative districts, the previous land register districts may be retained.

Notes

(1) In Germany, the whole territory is surveyed and divided into cadastral units (*Flurstücke*). The cadastral units are entered in the cadastral maps (*Liegenschaftskataster*), a public register operated by the cadastral authorities (*Katasterbehörden*). The cadastral maps are closely linked to the land register, as they provide an accurate description of the cadastral units which form the basis of the parcel (*Grundstück*), the fundamental unit of the land register. The parcel, which consists of one or several cadastral units (§6(4) GBV), is created by its entry in the land register.[126] The alteration of the composition of the parcel, be it the union of two or more separate parcels into one parcel (*Vereinigung*, §890(1) BGB, §5 GBO) or the entry of one piece of land as part of another parcel (*Zuschreibung*, §890(2) BGB, §6 GBO), requires a formal decision of the land register office.

(2) Each parcel receives a land register folio (*Realfoliensystem*, §3(1) GBO). This register folio constitutes the land register (§3(1) sentence 2 GBO). In Germany (but not in Austria[127]) it is also permissible to register several parcels of one owner that lie in the same district on one 'common folio' (*Zusammenschreibung*, *Personalfoliensystem*, §4(1) GBO). The land register folios may be kept in volumes or in loose-leaf form (§1(1) GBO).

(3) Since 1993[128] the state governments (*Landesregierungen*) are entitled to decide that the land register is kept in electronic form. The basic rules for the electronic land register are provided in §§126–34a GBO and §§61 *et seq* GBV. §134 GBO authorises the Federal Ministry of Justice to lay down further regulations by ministerial decree.

[126] The definition of the parcel was rendered by the Reichsgericht 12 March 1914, RGZ 84, 265: '[T]hat each part of the surface of the earth, which is spatially limited with respect to other parts and which is entered in a particular land register folio for itself or in a joint land register folio with a particular number within the parcel-index, is to be considered as independent parcel in the sense of the law of immovable property.'

This definition is generally accepted by German courts and literature: see Gursky in Bund et al, above n 106, at 259 *et seq*, para 16; Demharter, *Grundbuchordnung: GBO*, 27th edn (München, Beck, 2010) §2 at 43 *et seq*, para 15; Baur and Stürner, above n 114, §15 at 75, para 18; Kohler in Sächer and Rixecher, above n 14, before §873 at 110 *et seq*, para 3. Gursky in Bund et al, above n 106, at 259, para 16, however, indicates that the definition given by the Reichsgericht is, strictly speaking, insufficient, as §890 BGB, §3(4) GBO and §7(1) WEG allow for the entry of a parcel on several land register folios.

[127] But see the explanation concerning the group register (*Gruppenverzeichnis*) in the following.

[128] Registerverfahrensbeschleunigungsgesetz (RegVBG) of 20 December 1993, BGBl I p 2182.

(4) The Land Register Office is obliged to provide a land register folio for each parcel.[129] This means that each parcel must be entered in the land register (*Grundbuchszwang*). Parcels that are in public ownership (federal state, *Land*, communities, churches, etc), as well as watercourses, public roads and railways, however, pose an exception, as they are only entered in the land register upon request of the owner (§3(2) GBO). The right of superficies (*Erbbaurecht*)[130] and the apartment right (*Wohnungseigentum*)[131] are treated as an equivalent to a parcel ('*grundstücksgleiche Rechte*') and receive separate land register folios.

Each land register folio consists of the title (*Aufschrift*), the inventory (*Bestandsverzeichnis*) and three divisions (§4 GBV). The title indicates the court, the register district and the number of the register volume and the folio (§5 GBV). The inventory describes the size and the location of the parcel(s) and indicates the rights connected with the ownership of the parcel (§§6, 7 GBV). It contains the serial number of the parcel, the cadaster district and the cadastral number(s) of the cadastral unit(s), the commercial type (*Wirtschaftsart*), address and size of the parcel and gives information on the history of the composition of the parcel (division or union of whole parcels or parts of parcels in the past; *Abschreibungen, Zuschreibungen*). The first division (§9 GBV) contains the name, date of birth and address of the owner, as well as the date and legal basis for the acquisition. In case of co-ownership it also indicates the shares of the co-owners and in case of joint ownership the underlying legal relationship (§47 GBO). The second and third division contain the charges and restrictions (§§10, 11 GBV). Hypothecs, land charges (*Grundschulden*) and rent charges are, for reasons of clarity, separately entered in the third division and all the other property burdens (eg rights of servitude) and restrictions are entered in the second division of the land register.

(5) The *Austrian land register* is regulated by several specific statutes.[132] It consists of two registers: (i) the main register (*Hauptbuch*) for the actual entries with the collection of documents (*Urkundensammlung*) containing all the documents which served as the basis of an entry, and (ii) the register of deleted entries (*Verzeichnis der gelöschten Eintragungen*). In order to facilitate the access to the entries the land register further provides four auxiliary registers: the parcel-index (*Grundstücksverzeichnis*), the address-index (*Anschriftenverzeichnis*), the index of persons (*Personenverzeichnis*) indicating the parcel owners and the holders of a building right[133] and the group-index,[134] which allows checking of entries concerning a whole group of parcels (eg parcels which are part of a highway). All registers and

[129] See §116 GBO. The procedure is regulated in §§117–25 GBO.

[130] See §§14–17 Law on the Hereditary building Rights (G über das Erbbaurecht) of 15 January 1919, RGBl p 72.

[131] See §§7–9 WEG (Condominium Law).

[132] Grundbuchsgesetz (GBG, Land Register Law) BGBl 1955/39; Allgemeines Grundbuchsanlegungsgesetz (AllgGAG) BGBl 1930/2; Grundbuchsumstellungsgesetz (GUG) BGBl 1980/550; Liegenschaftsteilungsgesetz (LTG) BGBl 1930/3; Vermessungsgesetz (VermG) BGBl 1968/306.

[133] Upon regulation by the Federal Minister of Justice also persons who hold a registered right (eg hypothec, servitude) can be included in the index of persons (§4(1a) GUG as amended by BGBl I 2008/100).

[134] Provided by BGBl I 2008/100.

indexes are open for the public; only access to the index of persons is restricted.[135] All registers are kept electronically and it is provided that interaction with the land register can be conducted electronically. Notaries and attorneys are obliged to use the electronic filing system, which also includes the electronic submission of original documents.[136]

II.A.2.b Competent authority and legal review

Rechtspflegergesetz **8.64 (DE)**

§3 The following affairs are conferred on the registrar:

1. the affairs of the local court in their entirety, which are to be administered by the judge pursuant to the statutory provisions, with respect to

(h) land register matters, ...

§4 (1) The registrar takes any measures which are necessary for the settlement of the affairs conferred on him.

Grundbuchordnung (GBO) **8.65 (DE)**

§1 (1) The land registers, which may also be kept in loose-leaf form, are administered by the local courts (land register offices). ...

§71 (1) The decision of the land register office is subject to the judicial remedy of appeal.

(2) The appeal against a registration is not permissible. By way of appeal, however, can be demanded, that the land register office is ordered to register an objection pursuant to §53 or to carry out a cancellation.

§72 The appeal is decided by the appeal court [*Oberlandesgericht*] of the district where the land register office is situated.

§78 (1) Against the decision of the appeal court the judicial remedy of the appeal on a question of law [*Rechtsbeschwerde*] is permissible, if the appeal court has admitted the appeal in the decision.

(2) The appeal must be admitted, if

1. the legal matter is of fundamental importance or
2. the development of the law or the assurance of a consistent adjudication require the decision of the competent court [*Rechtsbeschwerdegericht*].

Notes

(1) The land register office (*Grundbuchamt*) is a department of the local court (*Amtsgericht*) of the judicial district where the parcel, which is the subject matter of the entry, is situated.

(2) The recording officer is the registrar (*Rechtspfleger*), a senior court officer (§2 Law on Registrars) who enjoys the independence of the judiciary (§9 Law on

[135] See §§5(4), 6(2) GUG.

[136] §§89b *et seq* GOG (Law on the organisation of the court system) and Regulation of the Federal Ministry of Justice on the eletronic filing system, BGBl II 2005/481 as amended by BGBl II 2011/220.

Registrars). The registrar has comprehensive decision-making powers. Decisions of the judge in land registration matters are a rare exception. The judge only decides if the registrar submits or is obliged to submit a case to the judge (§5 Law on Registrars), or if the party lodges a special appeal (*Erinnerung*) against the decision of the registrar (§11 Law on Registrars).

(3) The decision of the Land Register Office is subject to appeal (*Beschwerde*) to the appeal court (Oberlandesgericht) of the district where the Land Register Office is situated (§72 GBO). This decision can only be brought before the BGH with respect to questions of law that are of fundamental importance (§78 GBO).

(4) The judicial remedy of appeal is, however, not permissible if the contested decision of the Land Register Office is a registration (*Eintragung*, §71(2) GBO). The party whose interests are infringed by the incorrect entry is then entitled to apply for the correction of the land register (*Grundbuchberichtigung*; §§894 BGB *et seq*) and, in order to prevent the good-faith acquisition of the contested right by a third party,[137] to the entry of an objection (*Widerspruch*) in the land register (§§892, 899 BGB). The BGH, however, interprets §71(2) GBO in a narrow sense and, despite the wording of §71(2) GBO, applies it only to registrations that are encompassed by the public faith of the land register. Accordingly, it grants the remedy of the appeal (*Beschwerde*) also against registrations which, by their legal nature, cannot be the object of a public faith acquisition,[138] or where the specific contents of the land register (entry of an official objection by the land register office, no prior entry of the acquisition by a third party) exclude the possibility of a good faith acquisition by a third party.[139]

II.A.2.c Registration procedure

Introductory Note

In both countries, Germany and Austria, the process of registration follows strict rules arising from basic principles of land register law. These basic principles are the principle of party initiative (*Antragsprinzip*), the authorisation principle (*Konsensprinzip*), the priority principle and the sequency principle.

Principle of party initiative (Antragsprinzip) **8.66 (DE)**

§13 GBO (1) An entry shall only be granted upon application, in so far as the law does not otherwise provide. Everybody, whose right is affected by the entry or in whose favour the entry shall be granted, is entitled to file an application.

(2) The exact point in time, when the application reaches the land register office, shall be recorded on the application. ...

[137] For an explanation of the notion of 'public faith of the land register' and 'good faith acquisition' see II.A.2.e and f.

[138] BGH, 21 June 1957, BGHZ 25, 16.

[139] BGH, 16 April 1975, BGHZ 64, 194.

Authorisation principle (formelles und materielles Konsensprinzip)

§19 GBO An entry is executed if the person, whose right is affected by it, authorises it.

§20 GBO In the case of the conveyance of a parcel as well as in the case of the creation, modification of the content or conveyance of a hereditary building right the entry may only be executed if the required agreement of the entitled person and the other party is stipulated.

§29 GBO (1) An entry shall only be effected if the authorisation for registration or the other declarations as required for the entry are evidenced by public or publicly certified documents. Other prerequisites of the entry require the presentation of public documents, as far as they are not obvious for the land register office.

(3) Declarations or applications by a public authority, on the basis of which an entry shall be executed, must be signed and sealed or stamped.

Sequency principle

§39 GBO (1) An entry shall only be effected, if the person, whose right is affected by it, is registered as the entitled person.

Priority principle **8.67 (DE)**

§879 BGB (1) The order of priority of several rights that burden a parcel are determined according to the sequence of the entries if the rights are entered in the same section of the land register. With respect to rights that are registered in different sections, the right entered by stating an earlier date has priority; rights that are entered by stating the same date have the same priority.

(2) The entry is also decisive for the order of priority, if the agreement, which is according to §873 necessary for the acquisition of the right, was concluded only after the entry.

(3) A deviating determination of the order of priority must be registered in the Land Register.

Grundbuchordnung (GBO) **8.68 (DE)**

§17 If several entries are applied for, which affect the same right, the later filed entry must not be registered before the earlier filed application is effected. …

§45 (1) If several entries must be executed in the same section of the land register, they receive the order which corresponds to the sequence of the applications; if the applications have been filed at the same time, it must be recorded in the land register, that the entries have the same priority. …

Algemeines Bürgerliches Gesetzbuch **8.69 (AT)**

§440 If an owner has sold the same immovable property to two different persons, the one who applied first for the registration shall become the owner thereof.

Grundbuchgesetz (GBG) **8.70 (AT)**

§29 (1) The order of priority of an entry is determined by the point in time at which the application reached the land register court (§§438, 440 ABGB).

(2) Entries which were executed upon concurrently arriving applications have the same priority with respect to each other.

Notes

(1) With regard to registrations, the land register usually acts only on the *application of the party* or on the request of a public authority[140] (principle of party initiative, *Antragsprinzip*). *Ex officio* registrations pose a rare exception.[141] The registrar is bound by the content of the application and may only grant the entry exactly as applied for by the party. If the application does not meet the legal requirements, the registrar is obliged either to reject the application immediately or to request that the party correct or complete the application within a certain period of time (§18 GBO). Austrian law only allows for the correction of formal flaws of a submission (§82a GBG).

(2) Entries in the land register underlie the priority principle. The order of priority is determined by the point in time at which the application for the entry reached the land register, but German as well as Austrian law provide for several instruments for the alteration of the priority order by legal transaction.[142]

(3) According to §19 GBO, the entry requires the formal authorisation for registration (*Eintragungsbewilligung*) by the person whose right is affected by the entry. In order to receive an entry in the land register, the applicant thus needs not to prove the existence of the right per se, but must only show this formal declaration, as the law presumes that the person who issues this formal declaration actually conferred the underlying right. Consequently, the registrar is only obliged to check if the application meets the formal requirements as set forth by §§19 and 29 GBO (*formales Konsensprinzip*). §29 GBO provides that the declaration must be issued in the form of a public document or that the signatures are certified by a notary public.

(4) For the conveyance of the right of ownership of land and the creation, modification or conveyance of a hereditary building right §20 GBO, however, requires the presentation of the conveyance agreement[143] (*materielles Konsensprinzip*) which must also fulfil the formal requirements of §29 GBO. In this case the formal authorisation of registration (§19 GBO) must only be presented, if it is not covered by the contents of the conveyance agreement.[144]

(5) According to the public faith principle of §891 BGB,[145] it is legally presumed

[140] §38 GBO: '*In den Fällen, in denen nach gesetzlicher Vorschrift eine Behörde befugt ist, das Grundbuchamt um eine Eintragung zu ersuchen, erfolgt die Eintragung auf Grund des Ersuchens der Behörde.*'

[141] See eg §§18(2), 53 and 71(2) GBO.

[142] Germany: §879 (3) BGB: determination of priority (Rangvermerk), §880 BGB: subsequent change of priority (Rangänderung), §881 BGB: reservation of priority (Rangvorbehalt); Austria: §30 GBG: change of priority (Vorrangseinräumung), §58 GBG: reservation of priority (Rangvorbehalt).

[143] See §§873, 925 BGB.

[144] See Gursky in Bund et al, above n 106, at 406, para 253.

[145] For an explanation of the public faith of the land register see II.A.2.e and f.

that the person actually holds the right. Thus the registrar needs only to check whether the person who gives up a registered right or agrees to the limitation of such a right is entered in the land register (sequency principle, §39 GBO). An exception applies to the heir who intends to convey or give up his right (§40 GBO).

II.A.2.d Publicity of the land register

Grundbuchordnung (GBO) **8.71 (DE)**

§12 (1) Everybody, who shows a justified interest, is entitled to inspect the land register. The same applies to documents, to which the land register refers as supplement of an entry, as well as to applications for entry which have not yet been executed.

Grundbuchverfügung (GBV) **8.72 (DE)**

§43 (1) Representatives of domestic public authorities are entitled to inspect the land register and to request a copy without the need for showing a justified interest.
(2) The same applies to notaries as well as to attorneys, who want to inspect the land register upon proven order of a notary, to publicly appointed land surveyors and to holders of property rights, as far as the object of the inspection is the respective parcel. Irrespective of that, the inspection of the land register and the issue of copies from it are permissible, if the consent of the registered owner, given in the single case, is shown.

Grundbuchgesetz (GBG) **8.73 (AT)**

§7 (1) The land register is open to the public.

(2) Everybody is entitled to inspect the land register in the presence of an officer of the land register and to make copies or collect extracts from it; the registrar has to grant them.

Grundbuchsumstellungsgesetz (GUG) **8.74 (AT)**

§5 (4) Copies and information from the index of persons must be granted to the persons registered therein about the entries affecting them. In addition copies and information from the index of persons are to be granted only to those persons who show a legal interest, to the extent as justified thereby. The denial to grant a copy is subject to a court order [*Beschluss*]. …

§6 (2) The following are also entitled to inspect the index of persons:

1. notaries, … in succession matters …;

1a. attorneys, in order to identify registered rights of the deceased in their capacity as representative of the heirs and in order to grant copies and information to persons, who are registered in the index of persons, about the entries affecting them;

1b. notaries and attorneys to identify as representatives of the creditor registered rights of the debtor of an enforceable monetary claim;

2. the departments of the federal state, the state [*Land*] and the communities as

well as the social insurance authorities and the Association of the Social Insurance Authorities, as far as this is necessary for the compliance with their assigned duties and responsibilities.

LG Mannheim, 22 January 1992[146] **8.75 (AT)**

PUBLICITY OF THE LAND REGISTER

Terminated lease

The tenant whose landlord claims personal use in order to terminate the contract is entitled to inspect the inventory and the first division of the land register.

Facts: During eviction proceedings tenant A requested the inspection of the land register in order to show that her landlord, who claimed personal use, owns another apartment. If this allegation proved true the possessive action would be dismissed or the landlord would be obliged by law to offer A this apartment for tenancy. The application was rejected by the Land Register Office, but an appeal was brought against this.

Held: The tenant whose landlord claims personal use in order to terminate the contract has a justified interest in the sense of §12 GBO and is entitled to inspect the inventory and the first division of the land register.

Judgment: Pursuant to §12 GBO the inspection of the land register requires the existence of a justified interest. This is existent if the according application follows a rational interest justified by the circumstances; the interest as such may be of a legal, economic or mere factual nature … . This justified interest is to be granted to the claimant because of the pending eviction proceedings. …

Consequently, the present interest of the tenant to know the actual state of the land register only applies to the first division of the land register and the inventory referred to therein. The inspection of the land register normally encompasses all divisions of the land register. Literature … and courts …, however, admit a restriction of the inspection to particular divisions of the land register. Since in this case, according to the holding of the court of appeal, the justified interest of the plaintiff has been satisfied by granting an inspection of the first division in relation with the inventory, the inspection was to be restricted in this respect.

The present proceedings did not require the registered parcel owner to be heard by the court.

Note

This judgment is a good example of the interpretation of the legal interest provided by §12 GBO. Such interest need only be adduced (and not proved) by the applicant.[147] Although the land register office is not prohibited to give the landowner the opportunity to comment on the request of a third party to inspect the land register,[148] the parcel-owner has no right to be heard by the court, and, according

[146] NJW 1992, 2492.

[147] OLG Stuttgart, 17 January 1983, Rpfleger 1983, 272.

[148] BayObLG, 9 December 1992, NJW 1993, 1142.

to the BGH,[149] he has no right to appeal. Baur and Stürner[150] contest this position held by the BGH. According to their view, the constitutional right to informational self-determination, as outlined by the German Constitutional Court,[151] makes it necessary to interpret §12 GBO more narrowly and, at least in case of doubt, to grant the parcel-owner the right to be heard before the court and the right to appeal.

Bundesverfassungsgericht, 28 August 2000[152] **8.76 (DE)**

PUBLICITY OF THE LAND REGISTER

Wirtschaftswoche

The constitutional right of freedom of the press constitutes a legal interest in the sense of §12(1) GBO and entitles the press, in principle, to inspect the land register. The court is not obliged to hear the owner of the parcel.

Facts: The claimant was the editor of the economic magazine *Wirtschaftswoche*. Without further substantiation she filed an application at the land register office to inspect certain folios of the land register. The court requested the claimant specify the reasons for her application in order to show the existence of a legal interest according to §12(1) GBO. It explained that the inspection of an entry of the land register by a representative of the press requires a hearing of the owner of the concerned parcel and the balancing of the information interest of the press and the confidentiality interests of the affected owner. As the claimant refused to do so, the court dismissed the application. The claimant appealed without success and filed a constitutional complaint against the decision of the OLG Düsseldorf as court of last instance at the Federal Constitutional Court.

Held: The constitutional complaint is successful. The Bundesverfassungsgericht quashes the decision of the OLG Düsseldorf.

Judgment: The contested judgment violates Article 5(1) and (2) GG.

(a) The criterion for the following examination is the constitutional right of freedom of the press pursuant to Article 5(1) and (2) GG, the scope of protection of which is touched by the contested decision. The freedom of the press as guaranteed in Article 5(1) and (2) GG does not only guarantee the freedom of circulation of news and opinions; it rather protects the whole range of journalistic preparation activities, to which in particular the provision of information belongs. Only the basically unimpeded access to information allows the press to fulfil the role efficiently, which is assigned to it in a liberal democracy … . The Federal Constitutional Court has already outlined this with respect to the protection of the source of information or the informant, but also with respect to the access to public court hearings. Similarly there can exist a basic legitimate interest of the press regarding the access to data collections or registers—here to the land register—which have only limited access.

There is no use to discuss whether in addition to the constitutional right of freedom of the press the constitutional right of freedom of information is also affected by the contested decision. The land register is a source of information, which is open to everybody, even though only under certain conditions. A source of information is generally accessible, if it is technically qualified and dedicated to provide

[149] 6 March 1981, NJW 1981, 1563.
[150] Baur and Stürner, above n 114, §15 at 188, para 60.
[151] BVerfGE 65, 1.
[152] NJW 2001, 503.

information for the general public that is to say for an individually not definable group of people. As far as the state establishes the preconditions of the inspection in the GBO, the accessibility is constituted but not limited in a legal sense. The right to inspect depends on the factual preconditions of the GBO, notably on the explanation of a legitimate interest and within this scope also on governmental decisions regarding the application of the law. Whether this contradicts its qualification as generally accessible source of information is contested, but does not need to be decided in this place, since the right to gain information by the press is also protected by the freedom of the press.

According to §12(1) GBO everybody, who shows a legitimate interest, is entitled to inspect the land register. As the Federal Constitutional Court has already observed in another context, there are no concerns with respect to the constitutionality of this regulation. Also with regard to the freedom of the press there are no objections to this regulation, since the use of the indefinite legal term 'legitimate interest' gives enough leeway to the courts to take the significance of the freedom of the press adequately into account when interpreting and applying the regulation.

The Court of Appeal [*Oberlandesgericht*] made the right to inspection dependent from a specification of an interest of inspection, which is also provided by §12 GBO in the normal case of the inspection. ...

The precondition of specification of the legitimate interest, whereas specification is less than furnishing *prima facie* evidence, is not to be objected under constitutional law, as long as it restricts itself to the specification of an interest for information of the press. Since §12 GBO does not provide for a general right to inspect, the precondition of specification of a legitimate (not a 'legal') interest in the inspection ... is consistent and also applies, if the right to inspect is opened by an expanding interpretation for journalistic purposes. In the latter case, however, the requirements with respect to the legitimate interest itself and its specification need to take into account the peculiarity of a free press. The interest for information of the press if constitutionally granted and connected with its public function. It would be incompatible with the constitutional protection of the press, if the enforcement of the interest for information would depend on a governmental evaluation of the information request. The press must be able to decide on journalistic criteria, what it considers to be of value for the public interest and what not. The protection does not depend on the peculiarity and the quality standard of the press product or the reporting in detail. Rather, the interest for information as specified by the press—after examination of its existence without own evaluation—is to be considered as basis by the land registry for the following procedure.

Note and Question

Compare the German and Austrian rules concerning the right to inspect the land register. Do you think that it is necessary to restrict the publicity of the land register in order to protect the confidentiality interests of the land owner?

II.A.2.e Registrable rights and interests

Bürgerliches Gesetzbuch **8.77 (DE)**

§892 Public faith of the Land Register (1) In favour of the person who acquires a right in a parcel or a right in such a right by legal act, the contents of the Land

Register is presumed to be correct, unless an objection to the accuracy is registered or the inaccuracy is known to the acquirer. If the person entitled is restricted in favour of a particular person in his disposition of a right entered in the Land Register, the restriction is effective as against the acquirer only if it is apparent from the Land Register or known to the acquirer.

(2) If registration is necessary for the acquisition of the right, the knowledge of the acquirer at the date when the application for registration is made or, if the agreement required under §873 is reached only later, the date of agreement is conclusive.

Grundbuchordnung (GBO) **8.78 (DE)**

§54 Public charges as such, which rest on a parcel, are excluded from the registration in the land register, unless their registration is especially permitted or ordered by law.

Grundbuchgesetz (GBG) **8.79 (AT)**

§8 Types of entries

The entries in the land register are:

1. registrations (unconditional acquisitions of rights or extinctions—registrations or cancellations), which without further justification or
2. prenotations (conditional acquisitions of rights or extinctions—prenotations), which only on condition of their subsequent justification effect the acquisition, transfer, restriction or extinction of registered rights, or
3. mere notices.

§9 Objects of registration or prenotation

In the land register there may only be entered property rights and property charges, further the option to repurchase and the right of pre-emption (§§1070 and 1073 ABGB) as well as the lease (§1095 ABGB).

Notes

(1) Apart from §54 GBO, which restricts the registrability of public charges, German law does not provide for an explicit definition of the registrable rights and interests. Consequently, their definition must be derived from the purpose of the land register to give an accurate description of the rights to land in order to facilitate legal transactions of land.[153] According to §892 BGB, the scope of registrable rights and interests encompasses all rights in a parcel or rights to such rights and the relative restrictions in the disposition of a registered right. Registrable rights and interests thus comprise (i) property rights to land including the rights treated as an equivalent to a parcel (*grundstücksgleiche Rechte*), (ii) property rights on such rights, (iii) relative restrictions in the disposition of a registered right, (iv) the objection (*Widerspruch*, §899 BGB), (v) the priority notice (*Vormerkung*, §883 BGB) and (vi) the property right of pre-emption, also named 'option to purchase' in Chapter 3 (§§1094 *et seq* BGB). Not registrable are (i) relationships and charges

[153] Baur and Stürner, above n 114, §15 at 178, para 28

established by public law, (ii) rights that are not recognised by law as property rights, (iii) personal rights, (iv) personal data that do not enjoy the public faith of the land register (eg incapacity) and (v) absolute restrictions in the disposition of a registered right (eg legal restrictions in the disposition of farm land) or contractual restrictions in the disposition of a parcel.

(2) Austrian law provides for an explicit definition of the registrable rights and interests. According to §9 GBG, they comprise the property rights, which consist of ownership, hypothec, servitude, real burden (*Reallast*), apartment ownership and the right of supericies, and three personal rights (right of pre-emption, option to repurchase and the lease) which by its entry in the charges register obtain notice effects against third parties. Further registrable rights are the priority agreement (*Vorrangseinräumung*, §30 GBG) and the prohibition to alienate and/or burden a parcel according §364c ABGB (*Belastungs- und Veräußerungsverbot*). Contrary to German law, Austrian law distinguishes between three different types of entries, the registration (*Einverleibung*), the pre-notation (*Vormerkung*) and the notice (*Anmerkung*), which serve different functions. Registration and prenotation concern the creation and extinction of registrable property rights. The notice serves primarily the purpose of procuring certain effects, especially publicity effects, for specific, legally relevant circumstances. Examples are the notice that the holder of a registered right is restricted in the disposition of the right (eg minority, opening of insolvency proceedings), or the notice that a parcel or a right is subject to litigation.

II.A.2.f Effects of registration

(i) Effect between the parties

In Austrian and German law, the transfer of property rights by way of legal transaction requires the registration in the land register (constitutive effect; see II.A.1.a). Before registration the right belongs still to the transferor, while the acquirer has only a contractual claim against the transferor. The constitutive effect does not apply if the acquisition or cancellation of a property right is effected directly by the law itself or by judicial or administrative act. In this case the registration of the owner in the land register has only declaratory effect.

(ii) Third party effect
Public faith principle

Bürgerliches Gesetzbuch **8.80 (DE)**

§891 Legal presumption

(1) If a right has been entered in the Land Register for a person, it is presumed that the person is entitled to the right.

(2) If a registered right is deleted in the Land Register, it is presumed that the right does not exist.

§892 Public faith of the Land Register

(1) In favour of the person who acquires a right in a parcel or a right in such a right by legal transaction, the contents of the Land Register are presumed to be

correct, unless an objection to the accuracy is registered or the inaccuracy is known to the acquirer. If the person entitled is restricted in favour of a particular person in his disposition of a right entered in the Land Register, the restriction is effective as against the acquirer only if it is apparent from the Land Register or known to the acquirer.
(2) If registration is necessary for the acquisition of the right, the knowledge of the acquirer at the date when the application for registration is made or, if the agreement required under §873 is reached only later, the date of the agreement is conclusive.
§893 Legal transaction with the person registered
The provision in §892 applies correspondingly if, on the basis of this right, performance is made to the person for whom a right is registered in the Land Register, or if, on the basis of this right, between this person and another person a legal transaction that does not fall under the provision of §892 is made which contains a disposition of the right.

Algemeines Bürgerliches Gesetzbuch **8.81 (AT)**

§1500 The right which was acquired by acquisitive or extinctive prescription cannot be to the detriment of the person, who has acquired an object or a right in good faith of the public registers prior to the registration of the same.

Notes

(1) A fundamental feature of the German land register is the principle of public faith. The basis for the public faith in the land register is the legal presumption of the accuracy of the land register provided by §891 BGB. As a consequence, it is not the registered person, but the person who contests an entry, who bears the burden of proof that the land register is incorrect.[154]

(2) With regard to third persons, §§892 and 893 BGB provide that third persons are entitled to rely on the correctness of the land register (public faith principle). As a consequence, German law allows for the acquisition of property rights in good faith of the land register (*gutgläubiger Erwerb*) and the good faith acquisition of property rights free from burdens (*gutgläubiger lastenfreier Erwerb*). The public faith of the land register extends only to the existence or non-existence of registered rights, and rights to such rights, and the non-existence of relative restrictions in disposition. It does not encompass entries that indicate merely factual[155] or personal circumstances (eg size of a parcel, date of birth of the owner) and the existence or non-existence of personal rights to a parcel (eg a right of lease) or of rights, charges and restrictions that are not registrable per se. The public faith of the land register only applies to the acquisition or loss of property rights by legal transaction (between different persons), not if the acquisition or loss of a property right is effected by operation of law or by judicial or administrative act. According to §892(1) BGB, the acquirer's good faith is destroyed if he, or his agent acting

[154] See eg BGH, 23 March 1979, NJW 1979, 1656.
[155] It does, however, cover the description of the parcel in the cadastral map: LG Frankenthal, 12 October 1955, NJW 1956, 873.

on his behalf, positively knew that the land register is incorrect or if an objection (*Widerspruch*) is entered in the land register.

(3) These principles also apply *mutatis mutandis* to Austrian law. The acquisition in good faith of the land register is, however, only regulated indirectly by the provisions concerning the availability of the action for cancellation of a registered right (§62 GBG, *Löschungsklage*). Moreover, Austrian law is stricter than German law with regard to the good faith prerequisite, in that slight negligence already destroys the acquirer's good faith.[156] Moreover, according to case law, the acquisition in good faith of the land register does not cover the gratuitous acquisition of a property right.[157]

II.A.2.g The priority notice (*Vormerkung*)

Bürgerliches Gesetzbuch **8.82 (DE)**

§883 (1) To secure a claim to the grant or cancellation of a right in a parcel or in a right burdening a parcel or the alteration of the content or the priority of such a right, a priority notice may be entered in the Land Register. The registration of a priority notice is also admissible to secure a future or a conditional claim.

(2) A disposition that is made after the registration of the priority notice on the parcel or the right is ineffective to the extent that it would defeat or adversely affect the claim. This also applies, if the disposition is made by way of compulsory execution or enforcement of an attachment or by the insolvency administrator.

(3) The priority of the right to the grant of which the claim relates is determined according to the registration of the priority notice.

Notes

(1) A very common and important instrument of German law to secure the obligatory right to the acquisition of a property right to land is the priority notice (*Vormerkung*), a special entry in the land register that enables the acquirer to register his right notwithstanding subsequent adverse dispositions of the transferor. The priority notice requires the formal authorisation of the owner of the parcel, or the holder of the affected right, and the registration in the land register (§885 BGB). For the registration procedure, §29 GBO requires the notarial authentication of this declaration (or of the formal authorisation for registration according to §19 GBO).

(2) Austrian law does not provide for an instrument that is comparable to the German priority notice. Future and conditional claims cannot be registered at all.[158] The prenotation according to §438 ABGB (and §§35 *et seq* GBG), which is also called *Vormerkung*, serves also priority purposes, but has a rather restricted field of application. It only allows for preliminary registration if the document that serves as the basis for the registration (eg the sales contract) shows the general characteristics as provided by §26, 27 GBG, but lacks the specific contents of §§31 *et seq*

[156] OGH 7 April 1992, 4 Ob 523/92 JBl 1993, 186.

[157] See OGH 21 December 1989, 6 Ob 737/87 SZ 62/219, NZ 1990, 237; 18 February 2003, 4 Ob 189/02a JBl 2003, 584.

[158] OGH 28 April 1982, 3 Ob 18/82 SZ 55/58.

GBG, eg formal authorisation of registration, or notarial authentication. Once the missing requirements are presented, the so-called 'justification of the prenotation', the prenotated right becomes fully and retroactively effective. Another important instrument to grant a certain priority position to a future buyer or acquirer of a right of hypothec by the registered owner is the notice of priority (*Ranganmerkung*, §§53–56 GBG). The notice of priority is a tool of high practical importance and low costs, but limited in its application and only valid for one year from the date of its entry.

II.B ENGLISH LAW

II.B.1 THE TRANSFER OF PROPERTY RIGHTS IN LAND

English law distinguishes between two systems of transferring titles to land, the transfer by deeds (unregistered system) and the transfer by way of registration in the land register (registered system). The system of transfer by deeds is used for the transfer of titles that are not registered in the land register.[159] A deed is a written document which describes itself as a deed, is signed, and is attested by witnesses.[160] Traditionally, a deed needed to be sealed. This requirement, however, was abolished by the Law of Property (Miscellaneous Provisions) Act 1989.[161] Under the unregistered system, the purchaser of land must investigate the vendor's title in order to ensure that the vendor has power to sell the land and that it is not subject to undisclosed encumbrances. As this investigation must be repeated by each new purchaser it is time consuming and also costly. The system of transfer by deeds is nowadays in decline and will subsequently be completely replaced by the system of registration of title, as provided by the Land Registration Act 2002 (registered system).

Section 2 Law of Property (Miscellaneous Provisions) Act 1989 states the following formal requirements for contracts for the sale of land or other dispositions of any interest in land.[162] First, it must be made in writing. Second, it must incorporate all the terms which the parties have expressly agreed, either in one document or, where the contracts are exchanged, in each, and third, the document incorporating the terms must be signed by or on behalf of each party to the contract. A contract that does not meet these requirements is void. These formal requirements do not apply to short leases, to contracts made in the course of a public auction and contracts regulated under the Financial Services and Markets Act 2000.[163] A valid contract can be enforced by specific performance instead of the award of damages and, thus, gives the acquirer an immediate equitable interest in the object.

The Land Registration Act 2002 did not change this system. In addition to the paper-based conveyancing process, it provides for the legal framework to allow for

[159] See comprehensively C Harpum et al (eds), *Megarry & Wade: The Law of Real Property*, 8th edn (London, Sweet & Maxwell, 2012) 257–309 (unregistered conveyancing).

[160] Section 1(2) and (3) Law of Property (Miscellaneous Provisions) Act 1989.

[161] Section 1(1)(b).

[162] See Harpum et al, above n 159, 618 *et seq*.

[163] Section 2(5) Law of Property (Miscellaneous Provisions) Act 1989.

transferring and creating interests in land by electronic means ('electronic conveyancing'), a process that is now under implementation.[164]

II.B.2 THE LAND REGISTER

In England and Wales land registration is regulated by the Land Registration Act (LRA) 2002 and the Land Registration Rules 2003.[165] The new scheme replaces the former Land Registration Acts, the Land Registry Act 1862 and the Land Registration Act 1925,[166] which already provided a system of conveyancing by registration of title. In many parts of England and Wales this system was, until 1990, only optional, and thus allowed the continued use of the old common law method of conveyancing by deeds for unregistered land.

Although the majority of titles have since been registered, the existence of land with unregistered title still necessitates comprehensive rules for first registration of hitherto unregistered land. The LRA 2002, accordingly, provides for voluntary registration of title[167] and defines the events that trigger compulsory registration.[168] Although the LRA 2002 enhances first registration of all land with unregistered title, it does not provide for the immediate compulsory registration of all the remaining unregistered land. Consequently, the Law Commission stated on presentation of the LRA 2002 that total registration is rather

> a goal that should be sought within the comparatively near future. We, therefore, recommend that ways in which all the remaining land with unregistered title in England and Wales might be brought on to the register should be re-examined five years after the present Bill is brought into force.[169]

According to the Law Commission, the fundamental objective of the law is that

> the register should be a complete and accurate reflection of the state of the title of the land at any given time, so that it is possible to investigate title to land on line, with the absolute minimum of additional inquiries and inspections.[170]

In order to achieve this goal, the LRA 2002 seeks to create a conclusive register in order to eliminate as far as possible interests in land which are valid and enforcable even though they are not registered overriding interests.

[164] For further information on the actual status of the project see www.landregistry.gov.uk/e-conveyancing/publications/.
[165] For the genesis of the Bill, see *Land Registration for the Twenty-First Century: A Conveyancing Revolution* (2001) Law Com No 271 paras 1.15 *et seq.*
[166] Sch 13 LRA 2002.
[167] Part 2 ch 1 s 3 LRA 2002 (When title may be registered).
[168] Part 2 ch 1 s 4 LRA 2002 (When title must be registered) *et seq.*
[169] (2001) Law Com No 271, para 2.13.
[170] (2001) Law Com No 271, para 1.5.

II.B.2.a Organisation and structure of the land register

Land Registration Act 2002 **8.83 (E&W)**

Section 1 Register of title (1) There is to continue to be a register of title kept by the registrar.
(2) Rules may make provision about how the register is to be kept and may, in particular, make provision about—
(a) the information to be included in the register,
(b) the form in which information included in the register is to be kept, and
(c) the arrangement of that information.

Law Commission and HM Land Registry, Land Registration for the Twenty-first Century[171] **8.84 (E&W)**

Para 2.12 The register itself consists of three parts, namely
(1) The *Property Register*, which both describes the land and the estate comprised in the title and records the benefit of rights such as easements and covenants that are enjoyed by the property...;
(2) The *Proprietorship Register*, which records the nature of the title [That is whether it is absolute (as is usually the case) good leasehold, possessory or qualified. ...], the name, address and description of the proprietor, and any entries which affect his or her right to dispose of the land...; and
(3) The *Charges Register*, which records those encumbrances which burden the property... .

Notes

(1) Unlike Germany and Austria, which follow a strict territorial concept for the organisation of the land register, the English land register is structured according to relevant right ('estates vested in one proprietor'), namely estate in land, rentcharge, franchise, manor or *profit à prendre* in gross.[172] With respect to the internal structure of the register, however, namely its division into the three subregisters (property register, proprietor register and charges register) and the functions of these registers, there are many similarities between all three countries.

(2) The register is kept electronically. In order to facilitate access to information held by the register, the land register keeps several indices: the index under section 68 of the LRA 2002, providing for information on parcels of land,[173] the index of proprietors' names[174] and the day list,[175] showing the date and time of applications. In addition, the registrar must keep a register of cautions against first registration.[176]

[171] Law Commission and HM Land Registry, *Land Registration for the Twenty-first Century: A Consultative Document* (1998) Law Com No 254.
[172] See Rule 2 LRR 2003.
[173] Regarding registered estates or cautions relating to the land etc.
[174] Rule 11 LRR 2003.
[175] Rule 12 LRR 2003.
[176] S 19 LRA 2002.

II.B.2.b Competent authority and legal review

Land Registration Act 2002 **8.85 (E&W)**

Section 99 The land registry

(1) There is to continue to be an office called Her Majesty's Land Registry which is to deal with the business of registration under this Act.

(2) The land registry is to consist of—

(a) the Chief Land Registrar, who is its head, and

(b) the staff appointed by him;

and references in this Act to a member of the land registry are to be read accordingly.

(3) The Lord Chancellor shall appoint a person to be the Chief Land Registrar.

(4) Schedule 7 (which makes further provision about the land registry) has effect.

Section 107 The adjudicator

(1) The Lord Chancellor shall appoint a person to be the Adjudicator to Her Majesty's Land Registry.

(2) To be qualified for appointment under subsection (1), a person must have a 10 year general qualification (within the meaning of section 71 of the Courts and Legal Services Act 1990).

(3) Schedule 9 (which makes further provision about the adjudicator) has effect.

Section 108 Jurisdiction

(1) The adjudicator has the following functions—

(a) determining matters referred to him under section 73(7),[177] and

(b) determining appeals under paragraph 4 of Schedule 5.

(2) Also, the adjudicator may, on application, make any order which the High Court could make for the rectification or setting aside of a document which—

(a) effects a qualifying disposition of a registered estate or charge,

(b) is a contract to make such a disposition, or

(c) effects a transfer of an interest which is the subject of a notice in the register.

(3) For the purpose of subsection (2)(a), a qualifying disposition is—

(a) a registrable disposition, or

(b) a disposition which creates an interest which may be the subject of a notice in the register.

(4) The general law about the effect of an order of the High Court for the rectification or setting aside of a document shall apply to an order under this section.

Section 111 Appeals

(1) Subject to subsection (2), a person aggrieved by a decision of the adjudicator may appeal to the High Court.

[177] S 73(7) obliges the registrar to refer the decision of an objection that the registrar does not regard to be groundless and that cannot be disposed by agreement to the adjudicator.

Notes

(1) The land registration system in England and Wales is administered by Her Majesty's Land Registry, a public agency, which consists of an administrative headquarters in London and 24 district land registries.[178] Responsible for the whole system of registration is the Chief Land Registrar (registrar), who is appointed by the Lord Chancellor and assisted by his staff.[179] The registrar administers the registry and has ample powers to determine the applications made to the registry, especially with regard to first registration, where the registrar is entitled to examine and assess the applicant's title.[180] Subject to rules, the registrar may require a person to produce documents[181] and make orders about costs in relation to proceedings before him.[182] Such requirement or order is enforceable as an order of the court[183] and subject to appeal to the county court.[184] A specific procedure applies to objections.[185] If a person objects to an application to the registrar, the registrar is entitled to assess the objection and, if he decides that it is not groundless, he must give notice of the objection to the applicant. If it is not possible to dispose by agreement of the objection, the registrar must not determine the application, but has to refer the matter to the adjudicator.[186]

(2) The registrar is, pursuant to a court order or on his own accord, obliged (respectively entitled) to alter the register in order to correct a mistake (rectification), to bring the register up to date and to give effect to an estate, right or interest excepted from the effect of registration.[187] He is also able to alter the register for the purpose of removing a superfluous entry.[188] The registrar is obliged to pay indemnities according to Schedule 8 LRA 2002. He concludes the network access agreements[189] and provides for consultation and advisory service.

(3) The only rights of appeal from the registrar are provided by sections 75(4), 76(5) (appeal to the county court) and Schedule 5 paragraph 4 (appeal to the adjudicator) LRA 2002. Any other decision of the registrar is under judicial review.

(4) The office of Adjudicator of Her Majesty's Land Registry was introduced by the LRA 2002. It consists of the adjudicator, who is directly appointed by the Lord Chancellor, and his staff. As the adjudicator is not able to determine all the cases himself, Schedule 9 paragraph 4 LRA 2002 authorises the adjudicator to delegate his powers to members of his staff qualifying for the function.

(5) The adjudicator is wholly independent of HM Land Registry and exercises judicial powers. He determines (i) matters referred to him under section 73(7) LRA

[178] See (2001) Law Com No 271, para 2.10.
[179] S 99(3) LRA 2002. See also Sched 7 LRA 2002 which contains further rules concerning the holding of office and the remuneration of the Chief Land Registrar, the appointment of staff etc.
[180] Ss 9, 10 LRA 2002.
[181] S 75(1), (2) LRA 2002.
[182] S 76 LRA 2002.
[183] Ss 75(3), 76(4) LRA 2002.
[184] Ss 75(4), 76(5) LRA 2002.
[185] S 73 LRA 2002.
[186] S 73(7) LRA 2002.
[187] Sched 4 para 2(1)(c) LRA 2002.
[188] Sched 4 para 5(d) LRA 2002.
[189] See Sched 5 LRA 2002.

2002 (contested applications), (ii) hears appeals against decisions of the registrar with respect to entry into, or termination of, a network access agreement (Schedule 5 paragraph 4), and (iii) is entitled on application of a party to rectify or set aside conveyancing documents. A person aggrieved by a decision of the adjudicator has the right to appeal to the High Court. With regard to Schedule 5 paragraph 4 matters, only appeal on a point of law is possible.[190] In proceedings on a reference under section 73(7) LRA 2002, the adjudicator may, instead of deciding a matter himself, direct a party to a hearing before the court of either the entirety of the proceedings before him or one or more specific issues in those proceedings (such as a preliminary point of law).[191]

II.B.2.c Registration procedure

(i) First registration and registered dispositions

The LRA 2002 provides for comprehensive legislation for the first registration of unregistered land.[192] Registration may be voluntary (section 3 LRA) or compulsory triggered by certain events, namely the transfer of a legal estate in unregistered land or the creation or grant of a legal estate (section 4 LRA). According to section 5 LRA, the Lord Chancellor may by order amend section 4 LRA so as to add to the events that trigger first registration. If registration is compulsory, the responsible estate owner, or his successor in title, is obliged to apply for registration within 2 months from the date on which the relevant events occurs (section 6 LRA). This period may be extended by the registrar (section 6 subsection 5 LRA). Failure to register results in the loss of the legal estate (section 7 LRA) and liabiliy obligations (section 8 LRA). The transferee, however, retains the equitable interest in land.[193] Special provisions apply to land held by the Crown (demesne land) and grants out of demesne land (Part 7 LRA).

On first registration the applicant may receive different classes of title, depending on the assessment of the registrar. Section 9 provides three classes of title to freehold estates (fee simple absolute, qualified and possessory title)[194] and section 10 LRA provides four classes of title to leasehold estates (absolute title, good leasehold title, qualified title and possessory title). All titles may subsequently be upgraded by the registrar (sections 62(1)–(3) LRA), especially if the title has been entered in the register for at least 12 years and if the proprietor is in possession of the land (section 62(4), (5) LRA).

Persons who claim to be the owner of a qualifying estate or who are entitled to an interest affecting the qualifying estate are entitled to lodge a caution against first registration (sections 15–22 LRA). The caution ensures that the person entering the

[190] S 111(2) LRA 2002.
[191] S 110 LRA 2002.
[192] Part 2 LRA 2002.
[193] RJ Smith, *Property Law*, 7th edn (Harlow, Pearson Longman, 2011) 233.
[194] This classification reflects the validity of the title with respect to the probability that the title can be contested by a third person. See ss 9(2)–(5), 10 LRA 2002 and under II.B.2.f. On these terms see Chaper 3.

caution is informed of any application for first registration and thus gives him the opportunity to object to the registration or to protect his interests. Cautions against first registration are recorded on the cautions register kept by the registrar.

The rules on dispositions of registered land are provided in Part 3 LRA. Section 27(2) LRA enumerates the dispositions of a registered estate which are required to be completed by registration. Schedule 2 LRA provides for registration requirements. No registration is necessary for three transfers by operation of law: (i) a transfer on the death or insolvency of an individual proprietor, (ii) a transfer on the dissolution of a corporate proprietor and (iii) the creation of a legal charge which is a local land charge (section 27(5) LRA).

(ii) Registration procedure

Introductory Note

The registration procedure is extensively regulated by the Land Registration Rules 2003. They provide for comprehensive rules regarding the contents and form of applications and convey ample decision making and assessment powers to the registrar.

Land Registration Act 2002 **8.86 (E&W)**

Section 74 Effective date of registration An entry in the register in pursuance of—

(a) an application for registration of an unregistered legal estate, or

(b) an application for registration in relation to a disposition required to be completed by registration,

has effect from the time of the application.

II.B.3 PUBLICITY OF THE LAND REGISTER

Land Registration Act 2002 **8.87 (E&W)**

Section 66 Inspection of the registers etc (1) Any person may inspect and make copies of, or of any part of—

(a) the register of title,

(b) any document kept by the registrar which is referred to in the register of title,

(c) any other document kept by the registrar which relates to an application to him, or

(d) the register of cautions against first registration.

(2) The right under subsection (1) is subject to rules which may, in particular—

(a) provide for exceptions to the right, and

(b) impose conditions on its exercise, including conditions requiring the payment of fees.

Note

Section 66 LRA provides for open access to the land register and to any documents kept by the registrar. Contrary to section 112 of the Land Registration Act 1925 as substituted by the Land Registration Act 1988, which opened the land register to the general public for the first time,[195] this right also extends to documents regarding leases and charges kept by the registrar. The exercise of the access to the register is further specified by Part 13 of the Land Registration Rules 2003. Rules 136 and 137 of the Land Registration Rules 2003 restrict the inspection of the register with regard to documents designated by the registrar as exempt documents for containing prejudicial information. Access to the index of proprietors' names is also restricted. According to rule 11(3), a person may apply for a search in the index in respect of either his own name, or the name of a corporation aggregate, or the name of some other person in whose property he can satisfy the registrar that he is interested generally (eg as trustee in bankruptcy or personal representative).

II.B.3.a Registrable rights and interests

Land Registration Act 2002 **8.88 (E&W)**

Section 2 Scope of title registration

This Act makes provision about registration of title to—

(a) unregistered legal estates which are interests of any of the following kinds

(i) an estate in land,

(ii) a rentcharge,

(iii) a franchise,

(iv) a profit a prendre in gross, and

(v) any other interest or charge which subsists for the benefit of, or is a charge on, an interest the title to which is registered; and

(b) interests capable of subsisting at law which are created by a disposition of an interest the title to which is registered.

Section 27 Dispositions required to be registered

(2) In the case of a registered estate, the following are the dispositions which are required to be completed by registration—

(a) a transfer,

(b) where the registered estate is an estate in land, the grant of a term of years absolute—

(i) for a term of more than seven years from the date of the grant,

(ii) to take effect in possession after the end of the period of three months beginning with the date of the grant,

(iii) under which the right to possession is discontinuous, ...

(c) where the registered estate is a franchise or manor, the grant of a lease,

(d) the express grant or reservation of an interest of a kind falling within section 1(2)(a) of the Law of Property Act 1925, other than one which is capable of being registered under Commons Registration Act 1965,

[195] (2001) Law Com No 271, para 9.37: prior to this amendment the register could only be inspected by the registered proprietor or by an authorised person.

(e) the express grant or reservation of an interest of a kind falling within section 1 (2)(b) or (e) of the Law of Property Act 1925, and

(f) the grant of a legal charge.

(3) In the case of a registered charge, the following are the dispositions which are required to be completed by registration—

(a) a transfer, and

(b) the grant of a sub-charge.

(4) Schedule 2 to this Act (which deals with the relevant registration requirements) has effect.

Law of Property Act 1925 **8.89 (E&W)**

Section 1 (2) The only interests or charges in or over land which are capable of subsisting or of being conveyed or created at law are—

(a) An easement, right, or privilege in or over land for an interest equivalent to an estate in fee simple absolute in possession or a term of years absolute;

(b) A rentcharge in possession issuing out of or charged on land being either perpetual or for a term of years absolute;

(c) A charge by way of legal mortgage;...

Land Registration Act 2002 (notices and restrictions) **8.90 (E&W)**

Section 32 Nature and effect

(1) A notice is an entry in the register in respect of the burden of an interest affecting a registered estate or charge.

(2) The entry of a notice is to be made in relation to the registered estate or charge affected by the interest concerned.

(3) The fact that an interest is the subject of a notice does not necessarily mean that the interest is valid, but does mean that the priority of the interest, if valid, is protected for the purposes of sections 29 and 30.

Section 33 Excluded interests

No notice may be entered in the register in respect of any of the following—

(a) an interest under—

(i) a trust of land, or

(ii) a settlement under Settled Land Act 1925 ...

(b) a leasehold estate in land which—

(i) is granted for a term of years of three years or less from the date of the grant, and

(ii) is not required to be registered,

Section 40 Nature

(1) A restriction is an entry in the register regulating the circumstances in which a disposition of a registered estate or charge may be the subject of an entry in the register.

(2) A restriction may, in particular—

(a) prohibit the making of an entry in respect of any dispositions, or a disposition of a kind specified in the restriction;
(b) prohibit the making of an entry—
(i) indefinitely,
(ii) for a period specified in the restriction, or
(iii) until the occurrence of an event so specified.
(3) Without prejudice to the generality of subsection (2)(b)(iii), the event which may be specified include—
(a) the giving of notice,
(b) the obtaining of consent, and
(c) the making of an order by the court or registrar.
(4) The entry of a restriction is to be made in relation to the registered estate or charge to which it relates.

Section 41 Effect

(1) Where a restriction is entered in the register, no entry in respect of a disposition to which the restriction applies may be made in the register otherwise than in accordance with the terms of the restriction, subject to any order under subsection (2). ...

Notes

(1) Section 2 defines those rights that are subject to first registration, namely the fee simple and the lease, and, if the grantor is not registered, a rentcharge, a franchise and a *profit à prendre* in gross. Titles to freehold and leasehold estates may receive different classes of title on first registration depending on the quality of the title (sections 9, 10 LRA 2002).

(2) In respect to registered estates, the registrability of interests can be deduced from section 27(2) LRA 2002 which enumerates the dispositions by the registered proprietor which must be completed by registration. As a consequence, such dispositions constitute registrable interests, comprising the fee simple, leases granted for a period of seven years or more, future and discontinuous leases regardless of their length,[196] charges (mortgages)[197] including sub-charges, easements,[198] profits appurtenant to land and rentcharges.[199]

(3) Further types of entries are the notice and the restriction, methods to protect any interest affecting a registered estate on the register. Such interests are still called 'minor interests', according to section 3 LRA 1925, although the LRA 2002 no longer uses this term.[200] The notice has the effect that the purchaser is bound by

[196] Short leases are not registrable. They, however, may constitute overriding interests: Smith, above n 193, 252 *et seq*.

[197] The mortgage by demise or subdemise (long lease) is prohibited, see s 23(1)(a) LRA 2002.

[198] It is interesting to note that easements are only subject to compulsory registration, if expressly granted. Implied easements and easements arising by prescription do not have to be registered and constitute overriding interests. They may be protected by a notice. Voluntary registration is also possible. See Smith, above n 193, 239 *et seq*.

[199] Note that the new creation of rentcharges is severely restricted by the Rentcharges Act 1977.

[200] Smith, above n 193, 242.

the interest protected by the notice, while a restriction limits future entries on the register. If the restriction is not complied with, registration will be refused.

II.B.3.b Effect of registration—First registration

Land Registration Act 2002 **8.91 (E&W)**

Section 11 Freehold estates

…

(2) Registration with absolute title has the effect described in subsection (3) to (5).

(3) The estate is vested in the proprietor together with all interests subsisting for the benefit of the estate.

(4) The estate is vested in the proprietor subject only to the following interests affecting the estate at the time of registration—

(a) interests which are the subject of an entry in the register in relation to the estate,

(b) unregistered interests which fall within any of the paragraphs of Schedule 1, and

(c) interests acquired under the Limitation Act 1980 of which the proprietor has notice.

(5) If the proprietor is not entitled to the estate for his own benefit, or not entitled solely for his own benefit, then, as between himself and the persons beneficially entitled to the estate, the estate is vested in him subject to such of their interests as he has notice of.

(6) Registration with qualified title has the same effect as registration with absolute title, except that it does not affect the enforcement of any estate, right or interest which appears from the register to be excepted from the effect of registration.

(7) Registration with possessory title has the same effect as registration with absolute title, except that it does not affect the enforcement of any estate, right or interest adverse to, or in derogation of, the proprietor's title subsisting at the time of registration or then capable of arising.

Section 12 Leasehold estates

…

(2) Registration with absolute title has the effect described in subsection (3) to (5).

(3) The estate is vested in the proprietor together with all interests subsisting for the benefit of the estate.

(4) The estate is vested subject only to the following interests affecting the estate at the time of registration—

(a) implied and express covenants, obligations and liabilities incident to the estate,

(b) interests which are the subject of an entry in the register in relation to the estate,

(c) unregistered interests which fall within any of the paragraphs of Schedule 1, and

(d) interests acquired under the Limitation Act 1980 of which the proprietor has notice.

(5) If the proprietor is not entitled to the estate for his own benefit, or not entitled solely for his own benefit, then, as between himself and the persons beneficially entitled to the estate, the estate is vested in him subject to such of their interests as he has notice of.

(6) Registration with good leasehold title has the same effect as registration with

absolute title, except that it does not affect the enforcement of any estate, right or interest affecting, or in derogation of, the title of the lessor to grant the lease.

(7) Registration with qualified title has the same effect as registration with absolute title, except that it does not affect the enforcement of any estate, right or interest which appears from the register to be excepted from the effect of registration.

(8) Registration with possessory title has the same effect as registration with absolute title, except that it does not affect the enforcement of any estate, right or interest adverse to, or in derogation of, the proprietor's title subsisting at the time of registration or then capable of arising.

Section 37 Unregistered interests

(1) If it appears to the registrar that a registered estate is subject to an unregistered interest which—

(a) falls within any of the paragraphs of Schedule 1, and

(b) is not excluded by section 33,

he may enter a notice in the register in respect of the interest.

(2) The registrar must give notice of an entry under this section to such persons as rules may provide.

Section 71 Duty to disclose unregistered interests

Where rules so provide—

(a) a person applying for registration under Chapter 1 of Part 2 must provide to the registrar such information as the rules may provide about any interest affecting the estate to which the application relates which—

(i) falls within any of the paragraphs of Schedule 1, and

(ii) is of a description specified by the rules;

(b) a person applying to register a registrable disposition of a registered estate must provide to the registrar such information as the rules may provide about any unregistered interest affecting the estate which—

(i) falls within any of the paragraphs of Schedule 3, and

(ii) is of description specified by the rules.

Schedule 1—Unregistered interests which override first registration

Leasehold estates in land

1 A leasehold estate in land granted for a term not exceeding seven years from the date of the grant, except for a lease the grant of which falls within section 4(1) (d), (e) or (f).

Interests of persons in actual occupation

2 An interest belonging to a person in actual occupation, so far as relating to land of which he is in actual occupation, except for an interest under a settlement und the Settled Land Act 1925.

Easements and profits a prendre

3 A legal easement or profit à prendre.

Customary and public rights

4 A customary right.

5 A public right.

Local land charges

6 A local land charge

Mines and minerals

7–9 …

Miscellaneous[201]

10 A franchise.

11 A manorial right.

12 A right to rent which was reserved to the Crown on the granting of any freehold estate (whether or not the right is still vested in the Crown).

13 A non-statutory right in respect of an embankment or sea or river wall.

14 A right to payment in lieu of tithe.

16 A right in respect of the repair of a church chancel.

Note

The effect of first registration depends on the class of title. Registration of a freehold estate with absolute title means that the estate is vested in the registered proprietor. As explained in section 11 LRA 2002, the estate is only subject to (i) interests that are protected on the register (notices, restrictions, registered charges), (ii) overriding interests as described in Schedule 1,[202] (iii) adverse possession claims of which the proprietor has notice and (iv) obligations to persons with beneficial entitlements to the estate (eg deriving from a trust) of which he has notice. Qualified and possessory titles enjoy the same protection except with regard to the estates, rights or interests exempted from the effect of registration. This applies *mutatis mutandis* to leasehold estates.

II.B.3.c Effect of registration—Registered land

(i) Conclusiveness of the register

Land Registration Act 2002 **8.93 (E&W)**

Section 26—Protection of disponees (1) Subject to subsection (2), a person's right to exercise owner's powers in relation to a registered estate or charge is to be taken to be free from any limitation affecting the validity of a disposition.

(2) Subsection (1) does not apply to a limitation—

(a) reflected by an entry in the register, or

[201] Paras 10–14 of Schedule 1 cease to have effect 10 years after the Schedule came into force: s 117(1) LRA 2002.

[202] A further overriding interest is stated by s 90 LRA 2002 with respect to Public Private Partnership (PPP) leases relating to transport in London.

(b) imposed by, or under this Act.

(3) This section has effect only for the purpose of preventing the title of a disponee being questioned (and so does not affect the lawfulness of a disposition).

Law Commission and HM Land Registry,
Land Registration for the Twenty-first Century 2001[203] **8.94 (E&W)**

Para 4.10 First, the protection given to the disponee's title is complete and cannot be called into question. For example, if—

(1) W and X held land on a bare trust as nominee for Y, on terms that they could not make any disposition of the land without Y's written consent;

(2) Y, who was in actual occupation of the land held in trust, did not protect her interest by an entry of a restriction; and

(3) W and Z fraudulently charged the land to Z without Y's consent in breach of trust;

Z's charge would be valid and could not be called into question by Y. The fact that Y was in actual occupation at the time of the charge would not change this, because W and X's right to exercise owner's powers is taken to be free of limitation. It follows that Y cannot claim that her beneficial interest under the trust was an overriding interest because her prior consent to the charge was not obtained.

Para 4.11 Secondly, where the disposition is in fact unlawful, the consequences of that unlawfulness can be pursued so long as these do not call into question the validity of the disponee's title. The example may be given of trustees of land, A and B, who had limited powers of disposition, but who failed to enter a restriction on the register to reflect this fact. If they transferred the land to a buyer, C, in circumstances that were prohibited by the trust, they would commit a breach of trust. Furthermore, although C`s title could not be impeached, the protection given by Clause 26 does not extend to any independent forms of liability to which she might the subject. Thus if C knew of the trustee's breach of trust when the transfer was made, she might be personally accountable in equity for the knowing receipt of trust property transferred in breach of a trust.

Land Registration Act 2002 27 Dispositions required to be registered

(1) If a disposition of a registered estate or registered charge is required to be completed by registration, it does not operate at law until the relevant registration requirements are met.

58 Conclusiveness

(1) If, on the entry of a person in the register as the proprietor of a legal estate, the legal estate would not otherwise be vested in him, it shall be deemed to be vested in him as a result of the registration.

(2) Subsection 1 does not apply where the entry is made in pursuance of a registrable disposition in relation which some other registration requirement remains to be met.

[203] Law Commission and HM Land Registry, *Land Registration for the Twenty-first Century: A Conveyancing Revolution* (2001) Law Com No 271.

Schedule 3 Unregistered interests which override registered dispositions

Leasehold estates in land

1 A leasehold estate in land granted for a term not exceeding seven years from the date of the grant, except for—

(a) a lease the grant of which falls within section 4(1) (d), (e) or (f);

(b) a lease the grant of which constitutes a registrable disposition.

Interests of persons in actual occupation

2 An interest belonging at the time of the disposition to a person in actual occupation, so far as relating to land of which he is in actual occupation, except for—

(a) an interest under a settlement und the Settled Land Act 1925;

(b) an interest of a person of whom inquiry was made before the disposition and who failed to disclose the right when he could reasonably have been expected to do so;

(c) an interest—

(i) which belongs to a person whose occupation would not have been obvious on a reasonable careful inspection of the land at the time of the disposition, and

(ii) of which the person to whom the disposition is made does not have actual knowledge at that time;

(d) a leasehold estate in land granted to take effect in possession after the end of the period of three months beginning with the date of the grant and which has not taken effect in possession at the time of the disposition.

Easements and profits à prendre

3 (1) A legal easement or profit a prendre, except for an easement, or a profit a prendre which is not registered under the Commons Registration Act 1965, which at the time of the disposition—

(a) is not within the actual knowledge of the person to whom the disposition is made, and

(b) would not have been obvious on an reasonably careful inspection of the land over which the easement or profit is exercisable.

(2) The exception in sub-paragraph (1) does not apply if the person entitled to the easement or profit proves that it has been exercised in the period of one year ending with the day of the disposition.

Customary and public rights

4 A customary right.

5 A public right.

Local land charges

6 A local land charge

Mines and minerals

7–9 …

Miscellaneous[204] *10–16* …

[204] Paras 10–14 of Sched 3 cease to have effect 10 years after the Schedule came into force: s 117(1) LRA 2002.

Law Commission and HM Land Registry, Land Registration for the Twenty-first Century[205] **8.96 (E&W)**

Para 9.4 One of the most fundamental principles of registered conveyancing is that it is registration that vests the legal estate in the registered proprietor. Section 58 of the Act provides accordingly that if, on the entry of a person in the register as the proprietor of a legal estate, the legal estate would not otherwise be vested in him or her, it shall be deemed to be vested in him or her as a result of registration. Thus, for example, if a person is registered as proprietor on the strength of a forged transfer, the legal estate will vest in that transferee even though the transfer was a nullity.

Para 1.10 These changes will necessarily alter the perception of title to land. It will be the fact of registration and registration alone that confers title.

RJ Smith, Property Law[206] **8.97 (E&W)**

The effect of registration

LRA, s 29 states the effect of registered dispositions. So long as there is valuable consideration, any earlier unprotected interest is defeated by the transfer, unless that interest is overriding (as listed in Sched 3). This protection for registered dispositions is vitally important, as it establishes that the transferee (or other disponee) can safely rely upon the register. Several contrasts with first registration may be noted: the need for valuable consideration is introduced and there is no special protection for trust interests or adverse possession.

Several difficult problems emerge. Under the previous law, there was much debate as to whether the transferee must be in good faith. ... One problem to be considered ... concerns the effect of forged transfers. Three situations need to be distinguished, in each of which P is the original registered proprietor (not in actual occupation so as to have an overriding interest).

If A forges P's signature on a transfer to himself and is then registered, it seems obvious that A cannot be protected as a result of his fraudulent and criminal conduct, event though this is nowhere clearly stated in the legislation. The second situation is where A forges P's signature on a transfer to himself and, having obtained registration, later sells the land to B. Presuming that B is unaware of the forgery, he will obtain a good title to the land on being registered. This falls within the provision in s 29(1) that unprotected interests (here the claim of P, whose signature was forged) are defeated by a registered transfer.

The third, problem, situation is where A forges P's signature on a transfer direct to C, where C is registered and believes in good faith that she is buying from P. On the one hand, C has not been misled by the register. Instead, she has been duped by A into believing that she is dealing with P. Protecting C will reduce the incentive for purchasers to ensure that the documents are genuine. On the other hand, C has been registered as the new proprietor and it may be argued that, having paid for registration, she should obtain the same guarantee as any other purchaser.

[205] Law Commission and HM Land Registry, *Land Registration for the Twenty-first Century: A Conveyancing Revolution* (2001) Law Com No 271.

[206] Smith, above n 193, 240–41.

In assessing this, it should be remembered that overriding interests and rectification limit the effect of the purchaser's protection.

C faces two problems in relying on s 29. The first is that *Malory Enterprises Ltd v Cheshire Homes* (UK) *Ltd* [2002] Ch 216 at [65] has held that, under the pre-2002 law, there was no disposition where there was a forgery. If correct (the reasoning appears equally relevant to the 2002 Act), this means that s 29 cannot apply at all. Second, s 29 protects against unprotected interests 'affecting the estate immediately before the disposition'. In the case under discussion, P is registered prior to the transfer: there is no interest affecting P's estate to defeat! It might be replied that s 58 vests the legal title in C. That is correct, but it does not appear to protect against an adverse claim by P. The conclusion—somewhat surprising—is that the purchaser will not get a good title.

These issues will lose much of their significance as e-conveyancing is introduced. This is because the actions of lawyers in making electronic entries on the register will bind the proprietor regardless of whether they are authorised. Forgery in the conventional sense will not arise because there will be no transfer to be signed. The most common equivalent case is likely to be where A impersonates P and persuades a lawyer to act on (as it is thought) P's behalf. The purchaser, C, will obtain a good title.

A few points on specific dispositions should be added. An interesting rule for leases is that even short leases (ones that do not need to be registered) enjoy the benefits of registration. A separate point is that a transfer of a lease carries with it liability on covenants affecting the land. This means that, for example, a restrictive covenant binding a tenant in a lease need not be entered on the register. As regards easements, the benefits or registration apply even if the benefited land is not registered, so that the only entry is a notice on the grantor's title.

(ii) Priority

Land Registration Act 2002 **8.98 (E&W)**

Effects of dispositions on priority

Section 28 Basic rule

(1) Except as provided by sections 29 and 30, the priority of an interest affecting a registered estate or charge is not affected by a disposition of the estate or charge.

(2) It makes no difference for the purposes of this section whether the interest or disposition is registered.

Section 29 Effect of registered dispositions: estates

(1) If a registrable disposition of a registered estate is made for valuable consideration, completion of the disposition by registration has the effect of postponing to the interest under the disposition any interest affecting the estate immediately before the disposition whose priority is not protected at the time of registration.

(2) For the purposes of subsection (1), the priority of an interest is protected -

(a) in any case, if the interest—

(i) is a registered charge or the subject of a notice in the register,

(ii) falls within any of the paragraphs of Schedule 3, or

(iii) appears from the register to be excepted from the effect of registration, and

(b) in the case of a disposition of a leasehold estate, if the burden of the interest is incident to the estate.

(3) Subsection (2)(a)(ii) does not apply to an interest which has been the subject of a notice in the register at any time since the coming into force of this section.

(4) Where the grant of a leasehold estate in land out of a registered estate does not involve a registrable disposition, this section has effect as if—

(a) the grant involved such a disposition, and

(b) the disposition were registered at the time of the grant.

Section 30 Effect of registered dispositions: charges

(1) If a registrable disposition of a registered charge is made for valuable consideration, completion of the disposition by registration has the effect of postponing to the interest under the disposition any interest affecting the charge immediately before the disposition whose priority is not protected at the time of registration.

(2) For the purposes of subsection (1), the priority of an interest is protected -

(a) in any case, if the interest—

(i) is a registered charge or the subject of a notice in the register,

(ii) falls within any of the paragraphs of Schedule 3, or

(iii) appears from the register to be expected from the effect of registration, and

(b) in the case of a disposition of a charge which relates to a leasehold estate, if the burden of the interest is incident to the estate.

(3) Subsection (2)(a)(ii) does not apply to an interest which has been the subject of a notice in the register at any time since the coming into force of this section.

Harpum and Bignell, Registered Land[207] **8.99 (E&W)**

Para 3.27 Under s 28(1) of the LRA 2002, the basic rule of priority, which is subject to two important exceptions, is that the priority of an interest affecting the title to a registered estate or charge is not affected by a disposition of the estate or charge. It makes no difference for the purposes of this rule whether the interest or disposition is registered. In cases falling within the general rule, the priority of any interest in registered land is simply determined by the date of its creation. The first interest in time of creation prevails. ...

Para 3.29 The first exception to the basic rule of priority in s 28 (1) stated above is as follows. If a registrable disposition of a registered estate or charge is made for valuable consideration, completion of the disposition by registration has the effect of postponing to the interest under the disposition any interest affecting the estate or charge immediately before the disposition whose priority is not protected at the time of registration. ...

Para 3.34 Fifthly, the interrelationship of the basic rule and the special rule of priority needs to be understood. If an interest has priority over a subsequent interest under the basic rule, the person having that priority never needs to rely upon the special rule of priority applicable to registrable dispositions. The special rule enables a registered disponee to reverse priorities where there is in existence an unprotected interest

[207] C Harpum and J Bignell, *Registered Land. The New Law—The Land Registration Act 2002* (London, Jordan Publishing, 2002).

that has priority to his own interest under the basic rule. This can be illustrated by an example. W, the registered proprietor of freehold land charges the property to X Bank plc, which registers its registered charge. W then contracts to sell the land to Y, who protects her estate contract by entering a notice in the register of title of the land. Before the contract to sell can be completed, W defaults on the mortgage payments and X Bank plc exercises its powers of sale and contracts to sell the land to Z. Z takes the land free of Y's estate contract, even though it has been noted in the register. Z's priority derives from X Bank plc's charge which was created before Y's estate contract and therefore had priority over it. It should be noted, in this example, that only the basic rule of priority is in play. It is unnecessary to have recourse to the special rule of priority that is given to registrable dispositions.

(iii) Alteration

Land Registration Act 2002 **8.100 (E&W)**

Section 65 Alteration of register

Schedule 4 (which makes provision about alteration of the register) has effect.

Schedule 4

Alteration of the Register

Introductory

1 In this Schedule, references to rectification, in relation to alteration of the register, are to alteration which—

(a) involves the correction of a mistake, and

(b) prejudicially affects the title of a registered proprietor.

Alteration pursuant to a court order

2(1) The court may make an order for alteration of the register for the purpose of—

(a) correcting a mistake,

(b) bringing the register up to date, or

(c) giving effect to any estate, right or interest excepted from the effect of registration.

(2) An order under this paragraph has effect when served on the registrar to impose a duty on him to give effect to it.

3(1) This paragraph applies to the power under paragraph 2, so far as relating to rectification.

(2) If alteration affects the title of the proprietor of a registered estate in land, no order may be made under paragraph 2 without the proprietor's consent in relation to land in his possession unless—

(a) he has by fraud or lack of proper care caused or substantially contributed to the mistake, or

(b) it would for any other reason be unjust for the alteration not to be made.

(3) If in any proceedings the court has power to make an order under paragraph 2, it must do so, unless there are exceptional circumstances which justify its not doing so.

(4) In sub-paragraph (2), the reference to the title of the proprietor of a registered estate in land includes his title to any registered estate which subsists for the benefit of the estate in land.

4 …

Alteration otherwise than pursuant to a court order

5 The registrar may alter the register for the purpose of—

(a) correcting a mistake,

(b) bringing the register up to date,

(c) giving effect to any estate, right or interest excepted from the effect of registration, or

(d) removing a superfluous entry.

6(1) This paragraph applies to the power under paragraph 5, so far as relating to rectification.

(2) No alteration affecting the title of the proprietor of a registered estate in land may be made under paragraph 5 without the proprietor's consent in relation to land in his possession unless—

(a) he has by fraud or lack of proper care caused or substantially contributed to the mistake, or

(b) it would for any other reason be unjust for the alteration not to be made.

(3) If on an application for alteration under paragraph 5 the registrar has power to make the alteration, the application must be approved, unless there are exceptional circumstances which justify not making the alteration.

(4) In sub-paragraph (2), the reference to the title of the proprietor of a registered estate in land includes his title to any registered estate which subsists for the benefit of the estate in land.

…

Rectification and derivative interests

8 The powers under this Schedule to alter the register, so far as relating to rectification, extend to changing for the future the priority of any interest affecting the registered estate or charge concerned.

(iv) Indemnification

Land Registration Act 2002 **8.101 (E&W)**

Section 103 Indemnities

Schedule 8 (which makes provision for the payment of indemnities by the registrar) has effect.

Schedule 8

Indemnities

Entitlement

1 (1) A person is entitled to be indemnified by the registrar if he suffers loss by reason of—

(a) rectification of the register,

(b) a mistake whose correction would involve rectification of the register,

(c) a mistake in an official search,

(d) a mistake in an official copy,

(e) a mistake in a document kept by the registrar which is not an original and is referred to in the register,

(f) the loss or destruction of a document lodged at the registry for inspection or safe custody,

(g) a mistake in the cautions register, or

(h) failure by the registrar to perform his duty under section 50.

(2) For the purposes of sub-paragraph (1)(a)—

(a) any person who suffers loss by reason of the change of title under section 62 is to be regarded as having suffered loss by reason of rectification of the register, and

(b) the proprietor of a registered estate or charge claiming in good faith under a forged disposition is, where the register is rectified, to be regarded as having suffered loss by reason of such rectification as if the disposition had not been forged.

(3) No indemnity under sub-paragraph (1)(b) is payable until a decision has been made about whether to alter the register for the purpose of correcting the mistake; and the loss suffered by reason of the mistake is to be determined in the light of that decision.

Notes

(1) If the transfer of a right is performed by way of registration, it is the act of registration that confers the right. Registration thus has, like under Austrian and German law, constitutive effect ('no right without registration'). With respect to the parties concerned by the transaction, both excerpts show that registration may also have a legal effect on the parties themselves in that it transfers the right even when the transferee lacks true entitlement. RJ Smith, however, rightly points out that it would be not understandable if this would mean that even the transferee who acted in bad faith shall be protected. Both excerpts show that, for registered transactions, English law follows in a very extensive way the abstract transfer system.

(2) Registration in the land register has full third party effects. The protection of third parties is only limited by the priority of overriding interests and the rules on the rectification of the register.

(3) Compare the effects of registration of registered dispositions under English law to the good faith principle of the Austrian and German land register with respect to (i) the contracting parties; and (ii) a third party who acquires a legal right from the registered proprietor.

II.C FRENCH LAW

II.C.1 TRANSFER OF PROPERTY RIGHTS IN LAND

French law does not provide for specific rules for the transfer of property rights in land. According to the French consensual transfer system, ownership passes already with the contractual agreement of the parties without the need for further acts like transfer of possession or registration.[208] Like in Austria, but contrary to England and Germany, there is no general rule providing for formal requirements for the validity of contracts concerning the transfer of land.

Although French law does not rely on registration for the transfer procedure as such, it does provide for a land register. Contrary to Austria, Germany and England, registration in the land register, however, has no constitutive effect, but only a publicity function with regard to third parties (see below). Thus registration in the land register is not proof that the registered person is really legally entitled to the property right, as the land register neither has public faith like in Austria and Germany nor the guarantee function it has in England.

II.C.2 THE LAND REGISTER

The land register[209] is regulated in Articles 2426–57 Cciv and two decrees, decree no 55-22 from 4 January 1955 on the reform of the land register[210] and decree no 55-1350 from 14 October 1955 regulating the application of decree no 55-22. Articles 2426–39 Cciv contain the rules on the registration of priority rights and hypothecs (*privilèges et hypothèques*). Article 2449 Cciv regulates the public access to the land register, Article 2450 Cciv the liability of the registrar and Articles 2451–57 Cciv describe some general duties of the registrar. Decree no 55-22 regulates the registration of rights in immovables other than priority rights and hypothecs and contains the rules concerning the cadastre (*fichier immobilier*) and the duties of the registrar. These rules do not apply to Alsace-Lorraine that, due to historic reasons, has a land register similar to the German model.

The French land register follows a recordation system (compilation of documents, 'deeds register') and is traditionally organised according to the name of the land owner (personal register). In 1955, decree no 55-22 complemented this personal register with a parcel-register (*fichier immobilier*) and thus created a combined system that allows access to the register both by way of the name of the proprietor and the parcel.

II.C.2.a Organisation and structure of the land register

Decree no 55-22 **8.102 (FR)**

Section I: Creation of an entry for an immovable

Article 1 Required for each recording by the registrars of hypothecs is an parcel-entry (*fichier immobilier*) on which the recordings are mentioned of the name of

[208] See under I.

[209] For an introduction to the French land register, see P Malaurie and L Aynès, *Cours de droit civil IX: Les sûreté, la publicité foncière*, 10th edn (Paris, Éditions Cujas, 2000) 249 *et seq* and P Malaurie and L Aynès, *Cours de droit civil IV°: Les biens, la publicité foncière*, 5th edn (Paris, Éditions Cujas, 2002) 371 *et seq* and in German: M Ferid and H Sonnenberger, *Das Französische Zivilrecht*, vol II, 2nd edn (Heidelberg, Verlagsgesellschaft Recht und Wirtschaft mbH, 1986) 584–600.

[210] Law 23 March 1855, as amended by Decree no 55–22 from 4 January 1955 (*décret portant réforme de la publicité foncière*).

each owner and, per immovable, the excerpts of publicised documents, with reference to the classification in the archives.

The parcel-entry mentions, as it appears in the public documents, the current legal situation of the immovable.

Article 2 No change in the legal status of an immovable may be the subject-matter of a cadastral amendment, if the deed or the court decision that established the change was not first published on the parcel-entry.

Notes

(1) The land register consists of three main registers, (i) the *registre des inscriptions* for the registration of the documents concerning priority rights and hypothecs, (ii) the *registre des publications* for the registration of the documents concerning other property rights and (iii) the *registre des saisies immobilières* which serves execution purposes. All three registers constitute a compilation of parcel-related documents. The mode of entering these documents into the register is called *inscription* for priority rights and hypothecs and *publication* for other transfers.

(2) In addition to these main registers there are several auxiliary registers. According to Article 2453 Cciv, registrars are obliged to have a register in which they enter, day by day and in numerical order, the filings made with them of instruments, judicial decisions, schedules and, generally, of documents filed for the purpose of the execution of a formality of registration (*registre des dépôts*). This register is decisive for the date of the publication of a transaction and for the order of priority. The parcel-register (*fichier immobilier*) reflects the judicial situation of the parcels (Article 1(2) decree no 55-22). It consists of three indexes. The owner index (*fiches personnelles de propriétaire*) names in alphabetical order for each community the owners and indicates the parcels owned by each.[211] The parcel index (*fiches d'immeuble*, Article 10-12 decree no 55-1350) only covers urban parcels and gives details concerning nature, location and cultivation of the parcel (section I), allotments or divisions of the parcel (section II) and the relevant publications concerning the parcel (section III). The lot index (*fiches parcellaires*, Articles 8–9 decree no 55-1350) shows the publications of each lot by reference either to the parcel index or the published documents. The parcel register (*fichier immobilier*) is connected to the cadaster and Articles 17–31 decree no 55-1350 provide for the mechanism to ensure that *fichier immobilier* and cadaster are in conformity.

II.C.2.b Registration procedure, competent authority and legal review

Code civil **8.103 (FR)**

Article 2428 The registration of priority rights and hypothecs shall be made by the land registrar following the filing of two schedules dated, signed and certified to be corresponding to each other by the signatory of the certificate of identity provided for in Articles 5 and 6 from 4 January 1955; a decree in which the Conseil d'État shall determine the requirements as to form which the schedule designed to be kept

[211] Arts 4–7 decree no 55-1350.

in the land register must comply with. In the case where the registrant did not use a prescribed form, the registrar shall nevertheless accept the deposit, subject to the provisions of the penultimate paragraph of this Article.

However, in order to have judicial hypothecs or securities registered, a creditor shall present, either himself or through a third party, to the land registrar:

1° The original, an authentic office copy or a literal extract from the judicial decision giving rise to the hypothec, where the latter results from the provisions of Article 2123;

2° The authorisation of the court, the judicial decision or the instrument of title in matters of judicial provisional securities.

Each of the schedules contains exclusively the indications and notations provided by the decree of the Conseil d'Etat.

A filing shall be refused:

1° Failing the presentation of the title creating the security or the claim as to hypothecs and judicial securities;

2° Failing the mention of the certicification of the identity of the parties as provided by Articles 5 and 6 of the decree from 4 January 1955, or where the immovables are not individually designated, with indication of the *commune* where they are situated.

Where the registrar, after having accepted the filing, notices the omission of one of the mentions prescribed by this Article, or a discrepancy between, on the one hand, the statements relating to the identity of the parties or to the designation of the immovables contained in the schedule, and, on the other hand, those same statements contained in schedules or titles already recorded since 1 January 1956, the formality shall be rejected, unless the applicant regularises the schedule or produces the proof which establishes its accuracy, in which cases, the formality ranks on the date of the filing of the schedule noted in the register of filings.

A formality shall also be rejected where the schedules include an amount of secured claim greater than that which appears in the title as regards mortgaged and judicial securities, as well as in the case referred to in the first paragraph of this Article, where the applicant does not substitute a new schedule on a prescribed form to the schedule irregular as to form.

The decree above provided for shall determine the details of a refusal of a filing or of a rejection of a formality.

Article 2450 They [*conservateurs des hypothèques*] are responsible for the loss resulting:

1° From failure to record instruments and judicial decisions filed at their registries, and required registrations, any time that failure to record does not result from a decision of refusal or of rejection;

2° From the omission, in the certificates which they deliver, of one or several of the existing registrations, unless, in this latter case, the error comes from insufficient or inaccurate designations which may not be ascribed to them.

Article 2452 Except in the cases where they are entitled to refuse a filing or to reject a formality, in accordance with the provisions of statutes and regulations relating to land registration, registrars may not refuse or delay the fulfilment of a formality or the delivery of documents duly required, on pain of damages to the parties; for that purpose, memoranda of refusals or delays shall be, at the suit of the requiring party, forthwith drawn up, either by a judge of the lower court, or by a court usher of the court, or by another bailiff or a *notaire* with the assistance of two witnesses.

Decree no 55-22 **8.104 (FR)**

Article 3 No legal act or decision subject to publicity in an office of hypothecs may be published on the *fichier immobilier* if the title of the registrant or last right-holder has not previously been published in conformity with the provisions of this decree. An exception is provided to this rule if the right has been acquired without a title, notably by prescription or accession, or if the title of the registrant or last right-holder is anterior to 1 January 1956.

Article 26 When a document subject to publicity in an office of hypothecs has been subject to a refusal of deposit or a formal rejection, the recourse by the interested party against the decision of the *conservateur des hypothèques* is brought, within eight days of notification of this decision, before the president of the *tribunal de grande instance* in the jurisdiction in which the properties are situated. …

Article 34. 1. Notwithstanding all special contrary provisions, the publicity required by virtue of the preceding articles obligatorily gives rise to simultaneous deposit, at the office of hypothecs, of two execution copies, *verbatim* extracts or copies of the act or judicial decision to be published.

In the case of sales other than judicial ones, the execution copies, *verbatim* extracts or copies of the act must bear a standardised part, alone published in the *fichier immobilier*, which contains only the essential elements for publicity of the real rights and the basis for the salaries, taxes, duties and levies, according to the procedures fixed by decree in the Council of State.

One of these documents is sent to the depositor after the conservateur has adhibited a certificate attesting that the formality has been executed.

The other one, which must bear certification of the identity of the parties required by Articles 5 and 6, is kept at the office of hypothecs; a decree fixes the formal conditions that this document must satisfy.

2. Deposit is refused:

—If the execution copy, extract or copy that is to be kept at the office of hypothecs does not bear certification of the identity of the parties;

—If the immovables are not individually designed, with an indication of the *commune* where they are situated;

—In the case of non-compliance with the requirements of the decree provided in the last paragraph of 1;

—In the case of failure to submit the cadastral extract or the surveying documents referred to in the fifth paragraph of Article 7;

—In the case of non-production of the standardised part of the act referred to in the second paragraph of 1 of this article.

3. The formality is rejected if, after accepting the deposit, the *conservateur* discovers:

(a) Either the omission of one of the statements required by Articles 5, 6 and 7, subject to the right of the interested parties to redress material errors in the execution copy, extract or copy, by a corrective document taking effect on the date of its deposit;

(b) Or a conflict between, on the one hand, the statements relative to the identification of the parties or the designation of the immovables contained in the document to be published, and, on the other hand, the corresponding statements contained in the titles already published since 1 January 1956, excepting justification of the accuracy of the document to be published;

(c) Or, for sales other than judicial ones, the production of a standardised part not in conformity with the requirements of the second paragraph of 1 of the present article, subject to the right of the interested parties to redress material errors in that part.

4. Any appeal formulated against the refusal or rejection decision of the *conservateur* is subject to the rules fixed in Article 26.

5. Where it is mentioned in an act submitted for publicity, that it has had to be established urgently before receipt of the documents on the basis of which the persons and immovables have been designed, the errors or omissions relative to that designation may be rectified, prior to the demand of formality, by means of an additional statement adhibited by the drafter of the act further to the original draft or the original, either of an attestation established by discrete act where the act has already been registered; as regards bailiffs' acts, the statement may be added, by the interested bailiff or *avoué*, on the documents deposited at the office of hypothecs.

6. Where a judicial decision subject to publicity has been rendered without the documents referred to in 4 being communicated to the court, errors or omissions relative to designation of the persons and immovables can be, prior to the demand of formality, rectified or redressed by virtue of an order rendered on request by the president of the court that shall have ruled or by his delegate, on the request of the interested party, who must, to this effect, communicate the supporting documents. The president may, if he considers it necessary, remit the parties to appeal before the court.

Article 34-1 1. For the purposes of the second paragraph of 1 of Article 34, the standardised part relates in the order of the following statements:

—date and drafter of the act;

—legal qualification of the act supplemented, as the case may be, for complex operations, by a summary exposé relating the legal context of the provisions of the act submitted for publicity;

—the civil status of the parties to the act;

—complete designation of the immovables;

—references to publication of the title constituting the immediate origin of property;

—references to publication of the descriptive statement of division and any amendments for fractions of immovables. In the event that the act concerns two or more immovables whose immediate origin of property results from separate titles, each publication must mention the immovable concerned by that statement;

—as the case may be, other legal operations requiring to be subject to publication in the *fichier immobilier*;

—charges and conditions ;

—ownership, vacant possession;

—price and payment terms;

—declarations necessary for the liquidation, the base or audit of all taxes, duties, levies and salaries.

2. To enable verification of the application of 2 of Article 34, the standardised part must figure at the beginning of the execution copies, *verbatim* extracts or copies deposited and bear a closing statement.

Notes

(1) The land register is operated by an officer of the finance department, the so-called *conservateur des hypothèques*, who enjoys a rather independent status. He is financed by the imposed fees and, contrary to Germany, Austria and England, he is not covered by state liability but is personally liable for the damage he causes to the applicants.

(2) The *conservateur des hypothèques* does not evaluate the validity of the legal transaction that is to be published, but only controls two issues: (i) the *l'effet relatif* and (ii) whether the applications fulfill the formal requirements. The *effet relatif*[212] ensures, comparable to the German and Austrian sequency principle, that there are no gaps in the chain of the publications in the register. Contrary to Germany and Austria, an entry in the land register does not require the formal authorisation for registration (*Eintragungsbewilligung*) of the person who gives up (in order to transfer or cancel) a registered right, which—together with the act of registration—effectuates the transfer of the property right from the transferor to the transferee or acquirer. Accordingly, again unlike Austrian and German law, the *effet relatif* does not prevent the registration of two contravening acts, provided that both acquirers derive their right from the same registered person. An important example for such a constellation is the double sale of the same parcel by the owner.

(3) The *effet relatif* does not apply to the acquisition of a property right by way of operation of law, such as acquisitive prescription, accession or consolidation because of the death of the holder of a usufruct.[213] In this case, the published document must contain a simple declaration of the transferor specifying the way or the conditions of the acquisition or consolidation.

(4) On these grounds, no publication of the transferor (*effet relatif*) or formal default, the *conservateur* may refuse the publication, either immediately upon application (*refus de dépôt*[214]) or later, when the irregularity is only detected after entry in the *registre des dépôts* (*rejet de la formalité*[215]). The negative decision of the *conservateur des hypothèques* may be referred to the president of the *tribunal de grande instance* where the parcel is situated,[216] who either definitely refuses or rejects the application or decides that it must be duly executed. In this case, the application receives the priority status of the registration of the application in the *registre des dépôts*.

(5) The registration procedure is simple. The applicant, usually represented by the public notary, deposes in case of a publication the deed or judgment (in case of the *inscription* of a priority right or a hypothec also the so-called *bordereau*) that shall

[212] See Art 3 decree no 55-22, Arts 32 *et seq* decree no 55-1350.
[213] Art 35(1) decree no 55-1350.
[214] Art 34(2) decree no 55-22.
[215] Art 34(3) decree no 55-22.
[216] See Art 26 decree no 55-22.

be published both as original and copy at the office of the *conservateur*. One of these copies stays with the *conservateur* and the other is returned to the applicant.[217] Deeds that are registered in the land register must fulfil certain formal requirements. They need notarial authentication,[218] must state the last name, first name, address, date and place of birth, profession and the name of the spouse of each party[219] and give details of the parcel (type, location, size and cadastral denomination).[220]

II.C.2.c Publicity of the land register

Code civil **8.105 (FR)**

Article 2449 Land registrars are obliged to deliver to all those who so require a copy or extract of the documents, other than the schedules of registration, filed at their registry within the limit of fifty years preceding that of the demand, and a copy or extract of the subsisting registrations, or a certificate to the effect that there exists no document or registration coming within the scope of the request.

They are also obliged to deliver upon demand, within a period of ten days, copies of or extracts from the land register or a certificate to the effect that there exists no entry coming within the scope of the request.

Note

The land register is not directly open to the public. Interested persons, however, are entitled to claim (in writing) copies, extracts of documents or certificates attesting that there is no relevant entry from the registrar. Further details concerning the publicity of the register are regulated in Articles 38-1 *et seq* of decree no 55-1350.

II.C.2.d Registrable rights and interests

Decree no 55-22 **8.106 (FR)**

Article 28 Obligatorily to be published in the office of hypothecs at the location of the immovables are:

1° All acts, even carrying a suspensive condition, and all judicial decisions, effecting or recording between living persons:

(a) Change of ownership or constitution of immovable property rights other than priority rights and hypothecs, which are kept according to the terms laid down in the Civil Code;

(b) Lease for a term of more than twelve years, and, even for a lease of lesser duration, receipt or assignment of a sum equivalent to three years of rents or agricultural rents not due;

(c) Title to occupation of public land of the state or one of its public establishments constitutive of an immovable real rights delivered in application of Articles L34-1 to L34-9 of the *code du domaine de l'Etat* and Article 3 of law no 94-631 of 25 July 1994 as well as the assignment, transfer *mortis causa* or withdrawal of this title.

[217] Art 34(1) decree no 55-22.
[218] Art 4 decree no 55-22, Art 68 decree no 55-1350.
[219] Art 5 decree no 55-22 and Art 38 decree no 55-1350.
[220] Art 7 decree no 55-22, Art 17 *et seq* decree no 55-1350.

2° Acts between living persons drawn up separately to record clauses of temporary inalienability and all other restrictions on the right to dispose, as well as clauses liable to entail the rescission or cancellation or acts subject to publicity by virtue of 1°; likewise, judicial decision recording the existence of such clauses;

Judicial decisions laying down or amending the business rescue plan rendered in application of chapters II or III of law no 85-98 of 25 January 1985 relative to judicial rescue and liquidation of enterprises that lay down in application of Articles 70 or 89-1 of the aforementioned law the temporary inalienability of an immovable property contained in the plan.

3° Notarised attestations established in execution of Article 29 with a view to recording the transfer or constitution *mortis causa* of immovable real rights;

4° The judicial acts and decisions listed below where they relate to rights subject to publicity by virtue of 1°:

(a) Acts confirming agreements tainted with causes for nullity or rescission;

(b) Acts recording the fulfilment of a suspensive condition;

(c) Court applications seeking to obtain, and acts and decisions recording, the rescission, setting-aside, cancellation or rescission for unfair price of an agreement or a *mortis causa* disposal;

(d) Decisions rejecting the demands referred to in the preceding paragraph and waivers of rights of action and discontinuance of proceedings;

(e) Declaratory acts and decisions;

5° (repealed);

6° Agreements of indivision of immovable property;

7° The decision of the court recording the abandonment of land on account of a mortgage, provided for in Article 2174 of the Civil Code.

8° Acts that interrupt acquisitive prescription in conformity with Articles 2244 and 2248 of the Civil Code, and acts of renunciation of acquired prescription;

9° The documents, whose form and content will be fixed by decree, intended to record any change or modification in the surname or first names of physical persons, and changes of name, legal form or seat of companies, associations, trade unions and other legal entities, where these changes interest physical persons or legal entities in whose name a publicity formality has been carried out since 1 January 1956.

Article 37 1. May be published in the office of hypothecs of the location of the immovable properties concerning them, for the information of users:

1° Unilateral promises of sale and unilateral promises of lease for more than twelve years;

2° Agreements relative to the exercise of legal servitudes.

The acts or documents whose publicity is provided by the present article and extracts, execution copies or copies deposited at the office of mortgages for execution of the formality are subject to the general rules set down by the present decree, notably by Articles 4 to 7 and 34 concerning the form of acts, the identification of persons and things and the procedures for publicity.

2. May be published under the same conditions the documents listed below to which are annexed or in which are reproduced *verbatim* acts submitted or admitted for publicity, regardless of whether they have not been drawn up in authentic form:

1° Court applications seeking to obtain reiteration or realisation in authentic form of the said acts;

2° Notarised minute recording default or refusal of the contract partner or promising to proceed with the said reiteration or realisation;

3° Declaration, by notarised act, of the wish of the beneficiary of the act to demand the said reiteration or realisation.

The provisions of Article 30 are applicable as from the date of the formality, where this is followed, within a period of three years, by publication of an authentic act or judicial decision recording the reiteration or realisation. In the case of judicial proceedings, this period may be extended by the publication of one or more successive orders rendered to this effect by the president of the court seised.

Notes

(1) Article 28 decree no 55-22 lists the acts that must undergo publication in the land register.[221] It includes the creation and transfer of property rights by contract, lease contracts with duration of more than 12 years and judicial decisions regardless whether they are of a declaratory or constitutive nature. That the transfer is under a suspensive condition does not relieve from the duty to publication (Article 28 no 1 decree no 55-22), quite different from Austrian law, where a right that is under a suspensive condition cannot be registered at all, and to German law that only allows the registration of a priority notice (*Vormerkung*) but no registration of the right.

(2) Article 37 decree no 55-22 provides for the optional publication in the land register. Publication of acts listed in Article 37(1) decree no 55-22 serves mere information purposes. Article 37(2) decree no 55-22 goes further and allows the registration of an acquisition right in order to obtain a certain priority rank.

II.C.2.e Effect of registration

Decree no 55-22 **8.107 (FR)**

Article 30 1. The judicial acts and decisions subject to publicity by application of 1° of Article 28 are, if they have not been published, unenforceable against third parties who have acquired from the same party over the same property concurrent rights by virtue of acts or decisions subject to the same publicity obligation and that have been published, or have had priority rights or hypothecs registered. They are also unenforceable, if they have been published, where the acts, decisions, priority rights or hypothecs invoked by these third parties have previously been published.

Unable however to take advantage of this provision are third parties who were themselves charged with having concurrent rights published or their successors in universal title.

Successors in individual title to a right falling under 1° of Article 28, that have published the judicial act or decision, recording their own right, cannot have enforced against them *inter vivos* acts drawn up separately to record temporary inalienability clauses and any other restrictions on the right to dispose, or judicial decisions

[221] There are some further acts that need publication: see eg Art R143-23 Code rural et de la pêche maritime.

recording such clauses, where the said acts or decisions have been published after the publicity given to their own right.

Termination or revocation, cancellation or rescission for unfair price of a right falling under 1° of Article 28, where it produces a retroactive effect, is only enforceable against the successor in individual title to the destroyed right if the clause by virtue of which it has been invoked has previously been published or if the clause lies in the law.

2. Failure to publish acts of gift falling under Article 939 of the Civil Code remains enforceable under the conditions fixed by Article 941 of that code.

3. Failing publicity, there can never be enforced against third parties defined by the first paragraph of 1:

Leases, for a term greater than twelve years;

Acts effecting the assignment of rents or agricultural rents not due, for a period greater than three years.

4. Any person having an interest who, having published his own right, proves that he has suffered prejudice by reason either of the failure to publish before expiration of the legal period, or the incomplete or irregular publicity of one of the acts falling under 3° to 9° of Article 28, may demand damages.

However, the individual legatee of immoveable rights may, subject to the application of Articles 1035 and following of the Civil Code, assert publication of the notarised attestation against the successors in title of the deceased that have not previously published the judicial acts or decisions establishing concurrent rights in their favour. The individual legatee set aside by virtue of Articles 1035 and following of the Civil Code may, in the case that the *mortis causa* transfer depriving him of the object of the legacy has not been published, obtain damages if he has himself published his own right.

5. Claims seeking to have pronounced the rescission, revocation, cancellation or rescission for unfair price of rights resulting from acts subject to publicity are only admissible before the courts if they have themselves been published in conformity with the provisions of Article 28-4°, c, and if this publication is evidenced by a certificate from the conservateur or production of a copy of the claim bearing the mention of publicity.

Notes

(1) According to the French consensual system for the transfer of property rights, the failure to publish has no negative effect as regards the validity of the act between the parties and their successors, but only with respect to third parties. An act under Article 28(1) and (2) decree no 55-22 that is not published cannot be pleaded against a third party who acquired from the same person a contravening right on the same parcel (*inopposabilité des actes*), provided that the act of acquisition of the third party itself requires publication and further provided that the third party filed first for publication.[222] Case law also requires that the third party must not be in bad faith. Special rules apply to the transfer of property rights in immovables by way of gift (Article 941 Cciv).

[222] Art 30 no 1 decree no 55-22.

(2) Moreover, non-publication of an act by which a property right is acquired is a severe obstacle to the further transfer and burdening of this property right, as the *effet relatif* requires publication of the prior holder of the property right. The breach of the obligation to publish may also entail liability in tort.[223] In respect to acts listed in Article 28 no 3-9 decree no 55-22 only these sanctions apply.

(3) Priority rights and hypothecs need publication (*inscription*) in the *registre des inscriptions* of the land register in order to achieve third party effects (see Articles 2377, 2461, 2426 Cciv).

III. CREATION OF LIMITED PROPERTY RIGHTS

III.A CONTENT OF LIMITED PROPERTY RIGHTS

Introductory Notes

(a) The requirements for the valid creation of a limited property right are to a large degree similar to the requirements for the transfer of property. This has led the Dutch legislature to make an article in the Civil Code in which the requirements of transfer for the creation of a limited property right are referred to.

(b) In French law there is a doctrinal debate whether or not the creation of a limited property right amounts to original or derivative acquisition. The traditional French view is that since a limited property right is derived from a broader property right, the creation involves a transfer of certain privileges from that broader right so that the acquisition of a limited property right is derivative.[224] This is also the prevailing view in Dutch law[225] and, most probably, the prevailing view in Austrian law.[226]

(c) The two different views originate in the question whether or not the grantor of a limited property right transfers anything to the holder of the new limited property right. The limited property right as such did not exist before it was granted, which points to original acquisition. However, it is often said in French and Dutch law that a limited property right is derived from the superior right that it burdens, that a limited property right is a *démembrement* (literally: a part split off from the superior right).

(d) The German viewpoint combines the fact that the limited property right is

[223] See Art 30 no 4 decree no 55-22.

[224] O Deshayes, *Editions Dalloz*, 'Répertoire de droit civil, Ayant cause', no 82 (2008).

[225] Asser, Mijnssen, De Haan and Van Dam, Goederenrecht, *Algemeen Goederenrecht*, 15th edn (Deventer, 2006) no 195; HJ Snijders and EB Rank-Berenschot, *Goederenrecht*, 4th edn (Deventer, Kluwer 2007) no 299; A Pitlo, *Goederenrecht*, ed WHM Reehuis, AHT Heisterkamp, GE van Maanen and GT de Jong, 12th edn (Deventer, Kluwer, 2006) no 98; J Hijma and MM Olthof, *Compendium van het Nederlands vermogensrecht*, 9th edn (Deventer, Kluwer 2005) no 100.

[226] See for the creation of a pledge: H Koziol and R Welser, *Grundriss des bürgerlichen Rechts*, vol I, 13th edn, ed A Kletečka (Vienna, Manz 2006) 377 and Schwimann and M Hinteregger, *ABGB Praxiskommentar* (Vienna 2005) §451, no 2 and §456, no 1.

new and that at the same time it contains privileges which derive from the superior right which it burdens:

A von Tuhr, The General Part of German Private Law[227] **8.107 (DE)**

Succession in right is constitutive if not the entire right of the predecessor passes, but if from its content a right of lesser content originates and simultaneously passes to a different person. The original right could be called the mother-right, the derived right of lesser content: daughter-right. As the transferor keeps the mother-right, the constitutive succession is not a transfer but a burdening of the mother-right, which, as far as required by the daughter-right, cannot be exercised during the existence of the daughter-right. Since constitutive succession creates a right for the holder which did not exist with the predecessor and which often bears a special name, the succession is less obvious than in the case of translative succession; the succession is visible in that the content of the daughter-right is derived from the privileges contained in the mother-right: mostly the daughter-right consists of various privileges which are contained in the mother-right; sometimes the daughter-right has a negative content: it consists in that certain privileges contained in the mother-right cannot be exercised. The constitutive splitting off of rights is normally derivative [fn 19: through disposition of the holder of the mother-right (burdening)...], but in certain cases it can also be original [fn 20: prescription...].

A von Tuhr, The General Part of German Private Law[228] **8.108 (DE)**

There is original acquisition where the right of the acquirer does not depend on the right of a predecessor. That is always the case when a right with this content did not exist at the moment of acquisition. A contractual claim, for example, is acquired by way of original acquisition from the contract which created the claim.

Note

It may seem odd that acquisition of a contractual claim is original whereas acquisition of a limited property right is derivative. If we compare the owner of a plot of land who grants a servitude to an owner who grants a licence, a personal right to the use of his land, both rights, the property right and the personal right, might seem to derive from the owner's right of ownership. However, this is only true for the limited property right, which in principle cannot be created by grant if the grantor does not own the land. The contractual claim, on the other hand, comes into being even if the grantor is not the owner of the land. The reason is that the claim is not derived from the grantor's *ownership* but from the *contract* which he concluded with the grantee. As the contract did not exist before, the acquisition of the claim is original.

[227] A von Tuhr, *Der Allgemeine Teil des Deutschen Bürgerlichen Rechts*, 2nd vol (Munich/Leipzig 1914), 62–63.
[228] *Ibid*, p 41.

III.B CREATION OF LIMITED PROPERTY RIGHTS[229]

III.B.1 FRENCH LAW

Paul Ancel, Force of contracts[230] **8.109 (FR)**

Contracts giving rise to rights, besides personal rights, are generally only contracts that give rise to a subtraction of an existing right and they can be treated in the same way as contracts for transfer analysed above.

Footnote 70: the personal effect of a contract creating a right of hypothec is in that respect the same as a sale.

Note

The creation of limited property rights, a subtraction from existing property rights (*démembrement*), is made by contract. A property agreement or real agreement is not necessary. We have seen examples of this in Chapter 3 where, in French law a contract of lease also gives rise to the creation of a right of superficies. In order for third party effect, especially in case of immovables, registration is usually needed. The property right, however, is already created between the parties in the same way as the right of ownership can be transferred between them but will only have effect against third parties after registration.[231]

III.B.2 DUTCH LAW

Burgerlijk Wetboek **8.110 (NL)**

Article 3:98 Unless statute provides otherwise, all provisions of this division pertaining to the transfer of an object apply by way of analogy to the creation, transfer and abandonment of a limited property right on such object.

Parliamentary History, Book 3,
Clarification of Meijers to Article 3:98[232] **8.111 (NL)**

The creation of a limited property right can be considered as a way of transferring certain privileges from that right [the motherright]. As a result, it is laid down that the provisions on transfer of rights apply also to the creation of those rights.

[229] This paragraph was written by Bram Akkermans.

[230] P Ancel, Force obligatoire et contenu obligationnel du contrat, *Revue trimestrielle de droit civil* (*RTD Civ*) 1999, n 20.

[231] See B Akkermans, 'Concurrence of Ownership and Limited Property Rights' (2010) 18 *European Review of Private Law* 259 *et seq.*

[232] *Toelichting Meijers to Article 3:98, Parlementaire Geschiedenis van het Nieuwe Burgerlijk Wetboek*, Boek 3, p 404,

Notes

(1) The primary articles which are applicable by way of analogy are the Articles 3:83 and 3:84 BW. Article 3:83 BW lays down which things are transferable and Article 3:84 BW provides that for a valid transfer the transferor should have the right to dispose of the object in question, that the transfer should be based on a valid legal ground and that a valid act of transfer should take place. It means that the causal transfer system, which applies to the transfer of property, also applies to the creation of limited property rights.

(2) The parliamentary history of Article 3:98 BW shows that Meijers, the draftsman of this article, considered the creation of a limited property right as the transfer of certain rights comprised in the mother-right.

III.B.3 GERMAN LAW

In German law there is no provision comparable to Article 3:98 of the Dutch Civil Code. Yet it is generally acknowledged that the transfer system is, mutatis mutandis, applicable to the creation of limited property rights. For the creation of a right of usufruct on movables §1032 BGB, for example, refers to the paragraphs on the transfer of movables. Similarly, for the creation of a right of pledge §1274 refers to the paragraphs on transfer of movables. Apart from the formalities of creation, which may vary for each limited property right, the grantor should have the right to dispose and the creation is subject to the abstract transfer system, which entails that no valid legal ground is needed.[233]

III.B.4 AUSTRIAN LAW

Like German law Austrian law does not have a general provision comparable to Article 3:98 of the Dutch Civil Code, although Austrian law applies to the creation of limited propertry rights the same rules, mutatis mutandis, that apply to the transfer of property. For the creation of a pledge the Austrian civil code refers to the provisions on transfer (§450 ABGB). The grantor should have the right to dispose (§442 ABGB) and the creation is subject to the causal transfer system of Austrian law.[234]

[233] See for the applicability of the principle of abstractness to the creation of limited property rights on immovable property: JTh Füller, *Eigenständiges Sachenrecht* (Tübingen, Mohr Siebeck 2006) 197. See for the right of pledge: Staudinger–Wiegand, Vorbem zu §1204 *et seq* at 12, Nr 22.

[234] See for the creation of a pledge: H Koziol and R Welser, *Grundriss des bürgerlichen Rechts*, ed A Kletečka vol I, 13th edn (Vienna 2006) 377 and Schwimann and Hinteregger, above n 226, §451, no 2 and §456, no 1.

IV. COMPARATIVE OVERVIEW

IV.A TRANSFER OF PROPERTY RIGHTS IN LAND

The rules concerning the transfer of property rights for movables are also the basis for the transfer of property rights in land. Due to the high social and economic value of land, most countries have specific additional rules concerning the transfer agreement and provide for registration requirements in order to ensure the publicity of the transfer. In detail, these rules are different, as is the role of the land register for the transfer procedure.

German and English law already set up formal requirements for the conclusion of the contract. According to §311b(1) BGB, the contract for the transfer or acquisition of ownership to land needs notarial recordation, and section 2 of the Law of Property (Miscellaneous Provisions) Act 1989 states inter alia that contracts for the sale of land or other dispositions of any interest in land must be made in writing and signed by each party. A contract that does not meet these requirements is in both countries void. Austrian and French law do not provide for specific formalities for the conclusion of the contract as such. The contract, however, must fulfil certain requirements for the registration in the land register.

The German abstract transfer system, which also applies to the transfer of property rights in land, requires in addition to the contractual agreement (*Verpflichtungsgeschäft*) the conclusion of the real agreement (*dingliche Einigung*), which, together with the registration of the right in the land register, constitutes the *Verfügungsgeschäft*. For the acquisition and loss of ownership to land, including co-ownership and apartment right, the real agreement has a special name (*Auflassung*) and must fulfil specific formalities stipulated in §925 BGB in order to be legally effective.

In Austrian and German law, which are both representatives of the tradition system, the acquisition or cancellation of a property right in land by legal transaction makes the registration of the right in the land register a prerequisite. Before registration the acquirer has only a claim against the transferor. Registration of the property right in the land register thus has constitutive effect. This only applies when the right is transferred by legal transaction and not if a property right is acquired directly by the law itself or by judicial or administrative act. In this case the right is acquired upon effectiveness of the act and the registration in the land register only documents it (declaratory effect). In both countries the registration of the right in the land register requires a series of formal prerequisites which must strictly be observed.

In England (and Wales) the traditional system of transfer of titles to land by deeds (unregistered system) is subsequently being replaced by the transfer by way of registration in the land register (registered system). This is regulated by the Land Registration Act 2002, which enhances first registration of all land with hereto unregistered title. The Land Registration Act 2002 further provides for transferring titles to land electronically ('e-conveyancing'). It establishes a secure electronic network by which conveyancers (solicitors, licensed conveyancers) can access the land register and make changes to the register. This new system shall ensure the creation of a conclusive register by abolishing the time-lag ('registration gap') between the legal disposition and its registration. Like in Austria and Germany it is the right and not the holder of the right that is registered in the land register (title register) and registration in the land register has constitutive effect.

French law is very different. It has no specific formal rules for the transfer of property rights in land and does not rely on registration for the transfer procedure either. According to the French consensual transfer system, which also applies to the transfer of property rights in land, ownership passes already with the contractual agreement of the parties. Registration in the land register has no constitutive effect, but only a publicity function with regard to third parties.

IV.B THE LAND REGISTER

IV.B.1 ORGANISATION AND STRUCTURE OF THE LAND REGISTER

In Germany and Austria the land register has a territorial structure with the parcel as the basic entity of the register, while the English land register is structured according to rights ('estates vested in one proprietor'). The internal structure of the registers, its division into the sub-registers (property register, proprietor register and charges register), the functions of these registers and the auxiliary indices, are, however, quite similar. In Austria and England the registers are kept electronically, while in Germany the decision to keep the register in electronic form lies with the state governments.

In Austria and Germany the whole territory is divided into parcels, and all parcels, with few exceptions regarding parcels in public ownership in Germany, are entered in the land register. In England the process of registration of all titles to land is intended, but not yet completed. Accordingly, English law provides for comprehensive rules for first registration of hitherto unregistered land.

A less-developed system is provided by France. Contrary to the other countries, the French land register follows a recordation system providing for the compilation of documents regarding property rights (deeds register) and not for the registration of the right itself (title register). It is not organised according to parcel (Austria, Germany) or estate (England), but according to the name of the landowner (personal register). The land register consists of three separate registers, one for the compilation of documents concerning liens and hypothecs, a second for those concerning property rights and a third for execution purposes. Several auxiliary registers complement the main registers. Of these, the most important is the parcel register (*fichier immobilier*) which in its structure and contents resembles the land register in Austria, Germany and England, but lacks the legal implications attached to land register in these countries (constitutive effect and public faith in Austria and Germany respectively the guarantee effect in England).

IV.B.2 COMPETENT AUTHORITY, LEGAL REVIEW AND REGISTRATION PROCEDURE

In Austria and Germany the land register is situated at the local courts. It is part of the jurisdiction and decisions of the registrar are under full judicial review. In both countries the process of registration follows strict rules arising from several basic principles of land register law. These basic principles are the principle of party initiative (*Antragsprinzip*), the authorization principle (*Konsensprinzip*), the priority principle and the sequency principle.

The land registration system in England and Wales is administered by a public agency (Her Majesty's Land Registry). The Chief Land Registrar administers the land register and, contrary to the Austrian, German and French registrar who primarily check the compliance of the applications with formal rules, has ample decision-making powers. Decisions of the registrar are under judicial review, either before the adjudicator or a court.

In France, the land register is operated by an officer of the finance department (*conservateur des hypothèques*) who enjoys a rather independent status. He is financed by the imposed fees and, unlike in Austria, Germany and England, he is not covered by state liability but is personally liable for the damage he causes to the applicants. Negative decisions of the *conservateur des hypothèques* may be referred to the president of the *tribunal de grande instance* where the parcel is situated.

IV.B.3 PUBLICITY OF THE LAND REGISTER

The Austrian and English land register is open for the public. Only access to the index of proprietors' names is restricted. This is, however, not the case in Germany and France. In Germany it is necessary to show a legal interest in order to inspect the land register, and in France information is only given upon written request.

IV.B.4 EFFECTS OF REGISTRATION

In Austria and Germany it is legally presumed that the land register is correct and complete. This principle of public faith of the land register allows for the good faith acquisition of a non-existing real right and for the good faith acquisition of a real right free from an existing burden. The public faith of the land register extends only to the existence or non-existence of registered rights and not to entries that indicate merely factual or personal circumstances and applies only to the acquisition or loss of real rights by legal transaction. English law goes one step further. It does not only protect third persons who in good faith rely on the accuracy of the land register, but provides for the conclusiveness of the register (section 58 LRA 2002).

The French land register has neither public faith nor does it guarantee the correctness of an entry, but provides only for the publicity of the entry. It mainly protects the acquirer from a double sale by the transferor and is necessary for the further transfer and encumbrance of this property right. The breach of the obligation to publish may also entail the imposition of fines and liability in tort.

CONCISE BIBLIOGRAPHY

Asser, Mijnssen, De Haan and Van Dam, *Goederenrecht, Algemeen Goederenrecht*, 15th edn (Deventer, Kluwer 2006).

J Baur and R Stürner, *Sachenrecht*, 18th edn (München, Beck, 2009).

U Drobnig, 'Transfer of Property' in A Hartkamp et al (eds), *Towards a European Civil Code*, 4th edn (Alphen a/d Rijn, Kluwer Law International, 2011) ch 42.

C Harpum et al (eds), *Megarry & Wade: The Law of Real Property*, 8th edn (London: Sweet & Maxwell, 2012).

LPW van Vliet, *Transfer of Movables in German, French, English and Dutch Law* (Nijmegen, Ars Aequi Libri, 2000).

LPW van Vliet, 'Iusta Causa Traditionis and its History in European Private Law' (2003) 3 *European Review of private Law* 342–78.

LPW van Vliet, 'The Transfer of Moveables in Scotland and England' (2008) 12 *Edinburgh Law Review* 173–99.

CHAPTER NINE
DESTRUCTION

*Bram Akkermans, William Swadling, and Lars van Vliet**

This chapter deals with the sixth and final essential question of property law: how do property rights come to an end? Although property rights are created to last for a very long time, they can come to an end. This chapter explains the most common ways in which a property right can be destroyed. There is a close link to the fourth of the six essential questions, ie how are property rights created. Very often, where one person loses his property right another will acquire the right (derivative acquisition). However, it is also possible that a new property right comes into existence (original acquisition, see also Chapter 7).

I. INTRODUCTION

Previous chapters dealt with the creation and transfer of property rights; this chapter deals with the destruction of property rights. Generally speaking, there are two ways in which a property right can come to an end. The first is where the *res*, the object in respect of which the property right exists, is destroyed. The destruction of the *res* will also have the effect of bringing about the destruction of the property right itself. Second, property rights can be destroyed without destruction of the *res*, as, for example, through the doctrine of good faith purchase.

The destruction of property rights is not often given much attention by civil lawyers. In the approach taken by common lawyers much more attention is paid to this aspect of property law. However, in the civil law too the destruction of property rights occurs. This chapter looks at the destruction of property rights in civil

* William Swadling wrote the parts on English law in this chapter (III). Regarding the civil law systems, Lars van Vliet wrote the part on third party protection (II.B.2). Bram Akkermans wrote the other parts. The comparative remarks are a common effort.

law and common law. Because of the different approaches taken by the civil law and the common law, this chapter will first deal with civil law systems and, after that, deal with English law. In order to help comparison, the different sections are divided between cases involving destruction of the *res*, and destruction of the right without destruction of the *res*.

II. CIVIL LAW

II.A DESTRUCTION OF THE SUBJECT-MATTER OF THE RIGHT

Introductory Note

Destruction of the subject-matter of the right can happen in a number of ways. Although the most obvious is the painting which goes up in flames or the land which is engulfed by the sea, others are where the subject-matter is mixed with other physical objects, eg wine with wine; where it is used in some manufacturing process, such as flour which is baked into a cake; or where it is joined to another physical object, such as a handle affixed to a cup or bricks to land. It should be noted that two of the events which are destructive of rights, manufacture (*specificatio*) and mixing, are also constitutive of rights. They have therefore already been dealt with in Chapter 7.

II.A.1 FRENCH LAW

Code civil **9.1 (FR)**

Article 617 A right of usufruct is destroyed: ...

... By the total loss of the object on which the usufruct was created.

Article 623 Where a part only of an object subject to the right of usufruct is destroyed, the right of usufruct is preserved on what remains.

Article 624 Where a right of usufruct is created only on a building, and that building is destroyed by fire or other accident, or collapses from decay, the usufructuary does not have a right to use and enjoy the land or the materials.

Where the right of usufruct was created on a piece of land of which the building was a part, the *usufructuary* has the right to use and enjoy the land and the materials.

Article 625 Rights of use and habitation are created and destroyed in the same manner as the right of usufruct.

Article 703 Rights of servitude are destroyed when the objects are in such a condition that they can no longer be used.

Article 704 They revive when objects are restored in such a manner that they can be continue to be used unless so much time has already elapsed to give rise to the presumption that the servitude is destroyed, as is stated in Article 707.[1]

Article 1234 Obligations are extinguished:

[1] Art 707 Cciv can be found at 9.62 (FR).

By payment;

By novation;

By voluntary release;

By set-off;

By merger;

By the loss of the object;

By nullity or rescission;

By the effect of a resolutory condition, as was explained in the preceding Chapter; and

By the running of the statute of limitation, which will be the subject matter of a special title.

Note

Although Article 1234 Cciv is not directly concerned with property law, the provisions are of relevance in the case of a property right created on a claim. Although not all legal systems accept such a concept, French law certainly does. When, through the operation of the principle of specificity the claim that is the subject matter of a property right is destroyed, the property right can no longer exist.[2] For example, if a claim is paid and with that payment the claim comes to an end, the property right which was created on that claim must also cease to exist.[3]

II.A.2 GERMAN LAW

Bürgerliches Gesetzbuch **9.2 (DE)**

§362 (1) An obligation ceases to exist, when the performance that is due is performed to the creditor.

§1252 The right of pledge ceases to exist with the claim for which it was created.

Note

These two paragraphs deal with two different aspects of the effect of destruction of the subject-matter of a property right. When the subject-matter of a property right is a claim and the claim is paid, German law likewise holds that the property right on that claim must no longer exist. Moreover, when a claim over which a property security right is created ceases to exist, the property right that is accessory to that claim also ceases to exist. On accessority of property security rights, see Chapter 5.[4]

[2] On the principle of specificity, see Chaper 1.

[3] On the effect of claims as the subject-matter of a property right, see Chapter 4.

[4] Accessority is sometimes also referred to as accessoriness. On the two terms, see LPW van Vliet, 'Mortgages on Immovables in Dutch Law in Comparison to the German Mortgage and Land Charge' in M Hinteregger and T Boric (eds), *Sicherungsrechte an Immobilien im Europa* (Vienna and Berlin, Lit Verlag, 2009) 287–91. See also AJM Steven 'Accessoriness and Security over Land' [2009] *Edinburgh Law Review* 387.

II.A.3 DUTCH LAW

Hoge Raad, 17 February 1996[5] **9.3 (NL)**

Mulder qq v CLBN

NO PLEDGE ON CLAIM THAT IS SATISFIED

Payment of the claim

A right of pledge on a claim that is satisfied will be destroyed.

Facts: In 1985 a bank, CLBN, reached agreement with Connection on the assignment of all claims and future claims for security purposes to the bank. The introduction of the New Dutch Civil Code in 1992 transformed these assignments of claims into rights of silent pledge and the obligation to assign future claims in the creation of silent rights of pledge on the future claims. On 16 November 1992 the bank terminated the agreement. On 17 November 1992 Connection was declared insolvent. On 25 and 26 November 1992 the bank made its silent right of pledge public, transforming the right into a normal right of pledge. Connection, due to the insolvency proceedings, was represented by the trustee in bankruptcy Mulder.

During these events several claims, which had been the subject-matter of the rights of pledge, had been satisfied. Some of these claims had been paid before insolvency, either to the bank or to Connection. Some of these claims had been paid to the bank after the declaration of bankruptcy. Finally, some claims had also been paid to Mulder after the declaration of bankruptcy.

Held: A claim that has been paid to the rightful creditor will generally cease to exist. Before bankruptcy this was, because of the silent right of pledge, Connection. After bankruptcy the correct creditor was Mulder. However, upon notification of the silent right of pledge, the debtors could only pay their claim to the bank. Payment of claims before notification by the bank led to the destruction of the claims. Because the claims were destroyed, the right of pledge on these claims was also destroyed. Nevertheless, even though there was no right of pledge anymore, the bank kept its priority right over these claims.

Judgment: 3.3.3 By payment of a silently pledged claim to him who has capacity to take receipt of the payment, the claim is destroyed and hence also the right of pledge resting on the claim. …

3.4.2 Against the background of the legislative history of the law of silent pledges (below: 3.4.3) in this examination it must be presupposed that, in the case of the customary assignment in security of claims under the law applying before 1 January 1992 it is usual for the notification of the assignment required in Article 668 paragraph 2 (old) BW to be dispensed with. The claim belonged to the assignee even without that notification and did not form any part of the estate of the assignor. The trustee in bankruptcy was therefore liable to transfer to the assignee that which he might have received in satisfaction of the assigned debt.

3.4.3 In the treatment of the Introductory Act, further to the fear expressed by the Netherlands Association of Company Lawyers (Nederlands Genootschap van Bedrijfsjuristen) that the silent pledge would offer creditors a lesser security than the then customary possession in security, the assurance was given by the government that with the silent pledge—which had been opted for in accordance with the views of the Second Chamber—'practically the same result can be achieved as with possession in security', to which is added that the statutory rules are now such 'that existing finance mechanisms, despite the different technical statutory intention of the new

[5] NJ 1996, 471.

rules, can be continued without difficulty under the new law' (Parl History Book 3 (infr 3, 5 and 6), p 1197). The view primarily argued by the trustee in bankruptcy is hard to reconcile with these remarks by the government. According to this view, the silent pledgee, as long as he has not notified his right of pledge, cannot assert any claim to payments on the claims pledged to him that were received by the pledgor during the bankruptcy, because as a result of those payments, his right of pledge has been entirely destroyed whereas, if the silent pledgee is a bank, on the same ground there also is no cause to make an exception to the strict jurisprudential doctrine in the matter of set-off during and in view of bankruptcy. On this view there exists, in the event of the bankruptcy of the pledgor, between the position of the silent pledgee that has not notified, and that of a creditor that had had his debtor's claims transferred to him in security (see 3.4.2), an essential difference to the disadvantage of the silent pledgee. By contrast, the aforementioned remarks of the government are justified and furthermore preclude silent pledgees—in order to safeguard their position with a view to a possible bankruptcy of their pledgors—making early notification, if it is assumed that when the trustee in bankruptcy has collected a silently pledged claim, for which the pledged claim and hence the pledge right has been destroyed, the pledgee maintains his preference over the collected funds. It is true he must wait until the distribution list has become binding and he contributes to the bankruptcy costs on the basis of Art 182 paragraph 1 F, but he has a claim to satisfaction in the distribution in accordance with his preference as accorded to the right of pledge. Such is also in accordance with that stipulated in Article 58 F: sale by the trustee in bankruptcy of a pledged movable item destroys the right of pledge; however, the pledgor maintains his priority over the proceeds.

Notes

(1) This very complex case shows the operation of the general rule that a property right is destroyed when the thing in respect of which the property right exists ceases to exist.

(2) However, when the property right in question is a security right, in this case a right of pledge, the loss of the property right by destruction may be undesirable. Here, the Dutch Supreme Court was confronted with a situation in which it wanted to prevent banks from notifying their right of silent pledge, ie a right of pledge created in respect to a claim that is not notified to the debtor of that claim, in the realisation procedure. Notification is generally considered to have negative effects on the economy as it may signal uncreditworthiness. Thus, although the property right was destroyed upon payment of a claim to the correct creditor, the former holder of the right of pledge was able to enjoy his right of priority connected to the right of pledge when it existed.[6]

[6] Moreover, although not mentioned in this exerpt, the Dutch Supreme Court also decided that when the former holder of the right of pledge is a bank, it may additionally set-off the claim with other outstanding claims. Set-off, however, is not part of destruction of property rights, see ss 3.5.1. and 3.5.2.

II.B. DESTRUCTION OF THE RIGHT

Another, more complicated, way in which property rights can be destroyed is not by destruction of the object (*res*) in respect of which the property right was created, but by the destruction of the property right itself. Examples include prescription, third party protection, abandonment, merger and termination. Prescription offers a somewhat controversial case of destruction as civil law systems traditionally consider prescription as a way to create or transfer rights. However, where a right is gained through prescription, a right is also lost, ie destroyed.[7]

II.B.1 CREATION OF PROPERTY RIGHTS (ORIGINAL ACQUISITION)

Creation of property rights is dealt with in Chapter 7, 'Creation'. In some cases creation of a right follows the creation of a new object (*res*) and a completely new property right is created. However, there are also instances where a property right is created to the detriment of another property right that is destroyed. In order to ensure a coherent treatment of the subject matter, these instances of destruction are dealt with in Chapter 7.

II.B.2 THIRD PARTY PROTECTION (GOOD FAITH PURCHASE/ACQUISITION)

Introductory Notes

(a) In the following part we shall examine the rules of third party protection. As will be seen, most systems require that the acquirer give value in exchange for the right, though French law is an exception in this regard. For reasons of space, discussion is limited to the case of the acquisition of rights to goods from someone who does not have the best right to those goods. In civil law terms, therefore, what is entailed is acquisition from a non-owner.

(b) The relevant civil law jurisdictions, French, German, and Dutch law, differ as to their approach as to the effect of rules of third party protection. In some, it is an instance of the creation of a new right, while in others it is a case of a forced transfer of the right of the dispossessed 'owner'. In French law, for example, it is seen as an instance of the creation of a property right. The principal article on third party protection (Art 2276 Cciv) is part of a section in the Civil Code entitled '*de quelques prescriptions particulières*' (about some special cases of prescription). It is often described as a form of acquisitive prescription, though without a prescription period (instantaneous prescription).[8]

(c) In Dutch law, by contrast, purchase in good faith is regarded as an instance of transfer. Article 3:86 BW, which protects the acquirer in good faith, expressly provides that despite the fact that the transferor has no right to dispose of the goods, the transfer is valid under the conditions mentioned in the article. Although

[7] On prescription see Chapter 7.

[8] V Marcadé, *Explication du tit XX, LIV, III, du Code Napoléon (Prescription)* (Paris 1854) 246; G Baudry-Lacantinerie and A Tissier, *Traité théorique et pratique de droit civil, vol XXVIII (de la prescription)*, 3rd edn (Paris 1905) 660.

the non-owner is the transferor, ownership does not pass from him to the third party. Although the transferor was never the owner, the law allows him to effect a transfer of ownership from the true owner to the good faith purchaser.

(d) In German law the answer to the question whether the purchase in good faith creates new rights or transfers existing ones is controversial.[9] Arguably, it should be regarded as involving a transfer, for the acquisition contains all the requirements of a valid transfer in German law. In German law the provisions for the protection of a bona fide purchaser protect only against the transferor not having the right to dispose; they do not protect against other defects in the transfer.[10] If certain formalities have to be performed in order to transfer ownership, these formalities are also mandatory if the transferor has no right to dispose of the object.

(e) If in a causal transfer system the contract of sale underlying the transfer is void or is avoided, the transfer cannot be valid.[11] If third party acquisition were original, it would lead to the odd result that the transferee would acquire ownership despite the contract of sale being void. A transfer by an owner based on a void contract would not pass ownership but a transfer by a non-owner would.

(f) Another example is the protection good faith purchasers have against property rights burdening the acquired object. If the buyer of an object knows that the object is burdened by a pledge, but he does not know that the object does not belong to the seller, he may acquire ownership but burdened with a right of pledge. If the acquisition were original, the right of pledge would inevitably lapse and the bona fide purchaser would acquire the object free from any pre-existing rights.

(g) As will be seen below, there is no requirement in French law that the contract of sale be valid as a condition of good faith purchaser protection. This is consistent with the view that good faith purchase operates as creative of rights, rather than as a transfer.

II.B.2.a French law

Code civil **9.4 (FR)**

Article 2276 As regards movables possession counts as title.
Nevertheless, the person who has lost an object or from whom an object has been stolen is, up to three years from the day of the loss or theft, able to revindicate the object from the person in whose hands he finds it. This does not exclude the latter's remedy against the person from whom he obtained the object.[12]

(i) No requirement of valuable consideration in French law

As will be seen below, in German and Dutch law the protection is given only to

[9] A von Tuhr, *Der Algemeine Teil des deutschen Bürgerlichen Rechts*, vol 2.I (Munich and Leipzig, 1914) 52; M Wolff and L Raiser, *Sachenrecht*, 10th edn (Tübingen 1957) §69 IV; KH Schwab and H Prütting, *Sachenrecht*, 32nd edn (Munich 2006) no 441.

[10] The same applies to Dutch law.

[11] On the causal transfer system see Chapter 8.

[12] The passage 'from whom he obtained the object' is a rather free translation, as the text literally says: 'from whom he holds the object'. The translation expresses more clearly that the third party intended to acquire the object from the non-owner.

third parties who acquired the object in good faith and for valuable consideration. Whether or not the buyer has paid the purchase price is irrelevant. French law, on the other hand, does not require that the acquisition should be for valuable consideration.

(ii) Good faith

Cour de cassation, 16 June 1971[13] **9.5 (FR)**

Toulouse-Lautrec

Facts: X, an Art dealer, bought a few paintings by Henri de Toulouse-Lautrec for a very low price in suspicious circumstances. After his death, the owners of the paintings started proceedings against the Art dealer's wife and son to revindicate the paintings. The Court of Appeal held that the sale was suspect, that the Art dealer was not acting in good faith, and that he consequently had not acquired ownership under Article 2279 Cciv. One of the complaints raised by the wife and son was that the Court of Appeal had wrongly required them to show a sufficient legal ground for the acquisition. Another complaint was that the Court of Appeal had wrongly focused on X's bad faith and not on his wife and son's good faith and that vices which might affect the deceased's possession did not pass on to the heirs.

Held: The Court of Appeal did not hold that the defendants were required to show a sufficient legal ground for the invocation of Article 2279 Cciv, but it inferred from the sales contract that the father was a purchaser in bad faith. Moreover, the heir's possession has the same qualities and vices as the deceased's possession.

Judgment: On the first argument: considering that it results from the statements in the judgment appealed against that, in the dispute involving the spouses Z... Jacques Y... and Madeleine Gabrielle A... B... and the ownership of certain paintings, widow of Lucien X..., and her son Maxime X..., intervened on appeal to have it judged that the paintings in dispute belonged to them;

That they asserted that Lucien X..., the predecessor of the parties, had in good faith bought these paintings from a third party who was ostensibly a legitimate owner and therefore entitled to take advantage of the provisions of Article 2279 of the Civil Code.

That the court of appeal rejected the intervention of the jointly interested parties X..., considering that Lucien X... did not fulfil the conditions required for application of this article;

Considering that the judgment is therefore complained of for having thus ruled whereas the possessor is presumed to be in good faith for the application of the rule 'as regards movables, possession counts as title', such that it is for the alleged owner, who is in conflict with the possessor, to demonstrate both the bad faith of the latter and the equivocal character of his possession, the possessor never being compelled to demonstate the existence of a just title.

But considering that in stating that the jointly interested parties X... 'adduce no evidence of a puchase contracted by their predecessor in conditions leaving no doubt as to its validity, that the low price paid for the Toulouse-Lautrec works, whose quality he could not, as a knowledgeable professional, have been unaware of, confirms the obscure nature of the transaction entered into,that he wrote to his seller on 17 February 1959: "I have not yet been able to examine the works signed Lautrec that you have entrusted to my custody for sale" and that this letter

[13] 'Bulletin des arrêts de la *Cour de cassation*', Chambre civile 1 N 200 P 168.

prohibits the addition of faith to the purchase entries made to this police book on the preceding 12 February concerning four of the five works in dispute', the court of appeal, without compelling the jointly interested parties X... to demonstrate the existence of a just title, held, implicitly but necessarily, that Lucien X... acted in bad faith, which prohibited the the procurement of benefit to the latter of the provisions of the areforesaid Article 2279;

That thus the first argument could not be admitted; and on the second argument: considering that just as vainly it is complained of the judgment appealed against that it did not allow the widow of Lucien X... and Maxime X... to assert their own possession to benefit from Article 2279 of the Civil Code, whereas the character of the possession and the good faith of the possessor must, according to the argument, for the application of this article, be assessed in the person of him who invokes the possession and that the heir, who finds a movable item in his succession, holds from the commencement thereof the title that gives him the right of possession, such that the uncertainty, which might taint the title of the deceased does not necessarily taint the possession of the heir, if the revindicating owner does not demonstrate the latter's bad faith;

Considering, indeed, that contrary to an individual successor the heir succeeds to the vices in the possession of his prededessor;

That the bad faith of Lucien X... therefore prohibited his widow and his son, who succeeded him, from invoking the benefit of the rule 'as regards movables, possession counts as title';

That the second argument, too, must therefore be rejected.

Notes

(1) Note that Article 2279 has been renumbered 2276 in 2008.

(2) The judgment is interesting for several reasons. It first of all shows that good faith is required although the article does not state this. Moreover, it also shows that good faith is not only absent if the third party acquirer knew that he received the object from a non-owner, but that it is also absent if the third party should have known this.

(3) Secondly, the case shows that the qualities of the deceased's possession pass on to the heirs. The heir is a universal successor, that is to say, he succeeds to an entire patrimonium or estate or a percentage of it. On the other hand, a singular successor, such as a buyer, succeeds only in the title to one or more specific things. Unlike a singular successor, such as a buyer, the heir acquires the deceased's possession with all the qualities and vices pertaining to the deceased's possession, such as being a possessor in good or bad faith. The universal successor is regarded as succeeding the person of the deceased. It is an old Roman law rule (Inst 2,6,12) codified, for example, in Article 3:116 Dutch Civil Code. In the above case the heirs were seen as possessors in bad faith because their father, the predecessor in title, had bought in bad faith. See further, Chapter 8.

Cour de cassation civ 1e, 8 November 2007[14] **9.6 (FR)**

IMPORTANCE OF CAR DOCUMENTS FOR GOOD FAITH

Car documents (*carte grise*)

Photocopies of car documents may lead to good faith.

Facts: Gelva sold a car on hire-purchase to Deluc and Deluc lent the car to Alco-Hertz. The car belonged to Gelva. Alco-Hertz sold the car to the spouses X. The spouses claimed the release of the original car document of which they had received only photocopies. In a counter-claim Gelva revindicated the car. The spouses claimed that they had acquired ownership as purchasers in good faith.

Held: The Court of Appeal held that the spouses were purchasers in good faith because they had been given photocopies of the car document and other documents leading them to believe that the car belonged to the seller. By doing so the Court of Appeal, which has discretionary power to interpret the facts, did not infringe Article 2279 Cciv.

Judgment: On the sole argument, taken in its first branch:

Considering that the company Deluc, acquiring the rights of the company Gelva, objects that the judgment appealed against (Bordeaux, 19 June 2006) rejected its revindication action whereas, according to the argument, the benefit of the provisions of Article 2279 of the civil code supposes, on the part of him who asserts same, a non-equivocal possession of the item in dispute in name of its owner; that since the car document constitutes an indispensable accessory of an automobile, the possessor of a vehicle who claims to have 'acquired' it without procuring delivery of its car document necessarily has equivocal possession; that it results in the present case from the own findings of the judgment appealed against that the spouses X... never obtained the car document of the vehicle in dispute, which ruled out that their possession might be proper, from which it follows that the court of appeal disregarded Article 2279 of the Civil Code by false application;

Considering that, ruling on the revindication action raised by the owner of the vehicle, the court of appeal, acting within its absolute discretion, found that the spouses X.., to whom a photocopy of the car document had been delivered, accompanied by various documents leading one to believe that the company Alco Hertz was its owner, were possessors in good faith; that it rightly deduced therefrom that they had good cause to assert the benefit of Article 2279 of the Civil Code to oppose this action; from which it follows that the argument is not founded.

Notes

(1) Although the official car document, the *carte grise*, plays an important role in judging the purchaser's good faith, a buyer may be in good faith under French law even if he did not acquire or check the car document. In the above case the Court of Appeal held the purchaser to be in good faith on the basis that a *photocopy* of the car document had been given to the purchaser together with some other documents that could point to the seller being the owner of the car.

(2) In the case of professional sellers and buyers, the buyer may even be in good faith if the car documents clearly indicate that someone other than the seller owns

[14] No de pourvoi: 06-20.094.

the car, provided that the transaction is usual in that branch of trade.[15] This point of view seems to differ from Cour de cassation com 15 October 2002[16] in which the Cour de cassation upheld the Court of Appeal's judgment that the purchaser was not protected by Article 2279 Cciv if he did not acquire the car document. However, in Cour de cassation civ 1e, 14 May 1996[17] the Cour de cassation held that the third party acquirer should have received the car document, or at least should have checked whether the seller had the car document, which is slightly more lenient than 'should have received'. It seems that the Cour de cassation does not want to impose any strict rule on this point but rather leaves a lot of scope to the lower courts to judge which standard of good faith should be used in the case at hand. This would seem appropriate as the question of good faith largely is a question of fact.[18] The Cour de cassation in principle does not decide on questions of fact.

(iii) Stolen or lost goods

Code civil **9.7 (FR)**

Article 2277 Where the current possessor of a stolen or lost object has bought it at a fair or on a market, or at a public sale, or from a merchant selling similar objects, the original owner may have it returned to him only by reimbursing the possessor for the price that the object has cost him.

A lessor who, under Article 2332, revindicates the movables that have been removed without his consent and which have been bought in the same conditions, must likewise reimburse the buyer for the price which the things have cost him.

Cour de cassation civ 1e, 9 January 1996[19] **9.8 (FR)**

VIOLATION OF TRUST IS DIFFERENT FROM THEFT

Hispano-Suiza

A violation of trust is different from theft and does not entitle to a revindication under Article 2277 Cciv.

Facts: A very expensive classic car (a Hispano-Suiza) was stored in a garage by its owner, the claimant. The owner of the garage, the bailee, violated the trust put in him by the claimant and sold the car to a bona fide purchaser.

Held: As the car had not been stolen but rather the claimant's trust was violated, he was unable to revindicate the car from the bona fide purchaser. Article 2280 (now renumbered 2277) Cciv does not apply.

Judgment: On the sole argument, taken in its three branches:

Considering that M Y... objects that the appeal appealed against (Paris, 14 June 1993) declared that M X... was the owner of a Hispano-Suiza make of collector's automobile, misappropriated to his prejudice, and acquired by M X... from a garage-

[15] Cass com 24 April 2007, Bull 2007 IV no 115.

[16] Bull 2002 IV no 146, 165.

[17] Bull 1996 I no 199, 139.

[18] See Cass civ 1e, 23 March 1965, Bull civ I, no 206.

[19] No de pourvoi: 93-16700, Bull 1996 I no 22, 15.

owner; that the Court of Appeal is complained of as having not examined whether M X... had not voluntarily dispossessed himself by refraining from opposing the demand of M Y... for restitution of the automobile, placed under the authority of the justice authorities during the criminal prosecution, on the other hand, as having given priority to the possession of the third-party acquirer over the right of the original owner to whom possession was restored by a court decision, the judgment having thus disregarded Article 2279 of the Civil Code and reversed the onus of proof by causing the third-party acquirer to benefit from a presumption of good faith;

But considering that, by its own reasoning adopted from the judgment, the Court of Appeal, acting in its absolute discretion, held that M X... was the acquirer in good faith and that his dispossession had been involuntary, by reason of the seizure decision taken during the criminal investigation; it exactly deduced therefrom that he had remained in possession of the automobile, that this possession, free from vice, had had the effect of conferring upon him ownership of the automobile, and that M Y..., the victim of a violation of trust and not a theft, had no right to the action provided by Article 2280 of the Civil Code to obtain restitution by reimbursing the price paid by M X...;

That the Court of Appeal thereby, without reversing the onus of proof, legally justified its decision.

Notes

(1) Articles 2276 and 2277 Cciv postpone the acquisition of ownership by the third party in good faith where the owner has lost the object in question or where it has been stolen from him. The intention of the legislator was to make a distinction between cases in which possession of the object had been lost involutarily (loss and theft) and cases in which the owner had entrusted the object to another person who then violated the owner's confidence by acting in breach of the terms of the bailment.[20] The case shows clearly that the Cour de cassation upholds this distinction, deciding that Mr X was the victim not of theft but of a violation of trust and that consequently he cannot revindicate the car. It may be interesting to know that Mr X was actually Sir Peter Ustinov.

(2) Article 2277 Cciv applies only to cases in which the third party is in good faith. If he is not, revindication is always possible and does not underlie the limitations of Article 2277 Cciv.

Cour d'Appel de Lyon, 8 November 2001[21] **9.9 (FR)**

Antonio X v Mutuelle Macif Rhone Alpes

DEFINITION OF MARKET SALE

Renault Espace

A flea market is not a market in the sense of Article 2277 Cciv.

[20] See Cass civ 6 July 1886, *Lévy et Hachembourg v Moyse and Clausse*, DP 1887.1.25).
[21] No de pourvoi: 1999/07220.

Facts: A Renault car was bought at a flea market. The purchaser checked whether or not the car was registered as stolen or pledged. He paid the purchase price and took the car with him. It then turned out that the car was stolen and the purchaser was charged with buying stolen goods. The original owner's insurance company owns the car and revindicates the car. The buyer was later released and claimed to have become owner of the car through Article 2279 (now 2276) Cciv.

Held: A flea market is not a market in the sense of Article 2277 Cciv.

Judgment: Considering that the only term 'market' which can be applied to the case is a place where regular transactions are engaged in with established traders and not a flea market accessible to non-trader sellers notoriously known as a place for fencing stolen goods.

(iv) Actual possession

Code civil **9.10 (FR)**

Article 1141 If someone has obliged himself to give or deliver a purely movable object to two persons successively, the person who acquires actual possession is preferred and becomes its owner, even though his right to delivery is of a later date, provided, however, that he is in good faith.

Notes

(1) Article 1141 Cciv is about a double obligation to deliver the same movable object to two persons successively, eg a double sale. Where a specific and existing object is sold twice, ownership has already passed to the first buyer at the time of the second sale. This is the result of the so-called consensual transfer system of French law. However, Article 1141 Cciv makes an exception in that the person who first acquires possession of the object takes priority. A simple example would be the double sale of an object. Where the second buyer is the first to acquire actual possession (*possession réelle*) the second buyer becomes owner of the object despite the fact that ownership had already passed to the first buyer. The right of ownership of the first buyer lapses. This effect of Article 1141 Cciv takes place only if the second buyer was in good faith at the time he acquired possession. Of course, if the first buyer is the first to take delivery, Article 1141 Cciv is not needed, as we can simply follow the principal rule. The first buyer had already become owner as a result of the consensual transfer system.

(2) Why do Articles 1141 and 2276 Cciv require the bona fide third party to have acquired actual power over the object? It appears that there is no clear answer to the question. In the parliamentary debates on Article 2276 Cciv, the notoriously opaque *possession vaut titre* rule, no mention is made of the requirement. We should bear in mind that the requirement of *possession réelle* is not mentioned in the text of Article 2276. It is to be found only in Article 1141. However, as Article 1141 is merely a special application of the general Article 2276, French law accepted that *possession réelle* was required also when applying Article 2276. Unfortunately, the parliamentary history of Article 1141 is not very helpful either. It does not explain the requirement. According to Larombière the requirement of *possession réelle* in

Article 1141 Cciv indicates that the third party's possession should be unequivocal.[22] It ought to be *publique* (public), that is, recognisable to third parties.[23]

(3) In treatments about Article 2279 Cciv (now 2276) the requirement of *possession réelle* is often explained by reference to the requirements for acquisitive prescripion. And this is perhaps the key to understanding the requirement of actual possession. In the past a large number of authors regarded Article 2279 as a special instance of *usucapio* (acquisitive prescription): a form of prescription without a prescription period. It was normally called *prescription instantanée* (instant prescription).[24] The analogy was facilitated by the fact that Article 2279 had been placed in a section called *de quelques prescriptions particulières* (on various special cases of prescription). Acquisitive prescription requires, among other objects, that the possession should be *non équivoque* (unequivocal) (Art 2229 Cciv). According to these authors the same requirement applied to Article 2279.[25] So, perhaps the requirement of actual possession originated in applying by way of analogy the requirement of unequivocal possession originally written solely for acquisitive prescription.[26]

(4) Another explanation of the requirement of actual possession may be the fact that Article 2276 also gives a rule of procedural law: in the case of a conflict over who owns the object, the possessor is presumed to be the owner. The claimant who tries to revindicate the object has the burden of proof. Dross, however, has pointed out that although the requirement of possession is logical for the procedural function of Article 2276, the requirement is unjustified when Article 2276 is invoked to acquire ownership from a non-owner.[27]

W Dross, The single purpose of article 2279 Cciv[28] **9.11 (FR)**

Does the rule that regarding movables possession counts as title require that the person who relies on it gives evidence of a valid legal ground? From a historic point of view a positive answer seems obvious. Defending the idea that the possessor of a movable can acquire ownership of it not only by lapse of the ordinary thirty year's period but also in the Roman law period of three years numerous practitioners under the Old law have required the possessor to show a legal ground to support his possession. Regarding movables and immovables the shortening of the period required for prescription goes hand in hand with evidence of a legal ground. If one takes the view that in its acquisitive function article 2279 is never more than instantaneous prescription, this legal ground is *a fortiori* required. Some authors therefore require this from the possessor, for example Demolombe who writes: 'Article 2279

[22] L Larombière, *Théorie et pratique des obligations*, vol 1 (Brussels 1862) Art 1141, no 8.
[23] *Ibid*, Article 1141, no 8, 10, 12–14; G Baudry-Lacantinerie and L Barde, *Traité théorique et pratique de droit civil, vol XII (des obligations)*, part 1, 3rd edn (Paris 1906) no 410.
[24] See eg V Marcadé, Explication théorique et pratique du Code Civil, vol 12, 7th edn (Paris: Delamotte et fils 1874) 354; this theory is no longer current.
[25] G Baudry-Lacantinerie and L Barde, *Traité théorique et pratique de droit civil, vol XXVIII (de la prescription)*, 3rd edn (Paris 1905) no 849–850; M Planiol, G Ripert and M Picard, *Traité pratique de droit civil français, vol 3, Les Biens*, 2nd edn (Paris 1952) no 381 (who do not agree with this analogy).
[26] *Cf* F Zenati, 'Revindication mobilière' (1998) *Revue trimestrielle de droit civil* (*RTD Civ*) 408.
[27] See W Dross, 'Le singulier destin de l'article 2279 du code civil' (2006) *Revue trimestrielle de droit civil* (*RTD Civ*) 27. For the requirements of acquisitive prescription see Chapter seven.
[28] Ibid.

lays down a sort of acquisitive prescription, though without a prescription period; however, a legal ground is still required.' Marcadé accords with this, although he notes that saying that possession counts as title does not mean that it amount to prescription.

From a logical viewpoint this requirement, however, looks strange—and some authors have not hesitated to emphasise it before rejecting this requirement—exactly because possession gives such a title according to the maxim itself. ...

However, does this mean that every legal ground, of whatever nature, originating from a non-owner may be of benefit to the possessor? If proof is delivered that the defendant possesses relying on a putative legal ground, a void legal ground, or a legal ground incapable of transferring ownership, could the defendant then claim the right to keep the movable?

A negative answer seems obvious. The acquisitive function of Article 2279 has a direct connection to the idea of short prescription. Now, since regarding immovables someone who wishes to rely on a shortened prescription period has to show a legal ground which, even though it comes from a non-owner, should have certain qualities, the same should apply to someone who intends to win in proceedings for the return of a movable. It would follow from such a parallel that the revindicating party who shows that the possessor's title is declarative rather than translative, or a title of universal succession rather than singular succession, putative rather than real, void rather than valid, should win. ...

The legal ground of the possessor of the movable should be of a translative nature and should be a title of singular succession. ...

Regarding immovables shortened prescription is only possible if the legal ground relied on is real, that is to say, exists not only in the mind of the possessor: a putative title does not suffice. Case law takes a different approach in the application of Article 2279 with the blessing of doctrine which asserts that the title is only necessary for the appreciation of good faith. This is highly questionable since it is always said that the maxim is based on the interests of commerce. If the title is merely putative the interests of commerce are not at stake and on gets, also on this issue, on a slippery slope, which has already been criticised: it is good faith which one protects and not the interests of commerce.

The legal ground required for shortened prescription of an immovable should be valid, which means that it should not have a lack of formalily and should not be void. This latter requirement, according to the authors, should not be applied to Article 2279. However, it should be so applied if one believes German doctrine on this point, the reasoning of which takes as a starting point the sole rationale of the maxim, that is the protection of commerce. This consideration should lead to an equal treatment of a person who deals with a non-owner in a similar situation—but not a better and that is essential—and the situation in which he would be if he had dealt with the real owner of the movable. If it were accepted that despite voidness of the legal ground the possessor's acquisition cannot be questioned, the rule would protect him beyond what its rationale demands. An acquisition from a non-owner would turn out to be more favourable to the possessor than an acquisition from the true owner: he would only be exposed to an action by his transferor nullifying the acquisition, which the transferor will not start because, having sold the movable without right, he has not interest in doing so. However, the reasoning cannot convince for two reasons, one practical and one theoretical. ...

In conclusion, even if the requirement of a valid legal ground can be contested, the requirement of the legal ground being real, translative and leading to singular succession should be maintained. Doctrine often avoids every discussion on this point: if one claims that the title is just an element of good faith, the former dissolves in the latter so that the question which qualities are required becomes meaningless. However, while maintaining the acquisitive role given by doctrine to Article 2279 for cases of acquisition from an non-owner, these solutions would make it possible to take into account the interests of the revindicating party by allowing him on another terrain to attack the validity of the title the possessor relies on. Unfortunately, this is not yet the position taken by the majority of doctrine. Not only does the possessor have no duty to show a legal ground—which could be interpreted as a rule of burden of proof rather than a material rule—'but in addition,' think Planiol and Ripert, 'the proof which the revindicating party might deliver, that either the title is absent or the title does exist but is flawed, should be held ineffective.' Such a readical interpretation of Article 2279 is astonishing: what is left of the protection of commerce, the rationale of the text, if the possessor wins even if the revindicating party has proven that his counterparty does not have any legal ground for acquisition?

Note

Many French authors deny that where a bona fide possessor acquires ownership under Article 2276 Cciv ownership is transferred to the third party. They try to explain the third party's acquisition in different ways, for example by regarding it as an instance of instantaneous prescription. Dubertret, on the other hand, claims that it does amount to a transfer of ownership.[29]

Cour de cassation civ 1e, 25 March 1997[30] **9.12 (FR)**

Port autonome de Rouen and others v Le Foll and others

DOUBLE SALE

Rubble processor

The buyer first taking possession becomes owner.

Facts: The company Grande Paroisse sold to Port autonome de Rouen an industrial site with a rubble processor on it. Under the contract of sale the seller had a duty to have all buildings and constructions removed from the site. In anticipation of this contract the seller contracted the company ATD to remove the constructions. In addition the seller sold to ATD the rubble processor standing on the site. ATD started work before the contract of sale to Port autonome de Rouen was made. ATD sold the rubble processor on to the company Ciments Lafarge. In its turn Port autonome de Rouen sold the rubble processor on to the company Le Foll. The question is whether the first buyer (ATD) or the second buyer (Port autonome de Rouen) acquired ownership of the rubble processor.

Held: ATD was the first to acquire possession of the rubble processor. As a result, Port autonome de Rouen did not acquire ownership of the rubble processor. The Court of Appeal did not violate article 1141 Cciv.

[29] M. Dubertret, *Négociabilité et possession, Essai sur l'inopposabilité des vices de la propriété mobilière* (Paris, LGDJ, 2010) 248–49, no 354–56.

[30] No de pourvoi: 95-12705.

Judgment: Considering, on the second branch, that having found that ATD had commenced the demolition works on 4 June 1994, whereas Port autonome de Rouen only acquired the site by notarial deed of 24 June 1994, such that the taking of possession by ATD was prior to that of Port and not of its successor in title, the company Foll, the Court of Appeal, in holding that the company Ciments Lafarge, the acquirer of the rubble processor belonging to ATD, could assert its right of ownership against Port autonome de Rouen and Le Foll, far from violating Article 1141 of the Civil Code, in fact, on the contrary, made an exact application thereof; that it has thus legally justified its decision.

Note

In order to acquire ownership, the bona fide third party should have possession of the movable object as an owner, that is to say, he should think that he holds the object as an owner. Possession for the benefit of another person, which is often called *détention*, does not suffice. Moreover, the possession should give *actual power* over the object. This power may be exercised via another person holding the object for the benefit of the bona fide acquirer, such as a warehouseman, but indirect power exercised via the *seller* holding the object for the benefit of the bona fide acquirer (*constitutum possessorium*) does not suffice. Attornment by the warehouseman, who first held the object for the transferor and now attorns to the bona fide acquirer, suffices to give the bona fide acquirer actual possession of the object, even though physically the object has not been moved. It is vital that the seller should give up any possession over the object to the benefit of the third party.

Cour de cassation com, 28 November 1989[31] **9.13 (FR)**

SCPA v Agroshipping

REQUIRED LEVEL OF POSSESSION

Agroshipping

Third party holding for the pledge gives the pledge possession.

Facts: SCPA sold to Agroshipping a certain amount of grain under a retention of ownership clause. Agroshipping had the grain stored in a silo by a storage company Sonastock. Afterwards, Agroshipping pledged these goods to a bank, Crédit Lyonnais. When Agroshipping was declared insolvent the seller, SCPA, tried to revindicate the goods. Agroshipping had not yet paid the purchase price.

Held: The Court of Appeal held that the pledgee was in good faith and that he had acquired possession and that the pledgor had given up possession. As a court deciding the facts of the case the Court of Appeal could come to this decision. Moreover, it has rightly concluded that the pledgee could invoke the protection of Article 2279 Cciv.

Judgment: On the sole argument, taken in its three branches: ...

But considering, in the first place, that it is in the exercise of its absolute power of discretion the Court of Appeal held that the bank's possession was free of vices and that its acquisition of possession as well as the correlative dispossession of the

[31] No de pourvoi: 87-19626, Bull 1989, no 300, p 201.

debtor had manifested themselves in sufficiently apparent a manner, by delivery to a designed third party, so as to be recognizable to all;

Considering, in the second place, that the judges of the Court of Appeal have, acting in their absolute power of discretion, held that evidence of the bank's bad faith was not given and have rightly deduced therefrom that, presumed to be in good faith, the latter had good ground to invoke the benefit of Article 2279 of the Civil Code;

From which it follows that the argument is not founded in any of its branches.

Notes

(1) Here Article 2279 (now 2276) Cciv was invoked not in order to acquire ownership but to acquire a right of pledge. The protection of Article 2276 Cciv is here applied by way of analogy.

(2) Note that acquisition of actual possession was needed for two separate purposes: first, the creation of the possessory pledge; and, second, the protection of Article 2277 Cciv.

(3) A sufficient degree of possession was held to have passed to the third party, Crédit Lyonnais. The bailee holding the goods for the seller, Agroshipping, attorned to the third party, thus holding the goods henceforth for Crédit Lyonnais. By doing so Agroshipping gave up possession and transferred possession to Crédit Lyonnais. This is different from *constitutum possessorium* in which case the seller henceforth holds the goods for the buyer. The essential difference is that in the latter case the seller does not give up actual power over the goods. As we shall see in the following excerpt a third party who receives possession by way of *constitutum possessorium* cannot invoke the protection of Article 2277 Cciv.

(4) The above case is yet another example of the freedom of lower courts in deciding whether or not the third party was in good faith and whether or not the degree of possession was sufficient to create the pledge and rely on Article 2277 Cciv.

J-L Bergel, M Bruschi and S Cimamonti, Treatise on Civil Law, Property Law[32] **9.14 (FR)**

Possession must first of all be real, ie it must result from effective delivery of the thing and necessitates the thing being physically held. … By contrast, fictitious delivery or a constitutum possessorium does not give rise to possession which can be invoked against the revindicating party.

Cour de Cassation, 27 November 2001[33] **9.15 (FR)**

Cadéac-d'Arbaud v X

GOOD FAITH AND POSSESSION

[32] J-L Bergel, M Bruschi and S Cimamonti, *Traité de Droit Civil, Les Biens* (Paris, LGDJ 2010) no 224.

[33] No de pourvoi: 99-18335, Bull 2001, I, no 295, p 186.

Camille Claudel bronze

Good faith should be present at the time of the acquisition of actual possession.

Facts: In 1972 Mrs T bought from a bric-à-brac trader a number of objects for 20,000 FF, among which was a bronze statue. The statue was signed Camille Claudel but did not bear any caster's mark. The parties do not see it as authentic. In 1988, following the advice of F who estimated its worth between 120,000 and 300,000 FF, an antique dealer G bought the statue from T for 40,000 FF. Afterwards G sold the statue to F in order to have it auctioned. F was to pay 55,000 FF and 6% of the price on auction. On auction the statue was bought by Cadéac-d'Arbaud (C) for 1,450,000 FF. A suspensive condition of the sale was that C will get delivery only after payment and that C should receive a certificate of authenticity. As C has to finance the purchase with a loan, he cannot pay immediately. When C obtained the certificate identifying the statue as an original by Camille Claudel, the expert who issued the certificate informed C that Mrs T had started proceedings against her buyer to annul the sales contract for error and fraud, claiming restitution (in kind or in money) from any holder of the statue. Mrs T demanded seizure of the statue but her demand was dismissed. C then, pending proceedings, sold the statue to an American buyer who took the statue with him to the USA. The court of first instance and the Court of Appeal both held that the sale between T and G was void, that the voidness works against all subsequent buyers and that C cannot invoke Article 2279 Cciv. C claimed that he was in good faith at the moment he bought the statue and that this moment is decisive in the application of Article 2279 Cciv.[34]

Held: Under Article 2279 Cciv. the third party should be in good faith at the moment he receives actual possession over the object.

Judgment: On the two arguments together:

Considering that the judgment appealed against (Montpellier, 22 October 1997) is complained of for having declared binding on M. Cadéac-d'Arbaud, the acquirer at an auction for 1,450,000 francs of a bronze statue signed Camille Claudel, the voidness of its alienation by a previous owner for the initial price of 40,000 francs, and having ordered him, jointly and severally with the intermediate purchasers and the valuer and auctioneer, to compensate the loss resulting from the impossibility of restitution in kind of the object on the ground of a later sale to a purchaser residing in the United States, whereas, according to the first argument:

1° by disregarding the fact that the good faith necessary for acquisition by application of Article 2279 of the Civil Code is evaluated at the moment the sale is made, even if delivery of the thing, payment of the price or another suspensive event is not fulfilled, the Court of Appeal violated that provision; ...

But considering, on the first argument, that the good faith required by the mode of acquisition provided for by Article 2279 of the Civil Code, which does not affect the consent of the beneficiary but qualifies his possession, is evaluated at the time of effective entry into the same; that, in this way, the judges on the merits have pointed out that M Cadéac-d'Arbaud, who had become the acquirer on 11 December 1988, had learned between Christmas and New Year's Day, from the appraiser charged with establishing the authenticity of the object, that the former owner was going to go to court to contest the alienation she had agreed to, and that, by reason for the deferred payment, he had only been put in possession on 27 January 1989; that they deduced exactly therefrom that it had produced no acquisitive effect.

[34] The facts of the case are based on J-P Gridel (2002) *Recueil Dalloz* 671.

Code civil **9.16 (FR)**

Article 1599 The sale of an object of another is void: it can give rise to damages, where the buyer has ignored that the object belonged to someone else.

Cour de cassation 9 March 2005[35] **9.17 (FR)**

VOIDABLE SALE

Predeceased son

Sale of anothers property is voidable only at the instance of the buyer.

Facts: The facts cannot be inferred clearly from the judgment. Mrs X, with the required judicial permission, sold to Y the immovable property which had belonged to her predeceased son. She had been declared the only heir of her son. After her death the son of her predeceased son claimed to be the heir and invoked the nullity of the sale. The Court of Appeal held that Article 1599 of the Civil Code meant that the seller could not invoke the nullity but that the true owner could.

Held: The voidability of the sale of another's property can only be invoked by the buyer

Judgment: In deciding this way, whereas the action to nullify the sale of another's property can only be demanded by the acquirer and not by the true owner, who has an action of revindication, the Court of Appeal violated the above-mentioned text (Art 1599 Civil Code).

Notes

(1) The French Civil Code abolished one of the Roman law requirements for the transfer of ownership, namely the requirement of *traditio* (transfer of possession). This was often expressed by saying that the contract of sale itself passed ownership. It was commonly referred to as the *effet translatif des obligations*, the transferring effect of obligations. Of course, this transferring effect was unwelcome where the seller had sold goods which did not belong to him. The transfer by a non-owner should not pass ownership to the buyer. It was wrongly inferred that a valid contract *always* passed ownership to the acquirer by necessity, even if the seller did not own the object. The solution of the draftsmen was to provide that the sale by a non-owner was void, thus blocking the transferring effect of the contract. Acquisition by the third party should be possible only under Articles 2276 or 1141 Cciv.

(2) As the Civil Code only intended to abolish the requirement of *traditio*, it did not intend to abolish at the same time the requirement that the seller should have the right to dispose of the object sold. There is no logical necessity that a valid sale by a non-owner would pass ownership. French law could have provided that the contract of sale passes ownership only if the seller has the right to dispose of the object in question.

(3) French case law limits the scope of the article. Among other things, it reduced the effect of the article from voidness to voidability at the instance of the buyer

[35] Cass civ 3e, no 03-14.916, Bull 2005 III no 63, 56.

only.[36] The true owner of the object is able to revindicate his property even if the contract of sale between the non-owner and the third party has not been avoided. The avoidance is important only for the third party in his contractual relationship to the seller. It has no relevancy to the true owner.

II.B.2.b German law

Bürgerliches Gesetzbuch **9.18 (DE)**

§932 (1) As a result of a transfer under §929 the acquirer becomes owner even when the object did not belong to the transferor, unless he was not in good faith at the time he would acquire ownership under these provisions. In the case of §929 second sentence this applies only if the acquirer has acquired possession from the transferor. (2) The acquirer is not in good faith if he knew or due to gross negligence did not know that the object did not belong to the transferor.

Notes

(1) The second sentence of §929 BGB provides that where the acquirer is already in possession of the object, ownership of the object can be transferred by mere agreement without any transfer of possession being needed. The most common example is the case in which the acquirer held the object for the transferor, eg where the lessor sells and transfers the object to its lessee. §932 demands that in order to rely on third party protection the third party acquirer should have acquired possession from the transferor.

(2) It should be noted that in German law possession is an umbrella term covering both *possessio*, ie possession as an owner, and *detentio*, ie holding an object for another. This way of transfer is functionally equivalent to the *traditio brevi manu*, a transfer of possession by mere agreement (fictitious tradition), but an important difference is that in German law *brevi manu* is not regarded as a transfer of possession but rather as an exception to the requirement of transfer of possession.

Handelsgesetzbuch (HGB) **9.19 (DE)**

§366 (1) If a seller in the course of his busness transfers or pledges a movable object that does not belong to him, the provisions of the Civil Code to the benefit of those who acquire rights from a non-entitled person apply also when the good faith of the acquirer concerns transferor's or pledgor's right of disposal over the object. (2) When the object is burdened with a right of a third party, the provisions of the Civil Code to the benefit of those who acquire rights from a non-entitled person apply also when the good faith concerns the transferor's or pledgor's right to dispose of the object without conservation of the right. ...

[36] Civ 23 January 1832, *Fargeot v Laroche*, S 1832. 1. 666. Cass civ 1re, 17 July 1958, D 1958. 619 Cass civ 3e, 16 April 1973, Bull civ III, no 303; Cass civ 3e, 8 December 1999, Bull civ III, no 241. See Chr Albiges, 'Le véritable propriétaire demeure privé du droit d'agir en nullité de la vente de son bien par autrui' (2001) *Recueil Dalloz* 269 and S Petit, 'Vente de la chose d'autrui' (2007) *Recueil Dalloz* 3116.

Notes

(1) It should be noted that §932 BGB differs from §366 HGB,[37] the German Commercial Code, in that §932 BGB protects the acquirer's justified belief that the transferor was the *owner* of the object, whereas §366 HGB extends this protection to cases in which the acquirer knew that the transferor was not the owner but in which he justifiably believed that the transferor had *the right to transfer the object.* Therefore, if the transferor acts as an agent for the owner, and it turns out that the agent has acted beyond his authority or without any authority, the third party who knew that the tranferor was not the owner but a mere agent, may acquire ownership if he jusifiedly believed that the agent had sufficient authority to transfer ownership to him.[38] On the other hand, §932 BGB would protect the acquirer only if he justifiably believed that the agent was actually the *owner* of the object.

(2) Apart from this difference the same rules apply as in the Civil Code: §366 HGB refers to the rules on third party protection in the Civil Code. To give an example, §366 HGB will not protect in the case of stolen goods (§935 BGB).

(3) §366 HGB applies only if the seller is really acting as a commercial seller in the course of his business. If the seller is not so acting, the buyer's justified belief that he was so acting will not be protected.

(i) Good faith

BGH, 9 February 2005[39] **9.20 (DE)**

LEVEL OF GOOD FAITH

Truck's ownership documents

Common trade practices influence good faith.

Facts: The claimant, a financing and leasing company, bought a truck from dealer G, which the claimant leased to S. The truck had been sold to G by the defendant, the manufacturer, under a retention of ownership clause. The claimant paid the purchase price to G, but G did not pay his purchase price to the defendant. The truck's documents were held by the defendant's bank and were not given to G or the claimant. The claimant demanded delivery of the truck's documents. The claim was dismissed in first and second instance. The Court of Appeal held that the claimant was not a purchaser in good faith, as a financing and leasing company should have known that such retention of ownership clauses are very common.

Held: A company, such as the claimant, which buys trucks on a large scale, should have been aware of the common practice in trade that manufacturers sell to their dealers under a retention of ownership clause. The claimant is not a buyer in good faith and therefore did not acquire ownership of the truck. The claimant should have insisted on handing over of the truck documents.

[37] The *Handelsgesetzbuch* from 1897.

[38] This undoubtedly applies to a merchant who acts as a so-called indirect agent, acting in his own name rather than in the name of his principal. Many influential authors assert that the provision of §366 HGB can be applied also to a merchant who acts in the name of his principal (as a direct agent). See Münchener Kommentar HGB/Welter 2009, §366, Rn 42 and K Schmidt, *Handelsrecht*, 5th edn (Cologne, 1999) §23 III. Canaris is against this application to direct agency. See C-W Canaris, *Handelsrecht*, 24th edn (Munich, 2006) §27 I 4.

[39] VIII ZR 82/ 03, NJW 2005, 1365.

Judgment: The Court of Appeal held, rightly, that the payment claims last asserted by the claimant under §816 Abs 1 and §286 Abs 1 *BGB* ... in a total amount of DM98,750 = €50,490.07 are unfounded.

1. A claim by the claimant for delivery of the proceeds of disposal under §816 Abs 1 sentence 1 *BGB* would require that in the act of disposal and attendant transfer of ownership in the truck to a third party, the defendant had acted as an unentitled party. This is not the case. The defendant was still the owner of the vehicle at the time. In particular, it did not lose its ownership on the ground of the interim disposal of the truck by company G to the claimant. Company G did not become the owner of the vehicle for want of payment of the purchase price owing to the defendant's retention of ownership. Nor did G confer on the defendant any unlimited authority, to transfer ownership of the vehicle to a purchaser in the course of its business. Rather, company G only had authority to dispose of the truck upon payment of the purchase price to the defendant. Hence, the claimant could for its part only acquire ownership if it acted in good faith with regard to G's ownership of the truck (§932 Abs 1 sentence 1 *BGB*) or its power to dispose of the same (§366 Abs 1 *HGB*). The Court of Appeal rightly found that neither was the case. In so far as the Court of Appeal did not assume that the claimant could not in good faith believe that company G was the owner, the appeal does not raise any objections, nor any other causes for concern. The appeal pleads only for a review of the fact that the Court of Appeal rejected acquisition of ownership on the grounds of good faith acting in relation to the power to dispose of company G on the ground that the lack thereof had remained unknown to it through gross negligence (§§366 *HGB*, 932 Abs 2 *BGB*). However, it does not succeed on this ground. Gross negligence is in general understood as being an act in which the necessary standard of care in all the circumstances has not been fulfilled to an unusually great extent and in which things have remained unobserved that in the case in question everyone should have noticed. Whether gross negligence is to be imputed to the acquirer, is essentially a question of fact. ... Such a defect is neither displayed nor otherwise perceptible here. According to the case law of the *Bundesgerichtshof,* correctly cited by the Court of Appeal, as a rule the acquirer of a used car acts negligently when he does not demand examination of the vehicle registration document which is to be presented according to §25 Abs 4 sentence 2 *StVZO* in order to secure ownership or other rights over the vehicle each time the registration authority deals with the vehicle, especially in the case of notifications of changes in ownership (§27 Abs 3 *StVZO*), and thereby ought to protect the owner or other parties with real rights over the motor vehicle against acts of disposal by non-entitled parties. However, in the case—like here—of the acquisition of a new vehicle from an authorised motor vehicle dealer not recognised as being unreliable, the absence of the document is not unusual, for example because the document has yet to be issued. ... This latter proposition does not apply without limitation, however. Even in the case of the purchase of a new vehicle, the acquirer can lack good faith in the dealer's power to dispose in the circumstances of the individual case. So is it here. The Court of Appeal found without challenge, that in dealing with its dealers, the defendant regularly reserved ownership in the trucks sold by it until full delivery of the purchase price, that it accordingly restricted the power to dispose of the dealers and that it customarily held back the vehicle registration document or passed it to an escrow agent for the purposes of the document collection procedure in order to prevent a bona fide acquisition of ownership by third parties. Furthermore, the Court of Appeal

found without challenge, that as a financial lessor acting in the course of his business the claimant buys expensive commercial goods in large numbers and that its usual business also embraces the financing of trucks of considerable economic value. In these circumstances there is no cause to challenge the fact that in the trial on the facts the Court of Appeal accepted that the customary procedures in the relevant business dealings must have been known to the claimant and it must be accused of gross negligence, if it did not know the usual contractual arrangements between dealer and manufacturer and, accordingly, did not observe this in making payment of the purchase price to G.

Note

The text of §932(2) BGB demanding the absence of gross negligence (*grober Fahrlässigkeit*) seems to be more favourable to third parties than the equivalent French and Dutch provisions. However, case law does not demonstrate that this is true. It is very difficult or even impossible to know whether a certain case, in which a German judge held the purchaser to be in good faith, would have been decided differently by a French or Dutch judge. The facts of each case are different and perhaps even judges in the same country would have come to different conclusions. Yet, the above case at least shows that in the typical instance of sale of second-hand cars the purchaser cannot be in good faith if he did not check the car documents. In this respect German case law is equally demanding as French and Dutch case law, certainly not more lenient, as the text of §932 BGB would suggest.

(ii) Stolen and lost goods

Bürgerliches Gesetzbuch **9.21 (DE)**

§935 (1) The acquisition of ownership on the basis of §§932 to 934 does not have effect, when the object was stolen from the owner, was lost or otherwise went astray. Where the owner was only indirect possessor the same applies,if the possessor lost the object.

(2) These provisions do not apply to money or bearer documents [*Inhaberpapiere*] or to objects that are transferred by way of a public auction.

Notes

(1) Unlike Article 2277 Cciv, this provision does not confine the right to revindicate stolen and lost goods from the bona fide acquirer to a three-year period.

(2) The provision covers cases of so-called unwilling loss of possession. Like Article 2277 Cciv, §935 BGB makes a distinction between theft and embezzlement. Some but not all cases of embezzlement deprive the original owner of the possibility to revindicate the object from the bona fide third party. German law makes a difference between two different kinds of bailee. The first kind is a bailee who strictly has to obey orders in a relationship of subordinance, such as an employee. He is called a *Besitzdiener* (subordinate possessor) and has no possession in a legal sense of the word. His superior is regarded as the possessor. If this subordinate possessor embezzles the object, the superior possessor is seen as unwillingly having

lost the object, so that under §935 BGB he is able to revindicate.[40] The second kind of bailee is the *Besitzmittler* (the detentor), who has possession in the legal sense of the word which he exercises for the indirect possessor, the bailor. If the detentor embezzles the object, the loss is not regarded as unwilling. The owner willingly parted with his property by entrusting it to the bailee. As a result, he is unable to revindicate the object.[41]

(3) Different from Article 2277 Cciv the provision does not demand that in the case of revindication the owner should repay the purchase price to the bona fide purchaser.

(4) The notion of 'public auction' has been discussed in the following case.

BGH, 5 October 1989[42] **9.22 (DE)**

NOTION OF PUBLIC AUCTION IN §935 BGB

Hamburg City Seal

The auction in question was an auction in the sense of §935 BGB.

Facts: At an auction the defendant bought an old and valuable piece of Art: the fourth city seal of the City of Hamburg. Documents show that it had been used as long ago as 1306 to seal official documents. After the French annexation of Hamburg, the use of the seal was discontinued in 1810 and it was stored in the city archives. In 1944 the city archives were stored in a salt mine. When in 1945 the archives were brought back to Hamburg the seal and other objects turned out to be missing, probably stolen. The City of Hamburg, the claimant, now started proceedings against the defendant, an Art dealer, to revindicate the city seal. The defendant, however, claimed to have become owner under §935(2) BGB.

Held: The auction in question was a public auction in the sense of §935(2) BGB. Therefore the bona fide buyer became owner of the object. The City of Hamburg is unable to revindicate the object.

Judgment: In its action, the claimant has asserted its right of revindication as owner (§985 *BGB*). …

The Court of Appeal is of the view that the defendant acquired ownership in good faith. The seal does not constitute a *'res extra commercium'*, which is not capable of being legally transacted. Rather what is concerned is a so-called public thing in administrative use, in which civil law ownership can be founded. Whether a public law encumbrance can give rise to a revindication claim under public law, is not for examination in the procedure before the civil courts. The defendant is said to have acquired the seal in good faith at a public auction from a publicly appointed and sworn auctioneer for Art and antiques. As a result thereof, she acquired ownership under §935 II *BGB*. So-called voluntary auctions are also covered by §§935 II, 383 III *BGB*. There is nothing to evidence that the defendant grossly negligently failed to recognise the item acquired by her at the auction as the valuable original 14th century city seal. On the contrary, the defendant's conduct after her acquisition shows that she was uncertain about the significance and value of the item. Even if a prohibition against disposal could be inferred from the original public-law desti-

[40] See RG 18 May 1909, RGZ 71, 248, at 252–53.
[41] See BGH 20 September 2004, II ZR 318/02.
[42] IX ZR 265/88 (Köln), NJW 1990, 899.

nation of the seal, the bona fide legal acquisition by the defendant would prevail over that (§135 II *BGB*).

The appeal contends that public auctions within the meaning of §935 II *BGB* are only those cases of auction that have been especially named in a law; for it is argued that there is no objective ground to restrict the legal position of the true owner in the case of a voluntary auction. A voluntary auction, even if it is actually carried out publicly by a public auctioneer, could not justify an encroachment on ownership (Art 14 *GG*).

It was also argued that the Court of Appeal wrongly accepted that the defendant was not grossly negligent in being unaware of the value of the acquired item. According to the appeal the circumstances ought to have indicated with conspicuous clarity that an official seal was involved, possession of which had been lost by the council that had previously conducted dealings with the seal.

Ultimately, it was argued that the revindication claim was founded on the basis of §1007 II *BGB*, because possession of the seal had been lost by the claimant as the previous owner.

A corporeal good, that has become a public thing as a result of its being dedicated to an official purpose, here publication of official deeds by means of a seal, does not thereby become a '*res extra commercium*'. Rather it remains an object of private ownership and does not fall outside the ambit of the civil law. ... The view advanced by the claimant, that the seal, which has not been in further use for 179 years, is eternally incapable of passing into civil law ownership is not to be followed.

The law also allows bona fide acquisition of ownership in stolen, lost and otherwise dispossessed things in so far as they are sold by way of a public auction (§935 II *BGB*).

The acquirer of a thing is not in good faith when it is known or as a result of gross negligence unknown to him that a thing does not belong to the seller (§932 II *BGB*). Even the claimant did not contend that the defendant recognised the seal as real and knew its provenance. There is nothing to indicate that. Conduct is in general regarded as grossly negligent where the necessary standard of care has been breached to an unusually high degree given all circumstances and in which things have remained unobserved that in the case in question everyone should have noticed. Whether the acquirer of a thing has committed gross negligence is essentially a question of fact, which is only subject to subsequent examination in an appeal on points of law to the extent that there have been breaches of §286 *ZPO*, rules of logic or rules of experience.

As the court deciding the facts of the case, the Court of Appeal found that there existed no gross negligence in the case of the defendant's auction acquisition. Without being able to point to a procedural breach—the appeal here tries to impose its view in the place of that of the court deciding on the facts. This it may not do. The fact that the authenticity of the seal could easily be seen, as is averred by the appeal, cannot be inferred from the facts as found.

§383 III BGB gives a statutory definition of a public auction. In terms thereof, an auction by a bailiff or other official with authority to conduct an auction or by an officially appointed auctioneer must be carried out publicly, i.e. be accessible to anyone. Responsible for holding a public auction are the persons appointed by the state authorities according to §34b V *GewO* (*cf* new version of the *VersteigererVO* of 1.6.1976—BGBl I, 1345 1. *Cf* Art 7 of the *VO* of 28.11.1979—BGBl I, 1986). In so far as the conditions set forth in §383 III *BGB* are fulfilled, an acquisition at a voluntary auction is also protected according to §935 II *BGB*. ... That also applies to cases of public auctions not expressly named in the law. Trade and industry law provides for the public appointment of an auctioneer in order to give the public the possibility, 'to make use of such persons to whom statute attaches a particular creditworthiness in the exercise of their trade or who by virtue of the public appointment offer a particular guarantee of reliability and professional competence' (BVerwGE 5, 95 [96] = NJW 1957, 1248). 'Trust in a disposal carried out under official authority' should not be jeopardised in the case of an auction (Mot zum BGB III, 349). The owner is encumbered with the loss of his thing and the associated risk of ending up with nothing, even with the compensation claim he is entitled to against the seller, because contrary to this the interest of the third party, who is often economically affected by the disposal, in the validity of the auction sale demands a preference for the *bona fide* purchaser (Dünkel, p 70). The statutorily intended result of privileging a *bona fide* acquirer at a public auction is contained within the legally possible boundaries of the ownership guarantee under Article 14 I *GG*. That the auction here at which the defendant acquired the seal had been publicly announced and open to all has been found to be the case by the Court of Appeal and not cast into doubt by the appeal. However, the defendant then acquired ownership in good faith by the auction sale (§§932, 935 II *BGB*).

The petitionary revindication claim asserted by the appeal according to §1007 II *BGB* can be countered by the defendant's arguing that, as a result of the auction sale she has become the bona fide owner and hence is entitled to possession.

(iii) Actual possession

Bürgerliches Gesetzbuch **9.23 (DE)**

§933 If an object transferred under §930 [*constitutum possessorium*] does not belong to the transferor the acquirer will become owner when the object is handed over to him by the transferor, unless he is not in good faith at that moment.

Explanations for the Draft of a Civil Code for the German Nation, Book III[43] **9.24 (DE)**

Despite the lack of any explicit provision §306 HGB has always been understood in the sense that physical delivery is required, excluding a delivery in which the transferor keeps detention (constitutum possessorium). The draft follows this commercial law opinion. The owner who is threatened by bona fide acquisition should be protected against the fact that the loss of right to his detriment is hidden behind an act such as constitutum possessorium which is hardly noticeable. Out of consideration for the present tight of ownership this ownership continues and the revindication remains possible as long as the object remains in the hands of a person who is subject to the revindication and against whom an proceedings for revindication may already be pending (cf §238 ZPO), even if the possessor or holder has already tried to transfer through constitutum possessorium. This is not unfair to the bona fide acquirer

[43] *Motive zu dem Entwurfe eines Bürgerlichen Gesetzbuches für das Deutsche Reich*, Vol 3: *Sachenrecht* (Berlin and Leipzig 1888) 345.

because the fact that he allows the transferor's possession to continue means that he puts trust into the transferor, the risk of which bears on the acquirer.

Note

Unlike the parliamentary history of the French Civil Code the official explanations to the German Civil Code, the *Motive* and *Protokolle*, clearly indicate the reason for requiring actual possession.[44] As the *Motive* indicate §933 BGB accords with the traditional interpretation of §306 of the old Commercial Code of the German Confederation (*deutscher Bund*): the *Allgemeines Deutsches Handelsgesetzbuch* of 1861. The parallel provision of the new Commercial Code of 1897, still in force, is §366. This provision, like its predecessor, protects a bona fide purchaser who believed that a merchant was authorised to dispose. The old §306, although silent on this point, was interpreted so as to require the third party to have received actual possession. Case law and literature postponed third party protection in the case of *constitutum possessorium*.[45] Hence, the draftsmen of the Civil Code simply applied to the Civil Code a requirement which had already developed on the basis of the Commercial Code.[46] As we shall see below, the first of these reasons can also be found in the parliamentary history of the Dutch Civil Code.[47]

Bürgerliches Gesetzbuch **9.25 (DE)**

§934 If an object which is transferred under §931 does not belong to the transferor, the acquirer becomes owner at the time of assignment of the claim for restitution, where the transferor is indirect possessor of the object, and where the transferor has no possession the acquirer becomes owner when he acquires possession of the object from the third party. However, the acquirer does not become owner if at the time of the assignment of the claim for restitution or at the time of acquisition of possession the acquirer is not in good faith.

BGH, 27 March 1968[48] **9.26 (DE)**

CONSTITUTUM POSSESSORIUM FOLLOWED BY ATTORNMENT

Milling machine (Fräsmaschine)

Third party protection is available where the second party fully divests himself of his possession, even if his possession was mere indirect possession.

Facts: The claimant, a supplier of machines sold and delivered a milling machine to H under a retention of ownership clause. Part of the purchase price remained unpaid. H obtained a loan from C and transferred ownership of the machine to C by way of security (*fiducia cum creditore*). The transfer of

[44] See also Protokolle III, 3704.

[45] See K Cosack, *Lehrbuch des Handelsrechts*, 4th edn (Stuttgart, 1898) 149–50.

[46] For the equivalent interpretation of the modern §366, see K Schmidt, *Handelsrecht*, 5th edn (Cologne etc, 1999), §23 II 1 e.

[47] CJ van Zeben et al (eds), *Parlementaire Geschiedenis van het Nieuwe Burgerlijk Wetboek*, vol 3 (Deventer, 1981) 384.

[48] VIII ZR 11/66 (KG), BHGZ 50,45, (1968) NJW 1968, 1382.

possession took place by way of *constitutum possessorium*, so that H could continue to use the machine. Afterwards C transferred his claims against H and ownership of the machine to L in order to secure a loan given by L to C. In turn, L transferred all claims against C and ownership of the machine to the defendant. The required transfer of possession took place by H attorning to L, henceforth holding the machine for L. The claimant tries to revindicate the machine from the defendant. The court of first instance allowed the revindication. The Court of Appeal, however, dismissed the action. The Supreme Court upheld the court of appeal's decision.

Held: L had become owner of the machine as a result of third party protection. Consequently L could validly transfer ownership to the defendant. The claimant is therefore unable to revindicate the machine.

Judgment: II. The Court of Appeal accepts, nevertheless that L Ltd. has become the owner of the milling machine, and that it in turn effectively transferred ownership to the defendant. Contrary to the views of the appeal, there are no legal considerations to counter this. §4 of the contract of 24 August 1962 contains the statement of the parties, that they are agreed on the transfer of ownership and that trader C assigns his rights under the bailment between him and the debtor, H, to L Ltd. As is not denied by the appeal, this constitutes the necessary agreement within the meaning of §929 *BGB* and a substitute delivery within the meaning of §§931, 934 half-sentence 1 *BGB*. In such a case, according to the clear terms of the law, the assignee of the revindication claim—provided he is acting in good faith—immediately obtains ownership of the thing, forming the subject-matter of the contract, without a subsequent obtaining of direct possession having to be added thereto. That this result accords with the terms of §934 half-sentence 1 *BGB* is not denied by the appeal. Its view, that the provision of §934 half-sentence 1 should not be effective in cases such as the present one, because its application contradicts the principles of §933 *BGB*, is not to be followed.

III. 1. Rightly the Court of Appeal represents the position that it cannot be assumed, that a secured party, who, as trader C here, enters into a bailment with a non-owner, does not acquire indirect possession, because the transfer of ownership has gone wrong. This view, that the bona fide acquirer not only does not obtain ownership from a non-owner but also does not obtain any indirect possession through constructive possession, is represented in the literature under citation of §139 *BGB* by Wolff/Raiser *loc cit* (§69 II 2 c, fn 18). If it were correct, then C would not have been in a position to transfer indirect possession, so that a *bona fide* acquisition of ownership would have had to fail for want of the conditions under §934 half-sentence 1 *BGB*. In a previous judgment the adjudicative Senate has left open the issue of whether this opinion can be followed (cf Senate judgment of 21 April 1959—VIII ZR 148/58—NJW 1959, 1536 = WM 1959, 813). The question now requires an answer. At least for cases of the present kind, it is to be answered in the negative. The agreement about transfer for security purposes between H and C corresponds to the general case for such a contract, in that the party granting the security should continue in possession of the things and use them and keep them safe despite transfer of the collateral.

...

2. The other principles laid down by the legislator for the bona fide acquisition of ownership from a non-owner also do not preclude application of §934 half-sentence 1 *BGB* to the present case. The provisions of §§933, 934 *BGB* are governed by the principle that the legislator does not allow the creation of indirect possession to suffice for *bona fide* acquisition, but does allow its *transfer* to do so (cf *Westermann*, Sachenrecht, 5th edn, §48 II, 1, 2). Since an agreement of *constitutum*

possessorium does not *transfer* the seller's possession to the acquirer, the acquisition of direct possession must be an additional condition for a *bona fide* acquisition of ownership from the non-owner under §933 *BGB*. On the other hand, according to §870 BGB assignment of the claim to delivery flowing from a bailment transfers the seller's possession immediately, albeit only indirect possession. However, the law proceeds on the basis that indirect possession is assimilated to direct possession (*Westermann*, *loc cit*; cf also the case law on §934 half-sentence 2: *RG*, JW 32, 1212; Gruchot 53, 692; JW 08, 717; RGZ 89, 348, 349). This principle of assimilation and the fact that in the case of §§931, 934 half-sentence 1 *BGB* the seller divests himself entirely of his possession, whilst transfer by means of constitutum possessorium leaves possession with the seller, are the legislative ground for the law in §934 half-sentence 1 *BGB* deviating from the principle of visibility [*Sichtbarkeitsprinzip*] by way of derogation from the provisions in §933 *BGB*. It is in accordance with the legislator's will that the trust of a *bona fide* acquirer, which he places in an indirect possession evidenced by a bailment, should be just as protected as the trust in direct possession of the thing itself, provided that, as is required in both cases, the seller divests himself entirely of his possession (cf also *Baur*, Sachenrecht, 4th edn, §52 II, 4; *Westermann*, *loc cit*; see also Commission Protocols for the 2nd Reading of the Draft *BGB* [Prot p 209]). A contrary opinion has not, in so far as can be overseen, been represented in the case law of the Supreme Court. The view presented here also corresponds to the almost unanimous view in the literature (see apart from that already cited also BGB-*RGRK*, 11th edn, §934 note 4; *Staudinger*, BGB, 11th edn, §934 no 1 a; *Erman-Westermann*, BGB, 3rd edn, §934 note 1; *Heck*, Grundriß des Sachenrechts §56; *Serick*, *loc cit* vol II §23 I 7 and 8).

3. The considerations expressed by Böhmer (*Grundlagen der bürgerlichen Rechtsordnung*, II 2 §23 p 31 f—A, B, C) and also discussed by the Court of Appeal against an application of §934 half-sentence 1 *BGB* in accordance with its wording, are of the nature of legal policy. Böhmer particularly points out that adherence to the strict wording of the provision leads to results that do not accord with either the requirements of legal certainty and consistency nor the requirements of social justice and equity. He finds it unsustainable that in the application of §934 half-sentence 1 *BGB* the seller's retention of ownership has to give way to the security ownership of the lender, although both creditors have invested the same trust in the debtor. In his view, there is no reason to regard the interests of the 'true' lender in upholding his ownership as less worthy of protection than those of the loan-giver in securing his loan receivable. He particularly stresses that application of §934 half-sentence 1 *BGB* may not lead to circumvention of the rules in §933 *BGB*, in order, via §934 half-sentence 1 *BGB,* to achieve a situation in which the thing can in all cases and without risk remain where it is. Legal policy considerations do not, however, release the judge from his duty to apply the applicable law. In this the Senate does not exclude itself from the concerns raised by Böhmer. It is indeed remarkable that economically equivalent circumstances have to be judged differently, depending whether the one or the other provision (§933 or §934 half-sentence 1 *BGB*) is applicable, that thus the application of valid law leads to different results, the justification of which is not automatically evident. In a case like the present one this is particularly remarkable, because here the second secured party, who benefits from §934 half-sentence 1 *BGB*, was further removed from the item over which there was a retention of ownership than the first, which according to §933 *BGB* could not acquire any ownership. It is nonetheless decisive that the legislator

did not proceed arbitrarily with these differentiated regimes. Both regimes are, as stated above, governed by the principle that direct possession is to be equated to indirect possession and that, for bona fide acquisition of ownership, it is sufficient that the seller fully divests himself of his possession, regardless whether indirect or direct possession is concerned. In any event, this regime is not arbitrary, and hence the judge is not in a position to deviate from the intention clearly expressed by the legislator.

IV. Since the claimant has not refuted the statutorily presumed good faith of L Ltd, this company has become the owner of the milling machine and the claimant has thereby lost its retention of ownership.

Notes

(1) In Dutch law and French law the third and fourth party, L and the defendant company, respectively, would not have acquired ownership despite their good faith. The reason is that in Dutch and French law H, the original buyer, would not have acquired possession of the machine, H would have mere *detentio*. Consequently, H would have been unable to pass possession to C and C would have been unable to pass possession to L, which excludes any bona fide protection of L. Let us suppose that the above case were to be solved under Dutch or French law. A buyer of an object under a retention of ownership clause has no possession but mere *detentio* until the retention clause ends. He does not hold the object for his own benefit but he holds the object for the seller, respecting the seller's right of ownership. This is true even if the buyer does not realise that the seller is still the owner of the machine. The legal relationship of retention of ownership dictates this independently of the state of mind of the buyer. As a detentor the buyer is unable to pass possession to L. As *constitutum possessorium* is a way of *transferring* possession and possession can be transferred only by the possessor himself, the *constitutum possessorium* is invalid. In addition, the buyer cannot turn himself into a possessor (inversion of possession) without informing the seller and denying the latter's right of ownership (Article 3:111 BW and Article 2268 Cciv). Since C received no possession, the intended transfer of possession from C to L (by way of attornment by H to L) is also invalid. This invalidity prevents the then acquirer, L, from invoking the third party protection of Article 3:86 BW or Article 2276 Cciv. The same applies to the transfer between L and the defendant.

(2) The vital difference between Dutch and French law, on the one hand, and German law on the other hand, is that in German law the buyer H becomes possessor. Both Dutch, French and German law distinguish between a person holding the object for himself and the person holding the object for another person. Dutch and French law call the first person a possessor but call the second person a detentor rather than a possessor. German law uses the terms *Eigenbesitz* (possession for one's own benefit) and *Fremdbesitz* (possession for another's benefit), respectively, but uses the term *Besitz* (possession) as an umbrella term.[49] As in German law H is a possessor despite the retention of ownership clause: he is able to transfer possession

[49] LPW van Vliet, *Transfer of Movables in German, French, English and Dutch Law* (Nijmegen, 2000) §3.2.

by way of *constitutum possessorium* to C, who thereby becomes the next possessor. C in turn is able to transfer possession to L by ordering H to attorn to L.

(3) The different Dutch and French outcomes accord with the view of Böhmer discussed in the judgment. Böhmer's view is apparently shared by the German Supreme Court who at the same time feels unable to deviate from the text of the Civil Code which demands a different outcome to that which the Supreme Court finds appropriate. [50]

II.B.2.c Dutch law

Burgerlijk Wetboek **9.27 (NL)**

Article 3:86 (1) Despite the lack of power of the transferor to dispose, a transfer made in accordance with Articles 90, 91 or 93 of a movable object, that is not a registered thing, or a bearer or an order right, is valid if the transfer is for value and the acquirer was in good faith.

(2) If a thing mentioned in the previous paragraph that is transferred for value in accordance with Article 90, 91 or 93 is burdened with a limited property right which the acquirer neither knew of nor ought to have known of, this right ceases to exist in the case that the transfer was made under the same suspensive condition [*opschortende voorwaarde*] in the case that the transfer was made under which the delivery was made.

(3) Nevertheless, the owner of a movable object, who has lost possession thereof through theft, may, for the duration of three years, to be calculated from the day of the theft, reclaim his ownership, unless:

(a) the object was acquired by a natural person who does not act in the exercise of a profession or a business from a transferor whose business it is to sell to the public similar objects, other than as an auctioneer, on business premises that are intended for such a purpose, being an immovable object or a part thereof with the land that belongs thereto, and provided that the transferor acted in the normal course of his business; or

(b) it concerns money or bearer or order documents.

(4) Articles 316, 318 and 319 regarding the interruption of the prescription period of a claim apply to the period mentioned in the last paragraph mutatis mutandis.

Comparative Notes

(1) The article clearly shows that bona fide acquisition is regarded as a true transfer, a derivative acquisition rather than original acquisition. The non-owner is able to transfer the owner's right of ownership to the bona fide third party. Consequently, all requirements of a valid transfer, other than the requirement of the right to dispose, should be met.

(2) Like in French law (Article 2277 Cciv) and German law (§935 BGB) the case of theft gets special treatment. Whereas in German law bona fide acquisition seems to be excluded *eternally* in the case of theft, under Dutch and French

[50] J Wilhelm, *Sachenrecht*, 4th edn (Berlin, De Gruyter, 2010) no 987.

law the owner can only revindicate the stolen object within a time frame of three years. However, even in German law the stolen thing cannot be revindicated eternally, because after 10 years' possession the bona fide possessor acquires by way of prescription (§937 BGB) and after 30 years the action of revindication lapses as a result of limitation (§194 I read with §197 I no 1 BGB)

(3) Whereas in Dutch law the postponement of bona fide acquisition of objects is limited to stolen objects, French law applies this postponement also to lost objects. Similarly, the eternal exclusion of bona fide acquisition in German law is extended to objects which have been lost or otherwise went astray. Thus, in German and French law the protection of the owner in cases of involuntary loss is applied in more cases.

(4) Dutch, French and German law do not extend the special treatment of theft to cases of embezzlement because in the case of embezzlement possession was not lost involuntarily, but the owner's trust was violated.

(5) Dutch does not postpone bona fide acquisition for stolen money or bearer instruments. Similarly, the German exclusion of bona fide acquisition does not apply to stolen or lost money and bearer instruments.

(6) A notable difference between French and German law on the one hand, and Dutch law on the other hand, is that Dutch law protects only the third party who acquired for value (normally a buyer). Article 3:86 BW does not protect where goods are donated to a third party, even if the latter meets all other requirements for third party protection.

Unlike Article 2277 Cciv, the provision does not demand that in the case of revindication the owner should repay the purchase price to the bona fide purchaser. If a bona fide person buys the stolen object in a shop which normally sells these goods, under French law the owner can still revindicate within three years but only under the duty to reimburse to the sub-buyer the purchase price paid by him, whereas under Dutch law no revindication is possible in such as case. The owner's right given by French law to buy back his own object is often called the right of repurchase or the right of redemption.

Burgerlijk Wetboek **9.28 (NL)**

Article 3:87 (1) An acquirer who, within three years after his acquisition, is asked who transferred the thing to him, must without delay provide the data that is needed to find this person or which he, at the time of acquisition, could consider sufficient for that purpose. If he does not fulfil this obligation, he may not invoke the protection of Articles 86, 86a and 86b against an acquirer in good faith.

(2) The previous paragraph does not apply to money.

(i) Good faith

Burgerlijk Wetboek **9.29 (NL)**

Article 3:11 Good faith of a person, required for any legal effect, is not only lacking if he knew the facts or the right to which his good faith shall relate, but also if he, in the given circumstances, should have known of them. Impossibility of investigation does not prevent that the person who had good reasons to doubt is regarded as someone who should have known the facts or the right.

Hoge Raad, 7 October 2005[51] **9.30 (NL)**

Coppes v Van de Kolk

SALE OF A SECOND HAND CAR BY NON-OWNER

Second-hand Volvo

Good faith requires checking car documents.

Facts: Coppes sold a second-hand car to X on the condition of resale by X. The car documents remained with Coppes. X found a buyer for the car and sold and delivered the car to Van de Kolk. The buyer paid the purchase price partly to X and, on the instruction of X, to X's girlfriend. X did not pay his purchase price to Coppes and is later declared insolvent. Coppes then revindicated the car, asserting that he delivered the car to X under a retention of ownership clause. The buyer, Van de Kolk, claimed to have become owner of the car under Article 3:86 BW as a purchaser in good faith.

Held: The buyer of a second-hand car can be in good faith only if he has checked all the car documents. This rule is not confined to cases of theft and embezzlement.

Judgment: 3.3 On appeal, the court, which summed up Coppes's primary position as being that the delivery of the Volvo to X was effected under the suspensive condition of payment of the purchase price, hence under a retention of ownership, and that she subsidiarily invoked the right of revindication, rejected Coppes's arguments: according to the court, Van de Kolk was at the time of delivery of the Volvo on 17 August 2001 in good faith within the sense of both Art 3:86 and Art 7:42 BW. That which the court deliberated in that regard can, in so far as of importance now, be summed up as follows. The standard formulated by the Supreme Court in its judgment of 4 April 1986, no 12605, NJ 1986, 810, is not of application, for this standard is aimed at the protection of owners who have lost possession of their cars by theft or embezzlement, and neither the one nor the other is in question here (no 4.4). From the circumstance that X with the consent of Coppes had the Volvo in his custody with the intention that he should sell that car to someone such as Van de Kolk, it follows—proceeding from the retention of ownership stipulated by Coppes vis-à-vis X—that in the event that X should have informed Van de Kolk correctly and completely of his rights over the Volvo and his relationship with Coppes, it would have been sufficient for Van de Kolk's good faith that he had no reason to doubt that X would pay the purchase price for the Volvo over to Coppes (no 4.5). Coppes made insufficient representations to be able to conclude that Van de Kolk—in the case referred to in no 4.5—might not have acted in good faith (no 4.7). That X did not fully inform Van de Kolk about his rights over the Volvo and his relationship with Coppes does not imply that Coppes can still invoke the standard formulated in the said judgment (no 4.8).

3.4 Part 2.1, which the Supreme Court will deal with first, rightly claims that these statements manifest an incorrect summary regarding the provisions of Art 3:86 BW. In the aforementioned judgment of 4 April 1986, which relates to the

[51] NJ 2006, 351.

case where A voluntarily gives a car belonging to him, together with the car documents with the exception of the copy of part III, to B, who subsequently sells and delivers the car to C, who in turn sells and delivers to D, the Hoge Raad has ruled that—apart from exceptions—the acquirer of a second-hand car, if he wishes to be in good faith at the time of his acquisition, must have examined at least the car documents (the vehicle registration document and the copy of part III of the vehicle registration document) with a view to his predecessor's power of disposal. There is no reason to restrict this rule (whereby of course the successive amendments in Art 17 of the Kentekenreglement are to be taken into account) to the case—which according to the unchallenged opinion of the court in this appeal on a point of law does not arise here—where the owner of the car has lost possession thereof by theft or embezzlement.

(ii) Stolen property

Hoge Raad, 14 November 1997[52] **9.31 (NL)**

Uitslag v Wolterink

THE SELLER'S OFFICE SPACE

Caravan dealer

Movable caravan to be equalled with immovables for the application of Art 3:86(3) BW.

Facts: Koster was a professional trader in caravans. The company had its office space on a terrain where it stored all its caravans. The office space was itself a caravan. Koster sold one of the caravans to Wolterink, who sold the caravan on to Uitslag. Afterwards it was discovered that the caravan had been stolen from Buitenhuis. Buitenhuis's insurance company, to whom Buitenhuis transferred ownership of the caravan, revindicated the caravan from Uitslag who obeyed to the insurer's request and handed the caravan over. Uitslag then sued Wolterink for breach of contract claiming that Wolterink had not transferred ownership of the caravan to him. Uitslag claimed the purchase price from Wolterink. To his defence, however, Wolterink claimed that he did give ownership to Uitlslag because as a bona fide purchaser Wolterink received ownership under Article 3:86(3) BW which he transferred to Uitslag. However, Uitslag claimed that Article 3:86(3) BW did not protect Wolterink because Wolterink bought from Koster in a mobile office space.

Held: The Court of Appeal held that the office space, although it was a caravan, almost looked like an immovable building and that for the purposes of Article 3:86(3) BW it should be treated as equivalent to an immovable building. The fact that the office space was movable should not have restrained the Court of Apeal from its judgment. The judgment is understandable and is sufficiently explained.

Judgment: 3.3. The argument challenges the ruling of the Court that there is no reason to exclude the present transaction from the protection of Art 3:86 paragraph 3 BW, merely because the sales area is not permanently connected to the land (no 5.6), as incorrect or at least incomprehensible or insufficiently reasoned, since the requirement of 'business premises, being a built-upon immoveable property or a part thereof with the land belonging to the one or the other' laid down in this provision under a is not fulfilled.

3.4. As is apparent from the passages from the legislative history cited in the

[52] NJ 1998, 147.

opinion of the Advocate-General under 9, 10 and 11, Art 3:86 paragraph 3, opening words and under a concern weighing, on the one hand, of the interests of the consumer who buys a second-hand thing and, on the other hand, the interests of fighting crime. Here, the boundary is thus drawn that individual purchasers, provided the other requirements are met, deserve protection, if they—in the words of the Explanation to the third note of amendment, whereby Art 3:86 lid 3, opening words and under a, in so far as here of importance, received its present text—'have bought a thing in the normal course of trade for such things, whereby what is considered is particularly a purchase in a shop or other business with permanent business premises established in a fixed place' (Parliamentary History Book 3 (infr 3, 5 and 6), p 1223, last paragraph), where in principle they are not to expect stolen things. In this explanation, it is emphasised that the description is not limited to shops, and that it also covers a small plot of land provided with an office for the sale of caravans, but that it does not cover for instance the sale of things that are traded in a market on the street, from door to door, or in a pub (Parliamentary History Book 3 (infr 3, 5 and 6), p 1225, first paragraph).

3.5. Considering the scope of the present provision as set out above and also laid down by the Court in no 5.4 of its judgment, the Court has found in no 5.5 (a) that the caravan used as a point of sale was covered with wood down to the ground and that the entire thing at first sight gave the impression of being a wooden construction, (b) that it is not likely that the caravan can easily be transported away, although such will on the other hand not be entirely impossible, and (c) that there was no question of 'one-day trading', but on the contrary of a certain degree of continuity. On the basis of all the circumstances, the Court ruled that there was no reason for Wolterink not to trust that what was involved was normal trading whereby he did not need to expect stolen property, and there was therefore no reason to exclude the transaction between Koster and Wolterink from the protection of Art 3:86 paragraph 3. That the caravan used as a point of sale was not permanently connected to the ground is insufficient for this because, according to the Court, 'given the circumstances of the case, the present caravan can in any event be equated thereto in this regard,' whereby the Court expressed the view that the caravan must for the application of Art 3:86 paragraph 3 and hence with a view to the question of whether the purchaser Wolterink deserves the protection given by that provision, in the light of the circumstances of the case mentioned above under (a)-(c), be equated to an immovable property.

In doing so, the Court does not seem to have manifested an incorrect legal interpretation, but rather it—rightly—construed Art 3:86 paragraph 3 in consideration of the aim of that provision as stated above in 3.4. Namely, the sole fact that the caravan was not permanently connected to the ground, did not need to prevent the Court from ruling as it did. For the rest, the Court's judgment rests on an assessment of circumstances of a factual nature, so that it cannot be further tested for correctness in the appeal before the Supreme Court. It is not incomprehensible and needs no further reasoning.

The argument is therefore rejected.

(iii) Actual possession

Introductory Notes

(a) Like French and German law, Dutch law requires the bona fide acquirer to have actual power over the object in question. In the case of *constitutum possessorium* third party protection is postponed until the moment that the third party acquires actual power over the object. Of course, the third party should still be in good faith at that moment. As in French and German law actual possession includes indirect possession where a third party other than the seller holds the object for the acquirer (eg a warehouseman attorning from the seller to the buyer), but it excludes the case in which the seller himself holds the object for the acquirer (*constitutum possessorium*). It is therefore vital that the seller should give up any power over the object.

Differently from German law this result of excluding *constitutum possessorium* is not reached by one simple provision in the Civil Code but by two different rules. The reason is that Dutch law has no umbrella term for *possessio* and *detentio*. As a result, two different rules had to be made: one for the possessor and one for the detentor who transfers possession by way of *constitutum possessorium*. In both cases the purspose and the result of the rule is the same: postponing third party protection until actual power over the object is given to the acquirer, until the seller divests himself completely of any possessory link to the object.

(b) The rule applying to the detentor cannot be found in the Civil Code, it can only be inferred from different other provisions. Since Article 3:115 BW defines *constitutum possessorium* as a way of transferring possession and since possession can be transferred only by a possessor (in the strict Dutch sense of the word),[53] not by a detentor, a *constitutum possessorium* by a detentor will be void. Moreover, Article 3:111 BW prevents the detentor from attorning to a third party and from turning his detention into possession without noticing the person for whom he hold the thing. It is called the prohibition of interversion (*cf* the French notion of *interversion de titre* of Article 2268 Cciv). Article 3:86 BW protects only against the transferor not having the right to dispose of the object, it does not protect against voidness of the transfer or possession. This is not coincidence but rather a deliberate choice of the legislator.

(c) If, on the other hand, a possessor who does not own the object transfers possession by way of *constitutum possessorium*, the transfer is undoubtedly valid. Yet, Article 3:90(2) BW qualifies the effect of the transfer to some extent, as can be seen below.

Burgerlijk Wetboek **9.32 (NL)**

Article 3:90(2) If after the transfer the object remains in the hands of the transferor, the transfer works against a third party with an older right on the object only

[53] HR 4 June 1886, W 5305: 'Besides, for the delivery of an object by the seller into the possession of the buyer it should first of all be certain that in order for the seller to be able to transfer possession he should himself have possession ...'.

from the moment that the object comes into the hands of the acquirer, unless the holder of the older right agreed to the transfer.

Note

If B sells to C an object which he bought from A under a retention of ownership clause, A is the third party with the older right which Article 3:90(2) refers to; A still owns the object. The effect of Article 3:90(2) BW is that the legal act of transfer is invalid against the owner. However, a valid legal act of transfer is a vital requirement for third party acquisition. As noted above, Article 3:86 BW protects only against the transferor not having the right to dispose of the object, it does not protect against other defects, such as this one: a defective act of transfer. The result is that even though C purchased in good faith, he will acquire ownership only at the moment that the *constitutum possessorium* is followed by the handing over of actual power over the object. The defect of the act of transfer ends at that time, enabling the third party to invoke the third party protection of Article 3:86 BW. However, the third party should still be in good faith at that later moment.

Note

Although these reasons look self-evident at first sight, they are unconvincing.[54]

II.B.3 ABANDONMENT

The holder of a property right can generally do with his right as he wishes. This is particularly the case when the right provides a right to use. As a part of holding a property right the holder may decide to 'give up' his right. The 'giving up' of rights is known as abandonment. Abandonment is a slightly controversial subject and not all legal systems accept abandonment of all property rights. In civil law systems in particular abandonment of the right of ownership is problematic. In common law, too, abandonment of property rights is questionable.

One common example of abandonment is garbage that is placed on the street to be picked up. Abandoned objects generally become without ownership. They are a *res nullius* or a *res derelicta*.

Finally, apart from property rights, other rights can also be abandoned. Moreover, possession too can be abandoned, without the abandonment of ownership, which can lead to a loss of the right of ownership through extinctive or acquisitive prescription. On these types of prescription see sections II.B.1 and II.B.6 in this chapter. Usually, however, ownership and possession will be abandoned together.

II.B.3.a French law

Introductory Note

French law makes a distinction between objects that are abandoned and objects that are lost. Of objects that are lost (*choses perdues*) the right of ownership is not

[54] See LPW van Vliet, 'Acquisition and Loss of Ownership of Goods—Book VIII of the Draft Common Frame of Reference' (2011) 2 *Zeitschrift für Europäisches Privatrecht* 292–334 at 318–21.

lost by the owner. The same rules apply to wrecks, which are known in French as *épaves*. The owner does lose his right of ownership of object he abandons.[55]

(i) Abandonment of ownership

Cour de cassation civ 3e, 10 November 1987[56] **9.33 (FR)**

Servouze et Compagnie v Morin et Remaud and others

ABANDONMENT OF OWNERSHIP OF IMMOVABLE OBJECTS

Excavating materials

No one may be compelled by anyone to give up his ownership without consent.

Facts: Husband and wife D agreed in 1966 with company Servouze et Cie on the right for that company to extract materials from their parcel of land. The right to extract materials was sold by the husband and wife D on 15 April 1981 to the company Morin et Remaud. In order to safeguard its right, Servouze assigned its rights to excavate to the company Morin et Remaud and called for a guarantee of this right by the spouses D.

Some materials that had already been excavated were left on the land and a dispute arose as to the ownership of these materials. Servouze, who had excavated the materials, claimed ownership but did not immediately take these. In the court proceedings that followed, Servouze claimed the court proceedings unnecessarily delayed their right to take the materials. The court held that if Servouze did not take the materials after a certain period of time, these may be considered as abandoned. The court of appeal of Poitiers subsequently held against Servouze. The case went for appeal in cassation.

Held: No one may me deemed to simply have abandoned their ownership, certainly not automatically after a delay imposed by courts.

Judgment: Considering that the company Servouze also complains against the judgment for having ordered it to pay damages to the company Morin-Remaud and to the spouses D…, whereas, according to the argument, 'on the one hand, the summons of 15 April 1982 seeking to have a 'confirmation of the rights of the Company Servouze over the parcels of land (in dispute) … and the violation of the said rights by Etablissements Morin et Remaud'; that this summons, particularly, mentioned 'movements of materials of the Company Servouze and their covering by groundwork' and indicated 'that the extracted materials henceforth appeared unusable'; that in interpreting this summons as having no purpose other than to continue the exploitation and not to assert the rights of the Company Servouze over the stock of extracted materials, the Court of Appeal of Poitiers denatured the clear and precise terms thereof in disregard of the provisions of Article 4 of the *Nouveau Code de procédure civile*, and, on the other hand, the right to take part in proceedings only degenerates into abuse where it is exercised with the sole intention of causing harm and without appreciable benefit to its holder; that in recognising the rights of the Company Servouze over the materials already extracted that its action sought to safeguard, the Court of Appeal has not drawn the legal consequences of its own findings with regard to Article 1382 of the Civil Code; But considering that the Court of Appeal which has not denatured the summons and upheld the fault

[55] F Chabas, *Biens: Droit de Propriété et ses démembrements*, ed J Mazeaud et al, 8th edn, *Leçons de droit civil*, tome 2 (Paris, Montchrestien, 1994) 315–16.

[56] N 86-13500, JCP 1988.IV.23.

of the Company Servouze and that that company asserted an assigned right, has, in its hands, legally justified its decision; But on the second argument:

Having seen Article 545 of the Civil Code; Considering that no one can be forced to assign his property, except for reasons of public utility and providing there is a just indemnity paid beforehand; Considering that, after having imparted to the company Servouze a period of three months counting from service of this judgment to remove the extracted materials remaining on site, the judgment adds, that after that period the company will be considered as having abandoned ownership of the materials not removed;

That by ruling thus, without having found on the part of the owner company the manifestation of its will to abandon ownership of the materials, the Court of Appeal violated the aforementioned text; On these grounds, and without there being cause to rule on the third argument; quashes and cancels, but only in so far as it has said that the company Servouze should be considered as having abandoned ownership of the materials, the judgment rendered on 19 February 1986, between the parties, by the Court of Appeal of Poitiers; restores, accordingly, in this respect, the cause and the parties to the state in which they were before the said judgment and, in order that right be done, remits them before the Court of Appeal of Limoges, for this purpose designed by special deliberation conducted in Judge's Chambers.

Notes

(1) This case tells us two things. First of all, this case repeats implicitly that ownership cannot be lost through non-use in French law.[57] This was already dealt with in Chapter 7.[58]

(2) Secondly, we may interpret from this case that without the expressed intention (*la manifestation de sa volonté*) to give up ownership, the right of ownership cannot be abandoned. Contrary to loss of ownership through non-use, abandonment of ownership in French law is therefore possible.[59]

(ii) Effects of abandonment

Introductory Note

The moment an owner (successfully) abandons his right of ownership, from a property law point of view the object is no longer his problem.[60] Normally, one would assume that the right of ownership is lost, ie destroyed. However, in French law the Civil Code follows a different solution.

Code civil **9.34 (FR)**

Article 539 The things of persons who decease without heirs or whose inheritance is abandoned belong to the state.

Article 713 Things who do not have a master belong to the community on whose

[57] See Req 12 July 1905, DP 109.1.141, S 1907.1.273.

[58] See also Chapter 7.

[59] P Jourdain, G Marty, and P Raynaud, *Les Biens* (Paris, Dalloz, 1995) no 1585, 315–16.

[60] There might still be liability for the object, but the property right will be lost.

territory they are situated. However, the ownership is transfered *ex officio* to the State, if the community renounces to exercise its rights.

Article 714 There are objects which do not belong to anyone and the use of which is common to all.

The *lois de police* regulate how to enjoy them.

Cour de cassation civ 3e, 18 June 2003[61] **9.35 (FR)**

Directeur général des impôts v Association syndicale libre lotissement des Castors de l'Ermitage (l'ASL)

EFFECTS OF ABANDONMENT OF OWNERSHIP

Dissolving association

Abandonment of ownership of immovable objects leads to a transfer of that ownership to the French state.

Facts: In 1970 an association for the allotment of the Castors de l'Ermitage (ASL) was created for the management and maintenance of a piece of land. ASL acquired ownership of a piece of land bordering a green area. Eventually, ASL decided to dissolve itself and decided to abandon the parcel of land bordering the green area to the state. The director of taxes did not agree, and claimed ASL could own, but not so easily dispose of, land. What was left in the cassation procedure was the question whether ASL had indeed abandoned ownership.

Held: ASL has abandoned ownership by making a decision to that extent. Therefore the court of appeal has correctly applied Articles 539 and 713 of the Civil Code. Ownership has transferred to the State.

Judgment: failing acceptance of this voluntary disposition by its beneficiary, devolution of ownership of the piece of land in dispute was not realised and the members collectively remain the owners thereof; that by finding nevertheless that by application of Articles 539 and 713 of the Civil Code, the piece of land is vacant and ownerless and by virtue thereof devolves ipso iure to the State, the judges on the merits have made a correct application of the aforementioned texts;

But considering, that having found that there did not exist, in the statutes of ASL, any provision on the devolution of its goods in the case of dissolution and that it had, at the time of its dissolution, decided purely and simply to abandon the piece of land belonging to it, the court of appeal has rightly held that ownership of this ownerless good had devolved to the State by application of Articles 539 and 713 of the Civil Code;

Notes

(1) The effect of abandonment in French law is not the loss of a right of ownership in general, but a transfer of ownerhip to the French state. Objects that either become without an owner by operation of the law, eg in the case of succession without heirs, or objects that are intentionally abandoned, become owned by the state.

[61] Bull civ III, no 129, 115.

(2) The ownership does not necessarily also decide who is entitled to use the object. Article 714 Cciv provides a default answer.

(3) The case cited above shows an example of abandonment. By decision of the association the ownership is abandoned and will fall to the state. One question that may be asked is how the state becomes owner of the object in question. French law does not adhere to original acquisition in the case of abandonment, but accepts this as a transfer. Abandonment therefore leads to a derivative acquisition by the French state. The transfer in this case can likely be held to be a donation. The consent of the French state is therefore required.[62]

(4) Technically, abandonment of ownership in French law does not lead to a destruction of property rights, but to an acquisition by the state.

(iii) Special rules on abandonment

Introductory Note

Not only the right of ownership, but also other property rights can be abandoned in French law. Generally speaking the rules on abandonment follow the same rules as the abandonment of the right of ownership on the same object. However, the French Civil Code also provides some special rules.[63]

Code civil **9.36 (FR)**

Article 699 Even in the case where the owner of the land on which the right of servitude runs is compelled under the instrument of creation to make the works necessary for the use or preservation of a right of servitude at his own expense, he may always exempt himself from that burden by abandoning the servient land to the owner of the land that benefits from the existence of the right of servitude.

Article 2488 Prior charges and hypothecs are destroyed:

1° By extinguishment of the principal obligation except for the case provided for in Article 2422.

Note

These Articles offer examples of a special rule on abandonment from the Civil Code. The abandonment mentioned in these Articles is a unilateral act and therefore does not have to be accepted by the owner (of the dominant land in case of servitudes) to have effect.[64] The effect of a successful abandonment is the destruction of the property right.

[62] On this conclusion see P Malaurie and L Aynès, *Les Biens*, eds P Malaurie and L Aynès (2nd edn, Droit Civil; Paris, Defrénois, 2005) no 164, 51–52.

[63] *Ibid*, no 1128, 340.

[64] Req 11 May 1908, DP, 1908.I.365. *Ibid*, 340. A Breton, 'Théorie générale de la renonciation aux droits réels' [1928] *Revue trimestrielle de droit civil* (*RTD Civ*) 261–363, no 26, 294–95.

II.B.3.b German Law

Introductory Note

Abandonment of the right of ownership is also recognised in German law. It is known as *Dereliktion* in German. Generally a distinction in abandonment of ownership of movable and immovable objects is made.

(i) Abandonment of ownership of movable object

Bürgerliches Gesetzbuch **9.37 (DE)**

§959 A movable object becomes abandoned, when the owner, with the purpose of giving up the ownership, relinquishes possession of the object.

(ii) Abandonment of ownership of immovable objects

Introductory Note

Abandonment of ownership of immovable objects is more complicated in German law because of the system of registration. This system of registration is dealt with in Chapter 8. Generally stated, the German system is a positive system of registration, in which the register is considered to reflect the reality of ownership of land in Germany. Abandonment of ownership therefore has effects on the correctness of the land register.

Bürgerliches Gesetzbuch **9.38 (DE)**

§875 (1) The abandonment of a right in respect to a piece of land requires, in so far as the law does not provide otherwise, the declaration of the person holding the right that he abandons his right and the cancellation [*Löschung*] of the right in the land register. The declaration must be made to the land registration office or to the person for whose benefit it is made.
(2) Before the cancellation the person holding the right is only bound to his declaration if it has been made to the landed registration office or the person, for whose benefit it is made, has handed over an authorization of cancellation in accordance with the provisions of the Land Register Code.
§876 If a right in respect to a piece of land is burdened with the right of a third party, the abandonment of the right that burdens the land requires the permission of that third party. If the right that is to be abandoned belongs to the owner of another piece of land and that piece of land is burdened with a right of a third party, the permission of that third party is needed, unless the right is not affected by the abandonment. The permission must be declared to the land registration office or to the person for whose benefit the declaration is made; it cannot be withdrawn.

Note

These two paragraphs provide the general framework of rules on the abandonment of rights in respect to immovable objects.[65] It shows the involvement of the land register office (*Grundbuchambt*). Moreover, the position of third parties is explicitly dealt with.

Bürgerliches Gesetzbuch **9.39 (DE)**

§928 (1) The ownership of a piece of land may be abandoned by a declaration of abandonment made by the owner to the land registration office and by registration of the abandonment in the Land Register.
(2) The right to claim the abandoned piece of land is for the Tax Office of the Land in which the piece of land is situated. The Tax Office acquires the ownership by registration as owner in the Land Register.

Notes

(1) §928 BGB offers a specific rule on the abandonment of the right of ownership in respect to land. The rule in this article follows the general regime offered by §875 BGB.[66]

(2) The second section of §928 BGB shows that, as in French law, the German state has an interest in land ownership of which has been abandoned. However, contrary to the automatic rule in French law, the German state will acquire the right of ownership when the state decides to. Abandonment does not destroy the right of ownership of immovable objects, and property rights created on it remain in existence. The German state will therefore acquire ownership through derivative acquisition.[67]

(3) The right of the German state to acquire the ownership (*Aneignung*) does not have to be exercised by the state and can also be assigned to other persons.[68] There is discussion on the exact requirements for the assignment. A decision of the Reichsgericht states that the right could be assigned by agreement (*Abtretung*).[69] However, others argue that the requirements for the transfer of ownership of an immovable object should be followed.[70] A person other than with permission of the state can therefore not acquire the right of ownership of an abandoned immovable object in German law.[71]

[65] F Baur, JF Baur, and R Stürner, *Sachenrecht*, 17th edn (München, CH Beck'sche Verlagsbuchhandlung, 1999) 37.

[66] J Wilhelm, *Sachenrecht*, 2nd edn (Berlin and New York, Walter de Gruyter, 2002) 297–98.

[67] KH Schwab and H Prütting, *Sachenrecht. Ein Studienbuch*, 31st edn, Juridische Kurz-Lehrbücher (München, Verlag CH Beck, 2003) 143.

[68] Wilhelm, above n 66, 298.

[69] RGZ 82, 74. See *ibid*, 298.

[70] §925 BGB. *Ibid*, 298.

[71] HP Westermann, K-H Gursky, D Eickmann, *Sachenrecht. Ein Lehrbuch* (Heidelberg, CF Müller Verlag, 1998) 667.

(iii) Abandonment of property rights

Bürgerliches Gesetzbuch **9.40 (DE)**

§1064 To end a right of usufruct in relation to a movable object by way of legal act, a declaration of the usufructuary to the owner or the creator that he gives up the usufruct, suffices.

§1255 (1) For the abandonment by legal transaction of a right of pledge, a declaration by the creditor of the pledge to the pledgor or to the owner that he abandons his right, suffices.

(2) If the right of pledge is burdened with a right of a third party, the permission of that third party is required. The permission is to be declared to the person, for whose benefit it is made; it cannot be withdrawn.

§1183 To end a right of hypothec by way of a legal act, permission of the owner is required. The permission is to be declared before the Land register office or before the creditor; it is irrevocable.

Notes

(1) These paragraphs offer specific rules on the abandonment of property rights other than the right of ownership. These paragraphs offer procedures for the abandonment of property rights different from the normal procedure for abandonment of rights. Because there is always a relation between the holder of property right and the holder of right of ownership, from which the property right is derived, the notification of abandonment is generally aimed at the owner. Moreover, in some cases the permission of the owner is required for the abandonment to have effect.

(2) If the effect of abandonment of the property right is taken into account, the requirement of permission of the owner can be better understood. The return of the property right to the owner in German law has special effects. Through operation of §889 BGB, the property right will not be destroyed through mixing with the right of ownership. Instead an owner-property right is created. Permission of the owner for abandonment of the property right will destroy the right and will not make the right return to the owner as an owner-right.[72]

II.B.3.c Dutch law

Introductory Note

Dutch law also recognises the possibility to abandon property rights. A distinction should be made between the abandonment of the right of ownership and the abandonment of limited property rights.

[72] J von Staudinger and K-H Gursky, *J von Staudingers Kommentar zum Bürgerlichen Gesetzbuch mit Einfürungsgesetz und Nebengesetzen, Buch 3 Sachenrecht §§883–902* (Berlin, Sellier de Gruyter, 2002) 311–14.

(i) Abandonment of ownership of movable objects

Burgerlijk Wetboek **9.41 (NL)**

Article 5:18 The ownership of a movable object is lost, when the owner gives up possession with the purpose of ridding himself of the ownership.

Parliamentary History Book 5, 116 **9.42 (NL)**

M.v.A. II In the provisional report it is stated that the formulation 'possession renounces with the aim of divesting itself from ownership' is indeed very detailed. Is it, as is asked, not sufficient that the owner consciously renounce possession? The conscious renunciation of possession can only be effected by the owner, if he thereby also has the aim of renouncing ownership. It is desirable to have this expressed in the provision.

Note

In order to abandon ownership of movable objects in Dutch law it is not sufficient to leave the object somewhere, but the owner should also have the intention to give up his right of ownership.

(ii) Abandonment of Ownership of immovable objects

Burgerlijk Wetboek **9.43 (NL)**

Article 5:24 Immovable objects that do not have any other owner belong to the State.

Hoge Raad, 11 March 1966[73] **9.44 (NL)**

Nederlandse Antillen v Exploitatie Maatschappij

NO ABANDONMENT OF OWNERSHIP OF IMMOVABLE OBJECTS

The salt pond

Intention of the owner is required to abandon the right of ownership.

Facts: By Royal Decree of 21 June 1858 Perrinon received a concession to use a parcel of land on the Island of St Maarten for the duration of 80 years. Perrinon brought his rights into a company named Maatschappij tot Zoutwinning. On 17 May 1868, the Maatschappij tot Zoutwinning granted a right to use all its rights and concessions to the Exploitatie Maatschappij. This last company extracted salt from the parcel of land. In 1898 the Exploitatie Maatschappij acquired ownership of the parcel of land.

In 1940 the shareholders of the Exploitatie Maatschappij decided to liquidate the company. On 17 November 1945 the company registered the completion of the liquidation procedure and stated that the company had ceased to exist, but some accounting documents were not registered.

In 1947 the Dutch Antilles, claimant in this case, created a right of *emphyteusis* on behalf of Richardson. The Dutch Antilles claim to be owner of the parcel of land. The defendant, the Expoitatie Maatschappij, claimed it still owned the parcel of land. When the case came before the Dutch Supreme

[73] NJ 1966, 330.

Court, which is the highest competent court for the Dutch Antilles, the claimant argued the defendant had, with the liquidation, abandoned its right of ownership of the parcel of land.

Held: In order to abandon the right of ownership a specific intention to do so is required. Abandonment of ownership in respect to immovable objects is not possible in Dutch law.

Judgment: Considering that the sixth argument is likewise proposed in vain, since the, on this point applicable, BW of the Dutch Antilles in Art 569—just as the Dutch BW in Art 600—does state a rule, which creates the possibility, that a possessor abandon his possession, which with regard to immovable property simultaneously can have the consequence of loss of ownership, but, except for certain special cases, not arising in this proceeding, no provision, by virtue of which an owner of immovable property can effect abandonment of his right of ownership over that property;

That without such provision—which would then have to govern how the abandonment can be effected and how this can be recorded in the public registers—the possibility thereof cannot be accepted;

Asser, Mijnsen, Van Dam and Van Velten, Property Law 3-II, 129 **9.45 (NL)**

Absolute loss of ownership of immovable property at first sight appears not to be possible. Land always belongs to someone. Nor can one abandon ownership of a piece of land. The land does not become lost, not even when there is a question of flooding (article 5:29). The owner of the bed of the water acquires ownership of the flooded land. Thus there is also in this case said to be relative loss of ownership. Nonetheless, it is conceivable that an immovable property is destroyed, as a result of which ownership also becomes lost. One might think of a building that is situated on a piece of land over which building rights are conferred in favour of the owner of the building. This building is immovable and can be destroyed, for example by fire. The building rights continue in existence. Upon the erection of a new building, this will again belong to the party in whose favour the building rights were conferred [*opstaller*]. ...

Relative loss of ownership goes hand in hand with acquisition of ownership by another. In this regard, there must in the first place be considered a case of transfer, i.e. a transfer of ownership effected by delivery.

Notes

(1) Although the case provides the rule under the old Dutch Civil Code, it is still considered good law in the new Civil Code.[74] The Dutch Supreme Court has, more recently, followed the 1966 decision.[75]

(2) Abandonment of ownership of immovable objects in Dutch law has relative effect. By using the term ‘relative effect’, Dutch doctrine wants to express that abandonment of ownership of immovable objects does not lead to a destruction of the right of ownership. There is always another owner ready to acquire the right of ownership, whether this is another person or the Dutch state.

[74] C Asser et al, *Goederenrecht 3—II Zakelijke Rechten*, 14th edn, Mr C Asser’s Handleiding Tot De Beoefening Van Het Nederlands Burgerlijk Recht (Deventer, Kluwer, 2002) no 111, 130.

[75] HR 20 June 1997, (1999) NJ 301.

(iii) Abandonment of property rights other than ownership

Burgerlijk Wetboek **9.46 (NL)**

Article 3:82(2)(c) Limited property right are destroyed by:...
c Abandonment...

Article 3:98 Unless the law provides otherwise, everything that this Division provides on the transfer of things, is applicable mutatis mutandis to the creation, the assignment and the abandonment of a property right on such a thing

Article 3:224 If a usufructuary wishes to abandon his right at his own cost, due to the burdens and duties following from the right of usufruct, the person holding the principal entitlement to the thing is obliged to cooperate with this.**Article 5:82.** (1) If the owner of the dominant land wishes to abandon his right at his own costs, due to the burdens and obligations arising from the right of servitude, the owner of the servient land is obliged to cooperate with this.
(2) The deed of creation may provide otherwise for the duration of the first twenty years.

Note

Abandonment of property rights in Dutch law is therefore possible, but only in the same way as the property right on the same object was created. Abandonment of property rights therefore, unlike in French and German law, in principle requires the agreement by the owner.[76] In the proposal for Article 3:98 BW a second section was proposed in which abandonment of rights would be a unilateral act. However, the rules on termination, that can be made unilaterally, were considered sufficient.[77]

II.B.4 MERGER OF RIGHTS

(a) Property rights can be destroyed when they fall into the same hands as the property right from which they are derived. Usually this occurs when a limited property right and the right of ownership on the same object fall into the same hands. With this *concurrence* of ownership and property right, the rights and powers contained in the property right will mix with the rights and powers contained in the right of ownership, and it will be impossible to tell which rights and powers belong to the limited property rights anymore. Therefore, the property right will be considered to be destroyed.

(b) The way in which property rights are destroyed is connected to the way in which property rights are created. Therefore, in order to get a full overview of this subject, it should be looked at in relation to chapter seven dealing with creation of property rights.

[76] C Asser, FHJ Mijnssen, and P De Haan, *Goederenrecht 3—I Algemeen Goederenrecht*, ed FHJ Mijnssen and P De Haan, 14th edn, Mr C. Asser's Handleiding tot de beoefening van het Nederlands Burgerlijk Recht (Deventer, WEJ Tjeenk Willink, 2001) 11–13.

[77] CJ Van Zeben and JW Du Pon, *Parliamentaire Geschiedenis, Boek 5—Zakelijke Rechten*, ed CJ Van Zeben and JW Du Pon, Parlementaire Geschiedenis Van Het Nieuwe Burgerlijk Wetboek (Deventer, Kluwer, 1981) 306.

II.B.4.a French law

The concurrence of ownership and the limited property right that was created from that right of ownership in the same hands is known as *consolidation* in French law. The destruction of property rights follows directly from the method of creation of property rights in French law. In French law a property rights is a *démembrement* or subtraction from the right of ownership. When property right and ownership fall into the same hands, the part of the right of ownership that was temporarily subtracted mixes with the powers of the right of ownership that becomes complete again.

The issue of *consolidation* is hardly dealt with by the French Cour de Cassation. Instead, the French Civil Code provides provisions per property right dealing with the effects of concurrence of ownership and property rights.

(i) Merger of rights in French law

Code civil **9.47 (FR)**

Article 617 A usufruct is destroyed:
By the consolidation or vesting in the same person of the two capacities of usufructuary and of owner;

Article 705 A right of servitude is destroyed when the ownership of the servient land, and the ownership of the dominant land are united in the same hands.

Notes

(1) These two Articles from the French Civil Code offer the general regime for the destruction of property rights through merger of a limited property right with the right of ownership. The rule in Article 617 Cciv has been a particular cause for debate.[78]

(2) Generally it is held that when the original property right and the right of ownership fall into the same hands, the property right is destroyed through merger with the right of ownership. However, when the property right has been assigned to another person, the merger is not automatic. For the reasoning behind this deviation see the case below.

(ii) Exceptions to destruction of property rights through merger

Introductory Note

When the owner acquires a property right, or the holder of a property right himself acquires the right of ownership, destruction of the right might not be in order.[79] The problem with these types of acquisition is that the full set of powers in their original state must be reunited. When, for example, a right to a third party has been

[78] See Th Vialatte, 'L'effet extinctif de la réunion sur une même tête de qualités contraires et ses limites' [1978] *Revue trimestrielle de droit civil* (*RTD Civ*) 568–96, 568 *et seq*; B Losfeld, 'La consolidation. Réflexions sur un mode particulier d'extinction de l'usufruit' [2007] *Revue trimestrielle de droit civil* (*RTD Civ*) 1, 1 *et seq*.

[79] Losfeld, above n 78, no 41. See also B Akkermans, 'Concurrence of Ownership and Limited Property Rights' (2010) 18 *European Review of Private Law* 259.

granted on the same object in between, or when there is another holder of a property right on the same object, and this property right was created later than the property right that concurs with the right of ownership, destruction cannot be in order.

Cour de cassation civ 3e, 26 January 1972[80] **9.48 (FR)**
Société Méditeranneene de Courtage v Y and Z

CONCURRENCE OF OWNERSHIP AND PROPERTY RIGTHS

Lease by a usufructuary

A limited property right on which another right is created will not automatically be destroyed by concurrence of the property right and ownership into the same hands.

Facts: On 1 January 1962 widow X granted a lease to Y and Z of an immovable object on which she was holder of a right of usufruct. On 2 February 1968 the agreement was replaced with a new lease. On 2 May 1969 the Société Mediterranéene de Courtage acquired the right of ownership and the right of usufruct of the immovable object. The Société attempted to terminate the lease of 2 February 1968 on the ground that the lessor/usufructuary had not asked for permission of the owner for the lease, as is required by Article 595 Cciv. The lessees did not agree. During this stage of the proceedings the Cour de cassation was asked to consider whether the Court of Appeal had been right in granting the argument of the Société that the right of usufruct had been destroyed now that usufruct and ownership had fallen into the same hands.

Held: The right of usufruct was not destroyed by the acquisition of this right and the right of ownership into the same hands. The assignee of the right of usufruct is not the same has the holder of the right of usufruct himself. The right of lease is therefore not automatically void.

Judgment: But on the third branch of the same argument having seen Article 617 of the Civil Code;

Considering that by virtue of this text, the destruction of the usufruct by consolidation supposes the coming-together in the same hands of the two statuses of usufructuary and owner;

That in this regard, the assignee of the usufruct could not be assimilated to the usufructuary;

Considering that the judgment appealed against, to admit the action to cancel the lease raised by Societé Méditerranéenne de Courtage, holds that the assignment to the said société, by two separate acts, of the remainder interestes and the usufruct, by the two respective right-holders, destroyed the usufruct by consolidation;

That in ruling thus, wheras the conditions for destruction of the usufruct were not fulfilled and that, from the fact of the continued existence of this latter, the assignee of the usufruct was bound under guarantee vis-à-vis the tenant, the court of appeal violated the aforementioned text;

For these reasons and without there being need to rule on the second argument;

Quashes and cancels the judgment rendered between the parties on 17 March 1970, by the Court of Appeal of Montpellier;

[80] Bull civ III, no 69. D 1975, 22, n Penneau; JCP G 1972, II, 17104, n Goubeaux; [1972] *Revue trimestrielle de droit civil* (*RTD Civ*) 1972, 619, obs Bredin.

Thérèse Vialatte, The extinctive effect of the consolidation of contradictory qualities and its limits[81] **9.49 (NL)**

3.—If the right in question is not a personal right, but a property right, the effect produced by the coming-together in the same hands of contrary statuses is named 'consolidation', this being considered by many writers as analogous in relation to property rights to that which is commingling for personal rights. ...

It is interesting to observe that the only examples of survival of the right, found in the case law, concern either the right of lease or the mortgage, and that, although the solutions arrived at, in relation to the lease, can be extended to the situations where the extinguished right might be a property right (usufruct or servitude), they do not seem to have any raison d'être for a personal right. ....

12.—The solution, thus arrived at in relation to the lease, could apply, also, to the case of an immovable object sold by the bare owner to the usufructuary, or by the owner of the servient tenement to the owner of the dominant tenement.

The right of use and of enjoyment of the usufructuary impresses, 'in the common view', a depreciation on the immovable object over which it relates. Similarly, the existence of a servitude is a cause for a loss of value of the servient tenement since it imposes on the owner a restriction of his rights of ownership. Application of the objective concept of contractual loss [*lésion*], disregarding the personality of the acquirer, would therefore lead to valuing the immovable object taking account of the extinguished right, this extinction only being to the personality of the acquirer who has allowed the coming-together in one set of hands of contrary statuses.

Notes

(1) Although this case concerns a right of lease granted by the holder of a right of usufruct, and lease in French law is a personal right, the decision in this case is considered to be applicable to property rights in general. The case first of all establishes the rule that when a property right is in the hands of a third party a right will not automatically be destroyed through a merger with the right of ownership. The party in question was not the original usufructuary, but an assignee of the original usufructuary. In such a case, the court emphasises, there is no automatic operation of Article 617 Cciv.

(2) Secondly, when rights have been granted to third parties, the *consolidation*, ie the destruction of property rights through merger with the right of ownership, also cannot operate automatically. The reasoning behind this is best understood when the position of third parties that also have a right on the same object is taken into consideration. It is against this background that this excerpt of Vialatte should be understood.

(3) The solution of the Cour de cassation seems complicated. Instead, the court could perhaps have reasoned that rights on the same object were in the hands of a third party and that therefore the property right, in this case the right of usufruct, was not destroyed.

[81] Vialatte, above n 78, 574.

II.B.4.b German law

Introductory Notes

(a) The concurrence of property rights and the right of ownership in German law is known as *Konsolidation*. Generally, like in French law, a property right will be destroyed when it falls into the same hands as the right of ownership.

(b) However, the effects of concurrence of ownership and property rights will not always be fair to third parties that hold a right themselves on the limited property right that is destroyed. For example, a third party may hold a right of hypothec on a piece of land on which a right of *emphyteusis* was created earlier, and we assume the hypothec rests on the right of *emphyteusis*. When the holder of the right of *emphyteusis* acquires the right of ownership or vice versa, the right of hypothec, which was created on the right of *emphyteusis*, will be destroyed. To circumvent this undesirable effect, the German Civil Code provides a specific rule in respect to property rights on land.

(c) This paragraph will first deal with *Konsolidation* in German law and after that deal with the general exception for property rights on land offered by the German Civil Code.

(i) Merger of rights in German law

Bürgerliches Gesetzbuch **9.50 (DE)**

§1063 (1) The usufructuary [*Nießbraucher*] is entitled to possession of the object.

(2) In the exercise of his right of usufruct he must maintain the economic purpose of the object and must act according to the ordinary rules of business.

§1253 (1) The right of pledge ceases to exist if the creditor of the pledge returns the object to the pledgor or to the owner. A stipulation that the right of pledge will continue to exist is ineffective.

(2) If the object under pledge is in possession of the pledgor or of the owner, it is presumed that the object was returned to him by the creditor of the pledge. The presumption also applies, if the object under pledge is in possession of a third party who demanded possession of the object from the pledgor or the owner after the creation of the right of pledge.

§1256 (1) The right of pledge ceases to exist when it falls together with the right of ownership into the same hands. The right does not cease to exist as long as the claim, for which the right of pledge exists, is burdened with a right of a third party.

(2) The right of pledge is considered not to have ceased to exist, in so far as the owner has a legal interest in the continuation of the right.

(ii) Exceptions to destruction of property rights through merger

Bürgerliches Gesetzbuch **9.51 (DE)**

§889 A right on another's piece of land does not fall away when the owner of the land acquires the right or if the holder of the right receives the ownership of the same land.[82]

Explanations to the draft of a Civil Code for the German Nation, Book III §836 (now §889)[83] **9.52 (DE)**

How the right recognised in §836 [now §889, BGB] on an owner's object can be legally constructed, is not dealt with by the law. The construction is a task for legal science. Only this can be stated, that the often heard objection against the owner-hypothec, the owner cannot have a specific property right on the same object as his ownership, because the ownership already contains the advantages the specific property right provides, is not correct. Until now, the discussion results in the situation, that the owner, when the piece of land is transferred, can exercise his specific property right on the same piece of land and, when he remains to have ownership, dispose over it for the benefit of a third party, both advantages, the actual value of which should not be argued.

Notes

(1) As a result of the operation of §889 BGB, property rights that were created on an immovable object will not be destroyed when they fall into the same hands as the right of ownership. Moreover, in the system of the BGB it is even possible for an owner to create a property right on the object over which he also has ownership. The drafters of the BGB specifically recognised this possibility for a holder of a right of *Grundschuld* in §1196 BGB. The result is known as a *Eigentümergrundschuld* or owners-*Grundschuld.*

(2) How it is exactly possible that a property right is not destroyed through merger with the right of ownership in a *Konsolidation* remains unclear. The German legislator did not provide an answer.[84]

II.B.4.c Dutch Law

Introductory Notes

(a) Article 3:81(2) BW as quoted at the beginning of this chapter specifically states that property rights are destroyed through merger with the right of ownership.

(b) Also in Dutch law the position of third parties in respect to the destruction

[82] §889 BGB, 'Ein Recht an einem fremden Grundstück erlischt nicht dadurch, dass der Eigentümer des Grundstücks das Recht oder der Berechtigte das Eigentum an dem Grundstück erwirbt.'

[83] *Motive zu dem Entwurfe eines bürgerlichen Gesetzbuches für das Deutsche Reich—Sachenrecht*, III (Berlin, Verlag von J Guttentag, 1888) 205.

[84] See, for more information on the workings of §889 BGB, von Staudinger and Gursky, above n 72, 314. See, in English, B Akkermans, 'Concurrence of Ownership and Limited Property Rights' [2010] *European Review of Private Law* 259 *et seq.*

of property rights has been considered. However, the result of the discussion during the draft of the Dutch Civil Code is different from German law.

Burgerlijk Wetboek **9.53 (NL)**

Article 3:81(3) Renunciation and mixing of property rights do not have negative effect against those who have a property right on the property right that ceases to exist. Nor does mixing of property rights have positive effect on those who had a property right on the burdened object and were bound by the right that ceases to exist.

Parliamentary History, Book 3[85] **9.54 (NL)**

The rationale of the rule that a limited right is destroyed by merger, is that an obfuscation of the legal situation of things that is undesirable for the case law date would be the consequence, if after being merged with the principal right in one set of hands a limited right were legally to continue in existence without sufficient reason. Misunderstanding could then easily arise in respect to—for example, in the case of later transfer—what exactly was transferred. However, this ratio does not demand that the destruction of a limited right by merger should also have to extend to the disadvantage of limited rights established on that limited right; an exception that was already made in the draft in paragraph 3. But merger would work to the disadvantage of other limited rights also created on that object. This would mean immense, unjustified disadvantage to those in whose hands the merger occurs. Therefore, a second sentence is added to paragraph 3 in the amended draft, which extends that which is said in that paragraph with regard to merger with the rule that merger also does not work in favour of them whose limited right was created over the encumbered property after the right being destroyed. Those who acquire a limited right over the object prior to the establishment of the destroyed right, are not hereby named, because they also did not require to honour this right before the merger.

The third paragraph therefore maintains vis-à-vis the limited rights that at the moment of the merger rest on the right being destroyed by the merger or on the object thereby burdened, a legal situation as though the right being destroyed by merger were to have remained in existence. It also follows herefrom that the terms of this paragraph do not detract from the working at any time of another reason for destruction of that right, for instance the elapse of the time for which that right was created. Even if on the basis of Article 3.4.2.11 the principal entitled party will be able to abandon the prerogatives that he continues to draw even after the merger from the right being destroyed by merger on the basis of the second sentence of paragraph 3 …

From the new second sentence of the present paragraph 3, it now follows both that the mortgagee of, eg, a property burdened with a servitude will have to honour this servitude in the case of execution at a point in time after the dominant and servient tenement are merged in one hand, and that the usufructs of such a prop-

[85] CJ Van Zeben and JW Du Pon, *Boek 5—Zakelijke Rechten*, Parlementaire Geschiedenis Van Het Nieuwe Burgerlijk Wetboek (Deventer: Kluwer, 1981), p 310–311.

erty will after such merger have to continue to tolerate the servitude de facto being exercised by the owner of the two tenements. For the inverse case that the mortgage or the usufruct rests on the dominant tenement, one might compare the fourth paragraph of the explanation of Meijers on p 210(a). The import of the first sentence of paragraph 3 implies that it is also applicable in cases where the right being destroyed by abandonment or merger is a dependent right, linked to the right on which the limited right of another rests. The usufructuary of the dominant tenement can therefore continue to exercise the servitude that existed before the dominant and servient tenement came together in one hand. Thus, the pledgee of a claim secured by a mortgage can also exercise the mortgage right over the mortgaged property, after this has become property of his debtor (the creditor under the claim pledged in his favour) and thus the mortgage has been destroyed by merger with the property in his hand. And the situation is similar, where his debtor (the creditor under the claim pledged in his favour) has abandoned the mortgage

Notes

(1) The examples offered by the excerpt from the Dutch parliamentary history show that the exception of Article 3:81(3) BW was well considered.

(2) Note the similarities in approach to the problem in respect to third parties with the German discussion on *Konsolidation*. Remarkably, the outcome, especially the effect, is different from the German solution.

II.B.5 TERMINATION OF RIGHTS

Introductory Notes

(a) When property rights are created, sometimes arrangements are made in respect to when and how that property right will cease to exist. As a part of this agreement the property right may come to an end automatically, or it can be terminated by an act of the parties themselves.

(b) There is a strong link between termination and abandonment of property rights. In general abandonment of limited property rights, so not the right of ownership, requires permission by the owner. Termination, on the other hand, is generally a unilateral act for which no permission from the other party is required.

(c) Not all legal systems recognise the possibility to terminate a property right. Especially when extensive rules on abandonment of property rights exist. The primary example of such a legal system is German law, where the rules on abandonment of rights fulfil the functions termination of rights fulfil in other legal systems.

II.B.5.a French law

Code civil **9.55 (FR)**

Article 617 A usufruct is destroyed:
By the expiry of the time for which it was granted;

Article 2392 The rights of a creditor by way of antichresis are extinguished in particular: ... 2° Through anticipated restoration of the immovable to his owner.

Article 2488 Prior charges and mortgages are destroyed:

... 5° By the termination allowed by Article 2423, last paragraph and as far as provided for by this provision.

Article 2423 ... Where it [a hypothec] is granted for security of one or several future debts and for an an undetermined duration, the holder of the right of hypothec may at any time terminate the right subject to him giving three months' notice. Once terminated, the right still exists for security of pre-existing claims.

Notes

(1) Termination as a term is very broad. It can deal with a situation in which the contract creating the property right stipulates when the right is destroyed or the destruction can follow from operation of the law. Here the term expiry might be better. Secondly, termination can also occur when one of the parties, during the time the property right exists, decides to terminate the property right. It is this specific act for which the word termination should be used.

(2) These Articles show that generally French law allows the destruction of property rights through termination. The provisions on termination differ from the provisions on abandonment in the requirement of a period of notice for the termination.

II.B.5.b German Law

Termination of property rights in German law is not recognised. Instead, German law uses the rules on abandonment of property rights. For abandonment, see Section III.B.3. in this chapter.

II.B.5.c Dutch law

Burgerlijk Wetboek **9.56 (NL)**

Article 3:81 ... (2) Limited property right are destroyed by:

(d) renunciation [opzegging], if the right thereto has been granted by law or has been granted upon the creation of the right to the holder of the principal right, to the holder of the limited property right, or to both persons;

Article 5:78 A court may, on the request of the owner of the servient land modify or terminate a right of servitude:

(a) on the basis of unforeseen circumstances, which are of such a nature that following the requirements of reasonablness and fairness unaltered continuation of the right of servitude cannot be expected of the owner of the servient land;

(b) if at least twenty years after the creation of the right of servitude have passed and the unaltered continuation of the right of servitude is contrary to the general interest.

Article 5:79 A court may, on the request of the owner of the servient land, dissolve a right of servitude, if the exercise of that right has become impossible or the owner of the dominant land no longer has a reasonable interest in the exercise of the right, and it cannot be assumed that the possibility to exercise the right or the reasonable interest will return with that.

Article 5:87 (1) A right of *emphyteusis* can be terminated by the *emphyteuticarius*, unless the deed of creation provides otherwise.

(2) A right of *emphyteusis* can be terminated by the owner, if the *emphyteuticarius* is in default of payment of the canon for two consecutive years or fails to a serious extent in the performance of his obligations. The termination shall, under the penalty of nullity, be notified to those who are registered as holder of a property right or as seizor in the public registers within eight days. After the end of the right of *emphyteusis*, the owner is obliged to compensate the *emphyteuticarius* for the value that the *emphytheusis* has at that time, set-off with the costs he may claim from the *emphyteuticarius* arising out of the right of emphyteusis.

(3) A stipulation that deviates from the previous paragraph to the disadvantage of the *emphyteuticarius*, is void. In the deed of creation, the owner may be granted the right to terminate, except on the basis of a deficiency in the performance of his obligations by *emphyteuticarius*.

Article 5:97 (1) If twenty five years have passed since the creation of the right of *emphyteusis*, a court, on the request of the owner or the *emphyteuticarius*, may modify or terminate the right on the basis of changed circumstances, which are of such a nature that according to the requirements of reasonableness and fairness the unaltered continuation of the deed of creation can no longer be expected of the owner or the *emphyteuticarius*.

(2) A court may allow the request, subject to conditions determined by it.

(3) If a limited property right is created on the right of *emphyteusis* or the object, the request can only be allowed, if the holder of the limited property right is called to the procedure and the standard of paragraph 1 is also fulfilled in respect to him.

Notes

(1) Dutch law too explicitly allows termination of property rights, not only through a general provision but also specifically per property right.

(2) In Dutch law there is a relation between abandonment of property rights and termination. As we have seen above, abandonment of limited property rights in Dutch law generally requires consent of the owner. However, termination of a property right is, when termination is allowed, a unilateral act. In exchange for the unilateral character of the declaration a period of notice must be given, whereas abandonment can take effect immediately.[86]

II.B.6 EXTINCTIVE PRESCRIPTION

Introductory Notes

(a) When an object or a property right has not been used for a longer period of time one could ask the question whether the entitlement to that object or property right should still belong with the holder of the right. Perhaps someone else has been using the object in a way usually a right-holder would do. In Chapter 7,

[86] C Asser et al, *Goederenrecht 3—I Algemeen Goederenrecht*, 15th edn, Mr C. Asser's handleiding tot de beoefening van het Nederlands burgerlijk recht (Deventer, Kluwer, 2006) no 13–16.

Creation, we have seen that a property right can be acquired through the lapse of time under the heading acquisitive prescription.

(b) However, where a person acquires a right to an object through prescription, that person acquires a new property right. There is no transfer between the old and the new holder of a right. The person that held a right to that same object loses his right. There is, in other words, a destruction of the property right as well as the creation of a new right. Article 2219 of the French Civil Code states to this effect 'prescription is a way of acquiring or discharging oneself at the end of a certain amount of time, subject to conditions determined by law'.

(c) This section will focus on the ways in which a property right can be destroyed through lapse of time, known as extinctive prescription. There are two aspects that need to be highlighted. First, the property right itself can be destroyed through prescription. Secondly, sometimes the nature of the subject-matter of a right is so that this subject-matter can also be destroyed through prescription. This is so when the subject matter of a property right is, for example, a claim. In that case, as we have seen above in this chapter, the property right on that object may also be destroyed.

II.B.6.a French law

Since the introduction of the French Civil Code, the law on prescription has not been substantially altered. The French Civil Code offers specific rules for the prescription of certain property rights. Compared to the other prescription regimes offered in other legal systems, these French provisions are exceptional.

The rules on prescription in French law can be divided into two categories. First, there are rules on the prescription of claims protecting property rights. In respect to property rights, these claims are known as property claims. Secondly, property rights can be lost through the non-user of the right. After a certain period of non-user, the right-holder may lose his right.

(i) General rules on prescription

Code civil **9.57 (FR)**

Article 2262 All actions, real or personal, prescribe after thrity years, without he who claims the prescription is obliged to report a title or who can be opposed with an exception following from bad faith.

Article 2277 After five years, the following actions of payment prescribe:

Salaries;

Payments of pensions or life rents or alimoney payments;

Rents, farm rents and rental charges;

Interests or money lent, and generally all that is payable anually or at shorter periodic terms.

Actions to recover rent farm rent and rental charges also prescribe after five years.

Notes

These two Articles illustrate the simplicity of the basic rules on French prescription. In general all claims protecting rights prescribe after 30 years. In respect to property rights, proprietary claims fall under the general rules of Article 2262 Cciv.

Secondly, Article 2277 Cciv sets the prescription period of monetary claims at five years. Often, monetary claims are the subject-matter of property security rights. When, through prescription, the monetary claim is destroyed, the property right created on this claim is also destroyed.

(ii) Start of the prescription period

Code civil **9.58 (FR)**

Article 2260 Prescription is counted in days, not in hours.

Article 2261 It is acquired when the last day of the term is completed.

Note

As a general aspect of prescription, the time period for prescription is calculated in days. Therefore, usually the exact time the prescription starts to run is irrelevant.

(iii) Special rules

Introductory Note

Apart from these general rules on prescription, French law offers several special provisions dealing with prescription in specific cases.

Article 2 Declaration of the Rights of Man and of the Citizen 1789 **9.59 (FR)**

The aim of every political association is the conservation of natureal and imprescribable rights of man. These are libtery, ownership, certainty and the restistance to oppression.

Cour de Cassation Req 12 July 1905[87] **9.60 (FR)**

Le Cohu v Morvan

PRESCRIPTION OF OWNERSHIP AND REVINDICATION

The farmlands

The right of ownership cannot be lost through non-use, nor can the action of revindication be lost through prescription.

Facts: As a result of a judgment of 25 January 1854 two tenant farms were divided. The farm called Le Cohu-Morvan was allocated to the parties named Morvan; the farm called Le Cohu-Bodergat was allocated to the parties named Le Cohu. Due to the complicated factual situation of several parcels of

[87] DP 1907.I.141 obs Le Cons Pothier, S 1907.1.273, n de Wael.

land around the farms and to enable the use of these lands for farming, some of these lands were, by agreement between the farmers, allocated to the parties named Morvan.

From 1858 until 1894 the farmer of the lands that belonged to the farm Le Cohu-Bodergat was a person from the side of Morvan. This person farmed on the parts of the land allocated to the Morvan side by agreement. In order to restore this complicated situation Mr Morvan attempted to revindicate the land allocated to him by the agreement. Mrs Le Cohu refused the revindication and claimed that the land had been in possession of the Le Cohu side so long that the action for revindication had prescribed under Article 2262 Cciv.

Held: The right of ownership cannot be destroyed through the non-user of the right, nor can it be lost through prescription. The rule of Article 2262 Cciv therefore does not include the action of revindication.

Judgment: Considering that, despite the general nature of the terms of Art 2262, Cciv, which decides all actions, both real and personal, prescribe after thirty years, this text does not apply to the action for revindication raised by an owner dispossessed of his immovable property; that, since ownership does not become lost by non-use, the action for revindication which protects and sanctions this right can be exercised for as long as the defender does not prove that he has himself become the owner of the revindicated immovable object as a result of contrary possession, bringing together all the characters required for acquisitive prescription; from which it follows that, after having recognised that the possession opposed by the claimant in cassation was tainted with the fact the property was held subject to the right of another (*précarité*), the court of Rennes, in refusing to hold as prescribed the action for revindication founded on a title dating back more than thirty years, far from violating and falsely interpreting Arts 2241 and 2262, Cciv referred to in the argument, has, on the contrary, made correct application thereof;—rejects ...

Note

This case firmly established the general rule in French law that the right of ownership cannot be lost through extinctive prescription. It still applies today.

Commercial Code **9.61 (FR)**

Article L110-4 I. Obligations created in the trade between commercial parties and non-commercial parties prescribe after ten years if they are not subject to special rules on prescription that are more shortly.

II. All actions for payment prescribe :

1 For food for sailors on the order of a captain, or after a delivery ;

2 For the delivery of materials and other necessary objects for constructions, equipment and navigational equipment, one year after the deliveries;

3 For works made, one year after the works were made.

III. Actions of payment of salaries of officers, sailors and other members of a crew prescribe after five years in conformity with Article 2277 of the Civil Code.

Note

Some transactions are of such a special nature that the French legislature has opted to make special rules governing these relations. Among these are purely commercial relations, which are dealt with by the French Commercial Code. The

Commercial Code also dealt with transactions between one commercial party and one non-commercial party. This Article offers a special prescription regime.

Code civil **9.62 (FR)**

Article 617 A right of usufruct is destroyed:

By non-user of the right during thirty years; ...

Article 706 A right of servitude is destroyed by non-user during thirty years.

Article 707 The thirty years begin to run, according to the different kinds of servitudes, either from the day when one ceased to enjoy them, with respect to discontinuous servitudes, or from the day when an act contrary to the servitude has been performed, with respect to continuous servitudes.

Article 2488 Prior charges and mortgages are destroyed: ...

4 By prescription.

Prescription is acquired to a debtor, as to the object that is in his hands, by the time prescribed by the statute of limitations in respect of the actions which give a mortgage or a prior charge.

As to the property which is in the hands of a third party in possession, it is acquired by him by the time regulated for prescription of ownership for his benefit: in the case where prescription depends upon a title, it begins to run only from the day when that title has been recorded in the land registry of the situation of the immovables. Registrations made by a creditor do not interrupt the running of the prescription established by law in favour of the debtor or of the third party in possession.

Note

Depending on the type of property right, the French Civil Code provides specific rules for the precription procedure and periods.

II.B.6.b German law

Introductory Notes

(a) The German law of prescription operates on the basis of the extinctive prescription of claims to protect property rights (*Ansprüche*). When, for a certain period of time the holder of a right has not made use of the claim protecting his right, while the claim did arise, the holder may lose the possibility to use the claim through extinctive prescription. *De jure*, the result of this is not the loss of the property right, but the loss of the claim to protect the property right. However, in fact this leaves the property right unprotected. For example, the owner of a stolen object can, after a period of time, no longer claim his object back from the thief. This prescription does not deprive the owner of his right of ownership, but makes the right of ownership generally unenforceable.[88] Depending on the different nature of these claims, a different time period applies.

[88] It is possible that the claim can still be used against a specific person.

(b) In 2002 the German law of obligations was reformed. As a part of these reforms the law on prescription was modernised.[89] This modernisation did not so much alter the way in which prescription, extinctive prescription in particular operates, but simplified the different time periods. Before the reforms, depending on the nature of the claim that prescribed, time periods of 6 weeks, 3 and 6 months, 1, 2, 3, 4, 5 and 30 years applied. After the reforms, the standard time period was changed to 3 years and exceptions were standardised. Now the main time periods are 3, 5 and 30 years.

(i) General rules on prescription

Bürgerliches Gesetzbuch **9.63 (DE)**

§195 The regular prescription period is three years.

§196 Claims for the transfer of ownership in respect to a piece of land, as well as in respect to creation, assignment or termination of a right in respect to a piece of land or for the alteration of the content of such a right as well as the claims for the counter-performance of such prescribe after a period of ten years.

§197 (1) In so far as is not determined otherwise, the following claims prescribe after a period of 30 years:

1. Claims for the revendication of the right of ownership and other property rights. ...

Notes

(1) These general provisions from the German Civil Code show how, although the normal prescription period in German law is three years, the claim to protect property rights prescribes in 30 years. However, there are also claims following from holding property rights that prescribe after three years. These include the famous claim of §1004 that allows the holder of a property right to prevent or stop interference with his property right.[90]

(2) Claims arising from the creation or transfer of property rights indirectly relate to the property right, not as directly as the claim protecting the property right itself, and are in between the short and long time period. It is the claims mentioned in §197 BGB that are initiated against third parties. The claims in §196 BGB are between the parties creating or transferring the right.

(ii) Start of the prescription period

Bürgerliches Gesetzbuch **9.64 (DE)**

§199 (1) The regular prescription period starts to run at the end of the year, in which

1. the claim has arisen, and
2. the creditor acquires or, in the absence of gross negligence, should have acquired, knowledge of the circumstances giving rise to the claim and the identity of the debtor. ...

[89] *Gesetz zur Modernisierung des Schuldrechts* of 26 November 2001 (BGBl I page 3138).

[90] Schwab and Prütting, above n 67, 235.

(4) Other claims, such as claims for compensation for damage, prescribe without regard to the knowledge or grossly negligent knowledge after a period of ten years after they have arisen. …

Note

Note that this rule only applies for the general prescription term in German law. It softens the short three-year period and allows the person that risks losing his right some more time to react and stop the running of the prescription period.

Bürgerliches Gesetzbuch **9.65 (DE)**

§187 (1) If an event [*Ereignis*] or a certain moment during a day is decisive for the start of a period of time, for the calculation of the period time, the day on which the event or moment occurs is not included.
(2) If the start of a day is decisive for the start of a period of time, this day is included in the calculation of the period of time. The same applies for the day of birth in case of calculation of age.

§200 The prescription period that is applicable to claims that are not subject to the regular prescription period, starts at the moment the claim arises, in so far as another commencement of the prescription period is not provided. §199 paragraph (5) applies mutatis mutandis. …

Notes

(1) These provisions show that, when it comes to the exceptions to the general prescription rule of the German Civil Code, these are the provisions that apply to property rights, the prescription period starts to run from the moment the claim arises. Like in French law, the exact moment the time period starts to run is mostly irrelevant. The time period will start to run the day after the claim came into existence. When that day is a Sunday or a public holiday, the Civil Code states the time period starts running on the first working day following the Sunday or holiday.[91]

(2) When the running of the prescription period is stopped, §212 BGB states that a new prescription period starts to run the day after the old period was stopped.

(iii) Prescription of property rights on immovable objects

Bürgerliches Gesetzbuch **9.66 (DE)**

§902 (1) The claims protecting rights that have been registered are not subject to prescription. This does not apply to claims for recurrent performances in arrears or for compensation for damage.
(2) A right, against which an objection to accuracy has been registered in the land register, is equal to the right that is registered.

§901 If a right to another piece of land has been unlawfully cancelled in the land register, the right ceases to exist when the claim of the holder of the right against

[91] §193 BGB.

the owner has prescribed. The same applies, when a right that was created by operation of law on another piece of land was not registered in the land register.

Notes

(1) These two provisions show that it is important to make a distinction between those rights in respect to immovable objects that have been registered and those that have not. The registration system adhered to in Germany, which was dealt with in Chapter 8, does not allow the general loss of a property right through extinctive prescription.[92]

(2) If a right in respect to an immovable object is not registered, the registration system cannot prevent the loss of the action protecting that right through extinctive prescription. Therefore §901 BGB explicitly authorises this prescription and adds the destructive effect in respect to the property right in question.[93]

(iv) Specific rules on prescription

Bürgerliches Gesetzbuch **9.67 (DE)**

§216 (1) The prescription of a claim for which a right of hypothec, a shiphypothec or a right of pledge is created does not hindert he creditor to seek execution of his right on the land that is burdened by the right.

(2) When in order to secure a claim a right was provided, the retransfer cannot be demanded on the basis oft he prescription of a claim. When the right of ownership is reserved, a party may get out of the contract on the basis oft he precription oft he secured claim.

(3) Sections 1 and 2 do not apply tot he prescription of interests or other periodic payments.

§1028 (1) When on the burdened piece of land a plant is placed that interferes with a right of real servitude, the claim of the right holder of the real servitude to cease the interference with the right is subject to the rules on prescriptionm also when the servitude has been entered in the land registry. With the completion of the prescription the right of servitude ceases to exit, in so far as the plant interferes with the right.

Note

These paragraphs offers an example of a special property law prescription rule, in this case a right of hypothec and real servitude.

Other paragraphs in the BGB set special prescription periods for claims for, for example, the owner's claim for replacement of objects by the usufructuary (§1057 BGB, six months), and the pledgor's claim for replacement of objects by the pledgee (§1226 BGB, six months).

[92] Schwab and Prütting, above n 67, 95.
[93] Wilhelm, above n 66, 415–16.

II.B.6.c Dutch law

Dutch law also recognises the extinctive prescription of property rights. Like in German law, it is not the property rights itself, but the claims protecting the property rights that can no longer be invoked through prescription. As a result the property right generally remains with the original holder of the right, but its holder can no longer act to protect his right. It is because of this that Dutch law also recognises a special rule to remedy this situation (Article 3:105 BW).

(i) General rules on prescription

Burgerlijk Wetboek **9.68 (NL)**

Article 3:306 Unless the law provides otherwise, a claim prescribes after twenty years.
Article 3:307 (1) A claim for the performance of an obligation arising from a contract to do or to give something prescribes after the completion of a period of five years after the day, following the day on which the claim became enforceable.
(2) In case of an obligation to perform after an undetermined period of time, the prescription period mentioned in paragraph 1 will not commence until beginning of the day, following the day on which the creditor has notified to proceed to ,enforce the claim mentioned in paragraph 1 prescribes in any case after the completion of a period of twenty years after the beginning of the day, following the day on which the enforceability, if necessary after cancellation by the creditor, was at the earliest possible.
Article 3:308 Claims for the payment of interest and sums of money, life interest, dividends, lease payments, agricultural lease payments and anything else that must be paid within a year or a shorter period, prescribe after the completion of a period of five years after the day, following the day on which the claim became enforceable.

Note

The general rule on extinctive prescription in Dutch law is offered by Article 3:306 BW. The time period of 20 years applies, regardless of anything else. Moreover, for some claims, like in French and German law, specific time periods apply.

(ii) Start of the prescription period

Burgelijk Wetboek **9.69 (NL)**

Article 3:313 Unless the law provides otherwise, the prescription period for a claim for the performance of an obligation to give or to do something commences on the day, following the day on which immediate performance may be demanded.
Article 3:319 (1) By interruption of the prescription period of a claim, other than by initiating a demand that is followed by an award, a new prescription period commences from the following day. If a binding advice is requested and obtained, the new prescription period commences from the day on which the binding advice was rendered.
(2) The new prescription period is equal to the original, but not longer than five years. Nevertheless, the prescription will in no case have effect earlier than the day on which the original prescription period would have expired without the interruption.

Note

When the time period for prescription is stopped, Article 3:319 BW shows that from the day after that a new time period starts running. Therefore, it is possible, although unlikely, that a property right is destroyed after the running of the prescription period has been stopped once.

Hoge Raad, 8 May 1998[94] **9.70 (NL)**

Land Sachsen v C

START PRESCRIPTION PERIOD OF REVINDICATION OF STOLEN OBJECT

The stolen painting

The prescription period starts running from the moment another person than the owner starts acting as if he is possessor of the object.

Facts: In 1945 a painting known as *Klooster in een Landschap* was stolen in Germany, more specifically in what is now the Land Sachsen. In 1990 a buyer brought the painting to an auction house in Amsterdam to have it valued. The Land Sachsen seized the painting, claiming the painting was owned by Sachsen and not by the buyer. Therefore the Land Sachsen attempted to revindicate the painting. The buyer claimed to have acquired ownership through prescription. One of the questions before the Dutch Supreme Court was when the prescription period starts running. The answer to this question was needed to determine whether the buyer had indeed acquired ownership through acquisitive prescription. The Court of Appeal had held that Dutch law applied, and this part of the judgment was upheld by the Supreme Court.

Held: The prescription period starts running from the moment a person who is not the owner acts as if he is possessor of the object. The prescription period had therefore been completed.

Judgment: 3.5. Argument III attacks the view of the Court that, on the basis of the old BW applicable here, the prescription period in Art 2004 (old) BW started running as from the time of the involuntary loss of possession, which it is certain occurred more than 30 years ago.

The argument contends that fundamental principles of reasonableness and equity imply that an extinctive prescription period does not commence or can be completed before the creditor can assert his claim.

This argument, too, cannot succeed. The prescription period for revindication begins running as from the time that someone other than the owner carried out acts of possession in relation to the thing (HR 14 November 1969, NJ 1970, 283). Pursuant to the foregoing, the Court—not challenged in cassation—accepted that this was the case as from approximately 1950. The commencement of the aforementioned prescription period is namely not dependent on the moment that the owner acquired knowledge with regard to the facts that make it possible by means of revindication to demand the thing from a given person. The objection that the owner can therefore lose the right of revindication before has actually been able to level it against that person, is not decisive as against the demands of legal certainty in legal matters, which the institution of prescription is also intended to serve and which require that, after expiry of a fixed period running as from a fixed moment in

[94] NJ 1999, 44.

time, the thing can no longer be demanded on the ground of facts existing before the commencement of that period (cf HR 3 November 1995, RvdW 1995, 229 (NJ 1998, 380; reasoning)).

Note

This case offers an example of the application of the rules on prescription periods. It shows a very practical application of the rules by the Dutch Hoge Raad, that refuses to accept a subjective element, ie the state of mind of an acquirer, as a starting point.

(iii) Specific rules on prescription

Burgerlijk Wetboek **9.71 (NL)**

Article 3:105(1) He who possesses a thing at the point in time when the period of prescription of the claim aimed at ending that possession is completed, acquires that thing, even if his possession was not in good faith.

Note

Unlike German law, the Dutch law on extinctive prescription, which also operates on the basis of expiration of claims protecting property rights, adds an effect by operation of the law to the prescription of such a claim. Article 3:105 BW adds an effect of acquisitive prescription to a situation of extinctive prescription. On acquisitive prescription see Chapter 7.

Burgerlijk Wetboek **9.72 (NL)**

Article 3:323 (1) By completion of the prescription of a claim for the performance of an obligation, the rights of pledge and hypothec that secure it cease to exist.

(2) Neither does the prescription prevent that the right of pledge is exercised on the thing that is subject to the right, if this thing is a movable object, a bearer or order right or the bearer or order document was brought in the power of the pledgee or a third party.

(3) The claim for the performance of an obligation for which a right of hypothec was created, does not prescribe before twenty years have passed after the day following the day on which the right of hypothec was connected to the obligation.

Note

This article offers specific rules on the destruction of property security rights when the (monetary) claim, which is the subject matter of these property security rights, is destroyed through extinctive prescription.

Burgerlijk Wetboek **9.73 (NL)**

Article 3:106 When the prescription of a claim of the holder of a limited property right against the person with the principal entitlement to cease a state of affairs that interferes with the property right is completed, the limited property right ceases to exist, in for far as the exercise of the property right is obstructed by that state of affairs.

Note

The rule of Article 3:106 BW resembles the rule that is also offered in a more specific way by §1024 BGB. It shows the effect of the destruction of a claim for the protection of a property right in a special situation. Normally, the destruction of a claim protecting a property right will not automatically lead to the destruction of the property right itself. However, if the claim was for restoration of a situation in which the property right can be used, the holder of the property right can no longer use his right. This impossibility of using, or enjoying, the property right leads to a destruction of the property right based on Article 3:106 BW.

II.B.7 REALISATION OF A PROPERTY RIGHT

Introductory Notes

(a) Some property rights are specifically created to allow the holder to realise his right in case of a certain event. Usually this situation refers to property security rights such as pledge, hypothec or charges. Because these rights are created to secure the performance of a certain debt, the non-performance of the debtor will lead to the possibility for the holder of the right to take the object on which the right is created and sell it in order to satisfy the debt with the proceeds of the sale. Property security rights were dealt with in Chapter 5.

(b) Generally, when the holder of a property security right makes use of his right, the property right will come to an end. An example of this can be offered.

Bürgerliches Gesetzbuch **9.74 (DE)**

§1181 Destruction by realisation from the piece of land (1) If the creditor is satisfied from the piece of land, the right of hypothec ceases to exist.

(2) If the satisfaction of the creditor is made from one of the pieces of land that are burdened with a co-entitled hypothec [*Gesamthypothec*], the other pieces of land are also freed.

(3) The satisfaction out of the piece of land is equal to the satisfaction out of the belongings to which the right of hypothec applies.

II.B.8 DESTRUCTION SPECIFIC TO CERTAIN RIGHTS

As can be seen from the property rights that were dealt with in Chapters 3 and 5, there can be a large difference between the content of property rights. Because of these differences in content, sometimes there are specific rules on destruction that only apply to a specific property right. This section provides a short overview.

II.B.8.a French law

Code civil **9.75 (FR)**

Article 617 A right of usufruct is destroyed:
By the natural [repealed by implication] death of the usufructuary;
By the expiry of the time for which it was granted;
Article 2488 Prior charges and mortgages are destroyed:
1 By extinguishment of the principal obligation except for the case provided for in Article 2422.

II.B.8.b German law

Bürgerliches Gesetzbuch **9.76 (DE)**

§1061 The right of usufruct ceases to exist with the death of the usufructuary. When the right of usufruct is created for a legal person or a partnership with legal personality, it ceases to exist with these.

II.B.8.c Dutch law

Burgerlijk Wetboek **9.77 (NL)**

Article 3:258(1) When a thing that is subject to a right of pledge, as meant in Article 236 paragraph 1, comes into the power of the pledgor, the right of pledge is terminated, unless it was created in accordance with Article 237 paragraph (1).

III. COMMON LAW

The common law distinguishes between events which destroy the subject-matter of the right, and those which, though leaving the subject-matter intact, destroy only the right.

III.A DESTRUCTION OF SUBJECT-MATTER OF RIGHT

Destruction of the *res* will naturally destroy the right since it cannot now be said that there is a right against others in respect of a thing. Of course, there may be claims against third parties in tort or contract in respect of that destruction, but the essential fact remains that the property right formerly held by the claimant no longer exists. There are various ways in which the subject-matter of a right may be destroyed. The most obvious is a bolt of lightning or fire. Others might be mixing, manufacture and accession. It should be noted that some of these are dealt with in Chapter 7. That is because some, though not all, situations of destruction are also constitutive of rights. So, for example, the events of mixing and manufacture both destroy one set of rights and create new ones in their stead. Since these have been examined already, they will not be treated in this chapter. In fact, we are here only concerned with one instance of destruction of the subject-matter of the right, accession, which has no counterpart in the rules on creation.

III.A.1 ACCESSION

Introductory Note

An accession occurs when one thing becomes physically attached to another. Examples are the darning of sock with wool, the painting of a picture on canvas, or the erection of a building on land. The consequence of such an event is that the right in respect of the minor object, whatever it may be, is destroyed.

House of Lords, 1 May 1997[95] **9.78 (E&W)**

Elitestone Ltd v Morris

ACCESSION OF GOODS TO LAND

Wooden bungalows

Accession involves two factors, the degree of annexation to the land, and the object of the annexation.

Facts: The claimants held a fee simple title to land on which a number of wooden bungalows were erected, one of which was occupied by the defendants pursuant to an agreement described as a 'licence' and in return for an annual payment; the terms of the agreement permitted the defendants to enter upon the piece of land and 'to keep thereon a bungalow and to reside' in it. The main structure of the bungalow rested on concrete pillars which were attached to the ground. The bungalow could only be removed by being demolished. The claimants, successors in title to the original 'licensors', issued proceedings in the county court seeking possession from the occupiers of the land, including the defendant, Mr Morris. The assistant recorder refused the claim for possession, holding that the bungalow formed part of the land, with the result that the defendant occupied it under a lease of the land, and was therefore a protected tenant within the terms of the Rent Act 1977. The Court of Appeal allowed the claimants' appeal, holding that the bungalow was only a chattel, title to which remained vested in the defendant, and that the claimant had therefore only been granted a licence of the site, which did not attract the protection of the Rent Acts. The defendant appealed to the House of Lords.

Held: The bungalow had by accession become part of the land, with the result that the defendant occupied it under a lease. He therefore had the protection of the Rent Acts and the assistant recorder was right to refuse to grant an order for possession against him.

Judgment: Lord Lloyd of Berwick—The assistant recorder held, correctly, ... that the question in Mr Morris's case turned on whether or not the bungalow formed part of the realty. If it did, then Mr Morris was entitled to his declaration.

Having visited the site, the assistant recorder had this to say:

> 'While the house rested on the concrete pillars which were themselves attached to the ground, it seems to me clear that at least by 1985 and probably before, it would have been clear to anybody that this was a structure that was not meant to be enjoyed as a chattel to be picked up and moved in due course but that it

[95] [1997] 1 WLR 687.

should be a long-term feature of the realty albeit that, because of its construction, it would plainly need more regular maintenance.'

The Court of Appeal disagreed. Aldous LJ, who gave the leading judgment, was much influenced by the fact that the bungalow was resting by its own weight on concrete pillars, without any attachment. He was also influenced by the uncertainty of Mr Morris's tenure. Although Mr Morris had been in occupation since 1971, he was required to obtain an annual 'licence'. At first the licence fee was £3 a year. It rose to £10 in 1984, then to £52 in 1985, and finally to £85 in 1989. In 1990 the plaintiffs required a licence fee of £1,000: but Mr Morris ... declined to pay.

On these facts Aldous LJ inferred that it was the common intention of the parties that the occupiers should acquire the ownership of their bungalows, but the ownership of the sites should remain in the freeholders. On that footing Mr Morris's bungalow was to be regarded as a chattel. It was never annexed to the soil, so it never became part of the realty. It followed that the tenancy did not include the bungalow, and Mr Morris was not a protected tenant.

Unlike the judge, the Court of Appeal did not have the advantage of having seen the bungalow. ... The photographs show very clearly what the bungalow is, and especially what it is not. It is *not* like a Portakabin, or mobile home. The nature of the structure is such that it could not be taken down and re-erected elsewhere. It could only be removed by a process of demolition. This, as will appear later, is a factor of great importance in the present case. If a structure can only be enjoyed in situ, and is such that it cannot be removed in whole or in sections to another site, there is at least a strong inference that the purpose of placing the structure on the original site was that it should form part of the realty at that site, and therefore cease to be a chattel. ...

The question in the present appeal is whether, when the bungalow was built, it became part and parcel of the land itself. The materials out of which the bungalow was constructed, that is to say, the timber frame walls, the feather boarding, the suspended timber floors, the chipboard ceilings, and so on, were all, of course, chattels when they were brought onto the site. Did they cease to be chattels when they were built into the composite structure? The answer to the question, as Blackburn J pointed out in *Holland v Hodgson* (1872) LR 7 CP 328, depends on the circumstances of each case, but mainly on two factors, the degree of annexation to the land, and the object of the annexation.

Degree of annexation

The importance of the degree of annexation will vary from object to object. In the case of a large object, such as a house, the question does not often arise. Annexation goes without saying. So there is little recent authority on the point, and I do not get much help from the early cases in which wooden structures have been held not to form part of the realty, such as the wooden mill in *Rex v Otley* (1830) 1 B & Ad 161, the wooden barn in *Wansbrough v Maton* (1836) 4 A & E 884 and the granary in *Wiltshear v Cottrell* (1853) 1 E & B 674. But there is a more recent decision of the High Court of Australia which is of greater assistance. In *Reid v Smith* (1905) 3 CLR 656, 659 Griffith CJ stated the question as follows:

> 'The short point raised in this case is whether an ordinary dwelling-house, erected upon an ordinary town allotment in a large town, but not fastened to the soil, remains a chattel or becomes part of the freehold.'

The Supreme Court of Queensland had held that the house remained a chattel. But the High Court reversed this decision, treating the answer as being almost a matter of common sense. The house in that case was made of wood, and rested by its own weight on brick piers. The house was not attached to the brick piers in any way. It was separated by iron plates placed on top of the piers, in order to prevent an invasion of white ants. There was an extensive citation of English and American authorities. It was held that the absence of any attachment did not prevent the house forming part of the realty. Two quotations, at p 667, from the American authorities may suffice. In *Snedeker v Warring* (1854) 12 NY 170, 175 Parker J said: 'A thing may be as firmly affixed to the land by gravitation as by clamps or cement. Its character may depend upon the object of its erection.' In *Goff v O'Conner* (1855) 16 Ill 421, 423, the court said: 'Houses, in common intendment of the law, are not fixtures to, but part of, the land. ... This does not depend, in the case of houses, so much upon the particular mode of attaching, or fixing and connecting them with the land upon which they stand or rest, as it does upon the uses and purposes for which they were erected and designed.'

Purpose of annexation

Many different tests have been suggested, such as whether the object which has been fixed to the property has been so fixed for the better enjoyment of the object as a chattel, or whether it has been fixed with a view to effecting a permanent improvement of the freehold. This and similar tests are useful when one is considering an object such as a tapestry, which may or may not be fixed to a house so as to become part of the freehold: see *Leigh v Taylor* [1902] AC 157. These tests are less useful when one is considering the house itself. In the case of the house the answer is as much a matter of common sense as precise analysis. A house which is constructed in such a way so as to be removable, whether as a unit, or in sections, may well remain a chattel, even though it is connected temporarily to mains services such as water and electricity. But a house which is constructed in such a way that it cannot be removed at all, save by destruction, cannot have been intended to remain as a chattel. It must have been intended to form part of the realty. I know of no better analogy than the example given by Blackburn J in *Holland v Hodgson*:

> 'Thus blocks of stone placed one on the top of another without any mortar or cement for the purpose of forming a dry stone wall would become part of the land, though the same stones, if deposited in a builder's yard and for convenience sake stacked on the top of each other in the form of a wall, would remain chattels.'

Applying that analogy to the present case, I do not doubt that when Mr Morris's bungalow was built, and as each of the timber frame walls were placed in position, they all became part of the structure, which was itself part and parcel of the land. The object of bringing the individual bits of wood onto the site seems to be so clear that the absence of any attachment to the soil (save by gravity) becomes an irrelevance.

Finally I return to the judgment of the Court of Appeal. I need say no more about the absence of attachment, which was the first of the reasons given by the Court of Appeal for reversing the assistant recorder. The second reason was the intention which the court inferred from the previous course of dealing between the parties, and in particular the uncertainty of Mr Morris's tenure. ...

As to the second reason the Court of Appeal may have been misled by Blackburn J's use of the word 'intention' in *Holland v Hodgson*. But as the subsequent decision of the Court of Appeal in *Hobson v Gorringe* [1897] 1 Ch 182 made clear, and as the decision of the House in *Melluish v BMI (No 3) Ltd* [1996] AC 454 put beyond question, the intention of the parties is only relevant to the extent that it can be derived from the degree and object of the annexation. The subjective intention of the parties cannot affect the question whether the chattel has, in law, become part of the freehold, any more than the subjective intention of the parties can prevent what they have called a licence from taking effect as a tenancy, if that is what in law it is: see *Street v Mountford* [1985] AC 809.

I would allow this appeal and restore the order of the assistant recorder.

Lord Clyde delivered a separate speech in which he allowed the defendant's appeal.

Lords Browne-Wilkinson, Nolan and Nicholls of Birkenhead agreed with both speeches.

III.B DESTRUCTION OF RIGHT

III.B.1 LIMITATION

III.B.1.a Land

Limitation Act 1980 **9.79 (E&W)**

Section 15(1) No action shall be brought by any person to recover any land after the expiration of twelve years from the date on which the right of action accrued to him or, if it first accrued to some person through whom he claims, to that person.

Section 17 Subject to—

(a) section 18 of this Act; and

(b) section 75 of the Land Registration Act 1925;

at the expiration of the period prescribed by this Act for any person to bring an action to recover land (including a redemption action) the title of that person to the land shall be extinguished.

Court of Appeal, 21 July 1892[96] **9.80 (FR)**

Tichborne v Weir

LIMITATION

Limitation of a conveyance

The statutes of limitation do not effect a conveyance.

Facts: In 1802 the landlord's predecessor in title, Mrs Doughty, who held a fee simple title to a house, granted a lease of it to one Baxter for a term of 89 years at a yearly rent. The lease contained a covenant to repair. Baxter created an equitable mortgage of the lease by deposit with Giraud, and afterwards, in 1836, Giraud entered into possession of the premises without any acknowledgment to Baxter, who

[96] (1892) 67 LT 735, [1891–94] All ER Rep 449.

disappeared in 1836. Giraud remained in possession for 40 years until 1876, paying to the landlord the rent agreed in the lease to Baxter. In 1876, by a deed made between Giraud and the defendant reciting the lease granted by Mrs Doughty to Baxter and reciting that the premises were at that time legally vested in Giraud for the rest of the term, Giraud assigned all his estate and interest in the lease to the defendant, who then entered into possession and continued paying the same rent as Giraud till the end of the term in 1891, when he delivered up possession of the premises to the landlord, the successor in title of Mrs Doughty. The landlord sued the defendant for breach of the covenant to repair contained in the lease granted to Baxter. The question was whether section 34 of the Real Property Limitation Act 1833 had the effect of conveying the lease granted to Baxter to the defendant and with it the liability on the repairing covenant. Section 34 (the forerunner of section 17 of the Limitation Act 1980) provided:

> That at the determination of the period limited by this Act to any person for making an entry or distress, or bringing any writ of *quare impedit* or other action or suit, the right and title of such person to the land, rent, or advowson for the recovery whereof such entry, distress, action, or suit respectively might have been made or brought within such period, shall be extinguished.

Held: affirming the judgment of Cave J, that the effect of section 34 of the Real Property Limitation Act, 1833 was not to transfer to Giraud the right and title of Baxter, so that Giraud did not become subject to the covenant of the lease which he assigned to the defendant, but only to extinguish it by barring the remedy, and, consequently, the defendant was not liable under the covenant in the lease granted to Baxter.

Judgment: Lord Esher MR—The real point argued before us in this case is, whether the effect of s 34 of the Real Property Limitations Act, 1833, has been to transfer the lease formerly held by Baxter to Giraud, who for over twenty years had been in possession of the land without any acknowledgment to Baxter, who had equitably mortgaged the lease to him. The question is whether Giraud became subject to the covenants of the lease, and whether he has assigned the lease to the defendant. If the statute transferred the lease to Giraud, then Giraud became tenant of the landlord whether the landlord liked it or not. Reliance was placed on the words of the section, though it says not a word about transferring anything to anybody; it merely says the right 'shall be extinguished.' If that is all, the right of the man out of possession is extinguished so that he cannot eject the man who is in possession, but nothing is given to the latter by the statute. As no one can turn out the man in possession, his possession is the same in effect, as Lord St Leonards says in *Incorporated Society in Dublin v Richards* (1841) 1 Dr & War 258 as if he had a title conveyed to him.

But it is argued that cases have decided that a title is transferred by the statute. It is not said that there is any reported case which clearly decides that Giraud became under the statute a transferee of the lease; but it is contended that judges have used words which show that such is the case. The landlord relies on phrases used by Lord St Leonards, a very great real property lawyer; but they were used when he was speaking of a fee simple, and when no question was raised about a lease. The opinions of well-known writers of conveyancing textbooks are also opposed to the contentions put forward on behalf of the plaintiff. Textbooks written by living authors who are practising barristers are not quoted in the courts, but passages have been read from two books of great authority. Hayes in his own marginal note says in his book on *Conveyancing* (6th ed) vol 1, p 269: 'The statute does not convey but destroys the right.' Therefore, the matter comes to this. The words of the statute do not carry the proposition which is contended for, the reason of the thing is against it, there is an absence of judicial authority, and the views of well-known textbook writers are uniformly against it. All these reasons show that the effect of the statute is not that to right of one person is conveyed to another, but that the right is extinguished and destroyed. That being so, the judgment of Cave J is right, and this appeal must be dismissed.

Bowen LJ—I am of the same opinion. It seems to me that the whole of the argument addressed to us depends on the proposition that the statute transferred Baxter's rights and liabilities as against the landlord to Giraud. I think that the statute makes no transfer of any kind. Section 34 of the Real Property Limitations Act, 1833, says that, at the determination of the period limited by the Act to any person for making an entry or distress or bringing any writ of *quare impedit* or other action or suit, the right and title of such person to the land (which word includes a chattel interest) for the recovery whereof such entry, distress, action, or suit respectively might have been made or brought within such period, shall be extinguished. It is argued that the extinguishment of the title must have the effect of transferring the term to the man in possession, although there is no mention in the statute of any transfer.

The argument is really an overstraining of the words used by Lord St Leonards in *Incorporated Society in Dublin v Richards* and of Parke B in *Doe d Jukes v Sumner* (1845) 14 M & W 39 and a construing of them to mean more than what is said in the Act. It is true that the effect of the statute is not only to bar the remedy, but also to extinguish the title of the person out of possession, and in that sense the person in possession holds by virtue of the Act, but not by a fiction of a transfer of title. In *Dart's Vendors and Purchasers* (6th ed) vol 1, p 463, it is stated that

> 'Possession for a time exceeding the statutory limit not only bars the remedy, but also extinguishes the right of the original owner. It has been said that the effect of the Act is to make a parliamentary conveyance of the land to the person in possession after the statutory period has elapsed; but though it is true that the possessory owner, after the statutory limit has been passed, is placed by the Act in a position analogous to that which he would have occupied if the fee simple had been absolutely conveyed to him, yet his title under the Act is acquired solely by the extinction of the right of the prior rightful owner; not by any statutory transfer of the estate. If the statute operated as a sort of involuntary alienation of the estate of the rightful owner, the adverse possessor would take it subject to the subsisting charges; and wherever it was in settlement, his interest therein would constantly be varying according to the successive limitations of the settlement; but this is clearly not the operation of the statute.'

Similar language is used in *Hayes on Conveyancing*, p 269, and the reasoning there given is entirely germane to the matter. He says:

> 'We must not, however, confound the negative effect of the statute with the positive effect of a conveyance. In the example last considered, the rights of A and B do not become the rights of C under a species of involuntary alienation effected by the statute. If that hypothesis were adopted, it would follow that, when the bar became complete as against A, the tenant for life, C acquired a lawful estate pur autre vie; in short, that where the land is in settlement the adverse possessor would be from time to time invested with interests measured by those of the successive takers, whether chattel or freehold, and consequently be owner today of a short term of years, tomorrow, of the fee. Such is not the operation of the statute.'

That language is used in reference to a fee simple, but here we have not to deal with the fee.

From 1802 to the present time nothing has been done to bar any right of the original lessor. Giraud never acquired the fee simple, it was only as against Baxter that he acquired anything. The most that can be said is, that he acquired an absolute title to the land as against everybody but the landlord. He was not liable on the covenants in the lease. The arguments used in the books which I have read support the only view consistent with the statute. Only in one metaphorical sense can the section be said to give a title to land. ...

Kay LJ—... It was argued that the effect of the statute was to transfer the term from Baxter to Giraud, and so it would be vested in the defendant. Under the Real Property Limitations Act, 1833, s 34, 'the right and title' of Baxter 'to the land' (which by the interpretation clause includes chattel interest) was 'extinguished.' That is the operation of the section, and we are now asked to construe the Act so as to make it say that Baxter's right and title was transferred to Giraud. There is no authority for saying that this is the meaning of the Act. Great textbook writers may be quoted to show the general opinion of the profession at the time. Mr Dart and Mr Hayes are quite opposed to the correctness of the argument now put forward. Passages have been read from judgments in which the word 'transfer' has certainly been used. But in the first case cited, *Incorporated Society in Dublin v Richards*, the word is used by Lord St Leonards just after he had used the word 'extinguished;' and even if the detached sentences relied on be carefully read they are quite consistent with a meaning different from that which is attributed to them by the argument. The defendant got an estate in the land which he has admitted, by paying rent, is not the fee simple, and by operation of the statute Baxter's right to claim the term was extinguished. It follows that Giraud during the rest of the term was free from liability to Baxter or anyone claiming under him, but it does not follow that he acquired Baxter's estate. ...

III.B.1.b Goods

Limitation Act 1980 **9.81 (E&W)**

Section 3 (1) An action founded on tort shall not be brought after the expiration of six years from the date on which the cause of action accrued.

(2) Where any such cause of action has accrued to any person and the period prescribed for bringing that action has expired and he has not during that period recovered possession of the chattel, the title of that person to the chattel shall be extinguished.

Note

As these provisions demonstrate, the effect of limitation statutes in the common law is purely negative. Such statutes destroy, but do not convey, rights. However, an exception may exist in relation to titles to land which are registered, for by statute the dispossessor is given the ability to become registered with the title of the person he has dispossessed: see Land Registration Act 2002, section 97; Schedule 6.

III.B.2 SATISFACTION OF JUDGMENT IN CONVERSION

Torts (Interference with Goods) Act 1977 **9.82 (E&W)**

Section 5 Where damages for wrongful interference are, or would fall to be assessed on the footing that the claimant is being compensated—

(a) for the whole of his interest in the goods, or

(b) for the whole of his interest in the goods subject to a reduction for contributory negligence,

payment of the assessed damages ... extinguishes the claimant's title to that interest.

Note

There is no equivalent provision to this in respect of land, for the remedy of a person dispossessed of land is different to that of a person dispossessed of goods, in that a person dispossessed of land has a right to be put back in possession of the land itself, which accounts for the label *real* property in the common law.

III.B.3 GOOD FAITH PURCHASE

The starting point is that there is no general doctrine of good faith purchase in English law, either in the case of land or goods. The general rule is, somewhat unfelicitously, expressed in the maxim, *nemo dat quod non habet*. So, for example, the rule that good faith purchase for value is no defence to a claim in conversion of goods is enshrined in section 21(1) of the Sale of Goods Act 1979:

> Subject to this Act, where goods are sold by a person who is not their owner, and who does not sell them under the authority or with the consent of the owner, the buyer acquires no better title to the goods than the seller had, unless the owner of the goods is by his conduct precluded from denying the seller's authority to sell.

The question to be asked is when an exception will be made to this general rule, and good faith purchase operate as a defence to claims in respect of land or goods. Although there is no unequivocal case law on the question, it is assumed that good faith purchase when so available operates in the same way as does limitation and satisfaction of judgment in conversion by destroying the prior right, not transferring it to the person who would be otherwise a wrongdoer.

III.B.3.a Titles to money

Introductory Note

At common law, one who takes money, by which is meant coins or banknotes, for value given in good faith gets an absolute title to it. It is therefore both a general defence, in that it is not limited to any specific instances, and one which destroys all prior titles. As will be seen, other defences are different in this respect.

Court of King's Bench, 31 January 1758[97] **9.83 (E&W)**

Miller v Race

GOOD FAITH PURCHASE OF BANKNOTE

Banknote

Banknotes to be treated as money.

Facts: A Bank of England note of the value £21 10s 0d was stolen from its possessor, and the theft reported to the Bank of England. The plaintiff, an innkeeper, innocently exchanged coins of the same value for the stolen note. When he took it to the Bank to change it, it was taken from him by the defendant, one of the Bank's clerks, as a stolen note. He sued the defendant for conversion. It was argued that a banknote was not the equivalent of money, and should be treated as any other good, to which there was no general defence of good faith purchase.

Held: The prior title of the bank had been destroyed by the plaintiff's act of good faith purchase for value. Banknotes were to be treated in the same way as money, not as other goods.

Judgment: Lord Mansfield—declared that at the trial, he had no sort of doubt, but this action was well brought, and would lie against the defendant in the present case; upon the general course of business, and from the consequences to trade and commerce: which would be much incommoded by a contrary determination.

It has been very ingeniously argued by Sir Richard Lloyd for the defendant. But the whole fallacy of the argument turns upon comparing bank notes to what they do not resemble, and what they ought not to be compared to, viz to goods, or to securities, or documents for debts.

Now they are not goods, not securities, nor documents for debts, nor are so esteemed: but are treated as money, as cash, in the ordinary course and transaction of business, by the general consent of mankind; which gives them the credit and currency of money, to all intents and purposes. They are as much money, as guineas themselves are; or any other current coin, that is used in common payments, as money or cash.

They pass by a will, which bequeaths all the testator's money or cash; and are never considered as securities for money, but as money itself. Upon Lord Ailesbury's will, £900 in bank-notes was considered as cash. On payment of them, whenever a receipt is required, the receipts are always given as for money; not as for securities or notes.

So on bankruptcies, they cannot be followed as identical and distinguishable from money: but are always considered as money or cash.

It is a pity that reporters sometimes catch at quaint expressions that may happen to be dropped at the Bar or Bench; and mistake their meaning. It has been quaintly said, 'that the reason why money can not be followed is, because it has no earmark:' but this is not true. The true reason is, upon account of the currency of it: it can not be recovered after it has passed in currency. So, in case of money stolen, the true owner can not recover it, after it has been paid away fairly and honestly upon a valuable and bona fide consideration: but before money has passed in currency, an action may be brought for the money itself. There was a case in 1 G 1, at the sittings, *Thomas v Whip*, before Lord Macclesfield: which was an action

[97] (1758) 1 Burr 452.

upon assumpsit, by an administrator against the defendant, for money had and received to his use. The defendant was nurse to the intestate during his sickness; and, being alone, conveyed away the money. And Lord Macclesfield held that the action lay. Now this must be esteemed a finding at least.

Apply this to the case of a bank-note. An action may lie against the finder, it is true; (and it is not at all denied) but not after it has been paid away in currency. And this point has been determined, even in the infancy of bank-notes; for 1 Salk 126, M 10 W 3, at Nisi Prius, is in point. And Lord Chief Justice Holt there says that it is 'by reason of the course of trade; which creates a property in the assignee or bearer.' (And 'the bearer' is a more proper expression than assignee.)

Here, an inn-keeper took it, bona fide, in his business from a person who made an appearance of a gentleman. Here is no pretence or suspicion of collusion with the robber: for this matter was strictly inquired and examined into at the trial; and is so stated in the case, 'that he took it for a full and valuable consideration, in the usual course of business.' Indeed if there had been any collusion, or any circumstances of unfair dealing; the case had been much otherwise. If it had been a note for £1,000 it might have been suspicious: but this was a small note for £21 10s only: and money given in exchange for it.

III.B.3.b Title to goods other than money

There are currently four main situations in English law where good faith purchase operates as a defence to a claim for conversion or trespass to goods: sale by seller left in possession after the passing of title; sale by buyer given possession before the passing of title; sale of a voidable title; and purchase of title to car on credit. Until recently, there was a fifth, ancient exception, sale in *market overt*. It, however, was abolished by statute in 1994.

(i) Sale by seller in possession

Factors Act 1889 **9.84 (E&W)**

Section 2 Powers of mercantile agent with respect to disposition of goods

(1) Where a mercantile agent is, with the consent of the owner, in possession of goods or of the documents of title to goods, any sale, pledge, or other disposition of the goods, made by him when acting in the ordinary course of business of a mercantile agent, shall, subject to the provisions of this Act, be as valid as if he were expressly authorised by the owner of the goods to make the same; provided that the person taking under the disposition acts in good faith, and has not at the time of the disposition notice that the person making the disposition has not authority to make the same.

(2) Where a mercantile agent has, with the consent of the owner, been in possession of goods or of the documents of title to goods, any sale, pledge, or other disposition, which would have been valid if the consent had continued, shall be valid notwithstanding the determination of the consent: provided that the person taking under the disposition has not at the time thereof notice that the consent has been determined.

(3) Where a mercantile agent has obtained possession of any documents of title to goods by reason of his being or having been, with the consent of the owner, in

possession of the goods represented thereby, or of any other documents of title to the goods, his possession of the first-mentioned documents shall, for the purposes of this Act, be deemed to be with the consent of the owner.

(4) For the purposes of this Act the consent of the owner shall be presumed in the absence of evidence to the contrary.

Section 8. Disposition by seller remaining in possession

Where a person, having sold goods, continues, or is, in possession of the goods, or of the documents of title to the goods, the delivery or transfer by that person, or by a mercantile agent acting for him, of the goods or documents of title under any sale, pledge, or other disposition thereof, or under any agreement for sale, pledge or other disposition thereof, to any person receiving the same in good faith and without notice of the previous sale, has the same effect as if the person making the delivery or transfer were expressly authorised by the owner of the goods to make the same.

Note

The rule in section 8 of the Factors Act 1888 was also enacted in almost identical terms in section 25(1) of the Sale of Goods Act 1893, which in turn was replaced by section 24 of the Sale of Goods Act 1979. Section 8, however, still remains on the statute book.

Court of Appeal, 20 July 1971[98] **9.85 (E&W)**

Worcester Works Finance Ltd v Cooden Engineering Co Ltd

WRONGFUL SALE OF CAR SUBJECT TO HIRE-PURCHASE AGREEMENT

Wrongful sale

Possession for the purposes of the Factors Act need not be lawful possession.

Facts: In June 1966, the defendants sold a title to a car to a dealer who said he wanted it for a possible customer and who paid for it with a cheque for £525. On July 14, the dealer and one Millerick executed documents, the effect of which was that the plaintiffs, a finance company, understood that they had bought the title from the dealer, paying him £450 for it, and that they had let the car to Millerick under a hire-purchase contract. In fact, Millerick did nothing further under the agreement. The dealer, after the 'sale' to the plaintiffs, continued in possession of the car until August 1966, when the defendants, the original holders of the title, repossessed it after the dealer's cheque had been returned dishonoured. They did not sue him on the cheque. The dealer met the hire-purchase instalments for a time but then ceased to pay when about £315 was outstanding under the agreement. In 1968, the defendants made a hire-purchase agreement with a new party for the car. When that came to the knowledge of the finance company, they brought an action claiming against the defendants damages of £315 for conversion of the car to which they claimed to have a better title. The trial judge, Davies LJ, dismissed the claim on the ground that in August 1966 the dealer was a seller of the car who had continued in possession of it and by virtue of section 25(1) of the Sale of Goods Act 1893 (which replicated section 8 of the Factors Act 1888) had passed a good title to the defendants when they retook the car. The finance company was unsuccessful in its appeal to the Court of Appeal.

Held: 'Continues in possession' in section 25(1) of the Sale of Goods Act 1893 meant the seller continuing in physical possession of the goods, irrespective of the quality of his possession. Accordingly, as

[98] [1972] 1 QB 210.

the dealer was a seller of the car, who had continued in possession of it, albeit without the finance company's consent; and the retaking by the original owners constituted a 'disposition' in that there was a transfer of the property in the car by the seller to them; and there was evidence to support the finding that they retook in good faith and without actual notice of the dealer's sale to the finance company, all the requisites of section 25(1) were satisfied and the original owners had acquired a good title to the car.

Judgment: Lord Denning MR—This case raises again the question of which of two innocent people should suffer owing to the fraud of a third. ... Worcester Finance claimed that the car was theirs. Now they bring this action for damages for conversion. They have limited their claim to £315 0s 10d, which was the balance of the hire-purchase price. Worcester Finance rely on the documents which were executed, which on the face of them give them the title to the car. They claim £315 which is the balance outstanding, recoverable in conversion.

The Cooden company in answer rely on the provisions of section 25(1) of the Sale of Goods Act 1893. ... The Cooden company apply that section in this way: They say that Griffiths was a person who, having sold goods to the finance company, continued in possession of them.

The judge has found (and it is no longer disputed) that when the Cooden company delivered the car and logbook to Griffiths and received the cheque for £525, that was then a completed sale to Griffiths. That was in June of 1966. So Griffiths was the owner of the car at that time and was in possession of it. Then when Griffiths on July 14, 1966, invoiced the car to Worcester Finance, he was 'a person who had sold goods' to the finance company: and was thus within the opening words of section 25(1). So far there is no difference between the parties.

The question is whether Griffiths comes within the words: was he a person who 'continues or is in possession of the goods'? The material word here is 'continues.' The words 'or is' have been explained in a New Zealand case—*Mitchell v Jones* (1905) 24 NZLR 932—which was approved by the Privy Council in *Pacific Motor Auctions Pty Ltd v Motor Credits (Hire Finance) Ltd* [1965] AC 867. They refer only to a case where the person who sold the goods had not got the goods when he sold them, but they came into his possession afterwards. Those words 'or is' do not apply to this case, because Griffiths, at the time when he sold the car to Worcester Finance, was already in possession of it. The only relevant word is therefore 'continues.' Was Griffiths a person who, having sold goods, 'continues in possession of the goods'? Mr Jacob, who appears for Worcester Finance, submits that the words 'continues in possession' mean continues in *lawful* possession. He says that, after Griffiths sold the car to the finance company, he ought to have delivered it to the hirer Millerick: and that, by retaining it himself, he retained it unlawfully; and he was, vis-à-vis the finance company, a trespasser. He was in possession of it without their consent at all. In support of this contention Mr Jacob relied on two cases: *Staffs Motor Guarantee Ltd v British Wagon Co Ltd* [1934] 2 KB 305, applied in this court in *Eastern Distributors Ltd v Goldring (Murphy, Third Party)* [1957] 2 QB 600. In those cases it was held that the words 'continues in possession' mean continues in possession as seller and not as bailee: and accordingly, if the person who had sold goods continued in possession as a bailee, he did not 'continue in possession' within the meaning of the section. But those cases are no longer good law. They were disapproved by the Privy Council in *Pacific Motor Auctions Pty Ltd v Motor Credits (Hire Finance) Ltd* [1965] AC 867: and, although decisions of the Privy Council are not binding on this court, nevertheless when the Privy Council disapprove of a previous decision of this court, or cast doubt on it, then we are at liberty to depart from the previous decision. I am glad to depart from those earlier cases and to follow the Privy Council. The words 'continues in possession' refer to:

> 'the continuity of physical possession regardless of any private transactions between the seller and purchaser which might alter the legal title under which the possession was held': *per* Lord Pearce, at p 888.

It does not matter what private arrangement may be made by the seller with the purchaser—such as whether the seller remains bailee or trespasser, or whether he is lawfully in possession or not. It is sufficient if he remains continuously in possession of the goods that he has sold to the purchaser. If so, he can pass a good title to a bona fide third person, and the original purchaser will be ousted. But there must be a continuity of physical possession. If there is a substantial break in the continuity, as for instance, if the seller actually delivers over the goods to a purchaser who keeps them for a time, and then the seller afterwards gets them back, then the section might not apply.

Applying these principles it is plain that Griffiths was a person who, having sold goods to the finance company, 'continued in possession' of them until the time when they were retaken by the Cooden company.

The next question is whether the retaking by the Cooden company was 'the delivery or transfer' by Griffiths of the goods to the Cooden company under a 'disposition' thereof. Griffiths did not actually deliver or transfer the car to the Cooden company. But he acquiesced in their retaking it. That was, I think, tantamount to a delivery or transfer by him. But was it under a 'disposition' thereof?

Mr Jacob argued that there was no disposition here: there was, he said, only a retaking by the Cooden company. To my mind the word 'disposition' is a very wide word. In *Carter v Carter* [1896] 1 Ch 62, 67, Stirling J said that it extends 'to all acts by which a new interest (legal or equitable) in the property is effectually created.' That was under an entirely different statute, but I would apply that wide meaning in this section. When the Cooden company retook this car (because the cheque had not been met) there was clearly a transfer back to them of property in the goods. They would not thereafter be able to sue on the cheque. By retaking the goods they impliedly gave up their remedy on the cheque. That retransfer of the property back to the Cooden company was a 'disposition' within the section.

The last question is whether at the time when the Cooden company retook the car they received 'the same in good faith and without notice of the previous sale,' that is, without notice of the sale by Griffiths to the finance company. The word 'notice' here means actual notice, that is to say, knowledge of the sale or deliberately turning a blind eye to it. Our commercial law does not like constructive notice. It will have nothing to do with it. I am quite clear that the Cooden company acted in good faith without notice of the sale to the finance company. They had sold a car and been given a dud cheque for it; and were just retaking it.

So all the requisites of section 25(1) are satisfied. The retaking by the Cooden company has the same effect as if it was expressly authorised by Worcester Finance. It is equivalent to a transfer by Griffiths back to the Cooden company with the express authority of the finance company. So the Cooden company acquired a good title to the car.

This result is consonant with the object of section 25. Worcester Finance did not see the car at all. They did not take possession of it. They simply received documents from the dealer Griffiths and handed out money to him. They relied on his honesty. He was dishonest. He got £450 out of them by a trick. In contrast, the Cooden company actually had possession of the car—sold it to Griffiths—and when his cheque was dishonoured, they retook it. Plainly as a matter of commercial good sense the title should remain in the Cooden company and not in Worcester Finance. The Cooden company are protected by section 25. The car is theirs.

I think the judge was right in the conclusion to which he came, and I would dismiss the appeal.

Phillimore and Megaw LJJ gave concurring judgments.

(ii) Sale by buyer in possession before title passes

Factors Act 1889 **9.86 (E&W)**

Section 2 Powers of mercantile agent with respect to disposition of goods

As above.

Section 9 Disposition by buyer obtaining possession

Where a person, having bought or agreed to buy goods, obtains with the consent of the seller possession of the goods or the documents of title to the goods, the delivery or transfer, by that person or by a mercantile agent acting for him, of the goods or documents of title, under any sale, pledge, or other disposition thereof, or under any agreement for sale, pledge, or other disposition thereof, to any person receiving the same in good faith and without notice of any lien or other right of the original seller in respect of the goods, shall have the same effect as if the person making the delivery or transfer were a mercantile agent in possession of the goods or documents of title with the consent of the owner.

Court of Appeal, 22 July 1964[99] **9.87 (FR)**

Newtons of Wembley Ltd v Williams

SALE OF GOODS BY ONE NOT ENTITLED

Consent

An agent was in possession of goods with the consent of the seller even if that consent was later withdrawn.

Facts: The claimant, a second-hand car dealer, sold and delivered a car to a Mr Andrew on 15 June 1962, the payment being by cheque. The cheque to the claimant was dishonoured three days later, and they sent a 'stop' notice to the Hire Purchase Information Bureau claiming that the car was theirs from June 15; they also took all possible steps to trace Andrew, thereby admittedly avoiding the contract with him. The following month, Andrew sold the car in Warren Street, London for a cash payment to a purchaser, Biss. Very soon afterwards, Biss sold the car to the defendant, Williams. Williams, who took the car in good faith and without notice of any defect in Andrew's title, subsequently offered the car for sale, whereupon the Hire Purchase Information Bureau was informed, with the result that the claimants attempted unsuccessfully to seize the car. The claimants demanded the return of the car, and the defendant refused that demand. The claimants sued the defendant in detinue and conversion on the ground that they had avoided the sale to Andrews before he had sold the car in Warren Street in July,

[99] [1965] 1 QB 560.

so that he could not have passed a good title to Biss and Biss to the defendant. The defendant claimed the protection of sections 2 and 9 of the Factors Act 1889.

Held: That the defendant was entitled to the protection of the statute. The claimants having taken all available steps to recover the car and disaffirm the contract of sale upon the dishonour of Andrew's cheque, the contract was effectively rescinded even though they could not communicate notice of rescission to Andrew, so that at common law the title to the car revested in them. However, since Andrew had bought the car and since he had initially obtained possession of it with the claimants' consent, he was to be treated by virtue of section 9 of the Factors Act 1889 as if he were a mercantile agent in possession of it with the claimants' consent, which consent was by virtue of section 2(2) of the Act of 1889 to be deemed to continue notwithstanding that it had been revoked by the claimants' rescission of their contract. As the powers of a buyer in possession under section 9 of the Act of 1889 were no greater than those conferred by section 2(1) of the Act of 1889 on a mercantile agent, section 9 could not be invoked unless it be shown, not only that the person taking under the relevant disposition took in good faith and without notice of the original seller's rights, but also that the disposition was made in the ordinary course of business of a mercantile agent. Since Biss had bought the car from Andrew in Warren Street in good faith and without notice of the claimants' rights, and in view of the established street market in Warren Street for cash sales of secondhand cars, the sale by Andrew to Biss was made in the ordinary course of business of a mercantile agent and was accordingly effective to confer a good title on Biss and thence on the defendant.

Judgment: Sellers LJ—When the plaintiffs found on Monday, June 18, 1962, that the cheque was not to be met and that there was no probability of it being met as the bank account or accounts of the man Andrew were not in funds and there were many claims against them, they sought at once to recover the car and to rescind the contract. The judge found that they took all the available steps they could to recover the car and disaffirm the sale, and that the contract between the plaintiffs and Andrew was rescinded on or about June 20—rescinded by the unequivocal acts or conduct of the plaintiffs, applying the decision of this court in *Car & Universal Finance Co Ltd v Caldwell*: so that, whether the title to the car had ever passed to Andrew or not, it being a case clearly of false pretences, as the judge found, the title had revested in the plaintiffs by June 20, 1962. It may well be that the intention of the parties, if this was viewed as a bona fide transaction, was that the property in the car, the title to the car, had not passed in any case because it was not to pass by reason of a clause which provided that payment should be made on or before delivery and that until clearance of cheque or receipt of cash for the full purchase price by the plaintiffs the vehicle would remain their property. But it matters not: by June 20 the ownership of the car was with the plaintiffs. [His Lordship stated the facts occurring after June 20, 1962, and continued:] Both parties have claimed the car in these proceedings, and the matter came for consideration before Davies LJ, sitting at first instance as an additional judge of the Queen's Bench Division. He found that the defendant was entitled to retain the car. The plaintiffs appeal from that decision and seek to establish before this court that the defendant has no title to the car. The title the defendant seeks to advance is the title of Biss, when Biss was the buyer, or the purported buyer, of the car from Andrew in the Warren Street market on or about July 6, 1962.

Quite clearly, at common law, Andrew at that date had no title to give, and at common law Biss obtained no title. It was submitted before us that at that stage Andrew was a complete stranger in this matter, that the case is clear, and that possession should be given to the plaintiffs, or damages in lieu thereof. But in fact Andrew was not a complete stranger. Andrew had in fact the possession of the car, which had been given to him or which he had obtained when he acquired the car on the handing over of the cheque on June 15.

In those circumstances, notwithstanding the position at common law—or because of it—the defendant has relied on the Factors Act, 1889; and the question which arises in this case is whether the transaction between Andrew and Biss can be brought within the provisions of that Act.

I turn first to section 9. It is one of two sections, sections 8 and 9, dealing with dispositions by sellers and buyers of goods, section 8 dealing with the disposition by a seller remaining in possession, section 9 with disposition by a buyer obtaining possession. [His Lordship read section 9 and continued:] Andrew had bought the goods and obtained them with the consent of the plaintiffs. He had subsequently delivered them on a sale to Biss and, if Biss was a person receiving the same in good faith and without notice of any lien or other right of the original seller, then this section provides that the transaction shall have the same effect as if the person making the delivery, ie, Andrew, were a mercantile agent in possession of the goods or documents of title with the consent of the owner. So the first part of section 9 is complied with on the facts of this case, and the question arises whether the second part, the receiving of the goods in good faith (and it is not suggested that Biss had notice of any lien or other right of the original seller), has been complied with, and whether, treating Andrew as a mercantile agent, the requirements of section 9 in that respect have been complied with.

That requires a consideration in the first place of the question: What is a mercantile agent? In section 1(1), 'The expression 'mercantile agent' shall mean a mercantile agent having in the customary course of his business as such agent authority either to sell goods, or to consign goods for the purpose of sale, or to buy goods, or to raise money on the security of goods.' That description is to be applied to Andrew on the facts of this case.

Section 2(1) concerns the powers of a mercantile agent with respect to the disposition of goods. ... One of the points taken by the plaintiffs was that although at the outset Andrew was a person who had obtained, with the consent of the seller, possession of the goods, at the time when this transaction took place that consent no longer operated: it had been withdrawn by the rescission of the contract. But Andrew was in possession of the goods of the plaintiffs, a possession which he had obtained at the outset with their consent. Section 2(2) provides that 'Where a mercantile agent has, with the consent of the owner, been in possession of goods ... any sale ... which would have been valid if the consent had continued, shall be valid notwithstanding the determination of the consent. ...' That is an express provision which altered the law as it had been laid down in an earlier case some time in 1868. Notwithstanding that which the plaintiffs had done to terminate their contract and withdraw their consent, they had in fact—true, through inability to do otherwise—left the possession of their car with Andrew.

The only other question which arises is how far section 9, on its true construction, takes the ultimate sub-buyer (the defendant in the present case), relying, as he does, on what happened between Andrew and Biss. The judge treated section 9 as placing Andrew in the position of a mercantile agent, but with the obligation on the defendant of establishing not only that Biss took in good faith (I leave out the other requirement of no notice of the plaintiffs' rights; nothing arose on that), but also that in the transaction between Andrew and Biss (Andrew being treated as a mercantile agent in accordance with section 9), Andrew was 'acting in the ordinary course of business of a mercantile agent.' There is a possible construction, which was urged upon us by the defendant, that Andrew must be deemed to be acting under section 9 as a mercantile agent, that it must be assumed or deemed that he was acting in the ordinary course of business of a mercantile agent; and investigations were made in other parts of the Act of 1889, in particular section 8, to see whether any support could be had for that view.

Section 8 makes a different provision. It states that where a person, having sold goods, continues, or is, in possession of the goods and then sells them, then, providing the person who receives them does so in good faith and without notice of the previous sale, the transaction will have 'the same effect as if the person making the delivery or transfer were expressly authorised by the owner of the goods to make the same.' The words are different in section 9, and for myself I do not find much help, in constructing section 9, from looking at section 8, except for the fact that since they are different they are intended to have a different effect.

Before one takes too favourable a view for the sub-buyer and too harsh a view against the true owner of the goods as to the cases where section 9 can be invoked, one must remember that it is taking away the right which would have existed at common law, and for myself I should not be prepared to enlarge it more than the words clearly permitted and required. It seems to me that all that section 9 can be said clearly to do is to place the buyer in possession in the position of a mercantile agent when he has in fact in his possession the goods of somebody else, and it does no more than clothe him with that fictitious or notional position on any disposition of those goods. Section 2(1) makes it clear that the sub-buyer from a mercantile agent, to whom that section applies, has in order to obtain the full advantage of the subsection, to establish that the mercantile agent was acting in the ordinary course of business. It is said that that is a somewhat vague phrase, and we have been referred to some authorities with regard to that. It may be that in some cases precisely what is in 'the ordinary course of business' of a mercantile agent may call for some special investigation, but on the face of it it seems to me that it envisages a transaction by a mercantile agent and is to be derived from such evidence as is either known to the court or established by evidence as to what would be the ordinary course of business. …

The question arises here on the evidence whether this transaction is to be said to have been in the ordinary course of business of a mercantile agent. Counsel for the plaintiffs sought to establish that a transaction taking place in this somewhat unusual market, the street kerb in Warren Street, was, on the face of it, something which was not an ordinary business transaction in any way, by a mercantile agent or anybody else, but was to some extent suspect. But the judge had evidence about this and he said, and I think it is within the knowledge of the court, that there had been an established market in secondhand cars in this area on this very site for a long time. Although he said that he had some doubt at one time about the sale to Biss being in the ordinary course of business, for, as he pointed out, there were no business premises, the sale was in the street, and it was for cash, yet he came to the conclusion, which I think cannot be challenged, that there was in Warren Street and its neighbourhood an established street market for cash dealing in cars. When one looks at what took place in that area and finds the prospective buyer coming up and getting into contact with the prospective seller in regard to a car, with an offer and an acceptance, trial of the car and a looking over it and some questions asked and a delivery—I do not find anything to indicate that it was not in the ordinary course of business of a mercantile agent. It seems to me that the defendant has established that essential fact.

Pearson and Diplock LJJ agreed.

House of Lords, 21 April 1988[100] **9.88 (FR)**

National Employers' Mutual General Insurance v Jones

GOOD FAITH PURCHASE FROM A THIEF

Stolen car

The statutory protection of purchasers from those with inferior titles does not extend to stolen goods.

Facts: A car was stolen from a Miss Hopkin. The thief sold his (inferior) title to the car to one Lacey, who in turn sold on to Thomas, who sold it on to Autochoice (Bridgend) Ltd, who sold it on to Mid-Glamorgan Motors Ltd, who finally sold it on to the defendant, Jones. Miss Hopkins claimed against her insurers, the claimant, who paid out in return for an assignment to them of her rights against the various tortfeasors. The insurers thereupon sued Jones in conversion. He relied upon the defence in section 25 of the Sale of Goods Act 1979, essentially the same provision as that in section 9 of the Factors Act 1889. He was, he said, a buyer in good faith in possession with the consent of the person who had sold him the car, Mid-Glamorgan Motors. Accordingly, Mid-Glamorgan Motors were to be deemed as acting as agents of the owner, Miss Hopkins, when selling him the car, with the result that he was to be treated as having her title. He argued that the word 'owner' in section 25 was not to be equated with the word 'seller' because the legislature deliberately used two different words, not one.

Held: That the word 'owner' in section 25 of the Sale of Goods Act 1979 was to be read as the 'owner with whose consent the agent is in possession of the goods'. Accordingly, the statute furnished the defendant with no defence to the claimant's claim.

Judgment: Lord Goff of Chieveley—My Lords, this appeal raises a short, but nevertheless important, point of construction of two parallel statutory provisions, section 9 of the Factors Act 1889 and section 25(1) of the Sale of Goods Act 1979 (formerly section 25(2) of the Sale of Goods Act 1893). ....

Since the decision of the case turns on the construction of the two sections to which I have referred, I think it desirable first to set out the relevant statutory provisions. I take first the Factors Act 1889. The statute is expressed to be an Act to amend and consolidate the Factors Acts. For present purposes, the most relevant sections are section 2, 8 and 9. Section 2 falls under the sub-heading 'Dispositions by mercantile agents;' sections 8 and 9 fall under the sub-heading 'Dispositions by sellers and buyers of goods.' [His lordship then set out the sections].

Turning next to the Sale of Goods Act 1979, the most relevant sections are sections 21, 22(1), 24 and 25(1). These all fall under the sub-heading 'Transfer of title,' and provide: [his lordship then set out the relevant statutory provisions, which are set out above].

For the purposes of the present case, the sections directly in point are, as I have indicated, section 9 of the Factors Act 1889 and section 25(1) of the Sale of Goods Act 1979. These are in almost identical terms; the difference is not relevant to the decision in the present case. The argument of the appellant has been founded upon

[100] [1990] 1 AC 24.

these sections. I shall for convenience refer to section 9 of the Factors Act 1889. The submission was that Mid-Glamorgan Motors Ltd bought the car from Autochoice (Bridgend) Ltd, who gave possession of the car to them; and that Mid-Glamorgan Motors Ltd then delivered the car to the appellant under a sale, and the appellant received the same in good faith without notice of any lien or other right of the original seller in respect of the goods. Accordingly, by virtue of the section, such delivery shall have the same effect as if Mid-Glamorgan Motors Ltd were a mercantile agent in possession of the goods with the consent of the owner, ie (see section 2(1)) such sale shall be as valid as if Mid-Glamorgan Motors Ltd were expressly authorised by the owner to make the sale. It followed, submitted the appellant, that he acquired a good title to the car. This was the argument which found favour with Sir Denys Buckley, but was rejected by the judge in the county court, and by the majority of the Court of Appeal.

In order to consider the validity of this argument, it is necessary first to place the relevant statutory provisions in their legislative context. There have been five Factors Acts in all. The first was the Factors Act 1823. That Act was entitled:

> 'An Act for the better protection of the property of merchants and others, who may hereafter enter into contracts or agreements in relation to goods, wares or merchandises intrusted to factors or agents.'

The broad effect of the Act was that a person so entrusted with goods for the purpose of sale, who shipped such goods in his own name, should be deemed to be the true owner of them, so far as to entitle a bona fide consignee of the goods to a lien upon them in respect of money, etc, advanced to, or for the use of, the named shipper. The protection so conferred was, therefore, limited to the lien. But the whole basis of the protection was that the person adversely affected by the lien was a person who had entrusted the goods to the named shipper. It was this entrusting that constituted the named shipper a factor or agent; and it is no doubt because this constituted the basis of the legislation that it became known as the Factors Act 1823.

The next Act was the Factors Act 1825. This was entitled:

> 'An Act to alter and amend an Act for the better protection of the property of merchants and others, who may hereafter enter into contracts or agreements in relation to goods, wares or merchandise intrusted to factors or agents.'

By this Act, the protection conferred by the Factors Act 1823 was extended in two ways. First, it extended the protection conferred by the Factors Act 1823 to cases where it was not the goods, but the bills of lading or other documents of title, which had been entrusted to the factor or agent. Second, it conferred protection not only in the form of a lien in such cases and in the cases specified in the Factors Act 1823; it went further, and provided that contracts for the purchase of goods made with agents entrusted with those goods, should be 'binding upon and good against the owner of such goods.' This provision (to be found in section 4) was expressed to be subject to the following proviso:

> 'provided such contract ... be made in the usual and ordinary course of business, and that such person [the purchaser] ... shall not, when such contract is entered into ... have notice that such agent ... is ... not authorised to sell the said goods, wares and merchandise ...'

Now there can, in my opinion, be no doubt that 'the owner of such goods,' upon whom the contract made by the agent was binding, can refer only to the owner who had entrusted the goods to the agent. This is evident from the statutory purpose as demonstrated in the title to the Act, and from the proviso to section 4, quoted above, which focuses upon the requirement that the purchaser must not have notice that the agent was not *authorised* to *sell* the goods. It is evident that the whole Act, like its predecessor, was directed to giving protection to those who had dealt in good faith with factors or agents, to whom goods, or documents of title to goods, had been entrusted, to the extent that the rights of such persons should (so far as provided) override those of the owner who had so entrusted the goods or documents to the factor or agent. There is not the slightest indication in the statute that it was intended to take so radical a step as to depart (except in the limited circumstances I have indicated) from the cardinal principle of the law of property in chattels embodied in the Latin maxim nemo dat quod non habet, so as to enable a factor or agent, entrusted with goods by a thief or a purchaser from a thief, to give a good title to a bona fide purchaser from him, overriding the title of the true owner. Not surprisingly, it does not seem that any such argument was ever advanced under section 4 of the Factors Act 1825; if it had been, I cannot help but think that it would have been given very short shrift indeed.

The next Act was the Factors Act 1842. I need only mention this Act in passing. It was entitled 'An Act to amend the law relating to advances bona fide made to agents entrusted with goods;' and, as its title indicates, the intention was to extend the protection, conferred by the earlier Factors Acts, to persons who had made such advances in good faith, so as to validate any pledges, liens or other security granted upon the relevant goods or documents of title.

I come next to the Factors Act 1877, which is of some importance, for it legislated for the first time for the cases of vendors permitted to retain documents of title to goods, and vendees permitted to have such documents of title, after the sale. The Act was entitled simply 'An Act to amend the Factors' Acts,' and it was introduced by the following recital:

> 'Whereas doubts have arisen with respect to the true meaning of certain provisions of the Factors' Acts, and it is expedient to remove such doubts and otherwise to amend the said Acts, for the better security of persons buying or making advances on goods, or documents of title to goods, in the usual and ordinary course of mercantile business.'

For present purposes, the relevant sections are sections 3 and 4, which provide:

> '3. Where any goods have been sold, and the vendor or any person on his behalf continues or is in possession of the documents of title thereto, any sale, pledge, or other disposition of the goods or documents made by such vendor or any person or agent entrusted by the vendor with the goods or documents within the meaning of the principal Acts as amended by this Act so continuing or being in possession, shall be as valid and effectual as if such vendor or person were an agent or person entrusted by the vendee with the goods or documents within the meaning of the principal Acts as amended by this Act, provided the person to whom the sale, pledge, or other disposition is made has not notice that the goods have been previously sold.
>
> '4. Where any goods have been sold or contracted to be sold, and the vendee,

> or any person on his behalf, obtains the possession of the documents of title thereto from the vendor or his agents, any sale, pledge, or disposition of such goods or documents by such vendee so in possession or by any other person or agent entrusted by the vendee with the documents within the meaning of the principal Acts as amended by this Act shall be as valid and effectual as if such vendee or other person were an agent or person entrusted by the vendor with the documents within the meaning of the principal Acts as amended by this Act, provided the person to whom the sale, pledge, or other disposition is made has not notice of any lien or other right of the vendor in respect of the goods.'

Taking first section 3, it is, I think, of importance to observe that it provided that the 'sale, pledge, or other disposition of the goods or documents .... shall be as valid and effectual as if such vendor or person were an agent or person entrusted *by the vendee* with the goods or documents within the meaning of the principal Acts as amended by this Act ....' This can, I suppose, be described as a statutory hypothesis: but for me the significance of the provision is that it presupposes an *entrusting* by the *vendee* and an intention (consistent with the previous Factors Acts) that, by virtue of such entrusting, the title of the vendee may be adversely affected. Likewise, in section 4, we find a similar hypothesis—'as if such vendee or other person were an agent or person *entrusted* by the *vendor* with the documents'—plainly with the same policy in mind. Once again, it cannot sensibly be suggested that this Act, any more than the Factors Act 1825, was intended to affect adversely the title of a person from whom goods or documents of title had been stolen: the intention was only to affect adversely the title of one who had entrusted documents of title to another, though here the person so entrusted would not be a factor or agent, but a vendor or vendee entrusted with possession after a sale.

Such are the statutory precursors of the Factors Act 1889. This Act is, as I have already recorded, entitled simply 'An Act to amend and consolidate the Factors Acts.' There is no hint of any change of fundamental policy in the title; nor is there any preamble to the Act, in which any such change of policy would surely have been set out, had it been intended by Parliament to make such a change. As I have previously said, the relevant sections are sections 2, 8 and 9. Section 2 is concerned to provide for the validity of sales, pledges and other dispositions of goods by mercantile agents who are, 'with the consent of the owner,' in possession of the goods or of documents of title to the goods; such transactions, it is provided, shall be as valid as if the mercantile agents were expressly authorised 'by the owner of the goods to make the same.' Plainly, the owner of the goods here referred to is the owner with whose consent the agent is in possession of them. The section cannot be read as having the effect of adversely affecting the title of any person, other than the person who had entrusted the goods or documents of title to the mercantile agents; it cannot adversely affect the title of one from whom the goods had been stolen, whose goods have come into possession of the mercantile agent from the thief, or from a person deriving title from the thief. The policy underlying this section is, therefore, wholly consistent with the policy underlying the earlier Factors Acts.

I come therefore to sections 8 and 9. I will, for the sake of clarity set out the two sections again, in order to identify with initials the relevant actors in the drama. In section 8, I have identified the vendor as A; the first purchaser, who has allowed A to remain in possession of the goods or documents of title, I shall hereafter refer to as B1; and the second purchaser, to whom A has sold, pledged or otherwise disposed of the goods or documents of title, I have identified as B2. In section 9, I have identified the seller referred to in line 2 of the section as A; the person who bought or agreed to buy the goods from A, and who obtained possession of the goods or documents of title with A's consent, I have identified as B; and the person to whom B delivers or transfers the goods or documents of title under a sale, pledge or other disposal, or an agreement for the same, I have identified as C. Interpolating these initials, the sections read:

> '8. Where a person (A), having sold goods, continues, or is, in possession of the goods or of the documents of title to the goods, the delivery or transfer by that person (A), or by a mercantile agent acting for him, of the goods or documents of title under any sale, pledge, or other disposition thereof, or under any agreement for sale, pledge, or other disposition thereof, to any person (B2) receiving the same in good faith and without notice of the previous sale, shall have the same effect as if the person making the delivery or transfer were expressly authorised by the owner of the goods to make the same.
>
> '9. Where a person (B), having bought or agreed to buy goods, obtains with the consent of the seller (A) possession of the goods or the documents of title to the goods, the delivery or transfer, by that person (B) or by a mercantile agent acting for him, of the goods or documents of title, under any sale, pledge, or other disposition thereof, or under any agreement for sale, pledge, or other disposition thereof, to any person (C) receiving the same in good faith and without notice of any lien or other right of the original seller (A) in respect of the goods, shall have the same effect as if the person (B) making the delivery or transfer were a mercantile agent in possession of the goods or documents of title with the consent of the owner.'

These two sections, of course, go slightly further than sections 3 and 4 of the Factors Act 1877, in that they take effect not only when the relevant person ((A) in section 8, and (B) in section 9) is allowed to be in possession of the documents of title to the goods, but also when he is allowed to be in possession of the goods themselves. It is relevant to observe also that, whereas the statutory hypothesis at the end of sections 3 and 4 of the Factors Act 1877 refers to the transaction taking effect as if the person making the delivery or transfer was a person entrusted by the *vendee* with the goods or documents, or entrusted by the *vendor* with the documents, as the case may be, we now see, in section 8 and 9 of the Factors Act 1889, a different phraseology, referring not to the vendee (B1) or the vendor (A), but just to the 'owner of the goods' or 'the owner.' It is upon the slender foundation of this change of phraseology that the appellant, in the present case, has sought to build his argument that section 9 has the effect of adversely affecting the title, not only of a person (A) who has allowed another person (B) to be in possession of the relevant goods or documents, but also of anybody from whom the goods have been stolen, and whose goods have come into the possession of another who sells them.

For section 9 to have any such effect would constitute a change in policy of a fundamental kind, of which there is no evidence whatsoever in the remainder of the Act of 1889. I add for good measure that when, in 1893, section 9 was effectively incorporated (with changes which are immaterial for present purposes) as section 25(2) of the Sale of Goods Act of that year, it was incorporated into an Act of Parliament which expressly maintained the fundamental principle nemo dat quod non habet, in section 21(1) of the Act (now section 21(1) of the Act of 1979, quoted above). The succeeding sections enact what appear to be minor exceptions to that fundamental principle: yet, if the appellant's contention were to be correct, section 25(2) would have made not so much an exception to the principle, but would have substantially amounted to a reversal of it.

For the reasons I have set out, the statutory context provides overwhelming evidence that the legislature never intended, either in section 9 of the Factors Act 1889, or in section 25(2) of the Sale of Goods Act 1893 (or its successor, section 25(1) of the Sale of Goods Act 1979) to achieve the result contended for by the appellant. But there is further internal evidence, in the Act of 1889, that such a result can never have been intended.

Let me concentrate for a moment, not on section 9, but on section 8 of the Factors Act 1889. The submission for the appellant has to be that, when A has sold goods to B1, and B1 allows A to remain in possession of the goods after the sale, a subsequent sale by A to B2 will be effective to divest the title of a person from whom the goods have previously been stolen before they came into the hands of A. It is obvious that this can never have been the intention of the legislature. If it was, what was the relevance of the sale to B1, and the fact that B1 has allowed A to remain in possession? Assuming B1 to have acted in good faith, why should not A, whom I will assume to be the thief, give as good a title to B1 as to B2? Each is relying equally upon the possession of A of the goods. In truth, the whole section proceeds upon the assumption that the relevant owner of the goods, who is deemed to have authorised their delivery and transfer, is B1 - the person to whom the goods have been sold by A, and who has allowed A to remain in possession of them, and exactly the same point can be made in relation to section 9 itself. What is the relevance of the fact that B is in possession of the goods or documents of title with the permission of A? Again, there seems to be no good reason why C should get a good title, but that B (whom I assume to be acting in good faith) should not; each is simply relying, in good faith, upon the possession of his vendor.

Furthermore, if the construction of section 9 (and, by implication, section 8) urged by the appellant is correct, then we find a startling contrast between the policy underlying those two sections, and that underlying section 2. For section 2 goes no further than to divest the title of a person who has entrusted the mercantile agent with the possession of the relevant goods or documents of title; if sections 8 and 9 were to have the effect of divesting the title of a person from whom the goods have been stolen, and who has not entrusted them to the person who has purported to sell them to the purchaser, it is difficult to see why section 2 should have been so limited in its effect.

As a matter of construction of the relevant statutory provisions, therefore, I have reached the conclusion that the submission advanced by the appellant cannot be sustained. In my opinion, section 9 of the Factors Act 1889 must be read as providing that the delivery or transfer given by the intermediate transferor (B) shall have the same effect as if he was a mercantile agent in possession of the goods or documents of title with the consent of the owner who entrusted them to him (A). Such a construction is, in my opinion, to be derived from the terms of section 2(1) of the Act, to which section 9 evidently refers, and also from the legislative context which I have already discussed. The same construction must, of course, be placed upon section 25(1) of the Sale of Goods Act 1979.

I find myself fortified in this conclusion by a number of matters. First, so far as the researches of counsel have been able to ascertain, the suggestion that section 9 of the Act of 1889 should have the far-reaching effect now contended for by the appellant, has never before been advanced in an English court; in other words, the present case is preceded by almost a century of silence. Next, such statements of law in the authorities as can be interpreted as bearing upon the point appear to be unanimously against the appellant. I refer in particular to *Cahn v Pockett's Bristol Channel Steam Packet Co Ltd* [1889] 1 QB 643, 658-659, *per* Collins LJ, and *Folkes v King* [1923] 1 KB 282, 305-306, *per* Scrutton LJ. I would, however, add that the decision of the Court of Appeal in *Central Newbury Car Auctions Ltd v Unity Finance Ltd* [1957] 1 QB 371 and that of Pearson J in *Butterworth v Kingsway Motors* [1954] 1 WLR 1286, are both implicitly inconsistent with the appellant's submission. Third, there is Commonwealth authority directly in point. There is first the decision of Beattie J in *Elwin v O'Regan and Maxwell* [1971] NZLR 1124. That case was concerned with section 27(2) of the New Zealand Sale of Goods Act 1908, which is in the same terms as section 25(2) of the Sale of Goods Act 1893. Beattie J rejected an argument which was similar to that advanced by the appellant in the present case. There is also the decision of Moore J in *Brandon v Leckie* (1972) 29 DLR (3d) 633, a decision of the Alberta Supreme Court. That case arose under section 27(2) of the Alberta Sale of Goods Act 1970, which is in similar terms. He reached the same conclusion as Beattie J. Lastly, there is distinguished academic authority to the same effect. I refer in particular to *Atiyah, The Sale of Goods*, 7th ed (1985), pp 302-303, a passage relied upon both by Beattie J and by Moore J. In truth, all authority on the point is unanimously adverse to the contention of the appellant in the present case.

For these reasons, I would dismiss the appeal.

Lords Bridge of Harwich, Lowry, Brandon of Oakbrook, and Griffiths agreed.

(iii) Purchase in good faith and for value of a voidable title

Sale of Goods Act 1979 **9.89 (E&W)**

Section 23 Sale under a voidable title

When a seller of goods has a voidable title to them, but his title has not been avoided at the time of the sale, the buyer acquires a good title to the goods, provided he buys them in good faith and without notice of the seller's defect of title.

(iv) A special regime for cars on credit

Hire Purchase Act 1964 **9.90 (E&W)**

Section 27 Protection of purchasers of motor vehicles

(1) This section applies where a motor vehicle has been bailed or (in Scotland) hired under a hire-purchase agreement, or has been agreed to be sold under a conditional sale agreement, and, before the property in the vehicle has become vested in the debtor, he disposes of the vehicle to another person.

(2) Where the disposition referred to in subsection (1) above is to a private purchaser, and he is a purchaser of the motor vehicle in good faith without notice of the hire-purchase or conditional sale agreement (the 'relevant agreement') that disposition shall have effect as if the creditor's title to the vehicle has been vested in the debtor immediately before that disposition.

(3) Where the person to whom the disposition referred to in subsection (1) above is made (the 'original purchaser') is a trade or finance purchaser, then if the person who is the first private purchaser of the motor vehicle after that disposition (the 'first private purchaser') is a purchaser of the vehicle in good faith without notice of the relevant agreement, the disposition of the vehicle to the first private purchaser shall have effect as if the title of the creditor to the vehicle had been vested in the debtor immediately before he disposed of it to the original purchaser.

(4) Where, in a case within subsection (3) above—

(a) the disposition by which the first private purchaser becomes a purchaser of the motor vehicle in good faith without notice of the relevant agreement is itself a bailment or hiring under a hire-purchase agreement, and

(b) the person who is the creditor in relation to that agreement disposes of the vehicle to the first private purchaser, or a person claiming under him, by transferring to him the property in the vehicle in pursuance of a provision in the agreement in that behalf,

the disposition referred to in paragraph (b) above (whether or not the person to whom it is made is a purchaser in good faith without notice of the relevant agreement) shall as well as the disposition referred to in paragraph (a) above, have effect as mentioned in sub-section (3) above.

(5) The preceding provisions of this section apply—

(a) notwithstanding anything in [section 21 of the Sale of Goods Act 1979] (sale of goods by a person not the owner), but

(b) without prejudice to the provisions of the Factors Acts (as defined by [section 61(1) of the said Act of 1979] or of any other enactment enabling the apparent owner of goods to dispose of them as if he were the true owner.

(6) Nothing in this section shall exonerate the debtor from any liability (whether criminal or civil) to which he would be subject apart from this section; and, in a case where the debtor disposes of the motor vehicle to a trade or finance purchaser, nothing in this section shall exonerate—

(a) that trade or finance purchaser, or

(b) any other trade or finance purchaser who becomes a purchaser of the vehicle and is not a person claiming under the first private purchaser,

from any liability (whether criminal of civil) to which he would be subject apart from this section.

III.B.4 ESTOPPEL

Court of Appeal, 19 December 1894[101] **9.91 (E&W)**

Henderson v Williams

FRAUDULENTLY INDUCED ATTORNMENT

Induced by fraud

Defrauded vendor estopped from denying a valid attornment in favour of a good faith purchaser of title to the goods.

Facts: A person with a title to goods lying at a warehouse was induced by the fraud of one Fletcher, who pretended to be a reputable buyer, to instruct the warehouseman to transfer the goods to the order of Fletcher, and the goods were accordingly placed at his disposal. Fletcher then sold the goods to an innocent purchaser, who, before paying the price, obtained a statement from the warehouseman that he held the goods at the purchaser's order. On the discovery of Fletcher's fraud, the warehouseman refused to deliver the goods to the purchaser. In an action by the purchaser against the warehouseman.

Held: That the warehouseman, having attorned to the purchaser, was estopped from impeaching his title, that the refusal to deliver was a conversion.

Judgment: Lord Halsbury—... This is an action in which it is admitted that the warehouse-keeper is acting under the indemnity of Grey & Co, and I have thought it right to trace the question up to its source, and to treat Grey & Co, the true owners, as the persons who are the practical defendants in this case. Treating Grey & Co as the defendants in this case, I am of opinion that upon these facts they have no answer. The real truth is that Grey & Co are the persons who have permitted this fraud to be committed, by intrusting the goods to the order and disposition of Fletcher; and ... I think that it is not undesirable to refer to an American authority, ..., *Root v French*, in which, in the Supreme Court of New York, Savage CJ makes observations which seem to me to be well worthy of consideration. Speaking of a bonâ fide purchaser who has purchased property from a fraudulent vendee and given value for it, he says:

> 'He is protected in doing so upon the principle just stated, that when one of two innocent persons must suffer from the fraud of a third, he shall suffer, who, by his indiscretion, has enabled such third person to commit the fraud. A contrary principle would endanger the security of commercial transactions, and destroy that confidence upon which what is called the usual course of trade materially rests.'

It appears to me, therefore, that when once the correspondence is looked at upon which these goods were committed to Fletcher, to his order and disposition, and Fletcher was invested with a full power of disposition, it is impossible to argue that this was not a holding out, by the true owner of the goods, of Fletcher as capable of giving a good title. It is admitted that the present plaintiffs dealt bonâ fide with the person who was thus in the complete dominion of the property in question, and was, under these circumstances, and from this correspondence, held out by the true owners of the goods as the owner, and with whom therefore any contract made innocently by a bonâ fide purchaser for value would be protected.

[101] [1895] 1 QB 521.

Lindley LJ and A L Smith also gave judgment for the plaintiffs.

III.B.5 ABANDONMENT

Introductory Note

Although the rule is undoubtedly that it is impossible to abandon a title to land at common law, possibly a product of the feudal system, the rule with respect to titles to goods is unclear. There is no decision directly on point, and the academic authorities are divided.

St German, Dialogues Between a Doctor of Divinity and a Student of the Laws of England (1518), (Dialogue II, ch LI) **9.92 (E&W)**

Doctor: But yf a man in the see cast his goodes out of the shyp as forsaken: there be doctours hold that euery man may taken them laufully that wyl but otherwyse it is as they say if he throw them out for fere that they should ouercharge the shyp.

Student: There is no such law in this realme of goodes forsaken for though a man weiue the possession of his goodes & saith he forsaketh them yet by the law of the realme the property remayneth styll in hym & he may sease them after when he wyll.

Assize Court, 1614[102] **9.93 (E&W)**

Haynes' Case

ABANDONMENT OF GOODS

Gravedigging

A person cannot relinquish the property he has to his goods, unless they be vested in another.

Facts: One William Haynes dug up the graves of three men and one woman, in the night, and took their winding sheets from their bodies, and buried them again. He was charged with theft of the sheets.

Held: Conviction for theft upheld.

Judgment: It was resolved by the justices at Serjeants' Inn, Fleet-street, that the property of the sheets remain in the owners, that is, in him who had property therein, when the dead body was wrapped therewith; for the dead body is not capable of it. ... If apparel be put upon a boy, this is a gift in the law, for the boy hath capacity to take it; but a dead body being but a lump of earth hath no capacity: also, it is no gift to the person, but bestowed on the body for the reverence towards it, to express the hope of resurrection. Also a man cannot relinquish the property he hath to his goods, unless they be vested in another; and, accordingly, at the said assises he was severally indicted for taking each of these sheets: and the first indictment was of petty larceny, for which he was whipped; and at the same assises he was also indicted for the felonious taking the three other sheets,

[102] The exact date of decision of this case is unknown (1614) 12 Co Rep 113.

for which he had his clergy, and so escaped the sentence of death, which he well deserved, for this inhuman and barbarous felony.

Blackstone, Commentaries on the Laws of England, vol 1, 295 **9.94(E&W)**

A man that scatters his treasure into the sea, or upon the public surface of the earth, is construed to have absolutely abandoned his property, and returned it into the common flock, without any intention of reclaiming it: and therefore it belongs, as in a state of nature, to the first occupant, or finder.

Note

See also Blackstone 2 *Commentaries* 9 and 402.

IV. COMPARATIVE REMARKS

This chapter divides between the civil law and the common law. The reason for this is the existing differences in approach between the legal traditions. Nevertheless, there are also similarities, not only between the various civil law systems, but between the civil and common law. This section deals with some of those similarities and differences.

IV.A APPROACH

The notion of the 'destruction' of a right is not one generally treated by the civil law systems. However, this is not to say that civil law systems do not know of the destruction of rights, only that this question is usually dealt with in the context of the creation of another right. This can be seen in the case of the creation of new right through the manufacture of a new product from raw materials, and in the case of the creation of a new right through the lapse of time. Whether or not bona fide acquisition is also an example of destruction depends on its doctrinal analysis: is it a transfer or does it constitute original acquisition? If answered at all, this question is answered differently in the various civil law jurisdictions.

In 2005, the European Court of Human Rights handed down its decision in the case of *Pye v United Kingdom*. In this case, the Court considered the conformity of the rules on limitation with the constitutional right of ownership guaranteed by Article 1 of the First Protocol to the European Convention on Human Rights. The case raised many questions in civil law systems as to the constitutionality of the rules on extinctive prescription. *Pye v United Kingdom*, which will be dealt with in further detail in Chapter 10,[103] raised awareness that property rights can be destroyed in the several instances dealt with by this chapter.

[103] See on this case Chapter 7 (7.77 (E&W)), Chapter 10 (10.58 (ECHR)).

In English law, it is not uncommon to consider the issue of the destruction of rights, as shown by the cases used in this chapter. The increasing awareness of the destruction of rights has therefore brought the approach by civil and common lawyers closer together.

IV.B TERMINOLOGY

There seems to be a somewhat hidden difference (or, perhaps, at the end of the day it is no difference at all) in terminology used by the civil law and common law systems. Rules regarding bona fide purchase in English law are rules of third-party protection in civil law systems. Nevertheless, both systems approach the same question: how can we protect a party who does not know and could not know about a certain legal situation.

IV.C DESTRUCTION OF SUBJECT-MATTER

In both civil law and common law a property right in respect to an object will be destroyed when the object ceases to exist. This may happen, inter alia, through consumption, accession, mixture, or *specificatio*.

IV.D DESTRUCTION OF RIGHT

In both civil law and common law systems, though the object of the right remains extant, the property rights themselves are destroyed in similar situations, although differences also exist. These differences are mostly legal system specific and related to the legal framework of that system. For example, estoppel is a common law doctrine and therefore destruction of a property right as a consequence of estoppel is specific to that system. Another example is provided by the specific rules on the right of usufruct in, for instance, French law. As can be seen from Chapter 3, there is no right of usufruct in the common law law and consequently a specific rule concerning destruction of a right of usufruct is absent there.

IV.E TECHNIQUES OF DESTRUCTION

In general there are three ways in which property rights can be destroyed. A property right can be destroyed completely at the point when a new property right is created. A property right can be lost and therefore also destroyed in a more limited sense of the word, by a forced, ie involuntary, transfer to another party, though this is not a technique of the common law. Finally, a property right can also be lost completely, without the creation of a new property right.

IV.F PRESCRIPTION AND LIMITATION

All legal systems considered above have rules on the limitation of actions. After a certain lapse of time, actions may become statute barred. In civil law systems, this is called extinctive prescription, in common law systems limitation. Where only the right of action is statute barred, this is often called the 'weak' force of prescription: the property right does not lapse, only the action protecting the right. Where a non-owner has been in possession of the object for a long time, civil law systems may give ownership to this person after a certain lapse of time. In such a case prescription has what is known as 'strong' effect, destroying the former owner's property right. In civil law systems, this effect is reached by acquisitive prescription, which constitutes original acquisition rather than a transfer. The acquisition by the possessor necessarily entails the destruction of the former owner's property right. In English law, limitation may have both the weak and strong effect, save that it never transfers rights.

IV.G THIRD PARTY PROTECTION AND BONA FIDE PURCHASERS

A second similarity lies in the protection which in certain circumstances is given to a third party, as a civil lawyer would say, who acquires property from a party that was not capable or authorised to transfer a property right or, as a common lawyer would say, who acquired from someone in a situation where another person had a better right. It should be borne in mind that English law does not know the civilian concept of ownership and that, when the word is used in English cases or statutes, it must generally be read as a short-hand for 'person with the best title'. In English law, a person with an inferior title may pass his title to the goods to a third party, but any person with a better title will not lose his right to the goods. Generally, persons with better rights are protected, though in exceptional cases the bona fide third party is protected against this better title. In civil law terminology the non-owner may transfer possession of the goods to a third party, but not ownership of the goods, though in exceptional cases the third party is able to acquire ownership of those goods.

In such cases, the result of the application of these rules is that a party originally holding the right of ownership or the better title to the goods loses it.

In order for these rules to apply, the party acquiring the right must meet certain standards. In civil law systems this is the requirement of good faith; in English law the purchaser must be a bona fide purchaser for value without notice of the better title. This similarity in the approach is hidden behind the difference in terminology.

IV.H ABANDONMENT

Finally, a similarity lies in the ultimate right of disposition the holder has over his own property right. As was seen in Chapter 3, the holder of a property right is generally allowed to do with his right as he pleases within the limits of the law.

Part of this power concerns his right to abandon his right.[104] The right to abandon, the voluntary destruction of a property right, is therefore, though sometimes controversial, recognised.

However, differences exist in the effect of the abandonment. A general distinction between immovable objects or land and movable objects or goods must be made. Civil law systems generally recognise the right to abandon property rights in respect to movables. In the common law this is still a contested issue.

Immovable objects or land present more difficulties. In English law, abandonment of a property right in land is, because of the continued, though attenuated, existence of the feudal system, not permitted. In civil law systems, the return to the right of ownership after the abolition of the feudal system means that the state controls ownership of land. As a result, when abandonment is accepted, the state will hold a property right in respect to the immovable object. Dutch law offers the most restrictive approach, generally rejecting the third-party effect of an abandonment of property rights. Differences exist in the way in which the property right on behalf of the state is created after abandonment. This can either be creation of a new right or transfer of the existing right to the state.

CONCISE BIBLIOGRAPHY

W Dross, 'Le singulier destin de l'article 2279 du code civil' [2006] *Revue trimestrielle de droit civil* (*RTD Civ*) 27.

R Michaels, 'Erwerb vom Nichtberechtigten' in J. Basedow et al (eds), *Handwörterbuch des Europäischen Privatrechts*, vol 1 (Tübingen, Mohr Siebeck, 2009) 451–54.

M Prisching, *Gutgläubiger Erwerb an beweglichen Sachen im Rechtsvergleich* (Graz, Leykam, 2006).

AF Salomons, 'Good Faith Acquisition of Movables' in AS Hartkamp et al (ed.), *Towards a European Civil Code*, 4th edn (2011) 1065–82.

D Zeranski, 'Prinzipien und Systematik des gutgläubigen Erwerbs beweglicher Sachen' [2002] *Juristische Schulung* (*JuS*) 340.

[104] In Chapter 3 we also discussed the possibility that the holder of a property right destroys the object of his right. In such a situation, if successful, the property right on it will also be destroyed.

CHAPTER TEN
UNIFORM OR HARMONISED PROPERTY LAW

Bram Akkermans, Michael Milo and Vincent Sagaert

This final chapter deals with the unification and harmonisation of property law. The chapter offers an overview of the main areas in which there are international activities to deal with matters of property law. Harmonisation of property law is a complicated and controversial subject, because, as this casebook illustrates, there are many differences between property law systems. Nonetheless there are important initiatives already in place as well as in preparation that deal with matters of property law. This chapter will deal with both European and international initiatives, but with a focus on European Union law.

I. HARMONISATION OF PROPERTY LAW

I.A INTRODUCTION

Until recently, property law has not been subject to many unifying or harmonising efforts, not by formal supranational regulation nor by informal methods, such as the drawing up of principles, and neither has there been a lot of borrowing by national jurisdictions of foreign property law concepts.[1] Why would this be the case? The one overarching distinguishing characteristic of property rights is that they can be enforced against an indefinite number of people or—in other words—have an *erga omnes* effect. As such they are technically the opposite from personal rights to which specific persons are bound. This applies both to civil as well as to common law jurisdictions.[2] As was seen in the previous chapters in this casebook, the consequence is that property rights—since they affect the position of third parties—need to have a relatively high level of certainty and predictability. Because the interests of third parties need to be taken into account in property or insolvency conflicts, the national regulations of property law are mandatory, with a low level of party autonomy. Moreover, the regulation is usually very detailed and technical. National rules of private international law add to the picture. In international transactions choice of law—which would be the often-used option in contract law—is not the leading rule in property law issues. Instead the *lex situs* rule or *lex rei sitae*, the law of the legal system where the subject-matter of the property right is situated, determines the applicable law. Because of the importance and therefore the mandatory nature of property law, parties cannot generally deviate from this by contract. The diversity in these detailed mandatory property laws makes any effort of harmonisation of property law of now 28 legal systems a very cumbersome task.

I.B METHODS OF HARMONISATION

The focus is unmistakably changing. In particular, those areas relevant to international transactions, especially property security rights, have seen an increase in legislative activity.[3] But the current harmonising efforts go beyond the area of security rights. Harmonisation takes place in various ways. It may involve, for example, a binding international instrument, such as a ratified convention, a Regulation or a Directive at EU-level, or a non-binding international instrument (soft law), such as principles, model laws or legislative guides. Harmonisation also takes place at various levels. It may be top-down by international or national legislation or by

[1] JM Smits, *The Making of European Private Law* (Antwerp, Oxford, New York, Intersentia, 2002) 24–26, 245–70.

[2] FH Lawson and B Rudden, *The Law of Property* (Oxford, Oxford University Press, 2002); W Swadling, 'Property law' in P Birks (ed), *English Private Law*, vol I (Oxford, Oxford University Press, 2004) 204, §4.01; HP Westermann, *Sachenrecht* (Heidelberg, CF Müller Verlag, 1998) §3; F Terré and Ph Simler, *Droit civil. Les Biens* (Paris, Edition Dalloz, 2002) no 143.

[3] As had already been predicted, see eg A Gambaro, 'Perspectives on the Codification of the Law of Property' [1997] *European Review of Private Law* 497–504.

judicial decision setting or following international or foreign standards.[4] It may also be bottom-up by academic initiatives like the Study Group on a European Civil Code, the Common Core of European Private Law, or other academic research.[5]

I.C HARMONISING PROPERTY LAW

U Mattei, Basic Principles of Property Law, 18–19[6] **10.1 (INT)**

At first impression, after reading this brief historical account, one could think that the development of the civil law and the common law in the domain of property have nothing in common and that it is therefore useless to try to describe common developments. The leading institutional actors are so different that the results are bound to be different. For example, the naturalistic conception of property rights was never shared, on technical grounds, by common lawyers. In England, the structure of property rights has been determined through the courts by incrementally solving individual conflicts. In England, no revolution ever marked a clean break with the past legal order. Much of the rhetoric and structure of the law of real property still has feudal features. As a consequence often repeated in literature of comparative law, the common law notion of property right is not absolute when compared with the civil law. Indeed, the very word 'ownership' is of recent origin.

In the common law tradition, because of the practical needs of adjudication in courts of law, the notable divorce between property and liability which is a feature of the civil law 'absolute notion' never occurred. The structure of the law of nuisance shows this difference since it reflects the practical needs of creating boundaries between incompatible activities outside of a penetrating role of administrative regulation. In Anglo-American law, nuisance is a sort of synthesis between the law of property and the law of torts. The ownership of land in the common law is inherently limited by the need to use it in a reasonable way.

…

Nevertheless, if we compare homogeneous actors in the legal system we will find much more similar results than those we reach by comparing common law and civil law of property within monistic conceptions of the legal rule, as if property law was not a complex object of observation made by a plurality of competing legal formats. The very notion of the conception being more or less absolute loses much of its meaning. … [F]or example, the law of nuisance, despite many formal differences, is fundamentally similar if one considers it in its function of delimiting property rights in similar social and economic contexts, such as advanced Western capitalistic

[4] Eg A Watson, *Legal Transplants. An Approach to Comparative Law* (Edinburgh, Scottish Academic Press, 1973).

[5] A systematisation of methods towards uniformity has been offered, eg, by Smits, above n 1. He distinguishes between centralist and non-centralist methods of harmonisation. See particularly 6–28 and 35–71. On property law, see JHM van Erp, *European and National Property Law: Osmosis or Growing Antagonism?* 6th Walter Van Gerven Lecture (Groningen, Europa Law Publishing, 2006) and JHM van Erp, 'Deconstruction and Reconstruction of European Property Law: A Research Agenda' in E Cashin-Ritaine (ed), *Legal Engineering and Comparative Law/L'ingénierie juridique et le droit comparé. Rapports du colloque du 25e anniversaire de l'Institut Suisse De Droit Comparé Du 29 août 2008 à Lausanne* (Zurich and Basel, Schultess, 2009) 105.

[6] U Mattei, *Basic Principles of Property Law. A Comparative Legal and Economic Introduction* (London, Greenwood Press, 2000) 18–19.

systems. In other words, it is not that the owner in common law was bound while his civil law colleague was free. Put simply, historically variable limits to proprietary freedom are introduced by courts of law in the first context, while by public law regulation in the second. The latter kind of limits are simply easier for private law scholars (leading actors of the system) to ignore in a tradition in which the public law versus private law dichotomy is deeply rooted. They consequently find it harder to be reflected in the traditional definitions of ownership.

Notes

(1) Property law has traditionally been national law par excellence. National property law systems are very closed: they are for a large part mandatory law with little room for party autonomy as it involves interests of third parties. In international transactions the applicable law is determined by the jurisdiction where the object is situated (*lex rei sitae*). Probably due to this national and mandatory character property law has not seen many unifying or harmonisation projects, neither by formal supranational regulation, nor by informal methods, such as the drawing of principles.[7]

(2) The tendency, however, is unmistakably changing. There has been some borrowing by national jurisdictions of foreign property law concepts, and furthermore the application of the *lex rei sitae* seems also to take into account foreign interests protected through foreign property rights. The main harmonising focus regarding property law is particularly—not surprisingly—in those areas relevant to international transactions, of which (recognition of) security rights have drawn the largest attention.[8] But there is more to be found of interest.

(3) Constitutional law protects the arrangement of private property rights; it does so at the level of national constitutions, but also at the level of international treaties. Article 1, First Protocol of the European Convention of Human Rights (ECHR), which protects property rights (possessions) against expropriation, might have some unifying force, as private (property) law needs to be in conformity with the constitutional norms of the ECHR. This holds true as well for Article 8 ECHR which protects the right to housing and the right to a fair procedure, which protects the eviction of possessors of housing without a previous option of a court procedure (*cf* below, IV).

(4) Furthermore other conventions also deal with aspects of property law, of which the following are of importance: The Convention on the Law Applicable to Trusts and on their Recognition (1985) entered into force in the United Kingdom (1992), Italy (1992), Australia (1992), Canada (1993), the Netherlands (1996), Malta (1996), Luxemburg (2004), Switzerland (2007) and Monaco (2008).[9] The United Nations Convention on the Assignment of Receivables in International Trade (New York, 2001),[10] and the UNIDROIT Convention on International Factoring (Ottawa, 1988)[11] both deal with the transfer of claims. The international conventions with regard to

[7] Smits, above n 1, 24–26, 245–270.
[8] Gambaro, above n 3.
[9] www.hcch.net/index_en.php?act=conventions.text&cid=59.
[10] www.uncitral.org/uncitral/en/uncitral_texts/payments/2001Convention_receivables.html.
[11] www.unidroit.org/english/conventions/1988factoring/main.htm.

cultural property will be dealt with below in section VI. The Convention on International Interests in Mobile Equipment (Cape Town 2001) deals with a supranational security right in objects specified in protocols: aircrafts, satellites and trains.[12]

(5) Some model laws or legislative guides are dealing with property law aspects as well: the UNCITRAL Model Law on Cross-Border Insolvency (1997) and the UNCITRAL Legislative Guide on Insolvency Law (2004), deal with the recognition of foreign property rights in insolvency proceedings;[13] UNCITRAL has been working since 2002 on a Draft Legislative Guide on Secured Transactions;[14] the European Bank for Reconstruction and Development (EBRD) has since 1994 been developing a Model Law on Secured Transactions, which has been used by East European jurisdictions in their reform of their law on security rights.[15]

(6) The European Union has undertaken some harmonising activities in the field of property law, but there has been some doubt as to the EU's competence. A right of Euromortgage has been under discussion for over 30 years already, and is advocated by some (III.D.1); there is a Regulation on Insolvency Proceedings (Regulation 1346/2000, OJ L160/1: below III.C.3) which purports the recognition of retention of title and the regimen of property security rights; the European Union has also intervened in the harmonisation of the regimen of cultural objects (Directive 93/7/EEC, OJ L74/74; see below VI); the Directive on combating late payment in commercial transactions (Directive 35/2000/EC, OJ L200/35) contains a rather meagre provision regarding retention of title (III.C.2); the Directive on Financial Collateral Arrangements (Directive 47/2002/EC, OJ L168/43) deals with security rights and title transfer structures regarding financial collateral (III.C.4)

(7) Academic research in this area is proliferating. Apart from the increased attention of individual research on comparative property law, there are interesting and promising combined academic initiatives, of which the *Ius Commune* Casebooks for the Common Law of Europe is one example. The Principles of European Trust Law[16] aim to provide a systematic framework for trusts and trust-like devices. Chapter 11 of the Principles of European Contract Law deals with assignment of claims.[17] The Trento Common Core of European Private Law project[18] (VII.D) and the Study Group on a European Civil Code (VII.A.1) have embarked on drawing maps of—among other subjects—property law in European jurisdictions.

Apart from these harmonising efforts, there is perhaps a tendency for national property laws to open up to other jurisdictions and to be brought in line with international, especially financial-economic, developments, by importing foreign elements in national property law (legal transplants), either by legislation or by case law. In

[12] www.unidroit.org/english/conventions/mobile-equipment/main.htm; RM Goode, 'The Cape Town Convention on International Interests in Mobile Equipment' in AS Hartkamp et al (eds), *Towards a European Civil Code* (Nijmegen, Ars Aequi Libri, 2004) 757–67.

[13] www.uncitral.org/uncitral/en/uncitral_texts/insolvency.html.

[14] www.uncitral.org/uncitral/en/uncitral_texts/security.html.

[15] www.ebrd.com/country/sector/law/st/index.htm.

[16] DJ Hayton et al, *Principles of European Trust Law* (The Hague, Kluwer Law International; Deventer, WEJ Tjeenk Willink, 1999).

[17] http://frontpage.cbs.dk/law/commission_on_european_contract_law/index.html.

[18] www.jus.unitn.it/dsg/common-core/home.html.

the case of international transactions involving property law aspects, such as transfer of property or security rights, the national courts show—often, not always—a flexible approach in the application of the *lex rei sitae*, for example by giving foreign concepts a reasonable meaning within the framework of the applicable system of property law, by finding a national equivalent, particularly in the area of security rights. This will be demonstrated when dealing with private international law (see below, II).

I.D CONTENT OF THE CHAPTER

This chapter deals with some of the most important harmonising efforts in the area of property law. The application of the private international law rule of the *lex rei sitae* (or *lex situs*) to international transactions appears to be more flexible to foreign property rights (see below, II). The European Union (see below, III) has competence to harmonise private property laws, but this has been subject to debate. Harmonisation may be driven by the application of the free movement of goods, persons, services or capital (negative harmonisation) or following from specific (harmonising) Regulations and Directives (positive harmonisation). Important examples of the latter are Directive 2000/35/EC (renewed as Directive 2011/7/EU) on combating late payment in business transactions, the proposed Euromortgage and Regulation 1346/2000/EC on Insolvency Proceedings.

Positive law follows from many sources, international as well as national, formal as well as informal. Transparency and consistency is particularly a matter of concern for the European Union. A conceptual frame of reference may possibly be of assistance, and a Draft Common Frame of Reference has been published. Though not originally envisaged, aspects of property law have been included, such as transfer, security rights and trusts.

Property law operates in a society where fundamental rights are protected. In particular, the fundamental rights to property (Article 1 First Protocol to ECHR), the right to a fair procedure (Article 6 ECHR) and to the right to housing (Article 8 ECHR) have exercised influence on property law. Therefore this influence from fundamental rights is also dealt with (see below, IV).

International institutions have also exerted influence in the harmonisation of property laws. The International Institute for the Unification of Private Law (UNIDROIT)[19] has drafted conventions, model laws, principles and guides on various topics, of which some are relevant to property law. The following conventions deal with aspects of property law: the Convention on the Law Applicable to Trusts and on their Recognition (1985), which has been ratified by the civil law jurisdictions of Italy and The Netherlands; the United Nations Convention on the Assignment of Receivables in International Trade (New York, 2001), and the UNIDROIT Convention on International Factoring (Ottawa, 1988) which deal with the transfer of claims; the UNIDROIT Convention on International Financial Leasing (Ottawa,

[19] www.unidroit.org/dynasite.cfm?dsmid=103283.

1988), which provides for the recognition of the lessor's right in leased equipment in the lessee's insolvency; the UNESCO convention on Illicit Import, Export and Transfer of Ownership of Cultural Property 1970; the UNIDROIT Convention on Stolen or Illegally Exported Cultural Objects (Rome, 1995),[20] which deals with the international claims to return illegally exported cultural objects; the Convention on International Interests in Mobile Equipment (Cape Town 2001), which deals with a supranational security right in objects specified in protocols: aircrafts, satellites and trains.[21]

Some model laws and legislative guides deal with property law aspects as well: the UNCITRAL[22] Model Law on Cross-Border Insolvency (1997), which deals with the recognition of foreign property rights in insolvency proceedings; the UNCITRAL Legislative Guide on Insolvency Law (2004); UNCITRAL has issued a Legislative Guide on Secured Transactions in 2007, which was adopted by the general assembly of the United Nations in 2009; the EBRD Model Law on Secured Transactions.[23] We will particularly pay attention (see below, V) to the Convention on International Interests in Mobile Equipment (2001).

Finally, harmonisation often takes place at a number of levels at the same time. The protection of cultural property is a good example of this and will be dealt with in section VI of this chapter. The private initiatives of the study group on a European Civil Code (SGECC) and the Trento Common Core Project will be the last topic (see below, VII). At the end of the chapter some reflections on the future development of International and European property law are offered (see below, VIII).

II. PRIVATE INTERNATIONAL LAW AND PROPERTY LAW

Introductory Notes

(a) Property law, from a traditional viewpoint, is mainly national law and this starting point is only strengthened by the rules of private international law. National private international systems almost universally use the *lex rei sitae*—the legal system where the object is situated—as the determining factor to arrive at the applicable law to decide on property law aspects of an international case. Where party autonomy is accepted, as for example in Switzerland, the choice of law does not affect the position of third parties.[24] Application of the *lex rei sitae* rule may be detrimental to the functioning of, in particular, security rights created in property in one jurisdic-

[20] On which, see K Siehr, 'Vereinheitlichung des Mobiliarsachenrechts in Europa, insbesondere im Hinblick auf Kulturgüter' [1995] *Rabels Zeitschrift für Ausländisches und internationales Privatrecht* 454–68.
[21] Goode, above n 12, 757–767.
[22] www.uncitral.org/uncitral/en/index.html.
[23] www.ebrd.com/pages/sector/legal.shtml.
[24] E-M Kieninger, 'Introduction' in E-M Kieninger, *Security Rights in Movable Property in European Private Law* (Cambridge, Cambridge University Press, 2004) 17.

tion, which are subsequently exported to another legal system, where these security right need to take effect.[25]

(b) Particularly in case of property whose location constantly varies, such as aeroplanes, trains, cars and satellites, the *lex rei sitae* will not provide ex ante legal certainty. Yet—though there is a need for quantitative research—it seems there is a general tendency for increasing acceptance of the recognition of foreign security rights or retention of title constructions in national court decisions.[26] In the case of an international transaction involving claims (on claims, see Chapter 4), the situation is more complicated. In that case the Rome-I Regulation (Article 14), will apply, but the solutions reached are far from uniform. In the following, cases dealing with security rights and retention of title will be used to illustrate the effect of private international law in national property law.

Code civil **10.2 (FR)**

Article 3... Immovables, even those owned by foreigners, are governed by French law ...

Einführungsgesetez zum Bürgerliches Gesetzbuch (EGBGB) **10.3 (DE)**

Article 43(1) Rights in respect to an object (Sache) Rights in respect to an object are governed by the law of the State where the object is situated.

BGH, 20 June 1990[27] **10.4 (DE)**

APPLICABLE LAW TO ASSIGNMENT OF CLAIMS

Trinidad and Tobago

The law that applies to the claim that was assigned applies to the proprietary aspects of the assignment.

Facts: The Republic of Trinidad and Tobago agreed with a ship repair company to repair a ship belonging to the former Republic against payment of a large sum. The repair agreement was made subject to English law. The ship repair company contracted a credit with a financial institution (in order to pay the suppliers of the goods which were necessary for the ship repair). It assigned its claim against the Republic of Trinidad and Tobago to a credit institution. The claimant sold goods which were incorporated in the ship. The general conditions of the sales agreement provided for a security assignment of the claim also, to the amount of the sales price, which had not yet been paid.

Held: The law which applies to the claim which is the object of the assignment, applies to the proprietary aspects of the assignment of claims.

[25] Kieninger (*ibid*) mentions the example where the French Cour de cassation refused to recognise the German security ownership claim.

[26] Examples are the recognition of a Tanzanian floating charge as a Dutch *stil pandrecht* (silent or non-possessory pledge) in: HR 14 december 2001, (2002) NJ 241 (*Sisal II*).

[27] BGHZ 111, 376.

Judgment: Following consistent German case law and the leading doctrinal opinion, assignment, as is the case in the Swiss, Austrian, English and French private international law (cf the evidence provided by Von Bar, RabelsZ 1989, 462, 468 footnote 28)—must be governed by the law applicable to the claim (*Schuldstatut*). From that the effects of the exercise and the assignment of a right, that determines the legal relation, is governed. This is the right, which determines the legal relation, from which the claim arises. ...

In so far as the court of appeal based its confirming judgment on Article 33 section 2 EGBGB and the current revision objects that according to Article 220 section EGBGB is not applicable to newly created agreement before 1 September 1986, the date of entry into force of the new provisions of the EGBGB. For these the then applicable rules of private international law prevail, on which this decision cannot be made. Article 33 section 2 EGBGB under which the law applies to the assigned claim of the relation between the new creditor and the debtor, on the conditions under which the assignment can be opposed against the debtor, and on the effect of the performance by the debtor, merely codified the existing law. ...

In the interest of clarity of the law and legal certainty, as well with regard to Article 33 section 2 EGBGB that does not differentiate according to the nature of the claim or the purpose of the assignment, it seems necessary to treat the conditions and the effect of such an assignment together and make it subject to the law of the right, that forms the basis for the assigned claim according to law applicable to the the claim. This is therefore also decisive for the question of the ranking between concurrent assignments. ...

Burgerlijk Wetboek **10.5 (NL)**

10:127 Article 2. (1) Unless otherwise provided in the second and third paragraph, the property law rules (*goederenrechtelijk regime*) relating to an object are governed by the law of the state on whose territory the object is located.

10:128 Article 3. (1) The proprietary aspects of retention of title are governed by the law of the country in which the object is situated at the moment of delivery. This does not impede the obligations which arise according to the law which governs the contractual aspects of retention of title.

(2) However, parties may agree that the proprietary aspects of retention of title are governed by the law of the country to which the object is destined to be exported, if that law is more beneficial to the creditor than the law which would have been applicable according to the first section. This agreement will only have effect if the object is factually imported into the country of destination.

Hoge Raad, 16 May 1997[28] **10.6 (NL)**
Brandsma qq v Hansa

APPLICABLE LAW TO ASSIGNMENT OF CLAIMS

Chemicals under retention of title

Article 12 of the Rome Convention does not only apply to the obligatory aspects of the assignments, but also to its proprietary aspects.

Facts: A German seller sold and transferred under an extended retention of title clause (*verlängerter Eigentumsvorbehalt*) chemical products to a Dutch buyer, Bechem. The clause sought to assign in advance Bechem's future claims resulting from his subsequent sales to third parties of the chemical products. Bechem was declared insolvent. At that moment, neither Bechem had paid Hansa, nor had Senzora, one of Bechem's buyers, paid Bechem. Senzora paid the purchase price on a separate bank account. Have the claims been validly assigned to Hansa—as would be the case under German law, or are the claims caught by Bechem's insolvency—as would be the case under Dutch law? This depends on the applicable law. Hansa started legal proceedings against Brandsma, the trustee in Bechem's insolvency.

Held: The assignment of the claim is governed by German law, as the parties have agreed on the applicability of German law.

Judgment: The Rome Convention is according to its preamble based on the wish to go further in the field of private international law with the unification of the law already started within the European Community. In the light of this, when interpreting the scope of Article 12, one needs to assume that the Rome Convention intends to provide a wide, regulation that is as complete as possible for questions of international private law to which the legal conceptions covered by the Rome Convention may give rise. As concerns the rules for the choice of the applicable law for the legal conception of the assignment [*cessie*] contained in Article 12, It is therefore not self-evident that the contracting States should have wanted to shirk specific aspects of the assignment, which in some of the EC Member States are qualified to be of property law, from the uniform rules. ... This leads to the conclusion that the conflict rule contained in Article 12 does not only apply to the purely obligatory relation between the assignor and assignee, but also for proprietary aspects of the assignment.

Notes

(1) With this decision the Dutch Supreme Court has introduced party autonomy regarding the proprietary aspects of the assignment by recognising that the same conflict-of-law rule applies for the proprietary aspects of the assignment as for the obligatory aspects of it.

(2) Perhaps the underlying reason is the invalidity of the valid German transaction under Dutch substantive property law. In the first place transfers for security purposes are explicitly declared invalid by the 1992 Dutch Civil Code in Article 3:84 section 3.[29] Before 1992 transfers for security purposes were commonplace, as they still are in Germany. In the second place, after 1992 the assignment of claims

[28] (1998) NJ 585.

[29] Art 3:84(3) states: 'A legal act intended to transfer property for purposes of security ... does not constitute a valid cause for transfer of that property.' See also Chapter 5.

needed a notice to the debtor of the claim—which is not necessary according to German law, and neither was a requirement in Dutch law before 1992.[30] The consequence is that an otherwise prohibited (security) transaction under Dutch law, but authorised under Dutch law in this international setting, can now be executed in the Netherlands. This conflict-of-law rule opens up Dutch national property law by admitting that parties can chose a foreign property right, and has thus influenced the *numerus clausus* principle which underlies property law.[31]

(3) In addition, the Dutch legislature is modernising the rules of Dutch private international law. The Law on the Conflicts of Laws relating to Property Law (the *Wet Conflictenrecht Goederenrecht*) contains an innovation in Article 3 that allows parties exporting to another country, most notably Germany that recognises an extended retention of title (see Chapter 5), to already apply German law on an object situated in the Netherlands. The Law on the Conflicts of Laws relating to Property Law was an intermediary phase in the legislative process. The act is now repealed and the Article returned as Article 10:128 BW.

Court of Appeal 12 February 1923[32] **10.7 (E&W)**

Hills Dry Dock and Engineering Company Ltd v Credit Maritime et Fluvial de Belgique

The *Colorado*

A French hypothec on a vessel is equivalent to a maritime lien in English law.

Facts: The appellants were companies who had effected repairs to the French steamship *Colorado,* and, failing to obtain payment of their claim, had arrested the vessel in an action *in rem*, and in November, 1921, obtained judgment and an order for sale. The vessel was sold by the Marshal and the proceeds, about £6,000, paid into court. A caveat against payment out was entered by the respondents, the Credit Maritime et Fluvial de Belgique, mortgagees under a French deed of mortgage on the *Colorado*, for nearly £41,000.

Held: A French hypothec on a vessel is equivalent to a maritime lien in English law.

Judgment: Bankes LJ—It is said that, because in this judgment the bank's security is described as a mortgage deed, it must therefore, for all purposes of priority, be treated without further inquiry as an English mortgage and given priority as such. I do not agree with this suggestion. The judgment is expressed to be without prejudice to other claims against the vessel, and all questions of priorities are reserved. This, in my opinion, leaves the question quite open as to what the rights created by the so-called mortgage deed are. This question must be determined according to French law, as the contract was made in France, though the question of priority must be decided by English law. The reason for this rule is, I think, well and clearly stated in a passage in the judgment of Marshall CJ in *Harrison v Sterry* [FN8], where he says:

'The law of the place where a contract is made is, generally speaking, the law of

[30] But it has again been made possible since 2004 in Art 3:94(3).

[31] On *numerus clausus*, see Chapter 1.

[32] [1923] P102.

> the contract—ie, it is the law by which the contract is expounded. But the right of priority forms no part of the *107 contract itself. It is extrinsic, and is rather a personal privilege dependent on the law of the place where the property lies, and where the Court sits which is to decide the cause.'

The argument for the appellants in this Court, as I understood it, raised one question which is not referred to in the judgment of the learned judge. It was to the effect that the right created by a French mortgage, as the result of the amendment of art 191 of the Code de commerce by art 34 of the law of July 10, 1885, was a limited right only, and limited to a right to follow after the creditors given priority by art 191, among whom are creditors of the class of the Hills Dry Docks Company. I do not think that this contention is well founded. Both article and amendment appear to me to deal with remedies as opposed to rights, and they cannot, therefore, be taken into consideration for the purpose of ascertaining what the rights of the respondents are under the document referred to in these proceedings as the French mortgage. If this is the correct view, the only remaining question is whether the learned judge put the true interpretation upon the documents and upon the evidence of the French lawyer who was called to state what, by French law, the rights of the respondents were under the mortgage deed.

I do not think that the evidence left the question entirely free from doubt, but in my opinion the learned judge was quite justified upon the evidence in taking the view he did—namely, that the right created by the mortgage deed was a higher right than a mere right to proceed in rem, and though not capable of exact description in terms applicable to well-recognised English rights, it yet had attributes which entitled it to rank on a question of priorities in the same class as a maritime lien or the right created by an English mortgage. For these reasons the appeal, in my opinion, fails, and must be dismissed with costs.

Rome I Regulation. Voluntary assignment or contractual subrogation **10.8 (EU)**

Article 14 1. The relationship between assignor and assignee under a voluntary assignment or contractual subrogation of a claim against another person (the debtor) shall be governed by the law that applies to the contract between the assignor and assignee
under this Regulation.
2. The law governing the assigned or subrogated claim shall determine its assignability, the relationship between the assignee and the debtor, the conditions under which the assignment or subrogation can be invoked against the debtor and whether the debtor's obligations have been discharged.
3. The concept of assignment in this Article includes outright transfers of claims, transfers of claims by way of security and pledges or other security rights over claims.

Notes

(1) The *lex rei sitae* rule is applied in most legal systems, by legislation or case law, in order to determine the applicable law to corporeal movable objects. However, if the object of the property right is transported to another legal system than the one in which the security right has been created, it is possible that the foreign security

right is not known in the *numerus clausus* of the property law of the host legal system (that must be applied because of the *lex rei sitae*), and that in case of a conflict a court will have to decide on the possibility of enforcing the foreign security right. In that case, a court will have to assess whether there exists an equivalent right resembling the foreign property right in the national system, as it was done by the English Privy Council in the *Colorado* case.The result is known as a transformation or assimilation of the foreign property right in the national legal order.

(2) As emerges from the excerpts, it is much more difficult to determine the applicable law with regard to incorporeal things, such as receivables, as they do not have any actual *situs*.

The Dutch Supreme Court has introduced party autonomy regarding the proprietary aspects of the assignment by recognising that the same conflict-of-law rule applies for the proprietary aspects of the assignment as for the obligatory aspects of it. The consequence is that an otherwise forbidden (security) transaction under Dutch law, but authorised under foreign law, can now be executed in the Netherlands. This conflict-of-law rule opens up the national property law system by admitting that parties choose for a foreign property right. This solution is subject to criticism,[33] because it can lead to an almost unsolvable situation where two conflicting assignments have been effected under two different laws, and both laws provide for a different priority rule.

(3) German law takes a more traditional approach in applying the law applicable to the claim which is the object of the assignment.

(4) Large differences existing between the different legal systems have resulted in the silence of the Rome I Regulation (before that the Rome Convention), on the topic of the proprietary aspects of the assignment. It must be noticed that earlier drafts during the preparatory works of the Rome I Regulation provided for a conflict of law rule for the proprietary aspects, starting from 'the law of the country in which the assignor … has his habitual residence at the material time.' This rule is also applied in some national legal systems, such as Belgium, where Article 87 (3) of the PIL-Code provides that

> The creation of rights in rem in respect of a receivable as well as the effects of the transfer of the receivable on such rights is governed by the law of the State on territory of which the party that created the rights or that has transferred the rights had his habitual residence at the time of creation or transfer.

Comparative Remarks

(1) Property law systems are national and mandatory systems of law. The rules of private international law serve to protect the internal balance and coherence of these national mandatory systems of property law by applying the national system also to 'foreign elements' entering its territory. In this respect *lex rei sitae* is a protective measure.

[33] THD Struycken, 'The Proprietary Aspects of International Assignment of Debts and the Rome Covention, Art 12' [1998] *Lloyd's Maritime and Commercial Law Quarterly* 345–360.

(2) There is pressure on national legal systems, especially in the European Union, where there is an internal market that is based on the free movement of goods, persons, services and capital, to open up aspects of the legal system for some of these 'foreign elements'. Dutch law is traditionally at the forefront of modernisation and adaptation to the proper functioning of the EU internal market. The cases above illustrate the movement of the Dutch courts, and also the legislature, to allow some degree of party autonomy as regards the choice of applicable law.

(3) A more controversial question is whether the rules of national private international law can be maintained in the context of the internal market of the European Union. Some argue that the *lex rei sitae* requirement in the EU context should therefore be reconsidered.[34]

III. HARMONISATION AT THE LEVEL OF THE EUROPEAN UNION

III.A INTRODUCTION

The European Union is a special legal order in which there is an internal market. This internal market is a common marketplace for all Europeans on which there is freedom of movement of goods, persons, services and capital. Originally, the aim of the European integration project was mostly economic based and aimed at achieving an optimal functioning of the internal market. The co-operation between the Member States was then known as the European Economic Community (EEC). In 1992, with the Treaty of Maastricht, a European Union was created that covered the economic community, which was reformed and extended into the European Community, but also the European Coal and Steal Community (expired 23 July 2002) and the European Atomic Energy Community (EURATOM). The European Community was the most important of the three and offered a supranational legal order. Besides economic integration, the European Community also received competences in other areas such as social policy and consumer protection.

Over the years the European Community and the overarching European Union were further reformed until in 2007 the Treaty of Lisbon was signed that reformed European co-operation into the European Union as we now know it. This reform includes two international treaties, the Treaty of European Union (TEU) and the

[34] See eg E-M Kieninger, *Mobiliarsicherheiten Im Europäischen Binnenmarkt. Zum Einfluss Der Warenverkehrsfreiheit das nationale und international Sachenrecht Der Mitgliedstaaten* (Baden-Baden, Verlagsgesellschaft, 1996); E-M Kieninger, *Wettbewerb Der Privatrechtsordnungen Im Europäischen Binnenmarkt* (Tübingen, Mohr Siebeck, 2002); E-M Kieninger, 'European Regulation of Security Rights' in U Drobnig, HJ Snijders and EJ Zippro (eds), *Divergences of Property Law, An Obstacle to the Internal Market?* (München, Sellier European Law Publishers, 2006) 165–71; E-M Kieninger, 'Die Zukunft Des deutschen und europäischen Mobiliarkreditsicherungsrechts' [2008] *Archiv für die civilistische Praxis* 208; B Akkermans and E Ramaekers, 'Free Movement of Goods and Property Law' [2012] *European Law Journal* forthcoming; B Akkermans, 'Property Law and the Internal Market' in JHM van Erp, AF Salomons and B Akkermans (eds), *The Future of European Property Law* (München, Sellier European Law Publishers, 2012) 201 *et seq.*

Treaty on the Functioning of the European Union (TFEU), both of which are relevant to EU private law.

Competences are extremely important in EU law as the EU institutions cannot act without a specific legal basis in the, usually the TFEU, Treaty. Finding a legal basis, especially in the area of private law, let alone property law, is not always easy. Moreover, in the last decade the European Union has become subject to stricter requirements concerning the use of a correct legal basis.

The European Commission generally proposes EU legislation. Depending on the legal basis that is used, the European Parliament has an advising or much more substantial role in the legislative procedure. The Council of the European Union, also referred to as the Council of Ministers, is always involved and must agree to all acts of EU legislation. When legislation is made by the EU legislature, we refer to this as positive integration or positive harmonisation.

Besides positive harmonisation, there is also negative harmonisation in the European Union. In the internal market there is freedom of movement and the TFEU Treaty contains a series of prohibitions on restrictions of that freedom of movement. There is a limited harmonising effect from these provisions because it means that Member States are no longer allowed to protect their national legal order in a certain way. These prohibitions are negatively formulated, and hence we speak of negative harmonisation. In property law the effect of negative harmonisation mostly concerns the free movement of goods and the free movement of capital.

This section will deal with all these aspects of EU harmonisation of property law. First, we will take a look at positive harmonisation (section III.B), after which we will focus on negative harmonisation (section III.C).

III.B HARMONISATON BY ENACTMENT OF EU LEGISLATION

In order to make EU legislation, the European Commission must find an appropriate legal basis in the Treaty (III.B.2). Depending on the selected legal basis, the European Commission will choose to propose a Regulation, a Directive or another legislative act of EU law (III.B.1). After this the legislative procedure determined by the Article from the TFEU providing a legal basis will be followed. This last aspect falls outside the scope of this casebook.

III.B.1 LEGISLATIVE INSTRUMENTS: REGULATIONS AND DIRECTIVES

Treaty on the Functioning of the European Union **10.9 (EU)**

Article 288 To exercise the Union's competences, the institutions shall adopt regulations, directives, decisions, recommendations and opinions.

A regulation shall have general application. It shall be binding in its entirety and directly applicable in all Member States.

A directive shall be binding, as to the result to be achieved, upon each Member

State to which it is addressed, but shall leave to the national authorities the choice of form and methods.

A decision shall be binding in its entirety. A decision which specifies those to whom it is addressed shall be binding only on them.

Recommendations and opinions shall have no binding force.

Notes

(1) Depending on the legal basis that is selected (see below, II.B.2), the European Commission must make a proposal for a Regulation or for a Directive. This is an important choice. Regulations have direct application in the legal order of the Member States, and following the case law of the Court of Justice of the European Union (European Court of Justice or ECJ), these acts of EU law create rights and duties for individuals.[35] A Directive is directed at the Member States and must therefore be transformed into national law to create rights and duties for individuals.

(2) Directives are therefore less invasive measures of EU legislation than Regulations. It is precisely because of this that many acts of European private law have taken the form of Directives, granting discretionary power to the Member States to decide where a certain measure of EU law fits best into their national legal system.[36]

III.B.2 LEGAL BASIS OF UNIFICATION OR HARMONISATION

Introductory Note

As seen above, the foundation of EU legislation, Article 288 TFEU, provides for types of legislative instruments, but in order to act the European Commission needs to have a competence to issue legislation. This competence is not a general competence, but a functional one, directed towards the primary economic objective of the European Community to establish an internal market.[37]

Treaty on the Functioning of the European Union **10.10 (EU)**

Article 1 1. This Treaty organises the functioning of the Union and determines the areas of, delimitation of, and arrangements for exercising its competences.

2. This Treaty and the Treaty on European Union constitute the Treaties on which the Union is founded. These two Treaties, which have the same legal value, shall be referred to as 'the Treaties'.

Article 2 1. When the Treaties confer on the Union exclusive competence in a specific

[35] Case 26/62, *Van Gend & Loos (NV Algemene Transport- en Expeditie Onderneming) v Nederlandse Administratie der Belastingen* [1963] ECR 1; Case 6/64, *Costa v ENEL* [1964] ECR 585.

[36] On EU Private Law see C Twigg-Flesner (ed), *Cambridge Companion to EU Private Law* (Cambridge, Cambridge University Press, 2010).

[37] See Smits, above n 1, 7–15; P-C Müller-Graf, 'EC Directives as a Means of Private Law Unification' in Hartkamp et al, above n 12, 77–89; W van Gerven, 'The ECJ Case-law as a Means of Unification of Private Law' in Hartkamp et al, above n 12, 101–23. Of interest is also, specifically with regard to the CFR (see infra III G) MW Hesselink, JW Rutgers, T de Booys, 'The legal basis for an optional instrument on European contract law', Centre for European Contract Law, Working Paper Series No 2007/04, also available at http://papers.ssrn.com/sol3/papers.cfm?abstract_id=1091119.

area, only the Union may legislate and adopt legally binding acts, the Member States being able to do so themselves only if so empowered by the Union or for the implementation of Union acts.

2. When the Treaties confer on the Union a competence shared with the Member States in a specific area, the Union and the Member States may legislate and adopt legally binding acts in that area. The Member States shall exercise their competence to the extent that the Union has not exercised its competence. The Member States shall again exercise their competence to the extent that the Union has decided to cease exercising its competence. …

6. The scope of and arrangements for exercising the Union's competences shall be determined by the provisions of the Treaties relating to each area.

Article 3 1. The Union shall have exclusive competence in the following areas:

(a) customs union;

(b) the establishing of the competition rules necessary for the functioning of the internal market;

(c) monetary policy for the Member States whose currency is the euro;

(d) …

(e) common commercial policy.

2. The Union shall also have exclusive competence for the conclusion of an international agreement when its conclusion is provided for in a legislative act of the Union or is necessary to enable the Union to exercise its internal competence, or in so far as its conclusion may affect common rules or alter their scope.

Article 4 1. The Union shall share competence with the Member States where the Treaties confer on it a competence which does not relate to the areas referred to in Articles 3 and 6.

2. Shared competence between the Union and the Member States applies in the following principal areas:

(a) internal market;

(b) social policy, for the aspects defined in this Treaty;

(c) economic, social and territorial cohesion; …

(f) consumer protection; …

Note

As the excerpts show, competence is a difficult matter in EU Law. In some areas the European Union has exclusive competence, meaning that the Member States should no longe act in this area, but in most areas, including the policy area of the internal market, most relevant for EU property law, the competences are shared, meaning that both the European Union and the Member States have competences to act. For the European Union, this still requires finding a valid legal basis.

Treaty on European Union **10.11 (EU)**

Article 5 1. The limits of Union competences are governed by the principle of conferral. The use of Union competences is governed by the principles of subsidiarity and proportionality.

2. Under the principle of conferral, the Union shall act only within the limits of the competences conferred upon it by the Member States in the Treaties to attain the objectives set out therein. Competences not conferred upon the Union in the Treaties remain with the Member States.

3. Under the principle of subsidiarity, in areas which do not fall within its exclusive competence, the Union shall act only if and in so far as the objectives of the proposed action cannot be sufficiently achieved by the Member States, either at central level or at regional and local level, but can rather, by reason of the scale or effects of the proposed action, be better achieved at Union level.

The institutions of the Union shall apply the principle of subsidiarity as laid down in the Protocol on the application of the principles of subsidiarity and proportionality. National Parliaments ensure compliance with the principle of subsidiarity in accordance with the procedure set out in that Protocol.

4. Under the principle of proportionality, the content and form of Union action shall not exceed what is necessary to achieve the objectives of the Treaties.

The institutions of the Union shall apply the principle of proportionality as laid down in the Protocol on the application of the principles of subsidiarity and proportionality.

Note

Whenever the European Union wants to legislate in a certain area it must keep with the principle of subsidiarity, ie the principle ensuring the European Union does not claim competence it does not have on the basis of the treaty, and with the principle of proportionality, ie in legislating keep within the objectives set out in the Treaties and not go beyond these.

Treaty on the Functioning of the European Union **10.12 (EU)**

Article 26 1.The Union shall adopt measures with the aim of establishing or ensuring the functioning of the internal market, in accordance with the relevant provisions of the Treaties.

2. The internal market shall comprise an area without internal frontiers in which the free movement of goods, persons, services and capital is ensured in accordance with the provisions of the Treaties.

3. The Council, on a proposal from the Commission, shall determine the guidelines and conditions necessary to ensure balanced progress in all the sectors concerned.

Article 114 1. Save where otherwise provided in the Treaties, the following provisions shall apply for the achievement of the objectives set out in Article 26. The European Parliament and the Council shall, acting in accordance with the ordinary legislative procedure and after consulting the Economic and Social Committee, adopt the measures for the approximation of the provisions laid down by law, regulation or administrative action in Member States which have as their object the establishment and functioning of the internal market.

...

3. The Commission, in its proposals envisaged in paragraph 1 concerning health, safety, environmental protection and consumer protection, will take as a base a high level of protection, taking account in particular of any new development based

on scientific facts. Within their respective powers, the European Parliament and the Council will also seek to achieve this objective....

Article 115 Without prejudice to Article 114, the Council shall, acting unanimously in accordance with a special legislative procedure and after consulting the European Parliament and the Economic and Social Committee, issue directives for the approximation of such laws, regulations or administrative provisions of the Member States as directly affect the establishment or functioning of the internal market.

Notes

(1) These articles provide a possible legal basis for EU measures dealing with private law. These two articles (in the form of their predecessor Articles 95 and 94 EC Treaty, respectively) have been used as the basis for many rules of European Private Law. This includes for example the Directive on late payments and the Insolvency Regulation dealt with below (III.C.3).

(2) The reasoning of the European Commission has been to stress that the 28 European national legal systems differ very much and that therefore the functioning of the internal market is distorted because of this. However, it is not at all certain that the mere fact that there are differences between the private laws of the Member States does in fact hinder trade between Member States. There are strong proponents of this view,[38] but there is also a great deal of criticism.[39] Whether or not this really amounts to enough distortion to use Articles 114 or 115 TFEU as a legal basis remains to be seen. The use of their predecessors has been challenged by the Member States.

European Court of Justice, 10 May 2000[40] **10.13 (EU)**

Germany v Parliament and Council

POWER OF THE EUROPEAN UNION TO HARMONISE PRIVATE LAW

Tobacco advertising

The EU legislature does not have a general power to regulate the internal market.

Facts: Directive 98/43/EC of the European Parliament and of the Council of 6 July 1998 on the approximation of the laws, regulations and administrative provisions of the Member States relating to the advertising and sponsorship of tobacco products ([1992] OJ L213/9) was challenged by some Member States because the European legislator would have exceeded the powers conferred in Article 100a of the EC Treaty in adopting the Directive.

Held: Articles 100a, 57(2) and 66 of the EC Treaty do not constitute an appropriate legal basis for the Directive.

[38] Communication from the Commission to the Council and the European Parliament on European Contract law, COM (2001) 398, no 34; O Lando, 'Is Codification Needed in Europe?' [1993] *European Review of Private Law* 157–170, 159.

[39] See S Weatherill, 'Diversity between National Laws in the Internal Market' in Drobnig, Snijders and Zippro, 131 *et seq*.

[40] Case C-376/98 [2000] ECR I-8419.

Judgment: 83. Those provisions, read together, make it clear that the measures referred to in Article 100a (1) [Art 114 TFEU] of the Treaty are intended to improve the conditions for the establishment and functioning of the internal market. To construe that article as meaning that it vests in the Community legislature a general power to regulate the internal market would not only be contrary to the express wording of the provisions cited above, but would also be incompatible with the principle embodied in Article 3b of the EC Treaty (now article 5 EU) that the powers of the Community are limited to those specifically conferred on it.

84. Moreover, a measure adopted on the basis of Article 100a of the Treaty must genuinely have as its object the improvement of the conditions for the establishment and functioning of the internal market. If a mere finding of disparities between national rules and of the abstract risk of obstacles to the exercise of fundamental freedoms or of distortions of competition liable to result there from were sufficient to justify the choice of Article 100a as a legal base, judicial review of compliance with the proper legal basis might be nugatory. The Court would then be prevented from discharging the function entrusted to it by Article 164 of the EC Treaty (now Article 220 EC) of ensuring that the law is observed in the interpretation and application of the Treaty.

85. So, in considering whether Article 100a was the proper legal basis, the Court must verify whether the measure whose validity is at issue in fact pursues the objectives stated by the Community legislature. ...

Note

The ECJ therefore makes clear that there is no EU competence to unify or harmonise law on the mere basis of disparity in national laws.[41] The broad competences in the articles excerpted above are meant to be functional, directed towards the primary economic objective of the European Union to establish an internal market.[42] However, in order to use them, more is needed than the mere statement that the laws of the Member States are different.[43] The European Commission therefore now issues impact assessments, which are economic studies to investigate the current functioning of the internal market and the benefits for the internal market if changes are made by harmonising legislation. Such research results can then be used to use Articles 114 and 115 as a suitable legal basis.

Treaty on the Functioning of the European Union **10.14 (EU)**

Article 81 1. The Union shall develop judicial cooperation in civil matters having cross-border implications, based on the principle of mutual recognition of judgments

[41] See, *inter alia*, above n 39; S Weatherill, 'Competence and European private law' in C Twigg-Flesner (ed), *Cambridge Companion to European Union Private Law* (Cambridge, Cambridge University Press, 2010) 58 *et seq*.

[42] See Smits, above n 1, 7–15; Müller-Graf, above n 12, 77–89; W van Gerven, 'The ECJ Case-law as a Means of Unification of Private Law' in Hartkamp et al, above n 12, 101–23.

[43] See, eg, recital 5 in the preamble of Directive 85/577/EEC to protect the consumer in respect to contracts negotiated away from business premises (Doorstep Selling Directive), which states: 'and whereas such contracts and engagements are the subject of legislation which differs from one Member State to another; Whereas any disparity between such legislation may directly affect the functioning of the common market; whereas it is therefore necessary to approximate laws in this field'.

and of decisions in extrajudicial cases. Such cooperation may include the adoption of measures for the approximation of the laws and regulations of the Member States.

2. For the purposes of paragraph 1, the European Parliament and the Council, acting in accordance with the ordinary legislative procedure, shall adopt measures, particularly when necessary for the proper functioning of the internal market, aimed at ensuring:

(a) the mutual recognition and enforcement between Member States of judgments and of decisions in extrajudicial cases;

(b) the cross-border service of judicial and extrajudicial documents;

(c) the compatibility of the rules applicable in the Member States concerning conflict of laws and of jurisdiction;...

(e) effective access to justice;

(f) the elimination of obstacles to the proper functioning of civil proceedings, if necessary by promoting the compatibility of the rules on civil procedure applicable in the Member States;

Notes

(1) The predecessor to this Article, which was Article 65 EC Treaty, has been used in areas of international civil procedure and private international law to develop rules that serve the functioning of the internal market.[44] These include, for example, proposals for a certificate of succession and the European Small Claims Procedure[45]

(2) Article 81 mentions judicial co-operation in civil matters. This is a general objective and one could argue, although this is not entirely settled yet, that substantive harmonising efforts could also fall under this provision. However, seen the working of the Article, such a measure of EU law could only apply in cross-border cases, whereas measure adopted under Articles 114 and 115 TFEU could apply in both domestic and cross-border situations. This is a relevant question that is very much subject of the debate on European private law and raises important issues of non-discrimination. It is necessary to think about the possibility of where a certain rule would benefit parties in a cross-border setting, but not in a purely domestic setting.

Treaty on the Functioning of the European Union **10.15 (EU)**

Article 352 1. If action by the Union should prove necessary, within the framework of the policies defined in the Treaties, to attain one of the objectives set out in the Treaties, and the Treaties have not provided the necessary powers, the Council, acting unanimously on a proposal from the Commission and after obtaining the consent of the European Parliament, shall adopt the appropriate measures. Where

[44] See, on Art 67 EC Treaty, M Freudenthal, 'The Future of European Civil Procedure' [2003] *Electronic Journal of Comparative Law* 7.5, to be found at www.ejcl.org/ejcl/75/art75-6.html.

[45] Proposal for a Regulation of the European Parliament and of the Council on jurisdiction, applicable law, recognition and enforcement of decisions and authentic instruments in matters of succession and the creation of a European Certificate of Succession, COM(2009) 154 final; Regulation 861/2007/EC of the European Parliament and of the Council of 11 July 2007 establishing a European Small Claims Procedure.

the measures in question are adopted by the Council in accordance with a special legislative procedure, it shall also act unanimously on a proposal from the Commission and after obtaining the consent of the European Parliament. …
3. Measures based on this Article shall not entail harmonisation of Member States' laws or regulations in cases where the Treaties exclude such harmonisation. …

Note

(1) When Articles 114, 115 and 81 TFEU cannot be used, Article 352 TFEU (formally Article 308 EC Treaty) offers a provision of last resort on the basis of which measures of EU property law could be adopted. However, it is very important in this respect to consider paragraph 3 of Article 352 TFEU, which did not appear in the former version of Article 308 EC Treaty. This is especially relevant in the light of Article 345 TFEU (ex Article 295 EC Treaty), dealt with below (III.B.3).

(2) Article 352 TFEU has been used to adopt private law measures before, such as the European Company Statute.[46]

III.B.3 EXCLUSION OF PROPERTY LAW?—ARTICLE 345 TFEU

Property law faces a specific difficulty in Article 345 of the Treaty on the Functioning of the Internal Market. At first sight this article seems to prevent the European Union from acting in the area of property law.

Treaty on the Functioning of the European Union **10.16 (EU)**

Article 345 The Treaties shall in no way prejudice the rules in Member States governing the system of property ownership.

European Court of Justice 6 November 1984[47] **10.17 (EU)**

Robert Fearon Ltd v Irish Land Commission

COMPULSORY ACQUISITION BY PUBLIC BODIES

Fearon

Although Article 295 of the Treaty does not call into question the Member States' right to establish a system of compulsory acquisition by public bodies, such a system remains subject to the fundamental rule of non-discrimination which underlies the chapter of the Treaty relating to the right of establishment.

Facts: The purpose of both the Land Act 1933 and the Land Act 1965 of Ireland is to increase the size of holdings of land which, if that were not done, could not be exploited on an economic basis, to prevent land speculation, and, finally, to ensure as far as possible that the land belongs to those who work it. To achieve the latter objective, section 32(3) of the Land Act 1933, as amended by section 35 of the Land Act 1965, provides that the Irish Land Commission cannot exercise its powers of compul-

[46] Regulation 2157/2001/EC of 8 October 2001 on the Statute for a European company (SE).
[47] Case 182/83 [1984] ECR 3677.

sory acquisition against persons who have resided for more than one year within three miles of the land or against bodies corporate all of whose shareholders meet the same residence requirement. Five shareholders of Robert Fearon Ltd are British nationals, none of whom meets the residence requirement set out above.

Held: Article 52 of the Treaty does not prevent a Member State from making exemption from compulsory acquisition measures adopted under legislation governing the ownership of rural land subject to a requirement that nationals of other Member States who have taken part in the formation of a land-owning company reside on or near the land, if that residence requirement also applies to nationals of that Member State and if the powers of compulsory acquisition are not exercised in a discriminatory manner.

Judgment: 5. In its written observations, the Commission contends first of all that the system of compulsory acquisition by public bodies is part of the system of property ownership in Ireland and that Article 222 of the Treaty, according to which 'this Treaty shall in no way prejudice the rules in Member States governing the system of property ownership', would thus on its own justify a negative answer to the question put by the national court.

6. That conclusion cannot be accepted. By virtue of Article 54(3)(e) of the Treaty, the restrictions on the acquisition and use by a national of one Member State of land and buildings situated in another Member State are among those which are to be abolished with a view to the realisation of freedom of establishment. Similarly, the Council's 'programme general pour la suppression des restrictions a la liberte d 'établissement' (general programme for the abolition of restrictions on the freedom of establishment) of 18 December 1961 (*journal officiel* 1962, p 36) lists, among the restrictions on freedom of establishment to be abolished, provisions or practices which provide for less favourable rules for nationals of another Member State in regard to compulsory acquisition.

7. Consequently, although Article 222 of the Treaty does not call in question the Member States' right to establish a system of compulsory acquisition by public bodies, such a system remains subject to the fundamental rule of non-discrimination which underlies the chapter of the Treaty relating to the right of establishment. ...

European Court of Justice, 4 June 2002[48] **10.18 (EU)**

Commission v Belgium

EU CONFORMITY OF BELGIUM LEGISLATION

Golden Share

Article 345 TFEU cannot be invoked to protect the state's interest in a company, the system of property ownership is not exempted from the Treaty.

Facts: Belgium enacted a piece of legislation under which the Belgian state received a special share in the company Société nationale d'investissement. The state previously held more shares in that company, but upon privatisation, ie the sale of those state-owned shares to private individuals, the company was forced by Belgian law to provide the government with a so-called 'golden share'. This 'golden share' entitled the atate to prohibit transfers and takeovers made by the company, including a situation that the company was taken over, as well as the power to appoint two directors to the board of directors. The European Commission argued that these measures were against EU law, in particular the free movement of capital as companies must be able to be acquired by persons from other Member States (Article 73b

[48] Case C-503/99 [2002] ECR I-4809.

EC), the existence of such a 'golden share' therefore hinders the free movement of capital. Belgium argued that the ownership of shares concerns property law and that EU law under Article 345 TFEU (then 222 EC) determines that EU law is not applicable to property law matters.

Held: Article 345 TFEU does not exempt the system of property ownership of the Member States from the Treaty and the Article can therefore not be used to object to an interference of EU law with the ownership of shares.

Judgment: ... certain concerns may justify the retention by Member States of a degree of influence within undertakings that were initially public and subsequently privatised, where those undertakings are active in fields involving the provision of services in the public interest or strategic services (see today's judgments in Case C-367/98 *Commission* v *Portugal*, not yet published in the European Court Reports, paragraph 47, and Case C-503/99 *Commission* v *Belgium*, not yet published in the European Court Reports, paragraph 43).

44. However, those concerns cannot entitle Member States to plead their own systems of property ownership, referred to in Article 222 of the Treaty, by way of justification for obstacles, resulting from privileges attaching to their position as shareholder in a privatised undertaking, to the exercise of the freedoms provided for by the Treaty. As is apparent from the Court's case-law (Case C-302/97 *Konle* [1999] ECR I-3099, paragraph 38), that article does not have the effect of exempting the Member States' systems of property ownership from the fundamental rules of the Treaty.

B Akkermans and E Ramaekers, 'Article 345 TFEU (ex Article 295 EC). Its Meanings and Interpretations'[49] 10.19 (EU)

E Combining the Above: A Possible Interpretation of Article 345 TFEU

Taking all of the above into account it is possible to formulate a most likely interpretation of Article 345 TFEU to which the current use and interpretations by European legislature and courts can be tested. We will therefore return to the following interpretation in the conclusion to see whether the interpretation is sufficiently accurate or might need adaptation.

Article 345 TFEU, formerly Article 222 EEC, is an Article that limits, but not prevents, the application of the TFEU Treaty as a whole to the way in which rules of a Member State deal with the right of ownership of undertakings. The Article does not provide powers to the EU, nor does it give powers to the Member States. The conclusion can be drawn that Article 345 TFEU only concerns the private or public ownership of undertakings, with which the EU shall not concern itself and which can thus be regulated by the Member States themselves, especially since there is no apparent reason why the reference to undertakings was removed from the final version of the Article.

Notes

(1) At first sight Article 345 TFEU seems very clear and a literal or textual interpretation seems to provide a clear statement: EU law does not concern itself

[49] B Akkermans and E Ramaekers, 'Article 345 TFEU (Ex Article 295 EC). Its Meanings and Interpretations, [2010] *European Law Journal* 292, at 304–05.

with the law of property. However, the picture in reality is somewhat more complicated. Occasionally, the Article is used to block a certain development. For instance, the former European Commissioner for Enlargement Verheugen stated on questions asked to the European Parliament that the EU cannot concern itself with matters of property law.[50] In addition, in the work of the Directive (2000/35/EC) combating late payments Article 345 TFEU has been used as an argument not to move into the area of property law.[51] However, at the same time there is existing EU property law (see below, section III.C) and furthermore the ECJ takes a different approach. In fact, the ECJ has held in a number of cases that a restrictive interpretation of Article 345 TFEU does not hold true.[52] Moreover, further academic research seems to point at a different meaning of the Article and provide additional arguments to interpret the Article in a way other than just literally. The matter, however, remains somewhat controversial.

(2) It seems, however, more likely that this Article is meant to address the EU's competence in nationalisation and privatisation. It cannot be denied that the European Union interferes with property law to the extent that the internal market and that the non-discrimination principle are at stake, as is demonstrated by the *Fearon* and *Golden Share* cases. In this interpretation the Article refers to the principle of neutrality, which is an EU competition law principle, meaning that the Treaty does not judge whether a company is owned by the state or is in private hands. The first draft of the Article as well as the famous *Schuman declaration* from which the Article is derived, used the words 'the system of property ownership of *undertakings*' [emphasis added].[53] It seems therefore that the Article is neither an obstruction to the making of European property law, nor can it provide an argument for Member States to block the influence of EU law to national property law.

(3) The effect of that last part, the impossibility for Member States to block the influence of EU law on national property law potentially has very far-reaching effects. The ECJ makes it very clear in the *Golden Share* case that the rules of property ownership remain subject to the fundamental rules of the Treaty. With this statement the ECJ refers to the provisions on free movement, which, as will be seen below (III.E), can result in the inapplicability of measures of national property law because they, in effect, hinder the trade between Member States.

[50] Written Question E-0530/01 by Cristiana Muscardini (EPP) to the Commission (22 February 2001).

[51] Schweitzer, in E Grabitz and M Hilf, *Das Recht der Europäischen Union*, EL 28 (München, Beck, Oct 2005) Art 295; Bär-Bouyssière, in H von der Groeben and J Schwarze, *Kommentar zum Vertrag über die Europäischen Union und zur Gründung der Europäischen Gemeinschaft* (Baden-Baden, Nomos, 2004) Art 295 at 1–20.

[52] See W van Gerven, 'The ECJ Case-law as a Means of Unification of Private Law' in Hartkamp et al, above n 12, 101, fn 1. Akkermans and E Ramaekers, above n 49. See, for example, ECJ case C-309/96, *Annibaldi* [1997] ECR I-7493. In this case the European Court used Article 222 EEC (295 EC, 345 TFEU) as a barrier, but its justification for doing so is brief and incomprehensible.

[53] See, on this in particular, Akkermans and E Ramaekers, above n 49.

III.C EXISTING EU PROPERTY LAW

There is existing EU property law. Although the European Union has not directly sought to harmonise the entire or a very large area of property law, several EU legislative acts are in force that both directly and indirectly deal with matters of property law. Moreover, there is more EU property law in the making. This paragraph will deal with existing EU property law; the next (III.D) will deal with future EU property law, or property law in the making.

III.C.1 CULTURAL OBJECTS

Perhaps the first area of property law in which the European Union became active concerns the return of stolen cultural objects. These rules affect the rules on third party protection of bona fide purchasers dealt with in Chapter 9. The international and European regulation concerning cultural objects, also EU Directive 93/7/EEC, will be dealt with below in section VI.

III.C.2 LATE PAYMENTS[54]

Introductory Notes

(a) Directive 2011/7/EU of the European Parliament and of the Council of 16 February 2011 on combating late payments in commercial transactions replaces Directive 2000/35/EC combating late payment in commercial transactions. On 16 March 2011 the new Directive repealed the old. As far as the relevant property law provisions are concerned, not many changes have been made. We will therefore use the new 2011 version, under reference to the Articles in the 2001 version and still speak of the Directive meaning to refer to the 2011 version.

(b) The Directive aims to address the problem of late payment in business transactions, and in order to do so it obliges Member States to regulate more stringently the interest rates and the recovery procedures, but it also includes a rule on a retention of title or reservation of ownership device.

Directive 2011/7/EU **10.20 (EU)**

Recital 31 (old version n 21) It is desirable to ensure that creditors are in a position to exercise a retention of title on a non-discriminatory basis throughout the Community, if the retention of title clause is valid under the applicable national provisions designated by private international law.

Article 2. Definitions.

For the purposes of this Directive, the following definitions shall apply

…

(9) (old version (3)) 'Retention of title' means the contractual agreement according

[54] Dir 2000/35/EC, [2000] OJ L200/35; http://europa.eu.int/eur-lex/pri/en/oj/dat/2000/l_200/l_20020000808en00350038.pdf. The Directive has been renewed in 2011 (Dir 2011/7/EU, [2011] OJ L48/1), but there have been no changes regarding the retention of title provision.

to which the seller retains title to the goods in question until the price has been paid in full;...

Article 9 (old version 4). Retention of title.

1. Member States shall provide in conformity with the applicable national provisions designated by private international law that the seller retains title to goods until they are fully paid for if a retention of title has been expressly agreed between the buyer and the seller before the delivery of the goods.

2. Member States may adopt or retain provisions dealing with down payments already made by the debtor.

Notes

(1) In earlier drafts of the old Directive, the retention of title arrangement was much more substantial. During the political process negotiating the Directive the standards were considerably lowered. A retention of title should be expressly agreed upon; there is a referral to the applicable rule of national private international law; there is no longer a referral to the retention of title's effectivity in insolvency; and the effectivity of retention of title against third parties has disappeared. A prohibition of national formalities also disappeared from the Directive. This included, for example, the mandatory requirement to have the retention of title in a written document, containing a certain date.[55] The reason the European legislature took such a reserved stance on retention of title may probably have been the lack of time to undertake more in-depth study to the various national arrangements. No reasons are given in the published documents.[56] These national requirements have been challenged—see below the case of *Commission v The Italian Republic* (10.21 (EU)).

(2) The meaning of the current retention of title provision is not very extensive. It refers to the national rules of private international law, thereby referring to the national arrangements of substantive private law. Since all European jurisdictions already have a retention of title provision available, even effective in insolvency (see Chapter 5, on security interests) this Directive could have accomplished more.[57]

(3) The definition in the current version only mentions retention of title as a contractual arrangement; Article 9 refers to national law. Although it only provides a minimal approach it does remain relevant to property law, as Member States are and now remain obliged to offer a retention of title device in commercial transactions.

European Court of Justice, 26 October 2006[58] **10.21 (EU)**
Commission v Italian Republic

NATIONAL REQUIREMENTS TO RETENTION OF TITLE PROHIBITED BY DIRECTIVE 2000/35?

[55] As applies in Italy, Art 1524 Codice civile.

[56] As was suggested by E-M Kieninger, 'Der Eigentumsvorbehalt in der Verzugsrichtlinie – Chronik einer verpaßten Chance' in J Basedow et al, *Aufbruch nach Europa—75 Jahre Max Planck Institut für Privatrecht* (Tübingen, Mohr Siebeck, 2001) 151 *et seq*.

[57] *Ibid*.

[58] Case C-302/05 [2006] ECR I-10597.

Commission v Italy

National formal requirements to retention of title arrangements are not prohibited by Directive 2000/35.

Facts: The Commission of the European Communities sought a declaration from the Court that, by providing that a retention of title clause must be confirmed on individual invoices for successive supplies bearing a specific date that is prior to any attachment procedure and is duly entered in the accounting records in order for it to be enforceable against third party creditors of the buyer, the Italian Republic had failed to fulfil its obligations under Article 4(1) of Directive 2000/35/EC of the European Parliament and of the Council of 29 June 2000 on combating late payment in commercial transactions (OJ L200/35).

Held: The Italian arrangement regarding retention of title, containing formal requirements, is not precluded by Directive 2000/35.

Judgment: 29. In view of the wording of Article 4(1) of Directive 2000/35 and the purpose of that directive, it cannot be inferred from that provision that it is intended to affect any rules other than those which expressly provide, firstly, that it is possible for the seller and the buyer expressly to agree a retention of title clause before the goods are delivered and, secondly, that it is possible for the seller to retain title to the goods until they have been paid for in full.

30. Accordingly, the rules in question in the present case, which concern the enforceability of retention of title clauses against third parties, whose rights are not affected by Directive 2000/35, are still governed exclusively by the national legal orders of the Member States.

31. In those circumstances, by providing that a retention of title clause must be confirmed on individual invoices for successive supplies bearing a specific date that is prior to any attachment procedure and is duly entered in the accounting records in order for it to be enforceable against third party creditors of the buyer, the Italian Republic has not failed to fulfil its obligations under Article 4(1) of Directive 2000/35.

32. The Commission's action must therefore be dismissed.

Note

The minimal approach of the Directive is explicitly upheld by the ECJ.

III.C.3 INSOLVENCY PROCEEDINGS

Introductory Note

Regulation 1346/2000/EC of 29 May 2000 on insolvency proceedings,[59] as amended by the Regulation 694/2006/EC of 27 April 2006,[60] or the Insolvency Regulation, introduced a new set of rules with regard to insolvency proceedings with an international dimension. Its provisions have been largely taken over from the preceding Convention on Insolvency proceedings of 23 November 1995, which never entered into force due to political reasons: the BSE crisis, or mad-cow disease.[61] The Report

[59] [2000] OJ L160/1.
[60] [2006] OJ L100/1.
[61] See J Israël, *European Cross-border Insolvency Regulation: A Study of Regulation 1346/2000 on Insolvency Proceedings in the Light of a Paradigm of Co-operation and a Comitas Europaea* (Antwerp, Intersentia, 2005) 240–41.

on the Convention by Virgos and Schmit is therefore still of explanatory value.[62] Three sets of rules can roughly be distinguished:

1. rules with regard to the jurisdiction on insolvency proceedings, eg which Member State has the jurisdiction to start up an insolvency proceeding;
2. rules with regard to the enforcement and recognition of foreign European insolvency proceedings;
3. uniform rules with regard to conflict of laws. The Insolvency Regulation gives some rules on substantive law.

We will not deal with the first two categories, as they are outside the scope of property law.[63] However, some of the rules on substantive law contained in the third category largely influence the possibility to exercise and enforce property rights. The Regulation in particular affects property rights on land.[64]

Regulation 1346/2000/EC **10.22 (EU)**

Recital 25 There is a particular need for a special reference diverging from the law of the opening State in the case of rights in rem, since these are of considerable importance for the granting of credit. The basis, validity and extent of such a right in rem should therefore normally be determined according to the lex situs and not be affected by the opening of insolvency proceedings. The proprietor of the right in rem should therefore be able to continue to assert his right to segregation or separate settlement of the collateral security. Where assets are subject to rights in rem under the lex situs in one Member State but the main proceedings are being carried out in another Member State, the liquidator in the main proceedings should be able to request the opening of secondary proceedings in the jurisdiction where the rights in rem arise if the debtor has an establishment there. If a secondary proceeding is not opened, the surplus on sale of the asset covered by rights in rem must be paid to the liquidator in the main proceedings.

Article 5 Third parties' rights *in rem*.

1. The opening of insolvency proceedings shall not affect the rights in rem of creditors or third parties in respect of tangible or intangible, moveable or immoveable assets—both specific assets and collections of indefinite assets as a whole which change from time to time—belonging to the debtor which are situated within the territory of another Member State at the time of the opening of proceedings.

2. The rights referred to in paragraph 1 shall in particular mean:

(a) the right to dispose of assets or have them disposed of and to obtain satisfaction from the proceeds of or income from those assets, in particular by virtue of a lien or a mortgage;

[62] M Virgos and E Schmit, *Report on the Convention on Insolvency Proceedings*, Council Doc 6500/96, DRS 8 (CFC), May 3, 1996.

[63] For a more comprehensive analysis of the Insolvency Regulation: see G Moss (ed), *The EC regulation on insolvency proceedings: a commentary and annotated guide* (Oxford, Oxford University Press, 2002) 352; Israël, above n 61, 383.

[64] For an analysis of the impact of the Regulation on real property rights: M Veder, *Cross-border Insolvency Proceedings and Security Rights* (Deventer, Kluwer, 2004) 368.

(b) the exclusive right to have a claim met, in particular a right guaranteed by a lien in respect of the claim or by assignment of the claim by way of a guarantee;

(c) the right to demand the assets from, and/or to require restitution by, anyone having possession or use of them contrary to the wishes of the party so entitled;

(d) a right in rem to the beneficial use of assets.

3. The right, recorded in a public register and enforceable against third parties, under which a right in rem within the meaning of paragraph 1 may be obtained, shall be considered a right in rem.

4. Paragraph 1 shall not preclude actions for voidness, voidability or unenforceability as referred to in Article 4(2)(m).

Report on the Convention on Insolvency Proceedings[65] **10.23 (EU)**

97. Rights *in rem* can only properly fulfil their function insofar as they are not more affected by the opening of insolvency proceedings in other Contracting States than they would be by the opening of national insolvency proceedings. This aim could be achieved through alternative solutions which were in fact discussed in the working party. However, to facilitate the administration of the estate the simplicity of the formula laid down in the current Article 5 was preferred by the majority: insolvency proceedings do not affect rights in rem on assets located in other Contracting States.

98. The rule does not 'immunise' rights in rem against the debtor's insolvency. If the law of the State where the assets are located allows these rights in rem to be affected in some way, the liquidator (or any other person empowered to do so) may request secondary insolvency proceedings be opened in that State if the debtor has an establishment there. The secondary proceedings are conducted according to national law and allow the liquidator to affect these rights under the same conditions as in purely domestic proceedings. ...

103. This list is inspired in two main considerations. The first, that a right which exists only after insolvency proceedings have been opened, but not before, is not a right in rem for the purposes of Article 5 (which protect pre-existing rights).

The second, that a right in rem basically has two characteristics (see also the concept of rights in rem in the Member States in point 166 of the Schlosser Report on the 1968 Brussels Convention):

(a) its direct and immediate relationship with the asset it covers, which remains linked to its satisfaction, without depending on the asset belonging to a person's estate or on the relationship between the holder of the right in rem and another person;

(b) the absolute nature of the allocation of the right to the holder. This means that the person who holds a right in rem can enforce it against anyone who breaches or harms his right without his assent (eg such rights are typically protected by actions to recover); that the right can resist the alienation of the asset to a third party (it can be claimed erga omnes, with the restrictions characteristic of the protection of the bona fide purchaser); and that the right can thus resist individual enforcement by third parties and in collective insolvency proceedings (by its separation or individual satisfaction).

[65] Virgos and Schmit, above n 62.

104. A right in rem may not only be established with regard to specific assets but also with regard to assets as a whole. Security rights such as the 'floating charge' recognised in United Kingdom and Irish law can, therefore, be characterised as a right in rem for the purposes of the Convention. Likewise, rights characterised under national law as rights in rem over intangible assets or over rights are also included.

Notes

(1) The European legislature took into account the large differences between the legal systems of the Member States and therefore refers to 'rights *in rem*' in Article 5 of the Regulation but does not define what these are.[66] The classification of a right as a right *in rem*, or better as a property right, must be sought in national law, which, according to the conflict-of-law rules (in general, the *lex rei sitae*), governs property rights.

The only deviation from the above is found in Article 5(3), which for the purposes of Article 5, directly and independently of national law, considers any right entered in a public register and enforceable against third parties as a property rights (or right *in rem*).

(2) However, the rationale of Article 5 imposes certain limits to the national classifications of property rights. In order to facilitate the application of the Regulation and avoid doubts, Article 5(2) provides a list of types of rights that are normally considered by national laws as property rights. The justification of this list is revealed in paragraphs 103 and 104 of the Virgos Report, which preceded the Convention on Insolvency Proceedings (1995).[67]

(3) The applicable law governs the creation, validity and scope of these property rights, to be determined by the *lex rei sitae* at the relevant time. The creation, validity and scope cannot be affected by the opening of insolvency proceedings. This means that although the law of the Member State of the opening stipulates that all objects are part of the patrimony, the holder of a property right retains all his rights in respect of the objects in question. For instance, the holder of the property right may exercise the right to separate an object from the patrimony and, where necessary, to realise the asset individually to satisfy the claim. On the other hand, the liquidator, even if he is in possession of the object, cannot take any decision in respect to that object which might affect the property right validly created on it, without the consent of its holder.[68]

No restriction whatsoever contained in a national insolvency rule (suspension periods, prescription periods, formal requirements, lodging of claims, etc) can be opposed to a foreign security creditor.

(4) These provisions only deal with the situation in which the subject-matter of the property right is situated in another Member State than the Member State in which the insolvency proceedings are opened. The aim pursued by the legislature

[66] On the differences between property rights, see Chapters 3 and 4.

[67] The text of the Insolvency Regulation has, quasi-unamended, been copied from the Draft Treaty, which has not been adopted due to political circumstances.

[68] Virgos and Schmit, above n 62, 95.

is to increase the legal certainty of property rights. The Virgos/Schmit Report as cited above was literally transposed in the Insolvency Regulation.[69]

Regulation 1346/2000/EC **10.24 (EU)**

Article 7 Reservation of title (title retention)

1. The opening of insolvency proceedings against the purchaser of an asset shall not affect the seller's rights based on a reservation of title where at the time of the opening of proceedings the asset is situated within the territory of a Member State other than the State of opening of proceedings.
2. The opening of insolvency proceedings against the seller of an asset, after delivery of the asset, shall not constitute grounds for rescinding or terminating the sale and shall not prevent the purchaser from acquiring title where at the time of the opening of proceedings the asset sold is situated within the territory of a Member State other than the State of the opening of proceedings.
3. Paragraphs 1 and 2 shall not preclude actions for voidness, voidability or unenforceability as referred to in Article 4(2)(m).

Note

(1) Retention of title is, under the Insolvency Regulation, subject to the same set of rules as rights *in rem*. As a property right, a retention of title is not affected by the opening of an insolvency proceeding in another Member State than the one in which the object sold under title retention is situated.

(2) The most remarkable rule on retention of title is the uniform substantive rule contained in Article 7 (2), dealing with the insolvency of the seller under title retention. If the purchaser continues to make the payments agreed upon in the sales agreement, he shall acquire the ownership of the object once the condition for transfer of ownership (full payment of all secured claims) has been fulfilled. It conceals, in cross-border situations, the concept of the protection of the buyer under title retention. This protection has a property nature: although the objects belong to the insolvency patrimony, at the moment of the opening of the proceedings, the object can be extracted from the insolvency proceedings due to a later event (full payment). This proprietary protection of the buyer under title retention is also known as an *Anwartschaftsrecht* (see Chapter 3, section I.J.3)

(3) This rule also only applies if the object subject to retention of title is situated in another Member State then the Member State in which the insolvency proceeding were opened.

III.C.4 FINANCIAL COLLATERAL ARRANGEMENTS

Introductory Notes

(a) In June 2002 the European Parliament and the Council adopted Directive 2002/47/EC on Financial Collateral Arrangements. Financial collateral arrangements

[69] *Ibid*, 97–98.

are financial transactions between bank and other large financial institutions. They concern a very specific and technical area, also of property law, in which—generally speaking—banks lend money to each other in exchange for security. The term collateral refers to the objects that are provided as security. In case of these transactions the objects are intangible objects in the form of money, derivatives or other financial instruments.

(b) In this area contract law, and therefore party autonomy, is dominant, but matters of property law must necessarily be dealt with in order to make security arrangements work.

Directive 2002/47/EC **10.25 (EU)**

Recital 8 The *lex rei sitae* rule, according to which the applicable law for determining whether a financial collateral arrangement is properly perfected and therefore good against third parties is the law of the country where the financial collateral is located, is currently recognised by all Member States. Without affecting the application of this Directive to directly-held securities, the location of book entry securities provided as financial collateral and held through one or more intermediaries should be determined. If the collateral taker has a valid and effective collateral arrangement according to the governing law of the country in which the relevant account is maintained, then the validity against any competing title or interest and the enforceability of the collateral should be governed solely by the law of that country, thus preventing legal uncertainty as a result of other unforeseen legislation.

Recital 13 This Directive seeks to protect the validity of financial collateral arrangements which are based upon the transfer of the full ownership of the financial collateral, such as by eliminating the so-called re-characterisation of such financial collateral arrangements (including repurchase agreements) as security interests.

Article 2 Definitions

(a) 'financial collateral arrangement' means a title transfer financial collateral arrangement or a security financial collateral arrangement whether or not these are covered by a master agreement or general terms and conditions;

Article 5 Right of use of financial collateral under security financial collateral arrangements

1. If and to the extent that the terms of a security financial collateral arrangement so provide, Member States shall ensure that the collateral taker is entitled to exercise a right of use in relation to financial collateral provided under the security financial collateral arrangement.

2. Where a collateral taker exercises a right of use, he thereby incurs an obligation to transfer equivalent collateral to replace the original financial collateral at the latest on the due date for the performance of the relevant financial obligations covered by the security financial collateral arrangement.

Alternatively, the collateral taker shall, on the due date for the performance of the relevant financial obligations, either transfer equivalent collateral, or, if and to the extent that the terms of a security financial collateral arrangement so provide, set off the value of the equivalent collateral against or apply it in discharge of the relevant financial obligations.

3. The equivalent collateral transferred in discharge of an obligation as described in

paragraph 2, first subparagraph, shall be subject to the same security financial collateral agreement to which the original financial collateral was subject and shall be treated as having been provided under the security financial collateral arrangement at the same time as the original financial collateral was first provided.

4. Member States shall ensure that the use of financial collateral by the collateral taker according to this Article does not render invalid or unenforceable the rights of the collateral taker under the security financial collateral arrangement in relation to the financial collateral transferred by the collateral taker in discharge of an obligation as described in paragraph 2, first subparagraph.

5. If an enforcement event occurs while an obligation as described in paragraph 2 first subparagraph remains outstanding, the obligation may be the subject of a close-out netting provision.

Article 6 Recognition of title transfer financial collateral arrangements

1. Member States shall ensure that a title transfer financial collateral arrangement can take effect in accordance with its terms …

Notes

(1) A financial collateral arrangement under the Directive can take two forms: it may be a transfer for security purposes or a special right of pledge. These rights do not concern normal objects of property law, such the property security rights dealt with in Chapter 5, but these are special rights because they concern cash and derivatives. Like claims as subject matter of property rights, the nature of the property right is affected by the nature of the object (see Chapter 4).

(2) Under Article 5 the principle of the *lex commissoria*, the prohibition for the secured creditor to keep the object under security for himself has disappeared. This can be understood when two banks make a repurchase agreement, which would be a financial collateral arrangement, for 24 hours exchanging €500 million. When the debtor fails to fulfil his obligations, it would be strange if the creditor needed to sell the money to satisfy his debt with the proceeds of the sale of money.

(3) The financial collateral Directive thus creates a specific area of EU property law that generally only applies between large financial institutions.[70] However, Member States may enlarge the scope an apply the Directive also beyond its exact wording.

III.C.5 EMISSION RIGHTS

Introductory Notes

(a) On 13 October 2003 the European Parliament and the Council adopted Directive 2003/87/EC establishing a scheme for greenhouse gas emission allowance trading within the Community and amending Council Directive 96/61/EC. The Directive introduces 'emission rights' which are rights to emit carbon dioxide into the air. The Directive is part of the European Union's environmental policy, following the Kyoto Protocol. The general idea is to licence carbon dioxide (or greenhouse gas)

[70] Art 1 of Directive 2002/47/EC.

emission and to reduce the number of licences over time to stimulate the market either to emit less or to find more emission-efficient ways of production.

(b) Although at first sight the Directive has nothing to do with property law, the greenhouse gas emission right as such is a new object of property law. European Union law operates on different bases to national law. The ECJ protects the effectiveness of EU legislation, and therefore property rights held on greenhouse gas emission rights created under this Directive must not hinder the operation of the Directive. Some Member States therefore needed to adopt their rules to ensure the effective functioning of the Directive in its legal order.

Directive 2003/87/EC **10.26 (EU)**

Article 3 Definitions

(a) 'allowance' means an allowance to emit one tonne of carbon dioxide equivalent during a specified period, which shall be valid only for the purposes of meeting the requirements of this Directive and shall be transferable in accordance with the provisions of this Directive;

(b) 'emissions' means the release of greenhouse gases into the atmosphere from sources in an installation;

Article 12 Transfer, surrender and cancellation of allowances

1. Member States shall ensure that allowances can be transferred between:

(a) persons within the Community;

(b) persons within the Community and persons in third countries, where such allowances are recognised in accordance with the procedure referred to in Article 25 without restrictions other than those contained in, or adopted pursuant to, this Directive.

2. Member States shall ensure that allowances issued by a competent authority of another Member State are recognised for the purpose of meeting an operator's obligations under paragraph 3.

3. Member States shall ensure that, by 30 April each year at the latest, the operator of each installation surrenders a number of allowances equal to the total emissions from that installation during the preceding calendar year as verified in accordance with Article 15, and that these are subsequently cancelled.

4. Member States shall take the necessary steps to ensure that allowances will be cancelled at any time at the request of the person holding them.

Law on the Management of the Environment[71] **10.27 (NL)**

Article 16.42 1. Voidance, avoidance or rescission of the agreement that led to the transfer, has, after the transfer has been completed, no consequences for the validity of the transfer.

2. Every condition in relation to the transfer ends at the moment that transfer has been effected.

[71] *Wet Milieubeheer.*

3. In derogation from Article 228 of book 3 of the Civil Code a right of pledge cannot be created on an emission right

Notes

(1) Greenhouse gas emission rights are special rights that are generally subject to the system of property law. They are assignable and the rules on assignment, as we have seen in Chapter 4, generally rules of property law or rules in conformity to rules of property law, apply to these. The transfer of these emission rights can be problematic as the rights are intended to decrease in nature with the emission of greenhouse gas into the atmosphere. When, for example, 90% of the right has been used already, but the transfer becomes void or is avoided, a retro-transfer is impossible for 90%.

(2) Systems adhering to a causal system of transfer in which, as we have seen in Chapter 8, the validity of the transfer is dependent on the validity of the underlying agreement provide a legal cause ('title') to the transfer. Dutch law, as we saw in Chapter 8, adheres to a causal system, but because of the introduction of the Emission Trading Directive, paragraph 2 of Article 16.42 of the Law on the Management of the Environment introduces an abstract system of transfer, ie the invalidity of the underlying agreement (which is a condition too), will no longer affect the validity of the transfer.

(3) Also indirectly, therefore, measures of EU law can give rise to the creation of EU property law.[72]

III.D FUTURE EU PROPERTY LAW

In addition to existing EU property law, there is also EU property law under development. These are proposals, initiated by the European Commission, carried out by the Commission itself or by others at the request of the Commission, that have not been adopted into a final legislative form. These proposals are at different stages in the legislative, and sometimes even preparatory legislative, process. These initiatives deserve consideration as they give an indication of potential EU property law in the next decade(s).

They include the proposal for a right of Euromortgage, a European immovable property security right (III.D.1), regulations for succession and wills (III.D.2), matrimonial property law (III.D.3) and, perhaps most importantly, the Draft Common Frame of Reference (III.D.4), which is model legislation developed by academics at the request of the European Commission (see below, VII).

[72] On this see also JHM van Erp, 'De osmose van Nederlands en Europees goederenrecht' (2004) 10 (Special Issue)/no 94 *Nederlands Tijdschrift voor Burgerlijk Recht* (*NTBR*) 535; B Akkermans, 'The European Union Development of European Property Law' in C Godt (ed), *Hanse Law School in Perspective—Legal Teaching and Cross Border Research after Lisbon* (The Hague, Kluwer, 2011 forthcoming).

III.D.1 EUROMORTGAGE

Introductory Notes

(a) The European Commission has been looking for many years at whether a right of Euromortgage could be developed to overcome legal barriers to cross-border home loans.[73] A home loan is an EU term for a financial transaction whereby a private party borrows money from a bank for the acquisition of a property right in respect to land or another immovable object. The right of Euromortgage as envisaged originated from the International Union of the Latin Notariat (CNUF) and proposes the creation of a new property security right in the European Union, as an additional pan-European security right in respect to immovables, existing next to the national immovable property security rights.[74]

(b) In 2004, which are the latest European-generated statistics, it was demonstrated that only 1% of European citizens take out a property security for a home located in another Member State. Most of these buyers are people intending to become second homeowners or people living in border regions.

(c) After almost 30 years of debate, the European Commission released a Green Paper in 2005 in which it presented its ideas on the future European mortgage market.[75] Both before and after the Green Paper, the European Commission issued large economic studies into the mortgage markets of the Member States. One of these was carried out by the Forum Group on Mortgage Credit. Many other interested parties responded.[76]

(d) This Green Paper was followed by a White Paper in 2007 in which the Commission became more concrete and proposed measures to stimulate cross-border lending.[77] Both the Green Paper and the White Paper were issued before the financial crisis hit Europe by the end of 2007. The crisis meant that the European Commission needed its attention elsewhere and that proposals on mortgage markets were politically very sensitive.

(e) In 2011 the European Commission proposed a Directive on Mortgage Lending, which takes a more minimal approach than originally proposed in the 2005 Green Paper.[78]

[73] The first report dates from 1966, The Segré report can be found on the website of the European Commission at: http://ec.europa.eu/economy_finance/emu_history/documentation/chapter1/19661130en382develeurocapitm_a.pdf.

[74] B Foëx, 'L'Eurohypothèque' in F Wero (ed), *L'europeanisation du droit privé* (Fribourg, Editions Universitaires Fribourg Suisse, 1998) 482; H Wehrens, 'Real Security regarding Immovable Objects—Reflections on a Euromortgage' in Hartkamp et al, above n 12, 769–783.

[75] Green Paper, Mortgage Credit in the EU, COM(2005) 327 final.

[76] See the website of the European Commission on home loans at http://ec.europa.eu/internal_market/finservices-retail/home-loans/integration_en.htm.

[77] COM(2007) 807 final.

[78] Proposal of 31 March 2011 for a Directive of the European Parliament and of the Council on credit agreements relating to residential property, COM(2011) 142 final.

Green Paper—Mortgage Credit in the EU[79] **10.28 (EU)**

(6) The EU mortgage credit markets constitute a crucial aspect of the overall economy of all EU Member States. At the end of 2004, the value of outstanding residential mortgage loans represented about 40% of the EU GDP.

(7) Mortgage credit markets are amongst the most complex markets in which consumers engage. The 'value chain' of a mortgage transaction can involve different and specialised market players at each stage. Mortgage brokers, packagers of products, specialist/generalist lenders, issuers and purchasers of securities and bonds (including global investors), insurers, and even government agencies can be involved in the purchase of a single home by a single EU consumer. The importance of the EU mortgage credit markets cannot be overestimated in the recent, current and future economic climate.

(8) For most EU citizens, the purchase of their home represents the largest purchase in their lifetime. Most home purchases require a loan for part of the price. Such loans are usually, but not always, secured by a mortgage. This debt is likely to be the most significant on-going financial commitment for most EU households. That said, the equity in the home can represent a substantial asset which may have the potential to be used to finance consumption or retirement. Thus the level of mortgage debt and the contractual characteristics of that debt can play a direct role in the transmission of monetary policy and on economic activity as a whole. For example, contractual restrictions on or penalties for early repayment of the debt may delay the transmission of changes in interest rates and hinder refinancing in such circumstances. This relationship between the macro-economy and mortgage debt is highly significant, especially in flexible mortgage markets, as the slightest change in interest rates can have a significant effect on household budgets and spending capacity. This can have a noteworthy impact on debtors, with a potential knock-on effect, positive or negative, on their spending and asset levels.

(9) Most EU mortgage markets have been expanding rapidly in recent years. In many Member States outstanding mortgage debt is currently at historically high levels relative to GDP or household disposable income. The growth of mortgage lending has been fostered both by macro-economic factors (such as the fall in interest rates and the strong growth of house prices in some countries) and structural developments (such as the increasing liberalisation and integration of EU financial markets). However, what is apparent is that the EU mortgage credit markets, despite sharing some common trends, remain very diverse. Relative sizes vary, as does growth. Product variety, borrower profiles, distribution structures, loan durations, home-ownership rates and funding mechanisms differ considerably.

(10) These differences in mortgage and housing markets reflect Members States' attitude to regulation, economic history and cultural factors. Differences in outcomes are related to factors such as direct government intervention in housing markets (eg by means of fiscal incentives to home-ownership), prudential regulation (eg regulatory ceilings to Loan to Value Ratios), the level of competition in mortgage markets, housing rental market conditions (including the availability of social housing) and the perceived risk associated with mortgage lending (in particular, the costs and the time required to realise the collateral 's value in the event of default).

[79] COM(2005) 327 final.

(11) Many external sources and the Commission's on-going consultation support the view that these markets are not very integrated, notably in relation to the range of available products and cross-border mortgage activity, while price differences (spreads) are already relatively low. A recent study came to the conclusion that these markets were individual markets with their own characteristics and economic drivers. Also noted was little connection between national market participants in the primary and the secondary markets, other than global investors in mortgage bonds and mortgage backed securities (MBS). The level of direct cross-border sales is low, less than 1% of overall residential mortgage credit activity and largely confined to the purchase of holiday homes or border region purchases, both niche market sectors.

(12) So what are the potential benefits of such integration? The Commission's out-sourced study will present and quantify these potential benefits, which have been highlighted elsewhere already. An overall lower cost of the mortgage or home loan could be a prime potential benefit. Improved product completeness in ancillary products (eg example mortgage insurance products), as well as in core mortgage credit products (eg equity release products and flexible mortgages) is a potential benefit. The Commission follows with interest the emergence of such innovative products (they are currently present in only a handful of Member States), and is fully aware of the need to accompany such emergence with a high level of consumer protection. Another key benefit appears to be the potential to serve more borrowers, including those currently marginalised in many EU mortgage credit markets such as sub-prime borrowers (ie those with poor or incomplete credit ratings). As with integration in other financial services sectors, improved economies of scale are certainly possible. Diversification across borders and through increased use of the capital markets and insurance markets could also serve lower credit risk. Finally, there is potential for improved capital efficiency, that is, the capacity for capital to move to those markets where it is most needed and rewarded.

(13) As part of its assessment of the case for action in the EU mortgage credit markets, the Commission has analysed the 48 recommendations of the Forum Group on Mortgage Credit, which it created in March 2003 in order to assess the barriers to further integration of the EU mortgage credit markets and propose ways to address them. These recommendations cover most of the issues relevant to the integration of EU mortgage markets. The Commission is determined to make the best possible use of these recommendations in any action it may propose in the future. It is however clear that not all of these recommendations would require the same course of action and that some require more ground work before any decision can be made.

(14) The Commission shares the Forum Group's view that integration of EU mortgage credit markets necessitates addressing four main distinct but interrelated areas: consumer protection, legal issues, collateral and funding. This Green Paper examines these four areas. The Commission welcomes views on all issues covered in this Green Paper, on any further issues considered key to the increased integration and efficiency of the EU mortgage credit markets, and on their prioritisation....

Euromortgage

(47) The idea of a Euromortgage is not new. It is an attempt to create an EU-wide instrument for securing loans on property, that is, for the mortgage collateral, which can be used in a flexible way. Its proponents argue that its central aspect—the weakening of the link ('accessoriness') between the mortgage collateral and mortgage credit—would facilitate the creation and transfer of mortgages, thereby having

a beneficial impact on the mortgage credit market as a whole, in particular on its funding.

(48) The Commission is aware of market participant and academic led projects, aimed at designing a workable Euromortgage model in the form of a 26th regime. The Commission will review how these initiatives propose to deal with such a complex issue, which touches upon many other related areas such as property law and contract law.

The Commission invites views on the feasibility and desirability of the Euromortgage. It will, in any event, await the outcome of ongoing initiatives to inform its assessment of this issue. …

White Paper—Mortgage Credit in the EU[80] **10.29 (EU)**

The Treaty provides the basis for the creation of a single market and the abolition of obstacles to the free movement of goods, persons, services and capital. Evidence however shows that the single market for residential mortgages is far from integrated. Obstacles exist that restrict the level of cross-border activity on the supply and demand sides, thus reducing competition and choice in the market.

One study estimates the potential economic benefits from integrating EU mortgage markets as 0.7% of EU GDP and 0.5% of private consumption over the next ten years. The study suggests that these benefits could lower mortgage interest rates by up to 47 basis points by 2015, thereby reducing the interest payable on a EUR 100 000 mortgage loan by EUR 470 per year. Another study puts the benefits at 0.12–0.24% of EU GDP per annum. The estimated benefits, which could be slightly different today given the evolution of market conditions, arise from the increased efficiency of mortgage lenders and the availability of a wider range of products.

Limits to the potential for integration should however be acknowledged. The influence of factors such as language, distance, consumer preferences, or lender business strategies cannot be underestimated. However, other factors, which prevent the conduct of business or substantially raise the cost of business for offering or taking out a mortgage credit in another EU Member State, can be addressed by appropriate policy initiatives.

The Commission recognises that consumers predominantly shop locally for mortgage credit and that the majority will probably continue to do so for the foreseeable future. The integration of EU mortgage markets will therefore be essentially supply-driven, in particular through various forms of establishment in the Member State of the consumer.

Proposal for a Directive on Credit Agreements Relating to Residential Property[81] **10.30 (EU)**

Grounds for and objectives of the proposal

The present proposal has to be seen in the context of efforts to create an internal market for mortgage credit and against the background of the financial crisis.

[80] COM(2007) 807 final.

[81] Proposal of 31 March 2011 for a Directive of the European Parliament and of the Council on credit agreements relating to residential property, COM(2011) 142 final.

The financial crisis has had a substantial impact on EU citizens. Although an important contributing factor was the growth in securitisation, which allowed creditors to pass the risk of their lending portfolios to investors, consumers have faced the consequences first hand. Many have lost confidence in the financial sector and certain lending practices that used to prevail are now having a direct impact. As borrowers have found their loans increasingly unaffordable, defaults and foreclosures have risen. Addressing irresponsible lending and borrowing is therefore an important element in financial reform efforts.

For several years, the Commission has engaged in a comprehensive review of EU residential mortgages markets to ensure the efficient functioning of the single market. The White Paper on the integration of EU mortgage markets previously identified areas of direct relevance to responsible lending and borrowing (eg pre-contractual information, advice, assessment of creditworthiness, early repayment and credit intermediation) acting as barriers to the efficient functioning of the single market. These barriers prevent the pursuit of business or raise the cost of doing business in another Member State and lead to consumer detriment through low consumer confidence, higher costs and reduced customer mobility, both domestically and cross-border. In view of the problems brought to light in the financial crisis and in the context of efforts to ensure an efficient and competitive single market, the Commission undertook to come forward with measures on responsible lending and borrowing, including a reliable framework on credit intermediation. To this end, the objectives of the proposal are twofold. First, it aims to create an efficient and competitive single market for consumers, creditors and credit intermediaries with a high level of protection by fostering consumer confidence, customer mobility, cross-border activity of creditors and credit intermediaries, and a level playing field while respecting fundamental rights, particularly the right to the protection of personal data, enshrined in the *Charter of Fundamental Rights of the European Union*. Second, the proposal seeks to promote financial stability by ensuring that mortgage credit markets operate in a responsible manner…

Article 1 Subject Matter

The purpose of this Directive is to lay down a framework for certain aspects of the laws, regulations and administrative provisions of the Member States concerning credit agreements relating to residential immovable property for consumers and concerning certain aspects of the prudential and supervisory requirements for credit intermediaries and creditors.

Article 2 Scope

1. This Directive shall apply to the following credit agreements:

(a) Credit agreements which are secured either by a mortgage or by another comparable security commonly used in a Member State on residential immovable property or secured by a right related to residential immovable property.

(b) Credit agreements the purpose of which is to acquire or retain property rights in land or in an existing or projected residential building.

(c) Credit agreements the purpose of which is the renovation of the residential immovable property a person owns or aims to acquire, which are not covered by Directive 2008/48/EC of the European Parliament and of the Council of 23 April 2008. …

Notes

(1) The Green Paper was supplemented by a cost–benefit study published in August 2005 carried out on behalf of the Commission by independent external contractors from London Economics. According to the study, the value to the EU economy in 2005 of such increased integration over the following ten years was estimated at €94.6 billion, ie 0.89% of EU GDP. The study estimated that by 2015 integration of the EU mortgage credit market would raise EU GDP by 0.7% and private consumption by 0.5%.

(2) In 2006, the European Commission responded to the reactions it had received on the Green Paper.[82] Four main themes could be recognised. First, there was a clear message that there should be no integration for integration's sake. Many national mortgage markets are described as being generally efficient and competitive, and integrating the EU market should not be to their detriment. The need for a proper and robust impact assessment of any future measure is therefore deemed indispensable. Second, contributors also agreed that integration should not lead to standardisation. The diversity of mortgage products is seen as an asset that should not easily be sacrificed. Third, responses indicated that integration should not necessarily occur through harmonisation and alternatives to regulation should also be considered. Finally, according to contributions from all stakeholders, integration will be predominantly supply-driven rather than demand-driven. Few respondents believe that there is, at least in a foreseeable future, a substantial consumer appetite for actively looking cross-border.

(3) When the financial crisis hit the European Union at the end of 2007 the playing field changed completely. Where the European Commission had ventured directly into property law by proposing to consider the introduction of a right of Euromortgage, which is a proposal for a non-accessory immovable property security right, modelled inter alia after the German *Grundschuld* (see Chapter 5) that can be used throughout the European Union, the White Paper remains completely silent on the issue.[83] Instead the White Paper focuses on the contractual aspects of providing mortgage credit and attempts to leave the property aspects, ie the creation of a limited property security right, for the laws of the Member States. The financial crisis has shown the dangers of non-accessory property security rights, especially when these were used in securitisation transactions. German law, which served as a model for the Euromortgage idea, was forced to reintroduce aspects of accessority to protect debtors.[84]

(4) The 2011 proposal of the European Commission for a Directive on mortgage lending therefore only concerns the contractual aspects of mortgage lending. That is

[82] Feedback on the consultation on the green paper on mortgage credit (23 May 2006): http://ec.europa.eu/internal_market/finservices-retail/docs/home-loans/feedback_gp-en.pdf .

[83] H Wolfensteiner and OM Stöcker, 'A Non-accessory Security Right over Real Property for Central Europe' (2003) 8/1–2 *Notarius International* 118–24.

[84] On the German problems see C Clemente, 'Verwertung der nicht akzessorischen Grundschuld im Rahmen eines Forderungsverkaufs' (2007) 21 *Zeitschrift für Immobilienrecht* 737–46. *Gesetz zur Fortentwicklung der Finanzmarktstabilisierung* (Law on the further development of the stability of the financial market) of 17 July 2009, BGBI, IS 1980.

not to say the proposal will not have any effect on the property law aspects. Especially in Member States adhering to a consensual system of creation of property rights, but also in legal systems adhering to a causal tradition system, contractual aspects will have effect on the limited property rights that are created. Moreover, when cross-border lending is stimulated and more European Union citizens acquire land in other Member States, the market will call for further European harmonisation if necessary. The CROBECO project, Cross Border Electronic Conveyancing of Land, initiated by the European Land Registry Association (ELRA) and the EULIS, the European Land Information Service, offers a good example of such an initiative (see below, VII.E and VII.D, respectively)[85]

III.D.2 SUCCESSION AND WILLS

Introductory Notes

(a) The European Union is also active in fields that are not directly property law, but which are very closely related to it. We have seen such an example already in the form of the Insolvency Regulation above (III.C.3). The same applies to the activities relating to succession law. In 2006 the European Commission launched a Green Paper in which it proposed to deal with succession and wills in the internal market.[86] The reason for the Green Paper was the increased mobility of European citizens and the problems they encounter in dealing with inheritances when one of the involved parties lives or lived in another Member State. The European Commission aims to interfere in the private international laws of the Member States to ensure more legal certainty in cross-border succession matters. In 2009, the Green Paper was followed up by a Proposal for a Regulation of the European Parliament and of the Council on jurisdiction, applicable law, recognition and enforcement of decisions and authentic instruments in matters of succession and the creation of a European Certificate of Succession.[87]

(b) At the basis of the proposal is the abolition of the *lex rei sitae* requirement in favour of a limited choice of law. This choice is limited to a legal system to which the parties involved in the inheritance at stake are connected.

Proposal for a Regulation on Succession and Wills[88] **10.31 (EU)**

1.2 Grounds for and objectives of the proposal

The significance of cross-border successions within the European Union has been highlighted in the impact assessment attached to the proposal. The diversity of both the rules under substantive law and the rules of international jurisdiction or of applicable law, the multitude of authorities to which international succession matters can be referred and the fragmentation of successions which can result from these divergent rules are obstacles to the free movement of persons in the Union. Today, such

[85] See www.elra.eu/?page_id=636.
[86] Green Paper of 1 March 2006 on Succession and Wills, COM(2005) 65 final.
[87] COM(2009) 154 final.
[88] COM(2009) 154 final.

persons are therefore faced with considerable difficulties in asserting their rights with regard to an international succession. These divergent rules also prevent the full exercise of private property law, which, in accordance with the settled case law of the Court of Justice, forms an integral part of the fundamental rights which the Court ensures are respected. The objective of this proposal is to enable people living in the European Union to organise their succession in advance and effectively to guarantee the rights of heirs and/or legatees and of other persons linked to the deceased, as well as creditors of the succession. ...

Article 1 Scope

1. This Regulation shall apply to successions to the estates of deceased persons. It shall not apply to revenue, customs or administrative matters.

2. In this Regulation, 'Member State' means all the Member States with the exception of Denmark, [the United Kingdom and Ireland].

3. The following shall be excluded from the scope of this Regulation: ...

(d) questions relating to matrimonial property regimes and property regimes of relationships deemed by the law applicable to such relationships to have comparable effects to marriage; ...

(f) property rights, interests and assets created or transferred other than by succession by way of, for instance, gifts, such as in joint ownership with right of survival, pension plans, insurance contracts and or arrangements of a similar nature, without prejudice to Article 19(2)(j); ...

(i) the constitution, functioning and dissolving of trusts;

(j) the nature of rights *in rem*.

Article 16 General rule

Unless otherwise provided for in this Regulation, the law applicable to the succession as a whole shall be the law of the State in which the deceased had their habitual residence at the time of their death.

Article 17 Freedom of choice

1. A person may choose as the law to govern his succession as a whole the law of the State whose nationality he possesses at the time of making the choice or at the time of death. A person possessing multiple nationalities may choose the law of any of the States whose nationality he possesses at the time of making the choice.

2. The law shall be made expressly in a declaration in the form of a disposition of property upon death.

3. The substantive validity act whereby the choice of law was made shall be governed by the chosen law.

4. The modification or revocation of the choice of law shall meet the requirements as to form for the modification or revocation of a disposition of property upon death.

Notes

(1) The proposal for a Regulation will therefore, once entered into force, allow parties to choose the applicable law to their succession. This is an important deviation from the general rule of the laws of the Member States, which all adhere to the *lex rei sitae* rule to mandatorily determine the applicable law in property matters (see above, section II).

(2) Succession matters directly relate to property law, as succession is one of the ways in which property rights can be acquired (see Chapter 8). The last will and testament appoints heirs, ie persons who will receive property rights from the set of assets and debts of the deceased. Moreover, by last will or testament property relations can be created. This is done by a legacy, which is a specific provision in the last will directed at one or more of the heirs. The creation of such property relations is called *mortis causa*, or upon death. It can, for instance, be the creation of a specific trust or the providing of a right of usufruct by way of a legacy.

(3) Providing a choice of law can therefore potentially have very far-reaching consequences for the national systems of property law. Imagine an English citizen, living in Germany for most of his life, who passes away, leaving a last will with a choice of law for the law of England and Wales, in which he seeks to create a trust for one of his heirs. As a result German law needs to accommodate the creation of a trust under English law. Another example could be the creation of a right of usufruct under Dutch law, which, as we have seen in Chapter 3, provides more powers to the holder of the right than other legal systems, eg French law. The proposal for the Regulation addresses this matter rather briefly.

Comments on the Articles, Proposal for a Regulation on Succession and Wills **10.32 (EU)**

4.1. Chapter I: Scope of application and definitions

Article 1

The concept of 'succession' must be interpreted in an autonomous manner and encompasses all the elements of a succession, in particular its handover, administration and liquidation.

The exclusion of rights and properties created or transferred other than by means of succession to the estates of deceased persons covers not only the forms of joint property [joint tenancy] known under common law, but also all forms of gifts under civil law.

The exception envisaged for trusts is not an obstacle to the application to succession of the law governing it on the basis of this Regulation.

The Hague Convention of 1 August 1989 on the law applicable to succession to the estates of deceased persons.

Paragraph (j) stipulates that the Regulation applies to the acquisition of a right *in rem* relating to inherited property, but not to the content of such a right. The Regulation does not affect the '*numerus clausus*' of property law in the Member States, the classification of property and rights, and the determination of the prerogatives of the holder of such rights. As a consequence, it is not, in principle, valid to establish a right in rem without knowing the law of the place in which the property is located. The law on succession cannot lead to the introduction in the State in which the property is located of a property law clause, or the stripping of such clause, without the knowledge of the State. For example, usufruct cannot be introduced in a State which does not recognise it. However, this exception does not apply to the transfer of a right in rem recognised by the Member State in which the inherited property is located.

The publication of property rights, in particular the functioning of the land register and the effects of an entry or failure to make an entry in this register, is also excluded.

Notes

(1) It is thus the intention of the European legislature to leave the property law of the Member States unaffected. Whether this is possible remains doubtful as it is hard to conceive the applicability of another legal system to a succession than the home legal system, without imagining such conflicts of law arising.

(2) Moreover, the recognition of foreign property rights or property rights created under the law of another Member State is already subject to the provisions on free movement (see below, III.E). The possibility to choose another law as the applicable law to a succession will only provide an additional argument to apply the provisions of free movement to national property law.

(3) The effects of this will be harmonising immediately as Member States will have to accommodate foreign property rights into their own legal order.[89]

III.D.3 MATRIMONIAL PROPERTY LAW

Introductory Note

The European Union is also active in the area of matrimonial property law. With a Green Paper on Conflict of Laws in Matters Concerning Matrimonial Property Regimes, including the question of jurisdiction and mutual recognition, in 2006, the Commission moved directly into the area of property law.[90]

Green Paper on Conflicts of Laws in Matters Concerning Matrimonial Property Regimes[91] **10.33 (EU)**

2.2.2. The autonomy of the parties' will

Most of the Member States allow the spouses to choose the law applicable to the matrimonial property regime. If one envisages allowing such a choice in a future instrument, a limited number of connecting factors should obviously be provided for, in particular those involving an actual link with the spouses (eg the law of the State of the habitual residence or nationality of one or both spouses). The question whether the choice of applicable law should be subject to formalities and, if so, what formalities will also have to be considered.

There is also the question whether or not this agreement between spouses should be subject to a limitation in time, being applicable only in the event of the couple separating or while the parties are still living together. In that case, care must be taken not to undermine third parties' rights.

Question 5:

(a) Should there be the possibility for the spouses of choosing the law applicable

[89] On this see also Akkermans, above n 72.

[90] 17 July 2006, COM(2006) 400 final.

[91] Green Paper on Conflicts of Laws in Matters Concerning Matrimonial Property Regimes, 6.

to their matrimonial property regime? If so, what connecting factors can be taken into account to allow this choice?

(b) Should a multiple choice be allowed whereby some assets would be governed by one law and others by another law?

(c) Should it be possible to make or change this choice at any time, before and throughout the marriage or only at a specific time (at the time of dissolution of the marriage bond)?

Notes

(1) The European Commission is therefore considering introducing a choice of law, which would mean a deviation from the standard *lex rei sitae* rule applicable in the Member States. The effects would be similar to the effects described above in case of choice of law in succession cases.

(2) In matrimonial property relations generally no new property rights are created, but the spouses to a marriage share property rights between them.[92]

III.D.4 (DRAFT) COMMON FRAME OF REFERENCE

The Common Frame of Reference is a very extensive project, mostly covering matters of the law of obligations and, more specifically, contract law. There are, however, very interesting and important aspects of property law that are also dealt with. This section will deal with some of the most important property law aspects of the Common Frame of Reference Project. The text and Articles of the Draft Common Frame of Reference (DCFR) offer an important insight into the form and content of a future European private law, possibly also including the law of property, and on those grounds alone deserve to be dealt with. An elaborate discussion of these, especially a critical analysis, deserves to be made, but is beyond the scope of this casebook.

III.D.4.a Towards a Common Frame of Reference

Introductory Notes

(a) For over a decade, the European Commission has been working on the development of European private law. This mostly concerns contract law and consumer contract law, which are dealt with in other casebooks in this series.[93] From the end of the 1980s onwards, the European Union has adopted measures of contract law and

[92] On the property effects of the proposals as well as the question to enlarge the rules to civil unions and, possibly, cohabitation, see JHM van Erp, 'Matrimonial Property Regime and Patrimonial Aspects of Other Forms of Union: What Problems and Proposed Solutions? (Proposal for a Rome IV Regulation)', Advice to the Legal Affairs Committee of the European Parliament (JURI), 30 October 2010. See also Akkermans, above n 72.

[93] See H-W Micklitz, J Stuyck, E Terryn (general eds) and D Droshout (coordinating ed), with the collaboration of J-S Borghetti, S Cámara Lapuente, V Colaert, G Howells, E Poillot, P Rott, L Tichý, C Twigg-Flesner and T Van Dyck, *Cases, Materials and Text on Consumer Law* (Oxford, Hart Publishing, 2010) and H Beale, B Fauvarque-Cosson, J Rutgers, D Tallon and S Vogenauer, *Cases, Materials and Text on Contract Law* (Oxford, Hart Publishing, 2010).

consumer law that directly affect the private law systems of the Member States. This also includes, for example, the Late Payment Directive, dealt with above (III.C.2).

(b) Over the years the body of existing EU private law, also known as the contract law or consumer law *acquis communautaire* (or in short *acquis*), became very fragmented. Moreover, due the need to find a concrete legal basis in the Treaty, most legislation is very specific and not always was all legislation well co-ordinated. The European Commission therefore launched an action plan to bring more coherence into the body of European private law.

A More Coherent European Contract Law. An Action Plan, 12 February 2003[94] **10.34 (EU)**

The Commission communication on European contract law of July 2001 launched a process of consultation and discussion about the way in which problems resulting from divergences between national contract laws in the EU should be dealt with at European level. The present action plan maintains the consultative character of this process and presents the Commission's conclusions. It confirms the outcome of that process, i.e. that there is no need to abandon the current sector-specific approach. It also summarises the problems identified during the consultation process, which concern the need for uniform application of Community contract law as well as the smooth functioning of the internal market.

This action plan suggests a mix of non-regulatory and regulatory measures in order to solve those problems. In addition to appropriate sector-specific interventions, this includes measures:

—to increase the coherence of the Community acquis in the area of contract law,

—to promote the elaboration of EU-wide general contract terms, and

—to examine further whether problems in the European contract law area may require non-sectorspecific solutions such as an optional instrument.

In addition to continuing to put forward sector-specific proposals where these are required, the Commission will seek to increase, where necessary and possible, coherence between instruments, which are part of the Community contract law acquis, both in their drafting and in their implementation and application. Proposals will, where appropriate, take into account a common frame of reference, which the Commission intends to elaborate via research and with the help of all interested parties. This common frame of reference should provide for best solutions in terms of common terminology and rules, i.e. the definition of fundamental concepts and abstract terms like 'contract' or 'damage' and of the rules that apply, for example, in the case of non-performance of contracts. A review of the current European contract law acquis could remedy identified inconsistencies, increase the quality of drafting, simplify and clarify existing provisions, adapt existing legislation to economic and commercial developments which were not foreseen at the time of adoption and fill gaps in Community legislation which have led to problems in its application. The second objective of the common frame of reference is to form the basis for further reflection on an optional instrument in the area of European contract law. In order to promote the elaboration by interested parties of EU-wide general contract terms, the

[94] Communication from the Commission to the European Parliament and the Council, 'A More Coherent European Contract Law. An Action plan', [2003] OJ C63/1 [footnotes omitted].

Commission intends to facilitate the exchange of information on existing and planned initiatives both at a European level and within the Member States. Furthermore, the Commission intends to publish guidelines, which will clarify to interested parties the limits which apply. Finally, the Commission expects comments as to whether some problems may require non-sector-specific solutions, such as an optional instrument in the area of European contract law. The Commission intends to launch a reflection on the opportuneness, the possible legal form, the contents and the legal basis for possible solutions. …

41. Numerous contributions concerned problems as regards to the divergent national rules on contract law on the one hand and on the rules on transfer of property and securities concerning movable goods on the other hand. The national rules on the transition of property differ and therefore the moment of transition of property is different. Furthermore, this can also depend on the nature of the contract which, again, is different in national legal systems. It must be borne in mind that the possibility of a choice of law only concerns contractual rules, and not rules applicable to rights in rem, e.g. transition of property, where the applicable law is the *lex rei sitae*. Many businesses are not aware of this limitation. It has been pointed out that Community law (32) addresses part of the problem by providing for the validity of retention of title clauses, but it does not go beyond this.

42. Reservation of title is regulated differently from jurisdiction to jurisdiction and the effectiveness of relevant contract clauses varies accordingly. This applies even more to possible extensions where the reservation of title also covers, for example, a claim for the purchase price which arises upon a resale of the sold goods by the buyer or over products made from the sold goods. These extensions can also cover future claims or not only the purchase price of the specific goods delivered under a particular contract of sale, but all the buyer's outstanding indebtedness.

43. The divergence of rules often entails that, in the case of the sale of goods with reservation of title, the 'security' foreseen in the contract disappears at the moment when the good in question is brought across the border. It is generally observed that divergence of rules on securities creates a great risk for operators on the market. As a consequence for the supply side, the seller is forced to look to other forms of securities which are, such as bank guarantees, substantially more expensive and realistically speaking, unobtainable from the outset for SMEs. The result for the demand side is that trade credit provided by the seller to the buyer will be higher priced since the seller's risk is to a considerable degree increased or decreased depending upon the availability of proprietary security and its legal effectiveness. This risk can only be partially alleviated by costly legal opinions.

44. Similar problems have been mentioned in the financial services sector for granting trans-border credit, which is only possible if the corresponding securities are guaranteed.

It has been pointed out that the analysis of the validity of the cross-border transfer of securities necessitates costly in-depth legal expertise, which discourages from or impedes such cross-border transactions. In addition, it was mentioned that such analysis is rather time-consuming which, in cases of cross-border transactions to provide finance for re-capitalisation in order to prevent insolvency, might be a critical factor which prevents the whole operation.

45. Above all, some security instruments for movable goods are simply not known in other Member States and vanish if the secured goods are transferred across borders. An example given concerns the transfer of movable goods under the contractual

agreement of a *Sicherungsübereignung* from Germany to Austria. These differences also adversely affect the possibility of entering into cross border leasing contracts.

46. Contributions also indicated differences in national contract laws concerning credit assignments. The difference in rules on factoring was mentioned as a problem because the assignment of receivables is an important instrument for the financing of export transactions. In particular, some Member States restrict the assignment of future receivables or the bulk assignment of receivables, while others take a much more liberal stand in these matters. As a consequence, the factoring industry meets serious obstacles in some Member States, but is favoured by laws of others; this could lead to distortions of competition. Similar differences exist with regard to the validity of clauses contained in sales or service contracts that prohibit the assignment of claims arising from those contracts. Contributions emphasise that factoring companies are prevented from offering their services outside the Member State of their establishment by using one and the same type of contract throughout the whole of the Community. In any case, they would have to undertake a very careful analysis of different national laws.

Notes

(1) This Communication is the basis for what became a very large research project for a group of over 250 academics, developing model legislation for a future EU private law. The model legislation could be used, at the minimum level, as a 'toolbox' for future EU legislation in this area. This model legislation, known as the Common Frame of Reference, was developed by the Joined Network on European Private Law (CoPECL) comprising various research groups, including the Study Group on a European Civil Code (SGECC) and the Research Group on Existing EC Contract Law (*Acquis* Group) (see below, VII.A).

(2) This strategy was further developed in the 2004 Communication from the European Commission 'European Contract Law and the Revision of the Acquis: The Way Forward'.[95] As is made clear in the summary of the Commission's Action Plan cited above, it builds further on a consultation process, and it is intended to be carried out further through research and 'the help of all the interested parties'.

(3) Most importantly for the current discussion is the realisation of the researchers, to which the European Commission refers in paragraphs 42–46 in the excerpt above, that matters of property law are affected by the harmonisation of contract law. The study referred to was carried out under the auspices of Professors Christan Von Bar and Ulrich Drobnig.

C von Bar and U Drobnig (eds), Study on Property Law and Non-Contractual Liability Law as they Relate to Contract Law[96] **10.35 (EU)**

Executive Summary

This study deals with questions of law on the border lines between contract law on

[95] COM(2004) 651 final.

[96] C Von Bar and U Drobnig (eds), *Study on Property Law and Non-Contractual Liability Law as they Relate to Contract Law*, SANCO B5-1000/02/000574, 27. http://ec.europa.eu/consumers/cons_int/safe_shop/fair_bus_pract/cont_law/study.pdf.

the one side and non-contractual liability law and the law of property or things on the other. The study examines these questions of law for most of the legal systems of the European Union. This is conducted against the background of present considerations about approximating or possibly even harmonizing the European systems of contract law. Our study became necessary because the 'European Contract Law Project' has as its target an area of law which in all European jurisdictions is closely linked to tort law and property law, while at the same time the border lines between these two legal fields and contract law assume different contours from jurisdiction to jurisdiction. That essentially leads to two problematic domains, namely (i) which questions of demarcation and designation particularly need to be considered and decided if one intends to clarify what, in a European context, is to be understood by the notion of 'contract law', and (ii) which of those areas of law emerging at the end of this clarifying scrutiny of rules of a 'non-contract law' character have to be brought into consideration if one is contemplating an assessment of the possible success of approximation of laws merely in the 'contract' law realm. …

As regards property law the study shows in particular with the examples of transfer of ownership in movables and credit securities in which areas the added value of an approximation of laws limited to contract law threatens to remain minimal in comparison to the present legal situation, if at the same time concepts are not developed for a solution to those areas of law too. That is true from both a legal and an economic viewpoint. …

Note

The study concludes that there are areas of property law that are so affected by the development of rules on EU contract law that they should be included in the work towards the creation of EU private law. These areas include the transfer of ownership of movables, personal property security rights and trusts.

III.D.4.b General Provisions of the DCFR

SGECC and Acquis Group (eds), Draft Common Frame of Reference 2009 **10.36 (EU)**

Introduction 37. Matters of movable property law. The DCFR also covers some matters of movable property law, namely acquisition and loss of own- ership, proprietary security, and trust law. They form the content of Books VIII, IX and X and are published here for the first time. …

39. Reasons for the approach adopted. The coverage of the DCFR is thus considerably broader than what the European Commission seems to have in mind for the coverage of the CFR (see paragraph 59 below). The 'academic' frame of reference is not subject to the constraints of the 'political' frame of reference. While the DCFR is linked to the CFR, it is conceived as an independent text. The research teams began in the tradition of the Commission on European Contract Law but with the aim of extending its coverage. When this work started there were no political discussions underway on the creation of a CFR of any kind, neither for contract law nor for any other part of the law. Our contract with the Research Directorate-General to receive funding under the sixth European Frame- work Programme on Research reflects this; it obliges us to address all the matters listed above. The relatively broad coverage of the DCFR may be seen as advantageous also from a political perspective. Only

a comprehensive DCFR creates a concrete basis for the discussion of the coverage of the political CFR and thereby allows for an informed decision of the responsible political institutions. ...

The Underlying Principles of Freedom, Justice and Efficiency

Property

14. Limited scope for party autonomy. The principle of party autonomy has to be considerably modified in property law. Because proprietary rights affect third parties generally, the parties to a transaction are not free to create their own basic rules as they wish. They cannot, for example, define for themselves basic concepts like "possession". Nor are they free to modify the basic rules on how ownership can be acquired, transferred or lost. Under the DCFR they cannot even agree to an effective contractual prohibition on alienation. The free alienability of goods is important not only to the persons concerned but also to society at large. One type of freedom is restricted in order to promote another—and efficiency.

15. Recognition and enhancement of freedom in some respects. Within the essential limits just noted, the principle of party autonomy is reflected in Book VIII. It can be seen in the rule that the parties to a transfer of goods can generally determine by agreement the point in time when ownership passes, and in the rule that the consequences of the production of new goods out of another's goods or of the combination or commingling of goods belonging to different persons can be regulated by party agreement. The rules on proprietary security in Book IX can be seen as enhancing freedom (and efficiency) by opening up wide possibilities for the provision of non-possessory security, something which has not traditionally been possible in many legal systems. Similarly, the rules on trusts in Book X could enhance freedom by opening up possibilities for setting property aside for particular purposes (commercial, familial or charitable) in a flexible way which has been much used and much valued in some systems for a very long time and is gradually spreading to others. ...

36. Security a core aim. Security is a paramount value in relation to property law and pervades the whole of Book VIII. The rules in Chapter 6 on the protection of ownership and possession provide a particularly clear example. Indeed, in relation to the acquisition and loss of ownership in movables, certainty and predictability of outcome may sometimes be more important that the actual content of the rules. Different approaches, even fundamentally different approaches, can all lead to acceptable results. Again, however, different values have to be balanced against each other. Some methods of increasing security might, for example, inhibit easy transferabilty. And certainty has to be balanced against fairness, as can be seen very clearly in the rules in Book VIII on production, combination and commingling. It almost goes without saying that security is also a core aim of the Book on proprietary security. The whole objective is to enable parties to provide and obtain security for the proper performance of obligations. The rules are comprehensive and cover all types of proprietary security over moveable assets, including retention of ownership devices. They aim at maximum certainty by recommending a registration system for the effectiveness of a proprietary security against third parties.60 A large part of Book IX is concerned with the detailed regulation of this system. Its rules provide effective remedies for creditors wishing to enforce their security.

37. Protection of reasonable reliance and expectations. This value is strongly reflected in Book VIII. It can be seen most obviously in the rules on good faith acquisition from a person who has no right or authority to transfer ownership and

in the rules on the acquisition of ownership by continuous possession. In the Book on proprietary security this value is most obviously reflected in rules protecting the good faith acquisition of assets, or of security rights in assets, free from a prior security right.

38. The provision of effective remedies. This is just as important as in contract law but the remedies are different. They are designed to enable ownership and possession to be protected. So the owner is given a right to obtain or recover possession of the goods from any person exercising physical control over them. The possessor of goods is also given protective remedies against those who interfere unlawfully with the possession.

39. Protection of the status quo. This value lies behind some oft he rules in Book VIII designed to protect possession, particularly those for the protection of 'better possession'. ...

53. Importance of certainty. Certainty is so important in property law that there are fewer rules which rely overtly on justice than in the other branches of the law already discussed. However, the idea of treating like alike (specifically, treating all the creditors of the transferor alike) played an important part in the debates on the question of whether ownership should as a rule pass on the conclusion of the relevant contract (e. g. a contract for the sale of goods) or only on delivery of the goods or in accordance with another system. Moreover the notion of good faith plays a crucial role in the rules of Book VIII which deal with the acquisition of goods. Chapter 3 deals with good faith acquisition from a person who is not the owner. The main objective of those rules is the promotion of security by favouring the status quo but they are heavily qualified by notions of justice. The acquirer will get ownership only if the acquisition was in good faith. The position is the same in the rules on the acquisition of ownership by continuous possession. Justice is also an important element in the rules on the consequences of production, combinaion or commingling. It is not enough to produce an answer to the question of who owns the resulting goods. The result must also be fair. Where, for example, one person acquires ownership by producing something out of material owned by another, a fair result is achieved by giving the person who loses ownership a right to payment of an amount equal to the value of the material at the moment of production, secured by a proprietary security right in the new goods. This prevents the taking of an undue advantage at the expense of another. The only example of consumer protection in Book VIII is the rule on the ownership of unsolicited goods sent by a business to a consumer. Justice lies behind many of the rules in Book IX on proprietary security and particularly the rules on prior- ity and enforcement. In this context it means not only fairness as between the security provider and the secured creditor but also fairness between different secured creditors and indeed others having a proprietary right in the encumbered assets. The emphasis is on the protective aspect of justice and it is the security provider who often requires protection. There are provisions designed to afford particular protection to consumer security providers. Another aspect of justice is reflected in the rules on good faith acquisition of assets, or of security rights in assets, free from a prior security right...

Article I—1:101 Intended Field of Application

(1) These rules are intended to be used primarily in relation to contracts and other juridical acts, contractual and non-contractual rights and obligations and related property matters.

(2) They are not intended to be used, or used without modification or supplementation, in relation to rights and obligations of a public law nature or, except where otherwise provided, in relation to:

(a) the status or legal capacity of natural persons;

(b) wills and succession;

(c) family relationships, including matrimonial and similar relationships;

(d) bills of exchange, cheques and promissory notes and other negotiable instruments; …

(f) the ownership of, or rights in security over, immovable property …

(3) Further restrictions on intended fields of application are contained in later Books …

III.D.4.c Transfer of Ownership of Movables in the DCFR

SGECC and Acquis Group (eds), Draft Common Frame of Reference 2009 **10.37 (EU)**

Article VIII—1:101 Scope of application

(1) This Book applies to the acquisition, loss and protection of ownership of goods and to specific related issues.

(2) This Book does not apply to the acquisition or loss of ownership of goods by:

(a) universal succession, in particular under the law of succession and under company law;

(b) expropriation and forfeiture;

(c) separation from movable or immovable property;

(d) division of co-ownership, unless provided by VIII—2:306 (Delivery out of the bulk) or VIII—5:202 (Commingling);

(e) survivorship or accrual, unless covered by Chapter 5 of this Book;

(f) real subrogation, unless covered by Chapter 5 of this Book;

(g) occupation;

(h) finding; or

(i) abandonment.

(3) This Book applies to the acquisition and loss of ownership of goods by extra-judicial enforcement in the sense of Book IX or the equivalent. It may be applied, with appropriate adaptations, to the acquisition and loss of ownership of goods by judicial or equivalent enforcement…

Article VIII—1:201 Goods

'Goods' means corporeal movables. It includes ships, vessels, hovercraft or aircraft, space objects, animals, liquids and gases.

Article VIII—1:202 Ownership

'Ownership' is the most comprehensive right a person, the 'owner', can have over property, including the exclusive right, so far as consistent with applicable laws or rights granted by the owner, to use, enjoy, modify, de- stroy, dispose of and recover the property …

Article VIII—1:204 Limited proprietary rights
Limited proprietary rights in the sense of this Book are:

(a) security rights if characterised or treated as proprietary rights by Book IX or by national law;

(b) rights to use if characterised or treated as proprietary rights by other provisions of these model rules or by national law;

(c) rights to acquire in the sense of VIII—2:307(Contingent right of transferee under retention of ownership) or if characterised or treated as proprietary rights by other provisions of these model rules or by national law;

(d) trust-related rights if characterised or treated as proprietary rights by Book X or by national law.

Article VIII—2:101 Requirements for the transfer of ownership in general
(1) The transfer of ownership of goods under this Chapter requires that:

(a) the goods exist;

(b) the goods are transferable;

(c) the transferor has the right or authority to transfer the ownership;

(d) the transferee is entitled as against the transferor to the transfer of ownership by virtue of a contract or other juridical act, a court order or a rule of law; and

(e) there is an agreement as to the time ownership is to pass and the conditions of this agreement are met, or, in the absence of such agreement, delivery or an equivalent to delivery.

(2) For the purposes of paragraph (1)(e) the delivery or equivalent to de- livery must be based on, or referable to, the entitlement under the contract or other juridical act, court order or rule of law.

(3) Where the contract or other juridical act, court order or rule of law defines the goods in generic terms, ownership can pass only when the goods are identified to it. Where goods form part of an identified bulk, VIII—2:305 (Transfer of goods forming part of a bulk) applies. (4) Paragraph (1)(e) does not apply where ownership passes under a court order or rule of law at the time determined in it.

Article VIII—2:201 Effects of the transfer of ownership
(1) At the time determined by Section 1, ownership passes within the lim- its of the transferor's right or authority to dispose, with effect between the parties and with effect against third persons.

(2) The transfer of ownership does not affect rights and obligations be- tween the parties based on the terms of a contract or other juridical act, court order or rule of law, such as:

(a) a right resulting from the passing of risk;

(b) a right to withhold performance;

(c) a right to fruits or benefits, or an obligation to cover costs and charges; or

(d) a right to use or an obligation not to use or otherwise deal with the goods.

(3) The transfer of ownership does not affect rights of or against third parties under other rules of law, such as:

(a) any right of the transferor's creditors to treat the transfer as ineffective arising from the law of insolvency or similar provisions; or

(b) a right to claim reparation under Book VI (Non-contractual liability arising out of damage caused to another) from a third party damaging the goods.

(4) Where ownership has been transferred but the transferor still has a right to withhold delivery of the goods (paragraph (2)(b)), terminating the contractual relationship while exercising the right to withhold performance has retroactive proprietary effect in the sense of the following Article.

Article VIII—2:202 Effect of initial invalidity, subsequent avoidance, withdrawal, termination and revocation

(1) Where the underlying contract or other juridical act is invalid from the beginning, a transfer of ownership does not take place.

(2) Where, after ownership has been transferred, the underlying contract or other juridical act is avoided under Book II, Chapter 7, ownership is treated as never having passed to the transferee (retroactive proprietary effect).

(3) Where ownership must be re-transferred as a consequence of withdrawal in the sense of Book II, Chapter 5, or termination in the sense of Book III, Chapter 3, or revocation of a donation in the sense of Book IV.H, there is no retroactive proprietary effect nor is ownership re-transferred immediately. VIII—2:201 (Effects of the transfer of ownership) paragraph (4) remains unaffected.

(4) This Article does not affect any right to recover the goods based on other provisions of these model rules.

Article VIII—2:307 Contingent right of transferee under retention of ownership

Where the transferor retains ownership of the goods for the purposes of a 'retention of ownership device' in the sense of IX—1:103 (Retention of ownership devices: scope), the transferee's right to pay the price under the terms of the contract and the transferee's right to acquire ownership upon payment have effect against the transferor's creditors.

Notes

(1) Book VIII of the DCFR introduces a system of transfer of ownership of movable objects. The Book does not deal with immovables or land. The comments of the drafters to Book VIII state that

> Immovable property. Book VIII does not apply to immovable property. This converges with I—1:101 (Intended field of application) paragraph (2)(f). Practically, covering immovable property as well would have been unrealistic. It would have required, among other things, a complete analysis of European land registration systems, including rather technical and procedural details. The resulting rules could have been very different from those proposed for goods. For example, the importance of publicity and registration could have been weighed in a completely different way. A specific issue regarding the demarcation between movable and immovable property is, however, addressed in VIII—1:301 (Transferability) paragraph (2).[97]

(2) Book VIII adheres to a causal tradition system of transfer (see Chapter 8). The validity of the transfer is therefore dependent on the validity of the underlying

[97] See C von Bar et al (eds), *Principles Definitions and Model Rules of European Private Law. Draft Common Frame of Reference (DCFR)*, full edn (München, Sellier European Law Publishers, 2009) 4207.

agreement. In the Interim Outline Edition of the DCFR, a version of the text that was published in 2007, the rules on assignment of claims, which are dealt with in Book III of the DCFR, followed a different transfer regime than the regime foreseen for movable objects. In the final version of the DCFR this is corrected and assignment is also a causal system dealt with by Article III—5:118 DCFR.[98]

(3) Interestingly the DCFR and Book VIII, in particular Article VIII—1:204 DCFR, do not contain a definition of limited property rights. Instead, the DCFR leaves this matter to the Member States.

(4) There are exceptions to this, most notably in Article VIII—2:307 DCFR, is the introduction of a property acquisition right (see also Chapter 3, paragraph I.J.3). This special type of limited property right is unknown to most legal systems and stems from German law. In English law tpp the position of the acquirer of a right of ownership can be protected (see Chapter 3, II.A.10).[99]

III.D.4.d Personal Property Security Rights in the DCFR

SGECC and Acquis Group (eds), Draft Common Frame of Reference 2009 **10.38 (EU)**

Article IX—1:101 General rule

(1) This Book applies to the following rights in movable property based upon contracts for proprietary security:

(a) security rights; and

(b) ownership retained under retention of ownership devices.

(2) The rules of this Book on security rights apply with appropriate adaptations to:

(a) rights under a trust for security purposes;

(b) security rights in movable assets created by unilateral juridical acts; and

(c) security rights in movable assets implied by patrimonial law, if and in so far as this is compatible with the purpose of the law.

Article IX—1:102 Security right in movable asset

(1) A security right in a movable asset is any limited proprietary right in the asset which entitles the secured creditor to preferential satisfaction of the secured right from the encumbered asset.

(2) The term security right includes:

(a) limited proprietary rights of a type which is generally recognised as designed to serve as proprietary security, especially the pledge;

(b) limited proprietary rights, however named, that are based upon a contract for proprietary security and that are either intended by the parties to entitle the secured creditor to preferential satisfaction of the secured right from the encumbered asset or have this effect under the contract; and

[98] On the different versions see JHM van Erp, 'DCFR and Property Law: The Need for Consistency and Coherence' in R Schulze (ed), *Common Frame of Reference and Existing EC Contract Law* (Munich: Sellier European Law Publishers, 2008) 249 *et seq*.

[99] For a further discussion on these rules see LPW van Vliet, 'Acquisition and Loss of ownership of Goods—Book VIII of the Draft Common Frame of Reference' [2011] *Zeitschrift für Europäisches Privatrecht (ZEuP)* 292 *et seq*.

(c) other rights which are regarded as security rights under the rules of this Book, such as the right referred to in IX—2:114 (Right of retention of possession) and the rights covered by paragraph (3).

(3) A transfer or purported transfer of ownership of a movable asset which is made, on the basis of a contract for proprietary security, with the intention or the effect of securing satisfaction of a secured right can create only a security right in the asset for the transferee.

(4) Paragraph (3) applies in particular to:

(a) a security transfer of ownership of corporeal assets;

(b) a security assignment;

(c) a sale and lease-back; and

(d) a sale and resale.

Article IX—1:103 Retention of ownership devices: scope

(1) There is a 'retention of ownership device' when ownership is retained by the owner of supplied assets in order to secure a right to performance of an obligation.

(2) The term retention of ownership device includes:

(a) retention of ownership by a seller under a contract of sale;

(b) ownership of the supplier under a contract of hire-purchase;

(c) ownership of the leased assets under a contract of leasing, provided that according to the terms of the contract the lessee at the expiration of the lease period has an option to acquire ownership of, or a right to continue to use, the leased asset without payment or for merely nominal payment (financial leasing); and

(d) ownership of the supplier under a contract of consignment with the intention or the effect of fulfilling a security purpose.

Article IX—2:101 Methods of creation of security rights

A security right in a movable asset may be created: (a) by the security provider granting the security right to the secured creditor;

(b) by the secured creditor retaining the security right when transferring ownership of the asset to the security provider; or

(c) by the secured creditor relying on a right of retention of possession.

Article IX—2:102 Requirements for creation of security rights in general

The creation of a security right in a movable asset requires that:

(a) the asset exists;

(b) the asset is transferable;

(c) the secured right exists; and

(d) the additional requirements for the creation of a security right by granting, by retention or on the basis of a right of retention of possession are fulfilled.

Article IX—2:103 Possessory and non-possessory security rights

Unless otherwise agreed by the parties, the creation of a security right by contract does not require possession of the encumbered asset by the secured creditor.

Article IX—3:101 Effectiveness as against third persons

(1) A security right created according to Chapter 2 has no effects against the following classes of third persons:

(a) holders of proprietary rights, including effective security rights, in the encumbered asset;

(b) a creditor who has started to bring execution against those assets and who, under the applicable law, has obtained a position providing protection against a subsequent execution; and

(c) the insolvency administrator of the security provider, unless, subject to exceptions, the requirements of this Chapter are met.

(2) Where a security right that is effective against third persons according to the provisions of this Chapter is extended by virtue of the provisions of this Book without a need for an agreement to this effect to assets other than the assets that were originally encumbered, the extension of the security right is not subject to the requirements of this Chapter.

(3) A security right that had been acquired by a good faith acquisition in disregard of a retention of ownership device or an earlier security right in the asset to be encumbered is effective against the holder of the retention of ownership device or the holder of the earlier security right even if the requirements of this Chapter are not met. The effectiveness of the security right that had been acquired by a good faith acquisition against other third persons remains subject to the other rules of this Chapter.

Article IX—3:102 Methods of achieving effectiveness

(1) For security rights in all types of assets, effectiveness may be achieved by registration of the security right pursuant to Section 3.

(2) Effectiveness can also be achieved pursuant to Section 2:

(a) in the case of corporeal assets, by the secured creditor holding possession of the encumbered assets; or

(b) in the case of certain intangible assets, by the secured creditor exercising control over the encumbered assets.

Article IX—3:301 European register of proprietary security; other systems of registration or notation

(1) A registration that is required or allowed for any security right or retention of ownership device under the rules of this Book is to be effected in a European register of proprietary security, subject to paragraph (2).

(2) Where systems of registration or notation on title certificates for security rights in specific types of assets exist, the effectiveness of a security right to be registered or noted in these systems depends upon compliance with any mandatory rules applicable for these systems. For systems established under the national law of a member state, this rule is subject to IX—3:312 (Transitional provision in relation to entries in other systems of registration or notation under national law).

(3) An entry of security rights in financial instruments into a register maintained by or for the issuer of financial instruments or which under national law is determinative of title is not regarded as registration for the purposes of this Section but may constitute control if the requirements of IX—3:204 (Control over financial assets) paragraph (3) are complied with.

Notes

(1) Book IX of the DCFR uses a unitary model of security rights (see Chapter 5). It is inspired by the US system of Article 9 of the Uniform Commercial Code (UCC) also dealt with in Chapter 5. Book IX creates a new type of limited property right, a European Security Right (ESR) that can be created following the rules provided by the DCFR itself.

(2) The European Security Right can be a limited property security, such as is recognised and dealt with by the property laws of the Member States, but it can also be a retention of title. As we have seen in Chapter 5, a retention of title device is not always given the same status as a property security right.

(3) The system introduced by Book IX of the DCFR follows the US Article 9 UCC system. A European property security right is created between the parties, but must, in order to take effect, be published. Publication can be made by handing over possession of the object or thing provided as security, but can also be effected by registration of the European Property Security Right in the newly created Registry under Article IX—3:102 DCFR.

(4) The unitary approach of Book IX DCFR is another example of a unitary system of property security rights. Another interesting example of a unitary approach is offered by the model law of the EBRD on secured transactions.[100] The EBRD model rules are relevant as they were used to inspire legislatures in former socialist systems in developing new rules of private law. Interestingly, there is also a movement in the other direction, most notably in French law where in 2006 an explicit choice for a fragmented system of property security rights was made (see Chapter 5).

III.D.4.e Trusts in the DCFR

SGECC and Acquis Group (eds), Draft Common Frame of Reference 2009 **10.39 (EU)**

Article X—1:101 Trusts to which this Book applies

(1) This Book applies to trusts created under Chapter 2 (Constitution of trusts).

(2) With appropriate modifications this Book also applies to trusts:

(a) constituted by:

(i) a declaration to that effect set out in an enactment; or

(ii) a court order with prospective effect; or

(b) arising by operation of law set out in an enactment relating to a matter not determined by these rules.

(3) In this Book, 'court' includes a public officer or body, if authorised to act under the applicable national law, but does not include an arbitral tribunal.

Article X—1:201 Definition of a trust

A trust is a legal relationship in which a trustee is obliged to administer or dispose

[100] European Bank for Reconstruction and Development, Model Law on Secured Transactions (London, EBRD, 2004), to be found at www.ebrd.com/downloads/research/guides/secured.pdf.

of one or more assets (the trust fund) in accordance with the terms governing the relationship (trust terms) to benefit a beneficiary or advance public benefit purposes.

Article X—1:202 Special legal effects of a trust

(1) A trust takes effect in accordance with the rules in Chapter 10 (Relations to third parties) with the effect that the trust fund is to be regarded as a patrimony distinct from the personal patrimony of the trustee and any other patrimonies vested in or managed by the trustee.

(2) In particular (and except for some reason other than merely that the trust fund is vested in the trustee):

(a) the personal creditors of the trustee may not have recourse to the trust fund, whether by execution or by means of insolvency proceedings;

(b) the trust fund is not subject to rules allocating property rights on the basis of matrimonial or family relationships; and

(c) the trustee's successors are not entitled to benefit from the trust fund on the trustee's death.

Article X—2:101 Requirements for constitution

A trust is constituted in relation to a fund vested in the truster, without any further requirement, if:

(a) the truster declares an intention to constitute a trust in relation to that fund;

(b) the declaration satisfies the requirements set out in X—2:201 (Requirements for a declaration); and

(c) either X—2:102 (Constitution by transfer) or X—2:103 (Constitution without transfer) applies.

Article X—8:502 Vesting and divesting of trust assets

(1) Title to a trust asset vests in a person on appointment as a trustee, without a court order to that effect, if that title is:

(a) capable of transfer by agreement between a transferor and a transferee without the necessity for any further act of transfer or formality; or

(b) regarded under the applicable national law as vested in the trustees as a body.

(2) The vesting of an asset in a person who is appointed a trustee does not divest any continuing trustees.

(3) A person who resigns or is removed as a trustee is divested correspondingly.

Article X—10:101 Basic rule on creditors

(1) A person to whom a trustee owes a trust debt (a trust creditor) may satisfy that person's right out of the trust fund (in accordance with X—10:202 (Rights of trust creditors in relation to the trust fund)), but other creditors may not except in so far as these rules provide otherwise.

(2) Paragraph (1) does not affect any right of a creditor of a party to a trust to invoke a right of that party relating to the trust fund.

Notes

(1) Book X of the DCFR introduces a civil law trust. It is a trust that is heavily based on English law, but adapted to function also in a more civil law oriented

setting. As we noted in Chapter 6, there are also effective management devices in German and French law. The solution chosen by the DCFR is an intermediate version between the *Treuhand* and *Fiducie* on the one hand and the fully fledged English express trust on the other.

(2) The DCFR trust is of a contractual nature, but can be created by declaration. The trustee will hold the property entitlement to the trust objects and the beneficiary alone will be able to claim from these. There is, in other words, a separated patrimony from the private patrimony of the trustee from which the trustee's creditors must claim.

(3) Moreover, the DCFR contains provisions in case of misappropriation of trust objects (X—6:101 *et seq*), appointment of new trustees (X—8:401 DCFR) death of the trustee (X—8:504) and ways to end a DCFR trust relation (X—9:101 *et seq*).

(4) Of the three books of the DCFR dealing with aspects of property law, the book on trusts is usually considered the least likely to make it into actual EU legislation. Furthemore the comments of the drafters to this part of the DCFR are very limited.

III.D.4.f The next step: feasibility study of the expert group on EU contract law: towards and optional instrument?

Introductory Note

On 1 July 2010 the European Commission published a Green Paper on policy options towards a European contract law for consumers and businesses.[101] Almost at the same time the European Commission announced the establishment of an Expert Group on a Common Frame of Reference in the area of European contract law that would transform the DCFR into a proposal to the European Commission with which it could follow up one of the policy options suggested in the 2010 Green Paper.[102]

Green Paper on Policy Options Towards a European Contract Law **10.40 (EU)**

The Union could fill contract law gaps by adopting effective tools for the removal of market barriers relating to diverging contract laws. An instrument of European Contract Law, if sufficiently user-friendly and legally certain, could also serve as a model, in particular to international organisations which have taken the Union as a model for regional integration14. The Union could thus play a leading role in setting uniform international standards in this field, which could in turn give the European economy a competitive advantage in the world.

In order to carry out its mandate, the Commission has set up an Expert Group to study the feasibility of a user-friendly instrument of European Contract Law, capable of benefiting consumers and businesses which, at the same time, would provide for legal certainty. The Group will assist the Commission in selecting those parts of the DCFR which are directly or indirectly related to contract law, and in restructuring, revising and supplementing the selected provisions. It will also take into consideration

[101] COM(2010) 348 final.

[102] Commission Decision 2010/233/EU setting up the Expert Group on a Common Frame of Reference in the Area of European Contract Law.

other relevant sources in this area, as well as the contributions to the present consultation. The Group gathers the expertise from the Union's different legal traditions and stakeholders' interests. Members were selected from among reputable experts in the area of civil law, in particular contract law, and are acting independently and in the public interest. The results of the public consultation launched by this Green Paper will inform the on-going work of the Expert Group.

Option 1: Publication of the results of the Expert Group. …

Option 2: An official 'toolbox' for the legislator …

Option 3: Commission Recommendation on European Contract Law …

Option 4: Regulation setting up an optional instrument of European Contract Law …

Option 5: Directive on European Contract Law …

Option 6: Regulation establishing a European Contract Law …

Option 7: Regulation establishing a European Civil Code …

Notes

(1) The term 'property' does not appear in the Green Paper at all, and even when the Commission is writing about a European Civil Code and the areas it would cover, the term 'property' is avoided. It seems therefore that, for the moment, under the heading of the project on the common frame of reference, the law of property and therefore the work and the proposals on Books VIII, IX and X of the DCFR, are left aside.

(2) In the discussion and the debate that followed the publication of the Green Paper, it became clear that the European Commission favours Policy Option 4 on the creation of an optional instrument.[103] It is in this respect that the expert group did its work, although it was asked to refrain from choosing one of the policy options.

A European Contract Law for Consumers and Businesses: Publication of the results of the feasibility study carried out by the Expert Group on European contract law for stakeholders' and legal practitioners' feedback[104] **10.41 (EU)**

The working premises

The Commission asked the Expert Group to conduct a feasibility study on a draft instrument of European contract law whatever its legal form or nature. Given that the Commission had yet to take a formal position on any of the options set out in the Green Paper, the Expert Group was asked to work on an 'as if' basis drafting a study that could be used in different scenarios. …

Material scope of the feasibility study

The Commission asked the Expert Group to focus its feasibility study on a potential European contract law instrument covering sales contracts and service contracts

[103] See eg Speech/11/411 delivered by Justice Commissioner VP Viviane Reding at the Conference Towards a European Contract Law, Leuven 3 June 2011.

[104] Available at http://ec.europa.eu/justice/contract/files/feasibility-study_en.pdf.

associated with sales, such as installation or maintenance, provided by the seller or under the seller's responsibility (eg by a sub-contractor).

A self-standing instrument of European contract law

The Commission asked the Expert Group to conduct a feasibility study which would result in a self-standing and comprehensive text covering most aspects of a contractual relationship that would be of relevance for the contractual relationship in cross-border situations. Therefore certain topics which would be less relevant for cross-border contracts—such as rules on capacity, representation or assignment—were not covered by the Expert Group's work.

V. Next Steps

In its feasibility study, the Expert Group has delivered a text which strives to constitute a complete set of contract law rules covering those issues which, at a practical level, are relevant in a contractual relationship in the internal market of the European Union. It is now up to the Commission to decide if, how and to what extent this feasibility study could serve as a starting point for the preparation of a political follow-up initiative. In this sense the Commission services will use the Expert Group's text as a 'toolbox' in the preparation of a possible future initiative on European contract law.

Notes

(1) For the moment property law is excluded from the European Commission's initiative to develop an instrument of European private law. It seems that it is already politically controversial to propose what the expert group on the common frame of reference in European contract law is proposing, without including the law of property.

(2) That is, of course, not to state that the work of the drafters of the DCFR on Books VIII, IX and X were in vain. As we have seen in this section of this chapter, European property law is in the making and the books offer insights and concrete proposals to develop future European property law legislation.[105]

III.E HARMONISATION BY INTERNAL MARKET LAW OR BY CASE LAW OF THE ECJ

Internal market law has an effect of on the law of property. It would go well beyond the scope of this casebook to deal in any details with the way in which the ECJ has developed the law of the internal market. This section of the chapter will focus on the free movement of goods (III.E.1) and the free movement of capital (III.E.2) and will offer examples of how the law relating to these freedoms interferes with the national law of property of the Member States. Under each of these headings a

[105] On optional property law and pleading for the inclusion of property law into an EU's optional instrument, see JHM van Erp and B Akkermans, 'Optioneel Goederenrecht en IPR' in M Hesselink *et al* (eds), *Groenboek Europees Contractenrecht: naar een optioneel instrument?* (The Hague, Boom Juridische Uitgevers 2010) 105 *et seq.* Available at http://ec.europa.eu/justice/news/consulting_public/0052/contributions/59_nl.pdf.

case study is offered on the basis of an actual decision of the ECJ that may provide food for discussion and further thought.

III.E.1 FREE MOVEMENT OF GOODS AND PROPERTY LAW

Introductory Note

Next to the competence of the European Union to harmonise aspects of property law to serve the primary economic objective of the Union, there is also negative harmonisation. This harmonisation is based on Article 34 TFEU (ex Article 28 EC Treaty). ECJ case law on Article 34 has been important in achieving an internal market in the European Union,[106] by prohibiting import restrictions, but also *measures having equivalent effect* to import restrictions. When those measures fall within the ambit of Article 34 TFEU (III.E.1.a) they are prohibited unless a Member State is able to justify (III.E.1.b) its measures in the light of the principle of proportionality (III.E.1.d). The question may be raised whether mandatory national property law rules may be qualified as such (III.E.1.e). We will first look at Article 34 TFEU.

III.E.1.a Article 34 TFEU

Treaty on the Functioning of the European Union **10.42 (EU)**

Article 34 Quantitative restrictions on imports and all measures having equivalent effect shall be prohibited between Member States.

Note

(1) Article 34 TFEU makes a distinction between quantitative restrictions (QRs) and measures having the effect equivalent to a quantitative restriction (MEQR). QRs generally are restrictions on the number of products that can be imported into a Member State. MEQRs can be any measure that have the same *effect*. The ECJ has qualified and explained MEQRs in its *Dassonville* judgment as:

> All trading rules enacted by Member States which are capable of hindering, directly or indirectly, actually or potentially, intra-Community [now intra-Union] trade are to be considered as measures having an effect equivalent to quantitative.[107]

(2) When it comes to the law of property it is not immediately clear that a rule of property law hinders intra-Union trade. A simple example can illustrate that this can be the case. When a car is owned by a person in the Netherlands on which his bank holds a right of non-possessory pledge (see Chapter 5), and the owner drives his car to Germany where the property right must be exercised, eg in case of a default in payments to the bank, there is conflict between the Dutch rules on the realisation of the right of pledge (also dealt with in Chapter 5) and German law that will claim the applicable law under the *lex rei sitae* rule (see above, II).

[106] On which see P Craig and G de Burca, *EU Law. Text, Cases and Materials* (Oxford, Oxford University Press, 2003) 613 *et seq.*

[107] Case 8/74, *Procureur du Roi v Benoît and Gustave Dassonville* [1974] ECR 837.

The *lex rei sitae* will determine that German law applies to the car and therefore also the German *numerus clausus* of property rights (see Chapter 1). The German *numerus clausus* (see Chapter 3 and Chapter 5) does not recognise a non-possessory right of pledge. The combination of the rule of private international law, ie *lex rei sitae*, in combination with the application of substantive German property law, will therefore result in a loss of right for the bank, unless German law provides the Dutch bank with another property security right with the same ranking and more or less the same effectiveness.

(3) As was seen above (II) national rules of private international law normally provide an alternative for the holder of a foreign property right by transforming or assimilating the foreign property right into a national law equivalent right. However, in case of the Dutch non-possessory pledge, this is complicated as the German equivalent (see also Chapter 5) is ownership for security purposes. When the Dutch bank thus becomes security owner, the owner of the car will lose his right of ownership as there can be only one owner in German law (see Chapter 3).

(4) The normal method ECJ approach to this question was under the dichotomy it had developed in its *Keck and Mithouard* judgment.[108] This dichotomy was between rules relating to product characteristics, which would fall directly under the ambit of Article 34 TFEU, and rules relating to certain selling arrangements, such as Sunday trading rules, which would only fall under the prohibition of Article 34 if they were discriminatory in effect.[109]

European Court of Justice, 4 April 2009[110] **10.43 (EU)**

Commission v Italy

MARKET ACCESS TEST

Trailers

Measures adopted by a Member State, the object or effect of which is to treat products coming from other Member States less favourably, are to be regarded as measures having equivalent effect to quantitative restrictions on imports within the meaning of Article 28 EC, as are the measures referred to in paragraph 35 of the present judgment. Any other measure which hinders access of products originating in other Member States to the market of a Member State is also covered by that concept.

Facts: The Italian legislature adopted a law in which two- and three-wheel motor vehicles were prohibited from towing a trailer. An individual complained to the Italian Republic, claiming that the Italian law violated the free movement of goods under Article 34 TFEU. Italy argued that the rules it enacted related to the use of goods, rather than their characteristics. The Commission disagreed and brought proceedings to the ECJ.

Held: The prohibition does fall under Article 34 TFEU, but could, in this case be justified.

[108] Joined Cases C-267/91 and C-268/91, *Keck and Mithouard* [1993] ECR I-6097

[109] See P Craig and G de Burca, *EU Law. Texts, Cases and Materials*, 4th edn (Oxford, Oxford University Press, 2007) 690–95.

[110] Case C-110/05 [2009] ECR I-519.

Judgment: 33 It should be recalled that, according to settled case-law, all trading rules enacted by Member States which are capable of hindering, directly or indirectly, actually or potentially, intra-Community trade are to be considered as measures having an effect equivalent to quantitative restrictions and are, on that basis, prohibited by Article 28 EC (see, in particular, Dassonville, paragraph 5).

34 It is also apparent from settled case-law that Article 28 EC reflects the obligation to respect the principles of non-discrimination and of mutual recognition of products lawfully manufactured and marketed in other Member States, as well as the principle of ensuring free access of Community products to national markets (see, to that effect, Case 174/82 Sandoz [1983] ECR 2445, paragraph 26; Case 120/78 Rewe-Zentral ('Cassis de Dijon') [1979] ECR 649, paragraphs 6, 14 and 15; and Keck and Mithouard, paragraphs 16 and 17).

35 Hence, in the absence of harmonisation of national legislation, obstacles to the free movement of goods which are the consequence of applying, to goods coming from other Member States where they are lawfully manufactured and marketed, rules that lay down requirements to be met by such goods constitute measures of equivalent effect to quantitative restrictions even if those rules apply to all products alike (see, to that effect, 'Cassis de Dijon', paragraphs 6, 14 and 15; Case C-368/95 Familiapress [1997] ECR I-3689, paragraph 8; and Case C-322/01 Deutscher Apothekerverband [2003] ECR I-14887, paragraph 67).

36 By contrast, the application to products from other Member States of national provisions restricting or prohibiting certain selling arrangements is not such as to hinder directly or indirectly, actually or potentially, trade between Member States for the purposes of the case-law flowing from Dassonville, on condition that those provisions apply to all relevant traders operating within the national territory and that they affect in the same manner, in law and in fact, the marketing of domestic products and of those from other Member States. Provided that those conditions are fulfilled, the application of such rules to the sale of products from another Member State meeting the requirements laid down by that State is not by nature such as to prevent their access to the market or to impede access any more than it impedes the access of domestic products (see Keck and Mithouard, paragraphs 16 and 17).

37 Consequently, measures adopted by a Member State the object or effect of which is to treat products coming from other Member States less favourably are to be regarded as measures having equivalent effect to quantitative restrictions on imports within the meaning of Article 28 EC, as are the measures referred to in paragraph 35 of the present judgment. Any other measure which hinders access of products originating in other Member States to the market of a Member State is also covered by that concept.

B Akkermans and E Ramaekers, 'Free Movement of Goods and Property Law'[111] **10.44 (EU)**

All in all, since the *Trailers* case, there are five different categories of measures that fall under Article 34: (1) quantitative restrictions (QRs); (2) distinctly applicable MEQRs (MEQR a); (3) indistinctly applicable product characteristics (MEQR b); (4) any other measure hindering market access (MEQR c); and (5) certain selling arrangements

[111] Akkermans and E Ramaekers, above n 49.

(CSAs).[112] As regards the CSAs, a two-stage test is applied. If they do not meet the requirements from para. 16 of the *Keck* judgment, then they must be classified as a MEQR hindering market access (ie category 4). If they do meet the requirements from para 16 of *Keck* then the second test is whether they prevent or hinder market access. When yes, they again fall under category 4; when no, they are exempted from the scope of application of Article 34. This second test possibly includes a *de minimis* requirement,[113] so that only those CSAs that prevent or *substantially* hinder market access are caught under Article 34. ...

Notes

(1) In order for a measure of national law to be caught in the prohibition of Article 34 TFEU it minimally needs to provide a substantial hindrance to the internal market. The term *de minimis* refers to a doctrine of EU law stating that EU law should only act if there is an actual need to do so.

(2) Before we apply free movement of goods law to property law, we will turn to the justifications (III.E.1.b) and proportionality requirements (III.E.1.c).

III.E.1.b Article 36 TFEU

Treaty on the Functioning of the European Union **10.45 (EU)**

Article 36 The provisions of Articles 34 and 35 shall not preclude prohibitions or restrictions on imports, exports or goods in transit justified on grounds of public morality, public policy or public security; the protection of health and life of humans, animals or plants; the protection of national treasures possessing artistic, historic or archaeological value; or the protection of industrial and commercial property. Such prohibitions or restrictions shall not, however, constitute a means of arbitrary discrimination or a disguised restriction on trade between Member States.

[112] C Barnard, *The Substantive Law of the EU—The Four Freedoms*, 3rd edn (Oxford, Oxford University Press, 2010) 142.

[113] For now, this is an undecided issue. Traditionally, the ECJ's case law excludes a *de minimis* requirement for the free movement of goods, but a market access test without a *de minimis* requirement would leave very few—if any at all—national measures that would fall outside the scope of application of Art 34 TFEU and do therefore not need to be justified. As Spaventa indicates, 'those who advocated the market access test in the past have always attempted to qualify it so as to identify a threshold (through *de minimis* or notions such as a substantial hindrance to market access) below which national rules would not need to be justified'; E Spaventa, 'Leaving Keck Behind? The Free movement of Goods after the Rulings in Commission v Italy and Mickelsson and Roos' [2009] 34/6 *ELR* 923. See also Barnard, above n 112, 106–7 and 122.

European Court of Justice, 20 February 1979[114] **10.46 (EU)**

Rewe-Zentral AG v Bundesmonopolverwaltung für Branntwein

JUSTIFICATIONS FOR BREACHING ARTICLE 34 TFEU

Cassis de Dijon

Besides the grounds mentioned in Article 36 TFEU, mandatory requirements such as the effectiveness of fiscal supervision, the protection of public health, the fairness of commercial transactions and consumer protection may also be used to justify infringements of Article 34 TFEU.

Facts: The claimant in the national case underlying this preliminary question procedure at the ECJ wanted to import a shipment of Cassis de Dijon, blackcurrant liqueur, from France into Germany. The claimant applied for authorisation to do so, but this was denied by the Bundermonopolverwaltung für Branntwein because there was not enough alcohol content (15–20%) in the French liqueur for it to be marketed on the German market as liqueur under the then applying provisions of German law (minium 25%). The claimant argued that the German rules constituted an infringement of Article 34 TFEU (then Article 30 EEC Treaty). The German government argued that it needed to protect consumers and that its measures were therefore justified.

Held: The concept of 'measures having an effect equivalent to quantitative restrictions on imports' contained in Article 30 of the Treaty is to be understood to mean that the fixing of a minimum alcohol content for alcoholic beverages intended for human consumption by the legislation of a Member State also falls within the prohibition laid down in that provision where the importation of alcoholic beverages lawfully produced and marketed in another member state is concerned.

Judgment: 8 In the absence of common rules relating to the production and marketing of alcohol—a proposal for a regulation submitted to the council by the commission on 7 December 1976 (Official Journal C 309, p 2) not yet having received the council's approval—it is for the Member States to regulate all matters relating to the production and marketing of alcohol and alcoholic beverages on their own territory.

Obstacles to movement within the Community resulting from disparities between the national laws relating to the marketing of the products in question must be accepted in so far as those provisions may be recognized as being necessary in order to satisfy mandatory requirements relating in particular to the effectiveness of fiscal supervision, the protection of public health, the fairness of commercial transactions and the defence of the consumer.

9 The Government of the Federal Republic of Germany, intervening in the proceedings, put forward various arguments which, in its view, justify the application of provisions relating to the minimum alcohol content of alcoholic beverages, adducing considerations relating on the one hand to the protection of public health and on the other to the protection of the consumer against unfair commercial practices.

10 As regards the protection of public health the German Government states that the purpose of the fixing of minimum alcohol contents by national legislation is to avoid the proliferation of alcoholic beverages on the national market, in particular alcoholic beverages with a low alcohol content, since , in its view, such products may more easily induce a tolerance towards alcohol than more highly alcoholic beverages.

11 Such considerations are not decisive since the consumer can obtain on the

[114] Case 120/78 [1979] ECR 649.

market an extremely wide range of weakly or moderately alcoholic products and furthermore a large proportion of alcoholic beverages with a high alcohol content freely sold on the German market is generally consumed in a diluted form.

12 The German Government also claims that the fixing of a lower limit for the alcohol content of certain liqueurs is designed to protect the consumer against unfair practices on the part of producers and distributors of alcoholic beverages.

This argument is based on the consideration that the lowering of the alcohol content secures a competitive advantage in relation to beverages with a higher alcohol content, since alcohol constitutes by far the most expensive constituent of beverages by reason of the high rate of tax to which it is subject.

Furthermore, according to the German government, to allow alcoholic products into free circulation wherever, as regards their alcohol content, they comply with the rules laid down in the country of production would have the effect of imposing as a common standard within the community the lowest alcohol content permitted in any of the Member States, and even of rendering any requirements in this field inoperative since a lower limit of this nature is foreign to the rules of several Member States.

13 As the Commission rightly observed, the fixing of limits in relation to the alcohol content of beverages may lead to the standardization of products placed on the market and of their designations, in the interests of a greater transparency of commercial transactions and offers for sale to the public.

However, this line of argument cannot be taken so far as to regard the mandatory fixing of minimum alcohol contents as being an essential guarantee of the fairness of commercial transactions, since it is a simple matter to ensure that suitable information is conveyed to the purchaser by requiring the display of an indication of origin and of the alcohol content on the packaging of products.

14 It is clear from the foregoing that the requirements relating to the minimum alcohol content of alcoholic beverages do not serve a purpose which is in the general interest and such as to take precedence over the requirements of the free movement of goods, which constitutes one of the fundamental rules of the community.

In practice, the principle effect of requirements of this nature is to promote alcoholic beverages having a high alcohol content by excluding from the national market products of other member states which do not answer that description.

It therefore appears that the unilateral requirement imposed by the rules of a member state of a minimum alcohol content for the purposes of the sale of alcoholic beverages constitutes an obstacle to trade which is incompatible with the provisions of Article 30 of the Treaty.

There is therefore no valid reason why, provided that they have been lawfully produced and marketed in one of the member states, alcoholic beverages should not be introduced into any other Member State; the sale of such products may not be subject to a legal prohibition on the marketing of beverages with an alcohol content lower than the limit set by the national rules.

15 Consequently, the first question should be answered to the effect that the concept of 'measures having an effect equivalent to quantitative restrictions on imports' contained in Article 30 of the Treaty is to be understood to mean that the fixing of a minimum alcohol content for alcoholic beverages intended for human consumption by the legislation of a member state also falls within the prohibition laid down in that provision where the importation of alcoholic beverages lawfully produced and marketed in another member state is concerned.

Notes

(1) The statement that a certain measure of national law violates the prohibition of Article 34 TFEU does not mean it no longer applies in a certain case. The Member State will be allowed to justify the measure it imposes. It can do by making use of the grounds for justification mentioned in Article 36 TFEU, but it can also, in case of non-discriminatory measures, also known as indistinctly applicable measures, ie measures that do not make a distinction based on the country of origin of a certain good, use mandatory requirements (also called imperative requirements). These are additional grounds of justification for the Member State.

(2) This phase in the reasoning is important because the burden of proof now shifts from the trader to the Member State to show that its measures are actually in compliance with EU law.

III.E.1.c Proportionality

Introductory Note

A final requirement before the ECJ makes its decision in a case is whether the measure a Member State tries to justify is proportional to the aim pursued.

C Barnard, The Substantive Law of the EU. The Four Freedoms[115] **10.47 (EU)**

The Court has long emphasized that the measures taken by Member States must not only genuinely serve the purpose for which they are intended but they must also be proportionate to the risk presented by the import, with the burden of proving proportionality on the defendant state. The principle of proportionality comprises essentially two tests: a test of suitability and a test of necessity. As Tridimas explains, the first (suitability) refers to the relationship between the means and the ends: the means employed by the test must be suitable (or adequate or proportionate). As the Court put it in *United Foods,* there has to be a 'reasonable connexion' between the measures laid down by the authorities and the exercise of control. The second test (necessity) is one of weighing competing interests: the Court assesses the adverse consequences that the measure has on an interest worthy of legal protection and determines whether those consequences are justified in view of the importance of the objective pursued. Sometimes this second limb is viewed as having two distinct elements: whether there are other less restrictive means of producing the same result and, even if there are no less restrictive means, whether the measure, nevertheless, has an excessive effect on the applicant's interests.

Thus, using the medium of the proportionality principle, the court (usually the national court but sometimes the Court of Justice) performs a balancing exercise between the objectives pursued by the measure at issue and its adverse effects on individual freedom. While the Court may adopt a light touch review towards the objectives themselves, it is much stricter in its review of the means of achieving those objectives. ...

[115] Barnard, above n 112, 81.

Notes

(1) A measure that hinders intra-Union trade is thus prohibited under Article 34 TFEU if that measure cannot be justified and it cannot be proven that the measure is the most suitable and necessary (proportionality).

(2) Proportionality is the closing test of the approach of the ECJ to the free movement of goods. It can, because of its nature, only be decided on a case-by-case basis.

III.E.1.d Case study: free movement of goods and property law

Introductory Note

When we apply the free movement of goods to property law, as was already touched upon above (III.E.1), rules of national property law may be included in the scope of Article 34 TFEU and thus be prohibited to apply in a certain cross-border case.

EM Kieninger, Securities in Movable Property within the Common Market[116] **10.48 (EU)**

(ii) The *lex situs*-rule and its consequences for the enforcement of security rights which have been created under a different jurisdiction then where enforcement is sought

... The variety of security interests of which the preceding paragraph has tried to give an impression, exposes the creditor to a specific risk in international trade, namely the danger of loosing his security right through the change of the applicable law. The rule of private international law with respect to proprietary issues is the so-called lex situs—rule: Questions of property law are governed by the law of the situs where the collateral is situated at the relevant time. This rule is practically universally accepted and extends to immovables and movables alike. Whereas with immovables it is both natural and practical to apply the law of the country where the piece of land is situated, the operation is not as easy and practical when movable property is concerned. Movable property can move across borders and the question then arises, which of two laws should be applied—the law of the old *situs* or the law of the new one. At this point, two principles collide. On the one hand, property rights which have been validly created under the old *situs* should be upheld (*doctrine des droits acquis*), whereas on the other hand, the security right has to fit into the new *lex situs*, because the domestic trade at the new *situs* should not be confronted with unknown security rights, or rights which could not have been established in this way. Thus the new *lex situs*, with its principles of numerus clausus and publicity, very frequently forms a barrier to the recognition and enforcement of foreign security rights. ...

These considerations lead to the following question, which has so far only scarcely been discussed: Is there yet another solution to the problem of trans-border security rights in the European context, apart from harmonisation? ... Is the non-recognition of a foreign security right a 'measure having equivalent effect'? ...

Applying the *Oosthoek* formula, one has to reach the conclusion that the lex situs

[116] EM Kieninger, 'Securities in Movable Property within the Common Market' [1996] *European Review of Private Law* 43–66 [footnotes omitted].

rule, together with the various national regulations, which prevent the recognition of foreign security interests in a contract of sale, do represent a measure having equivalent effect within the meaning of article [34] if they cannot be justified by mandatory requirements. …

The list of mandatory requirements in the general interest which can justify a measure having equivalent effect is not closed. … Therefore it seems possible that the aims and principles of national law which prevent the recognition of foreign security rights may also be recognised as justifications.

The predominant reason for the *lex situs* rule is the protection of third parties who trust that property being on the territory of a certain jurisdiction can only be charged according to the laws of that jurisdiction. Private international law thus mirrors the principles of domestic property law of each jurisdiction and seeks to protect them from the outside world. Yet it would be premature to draw the conclusion that property law principles like the numerus clausus or the publicity of proprietary rights themselves are mandatory requirements. The publicity of proprietary rights in itself, for instance, is not indispensable for the functioning of a system of credit and security as the German example shows. It is, however, indispensable to create and to protect a certain order of property rights and a certain order of creditors. …

To justify a trade barrier it is not enough to refer to a mandatory requirement. According to the jurisdiction of the European Court, national restrictions must also pass the test of proportionality. In the context of security rights two elements of this test are of special importance: (i) the question whether the individual regulation is really capable of protecting the national order of creditors' rights, and (ii) whether the restriction is part of a coherent national order. … This may be illustrated by the French-German case mentioned in the beginning: The Bundesgerichtshof upheld a French *gage sur véhicule* and translated it into a German *Sicherungsübereignung* notwithstanding the fact that the German civil code expressly denies the validity of a non-possessory pledge. It argued that the principle of publicity could not be regarded as prohibiting the recognition of a foreign registered pledge because German law had itself derogated from it since the invention of the *Sicherungsübereignung*. This solution is not only the result of the doctrine of transposition; it is also required by European law. As German law no longer adhered to the principle of security rights, it could not justify the non-recognition of the French gage through the mandatory requirement of protecting the security of legal transactions on the domestic market. …

Note

Although Kieninger bases herself on older case law to some extent, her arguments are still completely valid and, with the ever-increasing volume of cross-border trade in the European Union, possibly more relevant than ever.

We can now turn to an actual example of the ECJ's approach to property law.

European Court of Justice, 7 March 1990[117] **10.49 (EU)**

H Krantz GmbH & Co v Ontvanger der Directe Belastingen and Staat der Nederlanden

DUTCH RIGHT TO SEIZURE IS NOT A MEQR

Krantz

Article 28 does not prohibit the national tax collector from seizing goods on the premises of the tax debtor, even if owned by a foreign supplier.

Facts: A German company Krantz sold and delivered a machine under a retention of title to a Dutch company. The machine was installed on the premises of the Dutch company. The machine was seized by the tax collector on the basis of a special right of the Dutch tax collector to seize property present on the premises, even if owned by third parties (*bodembeslag*). Krantz challenged the validity of this Dutch provision and argued it was against the free movement of goods dealt with by Article 34 TFEU (then Article 30 EEC Treaty).

Held: Article 28 of the Treaty, properly interpreted, does not prohibit national legislation which authorises the collector of direct taxes to seize goods, other than stocks, which are found on the premises of a taxpayer even if those goods are owned by a supplier established in another Member State.

Judgment: 9. As the Court has consistently held, initially in the judgement of 11 July 1974 in Case 8/74 Procureur du Roi v Dassonville [1974] ECR 837, all measures capable of hindering, directly or indirectly, actually or potentially, intra-community trade are to be regarded as measures having equivalent effect to quantitative restrictions.

10. It must, however, be observed that the national provision referred to by the national court applies without distinction to both domestic and imported goods, and does not seek to control trade with other Member States.

11. Furthermore, the possibility that nationals of other Member States would hesitate to sell goods on instalment terms to purchasers in the Member State concerned because such goods would be liable to seizure by the collector of taxes if the purchaser failed to discharge their Netherlands tax debts is too uncertain and indirect to warrant the conclusion that a national provision authorising such seizure is liable to hinder trade with other Member States.

12. Accordingly, the answer to the first question must be that Article [34] of the Treaty, properly interpreted, does not prohibit national legislation which authorises the collector of direct taxes to seize goods, other than stocks, which are found on the premises of a taxpayer even if those goods are from, and are the property of, a supplier established in another Member state.

Notes

(1) This is at first sight a disappointing judgment of the ECJ. Shortly summarised, the ECJ holds that it cannot establish a real substantive effect on the functioning of the internal market.

(2) Although generally not recognised, the case has given rise to a debate among

[117] Case C-69/88 [1990] ECR I-583.

EU lawyers whether a *de minimis* requirement applies to Article 34 TFEU. Generally this is denied.

(3) *Krantz*, however, is relevant because of the potential application it may have. Advocate General Darmon, who delivered an opinion in this case stated:

Opinion of AG Darmon to the Case C-69/88 Krantz **10.50 (EU)**

12. I propose to explain briefly my reasons for believing that the Invorderingswet has no bearing on imports. This law, which applies to movable property furnishing the place of residence of a person owing direct taxes irrespective of whether they originate in the Netherlands or elsewhere in the Community, does not cover stocks of raw materials, auxiliary materials, or finished products. Its scope is thus strikingly limited. Moreover, the Invorderingswet has no effect on the volume of demand from buyers on instalment terms. The only possible effect concerns the offering of goods on instalment terms by sellers, who might hesitate to enter into a contract with a buyer subject to Netherlands direct taxation. I should emphasize the merely hypothetical character of any 'reluctance' on the sellers' part, inasmuch as such reluctance could only relate to the materialization of an uncertain event —indeed, an event uncertain on two counts, since the risk of seizure of goods sold on instalment terms to a Netherlands buyer does not arise unless (i) that buyer also turns out to be a defaulting debtor of direct taxes, and (ii) the competent national authorities decide to resolve the situation by the seizure of property. Lastly, it may be added that in facing that risk (if any) all sellers are on the same footing, whether they are Netherlands nationals or from another Member State. …

16. The very broad definition of a 'measure having equivalent effect' formulated in the Dassonville judgment has since 1974 served as a constant point of reference for subsequent judgments on the subject. The inherent breadth of that definition and the Court's concern, apparent in its judgments, not to reduce its scope fully explain why businessmen have attempted to have a wide variety of measures treated as measures having equivalent effect to quantitative restrictions on imports, where such an effect however indirect and tenuous—cannot be altogether ruled out. The Court's judgment in Torfaen Borough Council, based on the Cinéthèque judgment, provides some clarification to the effect that restrictive effects on imports, if inherent in legislation pursuing goals permitted by the Treaty, cannot, unless they are disproportionate, cause a measure to be regarded as a measure having equivalent effect to quantitative restrictions. Thus a 'lower limit' for a measure having an equivalent effect to quantitative restrictions on imports is becoming discernible. The present case falls short of the 'lower limit to the lower limit', since the alleged effects on imports of the Invorderingswet cannot be substantiated in the first place.

Notes

(1) In other words, had the constellation of facts have been different, the ECJ could have decided otherwise.

(2) Imagine, once again the fictive case mentioned above of the enforcement of a Dutch non-possessory pledge in German property law. Would this have been the case, and the Dutch bank would have lost its right or the owner of the car would have lost his right, and this case had in particular applied between two commercial

sellers, the argument there is no substantial hindrance to cross-border trade seems difficult to follow. Moreover, under the new case law of the ECJ in the *Trailers* case (10.43 (EU)), the trader must now show a substantial hindrance to the access to the market.

(3) It remains controversial to argue in this direction, as there is no actual other ECJ case law. Most property lawyers stick with the existing positive law, but some also argue to go beyond that. A final excerpt in this section will hopefully offer food for discussion.

B Akkermans and E Ramaekers, Free Movement of Goods and Property Law[118] **10.51 (EU)**

The only case dealing with property law matters, *Krantz*, was decided under the EEC Treaty, therefore, before the creation of the European Union. As a result, the context of the decision was different than a case with a similar fact pattern today. The difference lies in the existence of the European Union. The Treaty of Maastricht is usually referred to as having given rise to cooperation in more than just economic areas. However, the Treaty also gave rise to the creation of the European Monetary Union and especially a further economic integration in the internal market. Moreover, the Treaties concluded after Maastricht, most notably the Lisbon Treaty—which entered into force on 1 December 2009—bring a strong emphasis on economic integration. This is not so much in the content of the Treaty Articles, which mostly remained the same, but more in the place the internal market takes in the policy of the Union.[119]

The Stockholm programme, the policy programme of the European Union for the next five years, focuses on Freedom, Security and Justice.[120] Under the heading of Justice the Council states that an area of justice must be consolidated so as to move beyond the current fragmentation.[121] This aim can be achieved through two different policies. First, there is an ongoing emphasis on mutual recognition.[122] Under this heading Member States are reminded of their duty to implement European law, but also to be aware of each other's legal systems. In respect to private law, this includes the recognition of (matrimonial) property rights from other Member States. Secondly, there is now a clear private law (named civil law in the Stockholm Programme) policy.[123] Civil justice, as it is known in European Union terminology, should be achieved by harmonisation, most notably of conflict of law rules. The programme states:

> 'The European Council considers that the process of harmonising conflict-of-law rules at Union level should also continue in areas where it is necessary, like separation and divorces. It could also include the area of company law, insurance contracts and security interests.'[124]

[118] Akkermans and Ramaekers, above n 34, conclusion.
[119] Art 34 TFEU, formally Art 28 EC and, before that, Art 30 EEC, has remained unchanged.
[120] The Stockholm Programme – An Open and Secure Europe Serving and Protecting the Citizens, Council of The European Union, 2 December 2009.
[121] *Ibid*, 4.
[122] *Ibid*, 22.
[123] *Ibid*, 24.
[124] *Ibid*, 24.

With that statement, property law, especially security rights, now seems more included than excluded from the European integration process. For a long time a debate has been had whether property law can be subject to harmonising efforts of the European Union. Article 345 TFEU in particular has played a significant role here. The Article states that the European Union Treaties shall in no way prejudice the system of property ownership of the Member States. However, research into the coming into being of this Article has shown that this Article does not form any obstacle to the development of European property law.[125]

The Stockholm Programme and further initiatives taken by the European Commission show that the European Union is slowly moving into the field of property law. This includes the financial collateral arrangements Directive, but also the newly proposed Regulation dealing with succession and matrimonial property rights.[126] Section 3.1 of the explanatory memorandum to the Regulation explains that the European Commission considered this to be property law.[127]

These developments show how European Union law more and more includes property law.[128] It shows how the European legal order has changed in the last decades. Moreover, as we dealt with above, the ECJ has also changed its approach towards fact patterns affecting the free movements of goods in the internal market. We now have an alternative approach to product characteristics and certain selling arrangements[129] in a market access test.[130] It seems, that market access is here to stay, as the Court, even applying a Keck-test, requires a hindrance to market access to allow Article 34 TFEU to be applicable. [131] However, and this must be stressed as well, the internal market law has not changed so much as to make all the early case law of the ECJ obsolete.

Taking these changes into account, it is time therefore to post the fundamental question: can the national closed systems of property law be maintained. The relationship between property law and internal market law has been commented on from a property law perspective much.[132] It is clear that if the Court would be asked to consider a situation we have referred to the Court is correct to be careful in accepting a violation of the free movement of goods. In the *Krantz* decision, both the Advocate General and the Court were careful to accept a substantial hindrance to intra-Union trade. Although the case concerned an unusual fact pattern because

[125] Akkermans and E Ramaekers, above n 49.

[126] See Proposal for a Regulation of the European Parliament and of the Council on jurisdiction, applicable law, recognition and enforcement of decisions and authentic instruments in matters of succession and the creation of a European Certificate of Succession, COM(2009) 154 final, recitals 5 and 6.

[127] This was further confirmed by Ms Salla Saastamoinen at the Conference on Cross-Border Successions, The New Commission Proposal: contents and way forward, 18 and 19 February 2010, Trier, *de auditu*.

[128] For a further overview see JHM van Erp and B Akkermans, 'European Union Property Law' in C Twigg-Flessner (ed), *Cambridge Companion of European Union Private Law* (Cambridge, Cambridge University Press 2010) 173–86.

[129] Case C-267/91, *Criminal Proceedings against Keck and Mithouard* [1993] ECR I-6097.

[130] See above, section II.2.

[131] Case C-405/98, *Gourmet International Products* [2001] ECR I-1795, para 18: 'It should be pointed out that, according to paragraph 17 of its judgment in *Keck and Mithouard*, if national provisions restricting or prohibiting certain selling arrangements are to avoid being caught by Article 30 of the Treaty, they must not be of such a kind as to prevent access to the market by products from another Member State or to impede access any more than they impede the access of domestic products.'

[132] See, eg, van Erp, above n 5, 6; B Akkermans, *The Principle of* Numerus Clausus *in European Property Law* (Antwerpen/Oxford/Portland, Intersentia, 2008) 518–20.

it concerned a special right of seizure of the Dutch tax author, there are clear indications to be taken from this case. The potential of cases resulting from a more general property law fact pattern on recognition of foreign property rights seems immense. However, in our view it is remarkable that the court seems to require a substantial rather than potential hindrance of intra-Union trade to establish a violation of Article 34 TFEU.[133]

This concerns the effect such a judgment could have had on property law. Taking a private lawyer's perspective, the essence of such a case concerns the recognition of a foreign property security right and thereby automatically the problem of ranking of several security rights—including a foreign security right—in insolvency proceedings. From this perspective such a case is not an 'unusual constellation of facts'. Rather, such property security rights frequently need to be taken into account in insolvency proceedings. As Klauer states: 'If the seller assumed that the buyer would stay solvent and willing to pay, then he would not need to create a security right. It is simply naive to assume, that the actions of a supplier would not be affected, if he had to fear that his security right would be lost or that its effectiveness would be diminished when crossing the border.'[134]

The submission that intra-Union trade would not be hindered too much, because the risk of losing a security right is too remote to actually lead to an increase in costs between parties has been criticised. Kieninger in particular has for many years put pressure on this submission.[135] Von Bar and Drobnig, in their study of property law and how it relates to contract law, offer evidence that foreign companies may be hesitant to trade with Dutch companies because of the existence of the right of seizure of the Tax authority.[136]

A fact pattern concerning the recognition of a foreign property right and the following transformation of that right into a national law equivalent should therefore be considered much less 'unusual' than is usually suggested. In our view Article 34 TFEU certainly applies to this situation, and—as Kieninger and Von Bar and Drobnig show—does lead to a substantial hindrance to market access.

Taking the above into consideration, such a fact pattern is likely to be decided in a different way by the Court. The ECJ is more likely to hold Article 34 TFEU violated and so help the development of the civil justice area. Whether this also includes the forced recognition of a foreign property right will depend on the further case proceedings. As we tried to illustrate above, there might be grounds for justification for non- or alternate recognition of foreign property rights, although these grounds are not likely to be deemed proportional by the Court. Two highly interesting aspects are connected to this observation. First, once the Court has opted for a violation of Article 34 TFEU because market access has been hindered, the burden of proof shifts from the trader to the Member State, which must now show its measure is

[133] In other words, whether the ECJ introduced a *de minimis* requirement. See Barnard, above n 112, 143–44.

[134] I Klauer, *Die Europäisierung Des Privatrechts—Der Eugh Als Zivilrichter* (Baden-Baden, Nomos, 1998) 91: 'Ginge der Verkäufer davon aus, dass der Käufer zahlungsfähig und zahlungswillig bleibt, so bräuchte er kein Sicherungsmittel zu vereinbaren. Es ist geradezu naiv anzunemen, es habe keinen Einfluss auf die Handlungsweise eines Lieferanten, wenn dieser befürchten muss, dass seine Sicherungsmittel beim Überschreiten der Grenze untergehen oder in ihrer Wirksamkeit beeinträchtigt werden' (translation by authors).

[135] Kieninger, 1996, 2002, 2006, 2008, above n 34.

[136] C von Bar and U Drobnig, *Study on Property Law and Non-contractual Liability Law as They relAte to Contract Law*, SANCO B5-1000/02/000574, at 527–29, 733.

justifiable, necessary and suitable.[137] Secondly, proportionality must be considered on a case-by-case basis.[138] Therefore, general submissions that property law is excluded from the scope of internal market law can no longer be made. Instead—and this seems to fit perfectly with the proposed Stockholm strategy under the new Lisbon Treaty—recognition of property rights validly created in another Member State benefits a well-functioning internal market.

The Stockholm programme offers a look into the future. If private law, property law in particular, is part of the legislative efforts and there seem to be no restrictions on the ECJ to apply internal market law to property law, the development of property law comes from two sides: positive and negative integration. Although the ECJ is criticised for this, it has been known before to help the development of controversial aspects of the integration process.[139] This connection we seek to make between the general EU policy and the ECJ is not so farfetched as it may seem at first sight. On several occasions the ECJ has held that property law is subject to the Internal Market.[140]

The idea of mutual recognition of property rights remains controversial as it touches on the national identity—as expressed through private law—of the Member States. Property law is in particular seen as a manifestation of the national authority, as a large part of it, mostly the law concerning ownership, forms the basis for succession and taxation. A decision forcing the Member States to recognise other property rights will have effects on the national systems of property law.[141] It is therefore better to approach this with harmonisation efforts, as these are undertaken in respect to property security rights.[142]

III.E.2 FREE MOVEMENT OF CAPITAL AND PROPERTY LAW

In addition to the free movement of goods, the free movement of capital is also of interest. This freedom can also apply to property law, but in a whole different area of property law than the free movement of goods. The free movement of capital mostly concerns the acquisition of ownership of land in another Member State. This section will describe some of the effects of the free movement of capital to property law.

[137] The latter two steps are part of the proportionality test, see Case 261/81, *Rau* [1982] ECR 3961 and Craig and de Burca, above n 109, 706–09.

[138] Barnard, above n 112, 171 *et seq.*

[139] R Herzog and L Gerken, 'Stop the European Court of Justice', EU Observer 10 September 2008, to be found at http://euobserver.com/9/26714.

[140] C-367/98, *Commission v Portugal* [2002] ECR I-4731; C-483/99, *Commission v France* [2002] ECR I-4781; and Case C-503/99 *Commission v Belgium* [2002] ECR I-4809.

[141] See, more elaborately, Akkermans, above n 132, 523 *et seq.*

[142] See, inter alia, E-M Kieniner, 'Evaluation: A Common Core? Convergences, Subsisting Differences and Possible Ways for Harmonisation' in E-M Kieninger (ed), *Security Rights in Movable Property in European Private Law* (Cambridge, Cambridge University Press, 2004) 647–73; C von Bar *et al* (eds), *Principles, Definitions and Model Rules of European Private Law. Draft Common Frame of Reference (DCFR)*, outline edn (München, Sellier European Law Publishers, 2008); HJ Snijders, 'Access to Civil Securities and Free Competition in the EU, A Plea for One European Security Right in Movables' in Drobnig, Snijders and Zippro, above n 34, 153–164.

III.E.2.a Freedom of Movement of Capital

Treaty on the Functioning of the European Union **10.52 (EU)**

Article 63 1. Within the framework of the provisions set out in this Chapter, all restrictions on the movement of capital between Member States and between Member States and third countries shall be prohibited.

2. Within the framework of the provisions set out in this Chapter, all restrictions on payments between Member States and between Member States and third countries shall be prohibited.

Directive 88/361/EEC **10.53 (EU)**

Preamble Whereas, since the full liberalization of capital movements could in some Member States, and especially in border areas, contribute to difficulties in the market for secondary residences; whereas existing national legislation regulating these purchases should not be affected by the entry into effect of this Directive;

Annex 1—Nomenclature In this Nomenclature, capital movements are classified according to the economic nature of the assets and liabilities they concern, denominated either in national currency or in foreign exchange.

The capital movements listed in this Nomenclature are taken to cover:

—all the operations necessary for the purposes of capital movements: conclusion and performance of the transaction and related transfers. The transaction is generally between residents of different Member States although some capital movements are carried out by a single person for his own account (eg transfers of assets belonging to emigrants),

—operations carried out by any natural or legal person (1), including operations in respect of the assets …

I—DIRECT INVESTMENTS …

3. Long-term loans with a view to establishing or maintaining lasting economic links. …

II—INVESTMENTS IN REAL ESTATE (not included under I).

A—Investments in real estate on national territory by non-residents.

B—Investments in real estate abroad by residents …

VIII—FINANCIAL LOANS AND CREDITS (not included under I, VII and XI) (1)

1. Short-term (less than one year)

2. Medium-term (from one to five years)

3. Long-term (five years or more)

A—Loans and credits granted by non-residents to residents

B—Loans and credits granted by residents to non-residents

IX—SURETIES, OTHER GUARANTEES AND RIGHTS OF PLEDGE

A—Granted by non-residents to residents

B—Granted by residents to non-residents …

Notes

(1) The freedom of movement of capital is relatively new to EU law. In the original 1957 EEC Treaty, the free movement of capital was mentioned, but not guaranteed in the same was as the other freedoms. This can be understood it we consider the process of economic integration that the EU Member States underwent. A customs union means abolishing all tariffs and levies on trade between Member States, but in order to ensure free movement of capital, much more co-operation is needed. It is therefore only in the 1980s the work that was started to move towards a European capital market and only with the 1992 Treaty of Maastricht that the freedom of movement of capital became protected by the EU Treaties.

(2) A definition of a capital movement as such is not provided by the Treaty, but the ECJ has held in the *Westdeutsche Landesbank Girozentrale v Stefan* decision:

> 5. The notion of capital movements is not defined by the EC Treaty. However, inasmuch as Article 73b of the Treaty substantially reproduces the contents of Article 1 of Council Directive 88/361/EEC of 24 June 1988 for the implementation of Article 67 of the Treaty (OJ 1988 L178, p 5), the nomenclature in respect of movements of capital used in Annex I to that directive still has the same indicative value, for the purposes of defining the notion of capital movements, as it did before the entry into force of Article 73b et seq of the Treaty, subject to the qualification, contained in the introduction to the nomenclature, that the list set out therein is not exhaustive (Case C-222/97 *Trummer and Mayer* [1999] ECR I-1661, paragraph 21).[143]

(3) The acquisition of ownership of land in another Member State, but also the financing of that acquisition, therefore falls under the protection of Article 63 TFEU. There are many interesting cases to discuss, such as the case of *Trummer and Mayer* on a right of hypothec expressed in German Deutschmarks in Austria,[144] but the next paragraph will, by way of an example of EU capital cases, deal with the acquisition of land in another Member State.

III.E.2.b Case Study: Austrian Land Law Regulations

European Court of Justice, 3 May 2002[145] **10.54 (EU)**

Hans Reisch and others v Bürgermeister des Landeshauptstadt Salzburg and others

ACQUISITION OF LAND AS A CAPITAL MOVEMENT

Reisch

A system of authorisation for the acquisition of land is contrary to Article 63 TFEU.

Facts: Mr Reisch was an Austrian national from another district than Salzburg, who sought to acquire ownership of a piece of land in the Salzburg district. Local Austrian legislation in force held that

[143] Case C-464/98, *Westdeutsche Landesbank Girozentrale v Friedrich Stefan* [2001] ECR I-173, para 5.

[144] Case C-222/97, *Trummer and Mayer* [1999] ECR I-1661.

[145] Joined Cases C-515/99, C-519/99 to C-524/99 and C-526/99 to C-540/99, *Hans Reisch and others v Bürgermeister des Landeshauptstadt Salzburg and others* [2002] ECR I-2157.

persons wishing to acquire a right of ownership of land had to notify the acquisition to obtain authorisation for the acquisition from the court. Such legislation was in force to prevent 'tourist colonies' from forming, and authorisation generally required that the land would be used as the primary residence of the acquirer. Mr Reisch and others argued that this measure of Austrian law violated the provisions on the free movement of capital. The Austrian government did not agree and further argued that EU law could not be applied here as Mr Reisch was an Austrian national acquiring ownership of land in Austria and that this was therefore a purely domestic situation to which EU law did not apply.

Held: A requirement of notification to obtain authorisation for the acquisition of ownership is against EU law.

Judgment: 25. However, that finding does not mean that there is no need to reply to the questions referred to the Court for a preliminary ruling in this case. In principle, it is for the national courts alone to determine, having regard to the particular features of each case, both the need for a preliminary ruling in order to enable them to give their judgment and the relevance of the questions which they refer to the Court (see Case C-448/98 Guimont [2000] ECR I-10663, paragraph 22). A reference for a preliminary ruling from a national court may be rejected by the Court only if it is quite obvious that the interpretation of Community law sought by that court bears no relation to the actual nature of the case or the subject-matter of the main action (see Case C-281/98 Angonese [2000] ECR I-4139, paragraph 18).

26. In this case, it is not obvious that the interpretation of Community law requested is not necessary for the referring court. Such a reply might be useful to it if its national law were to require that an Austrian national must be allowed to enjoy the same rights as those which a national of another Member State would derive from Community law in the same situation (Guimont, cited above, paragraph 23).

27. Accordingly, it is necessary to consider whether the provisions of the Treaty, interpretation of which is sought, preclude the application of national legislation such as that in issue in the main proceedings to the extent that it is applied to persons resident in other Member States.

Substance

28 It should be stated, as a preliminary point, that national legislation which regulates the acquisition of land for the purposes of prohibiting, in the interests of regional planning, the establishment of secondary residences in certain areas must comply with the provisions of the Treaty on the free movement of capital (Konle, cited above, paragraph 22).

29. First, as is apparent from Article 44(2)(e) EC, the right to acquire, use or dispose of immovable property on the territory of another Member State, which is the corollary of freedom of establishment (Case 305/87 Commission v Greece [1989] ECR 1461, paragraph 22), generates capital movements when it is exercised.

30. Secondly, as is clear from the nomenclature of capital movements set out in Annex I to Council Directive 88/361/EEC of 24 June 1988 for the implementation of Article 67 of the Treaty (repealed by the Treaty of Amsterdam) (OJ 1988 L178, p. 5), capital movements include investments in real estate on the territory of a Member State by non-residents. That nomenclature still has the same indicative value for the purposes of defining the notion of capital movements (see Case C-222/97 Trummer and Mayer [1999] ECR I-1661, paragraph 21, and Case C-464/98 Stefan [2001] ECR I-173, paragraph 5).

31. It is therefore necessary, as the referring court requests the Court to do, to determine the scope of the national measures in issue in the main proceedings in the light of Articles 56 EC to 60 EC.

32. It is not in dispute that those measures, by laying down a procedure of prior notification/authorisation for the acquisition of immovable property, restrict, by their very purpose, the free movement of capital (see, to that effect, Konle, cited above, paragraph 39).

33. Such restrictions may nevertheless be permitted if the national rules pursue, in a non-discriminatory way, an objective in the public interest and if they observe the principle of proportionality, that is if the same result could not be achieved by other less restrictive measures.

34. As regards the first requirement, it is apparent from paragraph 40 of the Konle judgment, cited above, that restrictions on the establishment of secondary residences in a specific geographical area, which a Member State imposes in order to maintain, for regional planning purposes, a permanent population and an economic activity independent of the tourist sector, may be regarded as contributing to an objective in the public interest. That finding can only be strengthened by the other concerns which may underly those same measures, such as protection of the environment. Moreover, it is apparent from the provisions of the SGVG that they do not discriminate between Austrian acquirers of title and persons resident in other Member States who exercise the freedoms guaranteed by the Treaty.

35. As regards the second requirement, the Court held, in paragraphs 44 to 48 of the Konle judgment, cited above, that a requirement of declaration prior to the purchase of building plots, coupled with the possibility of penalties for breach of the agreed declaration, for regional planning purposes, did comply with Community law. The procedure laid down by the SGVG is essentially declaratory in principle.

36. As the Austrian Government points out, it is only where the *Grundverkehrsbeauftragter* considers that there are grounds for believing that the property is not being used lawfully that he must refer the acquirer of title to the *Grundverkehrslandeskommission* for the transaction to be submitted to the authorisation procedure. That minimum requirement of prior notification has the advantage, unlike supervision procedures which are applied only a posteriori, of providing the acquirer of title with an element of legal certainty. Furthermore, it may be thought that prior examination is better suited to preventing certain damage, which is reparable only with difficulty, caused by hastily completed building projects. Thus, the formality of prior notification may be regarded as a step which is additional to the criminal sanctions and the action for annulment of the sale which the administrative authorities may bring before the national court. In those circumstances, this first aspect of the procedure instituted by the SGVG may be regarded as compatible with Community law.

37. As regards the procedure of prior authorisation before the *Grundverkehrslandeskommission*, by contrast, the Court has already held that restrictions on the free movement of capital resulting from the requirement of prior authorisation were able to be eliminated by means of an appropriate notification system without thereby detracting from the effective pursuit of the aims of those rules (see Joined Cases C-358/93 and C-416/93 Bordessa and Others [1995] ECR I-361, paragraph 27, and Joined Cases C-163/94, C-165/94 and C-250/94 Sanz de Lera and Others [1995] ECR I-4821, paragraphs 26 and 27).

38. In the main proceedings, given the opportunity for supervision which the prior notification scheme affords to the public authority, the existence of criminal sanctions and a specific action for annulment which may be brought before the national court should the project carried out fail to comply with the initial declaration, the prior authorisation procedure, which the *Grundverkehrsbeauftragter* alone

may initiate on the basis of mere presumptions, cannot be regarded as a measure which is strictly indispensable to prevent infringements of the legislation in issue in the main proceedings in respect of secondary residences. This is all the more so given that the competent authorities may make the grant of prior authorisation subject to requirements on which the SGVG does not impose any substantive restriction, and require the acquirer of title to provide security up to the value of the property.

39.The provisions of the SGVG relating to the prior authorisation procedure before the Grundverkehrslandeskommission therefore go beyond both that which is necessary to achieve the chosen regional planning objective and the measures which Member States are entitled to take, as set out in Article 58(1)(b) EC, to prevent infringements of their laws and regulations.

40. Accordingly, the reply to the referring court should be that Articles 56 EC to 60 EC:

—do not preclude a prior notification procedure such as that laid down by the scheme for the acquisition of land established by the SGVG;

—preclude a prior authorisation procedure such as that laid down by that scheme.

Notes

(1) *Reisch* offers a very interesting illustration of the application of the free movement of capital to the law of property. As we saw above (III.B.3) in the case law of the ECJ relating to Article 345 TFEU, although Member States are still free to regulate their property law system, they must do so within the boundaries set by the law of the internal market. This case offers an excellent example of a limitation of such freedom.

(2) It also shows that the ECJ will not refrain from answering a preliminary question just because there is a purely domestic situation at hand. This was also due to the somewhat controversial opinion of Advocate General Geelhoed in this case. To close this section on the effect of the law of the internal market on national property law, we will look at a section of this opinion.

Opinion of AG Geelhoed to Joined Cases C-515/99, C-519/99 to C-524/99 and C-526/99 to C-540/99 10.55 (EU)

31. A private individual acquiring a secondary residence may do so, firstly, with the aim of occupying it himself for part of the year. Activities relating to the free movement of persons will then be in issue: (the right of) residence in another Member State. Although secondary residences are usually occupied for only a limited period of the year, such occupancy none the less has something permanent about it. Furthermore, the occupancy of a secondary residence is relevant to the freedom to provide services. … The use of a secondary residence is bound to be accompanied by services provided for its private owner, for example, services connected with the residence itself, such as repairs, and services relating to tourist activities. Secondly, the private individual may not himself use the secondary residence he has acquired, but let it to others. He can then be regarded as a provider of services within the meaning of Article 50 EC. In a third, very common variant the secondary residence is intended for the owner's use for part of the year and is otherwise let to others. Fourthly, the immovable property may be acquired primarily as an investment or for

speculative reasons. In such cases the emphasis is not on its use as a secondary residence but on the expected increase in the value of the land. The free movement of capital is then at issue.

32. Land may also be acquired for professional purposes. Its use by the acquirer himself does not then, in principle, play any role. He will normally use the land to let secondary residences, in holiday parks, for example. The lessor, who will frequently offer a number of other (tourist) services besides residences to rent, can then be regarded as a provider of services. The main aim in acquisition for professional purposes may again be investment or speculation. The land is then acquired less with a view to its use for a secondary residence.

33. Finally, I would point out that the Salzburger Grundverkehrsgesetz of 1997 concerns the acquisition both of land on which buildings have already been constructed and of land where this is not yet the case. If no buildings are standing on the land at the time of acquisition, an acquirer wanting to be able to use it for a secondary residence will, of course, have to build on it. An acquirer who has a residence built on his land can be regarded as the person for whom a service is provided.

34. So much for the outline of the most common economic activities affected by the Salzburger Grundverkehrsgesetz of 1997. At this juncture I shall revert to the essential purpose of the legislation, namely the regulation of the use of immovable property for secondary residences. The main point is the way in which the land is used, whether by the acquirer himself or by a third party. This Opinion also focuses on the economic activities directly associated with that use of the land. Investment, or speculation in land, may be the acquirer's purpose, but these are not activities that the Salzburger Grundverkehrsgesetz seeks to address.

35. Finally, regardless of how land is used, the legislation in all cases affects the free movement of payments and capital. It concerns payment and capital transactions connected with the financing of the acquisition. In this context it affects both the actual investment in immovable property and the financing of that investment. I would point out that these effects are not intended by the legislation, but they none the less occur …

100. It is my view, in the fourth place, that the internal nature of cases such as the present is not very significant. It is mere coincidence that all of the parties in the cases referred to the Court are resident in the Member State of Austria. What is at issue here, after all, is investment in land in tourist areas. In such areas individuals or organisations from other Member States will often be similarly interested in acquiring immovable property in general. These cases also concern secondary residences, which are not, as a general rule, located at the acquirer's normal place of residence. This is the precise reason for the Austrian legislation here under discussion, which seeks to prevent the construction and use of secondary residences.

IV. HARMONISATION AT THE LEVEL OF THE COUNCIL OF EUROPE: ARTICLE 1 FIRST PROTOCOL OF THE EUROPEAN CONVENTION ON HUMAN RIGHTS

Introductory Notes

(a) Human rights (or fundamental rights) are laid down in national constitutions, but also in the ECHR, and, since 2010, in the Charter of Fundamental Rights of the European Union, which reaffirms the human rights in the ECHR.[146] The last decades there has been an increasing and highly debated influence of human rights law in private law. This is known as the constitutionalisation of private law.[147]

(b) Property law has been relatively less influenced. Yet there are undoubtedly some important developments to be taken into account. Developments in South Africa show that the social context in which traditional property law operates may just not suffice in itself to solve conflicts in an acceptable way: eviction of illegal squatters is no more possible on the basis of private law ownership alone, It should be judged in the perspective of the constitutional right to housing first, and only in that context does private ownership play a subordinate role. In this specific context of housing and eviction also in European situations, Article 8 ECHR plays an important role. Consequently the owner's power to evict is never unconditional, and should take the fundamental interests of the holder of the house into account.[148] This often involves also the application of the fundamental right to a fair procedure as laid down in Article 6 ECHR.[149]

(c) The most discussion has been caused by Article 1 of the First Protocol to the European Convention on the Protection of Human Rights.[150] This Article (P1-1) entails an international constitutional protection of property or possessions to the 47 Member States of the Council of Europe.[151] It needs to be stressed that the term property or possession has its own autonomous constitutional meaning.[152] The article makes the *taking* or *control of use of property* by the national state subject to certain criteria. The court tests whether there is a possession, and subsequently whether there is an infringement on this possession; the infringement then should be justified.

(d) Such a justification entails three aspects. The infringement should be lawful, it should pursue a legitimate aim in the public interest and it should be propor-

[146] [2010] OJ C83/02.

[147] See particularly G Brüggemeier, AC Ciacchi and G Comande, *Fundamental Rights and Private Law in the European Union*, vols I and II (Cambridge, Cambridge University Press, 2010).

[148] ECHR 27 May 2004, *Connors v UK*; ECHR 13 May 2008, *McCann v UK*.

[149] On this topic see particularly the seminal comparative analysis by AJ van der Walt, *Property in the Margins* (Oxford and Portland, Oregon, Hart Publishing, 2009).

[150] www.echr.coe.int/ECHR.

[151] www.coe.int/T/E/Com/About_Coe/Member_states/default.asp.

[152] ECHR 23 february 1995, *Gasus Dosier- und Fördertechnik GmbH v the Netherlands*, para 53: the concept of possession has 'an autonomous meaning which is certainly not limited to ownership of physical goods: certain other rights and interests constituting assets can also be regarded as "property rights" and thus "possessions" for the purpose of this provision'.

tional, striking a fair balance between the general public interest and the private interest in the protection of the individual's possession. If these criteria are not met, the national state will be held liable for infringements on this right to the peaceful enjoyment of possessions.

(e) However, the European Court of Human Rights always leaves the national state a wide margin of appreciation.[153] The margin of appreciation has particularly been stressed in case of horizontal application of human rights in private conflicts, The precise meaning of Article 1 First Protocol has been articulated in many cases. In most cases, the European Court of Human Rights gives a summary of the application of the Article. Particularly through recent case law the Article has exercised influence on national property law, but in the decision of 30 August 2007 (*Pye v UK*) the extent of this influence has been restricted.

IV.A ARTICLE 1 FIRST PROTOCOL ECHR

European Convention on Human Rights **10.56 (ECHR)**

Article 1 First Protocol Every natural or legal person is entitled to the peaceful enjoyment of his possessions.

No one shall be deprived of his possessions except in the public interest and subject to the conditions provided for by law and by the general principles of international law.

The preceding provisions shall not, however, in any way impair the right of a State to enforce such laws as it deems necessary to control the use of property in accordance with the general interest or to secure the payment of taxes or other contributions or penalties.

IV.B THE APPROACH OF THE EUROPEAN COURT OF HUMAN RIGHTS

European Court of Human Rights,
23 September 1982[154] **10.57 (ECHR)**

Sporrong and Lönnroth v Sweden

STRUCTURE OF ARTICLE 1 FIRST PROTOCOL—CLASSIFICATION

Sporrong and Lönnroth

Facts: In 1954, the Stockholm authorities burdened the land owned by the Sporrong Estate with a prohibition to build. In 1956, the same parcel of land was the object of a zonal expropriation permit covering 164 properties in order to build, over one of the main shopping streets in the centre of the capital, a viaduct leading to a major relief road. This prohibition to build and expropriation permit were

[153] The margin left to the national states is much less in case the infringed human right happens to be Art 6 or 8. See for Art 8 eg ECHR, 27 May 2004, *Connors v UK*, nos 82 and 83.

[154] No 7151/75.

extended at several instances, and only in 1979 did the government decide not to build the viaduct and, by consequence, cancelled the expropriation permit at the Council's request.

The same happened to Lonnroth; however, his land had only been the object of an expropriation permit since 1971 and a building prohibition since 1968. Both parties argued they had been deprived of the use of their property right to such an extent that they could no longer convey or burden the right themselves.

Held: There is no fair balance between the interference with the property rights and the requirements of general interest.

Judgment: 60. Although the expropriation permits left intact in law the owners' right to use and dispose of their possessions, they nevertheless in practice significantly reduced the possibility of its exercise. They also affected the very substance of ownership in that they recognised before the event that any expropriation would be lawful and authorised the City of Stockholm to expropriate whenever it found it expedient to do so. The applicants' right of property thus became precarious and defeasible.

The prohibitions on construction, for their part, undoubtedly restricted the applicants' right to use their possessions.

The Court also considers that the permits and prohibitions should in principle be examined together, except to the extent that analysis of the case may require a distinction to be drawn between them. This is because, even though there was not necessarily a legal connection between the measures (see paragraph 35 above) and even though they had different periods of validity, they were complementary and had the single objective of facilitating the development of the city in accordance with the successive plans prepared for this purpose.

There was therefore an interference with the applicants' right of property and, as the Commission rightly pointed out, the consequences of that interference were undoubtedly rendered more serious by the combined use, over a long period of time, of expropriation permits and prohibitions on construction.

2. The justification for the interference with the applicants' right of property

61. It remains to be ascertained whether or not the interference found by the Court violated Article 1 (P1-1).

That Article (P1-1) comprises three distinct rules. The first rule, which is of a general nature, enounces the principle of peaceful enjoyment of property; it is set out in the first sentence of the first paragraph. The second rule covers deprivation of possessions and subjects it to certain conditions; it appears in the second sentence of the same paragraph. The third rule recognises that the States are entitled, amongst other things, to control the use of property in accordance with the general interest, by enforcing such laws as they deem necessary for the purpose; it is contained in the second paragraph.

The Court must determine, before considering whether the first rule was complied with, whether the last two are applicable.

(a) The applicability of the second sentence of the first paragraph

62. It should be recalled first of all that the Swedish authorities did not proceed to an expropriation of the applicants' properties. The applicants were therefore not formally 'deprived of their possessions' at any time: they were entitled to use, sell, devise, donate or mortgage their properties.

63. In the absence of a formal expropriation, that is to say a transfer of ownership, the Court considers that it must look behind the appearances and investigate the realities of the situation complained of (see, mutatis mutandis, the Van Droog-

enbroeck judgment of 24 June 1982, Series A no 50, p 20, par 38). Since the Convention is intended to guarantee rights that are 'practical and effective' (see the Airey judgment of 9 October 1979, Series A no 32, p 12, par 24), it has to be ascertained whether that situation amounted to a de facto expropriation, as was argued by the applicants.

In the Court's opinion, all the effects complained of (see paragraph 58 above) stemmed from the reduction of the possibility of disposing of the properties concerned. Those effects were occasioned by limitations imposed on the right of property, which right had become precarious, and from the consequences of those limitations on the value of the premises. However, although the right in question lost some of its substance, it did not disappear. The effects of the measures involved are not such that they can be assimilated to a deprivation of possessions. The Court observes in this connection that the applicants could continue to utilise their possessions and that, although it became more difficult to sell properties in Stockholm affected by expropriation permits and prohibitions on construction, the possibility of selling subsisted; according to information supplied by the Government, several dozen sales were carried out (see paragraph 30 above).

There was therefore no room for the application of the second sentence of the first paragraph in the present case.

(b) The applicability of the second paragraph

64. The prohibitions on construction clearly amounted to a control of 'the use of [the applicants'] property', within the meaning of the second paragraph.

65. On the other hand, the expropriation permits were not intended to limit or control such use. Since they were an initial step in a procedure leading to deprivation of possessions, they did not fall within the ambit of the second paragraph. They must be examined under the first sentence of the first paragraph.

(c) Compliance with the first sentence of the first paragraph as regards the expropriation permits

66. The applicants' complaints concerned in the first place the length of the time-limits granted to the City of Stockholm, which they regarded as contrary to both Swedish law and the Convention.

67. The 1917 Act did not contain any provisions either on the length of the time-limit during which the expropriating authority had to institute judicial proceedings for the fixing of compensation for expropriation, or on the extension of the validity of permits.

According to the Sporrong Estate and Mrs. Lönnroth, it had been the established practice since the entry into force of the Act for the normal time-limit for service of a summons to appear before the Real Estate Court to be one year. Since the time-limits in the present case were as long as five and ten years respectively, it was alleged that there was no legal basis for the original permits; the same was said to apply to the three extensions of the permit affecting the property of the Sporrong Estate.

The respondent State replied that the issue and the extension of the permits were in conformity with Swedish law: it argued that since the Government were entitled to fix the period of validity of the original permit, they were also empowered, in the absence of any provision to the contrary, to extend it.

68. The Court does not consider that it has to resolve this difference of opinion over the interpretation of Swedish law. Even if the permits complained of were not

contrary to that law, their conformity therewith would not establish that they were compatible with the right guaranteed by Article 1 (P1-1).

69. The fact that the permits fell within the ambit neither of the second sentence of the first paragraph nor of the second paragraph does not mean that the interference with the said right violated the rule contained in the first sentence of the first paragraph.

For the purposes of the latter provision, the Court must determine whether a fair balance was struck between the demands of the general interest of the community and the requirements of the protection of the individual's fundamental rights (see, mutatis mutandis, the jugdment of 23 July 1968 in the 'Belgian Linguistic' case, Series A no 6, p 32, par 5). The search for this balance is inherent in the whole of the Convention and is also reflected in the structure of Article 1 (P1-1).

The Agent of the Government recognised the need for such a balance. At the hearing on the morning of 23 February 1982, he pointed out that, under the Expropriation Act, an expropriation permit must not be issued if the public purpose in question can be achieved in a different way; when this is being assessed, full weight must be given both to the interests of the individual and to the public interest.

The Court has not overlooked this concern on the part of the legislature. Moreover, it finds it natural that, in an area as complex and difficult as that of the development of large cities, the Contracting States should enjoy a wide margin of appreciation in order to implement their town-planning policy. Nevertheless, the Court cannot fail to exercise its power of review and must determine whether the requisite balance was maintained in a manner consonant with the applicants' right to 'the peaceful enjoyment of [their] possessions', within the meaning of the first sentence of Article 1 (P1-1).

70. A feature of the law in force at the relevant time was its inflexibility. With the exception of the total withdrawal of the expropriation permits, which required the agreement of the municipality, the law provided no means by which the situation of the property owners involved could be modified at a later date. The Court notes in this connection that the permits granted to the City of Stockholm were granted for five years in the case of the Sporrong Estate—with an extension for three, then for five and finally for ten years—and for ten years in the case of Mrs. Lönnroth. In the events that happened, they remained in force for twenty-three years and eight years respectively. During the whole of this period, the applicants were left in complete uncertainty as to the fate of their properties and were not entitled to have any difficulties which they might have encountered taken into account by the Swedish Government. The Commission's report furnishes an example of such difficulties. Mrs. Lönnroth had requested the Government to withdraw the expropriation permit. The City Council replied that the existing plans did not authorise any derogation; the Government, for their part, refused the request on the ground that they could not revoke the permit without the Council's express consent (see paragraph 21 above).

The Courts has not overlooked the interest of the City of Stockholm in having the option of expropriating properties in order to implement its plans. However, it does not see why the Swedish legislation should have excluded the possibility of re-assessing, at reasonable intervals during the lengthy periods for which each of the permits was granted and maintained in force, the interests of the City and the interests of the owners. In the instant case, the absence of such a possibility was all the less satisfactory in that the town-planning schemes underlying the expropriation permits and, at the same time, the intended use prescribed for the applicants' properties were modified on several occasions. ...

73. Being combined in this way, the two series of measures created a situation which upset the fair balance which should be struck between the protection of the right of property and the requirements of the general interest: the Sporrong Estate and Mrs Lönnroth bore an individual and excessive burden which could have been tendered legitimate only if they had had the possibility of seeking a reduction of the time-limits or of claiming compensation. Yet at the relevant time Swedish law excluded these possibilities and it still excludes the second of them.

In the Court's view, it is not appropriate at this stage to determine whether the applicants were in fact prejudiced (see, mutatis mutandis, the above-mentioned Marckx judgment, Series A no 31, p 13, par 27): it was in their legal situation itself that the requisite balance was no longer to be found.

74. The permits in question, whose consequences were aggravated by the prohibitions on construction, therefore violated Article 1 (P1-1), as regards both applicants.

Notes

(1) In this judgment, the European Court of Human Rights has set the structure of P1-1. It can be summarised in three rules:

- The first rule, which is of a general nature, annunciates the principle of peaceful enjoyment of possessions. This rule is set out in the first sentence of the first paragraph. It comprises, for example, expropriation permits.
- The second rule covers deprivation of possessions and subjects it to certain conditions. This rule appears in the second sentence of the same paragraph. The Court has already announced it will also take into account the so-called *de facto* expropriation, eg look behind the appearances and investigate the realities of the situation complained of, even if there has been no formal transfer of land to the authorities.[155]
- The third rule recognises that states are entitled, amongst other things, to control the use of property in accordance with the general interest, by enforcing such laws as they deem necessary for the purpose. This rule is contained in the second paragraph. It comprises inter alia building prohibitions.

(2) The second and third rule are an application of the first rule which underlies the respect for ownership. Therefore, the Court has first to investigate whether the second and third rule apply. If not, the Court will have recourse to the first rule, which has a subsidiary nature.

(3) The *Sporrong and Lonnröth* decision make clear that domestic rules on property law are also subject to a possible (international) constitutional appeal in Strasbourg, testing whether these national property laws are disproportional with respect to the individual interests involved.[156] The very possibility that national judicial decisions on private law may be appealed to the ECHR implies that also

[155] See, for a judgment with regard to a violation, on this basis: ECHR, 24 June 1993, *Papamichalopoulos and others v Greece*, no 14556/89.

[156] ECHR, 23 September 1982. See para 63.

in private (property) law the European convention and the decisions of the ECHR need to be taken into account, by the legislator, but also by the judiciary.

(4) The interference should not be disproportionately interfering in the individual's property interests, or, as it was framed in the *Sporrong* case, it should not upset the fair balance which should be struck between the protection of the right of property and the requirements of the general interest. The presence of compensation is material to the assessment whether the infringement is disproportionate, but there is no right to full compensation.[157] In case of a deprivation, the absence of compensation will normally lead to a violation of P1-1.

European Court of Human Rights,
23 February 1995[158] **10.57 (ECHR)**

Gasus Dosier- und Fordertechnik GmbH v The Netherlands

APPLICATION OF TAX COLLECTORS RIGHTS OF SEIZURE CONTRARY TO ARTICLE P1-1?

Gasus

There is no disproportional interference when the seller under title retention is subjected to a national tax collectors lien.

Facts: Atlas (The Netherlands) bought a concrete mixer from Gasus (Germany). Gasus delivered under a retention of title clause. The machine was installed on Atlas's premises. Gasus had only been partially paid when Atlas was declared insolvent. The machine was seized by the tax collector on the basis of a special right of seizure (*bodembeslag*) on property of third parties present on the premises of the tax debtor. Gasus tried to realise its retention of title. In the national procedure against the tax collector Gasus's claim was denied

Held: No violation of P 1-1.

Judgment: 53. The Court recalls that the notion 'possessions' (in French: *biens*) in Article 1 of Protocol No 1 (P1-1) has an autonomous meaning which is certainly not limited to ownership of physical goods: certain other rights and interests constituting assets can also be regarded as 'property rights', and thus as 'possessions', for the purposes of this provision (P1-1). In the present context it is therefore immaterial whether Gasus's right to the concrete-mixer is to be considered as a right of ownership or as a security right in rem. In any event, the seizure and sale of the concrete-mixer constituted an 'interference' with the applicant company's right 'to the peaceful enjoyment' of a 'possession' within the meaning of Article 1 of Protocol No 1 (P1-1). …

59. … The most natural approach, in the Court's opinion, is to examine Gasus's complaints under the head of 'securing the payment of taxes', which comes under the rule in the second paragraph of Article 1 (P1-1).

60. As follows from the previous paragraph, the present case concerns the right of States to enact such laws as they deem necessary for the purpose of 'securing the payment of taxes'. … In passing such laws the legislature must be allowed a

[157] ECHR, 21 February 1986, *James and others v United Kingdom*, no 8793/79, at 56.
[158] No 15375/89.

wide margin of appreciation, especially with regard to the question whether—and if so, to what extent—the tax authorities should be put in a better position to enforce tax debts than ordinary creditors are in to enforce commercial debts. The Court will respect the legislature's assessment in such matters unless it is devoid of reasonable foundation.

61. Section 16 (3) of the 1845 Act gave the tax authorities the power to recover tax debts against certain goods which, although in fact in the possession of their debtor—since they were on his premises and served as 'furnishings'—were owned, as a matter of law, by a third party. It thus dispensed the tax authorities from having to consider whether these goods were actually the property of the tax debtor. The purpose of the provision was obviously to facilitate the enforcement of tax debts, which in itself is clearly in the general interest.

62. According to the Court's well-established case-law, the second paragraph of Article 1 of Protocol No 1 (P1-1) must be construed in the light of the principle laid down in the Article's (P1-1) first sentence (see, among many other authorities, the above-mentioned AGOSI judgment, ibid). Consequently, an interference must achieve a 'fair balance' between the demands of the general interest of the community and the requirements of the protection of the individual's fundamental rights. The concern to achieve this balance is reflected in the structure of Article 1 (P1-1) as a whole, including the second paragraph: there must therefore be a reasonable relationship of proportionality between the means employed and the aim pursued. ...

66. The Court notes at the outset that the grant to the tax authorities of a power to recover tax debts against goods owned by certain third parties—such as a seller of goods who retains his title—does not in itself prompt the conclusion that a fair balance between the general interest and the protection of the individual's fundamental rights has not been achieved. The power of recovery against goods which are in fact in a debtor's possession although nominally owned by a third party is a not uncommon device to strengthen a creditor's position in enforcement proceedings; it cannot be held incompatible per se with the requirements of Article 1 of Protocol No 1 (P1-1). Consequently, a legislature may in principle resort to that device to ensure, in the general interest, that taxation yields as much as possible and that tax debts are recovered as expeditiously as possible. Nonetheless, it cannot be overlooked that, quite apart from the dangers of abuse, the character of legislation by which the State creates such powers for itself is not the same as that of legislation granting similar powers to narrowly defined categories of private creditors. Consequently, further examination of the issue of proportionality is necessary in this case.

67. In this connection, the Court also notes that in assessing the proportionality of the powers under section 16 (3) and their use in the present case it is immaterial that Gasus were a limited company with legal personality under German law and had their registered office in Germany. Gasus had sold and delivered their concrete-mixer to a purchaser based in the Netherlands and installed it on his premises. Gasus could therefore not have expected otherwise than that the effectiveness of their retention of title in the face of seizure depended on Netherlands law. ...

70. It is nonetheless true, as observed by the Commission, that the applicant company were engaged in a commercial venture which, by its very nature, involved an element of risk. ... Having allowed Atlas to pay the purchase price of the concrete-mixer in instalments, and being aware of the danger that Atlas might default on its payments, Gasus reserved their title to the concrete-mixer until the full price had been paid. This, under Netherlands law, provided them with a considerable degree

of security, as their claims to the concrete-mixer thus took priority over those of all other creditors except the tax authorities, who were entitled under section 16(3) of the 1845 Act to seize it and take the proceeds for the State.

Like the Commission, the Court considers that Gasus could have eliminated their risk altogether by declining to extend credit to Atlas: they could have stipulated payment of the entire purchase price in advance or else refused to sell the concrete-mixer in the first place. It also accepts that the applicant company might have obtained additional security, for example in the form of insurance or a banker's guarantee, which pass the risk on to another party.

Notes

(1) The terms possessions and property are equivalent, and are in the case law of the European Court in Strasbourg given a wide and autonomous meaning, as was made explicit in the *Gasus* (§53) decision. The autonomy implies that the Court does not follow any national private law definitions, but applies its own meaning to the definitions. The terms 'property' or 'possessions' do therefore not as such denote any specific significance for national property law. But is does encompass (and protects) also property rights, as in the present case, ownership.

(2) The interference should be lawful, pursuing a legitimate aim in the public interest, through proportionate means. In determining the legitimacy of the interference, the European Court leaves the national state a wide margin of appreciation. It will respect the legislature's judgment as to what is 'in the public interest' or necessary for securing the payment of taxes, unless that judgment be manifestly without reasonable foundation,[159] or, in the wording of this case, devoid of reasonable foundation (see §60 of the judgment).

(3) Since in this case there is no deprivation, but a control of use, the absence of compensation does not lead to disproportionality. There is no disproportionality in this case, the Court concludes, as Gasus could not have expected otherwise than the applicability of Dutch law (see §70 of the judgment), and as Gasus could have decided on another less risky transaction.

(4) Where the *Gasus* decision analysed the special right of seizure of the tax authority in the framework of the human right to property, the *Krantz* case of the ECJ (10.49 (EU)) tested this right of seizure against the framework of European law. Both courts held the right to be in line with the respective standards. It illustrates the possible restrained position of international courts in interfering too much with the national legal order and the discretionary legislative powers of the national authorities. Taxation is of course a sensitive area; but we will note that the European Court of Human Rights in particular will only reluctantly interfere with horizontal private law matters. It rather leaves this to the national judges.

(5) The standard P1-1 cases deal with the taking of property, or the regulation of the use of property by the national state. The national state is one of the parties in the conflict on the national level. However, in some cases private (horizontal)

[159] ECHR, 21 February 1986, *James and others v United Kingdom*, at 46.

property law conflicts have been subjected to the Court,[160] and on this basis it may particularly be argued that ECHR decisions may have an (perhaps even substantial) impact on private property law. The most recent and important one is ECHR 30 August 2007, *Pye v UK*.

IV.C CASE STUDY: *PYE V UK*

ECtHR, 30 August 2007[161] **10.58 (ECHR)**

Pye v UK

DEPRIVATION OF PROPERTY BY ADVERSE POSSESSION

Pye

Adverse possession is not in itself an infringement of Article P 1-1.

Facts: Pye was the holder of a fee simple of a plot of land measuring 25 hectares. The owners of property adjacent to the land, Mr and Mrs Graham ("the Grahams"), had occupied Pye's land under a grazing agreement until 31 December 1983. On 30 December 1983 a chartered surveyor acting for the applicants wrote to the Grahams noting that the grazing agreement was about to expire and thereby requiring them to vacate the land. In January 1984 Pye refused a request for a further grazing agreement for 1984. The Grahams remained in occupation at all times, continuing to use it for grazing. No request to vacate the land or to pay for the grazing was made. If it had been, all evidence pointed to the fact that the Grahams would happily have paid. In June 1984 Pye sold the standing crop of grass to the Grahams. In December 1984 the Grahams further inquired whether Pye would allow them to purchase more hay or have a further grazing agreement. No reply was received and the Grahams made no further attempt to contact Pye. From September 1984 onwards until 1999 the Grahams continued to use the whole of the disputed land for farming without permission.

The Grahams registered cautions at the Land Registry against the applicant companies' title on the ground that they had obtained title by adverse possession, under the Limitation Act 1980, which provides that a person (Pye) cannot bring an action to recover any land after the expiration of 12 years of adverse possession by another. Graham also relied on the Land Registration Act 1925, which provided that, after the expiry of the 12-year period, the registered proprietor (Pye) was deemed to hold the land in trust for the squatter (section 75 LRA 1925). There was no compensation available for Pye.

The High Court held in favour of the Grahams on 4 February 2000 ([2000] Ch 676). The Court of Appeal reversed the decision on the ground that the Grahams did not have the necessary intention to possess the land, and the applicant companies were therefore not 'dispossessed' thereof within the meaning of the 1980 Act. The Grahams appealed to the House of Lords, which allowed their appeal and restored the order of the High Court. Both in the High Court as well as in the House of Lords, the result reached was accompanied by criticism. Lord Bingham:

> While I am satisfied that the appeal must be allowed for the reasons given by my noble and learned friend, this is a conclusion which I (like the judge [Neuberger J] …) 'arrive at with no enthusiasm'.[162]

[160] ECHR, 15 November 2005, *Pye v UK*, no 44302/02 and ECHR, 21 February 1986, *James and others v United Kingdom* dealt with freehold; ECHR 23 February 1995, *Gasus Dosier- und Fördertechnik GmbH v the Netherlands*, no 15375/89 dealt with the (German retention of) ownership right; ECHR, 21 September 2004, *Schirmer v Poland*, no 68880/01 dealt with the Polish right of ownership; furthermore contractual claims, delictual (tort) claims, intellectual property rights, but also goodwill (ECHR, 26 June 1986, *Van Marle v The Netherlands*, n° 8543/79) have been tested by the ECHR in the context of purely private law disputes.

[161] No44302/02.

[162] *JA Pye (Oxford) Ltd and another v Graham and another* [2000] 3 All ER 865, at 867.

The European Court of Human Rights held on 15 November 2005, by four votes to three, that there had been a violation of Article 1 Protocol no 1. The application of the provisions of the 1925 and 1980 Acts to deprive Pye of his title to the registered land without compensation amounts to a deprivation of a possession and imposes an individual and excessive burden; it upsets the fair balance between the demands of the public interest, on the one hand, and Pye's right to the peaceful enjoyment of his possessions on the other. The case was referred to the Grand Chamber.

Held: Adverse possession is not in itself an infringement of P1-1.

Judgment: 57. The responsibility of the Government in the present case is therefore not direct responsibility for an executive or legislative act aimed at the applicant companies, but is rather their responsibility for legislation which is activated as a result of the inter-actions of private individuals: in the same way as the law in *James and others* was applied (and the Government were responsible for it) because private individuals had requested enfranchisement, in the present case the law was applied to the applicant companies only when the pre-existing conditions for the acquisition of title by adverse possession had been met.

60. … The Court agrees with the Chamber that there is nothing in principle to preclude the examination of a claim under Article 1 of Protocol No. 1 where the complaint is directed against legislation concerning property rights. …

63. It remains the case, however, that the applicant companies lost the beneficial ownership of 23 hectares of agricultural land as a result of the operation of the 1925 and 1980 Acts. The Court finds inescapable the Chamber's conclusion that Article 1 of Protocol No 1 is applicable. …

66. The statutory provisions which resulted in the applicant companies' loss of beneficial ownership were thus not intended to deprive paper owners of their ownership, but rather to regulate questions of title in a system in which, historically, 12 years' adverse possession was sufficient to extinguish the former owner's right to re-enter or to recover possession, and the new title depended on the principle that unchallenged lengthy possession gave a title. The provisions of the 1925 and 1980 Acts which were applied to the applicant companies were part of the general land law, and were concerned to regulate, amongst other things, limitation periods in the context of the use and ownership of land as between individuals. The applicant companies were therefore affected, not by a 'deprivation of possessions' within the meaning of the second sentence of the first paragraph of Article 1, but rather by a "control of use" of land within the meaning of the second paragraph of the provision. …

70. The Court finds that the existence of a 12-year limitation period for actions for recovery of land as such pursues a legitimate aim in the general interest.

71. As to the existence, over and above the general interest in the limitation period, of a specific general interest in the extinguishment of title and the attribution of new title at the end of the limitation period, the Court recalls that in discussing the public interest present in the case of *Jahn*, in the context of a deprivation of property, it stated that, 'finding it natural that the margin of appreciation available to the legislature in implementing social and economic policies should be a wide one [the Court] will respect the legislature's judgment as to what is "in the public interest" unless that judgment is manifestly without reasonable foundation'. … This is particularly true in cases such as the present one where what is at stake is a longstanding and complex area of law which regulates private law matters between individuals.

72. It is plain from the comparative material submitted by the parties that a

large number of member States possesses some form of mechanism for transferring title in accordance with principles similar to adverse possession in the common law systems, and that such transfer is effected without the payment of compensation to the original owner. …

74. It is a characteristic of property that different countries regulate its use and transfer in a variety of ways. The relevant rules reflect social policies against the background of the local conception of the importance and role of property. Even where title to real property is registered, it must be open to the legislature to attach more weight to lengthy, unchallenged possession than to the formal fact of registration. The Court accepts that to extinguish title where the former owner is prevented, as a consequence of the application of the law, from recovering possession of land cannot be said to be manifestly without reasonable foundation. There existed therefore a general interest in both the limitation period itself and the extinguishment of title at the end of the period.

75. … In other contexts, the Court has underlined that it is not in theory required to settle disputes of a private nature. It can nevertheless not remain passive, in exercising the European supervision incumbent on it, where a domestic court's interpretation of a legal act appeared 'unreasonable, arbitrary or … inconsistent … with the principles underlying the Convention' (*Pla and Puncernau v Andorra*, no 69498/01, §59, ECHR 2004-VIII). …

81. It is true that since the entry into force of the Land Registration Act 2002, the paper owner of registered land against whom time has been running is in a better position than were the applicant companies at the relevant time. The 2002 Act requires, in effect, the giving of notice to a paper owner before the expiry of the limitation period, to give him time, if he wishes, to take action to deal with the adverse possessor. It improves the position of the paper owner and, correspondingly, makes it more difficult for an adverse possessor to acquire a full 12 years' adverse possession. The provisions of the 2002 Act do not, however, apply to the present case, and the Court must consider the facts of the case as they are. In any event, legislative changes in complex areas such as land law take time to bring about, and judicial criticism of legislation cannot of itself affect the conformity of the earlier provisions with the Convention.

82. The Government contended that it could not be the role of Article 1 of Protocol No. 1 to protect commercial operators against their own failings. The Court regards this suggestion as related to those aspects of the Court's case-law which underline that the Court is not in theory required to settle disputes of a private nature, in respect of which States enjoy a wide margin of appreciation (see paragraph 75 above). In a case such as the present, where the Court is considering, principally, the statutory regime by which title is extinguished at the end of the limitation period, rather than the specific facts of the case, the relevance of the individual applicant's conduct is correspondingly restricted.

83. The applicant companies contended that their loss was so great, and the windfall to the Grahams so significant, that the fair balance required by Article 1 of Protocol No. 1 was upset. The Court would first note that, in the case of *James*, the Court found that the view taken by Parliament as to the tenant's 'moral entitlement' to ownership of the houses at issue fell within the State's margin of appreciation. In the present case, too, whilst it would be strained to talk of the 'acquired rights' of an adverse possessor during the currency of the limitation period, it must be recalled that the registered land regime in the United Kingdom is a reflection of a

long-established system in which a term of years' possession gave sufficient title to sell. Such arrangements fall within the State's margin of appreciation, unless they give rise to results which are so anomalous as to render the legislation unacceptable. The acquisition of unassailable rights by the adverse possessor must go hand in hand with a corresponding loss of property rights for the former owner. In *James and Others*, the possibility of "undeserving" tenants being able to make 'windfall profits' did not affect the overall assessment of the proportionality of the legislation (*James and Others* judgment, referred to above, §69), and any windfall for the Grahams must be regarded in the same light in the present case.

84. As to the loss for the applicant companies, it is not disputed that the land lost by them, especially those parts with development potential, will have been worth a substantial sum of money. However, limitation periods, if they are to fulfil their purpose (see paragraphs 67–74 above), must apply regardless of the size of the claim. The value of the land cannot therefore be of any consequence to the outcome of the present case.

85. In sum, the Court concludes that the fair balance required by Article 1 of Protocol No. 1 to the Convention was not upset in the present case.

FOR THESE REASONS, THE COURT

Holds by ten votes to seven that there has been no violation of Article 1 of Protocol No. 1 to the Convention.

Notes

(1) This decision overruled the Chamber decision of 15 November 2005. The Court makes clear that the it is retreating to a considerable extent from dealing with private property law arrangements. This may be caused by the difficulties the European Court of Human Rights has in dealing with private law conflicts. The Court decides in *individual* cases by scrutinising national legislation or even the application of national legislation by national judges.[163] It is not very clear what the binding force exactly is with regard to comparable cases in other jurisdictions and whether national authorities must adapt their national legislation or whether courts must create a new doctrine.

(2) In recent years the Court has been recognising more positive obligations. These positive duties for the states enhance the binding force of ECHR decisions.[164]

(3) The Grand Chamber classifies the cases in which a private law regulation is subject to their review as a fundamentally different one: the government is only indirectly and not directly responsible (paragraph 57). This is an important starting point, as it provides room for the Court to further underline the national margin of appreciation in its reasoning.

(4) There are some cases which offer precedence for this decision, but of more

[163] ECHR 13 July 2004, *Pla and Puncernau v Andorra*, no 69498/01, at 59, 62.

[164] See, eg, ECHR 30 November 2004, *Öneryildiz v Turkey*. On positive obligations, see OO Cherednychenko, 'Towards the Control of Private Acts by the European Court of Human Rights' [2006] *Maastricht Journal of European and Comparative Law* 2, at 4–5, and the further references. These positive obligations, but also general conclusions are difficult to distil from ECHR cases. If the ECHR decisions were to have an important position in the development of national private law, the ECHR certainly would need to pay far more attention to the arrangements of national law in a comparative perspective.

importance is the reasoning that, in paragraph 65, the loss of land was not through a statutory provision permitting the state to transfer or through a social policy, but rather through the *operation of the generally applicable rules on limitation periods for actions for recovery of land*, which are not intended to deprive, but to regulate questions of title. Private law arrangements are thus easily led towards proportionality.

(5) The Grand Chamber concludes the adverse possession arrangements to be proportionate (paragraphs 78–80). Of more importance is the Grand Chamber's fundamental approach to judging the proportionality—see paragraph 82. The Grand Chamber stresses its ambivalent position, that it 'is not in theory required to settle disputes of a private nature' but that at the same time it 'can nevertheless not remain passive, in exercising the European supervision incumbent on it, where a domestic court's interpretation of a legal act appeared unreasonable, arbitrary or … inconsistent … with the principles underlying the Convention'. The subsequent reasoning in the proportionality test shows that the European Court of Human Rights will not readily reach the conclusion of disproportionality.

IV.D EFFECTS OF ARTICLE 1 FIRST PROTOCOL ECHR ON NATIONAL PROPERTY LAW

It remains to be seen what the wider implications of Article 1 of the first protocol to the European Convention of Human Rights on the basis of these cases will be, and how it will develop. It seems that the in horizontal matters of property law the Court will not readily interfere in national arrangements.

The adoption of positive obligations under the more recent case law of the Court offers a more stringent requirement on the Contracting States to uphold the protection Article P1-1 ECHR offers. However, it is not very likely that parties will be able to obtain an injunction to force the state to prevent interference with their property rights.

V. HARMONISATION ON AN INTERNATIONAL LEVEL: UNIDROIT, UNCITRAL AND EBRD

V.A UNIDROIT: CAPE TOWN CONVENTION 2001 ON INTERESTS IN MOBILE EQUIPMENT

Introductory Notes

(1) An important role in the efforts towards an increasing harmonisation of private law can be attributed to the International Institute for the Unification of Private

Law (UNIDROIT).[165] This is an independent intergovernmental organisation with its headquarters in Rome. Its purpose is to study needs and methods for modernising, harmonising and co-ordinating private and, in particular, commercial law, as between states and groups of states.

(2) UNIDROIT has been set up in 1926 as an auxiliary organ of the League of Nations. The Institute was, following the demise of the League, re-established in 1940 on the basis of a multilateral agreement. It has contributed by different international Conventions (treaties) which were adopted within its framework on the harmonisation of private law. This also includes aspects of property law. As will be seen UNIDROIT played an important role in the development of common rules on cultural property (VI) Moreover, UNIDROIT has also been very active in the area of security rights on large mobile equipment, such as airplanes and trains. The Convention on International Interests in Mobile Equipment (2001) will be dealt with here.

(3) In 2001 UNIDROIT adopted a Convention on Interests in Mobile Equipment (CIME).[166] The objective of this Convention is to facilitate asset-based financing and leasing and other transactions with property impact with regard to interests in mobile equipment by establishing clear rules to govern them. The idea behind the Convention was that the equipment involved is transferred from one legal system to another legal system on a regular basis. Such movements generally create uncertainty concerns the creation and enforcement of property rights. For that purpose, the Convention seeks to establish a legal framework for international interests in such equipment and for that purpose to create an international registration system for their protection.

(4) The Convention has been ratified by 51 countries.[167]

UNIDROIT Convention on Interests in Mobile Equipment **10.59 (INT)**

Article 2 The international interest

1. This Convention provides for the constitution and effects of an international interest in certain categories of mobile equipment and associated rights.

[165] The homepage of this organisation is www.unidroit.org.

[166] For a more comprehensive analysis of the (draft) CIME: D Clancy and G Voss, 'Facilitating Asset-based Financing and Leasing of Aircraft Equipment through the Proposed Unidroit Convention' [1998] *Air&Space Law* 287–89; LS Clark, 'Reaching Prompt International Agreement on the Unidroit Convention and Aircraft Protocol: Public/Private sector' [1998] *Air&Space Law* 290–93; B Crans, 'The Unidroit Convention on International interests in Mobile Equipment and the Aircraft Equipment Protocol: Some Critical Observations' [1998] *Air&Space Law* 277–82; id, 'Analysing the Merits of the Proposed Unidroit Convention on International Interests in Mobile Equipment and the Aircraft Equipment Protocol on the Basis of a Fictional Scenario' [2000] *Air&Space Law* 51–56; CG Cuming, 'Hot Issues in the Development of the (Draft) Convention on International Interests in Mobile Equipment and the (Draft) Aircraft Equipment Protocol' [2000] *The International Lawyer* 1093–1105; E-M Kieninger, 'Effects in Insolvency of the International Interest in Mobile Equipment: A German Perspective' [1999] *UL Rev* 397–408; J Wool, 'The Next Generation of International Aviation Finance Law: An Overview of the Proposed Unidroit Convention on International Interests in Mobile Equipment as Applied to Aircraft Equipment' [1998] *Air&Space Law* 243–76; id, 'The Case for a Commercial Orientation to the Proposed UNIDROIT Convention as Applied to Aircraft Equipment' [1999] *UL Rev* 289–302.

[167] See www.unidroit.org/english/conventions/mobile-equipment/main.htm.

2. For the purposes of this Convention, an international interest in mobile equipment is an interest, constituted under Article 7, in a uniquely identifiable object of a category of such objects listed in paragraph 3 and designated in the Protocol:

(a) granted by the chargor under a security agreement;

(b) vested in a person who is the conditional seller under a title reservation agreement; or

(c) vested in a person who is the lessor under a leasing agreement.

An interest falling within sub-paragraph (a) does not also fall within sub-paragraph (b) or (c).

3. The categories referred to in the preceding paragraphs are:

(a) airframes, aircraft engines and helicopters;

(b) railway rolling stock; and

(c) space assets.

4. The applicable law determines whether an interest to which paragraph 2 applies falls within subparagraph (a), (b) or (c) of that paragraph.

5. An international interest in an object extends to proceeds of that object.

Article 3 Sphere of application

1. This Convention applies when, at the time of the conclusion of the agreement creating or providing for the international interest, the debtor is situated in a Contracting State.

2. The fact that the creditor is situated in a non-Contracting State does not affect the applicability of this Convention.

Notes

(1) These provisions reflect the compromise of the Convention between the *functional* approach of the US law systems, and the *conceptual* approach of the European continental legal systems.[168] On the one hand, US law does not make distinctions between the different categories of proprietary interests which can be established for security purposes (unitary system): any interest vested in order to protect a claim arising out of a credit transaction is to be considered as a security interest and creates the effects prescribed in Article 9 UCC.[169] On the other hand, the continental legal systems distinguish between the type of proprietary interests (fragmented system) created by the different security agreements (mortgage, pledge, ownership for security purposes), which justifies a different treatment on various issues, such as the validity requirements, publicity requirements, default remedies.

The CIME does not in itself determine into which of the two categories an agreement falls. That is left to the applicable law under the private international law rules of the state that has jurisdiction. For instance, a conditional sales agreement will be

[168] Explanatory Report, An overview of the convention, no 12. See also R Goode, 'The Unidroit Draft Mobile Equipment Convention: Confluence of Legal Concepts and Philosophies', in *Mélanges en l'honneur de Denis Tallon* (Paris, LGDJ, 1999) 75–76.

[169] See Art 1-201(37) and 9-202 Uniform Commercial Code. See Chapter 5.

characterised in the US as security agreement, while it will be characterised under the second category in most other legal systems.

(2) Article 2, paragraph 3 CIME provides the categories of assets on which the security rights which can be made subject to the CIME are created. All three categories involve means of transportation, which can easily change from one legal system to another legal system, in such way that parties are never sure which property regime will apply. The CIME gives a radical solution to this uncertainty: it is no less than the creation of a new international interest, so a new international property right which is subject to a uniform set of rules dealing with regard to the creation, enforcement and registration of the interest. The interest is not dependent upon rules of national law[170] or private international law. It is an autonomous right, with proper methods of creation, perfection and enforcement.

(3) The CIME only determines the framework of the proprietary rules with regard to the international interests on mobile equipment. The Convention has therefore been complemented with several Protocols specifying the rules on the different categories:

- Protocol to the Convention on International Interests in Mobile Equipment on Matters specific to Aircraft Equipment (Cape Town, 2001).[171]
- Protocol to the Convention on International Interests in Mobile Equipment on Matters specific to Railway Rolling Stock (Luxembourg, 2007).[172]

UNIDROIT Convention on Interests in Mobile Equipment **10.60 (INT)**

Chapter IV

The international registration system

Article 16 The International Registry

1. An International Registry shall be established for registrations of:

(a) international interests, prospective international interests and registrable non-consensual rights and interests;

(b) assignments and prospective assignments of international interests;

(c) acquisitions of international interests by legal or contractual subrogations under the applicable law;

(d) notices of national interests; and(e) subordinations of interests referred to in any of the preceding sub-paragraphs.

2. Different international registries may be established for different categories of object and associated rights.

3. For the purposes of this Chapter and Chapter V, the term 'registration' includes, where appropriate, an amendment, extension or discharge of a registration.

[170] It does not depend upon the existence of a functional equivalent in national law.

[171] See the text of the Protocol: www.unidroit.org/english/conventions/mobile-equipment/aircraftprotocol.pdf.

[172] See the text of the Protocol www.unidroit.org/english/conventions/mobile-equipment/railprotocol.pdf.

Article 17 The Supervisory Authority and the Registrar

1. There shall be a Supervisory Authority as provided by the Protocol.
2. The Supervisory Authority shall:

   (a) establish or provide for the establishment of the International Registry;

   (b) except as otherwise provided by the Protocol, appoint and dismiss the Registrar;

   (c) ensure that any rights required for the continued effective operation of the International Registry in the event of a change of Registrar will vest in or be assignable to the new Registrar;

   (d) after consultation with the Contracting States, make or approve and ensure the publication of regulations pursuant to the Protocol dealing with the operation of the International Registry;

   (e) establish administrative procedures through which complaints concerning the operation of the International Registry can be made to the Supervisory Authority;

   (f) supervise the Registrar and the operation of the International Registry;

   (g) at the request of the Registrar, provide such guidance to the Registrar as the Supervisory Authority thinks fit;

   (h) set and periodically review the structure of fees to be charged for the services and facilities of the International Registry;

   (i) do all things necessary to ensure that an efficient notice-based electronic registration system exists to implement the objectives of this Convention and the Protocol; and

   (j) report periodically to Contracting States concerning the discharge of its obligations under this Convention and the Protocol.

3. The Supervisory Authority may enter into any agreement requisite for the performance of its functions, including any agreement referred to in Article 27(3).
4. The Supervisory Authority shall own all proprietary rights in the data bases and archives of the International Registry.
5. The Registrar shall ensure the efficient operation of the International Registry and perform the functions assigned to it by this Convention, the Protocol and the regulations.

Chapter V

Other matters relating to registration …

Article 29 Priority of competing interests

1. A registered interest has priority over any other interest subsequently registered and over an unregistered interest.
2. The priority of the first-mentioned interest under the preceding paragraph applies:

   (a) even if the first-mentioned interest was acquired or registered with actual knowledge of the other interest; and

   (b) even as regards value given by the holder of the first-mentioned interest with such knowledge.

3. The buyer of an object acquires its interest in it:

   (a) subject to an interest registered at the time of its acquisition of that interest; and

(b) free from an unregistered interest even if it has actual knowledge of such an interest.

4. The conditional buyer or lessee acquires its interest in or right over that object:

(a) subject to an interest registered prior to the registration of the international interest held by its conditional seller or lessor; and

(b) free from an interest not so registered at that time even if it has actual knowledge of that interest.

5. The priority of competing interests or rights under this Article may be varied by agreement between the holders of those interests, but an assignee of a subordinated interest is not bound by an agreement to subordinate that interest unless at the time of the assignment a subordination had been registered relating to that agreement.

6. Any priority given by this Article to an interest in an object extends to proceeds.

7. This Convention:

(a) does not affect the rights of a person in an item, other than an object, held prior to its installation on an object if under the applicable law those rights continue to exist after the installation; and

(b) does not prevent the creation of rights in an item, other than an object, which has previously been installed on an object where under the applicable law those rights are created.

Article 30 Effects of insolvency

1. In insolvency proceedings against the debtor an international interest is effective if prior to the commencement of the insolvency proceedings that interest was registered in conformity with this Convention.

2. Nothing in this Article impairs the effectiveness of an international interest in the insolvency proceedings where that interest is effective under the applicable law.

3. Nothing in this Article affects:

(a) any rules of law applicable in insolvency proceedings relating to the avoidance of a transaction as a preference or a transfer in fraud of creditors; or

(b) any rules of procedure relating to the enforcement of rights to property which is under the control or supervision of the insolvency administrator.

Notes

(1) The Convention provides a very clear and simple *priority* rule: the first interest to be registered has priority over subsequently registered interests, and a registered interest has priority over an unregistered interest.[173] However, the Convention provides the possibility for states to make a declaration interfering with this priority rule. Firstly, a contracting state may at any time list the categories of non-consensual rights or interests which shall be registrable under this Convention.[174] Secondly, a contracting state may—according to Article 39—declare that a non-consensual right has priority over a registered international interest, but this declaration is subject to two conditions: (a) the non-consensual interest has, under the national law of that

[173] Art 29(1) CIME.
[174] Art 40 CIME.

state, priority over an interest in an aircraft object equivalent to that of the holder of a registered international interest; and (b) the non-consensual right cannot be registered in the International Registry under Article 40 CIME.

(2) The registration system of the CIME and its Protocols is remarkable. It is an international and autonomous registry, which is independent from the national registries existing in the Member States.[175] A different international registry is organised for each category involved (aircraft, railway rolling stock and space objects). Its goal is to provide for efficient, accurate and as simple as possible information to interested third parties. See, on national registration systems, Chapter 8.

UNIDROIT Convention on Interests in Mobile Equipment **10.61 (INT)**

Chapter IX

Assignments of associated rights and international interests; rights of subrogation

Article 31 Effects of assignment

1. Except as otherwise agreed by the parties, an assignment of associated rights made in conformity with Article 32 also transfers to the assignee:

(a) the related international interest; and

(b) all the interests and priorities of the assignor under this Convention.

2. Nothing in this Convention prevents a partial assignment of the assignor's associated rights. In the case of such a partial assignment the assignor and assignee may agree as to their respective rights concerning the related international interest assigned under the preceding paragraph but not so as adversely to affect the debtor without its consent.

3. Subject to paragraph 4, the applicable law shall determine the defences and rights of set-off available to the debtor against the assignee.

4. The debtor may at any time by agreement in writing waive all or any of the defences and rights of set-off referred to in the preceding paragraph other than defences arising from fraudulent acts on the part of the assignee.

5. In the case of an assignment by way of security, the assigned associated rights revest in the assignor, to the extent that they are still subsisting, when the obligations secured by the assignment have been discharged.

Article 32 Formal requirements of assignment

1. An assignment of associated rights transfers the related international interest only if it:

(a) is in writing;

(b) enables the associated rights to be identified under the contract from which they arise; and

(c) in the case of an assignment by way of security, enables the obligations secured

[175] CG Cuming, 'Considerations in the Design of an International Registry for Interests in Mobile Equipment' [1999] *UL Rev* 275–88; JHM van Erp, 'The Cape Town Convention: A Model for a European System of Security Interests Registration?' [2004[*European Review of Private Law* 91–110.

by the assignment to be determined in accordance with the Protocol but without the need to state a sum or maximum sum secured.

2. An assignment of an international interest created or provided for by a security agreement is not valid unless some or all related associated rights also are assigned.

3. This Convention does not apply to an assignment of associated rights which is not effective to transfer the related international interest.

Article 33 Debtor's duty to assignee

1. To the extent that associated rights and the related international interest have been transferred in accordance with Articles 31 and 32, the debtor in relation to those rights and that interest is bound by the assignment and has a duty to make payment or give other performance to the assignee, if but only if:

(a) the debtor has been given notice of the assignment in writing by or with the authority of the assignor; and

(b) the notice identifies the associated rights.

2. Irrespective of any other ground on which payment or performance by the debtor discharges the latter from liability, payment or performance shall be effective for this purpose if made in accordance with the preceding paragraph.

3. Nothing in this Article shall affect the priority of competing assignments.

Article 34 Default remedies in respect of assignment by way of security

In the event of default by the assignor under the assignment of associated rights and the related international interest made by way of security, Articles 8, 9 and 11 to 14 apply in the relations between the assignor and the assignee (and, in relation to associated rights, apply in so far as those provisions are capable of application to intangible property) as if references:

(a) to the secured obligation and the security interest were references to the obligation secured by the assignment of the associated rights and the related international interest and the security interest created by that assignment;

(b) to the chargee or creditor and chargor or debtor were references to the assignee and assignor;

(c) to the holder of the international interest were references to the assignee; and

(d) to the object were references to the assigned associated rights and the related international interest.

Article 35 Priority of competing assignments

1. Where there are competing assignments of associated rights and at least one of the assignments includes the related international interest and is registered, the provisions of Article 29 apply as if the references to a registered interest were references to an assignment of the associated rights and the related registered interest and as if references to a registered or unregistered interest were references to a registered or unregistered assignment.

2. Article 30 applies to an assignment of associated rights as if the references to an international interest were references to an assignment of the associated rights and the related international interest.

Note

These provisions must be read in the light of the nature of accessority of security rights. As we have seen in Chapter 5, security rights are gaining more and more autonomy in relation to the secured claim. This development seems to be reinforced by the CIME and its Protocols.

V.B UNCITRAL LEGISLATIVE GUIDES

The United Nations Commission on International Trade Law (UNCITRAL)[176] was established by the General Assembly of the United Nations in 1966 (Resolution 2205(XXI) of 17 December 1966). In establishing the Commission, the General Assembly recognised that disparities in national laws governing international trade created obstacles to the flow of trade, and it regarded the Commission as the vehicle by which the United Nations could play a more active role in reducing or removing these obstacles. UNCITRAL was charged with the general mandate to further the progressive harmonisation and unification of the law of international trade. The six working groups and their current topics are as follows:

Working Group I—Procurement
Working Group II—International arbitration and conciliation
Working Group III—Transport law
Working Group IV—Electronic commerce
Working Group V—Insolvency law
Working Group VI—Security interests

The latter two are of main importance for property law. With regard to insolvency law, the major accomplishment is the 2004—UNCITRAL Legislative Guide on Insolvency Law[177] and a Model Law on Cross-Border Insolvency.[178] With regard to security law, it should be noted that there exists a Draft—Legislative Guide on Secured Transactions. As this work is still in progress, we will not analyse it in more depth.[179]

V.C MODEL LAW ON SECURED TRANSACTIONS OF THE EUROPEAN BANK FOR RECONSTRUCTION AND DEVELOPMENT

As already mentioned above (I.C), the EBRD has issued a model law on secured transactions in 2004. This model law, accompanied by a commentary, proposes a unitary system of property security rights.[180]

[176] The homepage of the organisation is www.uncitral.org.
[177] www.uncitral.org/uncitral/en/uncitral_texts/insolvency/2004Guide.html.
[178] www.uncitral.org/uncitral/en/uncitral_texts/insolvency/1997Model.html.
[179] For the text of the Draft Legislative Guide: www.uncitral.org/uncitral/en/uncitral_texts/payments/Guide_securedtrans.html.
[180] See www.ebrd.com/pages/research/publications/guides/model.shtml.

VI. MULTI-LEVEL HARMONISATION? A CASE STUDY OF CULTURAL OBJECTS

Introductory Notes

(a) A very specific set of rules concerns cultural objects. These rules aim to preserve the national and cultural heritage of a country as much as possible. On an international level various conventions and directives have been issued: The Hague Convention for the Protection of Cultural Property in the Event of Armed Conflict (1954); the UNESCO Convention on the Means of Prohibiting and Preventing the Illicit Import, Export and Transfer of Ownership of Cultural Property (1970); The UNIDROIT-Convention on Stolen or Illegally Exported Cultural Objects (1995); and Directive 93/7/EEG of 15 March 1993 on the return of cultural objects unlawfully removed from the territory of a Member State. These instruments will be dealt with below. In pursuing the goal of protecting cultural objects, the legal rules affect property rights on these things in a twofold way.

(b) First of all, they restrict the powers of the owner both to use and to dispose of these objects. The owner of cultural property cannot export or transfer this specific object abroad without having obtained a prior authorisation of the national authorities.

(c) Secondly, if cultural objects have been brought or transferred abroad in violation of the applicable rules, the transferee can be obliged to make restitution. The national state to which heritage the property belongs can claim restitution—possibly going along with the payment of a compensation—out of the hands of the transferee. These rules largely affect the protection of the possessor in good faith of movables, as it exists in all legal systems (see Chapter 9).

(d) The rules on cultural objects are dispersed in the legal system. Numerous legal instruments govern this field of law. In this section, we will briefly analyse the way in which these different international instruments interact and—sometimes—interfere with each other.

(e) An observation must be made regarding terminology. As will become clear, the various legal instruments use different terminology. Thus we will encounter either property or objects. It is not in conformity with our casebook terminology (see Chapter 1), but the specific context will provide guidance as to the precise definitions.

The Hague Convention for the Protection of Cultural Property in the Event of Armed Conflict (1954)[181] **10.62 (INT)**

Article 1 Definition of cultural property

'Cultural property' shall cover, irrespective of origin or ownership:

[181] http://portal.unesco.org/en/ev.php-URL_ID=13637&URL_DO=DO_TOPIC&URL_SECTION=201.html. See for a general overview of this Convention: K Chamberlain, *War and Cultural Heritage: An Analysis of the 1954 Convention for the Protection of Cultural Property in the Event of Armed Conflict and its Two Protocols* (Leicester, Institute of Art and Law, 2004) 333.

(a) movable or immovable property of great importance to the cultural heritage of every people, such as monuments of architecture, art or history, whether religious or secular; archaeological sites; groups of buildings which, as a whole, are of historical or artistic interest; works of art; manuscripts, books and other objects of artistic, historical or archaeological interest; as well as scientific collections and important collections of books or archives or of reproductions of the property defined above;
(b) buildings whose main and effective purpose is to preserve or exhibit the movable cultural property defined in sub-paragraph (a) such as museums, large libraries and depositories of archives, and refuges intended to shelter, in the event of armed conflict, the movable cultural property defined in sub-paragraph (a);
(c) centers containing a large amount of cultural property as defined in sub-paragraphs (a) and (b), to be known as 'centers containing monuments'.

Article I-1-4 First Protocol
1. Each High Contracting Party undertakes to prevent the exportation, from a territory occupied by it during an armed conflict, of cultural property as defined in Article 1 of the Convention for the Protection of Cultural Property in the Event of Armed Conflict, signed at The Hague on 14 May, 1954.
2. Each High Contracting Party undertakes to take into its custody cultural property imported into its territory either directly or indirectly from any occupied territory. This shall either be effected automatically upon the importation of the property or, failing this, at the request of the authorities of that territory.
3. Each High Contracting Party undertakes to return, at the close of hostilities, to the competent authorities of the territory previously occupied, cultural property which is in its territory, if such property has been exported in contravention of the principle laid down in the first paragraph. Such property shall never be retained as war reparations.
4. The High Contracting Party whose obligation it was to prevent the exportation of cultural property from the territory occupied by it, shall pay an indemnity to the holders in good faith of any cultural property which has to be returned in accordance with the preceding paragraph.

Notes

(1) This Convention and its First Protocol have a rather limited scope: they impose an obligation on the parties to prevent the exportation of cultural objects from occupied territory, to take that property into its custody, and to return to the competent authorities of the formerly occupied territory, the illegally exported cultural property. They have an obligation to pay an indemnity to possessors in good faith.

(2) The Convention and its First Protocol have been ratified by 114 and 92 states, respectively.

UNESCO Convention on the Means of Prohibiting and Preventing the Illicit Import, Export and Transfer of Ownership of Cultural Property (1970) **10.63 (INT)**

Article 1 For the purposes of this Convention, the term 'cultural property' means property which, on religious or secular grounds, is specifically designated by each

State as being of importance for archaeology, prehistory, history, literature, art or science and which belongs to the following categories:

(a) Rare collections and specimens of fauna, flora, minerals and anatomy, and objects of palaeontological interest;

(b) property relating to history, including the history of science and technology and military and social history, to the life of national leaders, thinkers, scientists and artist and to events of national importance;

(c) products of archaeological excavations (including regular and clandestine) or of archaeological discoveries;

(d) elements of artistic or historical monuments or archaeological sites which have been dismembered;

(e) antiquities more than one hundred years old, such as inscriptions, coins and engraved seals;

(f) objects of ethnological interest;

(g) property of artistic interest, such as:

(i) pictures, paintings and drawings produced entirely by hand on any support and in any material (excluding industrial designs and manufactured articles decorated by hand);

(ii) original works of statuary art and sculpture in any material;

(iii) original engravings, prints and lithographs;

(iv) original artistic assemblages and montages in any material;

(h) rare manuscripts and incunabula, old books, documents and publications of special interest (historical, artistic, scientific, literary, etc.) singly or in collections;

(i) postage, revenue and similar stamps, singly or in collections;

(j) archives, including sound, photographic and cinematographic archives;

(k) articles of furniture more than one hundred years old and old musical instruments.

Article 6 The States Parties to this Convention undertake:

(a) To introduce an appropriate certificate in which the exporting State would specify that the export of the cultural property in question is authorised. The certificate should accompany all items of cultural property exported in accordance with the regulations;

(b) to prohibit the exportation of cultural property from their territory unless accompanied by the above-mentioned export certificate;

(c) to publicise this prohibition by appropriate means, particularly among persons likely to export or import cultural property.

Article 7 The States Parties to this Convention undertake:

(a) To take the necessary measures, consistent with national legislation, to prevent museums and similar institutions within their territories from acquiring cultural property originating in another State Party which has been illegally exported after entry into force of this Convention, in the States concerned. Whenever possible, to inform a State of origin Party to this Convention of an offer of such cultural property illegally removed from that State after the entry into force of this Convention in both States;

(b) (i) to prohibit the import of cultural property stolen from a museum or a religious or secular public monument or similar institution in another State Party to this

Convention after the entry into force of this Convention for the States concerned, provided that such property is documented as appertaining to the inventory of that institution;

(ii) at the request of the State Party of origin, to take appropriate steps to recover and return any such cultural property imported after the entry into force of this Convention in both States concerned, provided, however, that the requesting State shall pay just compensation to an innocent purchaser or to a person who has valid title to that property. Requests for recovery and return shall be made through diplomatic offices. The requesting Party shall furnish, at its expense, the documentation and other evidence necessary to establish its claim for recovery and return. The Parties shall impose no customs duties or other charges upon cultural property returned pursuant to this Article. All expenses incident to the return and delivery of the cultural property shall be borne by the requesting Party.

Article 8 The States Parties to this Convention undertake to impose penalties or administrative sanctions on any person responsible for infringing the prohibitions referred to under Articles 6(b) and 7(b) above.

Notes

(1) A more general approach than the previous 1954 Convention was taken by the 1970 UNESCO Convention. In order to ensure the integrity of cultural objects, the UNESCO Convention identifies three goals: (i) to stop the impoverishment of the cultural heritage of a nation through illicit import, export and transfer of ownership of cultural property; (ii) to agree that trade in cultural objects exported contrary to the law of the nation of origin is illicit; and (iii) to agree to prevent the importation of such objects and facilitate their return to source nations.

(2) The approach of this convention is more general than the Hague Convention (1954), as it is not restricted to the export from occupied territory.[182] The Convention addresses the more general problem of theft, clandestine excavation and illicit exports.[183] The 1970 Convention has been accepted or ratified by 109 states.

(3) This Convention only imposes obligations upon Member States, but does not govern the private law relations between private persons. UNIDROIT stepped in at request of UNESCO in the early 1980s to complement the public law arrangements of the UNESCO convention with private law instruments.[184]

(4) The purpose of the UNIDROIT Convention is to seek the harmonisation and coordination of the private laws of states and to pave the way for the gradual adoption of uniform rules of private law. Hence, it complements the UNESCO Convention (1970) by implementing rules that affect the property positions of private persons.

[182] S Gimbrère and T Pronk, 'The Protection of Cultural Property: From UNESCO to the European Community with Special Reference to The case of the Netherlands' [1992] *Netherlands Yearbook of International Law* 224–26; PJIM de Waart, 'Internationale bescherming van cultuurgoed als natuurlijke hulpbron' [1994] *Mededelingen Nederlandse vereniging voor Internationaal Recht*, at 9.

[183] See the recitals to the 1970 Convention. See for the entire text of the Convention: http://portal.unesco.org/en/ev.php-URL_ID=13039&URL_DO=DO_TOPIC&URL_SECTION=201.html.

[184] Unidroit Secretariat (Marina Schneider), 'Unidroit Convention on Stolen or Illegally Exported Cultural Objects: Explanatory Report' [2001] *Uniform Law Review* 3, 482.

The UNIDROIT Convention makes a fundamental distinction between (i) stolen cultural objects, thereby regulating the conflict of interests between the former possessor of such an object and a person acquiring it in good faith, and (ii) cultural objects unlawfully removed from their state of origin.

The 1995 UNIDROIT Convention on Stolen or Illegally Exported Cultural Objects (1995) **10.64 (INT)**

Article 3 (1) The possessor of a cultural object which has been stolen shall return it.
(2) For the purposes of this Convention, a cultural object which has been unlawfully excavated or lawfully excavated but unlawfully retained shall be considered stolen, when consistent with the law of the State where the excavation took place.
(3) Any claim for restitution shall be brought within a period of three years from the time when the claimant knew the location of the cultural object and the identity of its possessor, and in any case within a period of fifty years from the time of the theft.
(4) However, a claim for restitution of a cultural object forming an integral part of an identified monument or archaeological site, or belonging to a public collection, shall not be subject to time limitations other than a period of three years from the time when the claimant knew the location of the cultural object and the identity of its possessor.
(5) Notwithstanding the provisions of the preceding paragraph, any Contracting State may declare that a claim is subject to a time limitation of 75 years or such longer period as is provided in its law. A claim made in another Contracting State for restitution of a cultural object displaced from a monument, archaeological site or public collection in a Contracting State making such a declaration shall also be subject to that time limitation.
(6) A declaration referred to in the preceding paragraph shall be made at the time of signature, ratification, acceptance, approval or accession.
(7) For the purposes of this Convention, a 'public collection', consists of a group of inventoried or otherwise identified cultural objects owned by:

(a) a Contracting State;
(b) a regional or local authority of a Contracting State;
(c) a religious institution in a Contracting State; or
(d) an institution that is established for an essentially cultural, educational or scientific purpose in a Contracting State and is recognised in that State as serving the public interest.

(8) In addition, a claim for restitution of a sacred or communally important cultural object belonging to and used by a tribal or indigenous community in a Contracting State as part of that community's traditional or ritual use, shall be subject to the time limitation applicable to public collections.

Article 4 (1) The possessor of a stolen cultural object required to return it shall be entitled, at the time of its restitution, to payment of fair and reasonable compensation provided that the possessor neither knew nor ought reasonably to have known that the object was stolen and can prove that it exercised due diligence when acquiring the object.

(2) Without prejudice to the right of the possessor to compensation referred to in the preceding paragraph, reasonable efforts shall be made to have the person who transferred the cultural object to the possessor, or any prior transferor, pay the compensation where to do so would be consistent with the law of the State in which the claim is brought.

(3) Payment of compensation to the possessor by the claimant, when this is required, shall be without prejudice to the right of the claimant to recover it from any other person.

(4) In determining whether the possessor exercised due diligence, regard shall be had to all the circumstances of the acquisition, including the character of the parties, the price paid, whether the possessor consulted any reasonably accessible register of stolen cultural objects, and any other relevant information and documentation which it could reasonably have obtained, and whether the possessor consulted accessible agencies or took any other step that a reasonable person would have taken in the circumstances.

(5) The possessor shall not be in a more favourable position than the person from whom it acquired the cultural object by inheritance or otherwise gratuitously.

CHAPTER III—RETURN OF ILLEGALLY EXPORTED CULTURAL OBJECTS

Article 5 (1) A Contracting State may request the court or other competent authority of another Contracting State to order the return of a cultural object illegally exported from the territory of the requesting State.

(2) A cultural object which has been temporarily exported from the territory of the requesting State, for purposes such as exhibition, research or restoration, under a permit issued according to its law regulating its export for the purpose of protecting its cultural heritage and not returned in accordance with the terms of that permit shall be deemed to have been illegally exported.

(3) The court or other competent authority of the State addressed shall order the return of an illegally exported cultural object if the requesting State establishes that the removal of the object from its territory significantly impairs one or more of the following interests:

(a) the physical Preservation of the object or of its context;

(b) the integrity of a complex object;

(c) the preservation of information of, for example, a scientific or historical character;

(d) the traditional or ritual use of the object by a tribal or indigenous community, or establishers that the object is of significant cultural importance for the requesting State.

(4) Any request made under paragraph 1 of this article shall contain or be accompanied by such information of a factual or legal nature as may assist the court or other competent authority of the State addressed in determining whether the requirements of paragraphs 1 to 3 have been met.

(5) Any request for return shall be brought within a period of three years from the time when the requesting State knew the location of the cultural object and the identity of its possessor, and in any case within a period of fifty years from the date of the export or from the date on which the object should have been returned under a permit referred to in paragraph 2 of this article.

Article 6 (1) The possessor of a cultural object who acquired the object after it was illegally exported shall be entitled, at the time of its return, to payment by the requesting State of fair and reason compensation, provided that the possessor neither knew nor ought reasonably to have known at the time of acquisition that the object had been illegally exported.

(2) In determining whether the possessor knew or ought reasonably to have known that the cultural object had been illegally exported, regard shall be had to the circumstances of the acquisition, including the absence of an export certificate required under the law of the requesting State.

(3) Instead of compensation, and in agreement with the requesting State, the possessor required to return the cultural object to that State may decide:

(a) to retain ownership of the object; or

(b) to transfer ownership against payment or gratuitously to a person of its choice residing in the requesting State who provides the necessary guarantees.

(4) The cost of returning the cultural object in accordance with this article shall be borne by the requesting State, without prejudice to the right of that State to recover costs from any other person.

(5) The possessor shall not be in a more favourable position than the person from whom it acquired the cultural object by inheritance or otherwise gratuitously.

Notes

(1) The UNIDROIT Convention does not make any clear difference between voluntary and involuntary dispossession by the owner. This is different from the tradition in which some legal systems of the Romanistic legal family stand.[185] French and Belgian law allow the owner whose possession was involuntarily taken to revindicate during three years out of the hands of a possessor in good faith. In case of voluntary dispossession, however, revindication out of the hands of a possessor in good faith is always excluded. The UNIDROIT Convention adheres to a distinction based on a classification of the object as stolen.

(2) The Convention takes an innovative approach with regard to the content and proof of the good faith requirement. With regard to stolen goods, the Convention does not start from the presumption of good faith. The burden of proof of due diligence in case of theft is on the possessor.[186] If the possessor fails to prove this, he will not be entitled to compensation. 'It constitutes a departure from the rule in force in several legal systems that rely on a presumption of good faith', reveals the Explanatory Report.[187] Article 4 paragraph 4 enumerates circumstances which deserve particular attention in addressing the issue of due diligence: character of the parties, price paid, consultation of reasonably accessible registers and accessible agencies and steps which 'a reasonable person would have taken'.

[185] Comparative law has used the concept of legal family to classify national legal systems; yet this concept has been challenged as being too static, and the notion of legal tradition has taken a lead role. See HP Glenn, 'Legal Families and Legal Traditions' in M Reimann and R Zimmermann, *The Oxford Handbook of Comparative Law* (Oxford University Press, Oxford, 2006) 421–40.

[186] Explanatory Report to Art 4, (2001) 3 *UL Rev* 516, which also gives an insight into the meaning of good faith, by stating that in case of doubt, also an inquiry into the provenance of the object is needed.

[187] Explanatory Report to Art 4, parah 1, (2001) 3 *UL Rev* 516.

With regard to illegally exported objects, the burden of proof of good faith is left to be decided by the applicable law.[188] But also here at least some due diligence is required in order to qualify as good faith, as becomes clear from Article 6(2):

> [I]n determining whether the possessor knew or ought reasonably to have known that the cultural object had been illegally exported, regard shall be had to all the circumstances of the acquisition, including the absence of an export certificate required under the law of the requesting State.

Less diligence appears to be required, reveals the Explanatory Report.[189] Instead of compensation, with the agreement of the requesting state, the possessor in good faith is allowed to retain the ownership of the object or to transfer ownership to a person of his choice (Article 6(3)).

Directive 93/7/EEG of 15 March 1993 on the return of cultural objects unlawfully removed from the territory of a Member State 10.65 (EU)

Article 1(1) 'Cultural object' shall mean an object which:
—is classified, before or after its unlawful removal from the territory of a Member State, among the 'national treasures possessing artistic, historic or archaeological value' under national legislation or administrative procedures within the meaning of Article 36 of the Treaty,
and
—belongs to one of the categories listed in the Annex or does not belong to one of these categories but forms an integral part of:
—public collections listed in the inventories of museums, archives or libraries' conservation collection.
For the purposes of this Directive, 'public collections' shall mean collections which are the property of a Member State, local or regional authority within a Member States or an institution situated in the territory of a Member State and defined as public in accordance with the legislation of that Member State, such institution being the property of, or significantly financed by, that Member State or a local or regional authority;
—the inventories of ecclesiastical institutions.

Article 5 The requesting Member State may initiate, before the competent court in the requested Member State, proceedings against the possessor or, failing him, the holder, with the aim of securing the return of a cultural object which has been unlawfully removed from its territory.
Proceedings may be brought only where the document initiating them is accompanied by:
—a document describing the object covered by the request and stating that it is a cultural object,

[188] *Ibid.*
[189] *Ibid.*

—a declaration by the competent authorities of the requesting Member State that the cultural object has been unlawfully removed from its territory.

Article 6 The central authority of the requesting Member State shall forthwith inform the central authority of the requested Member State that proceedings have been initiated with the aim of securing the return of the object in question.
The central authority of the requested Member State shall forthwith inform the central authorities of the other Member States.

Article 7 1. Member States shall lay down in their legislation that the return proceedings provided for in this Directive may not be brought more than one year after the requesting Member State became aware of the location of the cultural object and of the identity of its possessor or holder.
Such proceedings may, at all events, not be brought more than 30 years after the object was unlawfully removed from the territory of the requesting Member State. However, in the case of objects forming part of public collections, referred to in Article 1 (1), and ecclesiastical goods in the Member States where they are subject to special protection arrangements under national law, return proceedings shall be subject to a time-limit of 75 years, except in Member States where proceedings are not subject to a time-limit or in the case of bilateral agreements between Member States laying down a period exceeding 75 years.
2. Return proceedings may not be brought if removal from the national territory of the requesting Member State is no longer unlawful at the time when they are to be initiated.

Article 8 Save as otherwise provided in Articles 7 and 13, the competent court shall order the return of the cultural object in question where it is found to be a cultural object within the meaning of Article 1 (1) and to have been removed unlawfully from national territory.

Article 9 Where return of the object is ordered, the competent court in the requested States shall award the possessor such compensation as it deems fair according to the circumstances of the case, provided that it is satisfied that the possessor exercised due care and attention in acquiring the object.
The burden of proof shall be governed by the legislation of the requested Member State.
In the case of a donation or succession, the possessor shall not be in a more favourable position than the person from whom he acquired the object by that means.
The requesting Member State shall pay such compensation upon return of the object.

Article 10 Expenses incurred in implementing a decision ordering the return of a cultural object shall be borne by the requesting Member State. The same applies to the costs of the measures referred to in Article 4 (4).

Article 11 Payment of the fair compensation and of the expenses referred to in Articles 9 and 10 respectively shall be without prejudice to the requesting Member State's right to take action with a view to recovering those amounts from the persons responsible for the unlawful removal of the cultural object from its territory.

Article 12 Ownership of the cultural object after return shall be governed by that law of the requesting Member State.

Article 13 This Directive shall apply only to cultural objects unlawfully removed from the territory of a Member State on or after 1 January 1993.

Article 14 1. Each Member State may extend its obligation to return cultural objects to cover categories of objects other than those listed in the Annex.

2. Each Member State may apply the arrangements provided for by this Directive to requests for the return of cultural objects unlawfully removed from the territory of other Member States prior to 1 January 1993.

Article 15 This Directive shall be without prejudice to any civil or criminal proceedings that may be brought, under the national laws of the Member States, by the requesting Member State and/or the owner of a cultural object that has been stolen.

Note

The completion of the EU internal market (foreseen) by 1 January 1993[190] needed to be accompanied by legislation on the protection of cultural objects. Yet Member States retain, under Article 36 TFEU, the right to define national treasures and to take the necessary measures to protect these (see above, III.E.1.b). Therefore the Directive on the return of cultural objects was enacted, which gives Member States instruments to secure the return to their territory of cultural objects which are classified as national treasures within the meaning of the said Article 36 TFEU and have been removed of their territory in breach of the abovementioned national measures or of Council Regulation (EEC) No 3911/92 of 9 December 1992 on the export of cultural goods.[191]

Cour de cassation, 16 June 1971[192] **10.66 (FR)**

GOOD FAITH—POSSESSION

Toulouse Lautrec

The professional trader in art cannot argue that he is possessor in good faith if he does not prove that he bought the artwork in good faith.

Judgment: Considering that by pronouncing that the consorts Blanc 'do not provide proof of a purchase concluded by their author/originator in circumstances which do not leave him with any doubts concerning its validity';

[190] On the basis of Art 14 EC Treaty.

[191] Recitals to Council Directive 93/7/EEC of 15 March 1993 on the return of cultural objects unlawfully removed from the territory of a Member State, [1993] OJ L74/74; Council Regulation 3911/92/EEC arranges uniform control (eg export licenses) on the export of cultural objects at the community's external borders. A further Regulation (752/93/EEC) dealt with requirements to national export licenses. Directive 93/7/EEC has been amended by Directive 96/100/EC, [1996] OJ L60/95 (dealing with small textual changes in the annex); Directive 2001/38/EC, [2001] OJ L187/43, deals with the annex and changes the monetary value to euros. Directive 93/7 is to be found at: http://europa.eu.int/eur-lex/lex/LexUriServ/LexUriServ.do?uri=CELEX:31993L0007:EN:HTML.

[192] Dalloz 1971, 566.

That the agreed small price for the works of Toulouse-Lautrec, of which he, an informed professional, could not ignore the quality, confirms the obscure character of the interfered transaction;

That he was writing to his vendor on 17 February 1959: 'I have not yet been able to see to the works signed Lautrec which you have entrusted in deposit at the sale' and that this letter prohibits to attach faith in the registrations of purchases made in the police book on the date of the foregoing 12 February concerning four of the five disputed works, the Court of Appeal has, without obliging the consorts Blanc to demonstrate the existence of a valid title, observed, in an implicit but necessary manner, the bad faith of Lucien Blanc, which prohibited to let him benefit from the clauses of the aforementioned Article 2279;

That thus the first ground should not be granted;

And regarding the second ground: Whereas also without success objection is raised against the judgment for not having admitted the widow of Lucien Bland and Maxime Blanc to benefit of their proper possession to benefit from Article 2279 of the Civil Code, whereas the character of the possession and the good faith of the possessor have to, according to the ground of appeal, in order for that article to apply, be assessed of the person that invokes the possession and the heir, who finds a piece of furniture in the succession, obtains from the opening of the succession the title which gives him the right to possess, in a manner, which could be equivalent to the title of the deceased does not necessarily affect the possession of the heir, if the revindicating owner does not demonstrate the bad faith of the latter;

Whereas, in fact, in contrast to the individual successor, the heir succeeds also the vices of the possession of its predecessor [*auteur*];

That the good faith of Lucien Blanc therefore prohibited his widow and his son, which succeeded him, to invoke the rule 'in the case of furniture, possession equates title' to their advantage;

That the second ground of appeal must therefore be rejected as well ...

Notes

(1) The conclusion to be drawn out of the preceding overview is that the various legal instruments, both national as well as international, seek to protect cultural objects in the public interest, but aim as well to protect the interests of bona fide purchasers. A balance is struck between protection of cultural heritage on the one hand and security of trade and the protection of private property rights in respect to cultural objects on the other hand. There are important differences as to the way these interests are balanced at a national and international level.

(2) Regarding the international instruments, the manner in which this balance is achieved differs in the UNIDROIT Convention and in the EU Directive. There are important differences in the content of good faith, in the burden of proof of good faith and, consequently, in the possessor's eligibility for compensation.[193]

[193] See on this topic particularly JM Milo and V Sagaert, 'Private Property Rights in Cultural Objects: Balancing Preservation of Cultural Objects and Certainty of Trade in Belgian and Dutch Law' in B Demarsin et al (eds), *Art and Law* (Brugge, die Keure, 2008) 468–93.

(3) The Directive, unlike the 1995 UNIDROIT Convention, does not solve the problem of content and burden of proof of the requirement of good faith itself. This issue is completely left to national Member States to deal with. It should be noted that in most Member States severe requirements are put forward, especially when the purchaser is a professional (see 10.66 (FR)).

(4) The effects of the Directive have been evaluated twice, in 2000 and in 2005.[194] The first report stressed improvements in co-operation between Member States and in traceability of cultural objects, due to lack of information. The European Parliament[195] as well as the Council[196] both proposed improvements to the efficiency of the Directive.[197]

(5) Cultural objects are an example of a specific topic that are regulated at various levels, international as well as national. The previous overview has shown that differences may continue to exist, even in case of harmonisation through a Directive. The coexistence of various international instruments and national jurisdictions and the continuing legal diversity provide a good example of what one might expect of any project aiming at uniformity of laws.

VII. THE ROLE OF ACADEMICS AND PRACTITIONERS IN THE HARMONISATION OF PROPERTY LAW

This chapter has dealt with harmonising efforts in the area of property law at a European, international and mixed level. We have already seen that some of these initiatives have been prepared, not by policymakers themselves, but by groups of academics. There are many more initiatives, especially in Europe, that deserve mentioning. This final section will deal with 'harmonising efforts' made by academics and practitioners. These efforts are not always directly aimed at harmonisation, but certainly have as the objective to work towards a better functioning of legal systems, at national, European and/or international level. We will start with the Joined Network on European Private Law (VII.A), of which the Study Group on a

[194] In 2000: Report from the Commission to the Council, the European Parliament and the European Economic and Social Committee on the Implementation of Council Regulation 3911/92/EEC on the export of cultural goods and Council Directive 93/7/EEC on the return of cultural objects unlawfully removed from the territory of a Member State, COM(2000) 0325 final. To be found at: http://europa.eu.int/eur-lex/lex/LexUriServ/LexUriServ.do?uri=CELEX:52000DC0325:EN:HTML. In 2005: Report from the Commission to the Council, the European Parliament and the European Economic and Social Committee. Second Report on the Implementation of Council Regulation 3911/92/EEC on the export of cultural goods and Council Directive 93/7/EEC on the return of cultural objects unlawfully removed from the territory of a Member State. Brussels, 21.12.2005 COM(2005) 675 final. To be found at: http://europa.eu.int/comm/enterprise/regulation/inst_sp/docs/dir937/com_2005_0675_F_EN.pdf.

[195] OJ C053 E/125.

[196] OJ C032/3.

[197] As expansion of the time limit of one year for the claim for return proceedings (Art 7(1)); campaign for public awareness; comprehensive public catalogues; an increase in co-operation between Member States.

European Civil Code is perhaps the most famous member (VII.A.1). After that we will turn to the EULIS project (VII.B), the CROBECO project (VII.C) and, finally, the Trento Common Core Project (VII.D).

VII.A THE JOINED NETWORK ON EUROPEAN PRIVATE LAW

In May 2005 a number of universities, institutions and other organisations created the Joined Network on European Private Law (CoPECL). The most important task of this network was to deliver a proposal for a Common Frame of Reference for a European contract law.[198] They have done so in the form of Common Principles of European Contract Law, hence the acronym CoPECL.

Principles are a term used very widely by academics to cover anything from underlying values, definitions, to model legislation. The 'principles' produced are usually accompanied by a set of notes and comments, whereby the comments seek to explain the intention of the drafters and the notes offer insights into the comparative research underlying the work of the drafters.

The CoPECL network comprises several groups:

- The Study Group on a European Civil Code (SGECC)
- The Research Group on Existing EC Contract Law (Acquis Group)
- The Project Group on a Restatement of European Insurance Contract Law (Insurance Group)
- The Association Henri Capitant together with the Société de Législation Comparée and de Conseil du Notariat
- The Common Core Group (Trento Common Core Group)
- The Research Group on the Economic Assessment of Contract Law Rules (Economic Impact Group)
- The Database Group
- The Academy of European Law (ERA)

Of these groups the first is the most relevant to our casebook; the Trento Common Core Group is dealt with under a separate heading (VII.D). The excellent work of the other groups has mainly concerned only contract law, but the Study Group on a European Civil Code has also ventured into property law, producing Principles of European Law (PEL) on transfer of ownership of movables, personal property security rights and trusts.[199] These books correspond to the topics dealt with by the DCFR above (III.D.4). The DCFR is a combination of the research results of the

[198] The network was funded, to this extent, by the European Commission under the Sixth General Framework Programme.

[199] B Lurger and W Faber, *Principles of European Law on Acquisition and Loss of Ownership of Goods (PEL Acq)* (München, Sellier European Law Publishers, 2011); U Drobnig, *Proprietary Security Rights in Movables (PEL Prop Sec)* (München, Sellier European Law Publishers, 2012 forthcoming); S Swann, *Trusts (PEL T)* (München, Sellier European Law Publishers, 2011).

Study Group on a European Civil Code and the Research Group on Existing EC Contract Law (*Acquis* Group).

VII.A.1 THE STUDY GROUP ON A EUROPEAN CIVIL CODE

Introductory Note

A main research group aiming to harmonise European private law is the Study Group on a European Civil Code (SGECC). It is a network of academics from across the EU, conducting comparative law research in private law in the various legal legal systems of the Member States.[200] The group purports to draft common European principles for the most important aspects of the law of obligations and for certain parts of property law in movables which are relevant for the functioning of the internal market. It is often called the Von Bar group after its president, Professor Christian von Bar.

Aims of the SGECC[201] **10.67 (EU)**

Aims

The aim of the Study Group is to produce a set of codified principles for the core areas of European private law (patrimonial law). Although the foundation for our work is detailed comparative law research, the principles which we are fashioning will represent more than a mere restatement of the existing law in the various EU jurisdictions from the standpoint of the predominant trends among the diverse legal regimes. Instead the Study Group seeks to formulate principles which constitute the most suitable private law rules for Europe-wide application.

The Study Group is not taking any one national law as a model which, with adaptation, is to be made the basis of European principles. We take the view that every legal system in the EU potentially has much to offer and the appropriateness of rules is determined on their merits rather than their national origin. Nor is the popularity of a rule necessarily decisive. While the fact that a rule or legal institution is widely shared naturally suggests its utility from a trans-national point of view, their deficiencies, in the light of legal developments, must also be considered. Improvements and alternative options may emerge in the process of analysis and in the attempt to find solutions which can bridge apparently polar approaches to the matter. In many cases the Principles will not be clearly reflected by existing law anywhere in the Member States. Instead they will represent innovations intended to build on the various national legal experiences and to avoid the problems which they have exposed.

Format of the Principles

The format of the draft text will reflect that which was adopted by the Commission on European Contract Law in the presentation of the Principles on European Contract Law. The Principles will take the form of a draft codification for the juris-

[200] The homepage of the organisation is www.sgecc.net.
[201] See www.sgecc.net/pages/en/introduction/101.scope.htm.

dictions of the European Union, complete with comments and illustrations explaining the provisions and how they apply and notes setting out their foundation in, derivation from or deviation from the existing laws.

Supporting possible legislative developments in the future

The Study Group is not concerned as such with political questions, such as implementation of the Principles in the form of EU legislation. Whether the Principles should take legislative form and, if so, in what manner and when are political questions which fall outside our remit. While our members have views on these subjects, they are really matters for wide public debate. The aim of the Study Group is to make a contribution to that debate by producing a possible legislative text. Our conviction is that the political case for a pan-European codification of patrimonial law or lesser measures (which might represent intermediate steps) is best tested against the background of an actual draft text which might form the basis for legislation. Whether or not such a text is ultimately to receive a political stamp of approval in any shape or form, it is a pre-requisite for that the enacted material has a rationally defensible foundation in the existing European private law. It is for this reason that drafting principles which might one day be made use of in European legislation must be carried out by legal experts with the benefit of and from the standpoint of current legal science.

The aim of the Study Group on a European Civil Code is therefore to determine (by means of scholarly comparative legal research) the extent to which the existing private law rules in the various legal systems of the Member States can be formulated in terms of shared legal principles. In order that any European legislative measure can thrive, if political support materialises, it is essential as a very minimum that the measure is supported by an academic consensus which regards the text as workable on an EU-wide arena, having regard to the different legal traditions of the constituent jurisdictions.

The non-legislative utility of the Principles

It would be fallacious to suppose that the essential reason for the work of the Study Group and the solitary value of the Principles will lie in the production of a text which can be fed raw into a cauldron of future political activity. The academic enterprise of researching the potential for codification of European private law and the considered process of restating contemporary principles common to the various legal systems in the Union is in itself a valuable contribution to legal science. As a concise, accessible and fully-annotated statement of private law principles with roots in all the different legal families of modern Europe, the draft text will constitute an unparalleled resource in comparative law for the benefit of judges, practising lawyers and jurists throughout the European Union and beyond. Besides its potential role in laying the first foundation of some conceivable legislative initiative, the Study Group envisages that its published output will serve the following primary purposes:

A. Accessible information about law in other EU jurisdictions

As a statement of the current law, the code may provide a first and efficient resource for lawyers requiring an overview of private law across the European Union. This may be of benefit to persons outside as well as inside the European Union who are contemplating business transactions or activities in Europe or with European partners and who require knowledge of the underlying private law in the various

Member States. In this way the restatement may contribute to the dismantlement of the potential barrier to beneficial economic activity which arises when essential legal knowledge is expensive or time-consuming to obtain.

B. Fostering the foreign law influence on domestic legal development: indirect legal integration in the EU

By showing in a comparative way how the various EU legal systems currently resolve problems in private law, the restatement will assist lawyers, judges, law reform bodies and legislators in legal argument and the development of existing law within their own jurisdiction. Conceivably, where national law is uncertain or considered doubtful or where its application has proved problematic, the restatement may incidentally help to foster a voluntary convergence of national laws. By outlining the case in favour of the mainstream position adopted in the European jurisdictions or the consensual European model solution, the Principles of European Patrimonial Law may influence national legal change towards a common European position. In this way the Principles may promote evolutionary legal integration, at least in marginal cases.

C. Supporting the development of EU law within the existing legal framework

In the context of Community law itself, the statement of principles of private law contained in the text produced by the Study Group may assist lawyers and the European Courts when, in accordance with the provisions of Union law and the jurisprudence of the court, it is necessary to derive principles of Community law from the principles of law common to the Member States. This is of particular relevance to the developing law of extra-contractual liability of the Community institutions under Art 288(1) of the EC Treaty (formerly Art 215 EC), where Community law imports as a source of law common principles of the national laws governing liability of administrative bodies. Those principles are themselves strongly influenced (at the very least) by the comparable private law in the legal systems of the Member States. However, the Principles of European Patrimonial Law would also be relevant as an aid to construction where Community legislation invokes general legal concepts in an undefined way and a uniform, pan-European meaning must be given to the legislation. In this way the Principles may assist both the European Court of Justice in construing existing legislation and the European legislative organs in formulating new legislation.

D. Facilitating party autonomy in formulating cross-border agreements

As a corpus of private law reflecting a reconciliation and fusion of varied legal traditions and private law rules in the European Union, the Principles may serve as a statement of principles which parties can voluntarily incorporate in the formation of cross-border agreements and in the voluntary resolution of claims including settlement by arbitration. The same holds for contracts entered into by EU institutions. The virtues of Principles of European Patrimonial Law in the form of a code in this regard are clear. Arrangement in terms of a coherent set of rules drafted with legislative enactment in mind, as opposed to purely discursive narration, will facilitate adoption and satisfy the standard of drafting expected in private agreements which are prepared professionally. Moreover, as a statement of the essential shared private law in Europe with a resonant echo in all the legal systems of the Member States, the code will offer the requisite neutrality and a certain equidistance from any one particular national legal system. Cross-border parties, seeking compromise between positions of domestic partiality, will be able to rely on the Principles as an impartial model and arbiter.

E. Promoting comparative law and understanding of foreign law in national legal education

Constituting a terse statement of European private law, the draft text and its commentary may provide a first resource for teaching in comparative legal studies and may help to foster understanding and communication among European lawyers trained in the distinct legal perspective provided by their own national system. In particular, in view of the difficulties of language and of acquiring abroad specialist material relating to smaller legal jurisdictions, the restatement may promote knowledge of the current private law of certain legal systems which might otherwise be neglected in teaching and scholarship elsewhere. In this context it should not be overlooked that knowledge of European private law has an immense role to play outside as well as inside the European Union.

Notes:

(1) From an organisational point of view, the work of the Study Group is conducted by two principal sets of bodies: (i) Working Teams, operating on a permanent basis with responsibility for research and proposals within the particular fields of private law assigned to them; and (ii) a Coordinating Group, a body of almost 50 academics from all the EU Member States which meets biannually and is charged with reviewing the content of submissions made by the Working Teams.[202] The following Working Teams have been operational:

Working Team on Sales, Services and Long-term Contracts
Working Team on Financial Services
Working Team on Credit Securities
Working Team on Extra-Contractual Obligations
Working Team on Rental of Movable Property
Working Team on Transfer of Movable Property
Working Team on Trust Law

(2) The work accomplished by three working groups is of principal importance for property law: (i) the Working Team on Credit Securities, which is established in Hamburg (Germany), under the supervision of Professor Ulrich Drobnig; (ii) the Working Team on Transfer of Movable Property, which is established in Salzburg, under the supervision of Professor Brigitta Lürger and Dr Wolfgang Faber; and (iii) the Working Team on Trust Law, which is established in Osnabrück, under the supervision of Dr. Stephen Swann. Land law has been explicitly excluded from the scope of the Study Group because, in the wordings of the Study Group itself, 'it would make little sense for the Study Group to commence its work by examining these areas of the law where the distinct legal cultures are likely to be relatively more entrenched in their heterogeneity'.[203]

[202] See www.sgecc.net/pages/en/organisation/index.overview.htm.
[203] www.sgecc.net/pages/en/introduction/101.scope.htm.

(3) At the end of 2008, the Study Group on a European Civil Code and the European Research Group on Existing EC Private Law (the *Acquis* Group) presented the first academic DCFR. On this, see above, III.D.4.

VII.B EULIS—EUROPEAN LAND INFORMATION SERVICE

The European Land Information Service or EULIS is a project initiated by land registry organisations in a number of EU Member States. These include Austria, Ireland, Lithuania, the Netherlands and Sweden, but with 15 more countries pending to be connected to the system. The EULIS system provides a link between the electronic land registry systems, enabling officials from one Member State to see information about parcels of land in another Member State.

Early on the initiative received attention by the European Commission and was mentioned in the Green Paper on Mortgage Credit in the EU dealt with above (10.28 (EU)) as a possible way forward (in section 69).

The challenge of the EULIS system is that the system will provide information in the land registry of another Member State in the language and format of that Member State. It is therefore difficult to know the exact content of a foreign land registry entry. The EULIS project offers a glossary of about 50 different terms in the languages of the participating countries, made by Registry officials, which offers more information.[204]

VII.C CROBECO—CROSS-BORDER ELECTRONIC CONVEYANCING OF LAND

A project initiated by the European Land Registry Association (ELRA) makes use of electronic land registration systems. Many EU Member States have, in the past decades, started a development towards electronic land recording or e-registration. Spain has one of the most advanced registration systems among the the EU Member State and together with the Dutch Land Registry (the *Kadaster*) a pilot project under the name Cross-Border Electronic Conveyancing of Land (CROBECO) was started.

The CROBECO project aims to make use of existing rules of private international law to choose the applicable law and enables parties from one Member State to conclude a contract and a deed of conveyance under their home legal system and then send the deed of conveyance, via the home land registry, to a foreign land registry where it is recorded and will have property effect, ie conveyance of the right of ownership. In the pilot project two Dutch buyers are able to conclude a written contract of sale and a deed of conveyance at a Dutch notary under Dutch law and send it off through the Dutch *Kadaster* to the Spanish land registry where it will effect a conveyance of ownership under Spanish law of a Spanish parcel of

[204] Moreover, the EULIS project connects to the E-Justice policy of the European Union and is likely to be developed much further in the coming years.

land.[205] The secret of success of the project lies in a standardised deed of conveyance that can be electronically generated into multiple language versions and relies on the trust between the land registry officials.

The CROBECO project is gaining attention and is promising to offer a possible way in which cross-border conveyancing can develop in the European Union without substantive EU legislative interference.[206] The CROBECO project is driven by practitioners but in strong collaboration with academics.[207]

VII.D THE TRENTO COMMON CORE PROJECT

Another important approach of the efforts that aims at an extensive dialogue between legal cultures is the Common Core Project, which is often referred to as 'Trento Common Core Project'. This project involves today more than 100 scholars mostly from Europe, the United States and South Africa.

The mission statement of the Common Core Project clarifies the difference in perspective between the different approaches of harmonisation, as they have been discussed before:

Mission Statement Common Core Project[208] **10.68 (INT)**

1) Goals—Legal Carthography

Stating it in very simple terms, we are seeking to unearth the common core of the bulk of European private law, ie, of what is already common, if anything, among the different legal systems of European Union member states. Such systems are differentiated not only by the civil law and the common law heritage, but also by a number of other Western legal traditions (or sub-traditions), according to the taxonomy one wishes to adopt. These differences impede our task, particularly if the perspective encompasses procedure and legal institutions where the divergence of legal tradition may be even more important. Consequently, we decided to limit our search to private law, within the general categories of contracts, torts, and property.

Such a common core must be revealed in order to obtain at least the mainlines of a reliable geographical map of the law of Europe. What the use of this map will be is of no concern to the cartographers who are drafting it. However, if reliable, it may become indispensable for whomever is entrusted with drafting European legislation. This may be particularly so in the process that appears to lead incrementally towards restatement and/or codification. …

While drafting a map is our immediate short-term concern, in the long run, this task is part of building a common European legal culture. Our culture-building task is

[205] See www.elra.eu/?page_id=636.

[206] See also http://mepli.blogspot.com/2010/11/crobeco-cross-border-electronic.html and http://mepli.blogspot.com/2011/02/crobeco-cross-border-electronic.html.

[207] Academic advisors to the project include this casebook's editors Professor Sjef van Erp and Dr Bram Akkermans.

[208] This text can be found at the homepage of the project: www.common-core.org.

shared by a number of projects, including the European Erasmus Student Exchange, and, on unofficial grounds, the creation of European law casebooks.

The idea underlying our project is that the best means to achieve an open legal space in Europe is through the creation of a model 'European law school' capable of shaping a truly common legal education. In order to do so some leading scholars in the field of comparative and European law have launched a project for the preparation of a series of casebooks on the common law of Europe. Our enterprise has been inspired mainly by the example of the United States. Despite the many relevant differences among state law, legal education is based on a single national model which produces lawyers capable of moving between states with no overwhelming difficulties. The authors of the European case book project declare that their project 'wishes to uncover common general principles which are already present in the living law of the European countries'; besides, 'rather than setting up a European law school, teaching materials are developed which can be used in such a law school, and in the curricula of other law schools as well, and by courts looking for rules and principles to decide a case, throughout Europe.'

This description shows the important similarities between the European Casebook and the Common Core Project. Both projects seek to identify the common features of private law in the European national legal systems, but it is not their goal to impose new rules and categories. They both are analytical, not openly prescriptive. Echoing the declaratory theory fashionable among common lawyers before Blackstone, 'the emphasis is not so much to create uniform rules as to find similar solutions and rules in the existing laws (and in they cannot be found, to state the differences) and to analyse and compare the legal reasoning behind them.'

But essentially what differentiates both projects is their target. The Common Core Project is aimed at scholars, while the European Casebook project is aimed at students. Producing suitable materials for didactic purposes implies that an accurate choice must be made between materials that will provide students (lacking or wishing to improve a specific comparative background) with the elements needed to understand legal systems different from their own. This selection is the province of academics. In fact, the idea of this group of scholars is to collect different materials in the form of a "cases and materials" text, i.e., to use cases, legislation, and legal doctrine materials, particularly in the form of short notes situating the other legal materials in their context. Ultimately, the goal is to provide students with a grasp of foreign law while educating them as common European lawyers. ...

5) Method—The common core approach in the European context

Method—The Lando Commission and the and Unidroit Principles

The fundamental characteristic of the first type of work is that it analyses the existing situation without trying in any way to force uniform solutions; its purpose is to provide the highest degree of precision a map of the relevant elements of different legal systems.

It is true that through the use of the comparative method many common features that remained obscure in traditional legal analysis will be unearthed, but this is because the instruments and techniques provide more accurate and correct analysis, not because they force convergence where it does not exist. Of course, more integration may follow from better knowledge, and therefore also the common core research may be considered as pushing indirectly towards more uniformity and less diversity. This is not however an objection that should impress us. Change following knowledge is a phenomenon that can be avoided only through obscurantism.

It is also true that common core research may be a useful instrument for legal harmonisation, in the sense that it provides reliable data to be used in devising new common solutions that may prove workable in practice. But this has nothing to do with the common core research in itself, which is devoted to produce reliable information, whatever its policy use might be.

This marks a strong difference between our project and any restatement-like enterprise. The latter involves the pursuit of rationality, harmony, and reform ideals, and this task implies the selection of the legal rules and materials that are best suited for the task. Whatever does not fit in a restatement-like framework is discarded. This is anathema for an analytical perspective: the very fact that rules and materials exist in a legal system requires that they be taken in consideration in the analysis and become part of the final 'map.'

This makes clear the distance between our research and the Lando project on the principles of European contract law, whose primary objective 'is to serve as a basis for a European Code of Contracts. They are intended as a fist step.' As O Lando himself explains, the principles of European contract law differ from the American Restatement on Contracts because they require a more radical approach. They do not simply select among several solutions extant in a single legal system. By having to provide workable solutions for a widely divergent legal environment, they sometimes embody rules that do not exist as such in any European legal system.

In spite of all these differences, however, the goals and the techniques of the two types of work (Lando and Restatement) are very much the same: they share the basic idea that they have to create new law (no matter how new in respect to the pre-existing legal situation), not simply analysing the existing one.

This normative attitude is shared also by the UNIDROIT principles on international commercial contracts. These are meant as 'soft' (ie, non-binding) law, and in this respect they are contrary to the idea of 'political' codification: they aim at promoting a uniform legal environment, not at imposing it through legislative means. Their philosophy assumes that differences between the legal systems are so great that they would defeat any attempt to impose uniformity.

The characteristic of having persuasive authority is common also to the principles of European contract law which, although meant to be finally embodied in one code, provide a common framework that functions as legal guidelines. The choice of a soft-law approach, however, does not eliminate the prescriptive nature of these projects: the change of the existing law has to be attained by indirect means, but the final aim remains legal change.

If we should sum up in one word the differences between the common core research and the common principles approach, that word might be 'scepticism'. The common core project, just as the Cornell project, uses value scepticism as the most important guideline: its aim is to provide a picture of the law existing in the European systems in a number of important areas which has to be as reliable and exact as possible. Whether this situation is legally efficient or rational is of no concern to the scholars involved. On the contrary, the projects whose main task is to promote common solutions to legal problems not only have to make a value-loaded selection, but are already imbedded in non sceptical values before the tension between uniformity and diversity. They try to find out, on the basis of comparative research, which solution may best regulate certain legal problems in a common way, discarding at the same time the possibility that core divergence (and certainly not only details) might be justified on many grounds.

Moreover, normative projects are also value-loaded in a different sense. Their choices cannot be made on nationalistic or chauvinistic grounds (as it can be for a piece of politically supported legislation), but of course they must be defended with reasons of general acceptability and rationality. Being by now lacking of political legitimacy, they end up advocating seemingly neutral ideas which have so far forced them into the narrow limits of areas of law, where no open value choices are to be made. Nevertheless, these areas cannot be neutral from the point of view of values: the rules that are finally selected must be coherent to the values that have been chosen as essential (or taken as a matter of course) by the participants, values that usually end up corresponding with market ideology. The common feature of the two kinds of enterprises is the use of comparative methods, but this common methodology serves diverging purposes, and consequently produces different results.

6) Method—European Civil Code

The idea of scepticism/neutrality is also relevant in the current debate on the feasibility and usefulness of a European civil code. There is strong disagreement among experts. Some of them think that a code is absolutely necessary in order to shape a truly common European law. Others think that this project is not feasible, either because the divergences among the national systems are still too strong (and this implies that in the future the situation may change, and a code may eventually be feasible), or because legal harmony can or must be attained with means other than a code.

The disagreement is not limited to technical legal aspects, it also involves the question on who is in charge of the choice of whether to have a code, and what materials to include in it. The European Parliament, by two 'Resolutions,' has endorsed the idea of a European code on private law, but the contents of such an action are not entirely clear. The first resolution uses both the terms 'harmonisation' and 'codification,' but these two have a different meaning. The first kind of actions implies the convergence of rules only to a limited extent, in order to attain a workable coordination among them. On the contrary, codification involves the creation of legal unity, thereby eliminating legal diversity.

The European Union, as shaped by the Treaty of Maastricht, has the task of creating an ever closer union among the peoples of Europe by attaining the economic and social aims set forth in the Treaty itself. This implies the possibility of enacting measures that provide a common legal framework, by eliminating legal differences that may hamper the development of a truly common European area. But it is far from clear whether the powers of the Union extend to the enactment of a code.

In fact, many scholars think that the principle of subsidiarity, embodied in the Treaty of Maastricht, bars such an action. The reference is to the principle by which in the fields where the EU does not have exclusive powers (and private law is definitely one of them), the Union can intervene only if the objectives cannot be sufficiently attained by State actions. Whether a European code is needed because several different national codes are not suited to regulate community legal relations is a highly debatable and debated issue. And the answer cannot be merely technical: it depends on the value assigned to legal pluralism as opposed to legal uniformity.

It is not our task to provide answers to this complex problem, but we hope that the result of our research will provide information that will be useful in evaluating the advantages and disadvantages of both positions. After all, in order to make a choice between pluralism and unity, the first step is to gain reliable knowledge of what is at stake.

The methodological awareness developed after five years of common core research also shows another important point that should be kept in mind in approaching the issue of European Codification. Some scholars are involved in a polemic that resembles in a somewhat Vichian way the nineteenth-century discussion between Savigny and Thibaut about German codification. In the present debate, 'Code' and 'Culture' appear still to be perceived as antithetic and exclusive of one another, as if in modern western societies enacted law could live without legal culture and the two could ignore each other.

An opposition that is similar to that between 'top down' and 'bottom up' reform. Indeed if there is one thing that the experience in the western legal tradition should have thought is that the opposition between top down and bottom up legal change is a false opposition. All legal changes have aspects of both. Law is in part politics (top down) and in part culture (bottom up). Put in other terms, institutional change is due in part to 'invisible hand' and in part to 'visible hand' phenomena. It is partially the local evolution of institutions, and partially the recognisable work of a political or professional elite, as Alan Watson has argued. Consequently, on the one hand, creating a code does not cancel the existence and the importance of other legal formants. Nor, on the other hand, an academic opposition to it is likely to be successful if the political conditions to do so exist. Certainly even if successful such opposition will not enlarge the domain of scholars over that of Brussels bureaucrats. A lot of European private law is already, if not codified in the civilian sense, at least enacted. More and more enactments are likely to occur. Such production of supernational law, short from making common core research useless, actually makes it even more necessary for the development of a somewhat homogeneous interpretive community.

Certainly even if the whole private law was codified there would be space for common core research at least until such a uniform interpretive community is fully developed.

Codification implies producing rules which are new for the whole or, at least, a part of legal actors in the systems concerned. Implementation of such rules needs a class of interpreters—judges, practitioners, scholars—acquainted with the new rules and with their rationales. The unavoidable lack of this knowledge in the short run, as well as—even in the long run—the strength of deeply rooted traditions as to different concepts, notions and their interrelations, may lead every effort of codification to a deadlock.

Hence, also as far as codification is concerned the real issue at stake is represented by the building of a common legal culture. An endeavour whose only tools seem to be, as we have already seen, a common legal education grounded upon the knowledge of what is common and what is different between the different European systems.

Note

The approach which is described in this excerpt is applied along different themes, which all appeal to national reporters. As far as property law is concerned, some of the discussion groups are:

- Trusts: the book with the national reports has been published as M Graziadei, U Mattei and L Smith, *Commercial Trusts in European Private Law* (Cambridge, Cambridge University Press, 2005).
- Security Rights in Immovable Property is still in progress and is co-ordinated by Professor C van der Merwe, Dr F Fiorentini and Professor G Watt.
- Transfer of Immovable Property is still in progress and is co-ordinated by Professor L Cooke and Professors L Martinez and A Pradi.
- Protection of Immovable Property is—since 2010—in progress and co-ordinated by Professor P Sparkes.

VIII. CONCLUDING REMARKS

At the end of this chapter some short concluding remarks are made that, we hope, may offer food for discussion and further research.

VIII.A MORE ACTIVITY THEN APPEARS AT FIRST SIGHT

There is more harmonisation going on in property law than might be expected at first sight. This is all the more so when considering the traditional mandatory rules of national property law. Property law systems are generally inward looking and protect their own rules by making effective use of the *lex rei sitae* rule. Creating harmonising rules is therefore difficult and always controversial. Development of harmonisation in the area of property law is therefore at a much slower pace than the developments in, for example, contract law.

VIII.B *LEX REI SITAE* IN DEMISE?

The application of the *lex rei sitae* rule in national private laws seems to have become more flexible in recognising foreign security rights and transfers in security. The result of this is that Member States themselves are bringing their laws more in conformity with each other. The best example of that we have perhaps seen in Chapter 6 dealing with management devices. The rise of non-possessory property security rights dealt with in Chapter 5 is also an example of this. Under this development it becomes easier for Member States to accommodate each other's property rights in their national legal order.

Member States are under pressure to do so, because the EU legislature is also moving into the field. In the area of succession and matrimonial property law there are serious considerations to replace the *lex rei sitae* with limited choice of law.

There are serious objections raised against this, especially from the viewpoint of legal certainly, but it seems a clear direction for international and European property law in the future.

VIII.C TOWARDS UNIFORM SYSTEMS OF PROPERTY SECURITY RIGHTS

When it comes to dealing with property security rights at an international level, it seems that the unitary system of property security rights, modelled after the famous Article 9 of the US Uniform Commercial Code, seems to be favoured. Although Member States maintain a fragmented system of property rights at a national level, internationally they also participate in uniform systems.

An interesting aspect of this development is the decrease in importance of the national property security rights. A similar development has occurred in the United States. When a national legal system grants a certain specific type of non-possessory security right, such a right will become recognised and enforced as a European Security Right or Article 9 UCC security right. The exact content of the property right remains relevant to the parties to the right only.

VIII.D FREE MOVEMENT OF GOODS OR PERSONS?

When thinking about harmonisation of property law it is easy to consider that movable objects are very capable of crossing borders and that therefore problems relating to the recognition and enforcement of these objects, as well as the property rights created on these, must be solved at a European or even more international level. However, the same applies to persons. In the European Union in particular there is an increasing movement of persons residing, either temporarily or permanently, in another Member State. These persons can experience problems relating to property law. This second aspect is also not so difficult to consider and problems with the free movement of persons must be solved. However, when these problems relate to matters of immovable property law (land), there are many other arguments, mostly dealing with legal certainty, that come into play.

VIII.E MOVABLES AND IMMOVABLES

Although at this moment projects relating to movable and intangible objects are in a more advanced state, projects dealing with land and immovable such as EULIS and CROBECO are gaining ground. It seems therefore that land is gaining ground, either through the free movement of persons (see VIII.D) or by, for example, receiving or providing services relating to land. Moreover, there is an increasing call to maintain the uniform systems of property law of the civil law Member States (see Chapter 1) and not move towards a situation in which there is land law and personal property law. On the other hand, a fragmented system of property law is reality in English law and could therefore also become the standard.

VIII.F EUROPEAN UNION PROPERTY LAW IN THE MAKING?

A final consideration of this casebook, after consideration of the similarities and differences between the property law systems of Austria, Belgium, France, Germany, the Netherlands and England and Wales dealt with by the earlier chapters, and the overview of the harmonising efforts presented in this chapter, is whether is desirable and if so possible to create an EU property law?

The answer to this question is not easy to answer at all and will very much depend on the person point of view of the reader. In some areas it is possible to find common ground, as the property laws of the Member States are already developing in the same direction (also towards each other), such as is the case with property security rights (Chapter 5) and trusts-like devices (Chapter 6). Moreover, there is also a strong similarity in the catalogue of available property rights (Chapter 3) and the way in which property rights are protected (Chapter 2), created (Chapter 7), transferred (Chapter 8) and destroyed (Chapter 9). By using common thought-patterns such as the principle of *numerus clausus* and the principle of transparency (Chapter 1) it becomes possible to discover common developments in the legal systems dealt with.

Of course, in order to make European Union property law not four or seven Member States are needed, but all 28 legal systems must be brought into line with each other. Much more work therefore needs to be done before we can conclusively come to an answer and, possibly, a proposal for an EU property law.

INDEX

INTRODUCTORY NOTE

References such as '138–9' indicate (not necessarily continuous) discussion of a topic across a range of pages. Wherever possible in the case of topics with many references, these have either been divided into sub-topics or only the most significant discussions of the topic are listed. Because the entire volume is about 'property law', the use of this term (and certain others occurring throughout the work) as an entry point has been restricted. Information will be found under the corresponding detailed topics.